[redacted]



**8B-7** (a) Adjusted cash balance, $5,607
**8B-8** (d) Vouchers payable, Dec. 31, $8,970
Bus. Dec. Prob. 8: No key figure

**9A-1** (a) Probable uncollectible accounts expense, $5,220
**9A-2** (b) Net accounts receivable, Jan. 31, $232,320
**9A-3** No key figure
**9A-4** No key figure
**9A-5** (c) Overstatement of Year 1 net income, $1,200
**9A-6** No key figure
**9A-7** No key figure
**9A-8** (b) Uncollectible accounts expense, $21,032
**9B-1** (b) Net accounts receivable, Jan. 31, $461,280
**9B-2** (b) Allowance for doubtful accounts, Dec. 31, $20,280
**9B-3** (a) May 26. Cash from discounting Davis note, $72,712
**9B-4** No key figure
**9B-5** (a) Note A. Maturity value, $20,600
**9B-6** (c) Total current assets, $21,595
**9B-7** June 30. Interest accrued Patten Company note payable, $100
**9B-8** (b) Amortization of discount on Copper-Weld, Inc. note, $420
Bus. Dec. Prob. 9: (a) Net income, $17,700

**10A-1** Gross profit percentage, Year 1, 33%
**10A-2** (a) (1) Inventory, fifo, $74,980
**10A-3** (a) (2) Lifo, $56,490; (b) Gross profit on sales, fifo, $338,360
**10A-4** (a) Gross profit rate, Year 4, 25%
**10A-5** (b) Cost ratio, 75%
**10A-6** (c) Gross profit on sales, $3,800
**10A-7** (a) Net income, Year 4, $75,000
**10B-1** Gross profit percentage, Year 1, 43%
**10B-2** (a) (1) Inventory, fifo, $14,060
**10B-3** (a) (1) Fifo, $188,300; (b) Gross profit on sales, lifo, $300,625
**10B-4** (a) Gross profit rate, Year 3, 34%
**10B-5** (a) Ending inventory at cost, $19,652
**10B-6** (c) Gross profit on sales, $670
**10B-7** (a) Net income, Year 9, $106,000
Bus. Dec. Prob. 10: (b) Gross profit $5,550

**11A-1** Year 2 Depreciation expense, $13,680
**11A-2** (a) Double-declining balance total, $135,164
**11A-3** (b) Land, $60,000
**11A-4** Depreciation for Year 2: (b) $78,400; (c) $72,000
**11A-5** (a) Accumulated depreciation Dec. 31, Year 9, $97,515
**11A-6** No key figure
**11A-7** (b) Machinery, Dec. 31, Year 11, $160,000
**11B-1** Depreciation expense, Year 3, $84,000
**11B-2** (b) Land, $90,000
**11B-3** Depreciation for Year 3: (b) $50,400; (c) $36,933
**11B-4** Depreciation expense, 1982, $96,000
**11B-5** (a) Accumulated depreciation, Dec. 31, Year 5, $168,030
**11B-6** (b) Machinery, Dec. 31, Year 8, $36,000

Bus. Dec. Prob. 11: (a) Depreciation in first three years, Bay Company, $37,500; Cove Company, $68,463

**12A-1** (a) Machine #3, gain on disposal, $4,000
**12A-2** (b) Cost basis, Machinery (new), $276,500
**12A-3** (b) Loss, $1,800
**12A-4** Depreciation expense, Year 3, $168,000
**12A-5** Amortization expense, patents, Year 10, $45,000
**12A-6** Depletion, Year 10, $552,000
**12A-7** (b) Paid for goodwill, $32,000
**12B-1** (a) Machine #2, gain on disposal, $6,000
**12B-2** (b) Cost basis, machinery (new), $296,000
**12B-3** (a) Depreciation expense, $8,800
**12B-4** Depreciation expense, Year 7, $20,150
**12B-5** No key figure
**12B-6** (a) Cost per ton, $11.60
**12B-7** (b) Revised earnings, Company X, $52,800; (c) price to be offered for Company X, $383,040
Bus. Dec. Prob. 12: No key figure

**13A-1** No key figure
**13A-2** No key figure
**13A-3** (b) Payroll taxes deducted from employees' earnings, $5,456.16
**13A-4** (c) Payroll taxes on employer, $3,315.20
**13A-5** (a) Net pay due, $5,604.90
**13B-1** No key figure
**13B-2** Payroll taxes on employer for year, $1,764
**13B-3** Accrued payroll, $8,848
**13B-4** (a) Earnings subject to FICA taxes, $60,603; (c) 6.7%
**13B-5** (c) Accrued payroll, $98,880
**13B-6** (a) Net pay due, $7,487.20
Bus. Dec. Prob. 13: No key figure

**14A-1** No key figure
**14A-2** (a) Profit under installment method, Year 1, $1 million
**14A-3** (a) Net income, cash basis, $47,900
**14A-4** (d) Decline in purchasing power of owner's equity, $8,000
**14A-5** Cost of goods sold—constant dollar basis, $212,500
Net loss—constant dollar basis, $4,500
**14B-1** No key figure
**14B-2** (a) Total sales revenue, $492,000
**14B-3** (a) Revised net income, Year 2, $107,100
**14B-4** (d) Increase in purchasing power of owner's equity, $7,000
**14B-5** Cost of goods sold—constant dollar basis, $315,000
Bus. Dec. Prob. 14: (b) (1) Net income, same accounting, Year 9, $60,000; (2) revised accounting, Year 9, $75,000

**15A-1** (b) Total assets, $220,800
**15A-2** (a) Net income, $54,000; (c) total assets, $217,720
**15A-3** (a) Share to Partner B, income $11,000
**15A-4** (d) Bonus, $50,000
**15A-5** (c) Bonus, $64,000

*(continued on back cover)*

# ACCOUNTING

## THE BASIS FOR BUSINESS DECISIONS

**McGraw-Hill Book Company**

New York St. Louis San Francisco Auckland Bogotá Hamburg Johannesburg London
Madrid Mexico Montreal New Delhi Panama Paris São Paulo Singapore
Sydney Tokyo Toronto

# ACCOUNTING
## THE BASIS FOR BUSINESS DECISIONS

FIFTH EDITION


**Walter B. Meigs,** Ph.D., C.P.A.
University of Southern California

**Robert F. Meigs,** D.B.A.
Professor of Accounting
School of Accountancy
San Diego State University

**ACCOUNTING: The Basis for Business Decisions**





34567890 KPKP 898765432

Library of Congress Cataloging in Publication Data

Meigs, Walter B

Accounting, the basis for business decisions.

Includes index.

1. Accounting. I. Meigs, Robert F., joint author.
II. Title.
HF5635.M49 1981 657 80-19756
ISBN 0-07-041551-X

This book was set in Century Schoolbook by York Graphic Services, Inc.
The editors were Donald G. Mason, Marjorie Singer, M. Susan Norton, and Elisa Adams;
the designer was Jo Jones;
the production supervisor was Dominick Petrellese.
The cover photograph was taken by Bjorn Bolstad/Photo Researchers, Inc.
Kingsport Press, Inc., was printer and binder.

# CONTENTS

# PREFACE

The environment of accounting is changing fast, and these environmental changes, such as continued inflation and the critical financial problems of many cities, affect the goals and the content of an introductory text in accounting. In order to function intelligently as a citizen as well as in a business of any size or type, every individual needs more than ever before a clear understanding of basic accounting concepts. In this fifth edition, we have tried to reflect the impact of inflation on accounting measurements and to suggest the direction of needed changes in accounting concepts and methods. The importance of adequate disclosure in the system of financial reporting is stressed, and attention is drawn to the need for improved accounting controls in all sectors of society.

Our goal is to present accounting as an essential part of the decision-making process for the voter, the taxpayer, the government official, the business manager, and the investor. This edition, like the preceding one, is designed for the first college-level course in accounting. In this course, instructors often recognize three general groups of students: those who stand at the threshold of preparation for a career in accounting, students of business administration who need a good understanding of accounting as an important element of the total business information system, and students from a variety of other disciplines who will find the ability to use and interpret accounting information a valuable accomplishment. During the process of revision the authors have tried to keep in mind the needs and interests of all three groups.

## New features in this edition

1 Illustrative cases—brief descriptions of interesting business situations which tie important concepts in the textbook to events in the "real world."

2 Increased emphasis on the interpretation and use of accounting information by decision makers.
3 Careful integration into the text and problems of the latest pronouncements of the Financial Accounting Standards Board, including FASB *Statement No. 33,* "Financial Reporting and Changing Prices."
4 The concept of present value, presented in clear and understandable terms, integrated into discussions of the valuation of assets and liabilities. Also, a new appendix following Chapter 18 summarizes in one location the various applications of present value and demonstrates the use of present value tables. Separate problem material accompanies this appendix.
5 Thorough review of all problem material to assure emphasis of key topics and to eliminate unnecessary mathematical complexity.
6 An increased number of single-concept problems and decision-oriented problems.
7 Increased emphasis on the impact of inflation upon accounting information.
8 New, open text design to enhance readability, with an increased number of diagrams to present concepts visually.
9 A discussion of the nature and purpose of reversing entries in Chapter 4.
10 An Instructor's Guide (separate from the Solutions Manual), with topical outlines of each chapter, an assignment guide indicating topics covered in each exercise and problem, and personal comments and observations by the authors on specific aspects of the text and of the introductory accounting course. Also included are solutions to the two parallel sets of Achievement Tests and Comprehensive Examinations.
11 Perspective—careful effort throughout the text and problems to utilize current and realistic prices, interest rates, and profit levels.

### Features carried forward from prior editions

Special qualities that are carried forward from prior editions include:

1 Respect for the needs of the student. Topics are covered in a depth which will qualify the student for subsequent course work in accounting.
2 Problem material developed and tested firsthand by the authors in their own classes for introductory accounting students.
3 Provocative problem material that raises a variety of interesting questions and carries the student far beyond routine drill.
4 For each chapter a business decision problem and a glossary of the key terms introduced or emphasized in the chapter. In addition, most chapters include a demonstration problem to assist students in developing skill in organizing the various elements of a problem into a useful format.

### New and extensively revised chapters

Many new topics are discussed in this fifth edition. For example Chapter 6, entitled Internal Control, now includes the major points of the Foreign Corrupt

Practices Act of 1977, which makes an adequate system of internal control legally mandatory. Chapter 14, dealing with the effects of inflation, covers the constant dollar and current cost disclosure requirements of *FASB Statement No. 33,* with emphasis on the interpretation of this information by users of financial statements. Chapter 18, on the subject of long-term liabilities, includes new up-to-date coverage of leases. Amortization of bond premium and discount is illustrated using both the straight-line and effective interest methods, and ample problem material is supplied covering both methods. Chapter 20, Income Taxes and Business Decisions, includes the many recent changes in tax law affecting both individuals and corporations.

In addition to covering new topics, we have revised many chapters to place greater emphasis upon the ***interpretation*** and ***use*** of accounting information. Chapter 17, dealing with such topics as earnings per share, extraordinary items, and discontinued operations, is extensively revised to emphasize the interpretation of this information by users of financial statements. An all new Chapter 19 covers marketable securities, use of the equity method, and consolidated financial statements in a single integrated discussion. The coverage of consolidated financial statements is designed to illustrate the basic concept of a consolidated entity and is far less detailed and mechanical than in prior editions. In Chapter 20, on income taxes, increased emphasis is given to tax planning and the impact of taxes upon business decisions. The chapters on cost accounting topics (Chapters 24 through 28) have been extensively revised to emphasize the use of cost information by managers in planning and controlling the activities of the business. Many of the problems in these chapters now require the student to make a business decision based upon accounting information.

## Emphasis and perspective

As in the previous editions we have attempted to present a balanced coverage of accounting from both financial and managerial viewpoints. Similarly, we have given continued attention to the problem of finding an ideal relation between an understanding of accounting procedures and the ability to use accounting information effectively. The role of electronic data processing is thoroughly recognized in the discussion of accounting systems (Chapter 7). However, students must understand, for example, how to make a journal entry by hand before they can instruct a computer to make it for them or before they can understand the journal-output of a computer. The discussion of accounting procedure throughout the book is geared to the objective of enhancing the student's grasp of the accounting process and its informational output.

## Supplementary materials

A full assortment of supplementary materials accompanies this text:

1 ***Solutions manual.*** A comprehensive manual containing answers to all review questions, exercises, Group A and Group B problems, and Business

Decision Problems contained in the text, along with complete answers to Practice Sets 1 and 2.

In the development of problem material for this book, special attention has been given to the inclusion of problems of varying length and difficulty. By referring to the time estimates, difficulty ratings, and problem descriptions in the ***Solutions Manual,*** instructors can choose problems that best fit the level, scope, and emphasis of the course they are offering.

*2* Two parallel sets of ***Achievement Tests*** and ***Comprehensive Examinations.*** Each set consists of eight Achievement Tests with each test covering two or three chapters; each Comprehensive Examination covers one-half of the entire text and may be used as a final examination. The availability of two parallel sets of tests makes it possible for an instructor to rotate examinations from year to year or to use two different examinations of equal difficulty and coverage in a single class.

*3* ***An instructor's guide.*** This new separate manual includes the following three sections for each chapter of the textbook:

*a* A brief topical outline of the chapter listing in logical sequence the topics the authors like to discuss in class.

*b* An assignment guide correlating specific exercises and problems with various topics covered in the chapter.

*c* Comments and observations.

The "Comments and observations" sections indicate the authors' personal views as to relative importance of topics and identify topics with which some students have difficulty. Specific exercises and problems are recommended to demonstrate certain points. Many of these sections include "Asides," introducing real-world situations (not included in the text) that are useful in classroom discussions. Also included are solutions to the parallel sets of Achievement Tests and Comprehensive Examinations.

*4* ***An examination question manual.*** With an abundance of test questions and exercises arranged chapter by chapter for the entire text, this examination booklet will be a most useful source for instructors who prefer to assemble their own examinations. The questions in this book are printed in an $8\frac{1}{2} \times 11$ format and can be torn out and copied to prepare individual examinations. All the true-false and multiple-choice questions in this manual are available on the EXAMINER system, a computerized test-generation system. Complete instructions for implementing the system are contained in the examination question manual.

*5* ***A self-study guide.*** Written by the authors, the ***Study Guide*** enables students to measure their progress by immediate feedback. This self-study guide includes an outline of the most important points in each chapter, an abundance of objective questions, and several short exercises for each chapter. In the back of the self-study guide are answers to questions and solutions to exercises to help students evaluate their understanding of the subject. The self-study guide will also be useful in classroom discussions and for review by students before examinations.

*6* ***Working papers.*** Two sets of problems for each chapter, Group A problems and Group B problems, are included in the text. The problems in the two groups are of similar difficulty and require about the same solution time. Soft-cover books of ***partially filled-in working papers*** are available for the Group A problems, as well as similar but separate workbooks for the Group B problems. Instructors may choose to alternate assignments, using Group A problems in one year or in one class and Group B problems in another. On these work sheets, the problem headings and some preliminary data have been entered to save students much of the mechanical pencil-pushing inherent in problem assignments. Also available are specially designed ***blank accounting forms,*** with a number of work sheets of each type appropriate for a course of typical assignments covering the entire book. All the working papers are in a new, improved format featuring wider money columns and the use of color.

7 ***Practice sets.*** The two practice sets available with the preceding edition have been completely revised. The first, Barker Office Supply, is for use after covering the first seven chapters of the book. The second, Skyline Corporation, may conveniently be used at any point after Chapter 18. Each practice set consists of a narrative of transactions and appropriate work sheets for preparing the solution. Each practice set is now bound in two books, making it more convenient for students to work with accounting forms and narrative.

8 ***Checklist of key figures for problems.*** This list appears on the front and back inside covers of this book. The purpose of the checklist is to aid students in verifying their problem solutions and in discovering their own errors.

9 ***Transparencies of problem solutions.*** This is a visual aid prepared by the publisher for the instructor who wishes to display in a classroom the complete solutions to any or all problems.

10 ***Additional transparencies for classroom illustrations.*** Sixteen special transparencies have been produced for use in the classroom to illustrate such concepts as closing entries, the preparation of a work sheet, and the use of controlling accounts and subsidiary ledgers.

11 ***A booklet of learning objectives.*** This brief statement of learning objectives for each chapter is designed to focus the student's attention on key principles and procedures. A clear understanding of these points will be especially helpful in following the chapters.

12 ***An audiotutorial system for the distant learner.*** The University of Mid-America has prepared thirteen half-hour television segments that correspond to the fifth edition of ***Accounting.*** These TV segments feature Robert Krulwich as the moderator for panel discussions covering accounting issues that are raised in the text chapters. In addition to the TV programs, audiotutorial students are furnished with a guide that coordinates the text, TV materials, Study Guide, and problems. Instructors utilizing this mode of instruction are furnished with a separate manual containing suggestions for organizing their course and for testing. Further details are available from the University of Mid-America, 1600 North 33d Street, P.O. Box 82006, Lincoln, Nebraska, 68501.

### Contributions by others

We want to express our sincere thanks to the many users of preceding editions who offered helpful suggestions for this edition. Especially helpful was the advice received from Scott Cracraft, Albion College; Irving L. Denton, North Virginia Community College, Annandale Campus; Robert Ford, Loma Linda University; Nicholas Genovese, Our Lady of Holy Cross College; Raymond A. Green, Texas Tech University; George C. Holdren, University of Nebraska, Lincoln; John P. Karbens, Chaminade University of Honolulu; Ron Lyons, California State Polytechnic University; Leslie L. McNelis, University of Texas at San Antonio; William D. Nichols, University of Notre Dame; Beth Reisig, George Mason University; Arthur T. Roberts, University of Baltimore; Charles Spector, State University of New York at Oswego; Dan Sullivan, Leeward Community College; DuWayne M. Wacker, The University of North Dakota; and Kathleen A. Wessman, Clayton Junior College.

We are keenly aware of the expert attention given this book and its many supplements by the editorial staff of McGraw-Hill, especially Marjorie Singer and Don Mason.

Our special thanks go to Professor Louis Geller of Queens College and Professor John J. Gorman of Rider College for assisting us in the proof stages of this edition by reviewing the end-of-chapter problems and text examples for accuracy.

To Professor Wai P. Lam, University of Windsor, we express our deep appreciation for his thorough review of both text and problems.

The assistance of Robert Graziano, Nicholas Gikas, and Steve Burns was most helpful in preparation of the manuscript.

We acknowledge with appreciation permission from the American Institute of Certified Public Accountants to quote from many of its pronouncements. All quotations are copyrighted by the American Institute of Certified Public Accountants.

We also are grateful to the Financial Accounting Standards Board which granted us permission to quote from FASB Statements, Discussion Memoranda, Interpretations, and Exposure Drafts. All quotations are copyrighted © by the Financial Accounting Standards Board, High Ridge Park, Stamford, Connecticut 06905, U.S.A., and are reprinted with permission. Copies of the complete documents are available from the FASB.

Walter B. Meigs

Robert F. Meigs

# ACCOUNTING
## THE BASIS FOR BUSINESS DECISIONS

# 1

# ACCOUNTING: THE LANGUAGE OF BUSINESS

What is accounting? Many people think of accounting as a highly technical field which can be understood only by professional accountants. Actually, nearly everyone practices accounting in one form or another on an almost daily basis. Accounting is the art of measuring, communicating, and interpreting financial activity. Whether you are preparing a household budget, balancing your checkbook, preparing your income tax return, or running General Motors, you are working with accounting concepts and accounting information.

Accounting has often been called the "language of business." In recent years, corporate profits have become a topic of considerable public interest. What are "corporate profits"? What levels of corporate profits are necessary to finance the development of new products, new jobs, and economic growth? One cannot hope to answer such questions without understanding the accounting concepts and terms involved in the measurement of income.

Since a language is a means of social communication, it is logical that a language should change to reflect changes in our environment, our life-styles, and our technology. Accounting, too, is a means of social communication in which changes and improvements are continually being made in order to communicate business information more efficiently. For example, as society has become increasingly interested in measuring the profitability of business organizations, accounting concepts and techniques have been changing to make such measurements more meaningful and more reliable.

We live in an era of accountability. Although accounting has made its most dramatic progress in the field of business, the accounting function is vital to every unit of our society. An individual must account for his or her income, and must file income tax returns. Often an individual must supply personal accounting information in order to buy a car or home, to qualify for a college scholarship, to secure a credit card, or to obtain a bank loan. Large corporations are accountable to their stockholders, to governmental agencies, and to the public. The federal government, the states, the cities, the school districts: all must use accounting as a basis for controlling their resources and measuring their accomplishments. Accounting is equally essential to the successful operation of a business, a university, a fraternity, a social program, or a city.

In every election the voters must make decisions at the ballot box on issues involving accounting concepts; therefore, some knowledge of accounting is needed by all citizens if they are to act intelligently in meeting the challenges of our society. The objective of this text is to help you develop your knowledge of accounting and your ability to use accounting information in making economic and political decisions.

## THE PURPOSE AND NATURE OF ACCOUNTING

The underlying purpose of accounting is to provide financial information about an economic entity. In this book the economic entity which we will be concentrating upon is a business enterprise. The financial information provided by an accounting system is needed by managerial decision makers to help them plan and control the activities of the economic entity. Financial information is also needed by ***outsiders***—owners, creditors, potential investors, the government, and the public—who have supplied money to the business or who have some other interest in the business that will be served by information about its financial position and operating results.

### A system for creating accounting information

In order to provide useful financial information about a business enterprise, we need some means of keeping track of the daily business activities and then summarizing the results in accounting reports. The methods used by a business to keep records of its financial activities and to summarize these activities in periodic accounting reports comprise the ***accounting system.***

The first function of an accounting system is to create a systematic record of the daily business activity, in terms of money. For example, goods and services are purchased and sold, credit is extended to customers, debts are incurred, and cash is received and paid out. These ***transactions*** are typical of business events which can be expressed ***in monetary terms,*** and must be entered in accounting records. The mere expression of an intent to buy goods or services in the future does not represent a transaction. The term ***transaction*** refers to a completed action rather than to an expected or possible future action. The ***recording*** of a transaction may be performed in many ways: that is, by writing with pen or pencil, by printing with mechanical or electronic equipment, or by punching holes or making magnetic impressions on cards or tape.

Of course, not all business events can be measured and described in monetary terms. Therefore, we do not show in the accounting records the appointment of a new chief executive, the signing of a labor contract, or the appearance of a new competing business on the scene.

In addition to compiling a narrative record of events as they occur, we ***classify*** transactions and events into related groups or categories. Classification enables us to reduce a mass of detail into compact and usable form. For example, grouping all transactions in which cash is received or paid out is a logical step in developing useful information about the cash position of a business enterprise.

To organize accounting information in a useful form, we ***summarize*** the classified information into accounting reports designed to meet the information needs of decision makers.

These three steps we have described—recording, classifying, and summarizing—are the means of creating accounting information. It is important, however, to recognize that the accounting process is not limited to the function of ***creating*** information. It also involves ***communicating*** this information to interested parties and ***interpreting*** accounting information as it relates to specific business decisions.

Often we will want to compare the financial statements of Company A with those of Company B. From this comparison, we can determine which company is the more profitable, which is financially stronger, and which offers the better chance of future success. You can benefit personally by making this kind of analysis of a company you are considering going to work for—or investing in.

## Communicating accounting information—Who uses accounting reports?

An accounting system must provide information to managers and also to a number of outsiders who have an interest in the financial activities of the business enterprise. The major types of accounting reports which are developed by the accounting system of a business enterprise and the parties receiving this information are illustrated in the following diagram:

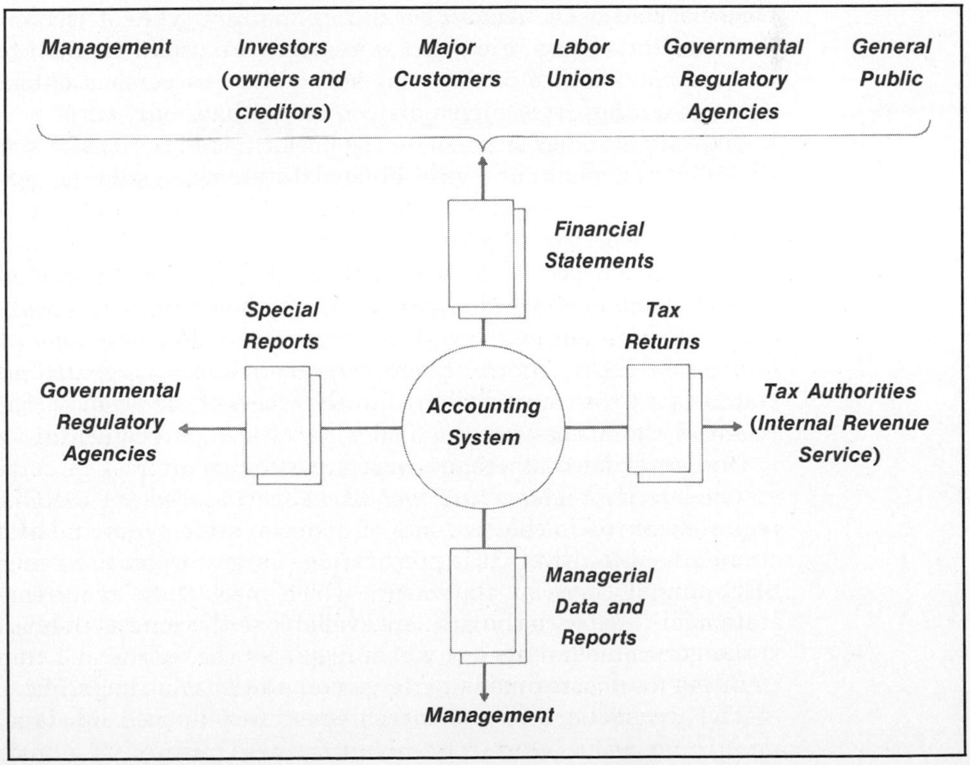

## Accounting information is user-oriented

The persons receiving accounting reports are termed the ***users*** of accounting information. The type of information that a specific user will require depends upon the kinds of decisions that person must make. For example, managers need detailed information about daily operating costs for the purpose of controlling the operations of the business and setting reasonable selling prices. Outsiders, on the other hand, usually need summarized information concerning resources on hand and information on operating results for the past year to use in making investment decisions, levying income taxes, or making regulatory decisions.

Since the information needs of various users differ, it follows that the accounting system of a business entity must be able to provide various types of accounting reports. The information in these reports must be presented in accordance with certain "ground rules" and assumptions, so that users of the reports will be able to interpret the information properly. For example, if a report indicates that a business owns land with an accounting value of $90,000, what does this dollar amount represent? Is it the original cost of the land to the business, the current market value of the land, or the assessed value for purposes of levying property taxes? Obviously the user of any accounting report needs to understand the standards and assumptions which have been used in preparing that report. In turn, the standards employed in the preparation of an accounting report must relate to the information needs of the user.

**Financial statements** Among the most important types of accounting reports are financial statements. Financial statements are useful to management and also are the main source of financial information to persons outside the business enterprise. These statements are concise, perhaps only three or four pages for a large business. They summarize the business transactions of a specific time period such as a month or a year. Financial statements show the ***financial position*** of the business at the time of the report and also the ***operating results*** by which the business arrived at this position.

The basic purpose of financial statements is to assist decision makers in evaluating the financial strength, profitability, and future prospects of a business entity. Thus, managers, investors, major customers, and labor all have a direct interest in these reports. Every large corporation prepares annual financial statements which are distributed to all owners of the business. In addition, these financial statements may be filed with various governmental agencies.

One governmental agency with a particular interest in corporate financial statements is the ***Securities and Exchange Commission*** (SEC). The SEC sets requirements as to the contents of financial statements and also the reporting standards followed in their preparation. Large corporations must file with the SEC annual financial statements which meet these requirements. Financial statements filed with the SEC are available to the general public. Thus, the SEC is the governmental agency which regulates the extent and the fairness of accounting disclosures made by large corporations to the public.

The accounting concepts, measurement techniques, and standards of presentation used in the preparation of financial statements are called ***generally accepted accounting principles.*** These principles continually change and evolve in response to changes in the business environment.

Developing accounting information in conformity with generally accepted accounting principles is called ***financial accounting,*** because this information is designed to summarize the financial position and operating results of a business entity. In the first part of this book we will emphasize financial accounting concepts rather than income tax rules, reports to regulatory agencies, or internal reports to management. As we shall see, financial accounting concepts apply to all types and sizes of business organizations. These concepts are useful to decision makers in both business and government in evaluating a wide range of economic issues.

**Income tax returns** The Internal Revenue Service, as well as certain state and local tax authorities, requires businesses and individuals to file annual income tax returns designed to measure taxable income. ***Taxable income*** is a legal concept defined by laws originating in Congress (or in state legislatures). Since Congress uses the income tax laws to achieve various social objectives as well as to finance the government, income tax laws are frequently modified or changed. Thus the rules used in preparing income tax returns may vary from one year to the next. In general, however, there is a close parallel between income tax laws and financial accounting concepts.

Businesses also must file tax returns for state and federal payroll taxes, federal excise taxes, and state sales taxes. The form and content of these reports is determined by the rules of the specific tax agency involved.

**Managerial data and reports** In addition to financial statements, management needs much detailed accounting data to assist it in planning and controlling the daily operations of the business. Management also needs specialized information for long-range planning and for major decisions such as the introduction of a new product or the closing of an older plant.

Determining the types of information most relevant to specific managerial decisions, and interpreting that information, is called ***managerial accounting.*** This topic is emphasized in the final chapters of this book.

**Reports to regulatory agencies** The activities of many business enterprises are regulated by various governmental agencies. For example, the Civil Aeronautics Board specifies the areas to be serviced by various airlines and the frequency of flights. The rates charged by companies which provide electricity, gas, water, and other public utilities usually are regulated by state utilities commissions.

Regulatory agencies often require special types of accounting information specifically tailored to their needs. For example, a state utilities commission making a decision as to whether to allow a rate increase by an electric company might request information about the cost to that company of producing electricity, the company's need to accumulate funds to provide service to outlying areas, and trends in population growth. In large part, however, reports to regulatory agencies are based upon generally accepted accounting principles.

## Using accounting information

Accounting extends beyond the process of creating records and reports. The ultimate objective of accounting is the ***use*** of this information, its analysis and interpretation. Accountants are always concerned with the significance of the figures they have produced. They look for meaningful relationships between events and financial results; they study the effect of various alternatives; and they search for significant trends that may throw some light on what will happen in the future.

Interpretation and analysis are not the sole province of the accountant. If managers, investors, and creditors are to make effective use of accounting information, they too must have some understanding of how the figures were put together and what they mean. An important part of this understanding is to recognize clearly the limitations of accounting reports. A business manager, an investor, or a creditor who lacks an understanding of accounting may fail to appreciate the extent to which accounting information is based upon ***estimates*** rather than upon precisely accurate measurements.

**The distinction between accounting and bookkeeping** Persons with little knowledge of accounting may also fail to understand the difference between accounting and bookkeeping. ***Bookkeeping*** means the recording of transactions, the record-making phase of accounting. The recording of transactions tends to be mechanical and repetitive; it is only a small part of the field of accounting and probably the simplest part. ***Accounting*** includes the design of accounting systems, preparation of financial statements, audits, cost studies, development of forecasts, income tax work, computer applications to accounting processes, and the analysis and interpretation of accounting information as an aid to making business decisions. A person might become a reasonably proficient bookkeeper in a few weeks or months; however, to become a professional accountant requires several years of study and experience.

## The work of accountants

Accountants tend to specialize in a given subarea of the discipline just as do attorneys and members of other professions. In terms of career opportunities, the field of accounting may be divided into three broad areas: (1) the public accounting profession, (2) private accounting, and (3) governmental accounting.

## Public accounting

***Certified public accountants*** are independent professional persons comparable to attorneys or physicians, who offer accounting services to clients for a fee. The ***CPA certificate*** is a license to practice granted by the state on the basis of a rigorous examination and evidence of practical experience. All states require that candidates pass an examination prepared and administered on a national basis twice each year by the American Institute of Certified Public Accountants. Requirements as to education and practical experience differ somewhat among the various states.

**Auditing** The principal function of CPAs is auditing. How do people outside a business entity—owners, creditors, government officials, and other interested parties—know that the financial statements prepared by a company's management are reliable and complete? In large part, these outsiders rely upon ***audits*** performed by a CPA firm which is ***independent*** of the company issuing the financial statements.

To perform an audit of a business, a firm of certified public accountants makes a careful study of the accounting system and gathers evidence both from within the business and from outside sources. This evidence enables the CPA firm to express its professional ***opinion*** as to the fairness and reliability of the financial statements. Persons outside the business, such as bankers and investors who rely upon financial statements for information, attach great importance to the annual ***audit report*** by the CPA firm. The ***independent*** status of a CPA firm retained to make an annual audit is just as important as its technical competence in assuring outsiders that the financial statements prepared by management disclose all relevant information and provide a fair picture of the company's financial position and operating results.

**Income tax services** An important element of decision making by business executives is consideration of the income tax consequences of each alternative course of action. The CPA is often called upon for "tax planning," which will show how a future transaction such as the acquisition of new equipment may be arranged in a manner that will hold income taxes to a minimum amount. The CPA is also frequently retained to prepare the federal and state income tax returns. To render tax services, the CPA must have extensive knowledge of tax statutes, regulations, and court decisions, as well as a thorough knowledge of accounting.

**Management advisory services** Auditing and income tax work have been the traditional areas of expertise for CPA firms, but the field of management advisory services is also important. When a CPA firm during the course of an audit discovers problems in a client's business, it is natural for the CPAs to make suggestions for corrective action. In response, the client often engages the CPAs to make a thorough investigation of the problem and to recommend new policies and procedures needed for a solution.

Public accounting firms gradually found themselves becoming more involved in management consulting work. Although this work often concerned accounting and financial matters, sometimes it dealt with organizational structure, statistical research, and a wide variety of problems not closely related to accounting. In recent years many CPA firms have created separate management advisory service departments which are staffed with mathematicians, industrial respects, however, accounting for governmental affairs requires a somewhat different approach because the objective of earning a profit is absent from public affairs. Universities, hospitals, churches, and other not-for-profit institutions also follow a pattern of accounting that is similar to governmental accounting.

**Internal Revenue Service** One of the governmental agencies which perform extensive accounting work is the Internal Revenue Service (IRS). The IRS handles the millions of income tax returns filed by individuals and corporations, and frequently performs auditing functions relating to these income tax returns and the accounting records on which they are based. Also, the IRS has been called upon to administer certain temporary economic controls, such as wage and price controls. These temporary controls have involved extensive and complex financial reporting by businesses, followed by review and audit by the IRS.

**Securities and Exchange Commission** Another governmental agency deeply involved in accounting is the Securities and Exchange Commission. The SEC reviews the financial statements of corporations which offer securities for sale to the public. In addition, the SEC has the legal power to require specific accounting methods and standards of financial disclosure for these companies.

Other governmental agencies employ accountants to prepare budgets and to audit the accounting records of various governmental departments and of private businesses which hold government contracts. Every agency of government at every level (federal, state, and local) must have accountants in order to carry out its responsibilities.

## Development of accounting standards—the FASB

Research to develop accounting principles and practices which will keep pace with changes in the economic and political environment is a major activity of professional accountants and accounting educators. In the United States four groups which have been influential in the improvement of financial reporting and accounting practices are the Financial Accounting Standards Board, the American Institute of Certified Public Accountants, the Securities and Exchange Commission, and the American Accounting Association.

Of special importance in establishing generally accepted accounting principles is the Financial Accounting Standards Board, known as the FASB. The FASB consists of seven full-time members, including representatives from public accounting, industry, and accounting education. In addition to conducting extensive research, the FASB issues ***Statements of Financial Accounting Standards,*** which represent authoritative expressions of generally accepted accounting principles.

Note that the FASB is part of the private sector of the economy and not a government agency. The development of accounting standards in the United States has traditionally been carried on in the private sector although the government, acting through the SEC, has exercised great influence on the FASB and other groups concerned with accounting research and standards of financial reporting.

The contribution of the FASB and the other groups mentioned above will be considered in later chapters. At this point we merely want to emphasize that accounting is not a closed system or a fixed set of rules, but a constantly evolving body of knowledge. As we explore accounting principles and related practices in this book, you will become aware of certain problems and conflicts for which fully satisfactory answers are yet to be developed. The need for further research is apparent despite the fact that present-day American accounting practices and standards of financial reporting are by far the best achieved anywhere at any time.

### Two primary business objectives

The management of every business must keep foremost in its thinking two primary objectives. The first is to earn a profit. The second is to stay solvent, that is, to have on hand sufficient cash to pay debts as they fall due. Profits and solvency, of course, are not the only objectives of business managers. There are many others, such as providing jobs for people, protecting the environment, creating new and improved products, and providing more goods and services at a lower cost. It is clear, however, that a business cannot hope to accomplish these objectives unless it meets the two basic tests of survival—operating profitably and staying solvent.

A business is a collection of resources committed by an individual or group of individuals, who hope that the investment will increase in value. Investment in any given business, however, is only one of a number of alternative investments available. If a business does not earn as great a profit as might be obtained from alternative investments, its owners will be well-advised to sell or terminate the business and invest elsewhere. A business that continually operates at a loss will eventually exhaust its resources and be forced out of existence. Therefore, in order to operate successfully and to survive, the owners or managers of an enterprise must direct the business in such a way that it will earn a reasonable profit.

Business concerns that have sufficient cash to pay their debts promptly are said to be ***solvent.*** In contrast, a company that finds itself unble to meet its obligations as they fall due is called ***insolvent.*** Solvency must also be ranked as a primary objective of any enterprise, because a business that becomes insolvent may be forced by its creditors to stop operations and end its existence.

### Accounting as the basis for business decisions

How do business executives know whether a company is earning profits or incurring losses? How do they know whether the company is solvent or insolvent, and whether it probably will be solvent, say, a month from today? The answer to both these questions in one word is ***accounting.*** Accounting is the process by which the profitability and solvency of a company can be measured. Accounting also provides information needed as a basis for making business decisions that will enable management to guide the company on a profitable and solvent course.

Stated simply, managing a business is a matter of deciding what should be done, seeing to it that the means are available, and getting people employed in the business to do it. At every step in this process, management is faced with alternatives, and every decision to do something or to refrain from doing something involves a choice. Successful managers must make the right choice when "the chips are down." In most cases the probability that a good decision will be made depends on the amount and validity of the information that the manager has about the alternatives and their consequences. However, it is seldom that all the information needed is either available or obtainable. Often a crystal ball in good working order would be helpful. As a practical matter, however, information which flows from the accounting records, or which can be developed by special analysis of accounting data, constitutes the basis on which a wide variety of business decisions should be made.

For specific examples of these decisions, consider the following questions. What prices should the firm set on its products? If production is increased, what effect will this have on the cost of each unit produced? Will it be necessary to borrow from the bank? How much will costs increase if a pension plan is established for employees? Is it more profitable to produce and sell product A or product B? Shall a given part be made or be bought from suppliers? Should an investment be made in new equipment? All these issues call for decisions that should depend, in part at least, upon accounting information. It might be reasonable to turn the question around and ask: What business decisions could be made intelligently ***without*** the use of accounting information? Examples would be hard to find.

In large-scale business undertakings such as the manufacture of automobiles or the operation of nationwide chains of retail stores, the top executives cannot possibly have close physical contact with and knowledge of the details of operations. Consequently, these executives must depend to an even greater extent than the small business owner upon information provided by the accounting system.

We have already stressed that accounting is a means of measuring the results of business transactions and of communicating financial information. In addition, the accounting system must provide the decision maker with ***predictive information*** for making important business decisions in a changing world.

## Internal control

Throughout this book, the fact that business decisions of all types are based at least in part on accounting data is emphasized. Management, therefore, needs assurance that the accounting data it receives are accurate and dependable. This assurance is provided in large part by developing a strong system of ***internal control.*** A basic principle of internal control is that no one person should handle all phases of a transaction from beginning to end. When business operations are so organized that two or more employees are required to participate in every transaction, the possibility of fraud is reduced and the work of one employee gives assurance of the accuracy of the work of another.

A system of internal control comprises all the measures taken by an organization for the purpose of (1) protecting its resources against waste, fraud, and inefficiency; (2) ensuring accuracy and reliability in accounting and operating data; (3) securing compliance with company policies; and (4) evaluating the level of performance in all divisions of the company.

A CPA firm in conducting an audit of a company will evaluate the adequacy of internal control in each area of the company's operations. The stronger the system of internal control, the more confidence the CPA can place in the integrity of the company's financial statements and accounting records. Consequently, the audit work can be performed more rapidly, with less detailed investigation of transactions, when internal controls are strong. The internal auditors also regard the study of internal control as a major part of their work. If internal controls are weak, the usual consequences are waste, fraud, inefficiency, and unprofitable operations.

## Forms of business organization

A business enterprise may be organized as a ***single proprietorship,*** a ***partnership,*** or a ***corporation.***

**Single proprietorship** A business owned by one person is called a single proprietorship. Often the owner also acts as the manager. This form of business organization is common for small retail stores and service enterprises, for farms, and for professional practices in law, medicine, and public accounting. The owner is personally liable for all debts incurred by the business. From an accounting viewpoint, however, the business is an entity separate from the proprietor.

**Partnership** A business owned by two or more persons voluntarily associated as partners is called a partnership. The organization of a partnership requires only an agreement among the persons joining together as partners.

The partnership agreement usually states how profits or losses shall be divided among the partners each year and the settlement to be made upon the withdrawal or death of a partner. Partnerships, like single proprietorships, are widely used for small businesses and for professional practices. A great many CPA firms are organized as partnerships. As in the case of a single proprietorship, a partnership is not legally an entity separate from its owners; consequently, a partner is personally responsible for the debts of the partnership. From an accounting standpoint, however, a partnership is a business entity separate from the personal activities of the partners.

**Corporation** A business organized as a separate legal entity with ownership divided into transferable shares of capital stock is called a corporation. Capital stock certificates are issued by the corporation to each stockholder showing the number of shares he or she owns. The stockholders are free to sell all or part of these shares to other investors at any time, and this ease of transfer adds to the attractiveness of investing in a corporation.

Persons wanting to form a new corporation must file an application with state officials for a corporate charter. When this application has been approved, the corporation comes into existence as a ***legal entity*** separate from its owners. The important role of the corporation in our economy is based on such advantages as the ease of gathering large amounts of money, transferability of shares in ownership, limited liability of owners, and continuity of existence.

Accounting principles and concepts of measurement apply to all three forms of business organization. In the first several chapters of this book, our study of basic accounting concepts will use as a model the single proprietorship, which is the simplest and most common form of business organization.

## FINANCIAL STATEMENTS: THE STARTING POINT IN THE STUDY OF ACCOUNTING

The preparation of financial statements is not the first step in the accounting process, but it is a convenient point to begin the study of accounting. The financial statements are the means of conveying to management and to interested outsiders a concise picture of the profitability and financial position of the business. Since these financial statements are in a sense the end product of the accounting process, the student who acquires a clear understanding of the content and meaning of financial statements will be in an excellent position to appreciate the purpose of the earlier steps of recording and classifying business transactions.

The two most widely used financial statements are the ***balance sheet*** and the ***income statement.***[1] Together, these two statements (perhaps a page each in length) summarize all the information contained in the hundreds or thousands of pages comprising the detailed accounting records of a business. In this introductory chapter and in Chapter 2, we shall explore the nature of the balance sheet, or statement of financial position, as it is sometimes called. Once we have become familiar with the form and arrangement of the balance sheet and with the meaning of technical terms such as ***assets, liabilities,*** and ***owner's equity,*** it will be as easy to read and understand a report on the financial position of a business as it is for an architect to read the blueprint of a proposed building. (We shall discuss the income statement in Chapter 3.)

### The balance sheet

The purpose of a balance sheet is to show the financial position of a business ***at a particular date.*** Every business prepares a balance sheet at the end of the year, and most companies prepare one at the end of each month. A balance sheet consists of a listing of the assets and liabilities of a business and of the owner's

---

[1] A third financial statement, called a ***statement of changes in financial position,*** will be discussed later.

equity. The following balance sheet portrays the financial position of the Westside Cleaning Company at December 31.

**Balance sheet shows financial position at a specific date**

***WESTSIDE CLEANING COMPANY***
***Balance Sheet***
***December 31, 19***

| *Assets* | | *Liabilities & Owner's Equity* | |
|---|---|---|---|
| Cash | $ 19,500 | Liabilities: | |
| Accounts receivable | 9,000 | Notes payable | $ 22,000 |
| Supplies | 500 | Accounts payable | 16,000 |
| Land | 21,000 | Salaries payable | 2,000 |
| Building | 44,500 | Total liabilities | $ 40,000 |
| Cleaning equipment | 13,000 | Owner's equity: | |
| Delivery equipment | 7,500 | Joe Crane, capital | 75,000 |
| Total assets | $115,000 | Total liabilities & owner's equity | $115,000 |

Note that the balance sheet sets forth in its heading three items: (1) the name of the business, (2) the name of the financial statement "Balance Sheet," and (3) the date of the balance sheet. Below the heading is the body of the balance sheet, which consists of three distinct sections: assets, liabilities, and owner's equity. The remainder of this chapter is largely devoted to making clear the nature of these three sections.

Another point to note about the form of a balance sheet is that cash is always the first asset listed; it is followed by receivables, supplies, and any other assets that will soon be converted into cash or consumed in operations. Following these items are the more permanent assets, such as land, buildings, and equipment.

The liabilities of a business are always listed before the owner's equity. Each liability (such as notes payable, accounts payable, and salaries payable) should be listed separately, followed by a total figure for liabilities.

**The business entity** The illustrated balance sheet refers only to the financial affairs of the business entity known as Westside Cleaning Company and not to the personal financial affairs of the owner, Joe Crane. Crane may have a personal bank account, a home, a car, a cattle ranch, and other property, but since these personal belongings are not a part of the cleaning business, they are not included in the balance sheet of this business unit.

In brief, ***a business entity is an economic unit which enters into business transactions that must be recorded, summarized, and reported. The entity is regarded as separate from its owner or owners;*** the entity owns its own property and has its own debts. Consequently, for each business entity, there should be a separate set of accounting records. A balance sheet and an income statement are intended to portray the financial position and the operating results of a single business entity. If the owner intermingles his or her personal affairs with the transactions of the business, the resulting financial statements will be misleading and will fail to describe the business fairly.

## Assets

***Assets are economic resources which are owned by a business and are expected to benefit future operations.*** Assets may have definite physical form such as buildings, machinery, or merchandise. On the other hand, some assets exist not in physical or tangible form, but in the form of valuable legal claims or rights; examples are amounts due from customers, investments in government bonds, and patent rights.

One of the most basic and at the same time most controversial problems in accounting is determining the dollar values for the various assets of a business.

**The cost principle** Assets such as land, buildings, merchandise, and equipment are typical of the many economic resources that will be used in producing income for the business. The prevailing accounting view is that such assets should be recorded at their cost. When we say that an asset is shown in the balance sheet at its ***historical cost,*** we mean the dollar amount originally paid to acquire the asset; this amount may be very different from what we would have to pay today to replace it. We have already described ***transactions*** as business events which can be measured in money and must be recorded in the accounting records. The price established in a transaction for the purchase of property or services is the cost to be recorded by the buyer. Thus, the "accounting value" or "valuation" of an asset means the cost of the asset to the entity owning it.

For example, let us assume that a business buys a tract of land for use as a building site, paying $40,000 in cash. The amount to be entered in the accounting records as the value of the asset will be the cost of $40,000. If we assume a booming real estate market, a fair estimate of the sales value of the land 10 years later might be $100,000. Although the market price or economic value of the land has risen greatly, the accounting value as shown in the accounting records and on the balance sheet would continue unchanged at the cost of $40,000. This policy of accounting for assets at their cost is often referred to as the ***cost principle*** of accounting.

In reading a balance sheet, it is important to bear in mind that the dollar amounts listed do not indicate the prices at which the assets could be sold, nor the prices at which they could be replaced. One useful generalization to be drawn from this discussion is that a balance sheet does not show "how much a business is worth."

**The going-concern assumption** It is appropriate to ask ***why*** accountants do not change the recorded values of assets to correspond with changing market prices for these properties. One reason is that the land and building used to house the business are acquired for ***use*** and not for resale; in fact, these assets cannot be sold without disrupting the business. The balance sheet of a business is prepared on the assumption that the business is a continuing enterprise, a "going concern." Consequently, the present estimated prices at which the land and buildings could be sold are of less importance than if these properties were intended for sale.

**The objectivity principle** Another reason for using cost rather than current market values in accounting for assets is the need for a definite, factual basis for valuation. The cost for land, buildings, and many other assets purchased for cash can be rather definitely determined. Accountants use the term ***objective*** to describe asset valuations that are factual and can be verified by independent experts. For example, if land is shown on the balance sheet at cost, any CPA who performed an audit of the business would be able to find objective evidence that the land was actually valued at the cost incurred in acquiring it. Estimated market values, on the other hand, for assets such as buildings and specialized machinery are not factual and objective. Market values are constantly changing and estimates of the prices assets could be sold for are largely a matter of personal opinion. Of course at the date an asset is acquired, the cost and market value are usually the same because the buyer would not pay more than the asset was worth and the seller would not take less than current market value. The bargaining process which results in the sale of an asset serves to establish both the current market value of the property and the cost to the buyer. With the passage of time, however, the current market value of assets is likely to differ considerably from the cost recorded in the owner's accounting records.

**Accounting for inflation** Severe worldwide inflation in recent years has raised serious doubts as to the adequacy of the conventional cost basis in accounting for assets. When inflation becomes very severe, historical cost values for assets simply lose their relevance as a basis for making business decisions. Proposals for adjusting recorded dollar amounts to reflect changes in the value of the dollar, as shown by a price index, have been considered for many years. However, stronger interest is being shown at present in balance sheets which would show assets at ***current appraised values*** or ***replacement costs*** rather than at historical cost. The British government has experimented extensively with the revision of corporate accounting to reflect inflation. The British approach proposes that year-end balance sheets show assets at their current value rather than at historical or original cost. Many companies in the Netherlands are now using some form of current-value accounting. In the United States, the Financial Accounting Standards Board requires that large corporations disclose the ***current replacement cost*** of certain assets as ***supplementary information*** to conventional cost-based financial statements.

Accounting concepts are not as exact and unchanging as many persons assume. To serve the needs of a fast-changing economy, accounting concepts and methods must also undergo continuous evolutionary change. As of today, however, the cost basis of valuing assets is still the generally accepted method.

The problem of valuation of assets is one of the most complex in the entire field of accounting. It is merely being introduced at this point; in later chapters we shall explore carefully some of the valuation principles applicable to the major types of assets.

### Liabilities

Liabilities are debts. All business concerns have liabilities; even the largest and most successful companies find it convenient to purchase merchandise and supplies on credit rather than to pay cash at the time of each purchase. The liability arising from the purchase of goods or services on credit is called an ***account payable,*** and the person or company to whom the account payable is owed is called a ***creditor.***

A business concern frequently finds it desirable to borrow money as a means of supplementing the funds invested by the owner, thus enabling the business to expand more rapidly. The borrowed funds may, for example, be used to buy merchandise which can be sold at a profit to the firm's customers. Or, the borrowed money might be used to buy new and more efficient machinery, thus enabling the company to turn out a larger volume of products at lower cost. When a business borrows money for any reason, a liability is incurred and the lender becomes a creditor of the business. The form of the liability when money is borrowed is usually a ***note payable,*** a formal written promise to pay a certain amount of money, plus interest, at a definite future time. An ***account payable,*** as contrasted with a ***note payable,*** does not involve the issuance of a formal written promise to the creditor, and it does not call for payment of interest. When a business has both notes payable and accounts payable, the two types of liabilities are shown separately in the balance sheet. The sequence in which these two liabilities are listed is not important, although notes payable are usually shown as the first item among the liabilities. A figure showing the total of the liabilities may also be inserted, as shown by the illustrated balance sheet on page 15.

The creditors have claims against the assets of the business, usually not against any particular asset but against the assets in general. The claims of the creditors are liabilities of the business and have priority over the claims of owners. Creditors are entitled to be paid in full even if such payment should exhaust the assets of the business, leaving nothing for the owner. The issue of valuation, which poses so many difficulties in accounting for assets, is a much smaller problem in the case of liabilities, because the amounts of most liabilities are specified by contract.

### Owner's equity

The owner's equity in a business represents the resources invested by the owner; it is equal to the total assets minus the liabilities. The equity of the owner is a residual claim because the claims of the creditors legally come first. If you are the owner of a business, you are entitled to whatever remains after the claims of the creditors are fully satisfied.

For example:

| | |
|---|---|
| *The Westside Cleaning Company has total assets of* . . . . . . . . . . . . . . . . . . | *$115,000* |
| *And total liabilities amounting to* . . . . . . . . . . . . . . . . . . . . . . . . . . . . . . . . | *40,000* |
| *Therefore, the owner's equity must equal* . . . . . . . . . . . . . . . . . . . . . . . . . | *$ 75,000* |

Suppose that the Westside Cleaning Company borrows $3,000 from a bank. After recording the additional asset of $3,000 in cash and recording the new liability of $3,000 owed to the bank, we would have the following:

| | |
|---|---|
| *The Westside Cleaning Company now has total assets of* . . . . . . . . . . . . . . . . | *$118,000* |
| *And total liabilities are now* . . . . . . . . . . . . . . . . . . . . . . . . . . . . . . . . . . . | *43,000* |
| *Therefore, the owner's equity still is equal to* . . . . . . . . . . . . . . . . . . . . . . . | *$ 75,000* |

It is apparent that the total assets of the business were increased by the act of borrowing money from a bank, but the increase in assets was exactly offset by an increase in liabilities, and the owner's equity remained unchanged. The owner's equity in a business ***is not increased*** by borrowing from banks or other creditors.

**Increases in owner's equity** If you begin a small business of your own, you will probably invest cash and possibly some other assets to get the business started. Later, as the business makes payments for rent, office equipment, advertising, salaries to employees, and other items, you may find it necessary to supply additional cash to the business. Hopefully, before long, the business will become self-sustaining. Whenever, as owner of the business, you transfer cash or other personally owned assets to the business entity, your ownership equity will increase. In summary, the owner's equity in a business comes from two sources:

**1** Investment by the owner
**2** Earnings from profitable operation of the business

Only the first of these two sources of owner's equity is considered in this chapter. The second source, an increase in owner's equity through earnings of the business, will be discussed in Chapter 3.

**Decreases in owner's equity** If you are the owner of a single proprietorship, you have the right to withdraw cash or other assets from the business at any time. Since you are strongly interested in seeing the business succeed, you will probably not make withdrawals that would handicap the business entity in operating efficiently. Once the business achieves momentum and financial strength, you may choose to make substantial withdrawals. Withdrawals are most often made by writing a check drawn on the company's bank account and payable to the owner. However, other types of withdrawals also occur, such as taking office equipment out of the business for personal use by the owner, or by causing cash belonging to the business to be used to pay a personal debt of the owner. Every withdrawal by the owner reduces the total assets of the business and reduces the owner's equity. In summary, decreases in the owner's equity in a business are caused in two ways:

1 Withdrawals of cash or other assets by the owner
2 Losses from unprofitable operation of the business

Only the first of these two causes of decrease in owner's equity is emphasized in this chapter. The second cause, a decrease in owner's equity through operating at a loss, will be considered in Chapter 3.

### The accounting equation

One of the fundamental characteristics of every balance sheet is that the total figure for assets always equals the total figure for liabilities and owner's equity. This agreement or balance of total assets with the total of liabilities plus owner's equity is one reason for calling this statement of financial position a ***balance sheet.*** But ***why*** do total assets equal the total of liabilities and owner's equity? The answer can be given in one short paragraph as follows.

The dollar totals on the two sides of the balance sheet are always equal because these two sides are merely two views of the same business resources. The listing of assets shows us ***what resources*** the business owns; the listing of liabilities and owner's equity tells us ***who supplied these resources*** to the business and how much each group supplied. Everything that a business owns has been supplied to it by the creditors or by the owner. Therefore, the total claims of the creditors plus the claim of the owner equal the total assets of the business.

The equality of assets on the one hand and of the claims of the creditors and the owner on the other hand is expressed in the equation:

*Fundamental accounting equation*

**Assets = Liabilities + Owner's Equity**
**\$115,000 = \$40,000 + \$75,000**

The amounts listed in the equation were taken from the balance sheet illustrated on page 15. A balance sheet is simply a detailed statement of this equation. To illustrate this relationship, compare the balance sheet of the Westside Cleaning Company with the above equation.

To emphasize that the equity of the owner is a residual element, secondary to the claims of creditors, it is often helpful to transpose the terms of the equation, as follows:

*Alternative form of equation*

**Assets − Liabilities = Owner's Equity**
**\$115,000 − \$40,000 = \$75,000**

Every business transaction, no matter how simple or how complex, can be expressed in terms of its effect on the accounting equation. A thorough understanding of the equation and some practice in using it are essential to the student of accounting.

Regardless of whether a business grows or contracts, this equality between the assets and the claims against the assets is always maintained. Any increase in the amount of total assets is necessarily accompanied by an equal increase on the other side of the equation, that is, by an increase in either the liabilities or the owner's equity. Any decrease in total assets is necessarily accompanied by a corresponding decrease in liabilities or owner's equity. The continuing equality of the two sides of the balance sheet can best be illustrated by taking a brand-new business as an example and observing the effects of various transactions upon its balance sheet.

### Effects of business transactions upon the balance sheet

Assume that James Roberts, a licensed real estate broker, decided to start a real estate business of his own, to be known as Roberts Real Estate Company. The planned operations of the new business call for obtaining listings of houses being offered for sale by owners, advertising these houses, and showing them to prospective buyers. The listing agreement signed with each owner provides that Roberts Real Estate Company shall receive at the time of sale a commission equal to 6% of the sales price of the property.

The new business was begun on September 1, when Roberts deposited $60,000 in a bank account in the name of the business, Roberts Real Estate Company The initial balance sheet of the new business then appeared as follows:

*Beginning balance sheet of a new business*

**ROBERTS REAL ESTATE COMPANY**
**Balance Sheet**
**September 1, 19__**

| Assets | | Owner's Equity | |
|---|---|---|---|
| Cash | $60,000 | James Roberts, capital | $60,000 |

Observe that the equity of the owner in the assets is designated on the balance sheet by the caption, James Roberts, capital. The word ***capital*** is the traditional accounting term used in describing the equity of the proprietor in the assets of the business.

**Purchase of an asset for cash** The next transaction entered into by Roberts Real Estate Company was the purchase of land suitable as a site for an office. The price for the land was $21,000 and payment was made in cash on September 3. The effect of this transaction on the balance sheet was twofold: first, cash was decreased by the amount paid out; and second, a new asset, Land, was acquired. After this exchange of cash for land, the balance sheet appeared as follows:

**ROBERTS REAL ESTATE COMPANY**
**Balance Sheet**
**September 3, 19__**

*Balance sheet totals unchanged by purchase of land for cash*

| Assets | | Owner's Equity | |
|---|---|---|---|
| Cash | $39,000 | James Roberts, capital | $60,000 |
| Land | 21,000 | | |
| Total assets | $60,000 | Total owner's equity | $60,000 |

**Purchase of an asset and incurring of a liability** On September 5 an opportunity arose to buy from OK Company a complete office building which had to be moved to permit the construction of a freeway. A price of $36,000 was agreed upon, which included the cost of moving the building and installing it upon the Roberts Company's lot. As the building was in excellent condition and would have cost approximately $80,000 to build, Roberts considered this a very fortunate purchase.

The terms provided for an immediate cash payment of $15,000 and payment of the balance of $21,000 within 90 days. Cash was decreased $15,000, but a new asset, Building, was recorded at cost in the amount of $36,000. Total assets were thus increased by $21,000 but the total of liabilities and owner's equity was also increased as a result of recording the $21,000 account payable as a liability. After this transaction had been recorded, the balance sheet appeared as shown below. Remember that cash is always the first asset listed in a balance sheet.

***ROBERTS REAL ESTATE COMPANY***
***Balance Sheet***
***September 5, 19__***

*Totals increased equally by purchase on credit*

| *Assets* | | *Liabilities & Owner's Equity* | |
|---|---|---|---|
| *Cash* | *$24,000* | *Liabilities:* | |
| *Land* | *21,000* | *Accounts payable* | *$21,000* |
| *Building* | *36,000* | *Owner's equity:* | |
| | | *James Roberts, capital* | *60,000* |
| *Total assets* | *$81,000* | *Total liabilities & owner's equity* | *$81,000* |

Note that the building appears in the balance sheet at $36,000, its cost to Roberts Real Estate Company. The estimate of $80,000 as the probable cost to construct such a building is irrelevant. Even if someone should offer to buy the building from the Roberts Company for $80,000 or more, this offer, if refused, would have no bearing on the balance sheet. Accounting records are intended to provide a historical record of ***costs actually incurred;*** therefore, the $36,000 price at which the building was purchased is the amount to be recorded.

**Sale of an asset** After the office building had been moved to the Roberts Company's lot, Roberts decided that the lot was much larger than was needed. The adjoining business, Carter's Drugstore, wanted more room for a parking area so, on September 10, Roberts Company sold the unused part of the lot to Carter's Drugstore for a price of $6,000. Since the sales price was computed at the same amount per foot as Roberts Company had paid for the land, there was neither a profit nor a loss on the sale. No down payment was required but it was agreed that the full price would be paid within three months. By this transaction a new asset, Accounts Receivable, was acquired, but the asset Land was decreased by the same amount; consequently, there was no change in the amount of total assets. After this transaction, the balance sheet appeared as follows:

*No change in totals by sale of land at cost*

**ROBERTS REAL ESTATE COMPANY**
**Balance Sheet**
**September 10, 19__**

| Assets | | Liabilities & Owner's Equity | |
|---|---|---|---|
| Cash | $24,000 | Liabilities: | |
| Accounts receivable | 6,000 | Accounts payable | $21,000 |
| Land | 15,000 | Owner's equity: | |
| Building | 36,000 | James Roberts, capital | 60,000 |
| Total assets | $81,000 | Total liabilities & owner's equity | $81,000 |

In the illustration thus far, Roberts Real Estate Company has an account receivable from only one debtor, and an account payable to only one creditor. As the business grows, the number of debtors and creditors will increase, but the Accounts Receivable and Accounts Payable designations will continue to be used. The additional records necessary to show the amount receivable from each individual debtor and the amount owing to each individual creditor will be explained in Chapter 7.

**Purchase of an asset on credit** A complete set of office furniture and equipment was purchased on credit from General Equipment, Inc., on September 14 for $5,400. As the result of this transaction the business owned a new asset, Office Equipment, but it had also incurred a new liability in the form of Accounts Payable. The increase in total assets was exactly offset by the increase in liabilities. After this transaction the balance sheet appeared as follows:

*Totals increased by acquiring asset on credit*

**ROBERTS REAL ESTATE COMPANY**
**Balance Sheet**
**September 14, 19__**

| Assets | | Liabilities & Owner's Equity | |
|---|---|---|---|
| Cash | $24,000 | Liabilities: | |
| Accounts receivable | 6,000 | Accounts payable | $26,400 |
| Land | 15,000 | Owner's equity: | |
| Building | 36,000 | James Roberts, capital | 60,000 |
| Office equipment | 5,400 | | |
| Total assets | $86,400 | Total liabilities & owner's equity | $86,400 |

**Collection of an account receivable** On September 20, cash of $1,500 was received as partial settlement of the account receivable from Carter's Drugstore. This transaction caused cash to increase and the accounts receivable to decrease by an equal amount. In essence, this transaction was merely the exchange of one asset for another of equal value. Consequently, there was no change in the amount of total assets. After this transaction, the balance sheet appeared as follows:

*ROBERTS REAL ESTATE COMPANY*
*Balance Sheet*
*September 20, 19__*

*Totals unchanged by collection of an account receivable*

| Assets | | Liabilities & Owner's Equity | |
|---|---|---|---|
| Cash | $25,500 | Liabilities: | |
| Accounts receivable | 4,500 | Accounts payable | $26,400 |
| Land | 15,000 | Owner's equity: | |
| Building | 36,000 | James Roberts, capital | 60,000 |
| Office equipment | 5,400 | | |
| Total assets | $86,400 | Total liabilities & owner's equity | $86,400 |

**Payment of a liability** On September 30 Roberts Real Estate Company paid $3,000 in cash to General Equipment, Inc. This payment caused a decrease in cash and an equal decrease in liabilities. Therefore the totals of assets and equities were still in balance. After this transaction, the balance sheet appeared as follows:

*ROBERTS REAL ESTATE COMPANY*
*Balance Sheet*
*September 30, 19__*

*Totals decreased by paying a liability*

| Assets | | Liabilities & Owner's Equity | |
|---|---|---|---|
| Cash | $22,500 | Liabilities: | |
| Accounts receivable | 4,500 | Accounts payable | $23,400 |
| Land | 15,000 | Owner's equity: | |
| Building | 36,000 | James Roberts, capital | 60,000 |
| Office equipment | 5,400 | | |
| Total assets | $83,400 | Total liabilities & owner's equity | $83,400 |

The transactions which have been illustrated for the month of September were merely preliminary to the formal opening for business of Roberts Real Estate Company on October 1. Since we have assumed that the business earned no commissions and incurred no expenses during September, the owner's equity at September 30 is shown in the above balance sheet at $60,000, unchanged from the original investment by Roberts on September 1. September was a month devoted exclusively to organizing the business and not to regular operations. In succeeding chapters we shall continue the example of Roberts Real Estate Company by illustrating operating transactions and considering how the net income of the business is determined.

## Effect of business transactions upon the accounting equation

A balance sheet is merely a detailed expression of the accounting equation, Assets = Liabilities + Owner's Equity. To emphasize the relationship between the accounting equation and the balance sheet, let us now repeat the September transactions of Roberts Real Estate Company to show the effect of each transaction upon the accounting equation. Briefly restated, the seven transactions were as follows:

**Sept.** **1** Began the business by depositing $60,000 in a company bank account.
**3** Purchased land for $21,000 cash.
**5** Purchased a building for $36,000, paying $15,000 cash and incurring a liability of $21,000.
**10** Sold part of the land at a price equal to cost of $6,000, collectible within three months.
**14** Purchased office equipment on credit for $5,400.
**20** Received $1,500 cash as partial collection of the $6,000 account receivable.
**30** Paid $3,000 on accounts payable.

In the table below, each transaction is identified by date; its effect on the accounting equation and also the new balance of each item are shown. Each of the lines labeled Balances contains the same items as the balance sheet previously illustrated for the particular date. The final line in the table corresponds to the amounts in the balance sheet at the end of September. Note that the equality of the two sides of the equation was maintained throughout the recording of the transactions.

| | Assets | | | | | | | | | = | Liabilities | + | Owner's Equity |
|---|---|---|---|---|---|---|---|---|---|---|---|---|---|
| | *Cash* | + | *Accounts Receivable* | + | *Land* | + | *Building* | + | *Office Equipment* | = | *Accounts Payable* | + | *James Roberts, Capital* |
| *Sept. 1* | +$60,000 | | | | | | | | | | | | +$60,000 |
| *Sept. 3* | −21,000 | | | | +$21,000 | | | | | | | | |
| *Balances* | $39,000 | | | | $21,000 | | | | | | | | $60,000 |
| *Sept. 5* | −15,000 | | | | | | +$36,000 | | | | +$21,000 | | |
| *Balances* | $24,000 | | | | $21,000 | | $36,000 | | | | $21,000 | | $60,000 |
| *Sept. 10* | | | +$6,000 | | −6,000 | | | | | | | | |
| *Balances* | $24,000 | | $6,000 | | $15,000 | | $36,000 | | | | $21,000 | | $60,000 |
| *Sept. 14* | | | | | | | | | +$5,400 | | +5,400 | | |
| *Balances* | $24,000 | | $6,000 | | $15,000 | | $36,000 | | $5,400 | | $26,400 | | $60,000 |
| *Sept. 20* | +1,500 | | −1,500 | | | | | | | | | | |
| *Balances* | $25,500 | | $4,500 | | $15,000 | | $36,000 | | $5,400 | | $26,400 | | $60,000 |
| *Sept. 30* | −3,000 | | | | | | | | | | −3,000 | | |
| *Balances* | $22,500 | + | $4,500 | + | $15,000 | + | $36,000 | + | $5,400 | = | $23,400 | + | $60,000 |

## USE OF FINANCIAL STATEMENTS BY OUTSIDERS

Through careful study of financial statements, it is possible for the outsider with training in accounting to obtain a fairly complete understanding of the financial position of the business and to become aware of significant changes that have occurred since the date of the preceding balance sheet. Bear in mind, however, that financial statements have limitations. As stated earlier, only those factors which can be reduced to monetary terms appear in the balance sheet. Let us consider for a moment some important business factors which are not set forth in financial statements. Perhaps a new competing store has just opened for business across the street; the prospect for intensified competition in the future will not be described in the balance sheet. As another example, the health, experience, and managerial skills of the key people in the management group may be extremely important to the success of a business, but these qualities cannot be measured and expressed in dollars in the balance sheet. Efforts to develop methods of accounting for the human resources of an organization presently constitute an important area of accounting research.

### Bankers and other creditors

Bankers who have loaned money to a business concern or who are considering making such a loan will be vitally interested in the balance sheet of the business. By studying the amount and kinds of assets in relation to the amount and payment dates of the liabilities, a banker can form an opinion as to the ability of the business to pay its debts promptly. The banker gives particular attention to the amount of cash and of other assets (such as accounts receivable) which will soon be converted into cash and then compares the amount of these assets with the amount of liabilities falling due in the near future. The banker is also interested in the amount of the owner's equity, as this ownership capital serves as a protecting buffer between the banker and any losses which may befall the business. Bankers are seldom, if ever, willing to make a loan unless the balance sheet and other information concerning the prospective borrower offer reasonable assurance that the loan can and will be repaid promptly at the maturity date.

Another important group making constant use of balance sheets consists of the credit managers of manufacturing and wholesaling firms, who must decide whether prospective customers are to be allowed to buy merchandise on credit. The credit manager, like the banker, studies the balance sheets of customers and prospective customers for the purpose of appraising their debt-paying ability. Credit agencies such as Dun & Bradstreet, Inc., make a business of obtaining financial statements from virtually all business concerns and appraising their debt-paying ability. The conclusions reached by these credit agencies are available to business concerns willing to pay for credit reports about prospective customers.

### Owners

The financial statements of corporations listed on the stock exchanges are eagerly awaited by millions of stockholders. A favorable set of financial statements may cause the market price of the company's stock to rise dramatically; an unfavorable set of financial statements may cause the "bottom to fall out" of the market price. Current dependable financial statements are one of the essential ingredients for successful investment in securities. Of course, financial statements are equally important in single proprietorships and partnerships. The financial statements tell the owners just how successful their business has been and summarize in concise form its present financial position.

### Others interested in financial information

In addition to owners, managers, bankers, and merchandise creditors, other groups making use of accounting data include governmental agencies, employees, investors, and writers for business periodicals. Some very large corporations have more than a million stockholders; these giant corporations send copies of their annual financial statements to each of these many owners. In recent years there has been a definite trend toward wider distribution of financial statements to all interested persons, in contrast to the attitude of a few decades ago when many companies regarded their financial statements as a confidential matter. This trend reflects an increasing awareness of the impact of corporate activities on all aspects of our lives and of the need for greater disclosure of information about the activities of business corporations.

The purpose of this discussion is to show the extent to which a modern industrial society depends upon accounting. Even more important, however, is a clear understanding at the outset of your study that accounting does not exist just for the sake of keeping a record or in order to fill out income tax returns and various other regulatory reports. These are but auxiliary functions. If you gain an understanding of accounting concepts, you will have acquired an analytical skill essential to the field of professional management. ***The prime and vital purpose of accounting is to aid decision makers in choosing among alternative courses of action.***

## KEY TERMS INTRODUCED IN CHAPTER 1

**Accounting equation** Assets equal liabilities plus owner's equity. A = L + OE.

**Accounting system** A financial information system which includes accounting forms, records, instruction manuals, flow charts, programs, and reports to fit the particular needs of the business.

**Accounts payable** Amounts which a company owes its creditors for goods and services purchased on credit.

**Accounts receivable** Amounts which a company expects to collect from its customers for goods and services sold to them on credit.

**American Institute of Certified Public Accountants (AICPA)** The national professional association of certified public accountants (CPAs). Carries on extensive research and is influential in improving accounting standards and practices.

**Assets** Economic resources (things of value) owned by a business which are expected to benefit future operations.

**Audit report** A report issued by a CPA expressing an independent professional opinion on the fairness and reliability of the financial statements of a business.

**Auditing** The principal activity of a CPA. Consists of an independent examination of the accounting records and other evidence relating to a business to support the expression of an impartial expert opinion about the reliability of the financial statements.

**Balance sheet** A financial statement which shows the financial position of a business entity by summarizing the assets, liabilities, and owner's equity at a specific date.

**Business entity** An economic unit that enters into business transactions that must be recorded, summarized, and reported. The entity is regarded as ***separate from its owner or owners.***

**Certificate in Management Accounting (CMA)** A designation granted to persons who have demonstrated competance in management accounting by passing an examination and meeting educational and experience requirements.

**Certified public accountants (CPAs)** Independent professional accountants licensed by a state to offer auditing and accounting services to clients for a fee.

**Controller** The chief accounting officer of a business.

**Corporation** A business organized as a separate legal entity and chartered by a state, with ownership divided into transferable shares of capital stock.

**Cost accounting** A specialized field of accounting concerned with determining and controlling the cost of particular products or processes.

**Cost principle** A widely used policy of accounting for assets at their original cost to the business.

**CPA certificate** A license to practice public accounting granted by a state on the basis of educational requirements, a rigorous examination, and (in most states) evidence of practical experience.

**Creditor** The person or company to whom a liability is owed.

**Financial Accounting Standards Board (FASB)** An independent group which conducts research in accounting and issues authoritative statements as to proper reporting of financial information.

**Financial statements** Reports which summarize the financial position and operating results of a business (balance sheet and income statement).

**Generally accepted accounting principles** The accounting concepts, measurement techniques, and standards of presentation used in financial statements. Examples include the cost principle, the going-concern assumption, and the objectivity principle.

**Going-concern assumption** An assumption by accountants that a business will continue to operate indefinitely unless specific evidence to the contrary exists, as, for example, impending bankruptcy.

**Internal control** All measures used by a business to guard against errors, waste, and fraud; to assure the reliability of accounting data; and to promote compliance with all company policies.

**Internal Revenue Service** A governmental agency charged with responsibility for collecting federal income taxes from individuals and corporations.

**Liabilities** Debts or obligations of a business. The claims of creditors against the assets of a business.

**Notes payable** Liabilities evidenced by a formal written promise to pay a certain amount of money plus interest at a future date. Usually arise from borrowing.

**Owner's equity** The excess of assets over liabilities. The amount of an owner's net investment in a business plus profits from successful operations which have been retained in the business.

**Partnership** A business owned by two or more persons voluntarily associated as partners.

**Securities and Exchange Commission (SEC)** A government agency which reviews the financial statements and other reports of corporations which offer securities for sale to the public. Works closely with the FASB and the AICPA to improve financial reporting practices.

**Single proprietorship** An unincorporated business owned by one person.

**Solvency** Having enough money to pay debts as they fall due.

**Tax accounting** The determination of taxable income, preparation of federal and state income tax returns, and planning of operations along lines that will hold tax payments to the legal minimum.

**Transactions** Business events which can be measured in money and which are entered in the accounting records.

**Withdrawals by owner** Amounts of cash or other assets removed from the business by the owner. Cause a decrease in owner's equity.

## DEMONSTRATION PROBLEM FOR YOUR REVIEW

An alphabetical list of the various items showing the financial condition of Wilson Company at September 30 appears below. Although the figure for the owner's equity is not given, it can be determined when all the items are arranged in the form of a balance sheet.

| | | | |
|---|---|---|---|
| *Accounts payable* | *$18,100* | *Land* | *$24,000* |
| *Accounts receivable* | *16,400* | *Notes payable* | *35,000* |
| *Building* | *39,200* | *Notes receivable* | *1,400* |
| *Cash* | *8,500* | *Office equipment* | *4,800* |
| *Delivery truck* | *3,000* | *Ralph Wilson, capital* | *?* |

On October 1, the following transactions occurred:

(1) Accounts payable of $8,000 were paid.

(2) The owner, Ralph Wilson, invested an additional $5,000 cash in the business.

(3) Office equipment was purchased at a cost of $1,000 to be paid for within 10

days. This equipment was almost new and was purchased from an attorney who had accepted a political appointment overseas. The equipment would have cost $1,500 if purchased through regular channels.

(4) One-quarter of the land was sold at cost. The buyer gave a promissory note for $6,000 due in 30 days. (Interest applicable to the note is to be ignored.)

**Instructions**

**a** Prepare a balance sheet at September 30, 19___.

**b** Prepare a balance sheet at October 1, 19___.

## SOLUTION TO DEMONSTRATION PROBLEM

**a**

***WILSON COMPANY***

***Balance Sheet***

***September 30, 19___***

| *Assets* | | *Liabilities & Owner's Equity* | |
|---|---|---|---|
| *Cash* | *$ 8,500* | *Liabilities:* | |
| *Notes receivable* | *1,400* | *Notes payable* | *$35,000* |
| *Accounts receivable* | *16,400* | *Accounts payable* | *18,100* |
| *Land* | *24,000* | *Total liabilities* | *$53,100* |
| *Building* | *39,200* | *Owner's equity:* | |
| *Office equipment* | *4,800* | *Ralph Wilson, capital* | *44,200* |
| *Delivery truck* | *3,000* | | |
| *Total assets* | *$97,300* | *Total liabilities & owner's equity* | *$97,300* |

**b**

***WILSON COMPANY***

***Balance Sheet***

***October 1, 19___***

| *Assets* | | *Liabilities & Owner's Equity* | |
|---|---|---|---|
| *Cash* | *$ 5,500* | *Liabilities:* | |
| *Notes receivable* | *7,400* | *Notes payable* | *$35,000* |
| *Accounts receivable* | *16,400* | *Accounts payable* | *11,100* |
| *Land* | *18,000* | *Total liabilities* | *$46,100* |
| *Building* | *39,200* | *Owner's equity:* | |
| *Office equipment* | *5,800* | *Ralph Wilson, capital* | *49,200* |
| *Delivery truck* | *3,000* | | |
| *Total assets* | *$95,300* | *Total liabilities & owner's equity* | *$95,300* |

## REVIEW QUESTIONS

**1** In broad general terms, what is the purpose of accounting?

**2** Why is a knowledge of accounting terms and concepts useful to persons other than professional accountants?

3 What is meant by the term ***business transaction?***

4 What are financial statements and how do they relate to the accounting system?

5 Explain briefly why each of the following groups is interested in the financial statements of a business:

  **a** Creditors
  **b** Potential investors
  **c** Labor unions

6 Distinguish between ***accounting*** and ***bookkeeping.***

7 What is the principal function of certified public accountants? What other services are commonly rendered by CPA firms?

8 Private accounting includes a number of subfields or specialized phases, of which cost accounting is one. Name four other such specialized phases of private accounting.

9 The SEC is concerned with the financial statements of what kind of business entity?

10 Is the Financial Accounting Standards Board (FASB) a government agency? What is its principal function?

11 One primary objective of every business is to operate profitably. What other primary objective must be met for a business to survive? Explain.

12 Not all the significant happenings in the life of a business can be expressed in monetary terms and entered in the accounting records. Identify two or more significant events affecting a business which could not be satisfactorily measured and entered in its accounting records.

13 Information available from the accounting records provides a basis for making many business decisions. List five examples of business decisions requiring the use of accounting information.

14 State briefly the purpose of a balance sheet.

15 Define assets. List five examples.

16 State briefly two proposals which have been made to enable accounting to function better during a period of inflation.

17 Define liabilities. List two examples.

18 Tom Ray, president of the Ray Company, was offered $500,000 cash for the land and buildings occupied by the business. These assets had been acquired five years ago at a price of $300,000. Ray refused the offer, but is inclined to increase the land and buildings to a total valuation of $500,000 in the balance sheet in order to show more accurately "how much the business is worth." Do you agree? Explain.

19 Explain briefly the concept of the ***business entity.***

20 State the accounting equation in two alternative forms.

21 The owner's equity in a business arises from what two sources?

22 Why are the total assets shown on a balance sheet always equal to the total of the liabilities and the owner's equity?

23 Can a business transaction cause one asset to increase or decrease without affecting any other asset, liability, or the owner's equity?

24 If a transaction causes total liabilities to decrease but does not affect the owner's equity, what change, if any, will occur in total assets?

25 Give examples of transactions that would:

  **a** Cause one asset to increase and another asset to decrease without any effect on the liabilities or owner's equity.
  **b** Cause both total assets and total liabilities to increase without any effect on the owner's equity.

## EXERCISES

*Ex. 1-1* The balance sheet items of Mack Company at December 31, 19___, are listed below in alphabetical order. You are to prepare a balance sheet (including a complete heading). Use a sequence for assets similar to that in the illustrated balance sheet on page 15.

| | | | |
|---|---|---|---|
| *Accounts payable* | *$10,200* | *Land* | *$ 27,000* |
| *Accounts receivable* | *19,500* | *Lou Mack, capital* | *115,800* |
| *Building* | *60,000* | *Office equipment* | *5,700* |
| *Cash* | *13,800* | | |

*Ex. 1-2* The items included in the balance sheet of Holt Company at December 31, 19___, are listed below in random order. You are to prepare a balance sheet (including a complete heading). Arrange the assets in the sequence shown in the balance sheet illustrated on page 15. You must compute the amount for Sandra Holt, capital.

| | | | |
|---|---|---|---|
| *Land* | *$30,000* | *Office equipment* | *$ 3,400* |
| *Accounts payable* | *14,600* | *Building* | *70,000* |
| *Accounts receivable* | *18,900* | *Cash* | *12,100* |
| *Sandra Holt, capital* | *?* | *Notes payable* | *65,000* |

*Ex. 1-3* The following transactions represent part of the activities of Malibu Company for the first month of its existence. Indicate the effect of each transaction upon the total assets of the business by use of the appropriate phrase: "increase total assets," "decrease total assets," "no change in total assets."

(1) The owner invested cash in the business.
(2) Purchased a typewriter for cash.
(3) Purchased a delivery truck at a price of $4,000, terms $500 cash and the balance payable in 24 equal monthly installments.
(4) Paid a liability.
(5) Borrowed money from a bank.
(6) Sold land for cash at a price equal to its cost.
(7) Sold land on account (on credit) at a price equal to its cost.
(8) Sold land for cash at a price in excess of its cost.
(9) Sold land for cash at a price less than its cost.
(10) Collected an account receivable.

*Ex. 1-4* **a** The assets of Atom Company total $160,000 and the owner's equity amounts to $40,000. What is the amount of the liabilities?

**b** The owner's equity of Wild Company appears on the balance sheet as $85,000 and is equal to one-third the amount of total assets. What is the amount of liabilities?

**c** The assets of Hot Line Company amounted to $75,000 on December 31 of Year 1 but increased to $105,000 by December 31 of Year 2. During this same period, liabilities increased by $25,000. The owner's equity at December 31 of Year 1 amounted to $50,000. What was the amount of owner's equity at December 31 of Year 2? Explain the basis for your answer.

*Ex. 1-5* For each of the following categories, state concisely a transaction that will have the required effect on elements of the accounting equation.

(1) Increase an asset and increase a liability.
(2) Decrease an asset and decrease a liability.
(3) Increase one asset and decrease another asset.
(4) Increase an asset and increase owner's equity.
(5) Increase one asset, decrease another asset, and increase a liability.

*Ex. 1-6* List the following four column headings on a sheet of notebook paper as follows:

| Transaction | Total Assets | Liabilities | Owner's Equity |
|---|---|---|---|

Next, you are to identify each of the following transactions by number on a separate line in the first column. Then indicate the effect of each transaction on the total assets, liabilities, and owner's equity by placing a plus sign (+) for an increase, a minus sign (−) for a decrease, or the letters (NC) for no change in the appropriate column.

(1) Purchased a typewriter on credit.
(2) Owner invested cash in the business.
(3) Purchased office equipment for cash.
(4) Collected an account receivable.
(5) Owner withdrew cash from the business.
(6) Paid a liability.
(7) Returned for credit some of the office equipment previously purchased on credit but not yet paid for.
(8) Sold land for cash at a price in excess of cost.
(9) Borrowed money from a bank.

As an example, transaction (1) would be shown as follows:

| Transaction | Total Assets | Liabilities | Owner's Equity |
|---|---|---|---|
| (1) | + | + | NC |

## PROBLEMS

### Group A

*1A-1* Listed below in random order are the items to be included in the balance sheet of Sun Basin Lodge at October 31, 19___. You are to prepare a balance sheet at October 31, using a sequence for assets similar to that in the illustrated balance sheet on page 15. Include a figure for total liabilities. The amount for John Chapman, capital, must be computed. Remember that the figure for total assets should appear on the same line as the amount for the total of liabilities and owner's equity.

| | | | |
|---|---|---|---|
| Notes payable | $91,000 | Accounts receivable | $ 3,150 |
| Land | 58,000 | Ski tow equipment | 48,500 |
| John Chapman, capital | ? | Office equipment | 1,225 |
| Cash | 2,225 | Accounts payable | 18,600 |
| Buildings | 86,000 | | |

**1A-2** While the accountant for Miller Company was on vacation, the balance sheet shown below was prepared by the owner of the business, Carl Miller, who had never studied accounting. Although the balance sheet appears to balance, it contains several errors in the location of items and in the headings. You are to prepare a corrected balance sheet using a sequence for assets similar to that shown in the illustrated balance sheet on page 15. Include a figure for total liabilities.

**MILLER COMPANY**
**For the Year Ended December 31, 19__**

| | | | |
|---|---|---|---|
| Land | $ 44,600 | Accounts payable | $127,604 |
| Building | 72,988 | Accounts receivable | 64,337 |
| Notes payable | 75,328 | Notes receivable | 40,000 |
| Carl Miller, capital | 50,102 | Office equipment | 14,268 |
| Cash | 10,016 | Delivery truck | 6,825 |
| Total assets | $253,034 | Total liabilities & owner's equity | $253,034 |

**1A-3** Five selected transactions of Canyon Company are summarized in the table below. The effect of each transaction upon the accounting equation is shown, and also the new balance of each item in the equation. For each of the transactions **(a)** through **(e),** you are to write a sentence explaining the nature of the transaction.

| | Assets | | | | | = Liabilities | + Owner's Equity |
|---|---|---|---|---|---|---|---|
| | Cash | + Accounts Receivable | + Land | + Building | + Office Equipment | = Accounts Payable | + J. Day, Capital |
| Balances | $3,000 | $9,000 | $8,000 | $21,000 | $3,000 | $4,000 | $40,000 |
| (a) | +500 | −500 | | | | | |
| Balances | $3,500 | $8,500 | $8,000 | $21,000 | $3,000 | $4,000 | $40,000 |
| (b) | | | | | +800 | +800 | |
| Balances | $3,500 | $8,500 | $8,000 | $21,000 | $3,800 | $4,800 | $40,000 |
| (c) | −200 | | | | | −200 | |
| Balances | $3,300 | $8,500 | $8,000 | $21,000 | $3,800 | $4,600 | $40,000 |
| (d) | −300 | | | | +900 | +600 | |
| Balances | $3,000 | $8,500 | $8,000 | $21,000 | $4,700 | $5,200 | $40,000 |
| (e) | +700 | | | | | | +700 |
| Balances | $3,700 | + $8,500 | + $8,000 | + $21,000 | + $4,700 | = $5,200 | + $40,700 |

**1A-4** Ames Office Services was organized on September 1 and completed the following transactions within a short time.

(1) J. Ames deposited $25,000 of personal funds in a bank account in the name of the new company.

(2) Purchased land and a building for a total price of $80,000, of which $30,000 was the value of the land and $50,000 was the value of the building. Paid $20,000 in cash and signed a note payable for the remaining $60,000.

(3) Bought office equipment on credit for $7,500 (30-day open account).

(4) Obtained a bank loan in the amount of $8,000. Signed a note payable.
(5) Paid $6,000 of the accounts payable.
(6) J. Ames invested an additional $2,000 of personal funds in the business by depositing cash in the company bank account.

**Instructions**

**a** Construct a tabular arrangement of the accounting equation similar to that illustrated on page 25. List the following assets, liabilities, and owner's equity as column headings: Cash, Land, Building, Office Equipment, Notes Payable, Accounts Payable, J. Ames, Capital.

**b** Use a separate line of the table to show the effects of each transaction on the assets, liabilities, and owner's equity. Identify each transaction by number along the left margin of the table. Show totals for all columns after transaction **(2)** and after each subsequent transaction.

*1A-5* During the period of organizing a business called Tony's Place, a balance sheet was prepared after each transaction. By studying these successive balance sheets, you can determine what transactions have occurred. You are to prepare a list of these transactions by date of occurrence. For example, the transaction leading to the balance sheet of October 1 could be described as follows: "On October 1, Tony Enrico invested $95,000 in cash and started the business called Tony's Place."

(1)

*TONY'S PLACE*
*Balance Sheet*
*October 1, 19__*

| Assets | | Owner's Equity | |
|---|---|---|---|
| Cash | $95,000 | Tony Enrico, capital | $95,000 |

(2)

*TONY'S PLACE*
*Balance Sheet*
*October 4, 19__*

| Assets | | Owner's Equity | |
|---|---|---|---|
| Cash | $60,000 | Tony Enrico, capital | $95,000 |
| Land | 35,000 | | |
| Total assets | $95,000 | Total owner's equity | $95,000 |

(3)

*TONY'S PLACE*
*Balance Sheet*
*October 26, 19__*

| Assets | | Liabilities & Owner's Equity | |
|---|---|---|---|
| Cash | $ 40,000 | Liabilities: | |
| Land | 35,000 | Notes payable | $ 50,000 |
| Building | 70,000 | Owner's equity: | |
| | | Tony Enrico, capital | 95,000 |
| Total assets | $145,000 | Total liabilities & owner's equity | $145,000 |

(4)

*TONY'S PLACE*
*Balance Sheet*
*November 10, 19__*

| Assets | | Liabilities & Owner's Equity | |
|---|---|---|---|
| Cash | $ 24,000 | Liabilities: | |
| Land | 35,000 | Notes payable | $ 40,000 |
| Building | 70,000 | Owner's equity: | |
| Equipment | 6,000 | Tony Enrico, capital | 95,000 |
| Total assets | $135,000 | Total liabilities & owner's equity | $135,000 |

*1A-6* The balance sheet items for Gremlin Auto Wash (arranged in alphabetical order) were as follows at August 1, 19__:

| | | | |
|---|---|---|---|
| Accounts payable | $ 4,000 | Land | $25,000 |
| Accounts receivable | 300 | Notes payable | 36,000 |
| Building | 20,000 | Supplies | 2,800 |
| Cash | 4,600 | Susan Young, capital | ? |
| Equipment | 26,000 | | |

During the next two days, the following transactions occurred:

**Aug. 2** Young invested an additional $15,000 cash in the business. The accounts payable were paid in full. (No payment was made on the notes payable.)

**Aug. 3** Equipment was purchased at a cost of $9,000 to be paid within 10 days. Supplies were purchased for $500 cash from another car-washing concern which was going out of business. These supplies would have cost $900 if purchased through normal channels.

**Instructions**

**a** Prepare a balance sheet at August 1, 19__.
**b** Prepare a balance sheet at August 3, 19__.

*1A-7* Hollywood Scripts is a service-type enterprise in the entertainment field, and its owner, Bradford Jones, has only a limited knowledge of accounting. Jones prepared the balance sheet below, which, although arranged satisfactorily, contains certain errors with respect to such concepts as the business entity and asset valuation.

*HOLLYWOOD SCRIPTS*
*Balance Sheet*
*November 30, 19__*

| Assets | | Liabilities & Owner's Equity | |
|---|---|---|---|
| Cash | $ 1,260 | Notes payable | $ 75,000 |
| Notes receivable | 4,500 | Accounts payable | 18,000 |
| Accounts receivable | 1,065 | Total liabilities | $ 93,000 |
| Land | 45,000 | Owner's equity: | |
| Building | 61,025 | Bradford Jones, capital | 45,958 |
| Office furniture | 6,843 | | |
| Other assets | 19,265 | | |
| Total assets | $138,958 | Total liabilities & owner's equity | $138,958 |

In discussion with Jones and by inspection of the accounting records, you discover the following facts.

(1) One of the notes receivable amounting to $3,000 is an IOU which Jones received in a poker game about ten years ago. The IOU bears only the initials B.K. and Jones does not know the name or address of the maker.
(2) Office furniture includes an antique desk purchased November 29 of the current year at a cost of $1,800. Jones explains that no payment is due for the desk until January and therefore this debt is not included among the liabilities.
(3) Also included in the amount for office furniture is a typewriter which cost $425 but is not on hand, because Jones gave it to a son as a birthday present.
(4) The "Other assets" of $19,265 represents the total amount of income taxes Jones has paid the federal government over a period of years. Jones believes the income tax law to be unconstitutional, and a friend who attends law school will help Jones recover the taxes paid as soon as he completes his legal education.
(5) The asset land was acquired at a cost of $25,000, but was increased to a valuation of $45,000 when a friend of Jones offered to pay that much for it if Jones would move the building off the lot.

**Instructions**

**a** Prepare a corrected balance sheet at November 30, 19___.
**b** For each of the five numbered items above, use a separate numbered paragraph to explain whether the treatment followed by Jones is in accord with generally accepted accounting principles.

## Group B

*1B-1* Prepare a balance sheet for the Sugarloaf Chalet as of June 30, 19___, from the random list of balance sheet items listed below. Use a similar sequence for assets as in the illustrated balance sheet on page 15. Include a figure for total liabilities. The figure for Karen Monday, capital, must be computed.

| | | | |
|---|---|---|---|
| *Accounts payable* | *$12,500* | *Snowmobiles* | *$ 8,200* |
| *Karen Monday, capital* | *?* | *Notes payable* | *60,000* |
| *Buildings* | *52,000* | *Equipment* | *25,000* |
| *Accounts receivable* | *11,250* | *Land* | *65,000* |
| *Cash* | *9,750* | | |

*1B-2* The items making up the balance sheet of Blue Sky Country at June 30 are listed below in tabular form similar to the illustration of the accounting equation on page 25.

| | Assets | | | | | | | = | Liabilities | | | + | Owner's Equity |
|---|---|---|---|---|---|---|---|---|---|---|---|---|---|
| | *Cash* | + | *Accounts Receivable* | + | *Automobiles* | + | *Office Equipment* | = | *Notes Payable* | + | *Accounts Payable* | + | *D. Hall, Capital* |
| *Balances* | *$6,500* | | *$58,400* | | *$6,000* | | *$3,800* | | *$20,000* | | *$25,200* | | *$29,500* |

During a short period after June 30, Blue Sky Country had the following transactions.

(1) Paid $1,200 of accounts payable.
(2) Collected $4,000 of accounts receivable.
(3) Bought office equipment at a cost of $5,700. Paid cash.
(4) Borrowed $10,000 from a bank. Signed a note payable for that amount.

(5) Purchased an automobile for $8,000. Paid $3,000 cash and signed a note payable for the balance of $5,000.

**Instructions**

**a** List the June 30 balances of assets, liabilities, and owner's equity in tabular form as shown above.

**b** Record the effects of each of the five transactions in the tabular arrangement illustrated above. Show the totals for all columns after each transaction.

***1B-3*** Five transactions of Barrel Company are summarized in the table below with each transaction identified by a number. The effect of each transaction upon the accounting equation is shown, and also the new balance of each item in the equation. For each of the transactions **(1)** through **(5)**, you are to write a sentence explaining the nature of the transaction.

| | Assets | | | | | | | | | = | Liabilities | + | Owner's Equity |
|---|---|---|---|---|---|---|---|---|---|---|---|---|---|
| | Cash | + | Accounts Receivable | + | Land | + | Building | + | Office Equipment | = | Accounts Payable | + | T. Lee, Capital |
| Balances | $2,000 | | $7,000 | | $29,000 | | $50,000 | | $7,000 | | $8,000 | | $87,000 |
| (1) | | | | | | | | | +700 | | +700 | | |
| Balances | $2,000 | | $7,000 | | $29,000 | | $50,000 | | $7,700 | | $8,700 | | $87,000 |
| (2) | +600 | | −600 | | | | | | | | | | |
| Balances | $2,600 | | $6,400 | | $29,000 | | $50,000 | | $7,700 | | $8,700 | | $87,000 |
| (3) | −400 | | | | | | | | | | −400 | | |
| Balances | $2,200 | | $6,400 | | $29,000 | | $50,000 | | $7,700 | | $8,300 | | $87,000 |
| (4) | −300 | | | | | | | | +1,300 | | +1,000 | | |
| Balances | $1,900 | | $6,400 | | $29,000 | | $50,000 | | $9,000 | | $9,300 | | $87,000 |
| (5) | +1,100 | | | | | | | | | | | | +1,100 |
| Balances | $3,000 | + | $6,400 | + | $29,000 | + | $50,000 | + | $9,000 | = | $9,300 | + | $88,100 |

***1B-4*** The following balance sheet of North Island, a business owned by William Madison, contains a number of errors in the placement of items and also in the headings. The dollar amounts of all items are correct. Prepare a corrected balance sheet, using a similar sequence for assets as in the illustrated balance sheet on page 15. Include a figure for total liabilities.

***NORTH ISLAND***

***For the Year Ended December 31, 19__***

| Assets | | Liabilities | |
|---|---|---|---|
| Cash | $ 10,850 | Notes payable | $ 40,000 |
| Accounts receivable | 52,750 | Accounts payable | 78,600 |
| Equity of owner | 38,700 | Delivery trucks | 12,750 |
| Land | 20,000 | Office equipment | 25,950 |
| Buildings | 35,000 | | |
| Total assets | $157,300 | Total liabilities & owner's equity | $157,300 |

***1B-5*** Helen Farr, a real estate broker, is sole proprietor of Condominiums, Etc. During the period of organizing the company, a balance sheet was prepared after each transaction. By studying this series of balance sheets, you can determine what transactions have occurred. You are to prepare a list of these transactions by date of occurrence. For example, the transaction leading to the balance sheet of July 1 could be described as follows: "On July 1, Helen Farr invested $120,000 cash and started the business of Condominiums, Etc."

**(1)**

**CONDOMINIUMS, ETC.**
**Balance Sheet**
**July 1, 19__**

| Assets | | Owner's Equity | |
|---|---|---|---|
| Cash | $120,000 | Helen Farr, capital | $120,000 |

**(2)**

**CONDOMINIUMS, ETC.**
**Balance Sheet**
**July 5, 19__**

| Assets | | Liabilities & Owner's Equity | |
|---|---|---|---|
| Cash | $ 69,600 | Liabilities: | |
| Land | 80,000 | Notes payable | $195,000 |
| Building | 165,400 | Owner's equity: | |
| | | Helen Farr, capital | 120,000 |
| Total assets | $315,000 | Total liabilities & owner's equity | $315,000 |

**(3)**

**CONDOMINIUMS, ETC.**
**Balance Sheet**
**July 18, 19__**

| Assets | | Liabilities & Owner's Equity | |
|---|---|---|---|
| Cash | $ 57,000 | Liabilities: | |
| Land | 80,000 | Notes payable | $195,000 |
| Building | 165,400 | Owner's equity: | |
| Office equipment | 12,600 | Helen Farr, capital | 120,000 |
| Total assets | $315,000 | Total liabilities & owner's equity | $315,000 |

**(4)**

**CONDOMINIUMS, ETC.**
**Balance Sheet**
**July 31, 19__**

| Assets | | Liabilities & Owner's Equity | |
|---|---|---|---|
| Cash | $ 33,200 | Liabilities: | |
| Land | 80,000 | Notes payable | $192,500 |
| Building | 165,400 | Owner's equity: | |
| Office equipment | 33,900 | Helen Farr, capital | 120,000 |
| Total assets | $312,500 | Total liabilities & owner's equity | $312,500 |

*1B-6* The following is a list of the balance sheet items of Rock Insurance Agency at May 31, 19___.

| | | | |
|---|---|---|---|
| *Accounts payable* | *$12,100* | *Cash* | *$ ?* |
| *Office equipment* | *7,200* | *Notes payable* | *10,000* |
| *J. Green, capital* | *52,900* | *Accounts receivable* | *15,400* |
| *Land* | *24,000* | *Building* | *26,000* |

Shortly after the above balance sheet date, the following transactions occurred.

**June 1** One-half of the land was sold at a price of $12,000, which was equal to its cost. A down payment of $2,000 cash was received on this date and the buyer agreed to pay the balance within 10 days.

**June 10** Cash in the amount of $10,000 was received from collection of an account receivable as final settlement from the buyer of the land. Also on this date, a cash payment of $1,100 was made on an account payable.

**Instructions**

**a** Prepare a balance sheet at May 31 from the list of balance sheet topics given in the first part of the problem. The amount for cash must be computed. Include an amount for total liabilities.

**b** Prepare a new balance sheet after the transaction of June 1, and a third balance sheet after the transactions on June 10.

*1B-7* John Mills resigned from a national firm of certified public accountants on October 1 to return home and begin a small public accounting practice. The following events all occurred during October while the business entity was being organized. Some of these events qualify as transactions; others do not. Some of the transactions are of a personal nature affecting the financial affairs of John Mills as an individual; others are business transactions affecting the business entity, John Mills, CPA. Thus, this problem calls for you to exercise judgment in applying the business entity concept and in recognizing transactions.

**Oct. 1** Sold personal investments consisting of government bonds and some General Motors stock for a total of $200,000 cash. Deposited $150,000 of this cash in a bank checking account in the name of the business, John Mills, CPA.

**Oct. 2** Because of concern over the prospects of severe inflation, Mills paid $50,000 for some gold bars and placed them in a personal safe deposit box rented at the local bank.

**Oct. 3** Purchased land with a small office building suitable for the new accounting practice. Total cost of the property was $180,000, of which $120,000 was allocable to land and $60,000 to building. A cash down payment of $100,000 was paid from the business bank account, and a note payable was issued for the balance calling for payment in five years or less.

**Oct. 4** A house painter came by the office and offered to paint the building during November if Mills in exchange would prepare the painter's income tax return at year-end. Mills agreed. The painter stated that the regular charge for painting the building would have been $600.

**Oct. 5** Purchased office equipment for cash of $6,500.

**Oct. 6** Mills moved a personal accounting library to the office with the purpose of investing this library as an asset of the business. Fair market value of the library was $1,200.

**Oct. 7** Mills worked eight hours on this date in arranging the office equipment and accounting library. The regular billing rate to clients was $40 an hour.

**Oct. 8** A well-known CPA firm opened an office directly across the street.

**Oct. 9** Mills agreed to employ a recent college graduate as staff assistant at a monthly salary of $1,500. The staff assistant was to report for work on November 1.

**Oct. 10** Mills purchased a dirt-track motorcycle to use on weekend trips, turning in an old motorcycle and paying a balance of $800 in cash.

**Oct. 11** Returned a defective chair included in the October 5 purchase of office equipment for full credit of $210. Received in exchange another model chair priced at $185 and a cash refund of $25, which was deposited in the business bank account.

**Oct. 12** On Sunday, while visiting a friend who was going out of business and entering military service, Mills had an opportunity to buy for $600 cash some office supplies which had originally cost $1,000. Mills used a personal check to pay for the supplies.

**Oct. 13** Mills brought to the office the office supplies purchased the previous day.

**Instructions**

**a** Prepare a list of those October events which do not qualify as transactions either for John Mills personally or for the business entity. Give reasons for your decision, such as "No present effect on assets or liabilities of Mills personally or of the business entity," or "Not completed action but merely the expression of an intent to do something in the future," or "Cannot be measured in dollars."

**b** Prepare a list of those October events which qualify as transactions but which are personal in nature, do not affect the business entity, and should not be included in the balance sheet of John Mills, CPA.

**c** Prepare a balance sheet at October 31 for the business entity, John Mills, CPA. The balance sheet should include only those October events which qualify as transactions affecting the business entity.

## BUSINESS DECISION PROBLEM 1

Case Company and Dale Company are in the same line of business and both were recently organized, so it may be assumed that the recorded costs for assets are close to current market values. The balance sheets for the two companies are as follows at October 31, 19___.

***CASE COMPANY***
***Balance Sheet***
***October 31, 19___***

| *Assets* | | *Liabilities & Owner's Equity* | |
|---|---|---|---|
| *Cash* | *$ 4,000* | *Liabilities:* | |
| *Accounts receivable* | *8,000* | *Notes payable* | |
| *Land* | *30,000* | *(due in 60 days)* | *$ 52,000* |
| *Building* | *50,000* | *Accounts payable* | *36,000* |
| *Office equipment* | *10,000* | *Total liabilities* | *$ 88,000* |
| | | *Owner's equity:* | |
| | | *Ted Case, capital* | *14,000* |
| *Total assets* | *$102,000* | *Total liabilities & owner's equity* | *$102,000* |

**DALE COMPANY**
**Balance Sheet**
**October 31, 19__**

| Assets | | Liabilities & Owner's Equity | |
|---|---|---|---|
| Cash | $20,000 | Liabilities: | |
| Accounts receivable | 40,000 | Notes payable | |
| Land | 16,000 | (due in 60 days) | $12,000 |
| Building | 20,000 | Accounts payable | 8,000 |
| Office equipment | 1,000 | Total liabilities | $20,000 |
| | | Owner's equity: | |
| | | Judy Dale, capital | 77,000 |
| Total assets | $97,000 | Total liabilities & owner's equity | $97,000 |

**Instructions**

**a** Assume that you are a banker and that each company has applied to you for a 90-day loan of $10,000. Which would you consider to be the more favorable prospect? Explain fully the factors affecting your decision.

**b** Assume that you are an investor considering the purchase of one or both of the companies. Both Ted Case and Judy Dale have indicated to you that they would consider selling their respective businesses. In either transaction you would assume the existing liabilities. For which business would you be willing to pay the higher price? Explain your answer fully. (It is recognized that, for either decision, additional information would be useful, but you are to reach your decisions on the basis of the information available.)

# 2

# RECORDING CHANGES IN FINANCIAL POSITION

Many business concerns have several hundred or even several thousand business transactions each day. It would obviously be impracticable to prepare a balance sheet after each transaction, and it is quite unnecessary to do so. Instead, the many individual transactions are recorded in the accounting records; and, at the end of the month or other accounting period, a balance sheet is prepared from these records. The purpose of this chapter is to demonstrate how business transactions are analyzed, entered in the accounting records, and stored for use in preparing balance sheets and other financial reports.

## The use of "accounts" for recording transactions

An accounting system includes a separate record for each item that appears in the balance sheet. For example, a separate record is kept for the asset cash, showing all the increases and decreases in cash which result from the many transactions in which cash is received or paid. A similar record is kept for every other asset, for every liability, and for owner's equity. The form of record used to record increases and decreases in a single balance sheet item is called an ***account,*** or sometimes a ***ledger account.*** All these separate accounts are usually kept in a loose-leaf binder, and the entire group of accounts is called a ***ledger.***

Today many businesses use computers for maintaining accounting records, and data may be stored on magnetic tapes rather than in ledgers. However, an understanding of accounting concepts is most easily acquired by study of a manual accounting system. The knowledge gained by working with manual accounting records is readily transferable to any type of automated accounting system. For these reasons, we shall use standard written accounting records such as ledger accounts as the model for our study of basic accounting concepts. These written records continue to be used by a great many businesses, but for our purposes they should be viewed as conceptual devices rather than as fixed and unchanging structural components of an accounting system.

## THE LEDGER

Ledger accounts are a means of accumulating in one place all the information about changes in specific assets, liabilities, and owner's equity. For example, a ledger account for the asset cash provides a record of the amount of cash receipts, cash payments, and the current cash balance. By maintaining a Cash account, management can keep track of the amount of cash available for meeting payrolls and for making current purchases of assets or services. This record of cash is also useful in planning future operations and in advance planning of applications for bank loans. The development of the annual budget requires estimating in advance the expected receipts and payments of cash; these estimates of cash flow are naturally based to some extent on the ledger accounts showing past cash receipts and payments.

In its simplest form, an account has only three elements: (1) a title, consisting of the name of the particular asset, liability, or owner's equity; (2) a left side, which is called the ***debit*** side; and (3) a right side, which is called the ***credit*** side. This form of account, illustrated below, is called a ***T account*** because of its resemblance to the letter T. More complete forms of accounts will be illustrated later.

***T account: a ledger account in simplified form***

| *Title of Account* | |
|---|---|
| ***Left or debit side*** | ***Right or credit side*** |

### Debit and credit entries

An amount recorded on the left or debit side of an account is called a ***debit,*** or a ***debit entry;*** an amount entered on the right or credit side is called a ***credit,*** or a ***credit entry.*** Accountants also use the words debit and credit as verbs. The act of recording a debit in an account is called ***debiting*** the account; the recording of a credit is called ***crediting*** the account. A debit to an account is also sometimes called a ***charge*** to the account; an account is debited or ***charged*** when an amount is entered on the left side of the account.

Students beginning a course in accounting often have preconceived but erroneous notions about the meanings of the terms debit and credit. For example, to some people unacquainted with accounting, the word credit may carry a more favorable connotation than does the word debit. Such connotations have no validity in the field of accounting. Accountants use ***debit*** to mean an entry on the left-hand side of an account, and ***credit*** to mean an entry on the right-hand side. The student should therefore regard debit and credit as simple equivalents of left and right, without any hidden or subtle implications.

To illustrate the recording of debits and credits in an account, let us go back to the cash transactions of Roberts Real Estate Company as illustrated in Chapter 1. When these cash transactions are recorded in an account, the receipts are listed in vertical order on the debit side of the account and the payments are listed on the credit side. The dates of the transactions may also be listed, as shown in the following illustration:

**Cash transactions entered in ledger account**

***Cash***

| | | | | |
|---|---|---|---|---|
| *9/1* | | *60,000* | *9/3* | *21,000* |
| *9/20* | 22,500 | *1,500* | *9/5* | *15,000* |
| | | 61,500 | *9/30* | *3,000* |
| | | | | 39,000 |

Note that the total of the cash receipts, $61,500, is in small-size figures so that it will not be mistaken for a debit entry. The total of the cash payments (credits), amounting to $39,000, is also in small-size figures to distinguish it from the credit entries. These ***footings,*** or memorandum totals, are merely a convenient step in determining the amount of cash on hand at the end of the month. The difference in dollars between the total debits and the total credits in an account is called the ***balance.*** If the debits exceed the credits the account has a ***debit balance***; if the credits exceed the debits the account has a ***credit balance.*** In the illustrated Cash account, the debit total of $61,500 is larger than the credit total of $39,000; therefore, the account has a debit balance. By subtracting the credits from the debits ($61,500 − $39,000), we determine that the balance of the Cash account is $22,500. This debit balance is noted on the debit (left) side of the account. The balance of the Cash account represents the amount of cash owned by the business on September 30; in a balance sheet prepared at this date, Cash in the amount of $22,500 would be listed as an asset.

**Debit balances in asset accounts** In the preceding illustration of a cash account, increases were recorded on the left or debit side of the account and decreases were recorded on the right or credit side. The increases were greater than the decreases and the result was a debit balance in the account.

All asset accounts normally have debit balances; in fact, the ownership of cash, land, or any other asset indicates that the increases (debits) to that asset have been greater than the decreases (credits). It is hard to imagine an account for an asset such as land having a credit balance, as this would indicate that the business had disposed of more land than it had acquired and had reached the impossible position of having a negative amount of land.

The balance sheets previously illustrated in Chapter 1 showed all the assets on the left side of the balance sheet. For your convenience in recalling the basic structure of a balance sheet, the fundamental accounting equation is again presented:

**Assets = Liabilities + Owner's Equity**

Remember that the balance sheet is simply a detailed statement of this equation, as shown by the following balance sheet:

***ROBERTS REAL ESTATE COMPANY***
***Balance Sheet***
***September 30, 19__***

| *Assets* | | *Liabilities & Owner's Equity* | |
|---|---|---|---|
| *Cash* | *$22,500* | *Liabilities:* | |
| *Accounts receivable* | *4,500* | *Accounts payable* | *$23,400* |
| *Land* | *15,000* | *Owner's equity:* | |
| *Building* | *36,000* | *James Roberts, capital* | *60,000* |
| *Office equipment* | *5,400* | | |
| *Total assets* | *$83,400* | *Total liabilities & owner's equity* | *$83,400* |

The fact that assets are located on the left side of the balance sheet is a convenient means of remembering the rule that an increase in an asset is recorded on the ***left*** (debit) side of the account, and also that an asset account normally has a debit (***left-hand***) balance.

***Any Asset Account***

*Asset accounts normally have debit balances*

| *(Debit)* | *(Credit)* |
|---|---|
| *Increase* | *Decrease* |

**Credit balances in liability and owner's equity accounts** Increases in liability and owner's equity accounts are recorded by credit entries and decreases in these accounts are recorded by debits. The relationship between entries in these accounts and their position on the balance sheet may be summed up as follows: (1) liabilities and owner's equity belong on the ***right*** side of the balance sheet; (2) an increase in a liability or an owner's equity account is recorded on the ***right*** (credit) side of the account; and (3) liability and owner's equity accounts normally have credit (***right-hand***) balances.

***Any Liability Account***
***or Owner's Equity Account***

*Liability and owner's equity accounts normally have credit balances*

| *(Debit)* | *(Credit)* |
|---|---|
| *Decrease* | *Increase* |

The diagram below emphasizes again the relationship between the position of an account in the balance sheet and the method of recording an increase or decrease in the account. The accounts used are those previously shown in the balance sheet (page 46) prepared for Roberts Real Estate Company.

*Diagram of balance sheet accounts*

***Balance Sheet Accounts***

| *(Left side of balance sheet)* Assets | = | *(Right side of balance sheet)* Liabilities + Owner's Equity |
|---|---|---|

**Cash**

| *(Debit)* | *(Credit)* |
|---|---|
| *Increase* | *Decrease* |

**Accounts Receivable**

| *(Debit)* | *(Credit)* |
|---|---|
| *Increase* | *Decrease* |

**Land**

| *(Debit)* | *(Credit)* |
|---|---|
| *Increase* | *Decrease* |

**Building**

| *(Debit)* | *(Credit)* |
|---|---|
| *Increase* | *Decrease* |

**Office Equipment**

| *(Debit)* | *(Credit)* |
|---|---|
| *Increase* | *Decrease* |

**Accounts payable**

| *(Debit)* | *(Credit)* |
|---|---|
| *Decrease* | *Increase* |

**James Roberts, Capital**

| *(Debit)* | *(Credit)* |
|---|---|
| *Decrease* | *Increase* |

**Concise statement of the rules of debit and credit** The rules of debit and credit, which have been explained and illustrated in the preceding sections, may be concisely summarized as follows:

*Mechanics of debit and credit*

| *Asset Accounts* | *Liability & Owner's Equity Accounts* |
|---|---|
| *Increases are recorded by debits* | *Increases are recorded by credits* |
| *Decreases are recorded by credits* | *Decreases are recorded by debits* |

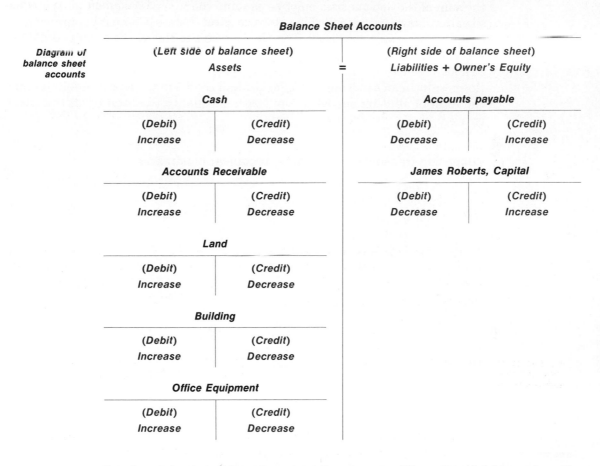

**Equality of debits and credits** Every business transaction affects two or more accounts. The ***double-entry system,*** which is the system in almost universal use, takes its name from the fact that ***equal debit and credit entries are made for every transaction.*** If only two accounts are affected (as in the purchase of land for cash), one account, Land, is debited and the other account, Cash, is credited for the same amount. If more than two accounts are affected by a transaction, the sum of the debit entries must be equal to the sum of the credit entries. This situation was illustrated when Roberts Real Estate Company purchased a building for a price of $36,000. The $36,000 debit to the asset account, Building, was exactly equal to the total of the $15,000 credit to the Cash account plus the $21,000 credit to the liability account, Accounts Payable. Since every transaction results in an equal amount of debits and credits in the ledger, it follows that the total of all debit entries in the ledger is equal to the total of all the credit entries.

## Recording transactions in ledger accounts: illustration

The procedure for recording transactions in ledger accounts will be illustrated by using the September transactions of Roberts Real Estate Company. Each transaction will first be analyzed in terms of increases and decreases in assets, liabilities, and owner's equity. Then we shall follow the rules of debit and credit in entering these increases and decreases in T accounts. Asset accounts will be shown on the left side of the page; liability and owner's equity accounts on the right side. For convenience in following the transactions into the ledger accounts, the letter used to identify a given transaction will also appear opposite the debit and credit entries for that transaction. This use of identifying letters is for illustrative purposes only and is not used in actual accounting practice.

**Transaction (a)** Roberts invested $60,000 cash in the business on September 1.

***Recording an investment in the business***

| *Analysis* | *Rule* | *Entry* |
|---|---|---|
| *The asset Cash was increased* | *Increases in assets are recorded by debits* | *Debit: Cash, $60,000* |
| *The owner's equity was increased* | *Increases in owner's equity are recorded by credits* | *Credit: James Roberts, Capital, $60,000* |

**Cash**

| | |
|---|---|
| *9/1 (a) 60,000* | |

**James Roberts, Capital**

| | |
|---|---|
| | *9/1 (a) 60,000* |

**Transaction (b)** On September 3, Roberts Real Estate Company purchased land for cash in the amount of $21,000.

*Purchase of land for cash*

| Analysis | Rule | Entry |
|---|---|---|
| *The asset Land was increased* | *Increases in assets are recorded by debits* | *Debit: Land, $21,000* |
| *The asset Cash was decreased* | *Decreases in assets are recorded by credits* | *Credit: Cash, $21,000* |

**Cash**

| | | | |
|---|---|---|---|
| 9/1 | 60,000 | 9/3 | (b) 21,000 |

**Land**

| | | | |
|---|---|---|---|
| 9/3 | (b) 21,000 | | |

**Transaction (c)** On September 5, Roberts Real Estate Company purchased a building from OK Company at a total price of $36,000. The terms of the purchase required a cash payment of $15,000 with the remainder of $21,000 payable within 90 days.

*Purchase of an asset, with partial payment*

| Analysis | Rule | Entry |
|---|---|---|
| *A new asset, Building, was acquired* | *Increases in assets are recorded by debits* | *Debit: Building, $36,000* |
| *The asset Cash was decreased* | *Decreases in assets are recorded by credits* | *Credit: Cash, $15,000* |
| *A new liability, Accounts Payable, was incurred* | *Increases in liabilities are recorded by credits* | *Credit: Accounts Payable, $21,000* |

**Cash**

| | | | |
|---|---|---|---|
| 9/1 | 60,000 | 9/3 | 21,000 |
| | | 9/5 | (c) 15,000 |

**Accounts Payable**

| | | | |
|---|---|---|---|
| | | 9/5 | (c) 21,000 |

**Building**

| | | | |
|---|---|---|---|
| 9/5 | (c) 36,000 | | |

**Transaction (d)** On September 10, Roberts Real Estate Company sold a portion of its land on credit to Carter's Drugstore for a price of $6,000. The land was sold at its cost, so there was no gain or loss on the transaction.

| | Analysis | Rule | Entry |
|---|---|---|---|
| Sale of land on credit (no gain or loss) | A new asset, Accounts Receivable, was acquired | Increases in assets are recorded by debits | Debit: Accounts Receivable, $6,000 |
| | The asset Land was decreased | Decreases in assets are recorded by credits | Credit: Land, $6,000 |

**Accounts Receivable**

| | | | |
|---|---|---|---|
| 9/10 | (d) 6,000 | | |

**Land**

| | | | |
|---|---|---|---|
| 9/3 | 21,000 | 9/10 | (d) 6,000 |

**Transaction (e)** On September 14, Roberts Real Estate Company purchased office equipment on credit from General Equipment, Inc., in the amount of $5,400.

| | Analysis | Rule | Entry |
|---|---|---|---|
| Purchase of an asset on credit | A new asset, Office Equipment, was acquired | Increases in assets are recorded by debits | Debit: Office Equipment $5,400 |
| | A new liability, Accounts Payable, was incurred | Increases in liabilities are recorded by credits | Credit: Accounts Payable, $5,400 |

**Office Equipment**

| | | | |
|---|---|---|---|
| 9/14 | (e) 5,400 | | |

**Accounts Payable**

| | | | |
|---|---|---|---|
| | | 9/5 | 21,000 |
| | | 9/14 | (e) 5,400 |

**Transaction (f)** On September 20, cash of $1,500 was received as partial collection of the account receivable from Carter's Drugstore.

| | Analysis | Rule | Entry |
|---|---|---|---|
| Collection of an account receivable | The asset Cash was increased | Increases in assets are recorded by debits | Debit: Cash, $1,500 |
| | The asset Accounts Receivable was decreased | Decreases in assets are recorded by credits | Credit: Accounts Receivable, $1,500 |

**Cash**

| | | | |
|---|---|---|---|
| 9/1 | 60,000 | 9/3 | 21,000 |
| 9/20 | (f) 1,500 | 9/5 | 15,000 |

**Accounts Receivable**

| | | | |
|---|---|---|---|
| 9/10 | 6,000 | 9/20 | (f) 1,500 |

**Transaction (g)** A cash payment of $3,000 was made on September 30 in partial settlement of the amount owing to General Equipment, Inc.

*Payment of a liability*

| Analysis | Rule | Entry |
|---|---|---|
| *The liability Accounts Payable was decreased* | *Decreases in liabilities are recorded by debits* | *Debit: Accounts Payable, $3,000* |
| *The asset Cash was decreased* | *Decreases in assets are recorded by credits* | *Credit: Cash, $3,000* |

**Cash**

| | | | |
|---|---|---|---|
| 9/1 | 60,000 | 9/3 | 21,000 |
| 9/20 | 1,500 | 9/5 | 15,000 |
| | | 9/30 | (g) 3,000 |

**Accounts Payable**

| | | | |
|---|---|---|---|
| 9/30 | (g) 3,000 | 9/5 | 21,000 |
| | | 9/14 | 5,400 |

## Running balance form of ledger account

The T form of account used thus far is very convenient for illustrative purposes. Details are avoided and we can concentrate on basic ideas. T accounts are also often used in advanced accounting courses and by professional accountants for preliminary analysis of a transaction. In other words, the simplicity of the T account provides a concise conceptual picture of the elements of a business transaction. In formal accounting records, however, more information is needed, and the T account is replaced in many manual accounting systems by a ledger account with special rulings, such as the following illustration of the Cash account for Roberts Real Estate Company:

*Ledger account with a balance column*

**Cash** — Account No.

| Date | | Explanation | Ref | Debit | Credit | Balance |
|---|---|---|---|---|---|---|
| 19— Sept. | 1 | | | 60000 00 | | 60000 00 |
| | 3 | | | | 21000 00 | 39000 00 |
| | 5 | | | | 15000 00 | 24000 00 |
| | 20 | | | 1500 00 | | 25500 00 |
| | 30 | | | | 3000 00 | 22500 00 |

The ***Date*** column shows the date of the transaction—which is not necessarily the same as the date the entry is made in the account. The ***Explanation*** column is needed only for unusual items, and in many companies it is seldom used. The ***Ref*** (Reference) column is used to list the page number of the journal in which the transaction is recorded, thus making it possible to trace ledger entries back to their source (a journal). The use of a ***journal*** is explained later in this chapter. In the ***Balance*** column of the account, the new balance is entered each time the account is debited or credited. Thus the current balance of the account can always be observed at a glance.

Although we will make extensive use of this three-column running balance form of account in later chapters, there will also be many situations in which we shall continue to use T accounts to achieve simplicity in illustrating accounting principles and procedures.

### The normal balance of an account

The running balance form of ledger account does not indicate specifically whether the balance of the account is a debit or credit balance. However, this causes no difficulty because we know that asset accounts normally have debit balances and that accounts for liabilities and owner's equity normally have credit balances.

The balance of any account normally results from recording more increases than decreases. In asset accounts, increases are recorded as debits, so asset accounts normally have debit balances. In liability and owner's equity accounts, increases are recorded as credits, so these accounts normally have credit balances.

Occasionally an asset account may temporarily acquire a credit balance, either as the result of an accounting error or because of an unusual transaction. For example, an account receivable may acquire a credit balance because of overpayment by a customer. However, a credit balance in the Building account could be created only by an accounting error.

### Sequence and numbering of ledger accounts

Accounts are usually arranged in the ledger in ***financial statement order,*** that is, assets first, followed by liabilities, owner's equity, revenue, and expenses. The number of accounts needed by a business will depend upon its size, the nature of its operations, and the extent to which management and regulatory agencies want detailed classification of information. An identification number is assigned to each account. A ***chart of accounts*** is a listing of the account titles and account numbers being used by a given business.

In the following list of accounts, certain numbers have not been assigned; these numbers are held in reserve so that additional accounts can be inserted in the ledger in proper sequence whenever such accounts become necessary. In this illustration, the numbers from 1 to 29 are used exclusively for asset accounts; numbers from 30 to 49 are reserved for liabilities; numbers in the 50s signify owner's equity accounts; numbers in the 60s represent revenue accounts and numbers from 70 to 99 designate expense accounts. The balance sheet accounts with which we are concerned in this chapter are numbered as shown in the following brief chart of accounts:

*System for numbering ledger accounts*

| ***Account Title*** | ***Account No.*** |
|---|---|
| ***Assets:*** | |
| *Cash* | *1* |
| *Accounts Receivable* | *2* |
| *Land* | *20* |
| *Building* | *22* |
| *Office Equipment* | *25* |
| ***Liabilities:*** | |
| *Accounts Payable* | *30* |
| ***Owner's Equity:*** | |
| *James Roberts, Capital* | *50* |

In large businesses with hundreds or thousands of accounts, a more elaborate numbering system is used. Some companies use a four-digit number for each ledger account; each of the four digits carries special significance as to the classification of the account.

**Sequence of asset accounts** At this point we need to give further attention to the sequence of accounts within the asset group. As shown in all the balance sheets illustrated thus far, cash is always listed first. It is followed by accounts receivable, notes receivable, and supplies. Next come the relatively permanent assets used in the business (often called ***plant assets***). Of this group, land is listed first and followed by buildings. After these two items, any order is acceptable for other assets used in the business, such as automobiles, furniture and fixtures, computers, lighting equipment, store equipment, etc.

## Flow of information through the accounting system

The term ***business transaction,*** as explained in Chapter 1, means ***a business event which can be expressed in money and must be recorded in the accounting records.*** Common examples are the payment or collection of cash, a purchase or sale on credit, and the withdrawal of assets by the owner of a business. Note that a transaction has an accounting value and has an influence on the financial statements. Events such as the opening of a competing business or the retirement of an employee, although possibly of importance to the business, are not considered to be transactions and are not entered in the accounts.

Business transactions are evidenced by ***business documents*** such as a check, a sales ticket, or a cash register tape. These business documents are the starting point for the flow of accounting information through the accounting system into the financial statements. In our description of the accounting process thus far, emphasis has been placed on the analysis of transactions in terms of debits and credits to ledger accounts. Although transactions ***could*** be entered directly in ledger accounts, it is much more convenient and efficient in a manual accounting system to record the information shown on business documents first in a ***journal*** and later to transfer the debits and credits to ledger accounts.

## THE JOURNAL

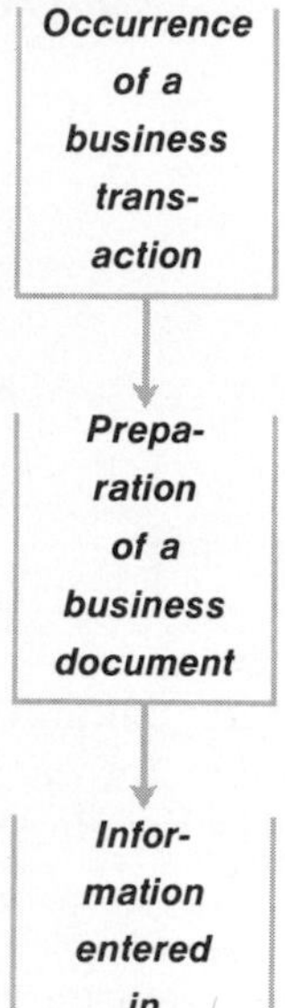


The *journal,* or book of original entry, is a chronological (day-by-day) record, showing for each transaction the debit and credit changes caused in specific ledger accounts. A brief explanation is also included for each transaction. At convenient intervals, the debit and credit entries recorded in the journal are transferred to the accounts in the ledger. The updated ledger accounts, in turn, serve as the basis from which the balance sheet and other financial statements are prepared. The flow chart on the left illustrates the sequence of steps by which information flows through the accounting system.

The unit of organization for the journal is the transaction, whereas the unit of organization for the ledger is the account. By making use of both a journal and a ledger, we can achieve several advantages which are not possible if transactions are recorded directly in ledger accounts:

1 ***The journal shows all information about a transaction in one place and also provides an explanation of the transaction.*** In a journal entry, the debits and credits for a given transaction are recorded together, but when the transaction is recorded in the ledger, the debits and credits are entered in different accounts. Since a ledger may contain hundreds of accounts, it would be very difficult to locate all the facts about a particular transaction by looking in the ledger. The journal is the record which shows the complete story of a transaction in one entry.

2 ***The journal provides a chronological record of all the events in the life of a business.*** If we want to look up the facts about a transaction of some months or years back, all we need is the date of the transaction in order to locate it in the journal.

3 ***The use of a journal helps to prevent errors.*** If transactions were recorded directly in the ledger, it would be very easy to make errors such as omitting the debit or the credit, or entering the debit twice or the credit twice. Such errors are not likely to be made in the journal, since the offsetting debits and credits appear together for each transaction. It is of course possible to forget to transfer a debit or credit from the journal to a ledger account, but such an error can be detected by tracing the entries in the ledger accounts back to the journal.

### The general journal: illustration of entries

Many businesses maintain several types of journals. The nature of operations and the volume of transactions in the particular business determine the number and type of journals needed. The simplest type of journal is called a ***general journal.*** It has only two money columns, one for debits and the other for credits; it may be used for all types of transactions.

The process of recording a transaction in a journal is called ***journalizing*** the transaction. To illustrate the use of the general journal, we shall now journalize the transactions of Roberts Real Estate Company which have been discussed previously.

*September journal entries for Roberts Real Estate Company*

*General Journal* — *Page 1*

| Date | | Account Titles and Explanation | LP | Debit | Credit |
|---|---|---|---|---|---|
| 19__ | | | | | |
| Sept. | 1 | Cash | 1 | 60,000 | |
| | | James Roberts, Capital | 50 | | 60,000 |
| | | Invested cash in the business. | | | |
| | 3 | Land | 20 | 21,000 | |
| | | Cash | 1 | | 21,000 |
| | | Purchased land for office site. | | | |
| | 5 | Building | 22 | 36,000 | |
| | | Cash | 1 | | 15,000 |
| | | Accounts Payable | 30 | | 21,000 |
| | | Purchased building to be moved to our lot. Paid part cash; balance payable within 90 days to OK Company. | | | |
| | 10 | Accounts Receivable | 2 | 6,000 | |
| | | Land | 20 | | 6,000 |
| | | Sold the unused part of our lot at cost to Carter's Drugstore. Due within three months. | | | |
| | 14 | Office Equipment | 25 | 5,400 | |
| | | Accounts Payable | 30 | | 5,400 |
| | | Purchased office equipment on credit from General Equipment, Inc. | | | |
| | 20 | Cash | 1 | 1,500 | |
| | | Accounts Receivable | 2 | | 1,500 |
| | | Collected part of receivable from Carter's Drugstore. | | | |
| | 30 | Accounts Payable | 30 | 3,000 | |
| | | Cash | 1 | | 3,000 |
| | | Made partial payment of the liability to General Equipment, Inc. | | | |

Efficient use of a general journal requires two things: (1) ability to analyze the effect of a transaction upon assets, liabilities, and owner's equity; and (2) familiarity with the standard form and arrangement of journal entries. Our primary interest is in the analytical phase of journalizing; the procedural steps can be learned quickly by observing the following points in the illustrations of journal entries shown above:

1 The year, month, and day of the first entry on the page are written in the date column. The year and month need not be repeated for subsequent entries until a new page or a new month is begun.
2 The name of the account to be debited is written on the first line of the entry and is customarily placed at the extreme left next to the date column. The amount of the debit is entered on the same line in the ***left-hand*** money column.
3 The name of the account to be credited is entered on the line below the debit entry and is ***indented,*** that is, placed about 1 inch to the right of the date column. The amount credited is entered on the same line in the ***right-hand*** money column.
4 A brief explanation of the transaction is usually begun on the line immediately below the last account credited. The explanation need not be indented.
5 A blank line is usually left after each entry. This spacing causes each journal entry to stand out clearly as a separate unit and makes the journal easier to read.
6 An entry which includes more than one debit or more than one credit (such as the entry on September 5) is called a ***compound journal entry.*** Regardless of how many debits or credits are contained in a compound journal entry, all the debits are customarily entered before any credits are listed.
7 The LP (ledger page) column just to the left of the debit money column is left blank at the time of making the journal entry. When the debits and credits are later transferred to ledger accounts, the numbers of the ledger accounts are listed in this column to provide a convenient cross reference with the ledger.

In journalizing transactions, remember that the exact title of the ledger accounts to be debited and credited should be used. For example, in recording the purchase of office equipment for cash, ***do not*** make a journal entry debiting "Office Equipment Purchased" and crediting "Cash Paid Out." There are no ledger accounts with such titles. The proper journal entry would consist of a debit to ***Office Equipment*** and a credit to ***Cash.***

A familiarity with the general journal form of describing transactions is just as essential to the study of accounting as a familiarity with plus and minus signs is to the study of mathematics. The journal entry is a ***tool*** for ***analyzing*** and ***describing*** the impact of various transactions upon a business entity. The ability to describe a transaction in journal entry form requires an understanding of the nature of the transaction and its effects upon the financial position of the business.

## Posting

The process of transferring the debits and credits from the general journal to the proper ledger accounts is called ***posting.*** Each amount listed in the debit column of the journal is posted by entering it on the debit side of an account in the ledger, and each amount listed in the credit column of the journal is posted to the credit side of a ledger account.

The mechanics of posting may vary somewhat with the preferences of the individual. The following sequence is commonly used:

1 Locate in the ledger the first account named in the journal entry.
2 Enter in the debit column of the ledger account the amount of the debit as shown in the journal.
3 Enter the date of the transaction in the ledger account.
4 Enter in the reference column of the ledger account the number of the journal page from which the entry is being posted.
5 The recording of the debit in the ledger account is now complete; as evidence of this fact, return to the journal and enter in the LP (ledger page) column the number of the ledger account or page to which the debit was posted.
6 Repeat the posting process described in the preceding five steps for the credit side of the journal entry.

**Illustration of posting** To illustrate the posting process, the journal entry for the first transaction of Roberts Real Estate Company is repeated at this point along with the two ledger accounts affected by this entry.

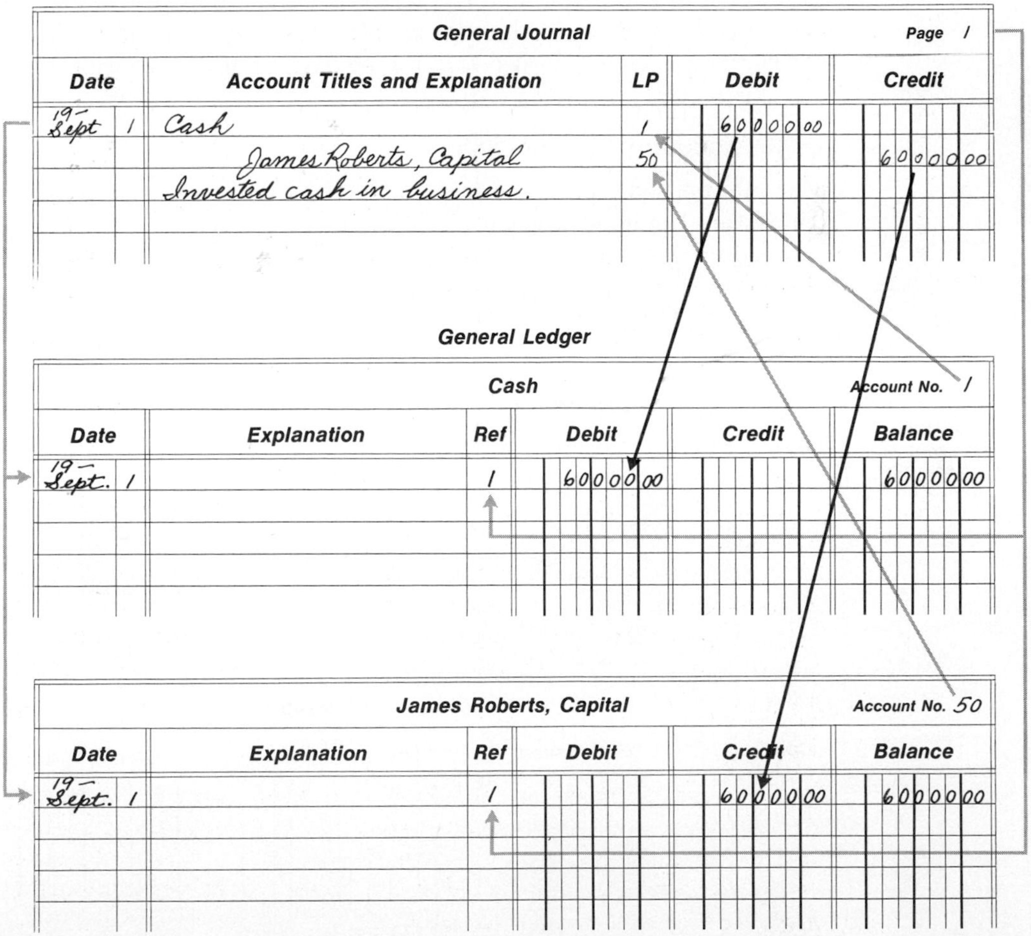

Note that the Ref (Reference) column of each of the two ledger accounts illustrated above contains the number 1, indicating that the posting was made from page 1 of the journal. Entering the journal page number in the ledger account and listing the ledger account number in the journal provide a cross reference between these two records. The audit of accounting records always requires looking up some journal entries to obtain more information about the amounts listed in ledger accounts. A cross reference between the ledger and journal is therefore essential to efficient audit of the records. Another advantage gained from entering in the journal the number of the account to which a posting has been made is to provide evidence throughout the posting work as to which items have been posted. Otherwise, any interruption in the posting might leave some doubt as to what had been posted.

Journalizing and posting by hand is a useful method for the study of accounting, both for problem assignments and for examinations. The manual approach is also followed in many small businesses. One shortcoming is the opportunity for error that exists whenever information is being copied from one record to another. In businesses having a large volume of transactions, the posting of ledger accounts is performed by accounting machines or by a computer, which speeds up the work and reduces errors. In these more sophisticated applications, transactions may be recorded simultaneously in both the journal and the ledger.

## Ledger accounts after posting

After all the September transactions have been posted, the ledger of Roberts Real Estate Company appears as shown below and on page 59. The accounts are arranged in the ledger in the same order as in the balance sheet, that is, assets first, followed by liabilities and owner's equity.

*Ledger showing September transactions*

**Cash** — Account No. 1

| Date | | Explanation | Ref | Debit | Credit | Balance |
|---|---|---|---|---|---|---|
| 19— Sept. | 1 | | 1 | 60,000.00 | | 60,000.00 |
| | 3 | | 1 | | 21,000.00 | 39,000.00 |
| | 5 | | 1 | | 15,000.00 | 24,000.00 |
| | 20 | | 1 | 1,500.00 | | 25,500.00 |
| | 30 | | 1 | | 3,000.00 | 22,500.00 |

**Accounts Receivable** — Account No. 2

| Date | | Explanation | Ref | Debit | Credit | Balance |
|---|---|---|---|---|---|---|
| 19— Sept. | 10 | | 1 | 6,000.00 | | 6,000.00 |
| | 20 | | 1 | | 1,500.00 | 4,500.00 |

**Land** — Account No. 20

| Date | | Explanation | Ref | Debit | Credit | Balance |
|---|---|---|---|---|---|---|
| 19— Sept. | 3 | | 1 | 21,000 00 | | 21,000 00 |
| | 10 | | 1 | | 6,000 00 | 15,000 00 |

**Building** — Account No. 22

| Date | | Explanation | Ref | Debit | Credit | Balance |
|---|---|---|---|---|---|---|
| 19— Sept. | 5 | | 1 | 36,000 00 | | 36,000 00 |

**Office Equipment** — Account No. 25

| Date | | Explanation | Ref | Debit | Credit | Balance |
|---|---|---|---|---|---|---|
| 19— Sept. | 14 | | 1 | 5,400 00 | | 5,400 00 |

**Accounts Payable** — Account No. 30

| Date | | Explanation | Ref | Debit | Credit | Balance |
|---|---|---|---|---|---|---|
| 19— Sept. | 5 | | 1 | | 21,000 00 | 21,000 00 |
| | 14 | | 1 | | 5,400 00 | 26,400 00 |
| | 30 | | 1 | 3,000 00 | | 23,400 00 |

**James Roberts, Capital** — Account No. 50

| Date | | Explanation | Ref | Debit | Credit | Balance |
|---|---|---|---|---|---|---|
| 19— Sept. | 1 | | 1 | | 60,000 00 | 60,000 00 |

## THE TRIAL BALANCE

Since equal dollar amounts of debits and credits are entered in the accounts for every transaction recorded, the sum of all the debits in the ledger must be equal to the sum of all the credits. If the computation of account balances has been accurate, it follows that the total of the accounts with debit balances must be equal to the total of the accounts with credit balances.

Before using the account balances to prepare a balance sheet, it is desirable to ***prove*** that the total of accounts with debit balances is in fact equal to the total of accounts with credit balances. This proof of the equality of debit and credit balances is called a ***trial balance.*** A trial balance is a two-column schedule listing the names and balances of all the accounts ***in the order in which they appear in the ledger***; the debit balances are listed in the left-hand column and the credit balances in the right-hand column. The totals of the two columns should agree. A trial balance taken from the ledger of Roberts Real Estate Company appears below.

***ROBERTS REAL ESTATE COMPANY***
***Trial Balance***
***September 30, 19__***

*Trial balance at month-end proves ledger is in balance*

| | | |
|---|---|---|
| Cash | $22,500 | |
| Accounts receivable | 4,500 | |
| Land | 15,000 | |
| Building | 36,000 | |
| Office equipment | 5,400 | |
| Accounts payable | | $23,400 |
| James Roberts, capital | | 60,000 |
| | $83,400 | $83,400 |

## Uses and limitations of the trial balance

The trial balance provides proof that the ledger is in balance. The agreement of the debit and credit totals of the trial balance gives assurance that:

**1** Equal debits and credits have been recorded for all transactions.
**2** The debit or credit balance of each account has been correctly computed.
**3** The addition of the account balances in the trial balance has been correctly performed.

Suppose that the debit and credit totals of the trial balance do not agree. This situation indicates that one or more errors have been made. Typical of such errors are (1) the entering of a debit as a credit, or vice versa; (2) arithmetic mistakes in balancing accounts; (3) clerical errors in copying account balances into the trial balance; (4) listing a debit balance in the credit column of the trial balance, or vice versa; and (5) errors in addition of the trial balance.

The preparation of a trial balance does not prove that transactions have been correctly analyzed and recorded in the proper accounts. If, for example, a receipt of cash were erroneously recorded by debiting the Land account instead of the Cash account, the trial balance would still balance. Also, if a transaction were completely omitted from the ledger, the error would not be disclosed by the trial balance. In brief, ***the trial balance proves only one aspect of the ledger, and that is the equality of debits and credits.***

Despite these limitations, the trial balance is a useful device. It not only provides assurance that the ledger is in balance, but it also serves as a convenient steppingstone for the preparation of financial statements. As explained in Chapter 1, the balance sheet is a formal statement showing the financial position of the business, intended for distribution to managers, owners, bankers, and various outsiders. The trial balance, on the other hand, is merely a working paper, useful to the accountant but not intended for distribution to others. The balance sheet and other financial statements can be prepared more conveniently from the trial balance than directly from the ledger, especially if there are a great many ledger accounts.

## Locating errors

In the illustration given, the trial balance was in balance. Every accounting student soon discovers in working problems, however, that errors are easily made which prevent trial balances from balancing. The lack of balance may be the result of a single error or a combination of several errors. An error may have been made in adding the trial balance columns or in copying the balances from the ledger accounts. If the preparation of the trial balance has been accurate, then the error may lie in the accounting records, either in the journal or in the ledger accounts. What is the most efficient approach to locating the error or errors? There is no single technique which will give the best results every time, but the following procedures, done in sequence, will often save considerable time and effort in locating errors.

1 Prove the addition of the trial balance columns by adding these columns in the opposite direction from that previously followed.
2 If the error does not lie in addition, next determine the exact amount by which the schedule is out of balance. The amount of the discrepancy is often a clue to the source of the error. If the discrepancy is divisible by 9, this suggests either a ***transposition*** error or a ***slide.*** For example, assume that the Cash account has a balance of $2,175, but in copying the balance into the trial balance the figures are ***transposed*** and written as $2,157. The resulting error is $18, and like all transposition errors is divisible by 9. Another common error is the slide, or incorrect placement of the decimal point, as when $2,175.00 is copied as $21.75. The resulting discrepancy in the trial balance will also be an amount divisible by 9.

   To illustrate another method of using the amount of a discrepancy as a clue to locating the error, assume that the Office Equipment account has a ***debit*** balance of $420, but that it is erroneously listed in the ***credit*** column of the trial balance. This will cause a discrepancy of two times $420, or $840, in the trial balance totals. Since such errors as recording a debit in a credit column are not uncommon, it is advisable, after determining the discrepancy in the trial balance totals, to scan the columns for an amount equal to exactly one-half of the discrepancy. It is also advisable to look over the transactions for an item of the exact amount of the discrepancy. An error may have been made by recording the debit side of the transaction and forgetting to enter the credit side.

3 Compare the amounts in the trial balance with the balances in the ledger. Make sure that each ledger account balance has been included in the correct column of the trial balance.
4 Recompute the balance of each ledger account.
5 Trace all postings from the journal to the ledger accounts. As this is done, place a check mark in the journal and in the ledger after each figure verified. When the operation is completed, look through the journal and the ledger for unchecked amounts. In tracing postings, be alert not only for errors in amount but also for debits entered as credits, or vice versa.

### Dollar signs

Dollar signs are not used in journals or ledgers. Some accountants use dollar signs in trial balances; some do not. In this book, dollar signs are used in trial balances. Dollar signs should always be used in the balance sheet, the income statement, and other formal financial reports. In the balance sheet, for example, a dollar sign is placed by the first amount in each column and also by the final amount or total. Many accountants also place a dollar sign by each subtotal or other amount listed below an underlining. In the published financial statements of large corporations, however, the use of dollar signs is often limited to the first and last figures in a column.

When dollar amounts are being entered in the columnar paper used in journals and ledgers, commas and periods are not needed. On unruled paper, commas and periods should be used. Most of the problems and illustrations in this book are in even dollar amounts. In such cases the cents column can be left blank, or if desired, zeros or dashes may be used.

### Accounting records in perspective

We have emphasized in this chapter the purpose of the journal and ledger and have explained how these accounting records are used. Now we need to consider how these records fit into the accounting process as a whole. It is important to keep in mind that accounting records are not an end in themselves. Just as the physician uses symbols and cryptic notations to write a prescription in the course of providing medical services, the accountant uses symbols and concise notations to interpret business transactions and to classify information about them. Although the prescription order written by the physician and the records created by the accountant are important and must be accurate and complete, they are only a means to an end. The goal of the physician is to restore the health of the patient. The goal of the accountant is to ***communicate accounting information to persons who will use this information as a basis for business decisions.*** These persons include managers, owners, investors, creditors, and governmental agencies. They want to know the financial position of the business as shown by the balance sheet. What resources (assets) does the business have and what debts (liabilities) does it owe? These persons also want to know how profitable the business has been, as shown by the income statement. Finally, they would like to know about the future prospects of the business. Looking into the future of a business involves much uncertainty, but the accumulating and interpreting of accounting information are vitally important elements of financial forecasting.

The use of journals and ledgers, along with the double-entry system and the various symbols and technical terms, has developed over a long period of time because these devices constitute an efficient ***information system.*** This information system absorbs each day the economic essence of many business transactions. After classifying and summarizing this mass of data, the accounting process produces concise financial statements for the use of decision makers. Remember that your study of the accounting model in the early chapters of this book will equip you to read financial statements with understanding and to make better decisions because you are familiar with the underlying accounting concepts and processes.

## KEY TERMS INTRODUCED IN CHAPTER 2

**Account** A record used to summarize all increases and decreases in a particular asset, such as Cash, or any other type of asset, liability, owner's equity, revenue, or expense.

**Account balance** The difference in dollars between the total debits and total credits in an account.

**Business documents** Original evidence of transactions, as for example, checks, sales tickets, and cash register tapes.

**Credit** An amount entered on the right-hand side of an account. A credit is used to record a decrease in an asset and an increase in a liability or owner's equity.

**Credit balance** The balance of an account in which the total amount of credits exceeds the total amount of debits.

**Debit** An amount entered on the left-hand side of an account. A debit is used to record an increase in an asset and a decrease in a liability or owner's equity.

**Debit balance** The balance of an account in which the total amount of debits exceeds the total amount of credits.

**Double-entry system** In recording transactions, the total dollar amount of debits must equal the total dollar amount of credits.

**Financial statement order** The usual sequence of accounts in a ledger; that is, assets first, followed by liabilities, owner's equity, revenue, and expenses.

**Footing** The total of amounts in a column.

**Journal** A chronological record of transactions, showing for each transaction the debits and credits to be entered in specific ledger accounts. The simplest type of journal is called a general journal.

**Journalizing** The process of recording a transaction in a journal. To journalize means to prepare an entry in a journal.

**Ledger** A loose-leaf book, file, or other record containing all the separate accounts of a business.

**Posting** The process of transferring information from the journal to individual accounts in the ledger.

**Trial balance** A two-column schedule listing the names and the debit or credit balances of all accounts in the ledger.

## DEMONSTRATION PROBLEM FOR YOUR REVIEW

**a** Drill Company was organized on July 1 and carried out a number of transactions during July before opening for business on August 1. The partially filled in journal for the company appears below and on page 65. You are to determine the titles of the accounts to be debited and credited to complete these July journal entries.

**b** Post the journal entries to the proper ledger accounts shown on pages 65 to 67. Insert the ledger account number in the LP column of the journal as each item is posted.

**c** Complete the following trial balance as of July 31, 19___:

***DRILL COMPANY***

***Trial Balance***

***July 31, 19___***

| | Debit | Credit |
|---|---|---|
| *Cash* | $ | |
| *Land* | | |
| *Building* | | |
| *Office equipment* | | |
| *Notes payable* | | $ |
| *Accounts payable* | | |
| *Howard Drill, capital* | | |
| | $ | $ |

***General Journal*** *Page 1*

| Date | | Account Titles and Explanations | LP | Debit | Credit |
|---|---|---|---|---|---|
| *19___* | | | | | |
| *July* | *1* | | | *50,000* | |
| | | | | | *50,000* |
| | | *Howard Drill opened a bank account in the name of the business by making a deposit of personal funds.* | | | |

**General Journal** Page 1

| Date | | Account Titles and Explanations | LP | Debit | Credit |
|---|---|---|---|---|---|
| 19__ | | | | | |
| July | 2 | | | 30,000 | |
| | | | | | 10,000 |
| | | | | | 20,000 |
| | | Purchased land. Paid one-third cash and issued a note payable for the balance. | | | |
| | 5 | | | 12,000 | |
| | | | | | 12,000 |
| | | Purchased a small portable building for cash. The price included installation on Drill Company's lot. | | | |
| | 12 | | | 2,500 | |
| | | | | | 2,500 |
| | | Purchased office equipment on credit from Suzuki & Co. | | | |
| | 28 | | | 1,000 | |
| | | | | | 1,000 |
| | | Paid part of account payable to Suzuki & Co. | | | |

**Cash** Account No. 1

| Date | | Explanation | Ref | Debit | Credit | Balance |
|---|---|---|---|---|---|---|
| 19— July | | | | | | |
| | | | | | | |
| | | | | | | |
| | | | | | | |

**Land** Account No. 20

| Date | | Explanation | Ref | Debit | Credit | Balance |
|---|---|---|---|---|---|---|
| | | | | | | |
| | | | | | | |
| | | | | | | |
| | | | | | | |

| Building | | | | | Account No. 22 |
|---|---|---|---|---|---|
| Date | Explanation | Ref | Debit | Credit | Balance |
| | | | | | |
| | | | | | |
| | | | | | |
| | | | | | |
| | | | | | |

| Office Equipment | | | | | Account No. 25 |
|---|---|---|---|---|---|
| Date | Explanation | Ref | Debit | Credit | Balance |
| | | | | | |
| | | | | | |
| | | | | | |
| | | | | | |
| | | | | | |

| Notes Payable | | | | | Account No. 30 |
|---|---|---|---|---|---|
| Date | Explanation | Ref | Debit | Credit | Balance |
| | | | | | |
| | | | | | |
| | | | | | |
| | | | | | |
| | | | | | |

| Accounts Payable | | | | | Account No. 32 |
|---|---|---|---|---|---|
| Date | Explanation | Ref | Debit | Credit | Balance |
| | | | | | |
| | | | | | |
| | | | | | |
| | | | | | |
| | | | | | |

| Howard Drill, Capital | | | | | | Account No. 50 |
|---|---|---|---|---|---|---|
| Date | | Explanation | Ref | Debit | Credit | Balance |
| | | | | | | |
| | | | | | | |
| | | | | | | |
| | | | | | | |

## SOLUTION TO DEMONSTRATION PROBLEM

a

*General Journal* — *Page 1*

| Date | | Account Titles and Explanations | LP | Debit | Credit |
|---|---|---|---|---|---|
| 19__ | | | | | |
| July | 1 | Cash | 1 | 50,000 | |
| | | Howard Drill, Capital | 50 | | 50,000 |
| | | Howard Drill opened a bank account in the name of the business by making a deposit of his personal funds. | | | |
| | 2 | Land | 20 | 30,000 | |
| | | Cash | 1 | | 10,000 |
| | | Notes Payable | 30 | | 20,000 |
| | | Purchased land. Paid one-third cash and issued a note payable for the balance. | | | |
| | 5 | Building | 22 | 12,000 | |
| | | Cash | 1 | | 12,000 |
| | | Purchased a small portable building for cash. The price included installation on Drill Company's lot. | | | |
| | 12 | Office Equipment | 25 | 2,500 | |
| | | Accounts Payable | 32 | | 2,500 |
| | | Purchased office equipment on credit from Suzuki & Co. | | | |
| | 28 | Accounts Payable | 32 | 1,000 | |
| | | Cash | 1 | | 1,000 |
| | | Paid part of account payable to Suzuki & Co. | | | |

**b**

**Cash** — Account No. 1

| Date | | Explanation | Ref | Debit | Credit | Balance |
|---|---|---|---|---|---|---|
| 19— July | 1 | | 1 | 50000 00 | | 50000 00 |
| | 2 | | 1 | | 10000 00 | 40000 00 |
| | 5 | | 1 | | 12000 00 | 28000 00 |
| | 28 | | 1 | | 1000 00 | 27000 00 |

**Land** — Account No. 20

| Date | | Explanation | Ref | Debit | Credit | Balance |
|---|---|---|---|---|---|---|
| 19— July | 2 | | 1 | 30000 00 | | 30000 00 |

**Building** — Account No. 22

| Date | | Explanation | Ref | Debit | Credit | Balance |
|---|---|---|---|---|---|---|
| 19— July | 5 | | 1 | 12000 00 | | 12000 00 |

**Office Equipment** — Account No. 25

| Date | | Explanation | Ref | Debit | Credit | Balance |
|---|---|---|---|---|---|---|
| 19— July | 12 | | 1 | 2500 00 | | 2500 00 |

**Notes Payable** — Account No. 30

| Date | | Explanation | Ref | Debit | Credit | Balance |
|---|---|---|---|---|---|---|
| 19— July | 2 | | 1 | | 20000 00 | 20000 00 |

**Accounts Payable** — Account No. 32

| Date | | Explanation | Ref | Debit | Credit | Balance |
|---|---|---|---|---|---|---|
| 19__ July | 12 | | 1 | | 2500 00 | 2500 00 |
| | 28 | | 1 | 1000 00 | | 1500 00 |

**Howard Drill, Capital** — Account No. 50

| Date | | Explanation | Ref | Debit | Credit | Balance |
|---|---|---|---|---|---|---|
| 19__ July | 1 | | 1 | | 50000 00 | 50000 00 |

c

**DRILL COMPANY**
**Trial Balance**
**July 31, 19__**

| | | |
|---|---|---|
| Cash | $27,000 | |
| Land | 30,000 | |
| Building | 12,000 | |
| Office equipment | 2,500 | |
| Notes payable | | $20,000 |
| Accounts payable | | 1,500 |
| Howard Drill, capital | | 50,000 |
| | $71,500 | $71,500 |

## REVIEW QUESTIONS

1 What is an account and how does it differ from a ledger?
2 In its simplest form, an account has only three elements or basic parts. What are these three elements?
3 What relationship exists between the position of an account on the balance sheet and the rules for recording increases in that account?
4 State briefly the rules of debit and credit as applied to asset accounts. As applied to liability and owner's equity accounts.
5 Is it true that favorable events are recorded by credits and unfavorable events by debits? Explain.
6 What relationship exists between journals and ledgers on the one hand and financial statements on the other?
7 Does the term ***debit*** mean increase and the term ***credit*** mean decrease? Explain.
8 What requirement is imposed by the double-entry system in the recording of any business transaction?
9 Explain precisely what is meant by each of the phrases listed below. Whenever

appropriate, indicate whether the left or right side of an account is affected and whether an increase or decrease is indicated.

**a** A debit of $200 to the Cash account
**b** Credit balance
**c** Credit side of an account
**d** A debit of $600 to Accounts Payable
**e** Debit balance
**f** A credit of $50 to Accounts Receivable
**g** A debit to the Land account

**10** For each of the following transactions, indicate whether the account in parentheses should be debited or credited, and give the reason for your answer.

**a** Purchased a typewriter on credit, promising to make payment in full within 30 days. (Accounts Payable)
**b** Purchased land for cash. (Cash)
**c** Sold an old, unneeded typewriter on 30-day credit. (Office Equipment)
**d** Obtained a loan of $5,000 from a bank. (Cash)
**e** James Brown began the business of Brown Sporting Goods Shop by depositing $20,000 cash in a bank account in the name of the business. (James Brown, Capital)

**11** How does a T account differ from a three-column running balance form of ledger account?

**12** For each of the following accounts, state whether it is an asset, a liability, or owner's equity; also state whether it would normally have a debit or a credit balance: (a) Office Equipment, (b) John Williams, Capital, (c) Accounts Receivable, (d) Accounts Payable, (e) Cash, (f) Notes Payable, (g) Land.

**13** List the following five items in a logical sequence to illustrate the flow of accounting information through the accounting system:

**a** Information entered in journal
**b** Preparation of a business document
**c** Financial statements prepared from ledger
**d** Occurrence of a business transaction
**e** Debits and credits posted from journal to ledger

**14** Compare and contrast a ***journal*** and a ***ledger.***

**15** Which step in the recording of transactions requires greater understanding of accounting principles: (a) the entering of transactions in the journal, or (b) the posting of entries to ledger accounts?

**16** When entering a transaction in a journal, which should be written first, the title of the account to be debited or the title of the account to be credited? Which is indented, the debit or the credit?

**17** What is a compound journal entry?

**18** State two facts about the sequence of accounts in a journal entry and the use of indentation which make it easy to distinguish between a debit and a credit.

**19** What purposes are served by a trial balance?

**20** In preparing a trial balance, an accounting student listed the balance of the Office Equipment account in the credit column. This account had a balance of $2,450. What would be the amount of the discrepancy in the trial balance totals? Explain.

**21** Are dollar signs used in journal entries? In ledger accounts? In trial balances? In financial statements?

**22** A student beginning the study of accounting prepared a trial balance in which two unusual features appeared. The Buildings account showed a credit balance of $20,000, and the Accounts Payable account a debit balance of $100. Considering each of these two abnormal balances separately, state whether the condition was the result of an error in the records or could have resulted from proper recording of an unusual transaction.

**23** During the first week of an accounting course, Student A expressed the opinion that a great deal of time could be saved if a business would record transactions directly in ledger accounts rather than entering transactions first in a journal and then posting the debit and credit amounts from the journal to the ledger. Student B agreed with this view but added that such a system should not be called a double-entry system since each transaction would be entered only once. Student C disagreed with both A and B, arguing that the use of a journal and a ledger was more efficient than entering transactions directly in ledger accounts. Furthermore, Student C argued that the meaning of a double-entry system did not refer to the practice of maintaining both a journal and ledger. Evaluate the statements made by all three students.

## EXERCISES

*Ex. 2-1* Analyze separately each of the following transactions using the format illustrated at the end of the exercise. In each situation, explain the debit portion of the transaction before the credit portion.

**a** On May 1, Laura Blair organized Blair Placement, an employment service, by opening a bank account in the company name with a deposit of $90,000.

**b** On May 3, purchased land and an office building for a total price of $124,000, of which $64,000 was applicable to the land and $60,000 was applicable to the building. A cash down payment of $50,000 was made and a note payable was issued for the balance of the purchase price.

**c** On May 6, office equipment was purchased on credit from Office Interiors at a price of $7,400. The account payable was to be paid by May 31.

**d** On May 7, a portion of the office equipment purchased on May 6 was found to be defective and was returned to Office Interiors. That company agreed that Blair Placement would not have to pay for the defective equipment, which had been priced at $800.

**e** On May 30, the remaining liability of $6,600 to Office Interiors was paid in full.

Note: The type of analysis to be made is shown by the following illustration, using transaction **a** as an example.

**a** (1) The asset Cash was increased. Increases in assets are recorded by debits. Debit Cash, $90,000.

(2) The owner's equity was increased. Increases in owner's equity are recorded by credits. Credit Laura Blair, Capital, $90,000.

*Ex. 2-2* The first six transactions of a newly organized company appear in the following T accounts.

**Cash**

| Debit | | Credit | |
|---|---|---|---|
| (1) | 23,000 | (2) | 12,000 |
| | | (3) | 5,000 |
| | | (5) | 1,000 |
| | | (6) | 4,500 |

**Office Equipment**

| Debit | | Credit | |
|---|---|---|---|
| (4) | 4,500 | | |

**Accounts Payable**

| Debit | | Credit | |
|---|---|---|---|
| (6) | 4,500 | (4) | 4,500 |

| Land | |
|---|---|
| (2) 12,000 | |

| Delivery Truck | |
|---|---|
| (5) 4,000 | |

| John Corning, Capital | |
|---|---|
| | (1) 23,000 |

| Building | |
|---|---|
| (3) 48,000 | |

| Notes Payable | |
|---|---|
| | (3) 43,000 |
| | (5) 3,000 |

For each of the six transactions in turn, indicate the type of accounts affected (asset, liability, or owner's equity) and whether the account was increased or decreased. Arrange your answers in the form illustrated for transaction (*1*), shown here as an example.

| | Account Debited | | Account Credited | |
|---|---|---|---|---|
| Transaction | Type of Account | Increase or Decrease | Type of Account | Increase or Decrease |
| (1) | Asset | Increase | Owner's equity | Increase |

*Ex. 2-3* Enter the following transactions in T accounts drawn on ordinary notebook paper. Label each debit and credit with the letter identifying the transaction. Prepare a trial balance at May 31.

(a) On May 10, Fred Rivero opened a bank account in the name of a new business, Sun Travel Service, by making a deposit of $90,000 cash.
(b) On May 13, purchased land for cash of $50,000.
(c) On May 18, a prefabricated building was purchased at a cost of $42,000. A cash payment of $33,000 was made and a note payable was issued for the balance.
(d) On May 20, office equipment was purchased at a cost of $3,000. A cash down payment of $1,000 was made, and it was agreed that the balance should be paid within 30 days.
(e) On May 30, paid $1,000 of the $2,000 liability arising from the purchase of office equipment on May 20.

*Ex. 2-4* Enter the following transactions in the two-column journal of Crystal Pool Service Company. Include a brief explanation of the transaction as part of each journal entry. Do not include in the explanation amounts or account titles since these are shown in the debit-credit portion of the entry.

**June 1** Acquired office equipment from Bell Company for $850 cash.
**June 3** Collected an account receivable of $2,000 from a customer, William Rinehart.
**June 4** Issued a check for $360 in full payment of an account payable to Chemical Supply Company.
**June 8** The owner, Ralph James, invested an additional $5,000 cash in the business.
**June 8** Borrowed $7,500 cash from the bank by signing a 90-day note payable.
**June 9** Purchased an adjacent vacant lot for use as parking space. The price was $62,000, of which $12,000 was paid in cash; a note payable was issued for the balance.

*Ex. 2-5* The single proprietorship of Andrew Duncan, CPA, had the following transactions, among others, during October. You are to record these transactions in a two-column general journal. Include an explanation as part of each entry.

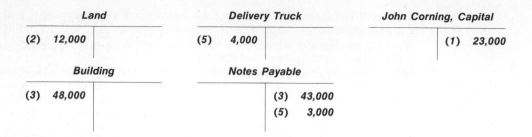

**Oct.** **1** Purchased office equipment on 30-day credit in the amount of $3,200.
**3** An office desk included in the office equipment purchased on October 1 proved to be defective and was returned for full credit of $400. This was the price at which Andrew Duncan, CPA, had purchased the desk.
**8** Collected an account receivable from a client, Coast Motel, in the amount of $900.
**9** Bought an automobile for use in the business. Paid cash, $6,400.
**18** Duncan invested $10,000 of personal funds in the business by making a deposit in the company bank account.
**22** Paid $1,000 on account in partial payment of the account payable which originated October 1 in acquiring office equipment.

*Ex. 2-6* The following accounts of Lakeland Real Estate Company at June 30, 19___, are listed below in alphabetical order. The amount in the account for Notes Payable has been purposely omitted. You are to prepare a trial balance with the proper heading and with the accounts listed in proper sequence. Indicate the balance for Notes Payable.

| | | | |
|---|---|---|---|
| *Accounts payable* | *$ 2,300* | *Judith Klein, capital* | *$58,400* |
| *Accounts receivable* | *15,300* | *Land* | *14,000* |
| *Automobile* | *4,900* | *Notes payable* | *?* |
| *Building* | *28,900* | *Office equipment* | *4,300* |
| *Cash* | *7,800* | | |

*Ex. 2-7* Some of the following errors would cause the debit and credit columns of the trial balance to have unequal totals. For each of the four paragraphs, write a statement explaining with reasons whether the error would cause unequal totals in the trial balance. Include in your explanations the dollar amounts of errors in trial balance totals or ledger account balances. Each paragraph is to be considered independently of the others.

**a** A check for $750 issued to pay an account payable was recorded by debiting Accounts Payable $750 and crediting Accounts Receivable $750.
**b** Collection of an account receivable in the amount of $500 was recorded by a debit to Cash for $500 and a debit to the owner's capital account for $500.
**c** A payment of $125 to a creditor was recorded by a debit to Accounts Payable of $125 and a credit to Cash of $25.
**d** A $950 payment for a typewriter was recorded as a debit to Office Equipment of $95 and a credit to cash of $95.

*Ex. 2-8* The trial balance prepared by Studio Patrol Service at December 31 was not in balance. In searching for the error, an employee discovered that a transaction for the purchase of a typewriter on credit for $530 had been recorded by a ***debit*** of $530 to the Office Equipment account and a ***debit*** of $530 to Accounts Payable. The Accounts Payable account had a large credit balance both before and after this $530 debit posting. The credit column of the incorrect trial balance had a total of $85,300.

In answering each of the following five questions, explain briefly the reasons underlying your answer and state the dollar amount of the error if any.

**a** Was the Office Equipment account overstated, understated, or correctly stated in the trial balance?
**b** Was the total of the debit column of the trial balance overstated, understated, or correctly stated?
**c** Was the Accounts Payable account overstated, understated, or correctly stated in the trial balance?
**d** Was the total of the credit column of the trial balance overstated, understated or correctly stated?
**e** How much was the total of the debit column of the trial balance before correction of the error?

# PROBLEMS

## Group A

*2A-1* Jensen Services, a single proprietorship owned by Paul Jensen, had the following transactions early in June:

(a) On June 1, collected cash of $2,400 from accounts receivable.
(b) On June 2, Paul Jensen made an additional investment in the business by depositing $2,000 cash in the company bank account.
(c) On June 3, made a payment of $1,200 on accounts payable.
(d) On June 4, bought office equipment on credit at a cost of $2,600.
(e) On June 6, bought additional office equipment for cash of $375.

**Instructions**

**a** Prepare an analysis of each of the above transactions. The form of analysis to be used is as follows, using transaction (a) as an example.

*a* (1) The asset Cash was increased. Increases in assets are recorded by debits. Debit Cash, $2,400.

(2) The asset Accounts Receivable was decreased. Decreases in assets are recorded by credits. Credit Accounts Receivable, $2,400.

**b** Prepare journal entries, including explanations, for the above transactions.

*2A-2* After several seasons of World Team tennis competition, Anne Peckham had saved enough money to start her own tennis school, to be known as Rancho Tennis College. During June, while organizing the business, Peckham kept only an informal record of transactions in the form of T accounts which she maintained on a large blackboard. Peckham asks you to develop from the T accounts a ledger using the standard three-column running balance form of accounts. She says that she will prepare journal entries for June from some rough notes she has kept but that she will need some assistance in establishing the running balance form of ledger accounts. The T accounts reflecting all June transactions are as follows:

***Cash*** 1

| | | | |
|---|---|---|---|
| *6/2* | *35,000* | *6/4* | *21,600* |
| | | *6/18* | *212* |
| | | *6/23* | *650* |

***Tennis Equipment*** 25

| | | | |
|---|---|---|---|
| *6/7* | *1,240* | | |
| *6/13* | *650* | | |

***Office Supplies*** 9

| | | | |
|---|---|---|---|
| *6/8* | *212* | | |

***Notes Payable*** 30

| | | | |
|---|---|---|---|
| | | *6/4* | *75,600* |

***Land*** 20

| | | | |
|---|---|---|---|
| *6/4* | *25,200* | | |

***Accounts Payable*** 31

| | | | |
|---|---|---|---|
| *6/18* | *212* | *6/7* | *1,240* |
| *6/23* | *650* | *6/8* | *212* |
| | | *6/13* | *650* |

**Tennis Courts** 22

| | | | |
|---|---|---|---|
| 6/4 | 72,000 | | |

**Anne Peckham, Capital** 50

| | | | |
|---|---|---|---|
| | | 6/2 | 35,000 |

**Instructions**

**a** Transfer the information shown by the T accounts to ledger accounts of the three-column running balance form.

**b** Prepare a trial balance at June 30 from the ledger accounts completed in part **a.**

*2A-3* Opinion Research Service was organized to conduct polls on various issues of interest to political candidates. The following alphabetical list shows the account balances at February 28, 19___.

| | | | |
|---|---|---|---|
| Accounts payable | $ 6,930 | Land | $ 86,900 |
| Accounts receivable | 4,625 | Notes payable | 275,000 |
| Automobiles | 12,600 | Notes receivable | 10,000 |
| Cameras | 2,200 | Office building | 120,200 |
| Cash | ? | Stationery & office supplies | 765 |
| Computer | 36,800 | Tape recorders | 3,800 |
| Furniture & fixtures | 12,250 | Taxes payable | 3,100 |
| Garage building | 48,000 | Technical library | 1,800 |
| | | Thelma Jones, capital | 66,820 |

**Instructions** Prepare a trial balance with the accounts arranged in the usual financial statement order. (Compute the balance for the Cash account so that the ledger will be in balance. In listing the relatively permanent assets used in the business, remember that land and buildings are listed before the other plant assets, such as cameras and automobiles, which may be in any order you prefer.)

*2A-4* The following T accounts summarize the information contained in the ledger of Call Company at October 31.

**Cash**

| | |
|---|---|
| 12,773 | 13,144 |
| 1,328 | 831 |
| 3,091 | |
| 778 | |

**Notes Payable**

| | |
|---|---|
| | 5,000 |

**Accounts Receivable**

| | |
|---|---|
| 1,244 | 3,091 |
| 4,318 | |
| 34,948 | |

**Accounts Payable**

| | |
|---|---|
| 12,144 | 454 |
| | 1,265 |
| | 11,965 |

**Land**

| | |
|---|---|
| 20,000 | |

**Taxes Payable**

| | |
|---|---|
| 731 | 946 |

| Building | |
|---|---|
| 32,000 | |

| Mortgage Payable | |
|---|---|
| | 28,000 |

| Furniture & Fixtures | |
|---|---|
| 2,500 | 328 |
| 7,300 | |

| Hunter Call, Capital | |
|---|---|
| | 50,000 |
| | 22,000 |

| Delivery Equipment | |
|---|---|
| 4,747 | 878 |

**Instructions** Determine the balances of the accounts and prepare a trial balance at October 31, 19___.

*2A-5* On October 1 Jon Linden, a licensed real estate broker, decided to organize a business, to be known as Linden Realty. The following events occurred during October:

**Oct. 1** Jon Linden opened a bank account in the name of the business by depositing personal savings of $60,000.

**Oct. 2** Purchased land and a small office building at a total price of $126,000. The terms of purchase required a cash payment of $46,000 and the issuance of a note payable for $80,000. The records of the property tax assessor indicated that the value of the building was one-half that of the land.

**Oct. 4** Sold a portion of the land at cost of $10,500 to an adjacent business, Community Medical Clinic, which wished to enlarge its parking lot. No down payment was required. Terms of the sale called for receipt of $2,000 within 10 days and the balance within 30 days.

**Oct. 10** Purchased office equipment on credit from Swingline Company in the amount of $2,100.

**Oct. 14** Received cash of $2,000 as partial collection of the receivable from Community Medical Clinic.

**Oct. 19** Paid $1,200 as partial settlement of the liability to Swingline Company.

The account titles and account numbers to be used are:

| | | | |
|---|---|---|---|
| *Cash* | 11 | *Office equipment* | 26 |
| *Accounts receivable* | 15 | *Notes payable* | 30 |
| *Land* | 21 | *Accounts payable* | 32 |
| *Building* | 23 | *Jon Linden, capital* | 50 |

**Instructions**

**a** Prepare journal entries for the month of October.
**b** Post to ledger accounts of the three-column running balance type.
**c** Prepare a trial balance at October 31.

*2A-6* After playing several seasons of professional football, Joe Bolt had saved enough money to start a business, to be called Number One Auto Rental. The transactions during March while the new business was being organized are listed below:

**Mar. 1** Joe Bolt invested $140,000 cash in the business by making a deposit in a bank account in the name of the new company.

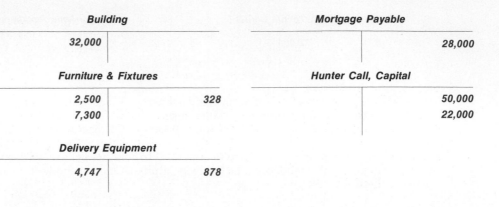

**Mar. 3** The new company purchased land and a building at a cost of $120,000, of which $72,000 was regarded as applicable to the land and $48,000 to the building. The transaction involved a cash payment of $41,500 and the issuance of a note payable for $78,500.

**Mar. 5** Purchased 20 new automobiles at $5,600 each from Fleet Sales Company. Paid $32,000 cash, and agreed to pay another $32,000 by March 26 and the remaining balance by April 15.

**Mar. 7** Sold an automobile at cost to Bolt's father-in-law, Howard Facey, who paid $2,400 in cash and agreed to pay the balance within 30 days.

**Mar. 8** One of the automobiles was found to be defective and was returned to Fleet Sales Company. The amount payable to this creditor was thereby reduced by $5,600.

**Mar. 20** Purchased office equipment at a cost of $4,480 cash.

**Mar. 26** Issued a check for $32,000 in partial payment of the liability to Fleet Sales Company.

The account titles and the account numbers used by the company are as follows:

| | | | |
|---|---|---|---|
| *Cash* | *10* | *Automobiles* | *22* |
| *Accounts receivable* | *11* | *Notes payable* | *31* |
| *Land* | *16* | *Accounts payable* | *32* |
| *Buildings* | *17* | *Joe Bolt, capital* | *50* |
| *Office equipment* | *20* | | |

**Instructions**

**a** Journalize the March transactions.
**b** Post to ledger accounts. Use the running balance form of ledger account.
**c** Prepare a trial balance at March 31.

*2A-7* The ledger accounts of Cheviot Hills Golf Club at September 30 are shown below in an alphabetical listing.

| | | | |
|---|---|---|---|
| *Accounts payable* | *$ 5,340* | *Lighting equipment* | *$ 52,900* |
| *Accounts receivable* | *1,300* | *Maintenance equipment* | *36,500* |
| *Building* | *64,200* | *Notes payable* | *390,000* |
| *Carol Martin, capital* | *264,060* | *Notes receivable* | *24,000* |
| *Cash* | *14,960* | *Office equipment* | *1,420* |
| *Fences* | *23,600* | *Office supplies* | *490* |
| *Golf carts* | *28,000* | *Sprinkler system* | *50,000* |
| *Land* | *375,000* | *Taxes payable* | *12,970* |

**Instructions**

**a** Prepare a balance sheet at September 30.
**b** Assume that immediately after the September 30 balance sheet was prepared, a tornado struck the golf course and destroyed the fences, which were not insured against this type of disaster. If the balance sheet were revised to reflect the loss of the fences, explain what other changes in the balance sheet would be required.

## Group B

*2B-1* After several years of experience as a real estate broker, Helen Finley organized her own firm on July 1 under the name of Helen Finley & Associates. During July the company had the following transactions prior to beginning regular operations.

(a) On July 1, Helen Finley opened a bank account in the name of the new company with a deposit of $150,000.
(b) On July 3, Helen Finley & Associates bought land for use in its operations at a total cost of $120,000. A cash down payment of $80,000 was made and a note payable was issued for the balance.
(c) On July 5, a movable building was purchased and installed on the lot at a cost of $38,000. Paid cash.
(d) On July 10, office equipment was purchased on credit from Dell Office Equipment at a cost of $2,200. The account payable was to be paid within 30 days.
(e) On July 31, a cash payment of $15,000 was made in partial settlement of the note payable issued on July 3.

**Instructions**

**a** Prepare an analysis of each of the above transactions. The form of analysis to be used is as follows, using transaction (a) above as an example.
  (1) The asset Cash was increased. Increases in assets are recorded by debits. Debit Cash, $150,000.
  (2) The owner's equity was increased. Increases in owner's equity are recorded by credits. Credit Helen Finley, Capital, $150,000.

**b** Prepare journal entries for the above five transactions. Include an explanation as a part of each journal entry.

*2B-2* The transactions of Valley Ice Skating Rink, a newly formed business, have been recorded by the owner, Casey Gaunt, in informally constructed T accounts. Gaunt asks you to transfer this information into ledger accounts of the three-column running balance type. He will prepare journal entries from memoranda and documents in his possession. The T accounts are shown below, with the related debits and credits representing each transaction identified by a letter as well as by date. [In transaction (*e*) on September 15, a motor originally included in the earlier purchase of equipment was sold on credit to a friend of Casey Gaunt's at its cost of $400.]

**Cash** 1

| | | | |
|---|---|---|---|
| 9/1 | (a) 25,000 | 9/3 | (b) 5,000 |
| 9/25 | (f) 300 | 9/29 | (g) 15,000 |

**Notes Payable** 30

| | | | |
|---|---|---|---|
| | | 9/3 | (b) 85,000 |

**Accounts Receivable** 4

| | | | |
|---|---|---|---|
| 9/15 | (e) 400 | 9/25 | (f) 300 |

**Accounts Payable** 31

| | | | |
|---|---|---|---|
| 9/29 | (g) 15,000 | 9/6 | (c) 20,000 |
| | | 9/12 | (d) 1,200 |

**Land** 20

| | | | |
|---|---|---|---|
| 9/3 | (b) 65,000 | | |

**Casey Gaunt, Capital** 50

| | | | |
|---|---|---|---|
| | | 9/1 | (a) 25,000 |

**Building** 22

| | | | |
|---|---|---|---|
| 9/3 | (b) 25,000 | | |

**Equipment** 25

| | | | |
|---|---|---|---|
| 9/6 | (c) 20,000 | 9/15 | (e) 400 |
| 9/12 | (d) 1,200 | | |

**Instructions**

**a** Transfer the information shown by the T accounts to ledger accounts of the three-column running balance type.

**b** Prepare a trial balance at September 30 from the ledger accounts completed in part **a.**

*2B-3* At March 31, an alphabetical list of the accounts of the Community Theater showed the following balances:

| | | | |
|---|---|---|---|
| Accounts payable | $ 14,125 | Notes payable | $64,100 |
| Accounts receivable | 500 | Notes receivable | 1,500 |
| Building | 133,000 | Office equipment | 2,625 |
| Cash | 11,100 | Stage equipment | 55,545 |
| Land | 118,000 | Supplies | 1,510 |
| Lighting equipment | 15,600 | Taxes payable | 1,750 |
| Mortgage payable (due 1990) | 220,000 | Tom Yamamoto, capital | ? |

**Instructions** Prepare a trial balance with the accounts arranged in the usual financial statement order. (Compute the balance for the owner's capital account so that the ledger will be in balance. Mortgage payable should appear last among the liabilities. In listing the relatively permanent assets used in the business, land and building should be listed before the other plant assets such as lighting equipment and stage equipment, which may be listed in any order you prefer.)

*2B-4* Kahala Secretarial Service is located in a suburban office building and provides typing, duplicating, and other services to the tenants of the building and to other clients. As of March 31, the ledger accounts contained entries as follows:

**Cash**

| | |
|---|---|
| 1,890.70 | 518.60 |
| 561.50 | 1,000.00 |
| 2,465.00 | 595.00 |
| 315.00 | 360.00 |

**Notes Payable**

| | |
|---|---|
| 1,000.00 | 14,000.00 |

**Accounts Receivable**

| | |
|---|---|
| 3,798.00 | 260.00 |
| 263.00 | 55.00 |
| 55.00 | |
| 190.50 | |
| 2,105.00 | |

**Accounts Payable**

| | |
|---|---|
| 318.60 | 232.35 |
| 200.00 | 318.60 |
| 360.00 | 890.00 |
| | 267.00 |
| | 511.35 |

**Office Supplies**

| | |
|---|---|
| 1,500.00 | |
| 250.00 | |
| 250.00 | |

**Taxes Payable**

| | |
|---|---|
| 265.00 | 1,465.00 |
| 330.00 | |

| Office Equipment | |
|---|---|
| 13,240.00 | |

| Jill Kahala, Capital | |
|---|---|
| | 15,084.40 |

| Delivery Equipment | |
|---|---|
| 6,200.00 | |

**Instructions** Determine the balances of the accounts and prepare a trial balance at March 31, 19___.

***2B-5*** Coast Property Management was started on November 1 by Jeanne Daly to provide managerial services for the owners of apartment buildings. The organizational period extended throughout November and included the transactions listed below.

**Nov. 1** Jeanne Daly opened a bank account in the name of the business with a deposit of $50,000 cash.

**Nov. 4** Purchased land and an office building for a price of $80,000, of which $38,400 was considered applicable to the land and $41,600 attributable to the building. A cash down payment of $24,000 was made and a note payable for $56,000 was issued for the balance of the purchase price.

**Nov. 7** Purchased office equipment on credit from Harvard Office Equipment, $4,400.

**Nov. 9** A typewriter (cost $560), which was part of the November 7 purchase of office equipment, proved defective and was returned for credit to Harvard Office Equipment.

**Nov. 11** Sold to Regent Pharmacy at cost one-third of the land acquired on November 4. No down payment was required. The buyer promised to pay one-half the purchase price of $12,800 within 10 days and the remainder by December 12.

**Nov. 18** Paid $1,600 in partial settlement of the liability to Harvard Office Equipment.

**Nov. 21** Received cash of $6,400 as partial collection of the account receivable from Regent Pharmacy.

The account titles and account numbers to be used are

| | | | |
|---|---|---|---|
| *Cash* | 11 | *Office equipment* | 25 |
| *Accounts receivable* | 15 | *Notes payable* | 31 |
| *Land* | 21 | *Accounts payable* | 32 |
| *Building* | 23 | *Jeanne Daly, capital* | 51 |

**Instructions**

**a** Prepare journal entries for the month of November.
**b** Post to ledger accounts of the three-column running balance form.
**c** Prepare a trial balance at November 30.

***2B-6*** James Gray, an attorney, resigned from a position with a large law firm to establish his own law practice. The business transactions during September while the new venture was being organized are listed below.

**Sept. 1** Gray opened a bank checking account in the name of the new firm, James Gray, Attorney at Law, by depositing $80,000.

**Sept. 3** Purchased a small office building located on a large lot for a total price of $160,000, of which $100,000 was applicable to the land and $60,000 to the building. A cash payment of $70,000 was made and a note payable was issued for the balance of purchase price.

**Sept. 7** Purchased a used calculating machine for $384, paying cash.

**Sept. 9** Purchased office furniture, filing cabinets, and a typewriter from Davidson Office Supply Co. at a cost of $3,960. A cash down payment of $720 was made, the balance to be paid in three equal installments due September 28, October 28, and November 28. The purchase was on open account and did not require signing of a promissory note.

**Sept. 10** A portion of the land purchased September 3 was sold for $36,000 to Douglass, Inc. The buyer made a down payment of $12,000 cash and agreed to pay the balance within 20 days. Since the land was sold at the same price per foot that Gray had paid for it, there was no gain or loss on the transaction.

**Sept. 28** Paid Davidson Office Supply Co. $1,080 cash as the first installment due on the account payable for office equipment.

**Sept. 30** Received $24,000 cash from Douglass, Inc., in full settlement of the account receivable created in the transaction of September 10.

**Instructions**

**a** Journalize the above transactions, then post to ledger accounts. Use the running balance form of ledger account. The account titles and the account numbers to be used are

| | | | |
|---|---|---|---|
| *Cash* | *10* | *Office equipment* | *23* |
| *Accounts receivable* | *16* | *Notes payable* | *32* |
| *Land* | *20* | *Accounts payable* | *35* |
| *Building* | *22* | *James Gray, capital* | *50* |

**b** Prepare a trial balance at September 30, 19___.

*2B-7* Educational TV was organized in February 19___, to operate as a local television station. The account titles and numbers used by the business are listed below:

| | | | |
|---|---|---|---|
| *Cash* | *11* | *Telecasting equipment* | *24* |
| *Accounts receivable* | *15* | *Film library* | *25* |
| *Supplies* | *19* | *Notes payable* | *31* |
| *Land* | *21* | *Accounts payable* | *32* |
| *Building* | *22* | *Alice Wilson, capital* | *51* |
| *Transmitter* | *23* | | |

The transactions for February were as follows:

**Feb. 1** Alice Wilson deposited $288,000 cash in a bank checking account in the name of the business, Educational TV.

**Feb. 2** Educational TV purchased the land, buildings, and telecasting equipment previously used by a local television station which had gone bankrupt. The total purchase price was $249,000, of which $90,000 was attributable to the land, $75,000 to the building, and the remainder to the telecasting equipment. The terms of the purchase required a cash payment of $179,000 and the issuance of a note payable for the balance.

**Feb. 5** Purchased a transmitter at a cost of $195,000 from AC Mfg. Co., making a cash down payment of $60,000. The balance, in the form of a note payable, was to be paid in monthly installments of $11,250, beginning February 15. (Interest expense is to be ignored.)

**Feb. 9** Purchased a film library at a cost of $31,995 from Modern Film Productions, making a down payment of $14,000 cash, with the balance on account payable in 30 days.

**Feb. 12** Bought supplies costing $2,925, paying cash.

**Feb. 15** Paid $11,250 to AC Mfg. Co. as the first monthly payment on the note payable created on February 5. (Interest expense is to be ignored.)

**Feb. 25** Sold part of the film library to City College; cost was $8,000 and the selling price also was $8,000. City College agreed to pay the full amount in 30 days.

**Instructions**

**a** Prepare journal entries for the month of February.
**b** Post to ledger accounts of the three-column running balance form.
**c** Prepare a trial balance at February 28, 19___.

## BUSINESS DECISION PROBLEM 2

Richard Fell, a college student with several summers' experience as a guide on canoe camping trips, decided to go into business for himself. To start this guide service, Fell estimated that at least $4,800 cash would be needed. On June 1, Fell organized Wilderness Canoe Trails by depositing $1,600 of personal savings in a bank account in the name of the business. Also on June 1, the business borrowed an additional $3,200 cash from John Fell (Richard's father) by issuing a three-year note payable. To help the business get started, John Fell agreed that no interest would be charged on the loan. The following transactions were also carried out by the business on June 1:

(1) Bought a number of canoes at a total cost of $6,200; paid $1,700 cash and agreed to pay the balance within 60 days.
(2) Bought camping equipment at a cost of $3,400 payable in 60 days.
(3) Bought supplies for cash, $800.

After the close of the season on September 10, Fell asked another student, Sharon Lee, who had taken a course in accounting, to help determine the financial position of the business.

The only record Fell had maintained was a checkbook with memorandum notes written on the check stubs. From this source Lee discovered that Fell had invested an additional $1,200 of savings in the business on July 1, and also that the accounts payable arising from the purchase of the canoes and camping equipment had been paid in full. A bank statement received from the bank on September 10 showed a balance on deposit of $2,840.

Fell informed Lee that all cash received by the business had been deposited in the bank and all bills had been paid by check immediately upon receipt; consequently, as of September 10 all bills for the season had been paid. However, nothing had been paid on the note payable.

The canoes and camping equipment were all in excellent condition at the end of the season and Fell planned to resume operations the following summer. In fact reservations had already been accepted from many customers who wished to return.

Lee felt that some consideration should be given to the wear and tear on the canoes and equipment but she agreed with Fell that for the present purpose the canoes and equipment should be listed in the balance sheet at the original cost. The supplies remaining on hand had cost $40 and Fell felt that a refund for this amount could be obtained if they were returned to the supplier.

Lee suggested that two balance sheets be prepared, one to show the condition of the business on June 1 and the other showing the condition on September 10. She also recommended to Fell that a complete set of accounting records be established.

**Instructions**

a Use the information in the first paragraph (including the three numbered transactions) as a basis for preparing a balance sheet dated June 1.

b Prepare a balance sheet at September 10. (Because of the incomplete information available, it is not possible to determine the amount of cash at September 10 by adding cash receipts and deducting cash payments throughout the season. The amount on deposit as reported by the bank at September 10 is to be regarded as the total cash belonging to the business at that date.)

c By comparing the two balance sheets, compute the change in owner's equity. Explain the sources of this change in owner's equity and state whether you consider the business to be successful. Also comment on the cash position at the beginning and end of the season. Has the cash position improved significantly? Explain.

# 3

# MEASURING BUSINESS INCOME

The earning of net income, or profits, is a major goal of almost every business enterprise, large or small. Profit is the ***increase in the owner's equity resulting from operation of the business.*** The opposite of profit, a decrease in owner's equity from operation of the business, is termed a ***loss.*** If you were to organize a small business of your own, you would do so with the hope and expectation that the business would operate at a profit, thereby increasing your ownership equity in the business. From the standpoint of the individual firm, profitable operation is essential if the firm is to succeed, or even to survive.

Operating profitably usually leads to an increase in total assets as well as in owner's equity. From the fundamental accounting equation (A = L + OE), we know that any transaction which changes total assets must also change either total liabilities or owner's equity. For example, borrowing money from a bank increases both total assets and total liabilities. Operating profitably increases owner's equity and this increase is usually accompanied by an increase in total assets. It is possible that the increase in owner's equity from profitable operations could be accompanied by a decrease in liabilities, but in the great majority of cases, operating profitably increases total assets along with the increase in owner's equity.

Profits may be retained in the business to finance expansion, or they may be withdrawn by the owner or owners. Some of the largest corporations have become large by retaining their profits in the business and using these profits for purposes of growth. Retained profits may be used, for example, to acquire new plant and equipment, to carry on research leading to new and better products, and to extend sales operations into new territories.

### Profits: public image versus economic function

In recent years, business profits have become a controversial issue. Critics often call corporate profits "excessive" and charge that profits are a major cause of rising prices. Such charges have received considerable publicity, and as a result many people have come to believe that business profits are something harmful to society. Actually, business profits perform a vital economic function in our economy, and a satisfactory level of business profits is generally associated with high employment, an improving standard of living, and an expanding national economy.

In a free market economy, profits assist in the efficient allocation of resources. When the demand for a particular product is much greater than the supply, the price consumers will pay for the product tends to rise. As the price rises, investors are attracted to that industry by the opportunity to earn greater than normal profits. The inflow of capital into the industry results in greater productive capacity, and supply of the product increases to meet demand.

Corporate profits may be viewed as the "return" to stockholders for having invested their resources in a particular company. When creditors lend money to a company, they expect to earn a reasonable rate of interest. When employees invest their time and labor, they expect to earn a reasonable wage. It is equally logical that stockholders, who supply financial resources to a business, should expect to earn a satisfactory return on their investment.

If business profits were reduced to insignificant levels, prices probably would rise rather than fall. Investors would stop providing capital to those industries in which profit opportunities were unsatisfactory. The resulting capital shortages would leave businesses unable to produce enough goods, causing production shortages, higher prices, and unemployment. Thus, a satisfactory level of business profits is essential to maintaining high levels of production and to financing economic growth.

When competition is restricted, profits may become "excessive." Excessive profits, just as excessive wages or excessive materials costs, can be harmful to the economy. Profits are excessive when they become unreasonably large in relation to the amounts of money invested and the degree of risk being taken by the owners of a business. The risk taken by owners of a business is the chance that future losses may decrease or even wipe out their investment. Once we have completed our study of how business profits are measured, we shall discuss some ways of appraising their adequacy.

### Net income

Since the drive for profits underlies the very existence of business organizations, it follows that a most important function of an accounting system is to provide information about the profitability of a business. Before we can measure the profits of a business, we need to establish a sharp, clear meaning for ***profits.*** Economists define profits as the amount by which an entity becomes ***better off*** during a period of time. Unfortunately, how much "better off" an entity has become may be largely a matter of personal opinion and cannot be measured ***objectively*** enough to provide a useful definition for accountants.

For this reason, accountants traditionally have looked to actual business transactions to provide objective evidence that a business has been profitable or unprofitable. For example, if a business buys an item for \$60 and promptly sells it for \$100 cash, we have objective evidence that the business has earned a profit of \$40. This policy of relying upon the objective evidence of completed transactions served accountants very well until the advent of continued severe inflation began to distort accounting measurements. We shall consider in later chapters some of the methods accountants are developing to compensate for the effects of inflation upon the income statement and balance sheet. Because the word ***profits*** has been used with various meanings by business managers and economists, accountants prefer to use the alternative term ***net income,*** and to define this term very carefully. ***Net income is the excess of the price of goods sold and services rendered over the cost of goods and services used up during a given time period.*** At this point, we shall adopt the technical accounting term ***net income*** in preference to the less precise term ***profits.***

To determine net income, it is necessary to measure for a given time period (1) the price of goods sold and services rendered and (2) the cost of goods and services used up. The technical accounting terms for these items comprising net income are ***revenue*** and ***expenses.*** Therefore, we may state that ***net income equals revenue minus expenses.*** To understand why this is true and how the measurements are made, let us begin with the meaning of revenue.

## Revenue

***Revenue is the price of goods sold and services rendered to customers.*** When a business renders services to its customers or delivers merchandise to them, it either receives immediate payment in cash or acquires an account receivable which will be collected and thereby become cash within a short time. The revenue for a given period is equal to the inflow of cash and receivables from sales made in that period. For any single transaction, the amount of revenue is a measurement of the asset values received from the customer.

Revenue causes an increase in owner's equity. The inflow of cash and receivables from customers increases the total assets of the company. On the other side of the accounting equation, the liabilities do not change, but the owner's equity is increased to match the increase in total assets. Thus revenue is the ***gross*** increase in owner's equity resulting from business activities. Bear in mind, however, that not every increase in owner's equity comes from revenue. As illustrated in Chapter 1, the owner's equity is also increased by the investment of assets in the business by the owner.

Various terms are used to describe different types of revenue; for example, the revenue earned by a real estate broker may be called ***Commissions Earned***; for a theater or stadium the term ***Admissions Revenue*** is appropriate; in the professional practice of lawyers, physicians, and CPAs, the revenue is called ***Fees***

***Earned***; and companies selling merchandise generally use the term ***Sales*** to describe their principal revenue account.

**Realization or recognition of revenue** Revenue is recognized and entered in the accounting records at the time services are rendered to a customer or when goods sold to a customer are delivered. The amount of revenue is equal to the cash received plus the accounts receivable acquired from customers buying on credit. Thus the ***point of sale*** is the time to recognize revenue, regardless of whether the customer pays cash or promises to pay later.

To illustrate the recognition of revenue, let us assume that a business begins operations in March and makes sales of merchandise or services to its customers in March as follows: sales for cash, $25,000; sales on credit (to be collected in April), $15,000. The revenue for March is $40,000, an amount equal to the ***cash received and to be received*** from March sales. When the accounts receivable of $15,000 are collected during April, they must not be counted a second time in measuring revenue for April. The act of collection causes an increase in the asset, Cash, and a corresponding decrease in the asset, Accounts Receivable. The amount of total assets remains unchanged, and, of course, there is no change in liabilities or owner's equity.

Another example of a cash receipt that does not represent revenue comes from borrowing. A business may obtain cash by borrowing from a bank. This increase in cash is offset by an increase in liabilities in the form of a note payable to the bank. The owner's equity is not affected by the borrowing transaction.

## Expenses

***Expenses are the cost of the goods and services used up in the process of obtaining revenue.*** Examples include salaries for employees, charges for newspaper advertising and for telephone service, and the wearing out (depreciation) of the building and office equipment. All these items are necessary to attract and serve customers and thereby to obtain revenue. Expenses are sometimes referred to as the "cost of doing business," that is, the cost of the various activities necessary to carry on a business. Since expenses are the cost of goods and services used up, they are also called ***expired costs.***

Expenses cause the owner's equity to decrease. Revenue may be regarded as the positive factor in producing net income, expenses as the negative factor. The relationship between expenses and revenue is a significant one; the expenses of a given month or other time period are incurred in order to generate revenue in that same period. The salaries earned by sales employees waiting on customers during July are applicable to July revenue and should be treated as July expenses, even though these salaries may not actually be paid to the employees until sometime in August.

As previously explained, revenue and cash receipts are not one and the same thing; similarly, expenses and cash payments are not identical. Examples of cash payments which are not expenses of the current period include the purchase of an office building for cash, the purchase of merchandise for later sale to customers, the repayment of a bank loan, and withdrawals of cash from the business by the owner. In deciding whether a given transaction should be regarded as an expense of the current period, it is often helpful to pose the following questions:

**1** Was the alleged "expense" incurred in order to produce revenue in the current period?
**2** Does the item in question reduce the owner's equity?

If the answer to both questions is Yes, the transaction does represent an expense.

### Withdrawals by the owner

The owner of an unincorporated business (James Roberts, in our continuing example) invests money in the enterprise and devotes all or part of his time to its affairs in the hope that the business will earn a profit. The owner does not earn interest on the money invested nor a salary for personal services. His incentive, rather than interest or salary, is the increase in owner's equity that will result if the business earns a net income.

An owner of an unincorporated business usually makes withdrawals of cash from time to time for personal use. These withdrawals are in anticipation of profits and are not regarded as an expense of the business. The withdrawal of cash by the owner is like an expense in one respect; it reduces the owner's equity. However, expenses are incurred for the purpose of generating revenue, and a withdrawal of cash by the owner does not have this purpose. From time to time the owner may also make additional investments in the business. The investment of cash and the withdrawal of cash by the owner may be thought of as exact opposites: the investment does not represent revenue; the withdrawal does not represent an expense. Investments and withdrawals of cash affect only balance sheet accounts and are not reported in the income statement.

Since a withdrawal of cash reduces the owner's equity, it ***could be*** recorded by debiting the owner's capital account (James Roberts, Capital, in our example). However, a clearer record is created if a separate ***drawing account*** (James Roberts, Drawing) is debited to record all amounts withdrawn. The drawing account is also known as a ***personal account.***

Debits to the owner's drawing account are required for any of the following transactions:

**1** Withdrawals of cash.
**2** Withdrawals of other assets. The owner of a clothing store, for example, may withdraw merchandise for his or her personal use. The amount of the debit to the drawing account would be for the cost of the goods which were withdrawn.
**3** Payment of the owner's personal bills out of company funds.

The disposition of the drawing account when financial statements are prepared will be illustrated later in this chapter.

### Matching revenue and expenses

To prepare an income statement and determine the net income for any particular time period, we use the ***matching principle.*** The word ***matching*** refers to the close relationship that exists between certain expenses and the revenue realized as a result of incurring those expenses. For example, assume that a real estate broker earned revenue of $30,000 in the form of commissions during a given year. Earning these commissions required the making of a great many telephone calls to clients, and the telephone bill for the year amounted to $1,500. Clearly the telephone expense is closely associated with the revenue realized and must be deducted along with other operating expenses such as advertising and office rent in determining net income for the year.

Note that timing is an important factor in matching revenue and expenses. Expenses are incurred in order to produce revenue. This year's expenses are associated with this year's revenue. We do not compare this year's expenses with last year's sales because there is no close relationship between the two. To carry out the matching principle and achieve a valid measurement of each period's net income, our accounting system must ensure that revenue is recognized when it is earned and that expenses are recorded in the period they are incurred.

In summary, revenue must be matched with the related expenses incurred in producing that revenue. In matching revenue and expenses in the income statement, we show first all the revenue earned and then deduct from the revenue all the expenses incurred in producing that revenue.

### Relating revenue and expenses to time periods

A balance sheet shows the financial position of the business at a given date. An income statement, on the other hand, shows the results of operations over ***a period of time.*** In fact, the concept of income is meaningless unless it is related to a period of time. For example, if the owner of a business says, "My business produces net income of $5,000," the meaning is not at all clear; it could be made clear, however, by relating the income to a time period, such as "$5,000 a week," "$5,000 a month," or "$5,000 a year."

**The accounting period** Every business concern prepares a yearly income statement, and most businesses prepare quarterly and monthly income statements as well. Management needs to know from month to month whether revenue is rising or falling, whether expenses are being held to the level anticipated, and how net income compares with the net income of the preceding month and with the net income of the corresponding month of the preceding year. The term ***accounting period means the span of time covered by an income statement.*** It may consist of a month, a quarter of a year, a half year, or a year.

Many income statements cover the calendar year ended December 31, but an increasing number of companies are adopting an annual accounting period ending with a month other than December. Generally a business finds it more convenient to end its annual accounting period during a slack season rather than during a time of peak activity. Any 12-month accounting period adopted by a business is called its ***fiscal year.*** A fiscal year ending at the annual low point of seasonal activity is said to be a ***natural business year.*** The fiscal year selected by the federal government for its accounting purposes begins on October 1 and ends 12 months later on September 30.

**Transactions affecting two or more accounting periods** The operation of a business entails an endless stream of transactions, many of which begin in one accounting period but affect several succeeding periods. Fire insurance policies, for example, are sometimes issued to cover a period of three years. In this case, the apportionment of the cost of the policy by months is an easy matter. If the policy covers three years (36 months) and costs, for example, $360, the insurance expense each month is $10.

Not all transactions can be so precisely divided by accounting periods. The purchase of a building, furniture and fixtures, machinery, a typewriter, or an automobile provides benefits to the business over all the years in which such an asset is used. No one can determine in advance exactly how many years of service will be received from such long-lived assets. Nevertheless, in measuring the net income of a business for a period of one year or less, the accountant must estimate what portion of the cost of the building and other long-lived assets is applicable to the current year. ***Since the apportionments for these transactions which overlap two or more accounting periods are in the nature of estimates rather than precise measurements, it follows that income statements should be regarded as useful approximations of annual income rather than as absolutely accurate determinations.***

If we assume a stable price level, the time period for which the measurement of net income can be most accurate is the entire life span of the business. When a business concern sells all its assets, pays its debts, and ends its existence, it would then theoretically be possible to determine with precision the net income for the time period from the date of organization to the date of termination. Such a theoretically precise measurement of net income, however, would be too late to be of much use to the owners or managers of the business. The practical needs of business enterprise are well served by income statements of reasonable accuracy that tell managers and owners each month, each quarter, and each year the results of business operation.

## Rules of debit and credit for revenue and expenses

Our approach to revenue and expenses has stressed the fact that revenue increases the owner's equity, and expenses decrease the owner's equity. The rules of debit and credit for recording revenue and expenses follow this relationship, and therefore the recording of revenue and expenses in ledger accounts requires only a slight extension of the rules of debit and credit presented in Chapter 2. The rule previously stated for recording increases and decreases in owner's equity was as follows:

Increases in owner's equity are recorded by credits.
Decreases in owner's equity are recorded by debits.

This rule is now extended to cover revenue and expense accounts:

Revenue increases owner's equity; therefore revenue is recorded by a credit.
Expenses decrease owner's equity; therefore expenses are recorded by debits.

## Ledger accounts for revenue and expenses

During the course of an accounting period, a great many revenue and expense transactions occur in the average business. To classify and summarize these numerous transactions, a separate ledger account is maintained for each major type of revenue and expense. For example, almost every business maintains accounts for Advertising Expense, Telephone Expense, and Salaries Expense. At the end of the period, all the advertising expenses appear as debits in the Advertising Expense account. The debit balance of this account represents the total advertising expense of the period and is listed as one of the expense items in the income statement.

Revenue accounts are usually much less numerous than expense accounts. A small business such as Roberts Real Estate Company in our continuing illustration may have only one or two types of revenue, such as commissions earned from arranging sales of real estate, and commissions earned from the rental of properties in behalf of clients. In a business of this type, the revenue accounts might be called Sales Commissions Earned and Rental Commissions Earned.

**Recording revenue and expense transactions: illustration** The organization of Roberts Real Estate Company during September has already been described. The illustration is now continued for October, during which month the company earned commissions by selling several residences for its clients. Bear in mind that the company does not own any residential property; it merely acts as a broker or agent for clients wishing to sell their houses. A commission of 6% of the sales price of the house is charged for this service. During October the company not only earned commissions but also incurred a number of expenses.

Note that each illustrated transaction which affects an income statement account also affects a balance sheet account. This pattern is consistent with our previous discussion of revenue and expenses. In recording revenue transactions, we debit the assets received and credit a revenue account. In recording expense transactions, we debit an expense account and credit the asset Cash, or a liability account if payment is to be made later. The transactions for October were as follows:

**Oct. 1** Paid $360 for publication of newspaper advertising describing various houses offered for sale.

Advertising expense incurred and paid

| Analysis | Rule | Entry |
|---|---|---|
| The cost of advertising is an expense | Expenses decrease the owner's equity and are recorded by debits | Debit: Advertising Expense, $360 |
| The asset Cash was decreased | Decreases in assets are recorded by credits | Credit: Cash, $360 |

**Oct. 6** Earned and collected a commission of $2,250 by selling a residence previously listed by a client.

Revenue earned and collected

| Analysis | Rule | Entry |
|---|---|---|
| The asset Cash was increased | Increases in assets are recorded by debits | Debit: Cash, $2,250 |
| Revenue was earned | Revenue increases the owner's equity and is recorded by a credit | Credit: Sales Commissions Earned, $2,250 |

**Oct. 16** Newspaper advertising was ordered at a price of $270, payment to be made within 30 days.

Advertising expense incurred; to be paid later

| Analysis | Rule | Entry |
|---|---|---|
| The cost of advertising is an expense | Expenses decrease the owner's equity and are recorded by debits | Debit: Advertising Expense, $270 |
| An account payable, a liability, was incurred | Increases in liabilities are recorded by credits | Credit: Accounts Payable, $270 |

**Oct. 20** A commission of $3,390 was earned by selling a client's residence. The sales agreement provided that the commission would be received in 60 days.

Revenue earned, to be collected later

| Analysis | Rule | Entry |
|---|---|---|
| An asset in the form of an account receivable was acquired | Increases in assets are recorded by debits | Debit: Accounts Receivable, $3,390 |
| Revenue was earned | Revenue increases the owner's equity and is recorded by a credit | Credit: Sales Commissions Earned, $3,390 |

*Salaries expense incurred and paid*

**Oct. 30** Paid salaries of $2,100 to office employees for services rendered during October.

| Analysis | Rule | Entry |
|---|---|---|
| *Salaries of employees are an expense* | *Expenses decrease the owner's equity and are recorded by debits* | *Debit: Office Salaries Expense, $2,100* |
| *The asset Cash was decreased* | *Decreases in assets are recorded by credits* | *Credit: Cash, $2,100* |

*Telephone expense incurred, to be paid later*

**Oct. 30** A telephone bill for October amounting to $144 was received. Payment was required by November 10.

| Analysis | Rule | Entry |
|---|---|---|
| *The cost of telephone service is an expense* | *Expenses decrease the owner's equity and are recorded by debits* | *Debit: Telephone Expense, $144* |
| *An account payable, a liability, was incurred* | *Increases in liabilities are recorded by credits* | *Credit: Accounts Payable, $144* |

*Withdrawal of cash by owner*

**Oct. 30** Roberts withdrew $1,800 cash for personal use.

| Analysis | Rule | Entry |
|---|---|---|
| *Withdrawal of assets by the owner decreases the owner's equity* | *Decreases in owner's equity are recorded by debits* | *Debit: James Roberts, Drawing, $1,800* |
| *The asset Cash was decreased* | *Decreases in assets are recorded by credits* | *Credit: Cash, $1,800* |

The journal entries to record the October transactions are as follows:

*October journal entries for Roberts Real Estate Company*

***General Journal*** — *Page 2*

| Date | | Account Titles and Explanation | LP | Debit | Credit |
|---|---|---|---|---|---|
| *19__* | | | | | |
| *Oct* | *1* | *Advertising Expense* | *70* | *360* | |
| | | *Cash* | *1* | | *360* |
| | | *Paid for newspaper advertising.* | | | |
| | *6* | *Cash* | *1* | *2,250* | |
| | | *Sales Commissions Earned* | *61* | | *2,250* |
| | | *Earned and collected commission by selling residence for client.* | | | |

**General Journal** — Page 2

| Date | | Account Titles and Explanation | LP | Debit | Credit |
|---|---|---|---|---|---|
| 19__ | | | | | |
| Oct | 16 | Advertising Expense | 70 | 270 | |
| | | Accounts Payable | 30 | | 270 |
| | | Ordered newspaper advertising; payable in 30 days. | | | |
| | 20 | Accounts Receivable | 2 | 3,390 | |
| | | Sales Commissions Earned | 61 | | 3,390 |
| | | Earned commission by selling residence for client; commission to be received in 60 days. | | | |
| | 30 | Office Salaries Expense | 72 | 2,100 | |
| | | Cash | 1 | | 2,100 |
| | | Paid office salaries for October. | | | |
| | 30 | Telephone Expense | 74 | 144 | |
| | | Accounts Payable | 30 | | 144 |
| | | To record liability for October telephone service. | | | |
| | 30 | James Roberts, Drawing | 51 | 1,800 | |
| | | Cash | 1 | | 1,800 |
| | | Withdrawal of cash by owner. | | | |

The column headings at the top of the illustrated journal page (***Date, Account Titles and Explanation, LP, Debit,*** and ***Credit***) are seldom used in practice. They are included here as an instructional guide but will be omitted from some of the later illustrations of journal entries.

## Sequence of accounts in the ledger

Accounts are located in the ledger in financial statement order; that is, the balance sheet accounts first (assets, liabilities, and owner's equity) followed by the income statement accounts (revenue and expenses). The usual sequence of accounts within these five groups is shown by the list at the top of page 95.

## Why are ledger accounts arranged in financial statement order?

Remember that a trial balance is prepared by listing the ledger account balances shown in the ledger, working from the first ledger page to the last. Therefore, if the accounts are located in the ledger in ***financial statement order,*** the same sequence will naturally be followed in the trial balance, and this arrangement

***Balance Sheet Accounts***

*Assets:*
- *Cash*
- *Marketable securities*
- *Notes receivable*
- *Accounts receivable*
- *Inventory (discussed in Chapter 5)*
- *Office supplies (unexpired insurance, prepaid rent, and other prepaid expenses discussed in Chapter 4)*
- *Land*
- *Buildings*
- *Equipment*
- *Other assets*

*Liabilities:*
- *Notes payable*
- *Accounts payable*
- *Salaries payable (and other short-term liabilities discussed in Chapter 4)*

*Owner's equity:*
- *John Smith, capital*
- *John Smith, drawing*

***Income Statement Accounts***

*Revenue:*
- *Commissions earned (fees earned, rent earned, sales, etc.)*

*Expenses: (No standard sequence of listing exists for expense accounts.)*
- *Advertising*
- *Salaries*
- *Rent*
- *Telephone*
- *Depreciation*
- *Various other expenses*

will make it easier to prepare the balance sheet and income statement from the trial balance. Also, this standard arrangement of accounts will make it easier to locate any account in the ledger.

## Ledger accounts for Roberts Real Estate Company: illustration

The ledger of the Roberts Real Estate Company after the October transactions have been posted is now illustrated. The accounts appear in financial statement order. To conserve space in this illustration, several ledger accounts appear on a single page; in actual practice, however, each account occupies a separate page in the ledger.

**Cash** — Account No. 1

| Date | | Explanation | Ref | Debit | Credit | Balance |
|---|---|---|---|---|---|---|
| 19— Sept | 1 | | 1 | 60,000 00 | | 60,000 00 |
| | 3 | | 1 | | 21,000 00 | 39,000 00 |
| | 5 | | 1 | | 15,000 00 | 24,000 00 |
| | 20 | | 1 | 1,500 00 | | 25,500 00 |
| | 30 | | 1 | | 3,000 00 | 22,500 00 |
| Oct | 1 | | 2 | | 360 00 | 22,140 00 |
| | 6 | | 2 | 2,250 00 | | 24,390 00 |
| | 30 | | 2 | | 2,100 00 | 22,290 00 |
| | 30 | | 2 | | 1,800 00 | 20,490 00 |

**Accounts Receivable** Account No. 2

| Date | | Explanation | Ref | Debit | Credit | Balance |
|---|---|---|---|---|---|---|
| 19— Sept | 10 | | 1 | 6000 00 | | 6000 00 |
| | 20 | | 1 | | 1500 00 | 4500 00 |
| Oct | 20 | | 2 | 3390 00 | | 7890 00 |

**Land** Account No. 20

| Date | | Explanation | Ref | Debit | Credit | Balance |
|---|---|---|---|---|---|---|
| 19— Sept | 3 | | 1 | 21000 00 | | 21000 00 |
| | 10 | | 1 | | 6000 00 | 15000 00 |

**Building** Account No. 22

| Date | | Explanation | Ref | Debit | Credit | Balance |
|---|---|---|---|---|---|---|
| 19— Sept | 5 | | 1 | 36000 00 | | 36000 00 |

**Office Equipment** Account No. 25

| Date | | Explanation | Ref | Debit | Credit | Balance |
|---|---|---|---|---|---|---|
| 19— Sept | 14 | | 1 | 5400 00 | | 5400 00 |

**Accounts Payable** Account No. 30

| Date | | Explanation | Ref | Debit | Credit | Balance |
|---|---|---|---|---|---|---|
| 19— Sept | 5 | | 1 | | 21000 00 | 21000 00 |
| | 14 | | 1 | | 5400 00 | 26400 00 |
| | 30 | | 1 | 3000 00 | | 23400 00 |
| Oct | 16 | | 2 | | 270 00 | 23670 00 |
| | 30 | | 2 | | 144 00 | 23814 00 |

**James Roberts, Capital** — Account No. 50

| Date | | Explanation | Ref | Debit | Credit | Balance |
|---|---|---|---|---|---|---|
| 19— Sept | 1 | | 1 | | 60000 00 | 60000 00 |
| | | | | | | |
| | | | | | | |

**James Roberts, Drawing** — Account No. 51

| Date | | Explanation | Ref | Debit | Credit | Balance |
|---|---|---|---|---|---|---|
| 19— Oct | 30 | | 2 | 1800 00 | | 1800 00 |
| | | | | | | |
| | | | | | | |

**Sales Commissions Earned** — Account No. 61

| Date | | Explanation | Ref | Debit | Credit | Balance |
|---|---|---|---|---|---|---|
| 19— Oct | 6 | | 2 | | 2250 00 | 2250 00 |
| | 20 | | 2 | | 3390 00 | 5640 00 |
| | | | | | | |
| | | | | | | |

**Advertising Expense** — Account No. 70

| Date | | Explanation | Ref | Debit | Credit | Balance |
|---|---|---|---|---|---|---|
| 19— Oct | 1 | | 2 | 360 00 | | 360 00 |
| | 16 | | 2 | 270 00 | | 630 00 |
| | | | | | | |
| | | | | | | |

**Office Salaries Expense** — Account No. 72

| Date | | Explanation | Ref | Debit | Credit | Balance |
|---|---|---|---|---|---|---|
| 19— Oct | 30 | | 2 | 2100 00 | | 2100 00 |
| | | | | | | |
| | | | | | | |
| | | | | | | |

| Telephone Expense | | | | | | Account No. 74 |
|---|---|---|---|---|---|---|
| Date | | Explanation | Ref | Debit | Credit | Balance |
| 19— Oct | 30 | | 2 | 144 00 | | 144 00 |

## Trial balance

The trial balance at October 31 was prepared from the preceding ledger accounts.

**ROBERTS REAL ESTATE COMPANY**
**Trial Balance**
**October 31, 19__**

*Proving the equality of debits and credits*

| | | |
|---|---|---|
| Cash | $20,490 | |
| Accounts receivable | 7,890 | |
| Land | 15,000 | |
| Building | 36,000 | |
| Office equipment | 5,400 | |
| Accounts payable | | $23,814 |
| James Roberts, capital | | 60,000 |
| James Roberts, drawing | 1,800 | |
| Sales commissions earned | | 5,640 |
| Advertising expense | 630 | |
| Office salaries expense | 2,100 | |
| Telephone expense | 144 | |
| | $89,454 | $89,454 |

## Recording depreciation at the end of the period

The preceding trial balance includes all the October expenses requiring cash payments such as salaries, advertising, and telephone service, but it does not include any depreciation expense. The term ***depreciation*** means the systematic allocation of the cost of an asset to expense over the accounting periods making up its useful life. Although depreciation expense does not require a monthly cash outlay, it is nevertheless an inevitable and continuing expense. Failure to make an entry for depreciation expense would result in ***understating*** the total expenses of the period and consequently in ***overstating*** the net income.

**Building** The office building purchased by Roberts Real Estate Company at a cost of $36,000 is estimated to have a useful life of 20 years. The purpose of the $36,000 expenditure was to provide a place in which to carry on the business and thereby to obtain revenue. After 20 years of use the building will be worthless and the original cost of $36,000 will have been entirely consumed. In effect, the company has purchased 20 years of "housing services" at a total cost of $36,000. A portion of this cost expires during each year of use of the building. If we assume that each year's operations should bear an equal share of the total cost (straight-line depreciation), the annual depreciation expense will amount to $\frac{1}{20}$ of $36,000, or $1,800. On a monthly basis, depreciation expense is $150 ($36,000 cost ÷ 240 months). There are alternative methods of spreading the cost of a depreciable asset over its useful life, some of which will be considered in Chapter 11.

The journal entry to record depreciation of the building during October follows:

***Recording depreciation of the building***

***General Journal*** ***Page 2***

| Date | | Account Titles and Explanation | LP | Debit | Credit |
|---|---|---|---|---|---|
| 19__ | | | | | |
| Oct | 31 | Depreciation Expense: Building | 76 | 150 | |
| | | Accumulated Depreciation: Building | 23 | | 150 |
| | | To record depreciation for October. | | | |

The depreciation expense account will appear in the income statement for October along with the other expenses of salaries, advertising, and telephone. The Accumulated Depreciation: Building account will appear in the balance sheet as a deduction from the Building account, as shown by the following illustration of a ***partial*** balance sheet:

***ROBERTS REAL ESTATE COMPANY***
***Partial Balance Sheet***
***October 31, 19__***

***Showing accumulated depreciation in the balance sheet***

| | | |
|---|---|---|
| Building (at cost) | $36,000 | |
| Less: Accumulated depreciation | 150 | $35,850 |

The end result of crediting the Accumulated Depreciation: Building account is much the same as if the credit had been made to the Building account; that is, the net amount shown on the balance sheet for the building is reduced from $36,000 to $35,850. Although the credit side of a depreciation entry ***could*** be made directly to the asset account, it is customary and more efficient to record such credits in a separate account entitled Accumulated Depreciation. The original cost of the asset and the total amount of depreciation recorded over the years can more easily be determined from the ledger when separate accounts are maintained for the asset and for the accumulated depreciation.

Accumulated Depreciation: Building is an example of a ***contra-asset account,*** because it has a credit balance and is offset against an asset account (Building) to produce the proper balance sheet valuation for the asset.

**Office equipment** Depreciation on the office equipment of Roberts Real Estate Company must also be recorded at the end of October. This equipment cost $5,400 and is assumed to have a useful life of 10 years. Monthly depreciation expense on the straight-line basis is, therefore, $45, computed by dividing the cost of $5,400 by the useful life of 120 months. The journal entry is as follows:

*General Journal* *Page 2*

*Recording depreciation of office equipment*

| Date | | Account Titles and Explanation | LP | Debit | Credit |
|---|---|---|---|---|---|
| *19__* | | | | | |
| *Oct* | *31* | *Depreciation Expense: Office Equipment . . . . . .* | *78* | *45* | |
| | | *Accumulated Depreciation: Office Equipment . . . . . . . . . . . . . . . . . . . .* | *26* | | *45* |
| | | *To record depreciation for October.* | | | |

No depreciation was recorded on the building and office equipment for September, the month in which these assets were acquired, because regular operations did not begin until October. Generally, depreciation is not recognized until the business begins active operation and the assets are placed in use. Accountants often use the expression "matching costs and revenues" to convey the idea of writing off the cost of an asset to expense during the time periods in which the business uses the asset to generate revenue.

The journal entry by which depreciation is recorded at the end of the month is called an ***adjusting entry.*** The adjustment of certain asset accounts and related expense accounts is a necessary step at the end of each accounting period so that the information presented in the financial statements will be as accurate and complete as possible. In the next chapter, adjusting entries will be shown for some other items in addition to depreciation.

### The adjusted trial balance

After all the necessary adjusting entries have been journalized and posted, an ***adjusted trial balance*** is prepared to prove that the ledger is still in balance. It also provides a complete listing of the account balances to be used in preparing the financial statements. The adjusted trial balance on page 101 differs from the trial balance shown on page 98 because it includes accounts for depreciation expense and accumulated depreciation.

## FINANCIAL STATEMENTS

### The income statement

When we measure the net income earned by a business we are measuring its economic performance—its success or failure as a business enterprise. The owner, the manager, and the company's banker are anxious to see the latest available income statement and thereby to judge how well the company is doing.

**ROBERTS REAL ESTATE COMPANY**
**Adjusted Trial Balance**
**October 31, 19__**

*Adjusted trial balance*

| | | |
|---|---|---|
| Cash | $20,490 | |
| Accounts receivable | 7,890 | |
| Land | 15,000 | |
| Building | 36,000 | |
| Accumulated depreciation: building | | $ 150 |
| Office equipment | 5,400 | |
| Accumulated depreciation: office equipment | | 45 |
| Accounts payable | | 23,814 |
| James Roberts, capital | | 60,000 |
| James Roberts, drawing | 1,800 | |
| Sales commissions earned | | 5,640 |
| Advertising expense | 630 | |
| Office salaries expense | 2,100 | |
| Telephone expense | 144 | |
| Depreciation expense: building | 150 | |
| Depreciation expense: office equipment | 45 | |
| | $89,649 | $89,649 |

If the business is organized as a corporation, the stockholders and prospective investors also will be keenly interested in each successive income statement. The October income statement for Roberts Real Estate Company appears as follows:

**ROBERTS REAL ESTATE COMPANY**
**Income Statement**
**For the Month Ended October 31, 19__**

*Income statement showing results of operations for October*

| | | |
|---|---|---|
| Sales commissions earned | | $5,640 |
| Expenses: | | |
| Advertising expense | $ 630 | |
| Office salaries expense | 2,100 | |
| Telephone expense | 144 | |
| Depreciation expense: building | 150 | |
| Depreciation expense: office equipment | 45 | 3,069 |
| Net income | | $2,571 |

This income statement consists of the last six accounts in the adjusted trial balance shown above. It shows that the revenue during October exceeded the expenses of the month, thus producing a net income of $2,571. Bear in mind, however, that our measurement of net income is not absolutely accurate or precise, because of the assumptions and estimates involved in the accounting process. We have recorded only those economic events which are evidenced by accounting transactions. Perhaps during October Roberts Real Estate Company has developed a strong interest on the part of many clients who are on the verge of buying or selling homes. This accumulation of client interest is an important step toward profitable operation, but is not reflected in the October 31 income statement because it is not subject to objective measurement. Remember also that in determining the amount of depreciation expense we had to estimate the useful life of the building and office equipment. Any error in our estimates is reflected in the net income reported for October. Despite these limitations, the income statement is of vital importance, and indicates that the new business has been profitable during the first month of its operation.

Alternative titles for the income statement include ***earnings statement, statement of operations,*** and ***profit and loss statement.*** However, ***income statement*** is by far the most popular term for this important financial statement. In summary, we can say that an income statement is used to evaluate the performance of a business by matching the revenue earned during a given time period with the expenses incurred in obtaining that revenue.

### The balance sheet

Previous illustrations of balance sheets have been arranged in the ***account form,*** that is, with the assets on the left side of the page and the liabilities and owner's equity on the right side. The balance sheet on page 103 is shown in ***report form,*** that is, with the liabilities and owner's equity sections listed below rather than to the right of the asset section. Both the account form and the report form are widely used.

The relationship between the income statement and the balance sheet is shown in the owner's equity section of the balance sheet. The owner's original capital investment of $60,000 was increased by reason of the $2,571 net income earned during October, making a total equity of $62,571. This equity was decreased, however, by the owner's withdrawal of $1,800 in cash at the end of October, leaving a final balance of $60,771.

Alternative titles for the balance sheet include ***statement of financial position*** and ***statement of financial condition.*** Although "balance sheet" may not be a very descriptive term, it continues to be the most widely used, perhaps because of custom and tradition.

In the Roberts Real Estate Company illustration, we have shown the two common ways in which the owner's equity in a business may be increased: (1) investment of cash or other assets by the owner, and (2) operating the business at a profit. There are also two ways in which the owner's equity may be decreased: (1) withdrawal of assets by the owner, and (2) operating the business at a loss.

## CLOSING THE ACCOUNTS

The accounts for revenue, expenses, and drawings are ***temporary proprietorship accounts*** used during the accounting period to classify and accumulate changes

**ROBERTS REAL ESTATE COMPANY**
**Balance Sheet**
**October 31, 19__**

*Balance sheet at October 31: report form*

**Assets**

| | | |
|---|---|---|
| Cash | | $20,490 |
| Accounts receivable | | 7,890 |
| Land | | 15,000 |
| Building | $36,000 | |
| Less: Accumulated depreciation | 150 | 35,850 |
| Office equipment | $ 5,400 | |
| Less: Accumulated depreciation | 45 | 5,355 |
| Total assets | | $84,585 |

**Liabilities & Owner's Equity**

| | | |
|---|---|---|
| Liabilities: | | |
| Accounts payable | | $23,814 |
| Owner's equity: | | |
| James Roberts, capital, Oct. 1, 19__ | $60,000 | |
| Net income for October | 2,571 | |
| Subtotal | $62,571 | |
| Less: Withdrawals | 1,800 | |
| James Roberts, capital, Oct. 31, 19__ | | 60,771 |
| Total liabilities & owner's equity | | $84,585 |

affecting the owner's equity. At the end of the period, we want to transfer the net effect of these various increases and decreases into the permanent account showing the owner's equity. We also want to reduce the balances of the temporary proprietorship accounts to zero, so that these accounts will again be ready for use in accumulating information during the next accounting period. These objectives are accomplished by the use of ***closing entries.***

Revenue and expense accounts are closed at the end of each accounting period by transferring their balances to a summary account called Income Summary. When the credit balances of the revenue accounts and the debit balances of the expense accounts have been transferred into one summary account, the balance of this Income Summary will be the net income or net loss for the period. If the revenue (credit balances) exceeds the expenses (debit balances), the Income Summary account will have a credit balance representing net income. Conversely, if expenses exceed revenue, the Income Summary will have a debit balance representing net loss.

As previously explained, all debits and credits in the ledger are posted from the journal; therefore, the closing of revenue and expense accounts requires the making of journal entries and the posting of these journal entries to ledger accounts. A journal entry made for the purpose of closing a revenue or expense account by transferring its balance to the Income Summary account is called a ***closing entry.*** This term is also applied to the journal entries (to be explained later) used in closing the Income Summary account and the owner's drawing account into the owner's capital account.

A principal purpose of the year-end process of closing the revenue and expense accounts is to reduce their balances to zero. Since the revenue and expense accounts provide the information for the income statement of ***a given accounting period,*** it is essential that these accounts have zero balances at the beginning of each new period. The closing of the accounts has the effect of wiping the slate clean and preparing the records for the recording of revenue and expenses during the succeeding accounting period.

It is common practice to close the accounts only once a year, but for illustration, we shall now demonstrate the closing of the accounts of Roberts Real Estate Company at October 31 after one month's operation.

**Closing entries for revenue accounts** Revenue accounts have credit balances. Closing a revenue account, therefore, means transferring its credit balance to the Income Summary account. This transfer is accomplished by a journal entry debiting the revenue account in an amount equal to its credit balance, with an offsetting credit to the Income Summary account. The only revenue account of Roberts Real Estate Company is Sales Commission Earned, which had a credit balance of $5,640 at October 31. The closing entry is as follows:

***Closing a revenue account***

***General Journal*** — ***Page 3***

| Date | | Account Titles and Explanation | LP | Debit | Credit |
|---|---|---|---|---|---|
| 19__ | | | | | |
| Oct | 31 | Sales Commissions Earned . . . . . . . . . . . . . . | 61 | 5,640 | |
| | | Income Summary . . . . . . . . . . . . . . . . . | 53 | | 5,640 |
| | | To close the Sales Commissions Earned account. | | | |

After this closing entry has been posted, the two accounts affected will appear as follows. A few details of account structure have been omitted to simplify the illustration; a directional arrow has been added to show the transfer of the $5,640 balance of the revenue account into the Income Summary account.

***Sales Commissions Earned*** — ***61***

| Date | | Exp. | Ref | Debit | Credit | Balance |
|---|---|---|---|---|---|---|
| Oct | 6 | | 2 | | 2,250 | 2,250 |
| | 20 | | 2 | | 3,390 | 5,640 |
| | 31 | To close | 3 | 5,640 | | -0- |

***Income Summary*** — ***53***

| Date | | Exp. | Ref | Debit | Credit | Balance |
|---|---|---|---|---|---|---|
| Oct | 31 | | 3 | | 5,640 | 5,640 |

**Closing entries for expense accounts** Expense accounts have debit balances. Closing an expense account means transferring its debit balance to the Income Summary account. The journal entry to close an expense account, therefore, consists of a credit to the expense account in an amount equal to its debit balance, with an offsetting debit to the Income Summary account.

There are five expense accounts in the ledger of Roberts Real Estate Company. Five separate journal entries could be made to close these five expense accounts, but the use of one ***compound journal entry*** is an easier, more efficient, time-saving method of closing all five expense accounts. A compound journal entry is an entry that includes debits to more than one account or credits to more than one account.

*Closing the various expense accounts by use of a compound journal entry*

*General Journal* — *Page 3*

| Date | | Account Titles and Explanation | LP | Debit | Credit |
|---|---|---|---|---|---|
| 19__ | | | | | |
| Oct | 31 | Income Summary | 53 | 3,069 | |
| | | Advertising Expense | 70 | | 630 |
| | | Office Salaries Expense | 72 | | 2,100 |
| | | Telephone Expense | 74 | | 144 |
| | | Depreciation Expense: Building | 76 | | 150 |
| | | Depreciation Expense: Office Equipment | 78 | | 45 |
| | | To close the expense accounts. | | | |

After this closing entry has been posted, the Income Summary account has a credit balance of $2,571, and the five expense accounts have zero balances, as shown on page 106.

**Closing the Income Summary account** The five expense accounts have now been closed and the total amount of $3,069 formerly contained in these accounts appears in the debit column of the Income Summary account. The commissions of $5,640 earned during October appear in the credit column of the Income Summary account. Since the credit entry of $5,640 representing October revenue is larger than the debit of $3,069 representing October expenses, the account has a credit balance of $2,571—the net income for October.

The net income of $2,571 earned during October causes the owner's equity to increase. The ***credit*** balance of the Income Summary account is, therefore, transferred to the owner's capital account by the closing entry on page 107.

**Expense accounts have zero balances after closing entries have been posted**

**Income Summary** — Account No. 53

| Date | | Explanation | Ref | Debit | Credit | Balance |
|---|---|---|---|---|---|---|
| 19__ | | | | | | |
| Oct | 31 | | 3 | | 5,640 | 5,640 |
| | 31 | | 3 | 3,069 | | 2,571 |

**Advertising Expense** — Account No. 70

| Date | | Explanation | Ref | Debit | Credit | Balance |
|---|---|---|---|---|---|---|
| 19__ | | | | | | |
| Oct | 2 | | 2 | 360 | | 360 |
| | 16 | | 2 | 270 | | 630 |
| | 31 | To close | 3 | | 630 | -0- |

**Office Salaries Expense** — Account No. 72

| Date | | Explanation | Ref | Debit | Credit | Balance |
|---|---|---|---|---|---|---|
| 19__ | | | | | | |
| Oct | 30 | | 2 | 2,100 | | 2,100 |
| | 31 | To close | 3 | | 2,100 | -0- |

**Telephone Expense** — Account No. 74

| Date | | Explanation | Ref | Debit | Credit | Balance |
|---|---|---|---|---|---|---|
| 19__ | | | | | | |
| Oct | 30 | | 2 | 144 | | 144 |
| | 31 | To close | 3 | | 144 | -0- |

**Depreciation Expense: Building** — Account No. 76

| Date | | Explanation | Ref | Debit | Credit | Balance |
|---|---|---|---|---|---|---|
| 19__ | | | | | | |
| Oct | 31 | | 2 | 150 | | 150 |
| | 31 | To close | 3 | | 150 | -0- |

**Depreciation Expense: Office Equipment** — Account No. 78

| Date | | Explanation | Ref | Debit | Credit | Balance |
|---|---|---|---|---|---|---|
| 19__ | | | | | | |
| Oct | 31 | | 2 | 45 | | 45 |
| | 31 | To close | 3 | | 45 | -0- |

**General Journal** — Page 3

*Net income earned increases the owner's equity*

| Date | | Account Titles and Explanation | LP | Debit | Credit |
|---|---|---|---|---|---|
| 19__ | | | | | |
| Oct | 31 | Income Summary | 53 | 2,571 | |
| | | James Roberts, Capital | 50 | | 2,571 |
| | | To close the Income Summary account for October by transferring the net income to the owner's capital account. | | | |

After this closing entry has been posted, the Income Summary account has a zero balance, and the net income earned during October appears in the owner's capital account as shown below:

**Income Summary** — Account No. 53

| | | | | | | |
|---|---|---|---|---|---|---|
| 19__ | | | | | | |
| Oct | 31 | Revenue | 3 | | 5,640 | 5,640 |
| | 31 | Expenses | 3 | 3,069 | | 2,571 |
| | 31 | To close | 3 | 2,571 | | -0- |

**James Roberts, Capital** — Account No. 50

| | | | | | | |
|---|---|---|---|---|---|---|
| 19__ | | | | | | |
| Sept | 1 | Investment by owner | 1 | | 60,000 | 60,000 |
| Oct | 31 | Net income for October | 3 | | 2,571 | 62,571 |

In our illustration the business has operated profitably with revenue in excess of expenses. Not every business is so fortunate; if the expenses of a business are larger than its revenue, the Income Summary account will have a debit balance. In case of a loss, the closing of the Income Summary account will require a debit to the owner's capital account and an offsetting credit to the Income Summary account. The owner's equity will, of course, be reduced by the amount of the loss debited to the capital account.

Note that the Income Summary account is used only at the end of the period when the accounts are being closed. The Income Summary account has no entries and no balance except during the process of closing the accounts at the end of the accounting period.

**Closing the owner's drawing account** As explained earlier in this chapter, withdrawals of cash or other assets by the owner are not considered as an expense of the business and, therefore, are not a factor in determining the net income for the period. Since drawings by the owner do not constitute an expense, the owner's drawing account is closed not into the Income Summary account but directly to the owner's capital account. The following journal entry serves to close the drawing account in the ledger of Roberts Real Estate Company at October 31.

*Drawing account is closed to owner's capital account*

**General Journal** — Page 3

| Date | | Account Titles and Explanation | LP | Debit | Credit |
|---|---|---|---|---|---|
| 19__ | | | | | |
| Oct | 31 | James Roberts, Capital . . . . . . . . . . . . . . . . . | 50 | 1,800 | |
| | | James Roberts, Drawing . . . . . . . . . . . . | 51 | | 1,800 |
| | | To close the owner's drawing account. | | | |

After this closing entry has been posted, the drawing account will have a zero balance, and the amount withdrawn by Roberts during October will appear as a deduction or debit entry in the capital account, as shown below:

*One account now shows total equity of owner*

**James Roberts, Drawing** — 51

| | | | | | | |
|---|---|---|---|---|---|---|
| 19__ | | | | | | |
| Oct | 30 | Withdrawal | 2 | 1,800 | | 1,800 |
| | 31 | To close | 3 | | 1,800 | -0- |

**James Roberts, Capital** — 50

| | | | | | | |
|---|---|---|---|---|---|---|
| 19__ | | | | | | |
| Sept | 1 | Investment by owner | 1 | | 60,000 | 60,000 |
| Oct | 31 | Net income for October | 3 | | 2,571 | 62,571 |
| | 31 | From owner's drawing account | 3 | 1,800 | | 60,771 |

**The closing process—in summary** Let us now summarize the process of closing the accounts.

1 Close the various revenue accounts by transferring their balances into the Income Summary account.
2 Close the various expense accounts by transferring their balances into the Income Summary account.
3 Close the Income Summary account by transferring its balance into the owner's capital account.
4 Close the owner's drawing account into the owner's capital account. (The balance of the owner's capital account in the ledger will now be the same as the amount of capital appearing in the balance sheet.)

The closing of the accounts may be illustrated graphically by use of T accounts as follows:

Diagram showing the closing of the accounts

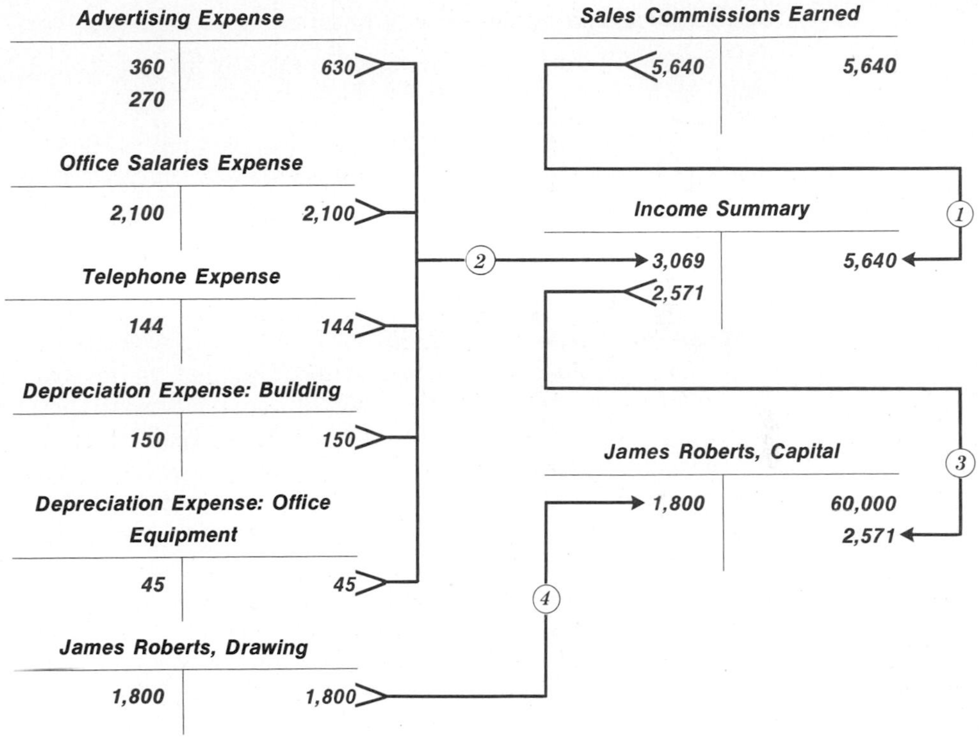


## After-closing trial balance

After the revenue and expense accounts have been closed, it is desirable to prepare an ***after-closing trial balance,*** which of course will consist solely of balance sheet accounts. There is always the possibility that an error in posting the closing entries may have upset the equality of debits and credits in the ledger. The after-closing trial balance, or ***post-closing trial balance*** as it is often called, is prepared from the ledger. It gives assurance that the accounts are in balance and ready for the recording of the transactions of the new accounting period. The after-closing trial balance of Roberts Real Estate Company follows:

**ROBERTS REAL ESTATE COMPANY**
*After-Closing Trial Balance*
*October 31, 19__*

Only the balance sheet accounts remain open

| | | |
|---|---|---|
| Cash | $20,490 | |
| Accounts receivable | 7,890 | |
| Land | 15,000 | |
| Building | 36,000 | |
| Accumulated depreciation: building | | $ 150 |
| Office equipment | 5,400 | |
| Accumulated depreciation: office equipment | | 45 |
| Accounts payable | | 23,814 |
| James Roberts, capital | | 60,771 |
| | $84,780 | $84,780 |

### Sequence of accounting procedures

The accounting procedures described to this point may be summarized in eight steps, as follows:

1 **Journalize transactions** Enter all transactions in the general journal, thus creating a chronological record of events.
2 **Post to ledger accounts** Post debits and credits from the general journal to the proper ledger accounts, thus creating a record classified by accounts.
3 **Prepare a trial balance** Prove the equality of debits and credits in the ledger.
4 **Make end-of-period adjustments** Draft adjusting entries in the general journal, and post to ledger accounts. Thus far we have illustrated only one type of adjustment: the recording of depreciation at the end of the period.
5 **Prepare an adjusted trial balance** Prove again the equality of debits and credits in the ledger.
6 **Prepare financial statements** An income statement is needed to show the results of operation for the period. A balance sheet is needed to show the financial position of the business at the end of the period.
7 **Journalize and post closing entries** The closing entries clear the revenue, expense, and drawing accounts, making them ready for recording the events of the next accounting period. The closing entries also transfer the net income or loss of the completed period to the owner's capital account.
8 **Prepare an after-closing trial balance** This step ensures that the ledger remains in balance after posting of the closing entries.

### Accrual basis of accounting versus cash basis of accounting

We now want to consider whether revenue should be recorded in the accounting period in which it is earned or in the period in which it is collected in cash. A parallel question is whether expenses should be recorded in the accounting period in which they are incurred or in the period in which they are paid. A business which recognizes revenue in the period in which it is earned and which deducts in the same period the expenses incurred in generating this revenue is using the ***accrual basis of accounting.***

Net income has meaning only when it is related to a specific period of time. Since net income is determined by offsetting expenses against revenue, both the expenses and the revenue used in the calculation must relate to the same time period. This matching or offsetting of related revenue and expenses gives a realistic picture of the profit performance of the business each period. The positive economic effect which revenue has on the business should be recognized at the time the revenue is earned (that is, at the time goods are sold and services are rendered to customers). The negative economic effect of expenses (that is, using up goods and services) should be recognized at the time these goods and services are consumed. The accrual basis is thus essential to income determination, and as we have already indicated, the measurement of income is a major objective of the whole accounting process.

The alternative to the accrual basis of accounting is the ***cash basis.*** Under cash basis accounting, revenue is not recorded until received in cash; expenses are assigned to the period in which cash payment is made. Most business concerns use the accrual method of accounting, but individuals and professionals (such as physicians and lawyers) usually maintain their accounting records on a cash basis.

The cash basis of accounting does not give a good picture of profitability. For example, it ignores uncollected revenue which has been earned and expenses which have been incurred but not paid. Throughout this book we shall be working with the accrual basis of accounting, except for that portion of Chapter 20 dealing with the income tax returns of individuals.

## KEY TERMS INTRODUCED OR EMPHASIZED IN CHAPTER 3

**Accounting period** The span of time covered by an income statement. One year is the accounting period for much financial reporting, but financial statements are also prepared by most companies for each quarter of the year and also for each month.

**Accrual basis of accounting** Calls for recording revenue in the period in which it is earned and recording expenses in the period in which they are incurred. The effect of events on the business is recognized as services are rendered or consumed rather than when cash is received or paid.

**Accumulated depreciation** A contra-asset account shown as a deduction from the related asset account in the balance sheet. Depreciation taken throughout the useful life of an asset is accumulated in this account.

**Adjusted trial balance** A listing of all ledger account balances after the amounts have been changed to include the adjusting entries made at the end of the period.

**Adjusting entries** Entries required at the end of the period to update the accounts before financial statements are prepared. Adjusting entries serve to apportion transactions properly between the accounting periods affected and to record any revenue earned or expenses incurred which have not been recorded prior to the end of the period.

**After-closing trial balance** A trial balance prepared after all closing entries have been made. Consists only of accounts for assets, liabilities, and owner's equity.

**Cash basis of accounting** Revenue is recorded when received in cash and expenses are recorded in the period in which cash payment is made. Fails to match revenue with related expenses and therefore does not lead to a logical measurement of income. Use is limited mostly to individual income tax returns and to accounting records of physicians and other professional firms.

**Closing entries** Journal entries made at the end of the period for the purpose of closing temporary accounts (revenue, expense, and drawing accounts) and transferring balances to the owner's capital account.

**Contra-asset account** An account with a credit balance which is offset against or deducted from an asset account to produce the proper balance sheet valuation for the asset.

**Depreciation** The systematic allocation of the cost of an asset to expense during the periods of its useful life.

**Drawing account** The account used to record the withdrawals of cash or other assets by the owner. Closed at the end of the period by transferring its balance to the owner's capital account.

**Expenses** The cost of the goods and services used up in the process of obtaining revenue. Sometimes referred to as ***expired costs.***

**Financial statement order** Sequence of accounts in the ledger: balance sheet accounts first (assets, liabilities, and owner's equity), followed by income statement accounts (revenue and expenses).

**Fiscal year** Any 12-month accounting period adopted by a business.

**Income statement** A report used to evaluate the performance of a business by matching its revenue and related expenses for a particular accounting period. Shows the net income or net loss.

**Income Summary account** The summary account in the ledger to which revenue and expense accounts are closed at the end of the period. The balance (credit balance for a net income, debit balance for a net loss) is transferred to the owner's capital account.

**Matching principle** The revenue earned during an accounting period is matched with the expenses incurred in generating this revenue.

**Net income** The excess of revenue earned over the related expenses for a given period.

**Report form balance sheet** A balance sheet in which the sections for liabilities and owner's equity are listed below the section for assets.

**Revenue** The price of goods sold and services rendered by a business. Equal to the inflow of cash and receivables in exchange for services rendered or goods delivered during the period.

**Temporary proprietorship accounts** The accounts for revenue, expenses, and withdrawals, used during the accounting period to classify changes affecting the owner's equity.

## DEMONSTRATION PROBLEM FOR YOUR REVIEW

Lane Insurance Agency began business on April 1, 19___. Assume that the accounts are closed and financial statements prepared each month. The company occupies rented office space but owns office equipment estimated to have a useful life of 10 years from date of acquisition, April 1. The trial balance for Lane Insurance Agency at June 30, 19___, is shown on page 113.

| | | |
|---|---|---|
| Cash | $ 1,275 | |
| Accounts receivable | 605 | |
| Office equipment | 6,000 | |
| Accumulated depreciation: office equipment | | $ 100 |
| Accounts payable | | 1,260 |
| Richard Lane, capital, May 31, 19__ | | 6,500 |
| Richard Lane, drawing | 1,000 | |
| Commissions earned | | 3,710 |
| Advertising expense | 500 | |
| Rent expense | 370 | |
| Telephone expense | 120 | |
| Salaries expense | 1,700 | |
| | $11,570 | $11,570 |

**Instructions**

**a** Prepare the adjusting journal entry to record depreciation of the office equipment for the month of June.

**b** Prepare an adjusted trial balance at June 30, 19__.

**c** Prepare an income statement for the month ended June 30, 19__, and a balance sheet in report form at June 30, 19__.

## SOLUTION TO DEMONSTRATION PROBLEM

**a** *Adjusting journal entry:*

| | | |
|---|---|---|
| Depreciation Expense: Office Equipment | 50 | |
| Accumulated Depreciation: Office Equipment | | 50 |
| To record depreciation for June ($6,000 ÷ 120 months). | | |

**b**

**LANE INSURANCE AGENCY**
**Adjusted Trial Balance**
**June 30, 19__**

| | | |
|---|---|---|
| Cash | $ 1,275 | |
| Accounts receivable | 605 | |
| Office equipment | 6,000 | |
| Accumulated depreciation: office equipment | | $ 150 |
| Accounts payable | | 1,260 |
| Richard Lane, capital | | 6,500 |
| Richard Lane, drawing | 1,000 | |
| Commissions earned | | 3,710 |
| Advertising expense | 500 | |
| Rent expense | 370 | |
| Telephone expense | 120 | |
| Salaries expense | 1,700 | |
| Depreciation expense: office equipment | 50 | |
| | $11,620 | $11,620 |

c

**LANE INSURANCE AGENCY**
**Income Statement**
**For the Month Ended June 30, 19__**

| | | |
|---|---|---|
| Commissions earned | | $3,710 |
| Expenses: | | |
| Advertising expense | $ 500 | |
| Rent expense | 370 | |
| Telephone expense | 120 | |
| Salaries expense | 1,700 | |
| Depreciation expense: office equipment | 50 | 2,740 |
| Net income | | $ 970 |

**LANE INSURANCE AGENCY**
**Balance Sheet**
**June 30, 19__**

**Assets**

| | | |
|---|---|---|
| Cash | | $1,275 |
| Accounts receivable | | 605 |
| Office equipment | $6,000 | |
| Less: Accumulated depreciation | 150 | 5,850 |
| Total assets | | $7,730 |

**Liabilities & Owner's Equity**

| | | |
|---|---|---|
| Liabilities: | | |
| Accounts payable | | $1,260 |
| Owner's equity: | | |
| Richard Lane, capital, May 31, 19__ | $6,500 | |
| Net income for June | 970 | |
| Subtotal | $7,470 | |
| Less: Withdrawals | 1,000 | |
| Richard Lane, capital, June 30, 19__ | | 6,470 |
| Total liabilities & owner's equity | | $7,730 |

## REVIEW QUESTIONS

1 What is the meaning of the term ***revenue?*** Does the receipt of cash by a business indicate that revenue has been earned? Explain.

2 What is the meaning of the term ***expenses?*** Does the payment of cash by a business indicate that an expense has been incurred? Explain.

3 The Milan Company, owned by Robert Gennaro, completed its first year of operation on December 31, 1983. State the proper heading for the first annual income statement.

4 Does a well-prepared income statement provide an exact measurement of net

income for the period, or does it represent merely an approximation of net income? Explain.

**5** How does depreciation expense differ from other operating expenses?

**6** Assume that a business acquires a delivery truck at a cost of $4,800. Estimated life of the truck is four years. State the amount of depreciation expense per year and per month. Give the adjusting entry to record depreciation on the truck at the end of the first month, and explain where the accounts involved would appear in the financial statements.

**7** Explain the rules of debit and credit with respect to transactions recorded in revenue and expense accounts.

**8** Supply the appropriate term (debit or credit) to complete the following statements.

**a** The owner's equity account, income summary account, and revenue accounts are increased by ____________ entries.

**b** Asset accounts and expense accounts are increased by ____________ entries.

**c** Liability accounts and owner's equity accounts are decreased by ____________ entries.

**9** Supply the appropriate term (debit or credit) to complete the following statements.

**a** When a business is operating profitably, the journal entry to close the Income Summary account will consist of a ____________ to that account and a ____________ to the owner's capital account.

**b** When a business is operating at a loss, the journal entry to close the Income Summary account will consist of a ____________ to that account and a ____________ to the owner's capital account.

**c** The journal entry to close the owner's drawing account consists of a ____________ to that account and a ____________ to the owner's capital account.

**10** All ledger accounts belong in one of the following five groups: asset, liability, owner's equity, revenue, and expense. For each of the following accounts, state the group in which it belongs. Also indicate whether the normal balance would be a debit or credit.

| | |
|---|---|
| **a** Fees Earned | **e** Building |
| **b** Notes Payable | **f** Depreciation Expense |
| **c** Telephone Expense | **g** Accumulated Depreciation: Building |
| **d** William Nelson, Drawing | |

**11** A service enterprise performs services in the amount of $500 for a customer in May and receives payment in June. In which month is the $500 of revenue recognized? What is the journal entry to be made in May and the entry to be made in June?

**12** Which of the following accounts should be closed by a debit to Income Summary and a credit to the account listed?

| | |
|---|---|
| James Harris, Drawing | Salaries Expense |
| Fees Earned | Accounts Payable |
| Advertising Expense | Depreciation Expense |
| Accounts Receivable | Accumulated Depreciation |

**13** Supply the appropriate terms to complete the following statements. ____________ and ____________ accounts are closed at the end of each accounting period by transferring their balances to a summary account called ____________ ____________. A ____________ balance in this summary account represents net income for the period; a ____________ balance represents a net loss for the period.

**14** Which of the ten accounts listed below are affected by closing entries at the end of the accounting period?

| | |
|---|---|
| Cash | James Miller, Drawing |
| Fees Earned | James Miller, Capital |
| Income Summary | Accumulated Depreciation |
| Accounts Payable | Accounts Receivable |
| Telephone Expense | Depreciation Expense |

**15** During its first year of operations, Appliance Repair Center performed services for customers as follows: for credit, $42,000; for cash, $50,000. During this first year expenses were incurred as follows: for cash, $65,000; on credit, $10,000. State the amount of the company's revenue, expenses, and net income for the year.

**16** The following ledger accounts are among those in the ledger of Daniel Drew, Surveyor. Which of these accounts would you expect to appear in the after-closing trial balance? Notes Receivable, Interest Expense, Cash, Salaries Expense, Daniel Drew, Drawing, Equipment, Fees Earned, Accumulated Depreciation, Office Supplies, Notes Payable, Depreciation Expense, Daniel Drew, Capital, Accounts Payable, Accounts Receivable, Rent Expense.

**17** How does the accrual basis of accounting differ from the cash basis of accounting? Which gives a more accurate picture of the profitability of a business? Explain.

## EXERCISES

*Ex. 3-1* John Grey & Company, a firm of real estate brokers, carried out the following transactions during the month of May. Which of these transactions represented revenue to the firm during the month of May? Explain.

**a** John Grey invested an additional $4,000 cash in the business.
**b** Collected $900 rent for May from a dentist to whom John Grey & Company rented part of its building.
**c** Arranged a sale of an apartment building owned by a client, James Robbins. The commission for making the sale was $9,000, but this amount would not be received until July 20 although the sale was completed in May.
**d** Collected cash of $1,500 from an account receivable. The receivable originated in April from services rendered to a client.
**e** Borrowed $8,000 from the National Bank, to be repaid in three months.

*Ex. 3-2* A business had the following transactions, among others, during January. Which of these transactions represented expenses for January? Explain.

**a** Paid $1,500 salary to a salesperson for time worked during January.
**b** Paid $210 for gasoline purchases for the delivery truck during January.
**c** Purchased a typewriter for $800 cash.
**d** Paid $2,000 in settlement of a loan obtained three months earlier.
**e** The owner withdrew $500 from the business for personal use.
**f** Paid a garage $200 for automobile repair work performed in November.

*Ex. 3-3* Supply the missing figures in the following five independent cases:

| | | |
|---|---|---|
| **a** | *Owner's equity at end of year* | *$ 77,900* |
| | *Owner's drawings during the year* | *12,400* |
| | *Net income for the year* | *16,600* |
| | *Owner's equity at beginning of year* | |
| **b** | *Net income for the year* | *$ 20,400* |
| | *Owner's equity at beginning of year* | *100,000* |
| | *Owner's equity at end of year* | |
| | *Owner's drawings during the year* | *15,500* |

| | | |
|---|---|---|
| c | *Net income for the year* | *$* |
| | *Owner's equity at end of year* | *32,100* |
| | *Owner's equity at beginning of year* | *26,500* |
| | *Owner's drawings during the year* | *10,400* |
| d | *Owner's drawings during the year* | *$* |
| | *Owner's equity at end of year* | *43,400* |
| | *Net income for the year* | *11,800* |
| | *Owner's equity at beginning of year* | *47,500* |
| e | *Owner's equity at beginning of year* | *$51,700* |
| | *Owner's equity at end of year* | *60,200* |
| | *Additional investment by owner during the year* | *10,000* |
| | *Net income for the year* | |
| | *Owner's drawings for the year* | *8,100* |

*Ex. 3-4* The income statement prepared by Grayling Company for the month of March showed net income of $18,500. In recording the transactions of the month, however, the accountant had made some errors. Study the following list of March transactions and identify any which were incorrectly recorded. Also give the journal entry as it should have been made. Finally, compute the correct amount of net income for the month of March.

a Earned a commission of $2,500 by selling a residence for a client. Commission to be received in 60 days. Recorded by debiting Commissions Earned and crediting Accounts Receivable.

b A payment of $250 for newspaper advertising was recorded by debiting Advertising Expense and crediting Accounts Receivable.

c Received but did not pay a bill of $285 for March telephone service. Recorded by debiting Telephone Expense and crediting Commissions Earned.

d Made an error in computing depreciation on the building for March. Recorded as $25. Should have been $250.

e Recorded the withdrawal of $1,600 by the owner, Howard Grayling, by debiting Salaries Expense and crediting Cash.

*Ex. 3-5* When beginning operations, Land Company established its ledger with the accounts arranged in alphabetical order, but found this sequence inconvenient for preparing financial statements. You are to rearrange the following alphabetical list of 21 ledger accounts in ***financial statement order*** so that Land Company may improve the organization of its ledger.

*Accounts Payable*
*Accounts Receivable*
*Accumulated Depreciation: Buildings*
*Accumulated Depreciation: Office Equipment*
*Advertising Expense*
*Buildings*
*Cash*
*Commissions Earned*
*Depreciation Expense: Buildings*
*Depreciation Expense: Office Equipment*
*Electricity Expense*
*Interest Payable*
*Land*
*Notes Payable*
*Notes Receivable*
*Office Equipment*
*Paul Ramon, Capital*
*Paul Ramon, Drawing*
*Rent Expense*
*Salaries Expense*
*Telephone Expense*

*Ex. 3-6* Label each of the following statements as true or false. Explain the reasoning underlying your answer and give an example of a ***transaction*** which supports your position.

**a** Every transaction that affects a balance sheet account also affects an income statement account.
**b** Every transaction that affects an income statement account also affects a balance sheet account.
**c** Every transaction that affects an expense account also affects an asset account.
**d** Every transaction that affects a revenue account also affects another income statement account.
**e** Every transaction that affects an expense account also affects a revenue account.

*Ex. 3-7* An employee of Service Company prepared the following closing entries from the ledger accounts for the year of 19___.

**a** Identify any errors which the employee made.
**b** Prepare correct closing entries for the business.

**Entry 1**

| | | |
|---|---|---|
| *Lawn Service Revenue* | *124,800* | |
| *Accumulated Depreciation* | *12,800* | |
| *Accounts Payable* | *43,200* | |
| *Income Summary* | | *180,800* |
| *To close accounts with credit balances.* | | |

**Entry 2**

| | | |
|---|---|---|
| *Income Summary* | *116,800* | |
| *Salaries Expense* | | *89,600* |
| *J. Doe, Drawing* | | *17,600* |
| *Advertising Expense* | | *6,400* |
| *Depreciation Expense* | | *3,200* |
| *To close accounts with debit balances.* | | |

**Entry 3**

| | | |
|---|---|---|
| *J. Doe, Capital* | *64,000* | |
| *Income Summary* | | *64,000* |
| *To close Income Summary account.* | | |

## PROBLEMS

### Group A

*3A-1* The March transactions of Boulevard Motors, an automobile repair shop, included the following:

(1) On March 1, paid rent for the month of March, $600.
(2) On March 3, at request of National Insurance, Inc., made repairs on car of Stanley West. Sent bill for $305 for services rendered to National Insurance, Inc. (Credit Repair Service Revenue.)
(3) On March 9, made repairs to car of H. F. Smith and collected in full the charge of $215.
(4) On March 14, placed advertisement in *Daily Star* to be published in issue of March 16 at cost of $75, payment to be made within 30 days.
(5) On March 25, received a check for $305 from National Insurance, Inc., representing collection of the receivable of March 3.

(6) On March 31, Wallace Addison, owner of Boulevard Motors, withdrew $1,800 from the business for personal use.

**Instructions**

**a** Write an analysis of each transaction. An example of the type of analysis desired is as follows:

(1) (a) Rent is an operating expense. Expenses are recorded by debits. Debit Rent Expense, $600.

(b) The asset Cash was decreased. Decreases in assets are recorded by credits. Credit Cash, $600.

**b** Prepare a journal entry (including explanation) for each of the above transactions.

*3A-2* Friendly Plumber performs repair work on both a cash and credit basis. Credit customers are required to pay within 30 days from date of billing. Revenue is recorded in an account entitled Repair Service Revenue. Among the June transactions were the following:

**June 1** Performed repair work for Arden Hardware, a credit customer. Sent bill for $247.

**June 2** Paid rent for June, $700.

**June 3** Purchased tools with estimated life of 10 years for $1,200 cash.

**June 10** Performed repairs for Harris Drugs and collected in full the charge of $510.

**June 15** Newspaper advertising to appear on June 18 was arranged at a cost of $250. Received bill from *Tribune* requiring payment within 30 days.

**June 18** Received payment in full of the $247 account receivable from Arden Hardware for our services on June 1.

**June 20** David Cohen, owner of Friendly Plumber, withdrew $1,000 cash from the business for personal use.

**June 30** Paid salary of $1,300 to office employee for services rendered during June.

**Instructions** Prepare a journal entry (including explanation) for each of the above transactions.

*3A-3* At year-end, Wildwood Park prepared the following adjusted trial balance.

***WILDWOOD PARK***

***Adjusted Trial Balance***

***December 31, 19__***

| | | |
|---|---|---|
| Cash | $ 12,500 | |
| Accounts receivable | 1,800 | |
| Equipment | 60,000 | |
| Accumulated depreciation: equipment | | $ 18,000 |
| Trucks | 30,000 | |
| Accumulated depreciation: trucks | | 10,000 |
| Roy Garcia, capital | | 72,000 |
| Roy Garcia, drawing | 20,000 | |
| Admissions revenue | | 160,000 |
| Advertising expense | 2,000 | |
| Rent expense | 34,000 | |
| Repairs expense | 5,200 | |
| Salaries expense | 79,000 | |
| Light & power expense | 4,500 | |
| Depreciation expense: equipment | 6,000 | |
| Depreciation expense: trucks | 5,000 | |
| | $260,000 | $260,000 |

**Instructions**

**a** Prepare journal entries to close the accounts. Use four entries: (1) to close the revenue account, (2) to close the expense accounts, (3) to close the Income Summary account, and (4) to close the owner's drawing account.

**b** Assume that in the following year, Wildwood Park again had $160,000 of admissions revenue, but that expenses increased to $170,000. Assuming that the revenue account and all the expense accounts had been closed into the Income Summary account at December 31, prepare a journal entry to close the Income Summary account.

*3A-4* Growers' Service closes its accounts and prepares financial statements at the end of each calendar year. The following adjusted trial balance was prepared at December 31 of the most recent year.

***GROWERS' SERVICE***
***Adjusted Trial Balance***
***December 31, 19__***

| | | |
|---|---|---|
| Cash | $ 7,300 | |
| Notes receivable | 4,500 | |
| Accounts receivable | 12,800 | |
| Land | 140,000 | |
| Building | 90,000 | |
| Accumulated depreciation: building | | $ 12,000 |
| Office equipment | 4,000 | |
| Accumulated depreciation: office equipment | | 1,600 |
| Notes payable | | 100,000 |
| Accounts payable | | 16,200 |
| Susan Lee, capital | | 132,300 |
| Susan Lee, drawing | 24,000 | |
| Commissions earned | | 88,000 |
| Advertising expense | 12,500 | |
| Insurance expense | 2,800 | |
| Utilities expense | 2,600 | |
| Salaries expense | 46,200 | |
| Depreciation expense: building | 3,000 | |
| Depreciation expense: office equipment | 400 | |
| | $350,100 | $350,100 |

**Instructions**

**a** Prepare an income statement for the year ended December 31.

**b** Prepare a balance sheet in report form at December 31. In the owner's equity section, show the changes in the owner's capital during the year as illustrated on page 103.

**c** Prepare closing entries at December 31. Use four entries as illustrated on pages 104–105 and 107–108.

*3A-5* Carl Smith, after several years of employment in the television industry, resigned from his job and invested his time and money in a new business, Village TV, which opened its doors to customers for the first time on July 1. The accounting policy followed is to close the accounts and prepare financial statements at the end of each month. A trial balance prepared at September 30 is shown below.

***VILLAGE TV***
***Trial Balance***
***September 30, 19___***

| | | |
|---|---|---|
| *Cash* | *$ 2,500* | |
| *Accounts receivable* | *1,500* | |
| *Land* | *40,000* | |
| *Building* | *60,000* | |
| *Accumulated depreciation: building* | | *$ 400* |
| *Repair equipment* | *6,000* | |
| *Accumulated depreciation: repair equipment* | | *200* |
| *Notes payable* | | *37,000* |
| *Accounts payable* | | *900* |
| *Carl Smith, capital* | | *70,000* |
| *Carl Smith, drawing* | *1,400* | |
| *Repair service revenue* | | *7,800* |
| *Advertising expense* | *140* | |
| *Repair parts expense* | *800* | |
| *Utilities expense* | *160* | |
| *Wages expense* | *3,800* | |
| | *$116,300* | *$116,300* |

Depreciation of the building is based on an estimated useful life of 25 years. Useful life of the repair equipment is estimated to be 5 years.

**Instructions**

**a** Prepare adjusting entries at September 30 to record depreciation for the month of September. (For the building, the calculation is: $60,000 ÷ 25 years × $\frac{1}{12}$.)

**b** Prepare an *adjusted* trial balance at September 30, 19___.

**c** Prepare an income statement for the month ended September 30, 19___, and a balance sheet in report form.

**d** If the company had overlooked the need for recording depreciation for September, what effect, if any, would this oversight have had upon the income statement and the balance sheet? (Use the terms "understated" and "overstated.")

**e** Smith wants to compare the earnings from the business with what he earned when working as a salaried employee. Before starting his own business, Smith had earned a monthly salary of $1,700 and had on deposit in a bank the amount of $70,000 which paid interest of $7,200 a year. Explain how the results of operations for September compare with the income (salary and interest) Smith would have received by continuing to work as a salaried employee and keeping the $70,000 savings in an interest-bearing bank account rather than investing it to start the business.

*3A-6* The operations of Sunset Realty consist of obtaining listings of houses being offered for sale by owners, advertising these houses, and showing them to prospective buyers. The company earns revenue in the form of commissions. The building and office equipment used in the business were acquired on January 1 of the current year and were immediately placed in use. Useful life of the building was estimated to be 30 years and that of the office equipment 8 years. The company closes its accounts monthly; on March 31 of the current year, the trial balance is as follows:

**SUNSET REALTY**
**Trial Balance**
**March 31, 19__**

| | Debit | Credit |
|---|---|---|
| Cash | $ 6,500 | |
| U.S. government bonds | 8,000 | |
| Accounts receivable | 5,000 | |
| Land | 25,000 | |
| Building | 72,000 | |
| Accumulated depreciation: building | | $ 400 |
| Office equipment | 24,000 | |
| Accumulated depreciation: office equipment | | 500 |
| Notes payable | | 81,000 |
| Accounts payable | | 10,000 |
| Ellen Norton, capital | | 46,100 |
| Ellen Norton, drawing | 2,000 | |
| Commissions earned | | 20,000 |
| Advertising expense | 900 | |
| Automobile rental expense | 700 | |
| Salaries expense | 13,300 | |
| Telephone expense | 600 | |
| | $158,000 | $158,000 |

**Instructions** From the trial balance and supplementary data given, prepare the following as of March 31, 19__.

**a** Adjusting entries for depreciation during March of building and of office equipment.
(Building: $72,000 cost ÷ 30 years × $\frac{1}{12}$ = one month's depreciation)
(Office equipment: $24,000 cost ÷ 8 years × $\frac{1}{12}$ = one month's depreciation)

**b** Adjusted trial balance.

**c** Income statement for the month of March and a balance sheet at March 31 in report form. In the owner's equity section of the balance sheet, show the changes in owner's capital during March as in the illustration on page 103.

**d** Closing entries.

**e** After-closing trial balance.

*3A-7* John Ryan organized Freeway Express on June 1, 19__, to provide long-distance moving of household furniture. During June the following transactions occurred:

**June 1** Ryan deposited $270,000 cash in a bank account in the name of the business, Freeway Express.

**June 3** Purchased land and building for a total price of $156,000, of which $60,000 was applicable to the land, and $96,000 to the building. Paid cash for full amount.

**June 5** Purchased three trucks from Dawson Motors at a cost of $40,000 each. A cash down payment of $50,000 was made, the balance to be paid by July 22.

**June 6** Purchased office equipment for cash, $4,800.

**June 6** Moved furniture for Mr. and Mrs. David Hart from San Diego to Boston for $4,000. Collected $1,000 in cash, balance to be paid within 30 days (credit Moving Service Revenue).
**June 11** Moved furniture for various clients for $9,800. Collected $4,400 in cash, balance to be paid within 30 days.
**June 15** Paid salaries to employees for first half of the month, $5,000.
**June 24** Moved furniture for various clients for a total of $6,480. Cash collected in full.
**June 30** Salaries expense for the second half of month amounted to $5,800.
**June 30** Received a gasoline bill for the month of June from Atlantic Oil Company in the amount of $6,200, to be paid before July 10.
**June 30** Received bill of $300 for repair work on trucks during June by Century Motor Company.
**June 30** The owner, John Ryan, withdrew $1,500 cash for personal use.

Ryan estimated a useful life of 20 years for the building, 4 years for the trucks, and 10 years for the office equipment.

The account titles to be used and the account numbers are as follows:

| | |
|---|---|
| *Cash* | *1* |
| *Accounts receivable* | *3* |
| *Land* | *5* |
| *Buildings* | *7* |
| *Accumulated depreciation:* | |
| *Buildings* | *8* |
| *Trucks* | *10* |
| *Accumulated depreciation:* | |
| *Trucks* | *11* |
| *Office equipment* | *13* |
| *Accumulated depreciation:* | |
| *Office equipment* | *14* |
| *Accounts payable* | *30* |
| *John Ryan, capital* | *50* |
| *John Ryan, drawing* | *51* |
| *Income summary* | *60* |
| *Moving service revenue* | *62* |
| *Salaries expense* | *70* |
| *Gasoline expense* | *72* |
| *Repairs expense* | *74* |
| *Depreciation expense:* | |
| *Buildings* | *76* |
| *Depreciation expense:* | |
| *Trucks* | *78* |
| *Depreciation expense:* | |
| *Office equipment* | *80* |

**Instructions**

**a** Prepare journal entries. (Number journal pages and enter the proper journal page number in the "Ref" column of the ledger accounts as each debit or credit is posted.)
**b** Post to ledger accounts. (As each journal entry is posted to the ledger, enter the identification number of the ledger account debited or credited in the "LP" column of the journal. This will show that the amount has been posted and will provide a cross reference between journal and ledger.)
**c** Prepare a trial balance as of June 30, 19___.
**d** Prepare adjusting entries for depreciation during June and post to ledger accounts. (For example, the depreciation computation for buildings is: $96,000 cost $\div$ 20 years $\times \frac{1}{12}$.)
**e** Prepare an adjusted trial balance.
**f** Prepare an income statement for June, and a balance sheet at June 30, in report form.
**g** Prepare closing entries and post to ledger accounts.
**h** Prepare an after-closing trial balance.

## Group B

*3B-1* The transactions during October for Pacific Plumbing Company included the following:

(1) On October 1, paid $640 cash for the month's rent.
(2) On October 3, made repairs for First National Bank and collected in full the charge of $1,014.
(3) On October 8, performed repair work for American Home Builders. Sent bill for $1,332 for services rendered.
(4) On October 15, placed an advertisement in the *Tribune* at a cost of $310 payment to be made within 30 days.
(5) On October 21, purchased equipment for $4,000 cash.
(6) On October 30, received a check for $1,332 from American Home Builders.
(7) On October 31, sent check to the *Tribune* in payment of liability incurred on October 15.
(8) On October 31, the owner, Lee Toguchi withdrew $1,600 cash for personal use.

**Instructions**

**a** Write an analysis of each transaction. An example of the type of analysis desired is as follows:

(1) (a) Rent is an operating expense. Expenses are recorded by debits. Debit Rent Expense, $640.

(b) The asset Cash was decreased. Decreases in assets are recorded by credits. Credit cash, $640.

**b** Prepare a journal entry (including explanation) for each of the above transactions.

*3B-2* Ski Flights provides transportation by helicopter for skiers, backpackers, and others to remote mountainous areas. Among the ledger accounts used by the company are the following:

| | |
|---|---|
| ***Cash*** | ***Advertising expense*** |
| ***Accounts payable*** | ***Fuel expense*** |
| ***Will Cane, capital*** | ***Rent expense*** |
| ***Will Cane, drawing*** | ***Repair & maintenance expense*** |
| ***Passenger fare revenue*** | ***Salaries expense*** |

Some of the January transactions of Ski Flights are listed below.

**Jan. 3** Paid $800 rent for the building for January.
**Jan. 4** Placed advertising in local newspapers for publication during January. The agreed price of $270 was payable within 10 days after the end of the month.
**Jan. 15** Cash receipts from passengers for the first half of January amounted to $4,825.
**Jan. 16** Will Cane, the owner, withdrew $1,800 cash for personal use.
**Jan. 16** Paid salaries to employees for services rendered in first half of January, $2,750.
**Jan. 29** Received a bill for fuel used from Western Oil Co., amounting to $985, and payable by February 10.
**Jan. 31** Paid $843 to Stevens Motors for repair and maintenance work during January.

**Instructions** Prepare a journal entry (including an explanation) for each of the above transactions.

*3B-3* An adjusted trial balance for Marina Center at December 31 appears below.

**MARINA CENTER**
**Adjusted Trial Balance**
**December 31, 19__**

| | | |
|---|---|---|
| Cash | $ 8,600 | |
| Accounts receivable | 12,000 | |
| Office equipment | 15,000 | |
| Accumulated depreciation: office equipment | | $ 3,000 |
| Accounts payable | | 6,000 |
| Raul Gomez, capital | | 24,600 |
| Raul Gomez, drawing | 18,000 | |
| Sales commissions earned | | 172,000 |
| Advertising expense | 41,500 | |
| Rent expense | 30,000 | |
| Salaries expense | 63,000 | |
| Utilities expense | 16,000 | |
| Depreciation expense: office equipment | 1,500 | |
| | $205,600 | $205,600 |

**Instructions**

**a** Prepare journal entries to close the accounts. Use four entries: (1) to close the revenue account, (2) to close the expense accounts, (3) to close the Income Summary account, and (4) to close the owner's drawing account.

**b** Does the amount of net income or net loss appear in the closing entries? Explain fully.

*3B-4* During the month of June, John Trent organized and began to operate an air taxi service to provide air transportation from a major city to a number of small towns not served by scheduled airlines. Transactions during the month of June were as follows:

**June 1** John Trent deposited $480,000 cash in a bank account in the name of the business, Trent Air Service.
**June 2** Purchased an aircraft for $356,400 and spare parts for $42,000, paying cash.
**June 4** Paid $540 cash to rent a building for June.
**June 10** Cash receipts from passenger fares revenue for the first 10 days amounted to $10,320.
**June 14** Paid $750 to Motor Maintenance Service for maintenance and repair service for June.
**June 15** Paid $2,880 salaries to employees for services rendered during first half of June.
**June 20** Cash receipts from passenger fares revenue for the second 10 days amounted to $12,250.
**June 30** Cash receipts from passenger fares revenue for the last 10 days of June amounted to $20,000.
**June 30** Paid $3,000 salaries to employees for services rendered during the second half of June.
**June 30** Trent withdrew $2,000 from business for personal use.
**June 30** Received a fuel bill from Phillips Oil Company amounting to $4,548 to be paid before July 10.

The account titles and numbers used by Trent Air Service are as follows:

| | | | |
|---|---|---|---|
| *Cash* | *11* | *Passenger fares revenue* | *51* |
| *Spare parts* | *14* | *Maintenance expense* | *61* |
| *Aircraft* | *21* | *Fuel expense* | *62* |
| *Accounts payable* | *31* | *Salaries expense* | *63* |
| *John Trent, capital* | *41* | *Rent expense* | *64* |
| *John Trent, drawing* | *42* | | |

**Instructions** Based on the foregoing transactions

**a** Prepare journal entries. (Number journal pages to permit cross reference to ledger.)

**b** Post to ledger accounts. (Number ledger accounts to permit cross reference to journal.) Enter ledger account numbers in the LP column of the journal as the posting work is done.

**c** Prepare a trial balance at June 30, 19___.

***3B-5*** Plaza Parking System was organized on March 1 for the purpose of operating an automobile parking lot. Included in the company's ledger are the following ledger accounts and their identification numbers.

| | | | |
|---|---|---|---|
| *Cash* | *11* | *Howard Ward, drawing* | *42* |
| *Land* | *21* | *Parking fees earned* | *51* |
| *Notes payable* | *31* | *Advertising expense* | *61* |
| *Accounts payable* | *32* | *Utilities expense* | *63* |
| *Howard Ward, capital* | *41* | *Salaries expense* | *65* |

The business was organized and operations were begun during the month of March. Transactions during March were as follows:

**Mar. 1** Howard Ward deposited $102,000 cash in a bank account in the name of the business, the Plaza Parking System.

**Mar. 2** Purchased land for $90,000, of which $54,000 was paid in cash. A short-term note payable (without interest) was issued for the balance of $36,000.

**Mar. 2** An arrangement was made with the Century Club to provide parking privileges for its customers. Century Club agreed to pay $660 monthly, payable in advance. Cash was collected for the month of March.

**Mar. 7** Arranged with Times Printing Company for a regular advertisement in the *Times* at a monthly cost of $114. Paid for advertising during March by check, $114.

**Mar. 15** Parking receipts for the first half of the month were $1,836, exclusive of the monthly fee from Century Club.

**Mar. 31** Received bill for light and power from Pacific Power Company in the amount of $78, to be paid before April 10.

**Mar. 31** Paid $720 to the parking attendant for services rendered during the month. (Payroll taxes are to be ignored.)

**Mar. 31** Parking receipts for the second half of the month amounted to $1,682.

**Mar. 31** Ward withdrew $1,080 for personal use.

**Mar. 31** Paid $12,000 cash on the note payable incurred with the purchase of land.

**Instructions**

**a** Journalize the March transactions.

**b** Post to ledger accounts. Enter ledger account numbers in the LP column of the journal as the posting work is done.

**c** Prepare a trial balance at March 31.

**d** Prepare an income statement and a balance sheet in report form. In the owner's equity section of the balance sheet, show the changes in the owner's capital during the period, as illustrated on page 103.

**3B-6** Home Repair is a new business which began operations on July 1. The company follows a policy of closing its accounts and preparing financial statements at the end of each month. A trial balance at September 30 appears below.

***HOME REPAIR***
***Trial Balance***
***September 30, 19__***

| | | |
|---|---|---|
| *Cash* | $ 2,500 | |
| *Accounts receivable* | 1,500 | |
| *Land* | 29,400 | |
| *Building* | 50,400 | |
| *Accumulated depreciation: building* | | $ 336 |
| *Repair equipment* | 7,500 | |
| *Accumulated depreciation: repair equipment* | | 250 |
| *Notes payable* | | 28,000 |
| *Accounts payable* | | 1,594 |
| *Paul Klein, capital* | | 58,800 |
| *Paul Klein, drawing* | 1,400 | |
| *Repair service revenue* | | 8,520 |
| *Advertising expense* | 150 | |
| *Repair parts expense* | 700 | |
| *Utilities expense* | 170 | |
| *Wages expense* | 3,780 | |
| | $97,500 | $97,500 |

Note that the trial balance includes two assets subject to depreciation: the building and the repair equipment. The accumulated depreciation accounts in the trial balance show the total depreciation for July and August; depreciation has not yet been recorded for September.

**Instructions**

**a** Prepare adjusting entries at September 30 to record depreciation. Use one entry to record depreciation on the building and a second entry to record depreciation on the repair equipment. The amounts of depreciation for September are $168 on the building and $125 on the repair equipment.

**b** Prepare an ***adjusted*** trial balance at September 30. (This will differ from the trial balance only by inclusion of the depreciation recorded in part **a**.)

**c** Prepare an income statement for the month ended September 30 and a balance sheet in report form. In the owner's equity section of the balance sheet, show the change in capital resulting from September operations.

**d** Prepare journal entries to close the accounts. Use four entries: (1) to close the revenue account, (2) to close the expense accounts, (3) to close the Income Summary account, and (4) to close the owner's drawing account.

**3B-7** Sarah Weiss, M.D., after completing her medical education, established her own practice on May 1. The following transactions occurred during the first month.

**May 1** Weiss opened a bank account in the name of the practice, Sarah Weiss, M.D., by making a deposit of $16,000.
**May 1** Paid office rent for May, $700.
**May 2** Purchased office equipment for cash, $7,200.

**May 3** Purchased medical instruments from Niles Instruments, Inc., at a cost of $12,000. A cash down payment of $2,000 was made and a note payable was signed which required a payment of $5,000 on June 3 of the current year and a final payment of $5,000 on July 3.

**May 3** Retained by Brandon Merchandising, Inc., to be on call for emergency service at a monthly fee of $400. The fee for May was collected in cash.

**May 15** Excluding the retainer of May 3, fees earned during the first 15 days of the month amounted to $1,600, of which $600 was in cash and $1,000 was in accounts receivable.

**May 15** Paid Mary Hester, R.N., her salary for the first half of May, $750.

**May 16** Dr. Weiss withdrew $975 for personal use.

**May 19** Treated Michael Tracy for injuries received in an accident during employment at Brandon Merchandising, Inc. Completed medical portions of insurance and industrial accident reports.

**May 27** Treated Cynthia Knight, who paid $25 cash for an office visit and who agreed to pay $35 on June 1 for laboratory medical tests completed May 27.

**May 31** Excluding the treatment of Cynthia Knight on May 27, fees earned during the last half of month amounted to $3,000, of which $1,100 was in cash and $1,900 was in accounts receivable.

**May 31** Paid Mary Hester, R.N., $750 salary for the second half of month.

**May 31** Received a bill from McGraw Medical Supplies in the amount of $640 representing the amount of medical supplies used during May. (Debit Medical Supplies Expense.)

**May 31** Paid utilities bill for the month, $150.

**Other information** Dr. Weiss estimated the useful life of medical instruments at 10 years and of office equipment at 12 years. The account titles to be used and the account numbers are as follows:

| | | | |
|---|---|---|---|
| *Cash* | *10* | *Sarah Weiss, drawing* | *41* |
| *Accounts receivable* | *13* | *Income summary* | *45* |
| *Medical instruments* | *20* | *Fees earned* | *49* |
| *Accumulated depreciation: medical instruments* | *21* | *Medical supplies expense* | *50* |
| *Office equipment* | *22* | *Rent expense* | *51* |
| *Accumlated depreciation: office equipment* | *23* | *Salaries expense* | *52* |
| *Notes payable* | *30* | *Utilities expense* | *53* |
| *Accounts payable* | *31* | *Depreciation expense: medical instruments* | *54* |
| *Sarah Weiss, capital* | *40* | *Depreciation expense: office equipment* | *55* |

**Instructions**

**a** Journalize the above transactions. (Number journal pages to permit cross reference to ledger.)

**b** Post to ledger accounts. (Use running balance form of ledger account. Number ledger accounts to permit cross reference to journal.)

**c** Prepare a trial balance at May 31, 19___.

**d** Prepare adjusting entries to record depreciation for the month of May and post to ledger accounts. (For medical instruments, cost $12,000 $\div$ 10 years $\times \frac{1}{12}$.)

**e** Prepare an adjusted trial balance.

**f** Prepare an income statement and a balance sheet in report form.

**g** Prepare closing entries and post to ledger accounts.

**h** Prepare an after-closing trial balance.

## BUSINESS DECISION PROBLEM 3

John Bell, owner of a small business called Top-Notch Company, has accepted a salaried position overseas and is trying to interest you in buying the business. Bell describes the operating results of the business as follows: "The business has been in existence for only 18 months, but the growth trend is very impressive. Just look at these figures."

| | *Cash Collections from Customers* |
|---|---|
| *First six-month period* | *$60,000* |
| *Second six-month period* | *80,000* |
| *Third six-month period* | *90,000* |

"I think you'll agree those figures show real growth," Bell concluded.

You then asked Bell whether sales were made only for cash or on both a cash and credit basis. He replied as follows:

"At first we sold both for cash and on open account. In the first six months we made total sales of $100,000 and 70% of those sales were made on credit. We had $40,000 of accounts receivable at the end of the first six-month period.

"During the second six-month period, we tried to discourage selling on credit because of the extra paper work involved and the time required to follow up on slow-paying customers. Our sales on credit in that second six-month period amounted to $35,000, and our total accounts receivable were down to $30,000 at the end of that period.

"During the third six-month period we made sales only for cash. Although we prefer to operate on a cash basis only, we did very well at collecting receivables. We collected in full from every customer to whom we ever sold on credit and we don't have a dollar of accounts receivable at this time."

**Instructions**

**a** To facilitate your reaching a decision, prepare a schedule comparing cash collections and sales data for each of the three 6-month periods under review. Use the following column headings:

| | *(1)* | *(2)* | *(3)* | *(4)* | *(5)* | *(6)* |
|---|---|---|---|---|---|---|
| | *Sales on Credit* | *Collections on Accounts Receivable* | *Ending Balance of Accounts Receivable* | *Total Cash Collections from Customers* | *Sales for Cash* | *(1) + (5) Total Sales* |
| *First six months* | | | | | | |
| *Second six months* | | | | | | |
| *Third six months* | | | | | | |

**b** Based upon your analysis in part **a**, do you consider Bell's explanation of the "growth trend" of cash collections to be a well-founded portrayal of the progress of the business? Explain fully any criticism you may have of Bell's line of reasoning.

# 4

# COMPLETION OF THE ACCOUNTING CYCLE

## Accounting periods and financial statements

For the purpose of making accounting measurements and preparing financial statements, the life of a business is divided into accounting periods of equal length. Because accounting periods are equal in length, we can compare the revenue and expenses of the current period with the revenue and expenses of prior periods and determine whether our operating results are improving or declining. Accounting thus provides a scorekeeping service. If this year's operations set a new record, the accounting system will tell us so.

As explained in Chapter 3, the ***accounting period*** means the span of time covered by an income statement. The usual accounting period for which complete financial statements are prepared and distributed to investors, bankers, and government agencies is one year. The measurement and reporting of taxable income to the Internal Revenue Service by corporations and individuals is also on an annual basis. However, most businesses also prepare quarterly and monthly financial statements so that management will be currently informed on the profitability of the business from month to month.

At the end of an accounting period, adjustments of some of the account balances in the ledger must be made before financial statements are prepared. Adjusting entries for depreciation are necessary, for example, because the recorded costs of buildings and office equipment are gradually expiring with the passage of time. Before financial statements are prepared, the accounts must be brought up to date with respect to depreciation and several other items.

To serve the needs of management, investors, bankers, and other groups, financial statements must be as complete and accurate as possible. The balance sheet must contain all the assets and liabilities at the close of business on the last day of the period. The income statement must contain all the revenue and expenses applicable to the period covered but must not contain any revenue or expenses relating to the following period. In other words, a precise ***cutoff*** of transactions at the end of the period is essential to the preparation of reliable financial statements. Adjusting entries are a means of achieving a precise cutoff of transactions on the last day of the period.

### Apportioning transactions between accounting periods

Some business transactions are begun and completed within a single accounting period, but many other transactions are begun in one accounting period and concluded in a later period. For example, a building purchased this year may last for 25 years; during each of those 25 years a fair share of the cost of the building should be recognized as expense. The making of ***adjusting entries*** to record the depreciation expense applicable to a given accounting period was illustrated in the preceding chapter. Let us now consider all types of transactions which overlap two or more accounting periods and therefore require adjusting entries.

## PRINCIPAL TYPES OF ADJUSTING ENTRIES

The various adjusting entries required at the end of the period may be classified into the following groups:

1 Recorded costs which must be apportioned between two or more accounting periods. Example: the cost of a building.
2 Recorded revenue collected in advance which must be apportioned between two or more accounting periods. Example: commissions collected in advance for services to be rendered this period and also in future periods.
3 Unrecorded expenses. Example: wages earned by employees after the last payday in an accounting period.
4 Unrecorded revenue. Example: commissions earned but not yet collected or billed to customers.

To demonstrate these various types of adjusting entries, the illustration of Roberts Real Estate Company will be continued for November. We shall consider in detail only those November transactions related to adjusting entries.

### Recorded costs apportioned between accounting periods

When a business makes an expenditure that will benefit more than one accounting period, the amount is usually debited to an asset account. At the end of each period which benefits from the expenditure, an appropriate portion of the cost is transferred from the asset account to an expense account. For example, let us consider payments for insurance and for office supplies.

**Prepaid expenses** Payments in advance are often made for such items as insurance, rent, and office supplies. At the end of the accounting period, a portion of the services or supplies probably will have expired or will have been consumed, but another portion will be unexpired or unused. That portion of the economic benefits from the expenditure which ***has expired or has been consumed is an expense of the current period.*** However, the ***unexpired or unused portion of the economic benefits from the expenditure represents an asset*** at the balance sheet date and will not become expense (expired cost) until a later accounting period.

**Insurance** On November 1, Roberts Real Estate Company paid $540 for a three-year fire insurance policy covering the building. This expenditure was debited to an asset account by the following journal entry:

***Expenditure for insurance policy recorded as asset***

| | | |
|---|---|---|
| *Unexpired Insurance* | 540 | |
|     *Cash* | | 540 |
| *Purchased three-year fire insurance policy.* | | |

Since this expenditure of $540 will protect the company against fire loss for three years, the cost of protection each year is $\frac{1}{3}$ of $540, or $180. The insurance expense applicable to each month's operations is $\frac{1}{12}$ of the annual expense, or $15. In order that the accounting records for November show insurance expense of $15, the following ***adjusting entry*** is required at November 30:

***Adjusting entry. Portion of asset expires (becomes expense)***

| | | |
|---|---|---|
| *Insurance Expense* | 15 | |
|     *Unexpired Insurance* | | 15 |
| *To record insurance expense for November.* | | |

This adjusting entry serves two purposes: (1) it apportions the proper amount of insurance expense to November operations and (2) it reduces the asset account so that the correct amount of unexpired insurance will appear in the balance sheet at November 30. What would be the effect on the income statement for November if the above adjustment were not made? The expenses would be understated by $15 and consequently the net income would be overstated by $15. The balance sheet also would be affected by failure to make the adjustment: the assets would be overstated by $15 and so would the owner's equity. The overstatement of the owner's equity would result from the overstated amount of net income transferred to Roberts' capital account when the accounts were closed at November 30.

**Office supplies** On November 2, Roberts Real Estate Company purchased enough stationery and other office supplies to last for several months. The cost of the supplies was $720, and this amount was debited to an asset account by the following journal entry:

***Expenditure for office supplies recorded as asset***

| | | |
|---|---|---|
| *Office Supplies* | 720 | |
|     *Cash* | | 720 |
| *Purchased office supplies.* | | |

No entries were made during November to record the day-to-day usage of office supplies, but on November 30 a careful count was made of the supplies still on hand. This count, or physical inventory, showed unused supplies with a cost of $600. It is apparent, therefore, that supplies costing $120 were used during November. On the basis of the November 30 count, an adjusting entry is made debiting an expense account $120 (the cost of supplies consumed during November), and reducing the asset account by $120 to show that only $600 worth of office supplies remained on hand at November 30. The ***adjusting entry*** follows:

***Adjusting entry. Portion of supplies used represents expense***

| | | |
|---|---|---|
| *Office Supplies Expense* | *120* | |
| *Office Supplies* | | *120* |
| *To record consumption of office supplies in November.* | | |

The Office Supplies account will appear in the balance sheet as an asset; the Office Supplies Expense account will be shown in the income statement. How would failure to make this adjustment affect the financial statements? In the income statement for November, the expenses would be understated by $120 and the net income overstated by the same amount. Since the overstated amount for net income in November would be transferred into the owner's capital account in the process of closing the accounts, the owner's equity section of the balance sheet would be overstated by $120. Assets also would be overstated because Office Supplies would be listed at $120 too much.

When payments for insurance, office supplies, and rent are expected to provide economic benefits for more than one accounting period, the advance payment is usually recorded by a debit to an asset account such as Unexpired Insurance, Office Supplies, or Prepaid Rent. However, the advance payment ***could*** be recorded by debiting an expense account such as Insurance Expense. At the end of the period, the adjusting entry would then consist of a debit to Unexpired Insurance and a credit to Insurance Expense. This alternative method would lead to the same amounts in the balance sheet and income statement as the method previously illustrated. Under both procedures, we would be treating as an expense of the current period the cost of the economic benefits consumed, and carrying forward as an asset the cost of the economic benefits applicable to future periods.

**Depreciation of building** The November 30 adjusting entry to record depreciation of the building used by Roberts Real Estate Company is exactly the same as the October 31 ***adjusting entry*** explained in Chapter 3.

***Adjusting entry. Cost of building is gradually converted to expense***

| | | |
|---|---|---|
| *Depreciation Expense: Building* | *150* | |
| *Accumulated Depreciation: Building* | | *150* |
| *To record depreciation for November.* | | |

This allocation of depreciation expense to November operations is based on the following facts: the building cost $36,000 and is estimated to have a useful life of 20 years (240 months). Using the straight-line method of depreciation, the portion of the original cost which expires each month is $\frac{1}{240}$ of $36,000, or $150.

The Accumulated Depreciation: Building account now has a credit balance of $300 as a result of the October and November credits of $150 each. The book value of the building is $35,700, that is, the original cost of $36,000 minus the accumulated depreciation of $300. The term ***book value*** means the net amount at which an asset is shown in the accounting records, as distinguished from its market value. ***Carrying value*** is an alternative term, with the same meaning as book value.

**Depreciation of office equipment** The November 30 adjusting entry to record depreciation of the office equipment is the same as the ***adjusting entry*** for depreciation a month earlier, as shown in Chapter 3.

***Adjusting entry. Cost of office equipment gradually converted to expense***

| | | |
|---|---|---|
| *Depreciation Expense: Office Equipment* | *45* | |
| *Accumulated Depreciation: Office Equipment* | | *45* |
| *To record depreciation for November.* | | |

Original cost of the office equipment was $5,400, and the estimated useful life was 10 years (120 months). Depreciation each month under the straight-line method is therefore $\frac{1}{120}$ of $5,400, or $45. What is the book value of the office equipment at this point? Original cost of $5,400 minus accumulated depreciation of $90 for two months leaves a book value of $5,310.

What would be the effect on the financial statements if the adjusting entries for depreciation of the building and office equipment were omitted at November 30? In the income statement the expenses would be understated by $195 ($150 depreciation of building and $45 depreciation of office equipment), and net income for the month would be overstated by $195. In the balance sheet the assets would be overstated by $195; the owner's equity would be overstated the same amount because of the $195 overstatement of the net income added to the capital account. If depreciation had not been recorded in either October or November, the overstatement in the balance sheet at November 30 would amount to $390 with respect both to assets and to owner's equity.

## Recorded revenue collected in advance apportioned between accounting periods

On November 1, Roberts Real Estate Company agreed to act as manager of some rental properties for a monthly fee of $300. The owner of the properties, John Day, was leaving the country on an extended trip and therefore paid the company for six months' service in advance. The journal entry to record the transaction on November 1 was

***Management fee collected but not yet earned***

| | | |
|---|---|---|
| *Cash* | *1,800* | |
| *Unearned Management Fees* | | *1,800* |
| *Collected in advance six months' fees for management of properties owned by John Day.* | | |

This receipt of cash does not represent revenue. By collecting in advance from the client, Roberts Real Estate Company becomes obligated to render services in the future. Revenue is earned only by the actual ***rendering*** of services to customers, or by the ***delivery*** of goods to them. This management fee will be earned gradually over a period of six months as Roberts Real Estate Company performs the required services. The $1,800 collected in advance is therefore credited to an ***unearned revenue*** account. Some accountants prefer the term ***deferred revenue.***

At the end of each month, an amount of $300 will be transferred from unearned revenue to a revenue account by means of an adjusting entry. The first in this series of transfers will be made at November 30 by the following ***adjusting entry.***

*Adjusting entry. To recognize earning of a part of management fee*

| | | |
|---|---|---|
| *Unearned Management Fees* | *300* | |
| *Management Fees Earned* | | *300* |
| *Fee earned by managing John Day property during November.* | | |

The $1,500 credit balance remaining in the Unearned Management Fees account represents an obligation to render $1,500 worth of services in five future months; therefore, it belongs in the balance sheet in the liability section. An unearned revenue account differs from other liabilities because it ordinarily will be settled by rendering services rather than by making a cash payment, but it nevertheless is a liability. The Management Fees Earned account is shown as revenue in the income statement for November.

## Unrecorded expenses

Adjusting entries are necessary at the end of each accounting period to record any expenses which have been incurred but not recognized in the accounts. Salaries of employees and interest on borrowed money are common examples of expenses which accumulate day by day but which may not be recorded until the end of the period. These expenses are said to ***accrue,*** that is, to grow or accumulate.

**Accrual of interest** On November 1, Roberts Real Estate Company borrowed the sum of $3,000 from a bank. Banks require every borrower to sign a ***promissory note,*** that is, a formal, written promise to repay the amount borrowed plus interest at an agreed future date. (Various forms of notes in common use and the accounting problems involved will be discussed more fully in Chapter 9.) The note signed by Roberts, with certain details omitted, is shown below.

*Note payable issued to bank*

$3,000 Los Angeles, California November 1, 19—

Three months *after date* I *promise to pay*

*to the order of* American National Bank

———Three thousand and no/100——— *dollars*

*for value received, with interest at* 12 percent per year

Roberts Real Estate Company

*By* James Roberts

The note payable is a liability of Roberts Real Estate Company, similar to an account payable but different in that a formal written promise to pay is required and interest is charged on the amount borrowed. A Notes Payable account is credited when the note is issued; the Notes Payable account will be debited three months later when the note is paid. Interest accrues throughout the life of the note payable, but it is not payable until the note matures on February 1. To the bank making the loan, the note signed by Roberts is an asset, a note receivable. The revenue earned by banks consists largely of interest charged to borrowers.

The journal entry made on November 1 to record the borrowing of $3,000 from the bank was as follows:

*Entry when bank loan is obtained*

| | | |
|---|---|---|
| ***Cash*** | ***3,000*** | |
| ***Notes Payable*** | | ***3,000*** |
| ***Obtained from bank three-month loan with interest at 12% a year.*** | | |

Three months later, Roberts Real Estate Company must pay the bank $3,090, representing repayment of the $3,000 note payable plus $90 interest ($\$3{,}000 \times .12 \times \frac{3}{12}$). The $90 is the total interest expense for the three months. Although no payment will be made for three months, one-third of the interest expense ($30) is ***incurred*** each month, as shown below.

*Accrual of interest*

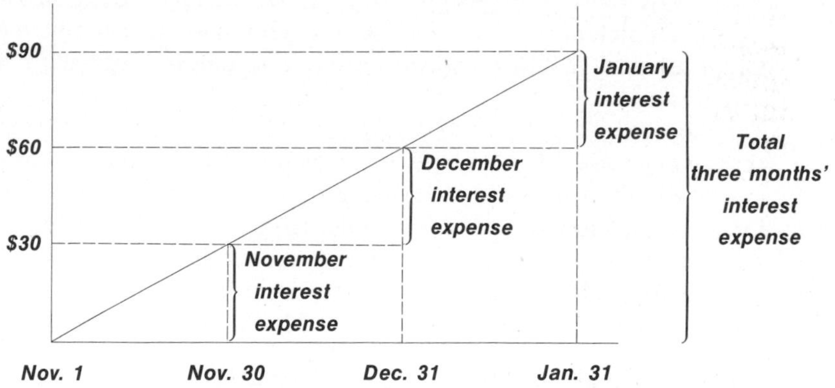


The following ***adjusting entry*** is made at November 30 to charge November operations with one month's interest expense and also to record the amount of interest owed to the bank at the end of November.

*Adjusting entry for interest expense incurred in November*

| | | |
|---|---|---|
| ***Interest Expense*** | ***30*** | |
| ***Interest Payable*** | | ***30*** |
| ***To record interest expense applicable to November.*** | | |

The debit balance in the Interest Expense account will appear in the November income statement; the credit balances in the Interest Payable and Notes Payable accounts will be shown in the balance sheet as liabilities. These two liability accounts will remain in the records until the maturity date of the loan, at which time a cash payment to the bank will wipe out both the Notes Payable account and the Interest Payable account.

**Accrual of salary** On November 20, Roberts hired Carl Nelson as a part-time salesman whose duties were to work evenings calling on property owners to secure listings of property for sale or rent. The agreed salary was $225 for a five-evening week, payable each Friday; payment for the first week was made on Friday, November 24. Personal income taxes and other taxes relating to payroll are ignored in this illustration.

Assume that the last day of the accounting period, November 30, fell on Thursday. Nelson had worked four evenings since being paid the preceding Friday and therefore had earned $180($\frac{4}{5} \times$ $225). In order that this $180 of November salary expense be reflected in the accounts before the financial statements are prepared, an ***adjusting entry*** is necessary at November 30.

*Adjusting entry for salaries expense incurred but unpaid at November 30*

| | | |
|---|---|---|
| *Sales Salaries Expense* | *180* | |
|     *Sales Salaries Payable* | | *180* |
| *To record salary expense and related liability to salesman for last four evenings' work in November.* | | |

The debit balance in the Sales Salaries Expense account will appear as an expense in the November income statement; the credit balance in the Sales Salaries Payable account is the amount owing to the salesman for work performed during the last four days of November and will appear among the liabilities in the balance sheet at November 30.

The next regular payday for Nelson will be Friday, December 1, which is the first day of the new accounting period. Since the accounts were adjusted and closed on November 30, all the revenue and expense accounts have zero balances at the beginning of business on December 1. The payment of a week's salary to Nelson will be recorded by the following entry on December 1:

*Payment of salary overlapping two accounting periods*

| | | |
|---|---|---|
| *Sales Salaries Payable* | *180* | |
| *Sales Salaries Expense* | *45* | |
|     *Cash* | | *225* |
| *Paid weekly salary to salesman.* | | |

Note that the net result of the November 30 accrual entry has been to split the salesman's weekly salary expense between November and December. Four days of the work week fell in November, so four days' pay, or $180, was recognized as November expense. One day of the work week fell in December so $45 was recorded as December expense.

No accrual entry is necessary for office salaries in Roberts Real Estate Company because Roberts regularly pays the office employees on the last working day of the month.

## Unrecorded revenue

The treatment of unrecorded revenue is similar to that of unrecorded expenses. Any revenue which has been earned but not recorded during the accounting period should be recognized in the accounts by means of an adjusting entry, debiting an asset account and crediting a revenue account. ***Accrued revenue*** is a term often used to describe revenue which has been accumulating during the period but which has not been recorded prior to the closing date.

On November 16, Roberts Real Estate Company entered into a management agreement with Henry Clayton, the owner of several small office buildings. The company agreed to manage the Clayton properties for a fee of $240 a month, payable on the fifteenth of each month. No entry is made in the accounting records at the time of signing a contract, because no services have yet been rendered and no change has occurred in assets or liabilities. The managerial duties are to begin immediately, but the first monthly fee will not be received until December 15. The following ***adjusting entry*** is therefore necessary at November 30:

***Adjusting entry for fees earned but uncollected***

| | | |
|---|---|---|
| *Management Fees Receivable* | *120* | |
| *Management Fees Earned* | | *120* |
| *To record accrued revenue from services rendered Henry Clayton during November.* | | |

The debit balance in the Management Fees Receivable account will be shown in the balance sheet as an asset. The credit balance of the Management Fees Earned account, including earnings from both the Day and Clayton contracts, will appear in the November income statement.

The collection of the first monthly fee from Clayton will occur in the next accounting period (December 15, to be exact). Of this $240 cash receipt, half represents collection of the asset account, Management Fees Receivable, created at November 30 by the adjusting entry. The other half of the $240 cash receipt represents revenue earned during December; this should be credited to the December revenue account for Management Fees Earned. The entry on December 15 is as follows:

***Management fee applicable to two accounting periods***

| | | |
|---|---|---|
| *Cash* | *240* | |
| *Management Fees Receivable* | | *120* |
| *Management Fees Earned* | | *120* |
| *Collected commission for month ended December 15.* | | |

The net result of the November 30 accrual entry has been to divide the revenue from managing the Clayton properties between November and December in accordance with the timing of the services rendered.

## Adjusting entries and the accrual basis of accounting

Adjusting entries help make accrual basis accounting work successfully. By preparing adjusting entries, we can recognize revenue in the accounting period in which it is earned and also bring into the accounts any unrecorded expenses which helped to produce that revenue. For example, an adjusting entry to record revenue which has been earned but has not been recorded or collected prior to the end of the period helps achieve our goal of an income statement which includes all the revenue earned in a given time period. Other adjusting entries cause expenses to be recorded in the accounting period in which the benefits from the expenditures are received, even though cash payment is made in an earlier or later period.

## THE WORK SHEET

The work necessary at the end of an accounting period includes construction of a trial balance, journalizing and posting of adjusting entries, preparation of financial statements, and journalizing and posting of closing entries. So many details are involved in these end-of-period procedures that it is easy to make errors. If these errors are recorded in the journal and in the ledger accounts, considerable time and effort can be wasted in correcting them. Both the journal and the ledger are formal, permanent records. They may be prepared manually in ink, produced on accounting machines, or printed by a computer. One way of avoiding errors in the permanent accounting records and also of simplifying the work to be done at the end of the period is to use a ***work sheet.***

A work sheet is a large columnar sheet of paper, especially designed to arrange in a convenient systematic form all the accounting data required at the end of the period. The work sheet is not a part of the permanent accounting records; it is prepared in pencil by accountants for their own convenience. If an error is made on the work sheet, it may be erased and corrected much more easily than an error in the formal accounting records. Furthermore, the work sheet is so designed as to minimize errors by automatically bringing to light many types of discrepancies which otherwise might be entered in the journal and posted to the ledger accounts. Dollar signs, decimal points, and commas are not used with the amounts entered on work sheets.

The work sheet may be thought of as a testing ground on which the ledger accounts are adjusted, balanced, and arranged in the general form of financial statements. The satisfactory completion of a work sheet provides considerable assurance that all the details of the end-of-period accounting procedures have been properly brought together. After this point has been established, the work sheet then serves as the source from which the formal financial statements are prepared and the adjusting and closing entries are made in the journal.

### Preparing the work sheet

A commonly used form of work sheet with the appropriate headings for Roberts Real Estate Company is illustrated on page 140. Note that the heading of the work sheet consists of three parts: (1) the name of the business, (2) the title Work Sheet, and (3) the period of time covered. The body of the work sheet contains five pairs of money columns, each pair consisting of a debit and a credit column. The procedures to be followed in preparing a work sheet will now be illustrated in five simple steps.

**1 Enter the ledger account balances in the Trial Balance columns** The titles and balances of the ledger accounts at November 30 are copied into the Trial Balance

Explanatory footnotes keyed to adjustments

**ROBERTS REAL ESTATE COMPANY**
**Work Sheet**
**For the Month Ended November 30, 19__**

| | Trial Balance | | Adjustments* | | Adjusted Trial Balance | | Income Statement | | Balance Sheet | |
|---|---|---|---|---|---|---|---|---|---|---|
| | Dr | Cr | Dr | Cr | Dr | Cr | Dr | Cr | Dr | Cr |
| Cash | 25,800 | | | | | | | | | |
| Accounts receivable | 6,990 | | | | | | | | | |
| Unexpired insurance | 540 | | | (a) 15 | | | | | | |
| Office supplies | 720 | | | (b) 120 | | | | | | |
| Land | 15,000 | | | | | | | | | |
| Building | 36,000 | | | | | | | | | |
| Accumulated depreciation: building | | 150 | | (c) 150 | | | | | | |
| Office equipment | 5,400 | | | | | | | | | |
| Accumulated depreciation: office equipment | | 45 | | (d) 45 | | | | | | |
| Notes payable | | 3,000 | | | | | | | | |
| Accounts payable | | 23,595 | | | | | | | | |
| Unearned management fees | | 1,800 | (e) 300 | | | | | | | |
| James Roberts, capital | | 60,771 | | | | | | | | |
| James Roberts, drawing | 1,500 | | | | | | | | | |
| Sales commissions earned | | 5,484 | | | | | | | | |
| Advertising expense | 1,275 | | | | | | | | | |
| Office salaries expense | 1,200 | | | | | | | | | |
| Sales salaries expense | 225 | | (g) 180 | | | | | | | |
| Telephone expense | 195 | | | | | | | | | |
| | 94,845 | 94,845 | | | | | | | | |
| Insurance expense | | | (a) 15 | | | | | | | |
| Office supplies expense | | | (b) 120 | | | | | | | |
| Depreciation expense: building | | | (c) 150 | | | | | | | |
| Depreciation expense: office equipment | | | (d) 45 | | | | | | | |
| Management fees earned | | | | (e) 300 | | | | | | |
| | | | | (h) 120 | | | | | | |
| Interest expense | | | (f) 30 | | | | | | | |
| Interest payable | | | | (f) 30 | | | | | | |
| Sales salaries payable | | | | (g) 180 | | | | | | |
| Management fees receivable | | | (h) 120 | | | | | | | |
| | | | 960 | 960 | | | | | | |

* Adjustments:
(a) Portion of insurance cost which expired during November.
(b) Office supplies used during November.
(c) Depreciation of building during November.
(d) Depreciation of office equipment during November.
(e) Earned one-sixth of the fee collected in advance on the Day properties.
(f) Interest expense accrued during November on note payable.
(g) Salesman's salary for last four days of November.
(h) Management fee accrued on Clayton contract in November.

**Enter the adjusted amounts in columns 5 and 6 of work sheet**

**ROBERTS REAL ESTATE COMPANY**
**Work Sheet**
**For the Month Ended November 30, 19__**

| | Trial Balance | | Adjustments* | | Adjusted Trial Balance | | Income Statement | | Balance Sheet | |
|---|---|---|---|---|---|---|---|---|---|---|
| | Dr | Cr | Dr | Cr | Dr | Cr | Dr | Cr | Dr | Cr |
| Cash | 25,800 | | | | 25,800 | | | | | |
| Accounts receivable | 6,990 | | | | 6,990 | | | | | |
| Unexpired insurance | 540 | | | (a) 15 | 525 | | | | | |
| Office supplies | 720 | | | (b) 120 | 600 | | | | | |
| Land | 15,000 | | | | 15,000 | | | | | |
| Building | 36,000 | | | | 36,000 | | | | | |
| Accumulated depreciation: building | | 150 | | (c) 150 | | 300 | | | | |
| Office equipment | 5,400 | | | | 5,400 | | | | | |
| Accumulated depreciation: office equipment | | 45 | | (d) 45 | | 90 | | | | |
| Notes payable | | 3,000 | | | | 3,000 | | | | |
| Accounts payable | | 23,595 | | | | 23,595 | | | | |
| Unearned management fees | | 1,800 | (e) 300 | | | 1,500 | | | | |
| James Roberts, capital | | 60,771 | | | | 60,771 | | | | |
| James Roberts, drawing | 1,500 | | | | 1,500 | | | | | |
| Sales commissions earned | | 5,484 | | | | 5,484 | | | | |
| Advertising expense | 1,275 | | | | 1,275 | | | | | |
| Office salaries expense | 1,200 | | | | 1,200 | | | | | |
| Sales salaries expense | 225 | | (g) 180 | | 405 | | | | | |
| Telephone expense | 195 | | | | 195 | | | | | |
| | 94,845 | 94,845 | | | | | | | | |
| Insurance expense | | | (a) 15 | | 15 | | | | | |
| Office supplies expense | | | (b) 120 | | 120 | | | | | |
| Depreciation expense: building | | | (c) 150 | | 150 | | | | | |
| Depreciation expense: office equipment | | | (d) 45 | | 45 | | | | | |
| Management fees earned | | | | (e) 300 | | 420 | | | | |
| | | | | (h) 120 | | | | | | |
| Interest expense | | | (f) 30 | | 30 | | | | | |
| Interest payable | | | | (f) 30 | | 30 | | | | |
| Sales salaries payable | | | | (g) 180 | | 180 | | | | |
| Management fees receivable | | | (h) 120 | | 120 | | | | | |
| | | | 960 | 960 | 95,370 | 95,370 | | | | |

* Explanatory notes relating to adjustments are the same as on page 142.

Land, Building, or Notes Payable in the illustrated work sheet) are entered in the Adjusted Trial Balance columns in exactly the same amounts as shown in the Trial Balance columns. After all the accounts have been extended into the Adjusted Trial Balance columns, this pair of columns is totaled to prove that no arithmetical errors have been made up to this point.

**4 Extend each amount in the Adjusted Trial Balance columns into the Income Statement columns or into the Balance Sheet columns** Assets, liabilities, and the owner's capital and drawing accounts are extended into the Balance Sheet columns; revenue and expense accounts are extended to the Income Statement columns. The process of extending amounts horizontally across the work sheet should begin with the account at the top of the work sheet, which is usually Cash. The cash figure is extended to the Balance Sheet debit column. Then the accountant goes down the work sheet line by line, extending each account balance to the appropriate Income Statement or Balance Sheet column. The likelihood of error is much less when each account is extended in the order of its appearance on the work sheet, than if accounts are extended in random order.

The extension of amounts horizontally across the work sheet is merely a sorting of the accounts making up the Adjusted Trial Balance into the two categories of income statement accounts and balance sheet accounts. The work sheet as it appears after completion of this sorting process is illustrated on page 145. Note that each amount in the Adjusted Trial Balance columns is extended to one and only one of the four remaining columns.

**5 Total the Income Statement columns and the Balance Sheet columns. Enter the net income or net loss as a balancing figure in both pairs of columns, and again compute column totals** The work sheet as it appears after this final step is shown on page 146.

The net income or net loss for the period is determined by computing the difference between the totals of the two Income Statement columns. In the illustrated work sheet, the credit column total is the larger and the excess represents net income:

| | |
|---|---|
| *Income Statement credit column total (revenue)* | *$5,904* |
| *Income Statement debit column total (expenses)* | *3,435* |
| *Difference: net income for period* | *$2,469* |

Note on the work sheet that the net income of $2,469 is entered in the Income Statement ***debit*** column as a balancing figure and also on the same line as a balancing figure in the Balance Sheet ***credit*** column. The caption Net Income is written in the space for account titles to identify and explain this item. New totals are then computed for both the Income Statement columns and the Balance Sheet columns. Each pair of columns is now in balance.

The reason for entering the net income of $2,469 in the Balance Sheet credit column is that the net income accumulated during the period in the revenue and expense accounts causes an increase in the owner's equity. If the balance sheet columns did not have equal totals after the net income had been recorded in the

**ROBERTS REAL ESTATE COMPANY**
**Work Sheet**
**For the Month Ended November 30, 19__**

Extend each adjusted amount to columns for income statement or balance sheet

| | Trial Balance | | Adjustments* | | Adjusted Trial Balance | | Income Statement | | Balance sheet | |
|---|---|---|---|---|---|---|---|---|---|---|
| | Dr | Cr | Dr | Cr | Dr | Cr | Dr | Cr | Dr | Cr |
| Cash | 25,800 | | | | 25,800 | | | | 25,800 | |
| Accounts receivable | 6,990 | | | | 6,990 | | | | 6,990 | |
| Unexpired insurance | 540 | | | (a) 15 | 525 | | | | 525 | |
| Office supplies | 720 | | | (b) 120 | 600 | | | | 600 | |
| Land | 15,000 | | | | 15,000 | | | | 15,000 | |
| Building | 36,000 | | | | 36,000 | | | | 36,000 | |
| Accumulated depreciation: building | | 150 | | (c) 150 | | 300 | | | | 300 |
| Office equipment | 5,400 | | | | 5,400 | | | | 5,400 | |
| Accumulated depreciation: office equipment | | 45 | | (d) 45 | | 90 | | | | 90 |
| Notes payable | | 3,000 | | | | 3,000 | | | | 3,000 |
| Accounts payable | | 23,595 | | | | 23,595 | | | | 23,595 |
| Unearned management fees | | 1,800 | (e) 300 | | | 1,500 | | | | 1,500 |
| James Roberts, capital | | 60,771 | | | | 60,771 | | | | 60,771 |
| James Roberts, drawing | 1,500 | | | | 1,500 | | | | 1,500 | |
| Sales commissions earned | | 5,484 | | | | 5,484 | | 5,484 | | |
| Advertising expense | 1,275 | | | | 1,275 | | 1,275 | | | |
| Office salaries expense | 1,200 | | | | 1,200 | | 1,200 | | | |
| Sales salaries expense | 225 | | (g) 180 | | 405 | | 405 | | | |
| Telephone expense | 195 | | | | 195 | | 195 | | | |
| | 94,845 | 94,845 | | | | | | | | |
| Insurance expense | | | (a) 15 | | 15 | | 15 | | | |
| Office supplies expense | | | (b) 120 | | 120 | | 120 | | | |
| Depreciation expense: building | | | (c) 150 | | 150 | | 150 | | | |
| Depreciation expense: office equipment | | | (d) 45 | | 45 | | 45 | | | |
| Management fees earned | | | | (e) 300 | | 420 | | 420 | | |
| | | | | (h) 120 | | | | | | |
| Interest expense | | | (f) 30 | | 30 | | 30 | | | |
| Interest payable | | | | (f) 30 | | 30 | | | | 30 |
| Sales salaries payable | | | | (g) 180 | | 180 | | | | 180 |
| Management fees receivable | | | (h) 120 | | 120 | | | | 120 | |
| | | | 960 | 960 | 95,370 | 95,370 | | | | |

* Explanatory notes relating to adjustments are the same as on page 142.

Completed work sheet

**ROBERTS REAL ESTATE COMPANY**
**Work Sheet**
**For the Month Ended November 30, 19__**

| | Trial Balance | | Adjustments* | | Adjusted Trial Balance | | Income Statement | | Balance sheet | |
|---|---|---|---|---|---|---|---|---|---|---|
| | Dr | Cr | Dr | Cr | Dr | Cr | Dr | Cr | Dr | Cr |
| Cash | 25,800 | | | | 25,800 | | | | 25,800 | |
| Accounts receivable | 6,990 | | | | 6,990 | | | | 6,990 | |
| Unexpired insurance | 540 | | | (a) 15 | 525 | | | | 525 | |
| Office supplies | 720 | | | (b) 120 | 600 | | | | 600 | |
| Land | 15,000 | | | | 15,000 | | | | 15,000 | |
| Building | 36,000 | | | | 36,000 | | | | 36,000 | |
| Accumulated depreciation: building | | 150 | | (c) 150 | | 300 | | | | 300 |
| Office equipment | 5,400 | | | | 5,400 | | | | 5,400 | |
| Accumulated depreciation: office equipment | | 45 | | (d) 45 | | 90 | | | | 90 |
| Notes payable | | 3,000 | | | | 3,000 | | | | 3,000 |
| Accounts payable | | 23,595 | | | | 23,595 | | | | 23,595 |
| Unearned management fees | | 1,800 | (e) 300 | | | 1,500 | | | | 1,500 |
| James Roberts, capital | | 60,771 | | | | 60,771 | | | | 60,771 |
| James Roberts, drawing | 1,500 | | | | 1,500 | | | | 1,500 | |
| Sales commissions earned | | 5,484 | | | | 5,484 | | 5,484 | | |
| Advertising expense | 1,275 | | | | 1,275 | | 1,275 | | | |
| Office salaries expense | 1,200 | | | | 1,200 | | 1,200 | | | |
| Sales salaries expense | 225 | | (g) 180 | | 405 | | 405 | | | |
| Telephone expense | 195 | | | | 195 | | 195 | | | |
| | 94,845 | 94,845 | | | | | | | | |
| Insurance expense | | | (a) 15 | | 15 | | 15 | | | |
| Office supplies expense | | | (b) 120 | | 120 | | 120 | | | |
| Depreciation expense: building | | | (c) 150 | | 150 | | 150 | | | |
| Depreciation expense: office equipment | | | (d) 45 | | 45 | | 45 | | | |
| Management fees earned | | | | (e) 300 | | 420 | | 420 | | |
| | | | | (h) 120 | | | | | | |
| Interest expense | | | (f) 30 | | 30 | | 30 | | | |
| Interest payable | | | | (f) 30 | | 30 | | | | 30 |
| Sales salaries payable | | | | (g) 180 | | 180 | | | | 180 |
| Management fees receivable | | | (h) 120 | | 120 | | | | 120 | |
| | | | 960 | 960 | 95,370 | 95,370 | 3,435 | 5,904 | 91,935 | 89,466 |
| Net Income | | | | | | | 2,469 | | | 2,469 |
| | | | | | | | 5,904 | 5,904 | 91,935 | 91,935 |

* Explanatory notes relating to adjustments are the same as on page 142.

credit column, the lack of agreement would indicate that an error had been made in the work sheet.

Let us assume for a moment that the month's operations had produced a loss rather than a profit. In that case the Income Statement debit column would exceed the credit column. The excess of the debits (expenses) over the credits (revenue) would have to be entered in the credit column in order to bring the two Income Statement columns into balance. The incurring of a loss would decrease the owner's equity; therefore, the loss would be entered as a balancing figure in the Balance Sheet *debit* column. The Balance Sheet columns would then have equal totals.

**Self-balancing nature of the work sheet** Why does the entering of the net income or net loss in one of the Balance Sheet columns bring this pair of columns into balance? The answer is short and simple. All the accounts in the Balance Sheet columns have November 30 balances with the exception of the owner's capital account, which still shows the October 31 balance. By bringing in the current month's net income as an addition to the October 31 capital, the capital account is brought up to date as of November 30. The Balance Sheet columns now prove the familiar proposition that assets are equal to the total of liabilities and owner's equity.

## Uses for the work sheet

**Preparing financial statements** Preparing the formal financial statements from the work sheet is an easy step. All the information needed for both the income statement and the balance sheet has already been sorted and arranged in convenient form in the work sheet. The income statement shown below contains the amounts listed in the Income Statement columns of the work sheet.

*Data taken from Income Statement columns of work sheet*

**ROBERTS REAL ESTATE COMPANY**
**Income Statement**
**For the Month Ended November 30, 19__**

| | | |
|---|---|---|
| Revenue: | | |
| Sales commissions earned | | $5,484 |
| Management fees earned | | 420 |
| Total revenue | | $5,904 |
| Expenses: | | |
| Advertising | $1,275 | |
| Office supplies | 120 | |
| Office salaries | 1,200 | |
| Sales salaries | 405 | |
| Telephone | 195 | |
| Insurance | 15 | |
| Depreciation: building | 150 | |
| Depreciation: office equipment | 45 | |
| Interest | 30 | |
| Total expenses | | 3,435 |
| Net income | | $2,469 |

The balance sheets previously illustrated have shown in the owner's equity section the changes during the month caused by the owner's withdrawals and by the net income or loss from operation of the business. A separate statement, illustrated below, is sometimes used to show the changes in the owner's equity during the period. When a separate statement is used, only the ending amount of the owner's capital account is shown in the balance sheet.

*Net income exceeded withdrawals by owner*

**ROBERTS REAL ESTATE COMPANY**
**Statement of Owner's Equity**
**For the Month Ended November 30, 19__**

| | |
|---|---|
| James Roberts, capital, Nov. 1, 19__ | $60,771 |
| Net income for November | 2,469 |
| Subtotal | $63,240 |
| Less: Withdrawals | 1,500 |
| James Roberts, capital, Nov. 30, 19__ | $61,740 |

*Compare these amounts with figures in Balance Sheet columns of work sheet*

**ROBERTS REAL ESTATE COMPANY**
**Balance Sheet**
**November 30, 19__**

**Assets**

| | | |
|---|---|---|
| Cash | | $25,800 |
| Accounts receivable | | 6,990 |
| Management fees receivable | | 120 |
| Unexpired insurance | | 525 |
| Office supplies | | 600 |
| Land | | 15,000 |
| Building | $36,000 | |
| Less: Accumulated depreciation | 300 | 35,700 |
| Office equipment | $ 5,400 | |
| Less: Accumulated depreciation | 90 | 5,310 |
| Total assets | | $90,045 |

**Liabilities & Owner's Equity**

| | |
|---|---|
| Liabilities: | |
| Notes payable | $ 3,000 |
| Accounts payable | 23,595 |
| Interest payable | 30 |
| Sales salaries payable | 180 |
| Unearned management fees | 1,500 |
| Total liabilities | $28,305 |
| Owner's equity: | |
| James Roberts, capital | 61,740 |
| Total liabilities & owner's equity | $90,045 |

**Recording adjusting entries in the accounting records** After the financial statements have been prepared from the work sheet at the end of the period, the ledger accounts are adjusted to bring them into agreement with the financial statements. This is an easy step because the adjustments have already been computed on the work sheet. The amounts appearing in the Adjustments columns of the work sheet and the related explanations at the bottom of the work sheet provide all the necessary information for the adjusting entries, as shown below, which are first entered in the journal and then posted to the ledger accounts.

*Adjustments on work sheet are entered in general journal*

***General Journal*** ***Page 5***

| Date | | Account Titles and Explanation | LP | Debit | Credit |
|---|---|---|---|---|---|
| 19__ | | | | | |
| Nov | 30 | Insurance Expense | | 15 | |
| | | Unexpired Insurance | | | 15 |
| | | Insurance expense for November. | | | |
| | 30 | Office Supplies Expense | | 120 | |
| | | Office Supplies | | | 120 |
| | | Office supplies used during November. | | | |
| | 30 | Depreciation Expense: Building | | 150 | |
| | | Accumulated Depreciation: Building | | | 150 |
| | | Depreciation for November. | | | |
| | 30 | Depreciation Expense: Office Equipment | | 45 | |
| | | Accumulated Depreciation: Office Equipment | | | 45 |
| | | Depreciation for November. | | | |
| | 30 | Unearned Management Fees | | 300 | |
| | | Management Fees Earned | | | 300 |
| | | Earned one-sixth of fee collected in advance for management of the properties owned by John Day. | | | |
| | 30 | Interest Expense | | 30 | |
| | | Interest Payable | | | 30 |
| | | Interest expense accrued during November on note payable. | | | |
| | 30 | Sales Salaries Expense | | 180 | |
| | | Sales Salaries Payable | | | 180 |
| | | To record expense and related liability to salesman for last four evenings' work in November. | | | |

*General Journal* *Page 5*

| Date | | Account Titles and Explanation | LP | Debit | Credit |
|---|---|---|---|---|---|
| | 30 | *Management Fees Receivable* . . . . . . . . . . . . | | *120* | |
| | | *Management Fees Earned* . . . . . . . . . . . . | | | *120* |
| | | *To record the receivable and related revenue earned for managing properties owned by Henry Clayton.* | | | |

**Recording closing entries** When the financial statements have been prepared, the revenue and expense accounts have served their purpose for the current period and should be closed. These accounts then will have zero balances and will be ready for the recording of revenue and expenses during the next fiscal period.

The journalizing and posting of closing entries were illustrated in Chapter 3. The point to be emphasized now is that the completed work sheet provides in convenient form all the information needed to make the closing entries. The preparation of closing entries from the work sheet may be summarized as follows:

**1** To close the accounts listed in the Income Statement credit column, debit the revenue accounts and credit Income Summary.

**2** To close the accounts listed in the Income Statement debit column, debit Income Summary and credit the expense accounts.

**3** To close the Income Summary account, transfer the balancing figure in the Income Statement columns of the work sheet ($2,469 in the illustration) to the owner's capital account. A profit is transferred by debiting Income Summary and crediting the capital account; a loss is transferred by debiting the capital account and crediting Income Summary.

**4** To close the owner's drawing account, debit the capital account and credit the drawing account. Note on the work sheet that the account, James Roberts, Drawing, is extended from the Adjusted Trial Balance debit column to the Balance Sheet debit column. It does not appear in the Income Statement columns because a withdrawal of cash by the owner is not regarded as an expense of the business.

The closing entries at November 30 are shown at the top of page 151.

## The accounting cycle

As stated at the beginning of this chapter, the life of a business is divided into accounting periods of equal length. In each period we repeat a standard sequence of accounting procedures beginning with the journalizing of transactions and concluding with an after-closing trial balance.

Because the work sheet includes the trial balance, the adjusting entries in preliminary form, and an adjusted trial balance, the use of a work sheet will modify the sequence of procedures given in Chapter 3, as follows:

*Closing entries derived from work sheet*

**General Journal** — *Page 6*

| Date | | Account Titles and Explanation | LP | Debit | Credit |
|---|---|---|---|---|---|
| 19__ | | | | | |
| Nov | 30 | Sales Commissions Earned | | 5,484 | |
| | | Management Fees Earned | | 420 | |
| | | Income Summary | | | 5,904 |
| | | To close the revenue accounts. | | | |
| | 30 | Income Summary | | 3,435 | |
| | | Advertising Expense | | | 1,275 |
| | | Office Salaries Expense | | | 1,200 |
| | | Sales Salaries Expense | | | 405 |
| | | Telephone Expense | | | 195 |
| | | Insurance Expense | | | 15 |
| | | Office Supplies Expense | | | 120 |
| | | Depreciation Expense: Building | | | 150 |
| | | Depreciation Expense: Office Equipment | | | 45 |
| | | Interest Expense | | | 30 |
| | | To close the expense accounts. | | | |
| | 30 | Income Summary | | 2,469 | |
| | | James Roberts, Capital | | | 2,469 |
| | | To close the Income Summary account. | | | |
| | 30 | James Roberts, Capital | | 1,500 | |
| | | James Roberts, Drawing | | | 1,500 |
| | | To close the owner's drawing account. | | | |

**1 Journalize transactions** Analyze business transactions as they occur and record them promptly in a journal.

**2 Post to ledger accounts** Transfer debits and credits from journal entries to ledger accounts.

**3 Prepare a work sheet** Begin with a trial balance of the ledger, enter all necessary adjustments, sort the adjusted account balances between income statement accounts and balance sheet accounts, and determine the net income or net loss.

**4 Prepare financial statements** Utilize the information in the work sheet to prepare an income statement, a statement of owner's equity, and a balance sheet.

**5 Adjust and close the accounts** Using the information in the work sheet as a guide, enter the adjusting entries in the journal. Post these entries to ledger accounts. Prepare and post journal entries to close the revenue and expense accounts into the Income Summary account and to transfer the net income or net loss to the owner's capital account. Also prepare and post a journal entry to close the owner's drawing account into the owner's capital account.

**6 Prepare an after-closing trial balance** Prove that equality of debit and credit balances in the ledger has not been upset by the adjusting and closing procedures.

The above sequence of accounting procedures constitutes a complete accounting process. The regular repetition of this standardized set of procedures in each accounting period is often referred as the ***accounting cycle.*** The procedures of a complete accounting cycle are illustrated below.

***Illustration of the accounting cycle***

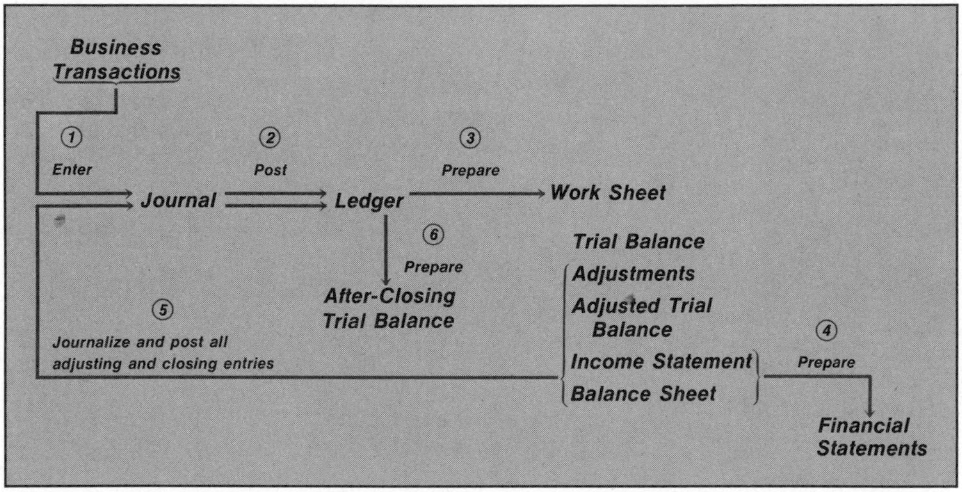


Note that the preparing of financial statements (Step 4) comes before entering adjusting and closing entries in the journal and posting these entries to the ledger (Step 5). This sequence reflects the fact that ***management wants the financial statements as soon as possible.*** Once the work sheet is complete, all information required for the financial statements is available. Top priority then goes to preparation of the financial statements.

In most business concerns the accounts are closed only once a year; for these companies the accounting cycle is one year in length. For purposes of illustration in a textbook, however, it is often convenient to assume that the entire accounting cycle is performed within the time period of one month. The completion of the accounting cycle is the occasion for preparing financial statements and closing the revenue and expense accounts.

## Preparing monthly financial statements without closing the accounts

Many companies which close their accounts only once a year nevertheless prepare ***monthly*** financial statements for managerial use. These monthly statements are prepared from work sheets, but the adjustments indicated on the work sheets are not entered in the accounting records and no closing entries are made.

Under this plan, the time-consuming operation of journalizing and posting adjustments and closing entries is performed only at the end of the fiscal year, but the company has the advantage of monthly financial statements. Monthly and quarterly financial statements are often referred to as ***interim statements,*** because they are in between the year-end statements. The annual or year-end statements are usually audited by a firm of certified public accountants; interim statements are usually unaudited.

## Reversing entries

Reversing entries are an optional bookkeeping procedure which may be carried out at year-end to simplify the recording of certain routine cash receipts and payments in the following period. As the name suggests, a ***reversing entry*** is the exact reverse of an adjusting entry. It contains the same account titles and dollar amounts as the related adjusting entry, but the debits and credits are the reverse of those in the adjusting entry and the date is the first day of the next accounting period.

Let us use as an example a small company on a five-day work week which pays its employees each Friday. Assume that the payroll is $600 a day or $3,000 for a five-day week. Throughout the year, the company's bookkeeper makes a journal entry each Friday as follows:

***Regular weekly entry for payroll***

| | | |
|---|---|---|
| *Salaries Expense* . . . . . . . . . . . . . . . . . . . . . . . . . . . . . . . . . . . . . . | *3,000* | |
| *Cash* . . . . . . . . . . . . . . . . . . . . . . . . . . . . . . . . . . . . . . . . . . . | | *3,000* |
| ***To record payment of salaries for the week.*** | | |

Next, let us assume that December 31, the last working day of Year 1, falls on Wednesday. All expenses of Year 1 must be recorded before the accounts are closed and financial statements prepared at December 31. Therefore, an adjusting entry must be made to record the salaries expense and the related liability to employees for the three days they have worked since the last payday. The adjusting entry for $1,800 (computed as 3 × $600 daily salary expense) is shown below:

***Adjusting entry at end of year***

| | | |
|---|---|---|
| *Salaries Expense* . . . . . . . . . . . . . . . . . . . . . . . . . . . . . . . . . . . . . . | *1,800* | |
| *Salaries Payable* . . . . . . . . . . . . . . . . . . . . . . . . . . . . . . . . . . . . . | | *1,800* |
| ***To record salaries expense and the related liability to employees for last three days worked in December.*** | | |

The closing of the accounts on December 31 will reduce the Salaries Expense account to zero, but the liability account, Salaries Payable, will remain open with its $1,800 credit balance at the beginning of the new year. On the next regular payday, Friday, January 2, the company's bookkeeper can record the $3,000 payroll by a debit of $1,800 to Salaries Payable, a debit of $1,200 to Salaries Expense, and a credit of $3,000 to Cash. However, splitting the debit side of the entry in this manner ($1,800 to the liability account and $1,200 to expense) requires more understanding and alertness from the bookkeeper than if the entry were identical with the other 51 payroll entries made during the year.

By making a reversing entry as of the first day of the new accounting period, we can simplify the recording of routine transactions and avoid the need for the company's employees to refer to prior adjusting entries for guidance. The reversing entry for the $1,800 year-end accrual of salaries would be dated January 1, Year 2, and would probably be made under the direction of the accountant responsible for the year-end closing of the accounts and preparation of financial statements. The entry would be as follows:

***Reversing entry makes possible . . .***

| | | | |
|---|---|---|---|
| *Jan. 1* | ***Salaries Payable*** | ***1,800*** | |
| | ***Salaries Expense*** | | ***1,800*** |
| | ***To reverse the accrual of salaries made on Dec. 31, Year 1.*** | | |

This reversing entry closes the Salaries Payable account by transferring the $1,800 liability to the credit side of the Salaries Expense account. Thus, the Salaries Expense account begins the new year with an abnormal credit balance of $1,800. On Friday, January 2, the normal payroll entry for $3,000 will be made to the same accounts as on every other Friday during the year.

***. . . regular payroll entry for first payday of new year***

| | | |
|---|---|---|
| ***Salaries Expense*** | ***3,000*** | |
| ***Cash*** | | ***3,000*** |
| ***Paid salaries for week ended Jan. 2, Year 2.*** | | |

After this January 2 entry has been posted, the ledger account for Salaries Expense will show a debit balance of $1,200, the result of this $3,000 debit and the $1,800 credit from the reversing entry on January 1. The amount of $1,200 is the correct expense for the two workdays of the new year at $600 a day. The results, of course, are exactly the same as if no reversing entry had been used and the company's bookkeeper had split the debit side of the January 2 payroll entry between Salaries Payable and Salaries Expense.

The ledger accounts for Salaries Expense and for Salaries Payable are shown below to illustrate the effect of posting the adjusting entry and the reversing entry.

***Salaries Expense***

| ***Year 1*** | | | | ***Debit*** | ***Credit*** | ***Balance*** |
|---|---|---|---|---|---|---|
| Various | | (51 weekly entries of $3,000) | | | | 153000 |
| Dec | 31 | Adjusting entry (3 days @ $600) | | 1800 | | 154800 |
| | 31 | To close at year-end | | | 154800 | -0- |
| Year | 2 | | | | | |
| Jan | 1 | Reversing entry | | | 1800 | 1800 cr |
| | 2 | Weekly payroll | | 3000 | | 1200 |

***Salaries Payable***

| ***Year 1*** | | | | ***Debit*** | ***Credit*** | ***Balance*** |
|---|---|---|---|---|---|---|
| Dec | 31 | Adjusting entry (3 days @ $600) | | | 1800 | 1800 |
| Year | 2 | | | | | |
| Jan | 1 | Reversing entry | | 1800 | | -0- |

**Which adjusting entries may be reversed?** Reversing entries may be used for ***any adjusting entry that accrues an expense*** (for example, interest expense, utilities expense, taxes expense, and salaries expense). Reversing entries also may be used for ***any adjusting entry that accrues revenue*** (for example, commissions earned but not yet collected or billed to customers, interest earned but not yet collected, and rent earned but not yet collected). Adjustments which accrue expenses or revenue bring liabilities or assets (receivables) into the records and ***are followed by payments or receipts of cash.*** This characteristic is helpful in identifying those adjusting entries which may be reversed.

Adjusting entries for depreciation ***are not reversed.*** Neither is the adjusting entry to apportion part of the cost of unexpired insurance to expense, nor the entry to apportion part of any asset to expense. Adjusting entries which recognize that a portion of revenue collected in advance has now been earned at the year-end are not reversed. Finally, remember that reversing entries are optional. They are a convenience in carrying out the accounting process, but are not essential to the application of accounting principles or the preparation of good financial statements.

## KEY TERMS INTRODUCED OR EMPHASIZED IN CHAPTER 4

**Accounting cycle** The sequence of accounting procedures performed during an accounting period. The procedures include journalizing transactions, posting, preparation of a work sheet and financial statements, adjusting and closing the accounts, and preparation of an after-closing trial balance.

**Accrued expenses** Expenses such as salaries of employees and interest on notes payable which have accumulated but are unpaid and unrecorded at the end of the period. Also called ***unrecorded expenses.***

**Accrued revenue** Revenue which has been earned during the accounting period but has not been collected or recorded prior to the closing date. Also called ***unrecorded revenue.***

**Book value** The net amount at which an asset is shown in accounting records. For depreciable assets, book value equals cost minus accumulated depreciation. Also called ***carrying value.***

**Carrying value** See book value.

**Deferred revenue** An obligation to render services or deliver goods in the future because of advance receipt of payment. Also called ***unearned revenue.***

**Interim statements** Financial statements prepared at intervals of less than one year. Usually quarterly and monthly statements.

**Prepaid expenses** Advance payments for such expenses as rent and insurance. The portion which has not been used up at the end of the accounting period is included in the balance sheet as an asset.

**Promissory note** A formal written promise to repay an amount borrowed plus interest at a future date.

**Reversing entries** An optional year-end bookkeeping technique consisting of the reversal on the first day of the new accounting period of those year-end adjusting entries which accrue expenses or revenue and thus will be followed by later cash payments or receipts. Purpose is to permit company personnel to record routine transactions in a standard manner without referring to prior adjusting entries.

**Unearned revenue** See deferred revenue.

**Unrecorded expenses** See accrued expenses.

**Unrecorded revenue** See accrued revenue.

**Work sheet** A large columnar sheet designed to arrange in convenient form all the accounting data required at the end of the period. Facilitates preparation of financial statements and the work of adjusting and closing the accounts.

## REVIEW QUESTIONS

**1** Which of the following statements do you consider most acceptable?
 **a** Adjusting entries affect balance sheet accounts only.
 **b** Adjusting entries affect income statement accounts only.
 **c** An adjusting entry may affect two or more balance sheet accounts or two or more income statement accounts, but cannot affect both a balance sheet account and an income statement account.
 **d** Every adjusting entry affects both a balance sheet account and an income statement account.

**2** The recording of depreciation involves two ledger accounts: Depreciation Expense and Accumulated Depreciation. Explain the purpose of each account; indicate whether it normally has a debit balance or a credit balance; and state where it appears in the financial statements.

**3** At the end of the current year, the adjusted trial balance of the Midas Company showed the following account balances, among others:

***Building, $31,600***

***Depreciation Expense: Building, $1,580***

***Accumulated Depreciation: Building, $11,060***

Assuming that straight-line depreciation has been used, what length of time do these facts suggest that the Midas Company has owned the building?

**4** The net income reported by Haskell Company for the year was $21,400, and the capital account of the owner, J. B. Haskell, stood at $36,000. However, the company had failed to recognize that interest amounting to $375 had accrued on a note payable to the bank. State the corrected figures for net income and for the owner's equity. In what other respect was the balance sheet of the company in error?

**5** Office supplies on hand in the Melville Company amounted to $600 at the beginning of the year. During the year additional office supplies were purchased at a cost of $1,560 and charged to the asset account Office Supplies. At the end of the year a physical count showed that supplies on hand amounted to $810. Give the adjusting entry needed at December 31.

**6** The X Company at December 31 recognized the existence of certain unexpired costs which would provide benefits to the company in future periods. Give examples of such unexpired costs and state where they would be shown in the financial statements.

**7** At year-end the adjusting entry to reduce the Unexpired Insurance account by the amount of insurance premium applicable to the current period was accidentally omitted. Which items in the income statement will be in error? Will these items be overstated or understated? Which items in the balance sheet will be in error? Will they be overstated or understated?

8 From the following list of ledger accounts, identify those which would ***not*** be included in an after-closing trial balance. Accounts Payable; Unearned Revenue; Commissions Receivable; Insurance Expense; Salaries Payable; Fees Earned; John Smith, Capital; Accumulated Depreciation; Depreciation Expense; Cash.

9 In performing the regular end-of-period accounting procedures, does the preparation of the work sheet precede or follow the posting of adjusting entries to ledger accounts? Why?

10 The Adjustments columns of the work sheet for Davis Company contained only three adjustments, as follows: depreciation of building, $3,600; expiration of insurance, $500; and salaries accrued at year-end, $4,100. If the Trial Balance columns showed totals of $600,000, what would be the totals of the Adjusted Trial Balance columns?

11 Should the Adjusted Trial Balance columns of the work sheet be totaled before or after the adjusted amounts are carried to the Income Statement and Balance Sheet columns? Explain.

12 In extending adjusted account balances from the Adjusted Trial Balance columns to the Income Statement and Balance Sheet columns, is there any particular sequence to be followed in order to minimize the possibility of errors? Explain.

13 Do the totals of the balance sheet ordinarily agree with the totals of the Balance Sheet columns of the work sheet?

14 Is a work sheet ever prepared when there is no intention of closing the accounts? Explain.

15 Does a statement of owner's equity cover a period of time or (like a balance sheet) show financial information for a single date? What elements does it include other than the amount of the owner's capital account?

16 The weekly payroll of Stevens Company amounts to $15,000 and employees are paid up to date every Friday. On January 1 of the current year, the Salaries Expense account showed a credit balance of $9,000. Explain the nature of the accounting entry or entries which probably led to this balance.

## EXERCISES

*Ex. 4-1* On September 1, Bar Company purchased a one-year fire insurance policy and recorded the payment of the full yearly premium of $4,800 by debiting Unexpired Insurance. The accounts were not adjusted or closed until the end of the calendar year. Prepare the necessary adjusting entry at December 31.

*Ex. 4-2* Mill Corporation adjusts and closes its accounts at the end of the calendar year. Prepare the adjusting entries required at December 31 based on the following information. (Not all of these items may require adjusting entries.)

**a** A bank loan had been obtained on October 1. Accrued interest on the loan at December 31 amounts to $1,200. No interest expense has been recorded.

**b** Depreciation of office equipment is based on estimated life of 10 years. The balance in the Office Equipment account is $26,400; no change has occurred in the account during the year.

**c** Interest receivable on United States government bonds owned at December 31 amounts to $1,920. This accrued interest has not been recorded.

**d** On December 31, an agreement was signed to lease a truck for 12 months beginning January 1 at a rate of 30 cents a mile. Usage is expected to be 1,500 miles per month and the contract specifies a minimum payment equivalent to 10,000 miles a year.

*Ex. 4-3* On Friday of each week, Ozark Company pays its sales personnel weekly salaries amounting to $100,000 for a five-day work week.

**a** Prepare the necessary adjusting entry at year-end, assuming that December 31 falls on Tuesday.

**b** Prepare the journal entry for payment by Ozark Company of a week's salaries to its sales personnel on Friday, January 3, the first payday of the new year. (Assume that no reversing entry was made.)

*Ex. 4-4* Among the ledger accounts used by Cottonwood Speedway are the following: Prepaid Rent, Rent Expense, Unearned Admissions Revenue, Admissions Revenue, Prepaid Printing, Printing Expense, Concessions Receivable, and Concessions Revenue. For each of the following items, write first the journal entry (if one is needed) to record the external transaction and secondly the adjusting entry, if any, required on March 31, the end of the fiscal year.

**a** On March 1, paid rent for the next four months at $25,000 per month.

**b** On March 2, sold season tickets for a total of $600,000. The season includes 60 racing days: 15 in March, 25 in April, and 20 in May.

**c** On March 3, an agreement was reached with Snack-Bars, Inc., allowing that company to sell refreshments at the track in return for 10% of the gross receipts from refreshment sales.

**d** On March 5, schedules for the 15 racing days in March and the first 10 racing days in April were printed and paid for at a cost of $10,000.

**e** On March 31, Snack-Bars, Inc., reported that the gross receipts from refreshment sales in March had been $135,000 and that the 10% owed to Cottonwood Speedway would be remitted on April 10.

*Ex. 4-5* Property Management Company manages apartment buildings for various owners who wish to be relieved of this responsibility. Among the ledger accounts in use are Cash, Unearned Management Fees, Management Fees, and Management Fees Receivable. On December 1, the company received a check for $12,000 from a client, Susan Hart, who was leaving for a six-month stay abroad. This check represented payment in advance for management of Hart's real estate properties during the six months of her absence. Explain how this transaction would be recorded, the adjustment, if any, to be made at December 31, and how this information would be shown in the year-end financial statements.

*Ex. 4-6* The following amounts are taken from consecutive balance sheets of Jensen Company.

| | Year 1 | Year 2 |
|---|---|---|
| Unexpired insurance | $ -0- | $1,200 |
| Unearned rental revenue | 5,500 | 4,000 |
| Interest payable | 100 | 800 |

The income statement for Year 2 of the Jensen Company shows the following items:

| | |
|---|---|
| Insurance expense | $ 700 |
| Rental revenue | 18,000 |
| Interest expense | 1,000 |

**Instructions** Determine the following amounts:

**a** Cash paid during Year 2 on insurance policies

**b** Cash received during Year 2 as rental revenue
**c** Cash paid during Year 2 for interest

*Ex. 4-7* Milo Company closes its accounts at the end of each calendar year. The company operates on a five-day work week and pays its employees up to date each Friday. The weekly payroll is regularly $5,000. On Tuesday, December 31, Year 1, an adjusting entry was made to accrue $2,000 salaries expense for the two days worked since the last payday. The company did not make a reversing entry. On Friday, January 3, Year 2, the regular weekly payroll of $5,000 was paid and recorded by the usual entry debiting Salaries Expense $5,000 and crediting Cash $5,000.

Were Milo Company's accounting records correct for Year 1? For Year 2? Explain two alternatives the company might have followed with respect to payroll at year-end. One of the alternatives should include a reversing entry.

## PROBLEMS

### Group A

*4A-1* Sierra Ski Bowl maintains its accounting records on a calendar-year basis. Using the year-end information shown below, you are to prepare all necessary adjusting journal entries at December 31.

(1) A one-year fire insurance policy had been purchased and paid for in full at a total premium of $1,800 on December 1 of the current year. The payment was debited to Unexpired Insurance.
(2) On December 31, the last day of the company's fiscal year, Sierra Ski Bowl signed an agreement to lease a truck from Olympic Rentals for the period of one year beginning January 1 at a rate of 24 cents per mile, with a minimum monthly charge of $240.
(3) Depreciation on the building for the year ended December 31 was $3,600.
(4) A portion of the land owned had been leased to an amusement park at a yearly rental of $14,400. One year's rent had been collected in advance at the date of the lease (December 16) and credited to Unearned Rental Revenue. (Recognize one-half month's rent as earned.)
(5) Another portion of the land owned had been rented on December 1 to a service station operator at an annual rate of $2,880. No rent had as yet been collected from this tenant.
(6) Accrued wages payable, $5,520.
(7) Accrued interest receivable on United States government bonds owned amounts to $990 as of December 31.
(8) A six-month bank loan in the amount of $72,000 had been obtained on October 31. No interest had been paid and no interest expense recorded. Accrued interest at December 31 amounted to $1,200.
(9) Accrued property taxes, $3,470.

**Instructions** From the information given above, draft the adjusting entries (including explanations) required at December 31.

*4A-2* The Foothill Music Festival uses a fiscal year ending June 30 and recognizes two types of revenue: Admissions Revenue and Concessions Revenue. The latter revenue comes from the sale of refreshments in the theater through a contract with a concessionaire. The events listed below in paragraphs (1) through (6) all occurred during June of the current year.

(1) On June 1, paid rent for six months at $1,200 per month. (Debit Prepaid Rent.)
(2) On June 2, sold season tickets to the Foothill Music Festival for a total of $15,600. Four different programs were included in the festival, scheduled to be presented as follows: Program no. 1, June 15–16; program no. 2, June 29–30; program no. 3, July 5–6; and program no. 4, July 19–20. (Credit Unearned Admissions Revenue.)
(3) On June 6, an agreement was reached with Harvey Lynn to sell refreshments in the theater. In return for the privilege, Lynn agreed to pay 5% of gross receipts to the management within three days after the conclusion of each program.
(4) On June 7, four program notes, one for each of the four programs, were printed at a total cost of $1,260. Cash was paid. (Debit Prepaid Printing.)
(5) On June 19, cash in the amount of $96 was received from Lynn, representing 5% of refreshment sales of $1,920 during program no. 1. (Credit Concessions Revenue.)
(6) On June 30, Lynn reported that total refreshment sales at program no. 2 amounted to $2,160. No cash was received at this time.

**Instructions** For each of the numbered paragraphs, you are to write first the journal entry (if one is required) to record the event, and secondly the related adjusting entry, if any, required at June 30, the end of the fiscal period.

***4A-3*** Kingspoint Motel maintains its accounting records on the basis of a calendar year. The following information is available as a source for adjusting entries at December 31.

(1) Salaries earned by employees but not yet paid amount to $10,860.
(2) As of December 31 the motel has earned $5,040 rental revenue from current guests who will not be billed until they are ready to check out. (Debit Rent Receivable.)
(3) On December 16, a suite of rooms was rented to a guest for six months at a monthly rental of $1,500. Rent for the first three months was collected in advance and credited to Unearned Rental Revenue.
(4) A one-year bank loan in the amount of $90,000 had been obtained on November 1. No interest has been paid and no interest expense has been recorded. The interest accrued at December 31 is $1,800.
(5) Depreciation on the motel for the year ended December 31 was $43,800.
(6) Depreciation on a station wagon owned by the motel was based on a four-year life. The station wagon had been purchased new on September 1 of the current year at a cost of $9,600.
(7) On December 31, Kingsport Motel entered into an agreement to host the National Building Suppliers Convention in June of next year. The motel expects to earn rental revenue of at least $15,000 from the convention.

**Instructions**

**a** From the information given above, draft the adjusting entries (including explanations) required at December 31.

**b** Assume that all necessary adjusting entries at December 31 have been recorded and that net income for the year is determined to be $300,000. How much net income would have been indicated by the accounting records if the company had failed to make the above adjusting entries? Show computations.

***4A-4*** Pension Consultants is a new firm organized January 1, 19___, to help other companies to develop employee pension plans which will meet the complex legal and accounting requirements imposed by federal regulations for all pension plans. Some clients of the company pay in advance for advisory services; others are billed after the services have been rendered. The company adjusts and closes its accounts ***each month.*** At May 31, the trial balance appeared as follows:

***PENSION CONSULTANTS***
***Trial Balance***
***May 31, 19__***

| | | |
|---|---|---|
| *Cash* | *$20,000* | |
| *Prepaid rent* | *3,000* | |
| *Office supplies* | *1,100* | |
| *Office equipment* | *10,800* | |
| *Accumulated depreciation: office equipment* | | *$ 400* |
| *Accounts payable* | | *2,000* |
| *Unearned revenue* | | *19,000* |
| *Kay Brett, capital* | | *16,000* |
| *Kay Brett, drawing* | *700* | |
| *Fees earned* | | *13,000* |
| *Telephone expense* | *800* | |
| *Travel expense* | *1,000* | |
| *Salaries expense* | *13,000* | |
| | *$50,400* | *$50,400* |

**Other data**

(a) The monthly rent was $600.
(b) Office supplies on hand May 31 amounted to $900.
(c) The office equipment was purchased on January 1. The useful life was estimated at 9 years.
(d) Fees of $4,000 were earned during the month by performing services for clients who had paid in advance. (Debit Unearned Revenue.)
(e) Pension advisory services rendered during the month but not yet collected or billed to clients amounted to $1,200. (Debit Pension Service Receivables.)
(f) Salaries earned by employees during the month but not yet paid amounted to $300.

**Instructions**

**a** Prepare adjusting entries.
**b** Prepare an adjusted trial balance. Accounts not appearing in the trial balance but used in the adjusting entries should be listed in the proper sequence in the adjusted trial balance. For example, Pension Service Receivables should be listed among the assets, and Rent Expense should be listed among the expense accounts.

***4A-5*** North Slope Engineering Consultants was organized January 1 to provide technical services to various oil companies in Alaska. The trial balance on page 162 was prepared at June 30 after six months of operations. The accounts are to be adjusted and closed for the first time at June 30.

**NORTH SLOPE ENGINEERING CONSULTANTS**
**Trial Balance**
**June 30, 19__**

| | | |
|---|---|---|
| Cash | $ 61,000 | |
| Prepaid office rent | 72,000 | |
| Supplies | 14,400 | |
| Instruments | 79,200 | |
| Notes payable | | $ 60,000 |
| Unearned fees | | 156,000 |
| Ronald Moulton, capital | | 131,200 |
| Ronald Moulton, drawing | 51,240 | |
| Fees earned | | 127,440 |
| Salaries expense | 194,400 | |
| Miscellaneous expense | 2,400 | |
| | $474,640 | $474,640 |

**Other data**

(a) Office rent for one year was paid on January 1, when the lease was signed.
(b) Supplies on hand on June 30 amounted to $2,880.
(c) Instruments were purchased on January 1. The useful life was estimated at 10 years.
(d) Accrued interest expense on notes payable was $600 at June 30.
(e) A number of clients obtained during the first six months of the company's operations had made advance payments for services to be rendered over a considerable period. As of June 30, value of services rendered and chargeable against Unearned Fees was $114,000.
(f) Services rendered and chargeable to other clients amounted to $44,400 as of June 30. No entries had yet been made to record the revenue earned by performing services for these clients. (Debit Fees Receivable.)
(g) Salaries earned by staff personnel but not yet paid amounted to $6,000 on June 30.

**Instructions**

**a** Prepare adjusting entries at June 30.
**b** Prepare an adjusted trial balance. (*Note:* You may find the use of T accounts helpful in computing the account balances after adjustments.)
**c** Prepare an income statement for the six-month period ended June 30, a statement of owner's equity, and a balance sheet.

***4A-6*** Bel Air Golf Course adjusts and closes its accounts at the end of each calendar year. Revenue is obtained from greens fees and also from a contract with a concessionaire who sells refreshments on the premises. At December 31, the information for adjustments was gathered and a work sheet was prepared. The first four columns of the work sheet contained the account balances and adjustments shown at the top of page 163.

| | Trial Balance | | Adjustments* | |
|---|---|---|---|---|
| | Dr | Cr | Dr | Cr |
| Cash | 10,920 | | | |
| Unexpired insurance | 2,520 | | | (a) 840 |
| Prepaid advertising | 1,200 | | | (b) 360 |
| Land | 450,000 | | | |
| Equipment | 57,600 | | | |
| Accumulated depreciation: equipment | | 9,600 | | (f) 4,800 |
| Notes payable | | 72,000 | | |
| Unearned revenue from concessions | | 9,000 | (d) 6,000 | |
| Walter Nelson, capital | | 371,000 | | |
| Walter Nelson, drawing | 18,000 | | | |
| Revenue from greens fees | | 220,000 | | |
| Advertising expense | 6,600 | | (b) 360 | |
| Water expense | 12,480 | | | |
| Salaries expense | 94,680 | | (e) 1,320 | |
| Repairs and maintenance expense | 21,000 | | | |
| Miscellaneous expense | 6,600 | | | |
| | 681,600 | 681,600 | | |
| Insurance expense | | | (a) 840 | |
| Interest expense | | | (c) 480 | |
| Interest payable | | | | (c) 480 |
| Revenue from concessions | | | | (d) 6,000 |
| Salaries payable | | | | (e) 1,320 |
| Depreciation expense: equipment | | | (f) 4,800 | |
| | | | 13,800 | 13,800 |

* Adjustments:
(a) $840 insurance expired during year.
(b) $360 prepaid advertising expired during year.
(c) $480 accrued interest expense on notes payable.
(d) $6,000 concession revenue earned during year.
(e) $1,320 of salaries earned but unpaid at December 31.
(f) $4,800 depreciation expense for year.

**Instructions** Using the data above, complete the work sheet by listing the appropriate amounts in the remaining six columns of the work sheet. Follow the work sheet format illustrated on page 146.

*4A-7* Research Associates is in the business of performing investigations and preparing financial analyses for business organizations and government agencies. Much of its work is done through a computer service center for which payment is made on an hourly basis. The company adjusts and closes its accounts monthly. At October 31, 19___, the account balances were as follows before adjustments were made.

| | |
|---|---|
| *Cash* | *$ 71,760* |
| *Research fees receivable* | |
| *Prepaid office rent* | *28,800* |
| *Prepaid computer rental* | *42,960* |
| *Office supplies* | *4,200* |
| *Office equipment* | *25,200* |
| *Accumulated depreciation: office equipment* | *600* |
| *Notes payable* | *24,000* |
| *Accounts payable* | *8,760* |
| *Interest payable* | |
| *Salaries payable* | |
| *Unearned research fees* | *114,600* |
| *Greg Green, capital* | *83,820* |
| *Greg Green, drawing* | *2,400* |
| *Research fees earned* | *16,200* |
| *Office salaries expense* | *5,040* |
| *Research salaries expense* | *58,320* |
| *Telephone expense* | *2,640* |
| *Travel expense* | *6,660* |
| *Office rent expense* | |
| *Computer rent expense* | |
| *Office supplies expense* | |
| *Depreciation expense: office equipment* | |
| *Interest expense* | |

**Other data**

(a) The amount in the Prepaid Office Rent account represented office rent for eight months paid in advance on October 1, when the lease was renewed.
(b) During October, 220 hours of computer time were used at a cost of $180 an hour.
(c) Office supplies on hand October 31 were determined by count to amount to $840.
(d) Office equipment was estimated to have a useful life of 7 years from date of purchase.
(e) Accrued interest on notes payable amounted to $96 on October 31.
(f) Services to clients amounting to $76,440 performed during October were chargeable against the Unearned Research Fees account.
(g) Services to clients who had not made advance payments and had not been billed amounted to $35,280 at October 31. (Debit Research Fees Receivable.)
(h) Salaries earned by research staff but not paid amounted to $5,160 on October 31.

**Instructions**

**a** Prepare a 10-column work sheet for the month ended October 31.
**b** Prepare an income statement, a statement of owner's equity, and a balance sheet.

*4A-8* Trade Winds Airlines provides passenger and freight service among some Pacific islands. The accounts are adjusted and closed each month. At June 30 the trial balance shown at the top of page 165 was prepared from the ledger.

**Other data**

(a) Monthly rent amounted to $3,000.
(b) Insurance expense for June was $3,900.

***TRADE WINDS AIRLINES***
***Trial Balance***
***June 30, 19__***

| | | |
|---|---|---|
| *Cash* | *$ 190,000* | |
| *Prepaid rent* | *54,000* | |
| *Unexpired insurance* | *47,300* | |
| *Prepaid maintenance service* | *22,500* | |
| *Spare parts* | *57,000* | |
| *Airplanes* | *810,000* | |
| *Accumulated depreciation: airplanes* | | *$ 77,000* |
| *Notes payable* | | *600,000* |
| *Unearned passenger revenue* | | *60,000* |
| *John Morgan, capital* | | *377,710* |
| *John Morgan, drawing* | *12,000* | |
| *Passenger revenue earned* | | *183,990* |
| *Gasoline expense* | *13,800* | |
| *Salaries expense* | *86,700* | |
| *Advertising expense* | *5,400* | |
| | *$1,298,700* | *$1,298,700* |

(c) All necessary maintenance work was provided by Ryan Air Service at a fixed charge of $7,500 a month. Service for three months had been paid for in advance on June 1. (Debit Maintenance Expense.)

(d) Spare parts used in connection with maintenance work amounted to $3,750 during the month. (Debit Maintenance Expense. Use two lines on work sheet for this expense account.)

(e) At the time of purchase, the remaining useful life of the airplanes, which were several years old, was estimated at 5,000 hours of flying time. During June, total flying time amounted to 160 hours. ($810,000 cost ÷ 5,000 hours = depreciation per hour flying time.)

(f) The Chamber of Commerce had purchased ***2,000 special tickets for $60,000.*** Note that the special price per ticket was $30. Each ticket allowed the holder one flight normally priced at $45. During the month 400 of these ***reduced-price tickets*** had been used by the holders. (Debit Unearned Passenger Revenue.)

(g) Salaries earned by employees but not paid amounted to $3,300 at June 30.

(h) Interest accrued on notes payable at June 30 amounted to $5,000.

**Instructions**

**a** Prepare a work sheet for the month ended June 30, 19__.

**b** Prepare an income statement, a statement of owner's equity, and a balance sheet. Follow the format illustrated on page 148.

**c** Prepare adjusting and closing journal entries.

*4A-9* The following events relating to salaries occurred in King Company near December 31, the end of the fiscal year.

**Dec. 27** Recorded payment of regular weekly salaries of $3,000.
**Dec. 31** Prepared an adjusting entry for accrued salaries of $1,200.
**Jan. 1** Made a reversing entry for accrued salaries.
**Jan. 3** Recorded payment of regular weekly salaries of $3,000.

King Company rents a portion of its building to a tenant for $2,100 a month payable in advance on the twenty-first of each month. The tenant is often late in making the payments. Year-end transactions relating to rent revenue were as follows.

**Dec. 31** Recorded accrued rent revenue of $700 for the period December 21–December 31.

**Jan. 1** Made a reversing entry for accrued rent revenue.

**Jan. 4** Recorded collection of $2,100 rent for period December 21–January 21.

**Instructions**

**a** Prepare journal entries (with explanations) for the four events relating to salaries.

**b** How much of the $3,000 in salaries paid on January 3 represents a January expense? Explain.

**c** Assume that no reversing entry was made by King Company; prepare the journal entry for payment of salaries on January 3.

**d** Prepare journal entries (with explanations) for the three events relating to rent revenue.

**e** How much of the $2,100 rent received on January 4 represents January revenue? Explain.

**f** Assume that no reversing entry was made by King Company with respect to rent; prepare the journal entry to record collection of $2,100 rent on January 4.

## Group B

*4B-1* The accounting records of Blue Mountain Resort are maintained on the basis of a fiscal year ending April 30. The following facts are to be used for making adjusting entries at April 30.

(1) Depreciation expense on the buildings for the year ended April 30 amounted to $42,375.

(2) A 36-month fire insurance policy had been purchased on April 1. The premium of $4,320 for the entire life of the policy had been paid on April 1 and recorded as Unexpired Insurance.

(3) A portion of the land owned had been leased on April 16 of the current year to a service station operator at a yearly rental rate of $12,000. One year's rent was collected in advance at the date of the lease and credited to Unearned Rental Revenue.

(4) A bus to carry guests to and from the airport had been rented beginning early on April 19 from Truck Rentals, Inc., at a daily rate of $60. No rental payment had yet been made.

(5) Among the assets owned by Blue Mountain Resort were government bonds in the face amount of $75,000. Accrued interest receivable on the bonds at April 30 was computed to be $2,925.

(6) A three-month bank loan in the amount of $300,000 had been obtained on April 1. No interest has yet been paid or recorded. Interest accrued at April 30 is $3,000.

(7) The company signed an agreement on April 30 to lease a truck from Ace Motors for a period of one year beginning May 1 at a rate of 30 cents a mile and with a clause providing for a minimum monthly charge of $900.

(8) Salaries earned by employees but not yet paid amounted to $9,900.

**Instructions** For each of the above paragraphs which warrants adjustment of the accounts, you are to prepare an adjusting journal entry. Include an explanation as part of each entry.

*4B-2* Gary Smith organized Safe Storage on January 1 for the purpose of leasing a large vacant building and renting space in this building to others for storage of industrial materials. The accounting policies of the company call for making adjusting entries and closing the accounts each month. Shown below is a trial balance and other information for use in preparing adjusting entries at January 31.

**SAFE STORAGE**
**Trial Balance**
**January 31, 19__**

| | | |
|---|---|---|
| Cash | $ 8,105 | |
| Unexpired insurance | 4,080 | |
| Office supplies | 405 | |
| Office equipment | 7,200 | |
| Notes payable | | $ 3,000 |
| Unearned storage fees | | 1,350 |
| Gary Smith, capital | | 11,795 |
| Gary Smith, drawing | 450 | |
| Storage fees earned | | 8,850 |
| Rent expense | 1,800 | |
| Telephone expense | 135 | |
| Salaries expense | 2,820 | |
| | $24,995 | $24,995 |

**Other data**

(a) The monthly insurance expense amounted to $400.
(b) The amount of office supplies on hand, based on a physical count on January 31, was $195.
(c) A $3,000 one-year note payable was signed on January 1. Interest accrued at January 31 was $30.
(d) The useful life of office equipment was estimated at 8 years.
(e) Certain clients chose to pay several months' storage fees in advance. It was determined that $480 of such fees was still unearned as of January 31.
(f) Several clients neglected to send in storage fees amounting to $330 for the month of January. These amounts have not been recorded but are considered collectible.
(g) Salaries earned by employees but not yet paid amounted to $240.

**Instructions** Based on the above trial balance and other information, prepare the adjusting entries (with explanations) needed at January 31.

*4B-3* Investors' Advisory Service was organized on June 1, 19__, to provide investment counseling to investors in securities. Some customers paid in advance on a subscription basis; others were billed after services were rendered. Assume that the company's accounts are adjusted and closed each month. The trial balance at October 31 follows:

***INVESTORS' ADVISORY SERVICE***
***Trial Balance***
***October 31, 19__***

| | | |
|---|---|---|
| *Cash* | *$13,000* | |
| *Prepaid rent* | *1,800* | |
| *Inventory of office supplies* | *500* | |
| *Office equipment* | *3,600* | |
| *Accumulated depreciation: office equipment* | | *$ 120* |
| *Accounts payable* | | *580* |
| *Unearned revenue* | | *6,000* |
| *Alice Bennett, capital* | | *12,000* |
| *Alice Bennett, drawing* | *300* | |
| *Fees earned* | | *5,000* |
| *Telephone expense* | *400* | |
| *Travel expense* | *100* | |
| *Salaries expense* | *4,000* | |
| | *$23,700* | *$23,700* |

**Other data**
(a) The monthly rent was $600.
(b) Office supplies on hand October 31 amounted to $325.
(c) The office equipment was purchased on June 1. The useful life was estimated at 10 years.
(d) Services rendered during the month and chargeable to Unearned Revenue (subscription basis) amounted to $1,500.
(e) Investment advisory services rendered during the month but not yet billed amounted to $280. (Debit Advisory Service Receivables.)
(f) Salaries earned by employees during the month but not yet paid amounted to $415.

**Instructions**
**a** Prepare adjusting entries at October 31.
**b** Prepare an adjusted trial balance.

***4B-4*** Stanley Wiley organized a drafting firm on January 1. At June 30, before the accounts were adjusted and closed for the first time, a trial balance was prepared as shown on page 169.

**Other data**
(1) Office rent of $6,000 for one year had been paid on January 1, when the lease was signed, and had been charged to Prepaid Office Rent.
(2) Drafting supplies on hand on June 30 amounted to $240.
(3) Drafting equipment was purchased on January 1. The useful life was estimated at 10 years.
(4) Accrued interest expense on notes payable was $50 as of June 30.
(5) A number of clients obtained during the first six months of the company's operations had made advance payments for services to be rendered over a considerable period. As of June 30, value of services rendered and chargeable against Unearned Fees was $9,500.

**BLUELINE DRAFTING SERVICE**
**Trial Balance**
**June 30, 19__**

| | | |
|---|---|---|
| Cash | $ 9,250 | |
| Prepaid office rent | 6,000 | |
| Inventory of drafting supplies | 1,200 | |
| Drafting equipment | 6,600 | |
| Notes payable | | $ 5,000 |
| Unearned fees | | 13,000 |
| Stanley Wiley, capital | | 15,100 |
| Stanley Wiley, drawing | 4,270 | |
| Fees earned | | 10,620 |
| Salaries expense | 16,200 | |
| Miscellaneous expense | 200 | |
| | $43,720 | $43,720 |

(6) Services rendered and chargeable to other clients amounted to $3,700 as of June 30. No entries had yet been made to record the revenue earned by performing services for these clients.
(7) Salaries earned by staff personnel but not yet paid amounted to $500 on June 30.

**Instructions**

**a** Prepare adjusting entries as of June 30.
**b** Prepare an adjusted trial balance. (***Note:*** You may find the use of T accounts helpful in computing the account balances after adjustments.)
**c** Prepare an income statement for the six-month period ended June 30, a statement of owner's equity, and a balance sheet.

*4B-5* The four-column schedule on page 170 represents the first four columns of a 10-column work sheet to be prepared for Miller's TV Repair Service for the month ended April 30, 19__. (The completed adjustment columns have been included to minimize the detail work involved.) These adjustments were derived from the following information available at April 30.
(a) Monthly rent expense, $300.
(b) Insurance expense for the month, $15.
(c) Advertising expense for the month, $150.
(d) Cost of supplies on hand, based on physical count on April 30, $390.
(e) Depreciation expense on equipment, $130 per month.
(f) Accrued interest expense on notes payable, $35.
(g) Salaries earned by employees but not yet paid, $175.
(h) Services amounting to $400 were rendered during April for customers who had paid in advance. This portion of the Unearned Revenue account should be regarded as earned as of April 30.

**MILLER'S TV REPAIR SERVICE**
**Work Sheet**
**For the Month Ended April 30, 19__**

| | Trial Balance | | Adjustments | |
|---|---|---|---|---|
| | Dr | Cr | Dr | Cr |
| Cash | 10,000 | | | |
| Prepaid rent | 900 | | | (a) 300 |
| Unexpired insurance | 255 | | | (b) 15 |
| Prepaid advertising | 590 | | | (c) 150 |
| Inventory of supplies | 630 | | | (d) 240 |
| Equipment | 11,700 | | | |
| Accumulated depreciation: equipment | | 1,040 | | (e) 130 |
| Notes payable | | 8,000 | | |
| Unearned revenue | | 1,200 | (h) 400 | |
| B. R. Miller, capital | | 12,665 | | |
| B. R. Miller, drawing | 1,500 | | | |
| Revenue from services | | 4,635 | | (h) 400 |
| Salaries expense | 1,965 | | (g) 175 | |
| | 27,540 | 27,540 | | |
| Rent expense | | | (a) 300 | |
| Insurance expense | | | (b) 15 | |
| Advertising expense | | | (c) 150 | |
| Supplies expense | | | (d) 240 | |
| Depreciation expense: equipment | | | (e) 130 | |
| Interest expense | | | (f) 35 | |
| Interest payable | | | | (f) 35 |
| Salaries payable | | | | (g) 175 |
| | | | 1,445 | 1,445 |

**Instructions** Prepare a 10-column work sheet utilizing the trial balance and adjusting data provided. Include at the bottom of the work sheet a brief explanation keyed to each adjusting entry.

*4B-6* Rolling Hills Golf Course obtains revenue from greens fees and also from a contract with a concessionaire who sells refreshments on the premises. The books are closed at the end of each calendar year; at December 31 the data for adjustments were compiled and a work sheet was prepared. The first four columns of the work sheet contained the account balances and adjustments shown on page 171.

**Instructions** Using the data on page 171, complete the work sheet by listing the appropriate amounts in the remaining six columns of the work sheet. Follow the format of the work sheet illustrated on page 146.

| | Trial Balance | | Adjustments* | |
|---|---|---|---|---|
| | Dr | Cr | Dr | Cr |
| Cash | 9,100 | | | |
| Unexpired insurance | 2,100 | | | (a) 700 |
| Prepaid advertising | 1,000 | | | (b) 300 |
| Land | 375,000 | | | |
| Equipment | 48,000 | | | |
| Accumulated depreciation: equipment | | 8,000 | | (f) 4,000 |
| Notes payable | | 110,000 | | |
| Unearned revenue from concessions | | 7,500 | (d) 5,000 | |
| Howard Catts, capital | | 268,000 | | |
| Howard Catts, drawing | 15,000 | | | |
| Revenue from greens fees | | 174,500 | | |
| Advertising expense | 5,500 | | (b) 300 | |
| Water expense | 10,400 | | | |
| Salaries expense | 78,900 | | (e) 1,100 | |
| Repairs and maintenance expense | 17,500 | | | |
| Miscellaneous expense | 5,500 | | | |
| | 568,000 | 568,000 | | |
| Insurance expense | | | (a) 700 | |
| Interest expense | | | (c) 400 | |
| Interest payable | | | | (c) 400 |
| Revenue from concessions | | | | (d) 5,000 |
| Salaries payable | | | | (e) 1,100 |
| Depreciation expense: equipment | | | (f) 4,000 | |
| | | | 11,500 | 11,500 |

*Adjustments:
(*a*) $700 insurance expired during year.
(*b*) $300 prepaid advertising expired at end of year.
(*c*) $400 accrued interest expense on notes payable.
(*d*) $5,000 concession revenue earned during year.
(*e*) $1,100 of salaries earned but unpaid at Dec. 31, 19___.
(*f*) $4,000 depreciation expense for year.

*4B-7* Oceanside Cinema closes its accounts each month. At November 30, the trial balance and other information given below and on page 172 were available for adjusting and closing the accounts.

**Other data**

(a) Advertising expense for the month, $3,750.
(b) Film rental expense for the month, $16,850.

(c) Depreciation expense on building, \$350 per month; on projection equipment, \$600 per month.
(d) Accrued interest on notes payable, \$100.
(e) The company's share of revenue from concessions for November, as reported by concessionaire, \$3,250. Check should be received by December 6.
(f) Salaries earned by employees but not paid, \$1,500.

**OCEANSIDE CINEMA**
**Trial Balance**
**November 30, 19__**

| | | |
|---|---|---|
| Cash | \$ 26,000 | |
| Prepaid advertising | 6,200 | |
| Prepaid film rental | 26,000 | |
| Land | 30,000 | |
| Building | 84,000 | |
| Accumulated depreciation: building | | \$ 1,750 |
| Projection equipment | 36,000 | |
| Accumulated depreciation: projection equipment | | 3,000 |
| Notes payable | | 15,000 |
| Accounts payable | | 4,400 |
| L. B. Jones, capital | | 166,150 |
| L. B. Jones, drawing | 4,250 | |
| Revenue from admissions | | 33,950 |
| Salaries expense | 8,700 | |
| Light and power | 3,100 | |
| | \$224,250 | \$224,250 |

**Instructions** Prepare
**a** A work sheet for the month ended November 30
**b** An income statement
**c** A statement of owner's equity
**d** A balance sheet

*4B-8* Resort Flying Service was organized on June 1 to offer air service for visitors to a famous island resort. The company follows the policy of adjusting and closing its accounts each month. At December 31, after seven months of operating experience, the trial balance on page 173 was prepared from the ledger.

**Other data**
(a) Monthly rent amounted to \$1,000.
(b) Insurance expense for December was \$1,300.
(c) All necessary maintenance work was provided by Cook Air Services at a fixed charge of \$2,500 a month. Service for three months had been paid for in advance on December 1.
(d) Spare parts used in connection with maintenance work amounted to \$1,250 during the month.
(e) At the time of purchase the remaining useful life of the aircraft, which were several years old, was estimated at 5,000 hours of flying time. During December, total flying time amounted to 160 hours.
(f) The Chamber of Commerce purchased 2,000 special price tickets for \$20,000.

Note that the special price per ticket is $10. Each ticket allowed the holder one flight normally priced at $15. During the month 400 of these ***reduced-price tickets*** had been used.

(g) Salaries earned by employees but not paid were $1,100 at December 31.

***RESORT FLYING SERVICE***
***Trial Balance***
***December 31, 19__***

| | | |
|---|---|---|
| Cash | $ 65,500 | |
| Prepaid rent | 18,000 | |
| Unexpired insurance | 15,600 | |
| Prepaid maintenance service | 7,500 | |
| Spare parts | 19,000 | |
| Aircraft | 270,000 | |
| Accumulated depreciation: aircraft | | $ 25,650 |
| Unearned passenger revenue | | 20,000 |
| Thomas White, capital | | 325,920 |
| Thomas White, drawing | 4,000 | |
| Passenger revenue earned | | 63,330 |
| Gasoline expense | 4,600 | |
| Salaries expense | 28,900 | |
| Advertising expense | 1,800 | |
| | $434,900 | $434,900 |

**Instructions**

**a** Prepare a 10-column work sheet for the month ended December 31.
**b** Prepare an income statement, a statement of owner's equity, and a balance sheet.
**c** Prepare adjusting and closing entries.

*4B-9* Timothy Property Management occupies a leased building on which it has paid rent in advance. Most of the company's revenue comes from managing office buildings and apartment buildings. Some clients pay Timothy in advance; these amounts are credited to Unearned Management Fees. Other clients pay only after services have been rendered for several months.

The company adjusts and closes its accounts at the end of each calendar year. At December 31, Year 5, selected ledger accounts ***before adjustment*** show the following balances:

| | Debit | Credit |
|---|---|---|
| Unearned management fees | | $ 3,000 |
| Management fees earned | | 94,000 |
| Prepaid rent | $12,000 | |
| Office supplies | 1,300 | |
| Notes payable | | 30,000 |
| Unexpired insurance | 2,500 | |
| Salaries expense | 33,000 | |
| Office equipment | 6,000 | |
| Accumulated depreciation: office equipment | | 1,200 |

The accountant for Timothy Property Management compiled the following information as a basis for adjusting entries at December 31, Year 5.

(1) Unearned management fees at December 31 amounted to $1,800.
(2) Management fees of $2,500 had been earned but not yet recorded or billed to customers.
(3) Prepaid rent on the building at December 31 was $3,000.
(4) Office supplies on hand per count at December 31, $300.
(5) Accrued interest payable on notes payable at December 31, $1,500.
(6) Unexpired insurance at December 31, $500.
(7) Accrued salaries owed to employees at December 31, $1,600.
(8) Depreciation expense for the year was based on an estimated 10-year life for the office equipment.

**Instructions**

**a** Prepare the adjusting entries needed at December 31.
**b** Which of the adjusting entries represent accruals of revenue or expense which will be followed by later cash collections or cash payments? List by identifying letter the adjusting entries of this type. Assuming that it is the company's policy to use ***reversing entries,*** determine which of the adjusting entries in part *a* may be reversed.
**c** Prepare the reversing entries.

## BUSINESS DECISION PROBLEM 4

Seven Souls Marina rents 50 slips in a large floating dock to owners of pleasure boats in the area. The marina also performs repair services on small craft.

Bob Mathews, a friend of yours, is convinced that recreational boating will become increasingly popular in the area and has entered into negotiations to buy Seven Souls Marina.

Bob does not have quite enough cash to purchase the business at the price the owner has demanded. However, the owner of the marina has suggested that Bob might purchase the marina with what cash he does have, and turn the net income of the business over to the retiring owner until the balance of the purchase price has been paid. A typical month's income for Seven Souls Marina is determined as follows:

| | | |
|---|---|---|
| ***Revenue:*** | | |
| ***Slip rentals*** | | ***$2,520*** |
| ***Repairs*** | | ***3,180*** |
| ***Total revenue*** | | ***$5,700*** |
| ***Operating expenses:*** | | |
| ***Wages*** | ***$1,920*** | |
| ***Insurance*** | ***36*** | |
| ***Depreciation expense: docks*** | ***960*** | |
| ***Depreciation expense: equipment*** | ***180*** | |
| ***Other expenses*** | ***240*** | ***3,336*** |
| ***Net income*** | | ***$2,364*** |

Bob is concerned about turning the whole net income of the business over to the former owner for the next several months, because he estimates that he and his family will need to keep at least $1,050 a month to meet their living expenses. In coming to you for advice, Bob explains that all revenue of Seven Souls Marina is collected when earned and that both wages and "other" expenses are paid when incurred. Bob does not understand, however, when depreciation expense must be paid or why there is any insurance expense when the insurance policies of the business have more than two years to run before new insurance must be purchased.

**Instructions**

**a** Advise Bob as to how much cash the business will generate each month. Support your position with a schedule of cash generated monthly; this schedule should begin with income as reported of $2,364 and show items to be added or subtracted in determining the cash generated monthly. Will this amount of cash enable Bob to withdraw $1,050 per month to meet his living expenses and also pay $2,364 per month to the former owner?

**b** Explain why insurance expense appears on the income statement of the business if no new policies will be purchased within the next two years.

# 5

# ACCOUNTING FOR PURCHASES AND SALES OF MERCHANDISE

The preceding four chapters have illustrated step by step the complete accounting cycle for Roberts Real Estate Company, a business rendering personal services. Service-type companies represent an important part of our economy. They include, for example, airlines, railroads, motels, travel agencies, theaters, golf courses, ski resorts, and professional football clubs. These enterprises receive commissions or fees for the services they provide and their net income is equal to the excess of commissions or fees earned over operating expenses incurred.

In contrast to the service-type business, ***merchandising companies,*** both wholesalers and retailers, earn revenue by selling goods or merchandise. Net income results if the revenue from sales exceeds (1) the cost of the goods sold and (2) the operating expenses. The term ***merchandise*** means goods acquired by a business for the purpose of resale to customers. In other words merchandise consists of the goods in which a business regularly deals.

## Income statement for a merchandising business

An income statement for a merchandising business consists of three main sections: (1) the revenue section, (2) the cost of goods sold section, and (3) the operating expenses section. This sectional arrangement is illustrated in the income statement on page 177 for a business dealing in sports equipment. Assume that the business of Olympic Sporting Goods consists of buying sports equipment from manufacturers and selling most of this merchandise to individual consumers at retail prices. However, the company also makes some sales at wholesale prices to colleges, health clubs, and small sports shops. To keep the illustration reasonably short, we shall use a smaller number of ledger accounts than generally would be used in a merchandising business.

*Note distinction between cost of goods sold and operating expenses*

***OLYMPIC SPORTING GOODS***
***Income Statement***
***For the Year Ended December 31, Year 10***

| | | |
|---|---|---|
| Gross sales | | $201,000 |
| Less: Sales returns & allowances | | 1,000 |
| Net sales | | $200,000 |
| Cost of goods sold: | | |
| Inventory, Jan. 1 | $ 25,000 | |
| Purchases | 125,000 | |
| Cost of goods available for sale | $150,000 | |
| Less: Inventory, Dec. 31 | 30,000 | |
| Cost of goods sold | | 120,000 |
| Gross profit on sales | | $ 80,000 |
| Operating expenses: | | |
| Salaries | $ 36,000 | |
| Advertising | 8,000 | |
| Telephone | 1,000 | |
| Depreciation | 4,000 | |
| Insurance | 1,000 | |
| Total operating expenses | | 50,000 |
| Net income | | $ 30,000 |

**Analyzing the income statement** How does this income statement compare in form and content with the income statement of the service-type business presented in preceding chapters? The most important change is the inclusion of the section entitled Cost of Goods Sold. Note how large the cost of goods sold is in comparison with other figures on the statement. The cost of merchandise sold during the year amounts to $120,000, or 60% of the year's net sales of $200,000. Another way of looking at this relationship is to say that for each dollar the store receives by selling goods to customers, the sum of 60 cents represents a recovery of the cost of the merchandise. This leaves a ***gross profit*** of 40 cents from each sales dollar, out of which the store must pay its operating expenses. In our illustration the operating expenses for the year were $50,000, that is, 25% of the net sales figure of $200,000. Therefore, the gross profit of 40 cents contained in each dollar of sales was enough to cover the operating expenses of 25 cents and leave a net income of 15 cents from each dollar of sales.

Of course the percentage relationship between sales and cost of goods sold will vary from one type of business to another, but, in all types of merchandising companies the cost of goods sold is one of the largest elements in the income statement. Accountants, investors, bankers, and business managers in general have the habit of mentally computing percentage relationships when they look at financial statements. Formation of this habit will be helpful throughout the study of accounting, as well as in many business situations.

In analyzing an income statement, we compare each item in the statement with the amount of net sales. The amount of net sales is regarded as 100%, and every other item or subtotal on the statement is expressed as a percentage of net sales. The cost of goods sold in most types of business will be between 60 and 80% of net sales. Conversely, the ***gross profit on sales*** (sales minus cost of goods sold) usually will vary between 40 and 20% of net sales.

**Appraising the adequacy of net income** The income statement for Olympic Sporting Goods on page 177 shows that a net income of $30,000 was earned during the year. Should this be regarded as an excellent, fair, or poor performance? Before reaching a conclusion, let us consider what this item of net income represents in an ***unincorporated*** business.

First, let us assume that the owner of Olympic Sporting Goods, Robert Riley, works full time as manager of the business. However, compensation for the personal services of the owner is not included among the expenses of the business, because he would be in a position to set his own salary at any amount he chose. The use of an arbitrarily chosen, unrealistic salary to the owner-manager would tend to destroy the significance of the income statement as a device for measuring the earning power of the business. Another reason may be that in the owner's own thinking he is not working for a salary when he manages his own business but is investing his time in order to make a profit. The net income of Olympic Sporting Goods must, therefore, be considered in part as the equivalent of a salary earned by the owner. If we assume that the owner could obtain employment elsewhere as a store manager at a salary of $20,000 a year, then we can reasonably regard $20,000 of the net income earned by Olympic Sporting Goods as compensation to Riley for personal services during the year.

Secondly, we must recognize that Riley, as owner of this small business, has invested his own savings, amounting to, say, $50,000. If, as an alternative to starting his own business, he had invested this $50,000 capital in high-grade securities, he might be receiving investment income of perhaps $4,000 a year.

After deducting from the $30,000 reported net income of Olympic Sporting Goods an assumed yearly salary of $20,000 to the owner and an estimated return on invested capital of $4,000, we have left a "pure profit" of $6,000. Economists often use the word ***profit*** to mean the residual pure profit remaining after deducting from the net income the estimated amounts needed to compensate the proprietor for his personal services and the use of his capital.

This residual element of profit is the all important incentive which induced Riley to risk his savings in a new business venture. The residual profit also is the reward for the time and effort which an owner must spend in planning, financing, and guiding a business, apart from the routine aspects of day-to-day management. Finally, the earning of $30,000 net income in one year provides no assurance that similar earnings, or for that matter any earnings will be forthcoming in another year. It would be somewhat rash to form an opinion about the adequacy of earning power of a business on the basis of such a short period of operating experience.

## Accounting for sales of merchandise

If merchandising companies are to succeed or even to survive, they must sell their goods at prices higher than they pay to the vendors or suppliers from whom they buy. The selling prices charged by a retail store must cover three things: (1) the cost of the merchandise to the store; (2) the operating expenses of the business such as advertising, store rent, and salaries of the sales staff; and (3) a net income to the business.

When a business sells merchandise to its customers, it either receives immediate payment in cash or acquires an account receivable which soon will be collected in cash. As explained in Chapter 3, the inflow of cash and receivables from sales of the current period is equal to the revenue for that period. Each cash sale is rung up on a cash register before the merchandise is handed to the customer. At the end of the day, the total shown by the cash register represents cash sales for the day and is recorded by a journal entry, as follows:

*Journal entry for cash sales*

| | | |
|---|---|---|
| ***Cash*** | ***900*** | |
| ***Sales*** | | ***900*** |
| ***To record the sale of merchandise for cash.*** | | |

The daily entering of cash sales in the journal tends to reduce the possibility of errors or dishonesty by employees in handling the cash receipts. In Chapter 7 a procedure will be described which provides a daily record of sales and cash receipts, yet avoids the making of a large number of postings to the Cash and Sales accounts.

For a sale of merchandise on credit, a typical journal entry would be:

*Journal entry for sale on credit*

| | | |
|---|---|---|
| ***Accounts Receivable*** | ***500*** | |
| ***Sales*** | | ***500*** |
| ***Sold merchandise on credit to Kay's Gift Shop; payment due within 30 days.*** | | |

Revenue from the sale of merchandise is considered as earned in the period in which the merchandise is delivered to the customer, even though payment in cash is not received for a month or more after the sale. Consequently, the revenue earned in a given accounting period may differ considerably from the cash receipts of that period.

The amount and trend of sales are watched very closely by management, investors, and others interested in the progress of a company. A rising volume of sales is evidence of growth and suggests the probability of an increase in earnings. A declining trend in sales, on the other hand, is often the first signal of reduced earnings and of financial difficulties ahead. The amount of sales for each year is compared with the sales of the preceding year; the sales of each month may be compared with the sales of the preceding month and also with the corresponding month of the preceding year. These comparisons bring to light significant trends in the volume of sales.

## Sales returns and allowances

Note that the key figure used in our analysis of the Olympic Sporting Goods income statement was ***net sales.*** Most merchandising companies allow customers to obtain a refund by returning merchandise which is found to be unsatisfactory. When customers find that merchandise purchased has minor defects, they may agree to keep such merchandise if an allowance is made on the sales price.

Refunds and allowances have the effect of reversing previously recorded sales and reducing the amount of revenue earned by the business. Thus, net sales is the revenue actually earned after giving consideration to sales returns and allowances. The journal entry to record sales returns and allowances is shown below:

*Journal entry for sales returns and allowances*

| | | |
|---|---|---|
| ***Sales Returns and Allowances*** | ***100*** | |
| ***Cash (or Accounts Receivable)*** | | ***100*** |
| ***Made refund for merchandise returned by customer.*** | | |

At the end of the accounting period, the amount accumulated in the Sales Returns and Allowances account will be shown in the income statement as a deduction from sales.

The use of a Sales Returns and Allowances account rather than recording refunds by direct debits to the Sales account is advisable because the accounting records then show both the total amount of sales and the amount of sales returns. Management is interested in the percentage relationship between goods sold and goods returned as an indication of customer satisfaction with the merchandise.

## Credit terms

For all sales of merchandise on credit, the terms of payment should be clearly stated, so that buyer and seller can avoid any misunderstanding as to the time and amount of the required payment. Credit terms differ between industries and also within an industry. Even within a single company, the credit terms offered may vary by type of customer. One common example of credit terms is "net 30 days" or "n/30," meaning that the net amount of the invoice or bill is due in 30 days. Another common form of credit terms is "10 e.o.m.," meaning payment is due 10 days after the end of the month in which the sale occurred.

## Sales discounts

Manufacturers and wholesalers often sell goods on credit terms of 30 to 60 days or more, but offer a discount for earlier payment. For example, the credit terms may be "2% 10 days, net 30 days." These terms mean that the authorized credit period is 30 days, but that the customer company may deduct 2% of the amount of the invoice if it makes payment within 10 days. On the invoice, these terms would appear in the abbreviated form "2/10, n/30"; this expression is read "2, 10, net 30." The 10-day period during which the discount is available is called the ***discount period.*** Because a sales discount provides an incentive to the customer to make an early cash payment, it is often referred to as a ***cash discount.***

For example, assume that Adams Company on November 3 sells merchandise for $1,000 on credit to Zipco, Inc., terms 2/10, n/30. At the time of the sale, the seller does not know if the buyer will take advantage of the discount by paying within the discount period; therefore, Adams Company records the sale at the full price by the following entry.

| | | | |
|---|---|---|---|
| *Nov. 3* | *Accounts Receivable* | *1,000* | |
| | *Sales* | | *1,000* |
| | *To record sale to Zipco, Inc., terms 2/10, n/30.* | | |

The customer now has a choice between saving $20 by paying within the discount period, or waiting a full 30 days and paying the full price. If Zipco mails its check on or before November 13, it is entitled to deduct 2% of $1,000 or $20, and settle the obligation for $980. If Zipco decides to forego the discount, it may postpone payment an additional 20 days until December 3 but must then pay $1,000.

Assuming that payment is made by Zipco on November 13, the last day of the discount period, the entry by Adams Company to record collection of the receivable is

| | | | |
|---|---|---|---|
| *Nov. 13* | *Cash* | *980* | |
| | *Sales Discount* | *20* | |
| | *Accounts Receivable* | | *1,000* |
| | *Collected from Zipco, Inc., for our sale of Nov. 3, less 2% cash discount.* | | |

If a customer returns a portion of the merchandise before making payment, the discount applies only to the portion of the goods kept by the customer. In the above example, if Zipco had returned $300 worth of goods out of the $1,000 purchase, the discount would have been applicable only to the $700 portion of the order which the customer kept.

**Reasons for sales discounts** From the viewpoint of the seller, the acceptance of $980 in cash as full settlement of a $1,000 account receivable represents a $20 reduction in the amount of revenue earned. By making this concession to induce prompt payment, the seller collects accounts receivable more quickly and is able to use the money collected to buy additional goods. A greater volume of business can be handled with a given amount of invested capital if this capital is not tied up in accounts receivable for long periods. There is also less danger of accounts receivable becoming uncollectible if they are collected promptly; in other words, the older an account receivable becomes, the greater the risk of nonpayment by the customer.

As previously explained, the allowing of a cash discount reduces the amount received from sales. On the income statement, therefore, sales discounts along with sales returns and allowances appear as a deduction from gross sales as shown below:

*Treatment of sales discounts on the income statement*

***Partial Income Statement***

| | | |
|---|---|---|
| *Gross sales* | | *$189,788* |
| *Less: Sales returns & allowances* | *$4,462* | |
| *Sales discounts* | *3,024* | *7,486* |
| *Net sales* | | *$182,302* |

## Accounting for the cost of goods sold

The cost of the merchandise sold during the year appears in the income statement as a deduction from the sales of the year. The merchandise which is ***available for sale but not sold*** during the year constitutes the inventory of merchandise on hand at the end of the year. The inventory is included in the year-end balance sheet as an asset.

How can the manager determine, at the end of a year, a month, or other accounting period, the quantity and the cost of the goods remaining on hand? How can management determine the cost of the goods sold during the period? These amounts must be determined before either a balance sheet or an income statement can be prepared. In fact, the determination of inventory value and of the cost of goods sold may be the most important single step in measuring the profitability of a business. There are two alternative aproaches to the determination of inventory and of cost of goods sold, namely, the ***perpetual inventory system*** and the ***periodic inventory system.***

## The perpetual inventory system

Automobile dealers and television stores sell merchandise of ***high unit value*** and make a relatively small number of sales each day. Because sales transactions are few and of substantial amount, it is easy to look up the cost of the individual automobile or television set being sold. Thus a cost figure can be recorded as the ***cost of goods sold*** for each sales transaction. Under this system, the records show the cost of each article in stock. Units added to inventory and units removed for delivery to customers are recorded on a daily basis—hence the name ***perpetual inventory system.*** When financial statements are to be prepared, the total cost of goods sold during the accounting period is easily determined by adding the costs recorded from day to day for the units sold.

The perpetual inventory system will be discussed in Chapter 10; at present we are concentrating upon the ***periodic inventory system*** used by many companies dealing in merchandise of low unit value.

## The periodic inventory system

In a business selling a variety of merchandise with low unit prices, the periodic inventory system may be more suitable than attempting to maintain perpetual inventory records of all items in stock. A business such as a drugstore may sell a customer a bottle of aspirin, a candy bar, and a tube of toothpaste. It is not practicable to look up in the records at the time of each sale the cost of such small items. Instead, stores which deal in merchandise of low unit value usually wait until the end of the accounting period to determine the cost of goods sold.

In the illustrated income statement of Olympic Sporting Goods on page 177, the cost of goods sold during the year was computed by the periodic inventory system, as follows:

*Computing cost of goods sold*

| | |
|---|---|
| *Inventory of merchandise at beginning of year* | *$ 25,000* |
| *Purchases* | *125,000* |
| *Cost of goods available for sale* | *$150,000* |
| *Less: Inventory at end of year* | *30,000* |
| *Cost of goods sold* | *$120,000* |

Every merchandising business has ***available for sale*** during an accounting period the merchandise on hand at the beginning of the period ***plus*** the merchandise purchased during the period. If all these goods were sold during the period, there would be no ending inventory, and cost of goods sold would be equal to the cost of goods available for sale. Normally, however, some goods remain unsold at the end of the period; ***cost of goods sold is then equal to the cost of goods available for sale minus the ending inventory of unsold goods.***

The cost of goods sold is an important concept which requires careful attention. To gain a thorough understanding of this concept, we need to consider the nature of the accounts used in determining the cost of goods sold.

## Beginning inventory and ending inventory

An inventory of merchandise consists of the goods on hand and available for sale to customers. In Olympic Sporting Goods, the inventory consists of golf clubs, tennis racquets, and skiing equipment; in a pet shop the inventory might include puppies, fish, and parakeets.

The goods on hand at the beginning of an accounting period are referred to as the ***beginning inventory***; the goods on hand at the end of the period are called the ***ending inventory.*** In our example of a year's operations of Olympic Sporting Goods, the beginning inventory on January 1 was $25,000 and the ending inventory on December 31 was $30,000. ***The ending inventory of one accounting period is the beginning inventory of the following period.*** Thus Olympic Sporting Goods' ending inventory of $30,000 at December 31 of Year 10 becomes its $30,000 beginning inventory for Year 11.

Determining the amount of the ending inventory is called "taking a physical inventory" and includes three steps. First, all items of merchandise in the store and stockrooms are counted; second, the quantity of each item is multiplied by the cost per unit; and third, the costs of the various kinds of merchandise are added together to get a total cost figure for all goods on hand.

The cost figure for ending inventory appears as an asset in the balance sheet and as a deduction in the cost of goods sold section of the income statement. It is brought into the accounting records by ***a closing entry debiting Inventory and crediting Income Summary.*** (This entry will be illustrated and explained more fully later in this chapter.) After the ending inventory has been recorded in the ledger, the Inventory account remains unchanged throughout the next accounting period. It represents both the ending inventory of the completed accounting period and the beginning inventory of the following period.

### Cost of merchandise purchased for resale

Under the periodic inventory system, the cost of merchandise purchased for resale to customers is recorded by debiting an account called Purchases, as shown below.

*Journal entry for purchase of merchandise*

| | | | |
|---|---|---|---|
| *Nov. 3* | *Purchases* | *10,000* | |
| | *Accounts Payable* | | *10,000* |
| | *Purchased merchandise from ABC Supply Co. Credit terms 2/10, n/30.* | | |

The Purchases account ***is used only for merchandise acquired for resale;*** assets acquired for use in the business (such as a delivery truck, a typewriter, or office supplies) are recorded by debiting the appropriate asset account, not the Purchases account. The Purchases account does not indicate whether the purchased goods have been sold or are still on hand.

At the end of the accounting period, the balance accumulated in the Purchases account represents the total cost of merchandise purchased during the period. This amount is used in preparing the income statement. The Purchases account has then served its purpose and it is closed to the Income Summary account. Since the Purchases account is closed at the end of each period, it has a zero balance at the beginning of each succeeding period.

**Purchase discounts** As explained earlier, manufacturers and wholesalers frequently grant a cash discount to customers who will pay promptly for goods purchased on credit. The selling company regards a cash discount as a ***sales discount;*** the buying company calls the discount a ***purchase discount.***

If the $10,000 purchase of November 3 shown above is paid for by Olympic Sporting Goods by November 13, the last day of the discount period, Olympic will save 2% of the price of the merchandise, or $200, as shown by the following entry:

| | | | |
|---|---|---|---|
| *Nov. 13* | *Accounts Payable* | *10,000* | |
| | *Purchase Discounts* | | *200* |
| | *Cash* | | *9,800* |
| | *Paid ABC Supply Co. for purchase of Nov. 3, less 2% cash discount.* | | |

The effect of the discount was to reduce the cost of the merchandise to Olympic Sporting Goods. The credit balance of the Purchase Discounts account should therefore be deducted in the income statement from the debit balance of the Purchases account.

Is it to the advantage of the buying company to settle the $10,000 liability within the discount period and thereby save $200. The alternative is for Olympic to conserve cash by postponing payment for an additional 20 days. The question may therefore be stated as follows: Does the amount of $200 represent a reasonable charge for the use of $9,800 for a period of 20 days? Definitely not; this charge is the equivalent of an annual interest rate of about 36%. (A 20-day period is approximately $\frac{1}{18}$ of a year; 18 times 2% amounts to 36%.[1]) Although interest rates vary widely, most businesses are able to borrow money from banks at an annual interest rate of 15% or less. Well-managed businesses, therefore, generally pay all invoices within the discount period even though this policy necessitates borrowing from banks in order to have the necessary cash available.

To be sure that every purchase of merchandise on credit is paid for before the discount period expires, many companies file approved invoices (bills) by date. For example, a folder dated January 15 will contain all invoices which must be paid on that date to qualify for discount. To pay an invoice ***before*** the last day of the discount period would be wasteful, because cash is a resource needed in the business.

**Purchase returns and allowances** When merchandise purchased from suppliers is found to be unsatisfactory, the goods may be returned, or a request may be made for an allowance on the price. A return of goods to the supplier is recorded as follows:

***Journal entry for return of goods to supplier***

| | | |
|---|---|---|
| *Accounts Payable* | *1,200* | |
| *Purchase Returns and Allowances* | | *1,200* |
| *To reduce liability to Jet Supply Co. by the cost of goods returned for credit.* | | |

It is preferable to credit Purchase Returns and Allowances when merchandise is returned to a supplier rather than crediting the Purchases account directly. The accounts then show both the total amount of purchases and the amount of purchases which required adjustment or return. Management is interested in the percentage relationship between goods purchased and goods returned, because the returning of merchandise for credit is an expensive, time-consuming process. Getting money back from the supplier provides only a partial recovery of the costs incurred. The time and effort spent in buying merchandise, in receiving and inspecting it, and in arranging for its return represent costly procedures. If these expenses are to be held to a minimum, management should be kept aware of the amount of returns and allowances. Excessive returns suggest inefficiency in the operation of the purchasing department and a need to find more dependable suppliers.

## The Transportation-in account

The cost of merchandise acquired for resale logically includes any transportation charges necessary to bring the goods to the purchaser's place of business. In some lines of business it is customary for the manufacturer to pay the cost of shipping merchandise to the retailer's store. In this case the manufacturer tries to set the price of the goods high enough to cover the transportation charges as well as all its other costs. Consequently, the cost of merchandise to the purchas-

[1] A more accurate estimate of interest expense on an annual basis can be obtained as follows: ($200 × 18) ÷ $9800 = 36.7%.

ing company normally includes the cost of transporting the goods, regardless of whether it pays the freight charges directly to the railroad or other carrier, or merely pays the seller a sufficiently high price to cover the cost of delivering the goods.

The journal entry to record the payment of transportation charges on inbound shipments of merchandise is as follows:

*Journalizing transportation charges on purchases of merchandise*

| | | |
|---|---|---|
| *Transportation-in* | *125* | |
| *Cash (or Accounts Payable)* | | *125* |
| *Air freight charges on merchandise purchased from Miller Brothers, Kansas City.* | | |

Since transportation charges are part of the ***delivered cost*** of merchandise purchased, the Transportation-in account is combined with the Purchases account in the income statement to determine the cost of goods available for sale.

Using a separate ledger account for transportation-in provides management with a clear record of the amount expended each period for inbound transportation. A knowledge of the amount and trend of each significant type of cost is a necessary first step if management is to control costs effectively. For example, detailed information concerning transportation costs would be important to management in making decisions between rail and air transportation, or in deciding whether to order in carload lots rather than in smaller quantities.

**Transportation charges on outbound shipments** Transportation charges on ***inbound*** shipments of merchandise must not be confused with transportation charges on ***outbound*** shipments of goods to customers. Freight charges and other expenses incurred in making deliveries to customers are regarded as selling expenses; these outlays are debited to a separate account entitled Delivery Expense and are not included in the cost of goods sold.

## F.O.B. shipping point and F.O.B. destination

The agreement between the buyer and seller of merchandise includes a provision as to which party shall bear the cost of transporting the goods. The term ***F.O.B. shipping point*** means that the seller will place the merchandise "free on board" the railroad cars or other means of transport, and that the buyer must pay transportation charges from that point. Many people in negotiating for the purchase of a new automobile have encountered the expression "F.O.B. Detroit," meaning that the buyer must pay the freight charges from the manufacturer's location in Detroit, in addition to the basic price of the car. In most merchandise transactions involving wholesalers or manufacturers, the buyer bears the transportation cost. Sometimes, however, as a matter of convenience, the seller prepays the freight and adds this cost to the amount billed to the buyer.

***F.O.B. destination*** means that the seller agrees to bear the freight cost. If the seller prepays the truckline or other carrier, the agreed terms have been met and no action is required of the buyer other than to pay the agreed purchase price of the goods. If the seller does not prepay the freight, the buyer will pay the carrier and deduct this payment from the amount owed the seller when making payment for merchandise purchased under terms of F.O.B. destination.

### Inventory theft and other losses

Under the periodic inventory system, it is assumed that all goods available for sale during the year are either sold or are on hand at year-end for the ending inventory. As a result of this assumption, the cost of merchandise lost because of shoplifting, employee theft, or spoilage will be included automatically in cost of goods sold. For example, assume that a store has goods available for sale which cost $600,000. Assume that shoplifters steal $10,000 worth of goods and that the ending inventory is $100,000. (If the thefts had not occurred, the ending inventory would have been $10,000 larger.) The cost of goods sold is computed at $500,000 by subtracting the $100,000 ending inventory from the $600,000 cost of goods available for sale. The theft loss is not shown separately in the income statement. In reality, cost of goods ***sold*** was $490,000, and cost of goods ***stolen*** was $10,000.

Although the periodic inventory system causes inventory losses to be included automatically in cost of goods sold, accountants have devised a method of estimating losses of merchandise from theft. This method is explained in Chapter 10.

### Accounting cycle for a merchandising business

An annual income statement showing the operations of Year 10 for Olympic Sporting Goods was presented at the beginning of this chapter. Now we will use Olympic's operations for the following year, Year 11, to illustrate a work sheet, financial statements, and closing entries.

### Work sheet for a merchandising business

A merchandising company, like the service business discussed in Chapter 4, uses a work sheet at the end of the period to organize the information needed to prepare financial statements and to adjust and close the accounts. The new elements in the work sheet for Olympic Sporting Goods on page 188 are the beginning inventory, the ending inventory, and the other merchandising accounts. The inventory accounts are shown in a distinctive color to help focus your attention on their treatment.

**Trial balance columns** The Trial Balance columns were prepared by listing the ledger account balances at December 31, Year 11. Notice that the Inventory account in the Trial Balance debit column still shows a balance of $30,000, the cost of merchandise on hand at the end of the prior year. No entries were made in the Inventory account during the current year despite the various purchases and sales of merchandise. The significance of the Inventory account in the trial balance is that it shows the amount of merchandise with which Olympic Sporting Goods began operations on January 1 of the current year.

***OLYMPIC SPORTING GOODS***
***Work Sheet***
***For the Year Ended December 31, Year 11***

| | Trial Balance | | Adjustments* | | Adjusted Trial Balance | | Income Statement | | Balance Sheet | |
|---|---|---|---|---|---|---|---|---|---|---|
| | Dr | Cr | Dr | Cr | Dr | Cr | Dr | Cr | Dr | Cr |
| Cash | 4,500 | | | | 4,500 | | | | 4,500 | |
| Accounts receivable | 3,500 | | | | 3,500 | | | | 3,500 | |
| Inventory, Jan. 1 | 30,000 | | | | 30,000 | | 30,000 | | | |
| Unexpired insurance | 4,000 | | | (b) 1,000 | 3,000 | | | | 3,000 | |
| Land | 30,000 | | | | 30,000 | | | | 30,000 | |
| Building | 60,000 | | | | 60,000 | | | | 60,000 | |
| Accumulated depreciation: building | | 12,000 | | (a) 3,000 | | 15,000 | | | | 15,000 |
| Notes payable | | 42,000 | | | | 42,000 | | | | 42,000 |
| Accounts payable | | 19,000 | | | | 19,000 | | | | 19,000 |
| Robert Riley, capital | | 54,000 | | | | 54,000 | | | | 54,000 |
| Robert Riley, drawing | 26,000 | | | | 26,000 | | | | 26,000 | |
| Sales | | 215,000 | | | | 215,000 | | 215,000 | | |
| Sales returns and allowances | 4,400 | | | | 4,400 | | 4,400 | | | |
| Sales discounts | 600 | | | | 600 | | 600 | | | |
| Purchases | 132,000 | | | | 132,000 | | 132,000 | | | |
| Purchase returns and allowances | | 3,700 | | | | 3,700 | | 3,700 | | |
| Purchase discounts | | 1,300 | | | | 1,300 | | 1,300 | | |
| Transportation-in | 3,000 | | | | 3,000 | | 3,000 | | | |
| Advertising expense | 9,000 | | | | 9,000 | | 9,000 | | | |
| Salaries expense | 37,000 | | | | 37,000 | | 37,000 | | | |
| Telephone expense | 1,100 | | | | 1,100 | | 1,100 | | | |
| Interest expense | 1,900 | | | | 1,900 | | 1,900 | | | |
| | 347,000 | 347,000 | | | | | | | | |
| Depreciation expense: building | | | (a) 3,000 | | 3,000 | | 3,000 | | | |
| Insurance expense | | | (b) 1,000 | | 1,000 | | 1,000 | | | |
| | | | 4,000 | 4,000 | 350,000 | 350,000 | | | | |
| Inventory, Dec. 31 | | | | | | | | 34,000 | 34,000 | |
| | | | | | | | 223,000 | 254,000 | 161,000 | 130,000 |
| Net income | | | | | | | 31,000 | | | 31,000 |
| | | | | | | | 254,000 | 254,000 | 161,000 | 161,000 |

**Note the treatment of the beginning inventory**

**Note the treatment of the ending inventory**

*Adjustments: (a) Depreciation of building during the year.
(b) Insurance premium expired during the year.

**Adjustment columns and Adjusted Trial Balance columns** The merchandising accounts usually do not require adjustment. Their balances are carried directly from the Trial Balance columns to the Adjusted Trial Balance columns.

Only two adjustments were necessary at December 31; one to record depreciation of the building and the other to record the insurance expense for the year. Salaries to employees and interest on the note payable were paid to date on December 31, so no accruals were needed for salaries or interest.

**Income Statement columns and Balance Sheet columns** The accounts which will appear in a company's income statement are the ones to be carried from the Adjusted Trial Balance columns to the Income Statement columns of the work sheet. These are the revenue accounts, cost of goods sold accounts, and operating expense accounts.

The revenue accounts are the Sales account, the Sales Returns and Allowances account, and the Sales Discounts account. The Sales account has been credited throughout the period with both cash and credit sales of merchandise. It has a credit balance which is carried from the Adjusted Trial Balance credit column of the work sheet to the Income Statement credit column.

Both the Sales Returns and Allowances account and the Sales Discounts account have debit balances which are carried to the Income Statement debit column, making these amounts offsets against or deductions from Sales. Since Sales Returns and Allowances and Sales Discounts are ***contra-revenue*** accounts or negative amounts of sales, it is logical that they should be offset against Sales, the primary revenue account.

The cost of goods sold accounts include three with debit balances: the beginning Inventory, Purchases, and Transportation-in. These three accounts are carried to the Income Statement debit column of the work sheet. Two of the cost of goods sold accounts in the trial balance have credit balances: the Purchase Returns and Allowances account and the Purchase Discounts account. These two accounts are carried to the Income Statement credit column of the work sheet so that they will appear as offsets to the Purchases account listed in the debit column.

**Recording the ending inventory on the work sheet** The key point to be observed in this work sheet is the method of recording the ***ending inventory.*** On December 31, Riley and his assistants took a physical inventory of all merchandise on hand. The entire inventory, priced at cost, amounted to $34,000. This ending inventory, dated December 31, does not appear in the trial balance; it is therefore written on the first available line below the trial balance totals. The amount of $34,000 is listed in the Income Statement credit column and also in the Balance Sheet debit column. By entering the ending inventory in the Income Statement ***credit*** column, we are in effect deducting it from the total of the beginning inventory, the purchases, and the transportation-in, all of which are extended from the trial balance to the Income Statement ***debit*** column.

One of the functions of the Income Statement columns is to bring together all the accounts involved in determining the cost of goods sold. The accounts with debit balances are the beginning Inventory, Purchases, and Transportation-in;

these accounts total $165,000. Against this total the three credit items of Purchase Returns and Allowances, $3,700, Purchase Discounts, $1,300, and ending Inventory, $34,000, are offset. The three accounts with debit balances exceed in total the three credit balances by an amount of $126,000; this amount is the cost of goods sold, as shown in the income statement on page 191.

The ending inventory is also entered in the Balance Sheet debit column of the work sheet, because this inventory of merchandise on December 31 will appear as an asset in the balance sheet bearing this date.

**Completing the work sheet** When all the accounts on the work sheet have been extended into the Income Statement or Balance Sheet columns, the final four columns should be totaled. The net income is computed and the work sheet completed in the same manner as illustrated in Chapter 4 for a service business.

## Financial statements

The work to be done at the end of the period is much the same for a merchandising business as for a service-type firm. First, the work sheet is completed; then, financial statements are prepared from the data in the work sheet; next, the adjusting and closing entries are entered in the journal and posted to the ledger accounts; and finally, an after-closing trial balance is prepared.[2] This completes the periodic accounting cycle.

**Income statement** The income statement on page 191 was prepared from the work sheet previously illustrated. Note particularly the arrangement of items in the cost of goods sold section of the income statement; this portion of the income statement shows in summary form most of the essential accounting concepts covered in this chapter.

**Statement of owner's equity** The statement of owner's equity shows the increase in owner's equity from the year's net income and the decrease from the owner's withdrawals during the year.

***OLYMPIC SPORTING GOODS***
***Statement of Owner's Equity***
***For the Year Ended December 31, Year 11***

***Which figure for owner's equity will appear in the balance sheet?***

| | |
|---|---|
| *Robert Riley, capital, Jan. 1* | *$54,000* |
| *Net income for the year* | *31,000* |
| *Subtotal* | *$85,000* |
| *Less: Withdrawals* | *26,000* |
| *Robert Riley, capital, Dec. 31* | *$59,000* |

[2] The journalizing of the two adjusting entries for Olympic Sporting Goods is not illustrated here because these entries are similar to those demonstrated in previous chapters.

**OLYMPIC SPORTING GOODS**
**Income Statement**
**For the Year Ended December 31, Year 11**

*This income statement consists of three major sections*

| | | | | |
|---|---|---|---|---|
| Gross sales | | | | $215,000 |
| Less: Sales returns and allowances | | | $ 4,400 | |
| Sales discounts | | | 600 | 5,000 |
| Net sales | | | | $210,000 |
| Cost of goods sold: | | | | |
| Inventory, Jan. 1 | | | $ 30,000 | |
| Purchases | | $132,000 | | |
| Less: Purchase returns and allowances | $3,700 | | | |
| Purchase discounts | 1,300 | 5,000 | | |
| Net purchases | | $127,000 | | |
| Add: Transportation-in | | 3,000 | | |
| Cost of goods purchased | | | 130,000 | |
| Cost of goods available for sale | | | $160,000 | |
| Less: Inventory, Dec. 31 | | | 34,000 | |
| Cost of goods sold | | | | 126,000 |
| Gross profit on sales | | | | $ 84,000 |
| Operating expenses: | | | | |
| Advertising | | | $ 9,000 | |
| Salaries | | | 37,000 | |
| Telephone | | | 1,100 | |
| Interest | | | 1,900 | |
| Depreciation | | | 3,000 | |
| Insurance | | | 1,000 | |
| Total operating expenses | | | | 53,000 |
| Net income | | | | $ 31,000 |

**Balance sheet** In studying the balance sheet on page 192, note that all items are taken from the Balance Sheet columns of the work sheet, but that the amount for Robert Riley, Capital is the December 31 balance of $59,000, computed as shown in the preceding statement of owner's equity.

## Closing entries

The entries used in closing revenue and expense accounts have been explained in preceding chapters. The only new elements in this illustration of closing entries for a merchandising business are the entries showing the elimination of the beginning inventory and the recording of the ending inventory. The beginning inventory is cleared out of the Inventory account by a debit to Income Summary and a credit to Inventory. A separate entry could be made for this purpose, but we can save time by making one compound entry which will debit the Income Summary account with the balance of the beginning inventory and with the balances of all temporary proprietorship accounts having debit balances. The

**OLYMPIC SPORTING GOODS**
**Balance Sheet**
**December 31, Year 11**

**Assets**

| | | |
|---|---|---|
| Cash | | $ 4,500 |
| Accounts receivable | | 3,500 |
| Inventory | | 34,000 |
| Unexpired insurance | | 3,000 |
| Land | | 30,000 |
| Building | $60,000 | |
| Less: Accumulated depreciation | 15,000 | 45,000 |
| Total assets | | $120,000 |

**Liabilities & Owner's Equity**

| | |
|---|---|
| Liabilities: | |
| Notes payable | $ 42,000 |
| Accounts payable | 19,000 |
| Total liabilities | $ 61,000 |
| Owner's equity: | |
| Robert Riley, capital | 59,000 |
| Total liabilities & owner's equity | $120,000 |

***temporary proprietorship accounts*** are those which appear in the income statement. As the name suggests, the temporary proprietorship accounts are used during the period to accumulate temporarily the increases and decreases in the proprietor's equity resulting from operation of the business. The entry to close out the beginning inventory and temporary proprietorship accounts with debit balances is illustrated below.

*Closing temporary proprietorship accounts with debit balances*

| | | | |
|---|---|---|---|
| Dec. 31 | Income Summary | 223,000 | |
| | Inventory (Jan. 1) | | 30,000 |
| | Purchases | | 132,000 |
| | Sales Returns and Allowances | | 4,400 |
| | Sales Discounts | | 600 |
| | Transportation-in | | 3,000 |
| | Advertising Expense | | 9,000 |
| | Salaries Expense | | 37,000 |
| | Telephone Expense | | 1,100 |
| | Interest Expense | | 1,900 |
| | Depreciation Expense | | 3,000 |
| | Insurance Expense | | 1,000 |
| | To close out the beginning inventory and the temporary proprietorship accounts with debit balances. | | |

The above entry closes (1) the accounts for beginning Inventory, Purchases, and Transportation-in; (2) the accounts for Sales Returns and Allowances, and for Sales Discounts; and (3) the operating expense accounts. Although the accounts for Sales Returns and Allowances and for Sales Discounts have debit balances, they are not expense accounts. In terms of account classification, they belong in the revenue group of accounts because they are offsets to the Sales account and appear in the income statement as deductions from Sales. After this first closing entry, the Inventory account has a zero balance. Therefore, it is time to record in this account the new inventory of $34,000 determined by count at December 31.

To bring the ending inventory into the accounting records after the stocktaking on December 31, we could make a separate entry debiting Inventory and crediting the Income Summary account. It is more convenient, however, to combine this step with the closing of the Sales account and any other temporary proprietorship accounts having credit balances, as illustrated in the following closing entry.

*Closing temporary proprietorship accounts with credit balances*

| | | | |
|---|---|---|---|
| *Dec. 31* | *Inventory (Dec. 31)* | *34,000* | |
| | *Sales* | *215,000* | |
| | *Purchase Returns and Allowances* | *3,700* | |
| | *Purchase Discounts* | *1,300* | |
| | *Income Summary* | | *254,000* |
| | *To record the ending inventory and to close all temporary proprietorship accounts with credit balances.* | | |

The remaining closing entries serve to transfer the balance of the Income Summary account to the owner's capital account and to close the drawing account, as follows:

*Closing the Income Summary account and owner's drawing account*

| | | | |
|---|---|---|---|
| *Dec. 31* | *Income Summary* | *31,000* | |
| | *Robert Riley, Capital* | | *31,000* |
| | *To close the Income Summary account.* | | |
| *Dec. 31* | *Robert Riley, Capital* | *26,000* | |
| | *Robert Riley, Drawing* | | *26,000* |
| | *To close the drawing account.* | | |

## Summary of merchandising transactions and related accounting entries

The transactions regularly encountered in merchandising operations and the related accounting entries may be concisely summarized as follows:

*Customary journal entries relating to merchandise*

| *Transactions during the Period* | *Related Accounting Entries: Debit* | *Credit* |
|---|---|---|
| *Purchase merchandise for resale* | *Purchases* | *Cash (or Accounts Payable)* |
| *Incur transportation charges on merchandise purchased for resale* | *Transportation-in* | *Cash (or Accounts Payable)* |
| *Return unsatisfactory merchandise to supplier, or obtain a reduction from original price* | *Cash (or Accounts Payable)* | *Purchase Returns and Allowances* |

| Transactions During the Period | Related Accounting Entries | |
|---|---|---|
| | Debit | Credit |
| Pay for merchandise within discount period | Accounts Payable | Cash and Purchase Discounts |
| Sell merchandise to customers | Cash (or Accounts Receivable) | Sales |
| Permit customers to return merchandise, or grant them a reduction from original price | Sales Returns and Allowances | Cash (or Accounts Receivable) |
| Collect account receivable within discount period | Cash and Sales Discounts | Accounts Receivable |
| **Inventory Procedures at End of Period** | | |
| Transfer the balance of the beginning inventory to the Income Summary account | Income Summary | Inventory |
| Take a physical inventory of goods on hand at the end of the period, and price these goods at cost | Inventory | Income Summary |

## Classified financial statements

The financial statements illustrated up to this point have been rather short and simple because of the limited number of accounts used in these introductory chapters. Now let us look briefly at a more comprehensive balance sheet for a merchandising business.

In the balance sheet of Graham Company illustrated on page 195 the assets are classified into three groups: (1) current assets, (2) plant and equipment, and (3) other assets. The liabilities are classified into two types: (1) current liabilities and (2) long-term liabilities. This classification of assets and liabilities is virtually a standard one throughout American business.

## The purpose of balance sheet classification

The purpose underlying a standard classification of assets and liabilities is to aid management, owners, creditors, and other interested persons in understanding the financial position of the business. Bankers, for example, would have a difficult time in reading the balance sheets of all the companies which apply to them for loans, if each of these companies followed its own individual whims as to the sequence and arrangement of accounts comprising its balance sheet. Standard practices as to the order and arrangement of a balance sheet are an important means of saving the time of the reader and of giving a fuller comprehension of the company's financial position. Some of the major balance sheet classifications are discussed briefly in the following section.

**Current assets** Current assets include cash, government bonds and other marketable securities, receivables, inventories, and prepaid expenses. To qualify for inclusion in the current asset category, an asset must be capable of being con-

***GRAHAM COMPANY***
***Balance Sheet***
***December 31, 19___***

***Assets***

| | | | |
|---|---|---|---|
| *Current assets:* | | | |
| *Cash* | | | *$ 14,500* |
| *U.S. government bonds* | | | *10,000* |
| *Notes receivable* | | | *2,400* |
| *Accounts receivable* | | | *26,100* |
| *Inventory* | | | *45,200* |
| *Prepaid expenses* | | | *1,200* |
| *Total current assets* | | | *$ 99,400* |
| *Plant and equipment:* | | | |
| *Land* | | *$100,000* | |
| *Building* | *$94,000* | | |
| *Less: Accumulated depreciation* | *1,920* | *92,080* | |
| *Store equipment* | *$ 9,400* | | |
| *Less: Accumulated depreciation* | *1,880* | *7,520* | |
| *Delivery equipment* | *$ 2,800* | | |
| *Less: Accumulated depreciation* | *700* | *2,100* | |
| *Total plant and equipment* | | | *201,700* |
| *Other assets:* | | | |
| *Land (future building site)* | | | *56,500* |
| *Total assets* | | | *$357,600* |

***Liabilities & Owner's Equity***

| | |
|---|---|
| *Current liabilities:* | |
| *Notes payable* | *$ 11,500* |
| *Accounts payable* | *19,040* |
| *Accrued expenses payable* | *1,410* |
| *Unearned revenue* | *1,100* |
| *Total current liabilities* | *$ 33,050* |
| *Long-term liabilities:* | |
| *Mortgage payable (due 1995)* | *25,000* |
| *Total liabilities* | *$ 58,050* |
| *Owner's equity:* | |
| *George Graham, capital* | *299,550* |
| *Total liabilities & owner's equity* | *$357,600* |

verted into cash within a relatively short period without interfering with the normal operation of the business. The period is usually one year, but it may be longer for those businesses having an operating cycle in excess of one year.

The term ***operating cycle*** means the average time period between the purchase of merchandise and the conversion of this merchandise back into cash. The series of transactions comprising a complete cycle often runs as follows: (1) purchase of merchandise, (2) sale of the merchandise on credit, (3) collection of the account receivable from the customer. The word ***cycle*** suggests the circular flow of capital from cash to inventory to receivables to cash again. This cycle of transactions in a merchandising business is portrayed in the following diagram.

*The operating cycle repeats continuously*

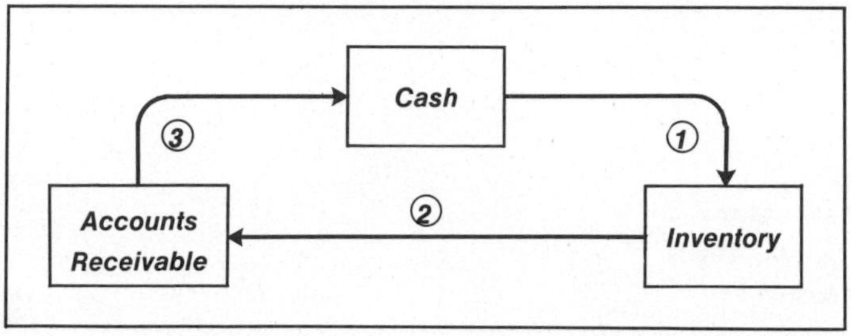


In a business handling fast-moving merchandise (a supermarket, for example) the operating cycle may be completed in a few weeks; for most merchandising businesses the operating cycle requires several months but less than a year.

The sequence in which current assets are listed depends upon their liquidity; the closer an asset is to becoming cash the higher is its liquidity. The total amount of a company's current assets and the relative amount of each type give some indication of the company's short-run, debt-paying ability.

**Current liabilities** Current liabilities are debts that are to be paid by use of current assets within the time period used to define current assets. This time period, as previously explained, is one year or one operating cycle, whichever is longer. Among the more common types of current liabilities are notes payable, accounts payable, taxes payable, salaries and wages payable, interest payable, and unearned revenue. Notes payable are usually listed first, followed by accounts payable; any sequence of listing is acceptable for other current liabilities.

To settle most types of current liabilities requires writing a check to the creditor; in other words, use of the current asset cash. A somewhat different procedure for settlement is followed for the current liability of unearned revenue. As explained in Chapter 4, unearned revenue is a liability which arises when money is received from customers in advance for goods or services to be delivered in the future. To meet such obligations usually will require using up current assets either through delivering merchandise to the customer or making payments to employees or others to provide the agreed services.

The key point to recognize is the relationship between current liabilities and current assets. Current liabilities must be paid in the near future and current assets must be available to make these payments. Comparison of the amount of current liabilities with the amount of current assets is an important step in appraising the ability of a company to pay its debts in the near future.

**Current ratio** Many bankers and other users of financial statements believe that for a business to qualify as a good credit risk, the total current assets should be about twice as large as the total current liabilities. In studying a balance sheet, a banker or other creditor will compute the ***current ratio*** by dividing total current assets by total current liabilities. The current ratio is a convenient measure of the short-run debt-paying ability of a business.

In the illustrated balance of Graham Company, the current assets of $99,400 are approximately three times as great as the current liabilities of $33,050; the current ratio is therefore 3 to 1, which would generally be regarded as a very strong current position. The current assets could shrink by two-thirds and still be sufficient for payment of the current liabilities. Although a strong current ratio is desirable, an extremely high current ratio (such as 4 to 1 or more) may signify that a company is holding too much of its resources in cash, marketable securities, and other current assets and is not pursuing profit opportunities as aggressively as it might.

**Working capital** The excess of current assets over current liabilities is called ***working capital***; the relative amount of working capital is another indication of short-term financial strength. In the illustrated balance sheet of Graham Company, working capital is $66,350, computed by subtracting the current liabilities of $33,050 from the current assets of $99,400. The importance of solvency (ability to meet debts as they fall due) was emphasized in Chapter 1. Ample working capital permits a company to buy merchandise in large lots, to carry an adequate stock of goods, and to sell goods to customers on favorable credit terms. Some companies have been forced out of business because of inadequate working capital, even though total assets were much larger than total liabilities.

## Classification in the income statement

A new feature to be noted in the illustrated income statement of Graham Company (page 198) is the division of operating expenses into the two categories of selling expenses and general and administrative expenses. Selling expenses include all expenses of storing merchandise, advertising and sales promotion, sales salaries and commissions, and delivering goods to customers. General and administrative expenses include the expenses of operating the general offices, the accounting department, the personnel office, and the credit and collection department.

This classification aids management in controlling expenses by emphasizing that certain expenses are the responsibility of the executive in charge of sales, and that other types of expenses relate to the business as a whole. Some expenses, such as depreciation of the building, may be divided between the two classifications according to the portion utilized by each functional division of the business.

Another feature to note in the income statement of the Graham Company is that interest earned on investments is placed after the figure showing income from operations. Other examples of such ***nonoperating revenues*** are dividends on shares of stock owned, and rent earned by leasing property not presently needed in the operation of the business.

The statement of owner's equity for Graham Company would be quite similar to the form illustrated earlier in this chapter.

**GRAHAM COMPANY**
**Income Statement**
**For the Year Ended December 31, 19__**

| | | | | |
|---|---|---|---|---|
| Gross sales | | | | $310,890 |
| Less: Sales returns & allowances | | | $ 3,820 | |
| Sales discounts | | | 4,830 | 8,650 |
| Net sales | | | | $302,240 |
| Cost of goods sold: | | | | |
| Inventory, Jan. 1 | | | $ 40,040 | |
| Purchases | | $212,400 | | |
| Less: Purchase returns & allowances | $2,400 | | | |
| Purchase discounts | 5,100 | 7,500 | | |
| Net purchases | | $204,900 | | |
| Add: Transportation-in | | 8,300 | | |
| Cost of goods purchased | | | 213,200 | |
| Cost of goods available for sale | | | $253,240 | |
| Less: Inventory, Dec. 31 | | | 45,200 | |
| Cost of goods sold | | | | 208,040 |
| Gross profit on sales | | | | $ 94,200 |
| Operating expenses: | | | | |
| Selling expenses: | | | | |
| Sales salaries | | $ 38,410 | | |
| Advertising | | 10,190 | | |
| Depreciation: building | | 840 | | |
| Depreciation: store equipment | | 940 | | |
| Depreciation: delivery equipment | | 700 | | |
| Insurance | | 1,100 | | |
| Miscellaneous | | 820 | | |
| Total selling expenses | | | $ 53,000 | |
| General and administrative expenses: | | | | |
| Office salaries | | $ 19,200 | | |
| Dues and subscriptions | | 750 | | |
| Depreciation: building | | 120 | | |
| Insurance | | 100 | | |
| Miscellaneous | | 930 | | |
| Total general and administrative expenses | | | 21,100 | |
| Total operating expenses | | | | 74,100 |
| Income from operations | | | | $ 20,100 |
| Interest earned on investments | | | | 300 |
| Net income | | | | $ 20,400 |

## Condensed income statement

The income statements prepared by different companies vary considerably in the amount of detail shown. An income statement of a large corporation intended for distribution to the public may be greatly condensed because the public presumably is not interested in the details of operations. A condensed income statement usually begins with ***net*** sales. The details involved in computing the cost of goods sold are also often omitted and only summary figures are given for selling expenses and general and administrative expenses. A condensed income statement for Graham Company follows:

*A condensed income statement*

***GRAHAM COMPANY***
***Income Statement***
***For the Year Ended December 31, 19___***

| | | |
|---|---|---|
| *Net sales* | | *$302,240* |
| *Cost of goods sold* | | *208,040* |
| *Gross profit on sales* | | *$ 94,200* |
| *Expenses:* | | |
| *Selling* | *$53,000* | |
| *General and administrative* | *21,100* | *74,100* |
| *Income from operations* | | *$ 20,100* |
| *Interest earned on investments* | | *300* |
| *Net income* | | *$ 20,400* |

## KEY TERMS INTRODUCED OR EMPHASIZED IN CHAPTER 5

**Beginning inventory** Goods on hand and available for sale to customers at the beginning of the accounting period.

**Cash discount** A reduction in price (usually 2% or less) offered by manufacturers and wholesalers to encourage customers to pay for merchandise within a specified discount period.

**Cost of goods sold** A computation appearing as a separate section of an income statement showing the cost of goods sold during the period. Computed by adding net delivered cost of merchandise purchases to beginning inventory to obtain cost of goods available for sale, and then deducting from this total the amount of the ending inventory. Usually equal to between 60 and 80% of net sales.

**Current assets** Cash and other assets that can be converted into cash within one year or the operating cycle (whichever is longer) without interfering with the normal operation of the business.

**Current liabilities** Any debts that must be paid within one year or the operating cycle (whichever is longer), with payment being made from current assets.

**Current ratio** Current assets divided by current liabilities. A measure of short-run debt-paying ability.

**Ending inventory** Goods still on hand and available for sale to customers at the end of the accounting period.

**F.O.B. destination** The seller bears the cost of shipping goods to the buyer's location.

**F.O.B. shipping point** The buyer of goods bears the cost of transportation from the seller's location to the buyer's location.

**General and administrative expenses** Expenses of the general offices, accounting department, personnel office, credit and collection department, and activities other than the selling of goods. A subdivision of operating expenses.

**Gross profit on sales** Revenue from sales minus cost of goods sold.

**Inventory (merchandise)** Goods acquired and held for sale to customers.

**Merchandise** Goods which a business buys for the purpose of selling to customers.

**Operating cycle** The average time period from the purchase of merchandise to its sale and conversion back into cash.

**Operating expenses** Include both selling expenses and general and administrative expenses. Deducted from gross profit on sales to determine net income.

**Periodic inventory system** A system of accounting for merchandise in which inventory at the balance sheet date is determined by counting and pricing the goods on hand. Cost of goods sold is computed by subtracting the ending inventory from the cost of goods available for sale.

**Perpetual inventory system** A system of accounting for merchandise that provides a continuous record showing the quantity and cost of all goods on hand.

**Physical inventory** The process of counting and pricing the merchandise on hand at a given date, usually the end of the accounting period.

**Purchases** An account used to record the cost of merchandise purchased for the purpose of sale to customers.

**Sales** The revenue account credited with the sales price of goods sold during the accounting period.

**Selling expenses** Expenses of marketing the product, such as advertising, sales salaries, and delivery of merchandise to customers. A subdivision of operating expenses.

**Working capital** Current assets minus current liabilities. Another measure of short-run, debt-paying ability.

## DEMONSTRATION PROBLEM FOR YOUR REVIEW

In this demonstration problem for a merchandising company, note that operations for the year result in a net loss. Since the revenue for the year is less than the expenses, the Income Summary account has a debit balance. The closing of the Income Summary account into the owner's capital account therefore will cause a decrease in the amount of the owner's capital.

The trial balance of Stone Supply Company at December 31, 19___, appears below. An inventory taken on December 31, 19___, amounted to $32,440. The following adjustments should be made:

(a) Depreciation of buildings, $4,100; of delivery equipment, $1,500.
(b) Accrued salaries: office, $845; sales, $950.
(c) Insurance expired, $250.
(d) Store supplies used, $1,000.

***STONE SUPPLY COMPANY***
***Trial Balance***
***December 31, 19___***

| | | |
|---|---|---|
| *Cash* | $ 9,310 | |
| *Accounts receivable* | 10,380 | |
| *Inventory, Jan. 1, 19___* | 28,650 | |
| *Store supplies* | 1,270 | |
| *Unexpired insurance* | 610 | |
| *Land* | 89,700 | |
| *Buildings* | 100,000 | |
| *Accumulated depreciation: buildings* | | $ 17,650 |
| *Delivery equipment* | 45,000 | |
| *Accumulated depreciation: delivery equipment* | | 14,800 |
| *Accounts payable* | | 22,450 |
| *Salaries payable* | | |
| *John Stone, capital* | | 285,165 |
| *John Stone, drawing* | 40,000 | |
| *Sales* | | 171,220 |
| *Sales returns & allowances* | 2,430 | |
| *Purchases* | 138,900 | |
| *Purchase returns & allowances* | | 1,820 |
| *Sales salaries expense* | 25,050 | |
| *Delivery expense* | 2,800 | |
| *Depreciation expense: delivery equipment* | | |
| *Office salaries expense* | 19,005 | |
| *Depreciation expense: buildings* | | |
| *Insurance expense* | | |
| *Store supplies expense* | | |
| | $513,105 | $513,105 |

**Instructions** Prepare a 10-column work sheet at December 31, 19___, with pairs of columns for Trial Balance, Adjustments, Adjusted Trial Balance, Income Statement, and Balance Sheet.

## SOLUTION TO DEMONSTRATION PROBLEM

**STONE SUPPLY COMPANY**
**Work Sheet**
**For the Year Ended December 31, 19___**

| | Trial Balance | | Adjustments* | | Adjusted Trial Balance | | Income Statement | | Balance Sheet | |
|---|---|---|---|---|---|---|---|---|---|---|
| | Dr | Cr | Dr | Cr | Dr | Cr | Dr | Cr | Dr | Cr |
| Cash | 9,310 | | | | 9,310 | | | | 9,310 | |
| Accounts receivable | 10,380 | | | | 10,380 | | | | 10,380 | |
| Inventory, Jan. 1, 19___ | 28,650 | | | | 28,650 | | 28,650 | | | |
| Store supplies | 1,270 | | | (d) 1,000 | 270 | | | | 270 | |
| Unexpired insurance | 610 | | | (c) 250 | 360 | | | | 360 | |
| Land | 89,700 | | | | 89,700 | | | | 89,700 | |
| Buildings | 100,000 | | | | 100,000 | | | | 100,000 | |
| Accum. depr.: buildings | | 17,650 | | (a) 4,100 | | 21,750 | | | | 21,750 |
| Delivery equipment | 45,000 | | | | 45,000 | | | | 45,000 | |
| Accum. depr.: del. eqpt. | | 14,800 | | (a) 1,500 | | 16,300 | | | | 16,300 |
| Accounts payable | | 22,450 | | | | 22,450 | | | | 22,450 |
| Salaries payable | | | | (b) 1,795 | | 1,795 | | | | 1,795 |
| John Stone, capital | | 285,165 | | | | 285,165 | | | | 285,165 |
| John Stone, drawing | 40,000 | | | | 40,000 | | | | 40,000 | |
| Sales | | 171,220 | | | | 171,220 | | 171,220 | | |
| Sales returns & allowances | 2,430 | | | | 2,430 | | 2,430 | | | |
| Purchases | 138,900 | | | | 138,900 | | 138,900 | | | |
| Purchase returns & allowances | | 1,820 | | | | 1,820 | | 1,820 | | |
| Sales salaries expense | 25,050 | | (b) 950 | | 26,000 | | 26,000 | | | |
| Delivery expense | 2,800 | | | | 2,800 | | 2,800 | | | |
| Depr. expense: del. eqpt. | | | (a) 1,500 | | 1,500 | | 1,500 | | | |
| Office salaries expense | 19,005 | | (b) 845 | | 19,850 | | 19,850 | | | |
| Depr. expense: buildings | | | (a) 4,100 | | 4,100 | | 4,100 | | | |
| Insurance expense | | | (c) 250 | | 250 | | 250 | | | |
| Store supplies expense | | | (d) 1,000 | | 1,000 | | 1,000 | | | |
| | 513,105 | 513,105 | 8,645 | 8,645 | 520,500 | 520,500 | | | | |
| Inventory, Dec. 31, 19___ | | | | | | | | 32,440 | 32,440 | |
| | | | | | | | 225,480 | 205,480 | 327,460 | 347,460 |
| Net loss | | | | | | | | 20,000 | 20,000 | |
| | | | | | | | 225,480 | 225,480 | 347,460 | 347,460 |

* Adjustments: (*a*) To record depreciation expense for the year.
(*b*) To record accrued salaries payable at Dec. 31, 19___.
(*c*) To record insurance expired.
(*d*) To record store supplies used.

## REVIEW QUESTIONS

1 During the current year, Green Bay Company made all sales of merchandise at prices in excess of cost. Will the business necessarily report a net income for the year? Explain.

2 Hi-Rise Company during its first year of operation had cost of goods sold of $90,000 and a gross profit equal to 40% of sales. What was the dollar amount of sales for the year?

3 In accounting for an unincorporated business, is it customary to include a salary to the owner as an expense of the business if he or she works full time for the business? Why or why not?

4 In appraising the adequacy of the net income of a small business in which the owner works on a full-time basis, the net income may be regarded as including three separate elements. What are these three elements?

5 Which of the following expenditures by Southside Drugstore should be recorded by a debit to the Purchases account?
**a** Purchase of a new delivery truck
**b** Purchase of a three-year insurance policy
**c** Purchase of merchandise from drug manufacturer
**d** Purchase of advertising space in local newspaper
**e** Payment in advance for three months' guard service by Security Patrol, Inc.

6 Supply the proper terms to complete the following statements:
**a** Net sales − cost of goods sold = _?_
**b** Beginning inventory + purchases − purchase returns and allowances − purchase discounts + transportation-in = _?_
**c** Cost of goods sold + ending inventory = _?_
**d** Cost of goods sold + gross profit on sales = _?_
**e** Net income + operating expenses = _?_

7 During the current year, Davis Corporation purchased merchandise costing $200,000. State the cost of goods sold under each of the following alternative assumptions:
**a** No beginning inventory; ending inventory $40,000
**b** Beginning inventory $60,000; no ending inventory
**c** Beginning inventory $58,000; ending inventory $78,000
**d** Beginning inventory $90,000; ending inventory $67,000

8 Zenith Company uses the periodic inventory system and maintains its accounting records on a calendar-year basis. Does the beginning or the ending inventory figure appear in the trial balance prepared from the ledger on December 31?

9 Compute the amount of cost of goods sold, given the following account balances: beginning inventory $40,000, purchases $84,000, purchase returns and allowances $4,500, purchase discounts $1,500, transportation-in $1,000, and ending inventory $36,000.

10 Explain the terms ***current assets, current liabilities,*** and ***current ratio.***

11 The Riblet Company has a current ratio of 3 to 1 and working capital of $60,000. What are the amounts of current assets and current liabilities?

12 Why is it advisable to use a Purchase Returns and Allowances account when a similar end result may be achieved by crediting the Purchases account when goods purchased are returned to the suppliers?

13 Which party (seller or buyer) bears the transportation costs when the terms of a merchandise sale are **(a)** F.O.B. shipping point; **(b)** F.O.B. destination?

14 Where does the account Transportation-in appear in the financial statements?

15 Is the normal balance of the Sales Returns and Allowances account a debit or a credit? Is the normal balance of the Purchase Returns and Allowances account a debit or a credit?

16 In which columns of the work sheet for a merchandising company does the ending inventory appear?

17 State briefly the difference between the ***perpetual*** inventory system and the ***periodic*** inventory system.

18 If cost of goods sold amounts to 65% of net sales of a merchandising business and net income amounts to 5% of net sales, what percentage of net sales is represented by operating expenses? What percentage of gross profit is included in each dollar of net sales?

19 An invoice dated October 21 bears credit terms of 2/10, n/30. What is the last day of the discount period? The last day of the credit period? Another invoice dated October 21 bears credit terms of 10 e.o.m. What is the last day of the credit period?

20 A cash discount affects both seller and buyer. What term describes a cash discount from the viewpoint of the seller? From the viewpoint of the buyer?

21 What single item on the income statement will, if added to the ending inventory, be equal to the cost of goods available for sale?

22 When the periodic inventory system is in use, how is the amount of inventory determined at the end of the period?

23 What is the purpose of a closing entry consisting of a debit to the Income Summary account and a credit to the Inventory account?

24 Describe a ***condensed income statement*** and indicate its advantages and possible shortcomings.

## EXERCISES

*Ex. 5-1* From the following list, select the appropriate items and compute the ***cost of goods available for sale.***

| | | | |
|---|---|---|---|
| *Purchases* | *$215,000* | *Purchase returns & allowances* | *$ 8,000* |
| *Sales* | *420,000* | *Purchase discounts* | *7,000* |
| *Transportation-in* | *10,000* | *Sales returns & allowances* | *12,000* |
| *Sales discounts* | *6,000* | *Beginning inventory* | *45,000* |

*Ex. 5-2* Use the following data as a basis for computing the amount of the beginning inventory.

| | |
|---|---|
| *Purchase returns and allowances* | *$ 6,880* |
| *Transportation-in* | *3,840* |
| *Cost of goods sold* | *67,040* |
| *Purchases* | *103,040* |
| *Ending inventory* | *61,520* |

*Ex. 5-3* Compute the amount of ***total*** purchases for the period, given the following data:

| | |
|---|---|
| *Sales* | *$200,000* |
| *Ending inventory* | *46,000* |
| *Purchase returns and allowances* | *2,500* |
| *Beginning inventory* | *50,000* |
| *Transportation-in* | *2,000* |
| *Cost of goods sold* | *150,000* |

*Ex. 5-4* During September, Mills Company made sales of merchandise on credit amounting to $203,200, of which $174,400 remain uncollected at September 30. Sales for cash during September amounted to $48,000 and an additional $158,400 was received from customers in payment for goods sold to them in prior months. Also during September, the Mills Company borrowed $57,600 cash from the Second National Bank. What was the total revenue for September?

*Ex. 5-5* The balance sheet of Hunt Company contained the following items, among others:

| | |
|---|---|
| *Cash* | *$ 37,600* |
| *Accounts receivable* | *148,000* |
| *Inventory* | *198,400* |
| *Store equipment (net)* | *192,000* |
| *Other assets* | *28,800* |
| *Mortgage payable (due in 3 years)* | *48,000* |
| *Notes payable (due in 10 days)* | *15,200* |
| *Accounts payable* | *138,400* |
| *Bob Hunt, capital* | *220,800* |

**Instructions**

**a** From the above information compute the amount of current assets and the amount of current liabilities.
**b** How much working capital does Hunt Company have?
**c** Compute the current ratio.

*Ex. 5-6* Hudson Company sold merchandise to River Company for $3,000; terms 2/10, n/30. River Company paid for the merchandise within the discount period. Both companies record invoices at the gross amounts.

**a** Give the journal entries by Hudson Company to record the sale and the subsequent collection.
**b** Give the journal entries by River Company to record the purchase and the subsequent payment.

*Ex. 5-7* Key figures taken from the income statement of Blue Spring Waters for two successive years are shown below:

| | *Year 5* | *Year 4* |
|---|---|---|
| *Sales* | *$320,000* | *$240,000* |
| *Cost of goods sold* | *240,000* | *168,000* |
| *Selling expenses* | *40,000* | *35,000* |
| *General and administrative expenses* | *16,000* | *17,800* |

**Instructions**

**a** The net income increased from $___ in Year 4 to $___ in Year 5.
**b** The net income as a percentage of sales was ___% in Year 4 and decreased to ___% of sales in Year 5.
**c** The gross profit on sales decreased from ___% in Year 4 to ___% in Year 5.

*Ex. 5-8* During its first year of operation, Clarington Company earned net income equal to 5% of net sales. The selling expenses were twice as large as net income but only one-half as large as general and administrative expenses, which amounted to $240,000. Prepare a condensed income statement for the first year of operation, which ended June 30, 19___.

*Ex. 5-9* Village Shop prepared a work sheet at December 31, Year 5. Shown below is the Income Statement pair of columns from that work sheet. To keep this exercise short, expense accounts have been combined. Use these work sheet data to prepare an income statement for the year ended December 31, Year 5.

| | Income Statement | |
|---|---|---|
| | Debit | Credit |
| Inventory, Dec. 31, Year 4 | 90,000 | |
| Sales | | 120,300 |
| Sales returns & allowances | 672 | |
| Purchases | 97,200 | |
| Purchase returns & allowances | | 7,200 |
| Transportation-in | 2,400 | |
| Selling expenses | 20,000 | |
| General and administrative expenses | 8,320 | |
| Inventory, Dec. 31, Year 5 | | 108,000 |
| | 218,592 | 235,500 |
| Net income | 16,908 | |
| | 235,500 | 235,500 |

*Ex. 5-10* Listed below in random order are some of the ledger account balances of Hong Kong Traders at December 31.

| | |
|---|---|
| Delivery equipment | $ 31,552 |
| Interest payable | 1,024 |
| Advance payments from customers | 5,760 |
| Notes payable (due in 90 days) | 64,000 |
| U.S. government bonds | 19,200 |
| Accounts receivable | 90,560 |
| Accounts payable | 59,200 |
| Interest receivable | 192 |
| Inventory | 244,640 |
| Accumulated depreciation: delivery equipment | 3,155 |
| Salaries payable | 2,560 |
| Cash | 43,040 |
| Land | 95,000 |
| Furniture & fixtures | 11,200 |

**Instructions**

**a** Compute the amount of ***working capital*** by arranging the ***appropriate*** items in the usual balance sheet sequence. A complete balance sheet is not required.

**b** Compute the current ratio and state whether you regard the company as being in a strong or a weak current position.

## PROBLEMS

### Group A

*5A-1* Shoreline Center uses the periodic inventory system and closes its accounts annually on June 30. A partial list of the company's transactions during May is shown below.

**May 1** Purchased merchandise from Pecos Baldy Company, $8,000. Terms, 2/10, n/30.
**May 2** Paid by check transportation charges on merchandise purchased from Pecos Baldy Company, $200.
**May 3** Cash sale of merchandise, $2,700.
**May 6** Purchased office equipment for use in business on credit from Steele Company, $2,777. Terms, net 30 days.
**May 9** Sold merchandise on account to Trent Construction Company, $3,960. Terms, net 30 days.
**May 10** Paid transportation charges on shipment to Trent Construction Company, $80.
**May 11** Paid Pecos Baldy Company within discount period for purchase made on May 1. Issued check for $7,840.
**May 11** Purchased merchandise for cash, $324.
**May 12** Returned defective equipment which cost $540 to Steele Company for credit.
**May 16** Sold merchandise on account to S. W. Hardy, $6,100. Terms 2/10, n/30.
**May 17** Granted a $100 allowance to S. W. Hardy on merchandise delivered on May 16, because of minor defects discovered in the merchandise.
**May 23** Agreed to cancel the account receivable from Trent Construction Company in exchange for their services in erecting a garage on our property. Construction completed today.
**May 26** Received check from S. W. Hardy within discount period in settlement of transaction of May 16. Customer took discount applicable to remaining balance after $100 allowance on May 17.
**May 28** Paid balance due Steele Company. (See transactions of May 6 and 12.)

**Instructions** Prepare a separate journal entry (including an explanation) for each of the above transactions.

*5A-2* Newport Beach is in the wholesale merchandise field and relies on the periodic inventory system. The income statement of the company for the first year ended June 30, 19___, contained the following items.

| | | | |
|---|---|---|---|
| *Gross profit on sales* | *$297,000* | *Transportation-in* | *$ 6,000* |
| *Depreciation expense* | *33,600* | *Purchases* | *559,100* |
| *Utilities expense* | *21,400* | *Ending inventory* | *?* |
| *Beginning inventory* | *110,000* | *Salaries expense* | *119,300* |
| *Sales returns & allowances* | *12,500* | *Insurance expense* | *3,700* |
| *Purchase returns & allowances* | *2,100* | *Miscellaneous expense* | *11,600* |
| *Advertising expense* | *26,400* | *Sales discounts* | *10,000* |
| *Sales* | *922,500* | *Purchase discounts* | *2,000* |

**Instructions**

a Prepare an income statement utilizing all the accounts listed above, including the determination of the amount of the ending inventory. Use the format illustrated on page 198.
b Compute the amount of net sales.
c Compute the gross profit percentage (gross profit on sales divided by net sales).
d Compute the percentage of net sales represented by the cost goods sold (cost of goods sold divided by net sales).
e Compute the percentage of net sales represented by net income (net income divided by net sales).

*5A-3* An alphabetical listing of the account balances of Four Seasons after its second complete year of operations is shown below. All necessary adjustments as of December 31 have been recorded and posted.

| | | | |
|---|---|---|---|
| *Accounts payable* | *$12,000* | *Prepaid insurance* | *$ 390* |
| *Accounts receivable* | *20,000* | *Property taxes expense* | *600* |
| *Accrued property taxes payable* | *580* | *Purchase discounts* | *1,280* |
| *Accumulated depreciation: equipment* | *2,275* | *Purchase returns and allowances* | *3,000* |
| *Cash* | *8,375* | *Purchases* | *129,835* |
| *Delivery expense* | *2,055* | *Rent expense* | *7,200* |
| *Depreciation expense* | *1,300* | *Salaries and wages expense* | *37,565* |
| *Equipment* | *7,960* | *Sales* | *211,820* |
| *Insurance expense* | *1,600* | *Sales discounts* | *1,820* |
| *Inventory, Jan. 1* | *26,780* | *Sales returns & allowances* | *4,000* |
| *Barry Jackson, capital* | *41,145* | *Selling commissions expense* | *8,000* |
| *Barry Jackson, drawing* | *5,600* | *Supplies* | *715* |
| *Notes receivable* | *3,500* | *Supplies expense* | *580* |
| | | *Transportation-in* | *4,225* |

The inventory, determined by count at December 31, was $19,560.

**Instructions**

a Prepare the income statement for the year ended December 31. Operating expenses are not to be subdivided between selling expenses and general and administrative expenses. Use the format of the income statement illustrated on page 198.
b Prepare all necessary journal entries to close the accounts at December 31.

*5A-4* Outrider Supplies, a successful small merchandising business, was purchased as a going concern by Roberta Conway on January 1, 1982. After one year of operation, the trial balance shown on page 209 was prepared:

A physical inventory was taken at the close of business December 31, 1982; this count showed merchandise on hand in the amount of $58,000.

**Other data**

(a) Property taxes accrued but not yet recorded, $1,800.
(b) A physical count showed supplies on hand of $840.
(c) The cost of insurance which had expired during the year was $560.
(d) Depreciation rates: 4% on buildings and 10% on equipment.

**OUTRIDER SUPPLIES**
**Trial Balance**
**December 31, 1982**

| | | |
|---|---|---|
| Cash | $ 8,000 | |
| Accounts receivable | 34,000 | |
| Inventory, Jan. 1, 1982 | 72,000 | |
| Supplies | 2,840 | |
| Unexpired insurance | 1,080 | |
| Land | 40,000 | |
| Buildings | 100,000 | |
| Equipment | 24,000 | |
| Accounts payable | | $ 56,620 |
| Roberta Conway, capital | | 170,000 |
| Roberta Conway, drawing | 15,000 | |
| Sales | | 390,500 |
| Sales returns & allowances | 8,000 | |
| Purchases | 232,000 | |
| Purchase returns & allowances | | 4,000 |
| Purchase discounts | | 1,680 |
| Transportation-in | 9,640 | |
| Selling commissions expense | 12,510 | |
| Delivery expense | 3,500 | |
| Salaries and wages expense | 59,230 | |
| Property taxes expense | 1,000 | |
| | $622,800 | $622,800 |

**Instructions**

**a** Prepare a 10-column work sheet at December 31.
**b** Prepare the journal entries to adjust the accounts at December 31.
**c** Prepare the journal entries required to close the accounts at December 31.

*5A-5* Shown on page 210 is a trial balance prepared from the ledger of Six Corners at December 31.

**Other data**

(a) The buildings were acquired early in Year 6 and are being depreciated over a 25-year useful life. The equipment is being depreciated over a 10-year useful life.
(b) Accrued salaries payable as of December 31 were $5,000.
(c) Examination of policies showed $600 unexpired insurance on December 31.
(d) Supplies on hand at December 31 were estimated to amount to $300.
(e) Inventory of merchandise on December 31, Year 7, was $44,600.

**Instructions**

**a** Prepare a 10-column work sheet at December 31, Year 7.
**b** Prepare an income statement, a statement of owner's equity, and a classified balance sheet.
**c** Prepare adjusting entries.
**d** Prepare closing entries.
**e** Compute the current ratio and the amount of working capital. Explain whether Six Corners appears to be an acceptable short-term credit risk.

*SIX CORNERS*
*Trial Balance*
*December 31, Year 7*

| | | |
|---|---|---|
| Cash | $ 29,800 | |
| Accounts receivable | 38,800 | |
| Inventory, Jan. 1, Year 7 | 59,000 | |
| Unexpired insurance | 1,800 | |
| Office supplies | 800 | |
| Land | 17,000 | |
| Buildings | 60,000 | |
| Accumulated depreciation: buildings | | $ 2,400 |
| Equipment | 16,000 | |
| Accumulated depreciation: equipment | | 4,800 |
| Accounts payable | | 52,000 |
| Jerry Wilson, capital | | 85,500 |
| Jerry Wilson, drawing | 8,000 | |
| Sales | | 326,000 |
| Sales returns & allowances | 4,100 | |
| Sales discounts | 1,100 | |
| Purchases | 192,000 | |
| Purchase returns & allowances | | 2,000 |
| Purchase discounts | | 1,600 |
| Transportation-in | 4,800 | |
| Salaries and wages expense | 40,000 | |
| Property taxes expense | 1,100 | |
| | $474,300 | $474,300 |

## Group B

*5B-1* Carleton Company uses the periodic inventory system. Sales are made on a variety of credit terms to various customers, and some sales are for cash. The company completed the following transactions among others during the month of January.

**Jan. 2** Sold merchandise on credit to Cable, Inc., $6,000. Terms, 2/10, n/30.
**Jan. 3** Purchased merchandise for cash, $1,065.
**Jan. 4** Sold merchandise to Tucker Company on credit, $1,200. Terms, 10 e.o.m.
**Jan. 6** Paid transportation charges on shipment to Tucker Company, $375.
**Jan. 8** Purchased office equipment from ABC Corporation for cash, $8,250.
**Jan. 12** Received check for $5,880 from Cable, Inc., as settlement within discount period for goods sold them on Jan. 2.
**Jan. 14** Permitted Tucker Company to return for credit $630 of the merchandise purchased on Jan. 4 (no reduction in the transportation charges paid on Jan. 6).
**Jan. 15** Sold merchandise for cash, $6,450.
**Jan. 16** Refunded $390 to a customer who had made a cash purchase on Jan. 15.
**Jan. 20** Purchased merchandise from Selzer Company on credit, $4,950. Terms 2/10, n/30.

**Jan. 21** Paid by check transportation charges on merchandise purchased from Selzer Company in the amount of $240.

**Jan. 23** Returned for credit of $450 merchandise purchased from Selzer Company (no reduction was allowed with respect to the transportation charges paid Jan. 21).

**Jan. 25** Purchased stationery and miscellaneous office supplies on open account, $705.

**Jan. 30** Made payment within discount period to Selzer Company for merchandise purchased Jan. 20. (Note that a portion of goods were returned for credit on Jan. 21.)

**Instructions** Prepare a separate journal entry (including an explanation) for each of the above transactions.

*5B-2* The income statement of Hamada Nurseries for the year ended December 31 contained the following items. The company is engaged in both the wholesale and retail sale of trees, shrubs, and plants. The periodic inventory system is in use.

| | | | |
|---|---|---|---|
| *Purchases* | *$258,000* | *Advertising expense* | *$11,000* |
| *Ending inventory* | *50,000* | *Sales returns & allowances* | *20,000* |
| *Beginning inventory* | *80,000* | *Purchase returns & allowances* | *10,000* |
| *Salaries expense* | *47,200* | *Delivery expense* | *8,000* |
| *Sales* | *425,200* | *Utilities expense* | *9,000* |
| *Insurance expense* | *2,800* | *Sales discounts* | *5,200* |
| *Depreciation expense* | *18,000* | *Purchase discounts* | *4,000* |
| *Transportation-in* | *6,000* | | |

**Instructions**

**a** Prepare an income statement utilizing all the accounts listed above. (Use the format illustrated on page 198.)

**b** Compute the gross profit percentage (gross profit on sales divided by net sales).

**c** Compute the percentage of net sales represented by cost of goods sold (cost of goods sold divided by net sales).

**d** Compute the percentage of net sales represented by net income (net income divided by net sales).

*5B-3* A four-column schedule consisting of the first four columns of a 10-column work sheet for Motorsport Supplies appears on page 212. The company uses the periodic inventory system and maintains its accounting records on a calendar-year basis. The completed Adjustments columns have been included in the work sheet to minimize the detail work involved. These adjustments were derived from the following information available at December 31.

(a) Depreciation expense for the year on store equipment, $2,200.
(b) Insurance premiums expired during the year, $1,400.
A physical inventory taken at December 31 showed the ending inventory to be $66,000.

**Instructions** Prepare a 10-column work sheet utilizing the trial balance and adjusting data provided. Follow the format illustrated on page 212. Include at the bottom of the work sheet a legend consisting of a brief explanation keyed to each adjusting entry.

**MOTORSPORT SUPPLIES**

| | Trial Balance | | Adjustments | |
|---|---|---|---|---|
| | Debit | Credit | Debit | Credit |
| Cash | 6,400 | | | |
| Accounts receivable | 16,000 | | | |
| Inventory, Jan. 1 | 60,000 | | | |
| Unexpired insurance | 4,400 | | | (b) 1,400 |
| Equipment | 22,000 | | | |
| Accumulated depreciation: equipment | | 6,600 | | (a) 2,200 |
| Accounts payable | | 20,400 | | |
| John Dawes, capital | | 82,800 | | |
| John Dawes, drawing | 20,000 | | | |
| Sales | | 529,000 | | |
| Sales returns & allowances | 21,000 | | | |
| Sales discounts | 8,000 | | | |
| Purchases | 368,000 | | | |
| Purchase returns & allowances | | 18,000 | | |
| Purchase discounts | | 6,000 | | |
| Transportation-in | 12,000 | | | |
| Advertising expense | 32,000 | | | |
| Rent expense | 25,000 | | | |
| Salaries expense | 68,000 | | | |
| | 662,800 | 662,800 | | |
| Depreciation expense | | | (a) 2,200 | |
| Insurance expense | | | (b) 1,400 | |
| | | | 3,600 | 3,600 |

*5B-4* After working in a managerial position for several years with a large corporation, Jill Ward bought a merchandising company, River Imports, on October 1, 1982. Ward had saved $30,000 over a period of years and had received an inheritance of $72,000, all of which she invested in the new business. Before taking this step, Ward had given considerable thought to the alternative of continuing in her present position, which paid her a salary of $23,400 a year, and investing her capital in high-grade securities, which she estimated would provide an average return of 8% on the amount invested.

River Imports uses the periodic inventory system and maintains its accounting records on the basis of a fiscal year ending September 30.

The trial balance on page 213 was taken from the records at September 30, 1983, after one year of operations.

The September 30, 1983, inventory by physical count was $34,800.

**Other data**

(a) Accrued property taxes, $1,200, not previously recorded.
(b) Supplies on hand, $600.
(c) Insurance expired during year, $800.
(d) Depreciation rates: 4% on building; 10% on equipment.

***RIVER IMPORTS***
***Trial Balance***
***September 30, 1983***

| | | |
|---|---|---|
| Cash | $ 6,000 | |
| Accounts receivable | 13,000 | |
| Inventory, Oct. 1, 1982 | 43,000 | |
| Supplies | 1,700 | |
| Unexpired insurance | 1,200 | |
| Land | 24,000 | |
| Building | 60,000 | |
| Equipment | 14,000 | |
| Accounts payable | | $ 27,400 |
| Jill Ward, capital | | 102,000 |
| Jill Ward, drawing | 15,000 | |
| Sales | | 240,800 |
| Sales returns & allowances | 1,600 | |
| Sales discounts | 1,000 | |
| Purchases | 140,000 | |
| Purchase returns & allowances | | 2,000 |
| Purchase discounts | | 1,400 |
| Transportation-in | 5,000 | |
| Selling commissions expense | 7,500 | |
| Delivery expense | 2,100 | |
| Salaries and wages expense | 36,000 | |
| Property taxes | 2,500 | |
| | $373,600 | $373,600 |

**Instructions**

**a** Prepare a 10-column work sheet at September 30, 1983. Use the format illustrated on page 188.

**b** Prepare a schedule comparing the net income from the business for the fiscal year ended September 30, 1983, with the net income Ward would have received by continuing as a salaried manager and investing her capital in securities. State your opinion, based on this comparative schedule, as to whether starting her own business was a good move for Jill Ward.

*5B-5* The trial balance on page 214 was prepared from the ledger of Arrowhead Company at December 31. The company maintains its accounts on a calendar year basis and closes the accounts only once a year. The periodic inventory system is in use.

**Other data**

(a) The depreciation rate on the building is 4%, based on a 25-year life.
(b) Unexpired insurance at the end of the year was determined to be $1,500.
(c) Office supplies unused and on hand at year-end amounted to $800.
(d) A physical inventory of merchandise at December 31, showed goods on hand of $140,000.

*ARROWHEAD COMPANY*
*Trial Balance*
*December 31, 19___*

| | | |
|---|---|---|
| *Cash* | *$ 20,000* | |
| *Accounts receivable* | *76,000* | |
| *Inventory, Jan. 1* | *160,000* | |
| *Unexpired insurance* | *4,000* | |
| *Office supplies* | *1,800* | |
| *Land* | *35,000* | |
| *Buildings* | *100,000* | |
| *Accumulated depreciation: buildings* | | *$ 20,000* |
| *Notes payable* | | *80,000* |
| *Accounts payable* | | *60,000* |
| *Richard Knight, capital* | | *194,800* |
| *Richard Knight, drawing* | *26,000* | |
| *Sales* | | *658,000* |
| *Sales returns and allowances* | *42,000* | |
| *Sales discounts* | *16,000* | |
| *Purchases* | *431,000* | |
| *Purchase returns and allowances* | | *23,000* |
| *Purchase discounts* | | *8,000* |
| *Transportation-in* | *10,000* | |
| *Advertising expense* | *5,000* | |
| *Salaries expense* | *110,000* | |
| *Utilities expense* | *7,000* | |
| | *$1,043,800* | *$1,043,800* |

**Instructions**

**a** Prepare a 10-column work sheet at December 31. Use the format illustrated on page 188.
**b** Prepare an income statement, a statement of owner's equity, and a ***classified*** balance sheet. The operating expenses need not be subdivided.
**c** Prepare adjusting entries and closing entries.

## BUSINESS DECISION PROBLEM 5

Jane Miller, an experienced engineer, is considering buying the Eastern Engineering Company at year-end from its current owner, Jack Peterson. Eastern Engineering Company has been a profitable business, earning about $54,000 each year. Jane Miller is certain she could operate the business just as profitably. The principal activity of the business has been the performance of engineering studies for government agencies interested in the development of air and water pollution control programs. Jane Miller comes to you with the balance sheet of Eastern Engineering Company shown on page 215 and asks your advice about buying the business.

***EASTERN ENGINEERING COMPANY***
***Balance Sheet***
***December 31, 19__***

| *Assets* | | *Liabilities & Owner's Equity* | |
|---|---|---|---|
| *Cash* | *$ 36,000* | *Notes payable* | *$ 54,000* |
| *U.S. government contract receivable* | *90,000* | *Accounts payable* | *16,200* |
| *Other contracts receivable* | *25,200* | *Wages payable* | *5,400* |
| *Equipment (net of depreciation)* | *81,000* | *J. Peterson, capital* | *210,600* |
| *Patents* | *54,000* | | |
| | *$286,200* | | *$286,200* |

Miller immediately points out, as evidence of the firm's solvency, that the current ratio for Eastern Engineering is 2 to 1. In discussing the specific items on the balance sheet, you find that the patents were recently purchased by Eastern, and Miller believes them to be worth their $54,000 cost. The notes payable liability consists of one note to the manufacturer of the equipment owned by Eastern, which Peterson had incurred five years ago to finance the purchase of the equipment. The note becomes payable, however, in February of the coming year. The accounts payable all will become due within 30 to 60 days.

Since Miller does not have enough cash to buy Peterson's equity in the business, she is considering the following terms of purchase: (1) Peterson will withdraw all the cash from the business, thus reducing his equity to $174,600, (2) Peterson will also keep the $90,000 receivable from the U.S. government, leaving his equity in the business at $84,600, and (3) by borrowing heavily, Miller thinks she can raise $84,600 in cash, which she will pay to Peterson for his remaining equity. Miller will assume the existing liabilities of the business.

**Instructions**

**a** Prepare a classified balance sheet for Eastern Engineering Company as it would appear immediately after Miller acquired the business, assuming that the purchase is carried out immediately on the proposed terms.

**b** Compute the current ratio and the working capital position of Eastern Engineering Company after Miller's purchase of the business.

**c** Write a memorandum to Miller explaining what problems she might encounter if she purchases the business as planned.

# 6

# INTERNAL CONTROL

## The meaning of internal control

Our discussion of a merchandising business in Chapter 5 emphasized the steps of the accounting cycle, especially the determination of cost of goods sold and the preparation of financial statements. In the present chapter we shall round out this discussion by considering the system of internal control by which management maintains control over the purchasing, receiving, storing, and selling of merchandise. Strong internal controls are needed not only for purchases and sales transactions, but for all other types of transactions as well. It is particularly important to maintain strong internal controls over transactions involving cash receipts and cash payments. In fact, the concept of internal control is so important that it affects all the assets of a business, all liabilities, the revenue and expenses, and every aspect of operations. ***The purpose of internal control is to aid in the efficient operation of a business.***

As defined in Chapter 1, the system of internal control includes all the measures taken by an organization for the purpose of (1) protecting its resources against waste, fraud, and inefficiency; (2) ensuring accuracy and reliability in accounting and operating data; (3) securing compliance with company policies; and (4) evaluating the level of performance in all divisions of the company.

## Internal control and business decisions

Many people think of internal control as a means of safeguarding cash and preventing theft, bribery, and other types of fraud. Although internal control is an important factor in protecting assets and preventing fraud, this is only a part of its role. Almost all business decisions are based at least in part upon accounting data. Examples of these decisions range from such minor daily actions as the authorizing of overtime work or the purchase of office supplies to such major actions as a change in product lines or a choice between leasing or buying a new building. The fact that business decisions are based on accounting data explains the importance of internal control, because ***the system of internal control provides assurance of the dependability of the accounting data relied upon in making decisions.***

### Internal control as a two-way communication system

The decisions made by management become company policy. To be effective, this policy must be communicated throughout the company and followed consistently. The results of the policies—the consequences of managerial decisions—must be reported back to management so that the soundness of company policies can be evaluated and a continuous updating process carried on.

Among the means of communication included in the system of internal control are organization charts, manuals of accounting policies and procedures, flow charts, forecasts, internal audit reports, job descriptions, purchase orders, interim financial statements, operating reports, and many other types of documentation. The term ***documentation*** refers to all the charts, forms, reports, and other business papers that guide and describe the working of a company's system of accounting and internal control.

In summary, a system of internal control extends throughout the organization. Like the nerves and nerve centers of a person, the internal control system provides direction to all activity and monitors the working of all units comprising a business organization.

### Objectives in the study of internal control

Our study of internal control at this point has two principal objectives: first, to explain the nature and importance of internal control; and second, to indicate the specific steps required to establish and maintain good internal control.

This chapter will not include detailed study of internal control measures applicable to specific topics such as cash, receivables, or inventories. Consideration of the internal controls needed for these and similar areas will appear in later chapters devoted to selected financial statement topics. Before reviewing in depth the internal controls over specific segments of a business, we need first to acquire an understanding of the principles underlying the entire system of internal control.

### Administrative controls and accounting controls

Internal controls are often viewed as falling into two major classes: administrative controls and accounting controls. ***Administrative controls*** are measures that apply principally to operational efficiency and compliance with established policies in all parts of the organization. For example, an administrative control may be a requirement that traveling salespersons submit reports showing the number of calls made on customers each day. Another example is a directive requiring airline pilots to have an annual medical examination, and another example, the requirement that factory employees wear identification badges. These internal administrative controls have no direct bearing on the reliability of the financial statements and other accounting reports. Consequently, administrative controls are not of direct interest to accountants and independent auditors.

***Internal accounting controls are measures that relate to protection of assets and to the reliability of accounting and financial reports.*** An example is the requirement that a person whose duties involve handling cash shall not also maintain accounting records. More broadly stated, the accounting function must be kept separate from the custody of assets. Another ***accounting control*** is the requirement that checks, purchase orders, and other documents be serially numbered. Still another example is the rule that a person who orders merchandise and supplies should not be the one to receive them and should not sign checks to pay for them.

When certified public accountants perform an audit of a company, they always study and evaluate the system of internal control. However, this work is concentrated on accounting controls rather than administrative controls, because the objective of the CPA is to form an opinion of the company's financial statements and it is the accounting controls which assure reliability in financial statements. An ***internal auditor,*** on the other hand, is interested in the operational efficiency of the company rather than the annual financial statements and therefore will study both administrative and accounting controls.

### Reliance by the CPA upon internal control

Before expressing an opinion on a company's financial statements, a CPA firm must gather evidence which supports each item in the balance sheet and income statement. This supporting evidence includes the ledgers, journals, and all kinds of business documents. The strength of the internal controls in force determines the reliability of the accounting records and of the entire accounting process. Therefore, a CPA firm encourages its clients to maintain strong internal control and makes recommendations for improvements in the system of internal control. A weakness in internal control does not necessarily mean that the accounting records are erroneous, but it does suggest to the CPA the ***possibility*** that the records supporting the financial statements may be in error.

### Strong internal control now required by law

In recent years, some American corporations have acknowledged making payments to foreign officials which could be interpreted as bribes. These payments in many cases were legal under the laws of the countries in which they were made, although they were not in conformity with American business ethics. In some cases, the top executives of the corporations involved were not aware that these transactions were taking place.

To put an end to such practices, the United States Congress passed the Foreign Corrupt Practices Act of 1977. This Act requires every corporation under the jurisdiction of the SEC to maintain a system of internal control sufficient to provide reasonable assurance that transactions are executed only with the knowledge and authorization of management. The Act also requires the system of internal control to limit the use of corporate assets to those purposes approved by management. Finally, the Act requires that accounting records of assets be compared at reasonable intervals with the assets actually on hand. These requirements are designed to prevent the creation of secret "slush funds" or other misuses of corporate assets. Violations of the Act may result in fines of up to $1 million and imprisonment of the responsible parties. Thus, a strong system of internal control, long recognized as vital to the operation of a large business, is now required by federal law.

The Foreign Corrupt Practices Act is actually much broader and more far-reaching than its name implies. One might assume from its name that a company without foreign operations and without corrupt practices would not be affected, but this is not the case. The Foreign Corrupt Practices Act has two major parts: one part deals with foreign bribes and the other consists of accounting provisions that affect every publicly owned corporation in the United States. These accounting provisions have already been used by the SEC to require greater responsibility by both corporate management and CPA firms in maintaining and evaluating strong systems of internal control.

### Impact of the Foreign Corrupt Practices Act on large corporations

The SEC has proposed that every publicly owned corporation report each year to its stockholders and to the SEC whether its system of internal control meets the objectives of the Foreign Corrupt Practices Act. The public report on internal control covers the entire year; it states whether any material weaknesses in internal control were pointed out by the CPA firm auditing the company and whether such weaknesses have been corrected.

In summary, the era ushered in by the Foreign Corrupt Practices Act is one in which top management of a large company must give high priority to maintaining a strong system of internal control. Every individual in a key position must be made to realize that the company is committed to clearly defined standards of business ethics and to carrying out only those transactions which conform to company policy. The proposed annual public report on internal control by a large corporation is to be examined by independent auditors to assure that it is documented and is consistent with the CPA firm's knowledge of the business. However, directors and officers of large corporations no longer can rely solely upon their internal auditors and independent auditors to test the system of internal control. Top management must make its own review of its system and continually carry on testing and monitoring of internal controls to meet its responsibilities as now defined by the SEC.

ILLUSTRATIVE CASE Because the Foreign Corrupt Practices Act makes it a crime not to maintain a reasonable system of internal control, many corporations have taken drastic action to protect themselves against the possibility of five-year jail terms for corporate officers. One large corporation doubled the size of its internal auditing staff, changed the Chief Internal Auditor's title to Vice President—Internal

Auditing, and doubled his salary. The company also paid a CPA firm a fee of $1.5 million to conduct a thorough study of the system of internal control. An officer explained: "We are determined to comply with the Foreign Corrupt Practices Act, but we're not clear as to just what compliance means. However, we feel that the sheer size of what we have spent for internal control is the best evidence that we are complying with the Act. We regard this expenditure as good insurance."

## GUIDELINES TO STRONG INTERNAL CONTROL

### Organization plan to establish responsibility for every function

An organization plan should indicate clearly the departments or persons responsible for such functions as purchasing, receiving incoming shipments, maintaining accounting records, approving credit to customers, and preparing the payroll. One person should be clearly responsible for each function. To illustrate the need for fixing responsibility, assume that all employees were given authority to make purchases for a business. The probable result would be duplication of orders, overstocking of some goods, and shortages of others. It would be difficult if not impossible, to determine who was at fault.

When an individual or department is assigned responsibility for a function, it is imperative that authority to make decisions also be granted. The assignment of responsibilities and all accounting and internal control policies should be in writing so that responsibility for poor performance cannot be shifted. The lines of authority and responsibility can conveniently be shown on an organization chart; a portion of an organization chart of a manufacturing company is illustrated on page 221.

As indicated in this organization chart, the direction of operations and custody of assets should be separate from the accounting function. An individual charged with the custody of assets or with the direction of operations may make errors or knowingly violate company policies; consequently, such individuals should not be involved in the accounting function because this would enable them to conceal such errors and irregularities.

### Control of transactions

If management is to direct the activities of a business according to plan, every transaction should go through four steps: It should be ***authorized, approved, executed,*** and ***recorded.*** For example, consider the sale of merchandise on credit. The top management of the company may ***authorize*** the sale of merchandise on credit to customers who meet certain standards. The manager of the credit and collection department may ***approve*** a sale of given dollar amount to a particular customer. The sales transaction is ***executed*** by preparing a sales invoice and delivering the merchandise to the credit customer. The sales transaction is ***recorded*** in the accounting department by debiting Accounts Receivable and crediting Sales.

Consider for a moment the losses that would probably be incurred if this

**Portion of an Organization Chart**

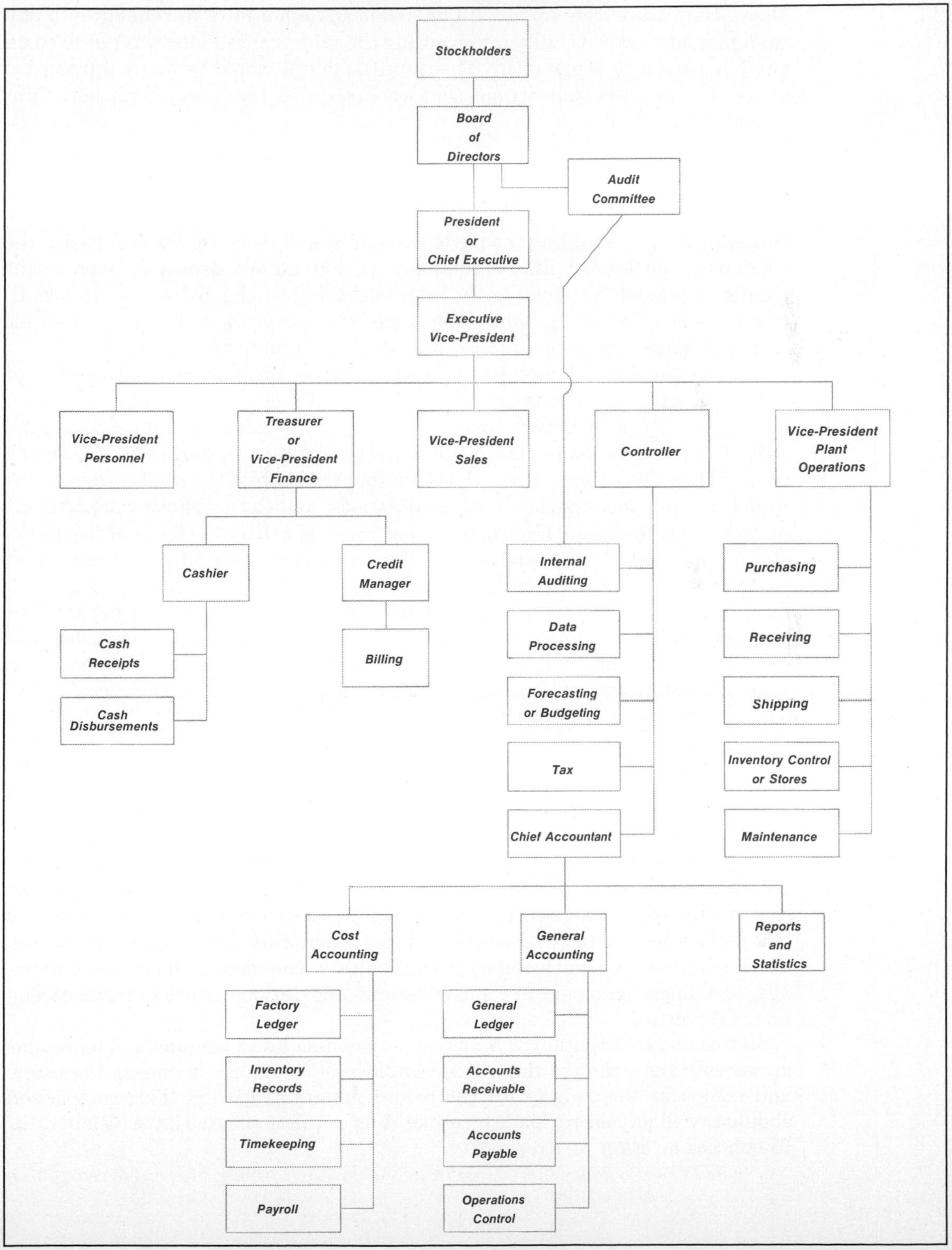

internal control of transactions did not exist. Assume, for example, that all employees in a store were free to sell on credit any amount of merchandise to any customer, and responsibility for recording the sales transactions was not fixed on any one person or department. The result no doubt would be many unrecorded sales; of those sales transactions that were recorded, many would represent uncollectible receivables.

### Subdivision of duties strengthens internal control

Procedures for controlling the purchase and sale of merchandise emphasize the subdivision of duties within a company so that no one person or department handles a transaction completely from beginning to end. When duties are divided in this manner, the work of one employee serves to verify that of another and any errors which occur tend to be detected promptly.

To illustrate the development of internal control through subdivision of duties, let us review the procedures for a sale of merchandise on account by a wholesaler. The sales department of the company is responsible for securing the order from the customer; the credit department must approve the customer's credit before the order is filled; the stock room assembles the goods ordered; the shipping department packs and ships the goods; and the accounting department records the transaction. Each department receives written evidence of the action of the other departments and reviews the documents describing the transaction to see that the actions taken correspond in all details. The shipping department, for instance, does not release the merchandise until after the credit department has approved the customer as a credit risk. The accounting department does not record the sale until it has received documentary evidence that (1) the goods were ordered, (2) the extension of credit was approved, and (3) the merchandise was shipped to the customer.

**Separation of accounting and custody of assets** An employee who has custody of an asset or access to an asset should not maintain the accounting record of that asset. The person having custody of an asset will not be inclined to waste it, steal it, or give it away if he or she is aware that another employee is maintaining a record of the asset. The employee maintaining the accounting record does not have access to the asset and therefore has no incentive to falsify the record. If one person has custody of assets and also maintains the accounting records, there is both opportunity and incentive to falsify the records to conceal a shortage. The diagram on page 223 illustrates how separation of duties creates strong internal control.

In this diagram Employee A has custody of assets and Employee B maintains an accounting record of the assets. Employee C periodically counts the assets and compares the count with the record maintained by B. This comparison should reveal any errors made by either A or B unless the two have collaborated to conceal an error or irregularity.

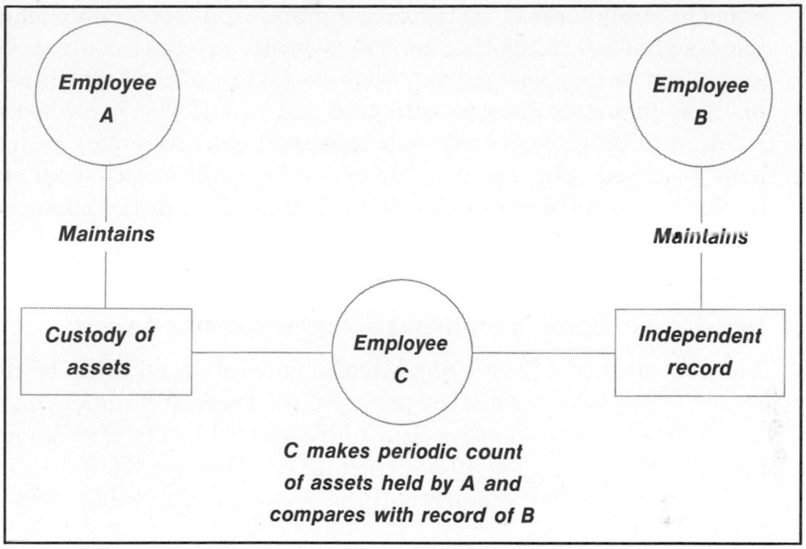


**Separation of responsibility for related transactions** When merchandise is sold to a customer on credit, the act of delivering the merchandise to the customer is closely related to the recording of the account receivable and to the later collection of the receivable. Responsibility for these related transactions should be assigned to different individuals or departments and documentary evidence should be created to record the action taken by each.

Assume for a moment, as an example of unsatisfactory internal control, that one employee was permitted to take the customer's order, approve the credit terms, get the merchandise from the stock room, deliver the goods to the customer, prepare the invoice, enter the transaction in the accounting records, and collect the account receivable. If this employee made errors, such as selling to poor credit risks, forgetting to enter the sale in the accounting records, or perhaps delivering more merchandise to the customer than was charged for, no one would know the difference. By the time such errors came to light, substantial losses would have been incurred.

**Prevention of fraud** If one employee is permitted to handle all aspects of a transaction, the danger of fraud is increased. Studies of fraud cases suggest that many individuals may be tempted into dishonest acts if given complete control of company property. Most of these persons, however, would not engage in fraud if doing so required collaboration with another employee. Losses through employee dishonesty occur in a variety of ways: merchandise may be stolen; payments by customers may be withheld; suppliers may be overpaid with a view to kickbacks to employees; and lower prices may be allowed to favored customers. The opportunities for fraud are almost endless if all aspects of a sale or purchase transaction are concentrated in the hands of one employee.

**Rotation of employees** To the extent practicable, rotation of employees from one job assignment to another may strengthen internal control. When employees know that other persons may soon be taking over their duties, they are more likely to maintain records with care and to follow established procedures. The rotation of employees may also bring to light any errors or irregularities that have occurred. This same line of reasoning indicates that all employees should be required to take annual vacations and all their duties should be performed by others during such vacation periods.

### Serially numbered documents—another control device

Another method of achieving internal control, in addition to the subdivision of duties, consists of having the printer include serial numbers on such documents as purchase orders, sales invoices, and checks. The use of serial numbers makes it possible to account for all documents. In other words, if a sales invoice is misplaced or concealed, the break in the sequence of numbers will call attention to the discrepancy.

### Competence of personnel

Even the best-designed system of internal control will not work satisfactorily unless the people assigned to operate it are competent. Each person involved must have a level of competence sufficient for the work assigned and a willingness to assume responsibility for performance. Competence and integrity of employees are in part developed through training programs, but they are also related to the policies for selection of personnel, the adequacy of supervision, and the complexity of the system.

### Financial forecasts

A financial forecast, as defined in Chapter 1, is a plan of operations for a future period. Specific goals are set for each division of the business as, for example, the expected volume of sales, the amounts of expenses, and the planned cash balance. Actual results achieved month by month can then be compared with the planned results and management's attention is promptly directed to any areas of substandard performance. The system of internal control is strengthened by the use of forecasts because errors or irregularities which cause actual results to differ from planned results will be identified and fully investigated.

### Internal auditing

In all large organizations an important element of internal control is the internal auditing staff. Internal auditors are professional-level employees with the responsibility of investigating throughout the company the efficiency of operations in every department or other organizational unit. They are continuously studying both administrative and accounting controls and reporting to top management on compliance with company standards and on problems which require strengthening of internal controls.

### Continuing review of the system of internal control

Business policies, products, and operating methods are in a constant state of change. Government regulations imposed on business (such as wage and price controls and a multitude of required reports) also are being constantly changed. Consequently, the system of internal control must continually be reviewed and updated if it is to function effectively. In the large corporation, the internal auditing staff devotes full time on a year-round basis to reviewing internal control and recommending changes. In all businesses, large or small, one major reason to retain a CPA firm to perform an annual audit is to benefit from a thorough independent evaluation of the system of internal control by competent professionals.

### Limitations of internal control

Although internal control is highly effective in increasing the reliability of accounting data and in protecting against fraud, no system of internal control is foolproof. Two or more dishonest employees working in collusion can defeat the system—temporarily. Carelessness by employees and misunderstanding of instructions can cause a breakdown in controls. The much-publicized Equity Funding management fraud case demonstrated that top management can circumvent the system of internal control for a considerable span of time if it is determined to do so.

### Internal control in the small business

Satisfactory internal control is more difficult to achieve in a small business than a large one because, with only a few employees, it is not possible to arrange extensive subdivision of duties. However, in many small businesses, internal control is unnecessarily weak because management does not understand the basic principles of internal control or neglects to give attention to the problem.

Some internal controls are suitable for even the smallest business, with only one or two employees. An example is the use of serial numbers on checks, sales invoices, and other documents to ensure that no document is misplaced and forgotten. Another example is insistence that documentary evidence be created to verify an invoice before it is paid, and that documents supporting the issuance of a check be marked paid when the check is issued.

An essential element in maintaining a reasonable degree of internal control in the small business is active participation by the owner-manager in strategic control procedures. These procedures will be considered in later chapters dealing with such topics as cash and receivables.

### Internal control in perspective

A description of internal control solely in terms of the prevention of fraud and the detection of errors represents too narrow a concept of this managerial technique. The building of a strong system of internal control is an accepted means of increasing operational efficiency.

In appraising the merits of various internal control procedures, the question of their cost cannot be ignored. Too elaborate a system of internal control may entail greater operating costs than are justified by the protection gained. For this reason the system of internal control must be tailored to meet the requirements of the individual business. Internal control measures which are appropriate in a large corporation (such as a professional staff of internal auditors) may be quite unrealistic for a small business. In most organizations, however, proper subdivision of duties and careful design of accounting procedures will provide a basis for adequate internal control and at the same time will contribute to efficient operation of the business.

### Fidelity bonds

Since no system of internal control can provide absolute protection against losses from dishonest employees, many companies require that employees handling cash or other negotiable assets be bonded. A ***fidelity bond*** is a type of insurance contract in which a bonding company agrees to reimburse an employer up to agreed dollar limits for losses caused by fraud or embezzlement by bonded employees. The term ***embezzlement*** refers to the fraudulent action of an officer or employee who takes for his own use cash or other assets with which he has been entrusted.

Fidelity bonds are not a substitute for internal control; they do little or nothing to assure reliable accounting data, to prevent wasteful inefficient use of company assets, or to encourage compliance with company policies. However, they are useful in protecting a company from losses due to embezzlement. Particularly in a small business with too few employees to permit much subdivision of duties, fidelity bonds may be very appropriate. It is often the most trusted employee who turns out to be an embezzler. The very fact that an employee is trusted completely may explain why he or she is given full access to cash and accounting records and assigned a combination of duties which makes large-scale embezzlement an easy matter.

## INTERNAL CONTROLS OVER THE PURCHASE AND SALE OF MERCHANDISE

### Business documents and procedures

Carefully designed business documents and procedures for using them are necessary to ensure that all transactions are properly authorized, approved, executed, and recorded. We have already considered the waste and confusion that would arise if every employee in a large business were authorized to purchase merchandise for the business and no standard forms or procedures had been provided to keep track of these purchases. The opportunity for fraud by dishonest employees, as well as for accidental errors and waste of resources, would be unlimited under such a haphazard method of operation.

Each step in ordering, receiving, and making payment for merchandise purchases should be controlled and recorded. A similar approach is necessary to establish control over the sales function. Various business documents are used to make sure that both buyer and seller have a clear understanding of the type, quantity, and price of merchandise, the terms of payment, and the method of delivery. Some of the most important of these business documents are

| Business Document | Initiated by | Sent to |
|---|---|---|
| Purchase requisition<br>Issued when quantity of goods on hand falls below established reorder point | Departmental sales managers or inventory control department | Purchasing department |
| Purchase order<br>Specifies prices, quantities, and method of transportation | Purchasing department | Original to selling company (vendor, supplier), copies to buyer's accounting, receiving, and finance departments |
| Invoice<br>Confirms that goods have been shipped and requests payment | Seller (supplier) | Accounting department of buying company |
| Receiving report<br>Based on count and inspection of goods received | Receiving department of buying company | Original to accounting department, copies to purchasing department and to department requisitioning goods |
| Invoice approval form | Accounting department of buying company | Finance department, to support issuance of check. Returned to accounting department with carbon copy of check. |

**Informal procedures in a small business** Very small companies of course are not divided into departments. The owner or manager may personally perform the purchasing function by placing orders with sales representatives of wholesalers and manufacturers. These sales representatives make regular visits to the store and may carry catalogs and samples to illustrate the products offered.

The owner-manager of a small store is sufficiently familiar with the stock of merchandise to know what items need to be replenished. A notebook record of items to be ordered may be maintained by writing down each day any items which the owner observes to be running low. A sales representative of a wholesaler or manufacturer who visits the store will write up the order in an order book. A copy of the order, showing the quantities and prices of all items ordered, is left with the store owner. Many small companies could easily improve their efficiency by consistent use of serially numbered business documents of the types outlined above, even though operations are not departmentalized.

### Purchase orders

In many businesses and especially in large organizations, the buying company uses its own purchase order forms. A purchase order of the Zenith Company issued to Adams Manufacturing Company is illustrated below.

***Serially numbered purchase order***

**PURCHASE ORDER** — ***Order No. 999***

***ZENITH COMPANY***
***10 Fairway Avenue, San Francisco, California***

***To:*** Adams Manufacturing Company — ***Date*** Nov. 10, 19__
19 Union Street — ***Ship via*** Jones Truck Co.
Kansas City, Missouri — ***Terms:*** 2/10, n/30

***Please enter our order for the following:***

| Quantity | Description | Price | Total |
|---|---|---|---|
| 15 sets | Model S irons | $60.00 | $900.00 |
| 50 dozen | X3Y Shur-Par golf balls | 7.00 | 350.00 |

***Zenith Company***

***By*** D.D. McCarthy

In large companies in which the functions of placing orders, receiving merchandise, and making payment are lodged in separate departments, several copies of the purchase order are usually prepared. The original is sent to the supplier; this purchase order is an authorization to deliver the merchandise and to submit a bill based on the prices listed. Carbon copies of the purchase order are usually routed to the accounting department, purchasing department, receiving department, and finance department.

Note that the illustrated purchase order bears a serial number, 999. When purchase orders are serially numbered, there can be no doubt as to how many orders have been issued. Each department authorized to receive copies of purchase orders should account for every number in the series, thus guarding against the loss or nondelivery of any document.

When merchandise is ordered by telephone, a formal written purchase order should nevertheless be prepared and sent to the supplier to confirm the verbal instuctions. Orders for office equipment, supplies, and other assets as well as merchandise should also be in writing to avoid misunderstanding and to provide a permanent record of the order.

The issuance of a purchase order does not call for any debit or credit entries in the accounting records of either the prospective buyer or seller. The company which receives an order does not consider (for accounting purposes) that a sale has been made until the merchandise is delivered. At that point ownership of the goods changes, and both buyer and seller should make accounting entries to record the transaction.

## Invoices

When a manufacturer or wholesaler receives an order for its products, it takes two actions. One is to ship the goods to the customer and the other is to send the customer an invoice. Many companies follow the policy that an invoice must be mailed to the customer on the day the goods are shipped. By the act of shipping the merchandise, the seller is giving up ownership of one type of asset, inventory; by issuing the invoice the seller is recording ownership of another form of asset, an account receivable.

An invoice contains a description of the goods being sold, the quantities, prices, credit terms, and method of shipment. The illustration below shows an invoice issued by Adams Manufacturing Company in response to the previously illustrated purchase order from Zenith Company.

*Invoice is basis for accounting entry*

***INVOICE***

***ADAMS MANUFACTURING COMPANY***
***19 Union Street***
***Kansas City, Missouri***

***Sold to*** Zenith Company — ***Invoice no.*** ***777***
10 Fairway Avenue — ***Invoice date*** Nov. 15, 19__
San Francisco, Calif. — ***Your order no.*** 999
***Shipped to*** Same — ***Date shipped*** Nov. 15, 19__
***Terms*** 2/10, n/30 — ***Shipped via*** Jones Truck Co.

| Quantity | Description | Price | Amount |
|---|---|---|---|
| 15 sets | Model S irons | $60.00 | $ 900.00 |
| 50 dozen | X3Y Shur-Par golf balls | 7.00 | 350.00 |
| | | | $1,250.00 |

From the viewpoint of the seller, an invoice is a ***sales invoice;*** from the buyer's viewpoint it is a ***purchase invoice.*** The invoice is the basis for an entry in the accounting records of both the seller and the buyer because it evidences the transfer of ownership of goods. At the time of issuing the invoice, the selling company makes an entry debiting Accounts Receivable and crediting Sales. The buying company however, does not record the invoice as a liability until after making a careful verification of the transaction, as indicated in the following section.

**Verification of invoice by purchaser** Upon receipt of an invoice, the purchasing company should verify the following aspects of the transaction:

**1** The invoice agrees with the purchase order as to prices, quantities, and other provisions.
**2** The invoice is arithmetically correct in all extensions of price times quantity and in the addition of amounts.
**3** The goods covered by the invoice have been received and are in satisfactory condition.

Evidence that the merchandise has been received in good condition must be obtained from the receiving department. It is the function of the receiving department to receive all incoming goods, to inspect them as to quality and condition, and to determine the quantities received by counting, measuring, or weighing. The receiving department should prepare a serially numbered report for each shipment received; one copy of this ***receiving report*** is sent to the accounting department for use in verifying the invoice.

The verification of the invoice in the accounting department is accomplished by comparing the purchase order, the invoice, and the receiving report. Comparison of these documents establishes that the goods described in the invoice were actually ordered, have been received in good condition, and were billed at the prices specified in the purchase order. To ensure that this comparison of documents is made in every case and that the arithmetical accuracy of the invoice is proved, it is customary to require an invoice approval form to be attached to each invoice and initialed by the employees performing each step in the verification work. Some companies prefer to use a rubber stamp imprint of this form to place the verification data directly on the vendor's invoice.

When these verification procedures have been completed, the invoice is recorded as a liability by an entry debiting the Purchases account and crediting Accounts Payable.

## Debit and credit memoranda (debit memos; credit memos)

In the process of verifying an invoice for merchandise purchased, the buyer sometimes finds discrepancies that require adjustment between buyer and seller. For example, there may be arithmetic errors in the invoice; merchandise may have been received in damaged condition; quantities of goods received may have been more or less than the quantities ordered or different from the quantities billed. If the discrepancy is merely an arithmetic error in the invoice or if a shipment contains goods that were not ordered, the purchasing company can easily make the required adjustment. Other situations, such as defects in merchandise, may require negotiation with the seller. In all cases when the purchasing company makes an adjustment, it must notify the seller of the details. It does so by sending the seller a ***debit memorandum*** or a ***credit memorandum.***

A debit memorandum (or debit memo) is a business document bearing the words "We debit your account." A debit memo issued by the buying company thus informs the seller that its account (an account payable) is being debited (reduced) in the records of the buyer, and explains the circumstances. A credit memo issued by the buyer has the opposite effect of informing the seller that its account is being credited (increased) on the buyer's records. Since an error in a purchase invoice may cause the total amount to be either overstated or understated, it is clear that a purchasing company may need to issue either a debit memo or a credit memo to correct the error. If the buying company issues a debit memo, it will record the action by ***debiting*** Accounts Payable and crediting Purchase Returns and Allowances. If the buying company issues a credit memo, it will debit Purchases and ***credit*** Accounts Payable.

All incoming merchandise should be counted and inspected in the receiving department of the buyer. If the buying company finds damaged or defective units in the shipment, it will get in touch with the seller to negotiate an adjustment. Pending a settlement, the buyer may record the invoice as a liability in the full amount of the invoice. When agreement is reached on an adjustment or a return of merchandise, the seller will issue a credit memo to the buyer. The seller will record the issuance of a credit memo by debiting Sales Returns and Allowances and crediting Accounts Receivable. On the seller's books, the account with the buyer is an account receivable, and must be credited in order to reduce it.

***Credit memorandum issued by seller of goods***

**ADAMS MANUFACTURING COMPANY**
**19 Union Street**
**Kansas City, Missouri**

**Credit memorandum no. 102**

**To:** Zenith Company **Date:** Nov. 22, 19__

10 Fairway Avenue

San Francisco, Calif.

***We credit your account as follows:***

Merchandise returned, 50 DLX gloves,
our invoice no. 825 .......... $450.00

The buyer, upon receipt of a credit memo from the seller, will debit Accounts Payable and credit Purchase Returns and Allowances. For example, if Zenith

Company (the buyer) receives a $450 credit memo from Adams Manufacturing Company (the seller), Zenith will record the receipt of the credit memorandum with the following entry:

*Entry based on receipt of credit memo*

| | | |
|---|---|---|
| ***Accounts Payable*** | ***450*** | |
| ***Purchase Returns & Allowances*** | | ***450*** |
| ***Received credit memo no. 102 from Adams Manufacturing Company to acknowledge reduction in our liability to them because of return of defective merchandise.*** | | |

In summary, a debit or credit memo may be issued by either the buyer or seller. The document takes its name from the party which issues it. If the issuer is debiting its account with the other party, the document is a ***debit*** memorandum. If the issuer is ***crediting*** its account with the other party, the document is a ***credit*** memorandum.

Strong internal control is needed over the issuance of credit memoranda. For example, a dishonest employee of the selling company might issue an unjustified credit memo and arrange to split the fraudulent amount with the buyer. To issue a credit memo is to surrender assets. Among internal control measures are (1) use of serially numbered credit memos with regular accounting for all numbers in the series, and (2) review and approval in writing of all credit memos by a designated official prior to their issuance. The individual authorized to originate credit memos should be an employee who does not have access to cash or to accounting records. The following case illustrates the problems which may result from failure to follow internal control procedures for credit memoranda.

ILLUSTRATIVE CASE Duncan & Co., certified public accountants, was making its first audit of Domino Corporation, a manufacturing business. The CPAs were informed by the controller of the client company that credit memos for merchandise returned by customers were issued only after employees in the receiving department had counted and inspected the returned merchandise and issued a serially numbered receiving report. This receiving report number was entered on the credit memo. In addition, written approval of the return was required to be obtained from Domino's sales department.

To determine whether this internal control was being followed consistently in practice, the auditors obtained from the files a random sample of credit memos. In comparing the dates of the credit memos with the dates of the related receiving reports, the auditors found that in numerous cases the credit memos had been issued several weeks before the return of the merchandise. In other instances, credit memos had been issued for merchandise which had never been returned by the customers. Most of the credit memos lacked any approval signature. The auditors questioned several employees who had prepared credit memos and found widespread disagreement as to the authorized procedures.

## Recording purchase invoices at net price

Most well-managed companies have a firm policy of taking all purchase discounts offered. The recording of purchase invoices at their gross amount and making payment of a reduced amount within the discount period was described in Chapter 5. Some companies which regularly take advantage of all available purchase discounts prefer the alternative method of recording purchase invoices at the net amount after discount rather than at the gross amount. If the amount which the buyer intends to pay is the invoice amount minus a cash discount, why not record this net amount as the liability at the time the invoice is received? For example, if Zenith Company receives a $10,000 purchase invoice bearing terms of 2/10, n/30, the entry could be

*Entry for purchase: net price method*

| | | | |
|---|---|---|---|
| *Nov. 3* | *Purchases* | *9,800* | |
| | *Accounts Payable* | | *9,800* |
| | *To record purchase invoice from Adams Manufacturing Company less 2% cash discount available.* | | |

Assuming that the invoice is paid within 10 days, the entry for the payment is as follows:

*Entry for payment: net price method*

| | | | |
|---|---|---|---|
| *Nov. 13* | *Accounts Payable* | *9,800* | |
| | *Cash* | | *9,800* |
| | *To record payment of $10,000 invoice from Adams Manufacturing Company less 2% cash discount.* | | |

Through oversight or carelessness, the purchasing company occasionally may fail to make payment of an invoice within the 10-day discount period. If such a delay occurred in paying the invoice from Adams Manufacturing Company, the full amount of the invoice would have to be paid rather than the recorded liability of $9,800. The journal entry to record the late payment on, say, December 3, is as follows:

*Entry for payment after discount period: net price method*

| | | | |
|---|---|---|---|
| *Dec. 3* | *Accounts Payable* | *9,800* | |
| | *Purchase Discounts Lost* | *200* | |
| | *Cash* | | *10,000* |
| | *To record payment of invoice and loss of discount by delaying payment beyond the discount period.* | | |

Under this method the cost of goods purchased is properly recorded at $9,800, and the additional payment of $200 caused by failure to pay the invoice promptly is placed in a special expense account designed to attract the attention of management. The gross price method of recording invoices described in Chapter 5 shows the amount of purchase discounts ***taken*** each period; the net price method now under discussion shows the amount of purchase discounts ***lost*** each period. The latter method has the advantage of drawing the attention of management to a breakdown in internal control. The fact that a purchase discount has been taken does not require attention by management, but a discount lost because of inefficiency in processing accounts payable does call for managerial investigation.

As previously suggested, inefficiency and delay in paying invoices should not be concealed by adding the penalty of lost discount to the cost of merchandise purchased. The purchases should be stated at the net price available by taking cash discounts; the Purchase Discounts Lost account should be shown in the income statement as an operating expense.

Both the gross price method and the net price method are acceptable and commonly used. In working problems the student should be alert for an indication of which method is to be used.

### Trade discounts

Many manufacturers and wholesalers publish annual catalogs in which their products are listed at suggested retail prices. Substantial reductions from the ***list prices*** (listed retail prices) are offered to dealers. These reductions from list prices (often as much as 30 or 40%) are called ***trade discounts.*** As market conditions change, the schedule of discounts is revised. This is a more convenient way to revise actual selling prices quickly than by publishing a new catalog.

Trade discounts are not recorded in the accounting records of either the seller or the buyer. A sale of merchandise is recorded at the actual selling price and the trade discount is merely a device for computing the actual sales price. From the viewpoint of the company purchasing goods, the significant price is not the list price but the amount which must be paid, and this amount is recorded as the cost of the merchandise.

For example, if a manufacturer sells goods to a retailer at a list price of $1,000 with a trade discount of 40%, the transaction will be recorded by the manufacturer as a $600 sale and by the retailer as a $600 Purchase. Because trade discounts are not recorded in the accounts they should be clearly distinguished from cash discounts.

### Control over approved invoices

The procedures for proper verification of a purchase invoice were described earlier in this chapter. After a purchase invoice has been approved for payment, it should be filed in a manner which assures that the required payment date will not be overlooked. For example, the invoice of November 3 from Adams Manufacturing Company could be placed in a "tickler file," a file with index cards bearing dates. Since this invoice must be paid by November 13 to take advantage of the cash discount, the invoice is filed in front of the index card for November 13. On that date the invoice is removed from the tickler file and sent to the cashier. The cashier prepares a check for $9,800 payable to Adams Manufacturing Company, enters the check number on the invoice approval form, and forwards both documents to the treasurer. The treasurer signs the check, mails it, and marks the invoice "Paid." The invoice and the attached approval sheet are then returned to the accounting department and placed in an alphabetical file of paid invoices.

### Sales taxes

Sales taxes are levied by many states and cities on certain retail sales. Usually certain classes of sales are exempt, notably food and some commodities, such as gasoline and cigarettes, already subject to special excise taxes. To restrict the practice of purchasing outside the state to avoid the tax, some states levy a supplementary ***use tax,*** applicable to goods purchased outside the state and brought in.

Typically a sales tax is imposed on the consumer, but the seller must collect the tax, file tax returns at times specified by law, and remit a percentage of the reported sales. The actual tax collected by the selling company from its customers may be greater or less than the amount paid to the government because no tax is collected on sales under a certain amount, and due to rounding of pennies, the tax collected on a given sale may be slightly more than the specified percentage.

A sales tax may be collected when a cash sale is made or it may be included in the charge to the customer's account on a credit sale. The liability to the governmental unit for sales taxes may be recorded at the time the sale is made as follows:

*Sales tax recorded at time of sale*

| | | |
|---|---|---|
| *Accounts Receivable (or Cash)* | *1,050* | |
| *Sales Tax Payable* | | *50* |
| *Sales* | | *1,000* |
| *To record sale of $1,000 subject to 5% sales tax.* | | |

Instead of recording the sales tax liability at the time of sale, some businesses prefer to credit the Sales account with the entire amount collected, including the sales tax, and to make an adjustment at the end of each period to reflect sales tax payable. For example, suppose that the total recorded sales for the period under this method were $315,000. Since the Sales account includes both the sales price and the sales tax (say, 5%), it is apparent that $315,000 is 105% of the actual sales figure. Actual sales are $300,000 ($315,000 ÷ 1.05) and the amount of sales tax due is $15,000. (Proof: 5% of $300,000 = $15,000.) The entry to record the liability for sales taxes would be

*Sales tax recorded as adjustment of sales*

| | | |
|---|---|---|
| *Sales* | *15,000* | |
| *Sales Tax Payable* | | *15,000* |
| *To remove sales taxes of 5% on $300,000 of sales from the Sales account, and reflect as a liability.* | | |

Any discrepancy between the tax due and the amount actually collected from customers, under this method, would be absorbed automatically in the net sales figure. If certain of the products being sold (such as food) are not subject to the tax, it is necessary to keep a record of taxable and nontaxable sales.

## KEY TERMS INTRODUCED OR EMPHASIZED IN CHAPTER 6

**Credit memorandum** A document issued to show a reduction in the amount owed by a customer because of goods returned, a defect in the goods or services provided, or an error.

**Debit memorandum** A document issued by a buyer to show a decrease in the amount previously recorded as owing to a seller. May also be issued by a seller to increase the amount previously recorded as receivable from a customer.

**Documentation** All the charts, forms, tapes, reports, and other business papers that guide and describe the working of a company's system of accounting and internal control.

**Embezzlement** Theft by a person of assets entrusted to him or her.

**Fidelity bond** A form of insurance contract in which a bonding company agrees to reimburse an employer for losses caused by theft by bonded employees.

**Financial forecast** A plan of operations for a future period with expected results expressed in dollars.

**Fraud** Dishonest acts intended to deceive, often involving the theft of assets and falsification of accounting records and financial statements.

**Internal accounting controls** Measures that relate to protection of assets and to the reliability of accounting information and financial statements.

**Internal administrative controls** A subcategory of internal controls which apply principally to operational efficiency and compliance with company policy and which do not bear directly on the dependability of financial statements.

**Internal auditing** An activity carried on in large organizations by a professional staff to investigate and evaluate the system of internal control on a year-round basis. Also to evaluate the efficiency of individual departments within the organization.

**Internal control** All measures used by a business to guard against errors, waste, or fraud and to assure the reliability of accounting data. Designed to aid in the efficient operation of a business and to encourage compliance with company policies.

**Invoice** An itemized statement of goods being bought or sold. Shows quantities, prices, and credit terms. Serves as the basis for an entry in the accounting records of both seller and buyer because it evidences the transfer of ownership of goods.

**Net price method** A policy of recording purchase invoices at amounts net of (reduced by) cash discounts.

**Organization chart** A diagram showing organizational lines of authority and responsibility, with emphasis on separation of functions.

**Purchase order** A serially numbered document sent by the purchasing department of a business to a supplier or vendor for the purpose of ordering materials or services.

**Receiving report** An internal form prepared by the receiving department for each incoming shipment showing the quantity and condition of goods received.

**Sales tax** A tax levied by most states and many cities on certain retail sales. Typically the seller must collect the tax and file returns with the taxing agency.

**Serial numbering of documents** The assignment of an unbroken sequence of numbers to a given class of documents, such as checks or invoices, so that the omission or loss of a document will be readily apparent.

**Trade discount** A percentage reduction from the list price of merchandise allowed to dealers by manufacturers and wholesalers; not recorded in the accounts because the net price is regarded as the actual sales price.

## REVIEW QUESTIONS

1 What is the purpose of a system of internal control? List four specific objectives which the measures included in a system of internal control are designed to achieve.

2 Criticize the following statement: "Internal control may be defined as all those measures which a business uses to prevent fraud."

3 Ross Corporation is a medium-sized business with 20 office employees. State two or three guidelines or principles which should be followed in assigning duties to the various employees so that internal control will be as strong as possible.

4 State a general principle to be observed in assigning duties among employees with respect to the purchase of merchandise so that strong internal control will be achieved.

5 Suggest a control device to protect a business against the loss or nondelivery of invoices, purchase orders, and other documents which are routed from one department to another.

6 Criticize the following statement: "In our company we get things done by requiring that a person who initiates a transaction follow it through in all particulars. For example, an employee who issues a purchase order is held responsible for inspecting the merchandise upon arrival, approving the invoice, and preparing the check in payment of the purchase. If any error is made, we know definitely whom to blame."

7 If a company obtains a fidelity bond protecting it against loss from dishonest actions on the part of any of its officers or employees, would it still be necessary for the company to maintain a system of internal control? Explain.

8 What is the principal difference between an audit by independent public accountants and the work done by internal auditors?

9 Explain why the operations and custodianship functions should be separate from the accounting function.

10 A system of internal control is often said to include two major types of controls: administrative controls and accounting controls. Explain the nature of each group and give an example of each.

11 A CPA makes a study and evaluation of internal controls as part of an annual audit. Is the CPA equally concerned with administrative controls and accounting controls? Explain.

12 Company A sells merchandise to B on credit and two days later agrees that B can return a portion of the merchandise. B does so. What document should Company A issue to record the return? What accounts on Company A's records are affected by this return of merchandise?

13 Blair Manufacturing Company sells appliances on both a wholesale and a retail basis and publishes an annual catalog listing products at retail prices. At what price should the sale be recorded when an item listed in the catalog at $400 is delivered to a wholesaler entitled to a 30% trade discount?

14 A company which has received a shipment of merchandise and a related invoice from the supplier sometimes finds it necessary to issue a debit memorandum. Describe a situation that would justify such action by the purchasing company.

15 Distinguish between a trade discount and a cash discount.

16 What accounting entry, if any, is required on the part of the company issuing a purchase order? On the part of the company receiving the purchase order?

17 Name three documents (business papers) which are needed by the accounting department to verify that a purchase of merchandise has occurred and that payment of the related liability should be made.

**18** Are publicly owned corporations which do business solely within the continental United States affected by the Foreign Corrupt Practices Act of 1977? Explain.

## EXERCISES

*Ex. 6-1* A strong system of internal control serves to protect a company's assets against waste, fraud, and inefficient use. Fidelity bonds provide a means by which a company may recover losses caused by dishonest acts of employees. Would it be reasonable for a company to maintain a strong system of internal control and also pay for a fidelity bond? Explain.

*Ex. 6-2* Jet Auto Supply Store received from a manufacturer a shipment of 200 gasoline cans. Harold Abbott, who handles all purchasing activities, telephoned the manufacturer and explained that only 100 cans were ordered. The manufacturer replied that two separate purchase orders for 100 cans each had recently been received from Jet Auto Supply Store. Harold Abbott is sure that the manufacturer is in error and is merely trying to justify an excess shipment, but he can find no means of proving the point. What is the missing element in internal control over purchases by Jet Auto Supply Store?

*Ex. 6-3* Robert Hale, owner of Hale Equipment, a merchandising business, explains to you how duties have been assigned to employees. Hale states: "In order to have clearly defined responsibility for each phase of our operations, I have made one employee responsible for the purchasing, receiving, and storage of merchandise. Another employee has been charged with responsibility for maintaining the accounting records and for making all collections from customers. I have assigned to a third employee responsibility for maintaining personnel records for all our employees and for timekeeping, preparation of payroll records, and distribution of payroll checks. My goal in setting up this organization plan is to have a strong system of internal control."

You are to evaluate Hale's plan of organization and explain fully the reasoning underlying any criticism you may have.

*Ex. 6-4* James Company sold merchandise to Bay Company on credit. On the next day, James Company received a telephone call from Bay Company stating that one of the items delivered was defective. James Company immediately issued credit memorandum no. 163 for $100 to Bay Company.

**a** Give the accounting entry required in James Company's records to record the issuance of the credit memorandum.

**b** Give the accounting entry required on Bay Company's accounting records when the credit memorandum is received. (Assume that Bay Company had previously recorded the purchase at the full amount of the seller's invoice and had not issued a debit memorandum.)

*Ex. 6-5* Taft Company received purchase invoices during July totaling $42,000, all of which carried credit terms of 2/10, n/30. It was the company's regular policy to take advantage of all available cash discounts, but because of employee vacations during July, there was confusion and delay in making payments to suppliers, and none of the July invoices was paid within the discount period.

**a** Explain briefly two alternative ways in which the amount of purchases might be presented in the July income statement.

**b** What method of recording purchase invoices can you suggest that would call to the attention of the Taft Company management the inefficiency of operations in July?

*Ex. 6-6* The Hasagami General Store operates in an area in which a 6% sales tax is levied on all products handled by the store. On cash sales, the salesclerks include the sales tax in the amount collected from the customer and ring up the entire amount on the cash register without recording separately the tax liability. On credit sales, the customer is charged for the list price of the merchandise plus 6%, and the entire amount is debited to Accounts Receivable and credited to the Sales account. On sales of less than one dollar, the tax collected is rounded to the nearest cent.

Sales tax must be remitted to the government quarterly. At March 31 the Sales account showed a balance of $152,360 for the three-month period ended March 31.

**a** What amount of sales tax is owed at March 31? (Round to nearest dollar.)
**b** Give the journal entry to record the sales tax liability on the books.

*Ex. 6-7* Give the journal entry, if any, to be prepared for each of these events:

**a** Received a telephone order from a customer for $1,800 worth of merchandise.
**b** Issued a purchase order to Mack Company for merchandise costing $2,500.
**c** Received the merchandise ordered from Mack Company and an invoice for $2,500; credit terms 2/10, n/30. The net price method is in use.
**d** Delivered the $1,800 of merchandise ordered in **a** above to the customer and mailed an invoice; credit terms 10 e.o.m.
**e** Mailed check to Mack Company in settlement for purchase in **c** above.
**f** Customer returned $400 of goods delivered in **d** above, which were unsatisfactory. A credit memorandum was issued for that amount.

## PROBLEMS

### Group A

*6A-1* At the Uptown Theater, the cashier is located in a box office at the front of the building. The cashier receives cash from customers and operates a ticket machine which ejects serially numbered tickets. The serial number appears on each end of the ticket. The tickets come from the printer in large rolls which fit into the ticket machine and are removed at the end of each cashier's working period.

After purchasing a ticket from the cashier, in order to be admitted to the theater a customer must hand the ticket to a doorman stationed some 50 feet from the box office at the entrance to the theater lobby. The doorman tears the ticket in half, opens the door for the customer, and returns the ticket stub to the customer. The other half of the ticket is dropped by the doorman into a locked box.

**Instructions**

**a** Describe the internal controls present in Uptown Theater's method of handling cash receipts.
**b** What steps should be taken regularly by the theater manager or other supervisor to make these internal controls work most effectively?
**c** Assume that the cashier and the doorman decided to collaborate in an effort to abstract cash receipts. What action might they take?
**d** On the assumption made in **c** of collaboration between the cashier and the doorman, what features of the control procedures would be most likely to disclose the embezzlement?

*6A-2* Redwood Products retained a firm of certified public accountants to devise a system of internal control especially suited to its operations. Assuming that the CPA firm has finished its work and the newly designed system of internal control is in use, answer fully the following questions:

**a** Will it be possible for any type of fraud to occur without immediate detection once the new system of internal control is in full operation?
**b** Describe two limitations inherent in any system of internal control that will prevent it from providing absolute assurance against inefficiency and fraud.

*6A-3* Dave Smith, an employee of Jones Company, is responsible for preparing checks to suppliers in payment for purchases of merchandise. Before submitting the checks to the treasurer for signature, Smith receives a copy of the purchase order, the receiving report, and the supplier's invoice. After determining that all three documents are in agreement and that no arithmetical errors exist, he fills in an invoice approval form and then prepares a check complete except for the treasurer's signature. Smith files the documents (purchase order, purchase invoice, receiving report, and invoice approval form) alphabetically by supplier. As a final step, he forwards the check to the treasurer for signature.

While trying to finish work early on Friday, December 31, Smith accidentally prepared for the treasurer's signature a check payable to Miller Company, a regular supplier, for $96,420, although the invoice and other documents indicated the amount payable was actually $69,420. Smith had previously made another error in recording the invoice, debiting the Purchases account when the debit should have been to Office Equipment because the invoice was for typewriters and other equipment to be used in the business and not to be sold to customers. The amount of this accounting entry agreed with the invoice but not with the check. The entry was as follows:

| | | |
|---|---|---|
| *Purchases* . . . . . . . . . . . . . . . . . . . . . . . . . . . . . . . . . . . . . . . . . . | *69,420* | |
| *Accounts Payable* . . . . . . . . . . . . . . . . . . . . . . . . . . . . . . . . . . . . | | *69,420* |
| *To record purchase invoice from Miller Company. Terms, cash upon delivery.* | | |

The check for $96,420 was forwarded to the treasurer, promptly signed, and entered in the accounting records as a debit to Accounts Payable and a credit to Cash in the amount of $96,420. The treasurer mailed the check to the supplier. The supplier did not notice the overpayment and deposited the check.

A physical inventory was taken at the close of business Dec. 31, and financial statements were prepared by Jones Company without discovery of the error. Net income for the year was $100,000 and the owner's capital at December 31 appeared in the balance sheet as $204,000.

On January 20, Smith was processing another invoice from Miller Company and discovered the previous overpayment error. Smith processed the new invoice in a normal manner and then informed Miller Company by telephone of the December overpayment, requesting that a refund check be mailed and the envelope marked for his attention. After receiving the refund check for $27,000, Smith went to a nearby town, opened a new bank account in the name of Jones Company and deposited the check. A short time later he withdrew the amount deposited, closed the bank account, and moved out of town leaving no forwarding address. Jones Company, a single proprietorship owned by Carl Jones, does not carry a fidelity bond on its employees.

**Instructions**

**a** Were the figures for net income and owner's capital correct as shown in the financial statements? (Keep in mind that the theft by Smith occurred in January.) Explain fully. If you consider these amounts incorrect, compute corrected amounts.

**b** Assuming that the facts about the overstated check, the refund, and the theft by Smith all came to light late in January, prepare the necessary adjusting entry or entries. Include a full explanation as part of such entries.

**c** Identify any weaknesses in the system of internal control indicated by the above events and make recommendations for improvements.

*6A-4* Lakeshore Sports sells sports equipment to retail stores and uses the periodic inventory system. The company prepared the following financial statements at December 31, the end of its fiscal year. (The section for operating expenses has been condensed to conserve space.)

**LAKESHORE SPORTS**
**Income Statement**
**For the Year Ended December 31, 19__**

| | | | |
|---|---|---|---|
| Gross sales | | | $480,000 |
| Less: Sales returns and allowances | | | 26,000 |
| Net sales | | | $454,000 |
| Cost of goods sold: | | | |
| Inventory, Jan. 1 | | $ 82,000 | |
| Purchases | $313,000 | | |
| Less: Purchase returns & allowances | 4,400 | | |
| Net purchases | $308,600 | | |
| Add: Transportation-in | 5,200 | | |
| Cost of goods purchased | | 313,800 | |
| Cost of goods available for sale | | $395,800 | |
| Less: Inventory, Dec. 31 | | 78,000 | |
| Cost of goods sold | | | 317,800 |
| Gross profit on sales | | | $136,200 |
| Operating expenses | | | 120,000 |
| Net income | | | $ 16,200 |

**LAKESHORE SPORTS**
**Balance Sheet**
**December 31, 19__**

**Assets**

| | | | |
|---|---|---|---|
| Current assets: | | | |
| Cash | | | $ 15,000 |
| Accounts receivable | | | 56,600 |
| Inventory | | | 78,000 |
| Prepaid expenses | | | 900 |
| Total current assets | | | $150,500 |
| Plant and equipment: | | | |
| Land | | $ 90,000 | |
| Buildings | $142,000 | | |
| Less: Accumulated depreciation | 12,000 | 130,000 | |
| Furniture & fixtures | $ 18,000 | | |
| Less: Accumulated depreciation | 2,000 | 16,000 | |
| Total plant and equipment | | | 236,000 |
| Total assets | | | $386,500 |

**Total Liabilities & Owner's Equity**

| | |
|---|---|
| ***Current liabilities:*** | |
| *Notes payable* | *$ 40,000* |
| *Accounts payable* | *45,000* |
| *Total current liabilities* | *$ 85,000* |
| ***Long-term liabilities:*** | |
| *Mortgage payable (due 1995)* | *170,000* |
| *Total liabilities* | *$255,000* |
| ***Owner's equity:*** | |
| *Jonathan Home, capital* | *131,500* |
| ***Total liabilities & owner's equity*** | *$386,500* |

The company's owner was disappointed in the year's net income, and retained Charles Field, a CPA, to review the system of internal control and examine the financial statements. During his investigation, conducted in January, Field discovered the following items requiring attention.

(1) Bill Smith, an employee whose duties included handling cash receipts, preparing credit memoranda, and maintaining accounting records, had fraudulently issued a credit memorandum for $6,000 to a customer, Mann Company. The credit memorandum had been recorded by a journal entry prepared by Smith on December 19 and posted to the ledger. Smith had placed a carbon copy of the credit memorandum in the file maintained for the customer. The credit memorandum indicated a return of merchandise by the customer, but actually no such return had occurred. Smith admitted that he had planned to split the $6,000 with his brother who was office manager for Mann Company. After the CPA discovered this irregularity, Jonathan Home, owner of Lakeshore Sports, contacted the owner of Mann Company, who agreed that no merchandise had been returned. He marked the credit memorandum "void" and returned it to Lakeshore Sports. He also discharged the office manager involved in the attempted fraud, and paid in full on January 20 for all purchases from Lakeshore Sports.

(2) A shipment of merchandise costing $12,000 had been received on December 26 and recorded as a purchase on that date. On December 28, some of this merchandise was found to be defective and was returned to the supplier. A credit memorandum for $3,600 was received from the supplier on December 30, but was filed away without any entry being made in the accounting records for the return of the merchandise.

(3) The sales transactions of December 31 consisting of $6,500 in sales on credit and $1,800 in cash sales had not been recorded before the accounts were closed for the year. The cash had been kept in the safe until January 3, when it was deposited at the bank. Both the credit sales and the cash sales made on December 31 were recorded by journal entries dated January 3 of the following year as though the sales had been made in January.

**Instructions**

**a** Set up T accounts for Cash, Accounts Receivable, Accounts Payable, Sales, Sales Returns and Allowances, and Purchase Returns and Allowances. List in these T accounts the balances given in the problem, then enter debits or credits to make corrections for the above three irregular items. Compute the new balances in the T accounts.

**b** Prepare a revised income statement for the year and a revised balance sheet at December 31 which will give effect to correction of the three items described in the problem. The owner's capital account should be increased or decreased by the amount of any change in the net income for the year.

**c** What weakness in internal control is suggested by Bill Smith's issuance of a fraudulent credit memorandum? Explain and make recommendations to strengthen the system of internal control.

*6A-5* The following transactions were completed by Modern Metals during the month of November 19___.

**Nov. 1** Purchased merchandise from Hayes Company, $8,000; terms 2/10, n/30.
**Nov. 7** Purchased merchandise from Joseph Corporation, $12,000; terms 2/10, n/30.
**Nov. 8** Merchandise having a list price of $1,200, purchased from Hayes Company, was found to be defective. It was returned to the seller, accompanied by debit memorandum no. 382.
**Nov. 17** Paid Joseph Corporation's invoice of November 7, less cash discount.
**Nov. 24** Purchased merchandise from Joseph Corporation, $7,600; terms 2/10, n/30.
**Nov. 30** Paid Hayes Company's invoice of November 1, taking into consideration the return of goods on November 8.

Assume that the merchandise inventory on November 1 was $32,960; on November 30, $31,260.

**Instructions**

**a** Journalize the above transactions, recording invoices at the net amount.
**b** Prepare the cost of goods sold section of the income statement.
**c** What is the amount of accounts payable at the end of November? What would the amount of accounts payable be at the end of November if Modern Metals followed the policy of recording purchase invoices at the gross amount?

*6A-6* The merchandising transactions of Pacific Wholesale Center for the month of July are detailed below. The company's policy is to take advantage of all cash discounts offered by suppliers; purchase invoices are recorded at the net amount. In making sales the company grants credit terms of 2/10, n/30, and strictly enforces the 10-day limitation for granting discounts. The amounts listed as cash sales are net of sales discounts.

**July 2** Sold merchandise to Fitch Co. for cash, $164,400.
**July 15** Sold merchandise on account to Ryan Furniture Co., $74,100.
**July 16** Purchased merchandise from Walden Supply Co., $94,800; terms 2/10, n/30 (to be recorded at net amount).
**July 16** Paid cash for transportation charges on goods received from Walden Supply Co., $3,630.
**July 18** Issued credit memorandum no. 361 to Ryan Furniture Co. for allowance on damaged goods, $2,100.
**July 24** Purchased merchandise from Potter Manufacturing Co., $85,500; terms 1/10, n/30 (to be recorded at net amount).
**July 25** Returned defective goods with invoice price of $4,500 to Potter Manufacturing Co., accompanied by debit memorandum no. 85.
**July 25** Received cash from Ryan Furniture Co. in full payment of account.
**July 26** Paid Walden Supply Co. account in full.

**Instructions**

**a** Record the above transactions in three-column, running balance ledger accounts. (Cash, Accounts Receivable, Accounts Payable, Sales, etc.) Journal entries are not required.
**b** Prepare a partial income statement for July showing sales and cost of goods sold (in detail), and gross profit on sales. Assume the inventory at June 30 to be $57,000 and at July 31 to be $69,600.
**c** What is the amount of accounts payable at July 31? What would be the amount of accounts payable at July 31 if the company followed a policy of recording purchase invoices at the gross amount?

## Group B

*6B-1* After spending several years as an executive for a large nationwide finance company, Charles Bell resigned in order to open his own finance business, called Happy Loan Company. The business consists of four very small offices in four cities a few miles apart. The activity of each office consists of making small loans to individual borrowers. The borrowers agree to repay the amount borrowed plus interest in monthly installments over a period of 36 months or less.

Charles Bell has his own office at one of the four loan offices and makes fairly frequent trips to the other offices to provide general supervision and to perform some internal auditing work. Early in the current year Bell called upon a firm of certified public accountants, explained that he was worried about the honesty of his employees, and made the following statement: "In the large nationwide loan company where I worked before starting my own business, we had over 500 offices scattered over 10 states. The system of accounting and internal control in that company made fraud absolutely impossible. I can describe the system to you in detail and I want you to install that system in my own company."

**Instructions**

**a** Explain how the CPA firm would probably respond to Bell's request that it install the large finance company's system of internal control in his new business.

**b** Comment on Bell's statement that the new system would make fraud absolutely impossible.

*6B-2* Edward Garvey, manager of Theater & Parks, Inc., made the following statement: "We consider the regular rotation of employee assignments to be an important element of a strong system of internal control. Consequently, we have our accounts receivable employee take over the work of our cashier every day from 11:30 to 12:30. Then the cashier takes over the position of the accounts receivable employee from 12:30 to 1:30 while that employee is given an hour off for lunch.

"We follow the same procedure with respect to the admission of customers to our theaters. The ticket seller in the box office will occasionally change places with the ticket taker at the door. This rotation policy also has the advantage of giving employees a better understanding of our system as a whole."

**Instructions** Evaluate Garvey's rotation of employees from the standpoint of maintaining strong internal control.

*6B-3* Jay Winkler, long-time office manager of Western Building Materials, prepares all purchase orders for merchandise in which the company deals. Winkler personally owns a large waterfront lot and during the current year he was having a marina constructed on this lot. The construction plans included boat slips, a large dock, a restaurant, and a marine supply store.

To obtain building materials for this project, Winkler fraudulently issued purchase orders in the name of Western Building Materials and instructed the suppliers to deliver the materials at his waterfront site. The suppliers did not question the propriety of these orders since they were accustomed to receiving from Western Building Supplies purchase orders signed by Winkler. When purchase invoices from the suppliers relating to these materials reached Western Building Materials, Winkler entered them in the accounting records as debits to Purchases and credits to Accounts Payable. On the appropriate dates, he prepared company checks payable to the suppliers and presented them to the treasurer of Western Building Materials for signature. Since the checks were payable to suppliers from whom Western Building Materials regularly made purchases, the treasurer signed and mailed the checks without question.

The accounting system used by Western Building Materials required that duplicate copies of purchase orders be attached to the related receiving reports and purchase invoices, and then filed alphabetically by vendor. Since there were no receiving reports for the materials that Winkler diverted to his marina, he removed from the files the purchase orders and related purchase invoices for these materials and concealed these documents in his desk. During the year, the billed price of the materials which Winkler ordered and diverted to his marina totaled $110,000. Of this total, all but $10,000 had been paid for at year-end by Western Building Materials and cash discounts of $2,000 had been taken. The remaining $10,000 in unpaid invoices were included in the year-end balance of accounts payable at the gross amount.

Western Building Materials uses the periodic inventory system. A complete physical inventory was taken on December 31. In an effort to prevent the theft of materials from having a conspicuous effect on the year's reported earnings, Winkler changed figures on the inventory count sheets, thereby causing the ending inventory to be overstated by $100,000.

Condensed financial statements for the company at December 31 of the current year appeared as follows:

**WESTERN BUILDING MATERIALS**
**Balance Sheet**
**December 31, 19__**

| Assets | | Liabilities & Owner's Equity | |
|---|---|---|---|
| Cash | $ 32,000 | Notes payable | $320,000 |
| Accounts receivable | 280,000 | Accounts payable | 260,000 |
| Inventory | 625,000 | Accrued salaries | 20,000 |
| Office equipment (net) | 5,000 | Total liabilities | $600,000 |
| Trucks (net) | 36,000 | Ralph West, capital | 378,000 |
| Totals | $978,000 | Totals | $978,000 |

**WESTERN BUILDING MATERIALS**
**Income Statement**
**For the Year Ended December 31, 19__**

| | | | | |
|---|---|---|---|---|
| Net sales | | | | $3,661,000 |
| Cost of goods sold: | | | | |
| Beginning inventory | | | $ 520,000 | |
| Purchases | | $3,225,000 | | |
| Less: Purchase ret. & all. | $72,000 | | | |
| Purchase discounts | 60,000 | 132,000 | 3,093,000 | |
| Cost of goods available for sale | | | $3,613,000 | |
| Less: Inventory, Dec. 31, 19__ | | | 625,000 | |
| Cost of goods sold | | | | 2,988,000 |
| Gross profit on sales | | | | $ 673,000 |
| Operating expenses: | | | | |
| Selling | | | $ 385,000 | |
| General and administrative | | | 265,000 | 650,000 |
| Net income | | | | $ 23,000 |

At an office party on New Year's Eve, Jay Winkler became somewhat intoxicated and confided to a secretary how he had acquired "free materials" to build a marina. The secretary reported this information to Ralph West, owner of the business, who immediately demanded an explanation from Winkler. Jay Winkler confessed to his dishonest actions and returned the purchase orders and purchase invoices he had removed from the files. Also on New Year's Eve, the marina being constructed by Winkler was completely destroyed by fire. There was no insurance in force, and Winkler had no other assets. Ralph West discharged Winkler and he left town without any forwarding address. Western Building Materials did not have a fidelity bond for its employees. Ralph West considers that the entire problem was caused by his failure to establish a satisfactory system of internal control. He does not attach any blame to the suppliers.

**Instructions**

**a** Compute the loss to Western Building Materials from Jay Winkler's dishonest actions. Show how you arrived at this amount.

**b** Prepare a corrected balance sheet and income statement. Delete from the cost of goods sold section of the income statement the purchased materials which in fact were never in the possession of the company. Also delete the purchase discount applicable to the $100,000 of diverted materials which had been paid for during the year. Include as a separate, nonoperating item, Loss from Material Shortages.

**c** Explain the weaknesses in the system of internal control which made possible concealment of the thefts by Winkler and recommend any appropriate improvements in the system.

***6B-4*** Pickett Fence completed the following transactions relating to the purchase of merchandise during the month of August 19___. It is the policy of the company to record all purchase invoices at the net amount and to pay invoices within the discount period.

**Aug. 1** Purchased merchandise from Rallis Company, $24,000; terms 2/10, n/30.
**Aug. 8** Purchased merchandise from Thomas Company, $36,000; terms 2/10, n/30.
**Aug. 8** Merchandise with a list price of $3,600 purchased from Rallis Company on August 1 was found to be defective. It was returned to the supplier accompanied by debit memorandum no. 118.
**Aug. 18** Paid Thomas Company's invoice of August 8, less cash discount.
**Aug. 25** Purchased merchandise from Thomas Company, $22,800; terms 2/10, n/30.
**Aug. 30** Paid Rallis Company's invoice of August 1, taking into consideration the return of defective goods on August 8.

The inventory of merchandise on August 1 was $98,880; on August 31, $93,780.

**Instructions**

**a** Journalize the above transactions, recording invoices at the net amount.

**b** Prepare the cost of goods sold section of the income statement.

**c** What is the amount of accounts payable at the end of August? What would be the amount of accounts payable at the end of August if Pickett Fence followed the policy of recording purchase invoices at the gross amount?

***6B-5*** Village Supply completed the following merchandising transactions during May. The company's policy calls for taking advantage of all cash discounts available to it from suppliers; purchase invoices are recorded at the ***net amount.*** In making sales, the company grants credit terms of 2/10, n/30, and strictly enforces the 10-day limitation. The amounts listed as cash sales below are net of sales discounts.

**May 3** Sold merchandise to Rich Company for cash, $32,880.
**May 16** Sold merchandise on account to Riverside Company, $14,820.

**May 16** Purchased merchandise from Hilton Supply Company, $18,900; terms 2/10, n/30 (to be recorded at the net amount).
**May 17** Paid transportation charges on goods received from Hilton Supply Company, $726.
**May 18** Issued credit memorandum no. 102 to Riverside Company for allowance on damaged goods, $420.
**May 24** Purchased merchandise from Pete Construction Co., $17,100; terms 1/10, n/30 (to be recorded at the net amount).
**May 25** Returned defective goods with invoice price of $900 to Pete Construction Co., accompanied by debit memorandum no. 122.
**May 26** Received cash from Riverside Company in full payment of account.
**May 26** Paid Hilton Supply Company account in full.

**Instructions**

**a** Record the above transactions in three-column running balance ledger accounts (Cash, Accounts Receivable, Accounts Payable, Sales, etc.). Journal entries are not required.

**b** Prepare a partial income statement for May showing sales and cost of goods sold (in detail), and gross profit on sales. Assume the inventory at April 30 to be $11,400 and the inventory at May 31 to be $13,920.

**c** What is the amount of accounts payable at May 31? What would be the amount of accounts payable at May 31 if the company followed a policy of recording purchase invoices at the gross amount?

## BUSINESS DECISION PROBLEM 6

Martin Company and Winter Company are both merchandising companies applying for nine-month bank loans in order to finance the acquisition of new equipment. Both companies are seeking to borrow the amount of $210,000 and have submitted the following balance sheets with their loan applications:

**MARTIN COMPANY**
**Balance Sheet**
**August 31, 19__**
**Assets**

| | | | |
|---|---|---|---|
| *Current assets:* | | | |
| Cash | | | $ 57,000 |
| Accounts receivable | | | 153,000 |
| Inventories | | | 162,000 |
| Short-term prepayments | | | 6,000 |
| Total current assets | | | $ 378,000 |
| *Plant and equipment:* | | | |
| Land | | $150,000 | |
| Building | $600,000 | | |
| Less: Accumulated depreciation | 90,000 | 510,000 | |
| Store equipment | $180,000 | | |
| Less: Accumulated depreciation | 45,000 | 135,000 | |
| Total plant and equipment | | | 795,000 |
| Total assets | | | $1,173,000 |

**Liabilities & Owner's Equity**

| | | | |
|---|---|---|---|
| **Current liabilities:** | | | |
| Accounts payable | | | $ 135,000 |
| Accrued wages payable | | | 45,000 |
| Total current liabilities | | | $ 180,000 |
| **Long-term liabilities:** | | | |
| Mortgage payable (due in 13 months) | | | 330,000 |
| Total liabilities | | | $ 510,000 |
| **Owner's equity:** | | | |
| Steve Martin, capital | | | 663,000 |
| Total liabilities & owner's equity | | | $1,173,000 |

**WINTER COMPANY**
**Balance Sheet**
**August 31, 19__**
**Assets**

| | | | |
|---|---|---|---|
| **Current assets:** | | | |
| Cash | | | $ 384,000 |
| U.S. government bonds | | | 210,000 |
| Accounts receivable | | | 603,000 |
| Inventories | | | 567,000 |
| Total current assets | | | $1,764,000 |
| **Plant & equipment:** | | | |
| Land | | $ 180,000 | |
| Building and equipment | $1,230,000 | | |
| Less: Accumulated depreciation | 180,000 | 1,050,000 | |
| Total plant & equipment | | | 1,230,000 |
| Total assets | | | $2,994,000 |

**Liabilities & Owner's Equity**

| | | | |
|---|---|---|---|
| **Current liabilities:** | | | |
| Notes payable | | | $ 600,000 |
| Accounts payable | | | 480,000 |
| Miscellaneous accrued liabilities | | | 180,000 |
| Total current liabilities | | | $1,260,000 |
| **Long-term liabilities:** | | | |
| Mortgage payable (due in 10 years) | | | 420,000 |
| Total liabilities | | | $1,680,000 |
| **Owner's equity:** | | | |
| Jack Winter, capital | | | 1,314,000 |
| Total liabilities & owner's equity | | | $2,994,000 |

Along with its balance sheet and loan application, Winter Company submitted to the bank a report issued by a national firm of certified public accountants. The report indicated that early in the year the CPA firm had been retained by Winter Company to make a special investigation of its system of internal control; the study resulted in a number of recommendations, all of which the company had promptly adopted.

**Instructions**

**a** Compute the current ratio and amount of working capital for each company as of August 31, 19___.

**b** Compute the current ratio and amount of working capital that each company would have after obtaining the bank loan and investing the borrowed cash in new equipment (assuming no other transactions affecting current accounts).

**c** From the viewpoint of a bank loan officer, to which company would you prefer to make a $210,000 nine-month loan? Explain. Include in your answer a discussion of the ability of each company to meet its obligations in the near future and also explain what bearing the CPA firm's report on internal control would have on your decision-making process as a bank loan officer.

# 7

# ACCOUNTING SYSTEMS: MANUAL AND EDP

In the early chapters of an introductory accounting book, basic accounting principles can be discussed most conveniently in terms of a small business with only a few customers and suppliers. This simplified model of a business has been used in preceding chapters to demonstrate the analysis and recording of the more common types of business transactions.

The recording procedures illustrated thus far call for recording each transaction by an entry in the general journal, and then posting each debit and credit from the general journal to the proper account in the ledger. We must now face the practical problem of streamlining and speeding up this basic accounting system so that the accounting department can keep pace with the rapid flow of transactions in a modern business.

Accounting systems in common use range from manual systems, which use special journals to streamline the journalizing and posting processes, to sophisticated computer systems which maintain accounting records on magnetic tape. The accounting system in use in any given company will be specially tailored to the size and information needs of the business.

## MANUAL ACCOUNTING SYSTEMS

In a large business there may be hundreds or even thousands of transactions every day. To handle a large volume of transactions rapidly and efficiently, it is helpful to group the transactions into like classes and to use a specialized journal for each class. This will greatly reduce the amount of detailed recording work and will also permit a division of labor, since each special-purpose journal can be handled by a different employee. The great majority of transactions (perhaps as much as 90 or 95%) usually fall into four types. These four types and four corresponding special journals are as follows:

| *Type of Transaction* | *Name of Special Journal* |
|---|---|
| *Sales of merchandise on credit* | *Sales journal* |
| *Purchases of merchandise on credit* | *Purchases journal* |
| *Receipts of cash* | *Cash receipts journal* |
| *Payments of cash* | *Cash payments journal* |

In addition to these four special journals, a ***general journal*** will be used for recording transactions which do not fit into any of the above four types. The general journal is the same book of original entry illustrated in preceding chapters; the adjective "general" is added merely to distinguish it from the special journals.

## Sales journal

Illustrated below is a sales journal containing entries for all sales on account made during November by the Seaside Company. Whenever merchandise is sold on credit, several copies of a sales invoice are prepared. The information listed on a sales invoice usually includes the date of the sale, the serial number of the invoice, the customer's name, the amount of the sale, and the credit terms. One copy of the sales invoice is used by the seller as the basis for an entry in the sales journal.

*Entries for sales on credit during November*

**Sales Journal** — Page 1

| Date | | Account Debited | Invoice No. | √ | Amount |
|---|---|---|---|---|---|
| 19__ | | | | | |
| Nov | 2 | John Adams | 301 | √ | 450 |
| | 4 | Harold Black | 302 | √ | 1,000 |
| | 5 | Robert Cross | 303 | √ | 975 |
| | 11 | H. R. Davis | 304 | √ | 620 |
| | 18 | C. D. Early | 305 | √ | 900 |
| | 23 | John Frost | 306 | √ | 400 |
| | 29 | D. H. Gray | 307 | √ | 11,850 |
| | | | | | 16,195 |
| | | | | | (5) (41) |

Note that the illustrated sales journal contains special columns for recording each of these aspects of the sales transaction, except the credit terms. If it is the practice of the business to offer different credit terms to different customers, a column may be inserted in the sales journal to show the terms of sale. In this illustration it is assumed that all sales are made on terms of 2/10, n/30; consequently, there is no need to write the credit terms as part of each entry. ***Only sales on credit are entered in the sales journal.*** When merchandise is sold for cash, the transaction is recorded in a ***cash receipts*** journal, which is illustrated later in this chapter.

**Advantages of the sales journal** Note that each of the above seven sales transactions is recorded on a single line. Each entry consists of a debit to a customer's account; the offsetting credit to the Sales account is understood without being written, because sales on account are the only transactions recorded in this special journal.

An entry in a sales journal need not include an explanation; if more information about the transaction is desired it can be obtained by referring to the file copy of the sales invoice. The invoice number is listed in the sales journal as part of each entry. The one-line entry in the sales journal requires much less writing than would be necessary to record a sales transaction in the general journal. Since there may be several hundred or several thousand sales transactions each month, the time saved in recording transactions in this streamlined manner becomes quite important.

Every entry in the sales journal represents a debit to a customer's account. Charges to customers' accounts should be posted daily so that each customer's account will always be up-to-date and available for use in making decisions relating to collections and to the further extension of credit. A check mark (✓) is placed in the sales journal opposite each amount posted to a customer's account, to indicate that the posting has been made.

Another advantage to the special journal for sales is the great saving of time in posting credits to the Sales account. Remember that every amount entered in the sales journal represents a credit to Sales. In the illustrated sales journal on page 251, there are seven transactions (and in practice there might be 700). Instead of posting a separate credit to the Sales account for each sales transaction, we can wait until the end of the month and make one posting to the Sales account for the total of the amounts recorded in the sales journal.

In the illustrated sales journal for November, the sales on account totaled $16,195. On November 30 this amount is posted as a credit to the Sales account, and the ledger account number for Sales (41) is entered under the total figure in the sales journal to show that the posting operation has been performed. The total sales figure is also posted as a debit to ledger account no. 5, Accounts Receivable. To make clear the reason for this posting to Accounts Receivable, an explanation of the nature of controlling accounts and subsidiary ledgers is necessary.

## Controlling accounts and subsidiary ledgers

In preceding chapters all transactions involving accounts receivable from customers have been posted to a single account entitled Accounts Receivable. Under this procedure, however, it is not easy to look up the amount receivable from a given customer. In practice, businesses which sell goods on credit ***maintain a separate account receivable for each customer.*** If there are 4,000 customers, this would require a ledger with 4,000 accounts receivable, in addition to the accounts for other assets, and for liabilities, owner's equity, revenue, and expenses. Such a ledger would be cumbersome and unwieldy. Also, the trial balance prepared from such a large ledger would be a very long one. If the trial balance showed the ledger to be out of balance, the task of locating the error or errors would be most difficult. All these factors indicate that it is not desirable to have too many accounts in one ledger. Fortunately, a simple solution is available; this solution is to divide up the ledger into several separate ledgers.

In a business which has a large number of accounts with customers and with creditors, it is customary to divide the ledger into three separate ledgers. All the accounts with ***customers*** are placed in alphabetical order in a separate ledger, called the ***accounts receivable ledger.*** All the accounts with ***creditors*** are arranged alphabetically in another ledger called the ***accounts payable ledger.*** Both of these ledgers are known as ***subsidiary ledgers,*** because they support and are controlled by the general ledger.

After thus segregating the accounts receivable from customers in one subsidiary ledger and placing the accounts payable to creditors in a second subsidiary ledger, we have left in the original ledger all the revenue and expense accounts and also all the balance sheet accounts except those with customers and creditors. This ledger is called the ***general ledger,*** to distinguish it from the subsidiary ledgers.

When the numerous individual accounts receivable from customers are placed in a subsidiary ledger, an account entitled Accounts Receivable continues to be maintained in the general ledger. This account shows the ***total amount due from all customers;*** in other words, this single ***controlling account*** in the general ledger takes the place of the numerous customers' accounts which have been removed to form a subsidiary ledger. The general ledger is still in balance be-

***Relationship of subsidiary ledgers to controlling accounts in general ledger***

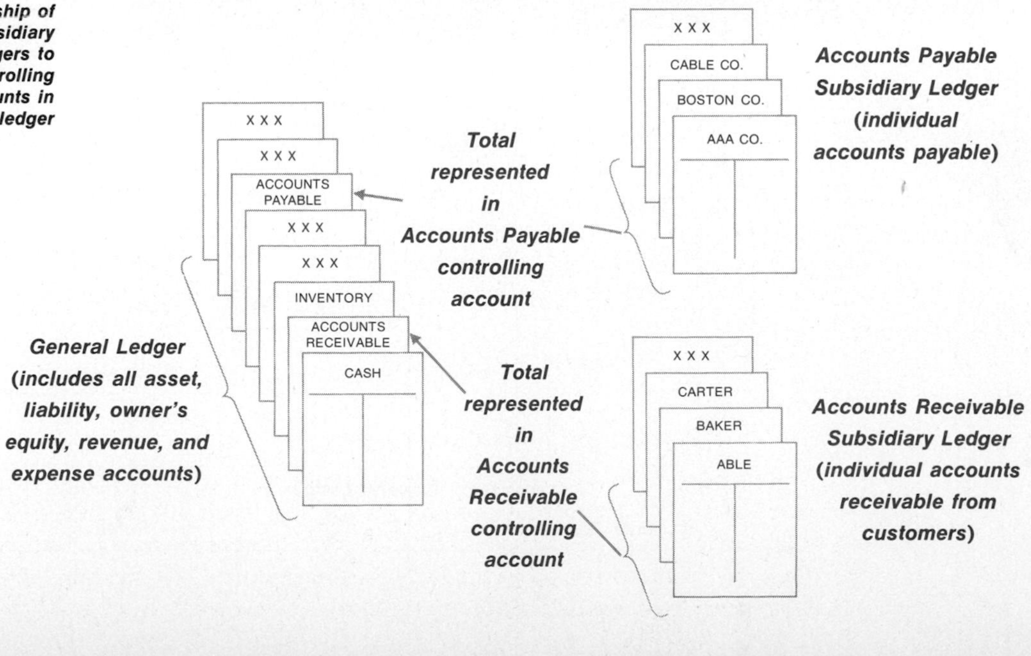

cause the controlling account, Accounts Receivable, has a balance equal to the total of the customers' accounts which were removed from the general ledger. Agreement of the controlling account with the sum of the accounts receivable in the subsidiary ledger also provides assurance of accuracy in the subsidiary ledger.

A controlling account entitled Accounts Payable is also kept in the general ledger in place of the numerous accounts with creditors which have been removed to form the accounts payable subsidiary ledger. Because the two controlling accounts represent the total amounts receivable from customers and payable to creditors, a trial balance can be prepared from the general ledger alone. The illustration on page 253 shows the relationship of the subsidiary ledgers to the controlling accounts in the general ledger:

**Posting to subsidiary ledgers and to controlling accounts** To illustrate the posting of subsidiary ledgers and of controlling accounts, let us refer again to the sales journal illustrated on page 251. Each debit to a customer's account is posted

***Subsidiary ledger posted daily; general ledger posted monthly***

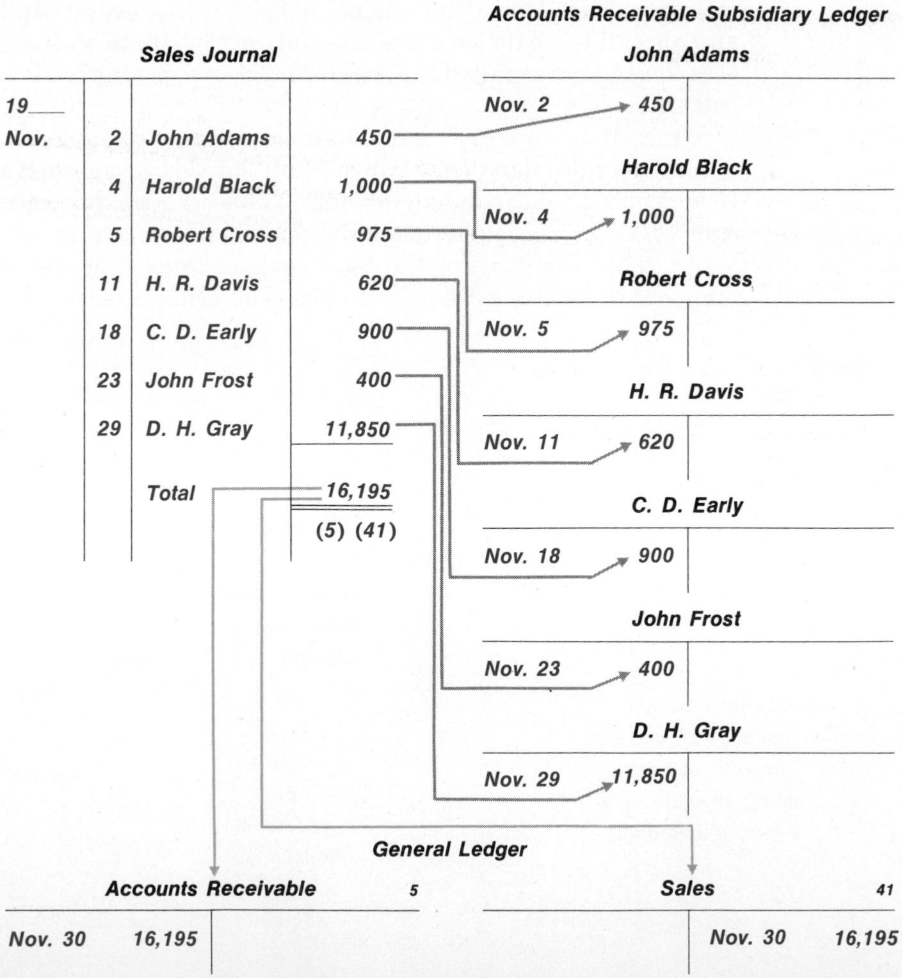

currently during the month from the sales journal to the customer's account in the accounts receivable ledger. The accounts in this subsidiary ledger are usually kept in alphabetical order and are not numbered. When a posting is made to a customer's account, a check mark (√) is placed in the sales journal as evidence that the posting has been made to the subsidiary ledger.

At month-end the sales journal is totaled. The total amount of sales for the month, $16,195, is posted as a credit to the Sales account and also as a debit to the controlling account, Accounts Receivable, in the general ledger. The controlling account will, therefore, equal the total of all the customers' accounts in the subsidiary ledger.

The diagram on page 254 shows the day-to-day posting of individual entries from the sales journal to the subsidiary ledger. The diagram also shows the month-end posting of the total of the sales journal to the two general ledger accounts affected, Accounts Receivable and Sales. Note that the amount of the monthly debit to the controlling account is equal to the sum of the debits posted to the subsidiary ledger.

## Purchases journal

The handling of purchase transactions when a purchases journal is used follows a pattern quite similar to the one described for the sales journal.

Assume that the purchases journal illustrated below contains all purchases of merchandise on credit during the month by the Seaside Company. The invoice date is shown in a separate column because the cash discount period begins on this date.

*Entries for purchases on credit during November*

***Purchases Journal*** *Page 1*

| *Date* | | *Account Credited* | *Invoice Date* | | √ | *Amount* |
|---|---|---|---|---|---|---|
| *19__* | | | *19__* | | | |
| *Nov* | *2* | *Alabama Supply Co.* | *Nov* | *2* | √ | *3,325* |
| | *4* | *Barker & Bright* | | *4* | √ | *700* |
| | *10* | *Canning & Sons* | | *9* | √ | *500* |
| | *17* | *Davis Co.* | | *16* | √ | *900* |
| | *27* | *Excelsior, Inc.* | | *25* | √ | *1,825* |
| | | | | | | *7,250* |
| | | | | | | *(50) (21)* |

The five entries are posted as they occur during the month as credits to the creditors' accounts in the subsidiary ledger for accounts payable. As each posting is completed a check mark (√) is placed in the purchases journal.

At the end of the month the purchases journal is totaled and ruled as shown in the illustration. The total figure, $7,250, is posted to two general ledger accounts as shown on the next page:

**1** As a debit to the Purchases account
**2** As a credit to the Accounts Payable controlling account

The account numbers for Purchases (50) and for Accounts Payable (21) are then placed in parentheses below the column total of the purchases journal to show that the posting has been made.

Under the particular system being described, the only transactions recorded in the purchases journal are ***purchases of merchandise on credit.*** The term ***merchandise*** means goods acquired for resale to customers. If merchandise is purchased for cash rather than on credit, the transaction should be recorded in the cash payments journal, as illustrated on pages 260 and 261.

The diagram below illustrates the day-to-day posting of individual entries from the purchases journal to the accounts with creditors in the subsidiary ledger for accounts payable. The diagram also shows how the column total of the purchases journal is posted at the end of the month to the general ledger accounts, Purchases and Accounts Payable. One objective of this diagram is to emphasize that the amount of the monthly credit to the control account is equal to the sum of the credits posted to the subsidiary ledger.

When assets other than merchandise are being acquired, as, for example, a delivery truck or an office desk for use in the business, the journal to be used depends upon whether a cash payment is made. If assets of this type are pur-

**Subsidiary ledger posted daily; general ledger posted monthly**

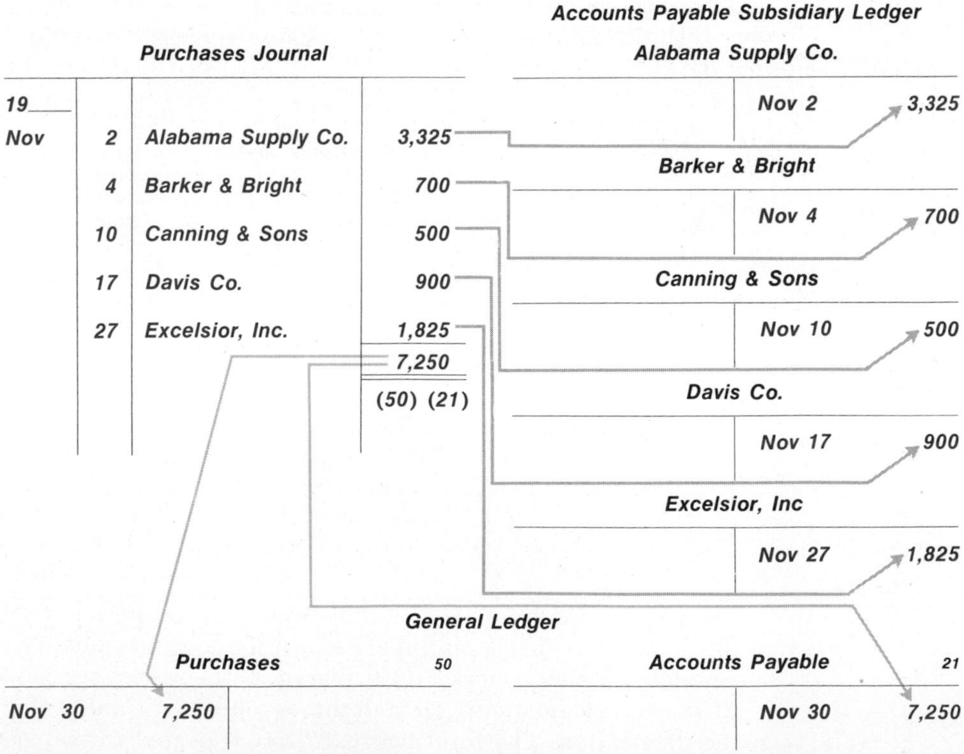

chased for cash, the transaction should be entered in the cash payments journal; if the transaction is on credit, the general journal is used. The purchases journal is not used to record the acquisition of these assets because the total of this journal is posted to the Purchases account and this account (as explained in Chapter 5) is used in determining the cost of goods sold.

### Cash receipts journal

***All transactions involving the receipt of cash are recorded in the cash receipts journal.*** One common example is the sale of merchandise for cash. As each cash sale is made, it is rung up on a cash register. At the end of the day the total of the cash sales is computed by striking the total key on the register. This total is entered in the cash receipts journal, which therefore contains one entry for the total cash sales of the day. For other types of cash receipts, such as the collection of accounts receivable from customers, a separate journal entry may be made for each transaction. The cash receipts journal illustrated on pages 258 and 259 contains entries for selected November transactions, all of which include the receipt of cash.

**Nov.** **1** R. B. Jones invested $75,000 cash to establish the Seaside Company.
**4** Sold merchandise for cash, $300.
**5** Sold merchandise for cash, $400.
**8** Collected from John Adams invoice of Nov. 2, $450 less 2% cash discount.
**10** Sold a small portion of land not needed in business for a total price of $7,000, consisting of cash of $1,000 and a note receivable for $6,000. The cost of the land sold was $5,000.
**12** Collected from Harold Black invoice of Nov. 4, $1,000 less 2% cash discount.
**20** Collected from C. D. Early invoice of Nov. 18, $900 less 2% cash discount.
**27** Sold merchandise for cash, $125.
**30** Obtained $4,000 loan from bank. Issued a note payable in that amount.

Note that the cash receipts journal illustrated on pages 258 and 259 has three debit columns and three credit columns as follows:

Debits:

1 Cash. This column is used for every entry, because only those transactions which include the receipt of cash are entered in this special journal.
2 Sales discounts. This column is used to accumulate the sales discounts allowed during the month. Only one line of the cash receipts book is required to record a collection from a customer who takes advantage of a cash discount.
3 Other accounts. This third debit column is used for debits to any and all accounts other than cash and sales discounts, and space is provided for writing in the name of the account. For example, the entry of November 10 in the illustrated cash receipts journal shows that cash and a note receivable were obtained when land was sold. The amount of cash received, $1,000, is entered in the Cash debit column, the account title Notes Receivable is written in the

Includes all transactions involving receipt of cash

**Cash Receipts Journal**

| Date | | Explanation | Debits | | | | |
|---|---|---|---|---|---|---|---|
| | | | Cash | Sales Discounts | Other Accounts | | |
| | | | | | Name | LP | Amount |
| 19__ | | | | | | | |
| Nov | 1 | Investment by owner | 75,000 | | | | |
| | 4 | Cash sales | 300 | | | | |
| | 5 | Cash sales | 400 | | | | |
| | 8 | Invoice Nov. 2, less 2% | 441 | 9 | | | |
| | 10 | Sale of land | 1,000 | | Notes Receivable | 3 | 6,000 |
| | 12 | Invoice Nov. 4, less 2% | 980 | 20 | | | |
| | 20 | Invoice Nov. 18, less 2% | 882 | 18 | | | |
| | 27 | Cash sales | 125 | | | | |
| | 30 | Obtained bank loan | 4,000 | | | | |
| | | | 83,128 | 47 | | | 6,000 |
| | | | (1) | (43) | | | (X) |

Other Accounts debit column and the amount of the debit to this account, $6,000. These two debits are offset by credit entries to Land, $5,000, and to Gain on Sale of Land, $2,000, in the Other Accounts credit column.

Credits:

1 Accounts receivable. This column is used to list the credits to customers' accounts as receivables are collected. The name of the customer is written in the space entitled Account Credited to the left of the Accounts Receivable column.

2 Sales. The existence of this column will save posting by permitting the accumulation of all sales for cash during the month and the posting of the column total at the end of the month as a credit to the Sales account (41).

3 Other accounts. This column is used for credits to any and all accounts other than Accounts Receivable and Sales. In some instances, a transaction may require credits to two accounts. Such cases are handled by using two lines of the special journal, as illustrated by the transaction of November 10, which required credits to both the Land account and to Gain on Sale of Land.

**Posting the cash receipts journal** It is convenient to think of the posting of a cash receipts journal as being divided into two phases. The first phase consists of the daily posting of individual amounts throughout the month; the second phase consists of the posting of column totals at the end of the month.

**Posting during the month** Daily posting of the Accounts Receivable credit col-

Page 1

| | Credits | | | | | |
|---|---|---|---|---|---|---|
| | Accounts Receivable | | | Other Accounts | | |
| Account Credited | √ | Amount | Sales | LP | Amount | |
| R. B. Jones, Capital | | | | 30 | 75,000 | |
| | | | 300 | | | |
| | | | 400 | | | |
| John Adams | √ | 450 | | | | |
| Land | | | | 11 | 5,000 | } |
| Gain on Sale of Land | | | | 40 | 2,000 | } |
| Harold Black | √ | 1,000 | | | | |
| C. D. Early | √ | 900 | | | | |
| | | | 125 | | | |
| Notes Payable | | | | 20 | 4,000 | |
| | | 2,350 | 825 | | 86,000 | |
| | | (5) | (41) | | (X) | |

umn is desirable. Each amount is posted to an individual customer's account in the accounts receivable subsidiary ledger. A check mark (√) is placed in the cash receipts journal alongside each item posted to a customer's account to show that the posting operation has been performed. When debits and credits to customers' accounts are posted daily, the current status of each customer's account is available for use in making decisions as to further granting of credit and as a guide to collection efforts on past-due accounts.

The debits and credits in the Other Accounts sections of the cash receipts journal may be posted daily or at convenient intervals during the month. If this portion of the posting work is done on a current basis, less detailed work will be left for the busy period at the end of the month. As the postings of individual items are made, the number of the ledger account debited or credited is entered in the LP (ledger page) column of the cash receipts journal opposite the item posted. Evidence is thus provided in the special journal as to which items have been posted.

**Posting column totals at month end** At the end of the month, the cash receipts journal is ruled as shown above and on page 258. Before posting any of the column totals, it is first important to prove that ***the sum of the debit column totals is equal to the sum of the credit column totals.***

After the totals of the cash receipts journal have been crossfooted, the following column totals are posted:

1 Cash debit column. Posted as a debit to the Cash account.
2 Sales Discounts debit column. Posted as a debit to the Sales Discounts account.
3 Accounts Receivable credit column. Posted as a credit to the controlling account, Accounts Receivable.
4 Sales credit column. Posted as a credit to the Sales account.

As each column total is posted to the appropriate account in the general ledger, the ledger account number is entered in parentheses just below the column total in the special journal. This notation shows that the column total has been posted and also indicates the account to which the posting was made. The totals of the Other Accounts columns in both the debit and credit sections of the special journal are not posted, because the amounts listed in the column affect various general ledger accounts and have already been posted as individual items. The symbol (X) is placed below the totals of these two columns to indicate that no posting is made.

## Cash payments journal

Another widely used special journal is the cash payments journal, sometimes called the ***cash disbursements journal,*** in which all payments of cash are recorded. Among the more common of these transactions are payments of ac-

***Includes all transactions involving payment of cash***

***Cash Payments Journal***

| | | | | Credits | | | | |
|---|---|---|---|---|---|---|---|---|
| | | | | | | Other Accounts | | |
| Date | | Check No. | Explanation | Cash | Purchase Discounts | Name | LP | Amount |
| 19__ | | | | | | | | |
| Nov | 1 | 101 | Paid November rent | 800 | | | | |
| | 2 | 102 | Purchased merchandise | 500 | | | | |
| | 8 | 103 | Invoice of Nov. 4, less 2% | 686 | 14 | | | |
| | 9 | 104 | Bought land and building | 70,000 | | Notes Payable | 20 | 30,000 |
| | 17 | 105 | Paid sales salaries | 3,600 | | | | |
| | 26 | 106 | Invoice of Nov. 16, less 2% | 882 | 18 | | | |
| | 27 | 107 | Purchased merchandise | 400 | | | | |
| | 28 | 108 | Purchased merchandise | 650 | | | | |
| | 29 | 109 | Newspaper advertisement | 50 | | | | |
| | 29 | 110 | Three-year ins. policy | 720 | | | | |
| | | | | 78,288 | 32 | | | 30,000 |
| | | | | (1) | (52) | | | (X) |

counts payable to creditors, payment of operating expenses, and cash purchases of merchandise.

The cash payments journal illustrated below contains entries for all November transactions of the Seaside Company which required the payment of cash.

**Nov.** **1** Paid rent on store building for November, $800.
**2** Purchased merchandise for cash, $500.
**8** Paid Barker & Bright for invoice of Nov. 4, $700 less 2%.
**9** Bought land, $65,000, and building, $35,000, for future use in business. Paid cash of $70,000 and signed a promissory note for the balance of $30,000. (Land and building were acquired in a single transaction.)
**17** Paid salesmen's salaries, $3,600.
**26** Paid Davis Co. for invoice of Nov. 16, $900 less 2%.
**27** Purchased merchandise for cash, $400.
**28** Purchased merchandise for cash, $650.
**29** Paid for newspaper advertising, $50.
**29** Paid for three-year insurance policy, $720.

Note in the illustrated cash payments journal that the three credit columns are located to the left of the three debit columns; any sequence of columns is satisfactory in a special journal as long as the column headings clearly distinguish debits from credits. The Cash column is often placed first in both the cash receipts journal and the cash payments journal because it is the column used in every transaction.

*Page 1*

| | Debits | | | | |
|---|---|---|---|---|---|
| | Accounts Payable | | | Other Accounts | |
| Account Debited | √ | Amount | Purchases | LP | Amount |
| Store Rent expense | | | | 54 | 800 |
| | | | 500 | | |
| Barker & Bright | √ | 700 | | | |
| Land | | | | 11 | 65,000 } |
| Building | | | | 12 | 35,000 } |
| Sales Salaries Expense | | | | 53 | 3,600 |
| Davis Co. | √ | 900 | | | |
| | | | 400 | | |
| | | | 650 | | |
| Advertising Expense | | | | 55 | 50 |
| Unexpired Insurance | | | | 6 | 720 |
| | | 1,600 | 1,550 | | 105,170 |
| | | (21) | (50) | | (X) |

Good internal control over cash disbursements requires that all payments be made by check. The checks are serially numbered and as each transaction is entered in the cash payments journal, the check number is listed in a special column provided just to the right of the date column. An unbroken sequence of check numbers in this column gives assurance that every check issued has been recorded in the accounting records.

The use of the six money columns in the illustrated cash payments journal parallels the procedures described for the cash receipts journal.

**Posting the cash payments journal** The posting of the cash payments journal falls into the same two phases already described for the cash receipts journal. The first phase consists of the daily posting of entries in the Accounts Payable debit column to the individual accounts of creditors in the accounts payable subsidiary ledger. Check marks (✓) are entered opposite these items to show that the posting has been made. If a creditor telephones to inquire about any aspect of his account, information on all purchases and payments made to date is readily available in the accounts payable subsidiary ledger.

The individual debit and credit entries in the Other Accounts columns of the cash payments journal may be posted daily or at convenient intervals during the month. As the postings of these individual items are made, the number of the ledger account debited or credited is entered in the LP (ledger page) column of the cash payments journal opposite the item posted.

The second phase of posting the cash payments journal is performed at the end of the month. When all the transactions of the month have been journalized, the cash payments journal is ruled as shown on pages 260 and 261, and the six money columns are totaled. The equality of debits and credits is then proved before posting.

After the totals of the cash payments journal have been proved to be in balance, the totals of the columns for Cash, Purchase Discounts, Accounts Payable, and Purchases are posted to the corresponding accounts in the general ledger. The numbers of the accounts to which these postings are made are listed in parentheses just below the respective column totals in the cash payments journal. The totals of the Other Accounts columns in both the debit and credit section of this special journal are not to be posted, and the symbol (X) is placed below the totals of these two columns to indicate that no posting is required.

## The general journal

When all transactions involving cash or the purchase and sale of merchandise are recorded in special journals, only a few types of transactions remain to be entered in the general journal. Examples include the purchase or sale of plant and equipment on credit, the return of merchandise for credit to a supplier, and the return of merchandise by customers for credit to their accounts. The general journal is also used for the recording of adjusting and closing entries at the end of the accounting period.

The following transactions of the Seaside Company during November could not conveniently be handled in any of the four special journals and were therefore entered in the general journal.

**Nov. 25** A customer, John Frost, was permitted to return for credit $50 worth of merchandise that had been sold to him on Nov. 23.

**28** The Seaside Company returned to a supplier, Excelsior, Inc., for credit $300 worth of the merchandise purchased on Nov. 27.

**29** Purchased for use in the business office equipment costing $1,225. Agreed to make payment within 30 days to XYZ Equipment Co.

***Transactions which do not fit any of the four special journals***

***General Journal*** — *Page 1*

| Date | | Account Titles and Explanation | LP | Dr | Cr |
|---|---|---|---|---|---|
| 19__ | | | | | |
| Nov | 25 | Sales Returns and Allowances | 42 | 50 | |
| | | Accounts Receivable, John Frost | 5/√ | | 50 |
| | | Allowed credit to customer for return of merchandise from sale of Nov. 23. | | | |
| | 28 | Accounts Payable, Excelsior, Inc. | 21/√ | 300 | |
| | | Purchase Returns and Allowances | 51 | | 300 |
| | | Returned to supplier for credit a portion of merchandise purchased on Nov. 27. | | | |
| | 29 | Office Equipment | 14 | 1,225 | |
| | | Accounts Payable, XYZ Equipment Co. | 21/√ | | 1,225 |
| | | Purchased office equipment on 30-day credit. | | | |

Each of the above entries includes a debit or credit to a controlling account (Accounts Receivable or Accounts Payable) and also identifies by name a particular creditor or customer. When a controlling account is debited or credited by a ***general journal entry,*** the debit or credit must be posted twice: one posting to the controlling account in the general ledger and another posting to a customer's account or a creditor's account in a subsidiary ledger. This double posting is necessary to keep the controlling account in agreement with the subsidiary ledger.

For example, in the illustrated entry of November 25 for the return of merchandise by a customer, the credit part of the entry is posted twice:

**1** To the Accounts Receivable controlling account in the general ledger; this posting is evidenced by listing the account number (5) in the LP column of the general journal.

**2** To the account of John Frost in the subsidiary ledger for accounts receivable; this posting is indicated by the check mark (√) placed in the LP (ledger page) column of the general journal.

### Showing the source of postings in ledger accounts

When a general journal and several special journals are in use, the ledger accounts should indicate the book of original entry from which each debit and credit was posted. An identifying symbol is placed opposite each entry in the reference column of the account. The symbols used in this text are as follows:

| | |
|---|---|
| S1 | meaning page 1 of the sales journal |
| P1 | meaning page 1 of the purchases journal |
| CR1 | meaning page 1 of the cash receipts journal |
| CP1 | meaning page 1 of the cash payments journal |
| J1 | meaning page 1 of the general journal |

### Subsidiary ledger accounts

The following illustration shows a customer's account in a subsidiary ledger for accounts receivable.

**Subsidiary ledger: account receivable**

***Name of Customer***

| Date | | | Ref | Debit | Credit | Balance |
|---|---|---|---|---|---|---|
| 19__ | | | | | | |
| July | 1 | | S1 | 400 | | 400 |
| | 20 | | S3 | 200 | | 600 |
| Aug | 4 | | CR7 | | 400 | 200 |
| | 15 | | S6 | 120 | | 320 |

The advantage of this three-column form of account is that it shows at a glance the present balance receivable from the customer. The current amount of a customer's account is often needed as a guide to collection activities, or as a basis for granting additional credit. In studying the above illustration note also that the Reference column shows the source of each debit and credit.

Accounts appearing in the accounts receivable subsidiary ledger are assumed to have debit balances. If one of these customers' accounts should acquire a credit balance by overpayment or for any other reason, the word ***credit*** should be written after the amount in the Balance column.

The same three-column form of account is also generally used for creditors' accounts in an accounts payable subsidiary ledger, as indicated by the following illustration:

**Subsidiary ledger: account payable**

***Name of Creditor***

| Date | | | Ref | Debit | Credit | Balance |
|---|---|---|---|---|---|---|
| 19__ | | | | | | |
| July | 10 | | P1 | | 625 | 625 |
| | 25 | | P2 | | 100 | 725 |
| Aug | 8 | | CP4 | 725 | | 0 |
| | 12 | | P3 | | 250 | 250 |

Accounts in the accounts payable subsidiary ledger normally have credit balances. If by reason of payment in advance or accidental overpayment, one of these accounts should acquire a debit balance, the word ***debit*** should be written after the amount in the Balance column.

As previously stated, both the accounts receivable and accounts payable subsidiary ledgers are customarily arranged in alphabetical order and account numbers are not used. This arrangement permits unlimited expansion of the subsidiary ledgers, as accounts with new customers and creditors can be inserted in proper alphabetical sequence.

## Ledger accounts

**The general ledger** The general ledger accounts of the Seaside Company illustrated next indicate the source of postings from the various books or original entry. The subsidiary ledger accounts appear on pages 267–269. To gain a clear understanding of the procedures for posting special journals, you should trace each entry in the illustrated special journals into the general ledger accounts and also to the subsidiary ledger accounts where appropriate. The general ledger accounts are shown in T-account form in order to distinguish them more emphatically from the accounts in the subsidiary ledgers.

Note that the Cash account contains only one debit entry and one credit entry, although there were many cash transactions during the month. The one debit, $83,128, represents the total cash received during the month and was posted from the cash receipts journal on November 30. Similarly, the one credit entry of $78,288 was posted on November 30 from the cash payments journal and represents the total of all cash payments made during the month.

*General ledger accounts*

**Cash** — 1

| | | | | | | | | | |
|---|---|---|---|---|---|---|---|---|---|
| 19__ | | | | | 19__ | | | | |
| Nov | 30 | | CR1 | 83,128 | Nov | 30 | | CP1 | 78,288 |

**Notes Receivable** — 3

| | | | | | | | | | |
|---|---|---|---|---|---|---|---|---|---|
| 19__ | | | | | | | | | |
| Nov | 10 | | CR1 | 6,000 | | | | | |

**Accounts Receivable** — 5

| | | | | | | | | | |
|---|---|---|---|---|---|---|---|---|---|
| 19__ | | | | | 19__ | | | | |
| Nov | 30 | | S1 | 16,195 | Nov | 25 | | J1 | 50 |
| | | | | | | 30 | | CR1 | 2,350 |

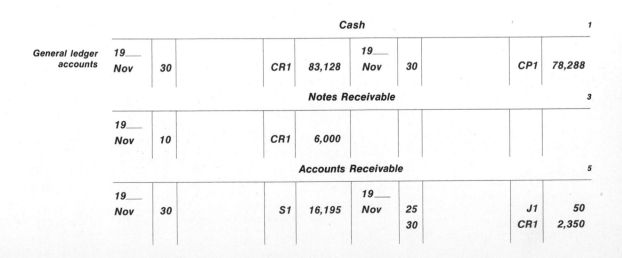

### Unexpired Insurance 6

| | | | | | | | | | |
|---|---|---|---|---|---|---|---|---|---|
| 19__ | | | | | | | | | |
| Nov | 29 | | CP1 | 720 | | | | | |

### Land 11

| | | | | | | | | | |
|---|---|---|---|---|---|---|---|---|---|
| 19__ | | | | | 19__ | | | | |
| Nov | 9 | | CP1 | 65,000 | Nov | 10 | | CR1 | 5,000 |

### Building 12

| | | | | | | | | | |
|---|---|---|---|---|---|---|---|---|---|
| 19__ | | | | | | | | | |
| Nov | 9 | | CP1 | 35,000 | | | | | |

### Office Equipment 14

| | | | | | | | | | |
|---|---|---|---|---|---|---|---|---|---|
| 19__ | | | | | | | | | |
| Nov | 29 | | J1 | 1,225 | | | | | |

### Notes Payable 20

| | | | | | | | | | |
|---|---|---|---|---|---|---|---|---|---|
| | | | | | 19__ | | | | |
| | | | | | Nov | 9 | | CP1 | 30,000 |
| | | | | | | 30 | | CR1 | 4,000 |

### Accounts Payable 21

| | | | | | | | | | |
|---|---|---|---|---|---|---|---|---|---|
| 19__ | | | | | 19__ | | | | |
| Nov | 28 | | J1 | 300 | Nov | 29 | | J1 | 1,225 |
| | 30 | | CP1 | 1,600 | | 30 | | P1 | 7,250 |

### R. B. Jones, Capital 30

| | | | | | | | | | |
|---|---|---|---|---|---|---|---|---|---|
| | | | | | 19__ | | | | |
| | | | | | Nov | 1 | | CR1 | 75,000 |

### Gain on Sale of Land 40

| | | | | | | | | | |
|---|---|---|---|---|---|---|---|---|---|
| | | | | | 19__ | | | | |
| | | | | | Nov | 10 | | CR1 | 2,000 |

### Sales 41

| | | | | | | | | | |
|---|---|---|---|---|---|---|---|---|---|
| | | | | | 19__ | | | | |
| | | | | | Nov | 30 | | CR1 | 825 |
| | | | | | | 30 | | S1 | 16,195 |

### Sales Returns and Allowances 42

| | | | | | | | | | |
|---|---|---|---|---|---|---|---|---|---|
| 19__ | | | | | | | | | |
| Nov | 25 | | J1 | 50 | | | | | |

**Sales Discounts** 43

| | | | | | | | | | |
|---|---|---|---|---|---|---|---|---|---|
| 19__ | | | | | | | | | |
| Nov | 30 | | CR1 | 47 | | | | | |

**Purchases** 50

| | | | | | | | | | |
|---|---|---|---|---|---|---|---|---|---|
| 19__ | | | | | | | | | |
| Nov | 30 | | CP1 | 1,550 | | | | | |
| | 30 | | P1 | 7,250 | | | | | |

**Purchase Returns and Allowances** 51

| | | | | | | | | | |
|---|---|---|---|---|---|---|---|---|---|
| | | | | | 19__ | | | | |
| | | | | | Nov | 28 | | J1 | 300 |

**Purchase Discounts** 52

| | | | | | | | | | |
|---|---|---|---|---|---|---|---|---|---|
| | | | | | 19__ | | | | |
| | | | | | Nov | 30 | | CP1 | 32 |

**Sales Salaries Expense** 53

| | | | | | | | | | |
|---|---|---|---|---|---|---|---|---|---|
| 19__ | | | | | | | | | |
| Nov | 17 | | CP1 | 3,600 | | | | | |

**Store Rent Expense** 54

| | | | | | | | | | |
|---|---|---|---|---|---|---|---|---|---|
| 19__ | | | | | | | | | |
| Nov | 1 | | CP1 | 800 | | | | | |

**Advertising Expense** 55

| | | | | | | | | | |
|---|---|---|---|---|---|---|---|---|---|
| 19__ | | | | | | | | | |
| Nov | 29 | | CP1 | 50 | | | | | |

**Accounts receivable ledger** The subsidiary ledger for accounts receivable appears as follows after the posting of the various journals has been completed.

*Customers' accounts*

**John Adams**

| | | | | | | |
|---|---|---|---|---|---|---|
| 19__ | | | | | | |
| Nov | 2 | | S1 | 450 | | 450 |
| | 8 | | CR1 | | 450 | 0 |

**Harold Black**

| | | | | | | |
|---|---|---|---|---|---|---|
| 19__ | | | | | | |
| Nov | 4 | | S1 | 1,000 | | 1,000 |
| | 12 | | CR1 | | 1,000 | 0 |

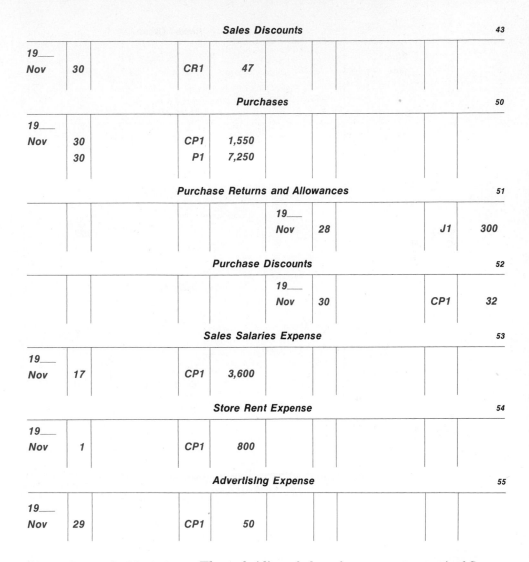

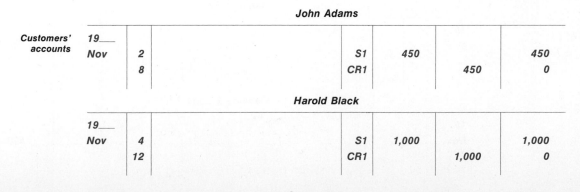

**Robert Cross**

| | | | | | | |
|---|---|---|---|---|---|---|
| 19__ | | | | | | |
| Nov | 5 | | S1 | 975 | | 975 |

**H. R. Davis**

| | | | | | | |
|---|---|---|---|---|---|---|
| 19__ | | | | | | |
| Nov | 11 | | S1 | 620 | | 620 |

**C. D. Early**

| | | | | | | |
|---|---|---|---|---|---|---|
| 19__ | | | | | | |
| Nov | 18 | | S1 | 900 | | 900 |
| | 20 | | CR1 | | 900 | 0 |

**John Frost**

| | | | | | | |
|---|---|---|---|---|---|---|
| 19__ | | | | | | |
| Nov | 23 | | S1 | 400 | | 400 |
| | 25 | | J1 | | 50 | 350 |

**D. H. Gray**

| | | | | | | |
|---|---|---|---|---|---|---|
| 19__ | | | | | | |
| Nov | 29 | | S1 | 11,850 | | 11,850 |

**Accounts payable ledger** The accounts with creditors in the accounts payable subsidiary ledger are as follows:

*Creditors' accounts*

**Alabama Supply Co.**

| | | | | | | |
|---|---|---|---|---|---|---|
| 19__ | | | | | | |
| Nov | 2 | | P1 | | 3,325 | 3,325 |

**Barker & Bright**

| | | | | | | |
|---|---|---|---|---|---|---|
| 19__ | | | | | | |
| Nov | 4 | | P1 | | 700 | 700 |
| | 8 | | CP1 | 700 | | 0 |

**Canning & Sons**

| | | | | | | |
|---|---|---|---|---|---|---|
| 19__ | | | | | | |
| Nov | 10 | | P1 | | 500 | 500 |

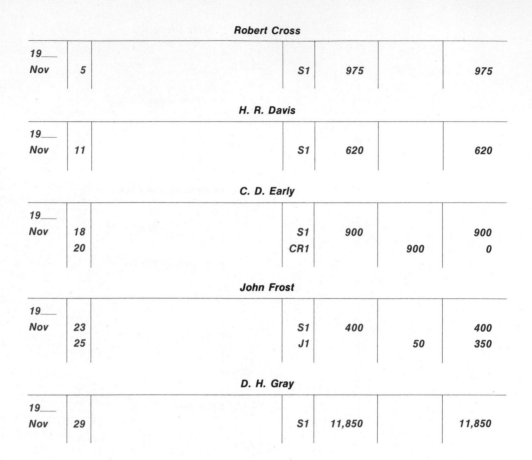

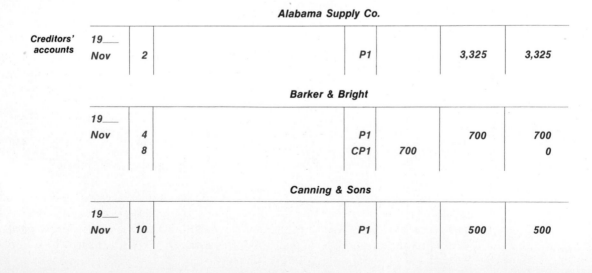

**Davis Co.**

| | | | | | | |
|---|---|---|---|---|---|---|
| 19__ | | | | | | |
| Nov | 17 | | P1 | | 900 | 900 |
| | 26 | | CP1 | 900 | | 0 |

**Excelsior, Inc.**

| | | | | | | |
|---|---|---|---|---|---|---|
| 19__ | | | | | | |
| Nov | 27 | | P1 | | 1,825 | 1,825 |
| | 28 | | J1 | 300 | | 1,525 |

**XYZ Equipment Co.**

| | | | | | | |
|---|---|---|---|---|---|---|
| 19__ | | | | | | |
| Nov | 29 | | J1 | | 1,225 | 1,225 |

## Proving the ledgers

At the end of each accounting period, proof of the equality of debits and credits in the general ledger is established by preparation of a trial balance, as illustrated in preceding chapters. When controlling accounts and subsidiary ledgers are in use, it is also necessary to prove that each subsidiary ledger is in agreement with its controlling account. This proof is accomplished by preparing a schedule of the balances of accounts in each subsidiary ledger and determining that the totals of these schedules agree with the balances of the corresponding controlling accounts. The Seaside Company's trial balance and schedules of accounts receivable and accounts payable appear on page 270.

## Variations in special journals

The number of columns to be included in each special journal and the number of special journals to be used will depend upon the nature of the particular business and especially upon the volume of the various kinds of transactions. For example, the desirability of including a Sales Discounts column in the cash receipts journal depends upon whether a business offers discounts to its customers for prompt payment.

A retail store may find that customers frequently return merchandise for credit. To record efficiently this large volume of sales returns, the store may establish a sales returns and allowances journal. A purchase returns and allowances journal may also be desirable if returns of goods to suppliers occur frequently.

Special journals should be regarded as laborsaving devices which may be designed with any number of columns appropriate to the needs of the particular business. A business will usually benefit by establishing a special journal for any type of transaction that occurs quite frequently.

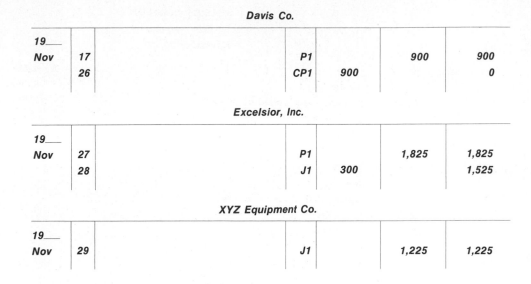

**SEASIDE COMPANY**
**Trial Balance**
**November 30, 19__**

*General ledger trial balance*

| | | |
|---|---|---|
| Cash | $ 4,840 | |
| Notes receivable | 6,000 | |
| Accounts receivable (see schedule below) | 13,795 | |
| Unexpired insurance | 720 | |
| Land | 60,000 | |
| Building | 35,000 | |
| Office equipment | 1,225 | |
| Notes payable | | $ 34,000 |
| Accounts payable (see schedule below) | | 6,575 |
| R. B. Jones, capital | | 75,000 |
| Gain on sale of land | | 2,000 |
| Sales | | 17,020 |
| Sales returns and allowances | 50 | |
| Sales discounts | 47 | |
| Purchases | 8,800 | |
| Purchase returns and allowances | | 300 |
| Purchase discounts | | 32 |
| Sales salaries expense | 3,600 | |
| Store rent expense | 800 | |
| Advertising expense | 50 | |
| | $134,927 | $134,927 |

**Schedule of Accounts Receivable**
**November 30, 19__**

*Subsidiary ledgers in balance with control accounts*

| | |
|---|---|
| Robert Cross | $ 975 |
| H. R. Davis | 620 |
| John Frost | 350 |
| D. H. Gray | 11,850 |
| Total (per balance of controlling account) | $13,795 |

**Schedule of Accounts Payable**
**November 30, 19__**

| | |
|---|---|
| Alabama Supply Co. | $3,325 |
| Canning & Sons | 500 |
| Excelsior, Inc. | 1,525 |
| XYZ Equipment Co. | 1,225 |
| Total (per balance of controlling account) | $6,575 |

### Direct posting from invoices

In many business concerns the efficiency of data processing is increased by posting sales invoices directly to the customers' accounts in the accounts receivable ledger rather than copying sales invoices into a sales journal and then posting to accounts in the subsidiary ledger. If the sales invoices are ***serially numbered,*** a file or binder of duplicate sales invoices arranged in numerical order may take the place of a formal sales journal. By accounting for each ***serial number,*** it is possible to be certain that all sales invoices are included. At the end of the month, the invoices are totaled on a calculator, and a general journal entry is made debiting the Accounts Receivable controlling account and crediting Sales for the total of the month's sales invoices.

Direct posting may also be used in recording purchase invoices. As soon as purchase invoices have been verified and approved, credits to the creditors' accounts in the accounts payable ledger may be posted directly from the purchase invoices.

The trend toward direct posting from invoices to subsidiary ledgers is mentioned here as further evidence that accounting records and procedures can be designed in a variety of ways to meet the individual needs of different business concerns.

## MECHANICAL ACCOUNTING SYSTEMS

The processing of accounting data may be performed manually, mechanically, or electronically. The term ***data processing*** includes the preparation of documents (such as invoices and checks) and the flow of the data contained in these documents through the major accounting steps of recording, classifying, and summarizing. A well-designed system produces an uninterrupted flow of all essential data needed by management for planning and controlling business operations.

### Unit record for each transaction

Our discussion has thus far been limited to a manual accounting system. One of the points we have emphasized is that an immediate record should be made of every business transaction. The ***medium*** used to make this record is usually a document or form, such as an invoice or a check. This concept of a unit record for each transaction is an important one as we consider the alternatives of processing these media by accounting machines, by punched cards, or by a computer. Regardless of whether we use mechanical or electronic equipment, the document representing a single transaction is a basic element of the accounting process.

### Use of office equipment in a manual data processing system

Manually kept records are a convenient means of demonstrating accounting principles, and they are also used by a great many small businesses. Strictly defined, a manual system of processing accounting data would call for handwritten journals, ledgers, and financial statements. Even in a small business with some handwritten records, however, the use of office machines and laborsaving devices such as cash registers, adding machines, desk calculators, and multicopy forms has become standard practice.

### Simultaneous preparation of documents, journals, and ledgers

Traditionally, each business transaction was recorded, copied, and recopied. A transaction was first evidenced by a document such as a sales invoice, then copied into a journal (book of original entry), and later posted to a ledger. This step-by-step sequence of creating accounting records is time-consuming and leaves room for the introduction of errors at each step. Whenever a figure, an account title, or an account number is copied, the danger of introducing errors exists. This is true regardless of whether the copying is done with pen and ink or by punching a machine keyboard. The copying process is subject to human errors. From this premise it follows that if several accounting records can be created by writing a transaction only once, the recording process will be not only faster but also more accurate.

### Accounting machines

The development of accounting machines designed to create several accounting records with a single writing of a transaction has progressed at a fantastic rate. Machines with typewriter keyboards and computing mechanisms were early developments useful in preparing journals, invoices, payrolls, and other records requiring the typing of names and the computation of amounts. ***Accounting machines*** is a term usually applied to mechanical or electronic equipment capable of performing arithmetic functions and used to produce a variety of accounting records and reports.

### Punched cards and tabulating equipment

Punched cards are a widely used medium for recording accounting data. Information such as amounts, names, account numbers, and other details is recorded by punching holes in appropriate columns and rows of a standard-sized card, usually by means of a ***key-punch machine.*** The information punched on the cards can then be read and processed by a variety of machines, including computers.

Every business receives original documents such as invoices and checks in many shapes and sizes. By punching the information on each such document into a card, we create a document of standard size which machines and computers can use in creating records and reports. For example, once the information on sales invoices has been punched into cards, these cards can be run through machines to produce a schedule of accounts receivable, an analysis of sales by product, by territory, and by each salesperson, and a listing of commissions earned by sales personnel.

Processing accounting data by means of punched cards may be viewed as three major steps, with specially designed machines for each step. The first step is that of recording data; a machine often used for this purpose is an electrically operated ***key punch*** with a keyboard similar to that of a typewriter.

The second major step is classifying or sorting the data into related groups or categories. For this step a machine called a ***sorter*** is used. The sorter reads the information on each punched card and then arranges the cards in a particular order, or sorts a deck of cards into groups based on the relationship of the data punched into the cards.

The third major step is summarizing the data. This step is performed by a ***tabulating machine,*** which has an ***output*** of printed information resulting from the classifying and totaling of the data on the cards.

## EDP ACCOUNTING SYSTEMS

The term ***electronic data processing*** (EDP) refers to the processing of data by electronic computers. A computer-based accounting system processes data in basically the same manner as does a manual or mechanical system. Transactions are initially recorded manually on source documents. The data from these source documents are then keypunched into punched cards which can be read by the computer. The computer processes the information and performs such routine tasks as printing journals (called transaction summaries), posting to ledger accounts, determining account balances, and printing financial statements and other reports.

The primary advantage of the computer is its incredible speed. The number of computations made by an electronic computer is measured in millions per second. In one minute, an electronic printer can produce as much printed material as the average typist in a full day. Because of this speed, ledger accounts may be kept continually up-to-date and current reports may be prepared quickly at any time to assist executives in making decisions.

### Elements of an EDP system

An electronic data processing system includes a computer, also called a ***central processing unit*** (CPU), and a number of related machines, which are often called ***peripheral equipment.*** The computer is the heart of the system; it performs the processing function which includes the storage of information, arithmetic computations, and control. The other two major elements are (1) ***input*** devices which prepare and insert information into the computer and (2) ***output*** devices which transfer information out of the computer to the accountant or other user. Both input and output devices perform the function of ***translation.*** The machines used to feed information into a computer translate the data into computer language; the output devices translate the processed data back into the language of written words, or of punched cards, paper tape, or magnetic tape.

*EDP system illustrated*

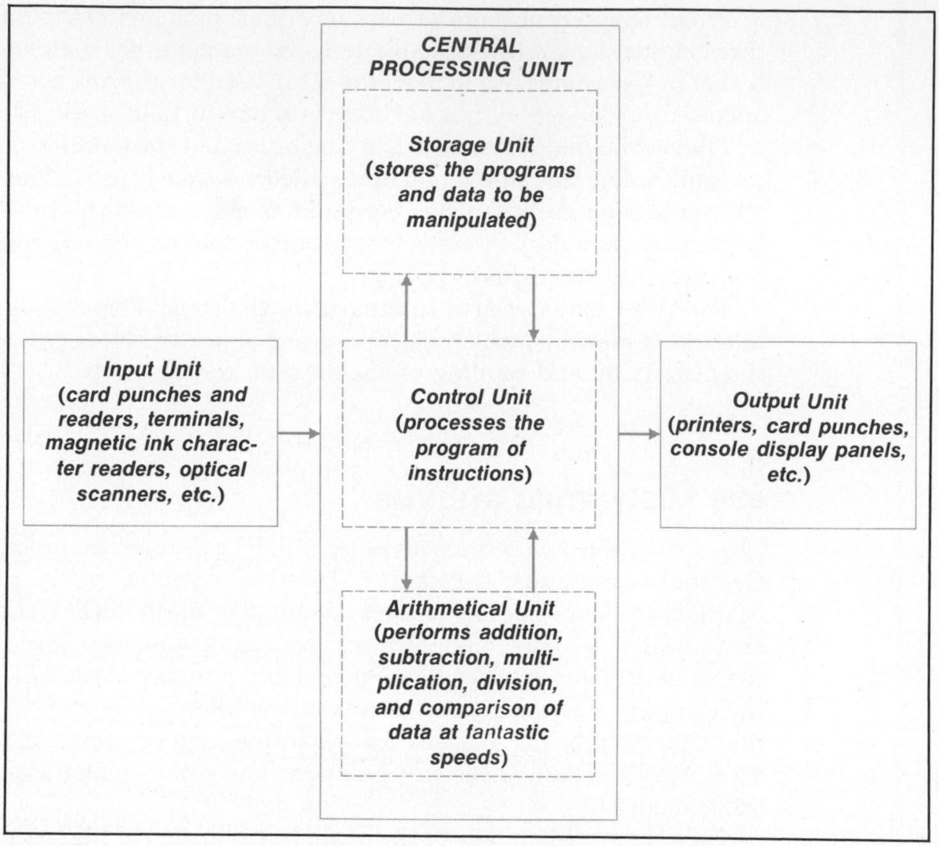


**Hardware and software** The machines and related equipment used in an EDP system are called ***hardware.*** All the other materials utilized in selecting, installing, and operating the system (except the operating personnel) are called ***software.*** Software includes not only the ***computer programs*** (the sequence of instructions given to the computer), but also feasibility studies, training materials such as films and manuals, studies of equipment requirements, and everything about the EDP system other than the hardware.

## Input devices

Among the input devices used to transfer instructions and accounting data into a computer are card readers, punched-paper-tape readers, magnetic-tape readers, character readers, and terminals. The card-reading device will either transmit information from punched cards into the memory unit of the computer or convert the information to paper or magnetic tape. Punched cards will be read by the card-reading devices at rates of several hundred or even several thousand per minute.

Punched-paper tape can be created as part of the process of recording transactions on cash registers or adding machines. This type of input medium is inexpensive to create and easy to use, but it does not permit the insertion of additional data or the making of corrections after the tape has been punched. Punched-tape readers deliver the data to the computer at high speeds. Both punched-card readers and paper-tape readers are usually connected directly to the computer and are described as part of the ***on-line*** (direct access) system. They offer the advantage of compatibility with nonelectronic equipment utilizing punched cards or tape.

Magnetic tape is a far faster means of feeding information into a computer and has the advantage of being easily stored. Corrections are also easily made on magnetic tape. Magnetic-tape reels are, however, more expensive than paper tape.

Character-reading machines are perhaps best known in the banking field. They read the account numbers printed in magnetic ink on checks and deposit tickets and convert these data into codes acceptable to the computer. Another type of character-reading device is the optical scanner, with a photoelectric cell which can read a printed document and convert the characters into computer language. This device makes unnecessary the costly step of translating printed matter into punched-card form.

***Terminals*** are keyboard devices which make it possible to enter limited amounts of data into an EDP system without punching the information into cards or tape as a preliminary step. Terminals are extremely slow in comparison with the operating capacity of the computer because they are manually operated. However, terminals have the advantage of allowing the various departments of a business to enter data directly into the accounting system, without having to send their source documents to an EDP department to be keypunched and read into the computer. Some retail stores use terminals in the sales departments to record each sale in the accounting records and to update the accounts receivable from customers. Terminals are also equipped with a printing device which permits output from the computer to be delivered immediately to the user of the terminal. The minicomputer and microcomputer systems now used by many small companies generally use a terminal resembling a typewriter as the principal input and output device.

## Output devices

The ***printer*** is the most important output device. It interprets the computer code and prints several hundred lines per minute, either at the computer center or at remote locations. The printer might be used to produce payroll checks, customers' statements, and many types of accounting reports.

Card-punching machines and paper-tape-punching machines can transfer data from the computer into punch cards and paper tape which later may be used as input data for subsequent analysis or processing.

## Processing operations in the computer

The processing operations performed by a computer include storage of information, arithmetic manipulation of data, and control. The computer receives and stores instructions and data; it calls this information from the memory or storage unit as required by the processing routine; it goes through arithmetic operations, makes comparisons of numbers, and takes the action necessary to produce the required output of information.

The term ***control*** describes the ability of the computer to guide itself through the processing operations utilizing detailed lists of instructions concerning the work to be done.

**Program** A ***program*** is a series of steps planned to carry out a certain process, such as the preparation of a payroll. Each step in the program is a command or instruction to the computer. A program for payroll might be compared with a very detailed written set of instructions given to an inexperienced employee assigned to the payroll function in a manual accounting system. A most important attribute of the computer is its ability to receive and store a set of instructions which controls its behavior.

The preparation of a computer program is a complicated and costly task. A company may employ its own programmers or may rely on outside organizations which specialize in such services.

## Differences between mechanical and electronic data processing systems

Mechanical data processing equipment such as electric calculators, mechanical accounting machines, and key-punch machines is extremely slow when compared with electronic equipment. The processing of data in the electronic system is accomplished by electric impulses traveling through electronic circuits. Such equipment functions hundreds of times faster than mechanical devices.

Another point of contrast is that the units of equipment comprising an EDP system are interconnected so that the processing of data is a continuous operation from the point of reading input data to the point of printing the report or other final result. On the other hand, a mechanical data processing system employs separate machines which do not communicate directly with each other. After each machine, such as a key punch, has performed its function, the output media (punched cards or paper tape) must be transported manually to another machine.

## Internal control and the computer

EDP equipment itself is highly reliable, and the possibility of errors caused by the hardware is very small. However, the use of reliable equipment does not eliminate entirely the possibilities of errors in the accounting records. Human beings create the information that goes into a computer, and human beings make mistakes. Errors may still be made in the preparation of source documents, such as invoices, checks, and credit memos. The process of keypunching data into punched cards is comparable to using a typewriter, and making errors is quite possible. Also, the computer program may contain errors which may cause the data to be processed improperly. To reduce the possibility of these types of errors, an EDP system should include both ***input controls*** and ***program controls.***

**Input controls** Input controls are the precautions taken to ensure that the data being entered into the computer are correct. One important input control is the manual preparation of ***control totals,*** representing the total dollar amount of all source documents sent to the EDP department for processing. The computer will add up the total dollar amount of all data processed and print this total as part of the computer output. The manually prepared control totals may then be compared to the total printed by the computer to ensure that all source documents sent to the EDP department have been processed.

Another input control is the use of a ***verifier key punch.*** When data are keypunched into punched cards, there is always the possibility of striking the wrong key, causing a keypunching error. A verifier key punch is used to keypunch the source data into the punched cards a second time; any differences between the first and second keypunching cause the machine to signal that an error has been made.

**Program controls** Program controls are error-detecting measures built into the computer program. An example of a program control is a ***limit test,*** which compares every item of data processed by the computer to a specified dollar limit. In the event an amount exceeds the dollar limit, the computer does not process that item and prints out an ***error report.*** A limit test is particularly effective in such computer applications as preparing paychecks, when it is known that none of the paychecks should be for more than a specified amount, such as $1,000.

Another example of a program control is an ***item count.*** The total number of punched cards to be processed by the computer is determined, and that total is entered as part of the input to the computer. The computer then counts the number of cards it processes, and if this number differs from the predetermined total, an error report is printed. This item count ensures that all the punched cards are actually processed by the computer.

**Separation of duties to prevent computer-related fraud** In Chapter 6 we emphasized that subdivision of duties is essential to strong internal control. if related duties are all lodged in the hands of one person, internal control is destroyed. Some spectacular fraud cases involving the use of computers have made clear the danger of having one person design the system and serve as both programmer and operator.

ILLUSTRATIVE CASE John Jones, a bank employee, developed a computer program which would identify all overdrawn checking accounts and prepare a list showing the depositors' names, account numbers, and the dollar amounts overdrawn. Jones was later assigned to work as operator of the bank's computer. While working in this capacity, he made a change in the program which caused the computer to ignore overdrafts in his own personal checking account. After inserting this patch in the computer program, Jones was able to overdraw his account in any amount without the overdraft coming to the attention of the bank's management. His fraud was discovered only when the computer broke down and a list of overdrawn accounts was prepared manually by other bank employees.

## Accounting applications of the computer

The use of electronic data processing equipment is possible for virtually every phase of accounting operations. Even a CPA firm, in conducting an annual audit, may use the computer as an audit tool. For this purpose the auditors may employ specially written computer programs to aid in their work of sampling and analyzing data to determine the fairness of the financial statements.

The most common application of the computer, however, is to process large masses of accounting data relating to routine repetitive operations such as accounts receivable, accounts payable, inventories, payrolls, and posting to ledger accounts.

**Payrolls** In a manual accounting system the preparation of payroll checks is usually separate from the maintenance of records showing pay rates, positions, time worked, payroll deductions, and other personnel data. An EDP system, however, has the capability of maintaining all records relating to payroll as well as turning out the required paychecks. Payroll processing is usually one of the first accounting operations to be placed on the computer.

The payroll procedure consists of determining for each employee the gross earnings, making deductions, computing net pay, preparing the payroll check, and maintaining a record of each individual's earnings. Also, the company needs a payroll summary for each period and usually a distribution of payroll costs by department, by product, or classified by the various productive processes. The payroll function has become increasingly complex and time-consuming in recent years because of the advent of social security taxes, income tax withholding, and other payroll deductions. Each employee must receive not only a payroll check but a statement showing the gross earnings, deductions, and net pay. The company's records must be designed to facilitate filing with the federal and state governments regular payroll reports showing amounts withheld for income taxes, unemployment insurance, and social security. The time and the expense required to prepare payrolls has risen in proportion to the need for more information. The demands by governments, labor unions, credit unions, and other outside agencies have added to the problem.

An EDP payroll system will not only maintain the necessary records, print the checks, and print these reports, but it can also keep management informed of the costs of various functions within the business. For example, data can be produced showing the work-hours and labor costs on each job, labor cost by department for each salesclerk, or the time required by different employees to perform similar work. In other words, much current information can be developed without significant extra expense that will provide management with a detailed breakdown of labor costs. The comparison below illustrates the efficiency of processing payrolls by EDP rather than manually:

*Payroll may be prepared either manually or by EDP*

| Function | Payroll Prepared Manually | Payroll Prepared by EDP |
|---|---|---|
| *1 Timekeeping* | *Fill in new set of records each period, making extensions manually.* | *Enter raw data on appropriate forms.* |
| *2 Computation of gross pay* | *Compute gross pay for each employee, perhaps with desk calculator, and enter manually in records.* | *Performed electronically.* |
| *3 Calculation of deductions* | *For each employee, refer to charts and make computations; enter manually in records.* | *Performed electronically.* |
| *4 Preparation of checks, earnings statements, and payroll register* | *Write by hand or type checks. Proofread and maintain controls.* | *Performed electronically.* |
| *5 Bank reconciliation* | *Reconcile payroll bank account per accounting records with monthly bank statement.* | *Performed electronically.* |
| *6 Reports to government* | *Prepare quarterly reports showing for each employee and in total amounts earned, deducted, and paid. Reconcile individual data with controls.* | *Performed electronically.* |
| *7 Managerial control data* | *Prepare distribution of hours and labor cost by department or by job. Other analyses may be needed.* | *Performed electronically.* |

**Computer-based journals and ledgers** As mentioned earlier in this chapter, computers also may be used to maintain the journals and ledgers and to prepare financial statements. Transactions and end-of-period adjustments still must be analyzed by persons possessing a knowledge of accounting principles. However, after these transactions have been analyzed and prepared in computer input form, the computer can be used to print the journals, post to the ledger accounts, and print the financial statements and other financial reports. The advantage of maintaining accounting records by computer is that the possibility of mathematical errors is greatly reduced, and the speed of the computer permits the records to be kept continuously up-to-date.

Other accounting applications of computers include forecasting the profit possibilities inherent in alternative courses of action, analyzing gross profit margins by department or by product line, and determining future cash requirements long in advance. Recent developments of accounting applications of the computer provide much more information about business operations than was available to management in the past.

### Computer service centers and time-sharing

A computer and related hardware are costly to buy or rent. The employment of personnel qualified to operate the equipment is also a major expense, especially for a small business. One way in which a small business can avoid investing large sums yet gain the operating efficiencies of EDP is to turn over its raw data to a bank, an accounting firm, or a computer center that offers EDP services on a fee basis. The small business may either keypunch its data and send the punched cards to the service center for processing or write the data on special forms and let the service center do the keypunching.

Another method of using EDP services without owning a computer is called ***time-sharing.*** Time-sharing refers to using a large central computer by means of a portable terminal, which is both an input and output device. Through these terminals, hundreds of businesses may make use of the same central computer. The company which owns the central computer sends each of these users a monthly bill, including a fixed monthly charge plus a per-minute charge for the actual time spent using the computer. Since the portable terminals communicate with the central computer using ordinary telephone lines, the terminals may be thousands of miles away from the central computer.

An advantage of time-sharing is the convenience of direct access to the computer through a portable terminal. A disadvantage, however, is that a terminal enters data into the computer using a manual keyboard. This is a relatively slow way of entering data into a computer. If large quantities of data must be processed, a computer service center may be less expensive than time-sharing.

### Do computers make decisions?

Computers can do only what they have specifically been told to do. Computers cannot make decisions in the sense of exercising judgment. They can choose among alternatives only by following the specific instructions contained in the program. When a computer encounters a situation for which it has not been programmed, it is unable to act. Computer programs must therefore be carefully tested to determine that they provide the computer with adequate instructions for all aspects of the data processing.

### Information systems

The automation of an accounting system speeds up the production and transmission of information. The term ***integrated data processing*** (IDP) describes the current trend of providing attachments for typewriters, accounting machines, cash registers, and other conventional equipment which will, as a by-product, produce perforated tape or cards acceptable to a computer. The typewriter, for example, when equipped with such attachments can be used not only to prepare conventional business documents but simultaneously to provide the same information in a form compatible with input requirements of a computer. The ***integration*** of processes for recording information in conventional form and concurrently providing input media for an EDP system eliminates the intermediate work of transferring information from invoices, checks, and other documents to the tape or cards acceptable for processing by the computer.

The integration of an accounting system requires that forms and procedures be designed not for the needs of a single department but rather as part of a complete ***information system*** for the entire business. To create such an integrated system, the accounting systems specialist tries to coordinate paper work and procedures in a manner that will provide a rapid and uninterrupted flow of all information needed in the conduct of the business as an entity.

## KEY TERMS INTRODUCED OR EMPHASIZED IN CHAPTER 7

**Accounts payable ledger** A subsidiary ledger containing an account with each supplier or vendor. The total of the ledger agrees with the general ledger controlling account, Accounts Payable.

**Accounts receivable ledger** A subsidiary ledger containing an account with each credit customer. The total of the ledger agrees with the general ledger controlling account, Accounts Receivable.

**Cash payments journal** A special journal used to record all payments of cash.

**Cash receipts journal** A special journal used to record all receipts of cash.

**Central processing unit (CPU)** Main section of a computer, including the storage unit, control unit, and arithmetic unit.

**Controlling account** A general ledger account which is supported by detailed information in a subsidiary ledger.

**Data processing** The preparation of documents and the flow of data contained in these documents through the major accounting steps of recording, classifying, and summarizing.

**Electronic data processing (EDP)** A system for processing data by use of electronic computers.

**Hardware** The machines and related equipment used in an EDP system.

**Input controls** Internal control measures to ensure accuracy of data entered into a computer (such as control totals, the total dollar amount of documents to be processed).

**Input devices** An element of a computer used to prepare and insert information into the computer.

**Output devices** An element of a computer which transfers information out of the computer to the accountant or other user.

**Program** Instructions to a computer consisting of a series of steps planned to carry out a certain process (such as payroll preparation).

**Program controls** Error-detecting measures built into a computer program (such as a limit test setting a maximum dollar amount, or item counts specifying the number of cards to be processed).

**Punched cards** An input device on which accounting data are recorded by using holes in columns and rows to represent numerical and alphabetical data.

**Purchases journal** A special journal used exclusively to record purchases of merchandise on credit.

**Sales journal** A special journal used exclusively to record sales of merchandise on credit.

**Software** All materials (except hardware) utilized in selecting, installing, and operating an EDP system.

**Subsidiary ledger** A supplementary record used to provide detailed information for a control account in the general ledger. The total of accounts in a subsidiary ledger equals the balance of the related control account in the general ledger.

**Terminals** Keyboard devices for entering information into a computer without first punching the information into punched cards or tape.

**Time-sharing** Use of a central computer through a terminal upon payment of a monthly fee by the subscriber.

## DEMONSTRATION PROBLEM FOR YOUR REVIEW

The Signal Corporation began operations on November 1, 19___. The chart of accounts used by the company included the following accounts, among others:

| | | | |
|---|---|---|---|
| *Cash* | *10* | *Purchases* | *60* |
| *Marketable securities* | *15* | *Purchase returns & allowances* | *62* |
| *Inventory of office supplies* | *18* | *Purchase discounts* | *64* |
| *Notes payable* | *30* | *Salaries expense* | *70* |
| *Accounts payable* | *32* | *Utilities expense* | *71* |

November transactions relating to the purchase of merchandise and to accounts payable are listed below, along with selected other transactions.

**Nov. 1** Purchased merchandise from Moss Co. for $3,000. Invoice dated today; terms 2/10, n/30.

**Nov. 3** Received shipment of merchandise from Wilmer Co. and invoice dated November 2 for $7,600; terms 2/10, n/30.

**Nov. 6** Purchased merchandise from Archer Company at cost of $5,600. Invoice dated November 5; terms 2/10, n/30.

**Nov. 9** Purchased marketable securities, $1,200.

**Nov. 10** Issued check to Moss Co. in settlement of invoice dated November 1, less discount.

**Nov. 12** Received shipment of merchandise from Cory Corporation and an invoice dated November 11 in amount of $7,100; terms net 30 days.

**Nov. 14** Issued check to Archer Company in settlement of invoice of November 5.

**Nov. 16** Paid cash for office supplies, $110.

**Nov. 17** Purchased merchandise for cash, $950.

**Nov. 19** Purchased merchandise from Klein Co. for $11,500. Invoice dated November 18; terms 2/10, n/30.
**Nov. 21** Purchased merchandise from Belmont Company for $8,400. Invoice dated November 20; terms 1/10, n/30.
**Nov. 24** Purchased merchandise for cash, $375.
**Nov. 26** Purchased merchandise from Brooker Co. for $6,500. Invoice dated today; terms 1/10, n/30.
**Nov. 28** Paid utilities, $150.
**Nov. 30** Paid salaries for November, $2,900.
**Nov. 30** Paid $2,600 cash to Wilmer Co. and issued 6%, 90-day promissory note for $5,000 in settlement of invoice dated November 2.

**Instructions**

**a** Record the transactions in the appropriate journals. Use a single-column purchases journal and a six-column cash payments journal.
**b** Indicate how postings would be made by placing ledger account numbers and check marks in the appropriate columns of the journals.
**c** Prepare a schedule of accounts payable at November 30 to prove that the subsidiary ledger is in balance with the controlling account.

## SOLUTION TO DEMONSTRATION PROBLEM

**a & b**

*Purchases Journal* — *Page 1*

| Date | | Account Credited | | Invoice Date | | √ | Amount |
|---|---|---|---|---|---|---|---|
| 19__ | | | | 19__ | | | |
| Nov | 1 | Moss Co. | (terms 2/10, n/30) | Nov | 1 | √ | 3,000 |
| | 3 | Wilmer Co. | (terms 2/10, n/30) | | 2 | √ | 7,600 |
| | 6 | Archer Company | (terms 2/10, n/30) | | 5 | √ | 5,600 |
| | 12 | Cory Corporation | (terms net 30) | | 11 | √ | 7,100 |
| | 19 | Klein Co. | (terms 2/10, n/30) | | 18 | √ | 11,500 |
| | 21 | Belmont Company | (terms 1/10, n/30) | | 20 | √ | 8,400 |
| | 26 | Brooker Co. | (terms 1/10, n/30) | | 26 | √ | 6,500 |
| | | | | | | | 49,700 |
| | | | | | | | (60)(32) |

**c**

***SIGNAL CORPORATION***
***Schedule of Accounts Payable***
***November 30, 19__***

| | |
|---|---|
| Belmont Company | $ 8,400 |
| Brooker Co. | 6,500 |
| Cory Corporation | 7,100 |
| Klein Co. | 11,500 |
| Total (per general ledger controlling account) | $33,500 |

The computer prepares the sales journal, posts to the accounts receivable ledger (maintained on magnetic tape), and performs an item count. Any discrepancy in the item count is printed out on an error report. A copy of the sales journal for each day is sent back to the accounting department for comparison with the daily control totals.

What control procedure will first detect the following independent errors?

**a** A sales invoice of $760 is accidentally keypunched as $7,600.

**b** A sales invoice is lost on the way from the accounting department to the EDP department.

**c** Several punched cards are lost before being processed by the computer.

## PROBLEMS

### Group A

***7A-1*** The accounting system used by Lake Company, a small business, includes journals and ledgers like those illustrated in Chapter 7. At November 30, the subsidiary ledger for accounts receivable consisted of the accounts with customers shown below. Note that postings to these accounts have been made from three different journals.

***L. Lawrence***

| Date | | Explanation | Ref | Debit | Credit | Balance |
|---|---|---|---|---|---|---|
| 19— | | | | | | |
| Nov | 3 | | S4 | 2240 | | 2240 |
| | 9 | | S4 | 4160 | | 6400 |
| | 27 | | CR2 | | 3840 | 2560 |

***M. Mooney***

| Date | | Explanation | Ref | Debit | Credit | Balance |
|---|---|---|---|---|---|---|
| 19— | | | | | | |
| Oct | 31 | Balance | | | | 20736 |
| Nov | 8 | | CR1 | | 12800 | 7936 |
| | 8 | | J1 | | 2560 | 5376 |
| | 28 | | CR2 | | 5376 | -0- |

***N. Nathan***

| Date | | Explanation | Ref | Debit | Credit | Balance |
|---|---|---|---|---|---|---|
| 19— | | | | | | |
| Oct | 31 | Balance | | | | 14080 |
| Nov | 10 | | J1 | | 3200 | 10880 |
| | 11 | | S4 | 8000 | | 18880 |
| | 30 | | CR2 | | 10240 | 8640 |

**O. Osmond**

| Date | | Explanation | Ref | Debit | Credit | Balance |
|---|---|---|---|---|---|---|
| 19— | | | | | | |
| Nov | 4 | | S4 | 2 8 1 6 0 | | 2 8 1 6 0 |
| | 29 | | S4 | 7 6 8 0 | | 3 5 8 4 0 |
| | 29 | | CR2 | | 2 8 1 6 0 | 7 6 8 0 |

**Instructions** You are to make the necessary entries in the general ledger controlling account, Accounts Receivable, for the month of November. Use a three-column, running balance form of ledger account. (Remember that a controlling account is posted on a daily basis for transactions recorded in the general journal, but is posted only at the end of the month for the *monthly totals* of special journals such as the sales journal and the cash receipts journal.)

Include in the controlling account the balance at October 31, the transactions from the general journal during November in chronological order, and the running balance of the account after each entry. Finally, make one posting for all sales on credit during November and one posting for all cash collections from credit customers during November. For each amount entered in the Accounts Receivable controlling account, the date and source (name of journal and journal page) should be listed. Use the symbols shown on page 264 to identify the various journals.

7A-2  The accounting system used by Airco, Inc., includes a general journal and four special journals for daily recording of transactions. Information recorded in these journals is posted to a general ledger and two subsidiary ledgers: one of the subsidiary ledgers contain accounts receivable and the other accounts payable. All three ledgers are in the three-column, running balance form. At September 30, the subsidiary ledger for accounts payable contained the accounts with creditors shown below. Note that postings to these accounts have been made from three different journals.

**R. Rodin**

| Date | | Explanation | Ref | Debit | Credit | Balance |
|---|---|---|---|---|---|---|
| 19— | | | | | | |
| Sept | 1 | | P1 | | 1 6 0 0 0 | 1 6 0 0 0 |
| | 20 | | P1 | | 1 2 8 0 0 | 2 8 8 0 0 |
| | 21 | Returned mdse. | J2 | 8 0 0 | | 2 8 0 0 0 |
| | 28 | | CP3 | 1 5 2 0 0 | | 1 2 8 0 0 |

**S. Smith**

| Date | | Explanation | Ref | Debit | Credit | Balance |
|---|---|---|---|---|---|---|
| 19— | | | | | | |
| Sept | 22 | | P1 | | 1 3 7 6 0 | 1 3 7 6 0 |

***T. Thorton***

| Date | | Explanation | Ref | Debit | Credit | Balance |
|---|---|---|---|---|---|---|
| 19— | | | | | | |
| Aug | 31 | Balance | | | | 960 |
| Sept | 15 | | CP3 | 960 | | -0- |
| | 16 | | P1 | | 3840 | 3840 |
| | 20 | | P1 | | 4800 | 8640 |

***U. Ullman***

| Date | | Explanation | Ref | Debit | Credit | Balance |
|---|---|---|---|---|---|---|
| 19— | | | | | | |
| Aug | 31 | Balance | | | | 35200 |
| Sept | 5 | Returned mdse. | J2 | 1920 | | 33280 |
| | 20 | | CP3 | 24000 | | 9280 |
| | 25 | | P1 | | 1600 | 10880 |

**Instructions** You are to prepare the general ledger controlling account, Accounts Payable, corresponding to the above subsidiary ledger accounts for the month of September. Use a three-column running balance form of ledger account. (Remember that a controlling account is posted on a daily basis for transactions recorded in the general journal, but is posted only at the end of the month for the ***monthly totals*** of special journals such as the purchases journal and the cash payments journal.)

Enter in the controlling account the beginning balance at August 31, the transactions from the general journal during September in chronological order, and the running balance of the account after each entry. Finally, make one posting for all purchases of merchandise on credit during September and one posting for all cash payments to suppliers during September. For each entry in the controlling account, show the date and source (journal and page number) of the item. Use the symbols shown on page 264 to identify the individual journals.

45 min

***7A-3*** The chart of accounts used by the Hunt Corporation included the following accounts, among others:

| | | | |
|---|---|---|---|
| ***Cash*** | ***10*** | ***Sales*** | ***50*** |
| ***Notes receivable*** | ***15*** | ***Sales returns & allowances*** | ***52*** |
| ***Accounts receivable*** | ***17*** | ***Sales discounts*** | ***54*** |
| ***Land*** | ***20*** | ***Purchases*** | ***60*** |
| ***Office equipment*** | ***25*** | ***Purchase returns & allowances*** | ***62*** |
| ***Notes payable*** | ***30*** | ***Interest revenue*** | ***82*** |
| ***Accounts payable*** | ***32*** | ***Gain on sale of land*** | ***85*** |

The sales activity, cash receipts, and certain other transactions for the month of June are presented below:

**June 1** Sold merchandise to Miley Company for cash, \$7,725.

**June 4** Sold merchandise to Presto Company, \$26,500. Invoice no. 618; terms 2/10, n/30.

**June 5** Received cash refund of \$3,400 for merchandise returned to a supplier.

**June 8** Sold merchandise to Topper Company for $13,500. Invoice no. 619; terms 2/10, n/30.
**June 9** Received a check from Hartman Company in payment of a $7,500 invoice, less 2% discount.
**June 11** Received $3,500 from Gray Company in payment of a past-due invoice.
**June 13** Received check from Presto Company in settlement of invoice dated June 4, less discount.
**June 16** Sold merchandise to Mexical Company, $13,000. Invoice no. 620; terms 2/10, n/30.
**June 16** Returned $3,000 of merchandise to supplier, ICM Corporation, for reduction of account payable.
**June 18** Purchased office equipment at a cost of $9,500; signing a 15%, 90-day note payable for the full amount.
**June 20** Sold merchandise to Johnston Company for $24,000. Invoice no. 621; terms 2/10, n/30.
**June 21** Mexical Company returned for credit $2,000 of merchandise purchased on June 16.
**June 23** Borrowed $75,000 cash from a local bank, signing a six-month note payable.
**June 25** Received payment in full from Mexical Company in settlement of invoice dated June 16, less return and discount.
**June 29** Sold land costing $95,000 for a price of $140,000. Terms of sale were $35,000 cash and a 12%, two-year note receivable for $105,000. (Credit Gain on Sale of Land for $45,000.)
**June 30** Collected from Johnston Company amount of invoice dated June 20, less 2% discount.
**June 30** Collected $40,600 in full settlement of a $40,000, 9%, 60-day note receivable held since May 1. (No interest revenue had been recorded on the note prior to this date).
**June 30** Received a 60-day, non-interest-bearing note from Topper Company in settlement of invoice dated June 8. ON FINAL-ONLY W/INTERE

**Instructions** Record the above transactions in the appropriate journals. Use a single-column sales journal, a six-column cash receipts journal, and a two-column general journal. Foot and rule the special journals and indicate how postings would be made by placing ledger account numbers and check marks in the appropriate columns of the journals.

*7A-4* Backpacker & Co. uses an accounting system that includes multicolumn special journals for cash receipts and cash payments. These journals are similar to those illustrated on pages 258–259 and 260–261. All the cash transactions during September are described below.

**Sept. 1** Cash purchase of merchandise, $6,848.
**Sept. 1** Paid Spalding Company invoice, $2,600 less 1% discount.
**Sept. 2** Cash sales of merchandise, $5,504.
**Sept. 2** Paid inbound freight charges on merchandise from Watkins Company, $326.
**Sept. 4** Purchased fixtures, $5,120, making a down payment of $1,280 and issuing a note payable for the balance.
**Sept. 5** Received $960 cash as partial collection of our $3,840 invoice to National Co. Also received a note receivable for the $2,880 balance of this invoice. (Use cash receipts journal.)
**Sept. 6** Paid Newcomb Company invoice, $4,500 less 2% discount.
**Sept. 7** Paid note due today, $9,600, and accrued interest amounting to $192.
**Sept. 10** Sold land costing $8,960 for $7,872. (Debit Loss on Sale of Land, $1,088.)

**Sept. 10** The owner, B. W. Hamilton, invested additional cash of $32,000 in the business.
**Sept. 12** Cash sales of merchandise, $4,243.
**Sept. 15** Paid September rent, $2,080.
**Sept. 15** Purchased U.S. government bonds, $6,400. (Debit U.S. Government Bonds.)
**Sept. 18** Cash purchase of merchandise, $4,640.
**Sept. 19** Paid gas and oil bill, $176, for automobile belonging to Mrs. B. W. Hamilton. (Car is not used in the business.)
**Sept. 20** Received $1,862 cash in full settlement of our invoice to Mesa Company after allowing 2% discount. (Face amount of invoice can be computed by dividing $1,862 by .98.)
**Sept. 21** Paid Mammoth Co. invoice, $5,200 less 2% discount.
**Sept. 23** Paid sales commissions of $2,528 to sales staff.
**Sept. 30** Received payment in full settlement of our $5,500 invoice to Presley Company, less 2% discount.
**Sept. 30** Paid monthly salaries, $6,000.

**Instructions**

**a** Enter the above transactions in the cash receipts journal and the cash payments journal.
**b** Foot and rule the journals.

*7A-5* Hill Center began business in October and established the following ledger accounts.

| | | | |
|---|---|---|---|
| *Cash* | *10* | *Sales returns & allowances* | *52* |
| *Notes receivable* | *14* | *Sales discounts* | *54* |
| *Accounts receivable* | *15* | *Purchases* | *60* |
| *Merchandise inventory* | *17* | *Purchase returns & allowances* | *62* |
| *Unexpired insurance* | *19* | *Purchase discounts* | *64* |
| *Land* | *20* | *Transportation-in* | *66* |
| *Building* | *21* | *Rent expense* | *70* |
| *Furniture and fixtures* | *24* | *Salaries expense* | *72* |
| *Notes payable* | *30* | *Taxes expense* | *74* |
| *Accounts payable* | *32* | *Supplies expense* | *76* |
| *Mortgage payable* | *36* | *Insurance expense* | *78* |
| *Ruth Hill, capital* | *40* | *Interest earned* | *80* |
| *Ruth Hill, drawing* | *42* | *Interest expense* | *83* |
| *Income summary* | *45* | *Loss on sale of land* | *84* |
| *Sales* | *50* | | |

The transactions during October were as follows:

**Oct. 1** The owner, Ruth Hill, deposited $81,000 in a bank account under the name, Hill Center.
**Oct. 4** Purchased land and building, paying $40,000 cash and signing a mortgage for the balance of $60,000. Estimated value of the land was $45,000.
**Oct. 6** Sold merchandise to Brad Parks, $6,800. Invoice no. 1, terms 2/10, n/60.
**Oct. 7** Purchased merchandise from Lakeview Company, $12,000. Invoice dated today; terms 2/10, n/30.
**Oct. 7** Sold merchandise for cash, $1,332.
**Oct. 7** Paid $486 for a two-year fire insurance policy. (Debit Unexpired Insurance.)
**Oct. 10** Paid freight charges of $369 on purchase from Lakeview Company.
**Oct. 12** Sold to ABC Corporation, $8,800. Invoice no. 2; terms 2/10, n/60.

**Oct. 13** Purchased merchandise for cash, $2,556.
**Oct. 15** Received payment from Brad Parks. Invoice no. 1, dated October 6, less 2% discount.
**Oct. 15** Purchased land for $30,000 cash.
**Oct. 16** Issued credit memorandum no. 1 to ABC Corporation, $800, for goods returned today by ABC Corporation.
**Oct. 17** Paid Lakeview Company invoice of October 7, less discount.
**Oct. 18** Purchased merchandise from Baker Company, $6,000. Invoice dated today; terms 2/10, n/30.
**Oct. 20** A portion of merchandise purchased from Baker Company was found to be substandard. After discussion with the vendor, a price reduction of $200 was agreed upon and a credit memo for this amount was received from Baker Company.
**Oct. 22** Received payment from ABC Corporation. Invoice no. 2, less return of merchandise on October 16 and discount on balance.
**Oct. 23** Purchased merchandise from Lakeview Company, $7,560. Invoice dated today; terms 2/10, n/60.
**Oct. 25** Sold for $29,000 cash the land purchased on October 15. (Debit Loss on Sale of Land, $1,000).
**Oct. 27** Sold merchandise for cash, $927.
**Oct. 28** Borrowed $5,400 from bank, issuing a note payable as evidence of indebtedness.
**Oct. 28** Paid Baker Company invoice of October 18, less allowance and discount.
**Oct. 30** Paid first installment on mortgage, $900. This payment included interest of $600.
**Oct. 30** Purchased merchandise for cash, $1,656.
**Oct. 31** Paid monthly salaries of $3,807.
**Oct. 31** Sold merchandise to Frank Sullivan, $4,950. Invoice no. 3; terms 2/10, n/60.

**Instructions**

**a** Enter the October transactions in the following journals:
Two-column general journal
One-column sales journal
One-column purchases journal
Six-column cash receipts journal
Six-column cash payments journal

**b** Foot and rule all special journals.

**c** Show how posting would be made by placing the ledger account numbers and check marks in the appropriate columns of the journals. This instruction includes placing ledger account numbers in the LP columns as well as under the totals for the month.

*7A-6* Sand Castle Company uses the following accounts (among others) in recording transactions:

| | | | |
|---|---|---|---|
| *Cash* | *10* | *Sales discounts* | *64* |
| *Notes receivable* | *14* | *Purchases* | *70* |
| *Accounts receivable* | *16* | *Purchase returns and allowances* | *72* |
| *Supplies* | *17* | *Purchase discounts* | *74* |
| *Unexpired insurance* | *18* | *Transportation-in* | *76* |
| *Equipment* | *26* | *Salaries expense* | *80* |
| *Notes payable* | *30* | *Supplies expense* | *84* |
| *Accounts payable* | *32* | *Insurance expense* | *86* |
| *Mortgage payable* | *40* | *Gain on sale of equipment* | *90* |
| *Sales* | *60* | *Interest expense* | *92* |
| *Sales returns and allowances* | *62* | | |

The schedules of accounts receivable and accounts payable for the company at October 31, 19___, are shown below:

***Schedule of Accounts Receivable***
***October 31, 19___***

| | |
|---|---|
| *Ace Contractors* | *$20,800* |
| *Reliable Builders, Inc.* | *8,750* |
| *Total* | *$29,550* |

***Schedule of Accounts Payable***
***October 31, 19___***

| | |
|---|---|
| *Durapave, Inc.* | *$30,000* |

The November transactions of Sand Castle Company were as follows:

**Nov. 2** Purchased merchandise on account from Durapave, Inc., $28,000. Invoice was dated today with terms of 2/10, n/30.

**Nov. 3** Sold merchandise to Ace Contractors $16,000. Invoice no. 428; terms 2/10, n/30.

**Nov. 4** Purchased supplies for cash, $875. (Debit the asset account, Supplies.)

**Nov. 5** Sold merchandise for cash, $5,600.

**Nov. 7** Paid the Durapave, Inc., invoice for $30,000, representing October purchases. No discount was allowed by Durapave, Inc., on this purchase.

**Nov. 10** Purchased merchandise from Tool Company, $32,500. Invoice dated November 9 with terms of 1/10, n/30.

**Nov. 10** Collected from Ace Contractors for invoice no. 428 for $16,000, less 2% discount, and for October sales of $20,800 on which the discount had lapsed.

**Nov. 12** Sold merchandise to Rex Company, $21,750. Invoice no. 429; terms 2/10, n/30.

**Nov. 14** Paid freight charges of $2,050 on goods purchased November 10 from Tool Company.

**Nov. 14** Sold equipment for $22,000, receiving cash of $1,500 and a note receivable for the balance. Equipment had been acquired recently at a cost of $20,000 for use in the business, but because of a change in plans, it was now being sold. (Credit Gain on Sale of Equipment, $2,000.)

**Nov. 15** Issued credit memorandum no. 38 upon return of $1,000 of merchandise by our customer, Rex Company.

**Nov. 18** Paid for one-year fire insurance policy, $1,425.

**Nov. 18** Purchased merchandise for cash, $7,625.

**Nov. 19** Paid the Tool Company invoice dated November 9, less the 1% discount.

**Nov. 20** Sold merchandise on account to Vincent Co., $13,650; invoice no. 430. Required customer to sign a 30-day, non-interest-bearing note. (Record this sale by a debit to Accounts Receivable, then transfer from Accounts Receivable to Notes Receivable by means of an entry in the general journal.)

**Nov. 22** Purchased merchandise for cash, $4,050.

**Nov. 22** Sold merchandise for cash, $4,675.

**Nov. 22** Received payment from Rex Company for invoice no. 429. Customer made deduction for credit memorandum no. 38 issued November 15, and a 2% discount.

**Nov. 23** Sold merchandise on account to Waite, Inc., $9,950. Invoice no. 431; terms 2/10, n/30.

**Nov. 25** Purchased merchandise from Smith Company, $26,500. Invoice dated November 24 with terms of 2/10, n/60.

**Nov. 26** Issued debit memorandum no. 42 for $2,125 to Smith Company because of shortage in merchandise delivered to us as compared with their invoice of November 24.

**Nov. 27** Purchased equipment having a list price of $60,000. Paid $10,000 down and signed a promissory note for the balance of $50,000.

**Nov. 30** Paid monthly salaries of $14,800 for services rendered by employees during November.

**Nov. 30** Paid monthly installment on mortgage, $3,500, of which $1,020 was interest expense.

**Instructions**

**a** Record the November transactions in the following journals:
 General journal—two columns
 Sales journal—one column
 Purchases journal—one column
 Cash receipts journal—six columns
 Cash payments journal—six columns

Foot and rule all special journals and show how postings would be made by placing ledger account numbers and check marks in the appropriate columns of the journals.

**b** Prepare a schedule of accounts receivable and accounts payable as of November 30, 19___.

*7A-7* The accounting records of Arrow Service include special journals for sales, purchases, cash receipts, and cash payments. All sales and all purchases are made on a credit basis. All transactions during September were recorded in the special journals; there were no entries in the general journal. The events of the month are reflected in summary form below by the after-closing trial balance of August 31 and the trial balance before adjustments a month later on September 30.

By close study of these trial balances, it is possible to determine the total amount of cash collected from customers during the month and the amount of cash received from other sources. Similarly, it is possible to determine the total amount of cash payments against accounts payable and the cash payments for other purposes such as acquisition of equipment, salaries, and other expenses.

| | After-Closing Trial Balance August 31 | | Trial Balance September 30 | |
|---|---|---|---|---|
| Cash | $ 56,960 | | $ 42,880 | |
| Accounts receivable | 76,800 | | 83,520 | |
| Inventory | 80,640 | | 80,640 | |
| Equipment | 112,000 | | 117,760 | |
| Accumulated depreciation: equipment | | $ 24,000 | | $ 24,000 |
| Accounts payable | | 62,400 | | 41,600 |
| Patrick Lewis, capital | | 240,000 | | 272,000 |
| Sales | | | | 54,400 |
| Purchases | | | 40,000 | |
| Salaries expense | | | 12,800 | |
| Advertising expense | | | 3,200 | |
| Supplies expense | | | 2,400 | |
| Property tax expense | | | 4,000 | |
| Miscellaneous expense | | | 4,800 | |
| | $326,400 | $326,400 | $392,000 | $392,000 |

**Instructions**

**a** Prepare a schedule showing all sources of cash receipts during September.
**b** Prepare a schedule showing the purpose of all cash payments made during September.
**c** Prepare one compound journal entry (general journal form) summarizing all September transactions involving the receipt of cash. The entry should include a debit to Cash and credits to other accounts for the amounts indicated in **a.**
**d** Prepare one compound journal entry (general journal form) summarizing all September transactions involving the payment of cash. The entry should include a credit to Cash and debits to other accounts for amounts indicated in **b.**

## Group B

***7B-1*** A manual accounting system similar to the one illustrated in Chapter 7 is used by Barnes Company. At September 30, the subsidiary ledger for accounts receivable included the following accounts with individual customers. Note that these accounts include postings from three different journals.

The purpose of this problem is to show the relationship between a controlling account and a subsidiary ledger. By studying the following subsidiary ledger accounts, you can determine what amounts should appear in the controlling account.

***A. Anderson***

| Date | | Explanation | Ref | Debit | Credit | Balance |
|---|---|---|---|---|---|---|
| 19— | | | | | | |
| Sept | 3 | | S4 | 560 | | 560 |
| | 9 | | S4 | 1040 | | 1600 |
| | 27 | | CR2 | | 960 | 640 |

***B. Brown***

| Date | | Explanation | Ref | Debit | Credit | Balance |
|---|---|---|---|---|---|---|
| 19— | | | | | | |
| Aug | 31 | Balance | | | | 5184 |
| Sept | 8 | | CR1 | | 3200 | 1984 |
| | 8 | | J1 | | 640 | 1344 |
| | 28 | | CR2 | | 1344 | -0- |

***C. Cathway***

| Date | | Explanation | Ref | Debit | Credit | Balance |
|---|---|---|---|---|---|---|
| 19— | | | | | | |
| Aug | 31 | Balance | | | | 3520 |
| Sept | 10 | | J1 | | 800 | 2720 |
| | 11 | | S4 | 2000 | | 4720 |
| | 30 | | CR2 | | 2560 | 2160 |

**D. Davis**

| Date | | Explanation | Ref | Debit | Credit | Balance |
|---|---|---|---|---|---|---|
| 19– | | | | | | |
| Sept | 4 | | S4 | 7040 | | 7040 |
| | 29 | | S4 | 1920 | | 8960 |
| | 29 | | CR2 | | 7040 | 1920 |

**Instructions** You are to prepare the general ledger controlling account, Accounts Receivable, for the month of September. Remember that a controlling account is posted on a daily basis for transactions recorded in the general journal, but is posted only at the end of the month for the ***monthly totals*** of special journals such as the sales journal and the cash receipts journal.

Include in the controlling account the balance at August 31, the September transactions from the general journal in chronological order, and the running balance of the account after each entry. Finally, make one posting to record total sales on credit for September and one posting to record total cash collections from customers during September. For each amount you enter in the Accounts Receivable controlling account, you should list the date and source (name of journal and journal page). Use the symbols shown on page 264 to identify the various journals. When the controlling account is completed, it should contain in summary form the information shown above in the customers' accounts in the subsidiary ledger.

***7B-2*** Carlox Corporation, a small retail store, uses a general journal and four special journals for daily recording of transactions. Information in these journals is posted to a general ledger and two subsidiary ledgers. One subsidiary ledger contains accounts receivable and the other accounts payable. All three ledgers are in the three-column, running balance form.

At May 30, the subsidiary ledger for accounts payable contained the following accounts with creditors.

**J. Johnson**

| Date | | Explanation | Ref | Debit | Credit | Balance |
|---|---|---|---|---|---|---|
| 19– | | | | | | |
| Apr | 30 | Balance | | | | 1440 |
| May | 14 | | CP2 | 1440 | | -0- |
| | 25 | | P3 | | 4000 | 4000 |
| | 28 | | P3 | | 6400 | 10400 |

**K. Kelly**

| Date | | Explanation | Ref | Debit | Credit | Balance |
|---|---|---|---|---|---|---|
| 19– | | | | | | |
| Apr | 30 | Balance | | | | 20160 |
| May | 2 | | J1 | 1600 | | 18560 |
| | 10 | | P3 | | 8000 | 26560 |
| | 25 | | CP2 | 18560 | | 8000 |

**L. Lewis**

| Date | | Explanation | Ref | Debit | Credit | Balance |
|---|---|---|---|---|---|---|
| 19— | | | | | | |
| May | 11 | | P3 | | 1920 | 1920 |
| | 14 | | P3 | | 3200 | 5120 |
| | 30 | | CP2 | 1920 | | 3200 |

**M. McKay**

| Date | | Explanation | Ref | Debit | Credit | Balance |
|---|---|---|---|---|---|---|
| 19— | | | | | | |
| May | 9 | | P3 | | 2880 | 2880 |
| | 12 | | P3 | | 3840 | 6720 |
| | 14 | | J1 | 320 | | 6400 |

**Instructions** Prepare a general ledger controlling account, Accounts Payable, corresponding to the above subsidiary ledger accounts for the month of May. Use a three-column running balance form of ledger account. (Remember that a controlling account is posted on a daily basis for transactions recorded in the general journal, but is posted only at the end of the month for the ***monthly totals*** of special journals such as the purchases journal and the cash payments journal.)

Enter in the controlling account the beginning balance at April 30, the transactions from the general journal during May in chronological order, and the running balance of the account after each entry. Finally, make one posting for all purchases of merchandise on credit during May and one posting for all cash payments to suppliers during May. For each entry in the controlling account, show the date and source (journal and page number) of the item. Use the symbols shown on page 264 to identify the various journals.

***7B-3*** Ozark Corporation has a chart of accounts which includes the following accounts, among others.

| | | | |
|---|---|---|---|
| ***Cash*** | ***10*** | ***Accounts payable*** | ***30*** |
| ***Office supplies*** | ***18*** | ***Purchases*** | ***50*** |
| ***Land*** | ***20*** | ***Purchase returns & allowances*** | ***52*** |
| ***Building*** | ***22*** | ***Purchase discounts*** | ***53*** |
| ***Notes payable*** | ***28*** | ***Salaries expense*** | ***60*** |

The December transactions relating to the purchase of merchandise for resale and to accounts payable are listed below along with selected other transactions.

**Dec. 1** Purchased merchandise from Sawyer Company at a cost of $9,380. Invoice dated today; terms 2/10, n/30.

**Dec. 4** Purchased merchandise from Bright Company for $30,200. Invoice dated December 3; terms 2/10, n/30.

**Dec. 5** Returned for credit to Sawyer Company defective merchandise having a list price of $2,880.

**Dec. 6** Received shipment of merchandise from Trojan Co. and their invoice dated December 5 in amount of $20,520. Terms net 30 days.

**Dec. 8** Purchased merchandise from Wayne Associates, \$24,480. Invoice dated today with terms 1/10, n/60.
**Dec. 10** Purchased merchandise from King Corporation, \$30,000. Invoice dated December 9; terms 2/10, n/30.
**Dec. 10** Issued check to Sawyer Company in settlement of balance resulting from purchase of December 1 and purchase return of December 5.
**Dec. 11** Issued check to Bright Company in payment of December 3 invoice.
**Dec. 18** Issued check to King Corporation in settlement of invoice dated December 9.
**Dec. 20** Purchased merchandise for cash, \$1,080.
**Dec. 21** Bought land, \$64,800, and building, \$144,000, for expansion of business. Paid cash of \$36,000 and signed a promissory note for the balance of \$172,800. (Land and building were acquired in a single transaction from R. M. Wilson.)
**Dec. 23** Purchased merchandise for cash, \$900.
**Dec. 26** Purchased merchandise from Taper Company for \$32,400. Invoice dated December 26, terms 2/10, n/30.
**Dec. 28** Paid cash for office supplies, \$270.
**Dec. 29** Purchased merchandise for cash, \$1,890.
**Dec. 31** Paid salaries for December, \$7,920.

**Instructions**

**a** Record the transactions in the appropriate journals. Use a single-column purchases journal, a six-column cash payments journal, and a two-column general journal. Foot and rule the special journals. Make all postings to the proper general ledger accounts and to the accounts payable subsidiary ledger.

**b** Prepare a schedule of accounts payable at December 31 to prove that the subsidiary ledger is in balance with the controlling account for accounts payable.

*7B-4* The accounting system of Westport Landing includes a general journal, four special journals, a general ledger, and two subsidiary ledgers. The chart of accounts includes the following accounts, among others.

| | | | |
|---|---|---|---|
| *Cash* | *10* | *Sales* | *50* |
| *Notes receivable* | *15* | *Sales returns & allowances* | *52* |
| *Accounts receivable* | *17* | *Sales discounts* | *54* |
| *Land* | *20* | *Purchases* | *60* |
| *Office equipment* | *25* | *Purchase returns & allowances* | *62* |
| *Notes payable* | *30* | *Interest revenue* | *82* |
| *Accounts payable* | *32* | *Gain on sale of land* | *85* |

Transactions in June involving the sale of merchandise and the receipt of cash are shown below, along with certain other selected transactions.

**June 1** Sold merchandise to Williams Company for cash, \$2,472.
**June 4** Sold merchandise to Bravo Company, \$8,500. Invoice no. 618; terms 2/10, n/30.
**June 5** Received cash refund of \$1,088 for merchandise returned to a supplier.
**June 8** Sold merchandise to Bradley Company for \$4,320. Invoice no. 619; terms 2/10, n/30.
**June 9** Received a check from Kamtex Company in payment of a \$2,400 invoice, less 2% discount.
**June 11** Received \$1,120 from Olympus Company in payment of a past-due invoice.
**June 13** Received check from Bravo Company in settlement of invoice dated June 4, less discount.

**June 16** Sold merchandise to XYZ Company, $4,040. Invoice no. 620; terms 2/10, n/30.
**June 16** Returned $960 of merchandise to supplier, King Company, for reduction of account payable.
**June 18** Purchased office equipment at a cost of $3,040, signing a 9%, 90-day note payable for the full amount.
**June 20** Sold merchandise to Armstrong Co. for $7,000. Invoice no. 621; terms 2/10, n/30.
**June 21** XYZ Company returned for credit $640 of merchandise purchased on June 16.
**June 23** Borrowed $24,000 cash from a local bank, signing a six-month note payable.
**June 25** Received payment in full from XYZ Company in settlement of invoice dated June 16, less return and discount.
**June 29** Sold land costing $30,400 for $11,200 cash and a note receivable for $33,600. (Credit Gain on Sale of Land for $14,400.)
**June 30** Collected from Armstrong Co. amount of invoice dated June 20, less 2% discount.
**June 30** Collected $12,992 in full settlement of a $12,800, 9%, 60-day note receivable held since May 1. (No interest revenue has yet been recorded.)
**June 30** Received a 60-day note receivable for $4,320 from Bradley Company in settlement of invoice dated June 8.

**Instructions** Record the above transactions in the appropriate journals. Use a single-column sales journal, a six-column cash receipts journal, and a two-column general journal. Foot and rule the special journals and indicate how postings would be made by placing ledger account numbers and check marks in the appropriate columns of the journals.

*7B-5* Frost Center uses multicolumn cash receipts and cash payments journals similar to those illustrated in this chapter. The cash activities for the month of May are presented below:

**May 1** The owner, R. J. Lopez, invested additional cash of $45,000 in the business.
**May 1** Purchased U.S. government bonds, $9,000. (Debit U.S. Government Bonds.)
**May 2** Paid May rent, $3,600. (Debit expense account.)
**May 2** Cash sales of merchandise, $12,300.
**May 4** Purchased fixtures, $10,500, making a down payment of $1,500 and issuing a note payable for the balance.
**May 9** Received $2,100 as partial payment of Bee Co. invoice of $6,300 and a note receivable for the balance.
**May 12** Paid Dallas Co. invoice, $9,000 less 2%.
**May 13** Sold land costing $7,500 for $8,850 cash. (Credit Gain on Sale of Land, $1,350.)
**May 15** Received $3,822 cash in settlement of our invoice to Bing Company after allowing 2% discount.
**May 19** Cash purchase of merchandise, $7,200.
**May 20** Paid note due today, $5,100, and accrued interest amounting to $102.
**May 21** Sold U.S. government bonds costing $3,000 for $2,925. (Debit Loss on Sale of Bonds, $75.)
**May 23** Paid installment on note payable due today, $1,440, of which $702 represented interest expense.
**May 25** Cash sales of merchandise, $9,045.
**May 25** Paid Post Company invoice, $9,900 less 2%.

**May 26** Purchased three-year fire insurance policy, $1,170.
**May 28** Cash purchase of merchandise, $6,450.
**May 30** Received cash in settlement of Baker Company invoice, $7,800, less 2%.
**May 31** Paid monthly salaries, $8,034.

**Instructions** Enter the above transactions in a six-column journal for cash receipts and a six-column journal for cash payments. Compute column totals and rule the journals. Determine the equality of debits and credits in column totals.

***7B-6*** Star Valley, a successful retail business, had the following transactions during November.

**Nov. 2** Purchased merchandise on account from Dunlop Co., $13,000. Invoice was dated today with terms of 2/10, n/30.
**Nov. 3** Sold merchandise to Filmore Company, $8,300. Invoice no. 428; terms 2/10, n/30.
**Nov. 4** Purchased supplies for cash, $300.
**Nov. 5** Sold merchandise for cash, $2,000.
**Nov. 9** Paid the Dunlop Co. invoice dated November 2.
**Nov. 10** Purchased merchandise from Burton Company, $11,700. Invoice dated November 9 with terms of 1/10, n/30.
**Nov. 10** Collected from Filmore Company for invoice no. 428, dated November 3.
**Nov. 12** Sold merchandise to Payless, Inc., $7,360. Invoice no. 429; terms 2/10, n/30.
**Nov. 14** Paid freight charges of $740 on goods purchased November 9 from Burton Company.
**Nov. 14** Sold land for $90,000, receiving cash of $20,000 and a note receivable for the balance. The land had been acquired at a cost of $75,000 for use in the business, but due to a change of plans was no longer needed. (Credit Gain on Sale of Land, $15,000.)
**Nov. 15** Issued credit memorandum no. 38 in favor of Payless, Inc., upon their return of $360 of merchandise.
**Nov. 18** Paid for one-year fire insurance policy, $1,400. (Debit Unexpired Insurance.)
**Nov. 18** Purchased merchandise for cash, $2,700.
**Nov. 19** Paid the Burton Company invoice dated November 9.
**Nov. 20** Sold merchandise on account to Peat Brothers, $7,000. Invoice no. 430. Required customer to sign a 30-day, non-interest-bearing note. (Record this sale by a charge to Accounts Receivable, then transfer from Accounts Receivable to Notes Receivable by means of an entry in the general journal.)
**Nov. 22** Purchased merchandise for cash, $1,500.
**Nov. 22** Sold merchandise for cash, $1,800.
**Nov. 22** Received payment from Payless, Inc., for invoice no. 429. Customer made deduction for credit memorandum no. 38 issued November 15.
**Nov. 25** Purchased merchandise from Amber Company, $9,500. Invoice dated November 24, with terms 2/10, n/60.
**Nov. 26** Issued debit memorandum no. 42 to Amber Company in connection with merchandise returned today to Amber amounting to $300.
**Nov. 27** Purchased equipment having a list price of $21,600. Paid $3,600 down and signed a promissory note for the balance of $18,000.
**Nov. 30** Paid monthly salaries of $5,300 for services rendered by employees during November.
**Nov. 30** Paid monthly installment on mortgage, $1,260, of which $370 was interest.

The following ledger accounts are used by Star Valley.

The accounting system of Leisure Clothing includes a sales journal, purchases journal, cash receipts journal, cash payments journal, and a general journal. As an internal control procedure, an officer of the company reviews and initials every entry in the general journal before the amounts are posted to the ledger accounts. Since the 10-day free trial policy has been in effect, hundreds of entries recording sales returns have been entered in the general journal each week. Each of these entries has been reviewed and initialed by an officer of the firm, and the amounts have been posted to Sales Returns & Allowances and to the Accounts Receivable control account in the general ledger, and also to the customer's account in the accounts receivable subsidiary ledger.

Since these sales return entries are so numerous, it has been suggested that a special journal be designed to handle them. This could not only save time in journalizing and posting the entries, but also eliminate the time-consuming individual review of each of these repetitious entries by an officer of the company.

**Instructions**

**a** How many amounts are entered in the general journal to describe a single sales return transaction? Are these amounts the same?

**b** Explain why these sales return transactions are suited to the use of a special journal. Explain in detail how many money columns the special journal should have, and what postings would have to be done either at the time of the transaction or at the end of the period.

**c** Assume that there were 3,000 sales returns during the month. How many postings would have to be made during the month if these transactions were entered in the general journal? How many postings would have to be made if the special journal you designed in **b** were used? (Assume a one-month accounting period.)

# 8

# THE CONTROL OF CASH TRANSACTIONS

## CASH

Accountants use the word ***cash*** to include coins, paper money, checks, money orders, and money on deposit with banks. However, cash does not include postage stamps, IOU's, or postdated checks.

In deciding whether a particular item comes within the classification of cash, the following rule is a useful one: ***Any medium of exchange which a bank will accept for deposit is included in cash.*** As an example, checks and money orders are accepted by banks for deposit and are considered as cash. Postage stamps and postdated checks are not acceptable for deposit at a bank and are not included in the accountant's definition of cash.

### Balance sheet presentation

Cash is a current asset. In fact, cash is the most current and most liquid of all assets. In judging whether other types of assets qualify for inclusion in the current assets section of the balance sheet, we consider the length of time required for the asset to be converted into cash.

The banker, credit manager, or investor who studies a balance sheet critically is always interested in the total amount of cash as compared with other balance sheet items, such as accounts payable. These outside users of a company's financial statements are not interested, however, in such details as the number of separate bank accounts, or in the distinction between cash on hand and cash in banks. A business that carries checking accounts with several banks will maintain a separate ledger account for each bank account. On the balance sheet, however, the entire amount of cash on hand and cash on deposit with the several banks will be shown as a single amount. One objective in preparing financial statements is to keep them short, concise, and easy to read.

Some bank accounts are restricted as to their use, so that they are not available for making payments to meet normal operating needs of the business. An example (discussed in Chapter 18) is a bond sinking fund, consisting of cash being accumulated by a corporation for the specific purpose of paying off bonded indebtedness at a future date and not available for any other use. A bank account located in a foreign country may also be restricted if monetary regulations prevent the transfer of funds between the two countries. Restricted bank accounts are not regarded as current assets because they are not available for use in paying current liabilities.

### Management responsibilities relating to cash

Efficient management of cash includes measures that will:

1 Prevent losses from fraud or theft
2 Provide accurate accounting for cash receipts, cash payments, and cash balances
3 Maintain a sufficient amount of cash at all times to make necessary payments, plus a reasonable balance for emergencies
4 Prevent unnecessarily large amounts of cash from being held idle in bank accounts which produce no revenue

Internal control over cash is sometimes regarded merely as a means of preventing fraud or theft. A good system of internal control, however, will also aid in achieving management's other objectives of accurate accounting for cash transactions and the maintenance of adequate but not excessive cash balances.

### Basic requirements for internal control over cash

Cash is more susceptible to theft than any other asset. Furthermore, a large portion of the total transactions of a business involve the receipt or disbursement of cash. For both these reasons, internal control over cash is of great importance to management and also to the employees of a business. If a cash shortage arises in a business in which internal controls are weak or nonexistent, every employee is under suspicion. Perhaps no one employee can be proved guilty of the theft, but neither can any employee prove his or her innocence.

On the other hand, if internal controls over cash are adequate, theft without detection is virtually impossible except through the collusion of two or more employees. To achieve internal control over cash or any other group of assets requires first of all that ***the custody of assets be clearly separated from the recording of transactions.*** Secondly, the recording function should be subdivided among employees, so that the work of one person is verified by that of another. This ***subdivision of duties*** discourages fraud, because collusion among employees would be necessary to conceal an irregularity. Internal control is more easily achieved in large companies than in small companies, because extensive subdivision of duties is more feasible in the larger business.

The major steps in establishing internal controls over cash include the following:

1 Separate the function of handling cash from the maintenance of accounting records. Employees who handle cash should not have access to the accounting records, and accounting personnel should not have access to cash.
2 Establish separate and specific routines to be followed in the handling of cash receipts, the making of cash payments, and the recording of cash transactions.
3 Require that all cash receipts be deposited daily in the bank and that all significant cash payments be made by check. Cash payments should ***not*** be made directly from cash receipts on hand.
4 Require that the validity and amount of every expenditure be verified before payment is made.
5 Separate the function of approving expenditures from the function of signing checks.

The application of these principles in building an adequate system of internal control over cash can best be illustrated by considering separately the topics of cash receipts and cash disbursements.

## Cash receipts

Cash receipts consist of two major types: cash received over the counter at the time of a sale and cash received through the mail as collections on accounts receivable.

**Use of cash registers** Cash received over the counter at the time of a sale should be rung up on a cash register, ***so located that the customer will see the amount recorded.*** If store operations can be so arranged that two employees must participate in each sales transaction, stronger internal control will be achieved than when one employee is permitted to handle a transaction in its entirety. In some stores this objective is accomplished by employing a central cashier who rings on a cash register the sales made by all salespeople.

At the end of the day, the store manager or other supervisor should compare the cash register tape, showing the total sales for the day, with the total cash collected.

**Use of prenumbered sales tickets** Internal control may be further strengthened by writing out a prenumbered sales ticket in duplicate at the time of each sale. The original is given to the customer and the carbon copy retained. At the end of the day an employee computes a total sales figure from these duplicate tickets, and also makes sure that no tickets are missing from the series. The total amount of sales as computed from the duplicate sales tickets is then compared with the total sales recorded on the cash register.

**Electronic checkout at the supermarket** Some large supermarkets have achieved faster checkout lines and stronger internal control by using electronic scanning equipment to read and record the price of all groceries passing the checkout counters. All of the 12,000 or so grocery items on the shelves bear a product code, consisting of a pattern of thick and thin vertical bars. At the checkout counter, the code on each item is read by a scanning laser. The code is sent instantaneously to a computer which locates the price and description of the item and flashes that information on a display panel in view of the customer and the checkout clerk. The description of the item and its price are also printed on the receipt tape given to the customer. Items such as fruit are not marked with a bar code, but are assigned a code number which is memorized by the checkout clerk. All the clerk needs to do is enter the code and place the fruit on a scale. The EDP equipment calculates the weight and price and prints all information on the tape.

Faster checkout means greater sales volume; in addition this system improves inventory control by giving management continuous information on what is being sold moment by moment, classified by product and by manufacturer. Comparison of these sales records with records of purchases will direct attention to any losses from theft or shoplifting.

**Cash received through the mail** The procedures for handling checks and currency received through the mail are also based on the internal control principle that two or more employees should participate in every transaction.

The employee who opens the mail should prepare a list of the checks received. In order that this list shall represent the total receipts of the day, the totals recorded on the cash registers may be added to the list. One copy of the list is forwarded with the cash (currency and checks) to the cashier, who will deposit in the bank all the cash received for the day. Another copy of the list is sent to the accounting department, which will record the amount of cash received.

At the close of business each day, the manager should determine that the total cash receipts recorded that day in the accounting records agree with the amount of the cashier's deposit, and also with the list of total cash receipts for the day.

**Cash over and short** In handling over-the-counter cash receipts, a few errors in making change will inevitably occur. These errors will cause a cash shortage or overage at the end of the day, when the cash is counted and compared with the reading on the cash register.

For example, assume that the total cash sales for the day as recorded by the cash register amount to $500, but that the cash in the drawer when counted amounts to only $490. The following entry would be made to record the day's sales and the cash shortage of $10.

*Recording cash shortage*

| | | |
|---|---|---|
| *Cash* | *490* | |
| *Cash Over and Short* | *10* | |
| *Sales* | | *500* |

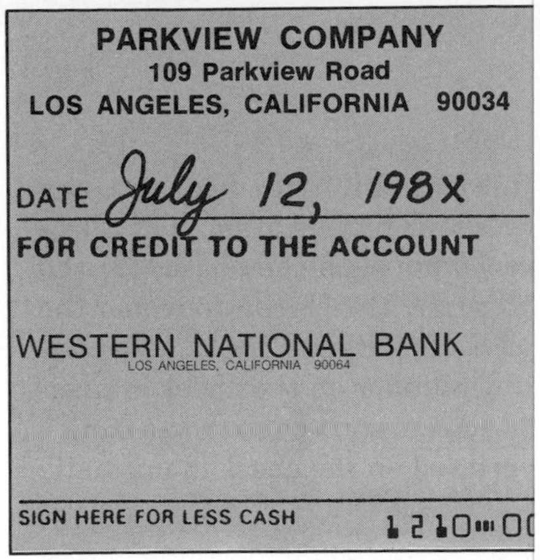
PARKVIEW COMPANY
109 Parkview Road
LOS ANGELES, CALIFORNIA 90034

DATE July 12, 198X
FOR CREDIT TO THE ACCOUNT

WESTERN NATIONAL BANK
LOS ANGELES, CALIFORNIA 90064

SIGN HERE FOR LESS CASH

The account entitled Cash Over and Short is debited with shortages and credited with overages. If the cash shortages during an entire accounting period are in excess of the cash overages, the Cash Over and Short account will have a debit balance and will be shown as miscellaneous ***expense*** in the income statement. On the other hand, if the overages exceed the shortages, the Cash Over and Short account will show a credit balance at the end of the period and should be treated as an item of miscellaneous ***revenue.***

### Cash disbursements

An adequate system of internal control requires that each day's cash receipts be deposited intact in the bank and that ***all disbursements be made by check.*** Checks should be prenumbered. Any spoiled checks should be marked "Void" and filed in sequence so that all numbers in the series can be accounted for.

Every transaction requiring a cash disbursement should be verified and approved before payment is made. Consider what might happen if a company merely paid without question every bill that arrived in the mail. Dishonest employees or outsiders could send the company invoices at excessive prices or could send invoices for goods and services which had never been ordered or delivered.

The official designated to sign checks should not be given authority to approve invoices for payment or to make entries in the accounting records. When a check is presented to a company official for signature, it should be accompanied by the approved invoice and voucher showing that the transaction has been fully verified and that payment is justified. When the check is signed, the supporting invoices and vouchers should be perforated or stamped "Paid" to eliminate any possibility of their being presented later in support of another check. If these rules are followed, it is almost impossible for a fraudulent cash disbursement to be concealed without the collusion of two or more persons.

In large companies which issue hundreds or thousands of checks daily, it is not practicable for a company official to sign each check manually. Instead, check-signing machines with various built-in control devices are used. This automation of the check-signing function does not weaken the system of internal control if attention is given to proper use of the machine and to control of the checks both before and after they pass through the check-signing machine.

ILLUSTRATIVE CASE Manning Corporation issued a great many checks every day but paid little attention to internal controls over its cash payments. Stacks of unissued checks were kept in an unlocked supply closet, along with styrofoam coffee cups. Because the number of checks issued was too great for the treasurer to sign them manually, a check-signing machine was used. This machine, after signing the checks, ejected them into a box equipped with a lock. In spite of warnings from the company's CPA firm, company officials found that it was "too inconvenient" to keep the box locked. Manning Corporation also failed to make any use of the check-counting device built into the check-signing machine. Although the company maintained very large amounts on deposit in checking accounts, it did not bother to reconcile bank statements for weeks or months at a time.

These weaknesses in internal control led to a crisis when a new employee was given a three-week-old bank statement and a bundle of paid checks and told to prepare a bank reconciliation. The new employee found that the bundle of paid

checks accompanyin
hand to support over
ning Corporation's C
transactions. This in
unrecorded checks h
checks had been issu
the company check-
carried out the theft

## BANK CHECKING A(

### Opening a bank acc

Virtually every busine
opened and maintaine
To open a personal che
the bank with identific
license.

For either a person
quires the new deposit
exactly as it will be wr
to sign checks on the a
card is kept on file b
familiar to bank emp
card. When a corporat
a resolution designati
copy of the resolution

The bank provides
each check imprinted
if desired. An identific
account is also printed
that transactions can
charged to the deposit
bered by the printer, a
checks used.

### Making deposits

The depositor fills ou
The deposit ticket illu
ited and the code num
for listing the amount
duplicate deposit tick
duplicate deposit ticke
of money turned over
internal control over c
of the duplicate deposi
the cashier or other
daily deposits of all c

bank, and should be added to the balance reported by the bank. Determine that any deposits in transit listed in last month's bank reconciliation are included as deposits in the current month's bank statement.

2 Arrange the paid checks in sequence by serial numbers and compare each check with the corresponding entry in the cash payments journal. (In the case of personal bank accounts for which the only record maintained is the checkbook, compare each paid check with the check stub.) Place a check mark in the depositor's cash payments journal opposite each entry for which a paid check has been returned by the bank. The unchecked entries should be listed in the bank reconciliation as ***outstanding checks to be deducted from the balance reported by the bank.*** Determine whether the checks listed as outstanding in the bank reconciliation for the preceding month have been returned by the bank this month. If not, such checks should be listed as outstanding in the current reconciliation.

3 Deduct from the balance per the depositor's records any debit memoranda issued by the bank which have not been recorded by the depositor. In the illustrated bank reconciliation on page 317, examples are the NSF check for $50.25 and the $2 service charge.

4 Add to the balance per the depositor's records any credit memoranda issued by the bank which have not been recorded by the depositor. An example in the illustrated bank reconciliation on page 317 is the credit of $500 collected by the bank in behalf of Parkview Company.

5 Prepare a bank reconciliation, reflecting the preceding steps, similar to the illustration on page 317.

6 Prepare journal entries for any items on the bank statement which have not yet been recorded in the depositor's accounts.

**Illustration of bank reconciliation** The July bank statement prepared by the bank for Parkview Company was illustrated on page 314. This statement shows a balance of cash on deposit at July 31 of $5,000.17. We shall assume that Parkview Company's records at July 31 show a bank balance of $4,172.57. Our purpose in preparing the bank reconciliation is to identify the items that make up the difference of $827.60 and to determine the correct cash balance.

Assume that the specific steps to be taken in preparing a bank reconciliation have been carried out and that the following reconciling items have been discovered:

1 A deposit of $310.90 mailed to the bank on July 31 does not appear on the bank statement.

2 A credit memorandum issued by the bank on July 30 in the amount of $500 was returned with the July bank statement and appears in the Deposits column of that statement. This credit represents the proceeds of a note receivable left with the bank by Parkview Company for the purpose of collection. The collection of the note has not yet been recorded by Parkview Company.

**3** Four checks issued in July or prior months have not yet been paid by the bank. These checks are:

| Check No. | Date | Amount |
|---|---|---|
| 801 | June 15 | $100.00 |
| 888 | July 24 | 10.25 |
| 890 | July 27 | 402.50 |
| 891 | July 30 | 205.00 |

**4** A debit memorandum issued by the bank on July 31 for a $2 service charge was enclosed with the July bank statement.

**5** Check no. 875 was issued July 20 in the amount of $85 but was erroneously listed on the check stub and in the cash payments journal as $58. The check, in payment of telephone service, was paid by the bank, returned with the July bank statement, and correctly listed on the bank statement as an $85 charge to the account. The Cash account is overstated because of this $27 error ($85 – $58).

**6** No entry has as yet been made in Parkview Company's accounts to reflect the bank's action on July 30 of charging against the account the NSF check for $50.25 drawn by J. B. Ball.

The July 31 bank reconciliation for Parkview Company follows:

***PARKVIEW COMPANY***

***Bank Reconciliation***

***July 31, 19___***

*Update and correct the balance per depositor's records*

| | | |
|---|---|---|
| Balance per depositor's records, July 31, 19___ | | $4,172.57 |
| Add: Note receivable collected for us by bank | | 500.00 |
| | | $4,672.57 |
| Less: Service charge | $ 2.00 | |
| NSF check of J. B. Ball | 50.25 | |
| Error on check stub no. 875 | 27.00 | 79.25 |
| Adjusted balance | | $4,593.32 |

*Update and correct the balance per bank statement*

| | | |
|---|---|---|
| Balance per bank statement, July 31, 19___ | | $5,000.17 |
| Add: Deposit of July 31 not recorded by bank | | 310.90 |
| | | $5,311.07 |
| Less: Outstanding checks | | |
| No. 801 | $100.00 | |
| No. 888 | 10.25 | |
| No. 890 | 402.50 | |
| No. 891 | 205.00 | 717.75 |
| Adjusted balance (as above) | | $4,593.32 |

The adjusted balance of $4,593.32 is the amount of cash owned by Parkview Company and is, therefore, the amount which should appear as cash in the July 31 balance sheet.

Note that the adjusted balance of cash differs from both the bank statement and the depositor's records. This difference is explained by the fact that neither set of records is up-to-date as of July 31, and also by the existence of an error on Parkview Company's records.

**Adjusting the records after the reconciliation** To make Parkview Company's records up-to-date and accurate, four journal entries affecting the Cash account are necessary for the four items that make up the difference between the $4,172.57 balance per the depositor's records and the adjusted balance of $4,593.32. These four reconciling items call for the following entries:

| | | |
|---|---|---|
| *Cash* | *500.00* | |
| *Notes Receivable* | | *500.00* |
| ***To record the note receivable collected for us by the bank.*** | | |
| *Miscellaneous Expense* | *2.00* | |
| *Cash* | | *2.00* |
| ***To record the service charge by the bank.*** | | |
| *Accounts Receivable, J. B. Ball* | *50.25* | |
| *Cash* | | *50.25* |
| ***To record as a receivable from J. B. Ball the amount of the NSF check returned to us by the bank.*** | | |
| *Telephone Expense* | *27.00* | |
| *Cash* | | *27.00* |
| ***To correct the error by which check no. 875 for an $85 payment for telephone service was recorded as $58 ($85 − $58 = $27).*** | | |

Instead of making four separate journal entries affecting the Cash account, one compound journal entry can be made to record all four of the above items. The journal entry (in general journal form) is as follows:

| | | |
|---|---|---|
| *Miscellaneous Expense* | *2.00* | |
| *Accounts Receivable, J. B. Ball* | *50.25* | |
| *Telephone Expense* | *27.00* | |
| *Cash* | *420.75* | |
| *Notes Receivable* | | *500.00* |
| ***To record a service charge by the bank, the return of an NSF check, the correction of an error in recording check no. 875, and the collection by the bank of a note receivable left by us for collection.*** | | |

## Petty cash

As previously emphasized, adequate internal control over cash requires that all receipts be deposited in the bank and all disbursements be made by check. However, every business finds it convenient to have a small amount of cash on hand with which to make some minor expenditures. Examples include payments for small purchases of office supplies, postage stamps, and taxi fares. Internal control over these small cash payments can best be achieved through a petty cash fund.

**Establishing the petty cash fund** To create a petty cash fund, a check is written for a round amount such as $50 or $100, which will cover the small expenditures to be paid in cash for a period of two or three weeks. This check is cashed and the money kept on hand in a petty cash box or drawer in the office.

The entry for the issuance of the check is:

*Creating the petty cash fund*

| | | |
|---|---|---|
| *Petty Cash* | *100* | |
| *Cash* | | *100* |
| *To establish a petty cash fund.* | | |

**Making disbursements from the petty cash fund** As cash payments are made out of the petty cash box, the custodian of the fund is required to fill out a ***petty cash voucher*** for each expenditure. A petty cash voucher shows the amount paid, the purpose of the expenditure, the date, and the signature of the person receiving the money. A petty cash voucher should be prepared for every payment made from the fund. The petty cash box should, therefore, always contain cash and/or vouchers totaling the exact amount of the fund.

The petty cash custodian should be informed that occasional surprise counts of the fund will be made and that he or she is personally responsible for the fund being intact at all times. Careless handling of petty cash has often been a first step toward large thefts; consequently, misuse of petty cash funds should not be tolerated.

**Replenishing the petty cash fund** Assume that a petty cash fund of $100 was established on June 1 and that payments totaling $89.75 were made from the fund during the next two weeks. Since the $100 originally placed in the fund is nearly exhausted, the fund should be replenished. To replenish a petty cash fund means to replace the amount of money that has been spent, thus restoring the fund to its original amount. A check is drawn payable to Petty Cash for the exact amount of the expenditures, $89.75. This check is cashed and the money placed in the petty cash box. The vouchers totaling that amount are perforated to prevent their reuse and filed in support of the replenishment check. The journal entry to record the issuance of the check will debit the expense accounts indicated by inspection of the vouchers, as follows:

*Replenishment of petty cash fund*

| | | |
|---|---|---|
| *Office Supplies Expense* | *40.60* | |
| *Telephone & Telegraph Expense* | *4.80* | |
| *Freight-in* | *6.00* | |
| *Postage Expense* | *25.25* | |
| *Miscellaneous Expense* | *13.10* | |
| *Cash* | | *89.75* |
| *To replenish the petty cash fund.* | | |

Note that ***expense accounts*** are debited each time the fund is replenished. The Petty Cash account is debited only when the fund is first established. There ordinarily will be no further entries in the Petty Cash account after the fund is established, unless the fund is discontinued or a decision is made to change its size from the original $100 amount.

The petty cash fund is usually replenished at the end of an accounting period, even though the fund is not running low, so that all vouchers in the fund are charged to expense accounts before these accounts are closed and financial statements prepared.

## The voucher system

One widely used method of establishing control over cash disbursements is the voucher system. This system provides that every transaction requiring a cash payment be verified and approved before a check is issued. A written authorization called a ***voucher*** is prepared for every expenditure, regardless of whether the expenditure is for payment of an expense, purchase of an asset, or payment of a liability.

A voucher is attached to each incoming invoice and given an identification number. The voucher (as illustrated on page 321) has spaces for listing the data from the invoice and specifying the ledger accounts to be debited and credited in recording the transaction. Space is also provided for approval signatures for each step in the verification and approval process. A completed voucher provides a description of the transaction and also of the work performed in verifying the liability and approving the cash disbursement.

Our purpose in preparing a voucher is to assure that the supplier's invoice is in agreement with our purchase order and our receiving report. The voucher provides an answer to such important questions as:

1 Are the goods and services charged to us on the supplier's invoice in accordance with our previously issued purchase order?
2 Have we actually received in good condition the quantities shown on the invoice?
3 Are all prices, computations, discounts, and credit terms on the invoice accurate?

If the answer to these questions is Yes, the invoice should be paid. The voucher provides written evidence that we ordered and received the goods or services we are being asked to pay for.

**Preparing a voucher** To illustrate the functioning of a voucher system, let us begin with the receipt of an invoice from a supplier. A voucher is prepared by filling in the appropriate blanks with information taken from the invoice, such as the invoice date, invoice number, amount, and the creditor's name and address. The voucher with the seller's invoice attached is then sent to the employees responsible for verifying the extensions and footings on the invoice and for comparing prices, quantities, and terms with those specified in the purchase order and receiving report. When completion of the verification process has been

***Use of voucher ensures verification of invoice***

**BROADHILL CORPORATION**
Chicago, Illinois

| | |
|---|---|
| | Voucher No. 241 |
| Pay to Black Company | Date May 1, 19— |
| 3160 Main Street | Date due May 10, 19— |
| Hilldale, Indiana | |

| | |
|---|---|
| Date of invoice April 30, 19— | Gross amount $ 1,000.00 |
| Invoice number 847 | Less: Cash discount 20.00 |
| | Net amount $ 980.00 |

**Approval**

| | Dates | Approved by |
|---|---|---|
| Extensions and footings verified | May 1, 19— | R.G. |
| Prices in agreement with purchase order | May 1, 19— | R.G. |
| Quantities in agreement with receiving report | May 1, 19— | R.G. |
| Credit terms in agreement with purchase order | May 1, 19— | R.G. |
| Account distribution & recording approved | William Cross (For Accounting Dept.) | |
| Approved for payment | Judith Davis (For Treasurer's Dept.) | |

***Reverse side of voucher***

| | | |
|---|---|---|
| | | Voucher No. 241 |
| Account distribution | | |
| | Amount | Date May 1, 19— |
| Purchases | $ 1,000.00 | |
| Transportation-in | | Date due May 10, 19— |
| Repairs | | |
| Heat, light, and power | | Payee Black Company |
| Advertising | | 3160 Main Street |
| Delivery expense | | Hilldale, Indiana |
| Misc. general expense | | Amount of invoice $ 1,000.00 |
| Telephone and telegraph | | Less: Cash discount 20.00 |
| Sales salaries | | Net amount $ 980.00 |
| Office salaries | | |
| | | Paid by check no. 632 |
| | | Date of check May 10, 19— |
| | | Amount of check $ 980.00 |
| Credit vouchers payable (total) | $ 1,000.00 | |
| Account distribution by KRD | | Entered in voucher register by A.J. |

evidenced by approval signatures of the persons performing these steps, the voucher and supporting documents are sent to an employee of the accounting department, who indicates on the voucher the accounts to be debited and credited.

The voucher is now reviewed by an accounting official to provide assurance that the verification procedures have been satisfactorily completed and that the liability is a proper one. After receiving this executive approval, the voucher is entered in a journal called a ***voucher register***.

## The voucher register

The voucher register shown below replaces the purchases journal described in Chapter 7. It may be thought of as an expanded purchases journal with additional debit columns for various types of expense and asset accounts.

In comparing the voucher register with a purchases journal, it should be emphasized that the purchases journal is used ***only*** to record purchases of merchandise on account. Consequently, every entry in a purchases journal consists of a debit to Purchases and a credit to Accounts Payable. The voucher register, on the other hand, is used to record ***all types of expenditures:*** for plant and equipment, for the payment of notes payable, for expenses, and for payroll as well as for purchases of merchandise. Every entry in the voucher register will consist of a credit to Vouchers Payable, but the debits may affect various asset and expense accounts. Occasionally the entry may require a debit to a liability account; for example, when a voucher is prepared to authorize the issuance of a check in payment of an existing mortgage or note payable.

Each voucher is entered in the voucher register in numerical order as soon as it is prepared and approved. When payment is made the number and date of the check are entered in the columns provided for this purpose. The total amount of unpaid vouchers may be determined from the register at any time merely by listing the "open" items, that is, vouchers for which no entry has yet been made in the Payment columns. The total of the unpaid vouchers appearing in the voucher register should agree with the total of the vouchers in the unpaid vouchers file at the same date.

*Voucher Register*

| Voucher No. | Date (19__) | | Creditor | Payment | | | Vouchers Payable, Cr | Purchases, Dr | Transportation-in, Dr |
|---|---|---|---|---|---|---|---|---|---|
| | | | | Date (19__) | | Check No. | | | |
| 241 | May | 1 | Black Company | May | 10 | 632 | 1,000 | 1,000 | |
| 242 | | 2 | Midwest Freight | | 3 | 627 | 50 | | 50 |
| 243 | | 4 | Ames Company | | 4 | 628 | 125 | | |
| 244 | | 5 | 1st Natl. Bank | | 5 | 629 | 8,080 | | |
| 245 | | 5 | Rathco, Inc. | | 6 | 631 | 1,200 | 1,200 | |
| 246 | | 5 | Midwest Freight | | 6 | 630 | 110 | | 110 |
| ~~~ | | | | | | | | | |
| 286 | | 30 | O. K. Supply Co. | | | | 70 | | |
| 287 | | 30 | J. Jones | | 30 | 665 | 210 | | |
| 288 | | 30 | Black Company | | | | 1,176 | 1,176 | |
| 289 | | 31 | Midwest Freight | | 31 | 666 | 90 | | 90 |
| 290 | | 31 | Payroll | | 31 | 667 | 1,865 | | |
| | | | | | | | 25,875 | 9,220 | 640 |
| | | | | | | | (21) | (51) | (52) |

The procedures for posting from the voucher register to the general ledger are similar to those previously described for other special journals. The letters VR are placed in the Reference column of a ledger account to show that the posting came from the voucher register.

The balance of the general ledger account, Vouchers Payable, should be reconciled at the end of the month with the total of the unpaid vouchers shown in the voucher register and also with the total of the vouchers in the unpaid vouchers file.

**Paying the voucher within the discount period** After the voucher has been entered in the voucher register, it is placed (with the supporting documents attached) in a tickler file according to the date of required payment. The voucher system emphasizes the required ***time for payment*** of liabilities rather than the identity of the creditors; for this reason, vouchers are filed by required date of payment. In computing future cash requirements of a business, the amount of a liability and the required date of payment are of basic significance; the identity of the payee has no bearing on the problem of maintaining a proper cash position.

Cash discount periods generally run from the date of the invoice. Since a voucher is prepared for each invoice, the required date of payment is the last day on which a check can be prepared and mailed to the creditor in time to qualify for the discount.

When the payment date arrives, an employee in the accounting department removes the voucher from the unpaid file, draws a check for signature by the

| *Advertising, Dr* | *Supplies, Dr* | *Repairs, Dr* | *Accrued Payroll, Dr* | *Other General Ledger Accounts* | | | |
|---|---|---|---|---|---|---|---|
| | | | | *Account Name* | *LP* | *Debit* | *Credit* |
| | | *125* | | | | | |
| | | | | *Notes Payable* | *25* | *8,000* | |
| | | | | *Interest Expense* | *79* | *80* | |
| | *70* | | | | | | |
| | | *210* | | | | | |
| | | | *1,865* | | | | |
| *510* | *470* | *335* | *3,800* | | | *10,900* | |
| *(61)* | *(14)* | *(74)* | *(24)* | | | *(x)* | |

treasurer, and records payment of the voucher in the check register (discussed in the following section of this chapter). An important feature of internal control is that the employee in the accounting department who prepares the check ***is not authorized to sign it.*** The unsigned check and the supporting voucher are now sent to the treasurer or other designated official in the finance department. The treasurer reviews the voucher, especially the approval signatures, and signs the check. Thus, the invoice is ***approved for payment*** in the accounting department, but the actual cash disbursement is made by the finance department. ***No one person or department is in a position both to approve invoices for payment and to issue signed checks.***

Once the check has been signed, the treasurer should mail it directly to the creditor. The voucher and all supporting documents are then perforated with a PAID stamp and are forwarded to the accounting department, which will note payment of the voucher in the voucher register and file the paid voucher. The purpose of perforating the voucher and supporting documents is to prevent the possibility of these same documents being used again in support of a duplicate payment. The operation of a voucher system is illustrated in the flow chart on page 325. Notes have been made on the illustration identifying the most important internal control features in the system.

## The check register

A check register is merely a simplified version of the cash payments journal illustrated in Chapter 7. When a voucher system is in use, ***checks are issued only in payment of approved and recorded vouchers.*** Consequently, every check issued is recorded by a debit to Vouchers Payable and a credit to Cash. The check register therefore contains a special column for debits to Vouchers Payable and a

***Check Register***

*Checks issued only in payment of approved vouchers*

| Check No. | Date (19__) | | Payee | Voucher No. | Vouchers Payable, Debit | Purchase Discounts, Credit | Cash, Credit |
|---|---|---|---|---|---|---|---|
| 627 | May | 3 | Midwest Freight | 242 | 50 | | 50 |
| 628 | | 4 | Ames Company | 243 | 125 | | 125 |
| 629 | | 5 | 1st National Bank | 244 | 8,080 | | 8,080 |
| 630 | | 6 | Midwest Freight | 246 | 110 | | 110 |
| 631 | | 6 | Rathco, Inc. | 245 | 1,200 | | 1,200 |
| 632 | | 10 | Black Company | 241 | 1,000 | 20 | 980 |
| 665 | | 30 | J. Jones | 287 | 210 | | 210 |
| 666 | | 31 | Midwest Freight | 289 | 90 | | 90 |
| 667 | | 31 | Payroll | 290 | 1,865 | | 1,865 |
| | | | | | 23,660 | 240 | 23,420 |
| | | | | | (21) | (53) | (1) |

*Operation of a Voucher System*

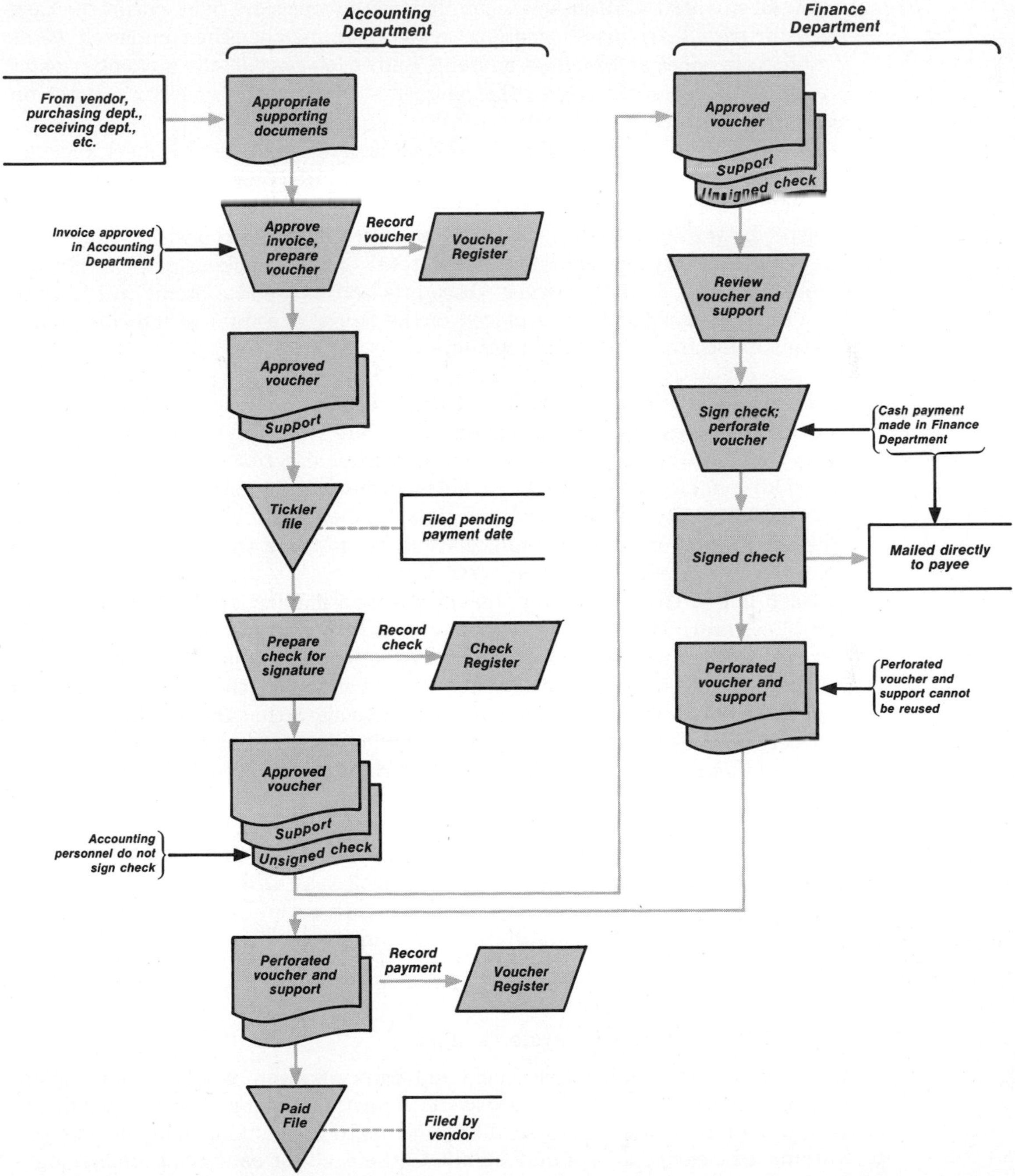

Cash credit column. The only other money column needed in this compact record is for credits to Purchase Discounts when invoices are paid within the cash discount period. In this illustration we are assuming that the company records purchase invoices at the gross amount. Shown on page 324 is a check register with entries corresponding to the payments listed in the voucher register on pages 322 and 323.

To record the payment of a voucher, an entry is made in the check register, and a notation of the check number and date is placed on the appropriate line in the voucher register. At the end of the month the column totals of the check register are posted as for other special journals; this posting consists of a debit to the Vouchers Payable account for the total of the vouchers paid during the month, a credit to the Purchase Discounts account, and a credit to the Cash account. The symbol CkR is placed in the ledger accounts to indicate that a posting came from the check register.

**The voucher register as a subsidiary ledger** When a voucher system is used to control liabilities and cash disbursements, there is no need to maintain an accounts payable subsidiary ledger such as the one described in Chapter 7. Since the traditional form of accounts payable ledger contains a separate account with every creditor, it requires a great deal of detailed posting and recording work. The elimination of this costly subsidiary ledger is one of the major savings to be achieved by adopting a voucher system.

Each line of the voucher register represents a liability account with an individual creditor. This liability account comes into existence when an invoice is received and a voucher is prepared and recorded, describing the amount owed under the terms of that invoice. When a voucher is paid, the check number and date are entered on the line for that voucher to show that the liability is ended. Inspection of the voucher register reveals which items have not been paid. A list of unpaid vouchers corresponds to a trial balance prepared from an accounts payable subsidiary ledger.

The voucher register thus serves a dual purpose; it is primarily a journal, but it also serves as the equivalent of a subsidiary ledger of liability accounts. However, the voucher register does not classify invoices by creditors; it does not show the total amount owed to a given creditor with several invoices outstanding. Neither does it show the total purchases from a given supplier over a period of time.

## Electronic funds transfer systems (EFTS)

Our discussion of cash transactions and bank accounts would be incomplete without mention of the many new systems for transferring funds electronically rather than by delivery of physical documents. In the banking field, for example, automated clearing houses may eliminate the need for banks to exchange bundles of customers' checks each day. If you pay your telephone bill by a check written on Bank A, the telephone company traditionally has deposited your check in its bank (Bank B). Bank B would then deliver your check and others like it to Bank A in order to collect. At the same time Bank A would be presenting a bundle of checks deposited with it but drawn on Bank B. In reality many banks, not just Bank A and Bank B, would be involved in this "clearing house" activity. Since the number of checks written each day is roughly 50 million, this exchange of paper represents a great opportunity for saving through electronic transfer of funds. Electronic equipment now exists which enables banks to transfer funds from the account of one depositor to the account of another without all this cumbersome exchange of paper.

Many other applications of electronic funds transfer are now in use. For example, a company may pay all its employees (if they agree) by delivering payroll information to its bank on magnetic tape. The bank's computer debits the employer's account and credits the bank account of each employee without any paper changing hands.

The further development of electronic funds transfer systems seems to be impeded more by government regulations, legislative barriers, and public attitudes than by lack of technology. A considerable portion of the public appears to be reluctant to move into a "checkless society."

## KEY TERMS INTRODUCED OR EMPHASIZED IN CHAPTER 8

**Bank reconciliation** A statement listing the items which make up the difference between the balance shown on the bank statement and the balance of cash according to the depositor's records.

**Bank service charge** An amount deducted from a depositor's checking account by the bank to cover the expense of maintaining a checking account or for special handling of such items as NSF checks.

**Bank statement** A monthly statement provided by the bank to the depositor, along with paid checks and notices of any bank charges and credits.

**Cash** Currency, coins, checks, money orders, and any other medium of exchange which a bank will accept for deposit and immediate credit to the depositor's account.

**Cash over and short** A ledger account used to accumulate the amounts by which actual cash receipts differ from the amount recorded on cash registers.

**Cash receipts** The inflow of cash to a business.

**Check register** A simplified version of the cash payments journal (see Chapter 7) used for recording cash payments when a voucher system is in use.

**Deposit ticket** A form filled out by the depositor listing the checks and currency being deposited. Each check is listed separately and identified by the code number of the bank on which it is drawn.

**Deposits in transit** Cash receipts which have been entered in the depositor's accounting records and mailed to the bank or left in the bank's night depository, but which reached the bank too late to be credited to the depositor's current monthly bank statement.

**Electronic funds transfer system** The electronic transfer of funds from the bank account of one depositor to the account of another without the delivery of checks. Many related applications are in use to reduce paper work in cash transactions.

**NSF check** A customer's check which was deposited but returned because of a lack of funds (Not Sufficient Funds) in the account on which the check was drawn.

**Outstanding checks** Checks issued by a business to suppliers, employees, or other payees but not yet presented to the bank for payment.

**Petty cash fund** A small amount of cash set aside for making minor cash payments for which writing of checks is not practicable.

**Petty cash voucher** A document prepared for each payment made from the petty cash fund. Serves as a receipt for the expenditure.

**Stop payment order** An order given by a depositor to a bank not to pay a particular check. To stop payment is appropriate when a check has been stolen, lost, or improperly issued.

**Voucher** A document prepared to authorize and describe an expenditure.

**Voucher register** A special journal used to record all liabilities which have been approved for payment.

**Voucher system** A method of controlling expenditures and the payment of liabilities. Requires that every liability be recorded as soon as it is incurred, and that checks be issued only in payment of approved liabilities.

## DEMONSTRATION PROBLEM FOR YOUR REVIEW

The information listed below is available in reconciling the bank statement for the White River Company on November 30, 19__.

(1) The ledger account for Cash showed a balance at November 30 of $7,766.64, including a $100 petty cash fund. Petty cash should be transferred to a separate account. The bank statement at November 30 indicated a balance of $9,734.70.

(2) The November 30 cash receipts of $5,846.20 had been mailed to the bank on that date and did not appear among the deposits on the November bank statement. The receipts include a check for $4,000 from a brokerage house for the sale of 150 shares of stock of the Axe Co. which cost $6,270. Neither the proceeds on the sale of stock nor the collections on accounts receivable ($1,846.20) has been recorded in the accounts of the White River Company.

(3) Included with the November bank statement was an NSF check for $220 signed by a customer, James Ruddock. This amount had been charged against the bank account on November 30.

(4) Of the checks issued in November, the following were not included among the paid checks returned by the bank:

| *Check No.* | *Amount* | *Check No.* | *Amount* |
|---|---|---|---|
| *924* | *$136.25* | *944* | *$ 95.00* |
| *940* | *105.00* | *945* | *716.15* |
| *941* | *11.46* | *946* | *60.00* |
| *943* | *826.70* | | |

(5) A service charge for $340 by the bank had been made in error against the White River Company account.

(6) A non-interest-bearing note receivable for $690 owned by the White River Company had been left with the bank for collection. On November 30 the company received a memorandum from the bank indicating that the note had been collected and credited to the company's account after deduction of a $5 collection charge. No entry has been made by the company to record collection of the note.

(7) A debit memorandum for $7.50 was enclosed with the paid checks at November 30. This charge covered the printing of checkbooks bearing the White River Company name and address.

**Instructions**

**a** Prepare a bank reconciliation at November 30.

**b** Prepare journal entries required at November 30 to bring the company's records up to date.

## SOLUTION TO DEMONSTRATION PROBLEM

a

***WHITE RIVER COMPANY***
***Bank Reconciliation***
***November 30, 19___***

| | | |
|---|---|---|
| *Balance per depositor's records, Nov. 30* | | *$ 7,766.64* |
| *Add: Proceeds on sale of stock* | *$4,000.00* | |
| *Collection on accounts receivable* | *1,846.20* | |
| *Note receivable collected by bank, $690, less collection charge, $5* | *685.00* | *6,531.20* |
| | | *$14,297.84* |
| *Less: Petty cash fund reported separately* | *$ 100.00* | |
| *NSF check, James Ruddock* | *220.00* | |
| *Charge by bank for printing checks* | *7.50* | *327.50* |
| *Adjusted balance* | | *$13,970.34* |
| *Balance per bank statement, Nov. 30* | | *$ 9,734.70* |
| *Add: Deposit of Nov. 30 not recorded by bank* | *$5,846.20* | |
| *Service charge made by bank in error* | *340.00* | *6,186.20* |
| | | *$15,920.90* |
| *Less: Outstanding checks on Nov. 30:* | | |
| *No. 924* | *$ 136.25* | |
| *No. 940* | *105.00* | |
| *No. 941* | *11.46* | |
| *No. 943* | *826.70* | |
| *No. 944* | *95.00* | |
| *No. 945* | *716.15* | |
| *No. 946* | *60.00* | *1,950.56* |
| *Adjusted balance (as above)* | | *$13,970.34* |

b *General Journal*

| | | | |
|---|---|---|---|
| *19__* | | | |
| *Nov. 30* | *Cash* | *6,531.20* | |
| | *Loss on Sale of Marketable Securities* | *2,270.00* | |
| | *Miscellaneous Expense* | *5.00* | |
| | *Investment in Marketable Securities* | | *6,270.00* |
| | *Notes Receivable* | | *690.00* |
| | *Accounts Receivable* | | *1,846.20* |
| | *To record increase in Cash account as indicated by bank reconciliation.* | | |
| *Nov. 30* | *Petty Cash* | *100.00* | |
| | *Miscellaneous Expense* | *7.50* | |
| | *Accounts Receivable, James Ruddock* | *220.00* | |
| | *Cash* | | *327.50* |
| | *To record cash disbursements as indicated by bank reconciliation and to record petty cash in a separate account.* | | |

## REVIEW QUESTIONS

**1** Does the expression "efficient management of cash" mean anything more than procedures to prevent losses from fraud or theft? Explain.

**2** If a company has checking accounts in three banks, should it maintain a separate ledger account for each? Should the company's balance sheet show the amount on deposit in each of the three checking accounts as a separate item? Explain.

**3** Mention some principles to be observed by a business in establishing strong internal control over cash receipts.

**4** Explain how internal control over cash transactions is strengthened by compliance with the following rule: "Deposit each day's cash receipts intact in the bank, and make all disbursements by check."

**5** List two items often encountered in reconciling a bank account which may cause cash per the bank statement to be larger than the balance of cash shown in the accounts.

**6** In the reconciliation of a bank account, what reconciling items necessitate a journal entry in the depositor's accounting records?

**7** Pico Stationery Shop has for years maintained a petty cash fund of $75, which is replenished twice a month.

**a** How many debit entries would you expect to find in the Petty Cash account each year?

**b** When would expenditures from the petty cash fund be entered in the ledger accounts?

**8** A check for $455 issued in payment of an account payable was erroneously listed in the cash payments journal as $545. The error was discovered early in the following month when the paid check was returned by the bank. What corrective action is needed?

**9** It is standard accounting practice to treat as cash all checks received from customers. When a customer's check is received, recorded, and deposited, but later returned by the bank marked NSF, what accounting entry or entries would be appropriate?

**10** Ringo Store sells only for cash and records all sales on cash registers before delivering merchandise to the customers. On a given day the cash count at the close of business indicated $10.25 less cash than was shown by the totals on the cash register tapes. In what account would this cash shortage be recorded? Would the account be debited or credited?

**11** Classify each of the numbered reconciling items listed below under one of the following headings: **(a)** an addition to the balance per depositor's records; **(b)** a deduction from the balance per depositor's records; **(c)** an addition to the balance per bank statement; **(d)** a deduction from the balance per bank statement.
(1) Deposits in transit
(2) Outstanding checks
(3) Customer's check deposited but returned by bank marked NSF
(4) Bank service charges
(5) Collection by bank of note receivable left with bank for collection in behalf of depositor

**12** Name three internal control practices relating to cash which would be practicable even in a small business having little opportunity for division of duties.

**13** With respect to a ***voucher system,*** what is meant by the terms ***voucher, voucher register,*** and ***check register?***

**14** What is the greatest single advantage of the voucher system?

**15** Randall Company uses a voucher system to control its cash disbursements. With respect to a purchase of merchandise, what three documents would need to be examined to verify that the voucher should be approved?

**16** Assume that a company using a general journal, a cash receipts journal, a cash payments journal, a sales journal, and a purchases journal decides to adopt a voucher system. Which of the five journals would be changed or replaced? Explain.

**17** On January 10 Susan Jones wrote a check for $500 and mailed it to Joe Smith in payment of a debt. On January 25, Smith called and asked to be paid, stating that no check had been received. Jones placed a stop payment order with her bank and wrote another check which she delivered personally to Smith.

**a** What information should Jones have given the bank in connection with the stop payment order in order that the bank could guard against paying the first check?

**b** In preparing a bank reconciliation at January 31, should Jones include on the outstanding check list the check on which payment had been stopped? Explain.

**c** If the first check was presented to the bank by a third person on February 15 and was cashed by the bank despite the existence of the stop payment order, would the loss fall on Jones, Smith, or the bank?

**18** In bidding for some surplus property offered at auction by a government agency, the Argus Company on December 28 drew a check for $3,000 and mailed it with the bid. The government agency on January 3 rejected the bid and returned the check. Should the $3,000 be included as cash in the December 31 balance sheet, which was prepared by the Argus Company on January 5 after the check had been returned? Explain.

## EXERCISES

*Ex. 8-1* Solana Corporation maintains a petty cash fund of $300. At December 31, the end of the company's fiscal year, the fund contained the following:

| | |
|---|---|
| *Currency and coins* | *$ 78.82* |
| *Expense vouchers:* | |
| *Taxi fares (Debit Travel Expense)* | *34.98* |
| *Office supplies expense* | *146.20* |
| *Contributions to Boy Scouts and others* | *40.00* |
| *Total* | *$300.00* |

Prepare the entry (in general journal form) to replenish the petty cash fund.

*Ex. 8-2* At July 31 the Cash account in the ledger of Art Mart, Inc., showed a balance of $36,500. The bank statement, however, showed a balance of $43,700 at the same date. If the only reconciling items consisted of a $2,400 deposit in transit, a bank service charge of $4, and 30 outstanding checks, what was the total amount of the outstanding checks?

*Ex. 8-3* At the end of the month Matson Company received a bank statement showing a balance of $28,000 on deposit. Among the reconciling items were outstanding checks totaling $5,800, bank service charges of $6, a deposit in transit of $4,400, and a memorandum showing that a $2,400 note receivable owned by Matson Company and left with the bank for collection had been collected and credited to the company's account.

**a** What is the adjusted amount of cash which should appear on the Matson Company's balance sheet?

**b** What was the balance per the depositor's records before making adjusting entries for any of the reconciling items?

*Ex. 8-4* The Warren Company established a petty cash fund of $150 on June 1. On June 20 the fund was replenished for the payments made to date as shown by the following petty cash vouchers: freight-in, $9.50; postage, $46; telephone expense, $3.20; repairs, $31.70; miscellaneous expense, $22. Prepare journal entries in general journal form to record the establishment of the fund on June 1 and its replenishment on June 20.

*Ex. 8-5* The petty cash fund of Wicker Company contained the following at December 31, 19___, the end of the fiscal year.

| | |
|---|---|
| *Cash on hand* | *$119.41* |
| *Expense vouchers:* | |
| *Flowers for funeral of deceased customer (Miscellaneous Expense)* | *20.40* |
| *Gift for purchasing agent of James Co. (Miscellaneous Expense)* | *27.09* |
| *Office supplies expense* | *13.10* |
| *Salary advance to employee* | *20.00* |
| *Total* | *$200.00* |

**a** Since there is a substantial amount of cash in the petty cash fund, is there any reason to replenish it at December 31? Explain.

**b** Prepare the entry (in general journal form) to replenish the petty cash fund.

*Ex. 8-6* Gray Rock Company uses a voucher system. You are to record the following transactions in ***general journal form*** (without explanations). Also indicate after each

entry the book of original entry in which the transaction would in practice be recorded.
(a) Voucher no. 100 prepared to purchase office equipment at cost of $4,000 from Coast Furniture Co.
(b) Check no. 114 issued in payment of voucher no. 100.
(c) Voucher no. 101 prepared to establish a petty cash fund of $150.
(d) Check no. 115 issued in payment of voucher no. 101.
(e) Voucher no. 102 prepared to replenish the petty cash fund which contained $40 cash, and receipts for postage $38, miscellaneous expense $54, and delivery service $18.
(f) Check no. 116 issued in payment of voucher no. 102. Check cashed and proceeds placed in petty cash fund.

## PROBLEMS

### Group A

*8A-1* Prepare a bank reconciliation for Marine Supply at July 31, 19___, from the information listed below. Use the form of reconciliation illustrated on page 317.
(1) Cash per the accounting records at July 31 amounted to $36,401; the bank statement at this date showed a balance of $32,251.
(2) The cash receipts of $5,464 on July 31 were mailed to the bank but not received by the bank during July.
(3) The paid checks returned by the bank included a stolen check for $882 which had been paid in error by the bank after the Marine Supply had issued a stop payment order to the bank. Note that the bank was at fault.
(4) The following memoranda accompanied the bank statement:
(a) A debit memo of $13 for service charges for July.
(b) A debit memo attached to a $680 check of a customer, Albert Davis, marked NSF.
(5) The following checks had been issued by Marine Supply but were not included among the paid checks returned by the bank: no. 167 for $1,369, no. 174 for $844, and no. 179 for $676.

*8A-2* The cash transactions and cash balances of Black Jack, Inc., for April, 19___, are summarized below.
(1) As of April 30, cash per accounting records was $7,709.12; per bank statement, $7,328.67.
(2) Cash receipts of $2,187.03 on April 30 were not deposited until May 1.
(3) The following memoranda accompanied the bank statement:
(a) A debit memo for service charges for the month of April, $7.56.
(b) A debit memo attached to a check of G. Herron, marked NSF, for $149.88.
(c) A credit memo for $1,452, representing the proceeds of a non-interest-bearing note collected by the bank for Black Jack, Inc. The note was for $1,464; the bank deducted a collection fee of $12.
(4) The following checks had been issued but were not included in the paid checks returned by the bank: no. 348 for $302.40, no. 351 for $124.32, and no. 356 for $85.30.

**Instructions**

**a** Prepare a bank reconciliation as of April 30.
**b** Draft in general journal form the journal entries necessary to adjust the accounts.
**c** State the amount of cash which should appear in the balance sheet at April 30.

*8A-3* Robert Smith, a trusted employee of Bluestem Products, found himself in personal financial difficulties and carried out the following plan to steal $1,000 from the company and to conceal the fraud.

Smith removed $1,000 in currency from the cash register. This amount represented the bulk of the cash received in over-the-counter sales during the three business days since the last bank deposit. Smith then removed a $1,000 check from the day's incoming mail; this check had been mailed in by a customer, Larry Jansen, in full payment of his account. Smith made no entry in the cash receipts journal for the $1,000 collection from Jansen but deposited the check in Bluestem Products' bank account in place of the $1,000 of over-the-counter cash receipts he had stolen. In order to keep Jansen from protesting when his month-end statement reached him, Smith made a general journal entry debiting Sales Returns and Allowances and crediting Accounts Receivable—Larry Jansen. Smith posted this entry to the two general ledger accounts affected and also to Jansen's account in the subsidiary ledger for accounts receivable.

**Instructions**

**a** Did these actions by Smith cause the general ledger to be out of balance or the subsidiary ledger to disagree with the control account? Explain.

**b** Several weaknesses in internal control apparently exist in Bluestem Products. Indicate the corrective actions needed.

*8A-4* Information necessary for the preparation of a bank reconciliation and related journal entries for the Stonehenge Corporation at November 30 is listed below:

(1) The balance per records of the Stonehenge Corporation is $10,423.09.

(2) The bank statement shows a balance of $9,154.57 as of November 30.

(3) Two debit memoranda accompanied the bank statement: one for $13 was for service charges for the month; the other for $864.60 was attached to an NSF check from Thomas Jones.

(4) The paid checks returned with the November bank statement disclosed two errors in the cash records. Check no. 832 for $923.48 had been erroneously recorded as $932.48 in the cash payments journal, and check no. 851 for $66.33 had been recorded as $33.66. Check no. 832 was issued in payment for a store display counter; check no. 851 was for advertising expense.

(5) A collection charge for $100.00 (not applicable to Stonehenge Corporation) was erroneously deducted from the account by the bank.

(6) Cash receipts of November 30 amounting to $625.25 were mailed to the bank too late to be included in the November bank statement.

(7) Checks outstanding as of November 30 were as follows: no. 860 for $160.00, no. 870 for $75.20, and no. 880 for $122.80.

**Instructions**

**a** Prepare a bank reconciliation at November 30.

**b** Prepare the necessary adjusting entries in general journal form.

*8A-5* Information necessary for the preparation of a bank reconciliation and related journal entries for the Green Valley Motel at March 31 is listed below.

(1) The balance per records of the Green Valley Motel is $17,244.02.

(2) The bank statement shows a balance of $21,278.29 as of March 31.

(3) Accompanying the bank statement was a check of D. Jones for $186.00, which was marked NSF by the bank.

(4) Checks outstanding as of March 31 were as follows: no. 84 for $1,841.02; no. 88 for $1,323.00; no. 89 for $16.26.

(5) Also accompanying the bank statement was a debit memorandum for $44.80 for safe deposit box rent; the bank had erroneously charged this item to the account of the Green Valley Motel.

(6) On March 29, the bank collected a non-interest-bearing note for Green Valley Motel. The note was for $2,963; the bank charged a collection fee of $8.40.
(7) A deposit of $2,008.50 was in transit; it had been mailed to the bank on March 31.
(8) In recording a $160 check received on account from a customer, Ross Company, the accountant for the Green Valley Motel erroneously listed the collection in the cash receipts journal as $16. The check appeared correctly among the deposits on the March bank statement.
(9) The bank service charge for March amounted to $5.31; a debit memo in this amount was returned with the bank statement.

**Instructions**

**a** Prepare a bank reconciliation at March 31.
**b** Prepare the necessary journal entries.

*8A-6* In order to handle small cash disbursements in an efficient manner, Whitehall Company established a petty cash fund on July 10, 19___. The company does not use a voucher system. The following transactions occurred relating to petty cash.

**July 10** A check for $300 was issued and cashed to establish a petty cash fund.
**July 31** A count of the fund at month-end disclosed the following:

| | |
|---|---|
| *Office supplies expense* | *$59.40* |
| *Postage expense* | *60.00* |
| *Travel expense* | *59.38* |
| *Miscellaneous expense* | *40.62* |
| *Currency and coin remaining in the fund* | *80.60* |

**July 31** A check was issued to replenish the petty cash fund.

**Instructions**

**a** Prepare entries in general journal form to record the above transactions.
**b** Explain why the petty cash fund should be replenished at the end of the accounting period even though the fund contains considerable cash.

*8A-7* Rancho Lumber Co. had never given much attention to internal control concepts and the internal controls over cash transactions were not adequate. Donna Jones, the cashier bookkeeper, handled cash receipts, made small disbursements from the cash receipts, maintained accounting records, and prepared the monthly reconciliations of the bank account.

At April 30, the statement received from the bank showed a balance on deposit of $30,510. The outstanding checks were as follows: no. 7062 for $371.16, no. 7183 for $306.00, no. 7284 for $470.61, no. 8621 for $315.34, no. 8623 for $613.80, and no. 8632 for $311.04. The balance of cash shown by the company's ledger account for Cash was $35,474.96, which included the cash on hand. The bank statement for April showed a credit of $360 arising from the collection of a note left with the bank; the company's accounts did not include an entry to record this collection.

Recognizing the weakness existing in internal control over cash transactions, Jones removed all the cash on hand in excess of $6,025.14, and then prepared the reconciliation shown on page 336 in an attempt to conceal this theft.

**Instructions**

**a** Determine how much cash Jones took. Prepare a bank reconciliation in a form which first shows the balance per the accounting records after adding the cash from collection of the note and, second, shows an adjusted bank balance after deducting the proper amount for all outstanding checks. The two adjusted balances will not agree; the difference is the amount of undeposited cash which should be on hand. Comparison of the undeposited cash which should be on hand

| | | |
|---|---|---|
| *Balance per accounting records, Apr. 30* | | *$35,474.96* |
| *Add: Outstanding checks:* | | |
| *No. 8621* | *$315.34* | |
| *No. 8623* | *613.80* | |
| *No. 8632* | *311.04* | *1,060.18* |
| | | *$36,535.14* |
| *Less: Cash on hand* | | *6,025.14* |
| *Balance per bank statement, Apr. 30* | | *$30,510.00* |
| *Less: Unrecorded credit* | | *360.00* |
| *True cash, Apr. 30* | | *$30,150.00* |

with the actual amount on hand of $6,025.14 will indicate the amount of the cash shortage.

**b** Explain how Jones attempted to conceal her theft in the improper bank reconciliation shown above. Your explanation may be in the form of a list of dollar amounts which add up to the total cash stolen by Jones.

**c** Suggest some specific internal control devices for the Rancho Lumber Co.

*8A-8* (If the partially filled-in working papers supplementing the text are not used, Problem 8A-8 should be omitted.)
The voucher system used by Blackwell, Inc., includes a voucher register and a check register similar to those illustrated on pages 322 and 323. At September 30, the following vouchers were in the unpaid file.

| *Date Due* | *Voucher No.* | *Creditor* | *Date of Invoice* | *Amount* | *Terms* |
|---|---|---|---|---|---|
| *Oct. 3* | *438* | *Brown Co.* | *Sept. 3* | *$1,800* | *n/30* |
| *Oct. 6* | *460* | *Gray, Inc.* | *Sept. 26* | *5,000* | *2/10,n/30* |

During October the following vouchers were prepared:

| *Date* | *Voucher No.* | *Payee* | *Amount* | *Terms* | *Account Distribution* |
|---|---|---|---|---|---|
| *Oct. 1* | *462* | *Ames Co.* | *$ 6,000* | *2/10,n/30* | *Purchases* |
| *7* | *463* | *Rapid Freight* | *300* | *cash* | *Transportation-in* |
| *10* | *464* | *Steel Desk* | *2,650* | *n/30* | *Office Equipment* |
| *12* | *465* | *Barco* | *5,600* | *2/10,n/30* | *Purchases* |
| *13* | *466* | *Rapid Freight* | *250* | *cash* | *Transportation-in* |
| *15* | *467* | *First Bank* | *11,400* | | *Notes Payable $10,000* |
| | | | | | *Interest Expense $1,400* |
| *17* | *468* | *Bell Co.* | *325* | *cash* | *Office Supplies* |
| *18* | *469* | *Ames Co.* | *1,000* | *2/10,n/30* | *Purchases* |
| *20* | *470* | *Tribune* | *280* | *cash* | *Advertising* |
| *25* | *471* | *Clip Co.* | *210* | *n/30* | *Office Supplies* |
| *29* | *472* | *AAA Service* | *550* | *n/30* | *Repairs* |
| *31* | *473* | *Payroll* | *12,000* | *cash* | *Accrued Payroll* |

The following checks were issued during October:

| Date | Check No. | Payee | Voucher No. | Amount |
|---|---|---|---|---|
| Oct. 3 | 601 | Brown Co. | 438 | $ 1,800 |
| 6 | 602 | Gray, Inc. | 460 | 4,900 |
| 7 | 603 | Rapid Freight | 463 | 300 |
| 11 | 604 | Ames Co. | 462 | 5,880 |
| 13 | 605 | Rapid Freight | 466 | 250 |
| 15 | 606 | First Bank | 467 | 11,400 |
| 17 | 607 | Bell Co. | 468 | 325 |
| 20 | 608 | Tribune | 470 | 280 |
| 22 | 609 | Barco | 465 | 5,488 |
| 28 | 610 | Ames Co. | 469 | 980 |
| 31 | 611 | Payroll | 473 | 12,000 |

**Instructions**

**a** Record the $6,800 of unpaid vouchers at September 30 in the general ledger liability account for Vouchers Payable, account no. 21.

**b** Enter individually the 12 October vouchers in a voucher register similar to the one illustrated in this chapter.

**c** Enter the 11 October checks in a check register similar to the one illustrated in this chapter. The date of each check and its serial number also should be listed in the appropriate columns of the voucher register for each voucher paid.

**d** Compute month-end totals of both the voucher register and the check register. Make the appropriate posting of totals to the general ledger account for Vouchers Payable, account no. 21. Prepare a list of unpaid vouchers at October 31. The total of this schedule should agree with the balance of the Vouchers Payable account in the general ledger.

## Group B

*8B-1* The information necessary for preparing a bank reconciliation for Hilltop Farms at November 30, 19___, appears below.

(1) As of November 30, cash per the accounting records was $32,496; per bank statement, $27,754.

(2) Cash receipts of $6,244 on November 30 were not deposited until December 1.

(3) Among the paid checks returned by the bank was a stolen check for $1,008 paid in error by the bank after Hilltop Farms had issued a stop payment order to the bank. Note that the bank was at fault.

(4) The following memoranda accompanied the bank statement:
(a) A debit memo for service charges for the month of November, $14.
(b) A debit memo attached to a $778 check of Frank Miller, marked NSF.

(5) The following checks had been issued but were not included in the paid checks returned by the bank: no. 921 for $1,564, no. 924 for $964, and no. 925 for $774.

**Instructions** Prepare a bank reconciliation for Hilltop Farms at November 30, 19___, in the form illustrated on page 317.

*8B-2* Portside, Inc., reports the following information concerning cash balances and cash transactions for the month of September:

(1) Cash balance per bank statement as of September 30 was $20,793.25.

(2) Two debit memoranda accompanied the bank statement: one for $4 was for service charges for the month; the other for $64.60 was attached to an NSF check from A. Smith.

(3) The paid checks returned with the September bank statement disclosed two errors in the cash records. Check no. 832 for $456.30 had been erroneously recorded as $465.30 in the cash payments journal, and check no. 851 for $77.44 had been recorded as $44.77. Check no. 832 was issued in payment for a store display counter; check no. 851 was for telephone expense. Note that both these errors were made by the depositor.

(4) A collection charge for $126.00 (not applicable to Portside, Inc.) was erroneously deducted from the account by the bank. Notice that this error was made by the bank.

(5) Cash receipts of September 30 amounting to $585.25 were mailed to the bank too late to be included in the September bank statement.

(6) Checks outstanding as of September 30 were as follows: no. 860 for $151.93, no. 867 for $82.46, and no. 869 for $123.61.

(7) The Cash account showed the following entries during September:

***Cash***

| | | | | | | | | | |
|---|---|---|---|---|---|---|---|---|---|
| *Sept* | *1* | *Balance* | | *18,341.82* | *Sept* | *30* | | *CD7* | *11,514.63* |
| | *30* | | *CR5* | *14,411.58* | | | | | |

**Instructions**

**a** Prepare a bank reconciliation at September 30.

**b** Prepare the necessary adjusting entries in general journal form.

*8B-3* Santa Rosa Winery maintains a petty cash fund to control small cash payments. The company does not use a voucher system. Shown below are the transactions involving the establishment of the fund and its replenishment at September 30, the end of the company's fiscal year:

**Sept. 12** A check for $360 was issued and cashed to establish a petty cash fund.

**Sept. 30** A count of the fund showed currency and coin of $96.11 remaining on hand. Petty cash vouchers in the fund were as follows:

| | |
|---|---|
| *Office supplies expense* | *$100.43* |
| *Postage expense* | *73.92* |
| *Telephone and telegraph expense* | *23.10* |
| *Miscellaneous expense* | *66.44* |

**Sept. 30** Although the fund had not been used fully, management wished to replenish the fund before the accounts were closed for the fiscal year. A check was therefore issued and cashed on this date in the amount necessary to replenish the fund.

**Instructions**

**a** Prepare journal entries in general journal form to record the establishment of the fund on September 12 and its replenishment on September 30.

**b** What would have been the effect, if any, on net income for the fiscal year ended September 30 if the company had forgotten to replenish the fund on September 30? Explain.

***8B-4*** The cash transactions and cash balances of Nightflite Express for July were as follows:

(1) The ledger account for Cash showed a balance at June 30 of $7,301.65.
(2) The cash receipts journal for July showed total cash received of $45,216.18.
(3) The credit to the Cash account posted from the cash payments journal at July 31 was $35,750.88.
(4) The cash received on July 31 amounted to $4,017.15. It was left at the bank in the night depository chute after banking hours on July 31 and was therefore not recorded by the bank on the July statement.
(5) The July bank statement showed a closing balance of $18,928.12.
(6) Also included with the July bank statement was a debit memorandum from the bank for $7.65 representing service charges for July.
(7) A credit memorandum enclosed with the July bank statement indicated that a non-interest-bearing note receivable for $4,545 from Rene Manes, left with the bank for collection, had been collected and the proceeds credited to the account of Nightflite Express.
(8) Comparison of the paid checks returned by the bank with the entries in the cash payments journal revealed that check no. 821 for $835.02 issued July 15 in payment for office equipment had been erroneously entered in the cash payments journal as $853.02.
(9) Examination of the paid checks also revealed that three checks, all issued in July, had not yet been paid by the bank: no. 811 for $861.12; no. 814 for $640.80; no. 823 for $301.05.
(10) Included with the July bank statement was a $180 check drawn by Howard Williams, a customer of Nightflite Express. This check was marked NSF. It had been included in the deposit of July 27 but had been charged back against the company's account on July 31.

**Instructions**

**a** Prepare a bank reconciliation for Nightflite Express at July 31. (Suggestion: As a first step compute the cash balance per the accounting records at July 31.)
**b** Prepare journal entries (in general journal form) to adjust the accounts at July 31. Assume that the accounts have not been closed.
**c** State the amount of cash which should appear on the balance sheet at July 31.

***8B-5*** At August 31, the balance of the Cash account in the ledger of Maui Traders was exactly equal to the ending balance shown on the bank statement. Since the two sets of records were in agreement at August 31, no bank reconciliation was needed at August 31.

The cash receipts journal and the cash payments journal maintained by Maui Traders showed transactions during September as listed on page 340. On October 1, Maui Traders received from its bank a bank statement covering the month of September. Enclosed with the bank statement were 23 checks paid by the bank during September and a $4.25 debit memorandum for service charges. The September bank statement appears on page 341.

**Cash Receipts**

| Date | | | Cash Dr |
|---|---|---|---|
| Sept | 1 | | 72.80 |
| | 3 | | 361.00 |
| | 6 | | 280.00 |
| | 8 | | 510.00 |
| | 10 | | 205.60 |
| | 13 | | 180.14 |
| | 15 | | 345.00 |
| | 17 | | 427.50 |
| | 20 | | 90.00 |
| | 22 | | 360.00 |
| | 24 | | 625.00 |
| | 27 | | 130.25 |
| | 29 | | 280.50 |
| | 30 | | 315.25 |
| | | | 4,183.04 |

**Cash Payments**

| Date | | | Ck. No. | Cash Cr |
|---|---|---|---|---|
| Sept | 1 | | 65 | 130.00 |
| | 1 | | 66 | 90.00 |
| | 1 | | 67 | 35.48 |
| | 2 | | 68 | 31.15 |
| | 4 | | 69 | 60.00 |
| | 4 | | 70 | 70.00 |
| | 5 | | 71 | 515.00 |
| | 9 | | 72 | 62.50 |
| | 10 | | 73 | 13.30 |
| | 10 | | 74 | 28.00 |
| | 13 | | 75 | 650.00 |
| | 19 | | 76 | 125.06 |
| | 19 | | 77 | 40.00 |
| | 19 | | 78 | 85.00 |
| | 20 | | 79 | 24.10 |
| | 21 | | 80 | 38.60 |
| | 22 | | 81 | 65.00 |
| | 22 | | 82 | 162.40 |
| | 23 | | 83 | 150.00 |
| | 26 | | 84 | 15.00 |
| | 28 | | 85 | 270.00 |
| | 28 | | 86 | 105.20 |
| | 28 | | 87 | 225.00 |
| | 28 | | 88 | 355.00 |
| | 30 | | 89 | 25.00 |
| | 30 | | 90 | 45.00 |
| | 30 | | 91 | 155.00 |
| | | | | 3,570.79 |

**Instructions**

**a** Compute the amount of cash at September 30 according to the depositor's records. Begin the computation with the balance of the general ledger account, Cash, at August 31, which is stated to be the same as the bank balance at that date. (See bank statement.)

**b** Prepare a bank reconciliation at September 30.

**c** Prepare a general journal entry to adjust the Cash account at September 30, based on information contained in the bank reconciliation in part **b**.

**BANK STATEMENT**

*Maui Traders*
*Lahaina, Maui*

**THE FIRST NATIONAL BANK OF MAUI**

*Vouchers Returned 24*

| Checks | | | Deposits | Date | Balance |
|---|---|---|---|---|---|
| | | | | Sept. 1 | 7,658.75 |
| 31.15 | 35.48 | 130.00 | 72.80 | Sept. 2 | 7,534.92 |
| 60.00 | | | 361.00 | Sept. 5 | 7,835.92 |
| 70.00 | 515.00 | | 280.00 | Sept. 7 | 7,530.92 |
| 90.00 | | | | Sept. 8 | 7,440.92 |
| 13.30 | 62.50 | | 510.00 | Sept. 9 | 7,875.12 |
| 28.00 | | | 205.60 | Sept. 12 | 8,052.72 |
| 650.00 | | | 180.14 | Sept. 14 | 7,582.86 |
| | | | 345.00 | Sept. 16 | 7,927.86 |
| 85.00 | | | 427.50 | Sept. 19 | 8,270.36 |
| 24.10 | 125.06 | | | Sept. 20 | 8,121.20 |
| 40.00 | 65.00 | | 90.00 | Sept. 21 | 8,106.20 |
| 162.40 | | | 360.00 | Sept. 23 | 8,303.80 |
| 15.00 | | | 625.00 | Sept. 26 | 8,913.80 |
| 355.00 | 270.00 | 225.00 | 130.25 | Sept. 28 | 8,194.05 |
| 155.00 | 25.00 | 4.25S | 280.50 | Sept. 30 | 8,290.30 |

*8B-6* Clay Company established a petty cash fund in January of the current year and carried out the following transactions relating to the fund. (The company does not use a voucher system.)

**Dec. 1** A check for $100 was issued and cashed to establish a petty cash fund.

**Dec. 15** The fund was replenished after a count which revealed the following cash and petty cash vouchers for disbursements:

| | |
|---|---|
| Office supplies expense | $15.70 |
| Postage expense | 26.00 |
| Travel expense | 31.25 |
| Miscellaneous expense | 8.40 |
| Telephone and telegraph expense | 12.70 |
| Currency and coin | 5.95 |

**Dec. 31** A count of the fund at year-end disclosed the following:

| | |
|---|---|
| *Office supplies expense* | *$23.76* |
| *Postage expense* | *24.00* |
| *Travel expense* | *23.75* |
| *Miscellaneous expense* | *16.25* |
| *Currency and coin* | *12.24* |

A check was issued on December 31 to replenish the petty cash fund. A second check for $50 was used to increase the amount of the fund to $150.

**Instructions**

**a** Prepare entries in general journal form to record the above transactions.

**b** Explain briefly why the petty cash fund should be replenished at the end of the accounting period even though the fund contains considerable cash.

*8B-7* The following information relates to the Truesdale Company's September 30 cash balance:

(1) As of September 30, cash per books was $5,810; per bank statement, $4,697.

(2) Cash receipts of $1,451 on September 30 were not deposited until October 1.

(3) Among the paid checks returned by the bank was a stolen check for $630 paid in error by the bank after Truesdale Company had issued a stop payment order to the bank.

(4) The following memoranda accompanied the bank statement:

(a) A debit memo for service charges for the month of September, $3.

(b) A debit memo attached to a $200 check from Susan Scott, marked NSF.

(5) The following checks had been issued but were not included among the paid checks returned by the bank: no. 921 for $326, no. 924 for $684, and no. 925 for $161.

**Instructions**

**a** Prepare a bank reconciliation as of September 30.

**b** Prepare the necessary adjusting journal entries.

*8B-8* (If the partially filled-in work sheets accompanying the text are not being used, Problem 8B-8 should be omitted.)

Lakeport Traders uses a voucher system to control its cash disbursements. The voucher register and check register are similar to those illustrated in this chapter. At November 30 the following vouchers were in the unpaid file:

| *Date Due* | *Voucher No.* | *Payee* | *Date of Invoice* | *Amount* | *Terms* |
|---|---|---|---|---|---|
| *Dec. 2* | *912* | *Stein Co.* | *Nov. 2* | *$ 6,500* | *n/30* |
| *Dec. 4* | *923* | *Four Corners* | *Nov. 24* | *10,000* | *2/10,n/30* |

The following vouchers were prepared during December:

| Date | Voucher No. | Payee | Amount | Terms | Account Distribution |
|---|---|---|---|---|---|
| Dec. 1 | 928 | Port Seven | $ 8,000 | 2/10,n/30 | Purchases |
| 4 | 929 | Expressline | 450 | cash | Transportation-in |
| 9 | 930 | Village Store | 210 | n/30 | Office Supplies |
| 12 | 931 | Classic Office | 3,800 | n/30 | Office Equipment |
| 14 | 932 | Ozark, Inc. | 12,000 | 2/10,n/30 | Purchases |
| 15 | 933 | Expressline | 625 | cash | Transportation-in |
| 17 | 934 | Pacific Bank | 21,900 | | Notes Payable, $20,000<br>Interest Expense, $1,900 |
| 22 | 935 | Torino, Inc. | 4,000 | 2/10,n/30 | Purchases |
| 22 | 936 | Herald | 650 | n/30 | Advertising Expense |
| 24 | 937 | Gulf Supply | 310 | n/30 | Office Supplies |
| 31 | 938 | Payroll | 14,600 | cash | Accrued Payroll |
| 31 | 939 | Petty Cash | 167 | cash | Office Supplies, $19<br>Advertising, $40<br>Transportation-in, $18<br>Postage Expense, $90 |

During December the following checks were issued:

| Date | Check No. | Payee | Voucher No. | Amount |
|---|---|---|---|---|
| Dec. 2 | 401 | Stein Co. | 912 | $ 6,500 |
| 4 | 402 | Four Corners | 923 | 9,800 |
| 4 | 403 | Expressline | 929 | 450 |
| 11 | 404 | Port Seven | 928 | 7,840 |
| 15 | 405 | Expressline | 933 | 625 |
| 17 | 406 | Pacific Bank | 934 | 21,900 |
| 24 | 407 | Ozark, Inc. | 932 | 11,760 |
| 31 | 408 | Payroll | 938 | 14,600 |
| 31 | 409 | Petty Cash | 939 | 167 |

**Instructions**

**a** Record the $16,500 of unpaid vouchers at November 30 in the general ledger liability account for Vouchers Payable, account no. 21.

**b** Enter individually the 12 December vouchers in a voucher register similar to the one illustrated in this chapter.

**c** Enter the nine December checks in a check register similar to the one illustrated in this chapter. The date of each check and its serial number also should be listed in the appropriate columns of the voucher register.

**d** Compute month-end totals of both the voucher register and the check register. Make the appropriate posting of totals to the Vouchers Payable ledger account mentioned in **a** above. Also prepare a schedule of unpaid vouchers at December 31.

## BUSINESS DECISION PROBLEM 8

June Davis inherited a highly successful business, Glacier Corporation, shortly after her twenty-second birthday and took over the active management of the business. A portion of the company's business consisted of over-the-counter sales for cash, but most sales were on credit and were shipped by truck. Davis had no knowledge of internal control practices and relied implicitly upon the bookkeeper-cashier, J. K. Wiley, in all matters relating to cash and accounting records. Wiley, who had been with the company for many years, maintained the accounting records and prepared all financial statements with the help of two assistants, made bank deposits, signed checks, and prepared bank reconciliations.

The monthly income statements submitted to Davis by Wiley showed a very satisfactory rate of net income; however, the amount of cash in the bank declined steadily during the first 18 months after Davis took over the business. To meet the company's weakening cash position, a bank loan was obtained and a few months later when the cash position again grew critical, the loan was increased.

On April 1, two years after Davis assumed the management of the company, Wiley suddenly left town, leaving no forwarding address. Davis was immediately deluged with claims of creditors who stated their accounts were several months past due and that Wiley had promised all debts would be paid by April 1. The bank telephoned to notify Davis that the company's account was overdrawn and that a number of checks had just been presented for payment.

In an effort to get together some cash to meet this emergency, Davis called on two of the largest customers of the company, to whom substantial sales on account had recently been made, and asked if they could pay their accounts at once. Both customers informed her that their accounts were paid in full. They produced paid checks to substantiate their payments and explained that Wiley had offered them reduced prices on merchandise if they would pay within 24 hours after delivery.

To keep the business from insolvency, Davis agreed to sell at a bargain price a half interest in the company. The sale was made to Helen Smith, who had had considerable experience in the industry. One condition for the sale was that Smith should become the general manager of the business. The cash investment by Smith for her half interest was sufficient for the company to meet the demands on it and continue operations.

Immediately after Smith entered the business, she launched an investigation of Wiley's activities. During the course of this investigation the following irregularities were disclosed:

(1) During the last few months of Wiley's employment with the company, bank deposits were much smaller than the cash receipts. Wiley had abstracted most of the receipts and substituted for them a number of worthless checks bearing fictitious signatures. These checks had been accumulated in an envelope marked "Cash Receipts—For Deposit Only."

(2) Numerous legitimate sales of merchandise on account had been charged to fictitious customers. When the actual customer later made payment for the goods, Wiley abstracted the check or cash and made no entry. The account receivable with the fictitious customer remained in the records.

(3) When checks were received from customers in payment of their accounts, Wiley had frequently recorded the transaction by debiting an expense account and crediting Accounts Receivable. In such cases Wiley had removed from the cash receipts an equivalent amount of currency, thus substituting the check for the currency and causing the bank deposit to agree with the recorded cash receipts.

(4) More than $3,000 a month had been stolen from petty cash. Fraudulent petty cash vouchers, mostly charged to the Purchases account, had been created to conceal these thefts and to support the checks cashed to replenish the petty cash fund.

(5) For many sales made over the counter, Wiley had recorded lesser amounts on the cash register or had not rung up any amount. He had abstracted the funds received but not recorded.

(6) To produce income statements that showed profitable operations, Wiley had recorded many fictitious sales. The recorded accounts receivable included many from nonexistent customers.

(7) In preparing bank reconciliations, Wiley had omitted many outstanding checks, thus concealing the fact that the cash in the bank was less than the amount shown by the ledger.

(8) Inventory had been recorded at inflated amounts in order to increase reported profits from the business.

**Instructions**

**a** For each of the numbered paragraphs, describe one or more internal control procedures you would recommend to prevent the occurrence of such fraud.

**b** Apart from specific internal controls over cash and other accounts, what general precaution could June Davis have taken to assure herself that the accounting records were properly maintained and the company's financial statements complete and dependable? Explain fully.

# 9

# RECEIVABLES AND PAYABLES

One of the key factors underlying the tremendous expansion of the American economy has been the trend toward selling all types of goods and services on credit. The automobile industry has long been the classic example of the use of retail credit to achieve the efficiencies of large-scale output. Today, however, in nearly every field of retail trade it appears that sales and profits can be increased by granting customers the privilege of making payment a month or more after the date of sale. The sales of manufacturers and wholesalers are made on credit to an even greater extent than in retail trade.

## ACCOUNTS RECEIVABLE

### The credit department

No business concern wants to sell on credit to a customer who will prove unable or unwilling to pay his or her account. Consequently, most business organizations include a credit department which must reach a decision on the credit worthiness of each prospective customer. The credit department investigates the debt-paying ability and credit record of each new customer and determines the maximum amount of credit to be extended.

If the prospective customer is a business concern as, for example, a retail store, the financial statements of the store will be obtained and analyzed to determine its financial strength and the trend of operating results. The credit department naturally prefers to rely upon financial statements which have been audited by certified public accountants.

Regardless of whether the prospective customer is a business concern or an individual consumer, the investigation by the credit department will probably include the obtaining of a credit report from a local credit agency or from a national credit-rating institution such as Dun & Bradstreet, Inc. A credit agency compiles credit data on individuals and business concerns, and distributes this information to its clients. Most companies that make numerous sales on credit find it worthwhile to subscribe to the services of one or more credit agencies.

### Uncollectible accounts

A business that sells its goods or services on credit will inevitably find that some of its accounts receivable are uncollectible. Regardless of how thoroughly the credit department investigates prospective customers, some uncollectible accounts will arise as a result of errors in judgment or because of unexpected developments. As a matter of fact, a limited amount of uncollectible accounts is evidence of a sound credit policy. If the credit department should become too cautious and conservative in rating customers, it might avoid all credit losses but, in so doing, lose profitable business by rejecting many acceptable customers.

### Reflecting uncollectible accounts in the financial statements

In measuring business income, one of the most fundamental principles of accounting is that ***revenue must be matched with the expenses incurred in generating that revenue.***

Uncollectible accounts expense is caused by selling goods on credit to customers who fail to pay their bills; such expenses, therefore, are incurred in the year in which the sales are made, even though the accounts receivable are not determined to be uncollectible until the following year. An account receivable which originates from a sale on credit in the year 1982 and is determined to be uncollectible sometime during 1983 represents an expense of the year 1982. Unless each year's uncollectible accounts expense is ***estimated*** and reflected in the year-end balance sheet and income statement, both of these financial statements will be seriously deficient.

To illustrate, let us assume that Arlington Corporation began business on January 1, Year 1, and made most of its sales on credit throughout the year. At December 31, Year 1, accounts receivable amounted to $200,000. On this date the management reviewed the status of the accounts receivable, giving particular study to accounts which were past due. This review indicated that the collectible portion of the $200,000 of accounts receivable amounted to approximately $190,000. In other words, management estimated that uncollectible accounts expense for the first year of operations amounted to $10,000. The following adjusting entry should be made at December 31, Year 1:

***Provision for uncollectible accounts***

| | | |
|---|---|---|
| *Uncollectible Accounts Expense* | *10,000* | |
| *Allowance for Doubtful Accounts* | | *10,000* |
| *To record the estimated uncollectible accounts expense for Year 1.* | | |

The Uncollectible Accounts Expense account created by the debit part of this entry is closed into the Income Summary account in the same manner as any other expense account. The Allowance for Doubtful Accounts which was credited in the above journal entry will appear in the balance sheet as a deduction from the face amount of the accounts receivable. It serves to reduce the accounts receivable to their ***realizable value*** in the balance sheet, as shown by the following illustration:

*How much is the estimated realizable value of the accounts receivable?*

***ARLINGTON CORPORATION***
***Partial Balance Sheet***
***December 31, Year 1***

| | | |
|---|---|---|
| *Current assets:* | | |
| *Cash* | | *$ 75,000* |
| *Accounts receivable* | *$200,000* | |
| *Less: Allowance for doubtful accounts* | *10,000* | *190,000* |
| *Inventory* | | *300,000* |
| *Total current assets* | | *$565,000* |

## The allowance for doubtful accounts

There is no way of telling in advance which accounts receivable will be collected and which ones will prove to be worthless. It is therefore not possible to credit the account of any particular customer to reflect our overall estimate of the year's credit losses. Neither is it possible to credit the Accounts Receivable controlling account in the general ledger. If the Accounts Receivable controlling account were to be credited with the estimated amount of doubtful accounts, this controlling account would no longer be in balance with the total of the numerous customers' accounts in the subsidiary ledger. The only practicable alternative, therefore, is to credit a separate account called Allowance for Doubtful Accounts with the amount estimated to be uncollectible.

In the preceding chapters accounts have repeatedly been classified into five groups: (1) assets, (2) liabilities, (3) owner's equity, (4) revenue, and (5) expenses. In which of these five groups of accounts does the Allowance for Doubtful Accounts belong? The answer is indicated by the position of the Allowance for Doubtful Accounts on the balance sheet. It appears among the assets and is used to reduce an asset (Accounts Receivable) from a gross value to a net realizable value. From the standpoint of account classification, the Allowance for Doubtful Accounts is, therefore, included in the asset category.

The Allowance for Doubtful Accounts is sometimes described as a ***contra-asset*** account, an ***offset*** account, an ***asset reduction*** account, a ***negative asset*** account, and most frequently of all, a ***valuation*** account. All these terms are derived from the fact that the Allowance for Doubtful Accounts is an account with a credit balance, which is offset against an asset account to produce the proper balance sheet value of an asset.

### Estimating uncollectible accounts expense

Before the accounts are closed and financial statements are prepared at the end of the accounting period, an estimate of uncollectible accounts expense must be made. This estimate will usually be based upon past experience, perhaps modified in accordance with current business conditions.

Since the allowance for doubtful accounts is necessarily an estimate and not a precise calculation, the factor of personal judgment may play a considerable part in determining the size of this valuation account. There is a fairly wide range of reasonableness within which the amount may be set. Most companies intend that the allowance shall be adequate to cover probable losses. The term ***adequate,*** when used in this context, suggests an amount somewhat larger than the minimum probable amount.

**Conservatism as a factor in valuing accounts receivable** The larger the allowance established for doubtful accounts, the lower the net valuation of accounts receivable will be. Some accountants and some business executives tend to favor the most conservative valuation of assets that logically can be supported. Accountants necessarily make decisions under conditions of uncertainty. Conservatism in the preparation of a balance sheet implies a tendency to resolve uncertainties in the valuation of assets by reporting assets at the lower end of the range of reasonable values rather than by establishing values in a purely objective manner.

The valuation of assets at conservative amounts is a long-standing tradition in accounting, stemming from the days when creditors were the major users of financial statements. From a theoretical point of view, the doctrine of balance sheet conservatism is difficult to support, but from the viewpoint of bankers and others who use financial statements as a basis for granting loans, conservatism in valuing assets has long been regarded as a desirable policy.

Assume that the balance sheet of Company A presents optimistic, exaggerated values for the assets owned. Assume also that this "unconservative" balance sheet is submitted to a banker in support of an application for a loan. The banker studies the balance sheet and makes a loan to Company A in reliance upon the values listed. Later the banker finds it impossible to collect the loan and also finds that the assets upon which the loan was based had been greatly overstated in the balance sheet. The banker will undoubtedly consider the overly optimistic character of Company A's balance sheet as partially responsible for the loss incurred by the bank. Experiences of this type have led creditors as a group to stress the desirability of conservatism in the valuation of assets.

In considering the argument for balance sheet conservatism, it is important to recognize that the income statement is also affected by the estimates made of uncollectible accounts expense. The act of providing a relatively large allowance for doubtful accounts involves a correspondingly heavy charge to expense. Setting asset values at a minimum in the balance sheet has the related effect of stating the current year's net income at a minimum amount.

## Two methods of estimating uncollectible accounts expense

The provision for uncollectible accounts is an estimate of expense sustained in the current year. Two alternative approaches are widely used in making the annual estimate of uncollectible accounts. One method consists of adjusting the valuation account to a new balance equal to the estimated uncollectible portion of the existing accounts receivable. This method is referred to as the ***balance sheet*** approach and rests on an ***aging of the accounts receivable.*** The adjusting entry takes into consideration the existing balance in the Allowance for Doubtful Accounts.

The alternative method requires an adjusting entry computed as a percentage of the year's net sales. This method may be regarded as the ***income statement*** approach to estimating uncollectible accounts expense. This ***percentage of sales*** method emphasizes the expense side of the adjustment and leaves out of consideration any existing balance in the valuation allowance account. If any substantial balance should accumulate in the Allowance for Doubtful Accounts, however, a change in the percentage figure being applied to sales might be appropriate. These two methods are explained below.

**Aging the accounts receivable** A past-due account receivable is always viewed with some suspicion. The fact that a receivable is past due suggests that the customer is either unable or unwilling to pay. The analysis of accounts receivable by age is known as aging the accounts, as illustrated by the schedule below.

***If you were credit manager . . . ?***

***Analysis of Accounts Receivable by Age***
***December 31, 19___***

| *Customer* | *Total* | *Not Yet Due* | *1–30 Days Past Due* | *31–60 Days Past Due* | *61–90 Days Past Due* | *Over 90 Days Past Due* |
|---|---|---|---|---|---|---|
| *A. B. Adams . . .* | *$ 500* | *$ 500* | | | | |
| *B. L. Baker . . . .* | *150* | | | *$ 150* | | |
| *R. D. Carl . . . . .* | *800* | *800* | | | | |
| *H. V. Davis . . . .* | *900* | | | | *$ 800* | *$ 100* |
| *R. M. Evans . . .* | *400* | *400* | | | | |
| *Others . . . . . . .* | *32,250* | *16,300* | *$10,000* | *4,200* | *200* | *1,550* |
| *Totals . . . . . .* | *$35,000* | *$18,000* | *$10,000* | *$4,350* | *$1,000* | *$1,650* |
| *Percentage . . .* | *100* | *51* | *29* | *12* | *3* | *5* |

This analysis of accounts receivable gives management a useful picture of the status of collections and the probabilities of credit losses. Almost half of the total accounts receivable are past due. The question "How long past due?" is pertinent, and is answered by the bottom line of the aging analysis. About 29% of the total receivables are past due from 1 to 30 days; another 12% are past due from 31 to 60 days; about 3% are past due from 61 to 90 days; and 5% of the total receivables consist of accounts past due more than three months. If an analysis of this type is prepared at the end of each month, management will be informed continuously on the trend of collections and can take appropriate action to ease or to tighten credit policy. Moreover, a yardstick is available to measure the performance of the persons responsible for collection activities.

The longer past due an account receivable becomes, the greater the likelihood that it will not be collected in full. In recognition of this fact, the analysis of receivables by age groups can be used as a stepping-stone in determining a reasonable amount to add to the Allowance for Doubtful Accounts. To determine this amount, we estimate the percentage of probable expense for each age group of accounts receivable. This percentage, when applied to the dollar amount in each age group, gives a probable expense for each group. By adding together the probable expense for all the age groups, the required balance in the Allowance for Doubtful Accounts is determined. The following schedule lists the group totals from the preceding illustration and shows how the total probable expense from uncollectible accounts is computed.

*Estimate of probable uncollectible accounts expense*

***Accounts Receivable by Age Groups***

| | Amount | Percentage Considered Uncollectible | Allowance for Doubtful Accounts |
|---|---|---|---|
| *Not yet due* | *$18,000* | *1* | *$ 180* |
| *1–30 days past due* | *10,000* | *3* | *300* |
| *31–60 days past due* | *4,350* | *10* | *435* |
| *61–90 days past due* | *1,000* | *20* | *200* |
| *Over 90 days past due* | *1,650* | *50* | *825* |
| *Totals* | *$35,000* | | *$1,940* |

This summary indicates that an allowance for doubtful accounts of $1,940 is required. Before making the adjusting entry, it is necessary to consider the existing balance in the allowance account. If the Allowance for Doubtful Accounts presently has a credit balance of, say, $500, the adjusting entry should be for $1,440 in order to bring the account up to the required balance of $1,940. This entry is as follows:

*Increasing allowance for doubtful accounts*

| | | | |
|---|---|---|---|
| *Uncollectible Accounts Expense* | | *1,440* | |
| *Allowance for Doubtful Accounts* | | | *1,440* |
| *To increase the valuation account to the estimated required total of $1,940, computed as follows:* | | | |
| *Present credit balance of valuation account* | *$ 500* | | |
| *Current provision for doubtful accounts* | *1,440* | | |
| *New credit balance in valuation account* | *$1,940* | | |

On the other hand, if the Allowance for Doubtful Accounts contained a ***debit*** balance of $500 before adjustment, the adjusting entry would be made in the amount of $2,440 ($1,940 + $500) in order to create the desired credit balance of $1,940. (The circumstances which could lead to a temporary debit balance in the Allowance for Doubtful Accounts will be explained later in this chapter.)

**Estimating uncollectible accounts as a percentage of net sales** An alternative approach preferred by some companies consists of computing the charge to uncollectible accounts expense as a percentage of the net sales for the year. The question to be answered is not "How large a valuation allowance is needed to reduce our receivables to realizable value?" Instead, the question is stated as "How much uncollectible accounts expense is associated with this year's volume of sales?" This method may be regarded as the ***income statement*** approach to estimating uncollectible accounts.

As an example, assume that for several years the expense of uncollectible accounts has averaged 1% of net sales (sales minus returns and allowances and sales discounts). At the end of the current year, before adjusting entries, the following account balances appear in the ledger:

| | Dr | Cr |
|---|---|---|
| *Sales* | | *$1,260,000* |
| *Sales returns and allowances* | *$40,000* | |
| *Sales discounts* | *20,000* | |
| *Allowance for doubtful accounts* | | *1,500* |

The ***net sales*** of the current year amount to $1,200,000; 1% of this amount is $12,000. The existing balance in the Allowance for Doubtful Accounts ***should be ignored in computing the amount of the adjusting entry,*** because the percentage of net sales method stresses the ***relationship between uncollectible accounts expense and net sales*** rather than the valuation of receivables at the balance sheet date. The entry is

*Provision for uncollectible accounts based on percentage of net sales*

| | | |
|---|---|---|
| *Uncollectible Accounts Expense* | *12,000* | |
| *Allowance for Doubtful Accounts* | | *12,000* |
| *To record uncollectible accounts expense of 1% of the year's net sales (.01 × $1,200,000).* | | |

If a company makes both cash sales and credit sales, it is better to exclude the cash sales from consideration and to compute the percentage relationship of uncollectible accounts expense to credit sales only.

This approach of estimating uncollectible accounts receivable as a percentage of credit sales is easier to apply than the method of aging accounts receivable. The aging of receivables, however, tends to give a more reliable estimate of uncollectible accounts because of the consideration given to the age and collectibility of the specific accounts receivable at the balance sheet date. Some companies use the income statement approach for preparing interim financial statements and internal reports but use the balance sheet method for preparing annual financial statements.

## Writing off an uncollectible account receivable

Whenever an account receivable from a specific customer is determined to be uncollectible, it no longer qualifies as an asset and should be written off. To ***write off*** an account receivable is to reduce the balance of the customer's account to zero. The journal entry to accomplish this consists of a credit to the Accounts Receivable controlling account in the general ledger (and to the customer's account in the subsidiary ledger), and an offsetting debit to the Allowance for Doubtful Accounts.

Referring again to the example of Arlington Corporation as shown on page 348, the ledger accounts were as follows after the adjusting entry for estimated uncollectible accounts had been made on December 31, Year 1:

| | |
|---|---|
| *Accounts receivable* | *$200,000* |
| *Less: Allowance for doubtful accounts* | *10,000* |

Next let us assume that on January 27, Year 2, a customer by the name of William Brown became bankrupt and the account receivable from him in the amount of $1,000 was determined to be worthless. The following entry should be made by Arlington Corporation:

*Writing off an uncollectible account*

| | | |
|---|---|---|
| *Allowance for Doubtful Accounts* | *1,000* | |
| *Accounts Receivable, William Brown* | | *1,000* |
| *To write off the receivable from William Brown as uncollectible.* | | |

The important thing to note in this entry is that the debit is made to the Allowance for Doubtful Accounts and ***not*** to the Uncollectible Accounts Expense account. The estimated expense of customer credit losses is charged to the Uncollectible Accounts Expense account at the end of each accounting period. When a particular account receivable is later ascertained to be worthless and is written off, this action does not represent an additional expense but merely confirms our previous estimate of the expense. If the Uncollectible Accounts Expense account were first charged with ***estimated*** credit losses and then later charged with ***proven*** credit losses, we would be double counting the actual uncollectible accounts expense.

After the entry writing off William Brown's account has been posted, the Accounts Receivable controlling account and the Allowance for Doubtful Accounts appear as follows:

*Both accounts reduced by write-off of worthless receivable*

***Accounts Receivable***

| | | | |
|---|---|---|---|
| *Year 1* | | *Year 2* | |
| *Dec. 31* | *200,000* | *Jan. 27 (Brown write-off)* | *1,000* |

***Allowance for Doubtful Accounts***

| | | | |
|---|---|---|---|
| *Year 2* | | *Year 1* | |
| *Jan. 27 (Brown write-off)* | *1,000* | *Dec. 31* | *10,000* |

Note that the ***net*** amount of the accounts receivable was unchanged by writing off William Brown's account against the Allowance for Doubtful Accounts. The write-off reduced the asset account by the same amount.

*Net value of receivables unchanged by write-off*

| *Before the Write-Off* | | *After the Write-Off* | |
|---|---|---|---|
| *Accounts receivable* | *$200,000* | *Accounts receivable* | *$199,000* |
| *Less: Allowance for doubtful accounts* | *10,000* | *Less: Allowance for doubtful accounts* | *9,000* |
| *Net value of receivables* | *$190,000* | *Net value of receivables* | *$190,000* |

The fact that writing off a worthless receivable against the Allowance for Doubtful Accounts does not change the net carrying value of accounts receivable shows that no expense is entered in the accounting records when an account receivable is written off. This example bears out the point stressed earlier in the chapter: ***Credit losses belong in the period in which the sale is made, not in a later period in which the account receivable is discovered to be uncollectible.***

**Write-offs seldom agree with previous estimates** The total amount of accounts receivable written off in a given year will seldom, if ever, be exactly equal to the estimated amount previously credited to the Allowance for Doubtful Accounts.

If the amounts written off as uncollectible turn out to be less than the estimated amount, the Allowance for Doubtful Accounts will continue to show a credit balance. If the amounts written off as uncollectible are greater than the estimated amount, the Allowance for Doubtful Accounts will acquire a ***temporary debit balance,*** which will be eliminated by the adjustment at the end of the period.

## Recovery of an account receivable previously written off

Occasionally a receivable which has been written off as worthless will later be collected in full or in part. Such collections are often referred to as ***recoveries*** of bad debts. Collection of an account receivable previously written off is evidence that the write-off was an error; the receivable should therefore be reinstated as an asset.

Let us assume, for example, that a past-due account receivable in the amount of $400 from J. B. Barker was written off by the following entry:

*Barker account considered uncollectible*

| | | |
|---|---|---|
| *Allowance for Doubtful Accounts* | *400* | |
| *Accounts Receivable, J. B. Barker* | | *400* |
| *To write off the receivable from J. B. Barker as uncollectible.* | | |

At some later date the customer, J. B. Barker, pays the account in full. The entry to restore Barker's account will be

*Barker account reinstated*

| | | |
|---|---|---|
| *Accounts Receivable, J. B. Barker* | *400* | |
| *Allowance for Doubtful Accounts* | | *400* |
| *To reverse the entry writing off J. B. Barker's account.* | | |

A separate entry will be made in the cash receipts journal to record the collection from Barker. This entry will debit Cash and credit Accounts Receivable, J. B. Barker.

### Direct charge-off method of recognizing uncollectible accounts expense

A few companies do not use a valuation allowance for accounts receivable. Instead of making adjusting entries to record uncollectible accounts expense on the basis of estimates, these companies recognize no uncollectible accounts expense until specific receivables are determined to be worthless. This method makes no attempt to match revenue and related expenses. Uncollectible accounts expense is recorded in the period in which individual accounts receivable are determined to be worthless rather than in the period in which the sales were made.

When the direct charge-off method is in use, the accounts receivable will be listed in the balance sheet at their gross amount, and ***no valuation allowance*** will be used. The receivables, therefore, are not stated at their probable realizable value.

In the determination of taxable income under present federal income tax regulations, both the direct charge-off method and the allowance method of estimating uncollectible accounts expense are acceptable. From the standpoint of accounting theory, the allowance method is much the better, for it enables expenses to be matched with related revenue and thus aids in making a logical measurement of net income.

### Credit card sales

Many retailing businesses avoid the risk of uncollectible accounts by making credit sales to customers who use well-known credit cards, such as American Express, Visa, and Master Charge. A customer who makes a purchase using one of these cards must sign a multipart form, which includes a ***credit card draft.*** A credit card draft is similar to a check which is drawn upon the funds of the credit card company rather than upon the personal bank account of the customer. The credit card company promptly pays cash to the merchant to redeem these drafts. At the end of each month, the credit card company bills the credit card holder for all the drafts it has redeemed during the month. If the credit card holder fails to pay the amount owed, it is the credit card company which sustains the loss.

By making sales through credit card companies, merchants receive cash more quickly from credit sales and avoid uncollectible accounts expense. Also, the merchant avoids the expenses of investigating customers' credit, maintaining an accounts receivable subsidiary ledger, and making collections from customers

**Bank credit cards** Some widely used credit cards (such as Visa and Master Charge) are issued by banks. When the credit card company is a bank, the retailing business may deposit the signed credit card drafts directly in its bank account, along with the currency and personal checks received from customers. Banks accept these credit card drafts for immediate deposit; consequently, a business making sales to customers using bank credit cards can enter these transactions in the accounting records as cash sales.

In exchange for handling the credit card drafts, the bank makes a monthly service charge which usually runs between $1\frac{1}{4}$ and $3\frac{1}{2}$% of the amount of the drafts deposited by the merchant during the month. This monthly service charge is automatically deducted from the merchant's bank account and appears with other bank service charges in the merchant's monthly bank statement.

**Other credit cards** When customers use nonbank credit cards (such as American Express, Diners' Club, and Carte Blanche), the retailing business cannot deposit the credit card drafts directly in its bank account. Instead of debiting Cash, the merchant records an account receivable from the credit card company. Periodically, the credit card drafts are mailed to the credit card company, which then sends a check to the merchant. Credit card companies, however, do not redeem the drafts at the full sales price. The agreement between the credit card company and the merchant usually allows the credit card company to take a discount of between $3\frac{1}{2}$ and 5% when redeeming the drafts.

To illustrate the procedures in accounting for these credit card sales, assume that Bradshaw Camera Shop sells a camera for $200 to a customer who uses a Quick Charge credit card. The entry would be

*Receivable is from the credit card company*

| | | |
|---|---|---|
| *Accounts Receivable, Quick Charge Co.* | *200* | |
|     *Sales* | | *200* |
| *To record sale to customer using Quick Charge credit card.* | | |

At the end of the week, Bradshaw Camera Shop mails credit card drafts totaling $1,200 to Quick Charge Co., which redeems the drafts less a 5% discount. When payment is received, the entry is

| | | |
|---|---|---|
| *Cash* | *1,140* | |
| *Credit Card Discount Expense* | *60* | |
|     *Accounts Receivable, Quick Charge Co.* | | *1,200* |
| *To record collection of account receivable from Quick Charge Co., less 5% discount.* | | |

The expense account, Credit Card Discount Expense, should be included among the selling expenses in the income statement of Bradshaw Camera Shop.

From a theoretical viewpoint, one might argue that the credit card discount expense should be recorded at the date of sale rather than at the date of collection. In this case, the sale of the camera for $200 would have been recorded by debiting Credit Card Discount Expense for $10 and Accounts Receivable, Quick Charge Co. for $190. Although this procedure would be theoretically preferable in terms of matching revenue with related expenses, it requires computing the discount expense separately for each sales transaction. For this reason, it is common practice to record the discount expense at the date of collection. Since the discount expense is small and collection usually occurs shortly after the date of sale, the difference between the two methods does not have a material effect upon the financial statements.

### Credit balances in accounts receivable

Customers' accounts in the accounts receivable subsidiary ledger normally have debit balances, but occasionally a customer's account will acquire a credit balance. This may occur because the customer overpays, pays in advance, or returns merchandise previously paid for. Any credit balances in the accounts receivable subsidiary ledger should be accompanied by the notation "Cr" to distinguish them from accounts with normal debit balances.

Suppose that the Accounts Receivable controlling account in the general ledger has a debit balance of $9,000, representing the following individual accounts with customers in the subsidiary ledger:

| | |
|---|---|
| *49 accounts with debit balance totaling* | *$10,000* |
| *1 account with a credit balance* | *1,000* |
| *Net debit balance of 50 customers' accounts* | *$ 9,000* |

One of the basic rules in preparing financial statements is that assets and liabilities should be shown at their gross amounts rather than being netted against each other. Accordingly, the amount which should appear as accounts receivable in the balance sheet is not the $9,000 balance of the controlling account, but the $10,000 total of the receivables with debit balances. The account with the $1,000 ***credit balance is a liability*** and should be shown as such rather than being concealed as an offset against an asset. The balance sheet presentation should be as follows:

| | | | |
|---|---|---|---|
| *Current assets:* | | *Current liabilities:* | |
| *Accounts receivable* | *$10,000* | *Credit balances in customers' accounts* | *$1,000* |

### Analysis of accounts receivable

What dollar amount of accounts receivable would be reasonable for a business making annual credit sales of $1,200,000? Comparison of the average amount of accounts receivable with the sales made on credit during the period indicates how long it takes to convert receivables into cash. For example, if annual credit sales of $1,200,000 are made at a uniform rate throughout the year and the accounts receivable at year-end amount to $200,000, we can see at a glance that the receivables represent one-sixth of the year's sales, or about 60 days of uncollected sales. Management naturally wants to make efficient use of the available capital in the business, and therefore is interested in a rapid "turnover" of accounts receivable. If the credit terms offered by the business in the above example were, say, 30 days net, the existence of receivables equal to 60 days' sales would warrant investigation. The analysis of receivables is considered more fully in Chapter 22.

## NOTES RECEIVABLE

### Definition of a promissory note

A promissory note is an unconditional promise in writing to pay on demand or at a future date a definite sum of money.

The person who signs the note and thereby promises to pay is called the ***maker*** of the note. The person to whom payment is to be made is called the ***payee*** of the note. In the illustration below, G. L. Smith is the maker of the note and A. B. Davis is the payee.

***Simplified form of promissory note***

$1,000 — Los Angeles, California — July 10, 19—

One month ***after date*** I ***promise to pay***

***to the order of*** A. B. Davis

-----One thousand and no/100------- ***dollars***

***payable at*** First National Bank of Los Angeles

***for value received, with interest at*** 12% per annum.

G. L. Smith

From the viewpoint of the maker, G. L. Smith, the illustrated note is a liability and is recorded by crediting the Notes Payable account. However, from the viewpoint of the payee, A. B. Davis, this same note is an asset and is recorded by debiting the Notes Receivable account. The maker of a note expects to pay cash at the maturity date; the payee expects to receive cash at that date.

### Nature of interest

Interest is a charge made for the use of money. To the borrower (maker of a note) interest is an expense; to the lender (payee of a note) interest is revenue.

**Computing interest** A formula used in computing interest is as follows:

**Principal × Rate of Interest × Time = Interest**

(Often expressed as **P × R × T = I**)

***Interest rates are usually stated on an annual basis.*** For example, the interest on a $1,000, one-year, 12% note is computed as follows:

**$1,000 × 0.12 × 1 = $120**

If the term of the note were only four months instead of a year, the interest charge would be $40, computed as follows:

$$\$1{,}000 \times 0.12 \times \tfrac{4}{12} = \$40$$

If the term of the note is expressed in days, the exact number of days must be used in computing the interest. ***The day on which a note is dated is not included; the day on which a note falls due is included.*** Thus, a note dated today and maturing tomorrow involves only one day's interest. As a matter of convenience in making calculations, it is customary to assume that a year contains 360 days. Suppose, for example, that a 60-day, 12% note for $1,000 is drawn on June 10. The interest charge could be computed as follows:

$$\$1{,}000 \times 0.12 \times \tfrac{60}{360} = \$20$$

The principal of the note ($1,000) plus the interest ($20) equals $1,020, and this amount (the ***maturity value***) will be payable on August 9. The computation of days to maturity is as follows:

| | |
|---|---|
| *Days remaining in June (30 − 10; date of origin is not included)* | *20* |
| *Days in July* | *31* |
| *Days in August to maturity date (date of payment is included)* | *9* |
| *Total days called for by note* | *60* |

**Prevailing interest rates** Interest rates, like the prices of goods and services, are always in a process of change. The Federal Reserve Board has a policy of deliberately causing interest rates to rise or fall in an effort to keep the economy running at a reasonable level of activity. Recently emphasis has been placed on raising interest rates in the hope of limiting inflation.

The rate of interest you receive by depositing money in a savings account at a bank or a savings and loan association depends on the length of time you agree to leave the deposit untouched. The lowest interest rate (presently 5 or 6% a year) applies to a passbook account which gives you the right to withdraw all or part of your deposit at any time. However, you can earn a higher rate of interest (perhaps 8 to 12% a year) if you agree to leave your money on deposit for, say, six months or a year or more.

If you obtain a long-term mortgage loan on a residence, you would presently pay about 12 or 14% as an annual interest rate. A business obtaining a loan from a bank may pay between 10 and 25% a year. Early in the 1980s interest rates were roughly double the rates which prevailed a few years earlier. The interest rate which banks charge on loans to the largest and strongest corporations is called the ***prime rate.*** Smaller companies and those not in a strong financial position may have to pay several percentage points more than the prime rate in order to obtain a bank loan.

Many retail stores charge interest on installment accounts at $1\frac{1}{2}$% a month, which is equivalent to 18% a year. Keep in mind that interest rates vary widely depending upon the nature of the loan and the financial strength of the borrower—and upon the fiscal policy of the federal government.

### Accounting for notes receivable

In some lines of business, notes receivable are seldom encountered; in other fields they occur frequently and may constitute an important part of total assets. Business concerns that sell high-priced durable goods such as automobiles and farm machinery often accept notes receivable from their customers. Many companies obtain notes receivable in settlement of past-due accounts receivable.

All notes receivable are usually posted to a single account in the general ledger. A subsidiary ledger is not essential because the notes themselves, when filed by due dates, are the equivalent of a subsidiary ledger and provide any necessary information as to maturity, interest rates, collateral pledged, and other details. The amount debited to Notes Receivable is always the ***face amount*** of the note, regardless of whether or not the note bears interest. When an interest-bearing note is collected, the amount of cash received will be larger than the face amount of the note. The interest collected is credited to an Interest Revenue account, and only the face amount of the note is credited to the Notes Receivable account.

**Illustrative entries** Assume that a 12%, 90-day note receivable is acquired from a customer, Marvin White, in settlement of an existing account receivable of $2,000. The entry for acquisition of the note is as follows:

***Note received to replace account receivable***

| | | |
|---|---|---|
| *Notes Receivable* | *2,000* | |
| *Accounts Receivable, Marvin White* | | *2,000* |
| *Accepted 12% 90-day note in settlement of account receivable.* | | |

The entry 90 days later to record collection of the note will be

***Collection of principal and interest***

| | | |
|---|---|---|
| *Cash* | *2,060* | |
| *Notes Receivable* | | *2,000* |
| *Interest Revenue* | | *60* |
| *Collected 12% 90-day note from Marvin White.* | | |

When a note is received from a customer at the time of making a sale of merchandise on account, two entries may be made, as follows:

***Sale may be run through accounts receivable when note is received from customer***

| | | |
|---|---|---|
| *Accounts Receivable, Russ Company* | *7,500* | |
| *Sales* | | *7,500* |
| *To record sale of merchandise on account.* | | |
| *Notes Receivable* | *7,500* | |
| *Accounts Receivable, Russ Company* | | *7,500* |
| *To record receipt of note from customer.* | | |

When this procedure is employed, the account with a particular customer in the subsidiary ledger for accounts receivable provides a complete record of all transactions with that customer, regardless of the fact that some sales may have been made on open account and others may have involved a note receivable. Having a complete history of all transactions with a customer on a single ledger card may be helpful in reaching decisions as to collection efforts or further extensions of credit.

**If the maker of a note defaults** A note receivable which cannot be collected at maturity is said to have been ***defaulted*** by the maker. Immediately after the default of a note, an entry should be made by the holder to transfer the amount due from the Notes Receivable account to an account receivable from the debtor.

Assuming that a 60-day, 12% note receivable for $1,000 from Robert Jones is not collected at maturity, the following entry would be made:

*Default of note receivable*

| | | |
|---|---|---|
| *Accounts Receivable, Robert Jones* | *1,020* | |
| *Notes Receivable* | | *1,000* |
| *Interest Revenue* | | *20* |
| *To record default by Robert Jones of a 12%, 60-day note.* | | |

The interest earned on the note is recorded as a credit to Interest Revenue and is also included in the account receivable from the maker. The interest receivable on a defaulted note is just as valid a claim against the maker as is the principal of the note; if the principal is collectible, then presumably the interest too can be collected.

By transferring past-due notes receivable into Accounts Receivable, two things are accomplished. First, the Notes Receivable account is limited to current notes not yet matured and is, therefore, regarded as a highly liquid type of asset. Secondly, the account receivable ledger card will show that a note has been defaulted and will present a complete picture of all transactions with the customer.

**Renewal of a note receivable** Sometimes the two parties to a note agree that the note shall be renewed rather than paid at the maturity date. If the old note does not bear interest, the entry could be made as follows:

*Renewal of note should be recorded*

| | | |
|---|---|---|
| *Notes Receivable* | *10,000* | |
| *Notes Receivable* | | *10,000* |
| *A 60-day, non-interest-bearing note from Bell Company renewed today with new 60-day, 14% note.* | | |

Since the above entry causes no change in the balance of the Notes Receivable account, a question may arise as to whether the entry is necessary. The renewal of a note is an important transaction requiring managerial attention; a general journal entry is needed to record the action taken by management and to provide a permanent record of the transaction. If journal entries were not made to record the renewal of notes, confusion might arise as to whether some of the notes included in the balance of the Notes Receivable account were current or defaulted.

**Adjustments for interest at end of period** Notes receivable acquired in one accounting period often do not mature until a following period. Interest is being earned throughout the life of the note, and this revenue should be apportioned between accounting periods on a time basis. At the end of an accounting period, interest earned to date on notes receivable should be accrued by an adjusting entry debiting the asset account, Interest Receivable, and crediting Interest Revenue. When the note matures and the interest is received in cash in the following period, the entry to be made consists of a debit to Cash, a credit to Interest Receivable for the amount of the accrual, and a credit to Interest Revenue for the remainder of the interest collected.

As explained in Chapter 4, some companies follow a policy of using reversing entries at year-end to simplify recording the later collection of interest applicable to two accounting periods. Under this optional policy, the reversing entry on January 1 would consist of a debit to Interest Revenue and a credit to Interest Receivable for the same amount as the prior adjusting entry. Later, when the interest is collected in cash, the collection will be recorded by a debit to Cash and a credit to Interest Revenue for the entire amount of interest received.

## Discounting notes receivable

Many business concerns which obtain notes receivable from their customers prefer to sell the notes to a bank for cash rather than to hold them until maturity. Selling a note receivable to a bank or finance company is often called ***discounting*** a note receivable. The holder of the note endorses the back of the note (as in endorsing a check) and delivers the note to the bank. The bank expects to collect the ***maturity value*** (principal plus interest) from the maker of the note at the maturity date, but if the maker fails to pay, the bank can demand payment from the endorser.

When a business endorses a note and turns it over to a bank for cash, it is promising to pay the note if the maker fails to do so. The endorser is therefore contingently liable to the bank. A ***contingent liability*** may be regarded as a potential liability which either will develop into a full-fledged liability or will be eliminated entirely by a future event. The future event in the case of a discounted note receivable is the payment (or default) of the note by the maker. If the maker pays, the contingent liability of the endorser is thereby ended. If the maker fails to pay, the contingent liability of the endorser becomes a real liability. In either case the period of contingent liability ends at the maturity date of the note.

The discounting of notes receivable with a bank may be regarded by a company as an alternative to borrowing by issuing its own note payable. To issue its own note payable to the bank would, of course, mean the creation of a liability; to obtain cash by discounting a note receivable creates only a contingent liability.

**Computing the proceeds** The amount of cash obtained from the bank by discounting a note receivable is termed the ***proceeds*** of the note. The proceeds are computed by applying an interest rate (termed the ***discount rate***) to the maturity value of the note for the time remaining before the note matures.

To illustrate, assume that on July 1 Retail Sales Company receives a 75-day, 12% note for $8,000 from Raymond Kelly. The note will mature on September 14 (30 days in July, 31 days in August, and 14 days in September). On July 16, Retail Sales Company discounts this note receivable with its bank, which charges a discount rate of 15% a year. How much cash will Retail Sales Company receive? The computation is as follows:

| | |
|---|---|
| *Face of the note* | *$8,000* |
| *Add: Interest from date of note to maturity ($8,000 × .12 × $\frac{75}{360}$)* | *200* |
| *Maturity value* | *$8,200* |
| *Less: Bank discount at 15% for the discount period of 60 days (July 16 to Sept. 14) ($8,200 × .15 × $\frac{60}{360}$)* | *205* |
| *Proceeds (cash received from bank)* | *$7,995* |

The entry made by Retail Sales Company to record the discounting of the Kelly note would be as follows:

| | | |
|---|---|---|
| *Cash* | *7,995* | |
| *Interest Expense* | *5* | |
| *Note Receivable* | | *8,000* |
| *Discounted Raymond Kelly note at bank at 15% annual interest rate. Maturity value $8,200 minus $205 discount equals proceeds of $7,995.* | | |

In this illustration, the cash of $7,995 received from the bank was less than the $8,000 face amount of the note. The proceeds received from discounting a note may be ***either more or less*** than the face amount of the note, depending upon the interest rates and time periods involved. The difference between the face amount of the note being discounted and the cash proceeds is usually recorded as either Interest Expense or Interest Revenue. If the proceeds are less than the face value, the difference is debited to Interest Expense. However, if the proceeds exceed the face value of the note, the difference is credited to Interest Revenue.

**Discounted note receivable paid by maker** Before the maturity date of the discounted note, the bank will notify the maker, Raymond Kelly, that it is holding the note. Kelly will therefore make payment directly to the bank.

**Discounted note receivable defaulted by maker** If Kelly should be unable to pay the note at maturity, the bank will give notice of the default to the endorser, Retail Sales Company, which immediately becomes obligated to pay, and will make the following entry to record the payment:

*This note is for the principal amount with interest stated separately*

The journal entry in Porter Company's accounting records for this borrowing is

*Face amount of note*

| | | |
|---|---|---|
| **Cash** | 10,000 | |
| **Notes Payable** | | 10,000 |
| ***Borrowed $10,000 for six months at 12% interest per year.*** | | |

Note that no liability is recorded for the interest charges when the note is issued. At the date that money is borrowed, the borrower has a liability only for the principal amount of the loan; the liability for interest charges comes into existence gradually over the life of the loan. At December 31, two months' interest expense has been incurred, and the following year-end adjusting entry is made:

*A liability arises for accrued interest*

| | | |
|---|---|---|
| **Interest Expense** | 200 | |
| **Interest Payable** | | 200 |
| ***To record interest expense incurred through year-end on 12% six-month note dated Nov. 1 ($10,000 × .12 × $\frac{2}{12}$ = $200).*** | | |

Assuming that the company does not use reversing entries, the entry to be made on May 1 when the note is paid will be

*Payment of principal and interest*

| | | |
|---|---|---|
| **Notes Payable** | 10,000 | |
| **Interest Payable** | 200 | |
| **Interest Expense** | 400 | |
| **Cash** | | 10,600 |
| ***To record payment of 12%, six-month note on maturity date and to recognize interest expense incurred since year-end ($10,000 × .12 × $\frac{4}{12}$ = $400).*** | | |

## Notes payable with interest charges included in the face amount

Instead of stating the interest rate separately as in the preceding illustration, the note payable issued by Porter Company could have been drawn so as to include the interest charge in the face amount of the note, as shown below:

*This note shows interest included in face amount of note*

Miami, Florida　　　　November 1, Year 1

Six months **after this date** Porter Company

**promises to pay to Security National Bank the sum of** $10,600

**Signed** John Caldwell

**Title** Treasurer

Note that the face amount of this note ($10,600) is greater than the amount borrowed ($10,000). Porter Company's liability at November 1 is only $10,000;

the other $600 included in the face amount of the note represents ***future interest charges.*** As interest expense is incurred over the life of the note, Porter Company's liability will grow to $10,600, just as in the preceding illustration.

The entry to record Porter Company's $10,000 borrowing from the bank at November 1 will be as follows for this type of note payable:

***Interest included in face of note***

| | | |
|---|---|---|
| ***Cash*** | ***10,000*** | |
| ***Discount on Notes Payable*** | ***600*** | |
| ***Notes Payable*** | | ***10,600*** |
| ***Issued to bank at 12% six-month note payable with interest charge included in face amount of note.*** | | |

The liability account, Notes Payable, was credited with the full face amount of the note ($10,600). It is therefore necessary to debit a ***contra-liability*** account, ***Discount on Notes Payable,*** for the future interest charges included in the face amount of the note. Discount on Notes Payable is shown in the balance sheet as a deduction from the Notes Payable account. In our illustration, the amounts in the balance sheet would be Notes Payable, $10,600, minus Discount on Notes Payable, $600, or a net liability of $10,000 at November 1.

**Discount on notes payable** The balance of the account Discount on Notes Payable represents ***interest charges applicable to future periods.*** As this interest expense is incurred, the balance of the discount account gradually is transferred into the Interest Expense account. Thus, at the maturity date of the note, Discount on Notes Payable will have a zero balance, and the net liability will have increased to $10,600. The process of transferring the amount in the Discount on Notes Payable account into the Interest Expense account is called ***amortization*** of the discount.

**Amortization of the discount** The discount on ***short-term*** notes payable usually is amortized by the straight-line method, which allocates a proportionate amount of the discount to interest expense in each accounting period.[1] If the $600 discount on the Porter Company note payable is amortized by the straight-line method, the discount will be transferred from the Discount on Notes Payable account into Interest Expense at the rate of $100 per month ($600 discount ÷ 6 months). Alternatively, we can compute the monthly interest expense by applying the rate of interest included in the face amount of the note (12% in our example) to the principal amount of the note, as follows: $\$10,000 \times 12\% \times \frac{1}{12} = \$100$.

Entries should be made to amortize an appropriate portion of the discount at the end of each accounting period and at the date the note matures. At Decem-

[1] When an interest charge is included in the face amount of a long-term note, the effective interest method of amortizing the discount is often used instead of the straight-line method. The effective interest method of amortization is discussed in Chapter 18.

ber 31, Year 1, Porter Company will make the following adjusting entry to recognize the two months' interest expense incurred since November 1.

*Amortization of discount*

| | | |
|---|---|---|
| *Interest Expense* | *200* | |
| *Discount on Notes Payable* | | *200* |
| *To record interest expense incurred to end of year on 12% six-month note dated Nov. 1 ($600 discount × $\frac{2}{6}$).* | | |

Note that the liability for accrued interest is recorded by crediting Discount on Notes Payable rather than Accrued Interest Payable. The credit to Discount on Notes Payable reduces the debit balance in this contra-liability account from $600 to $400, thereby increasing the ***net liability*** for notes payable by $200.

At December 31, Porter Company's net liability for the bank loan will appear in the balance sheet as shown below:

*Liability shown net of discount*

| | | |
|---|---|---|
| *Current liabilities:* | | |
| *Notes payable* | *$10,600* | |
| *Less: Discount on notes payable* | *400* | *$10,200* |

The net liability of $10,200 consists of the $10,000 principal amount of the debt plus the $200 interest which has accrued since November 1.

When the note matures on May 1, Year 2, Porter Company will recognize the four months' interest expense incurred since year-end and will pay the bank $10,600. The entry is

*Two-thirds of interest applicable to second year*

| | | |
|---|---|---|
| *Notes Payable* | *10,600* | |
| *Interest Expense* | *400* | |
| *Discount on Notes Payable* | | *400* |
| *Cash* | | *10,600* |
| *To record payment of six-month note due today and recognize interest expense incurred since year-end ($10,000 × 12% × $\frac{4}{12}$ = $400).* | | |

## Comparison of the two forms of notes payable

We have illustrated two alternative methods which Porter Company could use in accounting for its $10,000 bank loan, depending upon the form of the note payable. The journal entries for both methods, along with the resulting balance sheet presentations of the liability at November 1 and December 31, are summarized on page 369. Note that both methods result in Porter Company recognizing the same amount of interest expense and the same total liability in its balance sheet. The form of the note does not change the economic substance of the transaction.

| | Note written for $10,000 plus 12% interest | | | Note written with interest included in face amount | | |
|---|---|---|---|---|---|---|
| Entry to record borrowing on Nov. 1 | Cash | 10,000 | | Cash | 10,000 | |
| | Notes Payable | | 10,000 | Discount on Notes Payable | 600 | |
| | | | | Notes Payable | | 10,600 |
| Partial balance sheet at Nov. 1 | Current liabilities: | | | Current liabilities: | | |
| | Notes payable | | $10,000 | Notes payable | $10,600 | |
| | | | | Less: Discount on notes payable | 600 | $10,000 |
| Adjusting entry at Dec. 31 | Interest Expense | 200 | | Interest Expense | 200 | |
| | Interest Payable | | 200 | Discount on Notes Payable | | 200 |
| Partial balance sheet at Dec. 31 | Current liabilities: | | | Current liabilities: | | |
| | Notes payable | $10,000 | | Notes payable | $10,600 | |
| | Interest payable | 200 | $10,200 | Less: Discount on notes payable | 400 | $10,200 |
| Entry to record payment of note on May 1 | Notes Payable | 10,000 | | Notes Payable | 10,600 | |
| | Interest Payable | 200 | | Interest Expense | 400 | |
| | Interest Expense | 400 | | Discount on Notes Payable | | 400 |
| | Cash | | 10,600 | Cash | | 10,600 |

## The concept of present value applied to long-term notes

When a note payable is issued in exchange for cash, it is easy to determine whether an interest charge is included in the face amount of the note. Any difference between the face amount of the note and the amount of cash borrowed should be viewed as an interest charge. However, when a note is issued in exchange for other kinds of assets, such as land or equipment, the amount of interest (if any) included in the face amount of the note may be less apparent.

If a realistic rate of interest is stated separately in a long-term note, we may assume that no interest charge is included in the face amount. If no interest charge is specified, however, or if the specified interest rate is unrealistically low (such as 2% a year), a portion of the face amount of the note must be assumed to represent an interest charge. When such a note is issued or received, the transaction should be recorded at the ***present value*** of the note rather than at the face amount.

The concept of present value is based upon the "time value" of money—the idea that an amount of money which will not be received until some future date is equivalent to a smaller amount of money received today. The present value of a future cash receipt is the amount of money which, if received today, would be considered equivalent to the future receipt. The present value is always less than the future amount, because money available today can be invested to earn interest and thereby become equivalent to a larger amount in the future.[2]

When a note does not call for the payment of interest, the present value of the note is less than its face amount, because the face amount of the note will not be received until the maturity date. The difference between the present value of a note and its face amount should be viewed as an interest charge included in the face amount. Often we can determine the present value of a note by the fair market value of the asset acquired when the note is issued. Alternatively, the present value can be computed using mathematical techniques which will be discussed in later accounting courses.

The ***effective rate of interest*** associated with a note is that interest rate which will cause the note's present value to increase to the full maturity value of the note by the time the note matures.

## An illustration of notes recorded at present value

To illustrate the use of present value in transactions involving long-term notes, let us assume that on September 1, Everts Company buys equipment from Tru-Tool, Inc., by issuing a one-year note payable in the face amount of $330,000 with no mention of an interest rate. It is not logical to assume that Tru-Tool, Inc., would extend credit for one year without charging any interest. Therefore, some portion of the $330,000 face amount of the note should be regarded as a charge for interest. In the accounting records of Everts Company, the amount of this

---

[2]The concept of present value will be discussed further in Chapter 18.

interest charge should be debited to the contra-liability account Discount on Notes Payable, instead of being treated as part of the cost of the equipment.

If Everts Company were to debit Equipment and credit Notes Payable for the full $330,000 face amount of the note, the following errors would result: (1) the cost of the equipment and the amount of the related liability would be ***overstated*** by the amount of the interest charge included in the face amount of the note; (2) interest expense would be ***understated*** over the life of the note; and (3) depreciation expense would be ***overstated*** throughout the estimated service life of the equipment.

Let us assume that the regular sales price of this equipment is $300,000. In this case, the present value of the note is apparently $300,000, and the remaining $30,000 of the face amount represents a charge for interest. The rate of interest which will cause the $300,000 present value of the note to increase to the $330,000 maturity value in one year is 10%. Thus, the face amount of the note actually includes an interest charge computed at the effective interest rate of 10%.

Everts Company should use the present value of the note in determining the cost of the equipment and the amount of the related net liability, as shown by the following journal entry:

| | | |
|---|---|---|
| *Equipment* | *300,000* | |
| *Discount on Notes Payable* | *30,000* | |
|     *Notes Payable* | | *330,000* |
| *Purchased equipment for $300,000 by issuing a one-year note payable with a 10% interest charge included in the face amount.* | | |

Over the next 12 months, the $30,000 recorded as a discount on the note payable will be amortized into interest expense.

It is equally important for the selling company, Tru-Tool, Inc., to use the present value of the note in determining the amount of revenue to be recognized from the sale. The $30,000 interest charge included in the face amount of the note receivable from Everts Company represents ***unearned interest*** to Tru-Tool, Inc., and is ***not part of the sales price of the equipment.*** If Tru-Tool, Inc., were to treat the entire face amount of the note receivable as the sales price of the equipment, the result would be to overstate sales revenue and notes receivable by $30,000, and also to understate interest revenue by this amount over the life of the note. Tru-Tool, Inc., should record the sale at the present value of the note received, as shown below:

| | | |
|---|---|---|
| *Accounts Receivable, Everts Company* | *300,000* | |
|     *Sales* | | *300,000* |
| *To record sale of equipment to Evert Company.* | | |
| *Notes Receivable* | *330,000* | |
|     *Discount on Notes Receivable* | | *30,000* |
|     *Accounts Receivable, Everts Company* | | *300,000* |
| *Obtained from Everts Company a one-year note with a 10% interest charge included in the face amount.* | | |

Note that the interest charge included in the face amount of the note receivable is credited to ***Discount on Notes Receivable.*** This account represents unearned interest and is a contra-asset account which appears in the balance sheet as a deduction from notes receivable. As the interest is earned, the balance of the discount account will gradually be transferred into Interest Revenue. At December 31, Tru-Tool, Inc., will have earned four months' interest revenue and will make the following entry:

| | | |
|---|---|---|
| *Discount on Notes Receivable* | *10,000* | |
| *Interest Revenue* | | *10,000* |
| *To record interest earned from Sept. 1 through Dec. 31 on Everts Company note ($300,000 × 10% × $\frac{4}{12}$).* | | |

On September 1 of the following year, when the note receivable is collected from Everts Company, the required entry will be

| | | |
|---|---|---|
| *Cash* | *330,000* | |
| *Discount on Notes Receivable* | *20,000* | |
| *Interest Revenue* | | *20,000* |
| *Notes Receivable* | | *330,000* |
| *To record collection of Everts Company note and to recognize interest earned since year-end.* | | |

In an earlier era of accounting practice, failure to use the concept of present value in recording transactions involving long-term notes sometimes resulted in large overstatements of assets and sales revenue, especially by real estate development companies. In recognition of this problem, the Financial Accounting Standards Board now requires the use of present value in recording transactions involving ***long-term*** notes receivable or payable which do not bear reasonable stated rates of interest.[3]

When a note is issued for a short period of time, any interest charge included in its face amount is likely to be relatively small. Therefore, the use of present value is not required in recording normal transactions with customers or suppliers involving notes due within one year. Notes given or received in such transactions which do not specify an interest rate may be considered non-interest-bearing.

### Installment receivables

Another application of present value is found in the recording of ***installment sales.*** Many retailing businesses sell merchandise on installment sales plans, which permit customers to pay for their credit purchases through a series of periodic payments. The importance of installment sales is emphasized by a re-

---

[3] *APB Opinion No. 21,* "Interest on Receivables and Payables," AICPA (New York: 1971).

cent balance sheet of Sears, Roebuck, and Co., which shows about $6 billion of customer accounts receivable, nearly all of which call for collection in periodic monthly installments.

When merchandise is sold on an installment plan, substantial interest charges are usually added to the "cash selling price" of the product in determining the total dollar amount to be collected in the series of installment payments. The amount of sales revenue recognized at the time of sale, however, is limited to the ***present value*** of these installment payments. In most cases, the present value of these future payments is equal to the regular sales price of the merchandise. The portion of the installment account receivable which represents unearned finance charges is credited to the contra-asset account, Discount on Installment Receivables. The balance of this contra-asset account is then amortized into Interest Revenue over the length of the collection period.

Although the collection period for an installment receivable often runs as long as 24 to 36 months, such receivables are regarded as current assets if they correspond to customary credit terms of the industry. In published balance sheets, the Discount on Installment Receivables is often called Deferred Interest Income or Unearned Finance Charges. A typical balance sheet presentation of installment accounts receivable is illustrated below:

| | |
|---|---|
| *Trade accounts receivable:* | |
| *Accounts receivable* | *$ 75,040,500* |
| *Installment contracts receivable, including $31,000,000 due after one year* | *52,640,788* |
| | *$127,681,288* |
| *Less: Deferred interest income ($8,070,000) and allowance for doubtful accounts* | *9,942,600* |
| *Total trade accounts and notes receivable* | *$117,738,688* |

**Income tax aspects of installment sales** Current provisions of the federal income tax law permit sellers to spread the recognition of the gross profit from installment sales over the years in which collections are received. The result of this treatment is to postpone the recognition of taxable income and the payment of income tax. For financial statement purposes, however, the entire gross profit from installment sales is recognized ***in the period in which the sale occurs.*** The method of recognizing gross profit from installment sales for income tax purposes will be illustrated in Chapter 14. There are a number of other more complex issues relating to installment sales; these are covered in ***Modern Advanced Accounting*** of this series.

## KEY TERMS INTRODUCED OR EMPHASIZED IN CHAPTER 9

**Aging the accounts receivable** The process of classifying accounts receivable by age groups such as current, past due 1–30 days, past due 31–60 days, etc. A step in estimating the uncollectible portion of the accounts receivable.

**Allowance for Doubtful Accounts** A valuation account or contra account relating to accounts receivable and showing the portion of the receivables estimated to be uncollectible.

**Amortization of discount on notes payable** The process of gradually transferring the balance of the Discount on Notes Payable account (which represents future interest expense) into the Interest Expense account as the interest expense is incurred.

**Amortization of discount on notes receivable** The process of transferring the balance of the Discount on Notes Receivable account (which represents future interest revenue) into the Interest Revenue account as the interest revenue is earned.

**Contingent liability** A potential liability which either will develop into a full-fledged liability or will be eliminated entirely by a future event.

**Contra account** A ledger account which is deducted from or offset against a related account in the financial statements, for example, Allowance for Doubtful Accounts, Discount on Notes Payable, and Discount on Notes Receivable.

**Default** Failure to pay interest or principal of a promissory note at the due date.

**Direct charge-off method** A method of accounting for uncollectible receivables in which no expense is recognized until individual accounts are determined to be worthless. At that point the account receivable is written off with an offsetting debit to uncollectible accounts expense. Fails to match revenue and related expenses.

**Discount on Notes Payable** A contra-liability account representing any interest charges applicable to future periods included in the face amount of a note payable. Over the life of the note, the balance of the Discount on Notes Payable account is amortized into Interest Expense.

**Discount on Notes Receivable** A contra-asset account representing any unearned interest included in the face amount of a note receivable. Over the life of the note, the balance of the Discount on Notes Receivable account is amortized into Interest Revenue.

**Discounting notes receivable** Selling a note receivable prior to its maturity date.

**Effective interest rate** The rate of interest which will cause the present value of a note to increase to the maturity value by the maturity date.

**Installment sales** Sales on credit in which the customer agrees to make a series of installment payments, including substantial interest charges.

**Interest** A charge made for the use of money. The formula for computing interest is Principal × Rate of interest × Time = Interest ($P \times R \times T = I$).

**Maker (of a note)** A person or entity who issues a promissory note.

**Maturity date** The date on which a note becomes due and payable.

**Maturity value** The value of a note at its maturity date, consisting of principal plus interest.

**Notes payable** A liability evidenced by issuance of a formal written promise to pay a certain amount of money, usually with interest, at a future date.

**Notes receivable** A receivable (asset) evidenced by a formal written promise to pay a certain amount of money, usually with interest, at a future date.

**Payee** The person named in a promissory note to whom payment is to be made (the lender).

**Present value concept** Based upon the time value of money. The basic premise is that an amount of money which will not be received until a future date is equivalent to a smaller amount of money available today.

**Present value of a future cash receipt** The amount of money which an informed investor would pay today for the right to receive that future cash receipt. The present value is always less than the future amount, because money available today can be invested to earn interest and thereby become equivalent to a larger amount in the future.

**Principal amount** That portion of the maturity value of a note which is attributable to the amount borrowed or to the cost of the asset acquired when the note was issued, rather than being attributable to interest charges.

**Proceeds** The amount received from selling a note receivable prior to its maturity. Maturity value minus discount equals proceeds.

## DEMONSTRATION PROBLEM FOR YOUR REVIEW

The Monastery, Inc., sells custom wood furniture to decorators and the general public. Selected transactions relating to the company's receivables and payables for the month of August are shown below. The company uses the allowance method in accounting for uncollectible accounts.

**Aug. 1** Borrowed $48,000 from Central Bank by issuing a 90-day note payable with a stated interest rate of 15%.

**Aug. 5** Sold merchandise for $960 to R. Lucas on the installment plan. Lucas signed an installment contract requiring 12 monthly payments of $90 each, beginning September 5. (Record transaction by debiting Installment Contracts Receivable rather than Accounts Receivable.)

**Aug. 8** A $420 account receivable from S. Wilson was determined to be worthless and was written off.

**Aug. 10** Sold merchandise to Century Interiors on account, $15,200. It was agreed that Century Interiors would issue a 60-day, 8% note upon receipt of the merchandise and could deduct any freight it paid on the goods.

**Aug. 11** Received a 60-day note from StyleCraft Co. in settlement of $3,600 open account. Interest computed at the effective rate of 8% was included in the face amount of the note.

**Aug. 13** Received a letter from Century Interiors stating that it had paid $200 freight on the shipment of August 10. Enclosed was a 60-day, 8% note dated August 13 for $15,000.

**Aug. 16** Purchased land for $92,000, making a cash down payment of $20,000 and issuing a one-year note payable for the balance. The face amount of the note was $78,480, which included interest computed at an effective rate of 9%.

**Aug. 20** Received full payment from J. Porter of a $4,500, 60-day, 12% note dated June 21. Accrued interest receivable of $30 had been recorded in prior months.

**Aug. 23** Discounted the Century Interiors note dated August 13 at the bank. The bank discount rate of 9% was applied to the maturity value of the note for the 50 days remaining to maturity.

**Aug. 25** An account receivable of $325 from G. Davis had been written off in June; full payment was unexpectedly received from Davis.

**Aug. 29** Sales to ExtraCash credit card customers during August amounted to $14,800. (Summarize all credit card sales in one entry. ExtraCash Co. is not a bank.)

**Aug. 30** Collected cash from ExtraCash Co. for the August credit card sales, less a 5% discount charged by ExtraCash.

**Aug. 31** The Discount on Installment Receivables account is amortized to reflect $3,960 of finance charges earned during August.

**Aug. 31** As a result of substantial write-offs, the Allowance for Doubtful Accounts has a debit balance of $320. Aging of the accounts receivable indicates that the allowance account should have a $1,200 credit balance at the end of August.

**Instructions** Prepare journal entries to record the transactions listed above and to make any adjusting entries necessary at August 31.

## SOLUTION TO DEMONSTRATION PROBLEM

*General Journal*

| | | | | |
|---|---|---|---|---|
| *19__* | | | | |
| *Aug.* | *1* | *Cash* | *48,000* | |
| | | *Notes Payable* | | *48,000* |
| | | *Borrowed $48,000 from Central Bank; issued a 90-day, 15% note payable.* | | |
| | *5* | *Installment Contracts Receivable, R. Lucas* | *1,080* | |
| | | *Discount on Installment Receivables* | | *120* |
| | | *Sales* | | *960* |
| | | *Installment sale, due in 12 monthly installments of $90 each.* | | |
| | *8* | *Allowance for Doubtful Accounts* | *420* | |
| | | *Accounts Receivable, S. Wilson* | | *420* |
| | | *Wrote off uncollectible account from S. Wilson.* | | |
| | *10* | *Accounts Receivable, Century Interiors* | *15,200* | |
| | | *Sales* | | *15,200* |
| | | *Sale of merchandise on account.* | | |

| | | | |
|---|---|---|---|
| Aug. 11 | Notes Receivable | 3,648 | |
| | Discount on Notes Receivable | | 48 |
| | Accounts Receivable, StyleCraft Co. | | 3,600 |
| | Received 60-day note with interest at effective rate of 8% included in face amount in settlement of open account. | | |
| 13 | Notes Receivable | 15,000 | |
| | Delivery Expense | 200 | |
| | Accounts Receivable, Century Interiors | | 15,200 |
| | To record credit to Century Interiors for freight paid by them and receipt of 60-day, 8% note for balance of amount owed. | | |
| 16 | Land | 92,000 | |
| | Discount on Notes Payable | 6,480 | |
| | Notes Payable | | 78,480 |
| | Cash | | 20,000 |
| | Purchased land for $92,000, paying $20,000 cash and issuing a one-year note payable with a 9% interest charge included in the face amount. | | |
| 20 | Cash | 4,590 | |
| | Notes Receivable | | 4,500 |
| | Accrued Interest Receivable | | 30 |
| | Interest Revenue | | 60 |
| | Collected note from J. Porter, including $90 interest. | | |
| 23 | Cash | 15,010 | |
| | Notes Receivable | | 15,000 |
| | Interest Revenue | | 10 |
| | Discounted Century Interiors' note at bank, proceeds computed as follows: Maturity value $15,200 − bank charge of $190 ($15,200 × .09 × $\frac{50}{360}$) = $15,010. | | |
| 25 | Account Receivable, G. Davis | 325 | |
| | Allowance for Doubtful Accounts | | 325 |
| | To reinstate Davis receivable previously written off. | | |
| 25 | Cash | 325 | |
| | Accounts Receivable, G. Davis | | 325 |
| | To record collection of Davis account. | | |
| 29 | Accounts Receivable, ExtraCash Co. | 14,800 | |
| | Sales | | 14,800 |
| | To record credit card sales for August. | | |

| | | | |
|---|---|---|---|
| Aug. 30 | Cash | 14,060 | |
| | Credit Card Discount Expense | 740 | |
| | Accounts Receivable, ExtraCash Co. | | 14,800 |
| | *Collected August credit card sales invoices, less 5%.* | | |
| 31 | Discount on Installment Receivables | 3,960 | |
| | Interest Revenue | | 3,960 |
| | *To record finance charges earned on installment contracts receivable during August.* | | |
| 31 | Uncollectible Accounts Expense | 1,520 | |
| | Allowance for Doubtful Accounts | | 1,520 |
| | *To provide for estimated uncollectibles as follows:* | | |
| | Balance required . . . $1,200 | | |
| | Present balance (debit) . . . 320 | | |
| | Required increase in allowance . . . $1,520 | | |
| 31 | Interest Expense | 600 | |
| | Interest Payable | | 600 |
| | *To record interest expense on note payable to Central Bank ($48,000 × 15% × $\frac{30}{360}$).* | | |
| 31 | Discount on Notes Receivable | 16 | |
| | Interest Revenue | | 16 |
| | *To record interest earned through Aug. 31 on StyleCraft note receivable ($48 discount × $\frac{20}{60}$ = $16).* | | |
| 31 | Interest Expense | 270 | |
| | Discount on Notes Payable | | 270 |
| | *To amortize discount through Aug. 31 on one-year note payable dated Aug. 16 ($6,480 × $\frac{1}{12}$ × $\frac{1}{2}$).* | | |

## REVIEW QUESTIONS

1 Adams Company determines at year-end that its Allowance for Doubtful Accounts should be increased by $6,500. Give the adjusting entry to carry out this decision.

2 In making the annual adjusting entry for uncollectible accounts, a company may utilize a ***balance sheet approach*** to make the estimate or it may use an ***income statement approach.*** Explain these two alternative approaches.

3 At the end of its first year in business, Baxter Laboratories had accounts receivable totaling $148,500. After careful analysis of the individual accounts, the credit manager estimated that $146,100 would ultimately be collected. Give the journal entry required to reflect this estimate in the accounts.

4 In February of its second year of operations, Baxter Laboratories (Question **3** above) learned of the failure of a customer, Sterling Corporation, which owed

Baxter $800. Nothing could be collected. Give the journal entry to recognize the uncollectibility of the receivable from Sterling Corporation.

5 What is the ***direct charge-off method*** of handling credit losses as opposed to the ***allowance method?*** What is its principal shortcoming?

6 Morgan Corporation has decided to write off its account receivable from Brill Company because the latter has entered bankruptcy. What general ledger accounts should be debited and credited, assuming that the allowance method is in use? What general ledger accounts should be debited and credited if the direct charge-off method is in use?

7 Mill Company, which has accounts receivable of $309,600 and an allowance for doubtful accounts of $3,600, decides to write off as worthless a past-due account receivables for $1,500 from J. D. North. What effect will the write-off have upon total current assets? Upon net income for the period? Explain.

8 Describe a procedure by which management could be informed each month of the status of collections and the overall quality of the accounts receivable on hand.

9 What are the advantages to a retailer of making credit sales only to customers who use nationally recognized credit cards?

10 Alta Mine Co., a restaurant that had always made cash sales only, adopted a new policy of honoring several nationally known credit cards. Sales did not increase, but many of Alta Mine Co.'s regular customers began charging dinner bills on the credit cards. Has the new policy been beneficial to Alta Mine Co.? Explain.

11 Determine the maturity date of the following notes:
**a** A three-month note dated March 10
**b** A 30-day note dated August 15
**c** A 90-day note dated July 2

12 X Company acquires a 9%, 60-day note receivable from a customer, Robert Waters, in settlement of an existing account receivable of $4,000. Give the journal entry to record acquisition of the note and the journal entry to record its collection at maturity.

13 Distinguish between
**a** Current and long-term liabilities
**b** Estimated and contingent liabilities

14 Does a contingent liability appear on a balance sheet? If so, in what part of the balance sheet?

15 Jonas Company issues a 90-day, 12% note payable to replace an account payable to Smith Supply Company in the amount of $8,000. Draft the journal entries (in general journal form) to record the issuance of the note payable and the payment of the note at the maturity date.

16 Howard Benson applied to the City Bank for a loan of $20,000 for a period of three months. The loan was granted at an annual interest rate of 12%. Write a sentence illustrating the wording of the note signed by Benson if
**a** Interest is stated separately in the note.
**b** Interest is included in the face amount of the note.

17 With reference to Question **16** above, give the journal entry required on the books of Howard Benson for issuance of each of the two types of notes.

18 Rager Products sold merchandise to Baron Company in exchange for a one-year note receivable. The note was made out in the face amount of $13,189, ***including*** a 9% interest charge. Compute the amount of sales revenue to be recognized by Rager Products. (Hint: $13,189 equals 109% of sales amount.)

19 Sylmar Industries buys a substantial amount of equipment having an estimated service life of five years by issuing a two-year note payable. The note includes no mention of an interest charge. Explain the errors which will result in the future

| Entry | Date | Nature of Transaction |
|---|---|---|
| 1 | Omit date | To record sales of $482,800 in new territory during the year. All sales on credit. |
| 2 | Sept. 12 | To write off worthless receivable from European Desk Company. |
| 3 | Oct. 10 | To record collection from receiver in bankruptcy for Maple Furniture House and to write off remainder of receivable. |
| 4 | Oct. 15 | To write off as worthless receivable from Redwood Furniture Co. |
| 5 | Oct. 15 | To write off as worthless receivable from Heidelberg Co. |
| 6 | Nov. 2 | To reinstate receivable from Redwood Furniture Co. |
| 7 | Nov. 2 | To record collection of reinstated receivable from Redwood Furniture Co. |
| 8 | Nov. 2 | To reinstate receivable from Heidelberg Co. previously written off as worthless. |
| 9 | Nov. 2 | To record collection of reinstated receivable from Heidelberg Co. |
| 10 | Omit date | To write off worthless receivables amounting to $5,763, which originated in the old sales territory during the year. |
| 11 | Omit date | To record all sales for the year in the old sales territory, $2,619,360. |

**b** Open general ledger accounts for Uncollectible Accounts Expense and for the Allowance for Doubtful Accounts. Post the entries called for in **a** which affect these two accounts.

**c** Prepare the year-end adjusting entry to record the uncollectible accounts expense for the year. Include in the explanation portion of the journal entry your computation of expense in the old sales territory ($\frac{1}{4}$ of 1% of sales), and your computation of expense in the new sales territory (3% of sales). Also prepare the year-end closing entry to close the Uncollectible Accounts Expense account. Post both the adjusting entry and the closing entry to the two ledger accounts required in part **b** above.

## Group B

*9B-1* At December 31 last year, the balance sheet prepared by Pedro Montoya included $504,000 in accounts receivable and an allowance for doubtful accounts of $26,400. During January of the current year selected transactions are summarized as follows:

| | |
|---|---|
| *(1) Sales on account* | *$368,000* |
| *(2) Sales returns & allowances* | *7,360* |
| *(3) Cash payments by customers (no cash discounts)* | *364,800* |
| *(4) Account receivable from Acme Company written off as worthless* | *9,280* |

After a careful aging and analysis of all customers' accounts at January 31, it was decided that the allowance for doubtful accounts should be adjusted to a balance of $29,280 in order to reflect accounts receivable at net realizable value in the January 31 balance sheet.

**Instructions**

**a** Give the appropriate entry in general journal form for each of the four numbered items above and the adjusting entry at January 31 to provide for uncollectible accounts.

**b** Show the amounts of accounts receivable and the allowance for doubtful accounts as they would appear in a partial balance sheet at January 31.

**c** Assume that three months after the receivable from Acme Company had been written off as worthless, Acme Company won a large award in the settlement of patent litigation and immediately paid the $9,280 debt to Pedro Montoya. Give the journal entry or entries (in general journal form) to reflect this recovery of a receivable previously written off.

***9B-2*** The balance sheet prepared by Highland Products at December 31, Year 6, contained accounts receivable of $380,000 and an allowance for doubtful accounts of $10,000.

During Year 7, the company's sales volume reached a new high of $2,600,000; all sales during the year were made on credit. The total cash collections from customers in Year 7 (collections of accounts receivable) amounted to $2,500,000. Included in this figure for total collections was $5,000 representing the recovery in full of a $5,000 account receivable from Anthony Walker, a customer whose account had been written off as worthless late in Year 6. During Year 7, it was necessary to write off as worthless various customers' accounts totaling $11,000.

On December 1, Year 7, Highland Products sold for $216,000 a tract of land acquired as a possible building site several years earlier at a cost of $144,000. The land was now considered unsuitable as a building site. Terms of sale were $60,000 cash and a 12%, six-month note for $156,000. The buyer was a large corporation and the note was regarded as fully collectible. (Credit the profit on this transaction to Gain on Sale of Land.)

At December 31, Year 7, the accounts receivable included $60,000 of past-due accounts. After careful study of all past-due accounts, the management estimated that the probable loss contained therein was 20%, and that, in addition, 2% of the current accounts receivable should be regarded as doubtful of collection.

**Instructions**

**a** Prepare journal entries in general journal form for all transactions in Year 7 relating to accounts and notes receivable. (Five journal entries are needed: one to record all sales for the year; one to reinstate the Walker receivable; one to record total cash collections for the year; one to write off worthless accounts; and one to record the sale of the land at a profit.)

**b** Prepare two ledger accounts in three-column, running balance form—one a controlling account for Accounts Receivable, and the other for Allowance for Doubtful Accounts. Enter in these accounts the beginning balances for Year 7; then post the debits and credits indicated by the transactions of Year 7.

**c** Prepare the necessary adjusting journal entries at December 31, Year 7. Use one entry to provide for uncollectible accounts expense based on management's estimates and another entry to accrue interest on the note receivable.

**d** What amount should appear in the income statement for Year 7 as uncollectible accounts expense?

**e** Prepare a partial balance sheet at December 31, Year 7, showing under the heading of current assets the note receivable, the accounts receivable and the allowance for doubtful accounts, and the accrued interest receivable on the note.

***9B-3*** Indio Farm Supply sells to retail stores on 30-day open account, but requires customers who fail to pay invoices within 30 days to substitute promissory notes for their past-due accounts. No sales discount is offered. Among recent transactions were the following:

**Mar. 17** Sold merchandise to S. R. Davis on account, $72,000, terms n/30.

**Apr. 16** Received a 60-day, 10% note from Davis dated today in settlement of the open account of $72,000.

**May 26** Discounted the Davis note at the bank. The bank discount rate was 12% applied to the maturity value of the note for the 20 days remaining to maturity.

**June 15** Received notice from the bank that the Davis note due today was in default. Paid the bank the maturity value of the note. Since Davis has extensive business interests, the management of Indio Farm Supply is confident that no loss will be incurred on the defaulted note.

**June 25** Made a $48,000 loan to John Raymond on a 30-day, 15% note.

**Instructions**

**a** Prepare in general journal form the entries necessary to record the above transactions. (In making interest calculations, assume a 360-day year.)

**b** Prepare the adjusting journal entry needed at June 30, the end of the company's fiscal year, to record interest accrued on the two notes receivable. [Accrue interest at 10% per annum from date of default (June 15) on the maturity value of the Davis note.]

*9B-4* Arrowhead Corporation engaged in the following transactions involving notes payable during the fiscal year ended October 31. It is the company's policy to use a 360-day year for all interest calculations.

**June 6** Borrowed $6,000 from a long-time employee, C. W. Jones. Issued a 45-day, 12% note payable to Jones as evidence of the indebtedness.

**July 13** Purchased office equipment from New Company. This invoice amount was $9,000 and the New Company agreed to accept as full payment a 16%, three-month note for the invoiced amount.

**July 21** Paid the Jones note plus accrued interest.

**Sept. 1** Borrowed $126,000 from Security Bank at an interest rate of 16% per annum; signed a 90-day note with interest included in the face amount of the note.

**Oct. 1** Purchased merchandise in the amount of $5,400 from Post Co. Gave in settlement a 90-day note bearing interest at 18%.

**Oct. 13** The $9,000 note payable to New Company matured today. Paid the interest accrued and issued a new 30-day, 16% note to replace the maturing note.

**Instructions**

**a** Prepare journal entries (in general journal form) to record the above transactions.

**b** Prepare the adjusting entries needed at October 31, prior to closing the accounts. Use one adjusting entry to accrue interest on the two notes in which interest is stated separately (the Post Co. note and the New Company note). Use a separate adjusting entry to record interest expense accrued on the note with interest included in the face amount (the Security Bank note).

*9B-5* Three notes receivable, each in the amount of $20,000, were discounted by Electro-Magnet at its bank on May 10. The bank charged a discount rate of 12% per year, applied to the maturity value.

| *Date of Note* | *Annual Interest Rate, %* | *Life of Note* |
|---|---|---|
| *Note A—Apr. 10* | *12* | *3 months* |
| *Note B—Mar. 31* | *9* | *60 days* |
| *Note C—Mar. 11* | *16* | *90 days* |

**Instructions**

**a** From the above data, compute the proceeds of each note. Remember that all interest rates quoted are annual rates. In making interest calculations, assume a

360-day year. Answers should be rounded to the nearest cent wherever necessary. Arrange your solution in a schedule with three money columns, one for each note. List all data, such as date of note, life of note, maturity date, date of discounting at bank, discount period, interest rate on note, and discount rate charged at bank. Then in a section entitled Computations, enter amounts for the face amount of note, interest to maturity, maturity value, discount to be deducted, and proceeds.

**b** Prepare the journal entry needed on May 10 by Electro-Magnet to record the discounting of the three notes receivable. The discounting of the three notes may be treated as one transaction, and recorded in general journal form.

*9B-6* The following information concerning the receivables of the Bunker Corporation appeared in the accounts on December 1, Year 7. The company uses a 360-day year for all interest calculations.

| | |
|---|---|
| ***Accounts receivable:*** | |
| *C. L. Laurence* | *$ 2,425* |
| *E. D. Nemson* | *3,870* |
| *C. A. Shively* | *6,200* |
| *Total* | *$12,495* |
| ***Notes receivable:*** | |
| *A. P. Marra, 8%, 45-day note, dated Nov. 4, Year 7* | *$ 6,000* |
| *C. M. Hines, 9%, 90-day note, dated Nov. 30, Year 7* | *4,000* |
| *Total* | *$10,000* |
| ***Installment contracts receivable:*** | |
| *M. Moyers (monthly payment $150)* | *$ 2,850* |
| ***Unearned interest on installment contracts:*** | |
| *Applicable to M. Moyers contract* | *$ 386* |

During the month of December, the following additional transactions took place:

**Dec. 7** E. D. Nemson paid $870 on account and gave a 30-day, 8% note to cover the balance.

**Dec. 12** Received a 60-day, 8% note from C. L. Laurence in full settlement of his account.

**Dec. 19** A. P. Marra wrote that he would be unable to pay the note due today and included a check to cover the interest due and a new 30-day, 7% note renewing the old note. No accrued interest has been recorded in prior months.

**Dec. 28** Discounted the C. L. Laurence note at the bank. The proceeds on the note amounted to $2,432.

**Dec. 31** Received the monthly payment on the M. Moyers contract. The payment of $150 includes $20 of interest revenue earned during December. The interest charges included in the face amount of the installment contract had originally been credited to the contra-asset account, Unearned Interest on Installment Contracts.

**Instructions**

**a** Prepare five journal entries (in general journal form) for the five December transactions listed above.

**b** Prepare an adjusting entry at December 31 to accrue interest receivable on the three notes receivable on hand (the Nemson, Marra, and Hines notes). Include in the explanation portion of the adjusting entry the computations to determine the accrued interest on each of the three notes. Add these three accrued amounts to find the total amount for the adjusting entry.

**c** Prepare a partial balance sheet for Bunker Corporation at December 31 showing under the heading of current assets the notes receivable, accounts receivable, installment contracts receivable, unearned interest on installment contracts, and accrued interest receivable. Also add a footnote to disclose the amount of the contingent liability for the discounted note receivable.

*9B-7* During the fiscal year ending June 30 and shortly thereafter, Malibu Lake had the following transactions relating to notes payable.

**Feb. 6** Borrowed $10,000 from L. W. Smith and issued a 45-day, 16% note payable.
**Mar. 12** Purchased delivery truck from E-Z Company. Issued a 12%, three-month note payable for $15,000, the full cost of the truck.
**Mar. 23** Paid the note due today to L. W. Smith plus accrued interest.
**May 1** Borrowed the amount of $200,000 for 90 days from First Bank at an interest rate of 14% per year; signed a note payable with the interest included in the face amount of the note.
**May 31** Purchased merchandise for $7,500 from Patten Co. Issued a 90-day note bearing interest at 16% annually. (Use two entries: one to record the purchase with a credit to Accounts Payable, and the other to transfer the liability to Notes Payable.)
**June 12** The $15,000 note payable to E-Z Company matured today. Paid in cash the interest accrued and issued a new 30-day note bearing interest at 14% per annum to replace the maturing note. (Use one compound journal entry for this transaction.)
**June 30** End of fiscal year.
**July 12** Paid principal and interest of the 30-day, 14% note to E-Z Company dated June 12 which matured today.
**July 30** Paid in full the 90-day note to First Bank dated May 1 and maturing today.

**Instructions**

**a** Prepare journal entries (in general journal form) to record the six transactions dated prior to June 30. All interest rates quoted are annual rates. Use a 360-day year for interest computations.

**b** Prepare two adjusting entries at June 30 relating to interest expense. The first entry should accrue interest on the two notes with interest stated separately (the note to Patten Company and the note to E-Z Company). The explanation should include computations showing the amount of interest accrued on each note. The second adjusting entry should record interest on the First Bank note in which interest was included in the face amount.

**c** Prepare journal entries for the two transactions occurring in July.

*9B-8* During the three months ended June 30, Solar Corporation had the following transactions relating to notes payable.

**Apr. 1** Purchased equipment from Copper-Weld, Inc., for $13,000, making an $1,800 cash down payment and issuing a one-year note payable for the balance. The face amount of the note was $12,880, which included a 15% interest charge.
**Apr. 16** Gave $5,000 cash and a 90-day, 8% note to Lees Company in settlement of open account due today in the amount of $14,000.
**Apr. 25** Purchased equipment from ADM Company for $17,400, giving a 60-day, 9% note in settlement thereof.
**May 11** Borrowed $72,000 from Manufacturers Bank, giving a 90-day note as evidence of indebtedness. An interest charge computed at the effective rate of 17% per annum was included in the face amount of the note.

**June 15** Purchased merchandise on account from Phoenix Co., $18,000.

**June 18** Issued a 60-day note bearing interest at 9% in settlement of the Phoenix Co. account.

**June 24** Paid the 60-day, 9% note due to ADM Company, which matured today.

**Instructions**

a Prepare journal entries (in general journal form) to record the listed transactions for the three months ended June 30. (Use a 360-day year in computing interest.)

b Prepare adjusting entries to record the interest expense on notes payable through June 30. Prepare one adjusting entry to record the accrued interest payable on the two notes for which interest is stated separately (the Lees Company note and the Phoenix Co. note). The other adjusting entry should record the amortization of discount on the two notes in which interest is included in the face amount (the Copper-Weld, Inc., note and the Manufacturers Bank note).

c Prepare a partial balance sheet at June 30 reflecting the above transactions. Show Notes Payable to Bank (minus the discount) as one item and Notes Payable: Other (minus the discount) as a separate liability. Also include the accrued interest payable in the current liability section of the balance sheet.

## BUSINESS DECISION PROBLEM 9

Record House and Concert Sound are two companies engaged in selling stereo equipment to the public. Both companies sell equipment at a price 50% greater than cost. Customers may pay cash, purchase on 30-day accounts, or make installment payments over a 36-month period. The installment receivables include a three-year interest charge (which amounts to 30% of the sales price) in the face amount of the contract. Condensed income statements prepared by the companies for their first year of operations are shown below:

| | *Record House* | *Concert Sound* |
|---|---|---|
| *Sales* | *$387,000* | *$288,000* |
| *Cost of goods sold* | *210,000* | *192,000* |
| *Gross profit on sales* | *$177,000* | *$ 96,000* |
| *Operating expenses* | *63,000* | *60,000* |
| *Operating income* | *$114,000* | *$ 36,000* |
| *Interest earned* | *-0-* | *10,800* |
| *Net income* | *$114,000* | *$ 46,800* |

When Record House makes a sale of stereo equipment on the installment plan it immediately credits the Sales account with the face amount of the installment receivable. In other words, the interest charges are included in sales revenue at the time of the sale. The interest charges included in Record House's installment receivables originating in the first year amount to $72,000, of which $59,100 is unearned at the end of the first year. Record House uses the direct charge-off method to recognize uncollectible accounts expense. During the year, accounts receivable of $2,100 were written off as uncollectible, but no entry was made for $37,200 of accounts estimated to be uncollectible at year-end.

Concert Sound records sales revenue equal to the present value of its installment receivables and recognizes the interest ***earned during the year*** as interest revenue. Concert Sound provides for uncollectible accounts by the allowance method. The company recognized uncollectible accounts expense of $11,100 during the year and this amount appeared to be adequate.

**Instructions**

**a** Prepare a condensed income statement for Record House for the year, using the same methods of accounting for installment sales and uncollectible accounts as were used by Concert Sound. The income statement you prepare should contain the same seven items shown in the illustrated income statements. Provide footnotes showing the computations you made in revising the amount of sales and any other figures you decide to change.

**b** Compare the income statement you have prepared in part **a** to the one originally prepared by Record House. Which income statement do you believe better reflects the results of the company's operations during the year? Explain.

**c** What do you believe to be the key factor responsible for making one of these companies more profitable than the other? What corrective action would you recommend be taken by the less profitable company to improve future performance?

# 10

# INVENTORIES

## Some basic questions relating to inventories

In the previous chapters we have illustrated how the amount of inventory on hand at year-end is recorded in the accounts. Remember that the inventory figure appears in both the balance sheet and the income statement. In the balance sheet, inventory is often the largest current asset. In the income statement, inventory is subtracted from the cost of goods ***available*** for sale to determine the ***cost of goods sold*** during the period.

In our previous discussions, the dollar amount of the ending inventory was given with only a brief explanation as to how this amount was determined. The basis for the valuation of inventory, as for most other types of assets, is cost. We are now ready to explore the concept of ***cost*** as applied to inventories of merchandise.

Among the fundamental questions involved in accounting for inventories are these:

**1** What goods are to be included in inventory?
**2** How is the amount of the ending inventory determined?
**3** What are the arguments for and against each of several alternative methods of inventory valuation?
**4** What are the advantages of a perpetual inventory system?

## Periodic inventory system vs. perpetual inventory system

The distinction between a periodic inventory system and a perpetual inventory system was explained earlier in Chapter 5. To summarize briefly, a periodic system of inventory accounting requires that acquisitions of merchandise be recorded by debits to a Purchases account. At the date of a sales transaction, no entry is made to record the cost of the goods sold. Under the periodic inventory system, the inventory account is brought up-to-date only at the end of the accounting period when all the goods on hand are counted and priced.

The periodic inventory system is likely to be used by a business that sells a variety of merchandise with low unit prices, such as a drugstore or hardware store. To maintain perpetual inventory records in such a business would ordinarily be too time-consuming and expensive.

Companies that sell products of high unit value such as automobiles and television sets usually maintain a perpetual inventory system that shows at all times the amount of inventory on hand. As merchandise is acquired, it is added to an inventory account; as goods are sold, their cost is transferred out of inventory and into a cost of goods sold account. This continuous updating of the inventory account explains the name ***perpetual*** inventory system.

In the early part of this chapter we will use the periodic inventory system as a point of reference; in the latter part we will emphasize perpetual inventories.

## Inventory defined

One of the largest assets in a retail store or in a wholesale business is the inventory of merchandise, and the sale of this merchandise at prices in excess of cost is the major source of revenue. For a merchandising company, ***the inventory consists of all goods owned and held for sale in the regular course of business.*** Merchandise held for sale will normally be converted into cash within less than a year's time and is therefore regarded as a current asset. In the balance sheet, inventory is listed immediately after accounts receivable, because it is just one step further removed from conversion into cash than are the accounts receivable.

In manufacturing businesses there are three major types of inventories: ***raw materials, goods in process of manufacture,*** and ***finished goods.*** All three classes of inventories are included in the current asset section of the balance sheet.

To expand our definition of inventory to fit manufacturing companies as well as merchandising companies, we can say that inventory means "the aggregate of those items of tangible personal property which (1) are held for sale in the ordinary course of business, (2) are in process of production for such sale, or (3) are to be currently consumed in the production of goods or services to be available for sale."[1]

## Inventory valuation and the measurement of income

In measuring the gross profit on sales earned during an accounting period, we subtract the ***cost of goods sold*** from the total ***sales*** of the period. The figure for sales is easily accumulated from the daily record of sales transactions, but in many businesses no day-to-day record is maintained showing the cost of goods

[1] AICPA, *Accounting Research and Terminology Bulletins,* Final Edition (New York: 1961), p. 28.

sold.[2] The figure representing the cost of goods sold during an entire accounting period is computed at the end of the period by separating the ***cost of goods available for sale*** into two elements:

1 The cost of the goods sold
2 The cost of the goods not sold, which therefore comprise the ending inventory

This idea, with which you are already quite familiar, may be concisely stated in the form of an equation as follows:

*Finding cost of goods sold*

**Cost of Goods Available for Sale − Ending Inventory = Cost of Goods Sold**

Determining the amount of the ending inventory is the key step in establishing the cost of goods sold. In separating the ***cost of goods available for sale*** into its components of ***goods sold*** and ***goods not sold,*** we are just as much interested in establishing the proper amount for cost of goods sold as in determining a proper figure for inventory. Throughout this chapter you should bear in mind that the procedures for determining the amount of the ending inventory are also the means for determining the cost of goods sold. The valuation of inventory and the determination of the cost of goods sold are in effect the two sides of a single coin.

The American Institute of Certified Public Accountants has summarized this relationship between inventory valuation and the measurement of income in the following words: "A major objective of accounting for inventories is the proper determination of income through the process of matching appropriate costs against revenues."[3] The expression "matching costs against revenues" means determining what portion of the cost of goods available for sale should be deducted from the revenue of the current period and what portion should be carried forward (as inventory) to be matched against the revenue of the following period.

## Importance of an accurate valuation of inventory

The most important current assets in the balance sheets of most companies are cash, accounts receivable, and inventory. Of these three, the inventory of merchandise is usually much the largest. Because of the relatively large size of this asset, an error in the valuation of inventory may cause a material misstatement of financial position and of net income. An error of 20% in valuing the inventory may have as much effect on the financial statements as would the complete omission of the asset cash.

***An error in inventory will of course lead to other erroneous figures in the balance sheet,*** such as the total current assets, total assets, owner's equity, and

---

[2] As explained in Chap. 5, a company that maintains perpetual inventory records will have a day-to-day record of the cost of goods sold and of goods in inventory. Our present discussion, however, is based on the assumption that the periodic system of inventory is being used.
[3] AICPA, op. cit.

the total of liabilities and owner's equity. The error will also affect key figures in the income statement, such as the cost of goods sold, the gross profit on sales, and the net income for the period. Finally, it is important to recognize that ***the ending inventory of one year is also the beginning inventory of the following year.*** Consequently, the income statement of the second year will also be in error by the full amount of the original error in inventory valuation.

**Illustration of the effects of an error in valuing inventory** Assume that on December 31, 1983, the inventory of the Hillside Company is actually $100,000 but, through an accidental error, it is recorded as $90,000. The effects of this $10,000 error on the income statement for 1983 are indicated in the first illustration shown below, showing two income statements side by side. The left-hand set of figures shows the inventory of December 31, 1983, at the proper value of $100,000 and repre-

*Effect of error in inventory*

***HILLSIDE COMPANY***
***Income Statement***
***For the Year Ended December 31, 1983***

| | With Correct Ending Inventory | | With Incorrect Ending Inventory | |
|---|---|---|---|---|
| Sales | | $240,000 | | $240,000 |
| Cost of goods sold: | | | | |
| Beginning inventory, Jan. 1, 1983 | $ 75,000 | | $ 75,000 | |
| Purchases | 210,000 | | 210,000 | |
| Cost of goods available for sale | $285,000 | | $285,000 | |
| Less: Ending inventory, Dec. 31, 1983 | 100,000 | | 90,000 | |
| Cost of goods sold | | 185,000 | | 195,000 |
| Gross profit on sales | | $ 55,000 | | $ 45,000 |
| Operating expenses | | 30,000 | | 30,000 |
| Net income | | $ 25,000 | | $ 15,000 |

*Effect on succeeding year*

***HILLSIDE COMPANY***
***Income Statement***
***For the Year Ended December 31, 1984***

| | With Correct Beginning Inventory | | With Incorrect Beginning Inventory | |
|---|---|---|---|---|
| Sales | | $265,000 | | $265,000 |
| Cost of goods sold: | | | | |
| Beginning inventory, Jan. 1, 1984 | $100,000 | | $ 90,000 | |
| Purchases | 230,000 | | 230,000 | |
| Cost of goods available for sale | $330,000 | | $320,000 | |
| Less: Ending inventory, Dec. 31, 1984 | 120,000 | | 120,000 | |
| Cost of goods sold | | 210,000 | | 200,000 |
| Gross profit on sales | | $ 55,000 | | $ 65,000 |
| Operating expenses | | 33,000 | | 33,000 |
| Net income | | $ 22,000 | | $ 32,000 |

sents a correct income statement for the year 1983. The right-hand set of figures represents an incorrect income statement, because the ending inventory is erroneously listed as $90,000. Note the differences between the two income statements with respect to net income, gross profit on sales, and cost of goods sold. Income taxes have purposely been omitted in this illustration.

This illustration shows that an understatement of $10,000 in the ending inventory for the year 1983 caused an understatement of $10,000 in the net income for 1983. Next, consider the effect of this error on the income statement of the following year. The ending inventory of 1983 is, of course, the beginning inventory of 1984. The preceding illustration is now continued to show side by side a correct income statement and an incorrect statement for 1984. The ending inventory of $120,000 for the year 1984 is the same in both statements and is to be considered correct. Note that the $10,000 error in the beginning inventory of the right-hand statement causes an error in the cost of goods sold, in gross profit, and in net income for the year 1984.

**Counterbalancing errors** The illustrated income statements for 1983 and 1984 show that an understatement of the ending inventory in 1983 caused an understatement of net income in that year and an offsetting overstatement of net income for 1984. Over a period of two years the effects of an inventory error on net income will ***counterbalance,*** and the total net income for the two years together is the same as if the error had not occurred. Since the error in reported net income for the first year is exactly offset by the error in reported net income for the second year, it might be argued that an inventory error has no serious consequences. Such an argument is not sound, for it disregards the fact that accurate yearly figures for net income are a primary objective of the accounting process. Moreover, many actions by management and many decisions by creditors and owners are based upon ***trends*** indicated in the financial statements for two or more years. Note that the inventory error has made the 1984 net income appear to be more than twice as large as the 1983 net income, when in fact ***less*** net income was earned in 1984 than in 1983. Anyone relying on the erroneous financial statements would be greatly misled as to the trend of Hillside Company's earnings.

To produce dependable financial statements, inventory must be accurately determined at the end of each accounting period. The counterbalancing effect of the inventory error by the Hillside Company is illustrated below:

*Counterbalancing effect on net income*

| | | *With Inventory at Dec. 31, 1983, Understated* | |
|---|---|---|---|
| | ***With Inventory Correctly Stated*** | ***Reported Net Income Will Be*** | ***Reported Net Income Will Be Overstated (Understated)*** |
| *Net income for 1983* | *$25,000* | *$15,000* | *$(10,000)* |
| *Net income for 1984* | *22,000* | *32,000* | *10,000* |
| *Total net income for two years* | *$47,000* | *$47,000* | *$ -0-* |

**Relation of inventory errors to net income** The effects of errors in inventory upon net income may be summarized as follows:

1 When the ***ending*** inventory is understated, the net income for the period will be understated.
2 When the ***ending*** inventory is overstated, the net income for the period will be overstated.
3 When the ***beginning*** inventory is understated, the net income for the period will be overstated.
4 When the ***beginning*** inventory is overstated, the net income for the period will be understated.

## Taking a physical inventory

At the end of each accounting period the ledger accounts will show up-to-date balances for most of the assets. For inventory, however, the balance in the ledger account represents the ***beginning*** inventory, because no entry has been made in the Inventory account since the end of the preceding period. All purchases of merchandise during the present period have been recorded in the Purchases account. The ending inventory does not appear anywhere in the ledger accounts; it must be determined by a physical count of merchandise on hand at the end of the accounting period.

Establishing a balance sheet valuation for the ending inventory requires two steps: (1) determining the quantity of each kind of merchandise on hand, and (2) multiplying the quantity by the cost per unit. The first step is called ***taking the inventory;*** the second is called ***pricing the inventory.*** Taking inventory, or more precisely, taking a physical inventory, means making a systematic count of all merchandise on hand.

In most merchandising businesses the taking of a physical inventory is a year-end event. In some lines of business an inventory may be taken at the close of each month. It is common practice to take inventory after regular business hours or on Sunday. By taking the inventory while business operations are suspended, a more accurate count is possible than if goods were being sold or received while the count was in process.

**Planning the physical inventory** Unless the taking of a physical inventory is carefully planned and supervised, serious errors are apt to occur which will invalidate the results of the count. To prevent such errors as the double counting of items, the omission of goods from the count, and other quantitative errors, it is desirable to plan the inventory so that the work of one person serves as a check on the accuracy of another.

There are various methods of counting merchandise. One of the simplest procedures is carried out by the use of two-member teams. One member of the team counts and calls the description and quantity of each item. The other person lists the descriptions and quantities on an inventory sheet. (In some situations, a tape recorder is useful in recording quantities counted.) When all goods have been counted and listed, the items on the inventory sheet are priced at cost, and the unit prices are multiplied by the quantities to determine the valuation of the inventory.

To assure the accuracy of the recorded counts, a representative number of items should be recounted by supervisors. Some businesses make a practice of counting all merchandise a second time and comparing the quantities established by the different teams. The initials of the persons making both the first and the second counts should be placed on an inventory tag attached to each lot of merchandise counted. Once it is known that all merchandise has been tagged and that the counts are accurate, the tags are gathered and sent to the accounting office so that all the information can be summarized and the dollar valuation of inventory can be computed.

**Including all goods owned** All goods to which the company has title should be included in the inventory, regardless of their location. Title to merchandise ordinarily passes from seller to buyer at the time the goods are delivered. No question usually arises as to the ownership of merchandise on the shelves, in stock rooms, or in warehouses. A question of ownership often does arise, however, for merchandise en route from suppliers but not yet received on the last day of the year. A similar question of ownership concerns goods in the process of shipment to customers at year-end.

**Goods in transit** Do goods in transit belong in the inventory of the seller or of the buyer? If the selling company makes delivery of the merchandise in its own trucks, the merchandise remains its property while in transit. If the goods are shipped by rail, air, or other public carrier, the question of ownership of the goods while in transit depends upon whether the public carrier is acting as the agent of the seller or of the buyer. If the terms of the shipment are ***F.O.B.*** (free on board) ***shipping point,*** title passes at the point of shipment and the goods are the property of the buyer while in transit. If the terms of the shipment are ***F.O.B. destination,*** title does not pass until the shipment reaches the destination, and the goods belong to the seller while in transit. In deciding whether goods in transit at year-end should be included in inventory, it is therefore necessary to refer to the terms of the agreements with vendors (suppliers) and customers.

At the end of the year a company may have received numerous orders from customers, for which goods have been segregated and packed but not yet shipped. These goods generally should be included in inventory. An exception to this rule is found occasionally when the goods have been prepared for shipment but are being held for later delivery at the request of the customer.

**Passage of title to merchandise** The debit to Accounts Receivable and the offsetting credit to the Sales account should be made ***when title to the goods passes to the customer.*** It would obviously be improper to set up an account receivable and at the same time to include the goods in question in inventory. Great care is necessary at year-end to ensure that all last-minute shipments to customers are recorded as sales of the current year and, on the other hand, that no customer's order is recorded as a sale until the date when the goods are shipped. Sometimes, in an effort to meet sales quotas, companies have recorded sales on the last day of the accounting period, when in fact the merchandise was not shipped until early in the next period. Such practices lead to an overstatement of the year's earnings and are not in accordance with generally accepted principles of accounting.

Merchandise in inventory is valued at ***cost,*** whereas accounts receivable are stated at the ***sales price*** of the merchandise sold. Consequently, the recording of a sale prior to delivery of the goods results in an unjustified increase in the total assets of the company. The increase will equal the difference between the cost and the selling price of the goods in question. The amount of the increase will also be reflected in the income statement, where it will show up as additional earnings. An unscrupulous company, which wanted to make its financial statements present a more favorable picture than actually existed, might do so by treating year-end orders from customers as sales even though the goods were not yet shipped.

## Pricing the inventory

One of the most interesting and widely discussed problems in accounting is the pricing of inventory. Even those business executives who have little knowledge of accounting are usually interested in the various methods of pricing inventory, because inventory valuation has a direct effect upon reported net income. Federal income taxes are based on income, and the choice of inventory method may have a considerable effect upon the amount of income taxes payable. Federal income tax authorities are therefore very interested in the problem of inventory valuation and have taken a definite position on the acceptability of various alternative methods of pricing inventory.

In approaching our study of inventory valuation, however, it is important that we do not overemphasize the income tax aspects of the problem. It is true that one method of inventory valuation may lead to a substantially lower income tax liability than would another method, but there are other important considerations in pricing inventory apart from the objective of minimizing the current income tax burden.

Proper valuation of inventory is one part of a larger undertaking, that is, to measure net income properly and to provide all those persons interested in the financial position and operating results of a business with accounting data which are dependable and of maximum usefulness as a basis for business decisions.

Accounting for inventories involves determination of cost and of current fair value or replacement cost. An understanding of the meaning of the term ***cost*** as applied to inventories is a first essential in appreciating the complexity of the overall problem of inventory valuation.

## Cost basis of inventory valuation

"The primary basis of accounting for inventory is cost, which has been defined generally as the price paid or consideration given to acquire an asset. As applied to inventories, cost means in principle the sum of the applicable expenditures and charges directly or indirectly incurred in bringing an article to its existing condition and location."[4]

**Inclusion of indirect expenditures in inventory cost—a question of materiality** The starting point in determining the cost of inventory is the ***net invoice price*** of the goods in inventory. From a conceptual point of view, all indirect expenditures incurred in the acquisition of these goods should be added to the invoice prices in determining the cost of inventory. For example, part of the expenditure during the period for transportation-in is applicable to ending inventory and should be included in the inventory cost. In determining the cost of the ending inventory, many businesses add to the net invoice price of the goods a reasonable portion of the transportation charges incurred during the period.

In some lines of business, however, it is customary to price the year-end inventory without giving any consideration to transportation charges, because these charges are ***not material in amount.*** Although this practice results in a slight understatement of inventory cost, the understatement is so small that it does not affect the usefulness or reliability of the financial statements. Thus, the omission of transportation charges from the cost of inventory often may be justified by the factors of convenience and economy. Accounting textbooks stress theoretical concepts of cost and income determination. The student of accounting should be aware, however, that in many business situations a close ***approximation*** of cost will serve the purpose at hand. The extra work involved in developing more precise accounting data must be weighed against the benefits that will result.

If transportation-in is part of the cost of merchandise purchased, what about the other incidental charges relating to the acquisition of merchandise, such as the salary of the purchasing agent, insurance of goods in transit, cost of receiving and inspecting the merchandise, etc.? Although in theory these incidental charges should be identified and apportioned among the various items of merchandise purchased, the expense of computing cost on such a precise basis would usually outweigh the benefits to be derived. The costs of operating the purchasing department and the receiving department are customarily treated as expense of the period in which incurred, rather than being carried forward to another period by inclusion in the balance sheet amount for inventory.

## Inventory valuation methods

The prices of many kinds of merchandise are subject to frequent change. When identical lots of merchandise are purchased at various dates during the year, each lot may be acquired at a different cost price.

To illustrate the several alternative methods in common use for determining

---

[4] Ibid.

which purchase prices apply to the units remaining in inventory at the end of the period, assume the data shown below.

| | Number of Units | Cost per Unit | Total Cost |
|---|---|---|---|
| *Beginning inventory* | 100 | $ 80 | $ 8,000 |
| *First purchase (Mar. 1)* | 50 | 90 | 4,500 |
| *Second purchase (July 1)* | 50 | 100 | 5,000 |
| *Third purchase (Oct. 1)* | 50 | 120 | 6,000 |
| *Fourth purchase (Dec. 1)* | 50 | 130 | 6,500 |
| *Available for sale* | 300 | | $30,000 |
| *Units sold* | 180 | | |
| *Units in ending inventory* | 120 | | |

This schedule shows that 180 units were sold during the year and that 120 units are on hand at year-end to make up the ending inventory. In order to establish a dollar amount for cost of goods sold and for the ending inventory, we must make an assumption as to which units were sold and which units remain on hand at the end of the year. There are several acceptable assumptions on this point; four of the most common will be considered. Each assumption made as to the cost of the units in the ending inventory leads to a different method of pricing inventory and to different amounts in the financial statements. The four assumptions (and inventory valuation methods) to be considered are known as (1) specific identification, (2) average cost, (3) first-in, first-out, and (4) last-in, first-out.

Although each of these four methods will produce a different answer as to the cost of goods sold and the cost of the ending inventory, the valuation of inventory in each case is said to be at "cost." In other words, ***these methods represent alternative definitions of inventory cost.***

**Specific identification method** If the units in the ending inventory can be identified as coming from specific purchases, they ***may*** be priced at the amounts listed on the purchase invoices. Continuing the example already presented, if the ending inventory of 120 units can be identified as, say, 50 units from the purchase of March 1, 40 units from the purchase of July 1, and 30 units from the purchase of December 1, the cost of the ending inventory may be computed as follows:

*Specific identification method and . . .*

| | |
|---|---|
| *50 units from the purchase of Mar. 1 @ $90* | $ 4,500 |
| *40 units from the purchase of July 1 @ $100* | 4,000 |
| *30 units from the purchase of Dec. 1 @ $130* | 3,900 |
| *Ending inventory (specific identification)* | $12,400 |

The cost of goods sold during the period is determined by subtracting the ending inventory from the cost of goods available for sale.

*. . . cost of goods sold computation*

| | |
|---|---|
| *Cost of goods available for sale* | *$30,000* |
| *Less: Ending inventory* | *12,400* |
| *Cost of goods sold (specific identification method)* | *$17,600* |

A business may prefer not to use the specific identification method even though the cost of each unit sold could be identified with a specific purchase. The flow of cost factors may be more significant than the flow of specific physical units in measuring the net income of the period.

As a simple example, assume that a coal dealer purchased 100 tons of coal at $60 a ton and a short time later made a second purchase of 100 tons of the same grade of coal at $80 a ton. The two purchases are in separate piles and it is a matter of indifference as to which pile is used in making sales to customers. Assume that the dealer makes a retail sale of one ton of coal at a price of $100. In measuring the gross profit on the sale, which cost figure should be used, $60 or $80? To insist that the cost depended on which of the two identical piles of coal was used in filling the delivery truck is an argument of questionable logic.

A situation in which the specific identification method is more likely to give meaningful results is in the purchase and sale of such high-priced articles as boats, automobiles, and jewelry.

**Average-cost method** Average cost is computed by dividing the total cost of goods available for sale by the number of units available for sale. This computation gives a ***weighted-average unit cost,*** which is then applied to the units in the ending inventory.

*Average-cost method and . . .*

| | |
|---|---|
| *Cost of goods available for sale* | *$30,000* |
| *Number of units available for sale* | *300* |
| *Average unit cost* | *$ 100* |
| *Ending inventory (at average cost, 120 units @ $100)* | *$12,000* |

Note that this method, when compared with the specific identification method, leads to a different amount for cost of goods sold as well as a different amount for the ending inventory.

*. . . cost of goods sold computation*

| | |
|---|---|
| *Cost of goods available for sale* | *$30,000* |
| *Less: Ending inventory* | *12,000* |
| *Cost of goods sold (average-cost method)* | *$18,000* |

When the average-cost method is used, the cost figure of $12,000 determined for the ending inventory is influenced by all the various prices paid during the year. The price paid early in the year may carry as much weight in pricing the ending inventory as a price paid at the end of the year. A common criticism of the average-cost method of pricing inventory is that it attaches no more significance to current prices than to prices which prevailed several months earlier.

**First-in, first-out method** The first-in, first-out method, which is often referred to as ***fifo,*** is based on the assumption that the first merchandise acquired is the first merchandise sold. In other words, each sale is made out of the ***oldest*** goods in stock; ***the ending inventory therefore consists of the most recently acquired goods.*** The fifo method of determining inventory cost may be adopted by any business, regardless of whether or not the physical flow of merchandise actually corresponds to this assumption of selling the oldest units in stock. Using the same data as in the preceding illustrations, the 120 units in the ending inventory would be regarded as consisting of the most recently acquired goods, as follows:

*First-in, first-out method and . . .*

| | |
|---|---|
| *50 units from the Dec. 1 purchase @ $130* | *$ 6,500* |
| *50 units from the Oct. 1 purchase @ $120* | *6,000* |
| *20 units from the July 1 purchase @ $100* | *2,000* |
| *Ending inventory, 120 units (at fifo cost)* | *$14,500* |

During a period of ***rising prices*** the first-in, first-out method will result in a larger amount ($14,500) being assigned as the cost of the ending inventory than would be assigned under the average-cost method. When a relatively large amount is allocated as cost of the ending inventory, a relatively small amount will remain as cost of goods sold, as indicated by the following calculation:

*. . . cost of goods sold computation*

| | |
|---|---|
| *Cost of goods available for sale* | *$30,000* |
| *Less: Ending inventory* | *14,500* |
| *Cost of goods sold (first-in, first-out method)* | *$15,500* |

It may be argued in support of the first-in, first-out method that the inventory valuation reflects recent costs and is therefore a realistic value in the light of conditions prevailing at the balance sheet date.

**Last-in, first-out method** The last-in, first-out method, commonly known as ***lifo,*** is one of the most interesting methods of pricing inventories. The title of this method suggests that the most recently acquired goods are sold first, and that ***the ending inventory consists of "old" goods acquired in the earliest purchases.*** Although this assumption is not in accord with the physical movement of merchandise in most businesses, there is a strong logical argument to support the lifo method.

For the purpose of measuring income, the ***flow of costs*** may be more significant than the physical flow of merchandise. Supporters of the lifo method contend that the measurement of income should be based upon ***current*** market conditions. Therefore, current sales revenue should be offset by the ***current*** cost of the merchandise sold. Under the lifo method, the costs assigned to the cost of goods sold are relatively current, because they stem from the most recent purchases. Under the ***fifo*** method, on the other hand, the cost of goods sold is based on "older" costs.

Using the same data as in the preceding illustrations, the 120 units in the ending inventory would be priced as if they were the oldest goods available for sale during the period, as follows:

*Last-in, first-out method and . . .*

| | |
|---|---|
| *100 units from the beginning inventory @ $80* | *$8,000* |
| *20 units from the purchase of Mar. 1 @ $90* | *1,800* |
| *Ending inventory, 120 units (at lifo cost)* | *$9,800* |

Note that the lifo cost of the ending inventory ($9,800) is very much lower than the fifo cost ($14,500) of ending inventory in the preceding example. Since a relatively small part of the cost of goods available for sale is assigned to ending inventory, it follows that a relatively large portion must have been assigned to cost of goods sold, as shown by the following computation:

*. . . cost of goods sold computation*

| | |
|---|---|
| *Cost of goods available for sale* | *$30,000* |
| *Less: Ending inventory* | *9,800* |
| *Cost of goods sold (last-in, first-out method)* | *$20,200* |

**Comparison of the alternative methods of pricing inventory** We have now illustrated four common methods of pricing inventory at cost; the specific identification method, the average-cost method, the first-in, first-out method, and the last-in, first-out method. By way of contrasting the results obtained from the four methods illustrated, especially during a period of rapid price increases, let us summarize the amounts computed for ending inventory, cost of goods sold, and gross profit on sales under each of the four methods. Assume that sales for the period amounted to $27,500.

*Four methods of determining inventory cost compared*

| | *Specific Identification Method* | *Average-Cost Method* | *First-In, First-Out Method* | *Last-In, First-Out Method* |
|---|---|---|---|---|
| *Sales* | *$27,500* | *$27,500* | *$27,500* | *$27,500* |
| *Cost of goods sold:* | | | | |
| *Beginning inventory* | *$ 8,000* | *$ 8,000* | *$ 8,000* | *$ 8,000* |
| *Purchases* | *22,000* | *22,000* | *22,000* | *22,000* |
| *Cost of goods available for sale* | *$30,000* | *$30,000* | *$30,000* | *$30,000* |
| *Less: Ending inventory* | *12,400* | *12,000* | *14,500* | *9,800* |
| *Cost of goods sold* | *$17,600* | *$18,000* | *$15,500* | *$20,200* |
| *Gross profit on sales* | *$ 9,900* | *$ 9,500* | *$12,000* | *$ 7,300* |

This comparison of the four methods makes it apparent that during periods of ***rising prices,*** the use of lifo will result in lower reported profits and lower income taxes than would be the case under the other methods of inventory valuation. Perhaps for this reason many businesses have adopted lifo. Current income tax regulations permit virtually any business to use the last-in, first-out method in determining taxable income.[5]

During a period of ***declining prices,*** the use of lifo will cause the reporting of relatively large profits as compared with fifo, which will hold reported profits to a minimum. Therefore, the choice of an inventory pricing method may significantly affect the amount of income reported during prolonged periods of changing price levels.

**Which method of inventory valuation is best?** All four of the inventory methods described are regarded as acceptable accounting practices and all four are acceptable in the determination of taxable income. No one method of inventory valuation can be considered as the "correct" or the "best" method. In the selection of a method, consideration should be given to the probable effect upon the balance sheet, upon the income statement, upon the amount of taxable income, and upon such business decisions as the establishment of selling prices for goods.

The specific identification method has the advantage of portraying the actual physical flow of merchandise. However, this method permits manipulation of income by selecting which items to deliver in filling a sales order. Also, the specific identification method may lead to faulty pricing decisions by implying that identical items of merchandise have different economic values.

Identical items will have the same accounting values only under the average-cost method. Assume for example that a hardware store sells a given size nail for 65 cents per pound. The hardware store buys the nails in 100-pound quantities at different times at prices ranging from 40 to 50 cents per pound. Several hundred pounds of nails are always on hand, stored in a large bin. The average-cost method properly recognizes that when a customer buys a pound of nails it is not necessary to know exactly which nails the customer happened to select from the bin in order to measure the gross profit on the sale.

A shortcoming in the average-cost method is that changes in current replacement costs of inventory are concealed because these costs are averaged with older costs. As a result of this averaging, the reported gross profit may not reflect current market conditions. This problem is illustrated in the discussion of ***inventory profits*** later in this chapter.

The inflation of recent years is a strong argument for the use of the lifo method. When prices are rising drastically, the most significant cost data to use as a guide to sales policies are probably the ***current replacement costs*** of the goods being sold. The lifo method of inventory valuation comes closer than any of the other methods described to measuring net income in the light of current selling prices and replacement costs.

On the other hand, the use of lifo during a period of rising prices is apt to produce a balance sheet figure for inventory which is far below the current replacement cost of the goods on hand. The fifo method of inventory valuation will

---

[5]Income tax laws require the use of lifo for financial reporting if it is used for tax purposes.

lead to a balance sheet valuation of inventory more in line with current replacement costs.

Some business concerns which adopted lifo more than 30 years ago now show a balance sheet figure for inventory which is less than half the present replacement cost of the goods in stock. An inventory valuation method which gives significant figures for the income statement may thus produce misleading amounts for the balance sheet, whereas a method which produces a realistic figure for inventory on the balance sheet may provide less realistic data for the income statement.

The search for the "best" method of inventory valuation is rendered difficult because the inventory figure is used in both the balance sheet and the income statement, and these two financial statements are intended for different purposes. In the income statement the function of the inventory figure is to permit a matching of costs and revenue. In the balance sheet the inventory and the other current assets are regarded as a measure of the company's ability to meet its current debts. For this purpose a valuation of inventory in line with current replacement cost would appear to be more significant.

## Consistency in the valuation of inventory

The ***principle of consistency*** is one of the basic concepts underlying reliable financial statements. This principle means that once a company has adopted a particular accounting method, that company should follow that method consistently rather than switch methods from one year to the next. Consider the consequences if we were to ignore the principle of consistency in accounting for inventories. A company could cause its net income for any given year to increase or decrease merely by changing its method of inventory valuation. The principle of consistency does not mean that every company in an industry must use the same accounting method; it does mean that a given company should not switch year after year from one accounting method to another.

Bear in mind that a company has considerable latitude in selecting a method of inventory valuation best suited to its needs. The principle of consistency comes into play after a given method has been selected. We have already illustrated in the example on page 405 how different methods can produce differences in reported income. Consequently, a change from one inventory method to another will usually cause reported income to change significantly in the year in which the change is made. Frequent switching of methods would make the income statements undependable as a means of portraying trends in operating results. Because of the principle of consistency, the user of financial statements is able to assume that the company has followed the same accounting methods it used in the preceding year. Thus, the value of financial statements is increased because they enable the user to make reliable comparisons of the results achieved from year to year.

The principle of consistency does not mean that a business can ***never*** change its method of inventory valuation. However, when a change is made, the effects of the change upon reported net income should be ***disclosed fully*** in the footnotes accompanying the financial statements.[6] ***Adequate disclosure*** of all information necessary for the proper interpretation of financial statements is another basic principle of accounting. Even when the same method of inventory pricing is being followed consistently, the financial statements should include a disclosure of the pricing method in use.

### The environment of inflation

We have previously discussed the relationship between the valuation of assets in the balance sheet and the recognition of costs and expenses in the income statement. As assets are sold or used up, their cost is removed from the balance sheet and recognized in the income statement as a cost or expense. In the case of inventory, the cost of units sold is transferred from the balance sheet to the income statement as cost of goods sold. In the case of depreciable assets, such as a building, the cost is gradually transferred to the income statement as depreciation expense. This flow of costs is illustrated below:

***Historical costs appear in both balance sheet and income statement***

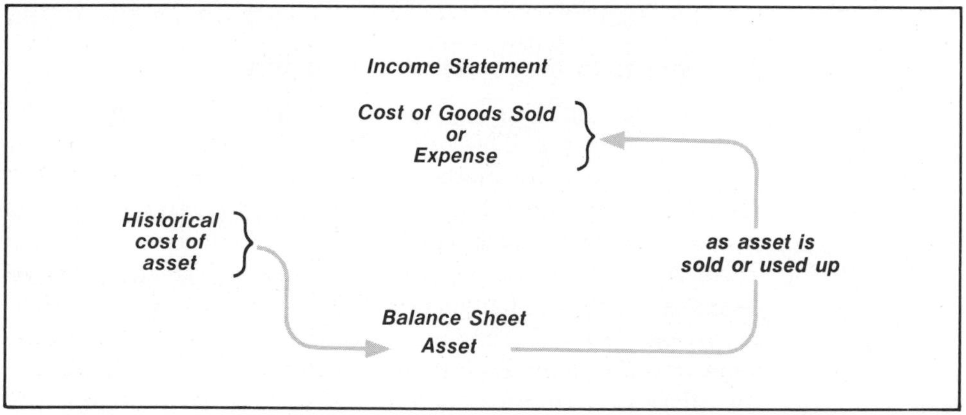


A period of sustained inflation causes some distortion in financial statements which are based upon historical costs. Rising price levels may cause assets to be valued in the balance sheets at amounts substantially below their current replacement cost. Similarly, the cost assigned to the income statement as these assets are sold or used up tends to understate the cost to the business of replacing these assets.

The inflationary policies and high income tax rates of recent years have stimulated the interest of business management in the choice of inventory methods. Most business executives and government officials expect the trend of rising prices to continue; in other words, an environment of inflation has come to be considered as normal. The lifo method of inventory valuation causes reported net income to reflect the increasing cost of replacing the merchandise sold during

[6]A change in the method of inventory valuation also requires the approval of the Internal Revenue Service.

the year and also tends to avoid basing income tax payments on an exaggerated measurement of taxable income. Therefore, the existence of inflation is an argument for the lifo method of inventory.

### Inventory profits

Many accountants believe that the use of fifo or of average cost during a period of inflation results in the reporting of overstated profits and consequently in the payment of excessive income taxes. Profits are considered to be overstated because under both the fifo and average-cost methods, the gross profit is computed by subtracting "old" inventory costs rather than current replacement costs from sales revenue. These old costs are relatively low, resulting in a high reported gross profit. However, the company must pay the higher current cost in order to replenish its inventory.

To illustrate this concept, assume that TV Sales Shop has an inventory of 20 television sets which were acquired at an average cost of $270. During the current month, 10 television sets are sold for cash at a sales price of $350 each. Using the average-cost method to value inventory, the company will report the following gross profit for the month:

| | |
|---|---|
| *Sales (10 × $350)* | *$3,500* |
| *Cost of goods sold (10 × $270)* | *2,700* |
| *Gross profit on sales* | *$ 800* |

However, TV Sales Shop must replace its inventory of television sets to continue in business. Because of inflation, TV Sales Shop can no longer buy 10 television sets for $2,700. Let us assume that the current replacement cost of television sets is $325 each; TV Sales Shop must pay $3,250 to replenish its inventory. Thus, TV Sales Shop is able to keep only $250 ($3,500 − $3,250) of the reported $800 gross profit; the remaining $550 has to be reinvested in inventory because of the increasing cost of television sets. This $550 would be considered a fictitious profit, or an ***inventory profit,*** by many accountants and business executives.

The inventory profit included in the reported net income of a business may be computed by deducting the cost of goods sold shown in the income statement from the ***replacement cost*** (computed at the date of sale) of these goods.

In periods of rapid inflation, a significant portion of the reported net income of companies using fifo or average cost may actually be inventory profits. The net income of companies using lifo will include much less inventory profit because lifo causes more current costs to be included in the cost of goods sold.

### FASB Statement No. 33—Disclosing the effects of inflation

In an effort to compensate for the distortions in financial statements caused by inflation, the Financial Accounting Standards Board recently adopted ***State-***

***ment No. 33,*** "Financial Reporting and Changing Prices."[7] This Statement requires large corporations to disclose the extent to which historical costs appearing in both the balance sheet and the income statement understate current price levels. These disclosures can be in a footnote to the historical cost–based financial statements, or in a special set of supplementary financial statements. This information thus ***supplements*** rather than replaces the use of historical cost as a basis of accounting.

One requirement of Statement No. 33 is that large corporations disclose what it would cost to ***replace*** their inventories at year-end and what their cost of goods sold would be if computed by using the ***current replacement cost*** at the date of sale. The disclosure of the cost of goods sold computed on the basis of replacement cost has revealed that a substantial portion of the net income reported by many large corporations ***is actually inventory profit.*** In other words, net income tends to be ***overstated*** when companies rely solely on historical cost values during a period of inflation.

The FASB's action to require disclosure of replacement cost information may prove to be one of the most significant changes in accounting practice in many years. Some accountants view it as a major step away from cost-based accounting toward current-value accounting. At present, only very large corporations are required to make the disclosures called for in Statement No. 33, but the FASB encourages smaller companies to comply on a voluntary basis. Statement No. 33 calls for many disclosures in addition to the replacement cost of inventories and the cost of goods sold. These other disclosure requirements, including general price level adjustments and replacement costs of plant assets, are discussed in later chapters of this text.

## The lower-of-cost-or-market rule (LCM)

Although cost is the primary basis for valuation of inventories, circumstances may arise under which inventory may properly be valued at less than its cost. If the ***utility*** of the inventory has fallen below cost because of a decline in the price level, a loss has occurred. This loss may appropriately be recognized as a loss of the current period by reducing the accounting value of the inventory from cost to a lower level designated as market. The word ***market*** as used in this context means ***current replacement cost.*** For a merchandising company, ***market*** is the amount which the concern would have to pay at the present time for the goods in question, purchased in the customary quantities through the usual sources of supply and including transportation-in. To avoid misunderstanding, the rule might better read "lower of actual cost or replacement cost."

In the early days of accounting when the principal users of financial statements were creditors and attention was concentrated upon the balance sheet, conservatism was a dominant consideration in asset valuation. The lower-of-cost-or-market rule was then considered justifiable because it tended to produce

[7] FASB, *Statement No. 33,* "Financial Reporting and Changing Prices" (Stamford, Conn.: 1979).

a "safe" or minimum value for inventory. The rule was widely applied for a time without regard for the possibility that although replacement costs had declined, there might be no corresponding and immediate decline in selling prices.

As the significance of the income statement has increased, considerable dissatisfaction with the lower-of-cost-or-market rule has developed. If ending inventory is written down from cost to a lower market figure but the merchandise is sold during the next period at the usual selling prices, the effect of the write-down will have been to reflect a fictitious loss in the first period and an exaggerated profit in the second period. Arbitrary application of the lower-of-cost-or-market rule ignores the historical fact that selling prices do not always drop when replacement prices decline. Even if selling prices do follow replacement prices downward, they may not decline by a proportionate amount.

Because of these objections, the lower-of-cost-or-market rule has undergone some modification and is now qualified in the following respects. If the inventory can probably be sold at prices which will yield a ***normal profit,*** the inventory should be carried at cost even though current replacement cost is lower. Assume, for example, that merchandise is purchased for $1,000 with the intention of reselling it to customers for $1,500. The replacement cost then declines from $1,000 to $800, but it is believed that the merchandise can still be sold to customers for $1,450. In other words, the normal anticipated profit has shrunk by $50. The carrying value of the inventory could then be written down from $1,000 to $950. There is no justification for reducing the inventory to the replacement cost of $800 under these circumstances.

Another qualification of the lower-of-cost-or-market rule is that inventory should never be carried at an amount greater than ***net realizable value,*** which may be defined as prospective selling price minus anticipated selling expenses. Assume, for example, that because of unstable market conditions, it is believed that goods acquired at a cost of $500 and having a current replacement cost of $450 will probably have to be sold for no more than $520 and that the selling expenses involved will amount to $120. The inventory should then be reduced to a carrying value (net realizable value) of $400, which is less than current replacement cost.

**Application of the lower-of-cost-or-market rule** The lower of cost or market for inventory is often computed by determining the cost and the market figures for each item in inventory and using the lower of the two amounts in every case. If, for example, item A cost $100 and replacement cost is $90, the item should be priced at $90. If item B cost $200 and replacement cost is $225, this item should be priced at $200. The total cost of the two items is $300 and total replacement cost is $315, but the total inventory value determined by applying the lower-of-cost-or-market rule to each item in inventory is only $290. This application of the lower-of-cost-or-market rule is illustrated by the tabulation on page 412.

If the lower-of-cost-or-market rule is applied item by item, the carrying value of the above inventory would be $10,600. However, an alternative and less rigorous version of the lower-of-cost-or-market rule calls for applying it to the total of

*Application of Lower-of-Cost-or-Market Rule, Item-by-Item Method*

*Pricing inventory at lower of cost or market*

| | | Unit Cost | | Total Cost | | |
|---|---|---|---|---|---|---|
| *Item* | *Quantity* | *Cost* | *Market* | *Cost* | *Market* | *Lower of Cost or Market* |
| A | 10 | $100 | $ 90 | $ 1,000 | $ 900 | $ 900 |
| B | 8 | 200 | 225 | 1,600 | 1,800 | 1,600 |
| C | 50 | 50 | 60 | 2,500 | 3,000 | 2,500 |
| D | 80 | 90 | 70 | 7,200 | 5,600 | 5,600 |
| *Totals* | | | | $12,300 | $11,300 | $10,600 |

the entire inventory rather than to the individual items. If the above inventory is to be valued by applying the lower-of-cost-or-market rule to the total of the inventory, the balance sheet amount for inventory is determined merely by comparing the total cost of $12,300 with the total replacement cost of $11,300 and using the lower of the two figures. Still another alternative method of using the lower-of-cost-or-market concept is to apply it to categories of the inventory rather than item by item. Each of these alternative methods of applying the lower-of-cost-or-market rule is acceptable in current accounting practice, although once a method has been selected it should be followed consistently from year to year.

## Gross profit method of estimating inventories

The taking of a physical inventory is a time-consuming and costly job in many lines of business; consequently, a physical inventory may be taken only once a year. Monthly financial statements are needed, however, for intelligent administration of the business, and the preparation of monthly statements requires a determination of the amount of inventory at the end of each month. In many cases this dilemma may be solved satisfactorily by estimating the inventory each month by using the ***gross profit method.***

The gross profit method of estimating inventory is based on the assumption that the rate of gross profit remains the same from one accounting period to the next. This assumption is a realistic one for many fields of business. When the gross profit rate is known, the ending inventory can be estimated by the following procedures:

1 Determine the cost of goods available for sale from the general ledger records of beginning inventory and net purchases.
2 Estimate the cost of goods sold by reducing the net sales figure by the usual gross profit rate.
3 Subtract the cost of goods sold from the cost of goods available for sale to find the estimated ending inventory.

To illustrate, assume that Metro Hardware Co. has a beginning inventory of $50,000 on January 1. During the month of January, net purchases amount to $8,000 and net sales total $20,000. Assuming that the company's normal gross profit rate is 40% of net sales, the inventory on hand at January 30 may be estimated as follows:

| | | |
|---|---|---|
| | *Beginning inventory (Jan. 1)* | *$50,000* |
| | *Net purchases* | *8,000* |
| *Step 1 . . .* | *Cost of goods available for sale* | *$58,000* |
| *Step 2 . . .* | *Less: Estimated cost of goods sold (60%* of $20,000 net sales)* | *12,000* |
| *Step 3 . . .* | *Estimated ending inventory (Jan. 31)* | *$46,000* |

*Since the gross profit rate is 40%, the cost of goods sold must equal 60% of net sales.

The gross profit method of estimating inventory has several uses apart from the preparation of monthly financial statements. This technique may be used after the taking of a physical inventory to confirm the overall reasonableness of the amount determined by the counting and pricing process. In the event of a fire which destroys the inventory, the approximate amount of goods on hand at the date of the fire may also be computed by the gross profit method.

## The retail method of inventory valuation

The retail method of estimating ending inventory is somewhat similar to the gross profit method. It is widely used by chain stores, department stores, and other types of retail business. Goods on sale in retail stores are marked at the retail prices; it is therefore more convenient to take inventory at current retail prices than to look up invoices to find the unit cost of each item in stock. After first determining the value of the inventory at retail price, the next step is to convert the inventory to cost price by applying the ratio prevailing between cost and selling price during the current period. This method of approximating an inventory may also be carried out by using data from the accounts without taking any physical count of the goods on hand. The underlying basis for the ***retail method*** of inventory valuation is the ratio of cost to selling price for the ***current period,*** whereas the ***gross profit method*** of estimating inventory rests on the rate of gross profit experienced in ***preceding periods.***

When the retail method of inventory is to be used, it is necessary to maintain records of the beginning inventory and of all purchases during the period in terms of selling price as well as at cost. Goods available for sale during the period can then be stated both at cost and at selling price. By deducting the sales for the period from the sales value of the goods available for sale, the ending inventory at selling price may be determined without the need for a physical count. The ending inventory at selling price is then converted to a cost basis by using the percentage ratio of cost to selling price for the current period.

In practice, the application of this method may be complicated because the originally established sales prices are modified by frequent price markups and markdowns. These frequent changes in retail price present some difficulties in determining the correct rate to use in reducing the inventory from selling price to cost. The following illustration shows the calculation of inventory by the retail method, without going into the complications which would arise from markups and markdowns in the original retail selling price.

*Used by many department stores*

| | Cost Price | Selling Price |
|---|---|---|
| *Beginning inventory* | *$20,000* | *$30,000* |
| *Net purchases during the month* | *11,950* | *15,000* |
| *Goods available for sale* | *$31,950* | *$45,000* |
| *Less: Net sales for the month* | | *20,000* |
| *Ending inventory at selling price* | | *$25,000* |
| *Cost ratio ($31,950 ÷ $45,000)* | | *71%* |
| *Ending inventory at cost (71% × $25,000)* | *$17,750* | |

## Perpetual inventory system

Companies which deal in merchandise of high unit cost, such as television sets or outboard motors, find a perpetual inventory system worthwhile and efficient. Since inventory may be one of the largest assets in a business and has a rapid rate of turnover, strong internal control is especially important. A perpetual inventory system, if properly designed and operated, can provide the strongest possible internal control over the inventory of merchandise. The key feature of a perpetual inventory system is that the records show continuously the amount of inventory on hand and the cost of goods sold. Large companies that maintain their accounting records electronically are in a good position to carry on continuous updating of inventory records.

## Internal control and perpetual inventory systems

A perpetual inventory system has the potential of providing excellent internal control. However, the fact that perpetual inventory records are in use does not automatically guarantee strong internal control. Such basic internal control concepts as the subdivision of duties, the control of documents by serial numbers, and separation of the accounting function from the custody of assets are essential elements with either the perpetual or periodic inventory systems.

ILLUSTRATIVE CASE Par-Flite, a manufacturer of golf equipment, maintained an inventory of several thousand sets of golf clubs. The clubs were kept in a storeroom with barred windows and doors under the supervision of John Adams. Adams was also responsible for maintaining detailed perpetual inventory records of the golf clubs in the storeroom. Another employee acquired an unauthorized key to the storeroom and began stealing large numbers of clubs. Adams discovered that the quantities on hand did not agree with the perpetual records he maintained. Afraid that his records would be criticized as highly inaccurate, he made numerous changes in the records so they would agree with quantities of golf clubs on hand. The theft of clubs continued and large losses were sustained before the inventory shortage came to the attention of management.

If the person maintaining inventory records had not also been responsible for physical custody of the merchandise, there would have been no incentive or opportunity to conceal a shortage by falsifying the records. Satisfactory internal control over inventories requires that the accounting function be separate from the custody of assets. Frequent comparison of quantities of merchandise on hand with the quantities shown by the perpetual inventory records should be made by employees who do not have responsibility either for custody of assets or for maintenance of records.

## Perpetual inventory records

The information required for a perpetual inventory system can be processed electronically or manually. In a manual system a subsidiary record card, as shown below, is used for each type of merchandise on hand. If the company has 100 different kinds of products in stock, then 100 inventory record cards will make up the subsidiary inventory record. Shown below is an inventory record card for item XL-2000.

***Perpetual inventory record card***

*Item* XL-2000 *Maximum* 20

*Location* Storeroom 2 *Minimum* 8

| | PURCHASED | | | SOLD | | | BALANCE | | |
|---|---|---|---|---|---|---|---|---|---|
| Date | Units | Unit Cost | Total | Units | Unit Cost | Total | Units | Unit Cost | Balance |
| Jan. 1 | | | | | | | 12 | $50.00 | $600.00 |
| 7 | | | | 2 | $50.00 | $100.00 | 10 | 50.00 | 500.00 |
| 9 | 10 | $55.00 | $550.00 | | | | 10 | 50.00 | |
| | | | | | | | 10 | 55.00 | 1,050.00 |
| 12 | | | | 8 | 50.00 | 400.00 | 2 | 50.00 | |
| | | | | | | | 10 | 55.00 | 650.00 |
| 13 | | | | 2 | 50.00 | 100.00 | | | |
| | | | | 1 | 55.00 | 55.00 | 9 | 55.00 | 495.00 |

On this card, the quantity and cost of units received will be listed at the date of receipt; the quantity and cost of units sold will be recorded at the date of sale; and after each purchase or sales transaction, the balance remaining on hand will be shown. This running balance will be shown in number of units, cost per unit, and total dollar amount.

The information on the illustrated inventory record shows that the first-in, first-out basis of pricing the inventory is being used. After the sale of two units on January 7, the remaining inventory consisted of 10 units at a cost of $50 each. The purchase on January 9 of 10 units carried a unit cost of $55, rather than $50, hence must be accounted for separately. The balance on hand after the January 9 purchase appears on two lines: 10 units at $50 and 10 units at $55. When eight units were sold on January 12, they were treated as coming from the oldest stock on hand and therefore had a cost of $50 each. The balance remaining on hand then consisted of two units at $50 and 10 units at $55. When three units were sold on January 13, the cost consisted of two units at $50 and one unit at $55. The remaining inventory of nine units consists of the most recently acquired units with a cost of $55 each.

Perpetual inventory records may also be maintained on a last-in, first-out basis or on an average-cost basis, but these systems involve some complexities which are considered in advanced accounting courses.

Control over the amount invested in inventory can be strengthened by listing on each inventory card the maximum and minimum quantities that should be kept in stock. By maintaining quantities within these limits, overstocking and out-of-stock situations can be avoided.

**General ledger entries for a perpetual inventory system** The general ledger controlling account entitled ***Inventory*** is continuously (perpetually) updated when a perpetual inventory system is in use. This Inventory account controls the many subsidiary record cards discussed above. A continuously updated Cost of Goods Sold account is also maintained in the general ledger.

The purchase of merchandise by a company using a perpetual inventory system requires a journal entry affecting general ledger controlling accounts as follows:

| | | |
|---|---|---|
| *Inventory* | *550* | |
|     *Accounts Payable, Lake Company* | | *550* |
| *To record purchase of merchandise on credit.* | | |

This purchase transaction would also be recorded in the subsidiary ledger (the perpetual inventory cards) showing the quantity of each kind of merchandise purchased. The $550 purchase from Lake Company might affect only one or perhaps a dozen of the subsidiary records, depending on how many types of merchandise were included in this purchase transaction.

For every sales transaction, we can determine the cost of the goods sold by referring to the appropriate perpetual inventory card record. Therefore, at the time of a sale, we can record both the amount of the selling price and the ***cost*** of the goods sold, as illustrated in the following pair of related entries.

| | | |
|---|---|---|
| *Accounts Receivable, J. Williams* | *140* | |
|     *Sales* | | *140* |
| *To record the sale of merchandise on credit.* | | |

| | | |
|---|---|---|
| *Cost of Goods Sold* | *100* | |
|     *Inventory* | | *100* |
| *To record the cost of goods sold and the related decrease in inventory.* | | |

To avoid making a large number of entries in the general journal, a special column can be entered in the sales journal to show the cost of the goods involved in each sales transaction. At the end of the month the total of this "Cost" column can be posted as a debit to Cost of Goods Sold and a credit to Inventory.

A company maintaining perpetual inventory records will also conduct a physical count of all merchandise once a year and compare the amount of the physical inventory with the perpetual inventory records. An adjusting entry can be made to bring the inventory records into agreement with the physical inventory. For example, if shoplifting or other factors have caused an inventory shortage, the adjusting entry will consist of a debit to the loss account, Inventory Shortage, and a credit to Inventory.

When a perpetual inventory system is in use, the Inventory account is increased by purchases of merchandise. It is decreased by the cost of goods sold, by purchase returns and allowances, and by purchase discounts. At the end of the year the dollar balances of all the subsidiary inventory record cards should be added to see that the total is in agreement with the general ledger controlling account. The only adjustment necessary at year-end will be to correct the Inventory controlling account and the subsidiary records for any discrepancies indicated by the taking of a physical inventory.

The advantages of a perpetual inventory system as indicated in the preceding discussion include:

1 Stronger internal control. By comparing the physical inventory with the perpetual records, management will be made aware of any shortages or errors and can take corrective action.
2 A physical inventory can be taken at dates other than year-end, or it can be taken for different products or different departments at various dates during the year, since the perpetual records always show the amounts which ***should*** be on hand.
3 Quarterly or monthly financial statements can be prepared more readily because of the availability of dollar amounts for inventory and cost of goods sold in the accounting records.

## KEY TERMS INTRODUCED OR EMPHASIZED IN CHAPTER 10

**Average-cost method** A method of inventory valuation. Weighted-average unit cost is computed by dividing the total cost of goods available for sale by the number of units available for sale.

**Consistency in inventory valuation** An accounting standard that calls for the use of the same method of inventory pricing from year to year, with full disclosure of the effects of any change in method. Intended to make financial statements comparable.

**Cost of inventory** The price paid for the inventory plus the costs of bringing the goods to the point where they are offered for sale.

**First-in, first-out (fifo)** A method of computing the cost of inventory and the cost of goods sold based on the assumption that the first merchandise acquired is the first merchandise sold, and that the ending inventory consists of the most recently acquired goods.

**F.O.B. destination** A term meaning the seller bears the cost of shipping goods to the buyer's location. Title to the goods remains with the seller while the goods are in transit.

**F.O.B. shipping point** The buyer of goods bears the cost of transportation from the seller's location to the buyer's location. Title to the goods passes at the point of shipment and the goods are the property of the buyer while in transit.

**Gross profit method** A method of estimating the cost of the ending inventory based on the assumption that the rate of gross profit remains approximately the same from year to year.

**Inventory** Goods acquired or produced for sale in the regular operation of a business. Goods in which a business deals.

**Inventory profits** The amount by which the cost of replacing goods sold (computed at the date of sale) ***exceeds*** the reported cost of goods sold. Many accountants consider inventory profits to be a "fictitious" profit, because this amount usually must be reinvested in inventories and therefore is not available for distribution to stockholders.

**Last-in, first-out (lifo) method** A method of computing the cost of goods sold by use of the prices paid for the most recently acquired units. Ending inventory is valued on the basis of prices paid for the units first acquired.

**Lower-of-cost-or-market method** A method of inventory pricing in which goods are valued at original cost or replacement cost (market), whichever is lower.

**Net realizable value** The prospective selling price minus anticipated selling expenses. Inventory should not be carried at more than net realizable value.

**Perpetual inventory system** Provides a continuous (perpetual) running record of the goods on hand. As goods are sold their cost is transferred to a Cost of Goods Sold account.

**Physical inventory** A systematic count of all goods on hand, followed by the application of unit prices to the quantities counted and development of a dollar value for ending inventory.

**Retail method** A method of estimating inventory in a retail store based on the assumption that the cost of goods on hand bears the same percentage relationship to retail prices as does the cost of all goods available for sale to the original retail prices. Inventory is first priced at retail and then converted to cost by application of a cost-to-retail percentage.

**Specific identification method** A method of pricing inventory by identifying the units in the ending inventory as coming from specific purchases.

## REVIEW QUESTIONS

1 Which of the seven items listed below are used in computing the ***cost of goods available for sale?***

- a Ending inventory
- b Sales
- c Beginning inventory
- d Purchases
- e Transportation-in
- f Purchase returns and allowances
- g Delivery expense

2 Through an error in counting of merchandise at December 31, Year 4, the Trophy Company overstated the amount of goods on hand by $8,000. Assuming that the error was not discovered, what was the effect upon net income for Year 4? Upon owner's equity at December 31, Year 4? Upon net income for Year 5? Upon owner's equity at December 31, Year 5?

3 Is the establishment of an appropriate valuation for the merchandise inventory at the end of the year more important in producing a dependable income statement, or in producing a dependable balance sheet?

4 Explain the meaning of the term ***physical inventory.***

5 Near the end of December, Hadley Company received a large order from a major customer. The work of packing the goods for shipment was begun at once but could not be completed before the close of business on December 31. Since a written order from the customer was on hand and the goods were nearly all packed and ready for shipment, Hadley felt that this merchandise should not be included in the physical inventory taken on December 31. Do you agree? What is probably the reason behind Hadley's opinion?

6 During a prolonged period of rising prices, will the fifo or lifo method of inventory valuation result in higher reported profits?

7 Throughout several years of strongly rising prices, Company A used the lifo method of inventory valuation and Company B used the fifo method. In which company would the balance sheet figure for inventory be closer to current replacement cost of the merchandise on hand? Why?

8 You are making a detailed analysis of the financial statements and accounting records of two companies in the same industry, Adams Company and Bar Company. Price levels have been rising steadily for several years. In the course of your investigation, you observe that the inventory value shown on the Adams Company balance sheet is quite close to the current replacement cost of the merchandise on hand. However, for Bar Company, the carrying value of the inventory is far below current replacement cost. What method of inventory valuation is probably used by Adams Company? By Bar Company? If we assume that the two companies are identical except for the inventory valuation method used, which company has probably been reporting higher net income in recent years?

9 Why do some accountants consider the net income reported by businesses during a period of rising prices to be overstated?

10 Assume that a business uses the first-in, first-out method of accounting for inventories during a prolonged period of inflation and that the business pays dividends equal to the amount of reported net income. Suggest a problem that may arise in continued successful operation of the business. What does this situation have to do with "inventory profits"?

11 The Financial Accounting Standards Board requires large corporations to disclose the cost of replacing their inventories and to disclose what their cost of goods sold would be if computed by using replacement costs. Do you think this policy indicates that corporate profits have tended to be overstated or understated in recent years? Explain.

12 Explain the meaning of the term ***market*** as used in the expression "lower of cost or market."

13 One of the items in the inventory of Grayline Stores is marked for sale at $125. The purchase invoice shows the item cost $95, but a newly issued price list from the manufacturer shows the present replacement cost to be $90. What inventory valuation should be assigned to this item if Grayline Stores follows the lower-of-cost-or-market rule?

14 Explain the usefulness of the ***gross profit method*** of estimating inventories.

15 A store using the ***retail inventory method*** takes its physical inventory by applying current retail prices as marked on the merchandise to the quantities counted. Does this procedure indicate that the inventory will appear in the financial statements at retail selling price? Explain.

16 Estimate the ending inventory by the gross profit method, given the following data: beginning inventory $40,000, net purchases $100,000, net sales $106,667, average gross profit rate 25% of net sales.

17 Summarize the difference between the ***periodic system*** and the ***perpetual system*** of accounting for inventory. Which system would usually cost more to maintain? Which system would be most practicable for a restaurant, a retail drugstore, a new car dealer?

18 Identify each of the four statements shown below as true or false. In the accounting records of a company using a perpetual inventory system:

**a** The Inventory account will ordinarily remain unchanged until the end of an accounting period.

**b** The Cost of Goods Sold account is debited with the sales price of merchandise sold.

**c** The Inventory account and the Cost of Goods Sold account will both normally have debit balances.

**d** The Inventory account and the Cost of Goods Sold account will normally have equal but offsetting balances.

## EXERCISES

*Ex. 10-1* The condensed income statements prepared by Blaze Company for two years are shown below:

| | Year 2 | Year 1 |
|---|---|---|
| Sales | $183,400 | $168,000 |
| Cost of goods sold | 106,400 | 134,400 |
| Gross profit on sales | $ 77,000 | $ 33,600 |
| Operating expenses | 28,000 | 28,000 |
| Net income | $ 49,000 | $ 5,600 |

The inventory at the end of Year 1 was understated by $16,800, but the error was not discovered until after the accounts had been closed and financial statements prepared at the end of Year 2. The balance sheets for the two years showed owner's equity of $71,400 at the end of Year 1 and $86,800 at the end of Year 2.

Compute the correct net income figures for Year 1 and Year 2 and the gross profit percentage for each year based on corrected data. What correction, if any, should be made in owner's equity at the end of Year 1 and at the end of Year 2?

*Ex. 10-2* The beginning inventory balance of item X on January 1 and the purchases of this item during the current year were as follows:

| | | | | |
|---|---|---|---|---|
| Jan. 1 | Beginning inventory | 500 units | @ $10.00 | $ 5,000 |
| Feb. 23 | Purchase | 1,600 units | @ $11.00 | 17,600 |
| Apr. 20 | Purchase | 1,000 units | @ $11.20 | 11,200 |
| May 4 | Purchase | 1,000 units | @ $11.60 | 11,600 |
| Nov. 30 | Purchase | 400 units | @ $12.50 | 5,000 |
| Totals | | 4,500 units | | $50,400 |

At December 31 the ending inventory consisted of 675 units.

Determine the cost of the ending inventory, based on each of the following methods of inventory valuation:

**a** Average cost
**b** First-in, first-out
**c** Last-in, first out

*Ex. 10-3* Marantz Corporation sells only one product; sales and purchases occur at a uniform rate throughout the year. The following items appear in the company's financial statements for Year 4:

| | |
|---|---|
| Purchases | $2,000,000 |
| Cost of goods sold | 1,900,000 |
| Inventory, Jan. 1, Year 4 (fifo basis) | 520,000 |
| Inventory, Dec. 31, Year 4 (fifo basis) | 620,000 |

A footnote to the financial statements disclosed that the replacement cost of inventory at December 31, Year 4, was $650,000 and that the cost of goods sold computed using replacement costs at the date of sale amounted to $2,150,000.

**a** Compute the amount of inventory profit included in Marantz Corporation's reported operating results for Year 4.
**b** Did the number of units in Marantz Corporation's inventory increase or decrease during Year 4? Explain your reasoning.

*Ex. 10-4* Ruger Company has compiled the following information concerning items in its inventory at December 31:

| | | Unit Cost | |
|---|---|---|---|
| Item | Quantity | Cost (fifo) | Market |
| A | 120 | $ 46 | $ 50 |
| B | 70 | 160 | 136 |
| C | 62 | 100 | 110 |
| D | 81 | 280 | 290 |

Determine the total inventory value to appear on Ruger Company's balance sheet under the lower-of-cost-or-market rule, assuming **(a)** that the rule is applied to inventory as a whole and **(b)** that the rule is applied on an item-by-item basis.

*Ex. 10-5* When Ellen Sharp arrived at her store on the morning of May 29, she found empty shelves and display racks; thieves had broken in during the night and stolen the entire inventory. Sharp's accounting records showed that she had $48,000 inventory on May 1 (cost value). From May 1 to May 29, she had made sales of $192,000 and purchases of $151,200. The gross profit during the past several years had consistently averaged 30% of sales. Sharp wishes to file an insurance claim for the theft loss. What is the estimated cost of her inventory at the time of the theft? Show computations.

*Ex. 10-6* Vagabond Shop wishes to determine the approximate month-end inventory using data from the accounting records without taking a physical count of merchandise on hand. From the following information, estimate the cost of the September 30 inventory by the retail method of inventory valuation.

| | Cost Price | Selling Price |
|---|---|---|
| Inventory of merchandise, Aug. 31 | $264,800 | $400,000 |
| Purchases (net) during September | 170,400 | 240,000 |
| Sales (net) during September | | 275,200 |

*Ex. 10-7* Santa Cruz Wholesale Company uses a ***perpetual inventory system.*** On January 1, the Inventory account had a balance of $87,500. During the first few days of January the following transactions occurred.

**Jan. 2** Purchased merchandise on credit from Bell Company for $12,500.

**Jan. 3** Sold merchandise for cash, $9,000. The cost of this merchandise was $6,300.

**a** Prepare entries in general journal form to record the above transactions.

**b** What was the balance of the Inventory account at the close of business January 3?

*Ex. 10-8* Stream Bicycle Shop uses the first-in, first-out method of inventory valuation. At the end of the current year the shop had exactly the same number of bicycles in stock as at the beginning of the year, and the same proportion of each model. However, the year had been one of severe inflation and the cost of the ending inventory was shown in the accounts at $12,000 whereas the cost of the beginning inventory had been only $8,000. The net income reported by the shop for the year was $15,000. Comment on the validity of the reported net income and indicate what adjustment might be reasonable to give the owner a realistic picture of the results of the year's operations.

## PROBLEMS

### Group A

*10A-1* Hollywood Costume Co. is being offered for sale as a going concern. Its income statements for the last three years include the following key figures:

| | Year 3 | Year 2 | Year 1 |
|---|---|---|---|
| Net sales | $540,000 | $520,000 | $500,000 |
| Cost of goods sold | 356,400 | 348,800 | 345,000 |
| Gross profit on sales | $183,600 | $171,200 | $155,000 |
| Gross profit percentage | 34% | 33%* | 31% |

*Rounded to the nearest full percentage point.

In discussions with prospective buyers, the owners are emphasizing the rising trends of gross profit and gross profit percentage as very favorable factors.

Assume that you are retained by a prospective purchaser of the business to make an investigation of the fairness and reliability of Hollywood Costume Co.'s accounting records and financial statements. You find everything in order except for the following: (1) An arithmetical error in the computation of inventory at the end of Year 1 had caused a $10,000 understatement in that inventory; and (2) a duplication of figures in the computation of inventory at the end of Year 3 had caused an overstatement of $27,000 in that inventory. The company uses the periodic inventory system and these errors had not been brought to light prior to your investigation.

**Instructions**

**a** Prepare a revised three-year schedule along the lines of the one illustrated above.

**b** Comment on the trend of gross profit and gross profit percentage before and after the revision.

***10A-2*** Information relating to the inventory quantities, purchases, and sales of a certain type of capacitor by Morton Electronics during Year 4 is shown below:

| | Number of Units | Cost per Unit | Total Cost |
|---|---|---|---|
| Inventory, Jan. 1, Year 4 | 8,000 | $5.89 | $ 47,120 |
| First purchase (Mar. 15) | 10,300 | 6.20 | 63,860 |
| Second purchase (June 6) | 12,400 | 6.60 | 81,840 |
| Third purchase (Sept. 20) | 9,600 | 6.80 | 65,280 |
| Fourth purchase (Dec. 31) | 7,700 | 7.00 | 53,900 |
| Goods available for sale | 48,000 | | $312,000 |
| Units sold during Year 4 | 37,200 | | |
| Inventory, Dec. 31, Year 4 | 10,800 | | |

**Instructions**

**a** Compute the cost of the December 31, Year 4, inventory and the cost of goods sold for the capacitors in Year 4 using:
(1) The first-in, first-out method
(2) The last-in, first-out method
(3) The average-cost method

**b** Which of the three inventory pricing methods provides the most realistic balance sheet valuation of inventory in light of the current replacement cost of the capacitors? Does this same method also produce the most realistic measure of income in light of the costs being incurred by Morton Electronics to replace the capacitors when they are sold? Explain.

***10A-3*** Milage Plus, Inc., specializes in the sale of a single product. During Year 9, 106,000 units were sold for a total price of $800,000. The inventory at January 1, Year 9, consisted of 9,100 units valued at cost of $36,400. Purchases during the year were as follows: 20,000 units @ $4.10; 30,000 units @ $4.25; 50,000 units @ $4.60; and 10,900 units @ $5.00.

**Instructions**

**a** Compute the December 31, Year 9, inventory using:
(1) The first-in, first-out method
(2) The last-in, first-out method
(3) The average-cost method

**b** Prepare partial income statements for each of the above three methods of pricing inventory. The income statements are to be carried only to the determination of gross profit on sales.

**c** Which of the three methods of pricing inventory would be most advantageous from an income tax standpoint during a period of rising prices? Comment on the significance of the inventory figure under the method you recommend with respect to current replacement cost.

***10A-4*** The entire inventory of Airbrush Shirt Company was destroyed by fire on April 19, Year 5. The company does not maintain perpetual inventory records, and the last physical inventory had been taken on December 31, Year 4. Therefore, an estimate of the inventory value at April 19 must be prepared in order to file an insurance claim.

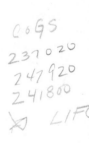

The following partial income statement for Year 4 is available to aid you in estimating the amount of inventory at the date of the fire:

***AIRBRUSH SHIRT COMPANY***
***Income Statement***
***For the Year Ended, December 31, Year 4***

| | | |
|---|---|---|
| ***Net sales*** | | ***$397,000*** |
| ***Cost of goods sold:*** | | |
| ***Inventory, Jan. 1, Year 4*** | ***$122,500*** | |
| ***Purchases*** | ***315,000*** | |
| ***Cost of goods available for sale*** | ***$437,500*** | |
| ***Less: Inventory, Dec. 31, Year 4*** | ***140,000*** | ***297,500*** |
| ***Gross profit on sales*** | | ***$ 99,500*** |

**Other data** The sales figure in the above income statement does not include $13,000 sales value of merchandise sold to a customer late in the day on December 31. This sale was erroneously recorded as occurring on the following business day, which was January 2, Year 5. Also, the $10,000 cost of this merchandise was erroneously included in the figure for inventory at December 31, Year 4.

Records salvaged from the fire revealed the merchandise transactions from December 31, Year 4, to the date of the fire to be: net sales, $181,500 (including the $13,000 sale erroneously recorded on January 2); and net purchases, $108,000.

**Instructions**

**a** Prepare a report directed to the insurance adjuster summarizing your findings. Include an estimate of the inventory value as of the date of the fire and a computation of the applicable gross profit rate.

**b** Explain how the gross profit method of estimating inventories may be used other than in case of a fire loss.

***10A-5*** Porterfield's, a retail store, carries a wide range of merchandise consisting mostly of articles of low unit price. The selling price of each item is plainly marked on the merchandise. At each year-end, the company has taken a physical count of goods on hand and has priced these goods at cost by looking up individual purchase invoices to determine the unit cost of each item in stock. Stevens, the store manager, is anxious to find a more economical method of assigning dollar values to the year-end inventory, explaining that it takes much more time to price the inventory than to count the merchandise on hand.

By analyzing the accounting records you are able to determine that net purchases of merchandise in Year 4 totaled $1,330,000; the retail selling price of this merchandise was $1,750,000. At the end of Year 4, a physical inventory showed goods on hand priced to sell at $375,000. This represented a considerable increase over the inventory of a year earlier. At December 31, Year 3, the inventory on hand had appeared in the balance sheet at cost of $170,000, although it had a retail value of $250,000.

**Instructions**

**a** Outline a plan whereby the inventory can be computed without the necessity of looking up individual purchase invoices. List step by step the procedures to be followed. Ignore the possibility of markups and markdowns in the original retail price of merchandise.

**b** Compute the cost of the inventory at December 31, Year 4, using the method described in **a.**

**c** Explain how the inventory method you have described can be modified for the preparation of monthly financial statements when no physical count of inventory is taken.

**10A-6** Oaktree Wholesale Company uses a perpetual inventory system, including a perpetual inventory record card for each of the 60 types of products it keeps in stock. The following transactions show the purchases and sales of one of these products (XK3) during September.

| | | |
|---|---|---|
| Sept. 1 | *Balance on hand, 50 units, cost $60 each* | $3,000 |
| 4 | *Purchase, 20 units, cost $65 each* | 1,300 |
| 8 | *Sale, 35 units, sales price $100 each* | 3,500 |
| 9 | *Purchase, 40 units, cost $65 each* | 2,600 |
| 20 | *Sale, 60 units, sales price $100 each* | 6,000 |
| 25 | *Purchase, 40 units, cost, $70 each* | 2,800 |
| 30 | *Sale, 5 units, sales price $110 each* | 550 |

**Instructions**

**a** Record the beginning inventory, the purchases, the cost of goods sold, and the running balance on an inventory record card like the one illustrated on page 415. Use the first-in, first-out method.

**b** Assume that all sales were made on credit. Compute the total sales and total cost of goods sold of product XK3 for September. Prepare an entry in general journal form to record these sales and a second entry to record the cost of goods sold for September.

**c** Compute the gross profit on sales of product XK3 for the month of September.

**10A-7** Income statements prepared by Sunflower Paints for Year 4 and Year 5 are shown below. The periodic inventory system is being used.

| | Year 5 | Year 4 |
|---|---|---|
| *Net sales* | $700,000 | $660,000 |
| *Cost of goods sold:* | | |
| *Beginning inventory* | $240,400 | $240,000 |
| *Net purchases* | 444,740 | 409,160 |
| *Cost of goods available for sale* | $685,140 | $649,160 |
| *Ending inventory* | 241,000 | 240,400 |
| *Cost of goods sold* | $444,140 | $408,760 |
| *Gross profit on sales* | $255,860 | $251,240 |
| *Expenses* | 180,000 | 170,100 |
| *Net income* | $ 75,860 | $ 81,140 |

The owner's equity as shown in the company's balance sheet was as follows: December 31, Year 3, $350,000; December 31, Year 4, $431,140; and December 31, Year 5, $507,000.

Early in Year 6, Alan Frank, accountant for Sunflower Paints, made a review of the documents and procedures used in taking the physical inventory at December 31 for both Year 4 and Year 5. His investigation disclosed the two questionable items listed below:

(1) Merchandise shipped to a customer on December 31, Year 4, F.O.B. shipping point, was included in the physical inventory taken that date. The cost of the merchandise was $2,900 and the sales price was $3,600. Because of the press of year-end work, the sales invoice was not prepared until January 6, Year 5. On that date the sale was recorded as a January transaction by entry in the sales journal, and the sales invoice mailed to the customer.

(2) Merchandise costing $6,840 which had been received on December 31, Year 4, had been included in the inventory taken on that date, although the purchase was

*(handwritten margin notes:)* OE 3 = 350,000  Adj NE 4  75,000  425,000  Corr OE 4  yrs + 82,000  507,000  OE

not recorded until January 8 when the vendor's invoice arrived. The invoice was then recorded in the purchases journal as a January transaction.

**Instructions**

**a** Prepare corrected income statements for the years ended December 31, Year 4 and Year 5. (You may find it helpful to set up T accounts for Sales, Year 4, and Sales, Year 5; Purchases, Year 4, and Purchases, Year 5; and Inventory, December 31, Year 4.)

**b** Compute corrected amounts for owner's equity at December 31, Year 4 and Year 5. Assume no withdrawals were made by the owner in Year 4 or Year 5.

## Group B

**10B-1**  Fantasy Ventures is being offered for sale as a going concern. Its income statements for the last three years include the following key figures.

|  | Year 3 | Year 2 | Year 1 |
|---|---|---|---|
| Net sales | $430,000 | $425,000 | $400,000 |
| Cost of goods sold | 240,800 | 243,000 | 240,000 |
| Gross profit on sales | $189,200 | $182,000 | $160,000 |
| Gross profit percentage | 44% | 43%* | 40% |

*Rounded to nearest full percentage point.

In discussions with prospective buyers, the owners are emphasizing the rising trends of gross profit and gross profit percentage as very favorable factors.

Assume that you are retained by a prospective purchaser of the business to make an investigation of the fairness and reliability of Fantasy Ventures' accounting records and financial statements. You find everything in order except for the following: (1) The inventory was understated by $12,000 at the end of Year 1 and (2) it was overstated by $21,500 at the end of Year 3. The company uses the periodic inventory system and these errors had not been brought to light prior to your investigation.

**Instructions**

**a** Prepare a revised three-year schedule along the lines of the one illustrated above.

**b** Comment on the trend of gross profit and gross profit percentage before and after the revision.

**10B-2**  Information relating to the inventory quantities, purchases, and sales of an 8-inch speaker unit by The Audio Shop during 19X4 is shown below:

|  | Number of Units | Cost per Unit | Total Cost |
|---|---|---|---|
| Inventory, Jan. 1, 19X4 | 900 | $10.00 | $ 9,000 |
| First purchase (Apr. 3) | 1,180 | 10.20 | 12,036 |
| Second purchase (July 7) | 800 | 10.35 | 8,280 |
| Third purchase (Oct. 22) | 620 | 10.70 | 6,634 |
| Fourth purchase (Dec. 15) | 1,000 | 10.85 | 10,850 |
| Goods available for sale | 4,500 |  | $46,800 |
| Units sold during 19X4 | 3,200 |  |  |
| Inventory, Dec. 31, 19X4 | 1,300 |  |  |

**Instructions**

**a** Compute the cost of the December 31, 19X4, inventory and the cost of goods sold for the 8-inch speaker units in 19X4 using:

(1) The first-in, first-out method
(2) The last-in, first-out method
(3) The average-cost method

**b** Which of the three inventory pricing methods provides the most realistic balance sheet valuation of inventory in light of the current replacement cost of the speaker units? Does this same method also produce the most realistic measure of income in light of the costs being incurred by The Audio Shop to replace the speakers when they are sold? Explain.

*10B-3* Water Massage, Inc., sells only one product. During the current year, 77,500 units were sold for total sales revenue of $930,000. The beginning inventory at January 1 consisted of 15,000 units valued at cost of $112,500. Purchases during the year were as follows: 20,000 units at $7.75; 28,500 units at $8.00; 21,000 units at $8.30; and 15,500 units at $8.40.

**Instructions**

**a** Compute the year-end (December 31) inventory using:
(1) The first-in; first-out method
(2) The last-in, first-out method
(3) The average-cost method

**b** Prepare partial income statements for each of the above three methods of pricing inventory. The income statements are to be carried only to the determination of gross profit on sales.

**c** Which of the three methods of pricing inventory would be most advantageous from an income tax standpoint during a period of rising prices? Comment on the significance of the inventory figure under the method you recommend with respect to current replacement cost.

*10B-4* On May 15, Year 4, an early morning fire destroyed the entire inventory of Suburban Associates. The inventory was stored in a rented warehouse; the offices occupied by the company were not damaged and the accounting records were intact. Suburban Associates did not maintain perpetual inventory records, and the last physical inventory taken had been on December 31 of the prior year.

An estimate of the inventory value at May 15, the date of the fire, must be prepared in order to file an insurance claim. The following income statement for the prior year is available to aid you in estimating the amount of the inventory at the date of the fire.

***SUBURBAN ASSOCIATES***
***Income Statement***
***For the Year Ended December 31, Year 3***

| | | |
|---|---|---|
| *Net sales* | | *$740,000* |
| *Cost of goods sold:* | | |
| *Inventory, Jan. 1* | *$144,000* | |
| *Purchases* | *520,000* | |
| *Cost of goods available for sale* | *$664,000* | |
| *Less: Inventory, Dec. 31* | *163,000* | *501,000* |
| *Gross profit on sales* | | *$239,000* |
| *Expenses* | | *149,000* |
| *Net income* | | *$ 90,000* |

**Other data** Included in the purchases figure shown in the income statement was $12,600 of office equipment which Suburban Associates had acquired late in December for its own use from a competing concern which was quitting business. The accountant of Suburban Associates had not understood the nature of this transaction and had recorded it by debiting the Purchases account. The office equipment, however, was not included in the inventory at December 31, Year 3.

The accounting records revealed the merchandise transactions from December 31, Year 3, to the date of the fire to be: sales, \$306,000; sales returns and allowances, \$2,700; transportation-in, \$1,800; purchases, \$196,200; purchase returns and allowances, \$3,600.

**Instructions**

**a** Prepare a report directed to the insurance adjuster summarizing your findings. Include an estimate of the inventory value as of the date of the fire and a computation of the applicable gross profit rate.

**b** Explain how the gross profit method of estimating inventories may be used other than in case of a fire loss.

*10B-5* Toy Castle, a retail business, had net sales during January of \$32,600. Purchases of merchandise from suppliers during January amounted to \$20,620. Of these January purchases, invoices totaling \$13,620 were paid during the month; the remaining January invoices totaling \$7,000 were still unpaid at January 31. The merchandise purchased during January had a retail sales value of \$29,500.

On January 1 the merchandise on hand represented a cost of \$21,200 as determined by the year-end physical inventory. The retail sales value of this inventory was \$32,000. The retail selling price was plainly marked on every item of merchandise in the store.

At January 31 the manager of Toy Castle wished to estimate the cost of inventory on hand without taking time to count the merchandise and look up the cost prices as shown on purchase invoices.

**Instructions**

**a** Use the retail inventory method to estimate the cost of the inventory at January 31.

**b** What effect, if any, does the fact that January purchase invoices in the amount of \$7,000 were unpaid at January 31 have upon the determination of the amount of inventory at January 31?

*10B-6* A perpetual inventory system is used by Vista Company and an inventory record card is maintained for each type of product in stock. The following transactions show the beginning inventory, the purchases, and the sales of product KR9 for the month of May.

| | | | |
|---|---|---|---|
| May | 1 | *Balance on hand, 20 units, cost \$40 each* | *\$800* |
| | 5 | *Sale, 8 units, sales price \$60 each* | *480* |
| | 6 | *Purchase, 20 units, cost \$45 each* | *900* |
| | 21 | *Sale, 10 units, sales price \$60 each* | *600* |
| | 31 | *Sale, 15 units, sales price \$65 each* | *975* |

**Instructions**

**a** Record the beginning inventory, the purchases, the cost of goods sold, and the running balance on an inventory record card like the one illustrated on page 415. Use the first-in, first-out method.

**b** Assume that all sales were made on credit. Compute the total sales and the total cost of goods sold of product KR9 for May. Prepare an entry in general journal form to record these sales and a second entry to record the cost of goods sold for the month of May.

**c** Compute the gross profit on sales of product KR9 for the month of May.

*10B-7* The owner's equity as shown in the balance sheets prepared by Video Games for the last three years was as follows: December 31, Year 8, \$560,000; December 31, Year 9, \$676,500; and December 31, Year 10, \$787,800.

The income statements for Years 9 and 10 were as follows:

| | Year 10 | Year 9 |
|---|---|---|
| *Net sales* | *$879,500* | *$835,500* |
| *Cost of goods sold:* | | |
| *Beginning inventory* | *$123,400* | *$110,200* |
| *Net purchases* | *540,200* | *501,200* |
| *Cost of goods available for sale* | *$663,600* | *$611,400* |
| *Ending inventory* | *140,600* | *123,400* |
| *Cost of goods sold* | *$523,000* | *$488,000* |
| *Gross profit on sales* | *$356,500* | *$347,500* |
| *Expenses* | *245,200* | *231,000* |
| *Net income* | *$111,300* | *$116,500* |

Samuel Peterson, accountant for Video Games, decided early in Year 11 to make a review of the documents and procedures used in taking the physical inventory at December 31, Year 9 and Year 10. His investigation revealed two questionable items as indicated below:

(1) Merchandise shipped to a customer on December 31, Year 9, F.O.B. shipping point, was included in the physical inventory at December 31, Year 9. The cost of the merchandise was $2,800 and the sales price was $4,500. Because of the press of year-end work, the sales invoice was not prepared until January 8, Year 10. On that date the sale was recorded as a January, Year 10, transaction in the sales journal, and the invoice was mailed to the customer.

(2) Merchandise with a cost of $12,200 which had been received on December 31, Year 9, had been included in the inventory taken on that date, although the purchase was not recorded until January 8, Year 10, when the vendor's invoice arrived. The invoice was then recorded in the purchases journal as a January transaction.

**Instructions**

**a** Prepare corrected income statements for the periods ended December 31, Year 9 and Year 10. (You may find it helpful to set up T accounts for sales, Year 9, and Sales, Year 10; Purchases, Year 9, and Purchases, Year 10; and Inventory, December 31, Year 9.)

**b** Compute corrected amounts for owner's equity at December 31, Year 9 and Year 10. (No withdrawals were made by the owner during these two years.)

## BUSINESS DECISION PROBLEM 10

You are the sales manager of Import Motors, an automobile dealership specializing in European imports. Among the automobiles in Import Motors' showroom are two Italian sports cars, which are identical in every respect except for color; one is red and the other white. The red car had been ordered last February, at a cost of $6,300 American dollars. The white car had been ordered early last March, but because of a revaluation of the Italian lira relative to the dollar, the white car had cost only $5,850 American dollars. Both cars arrived in the United States on the same boat and had just been delivered to your showroom. Since the cars were identical except for color and both colors were equally popular, you had listed both cars at the same suggested retail price, $9,000.

Smiley Miles, one of your best salesmen, comes into your office with a proposal. He has a customer in the showroom who wants to buy the red car for $9,000. However, when Miles pulled the inventory card on the red car to see what options were included, he happened to notice the inventory card of the white car. Import Motors, like most automobile dealerships, uses the specific identification method to value inventory. Consequently, Miles noticed that the red car had cost $6,300, while the white one had cost Import Motors only $5,850. This gave Miles the idea for the following proposal.

"If I sell the red car for $9,000, Import Motors makes a gross profit of $2,700. But if you'll let me discount that white car $150, I think I can get my customer to buy that one instead. If I sell the white car for $8,850, the gross profit will be $3,000, so Import Motors is $300 better off than if I sell the red car for $9,000. Since I came up with this plan, I feel I should get part of the benefit, so Import Motors should split the extra $300 with me. That way, I'll get an extra $150 commission, and the company still makes $150 more than if I sell the red car."

**Instructions**

**a** Prepare a schedule which shows the total revenue, cost of goods sold, and gross profit to Import Motors if ***both*** cars are sold for $9,000 each.

**b** Prepare a schedule showing the revenue, cost of goods sold, and gross profit to Import Motors if both cars are sold but Miles' plan is adopted and the white car is sold for $8,850. Assume the red car is still sold for $9,000. To simplify comparison of this schedule to the one prepared in part **a**, include the extra $150 commission to Miles in the cost of goods sold of the part **b** schedule.

**c** Write out your decision whether or not to accept Miles's proposal, and explain to Miles why the proposal either would or would not be to the advantage of Import Motors. (Hint: Refer to your schedules prepared in parts **a** and **b** in your explanation.)

# 11

# PLANT AND EQUIPMENT: DEPRECIATION

## PLANT AND EQUIPMENT

The term ***plant and equipment*** is used to describe long-lived assets acquired for use in the operation of the business and not intended for resale to customers. Among the more common examples are land, buildings, machinery, furniture and fixtures, office equipment, and automobiles. A delivery truck in the showroom of an automobile dealer is inventory; when this same truck is sold to a drugstore for use in making deliveries to customers, it becomes a unit of plant and equipment.

The term ***fixed assets*** has long been used in accounting literature to describe all types of plant and equipment. This term, however, has virtually disappeared from the published financial statements of large corporations. ***Plant and equipment*** appears to be a more descriptive term. Another alternative title used on many corporation balance sheets is ***property, plant, and equipment.***

### Plant and equipment represent bundles of services to be received

It is convenient to think of a plant asset as a bundle of services to be received by the owner over a period of years. Ownership of a delivery truck, for example, may provide about 100,000 miles of transportation. The cost of the delivery truck is customarily entered in a plant and equipment account entitled Delivery Truck, which in essence represents payment in advance for several years of transportation service. Similarly, a building may be regarded as payment in advance for several years' supply of housing services. As the years go by, these services are utilized by the business and the cost of the plant asset is gradually transferred into depreciation expense.

An awareness of the similarity between plant assets and prepaid expenses is essential to an understanding of the accounting process by which the cost of plant assets is allocated to the years in which the benefits of ownership are received.

## Major categories of plant and equipment

Plant and equipment items are often classified into the following groups:

1 Tangible plant assets. The term ***tangible*** denotes physical substance, as exemplified by land, a building, or a machine. This category may be subdivided into two distinct classifications:
  a Plant property subject to depreciation; included are plant assets of limited useful life such as buildings and office equipment.
  b Land. The only plant asset not subject to depreciation is land, which has an unlimited term of existence.
2 Intangible assets. Examples are patents, copyrights, trademarks, franchises, organization costs, leaseholds, and goodwill. Current assets such as accounts receivable or prepaid rent are not included in the intangible classification, even though they are lacking in physical substance. The term ***intangible assets*** is used to describe assets which are used in the operation of the business but have no physical substance, and are noncurrent.

## Accounting problems relating to plant and equipment

Some major accounting problems relating to plant and equipment are indicated by the following questions:

1 How is the cost of plant and equipment determined?
2 How should the costs of plant and equipment be allocated against revenue?
3 How should expenditures for repairs and maintenance be treated?
4 How does inflation affect the measurement of depreciation expense?
5 Should financial statements include disclosure of depreciation computed on the basis of replacement cost?
6 How should disposal of plant assets be recorded?

We are presently concerned with answering the first of these questions; an understanding of how the cost of plant and equipment is determined will be helpful in subsequent study of depreciation.

## Determining the cost of plant and equipment

The cost of plant and equipment includes all expenditures reasonable and necessary in acquiring the asset and placing it in a position and condition for use in the operations of the business. Only ***reasonable*** and ***necessary*** expenditures should be included. For example, if the company's truck driver receives a traffic ticket while hauling a new machine to the plant, the traffic fine is ***not*** part of the cost of the new machine. If the machine is dropped and damaged while being unloaded, the cost of repairing the damage should be recognized as expense in the current period and should ***not*** be added to the cost of the machine.

Cost is most easily determined when an asset is purchased for cash. The cost of the asset is then equal to the cash outlay necessary in acquiring the asset plus any expenditures for freight, insurance while in transit, installation, trial runs, and any other costs necessary to make ***the asset ready for use.*** If plant assets are purchased on the installment plan or by issuance of notes payable, the interest element or carrying charge should be recorded as interest expense and ***not*** as part of the cost of the plant assets.

This principle of including in the cost of a plant asset all the incidental charges necessary to put the asset in use is illustrated by the following example. A factory in Minneapolis orders a machine from a San Francisco tool manufacturer at a list price of $10,000, with terms of 2/10, n/30. A sales tax of 6% must be paid, also freight charges of $1,250. Transportation from the railroad station to the factory costs $150, and installation labor amounts to $400. The cost of the machine to be entered in the Machinery account is computed as follows:

***Items included in cost of machine***

| | |
|---|---|
| *List price of machine* | *$10,000* |
| *Less: Cash discount (2% × $10,000)* | *200* |
| *Net cash price* | *$ 9,800* |
| *Sales tax (6% × $9,800)* | *588* |
| *Freight* | *1,250* |
| *Transportation from railroad station to factory* | *150* |
| *Installation labor* | *400* |
| *Cost of machine* | *$12,188* |

Why should all the incidental charges relating to the acquisition of a machine be included in its cost? Why not treat these incidental charges as expenses of the period in which the machine is acquired?

The answer is to be found in the basic accounting principle of ***matching costs and revenue.*** The benefits of owning the machine will be received over a span of years, 10 years, for example. During those 10 years the operation of the machine will contribute to revenue. Consequently, the total costs of the machine should be recorded in the accounts as an asset and allocated against the revenue of the 10 years. All costs incurred in acquiring the machine are costs of the services to be received from using the machine.

**Land** When land is purchased, various incidental costs are generally incurred, in addition to the purchase price. These additional costs may include commissions to real estate brokers, escrow fees, legal fees for examining and insuring the title, delinquent taxes paid by the purchaser, and fees for surveying, draining, clearing, grading, and landscaping the property. All these expenditures are part of the cost of the land. Special assessments for local improvements, such as the paving of a street or the installation of sewers, should also be charged to the Land account, for the reason that a more or less permanent value is being added to the land.

***Apportionment of a lump-sum purchase*** Separate ledger accounts are necessary for land and buildings, because buildings are subject to depreciation and land is not. The treatment of land as a nondepreciable asset is based on the premise that land used as a building site has an unlimited life. When land and building are purchased for a lump sum, the purchase price must be apportioned between the land and the building. An appraisal may be necessary for this purpose. Assume, for example, that land and a building are purchased for a bargain price of $100,000. The apportionment of this cost on the basis of an appraisal may be made as follows:

*Apportioning cost between land and building*

| | Value per Appraisal | Percentage of Total | Apportionment of Cost |
|---|---|---|---|
| *Land* | *$ 48,000* | *40%* | *$ 40,000* |
| *Building* | *72,000* | *60%* | *60,000* |
| *Total* | *$120,000* | *100%* | *$100,000* |

Sometimes a tract of land purchased as a building site has on it an old building which is not suitable for the buyer's use. The Land account should be charged with the entire purchase price ***plus any costs incurred in tearing down or removing the building.*** Proceeds received from sale of the materials salvaged from the old building are recorded as a credit in the Land account.

Land acquired as a future building site should be reported under Investments or under Other Assets, rather than as part of Plant and Equipment, because it is not currently being used in operations.

**Land improvements** Improvements to real estate such as driveways, fences, parking lots, and sprinkler systems have a limited life and are therefore subject to depreciation. For this reason they should be recorded not in the Land account but in a separate account entitled Land Improvements. On the other hand, any improvements such as grading or leveling, which will last indefinitely and are not to be depreciated, are entered in the Land account.

**Buildings** Old buildings are sometimes purchased with the intention of repairing them prior to placing them in use. Repairs made under these circumstances are charged to the Buildings account. After the building has been placed in use, ***ordinary repairs*** are considered as maintenance expense when incurred.

When a building is constructed by the business itself, rather than being purchased, cost includes the materials and labor used plus an equitable portion of overhead or other indirect costs, such as executive salaries. Any other outlays specifically relating to the construction such as architectural fees, insurance during the construction period, and building permits should also be included in the cost of the building. A building or machine constructed by a company for its own use should be recorded in the accounts at cost, not at the price which might have been paid to outsiders if the asset had been acquired through purchase.

## Capital expenditures and revenue expenditures

The term ***expenditure*** means making a payment or incurring an obligation to make a future payment for an asset or service received. The acquisition of an asset (such as an automobile) or of a service (such as repairs to the automobile) may be for cash or on credit. In either situation the transaction is properly referred to as an expenditure.

Expenditures for the purchase or expansion of plant assets are called ***capital expenditures*** and are recorded in asset accounts. Expenditures for ordinary repairs, maintenance, fuel, and other items necessary to the ownership and use of plant and equipment are called ***revenue expenditures*** and are recorded by debits to expense accounts. The charge to an expense account is based on the assumption that the benefits from the expenditure will be used up in the current period, and the cost should therefore be deducted from the revenue of the current period in determining the net income.

A business may purchase many items which will benefit several accounting periods, but which have a relatively low cost. Examples of such items include auto batteries, wastebaskets, and pencil sharpeners. Such items are theoretically capital expenditures, but if they are recorded as assets in the accounting records it will be necessary to compute and record the related depreciation expense in future periods. We have previously mentioned the idea that the extra work involved in developing more precise accounting information should be weighed against the benefits that result. Thus, for reasons of convenience and economy, expenditures which are ***not material*** in dollar amount are treated in the accounting records as expenses of the current period. In brief, ***any material expenditure that will benefit several accounting periods is considered a capital expenditure. Any expenditure that will benefit only the current period or that is not material in amount is referred to as a revenue expenditure.***

Careful distinction between capital and revenue expenditures is important in the determination of net income. If the cost of constructing a new building, for example, is recorded as ***ordinary repairs expense*** (a revenue expenditure), the net income of the current period will be understated. The net income of future periods will be overstated because of the absence of depreciation expense applicable to the unrecorded asset.

Many companies develop formal policy statements defining capital and revenue expenditures as a guide toward consistent accounting practice from year to year. These policy statements often set a minimum dollar limit for a capital expenditure (such as $100 or $200).

Among the more common types of ***capital expenditures*** are:

1 Acquisition cost of plant and equipment, including freight, sales tax, and installation charges. When secondhand property is purchased, the cost of any repairs made to put the property in good operating condition ***before*** placing it in use is also considered as a capital expenditure and is charged to the asset account.
2 Additions. If a building is enlarged by adding a new wing or a mezzanine floor, the benefits from the expenditure will be received over a period of years, and the outlay should be debited to the asset account.
3 Betterments. The replacement of a stairway with an escalator is an example of an expenditure for a betterment or improvement which will yield benefits over a period of years and should therefore be charged to the asset account.

Among the more common types of ***revenue expenditures*** relating to plant and equipment are the repairs, maintenance, lubrication, cleaning, and inspection necessary to keep an asset in good working condition. The term ***ordinary repairs*** is often used to include all expenditures of this type. The cost of replacing small component parts of an asset (such as window panes in a building or tires and battery in an automobile) are also included in ordinary repairs.

Any expenditure made for the purpose of maintaining a plant asset in normally efficient working condition is an expense and will appear on the income statement as a deduction from the revenue of the current period. The treatment of an expenditure as a deduction from the revenue of the current period is the reason for the term revenue expenditure.

**Effect of errors in distinguishing between capital and revenue expenditures** Because a capital expenditure is recorded by debiting an asset account, the transaction has no immediate effect upon net income. However, the depreciation of the amount entered in the asset account will be reflected as an expense in future periods. A revenue expenditure, on the other hand, is recorded by debiting an expense account and therefore represents an immediate deduction from earnings in the current period.

If a capital expenditure is erroneously recorded as a revenue expenditure, as, for example, the cost of a new typewriter charged to the Office Expense account, the result will be an understatement of the current year's net income. If the error is not corrected, the net income of subsequent years will be overstated because no depreciation expense will be recognized during the years in which the typewriter is used.

If a revenue expenditure is erroneously treated as a capital expenditure, as, for example, a payment for truck repairs charged to the asset account, Delivery Truck, the result will be an overstatement of the current year's net income. If the error is not corrected, the net income of future years will be understated because of excessive depreciation charges based on the inflated amount of the Delivery Truck account.

These examples indicate that a careful distinction between capital and revenue expenditures is essential to attainment of one of the most fundamental objectives of accounting—the determination of net income for each year of operation of a business.

ILLUSTRATIVE CASE During an annual audit of Bowden Company, a CPA firm was reviewing entries in the general journal. An entry that caught the attention of Carol Jones, CPA, consisted of a debit to Office Furniture and a credit to Notes Payable for $42,000. Upon investigation, Jones learned that the transaction was the acquisition of a hand-carved clock from James Burns, a long-time employee. Burns had retired after 40 years of distinguished service with Bowden Company. His hobby for many years had been the building of hand-carved clocks. At the time of his retirement, the Company, at its president's suggestion, purchased one of the clocks from Burns at a price of $42,000, giving in payment the company's 12%, five-year note payable.

The investigation of the transaction by Carol Jones indicated that the commercial value of the clock was about $400. Jones therefore advised the company to transfer the $42,000 expenditure out of the Office Furniture account and into Employee Compensation.

### Extraordinary repairs

The term ***extraordinary repairs*** has a specific meaning in accounting terminology; it means a reconditioning or major overhaul that will extend the useful life of a plant asset beyond the original estimate. For example, a new automobile may be depreciated on the basis of an estimated useful life of four years. Assume that after three years of use, a decision is made to install a new engine in the automobile and thereby to extend its overall useful life from the original estimate of four years to a total of six years.

An extraordinary repair of this type may be recorded by debiting the Accumulated Depreciation account. This entry is sometimes explained by the argument that the extraordinary repair cancels out some of the depreciation previously recorded. The effect of this reduction (debit entry) in the Accumulated Depreciation account is to ***increase*** the carrying value of the asset by the cost of the extraordinary repair. Since an extraordinary repair causes an increase in the carrying value of the asset and has no immediate direct effect upon net income, it may be regarded as a form of capital expenditure.

To expand the above example of an extraordinary repair to an automobile, assume the following data: on January 1, 1982, a new automobile was acquired at a cost of $8,000; estimated useful life, four years; salvage value, zero; annual depreciation expense, $2,000. Three years later on December 31, 1984, extraordinary repairs (a new engine) were made at a cost of $2,200. Estimated useful life of the automobile beyond this date was thereby increased from the original estimate of one year to a revised estimate of three more years. The ledger accounts will appear as follows after recording these events.

*Extraordinary repair charged to Accumulated Depreciation*

**Automobile**

| | | | |
|---|---|---|---|
| *Jan. 1, 1984* | *8,000* | | |

**Accumulated Depreciation**

| | | | |
|---|---|---|---|
| *Dec. 31, 1984* | *2,200* | *Dec. 31, 1982* | *2,000* |
| | | *Dec. 31, 1983* | *2,000* |
| | | *Dec. 31, 1984* | *2,000* |

The carrying value of the automobile is now $4,200, and the balance sheet presentation will be as follows on December 31, 1984.

*Increased book value for depreciable asset*

| | | |
|---|---|---|
| *Plant and equipment:* | | |
| *Automobile* . . . . . . . . . . | *$8,000* | |
| *Less: Accumulated depreciation* . . . . . . | *3,800* | *$4,200* |

In the remaining three years of estimated life for the automobile, the annual depreciation expense will be $1,400 (carrying value $4,200 ÷ 3). Three years later at the end of 1987, the automobile will be fully depreciated, and the Accumulated Depreciation account (illustrated below) will show a credit balance of $8,000 (credits of $10,200 less debits of $2,200).

*Total depreciation equals total cost incurred*

**Accumulated Depreciation**

| | | | |
|---|---|---|---|
| Dec. 31, 1984 | 2,200 | Dec. 31, 1982 | 2,000 |
| | | Dec. 31, 1983 | 2,000 |
| | | Dec. 31, 1984 | 2,000 |
| | | Dec. 31, 1985 | 1,400 |
| | | Dec. 31, 1986 | 1,400 |
| | | Dec. 31, 1987 | 1,400 |

The valuation account, Accumulated Depreciation, now exactly offsets the asset account and no more depreciation can be taken. Observe that the total depreciation recorded during the six years the automobile was in use amounts to $10,200; this agrees exactly with the total expended for the automobile and for the extraordinary repair. In other words, these two capital expenditures have been transformed into expense over a period of six years, during which the business was receiving the benefits from the expenditures.

## DEPRECIATION

### Allocating the cost of plant and equipment over the years of use

Plant assets, with the exception of land, are of use to a company for only a limited number of years, and the cost of each plant asset is allocated as expense among the years in which it is used. Accountants use the term ***depreciation*** to describe this gradual conversion of the cost of a plant asset into expense. Depreciation, as the term is used in accounting, does not mean the decrease in market value of a plant asset over a period of time. ***Depreciation means the allocation of the cost of a plant asset to the periods in which services are received from the asset.***

When a delivery truck is purchased, its cost is first recorded as an asset. This cost becomes expense over a period of years through the accounting process of depreciation. When gasoline is purchased for the truck, the price paid for each tankful is immediately recorded as expense. In theory, both outlays (for the truck and for a tank of gas) represent the acquisition of assets, but since it is reasonable to assume that a tankful of gasoline will be consumed in the accounting period in which it is purchased, we record the outlay for gasoline as an expense immediately. It is important to recognize, however, that ***both the outlay for the truck and the payment for the gasoline become expense in the period or periods in which each renders services.***

A separate Depreciation Expense account and a separate Accumulated Depreciation account are generally maintained for each group of depreciable assets such as factory buildings, delivery equipment, and office equipment so that a proper allocation of depreciation expense can be made between functional areas of activity such as sales and manufacturing. Depreciation on manufacturing facilities is not necessarily an expense of the period in which it is recorded; the depreciation charge is first embodied in the inventory of finished goods manufactured, and the cost of this inventory is later deducted from revenue as an expense of the period when the goods are sold.

Depreciation differs from most expenses in that it does not require a cash payment at or near the time it is recorded. The entry to record depreciation (a debit to Depreciation Expense and a credit to Accumulated Depreciation) has no effect on current assets or current liabilities. However, when depreciable assets wear out, a large cash payment must be made in order to replace them.

Because of the noncash nature of depreciation expense and because the dollar amount is materially affected by the depreciation method selected, it is desirable that the total amount of depreciation expense for the year be disclosed in the income statement.

### Depreciation not a process of valuation

Accounting records do not purport to show the constantly fluctuating market values of plant and equipment. Occasionally the market value of a building may rise substantially over a period of years because of a change in the price level, or for other reasons. Depreciation is continued, however, regardless of the increase in market value. The accountant recognizes that the building will render useful services for only a limited number of years, and that its full cost must be allocated as expense of those years regardless of fluctuations in market value.

The ***book value*** or ***carrying value*** of a plant asset is its cost minus the related accumulated depreciation. Plant assets are shown in the balance sheet at their book values, representing the portion of their cost which will be allocated to expense in future periods. Accumulated depreciation represents the portion of the assets' cost which has already been recognized as expense.

### Accumulated depreciation does not consist of cash

Many readers of financial statements who have not studied accounting mistakenly believe that accumulated depreciation accounts represent money accumulated for the purpose of buying new equipment when the present equipment wears out. Perhaps the best way to combat such mistaken notions is to emphasize that a credit balance in an accumulated depreciation account represents the ***expired cost*** of assets acquired in the past. The amounts credited to the accumulated depreciation account could, as an alternative, have been credited directly to the plant and equipment account. An accumulated depreciation account has a ***credit*** balance; it does not represent an asset; and it cannot be used in any way to pay for new equipment. To buy a new plant asset requires cash; the total amount of cash owned by a company is shown by the asset account for cash.

## Causes of depreciation

There are two major causes of depreciation, physical deterioration and obsolescence.

**Physical deterioration** Physical deterioration of a plant asset results from use, and also from exposure to sun, wind, and other climatic factors. When a plant asset has been carefully maintained, it is not uncommon for the owner to claim that the asset is as "good as new." Such statements are not literally true. Although a good repair policy may greatly lengthen the useful life of a machine, every machine eventually reaches the point at which it must be discarded. In brief, the making of repairs does not lessen the need for recognition of depreciation.

**Obsolescence** The term ***obsolescence*** means the process of becoming out of date or obsolete. An airplane, for example, may become obsolete even though it is in excellent physical condition; it becomes obsolete because better planes of superior design and performance have become available. Obsolescence relates to the capacity of a plant asset to render services to a particular company for a particular purpose.

The usefulness of plant assets may also be reduced because the rapid growth of a company renders such assets inadequate. Inadequacy of a plant asset may necessitate replacement with a larger unit even though the asset is in good physical condition and is not obsolete. Obsolescence and inadequacy are often closely associated; both relate to the opportunity for economical and efficient use of an asset rather than to its physical condition. Obsolescence is probably a more significant factor than physical deterioration in putting an end to the usefulness of most depreciable assets. Current accounting practice, however, does not usually attempt to separate the effects of physical deterioration and obsolescence.

## Methods of computing depreciation

A business need not use the same method of depreciation for all its various assets. For example, a company may use straight-line depreciation on some assets and a declining-balance method for other assets. Management also has the option of using different methods of depreciation in the accounting records and financial statements than are employed in the determination of taxable income. The most widely used methods (straight-line, units-of-output, declining-balance, and sum-of-the-years'-digits) are explained and illustrated in the following sections.

**Straight-line method** The simplest and most widely used method of computing depreciation is the straight-line method. This method was described in Chapter 3 and has been used repeatedly in problems throughout this book. Under the straight-line method, an equal portion of the cost of the asset is allocated to each period of use; consequently, this method is most appropriate when usage of an asset is fairly uniform from year to year.

The computation of the periodic charge for depreciation is made by deducting the estimated ***residual*** or ***salvage value*** from the cost of the asset and dividing the remaining ***depreciable cost*** by the years of estimated useful life. For example, if a depreciable asset has a cost of $5,200, a residual value of $400, and an estimated useful life of four years, the annual computation of depreciation expense will be as follows:

$$\frac{\text{Cost} - \text{Residual Value}}{\text{Years of Useful Life}} = \frac{\$5{,}200 - \$400}{4} = \$1{,}200$$

This same depreciation computation is shown below in tabular form.

*Computing depreciation by straight-line method*

| | |
|---|---|
| *Cost of the depreciable asset* | *$5,200* |
| *Less: Estimated residual value (amount to be realized by sale of asset when it is retired from use)* | *400* |
| *Total amount to be depreciated (depreciable cost)* | *$4,800* |
| *Estimated useful life* | *4 years* |
| *Depreciation expense each year ($4,800 ÷ 4)* | *$1,200* |

The following schedule summarizes the accumulation of depreciation over the useful life of the asset. The amount to be depreciated is $4,800 (cost of $5,200 minus estimated residual value of $400).

*Constant annual depreciation expense*

***Depreciation Schedule: Straight-Line Method***

| *Year* | *Computation* | *Depreciation Expense* | *Accumulated Depreciation* | *Book Value* |
|---|---|---|---|---|
| | | | | *$5,200* |
| *First* | *($\frac{1}{4}$ × $4,800)* | *$1,200* | *$1,200* | *4,000* |
| *Second* | *($\frac{1}{4}$ × $4,800)* | *1,200* | *2,400* | *2,800* |
| *Third* | *($\frac{1}{4}$ × $4,800)* | *1,200* | *3,600* | *1,600* |
| *Fourth* | *($\frac{1}{4}$ × $4,800)* | *1,200* | *4,800* | *400* |
| | | *$4,800* | | |

Depreciation rates for various types of assets can conveniently be stated as percentages. In the above example the asset had an estimated life of four years, so the depreciation expense each year was $\frac{1}{4}$ of the depreciable amount. The fraction "$\frac{1}{4}$" is of course equivalent to an annual rate of 25%. Similarly, an asset with a 20-year life would call for annual depreciation expense of $\frac{1}{20}$, or 5%. A 10-year life would require a depreciation rate of $\frac{1}{10}$, or 10% and an eight-year life a depreciation rate of $\frac{1}{8}$, or $12\frac{1}{2}$%.

In the preceding illustration we assumed that the company maintained its accounts on a calendar-year basis and that the asset was acquired on January 1, the beginning of the accounting period. If the asset had been acquired sometime during the year, on October 1 for example, it would have been in use for only three months, or $\frac{3}{12}$ of a year. Consequently, the depreciation to be recorded at December 31 would be only $\frac{3}{12}$ of $1,200, or $300. Stated more precisely, the depreciation expense in this situation is computed as follows: $\frac{3}{12} \times 25\% \times \$4{,}800 = \$300$.

In practice, the possibility of residual value is sometimes ignored and the annual depreciation charge computed by dividing the total cost of the asset by the number of years of estimated useful life. This practice may be justified in those cases in which residual value is not material and is difficult to estimate accurately. Under this approach the yearly depreciation expense in the above example would be $5,200 ÷ 4, or $1,300. The percentage rate would still be 25%, since one-fourth of the depreciable amount becomes expense each year.

**Units-of-output method** For certain kinds of assets, more equitable allocation of the cost can be obtained by dividing the cost (minus salvage value, if significant) by the estimated units of output rather than by the estimated years of useful life. A truck line or bus company, for example, might compute depreciation on its vehicles by a mileage basis. If a truck costs $11,000 and has a residual value of $1,000 and a useful life of 100,000 miles, the depreciation rate per mile of operation is 10 cents ($10,000 ÷ 100,000). This calculation of the depreciation rate may be stated as follows:

$$\frac{\text{Cost} - \text{Residual Value}}{\text{Estimated Units of Output (Miles)}} = \text{Depreciation per Unit of Output (Mile)}$$

or

$$\frac{\$11{,}000 - \$1{,}000}{100{,}000 \text{ miles}} = \$0.10 \text{ depreciation per mile}$$

At the end of each year, the amount of depreciation to be recorded would be determined by multiplying the 10-cent rate by the number of miles the truck had operated during the year. This method is suitable only when the total units of output of the asset over its entire useful life can be estimated with reasonable accuracy.

**Accelerated depreciation methods** The term ***accelerated depreciation*** means recognition of relatively large amounts of depreciation in the early years of use and reduced amounts in the later years. Many types of plant and equipment are most efficient when new and therefore provide more and better services in the early years of useful life. If we assume that the benefits derived from owning an asset are greatest in the early years when the asset is relatively new, then the amount of the asset's cost which we allocate as depreciation expense should be greatest in these same years. This is consistent with the basic accounting concept of matching costs with related revenue. Another reason for using accelerated depreciation is the pleasing prospect of reducing the current year's income tax burden by recognizing a relatively large amount of depreciation expense.

***Declining-balance method*** For income tax purposes one of the acceptable methods of "rapid write-off" of depreciable assets consists of doubling the normal rate of depreciation and applying this doubled rate each year to the undepreciated cost (book value) of the asset. The term ***double-declining-balance*** is often applied to this form of accelerated depreciation.

Assume, for example, that an automobile is acquired for business use at a cost of $8,000. Estimated useful life is four years; therefore, the depreciation rate under the straight-line method would be 25%. To depreciate the automobile by the double-declining-balance method, we double the straight-line rate of 25% and apply the doubled rate of 50% to the book value. Depreciation expense in the first year would then amount to $4,000. In the second year the depreciation expense would drop to $2,000, computed at 50% of the remaining book value of $4,000. In the third year depreciation would be $1,000, and in the fourth year only $500. The following table shows the allocation of cost under this method of depreciation.

***Depreciation Schedule: Declining-Balance Method***

*Accelerated depreciation: declining-balance*

| Year | Computation | Depreciation Expense | Accumulated Depreciation | Book Value |
|---|---|---|---|---|
| | | | | $8,000 |
| First | (50% × $8,000) | $4,000 | $4,000 | 4,000 |
| Second | (50% × $4,000) | 2,000 | 6,000 | 2,000 |
| Third | (50% × $2,000) | 1,000 | 7,000 | 1,000 |
| Fourth | (50% × $1,000) | 500 | 7,500 | 500 |

If the automobile is continued in use beyond the estimated life of four years, depreciation may be continued at the 50% rate on the book value. In the fifth year, for example, the depreciation expense would be $250 (50% × $500), and in the sixth year $125 (50% × $250). When the double-declining-balance method is used, the cost of a depreciable asset will never be entirely written off as long as the asset continues in use. Perhaps because of the existence of this undepreciated balance of original cost, the tax regulations do not require any deduction from original cost for residual value when this method of depreciation is used. However, if the asset has a residual value, depreciation must stop at this point. For example, if the $8,000 automobile illustrated above has a residual value of $800, the depreciation for the fourth year would be restricted to $200, which is the amount of depreciation required to reduce the carrying value of the automobile to its residual value. In working accounting problems involving the double-declining-balance method of depreciation, remember that depreciation expense is computed as a percentage of full original cost; residual value is not deducted.

If the asset in the above illustration had been acquired on April 1 rather than on January 1, depreciation for only nine months (April–December) would be recorded in the first year. The computation would be $\frac{9}{12}$ × (50% × $8,000), or $3,000. For the next calendar year the calculation would be 50% × ($8,000 − $3,000), or $2,500.

***Sum-of-the-years'-digits method*** This is another method of allocating a large portion of the cost of an asset to the early years of its use. The depreciation rate to be used is a fraction, of which the numerator is the remaining years of useful life (as of the beginning of the year) and the denominator is the sum of the years of useful life. Consider again the example of an automobile costing $8,000, having an estimated life of four years and an estimated residual value of $800. (Present income tax regulations require that residual value be taken into account when either the straight-line method or the sum-of-the-years'-digits method of depreciation is used.) Since the asset has an estimated life of four years, the denominator of the fraction will be 10, computed as follows: $1 + 2 + 3 + 4 = 10$. For the first year, the depreciation will be $\frac{4}{10} \times$ $7,200, or $2,880. For the second year, the depreciation will be $\frac{3}{10} \times$ $7,200, or $2,160; in the third year $\frac{2}{10} \times$ $7,200, or $1,440; and in the fourth year, $\frac{1}{10} \times$ $7,200, or $720. In tabular form this depreciation program will appear as follows:

***Depreciation Schedule: Sum-of-the-Years'-Digits Method***

*Accelerated depreciation: sum-of-the-years'-digits*

| *Year* | *Computation* | *Depreciation Expense* | *Accumulated Depreciation* | *Book Value* |
|---|---|---|---|---|
| | | | | *$8,000* |
| *First* | *($\frac{4}{10}$ × $7,200)* | *$2,880* | *$2,880* | *5,120* |
| *Second* | *($\frac{3}{10}$ × $7,200)* | *2,160* | *5,040* | *2,960* |
| *Third* | *($\frac{2}{10}$ × $7,200)* | *1,440* | *6,480* | *1,520* |
| *Fourth* | *($\frac{1}{10}$ × $7,200)* | *720* | *7,200* | *800* |

Assume that the asset being depreciated by the sum-of-the-years'-digits method was acquired on April 1 and the company maintains its accounts on a calendar-year basis. Since the asset was in use for only nine months during the first accounting period, the depreciation to be recorded in this first period will be for only $\frac{9}{12}$ of a full year, that is, $\frac{9}{12} \times$ $2,880, or $2,160. For the second accounting period the depreciation computation will be:

| | |
|---|---|
| *$\frac{3}{12}$ × ($\frac{4}{10}$ × $7,200)* | *$ 720* |
| *$\frac{9}{12}$ × ($\frac{3}{10}$ × 7,200)* | *1,620* |
| *Depreciation expense, second period* | *$2,340* |

A similar pattern of allocation will be followed for each accounting period of the asset's life.

**Depreciation for fractional periods** In the case of depreciable assets acquired sometime during the year, it is customary to figure depreciation to the nearest month. For example, if an asset is acquired on July 12, depreciation would be computed from July 1; if the asset had been acquired on July 18 (or any other date in the latter half of July), depreciation would be recorded for only five months (August through December) for the current calendar year.

Some businesses prefer to begin depreciation on the first of the month following the acquisition of a depreciable asset. This method, or any one of many similar variations, is acceptable so long as it is followed consistently.

## Revision of depreciation rates

Depreciation rates are based on estimates of the useful life of assets. These estimates of useful life are seldom precisely correct and sometimes are grossly in error. Consequently, the annual depreciation expense based on the estimated useful life may be either excessive or inadequate. What action should be taken when, after a few years of using a plant asset, it is decided that the asset actually is going to last for a considerably longer or shorter period than was originally estimated? When either of these situations arises, a revised estimate of useful life should be made and the periodic depreciation expense decreased or increased accordingly.

The procedure for correcting the depreciation program may be stated in a very few words: ***Spread the remaining undepreciated cost of the asset over the years of remaining useful life.*** The annual depreciation expense is increased or decreased sufficiently so that the depreciation program will be completed in accordance with the revised estimate of remaining useful life. The following data illustrate a revision which increases the estimate of useful life and thereby decreases the annual depreciation expense.

*Data prior to revision of depreciation rate*

| | |
|---|---|
| *Cost of asset* | *$10,000* |
| *Estimated useful life (no residual value)* | *10 years* |
| *Annual depreciation expense (prior to revision)* | *$ 1,000* |
| *Accumulated depreciation at end of six years ($1,000 × 6)* | *$ 6,000* |

At the beginning of the seventh year, it is decided that the asset will last for eight more years. The revised estimate of useful life is, therefore, a total of 14 years. The depreciation expense to be recognized for the seventh year and for each of the remaining years is $500, computed as follows:

*Revision of depreciation program*

| | |
|---|---|
| *Undepreciated cost at end of sixth year ($10,000 − $6,000)* | *$4,000* |
| *Revised estimate of remaining years of useful life* | *8 years* |
| *Revised amount of annual depreciation expense ($4,000 ÷ 8)* | *$ 500* |

The method described above for the revision of a depreciation program is generally used and is acceptable in the determination of taxable income. The Financial Accounting Standards Board also supports this approach for financial reporting purposes.

## Depreciation and income taxes

Different methods of depreciation may be used for the purpose of preparing financial statements and the purpose of preparing income tax returns. Many large corporations use straight-line depreciation in their financial statements, because this permits reporting higher earnings which in turn suggests that management is doing an efficient job. For income tax purposes, however, many businesses use an accelerated depreciation method.

**a** Based solely on the above information, about how much cash would you expect Jewel Company to have today? Explain the basis for your answer. (Bear in mind that the company had $15,000 cash after paying for the plant and equipment 20 years ago and that depreciation is a noncash expense.)

**b** What is the prospect for Jewel Company being able to pay for the new plant and equipment it needs? Include specific dollar amounts in your answer.

**c** On what grounds might the accounting measurement of net income by Jewel Company be criticized in the light of 20 years of operation in an inflationary environment?

## PROBLEMS

### Group A

*11A-1* Grain Products uses straight-line depreciation on all its depreciable assets. The accounts are adjusted and closed at the end of each calendar year. On January 2, Year 1, the corporation purchased machinery for cash at a cost of $143,280. Useful life was estimated to be 10 years and residual value $6,480.

After almost three years of using the machinery, the company decided in Year 3 that, in view of technological changes in the industry, the total estimated useful life of the machinery should be revised from 10 years to six years and that the residual scrap value estimate should be lowered from $6,480 to $4,320. The revised estimate of useful life was made prior to recording depreciation for the year ended December 31, Year 3.

**Instructions** Prepare general journal entries in chronological order for the above events, beginning with the purchase of the machinery on January 2, Year 1. Show separately the depreciation for each year from Year 1 to Year 3, inclusive.

*11A-2* Fontana Corporation, a newly organized business, purchased equipment at a cost of $146,560. The estimated life of these assets is five years and the residual value $2,560. The company is considering whether to use straight-line depreciation, the sum-of-the-years'-digits method, or the double-declining-balance method. Consideration is also being given to the possibility of using one method for the preparation of income tax returns and another method for financial statements to be sent to bankers and investors.

The president of Fontana Corporation informs you that the company wants to keep income taxes at a minimum during the coming year (Year 1), but to report the largest possible earnings in the company's first annual financial statements. The president believes that reporting high earnings in the first year will be helpful in obtaining bank loans or raising capital from other sources.

**Instructions**

**a** Compute the annual depreciation expense throughout the five-year life of the equipment under each of the three methods under consideration. (Use a work sheet with three money columns headed, respectively, Straight-line, Sum-of-the-years'-digits, and Double-declining-balance. Also show the total depreciation under each method and show in footnotes how the calculations were made.) Round off depreciation calculations to the nearest dollar.

**b** Advise the president of Fontana Corporation which method of depreciation should be used for income tax purposes and which method for the company's financial statements in order to achieve the stated objectives of holding income taxes to a minimum in Year 1 while showing the maximum earnings in the company's financial statements.

*11A-3* Included in the ledger of Angus-Lee was an account entitled Property, which had been used to record a variety of expenditures. At the end of Year 5, the Property account showed the following entries:

| | | |
|---|---|---|
| ***Debit entries:*** | | |
| *4/3 Amount paid to acquire building site* | | *$ 62,500* |
| *4/15 Cost of removing old unusable building from site* | | *5,000* |
| *9/30 Contract price for new building completed Sept. 30* | | *200,000* |
| *9/30 Insurance, inspection fees, and other costs directly related to construction of new building* | | *10,000* |
| *Total debits* | | *$277,500* |
| ***Credit entries:*** | | |
| *4/15 Proceeds from sale of old lumber and other material from demolition of old building* | *$ 7,500* | |
| *12/31 Depreciation for Year 5, computed at 5% of balance in Property account ($270,000). Debit was to Depreciation Expense* | *13,500* | |
| *Total credits* | | *21,000* |
| *12/31 Balance in Property account at year-end* | | *$256,500* |

**Instructions**

a Identify four errors made by Angus-Lee in accounting for plant assets and depreciation.

b Prepare a two-column schedule with column headings of Land and Buildings. Use this schedule to classify properly the debits and credits (other than depreciation) which Angus-Lee entered in its account entitled Property. For example, use the first line of your schedule to show in which account the debit of April 3 should be recorded.

Land 60,000

c Prepare a compound journal entry to correct the accounts according to the classification developed in **b.** This correcting entry should include a credit for $256,500 to close the Property account and replace it with more descriptive accounts. The entry will also include adjustment of the incorrect treatment of depreciation. Estimated life of the new building was 20 years; depreciation should be recognized for the three months the building was in use during the current year, using the straight-line method. The revenue and expense accounts have not been closed for the current year.

*11A-4* New machinery was acquired by White Company at a cost of $300,000. Useful life of the machinery was estimated to be five years, with residual salvage value of $6,000.

**Instructions** Compute the annual depreciation expense throughout the five-year life of the machinery under each of the following methods of depreciation:

a Straight-line

b Sum-of-the-years'-digits

c Double-declining-balance (Round calculations to nearest dollar.)

*11A-5* In the last few years Jayhawk Corporation has acquired four machines. At the time of acquiring each machine, different personnel were employed in the accounting department; consequently, various methods of depreciation have been adopted for the several machines. Information concerning the four machines may be summarized as follows:

| Machine | Date Acquired | Cost | Estimated Useful Life, Years | Estimated Residual Value | Method of Depreciation |
|---|---|---|---|---|---|
| A | Jan. 1, Year 8 | $ 97,200 | 6 | None | Declining-balance |
| B | June 30, Year 8 | 151,200 | 8 | 10% | Straight-line |
| C | Jan. 1, Year 9 | 100,800 | 10 | $1,800 | Sum-of-the-years'-digits |
| D | Jan. 1, Year 10 | 118,800 | 12 | None | Declining-balance |

**Instructions**

**a** Compute the amount of accumulated depreciation, if any, on each machine owned at December 31, Year 9. For machines A and D, assume that the depreciation rate was double the rate which would be applicable under the straight-line method.

**b** Prepare a depreciation schedule for use in the computation of the Year 10 depreciation expense. Use the following column headings:

| Machine | Method of Depreciation | Date of Acquisition | Cost | Estimated Residual Value | Amount to Be Depreciated | Useful Life, Years | Accumulated Depreciation, Dec. 31, Year 9 | Depreciation Expense, Year 10 |
|---|---|---|---|---|---|---|---|---|

**c** Prepare a journal entry to record the Year 10 depreciation expense.

*11A-6* On March 31, Year 1, Limestone Company purchased new machinery at a cost of $140,800. Depreciation has been computed by the straight-line method based on an estimated useful life of five years and residual scrap value of $12,800.

On January 2, Year 4, extraordinary repairs (which were almost equivalent to a rebuilding of the machinery) were performed at a cost of $30,400. Because of the thoroughgoing nature of these repairs, the normal life of the machinery was extended materially. The revised estimate of useful life was four years from January 1, Year 4.

**Instructions** Prepare journal entries to record the original purchase of the machinery; the provision for depreciation on December 31, Year 1, Year 2, and Year 3; the expenditure for the extraordinary repairs in January, Year 4; and the provision for depreciation on December 31, Year 4. Assume payment in cash for the machine and for the extraordinary repairs.

*11A-7* On July 1, Year 10, Skybolt, Inc., purchased a new machine at the advertised price of $144,000. The terms of payment were 2/10, n/30 and payment was made immediately, thus taking the available discount. The payment included a 4% state sales tax. On July 3, the machine was delivered; Skybolt, Inc., paid freight charges of $3,155.20 and assigned its own employees to the task of installation. The labor costs for installing the machine amounted to $10,080. During the process of installation, carelessness by a workman caused damage to an adjacent machine, with resulting repairs of $1,280.

On November 10, Year 10, after more than four months of satisfactory operations, the machine was thoroughly inspected, cleaned, and oiled at a cost of $1,680.

The useful life of the machine was estimated to be 10 years and the residual scrap value zero. The policy of Skybolt, Inc., is to use straight-line depreciation and to begin depreciation as of the first of the month in which a plant asset is acquired. During Year 10 and Year 11, however, numerous changes in the company's accounting personnel were responsible for a number of errors and deviations from policy.

At December 31, Year 11, the unaudited financial statements of Skybolt, Inc., showed the machine to be carried at a cost of $141,120 and the accumulated depreciation as $21,168. Net income reported for Year 10 was $396,800 and for Year 11 it was $442,400.

**Instructions**

**a** Prepare correct journal entries for all the above transactions from July 1 to December 31, Year 10. Include the year-end entry for depreciation and the related closing entry. The sales tax was $5,644.80.

**b** Compute the correct balances for the Machinery account and for the Accumulated Depreciation: Machinery account at December 31, Year 11.

**c** Compute revised figures for net income for Year 10 and Year 11. Disregard income taxes.

## Group B

*11B-1* Old Dominion Company adjusts and closes its accounts at the end of each calendar year and uses the straight-line method of depreciation on all its plant and equipment. On January 1, Year 1, machinery was purchased for cash at a cost of $427,350. Useful life was estimated to be 10 years and residual value $7,350.

Three years later in December, Year 3, after steady use of the machinery, the company decided that because of rapid technological change, the estimated total useful life should be revised from 10 years to 6 years. No change was made in the estimate of residual value. The revised estimate of useful life was decided upon prior to recording depreciation for the period ended December 31, Year 3.

**Instructions** Prepare journal entries in chronological order for the above events, beginning with the purchase of the machinery on January 1, Year 1. Show separately the depreciation for each year from Year 1 to Year 3, inclusive.

*11B-2* Hillside Company early in the current year purchased some hilly land with old abandoned buildings. The old buildings were removed, the land was leveled, and a new building was constructed. The company moved from its former rented quarters into the new building on October 1. Transactions relating to these events were recorded in an account entitled Property, which contained the following entries at the end of the current year. (See entries at top of page 458.)

**Instructions**

**a** List the errors made in the application of accounting principles or practices by Hillside Company.

**b** Prepare a three-column schedule with column headings of Entertainment Expense, Land, and Buildings. Use this schedule to classify properly the debits and credits (other than depreciation) which Hillside Company entered in its account entitled Property. For example, use the first line of your schedule to show in which account the debit of March 9 should be recorded.

**c** Prepare a compound journal entry to correct the accounts according to the classification developed in **b.** This correcting entry should include a credit for $392,400 to close the Property account and replace it with more descriptive accounts. The entry will also include adjustment of the incorrect treatment of depreciation. Estimated life of the new building was 25 years; depreciation should be recognized for the three months the building was in use during the current year, using the straight-line method. The revenue and expense accounts have not been closed for the current year.

| | | |
|---|---|---|
| ***Debit entries:*** | | |
| *3/9 Purchase for cash of building site* | | *$ 68,750* |
| *4/28 Payment for demolition of old building* | | *7,500* |
| *5/15 Payment for leveling of land* | | *25,000* |
| *9/28 Payment for insurance on building during construction* | | *15,000* |
| *9/28 Payment for new building completed today* | | *300,000* |
| *10/7 Payment to caterer for office party for employees, customers, and friends to celebrate the move to new building* | | *3,750* |
| *Total debits* | | *$420,000* |
| ***Credit entries:*** | | |
| *4/28 Cash received from sale of materials from demolished building* | *$11,250* | |
| *12/31 Depreciation for the current year, computed at 4% of balance in Property account ($408,750). Debit was to Depreciation Expense* | *16,350* | |
| *Total credits* | | *27,600* |
| *12/31 Balance in Property account at year-end* | | *$392,400* |

*11B-3* Del Mar Electronics acquired new equipment with an estimated useful life of five years. Cost of the equipment was $256,480 and the residual salvage value was estimated to be $4,480.

**Instructions** Compute the annual depreciation expense throughout the five-year life of the equipment under each of the following methods of depreciation:

**a** Straight-line
**b** Sum-of-the-years'-digits
**c** Double-declining-balance (Round computations to the nearest dollar.)

*11B-4* Insulation Systems acquired a new machine on April 1, 1981, at a cost of $528,000. The company has used the straight-line method of depreciation based on an estimated life of five years and a residual salvage value of $48,000.

On January 2, 1984, after almost three years of use, extraordinary repairs were made on the machine at a cost of $114,000. The repairs were virtually the equivalent of rebuilding the machine, and management believed that this thorough reconditioning would extend the normal life of the machine substantially. The revised estimate of useful life was four years from January 1, 1984.

**Instructions** Prepare general journal entries to record the original purchase of the machine; the provision for depreciation on December 31, 1981, 1982, and 1983; the expenditure for the extraordinary repairs in 1984; and the provision for depreciation on December 31, 1984. Assume payment in cash for the machine and for the extraordinary repairs.

*11B-5* During the last few years, Sunhill Corporation has acquired four costly machines but has given little consideration to depreciation policies. At the time of acquisition of each machine, a different accountant was employed; consequently, various methods of depreciation have been adopted for the several machines. Information concerning the four machines appears on page 459.

| Machine | Date Acquired | Cost | Estimated Useful Life, Years | Estimated Residual Value | Method of Depreciation |
|---|---|---|---|---|---|
| A | Jan. 1, Year 4 | $145,800 | 6 | None | Declining-balance |
| B | June 30, Year 4 | 302,400 | 8 | 10% | Straight-line |
| C | Jan. 1, Year 5 | 201,600 | 10 | $3,600 | Sum-of-the-years'-digits |
| D | Jan. 1, Year 6 | 237,600 | 12 | None | Declining-balance |

**Instructions**

**a** Compute the amount of accumulated depreciation, if any, on each machine at December 31, Year 5. For machines A and D, assume that the depreciation rate was double the rate which would be applicable under the straight-line method.

**b** Prepare a depreciation schedule for use in the computation of the depreciation expense. Use the following column headings:

| Machine | Method of Depreciation | Date of Acquisition | Cost | Estimated Residual Value | Amount to Be Depreciated | Useful Life, Years | Accumulated Depreciation, Dec. 31, Year 5 | Depreciation Expense, Year 6 |
|---|---|---|---|---|---|---|---|---|

**c** Prepare a journal entry to record the depreciation expense for Year 6.

*11B-6* Rialto Corporation purchased new machinery on July 1, Year 7, at the advertised price of $32,500. The terms of payment were 2/10, n/30 and payment was made immediately, including a 4% state sales tax on $31,850. On July 3, the machinery was delivered; Rialto Corporation paid freight charges of $608 and assigned its own employees to the task of installation. The labor costs for installing the machinery amounted to $2,268. During the process of installation, carelessness by a workman caused damage to an adjacent machine, with resulting repairs of $288.

On October 15, after more than three months of satisfactory operation, the machinery was thoroughly inspected, cleaned, and oiled at a cost of $378.

The useful life of the machinery was estimated to be 10 years and the residual scrap value to be zero. The policy of the Rialto Corporation is to use straight-line depreciation and to begin depreciation as of the first of the month in which a plant asset is acquired. During Year 7 and Year 8, however, numerous changes in the company's accounting personnel were responsible for a number of errors and deviations from policy.

Depreciation expense recorded on the machinery for Year 7 was $1,593 and for Year 8, $3,185. At December 31, Year 8, the unaudited financial statements of the Rialto Corporation showed the machinery to be carried at a cost of $31,850 and the accumulated depreciation as $4,778. Net income reported for Year 7 was $89,280 and for Year 8, $99,540.

**Instructions**

**a** Prepare entries in general journal form for all the above transactions from July 1 to December 31, Year 7. Include the year-end entry for depreciation and the related closing entry.

**b** Compute the correct balances for the Machinery account and for accumulated depreciation at December 31, Year 8.

**c** Compute revised figures for net income for Year 7 and Year 8. (The only errors in the reported net income figures are those indicated by information given in the problem.) Use a separate column for each year and begin with the reported net income for each year, followed by the necessary additions and deductions to arrive at corrected net income for each year. Disregard income taxes.

## BUSINESS DECISION PROBLEM 11

Samuel Slater is interested in buying a manufacturing business and has located two similar companies being offered for sale. Both companies are single proprietorships which began operations three years ago, each with invested capital of $400,000. A considerable part of the assets in each company is represented by a building with an original cost of $100,000 and an estimated life of 40 years, and by machinery with an original cost of $200,000 and an estimated life of 20 years. Residual value is negligible.

Bay Company uses straight-line depreciation and Cove Company uses fixed-percentage-on-declining-balance depreciation (double the straight-line rate). In all other respects the accounting policies of the two companies are quite similar. Neither company has borrowed from banks or incurred any indebtedness other than normal trade payables. The nature of products and other characteristics of operations are much the same for the two companies.

Audited financial statements for the three years show net income as follows:

| *Year* | *Bay Company* | *Cove Company* |
|---|---|---|
| *1* | *$ 62,000* | *$ 59,000* |
| *2* | *65,200* | *63,200* |
| *3* | *68,400* | *66,900* |
| *Totals* | *$195,600* | *$189,100* |

Slater asks your advice as to which company to buy. They are offered for sale at approximately the same price, and Slater is inclined to choose Bay Company because of its consistently higher earnings. On the other hand, the fact that Cove Company has more cash and a stronger working capital position is impressive. The audited financial statements show that withdrawals by the two owners have been approximately equal during the three-year life of the two companies.

**Instructions**

**a** Compute the depreciation recorded by each company in the first three years. Round off depreciation expense for each year to the nearest dollar.

**b** Write a memorandum to Slater advising which company in your judgment represents the more promising purchase. Give specific reasons to support your recommendation. Include a recomputation of the earnings of Cove Company by using straight-line depreciation in order to make its income statements comparable with those of Bay Company. Compare the earnings of the two companies year by year after such revision to a uniform basis.

# 12

# PLANT AND EQUIPMENT, NATURAL RESOURCES, AND INTANGIBLES

## Disposal of plant and equipment

When depreciable assets are disposed of at any date other than the end of the year, an entry should be made to record depreciation for the fraction of the year ending with the date of disposal. In the following illustrations of the disposal of items of plant and equipment, it is assumed that any necessary entries for fractional-period depreciation have been recorded.

As units of plant and equipment wear out or become obsolete, they must be scrapped, sold, or traded in on new equipment. Upon the disposal or retirement of a depreciable asset, the cost of the property is removed from the asset account, and the accumulated depreciation is removed from the related valuation account. Assume, for example, that office equipment purchased 10 years ago at a cost of $5,000 has been fully depreciated and is no longer useful. The entry to record the scrapping of the worthless equipment is as follows:

***Scrapping fully depreciated asset***

| | | |
|---|---|---|
| *Accumulated Depreciation: Office Equipment* | *5,000* | |
| *Office Equipment* | | *5,000* |
| *To remove from the accounts the cost and the accumulated depreciation on fully depreciated office equipment now being scrapped. No salvage value.* | | |

Once an asset has been fully depreciated, no more depreciation should be recorded on it, even though the property is in good condition and is continued in use. The objective of depreciation is to spread the ***cost*** of an asset over the periods of its usefulness; in no case can depreciation expense be greater than the amount paid for the asset. When a fully depreciated asset is continued in use beyond the original estimate of useful life, the asset account and the Accumulated Depreciation account should remain in the accounting records without further entries until the asset is retired.

**Gains and losses on disposal of plant and equipment** The *book value* (or *carrying value*) of a plant asset is its cost minus the total recorded depreciation, as shown by the Accumulated Depreciation account. For a fully depreciated asset with no salvage value, the book value is zero, since the credit balance in the Accumulated Depreciation account exactly offsets the debit balance in the asset account. If a depreciable asset is discarded before it is fully depreciated and there is no salvage value, a loss results in an amount equal to the book value of the asset. Since the residual value and useful life of plant assets are only estimates, it is not uncommon for plant assets to be sold at a price which differs from their book value at the date of disposal. When plant assets are sold, ***any gain or loss on the disposal is computed by comparing the book value with the amount received from the sale.*** A sales price in excess of the book value produces a gain; a sales price below the book value produces a loss. These gains or losses, if material in amount, should be shown as a separate item in the income statement in computing the income from operations.

***Disposal at a price above book value*** Assume that a machine originally cost $10,000 and that, after several years of use, depreciation has been recorded in the total amount of $8,000. The machine therefore has a book value (or undepreciated cost) of $2,000. Next, let us assume that this machine with a book value of $2,000 is sold for $3,000 cash. Since we are receiving $3,000 in cash, or $1,000 more than the book value of the machine, a gain of $1,000 is realized on the disposal of this asset. The entry to record this disposal of a plant asset is as follows:

*Gain on disposal of plant asset*

| | | |
|---|---|---|
| Cash | 3,000 | |
| Accumulated Depreciation: Machinery | 8,000 | |
| Machinery | | 10,000 |
| Gain on Disposal of Plant Assets | | 1,000 |
| To record sale of machinery at a price above book value. | | |

***Disposal at a price below book value*** Now assume that the same machine is sold for $500. The journal entry in this case would be as follows:

*Loss on disposal of plant asset*

| | | |
|---|---|---|
| Cash | 500 | |
| Accumulated Depreciation: Machinery | 8,000 | |
| Loss on Disposal of Plant Assets | 1,500 | |
| Machinery | | 10,000 |
| To record sale of machinery at a price below book value. | | |

***Disposal at a price equal to book value*** As a third example, assume that this same machine is sold for $2,000, the exact amount of its book value. The disposal of a depreciable asset at a price equal to book value would result in neither a gain nor a loss. The entry would be as follows:

*No gain or loss when disposal price equals book value*

| | | |
|---|---|---|
| *Cash* | *2,000* | |
| *Accumulated Depreciation: Machinery* | *8,000* | |
| *Machinery* | | *10,000* |
| *To record sale of machinery at a price equal to book value.* | | |

**Depreciation for fractional period before disposal** Most disposals of plant and equipment occur at dates other than the year-end. In such cases it is necessary to record depreciation for the fraction of the year ending with the date of disposal. Assume that straight-line depreciation is being used and that the accounts showed the following balances at December 31.

| | |
|---|---|
| *Office equipment* | *$20,000* |
| *Accumulated depreciation: office equipment* | *16,000* |

The credit balance of $16,000 in the Accumulated Depreciation account was the result of eight annual credits of $2,000 each. On the following March 31, the office equipment was sold for $1,000. No depreciation had been recorded since the accounts were adjusted and closed on December 31. Two entries are necessary at the time of disposing of the office equipment: one to record depreciation for the three months ending with the date of disposal, and a second to record the sale of the equipment.

*Record depreciation to date of disposal*

| | | |
|---|---|---|
| *Depreciation Expense: Office Equipment* | *500* | |
| *Accumulated Depreciation: Office Equipment* | | *500* |
| *To record depreciation for the three months prior to disposal of office equipment ($2,000 × $\frac{1}{4}$).* | | |

*. . . then record sale of the equipment*

| | | |
|---|---|---|
| *Cash* | *1,000* | |
| *Accumulated Depreciation: Office Equipment* | *16,500* | |
| *Loss on Disposal of Plant Assets* | *2,500* | |
| *Office Equipment* | | *20,000* |
| *To record sale of office equipment at less than book value.* | | |

## Trading in used assets on new

Certain types of depreciable assets, such as automobiles and office equipment, are customarily traded in on new assets of the same kind. The trade-in allowance granted by the dealer may differ materially from the book value of the old asset. If the dealer grants a trade-in allowance in excess of the book value of the asset being traded in, there is the suggestion of a gain being realized on the exchange. The evidence of a gain is not conclusive, however, because the list price of the new asset may purposely have been set higher than a realistic cash price to permit the offering of inflated trade-in allowances.

***For the purpose of determining taxable income, no gain or loss is recognized when a depreciable asset is traded in on another similar asset.*** The tax regulations provide that ***the cost of the new asset shall be the sum of the book value of the old asset traded in plus the additional amount paid or to be paid in acquiring the new asset.***

To illustrate the handling of an exchange transaction in this manner, assume that a delivery truck is acquired at a cost of $8,000. The truck is depreciated on the straight-line basis with the assumption of a five-year life and no salvage value. Annual depreciation expense is ($8,000 ÷ 5), or $1,600. After four years of use, the truck is traded in on a new model having a list price of $10,000. The truck dealer grants a trade-in allowance of $2,400 for the old truck; the additional amount to be paid to acquire the new truck is, therefore, $7,600 ($10,000 list price minus $2,400 trade-in allowance). The ***cost basis*** of the new truck is computed as follows:

*Trade-in: cost of new equipment*

| | |
|---|---|
| *Cost of old truck* | *$8,000* |
| *Less: Accumulated depreciation ($1,600 × 4)* | *6,400* |
| *Book value of old truck* | *$1,600* |
| *Add: Cash payment for new truck (list price, $10,000 − $2,400 trade-in allowance)* | *7,600* |
| *Cost basis of new truck* | *$9,200* |

The trade-in allowance and the list price of the new truck are not recorded in the accounts; their only function lies in determining the amount which the purchaser must pay in addition to turning in the old truck. The journal entry for this exchange transaction is as follows:

*Entry for trade-in*

| | | |
|---|---|---|
| *Delivery Truck (new)* | *9,200* | |
| *Accumulated Depreciation: Delivery Truck (old)* | *6,400* | |
| *Delivery Truck (old)* | | *8,000* |
| *Cash* | | *7,600* |
| *To remove from the accounts the cost of old truck and accumulated depreciation thereon, and to record new truck at cost equal to book value of old truck traded in plus cash paid.* | | |

Note that the method used above to record the trade-in of an old productive asset for a new one is different from the usual assumption that the cost of a newly acquired asset is equal to its implied cash price. The reason (as approved by the Financial Accounting Standards Board) for not recognizing a gain on a trade-in is that revenue is not realized merely by the act of substituting a new productive asset for an old one. Revenue flows from the production and sale of the goods or services which the productive asset makes possible.[1] The nonrecognition of a suggested gain on a trade-in causes the recorded cost of the new asset to be less than if the gain were recognized. Consequently, depreciation expense will be less because of the reduced amount recorded as cost of the new asset, and the net income in future years will be correspondingly greater.

[1] *APB Opinion No. 29,* "Accounting for Nonmonetary Transactions," AICPA (New York: 1973).

Although income tax regulations and financial accounting rules are alike in not recognizing a ***gain*** on a trade-in, they differ in the case of a trade-in which involves a material loss. Tax regulations do not permit recognition of the loss, but for financial statements the loss should be recognized. For example, assume that a company trades in old machinery on new machinery priced at $600,000. The old machinery originally cost $400,000 and accumulated depreciation amounts to $300,000. Thus the old machinery has a book value of $100,000. However, assume that the trade-in allowance on the old machinery is only $10,000. To give up machinery carried in the accounts at a book value of $100,000 and receive only a $10,000 trade-in allowance indicates a very material loss of $90,000. Perhaps the depreciation taken on the old machinery was too low; that is, based on too long an estimated useful life. In any event, material losses should be recognized as soon as they become apparent. The journal entry for the trade-in transaction should recognize the loss as follows:

| | | |
|---|---|---|
| *Machinery (new)* | *600,000* | |
| *Accumulated Depreciation: Machinery (old)* | *300,000* | |
| *Loss on Trade-in of Plant Assets* | *90,000* | |
| *Machinery (old)* | | *400,000* |
| *Cash* | | *590,000* |
| *To recognize for financial reporting purposes a material loss on trade-in of machinery. Loss not recognized in determining taxable income.* | | |

If a trade-in transaction involved only a very small loss, most companies would probably follow the income tax rules and not recognize the loss. This treatment would avoid the need for a double record of depreciable assets and depreciation expense, and the departure from financial accounting rules would be permissible if the amount of the loss was not material.

## Maintaining control over plant and equipment: subsidiary ledgers

Unless internal controls over plant and equipment are carefully designed, many units of equipment are likely to be broken, discarded, or stolen without any entry being made in the accounting records for their disposal. The asset accounts will then be overstated, and depreciation programs for such missing units of equipment will presumably continue. Consequently, net income will be misstated because of the omission of losses on retirement of plant assets and because of erroneous depreciation charges.

One important control device which guards against failure to record the retirement of assets is the use of controlling accounts and subsidiary ledgers for plant and equipment. The general ledger ordinarily contains a separate asset account and related depreciation accounts for each major classification of plant assets, such as land, buildings, office equipment, and delivery equipment. For example, the general ledger will contain the account Office Equipment, and also, the related accounts Depreciation Expense: Office Equipment, and Accumulated Depreciation: Office Equipment. The general ledger account, Office Equipment, contains entries for a variety of items: typewriters, filing cabinets, dictaphones, desks, etc. It is not possible in this one general ledger account to maintain adequate information concerning the cost of each item, its estimated useful life, book value, insured value, and other data which may be needed by management as a basis for decisions on such issues as replacement, insurance, and taxation.

A ***subsidiary ledger*** should therefore be established for office equipment, and for each of the other general ledger accounts which represents many separate units of plant property. The subsidiary ledger in a manual accounting system may consist of a card file, with a separate card for each unit of property, such as a typewriter or desk. Each card shows the name of the asset, identification number, and such details as date of acquisition, cost, useful life, depreciation, accumulated depreciation, insurance coverage, repairs, and gain or loss on disposal. The general ledger account, Office Equipment, serves as a control; the balance of this controlling account is equal to the total cost of the items in the subsidiary ledger for office equipment. The general ledger account, Accumulated Depreciation: Office Equipment, is also a controlling account; its balance is equal to the total of the accumulated depreciation shown on all the cards in the office equipment ledger. Every acquisition of office equipment is entered in the controlling account and also on a card in the subsidiary ledger. Similarly, every disposal of an item of office equipment is entered in both the controlling account and the subsidiary ledger.

Each card in a subsidiary ledger for plant and equipment shows an identification number which should also appear in the form of a metal tag attached to the asset itself. Consequently, a physical inventory of plant and equipment can be taken and will prove whether all units of equipment shown by the records are actually on hand and being used in operations.

Other advantages afforded by a plant and equipment ledger are the ready availability of information for the periodic computation of depreciation, and for entries to record the disposal of individual items of property. A better basis is also available for supporting the data in tax returns, for obtaining proper insurance coverage, and for supporting claims for losses sustained on insured property. In well-managed companies, it is standard practice to control expenditures for plant and equipment by preparing a budget of all planned acquisitions for at least a year in advance. A first essential to the preparation of such a budget is a detailed record showing the assets presently owned, their cost, age, and remaining useful life.

## NATURAL RESOURCES

### Accounting for natural resources

Mining properties, oil and gas wells, and tracts of standing timber are leading examples of natural resources or "wasting assets." The distinguishing characteristics of these assets are that they are physically consumed and converted into inventory. In a theoretical sense, a coal mine might even be regarded as an "underground inventory of coal"; however, such an inventory is certainly not a current asset. In the balance sheet, mining property and other natural resources are usually listed as a separate group of tangible assets.

Natural resources should be recorded in the accounts at cost. As the resource is removed through the process of mining, cutting, or pumping, the asset account must be proportionately reduced. The carrying value (book value) of a coal mine, for example, is reduced by a small amount for each ton of coal mined. The original cost of the mine is thus gradually transferred out of the asset account and becomes part of the cost of the coal mined and sold.

The cost of a mine or other natural resource may include not only the purchase price but also payments for surveying and various exploratory and developmental activities. Many companies in such industries as oil, gas, and mining carry on a continuous program of exploration and development as, for example, the much-discussed development of offshore oil fields. Since expenditures for exploration and development thus become normal and continuous, these payments are generally charged to expense in the year in which the exploration or development is performed. If the payments for exploration and development were reasonably certain to produce future revenue, the theoretically preferable accounting policy would be to capitalize these costs so that they could be matched against the related revenue which they would produce in later years.

**Depletion** The term ***depletion*** is used to describe the pro rata allocation of cost of a natural resource to the units removed. Depletion is computed by dividing the cost of the natural resource (minus any residual value) by the estimated available number of units, such as barrels of oil or tons of coal. The depletion charge per unit is then multiplied by the number of units actually removed during the year to determine the total depletion charge for that period.

To illustrate the computation of depletion expense, assume that the sum of $10,100,000 is paid for a coal mine believed to contain 1 million tons of coal. Residual value of the mine after removal of all the coal is estimated to be $100,000. Cost of the mine minus the residual value is $10,000,000, the amount subject to depletion. The depletion charge per unit is $10,000,000 ÷ 1,000,000 tons, or $10 a ton. If we assume that 200,000 tons of coal were mined and sold during the first year of operation, the depletion charge for the year would be $10 × 200,000 tons or $2,000,000. The journal entry necessary at the end of the year to record depletion of the mine would be as follows:

*Recording depletion*

| | | |
|---|---|---|
| *Depletion Expense* | *2,000,000* | |
| *Accumulated Depletion: Coal Mine* | | *2,000,000* |
| *To record depletion expense for the year; 200,000 tons mined @ $10 per ton.* | | |

In reporting natural resources in the balance sheet, accumulated depletion should be deducted from the cost of the property. A recent balance sheet of Anaconda Company, for example, reports its natural resources as follows:

*Natural resources in the balance sheet*

| | |
|---|---|
| ***Mines and mining claims, water rights and lands, less accumulated depletion of $149,874,000*** | ***$138,410,000*** |
| ***Timberlands and phosphate and gravel deposits, less accumulated depletion of $5,602,000*** | ***2,111,000*** |

Depletion expense in a mining business might be compared with the Purchases account in the ledger of a retail store. The Purchases account represents part of the cost to the store of the goods available for sale; the Depletion Expense account in a mining company represents a part of the cost of the coal or other product available for sale.

For example, if all the coal produced this year by a mining company is sold this year, it is apparent that the cost of the coal (including depletion) will be deducted from this year's revenue. However, it is quite possible that some of the coal produced this year will not be sold this year and will still be on hand at December 31. In this case, the unsold coal is inventory and all the costs of producing it (labor, depletion, etc.) will be included in the Inventory account. The costs carried over as year-end inventory will become part of the cost of goods sold next year and thus will be deducted from next year's revenue.

In other words, ***depletion is recorded in the year in which the coal is taken out of the ground.*** The depletion is part of the cost of the product. If the product is held as inventory until the following year rather than being sold in the year produced, the depletion applicable to the units held as inventory will be carried forward as part of the inventory value. Of course the cost of the inventory of coal or other extracted product on hand at the end of the year includes not only the depletion charge but also the labor cost and other expenditures incurred in bringing the coal to the surface.

**Percentage depletion versus cost depletion** For the determination of taxable income, the Internal Revenue Code permits a deduction for depletion expense equal to a specified ***percentage of the revenue*** from production from a few mineral deposits such as gold, silver, lead, and zinc ore. Depletion as a percentage of revenue was formerly allowed for the oil and gas industry, but this provision of the tax laws was repealed by Congress except for certain small producers.

Depletion computed as a percentage of revenue ***is used only for income tax purposes, not for financial statements.*** In terms of generally accepted accounting principles, depletion is always based on the ***cost*** of the mine or other natural resource.

**Depreciation of buildings and equipment closely related to natural resources** Buildings and equipment installed at a mine or drilling site may be useful only at that particular location. Consequently, such assets should be depreciated over their normal useful lives, or over the life of the natural resource, ***whichever is shorter.*** Often depreciation on such assets is computed using the units-of-output method, thus relating the depreciation expense to the rate at which units of the natural resource are removed.

For example, assume that a building costing $205,000 and having a normal useful life of 20 years is erected at the site of a mine estimated to contain 100,000 tons of ore. Once the mine is exhausted, the building will have only scrap value, say, $5,000. Production of ore is being carried on at a rate which will probably exhaust the mine within four to six years. Consequently, the useful life of the building will be only four to six years. During the first year after construction of the building, ore is mined in the amount of 25,000 tons. How much depreciation should be recognized on the building?

In this situation, depreciation of the building should be based on the life of the mine, and computed in the same manner as depletion. Cost, $205,000, minus residual or scrap value, $5,000, equals a depreciable cost of $200,000. This $200,000 divided by the 100,000 tons of ore to be produced over the life of the mine equals a depreciation rate of $2 for each ton produced. In the first year, we assumed production of 25,000 tons; therefore, depreciation would be $2 × 25,000 tons, or $50,000 for the first year. The formula may be stated concisely as follows:

$$\frac{\text{Cost} - \text{Residual Value}}{\text{Estimated Total Units}} = \text{Depreciation Cost per Unit}$$

## INTANGIBLE ASSETS

### Characteristics

As the word ***intangible*** suggests, assets in this classification have no physical substance. Leading examples are goodwill, leaseholds, patents, and trademarks. Intangible assets are classified in the balance sheet as a subgroup of plant assets. However, not all assets which lack physical substance are regarded as intangible assets. An account receivable, for example, or a short-term prepayment is of nonphysical nature but is classified as a current asset and is not regarded as an intangible. In brief, ***intangible assets are assets which are used in the operation of the business but which have no physical substance and are noncurrent.***

The basis of valuation for intangible assets is cost. In some companies, certain intangible assets such as trademarks may be of great importance but may have been acquired without the incurring of any cost. An intangible asset should appear in the balance sheet ***only*** if a cost of acquisition or development has been incurred.

However, accounting for an intangible asset is rendered somewhat difficult because the lack of physical substance makes evidence of its existence more elusive, may make its value more debatable, and may make the length of its useful life more questionable. These characteristics of intangible assets suggest that realizable value may be undeterminable or even nonexistent. Perhaps because of the lack of clear support for precise valuation of intangibles, many companies choose to carry their intangible assets on the balance sheet at a nominal valuation of $1; Jantzen, Inc., and Polaroid Corporation are prominent examples.

There is little doubt, however, that in some companies the intangible assets, such as goodwill or a franchise, are vitally important to profitable operations. The carrying of intangible assets on the balance sheet is justified only when there is good evidence that future earnings will be derived from these assets.

### Operating expenses versus intangible assets

Many types of expenditures offer at least a half promise of yielding benefits in subsequent years, but the evidence is so doubtful and the period of usefulness so hard to define that most companies treat these expenditures as expense when incurred. Another reason for charging these outlays to expense is the practical difficulty of separating them from the recurring expenses of current operations.

Examples are the expenditures for intensive advertising campaigns to introduce new products, and the expense of training employees to work with new types of machinery or office equipment. There is little doubt that some benefits from these outlays continue beyond the current period, but because of the uncertain duration of the benefits, it is almost universal practice to treat expenditures of this nature as expense of the current period.

### Amortization

The term ***amortization*** is used to describe the systematic write-off to expense of the cost of an intangible asset over the periods of its economic usefulness. The usual accounting entry for amortization consists of a debit to Amortization Expense and a credit to the intangible asset account. There is no theoretical objection to crediting an accumulated amortization account rather than the intangible asset account, but this method is seldom encountered in practice.

For many years some accountants argued that certain intangibles, such as trademarks, had ***unlimited*** useful lives and therefore should not be amortized. However, the FASB supports the view that the value of intangible assets existing at any one date eventually disappears, and that ***all*** intangible assets must be amortized over their useful lives.[2]

Although it is difficult to estimate the useful life of an intangible such as goodwill, it is highly probable that such an asset will not contribute to future earnings on a permanent basis. The cost of the intangible asset should, therefore, be deducted from revenue during the years in which it may be expected to aid in producing revenue.[3] The maximum period of amortization cannot exceed 40 years under the rules presently enforced by the Financial Accounting Standards Board.[4] The straight-line method of amortization is generally used for intangible assets.

**Arbitrary write-off of intangibles** Arbitrary, lump-sum write-off of intangibles (leaving a nominal balance of $1 in the accounts) is a practice sometimes found

---

[2] *APB Opinion No. 17,* "Intangible Assets," AICPA (New York: 1970), par. 27.
[3] Present tax regulations do not permit the amortization of goodwill in computing taxable income.
[4] *APB Opinion No. 17,* par. 29.

in companies which have not adopted a systematic amortization program. Arguments for this practice emphasize the element of conservatism, the practical difficulty of estimating an appropriate period for amortization, and the absence of any realizable value for intangibles. Accountants generally agree that whenever any event occurs which indicates that an intangible has lost all value, immediate write-off of the entire cost is warranted regardless of whether an amortization program has previously been followed.

On the other hand, arbitrary write-offs of valuable, revenue-producing intangible assets are no more in accordance with accounting theory than would be the arbitrary write-off of land or buildings.

## Goodwill

Business executives used the term ***goodwill*** in a variety of meanings before it became part of accounting terminology. One of the most common meanings of goodwill in a nonaccounting sense concerns the benefits derived from a favorable reputation among customers. To accountants, however, goodwill has a very specific meaning not necessarily limited to customer relations. It means the ***present value of future earnings in excess of the normal return on net identifiable assets.*** Above-average earnings may arise not only from favorable customer relations but also from such factors as location, monopoly, manufacturing efficiency, and superior management.

The phrase ***normal return on net identifiable assets*** requires explanation. Net assets means the owner's equity in a business, or assets minus liabilities. Goodwill, however, is not an ***identifiable*** asset. The existence of goodwill is implied by the ability of a business to earn an above-average return; however, the cause and precise dollar value of goodwill are largely matters of personal opinion. Therefore, ***net identifiable assets*** means all assets except goodwill minus liabilities. A ***normal return*** on net identifiable assets is the rate of return which investors demand in a particular industry to justify their buying a business at the ***fair market value*** of its net identifiable assets. A business has goodwill when investors will pay a higher price because the business earns more than the normal rate of return.

Assume that two businesses in the same line of trade are offered for sale and that the normal return on the fair market value of net identifiable assets in this industry is 12% a year. The relative earning power of the two companies during the past five years is shown below:

| | Company X | Company Y |
|---|---|---|
| *Fair market value of net identifiable assets* | *$1,000,000* | *$1,000,000* |
| *Normal rate of return on net assets* | *12%* | *12%* |
| *Average net income for past five years* | *$ 120,000* | *$ 160,000* |
| *Normal earnings, computed as 12% of net identifiable assets* | *120,000* | *120,000* |
| *Earnings in excess of normal* | *$ -0-* | *$ 40,000* |

An investor would be willing to pay $1,000,000 to buy Company X, because Company X earns the normal 12% return which justifies the fair market value of its net identifiable assets. Although Company Y has the same amount of net identifiable assets, an investor would be willing to pay ***more*** for Company Y than for Company X because Company Y has a record of superior earnings which will presumably continue for some time in the future. The extra amount that a buyer would pay to purchase Company Y represents the value of Company Y's goodwill.

**Estimating goodwill** How much will an investor pay for goodwill? Above-average earnings in past years are of significance to prospective purchasers only if they believe that these earnings will continue after they acquire the business. Investors' appraisals of goodwill, therefore, will vary with their estimates of the future earning power of the business. Very few businesses, however, are able to maintain above-average earnings for more than a few years. Consequently, the purchaser of a business will usually limit any amount paid for goodwill to not more than four or five times the amount by which annual earnings exceed normal earnings.

Arriving at a fair value for the goodwill of a going business is a difficult and subjective process. Any estimate of goodwill is in large part a matter of personal opinion. The following are several methods which a prospective purchaser might use in estimating a value for goodwill:

1 Negotiated agreement between buyer and seller of the business may be reached on the amount of goodwill. For example, it might be agreed that the fair market value of net identifiable assets is $1,000,000 and that the total purchase price for the business will be $1,180,000, thus providing a $180,000 payment for goodwill.

2 Goodwill may be determined as a multiple of the amount by which average annual earnings exceed normal earnings. Referring to our example involving Company Y, a prospective buyer may be willing to pay four times the amount by which average earnings exceed normal earnings, indicating a value of $160,000 (4 × $40,000) for goodwill. The purchase price of the business, therefore, would be $1,160,000.

   The multiple applied to the excess annual earnings will vary widely from perhaps 1 to 10. An investor who pays four times the excess earnings for goodwill must, of course, expect these earnings to continue for at least four years.

3 Goodwill may be estimated by ***capitalizing*** the amount by which average earnings exceed normal earnings. Capitalizing an earnings stream means dividing those earnings by the investor's required rate of return. The result is the maximum amount which the investor could pay for the earnings and have them represent the required rate of return on the investment. To illustrate, assume that the prospective buyer decides to capitalize the $40,000 annual excess earnings of Company Y at a rate of 20%. This approach results in a $200,000 estimate ($40,000 ÷ .20 = $200,000) for the value of goodwill. (Note that $40,000 per year represents a 20% return on a $200,000 investment.)

   A weakness in the capitalization method is that ***no provision is made for the recovery*** of the investment. If the prospective buyer is to earn a 20% return on the $200,000 investment in goodwill, either the excess earnings must continue ***forever*** (an unlikely assumption) or the buyer must be able to recover the $200,000 investment at a later date by selling the business at a price above the fair market value of net identifiable assets.

**Recording goodwill in the accounting records** Goodwill is recorded in the accounting records ***only when it is purchased;*** this situation usually occurs only when a going business is purchased in its entirety. After the fair market values of all identifiable assets have been recorded in the accounting records of the new owners, any additional amount paid for the business may properly be debited to an asset account entitled Goodwill. This intangible asset must then be amortized over a period not to exceed 40 years, although a much shorter amortization period usually is appropriate.

Many businesses have never purchased goodwill but have generated it internally through developing good customer relations, superior management, or other factors which result in above-average earnings. Because there is no objective means of determining the dollar value of goodwill unless the business is sold, internally developed goodwill is ***not recorded*** in the accounting records. Thus, goodwill may be a very important asset of a successful business but may not even appear in the company's balance sheet.

## Leased property

Many companies lease land, buildings, airplanes, trucks, computers, and other equipment rather than buying these assets. The owner of the property is the ***lessor;*** the tenant or company obtaining the use of the property is the ***lessee.*** The rights transferred to the lessee under a lease contract are described as a ***leasehold.***

Some leases merely provide for regular monthly payments of rent; in these cases a leasehold account is not used. The lessee making monthly payments to the lessor debits these payments to Rent Expense. Sometimes a lease agreement covering several years is so drawn as to require the payment in advance of the final year's rent. Rent payments for all but the final year may be made on a month-to-month basis. In this case the Leasehold account will be debited with the advance payment of the final year's rent at the time the lease is signed, and this amount will remain in the account until the final year of the lease, at which time the advance payment will be transferred to the Rent Expense account.

There are two methods of accounting for leased property, depending upon the terms of the lease. Under one method, the ***lessee*** views the periodic lease payments as rent expense and does not record the leased property as an asset in the accounting records. Under the other method, lease agreements are viewed as creating both an asset and a liability, which are recorded in the accounts of the lessee at the ***present value*** of the future lease payments. The asset, which might be called ***leased equipment,*** will appear in the balance sheet with other types of plant and equipment and will be depreciated over the life of the lease. Accounting for leases will be discussed further in Chapter 18.

### Leasehold improvements

Most long-term leases of land and buildings usually state that any improvements to the property, such as an air-conditioning system or an escalator, must be paid for by the lessee. However, these improvements become part of the property. They revert to the lessor at the end of the lease and cannot be removed by the tenant. Consequently, the costs of improvements on leased property should be recorded in a Leasehold Improvements account and amortized to expense during the remaining life of the lease or of the estimated useful life of the improvement, whichever is shorter. This procedure is usually followed even though the lessee has an option to renew the lease, because there is no assurance in advance that conditions will warrant the exercise of the renewal clause.

### Patents

A patent is an exclusive right granted by the federal government for manufacture, use, and sale of a particular product. The purpose of this exclusive grant is to encourage the invention of new machines and processes. When a company acquires a patent by purchase from the inventor or other holder, the purchase price should be recorded by debiting the intangible asset account Patents. The cost of a successful lawsuit to defend the validity of a patent is also capitalized by charge to the Patents account. The legal costs of defending a patent in a court case are sometimes greater than the cost of developing the patent.

Patents are granted for a period of 17 years, and the period of amortization must not exceed that period. However, if the patent is likely to lose its usefulness in less than 17 years, amortization should be based on the shorter period of estimated useful life. Assume that a patent is purchased from the inventor at a cost of $100,000, after five years of the legal life have expired. The remaining ***legal*** life is, therefore, 12 years, but if the estimated ***useful*** life is only four years, amortization should be based on this shorter period. The entry to be made to record the annual amortization expense would be:

*Entry for amortization of patent*

| | | |
|---|---|---|
| *Amortization Expense: Patents* | *25,000* | |
| *Patents* | | *25,000* |
| *To amortize cost of patent on a straight-line basis and estimated life of four years.* | | |

### Copyrights

A copyright is an exclusive right granted by the federal government to protect the production and sale of literary or artistic materials for the life of the creator plus 50 years. The cost of obtaining a copyright in some cases is minor and therefore is chargeable to expense when paid. Only when a copyright is purchased will the expenditure be material enough to warrant capitalization and spreading over the useful life. The revenue from copyrights is usually limited to only a few years, and the purchase cost should, of course, be amortized over the years in which the revenue is expected.

### Franchises

A franchise is a right granted by a company or a governmental unit to conduct a certain type of business in a specific geographical area. An example of a franchise is the right to operate a McDonald's restaurant in a specific neighborhood. Another example is an airline route granted by the Civil Aeronautics Board authorizing a particular airline to operate between, say, Denver and Honolulu. Franchises are often written for a specified number of years and many such agreements include a provision for renewal.

The franchises granted by some corporations carry other benefits to the franchisees (holders of the franchises). For example, a local Chevrolet dealer benefits from the national advertising programs of the company. The company or governmental unit granting a franchise often imposes certain operating standards on the franchisee in order to maintain a reputation for high quality of products or services. The cost of franchises varies greatly and often may be quite substantial. When the cost of a franchise is small, it may be charged immediately to expense, but if the cost is substantial, it should be capitalized. Amortization should be based on the life of the franchise but must not exceed 40 years.

### Trademarks and trade names

Coca Cola's distinctive bottle is an example of a trademark known around the world. A trademark is a word, symbol, or design that identifies a product or group of products. A permanent exclusive right to the use of a trademark, brand name, or commercial symbol may be obtained by registering it with the federal government. The costs of developing a trademark or brand name often consist of advertising campaigns which should be treated as expense when incurred. If a trademark or trade name is purchased, however, the cost may be substantial. Such cost should be capitalized and amortized to expense over a period of not more than 40 years. If the use of the trademark is discontinued or its contribution to earnings becomes doubtful, any unamortized cost should be written off immediately.

### Other intangibles and deferred charges

Many other types of intangible assets are found in the published balance sheets of large corporations. Some examples are formulas, processes, name lists, and film rights.

Intangibles, particularly those with limited lives, are sometimes classified as "deferred charges" in the balance sheet. A ***deferred charge*** is an expenditure that is expected to yield benefits for several accounting periods, and should be amortized over its estimated useful life. Included in this category are such items as bond issuance costs, plant rearrangement and moving costs, start-up costs, and organization costs. The distinction between intangibles and deferred charges is not an important one; both represent "bundles of services" in the form of long-term prepayments awaiting allocation to those accounting periods in which the services will be consumed.

### Research and development costs

The spending of billions of dollars a year on research and development leading to all kinds of new products is a striking characteristic of American industry. In the past, some companies treated all research and development costs as expense in the year incurred; other companies in the same industry recorded these costs as intangible assets to be amortized over future years. This diversity of practice prevented the financial statements of different companies from being comparable.

The lack of uniformity in accounting for research and development was ended when the Financial Accounting Standards Board ruled that all research and development expenditures should be charged to expense when incurred.[5] The action by the FASB was favorably received because it reduced the number of alternative accounting practices and helped make financial statements of different companies more comparable. Incidentally, the FASB Statement did not apply to the development costs unique to companies developing natural resources, as discussed on page 467.

## KEY TERMS INTRODUCED OR EMPHASIZED IN CHAPTER 12

**Amortization** The systematic write-off to expense of the cost of an intangible asset over the periods of its economic usefulness.

**Book value** The cost of a plant asset minus the total recorded depreciation, as shown by the Accumulated Depreciation account. The remaining undepreciated cost, also known as ***carrying value.***

**Copyright** An exclusive right granted by the federal government to protect the production and sale of literary or artistic materials.

**Deferred charge** An expenditure expected to yield benefits for several accounting periods and therefore capitalized and written off during the periods benefited.

**Depletion** Allocating the cost of a natural resource to the units removed as the resource is mined, pumped, cut, or otherwise consumed.

**Goodwill** The present value of expected future earnings of a business in excess of the earnings normally realized in the industry. Recorded when a business entity is purchased at a price in excess of the fair value of its tangible assets and identifiable intangible assets less liabilities.

**Intangible assets** Those assets which are used in the operation of a business but which have no physical substance and are noncurrent.

**Lessee** The tenant of leased property.

**Lessor** The owner of leased property.

**Natural resources** Mines, oil fields, standing timber, and similar assets which are physically consumed and converted into inventory.

---

[5] Financial Accounting Standards Board, *Statement of Financial Accounting Standards No. 2,* "Accounting for Research and Development Costs," (Stamford, Conn.: 1974), par. 12.

**Net assets** Assets minus liabilities. Equal to owner's equity.

**Net tangible assets** Total of all assets (except the intangibles) minus liabilities.

**Patent** The exclusive right granted by the federal government for the manufacture, use, and sale of a particular product.

## REVIEW QUESTIONS

1 Century Company traded in its old computer on a new model. The trade-in allowance for the old computer is greater than its book value. Should Century Company recognize a gain on the exchange in computing its taxable income or in determining its net income for financial reporting? Explain.

2 Fargo Corporation traded in an old machine on a similar new one, but received a trade-in allowance less than the book value of the old machine. The Internal Revenue Service did not permit the company to recognize any loss on the transaction in computing its taxable income. How will Fargo benefit in future years for income tax purposes as a result of the indicated loss on the trade-in not being allowed by the IRS?

3 Describe briefly three situations in which debit entries may properly be made in accumulated depreciation accounts.

4 Student A asserts that when a depreciable plant asset is to be sold a first step is to record depreciation for the fractional period to the date of sale. Student B argues that an entry for depreciation at the date of disposing of the asset is inefficient because in his opinion it is more convenient to make all depreciation entries at the end of the year. At that time he would take into consideration that certain depreciable assets had been in use for only a portion of the year prior to their disposal. Evaluate these arguments.

5 Topeka Corporation maintains a general ledger controlling account for office equipment. This controlling account is supported by a subsidiary ledger in the form of a card file with a card for each unit of equipment. On 30 of these cards, the accumulated depreciation is equal to the cost of the asset. Assuming that the 30 items represented by the cards are still in regular use, should additional depreciation be recorded on them? When should these 30 cards be removed from the subsidiary ledger, and the cost and accumulated depreciation be removed from the general ledger accounts?

6 What is the term used to describe the pro rata allocation of the cost of a mine or other natural resource to the units removed during the year?

7 Lead Hill Corporation recognizes $1 of depletion for each ton of ore mined. During the current year the company mined 600,000 tons but sold only 500,000 tons, as it was attempting to build up inventories in anticipation of a possible strike by employees. How much depletion should be deducted from revenue of the current year?

8 Under what circumstances does good accounting call for a mining company to depreciate a plant asset over a period shorter than the normal useful life?

9 Define ***intangible assets.*** Would an account receivable arising from a sale of merchandise under terms of 2/10, n/30 qualify as an intangible asset under your definition?

10 The James Electric Shop obtained its store building under a 10-year lease at $400 a month. The lease agreement required payment of rent for the tenth year at the time of signing the lease. All other payments were on a monthly basis. Give the

journal entry required at the date of signing the lease when James wrote a check for $5,200, representing payment of the current month's rent and the $4,800 applicable to the tenth year of the lease. What entries, if any, are indicated for the tenth year of the lease?

**11** Under what circumstances should goodwill be recorded in the accounts?

**12** In reviewing the financial statements of Digital Products Co. with a view to investing in the company's stock, you notice that net tangible assets total $1 million, that goodwill is listed as $100,000, and that average earnings for the past five years have been $20,000 a year. How would these relationships influence your thinking about the company?

**13** Space Research Company paid $500,000 cash to acquire the entire business of Saturn Company, a strong competitor. In negotiating this lump-sum price for the business, a valuation of $60,000 was assigned to goodwill, representing four times the amount by which Saturn Company's annual earnings had exceeded normal earnings in the industry. Assuming that the goodwill is recorded in the accounts of Space Research Company, should it remain there permanently or be amortized? What basis of amortization might be used?

**14** Current accounting standards require that the cost of various types of intangible assets be amortized by regular charges against earnings. Over what period of time should amortization extend? (Your answer should be in the form of a principle or guideline rather than a specific number of years.)

**15** Several years ago March Metals purchased for $120,000 a well-known trademark for padlocks and other security products. After using the trademark for three years, March Metals discontinued it altogether when the company withdrew from the lock business and concentrated on the manufacture of aircraft parts. Amortization of the trademark at the rate of $3,000 a year is being continued on the basis of a 40-year life, which the owner of March Metals says is required by accounting standards. Do you agree? Explain.

## EXERCISES

*Ex. 12-1* A machine that originally cost $48,000 on January 1, Year 1, was depreciated on the straight-line basis. Estimated useful life was eight years with no residual value. After five years and four months of use, the machine was sold on April 30, Year 6, for cash of $20,000. Depreciation was last recorded at December 31, Year 5.

Determine **(a)** the depreciation for the fractional period from January 1 to April 30 of Year 6; **(b)** the book value of the machine at April 30, the date of sale; **(c)** the gain or loss on the disposal of the machine. **(d)** Also prepare the journal entry to record the sale of the machine at April 30, Year 6.

*Ex. 12-2* An airplane with a book value of $30,000 was traded in on a new airplane with a list price of $300,000. The trade-in allowance (not necessarily the fair market value) for the old airplane was $48,000.

**a** How much cash must be paid for the new airplane?

**b** What is the cost basis of the new airplane for income tax purposes?

**c** How much depreciation should be recorded on the new airplane for the first year of use, assuming a four-year life, a residual value of $42,000, and the use of straight-line depreciation?

*Ex. 12-3* Dell Company traded in an old machine on a similar new one. The original cost of the old machine was $30,000 and the accumulated depreciation was $24,000. The list price of the new machine was $40,000 and the trade-in allowance was $8,000. What amount must Dell pay? Compute the indicated gain or loss (regardless of whether it should be recorded in the accounts). Compute the cost basis of the new machine to be used in figuring depreciation for determination of income subject to federal income tax.

*Ex. 12-4* A tractor which cost $24,800 had an estimated useful life of five years and an estimated salvage value of $4,800. Straight-line depreciation was used. Give the entry required by each of the following alternative assumptions:

**a** The tractor was sold for cash of $15,000 after two years' use.

**b** The tractor was traded in after three years on another tractor with a list price of $36,000. Trade-in allowance was $14,600. The trade-in was recorded in a manner acceptable for income tax purposes.

**c** The tractor was scrapped after four years' use. Since scrap dealers were unwilling to pay anything for the tractor, it was given to a scrap dealer for his services in removing it.

*Ex. 12-5* Yellow Knife Mines started mining activities early in Year 1. At the end of the year its accountant prepared the following summary of its mining costs:

| | |
|---|---|
| *Labor* | *$2,380,000* |
| *Materials* | *245,000* |
| *Miscellaneous* | *539,280* |

These costs do not include any charges for depletion or depreciation. Data relating to assets used in mining the ore follow:

| | |
|---|---|
| *Cost of mine (estimated deposit, 10 million tons; residual value of the mine estimated at $420,000)* | *$2,100,000* |
| *Buildings (estimated life, 15 years; no residual value)* | *184,800* |
| *Equipment (useful life, six years regardless of number of tons mined; residual value $42,000)* | *336,000* |

During the year 800,000 tons (8%) of ore were mined, of which 600,000 tons were sold. It is estimated that it will take at least 15 years to extract the ore.

Determine the cost that should be assigned to the inventory of unsold ore at the end of Year 1.

*Ex. 12-6* During the past several years the net sales of Hawthorne Company have averaged
Ass. – $4,500,000 annually and net income has averaged 6% of net sales. At the present time the company is being offered for sale. Its accounting records show net assets (total assets minus all liabilities) to be $1,500,000.

An investor negotiating to buy the company offers to pay an amount equal to the book value for the net assets and to assume all liabilities. In addition, the investor is willing to pay for goodwill an amount equal to net earnings in excess of 15% on net assets, capitalized at a rate of 25%.

On the basis of this agreement, what price should the investor offer for the Hawthorne Company?

## PROBLEMS

### Group A

*12A-1* Angus Company, which maintains its accounts on a calendar-year basis, acquired three machines on January 1 of Year 10. Data concerning cost, depreciation, and disposal of the three machines were as follows:

| | Machine No. 1 | Machine No. 2 | Machine No. 3 |
|---|---|---|---|
| *Method of depreciation* | *Straight-line* | *Sum-of-the-years' digits* | *Double-declining balance* |
| *Cost* | *$21,000* | *$32,000* | *$64,000* |
| *Residual value* | *$ 1,000* | *$ 2,000* | *$ 4,000* |
| *Estimated useful life* | *5 years* | *5 years* | *8 years* |
| *Date of disposal* | *June 30, Year 10* | *Jan. 1, Year 12* | *Jan. 1, Year 12* |
| *Proceeds from disposal* | *$ -0-* | *$17,000* | *$40,000* |

Machine no. 1 was completely destroyed by fire on June 30, Year 10, after only six months of use. Machines no. 2 and no. 3 were sold for cash on January 1, Year 12, when Angus Company decided to lease larger, more efficient machines.

**Instructions**

**a** Prepare three subsidiary ledger cards, one for each of the three machines. Each card should show the following:

| | | |
|---|---|---|
| *Machine no.* | ______________ | |
| *Date of acquisition* | ______________ | |
| *Cost* | *$* ______________ | |
| *Residual value* | *$* ______________ | |
| *Estimated useful life* | ______________ | |
| *Method of depreciation* | ______________ | |
| *Depreciation by years* | *Year 10 $* __________ | *Year 11 $* __________ |
| *Accumulated depreciation* | *Dec. 31, Year 10 $* ______ | *Dec. 31, Year 11 $* ______ |
| *Date of disposal* | ______________ | |
| *Proceeds of disposal* | *$* ______________ | |
| *Book value at date of disposal* | *$* ______________ | |
| *Gain or loss on disposal* | *$* ______________ | |

**b** Prepare general journal entries in chronological order for Years 10, 11, and 12 to record the acquisition, depreciation, and disposal of the three machines. Use only one account for Depreciation Expense and one account for Accumulated Depreciation. Include in the explanation portion of the journal entries the details of the computations for each machine.

*12A-2* Several years ago Coastline Service acquired some machinery at a cost of $108,000. The company has used straight-line depreciation and an estimated useful life of 10 years. No provision was made for salvage value because the expected cost of removing the machinery at the end of its useful life was at least as much as might be received as salvage.

After several years of using the machinery, Coastline Service traded it in on April 1 on new machinery priced at $262,000. The trade-in allowance for the old machinery amounted to $4,400. Accumulated depreciation on the old machinery was $86,400 at December 31 prior to the year of the trade-in. No depreciation had been recorded between the closing of the accounts at December 31 and the exchange for the new machinery on April 1. The remainder of the trade-in transaction consisted of a $36,000 cash payment and the signing of a 12% one-year note payable for the balance of the purchase price of the new machine.

**Instructions** Prepare entries in general journal form to record the following:

**a** Depreciation for the fraction of a year prior to the April 1 transaction.

**b** The acquisition of the new machinery on April 1 under the rules acceptable for income tax purposes.

**c** The acquisition of the new machinery on April 1 under the assumption that gain or loss is to be recognized and that the trade-in allowance represents the fair market value of the old machinery being traded in.

*12A-3* Blue Hills, Inc., a manufacturer, showed the following information in its ledger account for Machinery for the current year.

| | | |
|---|---|---|
| *Jan. 2* | *Acquired four identical machines @ $21,600 each* | *$86,400* |
| *Jan. 4* | *Installation costs* | *2,880* |
| | *Total debits* | *$89,280* |
| *Dec. 31* | *Less: Credit for proceeds from sale of one machine* | *16,560* |
| *31* | *Balance in Machinery account* | *$72,720* |

The corporation's policy for depreciating the machines is to use the straight-line method with an estimated useful life of five years and an estimated residual value of $2,520 per machine. The December 31 transaction for the sale of one machine was recorded by a debit to Cash for the full sales price of $16,560 and a credit to Machinery for $16,560.

**Instructions**

**a** Prepare one journal entry at December 31 to record depreciation expense for the year on all four machines.

**b** What was the amount of the gain or loss on the sale of the machine on December 31? Show computations.

**c** Prepare one journal entry to ***correct the accounts*** at December 31. In drafting your correcting entry, give consideration to the debit and credit already entered in the accounts on December 31 to record the sale of one of the machines. Your entry should reduce the Machinery account and the Accumulated Depreciation account and should record the gain or loss on the disposal of the machine which was not recognized in the entry made at the time of the sale.

*12A-4* Century Associates adjusts and closes its accounts at the end of each calendar year and uses the straight-line method of depreciation on all its plant and equipment. On January 1, Year 1, machinery was purchased for cash at a cost of $854,700. Useful life was estimated to be 10 years and residual value $14,700.

Three years later in December, Year 3, after steady use of the machinery, the company decided that because of rapid technological change, the estimated total useful life should be revised from 10 years to 6 years. No change was made in the estimate of residual value. The revised estimate of useful life was decided upon prior to recording depreciation for the period ended December 31, Year 3.

On June 30, Year 4, Century Associates decided to lease new, more efficient machinery; consequently, the machinery described above was sold on this date for $510,000 cash.

**Instructions** Prepare journal entries to record the purchase of the machinery, the recording of depreciation for each of the four years, and the disposal of the machinery on June 30, Year 4. Do not prepare closing entries.

*12A-5* A new patent was purchased by Lincoln Company from the inventor immediately after its issuance on January 2, Year 10. The full price of $400,000 was paid in cash.

The patented device was promptly put to use in Lincoln's production operations. Although the legal life of the patent was 17 years, the company estimated that technological changes in its industry would limit the economic usefulness of the patent to 10 years.

On March 1, Year 10, the company paid $50,000 in legal fees for the services of attorneys who successfully defended an infringement suit against the patent.

In December of Year 12, Lincoln Company decided that the ***total*** useful life of the patent would be limited to five years rather than the original estimate of 10 years. This decision was reached before amortization was recorded for Year 12.

**Instructions** Prepare journal entries to record the above events relating to the acquisition and amortization of the patent from January 2, Year 10, through December 31, Year 12. Remember that Lincoln Company recorded amortization for two years (Year 10 and Year 11) before the decision was made as to a shorter useful life.

***12A-6*** Cactus Oil, an established company, borrowed $9 million from Sage National Bank on January 1, Year 10, issuing a note payable due in five years, with interest at 10% payable annually on December 31. Also on January 1, Year 10, the company purchased for $4,800,000 cash an oil field estimated to contain at least 2 million barrels of oil. Equipment estimated to last for the productive life of the oil wells, and having no scrap value, was also acquired for cash on January 1 at a cost of $160,000. This equipment would have no economic usefulness after exhaustion of the oil field; therefore it was to be depreciated on a units-of-output basis.

During January the company spent $750,000 in developing the field, and several shallow wells were brought into production. The established accounting policy of the company was to treat drilling and development expenditures of this type as expense of the period in which the work was done.

Construction of a pipeline was completed on May 1, Year 10, and the full cost of $1,440,000 was paid in cash. Although this pipeline was physically capable of being used for many years, its economic usefulness was limited to the productive life of the wells. Therefore, the depreciation method used was based on the estimated number of barrels of oil to be produced.

Operating expenses incurred during Year 10 (other than depreciation and depletion) amounted to $960,000, and 230,000 barrels of oil were produced and sold. (The journal entry for the operating expenses should be dated December 31. Debit Operating Expenses. Depletion expense and depreciation expense also should be recorded at December 31. Compute depletion expense by calculating a depletion rate per barrel and multiplying this rate by the 230,000 barrels produced. Compute depreciation of the equipment and of the pipeline in the same manner: that is, compute the depreciation expense per barrel and multiply this rate by the 230,000 barrels representing the production of Year 10.) Entries for sales of oil are to be omitted.

Cash operating expenses for Year 11 amounted to $1,500,000. Oil production totaled 800,000 barrels, of which all but 80,000 barrels were sold during the year. (Ending inventory should be valued at 10% of the year's production costs including depletion and depreciation; 80,000 barrels in inventory represents 10% of the 800,000 barrels produced.)

**Instructions** Prepare journal entries to record the transactions of Year 10 and Year 11. The sequence of entries should be in the following pattern:

| | |
|---|---|
| **Jan. 1, Year 10** | Entries for obtaining the loan, buying the oil property, and buying the equipment. |
| **Jan. 31** | Record development expense. |
| **May 1** | Record cost of constructing pipeline. |
| **Dec. 31** | Record operating expenses for the year. |
| **Dec. 31** | Record depletion expense based on per-barrel rate. |
| **Dec. 31** | Record depreciation of equipment based on per-barrel rate. |

| | |
|---|---|
| Dec. 31 | Record depreciation of pipeline based on per-barrel rate. |
| Dec. 31 | Record payment of interest expense on note payable. |
| Dec. 31, Year 11 | Record cash operating expenses for Year 11. |
| Dec. 31 | Record depletion expense (800,000 barrels produced) |
| Dec. 31 | Record depreciation of equipment (800,000 barrels produced) |
| Dec. 31 | Record depreciation of pipeline (800,000 barrels produced) |
| Dec. 31 | Record payment of interest on bank loan. |
| Dec. 31 | Set up cost of year-end inventory of 80,000 barrels of oil. (Credit the various expense accounts to which the year's production costs were charged.) |

*12A-7* Classic Furniture is considering purchasing the net assets, exclusive of cash, of Antique Reproductions on January 2, Year 7. Antique Reproductions, a single proprietorship owned by Francis Taylor, has been in business for six years and has reported an average annual net income of $41,000 during this period.

After any necessary adjustments have been made to the accounting records of Antique Reproductions, Classic Furniture will pay a price equal to the book value of net assets, excluding the cash of $35,000, plus an amount for goodwill. Classic Furniture will assume all liabilities of Antique Reproductions. The goodwill is to be determined as four times the amount by which average earnings exceed a normal rate of return of 12% on the present net identifiable assets (owner's equity less goodwill) of Antique Reproductions. The purchase plan calls for Classic Furniture to make a cash down payment of $100,000 and issue a promissory note for the balance of the purchase price.

The balance sheet for Antique Reproductions on December 31, Year 6, follows:

***Assets***

| | | | |
|---|---|---|---|
| *Cash* | | | $ 35,000 |
| *Other current assets* | | | 71,000 |
| *Plant and equipment:* | | | |
| *Land* | | $113,600 | |
| *Buildings* | $146,400 | | |
| *Less: Accumulated depreciation* | 38,400 | 108,000 | |
| *Equipment* | $186,000 | | |
| *Less: Accumulated depreciation* | 117,000 | 69,000 | 290,600 |
| *Patent* | | | 54,000 |
| *Goodwill* | | | 15,000 |
| *Total assets* | | | $465,600 |

***Liabilities & Owner's Equity***

| | |
|---|---|
| *Accounts payable* | $ 74,000 |
| *Long-term liabilities:* | |
| *Mortgage note payable* | 110,000 |
| *Francis Taylor, capital* | 281,600 |
| *Total liabilities & owner's equity* | $465,600 |

**Other data**

(1) The $15,000 of goodwill was recorded in the accounts three years ago when Taylor decided that the increasing profitability of the business should be

The December 31 transaction for the sale of one machine was recorded by a debit to Cash for the $8,000 received from the sale and a credit to Office Equipment for $8,000.

Company policy calls for the depreciation of the data processing machines on a straight-line basis with an estimated useful life of five years and an estimated residual value of $1,000 per machine.

**Instructions**

**a** Prepare one journal entry at December 31 to record depreciation for the year on all four machines.

**b** What was the amount of gain or loss on the sale of the machine on December 31? Show computations.

**c** Prepare one journal entry to ***correct the accounts*** at December 31. In drafting your correcting entry, give consideration to the debit and credit already entered in the accounts on December 31 to record the sale of one of the machines. Your entry should reduce the Office Equipment account and the Accumulated Depreciation account and should record the gain or loss on the disposal of the machine which was not recognized in the entry made at the time of the sale.

*12B-4* Custom Research acquired equipment on July 1, Year 4, at a cost of $103,480. Useful life was estimated to be 10 years and scrap value $4,680. Custom Research depreciates its plant assets by the straight-line method and closes its accounts annually on June 30.

On June 30, Year 7, after considerable experience with the equipment, the company decided that the estimated total life should be revised from 10 years to 6 years and the residual scrap value lowered from $4,680 to $3,120. This revised estimate was made prior to recording depreciation for the fiscal year ended June 30, Year 7.

On December 31, Year 8, the equipment was sold for $17,810 cash.

**Instructions** Prepare journal entries to record all the above transactions and the depreciation expense from July 1, Year 4, to December 31, Year 8. (Use the word "Equipment" as the title of the asset account.)

*12B-5* Scuba Gear maintains its accounting records on the basis of a fiscal year beginning July 1 and ending June 30. On July 1 the company leased a store building from Tucker Investment for a period of 10 years for a total contractual amount of $624,000. Terms of the lease called for an immediate cash payment of $62,400, representing rent for the final year of the 10-year lease period. Also on July 1, Scuba Gear (the lessee) paid $5,200 for the current month's rent and agreed to pay rent monthly in advance during the first nine years of the lease. The lease also provided that Scuba Gear must pay for any repairs or improvements it wished to make. These improvements could not be removed and would revert to the lessor at the end of the lease.

An escalator was immediately installed by the lessee at a cost of $41,600, paid in cash. The normal life of the escalator was stated by the manufacturer to be 20 years. Some lighting fixtures were also installed at a cost of $5,200 paid in cash, for which the estimated life was five years.

**Instructions** Prepare journal entries to record:

**a** Payment of $67,600, representing $5,200 rent for July and $62,400 for the final year's rent under the 10-year lease contract.

**b** Payment for the escalator and lighting fixtures.

**c** First annual amortization of the cost of the escalator.

**d** First annual amortization of the cost of the lighting fixtures.

**e** Final disposition of the $62,400 advance payment of rent applicable to the tenth year of the lease.

*12B-6* Wildcat Mines acquired a coal mine on January 1, Year 10, for a cash price of $5,000,000. Estimates by an independent firm of consulting engineers indicated that the mine contained 1,000,000 tons of coal.

The equipment needed to extract the coal from the mine was purchased January 2, Year 10, for $615,000 cash. This equipment is expected to last for the life of the mine and to have a residual scrap value of $15,000. Depreciation of the equipment is to be computed by the units-of-output method.

During Year 10, a total of 150,000 tons of coal were mined. Of this total, 100,000 tons were sold and 50,000 tons remained in inventory at year-end. Production expenses during the year (other than depreciation and depletion) amounted to $900,000 and were paid in cash. Debit Production Expenses, under date of December 31.

On January 1, Year 11, Wildcat Mines sold the mine, including the equipment and the inventory of 50,000 tons of coal, for a total price of $6,000,000 in cash.

**Instructions**

**a** Compute the cost per ton of coal produced in Year 10. (Cost per ton equals depletion cost per ton plus depreciation cost per ton plus other production costs per ton.) Show the computations in an orderly manner with each element identified.

**b** Compute the cost of the ending inventory of 50,000 tons of coal.

**c** Prepare general journal entries to record the transactions described for Year 10. Entries for sales are to be omitted. Prepare the adjusting entries at December 31, Year 10, to record depletion of the mine and depreciation of the equipment. Record the ending inventory of coal; the offsetting credits should be to the three expense accounts containing the year's production costs.

**d** Prepare a compound journal entry to record the sale of the mine, equipment, and inventory on January 1, Year 11.

*12B-7* Ruth Barnes, an experienced executive in retail store operation, is interested in buying an established business in the retail clothing field. She is now attempting to make a choice among three similar concerns which are available for purchase. All three companies have been in business for five years. The balance sheets presented by the three companies may be summarized as follows:

| *Assets* | *Company X* | *Company Y* | *Company Z* |
|---|---|---|---|
| *Cash* | *$ 24,000* | *$ 24,000* | *$ 40,000* |
| *Accounts receivable* | *185,600* | *190,400* | *217,600* |
| *Inventory* | *352,000* | *288,000* | *288,000* |
| *Plant assets (net)* | *110,400* | *128,000* | *80,000* |
| *Goodwill* | | *4,800* | |
| | *$672,000* | *$635,200* | *$625,600* |
| *Liabilities & Owner's Equity* | | | |
| *Current liabilities* | *$284,800* | *$296,000* | *$320,000* |
| *Owner's equity* | *387,200* | *339,200* | *305,600* |
| | *$672,000* | *$635,200* | *$625,600* |

The average net earnings of the three businesses during the past five years had been as follows: Company X, $59,200; Company Y, $51,200; and Company Z, $54,400.

With the permission of the owners of the three businesses, Barnes arranged for a certified public accountant to examine the accounting records of the companies. This investigation disclosed the following information:

**Accounts receivable** In Company X, no provision for uncollectible accounts had been made at any time, and no accounts receivable had been written off. Numerous past-due receivables were in the accounts, and the estimated uncollectible items which had accumulated during the past five years amounted to $16,000. In both Company Y and Company Z, the receivables appeared to be carried at net realizable value.

**Inventories** Company Y had adopted the first-in, first-out method of inventory valuation when first organized but had changed to the last-in, first-out method after one year. As a result of this change in method of accounting for inventories, the present balance sheet figure for inventories was approximately $32,000 less than replacement cost. The other two companies had used the first-in, first-out method continuously, and their present inventories were approximately equal to replacement cost.

**Plant and equipment** In each of the three companies, the plant assets included a building which had cost $80,000 and had an estimated useful life of 25 years with no residual scrap value. Company X had taken no depreciation on its building; Company Y had used straight-line depreciation at 4% annually; and Company Z had erroneously depreciated its building by applying a constant rate of 4% to the undepreciated balance. (Note that the depreciation method used by Company Z was not accelerated depreciation, because the straight-line rate was not increased. Company Z merely made a basic error in its attempt to use straight-line depreciation.) All plant assets other than buildings had been depreciated on a straight-line basis (correctly applied) in all companies. Barnes believed that the book value of the plant assets in all three companies would approximate fair market value if depreciation were computed uniformly on a straight-line basis.

**Goodwill** The item of goodwill, $4,800, on the balance sheet of Company Y represented the cost of a nonrecurring advertising campaign conducted during the first year of operation.

Barnes is willing to pay for net tangible assets (except cash) at book value, plus an amount for goodwill equal to three times the average annual net earnings in excess of 10% on the net tangible assets. Cash will not be included in the transfer of assets.

**Instructions**

**a** Prepare a revised summary of balance sheet data after correcting all errors made by the companies. In addition to correcting errors, make the necessary changes to apply straight-line depreciation and first-in, first-out inventory methods in all three companies. Round all amounts to the nearest dollar. (In computing the correct amount for net plant assets of Company Z, the following approach may be helpful. First, compute the total depreciation actually taken by Company Z under its erroneous use of straight-line depreciation; next, compute the correct depreciation for the five-year period under straight-line depreciation; finally compare these two totals and use the difference as an adjustment of the net plant assets of Company Z.)

**b** Determine revised amounts for average net earnings of the three companies after taking into consideration the correction of errors and changes of method called for in **a** above.

**c** Determine the price which Barnes should offer for each of the businesses.

## BUSINESS DECISION PROBLEM 12

Jane Carr, president of Carr Home Products Corporation, states that her company has spent nearly a half million dollars during the current year on special advertising campaigns to introduce new products. "The campaigns were begun and completed during the current year," she explains, "but I believe we will be selling these new products for many years in the future. Consequently, I wanted to show the cost of this advertising as an intangible asset on the balance sheet and amortize it over, maybe, 10 years. However, the CPA firm that audits our company insisted on treating this advertising as a charge against this year's operations."

**Instructions**

**a** Is Carr's argument that benefits will be received in future years from the advertising this year to introduce new products a logical and valid one? Explain.

**b** Would Carr's argument for showing the advertising expenditures as an intangible asset be stronger if the bills for the advertising were still unpaid at December 31 and appeared on the year-end balance sheet as a current liability? Give reasons for your answer.

**c** What is the position of the Financial Accounting Standards Board with respect to expenditures for developing intangible assets which are not specifically identifiable?

**d** On balance, what is your conclusion as to whether the advertising expenditures should be an expense of the current year or listed as intangible assets on the balance sheet?

# 13

# PAYROLL ACCOUNTING

Labor costs and related payroll taxes constitute a large and constantly increasing portion of the total costs of operating most business organizations. In the commercial airlines, for example, labor costs traditionally have represented 40 to 50% of total operation costs.

The task of accounting for payroll costs would be an important one simply because of the large amounts involved; however, it is further complicated by the many federal and state laws which require employers to maintain certain specific information in their payroll records not only for the business as a whole but also for each individual employee. Frequent reports of total wages and amounts withheld must be filed with government agencies. These reports are prepared by every employer and must be accompanied by payment to the government of the amounts withheld from employees and of the payroll taxes levied on the employer.

A basic rule in most business organizations is that every employee must be paid on time, and the payment must be accompanied by a detailed explanation of the computations used in determining the net amount received by the employee. The payroll system must therefore be capable of processing the input data (such as employee names, social security numbers, hours worked, pay rates, overtime, and taxes) and producing a prompt and accurate output of paychecks, payroll records, withholding statements, and reports to government agencies. In addition, the payroll system must have built-in safeguards against overpayments to employees, the issuance of duplicate paychecks, payments to fictitious employees, and the continuance on the payroll of persons who have been terminated as employees.

## Internal control over payrolls

The requirements for a payroll system as described in the preceding section indicate the need for strong internal control over payrolls. The large dollar amounts involved; the need for fast, accurate processing of data; the requirement of prompt, regular distribution of payroll checks; the required reports to government—all these factors point to the need for strong internal controls, regardless of whether the business entity is a small one with a manual accounting system or a larger organization using electronic equipment.

Some specific characteristics of present-day payroll accounting reduce the likelihood of payroll frauds, which in the past were common and often substantial. These helpful factors include the required frequent filing of payroll data with the government, and the universal use of employer identification numbers and employees' social security numbers. For example, "padding" a payroll with fictitious names is more difficult when social security numbers must be on file for every employee, individual earnings records must be created, and quarterly reports must be submitted to the Internal Revenue Service, showing for every employee the gross earnings, social security taxes, and income tax withheld.

The repetitive nature of payroll preparation makes it an especially suitable area for use of a computer. However, the widespread use of computers for processing payroll does not mean that the threat of payroll fraud has disappeared. The separation and subdivision of duties is still essential. For the company with an EDP system, adequate internal control over payrolls demands clear separation of the functions of systems analysts, programmers, key-punch operators, computer operators, librarians, and control group personnel. If this segregation of duties is not maintained, the opportunity exists for payroll fraud on a gigantic scale. The fact that virtually all phases of payroll accounting can be handled rapidly by a computer may have induced some companies to place less emphasis on the separation of duties essential to strong internal control.

ILLUSTRATIVE CASE One recent payroll fraud case in a huge company was linked with a well-publicized change in income tax rates. Knowing that employees expected a change in the amount of tax withheld on the officially scheduled date, a computer operator with wide latitude of duties purposely overstated each employee's tax by a few cents and diverted to himself the aggregate of these amounts. Since a very large labor force was involved, the dollar amount of the fraud was quite substantial. This irregularity would not have been possible if reasonable standards for subdivision of duties had been maintained.

In most organizations the payroll activities include the functions of (1) employing workers, (2) timekeeping, (3) payroll preparation and record keeping, and (4) the distribution of pay to employees. Internal control will be strengthened if each of these functions is handled by a separate department of the company.

**Employment (personnel) department** The work of the employment or personnel department may begin with screening of applicants. For those applicants who appear acceptable, interviews are arranged with the line supervisor for whom

the practice of public accounting and accept a position as controller of a company, he or she would become an employee. Another example of independent contractors is that of typists who, using their own typewriters, supplies, and office space, type term papers for college students for a fee. The ***fees*** paid to independent contractors are distinct from ***salaries*** and ***wages;*** they are not included in payroll records and are not subject to withholding.

Compensation to employees on an hourly rate or on a piecework basis is usually called ***wages.*** Compensation on a monthly or yearly basis is usually referred to as ***salary.*** The ***hourly payroll*** for wages is often prepared separately from the ***monthly salary payroll*** as a matter of convenience in computation, but both are subject to the same tax rules. In practice, one often finds the terms ***wages*** and ***salaries*** used interchangeably.

### Employee earnings

Employers engaged in interstate commerce are required by the Federal Fair Labor Standards Act (also known as the Wages and Hours Law) to pay overtime at a minimum rate of $1\frac{1}{2}$ times the regular rate for hours worked in excess of 40 per week. Many companies also pay overtime premium rates for night shifts and for work on Sundays and holidays. Since wages earned are now commonly based on hours worked at various rates, the function of timekeeping has become of increased importance. Time clocks and time cards are widely used in compiling the detailed information required for payroll purposes.

### Deductions from earnings of employees

The take-home pay of most employees is much less than the gross earnings. Major factors explaining this difference between the amount earned and the amount received are social security taxes, federal income taxes withheld, and other deductions discussed below.

### Social security taxes (FICA)

Under the terms of the Social Security Act, qualified workers who retire after reaching a specified age receive monthly retirement payments and Medicare benefits. Benefits are also provided for the family of a worker who dies before or after reaching this retirement age. Funds for the operation of this program are obtained through taxes levied under the Federal Insurance Contributions Act, often referred to as FICA taxes, or simply as ***social security taxes.***

Employers are required by the Federal Insurance Contributions Act to withhold a portion of each employee's earnings as a contribution to the social security program. A tax at the same rate is levied against the employer. For example, assume that an employee earns $20,000 subject to FICA taxes of 6%. The employer will withhold $1,200 ($20,000 × .06) from the employee's earnings. The employer will then pay to the government the amount of $2,400, consisting of the $1,200 withheld from the employee plus an additional $1,200 of FICA tax on the employer.

Our discussion is focused on FICA taxes on employers and employees. However, self-employed persons such as independent contractors and proprietors of small businesses also must pay FICA taxes.

Two factors are involved in computing the FICA tax: the ***base*** or amount of earnings subject to the tax, and the ***rate*** which is applied to the base. Both the ***base*** and the ***rate*** have been increased many times in recent years and probably will continue to be changed in future years. The following table indicates that individuals were required to pay approximately 53 times as much in 1980 as they were in 1937 when the social security plan was started.

| *Year* | *Base (Earnings Subject to FICA Tax)* | *Tax Rate* | *Amount of Tax* |
|---|---|---|---|
| *1937* | *$ 3,000* | *1.0%* | *$ 30* |
| *1951* | *3,600* | *1.5%* | *54* |
| *1966* | *6,600* | *4.2%* | *277* |
| *1972* | *9,000* | *5.2%* | *468* |
| *1977* | *16,500* | *5.85%* | *965* |
| *1980* | *25,900* | *6.13%* | *1,588* |
| *1990* | *?* | *?* | *?* |

These changes in rates and in the base do not affect the accounting principles or procedures involved. For illustrative purposes in this book, we shall assume the rate of tax to be 6% on both the employee and the employer, applicable to a base of $26,000 (the first $26,000 of wages received by each employee in each calendar year). This assumption of round amounts for both the tax and the base is a convenient one for the purpose of illustrations and for the solution of problems by the student, regardless of frequent changes in the rate and base.

An example may clarify the expression "subject to FICA tax." Assume that during a year when a $26,000 base prevails, you earn $30,000 in salary. You would have to pay the 6% FICA tax on $26,000 of your salary. You would not pay FICA tax on the $4,000 by which your salary exceeded the $26,000 base.

### Federal income taxes

Our pay-as-you-go system of federal income tax requires employers to withhold a portion of the earnings of their employees. The amount withheld depends upon the amount of the earnings and upon the number of income tax exemptions claimed by the employee. For each income tax exemption, the employee is entitled to a withholding allowance currently amounting to $1,000. Each withholding allowance thus causes $1,000 of yearly earnings to be exempt from income tax. On a federal income tax return, one exemption is allowed for oneself, one for a spouse, and one for each dependent. Thus a married couple with three dependent children would be entitled to five exemptions and would qualify for five withholding allowances. Each new employee is asked to file a withholding allowance certificate (Form W-4) as illustrated below.

Form **W-4** (Rev. October 1979)

Department of the Treasury—Internal Revenue Service

**Employee's Withholding Allowance Certificate**

Print your full name ▶ RITA MILLER | Your social security number ▶ 572 : 19 : 4627

Address (including ZIP code) ▶ 403 COLLEGE AVE. RENO, NEVADA 89504

Marital status: ☐ Single ☒ Married ☐ Married, but withhold at higher Single rate

**Note:** *If married, but legally separated, or spouse is a nonresident alien, check the single block.*

1 Total number of allowances you are claiming (from line F of the worksheet on page 2) . . . . . . . . . . . 2

2 Additional amount, if any, you want deducted from each pay (if your employer agrees) . . . . . . . . . . . $

3 I claim exemption from withholding because (see instructions and check boxes below that apply):

a ☐ Last year I did not owe any Federal income tax and had a right to a full refund of ALL income tax withheld, AND

b ☐ This year I do not expect to owe any Federal income tax and expect to have a right to a full refund of ALL income tax withheld. If both a and b apply, enter "EXEMPT" here . . . . . . . . . . . . . . . . ▶

c If you entered "EXEMPT" on line 3b, are you a full-time student? . . . . . . . . . . . . . . . ☐ Yes ☐ No

Under the penalties of perjury, I certify that I am entitled to the number of withholding allowances claimed on this certificate, or if claiming exemption from withholding, that I am entitled to claim the exempt status.

Employee's signature ▶ Rita Miller Date ▶ January 2, 198X

Employer's name and address (including ZIP code) (FOR EMPLOYER'S USE ONLY): Wilton Company, 690 Delta Drive, Reno, Nevada 89504

Employer identification number: 95-2215683

The withholding allowance certificate (Form W-4) states the number of allowances claimed. If the number of dependents changes, the employee may file a new certificate. Persons over sixty-five or blind are entitled to additional allowances. (More extensive consideration of exemptions and other aspects of federal income taxes will be discussed in Chapter 20.) The allowance certificate is given to the employing company so that it will be able to compute the proper amount of tax to be withheld. As a matter of convenience to employers, the government provides withholding tax tables which indicate the amount to withhold for any amount of earnings and any number of withholding allowances.

Present regulations provide a graduated system of withholding, designed to make the amount of income tax withheld approximate the individual's tax liability at the end of the year. Because persons in higher income brackets are subject to higher rates of taxation, the withholding rates are correspondingly higher for them. There is no ceiling with respect to the amount of salary subject to income tax.

Most states and cities which levy income taxes also require the employer to withhold the tax from employees' earnings. Because such situations involve a variety of rates, they will not be discussed here.

### Other deductions from employees' earnings

In addition to the compulsory deductions for taxes, many other deductions are voluntarily authorized by employees. Union dues and insurance premiums already have been mentioned as examples of payroll deductions. Others include charitable contributions, retirement programs, savings bond purchases, and pension plans.

### Employer's responsibility for amounts withheld

In withholding amounts from an employee's earnings for either voluntary or involuntary deductions, the employer acts merely as a collection agent. The amounts withheld are paid to the designated organization, such as a government agency or labor union. The employer is also responsible for maintaining accounting records which will enable it to file required reports and make timely payments of the amounts withheld. From the employer's viewpoint, the amounts withheld from employees' earnings represent current liabilities. A statement of earnings and deductions is usually prepared by the employer and given to the employee with each paycheck or pay envelope to explain how the net pay was determined.

### Illustration: computation of employee's net pay

This illustration shows the deductions which typically may explain the difference between ***gross earnings*** for a pay period and the "take-home" pay, or net amount received by an employee. The deductions are in part based upon the two withholding allowances indicated in Rita Miller's Employee's Withholding Allowance Certificate illustrated previously. The pay period is for the month of May. Remember that state income taxes have purposely been omitted from our illustration.

***Total earnings minus deductions equal take-home pay***

| | | |
|---|---|---|
| *Gross earnings of employee Miller for the month* | | *$2,500.00* |
| *Deductions:* | | |
| *FICA tax (assume 6%)* | *$150.00* | |
| *Federal income tax* | *492.80* | |
| *Retirement plan (assume 4%)* | *100.00* | |
| *Group insurance* | *42.20* | |
| *Total deductions from Miller's earnings* | | *785.00* |
| *Net take-home pay for the month for employee Rita Miller* | | *$1,715.00* |

In the preceding illustration, the inclusion of the FICA deduction shows that Rita Miller's earnings thus far in the calendar year had not reached the $26,000 maximim earnings assumed to be subject to FICA taxes. Since Miller earns $2,500 a month, her take-home pay of $1,715 can be expected to rise by $150 after November when her gross earnings will have passed the $26,000 base amount subject to FICA taxes.

The amount of federal income tax withheld, $492.80, was determined by reference to the monthly wage bracket for a married taxpayer with two withholding allowances, as shown in the withholding tables published by the Internal Revenue Service. These tables show the amounts to be withheld for employees at various wage levels and for varying numbers of withholding allowances. A small section of a withholding table is shown on page 498; the amount applicable to Rita Miller in our illustration is circled.

**MARRIED Persons — MONTHLY Payroll Period**

| And the wages are— | | And the number of withholding allowances claimed is— | | | | | | | | | | |
|---|---|---|---|---|---|---|---|---|---|---|---|---|
| At least | But less than | 0 | 1 | 2 | 3 | 4 | 5 | 6 | 7 | 8 | 9 | 10 or more |
| | | The amount of income tax to be withheld shall be— | | | | | | | | | | |
| $2,160 | 2,200 | 443.70 | 417.00 | 390.40 | 365.20 | 341.80 | 318.50 | 295.20 | 272.00 | 252.00 | 232.00 | 212.00 |
| 2,200 | 2,240 | 456.50 | 429.80 | 403.20 | 376.50 | 353.00 | 329.70 | 306.40 | 283.00 | 261.60 | 241.60 | 221.60 |
| 2,240 | 2,280 | 469.30 | 442.60 | 416.00 | 389.30 | 364.20* | 340.90 | 317.60 | 294.20 | 271.20 | 251.20 | 231.20 |
| 2,280 | 2,320 | 482.10 | 455.40 | 428.80 | 402.10 | 375.40 | 352.10 | 328.80 | 305.40 | 282.10 | 260.80 | 240.80 |
| 2,320 | 2,360 | 494.90 | 468.20 | 441.60 | 414.90 | 388.20 | 363.30 | 340.00 | 316.60 | 293.30 | 270.40 | 250.40 |
| 2,360 | 2,400 | 507.70 | 481.00 | 454.40 | 427.70 | 401.00 | 374.50 | 351.20 | 327.80 | 304.50 | 281.20 | 260.00 |
| 2,400 | 2,440 | 521.10 | 493.80 | 467.20 | 440.50 | 413.80 | 387.20 | 362.40 | 339.00 | 315.70 | 292.40 | 269.60 |
| 2,440 | 2,480 | 535.90 | 506.60 | 480.00 | 453.30 | 426.60 | 400.00 | 373.60 | 350.20 | 326.90 | 303.60 | 280.20 |
| 2,480 | 2,520 | 550.70 | 519.80 | 492.80 | 466.10 | 439.40 | 412.80 | 386.10 | 361.40 | 338.10 | 314.80 | 291.40 |
| 2,520 | 2,560 | 565.50 | 534.60 | 505.60 | 478.90 | 452.20 | 425.60 | 398.90 | 372.60 | 349.30 | 326.00 | 302.60 |
| 2,560 | 2,600 | 580.30 | 549.40 | 518.60 | 491.70 | 465.00 | 438.40 | 411.70 | 385.00 | 360.50 | 337.20 | 313.80 |
| 2,600 | 2,640 | 595.10 | 564.20 | 533.40 | 504.50 | 477.80 | 451.20 | 424.50 | 397.80 | 371.70 | 348.40 | 325.00 |
| 2,640 | 2,680 | 609.90 | 579.00 | 548.20 | 517.40 | 490.60 | 464.00 | 437.30 | 410.60 | 384.00 | 359.60 | 336.20 |
| 2,680 | 2,720 | 624.70 | 593.80 | 563.00 | 532.20 | 503.40 | 476.80 | 450.10 | 423.40 | 396.80 | 370.80 | 347.40 |
| 2,720 | 2,760 | 639.50 | 608.60 | 577.80 | 547.00 | 516.20 | 489.60 | 462.90 | 436.20 | 409.60 | 382.90 | 358.60 |

The other two deductions from gross earnings (for a retirement plan and for group insurance) were voluntary and had been authorized in writing by Rita Miller.

### Payroll records and procedures

Although payroll records and procedures vary greatly according to the number of employees and the extent of automation in processing payroll data, there are a few fundamental steps common to payroll work in most organizations. One of these steps taken at the end of each pay period is the preparation of a payroll showing the names and earnings of all employees. The information entered in this payroll record (sometimes called a ***payroll register***) will include the authorized rate of pay for each employee and the number of hours worked, taken from time cards or similar documents. After separating the regular hours from overtime hours and applying appropriate pay rates for each category, the total taxable earnings are determined. Federal income tax, FICA tax, state income tax if any, and any items authorized by the employee are then deducted to arrive at the net amount payable. When the computation of the payroll record has been completed, the next step is to reflect the expense and the related liabilities in the ledger accounts. A general journal entry such as shown below may be made to bring into the accounts the information summarized in the payroll register. (This entry does not include payroll taxes on the employer.)

***Journal entry to record payroll***

| | | |
|---|---|---|
| *Sales Salaries Expense* | *4,800* | |
| *Office Salaries Expense* | *3,200* | |
|     *FICA Tax Payable (6% of $8,000)* | | *480* |
|     *Liability for Income Tax Withheld* | | *1,280* |
|     *Liability for Group Insurance Withheld* | | *150* |
|     *Accrued Payroll* | | *6,090* |
| *To record the payroll for the period Jan. 1–Jan. 15.* | | |

The two debits to expense accounts indicate that the business has incurred salaries expense of $8,000; however, only $6,090 of this amount will be paid to the employees on payday. The payment will be recorded by a debit to Accrued Payroll and a credit to Cash. The remaining $1,910 (consisting of deductions for taxes and insurance premiums withheld) is lodged in liability accounts. Payment of these liabilities will be made at various later dates.

**Payment of employees** The preceding section illustrated the recording of the payroll and showed the sum of $6,090 in a current liability account entitled Accrued Payroll. The procedures for the actual payment to employees to discharge this liability will depend upon whether the company pays salaries by checks on the regular bank account, by checks drawn on a special bank account, or in cash. These payment procedures also depend on whether a voucher system is in use.

Many companies find it convenient to establish a separate payroll bank account. At the close of each pay period, a check is drawn on the general bank account for the entire amount of the payroll and deposited in the payroll bank account. Paychecks to individual employees are then drawn on the payroll bank account, which is immediately reduced to zero. If the voucher system is in use, a voucher for the payroll would be prepared and recorded in the voucher register as a debit to Payroll Bank Account and a credit to Vouchers Payable in the amount of $6,090.[1] The transfer of the funds would then be carried out by issuing a check on the general bank account and recording the disbursement in the check register by a debit to Vouchers Payable and a credit to Cash.

**Payment of employees in cash** Payment of salaries in cash affords less internal control than the use of checks, but is preferred by a few companies in locations where banks or other check-cashing facilities are not readily available. The recording procedures do not differ significantly from those previously described; a voucher is prepared for the amount of the payroll, and a single check drawn and cashed to obtain the cash to fill the individual pay envelopes. As previously mentioned, a statement of earnings and deductions is usually furnished to the employee each payday. When payment is made by check, this information is printed on a stub attached to the paycheck. When wages are paid in cash, the information may be printed on the pay envelope.

**Wage and tax statement** By January 31 each year, employers are required to furnish every employee with a Wage and Tax Statement (Form W-2), illustrated on page 500. This form shows gross earnings for the preceding calendar year and the amounts withheld for FICA tax and income taxes. The employer sends one copy of this form to the Director of Internal Revenue and gives three copies to the employee. When the employee files a federal income tax return, he or she must attach a copy of the withholding statement. A copy also must be attached

---

[1] No vouchers need be prepared at this time for the $1,910 of liabilities resulting from deductions. Vouchers will be prepared prior to the time for payment of these liabilities.

| | | | |
|---|---|---|---|
| 1 Control number | 222 | 2 Employer's State number 214-5176-0 | |
| 3 Employer's name, address, and ZIP code<br>Wilton Company<br>690 Delta Drive<br>Reno, Nevada 89504 | 4 Subtotal Correction Void<br>☐ ☐ ☐<br>5 Employer's identification number<br>95-22125683<br>6 Advance EIC payment | 7 | |
| 8 Employee's social security number<br>572-19-4627 | 9 Federal income tax withheld<br>$5,913.60 | 10 Wages, tips, other compensation<br>$30,000.00 | 11 FICA tax withheld<br>$1,560.00 |
| 12 Total FICA wages<br>$26,000.00 | | | |
| 13 Employee's name (first, middle, last) and address<br>Rita Miller<br>403 College Ave.<br>Reno, Nevada 89504 | 14 Pension plan coverage? Yes/No<br>Yes | 15 | 16 FICA tips |
| | 18 State income tax withheld | 19 State wages, tips, etc. | 20 Name of state<br>Nevada |
| | 21 Local income tax withheld | 22 Local wages, tips, etc. | 23 Name of locality |
| | Copy B To be filed with employee's FEDERAL tax return<br>This information is being furnished to the Internal Revenue Service. | | |

Form **W-2 Wage and Tax Statement 1979** Department of the Treasury—Internal Revenue Service

to the state income tax return. (Since our discussion does not include state income taxes, none is shown on the illustrated Form W-2.)

**Employer's quarterly federal tax return** A business must use the calendar year in accounting for payroll taxes even though it uses a fiscal year for its financial statements and its income tax return. Four times a year, the employer is required to report to the government the amounts withheld from employees' pay for federal income taxes and FICA taxes. The FICA tax on the employer (see page 502) is also shown on the same report form. A copy of this widely used report, known as Form 941, is illustrated on page 501. It shows the total wages paid, the wages subject to FICA taxes, the amount of FICA taxes, and the amount of federal income taxes withheld. The report must be filed during the month following the close of each quarter.

**Payment of payroll taxes** If the amounts withheld from employees plus the payroll taxes on the employer are significant in amount, they must be deposited at weekly or monthly intervals. Only a very small business with less than $200 of taxes involved may wait until the end of the quarter to make payment. The key point of the schedule for deposits is that the government insists on current payment from the employer of all payroll taxes and income taxes withheld.

**Individual earnings records for employees** At the end of each payroll period, it is essential to have available the cumulative amount of each employee's earnings for the year to date. Otherwise, the employer would not know whether FICA taxes should be withheld from the employee's earnings during the current week or month. An individual Employee Earnings Record is illustrated on page 502. The payroll data to update this individual record are taken at the end of each pay period from a line in the payroll register.

Form **941**
(Rev. July 1979)
Department of the Treasury
Internal Revenue Service

## Employer's Quarterly Federal Tax Return

| | | |
|---|---|---|
| Your name, address, employer identification number, and calendar quarter of return. (If not correct, please change) | Name (as distinguished from trade name): John Wilton<br>Trade name, if any: Wilton Company<br>Address and ZIP code: 690 Delta Drive, Reno, Nevada 89504 | Date quarter ended: September 30, 198X<br>Employer identification number: 95-2215683 |

T / FF / FD / FP / I / T

If address is different from prior return, check here ▶ ☐

| Line | | Amount | |
|---|---|---|---|
| 1 | Number of employees (except household) employed in the pay period that includes March 12th (complete for first quarter only) | | |
| 2 | Total wages and tips subject to withholding, plus other compensation → | 18,224 | 88 |
| 3 | Total income tax withheld from wages, tips, annuities, gambling, etc. (see instructions) | 4,607 | 80 |
| 4 | Adjustment of withheld income tax for preceding quarters of calendar year | | |
| 5 | Adjusted total of income tax withheld → | 4,607 | 80 |
| 6 | Taxable FICA wages paid $3,224.88 multiplied by 12.26% = TAX | 395 | 37 |
| 7 | Taxable tips reported $ multiplied by 6.13% = TAX | | |
| 8 | Total FICA taxes (add lines 6 and 7) → | 395 | 37 |
| 9 | Adjustment of FICA taxes (see instructions) (fractions only) | | 01 |
| 10 | Adjusted total of FICA taxes → | 395 | 38 |
| 11 | Total taxes (add lines 5 and 10) | 5,003 | 18 |
| 12 | Advance earned income credit (EIC) payments, if any (see instructions) | | |
| 13 | Net taxes (subtract line 12 from line 11) | 5,003 | 18 |

**Record of Federal Tax Deposits (See instructions on page 4)**

| Deposit period ending: | | I. Tax liability for period | II. Date of deposit | III. Amount deposited |
|---|---|---|---|---|
| Overpayment from previous quarter | | | | |
| First month of quarter | 1st through 7th day | | | |
| | 8th through 15th day | | | |
| | 16th through 22d day | | | |
| | 23d through last day | | | |
| A First month total | A | 1,723.56 | 8-1-8X | 1,723.56 |
| Second month of quarter | 1st through 7th day | | | |
| | 8th through 15th day | | | |
| | 16th through 22d day | | | |
| | 23d through last day | | | |
| B Second month total | B | 1,646.18 | 9-11-8X | 1,646.18 |
| Third month of quarter | 1st through 7th day | | | |
| | 8th through 15th day | | | |
| | 16th through 22d day | | | |
| | 23d through last day | | | |
| C Third month total | C | 1,633.44 | 10-5-8X | 1,633.44 |
| D Total for quarter (add items A, B, and C) | | 5,003.18 | | 5,003.18 |
| E Final deposit made for quarter. (Enter zero if the final deposit made for the quarter is included in item D) | | | | |

| Line | | Amount | |
|---|---|---|---|
| 14 | Total deposits for quarter (including final deposit made for quarter) and overpayment from previous quarter. (See instructions for deposit requirements on page 4)<br>Note: *If undeposited taxes at the end of the quarter are $200 or more, deposit the full amount with an authorized financial institution or a Federal Reserve bank according to the instructions on the back of the Federal Tax Deposit Form 501. Enter this deposit in the Record of Federal Tax Deposits and include it on line 14.* | 5,003 | 18 |
| 15 | Undeposited taxes due (subtract line 14 from line 13—this should be less than $200). Pay to Internal Revenue Service and enter here → | 0 | 00 |

16 If line 14 is more than line 13, enter overpayment here ▶ $ and check if to be: ☐ Applied to next return, or ☐ Refunded.

17 If you are not liable for returns in the future, write "FINAL." (See instructions) ▶ Date final wages paid ▶

Under penalties of perjury, I declare that I have examined this return, including accompanying schedules and statements, and to the best of my knowledge and belief it is true, correct, and complete.

Date ▶ October 5, 198X Signature ▶ *John Wilton* Title ▶ *Owner*

**Please file this form with your Internal Revenue Service Center (see instructions on "Where to File").** Form **941** (Rev. 7-79)

This detailed record also shows for each employee the gross earnings for each pay period, the deduction for FICA tax, the income tax withheld, other deductions authorized by the employee, and the amount of net pay. These employee earnings records are used by employers in preparing the quarterly and annual

**Employee Earnings Record**

Name Rita Miller
Address 403 College ave.
Reno, NV. 89504
Position Supervisor
Married X Single
Number of exemptions 2

Social security no. 572-19-4627
Date of birth January 19, 195X
Date employed July 19, 198X
Date terminated
Reason for termination
Rate of pay $2,500 month

| Pay Period Ended | Hours Worked: Regular | Hours Worked: Overtime | Earnings: Regular | Earnings: Overtime | Earnings: Gross Pay | Earnings: Cumulative | Deductions: FICA Tax | Deductions: Federal Income Tax | Deductions: Other | Net Pay | Check No. |
|---|---|---|---|---|---|---|---|---|---|---|---|
| 198X 1-31 | | | | | 2,500.00 | 2,500.00 | 150.00 | 492.80 | 142.20 | 1,715.00 | 309 |
| 2-28 | | | | | 2,500.00 | 5,000.00 | 150.00 | 492.80 | 142.20 | 1,715.00 | 398 |
| 3-31 | | | | | 2,500.00 | 7,500.00 | 150.00 | 492.80 | 142.20 | 1,715.00 | 481 |
| Total 1st Qtr. | | | | | 7,500.00 | 7,500.00 | 450.00 | 1,478.40 | 426.60 | 5,145.00 | |
| | | | | | | | | | | | |
| | | | | | | | | | | | |
| | | | | | | | | | | | |
| Totals Year | | | | | 30,000.00 | 30,000.00 | 1,560.00 | 5,913.60 | 1,706.40 | 20,820.00 | |

reports which they must file with federal and state authorities. A variety of other uses may occur such as calculating bonuses, or proving compliance with the Federal Wages and Hours Law.

## Payroll taxes on the employer

The discussion of payroll taxes up to this point has dealt with taxes levied on employees and withheld from their pay. From the viewpoint of the employing company, such withheld taxes are significant because they must be accounted for and remitted in a timely manner to the appropriate government agencies. However, ***payroll taxes are also levied on the employer.*** These taxes on the employer are expenses of the business and ***are recorded by debits to expense accounts,*** just as in the case of property taxes or license fees for doing business.

**Social security (FICA) tax** The employer is taxed to help finance the social security program. The tax is figured at the same rate and on the same amount of earnings used to compute FICA tax on employees. (In all problems and illustrations in this book, the tax is assumed to be 6% on the first $26,000 of gross earnings by each employee in each calendar year.)

**Federal unemployment insurance tax** Unemployment insurance is another part of the national social security program designed to offer temporary relief to unemployed persons. The FUTA tax (Federal Unemployment Tax Act) is levied on ***employers only*** and is not deducted from the wages of employees. The FUTA tax (also known as "unemployment compensation" or UC) applies to approximately the same classes of employment as the FICA tax. The rates of tax and the wage base subject to the tax are changed from time to time. For purposes of illustration in this book, we shall assume that employers are subject to federal unemployment tax at the rate of 3.4% on the first $6,000 of ***each employee's earnings*** in each calendar year. However, the employer may take a credit against this tax (not in excess of 2.7% of the first $6,000 of each employee's wages) for amounts that are paid into state unemployment funds. As a result, an employer may be subject to a ***federal*** tax of only 0.7% on wages up to $6,000 per employee.

**State unemployment compensation tax** All the states participate in the federal-state unemployment insurance program. Although the state laws vary somewhat as to types of covered employment, the usual rate of tax is 2.7% of the first $6,000 of earnings by each employee during a calendar year. Under this provision, the employer actually makes payment of the larger part of the FUTA tax directly to state governments which carry out the federal-state unemployment insurance program.

This arrangement means that the FUTA tax is divided into two parts: the larger part, or 2.7% (.90 × .03), of the first $6,000 of wages paid going to the state and the remainder to the federal government. Some states use a merit-rating plan enabling those employers who maintain stable work forces to pay a reduced rate of state unemployment tax. Under the merit-rating plans of some states, an employer whose employees have applied for little or no unemployment compensation may be rewarded with a rate of perhaps 1 to 2% rather than the standard 2.7%. In computing the federal unemployment compensation tax, the employer company will still receive credit for the full 2.7% it would have been required to pay the state if it had not qualified as a superior risk.

**Accounting entry for employer's payroll taxes** The entry to record the employer's payroll taxes is usually made at the same time the payroll is recorded. To illustrate, let us use again the $8,000 payroll first used on page 498 in the discussion of amounts withheld from employees; this time, however, we are illustrating taxes levied on the ***employer***. (None of the employees has earned over $6,000 since this is the first pay period of the current year.)

***Journal entry to record payroll taxes on employer***

| | | |
|---|---|---|
| *Payroll Taxes Expense* | *752* | |
| *FICA Tax Payable (6% of $8,000)* | | *480* |
| *State Unemployment Tax Payable (2.7% of $8,000)* | | *216* |
| *Federal Unemployment Tax Payable (0.7% of $8,000)* | | *56* |
| *To record payroll taxes on employer for period ended Jan. 15.* | | |

Thus the total payroll expense for the employer is $8,752, which consists of wages of $8,000 and payroll taxes of $752.

### Accrual of payroll taxes at year-end

The payroll taxes levied against an employer become a legal liability when wages are actually paid, rather than at the time the services by employees are rendered. If the wages earned in a given accounting period are paid in the same period, the payroll tax expense is clearly applicable to that period. However, at year-end, most businesses make an adjusting entry to accrue wages earned by employees but not payable until the following period. Should the related payroll taxes on the employer also be accrued? Logically, both wages and taxes on such wages are an expense of the period in which the wages are earned and should therefore be accrued. However, as a practical matter, many businesses do not accrue the payroll tax expense because legally the liability does not come into being until the following year when the wages are paid. In determining income subject to federal income tax, the legal concept prevails, and payroll tax cannot be deducted until the period in which paid. As a matter of convenience, many companies want their accounting records and their income tax returns to agree as closely as possible; therefore such companies prefer ***not to accrue*** payroll tax on employers. This conflict between the logic of accounting principles and the administrative conveniences built into tax laws appears in many other areas of accounting apart from payroll taxes.

### Presentation of payroll taxes in the financial statements

The payroll taxes levied on the employer and the taxes withheld from employees are current liabilities of the business until payment to the government is made. The following accounts are, therefore, classified in the balance sheet as current liabilities: FICA Taxes Payable, Federal Unemployment Taxes Payable, State Unemployment Taxes Payable, and Liability for Income Tax Withheld.

Payroll Taxes Expense appears in the income statement: it may be apportioned between selling expenses and general expenses on the basis of the amount of payroll originating in each functional division. Thus, payroll taxes on salaries of the sales staff are classified as a selling expense, and payroll taxes on office salaries are classified as a general and administrative expense.

## KEY TERMS INTRODUCED OR EMPHASIZED IN CHAPTER 13

**Employee's earnings record** A record maintained for each employee summarizing gross earnings, deductions, net pay, and other payroll information.

**Employee's Withholding Allowance Certificate (W-4)** A federal form prepared by the employee and given to the employer stating the number of withholding exemptions claimed. Used in determining the amount of income tax to be withheld from the employee's pay.

**Employer's Quarterly Federal Tax Return (Form 941)** A report prepared every three months by the employer to provide the federal government with a record of all wages paid, amounts withheld, and amounts of tax on both employees and employer.

**Federal Unemployment Compensation Tax (FUTA)** A tax imposed on the employer by the Federal Unemployment Tax Act based on amount of payrolls. Designed to provide temporary payments to unemployed persons.

**FICA tax** Payroll tax imposed by the Federal Insurance Contribution Act on both employer and employees. Used to finance the social security program of monthly retirement payments and Medicare benefits. Benefits also are paid to the family of a worker who dies before reaching retirement age.

**Gross earnings** Total amount earned by an employce before deductions such as social security taxes, federal income tax withheld, and any voluntary deductions.

**Independent contractor** A person or firm providing services to a company for a fee or commission. Not controlled or supervised by the client company. Not subject to payroll taxes.

**Payroll** A record listing the names of employees during a given pay period, the rates of pay, time worked, gross earnings, deductions for taxes and any other amounts withheld, and net pay.

**Payroll register** A form of payroll record showing for each pay period all payroll information for employees individually and in total.

**Salaries** Compensation on a monthly or yearly basis to employees performing administrative, managerial, or professional duties.

**State unemployment compensation tax** A tax generally levied on employers only and based on payrolls. A part of the joint federal-state program to provide payments to unemployed persons. (In a few states a tax is also levied on employees.)

**Wage and Tax Statement (W-2 Form)** A form furnished by the employer to every employee showing the employee's gross earnings for the calendar year and the amounts withheld for FICA taxes and income taxes.

**Wages** Compensation to employees computed at an hourly rate or on a piecework basis.

**Withholding tables** Tables provided by federal and state governments showing amounts of federal and state income taxes to be withheld from employees' pay.

## REVIEW QUESTIONS

**1** Name the federal taxes that most employers are required to withhold from employees. What account or accounts would be credited with the amounts withheld?

**2** Distinguish between an employee and an independent contractor. Why is this distinction important with respect to payroll accounting?

**3** Explain which of the following taxes relating to an employee's wages are borne by the employee and which by the employer:
- **a** FICA taxes
- **b** Federal unemployment compensation taxes
- **c** State unemployment compensation taxes
- **d** Federal income taxes

**4** List four kinds of information which constitute input to the payroll accounting system and four kinds of information included in the output of the payroll system.

5 That type of payroll fraud known as "padding" a payroll is a more difficult maneuver under today's payroll accounting practices than it was a generation or more ago. What present-day factors make the padding of payrolls a complex and more difficult type of fraud?

6 Is the Salary Expense account equal to "take-home" pay or to gross earnings? Why?

7 When and for what purpose is an Employee's Withholding Allowance Certificate obtained?

8 What purposes are served by maintaining a detailed earnings record for each employee?

9 Are the payroll taxes levied against employers considered a legal liability and a deductible expense in the period the wages are earned by the employees or in the period the wages are paid?

10 Explain two methods which have been used repeatedly by the federal government in increasing the amount of FICA taxes over the years.

11 John Adams earns $7 an hour and works a varying number of hours in each pay period. What documents or materials would an employer need to use in determining the amount of income tax to withhold from Adams's pay?

12 William Smith is employed at a monthly salary of $2,200. He is married and claims two withholding allowances on his W-4 form. Use the withholding table on page 498 to determine the amount of federal income tax which will be withheld from Smith's monthly paycheck.

## EXERCISES

*Ex. 13-1* The payroll of Fields Company may be summarized as follows:

| | |
|---|---|
| *Gross earnings of employees* | *$400,000* |
| *Employee earnings not subject to FICA tax* | *48,000* |
| *Employee earnings not subject to FUTA tax* | *75,000* |

Assuming that the payroll is subject to an FICA tax rate of 6%, a 2.7% state unemployment tax rate, and an FUTA tax rate of .7 of 1%, compute the amount of the Fields Company's ***payroll tax expense*** for the year, showing separately the amount of each of the three taxes. (Note: Taxes on employees are not involved in this exercise.)

*Ex. 13-2* Windsor Milling Company had 100 employees throughout the current year. The lowest-paid employee had gross earnings of $8,000. Assume that the Federal Unemployment Tax Act specifies a rate of 3.4% on the first $6,000 of gross earnings, and that the state unemployment tax is 2.7% of the same base. The employer is permitted to take as a credit against the federal tax the 2.7% of wages paid to the state. Compute the following:

**a** The state unemployment tax for the year
**b** The federal unemployment tax for the year
**c** The total unemployment tax for the year

*Ex. 13-3* Arthur Ward's base rate of pay as a machinist is $12 an hour and he is entitled to time and one-half for overtime. During the week ended December 10, he worked 50 hours. His cumulative earnings for the year prior to the current week had been $25,600. The federal income tax withheld for the current week was $138.30. Prepare a schedule showing for Ward his earnings for the current week, deductions, and net pay. Assume the FICA tax rate to be 6% and the base to be $26,000.

*Ex. 13-4* Diane Hill was employed as a chemist throughout the year at Metal Industries. Her monthly salary was $2,225 during the first six months of the year; on July 1 her salary was increased to $2,500 monthly. Hill is married and claims one withholding allowance on the W-4 form filed with her employer. Assume that FICA tax is 6% on the first $26,000 earned in a calendar year.

Compute Diane Hill's deductions for FICA taxes and federal income tax withheld and her net pay for the month of June and for the month of December. (Refer to the withholding tables on page 498 to determine the amounts of income tax withheld.)

*Ex. 13-5* Ruth Cohen is employed at a base rate of $5 an hour by a company subject to the Fair Labor Standards Act (Wages and Hours Law). The only deductions for Cohen are FICA taxes and $39.80 for federal income taxes. During the first week in January Cohen worked 45 hours. You are to prepare a schedule showing her regular pay, overtime premium pay, gross earnings for the week, FICA tax deduction (assume a 6% rate), federal income tax deduction, and net pay.

*Ex. 13-6* The payroll record of Miller Company for the week ended January 7 showed the following amounts for total earnings: sales employees $8,800; office employees $7,200. Amounts withheld consisted of FICA taxes at a 6% rate on all earnings for this period, federal income taxes $1,920, and medical insurance $600.

**a** After computing the amount of FICA taxes withheld, prepare a general journal entry to record the payroll. Do not include taxes on the employer.

**b** Prepare a general journal entry to record the payroll taxes expense to Miller Company relating to this payroll. Assume that the federal unemployment tax rate is 3.4% of the first $6,000 paid each employee, and that 2.7% of this tax is payable to the state. No employee received more than $6,000 in this first pay period of the year.

*Ex. 13-7* A foreman in the factory of Barton Products, a large manufacturing company, discharged an employee but did not notify the personnel department of this action. The foreman then began forging the employee's signature on time cards. When giving out paychecks, the foreman diverted to his own use the paychecks drawn payable to the discharged worker. What internal control measure would be most effective in preventing this fraudulent activity?

## PROBLEMS

### Group A

*13A-1* Char Burger, a chain of 10 drive-in hamburger stands, is a sole proprietorship owned by Betty Lee. Although Lee has other business interests, she devotes a portion of her time to management of the drive-in chain. A manager is employed at each of the 10 locations and the number of employees at each location varies from six to twelve.

The manager of each unit prepares payroll sheets each week showing hours worked as reported by the employees on time cards which are approved by the manager. Each manager's salary is also listed on the weekly payroll. Upon completion of the payroll, the manager pays all employees and him- or herself in cash. Each employee acknowledges receipt of payment by signing the payroll sheet.

Employees at each branch are employed and terminated by the local managers, who also set wage rates. The salaries of the managers are authorized by Betty Lee.

Each week the payroll sheets are mailed by the managers to Lee, whose secretary prepares individual earnings records for each employee and compiles federal and state tax returns from the weekly payroll sheets.

**Instructions**

**a** Write a paragraph evaluating the adequacy of internal controls over payrolls. State the specific practices, if any, which you think should be changed.

**b** List four specific ways in which payroll fraud could be carried on by the manager of any of the 10 drive-ins.

*13A-2* The payroll records of Copper Kettle for the first week in January showed total salaries earned by employees of $12,000. This total included $7,000 of salaries to sales employees and $5,000 to office employees.

The amounts withheld from employees' pay consisted of FICA taxes computed at an assumed rate of 6%, federal income taxes of $1,150, and group insurance premiums of $140.

**Instructions**

**a** Prepare a general journal entry to summarize the above payroll and the deductions from the earnings of employees. Payroll taxes on the employer are not to be included in this entry.

**b** Prepare a general journal entry to summarize the payroll taxes on the ***employer*** associated with the above payroll. Assumed tax rates are as follows: FICA tax of 6%, state unemployment tax of 2.7%, and a federal unemployment tax of .7%.

**c** What is the amount of the total payroll expense of Copper Kettle for the first week in January? Show computations.

*13A-3* Denver Company is located in a state which permits a company to pay a reduced state unemployment tax rate if the company's employees have collected little unemployment insurance. Denver Company has an excellent record of maintaining a stable work force and therefore qualifies under the merit plan for a rate of 1.2% rather than the usual 2.7% of gross earnings.

The employees' earnings records thus far in the current year are as follows:

| *Employee* | *Cumulative Earnings* | *Employee* | *Cumulative Earnings* |
|---|---|---|---|
| *Arthur, D. S.* | *$14,322* | *Hamilton, A. J.* | *$ 8,771* |
| *Barnett, S. T.* | *11,868* | *Monday, M. D.* | *17,328* |
| *Darwin, E. G.* | *2,550* | *Saunders, K. U.* | *3,930* |
| *Greer, C. K.* | *6,167* | *Taylor, M. E.* | *30,065* |

FICA taxes are assumed to be 6% on the first $26,000 of an employee's gross earnings. The federal unemployment tax is assumed to be 3.4% of the first $6,000 of gross earnings, but with credit to the employer for a maximum of 2.7% of gross earnings for state unemployment taxes.

**Instructions**

**a** Prepare a schedule showing for each employee the cumulative earnings, the earnings subject to unemployment compensation tax, and the earnings subject to FICA taxes for the year to date. Columnar headings for the schedule should be as follows:

| | | *Earnings Subject to* | |
|---|---|---|---|
| *Employee* | *Cumulative Earnings* | *Unemployment Taxes* | *FICA Taxes* |

**b** Compute the total payroll taxes ***deducted*** from the earnings of employees as a group for the year to date.

**c** Compute the total payroll taxes expense of Denver Company, and the percentage of total payroll represented by payroll taxes expense. (Round off to the nearest tenth of a percent.)

*13A-4* During the week ended December 31, the gross earnings of the employees of Sunbelt Financial amounted to $80,000. In accord with established company policy, all employees will be paid for this week's work on January 3. The company adjusts and closes its accounts on December 31.

With respect to payroll, the income tax withholding for the last week of December amounted to $11,200. FICA taxes (6% each on employer and employee) were applicable to only $48,000 of the $80,000 payroll, and unemployment taxes (2.7% state and .7 of 1% federal) were applicable to only $12,800 of the gross earnings for this last week of the year.

**Instructions**

**a** In making the adjusting entry for unpaid wages at December 31, should the payroll taxes be accrued? Explain fully.

**b** Assume that the company wishes to have its accounting records agree with rules by the Internal Revenue Service as to the timing of expense deductions for payroll taxes in computing income tax returns. In accordance with this policy, what amount should appear in the balance sheet at December 31 to reflect the liability arising from wages earned by employees during the last week of the year?

**c** Assume that the company wishes to accrue all payroll expenses at the year-end, regardless of the deductibility of payroll taxes under income tax rules. Prepare journal entries to record the payroll at December 31 including amounts withheld from employees and payroll taxes on the employer.

*13A-5* Two of the employees of Window Craft receive monthly salaries; the remaining three employees are paid an hourly rate with provision for time and one-half for overtime. The basic data for the May 31 payroll are given below:

| Employee | Hours: Reg | Hours: OT | Pay Rate | Compensation to April 30 | Gross Pay Due for May | Federal Income Tax Withheld |
|---|---|---|---|---|---|---|
| Allen | 160 | 15 | $ 8.00/hr | $ 6,000 | $1,460 | $ 275 |
| Benson | 160 | | 7.00/hr | 4,000 | 1,120 | 230 |
| Cramer | 160 | 12 | 5.00/hr | 3,560 | 890 | 125 |
| Dodson | Salary | | 1,440.00/mo | 5,760 | 1,440 | 300 |
| Eller | Salary | | 3,000.00/mo | 12,000 | 3,000 | 505 |
| Total | | | | | $7,910 | $1,435 |

**Other data** Compensation of Dodson and Eller is considered an administrative expense; the balance of the earnings is chargeable to Shop Wages. Payroll taxes apply as follows: FICA, 6% up to maximum of $26,000; state unemployment, 2.7% up to maximum of $6,000; federal unemployment, .7% up to maximum of $6,000. Window Craft has group insurance and a retirement plan under which all employees contribute 5% of their gross pay and the company matches this contribution. Both employees' and employer's contributions are deposited with the Reliable Insurance Company at the end of each month.

**Instructions**

**a** Prepare a payroll register for May using the following columns:

| Employee | Gross Pay | Amount Subject to: Unemployment Taxes | Amount Subject to: FICA Tax | Federal Income Tax Withheld | FICA Tax Withheld | Retirement Deduction | Net Pay Due |
|---|---|---|---|---|---|---|---|

**b** Explain how the gross pay for Cramer was computed for the month of May.

**c** Explain why the federal income taxes withheld for Allen are less than those withheld for Dodson despite the fact that Allen received a higher gross compensation.

**d** Prepare in general journal form the entry to record the payroll for the month of May and the amounts withheld from employees. (Do not include payroll taxes on employer in this entry.)

**e** Prepare in general journal form the entry to record the employer's payroll taxes and insurance plan contributions for the month of May. (The account to be debited for the expense to the employer of contributions for group insurance and retirement may be entitled Group Insurance and Retirement Expense.)

## Group B

*13B-1* Friendly Finance Company makes small loans through a network of more than 100 branch offices in several states. A branch manager is in charge of each office and the number of employees under the manager's supervision is usually from four to seven. Each branch manager prepares a weekly payroll sheet, including his or her own salary. All employees are paid from cash on hand. The employees sign the payroll sheet signifying receipts of their salaries. Hours worked by hourly personnel are inserted in the payroll sheet from time cards prepared by the employees and approved by the manager.

The weekly payroll sheets are sent to the home office along with other accounting statements and reports. The home office compiles employee earnings records and prepares all federal and state salary reports from the payroll sheets.

Salaries are established by home office job evaluation schedules. Salary adjustments, promotions, and transfers of full-time employees are approved by a home office salary committee based upon recommendations of branch managers and area supervisors. Branch managers advise the salary committee of new full-time employees and terminations. Part-time and temporary employees are hired without referral to the salary committee.

**Instructions** After evaluation of the company's payroll system, especially the internal control features, suggest five ways in which the branch managers might carry out payroll fraud.

*13B-2* Gary Norton, an accountant employed by Land Corporation, earned $30,000 in the calendar year just ended. His salary was unchanged throughout the year and was paid monthly in the amount of $2,500. Norton is married, has one child, and claimed three withholding allowances on the W-4 form filed with his employer. The federal income tax withheld from Norton's monthly salary can be determined by reference to the withholding table on page 498. Assume that FICA taxes are 6% of wages up to $26,000 and that federal unemployment taxes are 3.4% on the first $6,000 of each year's gross earnings. However, a credit against this FUTA tax is permitted the employer for payment to the state of 2.7% of wages up to $6,000 a year. Also withheld from Norton's paychecks was a monthly deduction of $50 authorized by Norton for group insurance. Note that the total of this deduction for the year was $600.

**Instructions**

**a** Determine the amount of federal income tax withheld ***during the entire year*** from Norton's paychecks.

**b** Prepare two general journal entries summarizing the payroll transactions with employee Norton for the ***entire year.*** (Do not show monthly amounts.) The first entry should summarize the gross pay and deductions for Norton, but should not include payroll taxes on the employer. Ignore any payments of tax or insurance during the year and let the liability accounts show the totals for the year. Credit Cash for the amount paid to Norton.

In a second entry, record the payroll taxes on the employer for the entire year. Again, ignore any payments of tax during the year and let the liability accounts show the totals for the year.

**c** Compute the total yearly cost (including taxes) to Land Corporation of having Norton on the payroll at an annual salary of $30,000.

***13B-3*** During January, Black Sands, Inc., incurred salaries expense of $11,200, classified as follows: $8,000 of salaries expense for the sales force and $3,200 salaries expense for office personnel.

FICA taxes were withheld from employees' earnings at an assumed rate of 6%. Other amounts withheld were $1,500 for federal income taxes and $180 for group insurance premiums.

**Instructions**

**a** Prepare a general journal entry to record the payroll and the deductions from employees' earnings. Do not include payroll taxes on the employer in this journal entry.

**b** Prepare a general journal entry to record the payroll taxes on the ***employer*** as a result of the above payroll. Assume an FICA tax of 6%, a state unemployment tax of 2.7%, and a federal unemployment tax of .7% on the entire payroll.

**c** What is the total payroll expense of Black Sands, Inc., for January? Show computations.

***13B-4*** Because of its record of stable employment, Marine Associates qualifies under a state merit-rating plan which permits a company to pay a reduced state unemployment tax rate if its employees have collected little or no unemployment insurance. Marine Associates qualifies under the merit-rating plan for a rate of 1.2% rather than the usual 2.7% of gross earnings.

The employees' earnings records so far in the current year are as follows:

| *Employee* | *Cumulative Earnings* | *Employee* | *Cumulative Earnings* |
|---|---|---|---|
| *Axler, C. F.* | *$8,593* | *Hart, P. W.* | *$ 5,261* |
| *Cox, R. M.* | *7,121* | *Kelly, P. T.* | *29,890* |
| *Ford, G. A.* | *1,530* | *Loe, S. B.* | *2,358* |
| *Gamble, E. H.* | *3,701* | *Pratt, L. M.* | *6,039* |

The FICA taxes are assumed to be 6% on the first $26,000 of gross earnings. The rate of federal unemployment tax is assumed to be 3.4% on the first $6,000 of gross earnings, but with credit to the employer for a maximum of 2.7% of gross earnings for state unemployment taxes.

**Instructions**

**a** Prepare a three-column schedule showing for each employee the following accounts: cumulative earnings (as given), earnings subject to unemployment compensation tax, and earnings subject to FICA taxes. As an example, the first line of the schedule would show for Axler, C. F. the following three amounts: $8,593, $6,000, and $8,593.

**b** Some payroll taxes are levied on the employee and some on the employer. Use the information shown in **a** above to compute the total payroll taxes ***deducted*** from the earnings of the employees as a group. (Income taxes are not involved in this problem.)

**c** Compute the total payroll taxes levied on the employer, Marine Associates, and the percentage of the total payroll represented by this payroll tax. Round amounts to the nearest tenth of a percent.

*13B-5* Santa Fe Trail adjusts and closes its accounts on a calendar-year basis. During the week ended December 31, the gross earnings of the company's office employees amounted to $120,000. Under established company policy, the payment of this payroll would be made to employees on January 3.

The federal income tax to be withheld from the earnings of employees during the last week of December amounted to $16,800. The FICA taxes (6% each on employer and employee) were applicable to only $72,000 of the $120,000 payroll, and unemployment taxes (2.7% state and .7 of 1% federal) were applicable to only $19,200 of the gross earnings for the last week of the year.

**Instructions**

**a** In making the adjusting entry for unpaid salaries at December 31, should the payroll taxes be accrued? Explain fully.

**b** Santa Fe Trail, like many other concerns, prefers to have its accounting records agree with rules by the Internal Revenue Service as to the timing of expense deductions for payroll taxes in computing income taxes payble. In accordance with this company policy, what amount should appear in the balance sheet at December 31 to reflect the liability arising from salaries earned by employees during the last week of the year?

**c** Assume that the company wishes to accrue all payroll expenses at the year-end, regardless of the deductibility of payroll taxes under income tax rules. Prepare two journal entries to accrue the payroll at December 31. In the first entry include amounts withheld from employees. In the second entry show payroll taxes on the employer.

*13B-6* Century Plaza has six employees; two are paid monthly salaries and the other four are paid an hourly rate with provision for time and one-half for overtime. The basic data for the July 31 payroll follows:

| Employee | Hours Reg | Hours OT | Pay Rate | Compensation to June 30 | Gross Pay Due for July | Federal Income Tax Withheld |
|---|---|---|---|---|---|---|
| Rausch | 160 | 14 | $ 5.40 hr | $ 5,580 | $ 977.40 | $ 96.66 |
| Sims | 160 | | 6.30 hr | 6,120 | 1,008.00 | 110.52 |
| Tyler | 160 | 20 | 10.00 hr | 4,410 | 1,900.00 | 310.10 |
| Ulmer | Salary | | 1,296.00 mo | 7,776 | 1,296.00 | 97.50 |
| Vincent | 160 | | 4.05 hr | 1,200 | 648.00 | 62.80 |
| Wayne | Salary | | 4,800.00 mo | 28,800 | 4,800.00 | 1,370.80 |

**Other data** Compensation of Ulmer and Wayne is considered an administrative expense; the balance of the earnings is chargeable to Shop Wages. Payroll taxes apply as follows: FICA, 6% up to maximum of $26,000; state unemployment, 2.7% up to maximum of $6,000; federal unemployment, .7% up to maximum of $6,000. Century Plaza has group insurance and a retirement plan under which all employees contribute 7% of their gross pay and Century Plaza matches this contribution. Both employees' and employer's contributions are deposited with the National Insurance Company at the end of each month. (Round calculations to the nearest cent and disregard one-cent discrepancies due to rounding.)

**Instructions**

a Prepare a payroll record for July, using the following columns:

| Employee | Gross Pay | Amount Subject to: Unemployment Taxes | Amount Subject to: FICA Tax | Federal Income Tax Withheld | FICA Tax Withheld | Retirement Deduction | Pay Due |
|---|---|---|---|---|---|---|---|

b Explain how the gross pay for Tyler was computed for the month of July.

c Explain why the federal income taxes withheld for Ulmer are less than those withheld for Sims despite the fact that Ulmer received a higher gross compensation.

d Prepare in general journal form the entry to record the payroll for the month of July and the amounts withheld from employees.

e Prepare in general journal form the entry to record the employer's payroll taxes and insurance plan contributions for the month of July.

## BUSINESS DECISION PROBLEM 13

The payroll procedures of Metals, Inc., a manufacturing concern with 80 factory employees, may be summarized as follows:

1 Applicants are interviewed and hired by Carl Olson, the factory superintendent. He obtains an employee's Withholding Allowance Certificate (a W-4 form) from each new employee and writes on it the hourly rate of pay to be used. The superintendent gives this certificate to a payroll clerk as notice that a new employee has been added.

2 When hourly pay rate changes are made, the superintendent advises the payroll clerk verbally of the new rate for the employee(s) affected.

3 Blank time cards are kept in a box at the factory entrance. On Mondays each employee takes a time card, writes in his or her name, and makes pencil notations during the week of hours of arrival and departure. At the end of the week, the employee returns the card to the box.

4 The completed cards are taken from the box on Monday mornings. Two payroll clerks divide the cards alphabetically between them; compute the gross pay, deductions, and net pay; post the information to the employees' individual earning records; and prepare and number the payroll checks.

5 The payroll checks are signed by the chief accountant and given to the superintendent, who distributes them to employees and holds those for any absent employees.

6 The payroll bank account is reconciled by the chief accountant, who also prepares the quarterly and annual payroll tax reports.

**Instructions** With the objective of improving the system of internal control over the hiring practices and payroll procedures of Metals, Inc., you are to recommend any basic changes needed in organization, equipment, forms, and procedures. Then list at least six specific hiring practices and payroll procedures which you believe should be instituted.

# 14

# ACCOUNTING PRINCIPLES AND CONCEPTS; EFFECTS OF INFLATION

Throughout this book we try to explain the theoretical roots of each new accounting principle or standard as it comes under consideration. When you travel through new territory, however, you may find it useful to pause at some intermediate stage in your trip to consider what you have seen and to sort out your observations into some meaningful overall impression. This seems an appropriate point in our discussion of accounting for such a pause. You now have an overview of the accounting process and should be better prepared to understand how accounting procedures are shaped by theoretical concepts.

## Need for recognized accounting standards

The basic objective of financial statements is to provide information about a business enterprise; information that will be useful in making economic decisions. Investors, managers, economists, bankers, labor leaders, and government administrators all rely upon financial statements and other accounting reports in making the decisions which shape our economy. Therefore, it is of vital importance that the information contained in financial statements be highly reliable and clearly understood. Also, it is important for financial statements to be prepared in a manner which permits them to be compared fairly with prior years' statements and with financial statements of other companies. In short, we need a well-defined body of accounting principles or standards to guide accountants in preparing financial statements with the characteristics of ***reliability, understandability,*** and ***comparability.***

## Generally accepted accounting principles

The principles which constitute the "ground rules" for financial reporting are termed ***generally accepted accounting principles.*** Accounting principles are also referred to as ***standards, assumptions, postulates, and concepts.*** The various terms used to describe accounting principles indicate the many efforts which have been made to develop a satisfactory framework of accounting theory.[1] For example, the word ***standards*** was chosen rather than ***principles*** when the Financial Accounting Standards Board replaced the Accounting Principles Board as the top rule-making body of the accounting profession. The efforts to construct a satisfactory body of accounting theory are still in process, because accounting theory must continually change with changes in the business environment and changes in the needs of financial statement users.

Accounting principles are not rooted in laws of nature, as are the laws of the physical sciences. Rather, accounting principles are developed in relation to what we consider to be the most important objectives of financial reporting. For example, in recent years accountants as well as business executives have recognized that part of the "cost" to society of conducting certain types of economic activity includes the pollution of air and water and other damage to the environment. Research is currently being undertaken to develop accounting principles for the identification and measurement of these "social costs."

## The conceptual framework project

The most recent effort to develop a comprehensive framework for financial accounting and reporting is the conceptual framework project currently being carried on by the Financial Accounting Standards Board. The FASB has described the framework which it hopes to develop as ". . . a ***constitution,*** a coherent system of interrelated objectives and fundamentals that can lead to consistent standards and that prescribe the nature, function, and limits of financial accounting and financial statements."[2]

It is difficult to predict the extent to which the conceptual framework project may affect the basic concepts and principles currently used in developing accounting information. Perhaps the changes will be few; on the other hand, the proposed changes could be as major as a departure from historical cost as the basis for asset valuation and income determination. In any case, the conceptual framework project is indicative of the continuing effort within the accounting profession to improve the relevance and reliability of accounting information.

## Authoritative support for accounting principles

To qualify as "generally accepted," an accounting principle must usually receive "substantial authoritative support." The most influential authoritative groups in this country include (1) the American Institute of Certified Public Account-

---

[1] See, for example, *Accounting Research Study No. 1,* "The Basic Postulates of Accounting," AICPA (New York: 1961); *Accounting Research Study No. 3,* "A Tentative Set of Broad Accounting Principles for Business Enterprises," AICPA (New York: 1962); and the series of *Statements of Financial Accounting Concepts* issued by the FASB.

[2] *FASB Discussion Memorandum,* "Conceptual Framework for Financial Accounting and Reporting: Elements of Financial Statements and Their Measurement," FASB (Stamford, Conn: 1976).

ants (AICPA), the professional association of licensed CPAs; (2) the Financial Accounting Standards Board which includes representatives from public accounting, industry, education, and government; and (3) the Securities and Exchange Commission (SEC), an agency of the federal government established to administer laws and regulations relating to the publication of financial information by corporations whose stock is publicly owned.[3] Also important in the development of accounting theory has been the American Accounting Association, an organization of accounting educators.

**American Institute of Certified Public Accountants (AICPA)** The AICPA has long been concerned with stating and defining accounting principles because its members daily face the problem of making decisions about generally accepted principles as they perform audits and other professional work. Some years ago, the AICPA established the Accounting Principles Board, which issued 31 formal ***Opinions*** on specific accounting practices and also issued broad ***Statements*** designed to improve the quality of financial reporting. In 1973, the Accounting Principles Board was replaced by the Financial Accounting Standards Board. However, the Opinions and Statements of the APB ***remain in effect.***

**Financial Accounting Standards Board (FASB)** The FASB was established by the AICPA as an independent body to assume the responsibilities of the former Accounting Principles Board. The FASB consists of seven full-time members, including representatives from public accounting, industry, government, and accounting education.

Lending support to the FASB are an advisory council and a large research staff. The FASB is authorized to issue ***Statements of Financial Accounting Standards,*** which represent expressions of generally accepted accounting principles. As discussed earlier in this chapter, the FASB is also attempting to develop a broad conceptual framework for financial accounting and reporting.

**Securities and Exchange Commission (SEC)** The SEC has legal authority to establish accounting principles and disclosure requirements for all large, publicly owned corporations. The views of the Commission on various accounting issues are published in the SEC's ***Accounting Series Releases,*** or ***ASRs.*** In the past, the SEC has tended to adopt or to modify the recommendations of the FASB, rather than to develop its own independent set of accounting principles.

**American Accounting Association (AAA)** The AAA has sponsored a number of research studies and monographs in which individual authors and Association

[3]Other professional organizations which have influenced the development of accounting principles are the National Association of Accountants and the Financial Executives Institute. In addition to the SEC, the following government regulatory agencies influence financial reporting of business units falling under their jurisdiction: Federal Power Commission, Interstate Commerce Commission, Civil Aeronautics Board, and Federal Communications Commission.

committees attempt to summarize accounting principles. These statements have had considerable influence on the thinking of accounting theorists and practitioners. However, the AAA lacks the power of the FASB to impose its collective view on accounting practice; it therefore exercises its influence through the prestige of its authors and the persuasiveness of their views.

In addition to the above sources, "substantial authoritative support" may include widespread use of an accounting practice within a particular industry, or general recognition of a practice in the accounting literature.

Because accounting principles must evolve with changes in the business environment, there is no complete list of generally accepted accounting principles. There is, however, a consensus among accountants and informed users of financial statements as to what these principles are. Most accounting principles are applicable to profit-making organizations of any size and form. We shall now discuss briefly the major principles that govern the accounting process and comment on some areas of controversy.

## The accounting entity concept

One of the basic principles of accounting is that information is compiled for a clearly defined accounting entity. An accounting entity is any ***economic unit*** which controls resources and engages in economic activities. An individual is an accounting entity. So is a business enterprise, whether organized as a proprietorship, partnership, or corporation. Governmental agencies are accounting entities, as are all nonprofit clubs and organizations. An accounting entity may also be defined as an identifiable economic unit ***within a larger accounting entity.*** For example, the Chevrolet Division of General Motors Corporation may be viewed as an accounting entity separate from GM's other activities.

The basic accounting equation, Assets = Liabilities + Owner's Equity, reflects the accounting entity concept since the elements of the equation relate ***to the particular entity whose economic activity is being reported in the financial statements.*** Although we have considerable flexibility in defining our accounting entity, we must be careful to use the ***same definition*** in the measurement of assets, liabilities, owner's equity, revenue, and expense. An income statement would not make sense, for example, if it included all the revenue of General Motors Corporation but listed only the expenses of the Chevrolet Division.

Although the entity concept appears straightforward, it can pose some judgmental allocation problems for accountants. Assume, for example, that we want to prepare an income statement for only the Chevrolet Division of General Motors. Also assume that a given plant facility is used in the production of Chevrolets, Pontiacs, and school buses. How much of the depreciation on this factory building should be regarded as an expense of the Chevrolet Division? We will discuss the solution to such problems in later chapters; however, the importance of the entity concept in developing meaningful financial information should be clear.

### The going-concern assumption

An underlying assumption in accounting is that an accounting entity will continue in operation for a period of time sufficient to carry out its existing commitments. The assumption of continuity, especially in the case of corporations, is in accord with experience in our economic system. This assumption leads to the concept of the ***going concern.*** In general, the going-concern assumption justifies ignoring immediate liquidating values in presenting assets and liabilities in the balance sheet.

For example, suppose that a company has just purchased a three-year insurance policy for $5,000. If we assume that the business will continue in operation for three years or more, we will consider the $5,000 cost of the insurance as an asset which provides services (freedom from risk) to the business over a three-year period. On the other hand, if we assume that the business is likely to terminate in the near future, the insurance policy should be recorded at its cancellation value—the amount of cash which can be obtained from the insurance company as a refund on immediate cancellation of the policy, which may be, say, $4,500.

Although the assumption of a going concern is justified in most normal situations, it should be dropped when it is not in accord with the facts. Accountants are sometimes asked to prepare a statement of financial position for an enterprise that is about to liquidate. In this case the assumption of continuity is no longer valid and the accountant drops the going-concern assumption and reports assets at their current liquidating value and liabilities at the amount required to settle the debts immediately.

### The time period principle

We assume an indefinite life for most accounting entities. But accountants are asked to measure operating progress and changes in economic position at relatively short time intervals during this indefinite life. Users of financial statements need periodic measurements for decision-making purposes.

The need for frequent measurements creates many of the accountant's most challenging problems. Dividing the life of an enterprise into time segments, such as a year or a quarter of a year, requires numerous estimates and assumptions. For example, estimates must be made of the useful lives of depreciable assets and assumptions must be made as to appropriate depreciation methods. Thus periodic measurements of net income and financial position are at best only informed estimates. The tentative nature of periodic measurements should be understood by those who rely on periodic accounting information.

### The monetary principle

The monetary principle means that money is used as the basic measuring unit for financial reporting. Money is the common denominator in which accounting measurements are made and summarized. The dollar, or any other monetary unit, represents a unit of value; that is, it reflects ability to command goods and services. Implicit in the use of money as a measuring unit is the ***assumption that the dollar is a stable unit of value,*** just as the mile is a stable unit of distance and an acre is a stable unit of area.

Having accepted money as a measuring unit, accountants freely combine dollar measures of economic transactions that occur at various times during the life of an accounting entity. They combine, for example, a $20,000 cost of equipment purchased in 1970 and the $40,000 cost of similar equipment purchased in 1980 and report the total as a $60,000 investment in equipment.

Unlike the mile and the acre, which are stable units of distance and area, the dollar ***is not a stable unit of value.*** The prices of goods and services in our economy change over time. When the ***general price level*** (a phrase used to describe the average of all prices) increases, the value of money (that is, its ability to command goods and services) decreases.

Despite the steady erosion in the purchasing power of the dollar in the United States during the last 40 years, accountants have continued to prepare financial statements in which the value of the dollar is assumed to be stable. This unrealistic assumption is one of the reasons why financial statements are viewed by some critics as misleading. Accounting principles are currently evolving toward restatement of accounting information for the changing value of the dollar and toward the preparation of supplementary statements showing current replacement costs. The adjustment of accounting information to reflect the effects of inflation will be discussed in a subsequent section of this chapter.

### The objectivity principle

The term ***objective*** refers to measurements that are unbiased and subject to verification by independent experts. For example, the price established in an arm's-length transaction is an objective measure of exchange value at the time of the transaction. It is not surprising, therefore, that exchange prices established in business transactions constitute much of the raw material from which accounting information is generated. Accountants rely on various kinds of evidence to support their financial measurements, but they seek always the most objective evidence available. Invoices, contracts, paid checks, and physical counts of inventory are examples of objective evidence.

If a measurement is objective, 10 competent investigators who make the same measurement will come up with substantially identical results. However, 10 competent accountants who set out independently to measure the net income of a given business would ***not*** arrive at an identical result. Despite the goal of objectivity, it is not possible to insulate accounting information from opinion and personal judgment. The cost of a depreciable asset can be determined objectively but not the periodic depreciation expense. To measure the cost of the asset services that have been used up during a given period requires estimates of the residual value and service life of the asset and judgment as to the depreciation method that should be used. Such estimates and judgments can produce significant variations in net income.

Objectivity in accounting has its roots in the quest for reliability. Accountants want to make their economic measurements reliable and, at the same time, as relevant to decision makers as possible. Where to draw the line in the trade-off between ***reliability*** and ***relevance*** is one of the crucial issues in accounting theory. The need for reliable and verifiable data is an important constraint, particularly with respect to information reported to outsiders. Thus, accountants are constantly faced with the necessity of compromising between what users of financial information would like to know and what it is possible to measure with a reasonable degree of reliability.

## Asset valuation: the cost principle

Both the balance sheet and the income statement are extensively affected by the cost principle. Assets are initially recorded in the accounts at cost, and no adjustment is made to this valuation in later periods, except to allocate a portion of the original cost to expense as the assets expire. At the time an asset is originally acquired, cost represents the "fair market value" of the goods or services exchanged, as evidenced by an arm's-length transaction. With the passage of time, however, the fair market value of such assets as land and buildings may change greatly from their historical cost. These later changes in fair market value generally have been ignored in the accounts, and the assets have continued to be valued in the balance sheet at historical cost (less the portion of that cost which has been allocated to expense).

Increasing numbers of professional accountants believe that current market values should be used as the basis for asset valuation rather than historical cost. These accountants argue that current values would result in a more meaningful balance sheet. Also, they claim that current values should be allocated to expense to represent fairly the cost to the entity of the goods or services consumed in the effort to generate revenue.

The cost principle is derived from the principle of ***objectivity.*** Those who support the cost principle argue that it is important that users have confidence in financial statements, and this confidence can best be maintained if accountants recognize changes in assets and liabilities only on the basis of completed transactions. Objective evidence generally exists to support cost, but evidence supporting current values may be less readily available.

## Measuring revenue: the realization principle

When should revenue be recognized? Under the assumptions of accrual accounting, revenue should be recognized "when it is earned." However, the "earning" of revenue usually is an extended ***economic process*** and does not actually take place at a single point in time.

Some revenue, such as interest earned, is directly related to time periods. For this type of revenue, it is easy to determine how much revenue has been earned by computing how much of the earning process is complete. However, the earning process for sales revenue relates to ***economic activity*** rather than to a specific period of time. In a manufacturing business, for example, the earning process involves (1) acquisition of raw materials, (2) production of finished goods, (3) sale of the finished goods, and (4) collection of cash from credit customers.

In the manufacturing example, there is little objective evidence to indicate how much revenue has been earned during the first two stages of the earning process. Accountants therefore usually do not recognize revenue until the revenue has been ***realized.*** Revenue is realized when both of the following conditions are met: (1) the earning process is ***essentially complete*** and (2) ***objective evidence*** exists as to the amount of revenue earned.

In most cases, the realization principle indicates that revenue should be recognized ***at the time of the sale of goods or the rendering of services.*** Recognizing revenue at this point is logical because the firm has essentially completed the earning process and the realized value of the goods or services sold can be measured objectively in terms of the price billed to customers. At any time prior to sale, the ultimate realizable value of the goods or services sold can only be estimated. After the sale, the only step that remains is to collect from the customer, and this is usually a relatively certain event.

In Chapter 3, we described a complete ***cash basis*** of income measurement whereby revenue is recognized only when cash is collected from customers and expenses are recorded only when cash is actually paid out. Cash basis accounting ***does not conform*** to generally accepted accounting principles, but it is widely used by individuals in determining their ***taxable*** income. (Remember that the accounting methods used in income tax returns often differ from those used in financial statements.)

**The installment method** Companies selling goods on the installment plan sometimes use the installment method of accounting for income tax purposes. Under the installment method, the seller recognizes the gross profit on sales gradually over an extended time span as the cash is actually collected from customers. If the gross profit rate on installment sales is 30%, then out of every dollar collected on installment receivables, the sum of 30 cents represents gross profit.

To illustrate, assume that on December 15, Year 1, a retailer sells for $400 a television set which cost $280, or 70% of the sales price. The terms of the sale call for a $100 cash down payment with the balance payable in 15 monthly installments of $20 each, beginning on January 1, Year 2. (Interest charges are paid separately and can be ignored in this illustration.) The collections of cash and recognition of profit under the installment method are summarized below:

*Installment method illustrated*

| *Year* | *Cash Collected* | – | *Cost Recovery, 70%* | = | *Profit Earned, 30%* |
|---|---|---|---|---|---|
| *1* | *$100* | | *$ 70* | | *$ 30* |
| *2* | *240* | | *168* | | *72* |
| *3* | *60* | | *42* | | *18* |
| *Totals* . . . . . . . | *$400* | | *$280* | | *$120* |

This method of profit recognition exists largely because it is allowed for income tax purposes; it postpones the payment of income taxes until cash is collected from customers. From an accounting viewpoint, there is little theoretical justification for delaying the recognition of profit beyond the point of sale. Therefore, the installment method is seldom used in financial statements.[4]

**Percentage-of-completion: an exception to the realization principle** Under certain circumstances, accountants may depart from the realization principle and recognize income during the production process. An example arises in the case of long-term construction contracts, such as the building of a dam over a period of 10 years. Clearly the income statements of a company engaged in such a project would not be useful to managers or investors if no profit or loss were reported until the dam was finally completed. The accountant therefore estimates the portion of the dam completed during each accounting period, and recognizes the gross profit on the project ***in proportion*** to the work completed. This is known as the percentage-of-completion method of accounting for long-term contracts.

The percentage-of-completion method works as follows:

1 An estimate is made of the total costs to be incurred and the total profit to be earned over the life of the project.
2 Each period, an estimate is made of the portion of the total project completed during the period. This estimate is usually made by expressing the costs incurred during the period as a percentage of the estimated total cost of the project.
3 The percentage figure determined in step **2** is applied to the estimated total profit on the contract to compute the amount of profit applicable to the current accounting period.
4 No estimate is made of the percentage of work during the final period. In the period in which the project is completed, any remaining profit is recognized.

To illustrate, assume that Reed Construction Company enters into a contract to build an irrigation canal at a price of $5,000,000. The canal will be built over a three-year period at an estimated total cost of $4,000,000. Therefore, the estimated total profit on the project is $1,000,000. The following schedule shows the actual costs incurred and the amount of profit to be recognized in each of the three years using the percentage-of-completion method:

***Profit recognized as work progresses***

| *Year* | *(A)* *Actual Costs Incurred* | *(B)* *Percentage of Work Done in Year* *(Column A ÷ $4,000,000)* | *(C)* *Profit Considered Earned* *($1,000,000 × Column B)* |
|---|---|---|---|
| *1* | *$ 600,000* | *15* | *$150,000* |
| *2* | *2,000,000* | *50* | *500,000* |
| *3* | *1,452,000* | * | *298,000 balance* |
| *Totals* . . . . . . . . . . | *$4,052,000* | | *$948,000* |

*Balance required to complete the contract.

[4]Under generally accepted accounting principles, use of the installment method is permissible only when the amounts likely to be collected on installment sales are so uncertain that no reasonable basis exists for estimating an allowance for doubtful accounts.

The percentage of the work completed during Year 1 was estimated by dividing the actual cost incurred in the year by the estimated total cost of the project ($600,000 ÷ $4,000,000 = 15%). Because 15% of the work was done in Year 1, 15% of the estimated total profit of $1,000,000 was considered earned in that year ($1,000,000 × 15% = $150,000). Costs incurred in Year 2 amounted to 50% of the estimated total costs ($2,000,000 ÷ $4,000,000 = 50%); thus, 50% of the estimated total profit was recognized in Year 2 ($1,000,000 × 50% = $500,000). Note that no percentage of work completed figure was computed for Year 3. In Year 3, the total actual cost is known ($4,052,000), and the actual total profit on the contract is determined to be $948,000 ($5,000,000 – $4,052,000). Since profits of $650,000 were previously recognized in Years 1 and 2, the remaining profit ($948,000 – $650,000 = $298,000) must be recognized in Year 3.

Although an expected ***profit*** on a long-term construction contract is recognized in proportion to the work completed, a different treatment is accorded to an expected ***loss.*** If at the end of any accounting period it appears that a loss will be incurred on a contract in progress, the ***entire loss should be recognized at once.***

The percentage-of-completion method should be used only when the total profit expected to be earned can be ***reasonably estimated in advance.*** If there are substantial uncertainties in the amount of profit which will ultimately be earned, no profit should be recognized until ***production is completed.*** This approach is often referred to as the ***completed-contract method.*** If the completed-contract method had been used in the preceding example, no profit would have been recognized in Years 1 and 2; the entire profit of $948,000 would be recorded in Year 3 when the contract was completed and actual costs known.

## Measuring expenses: the matching principle

Revenue, the gross increase in net assets resulting from the production or sale of goods and services, is offset by expenses incurred in bringing the firm's output to the point of sale. Examples of expenses relating to revenue are the cost of merchandise sold, the expiration of asset services, and out-of-pocket expenditures for operating costs. The measurement of expenses occurs in two stages: (1) measuring the ***cost*** of goods and services that will be consumed or expire in generating revenue and (2) determining ***when*** the goods and services acquired have contributed to revenue and their cost thus ***becomes an expense.*** The second aspect of the measurement process is often referred to as ***matching costs and revenue*** and is fundamental to the ***accrual basis*** of accounting.

Costs are matched with revenue in two major ways:

**1 In relation to the product sold or service rendered** If goods or services can be related to the product or service which constitutes the output of the enterprise, its cost becomes an expense when the product is sold or the service rendered to customers. The cost of goods sold in a merchandising firm is a good example of this type of expense. Similarly, a commission paid to a real estate salesperson by a real estate brokerage office is an expense directly related to the revenue generated by the salesperson.

**2 In relation to the time period during which revenue is earned** Some costs incurred by businesses cannot be directly related to the product or service output of the firm. Expired fire insurance, property taxes, depreciation on a building, the salary of the president of the company—all are examples of costs incurred in generating revenue which cannot be related to specific transactions. The accountant refers to this class of costs as ***period costs,*** and charges them to expense by associating them with the ***period of time*** during which they are incurred and presumably contribute to revenue, rather than by associating them with specific revenue-producing transactions.

## The consistency principle

The principle of ***consistency*** implies that a particular accounting method, once adopted, will not be changed from period to period. This assumption is important because it assists users of financial statements in interpreting changes in financial position and changes in net income.

Consider the confusion which would result if a company ignored the principle of consistency and changed its method of depreciation every year. The company could cause its net income for any given year to increase or decrease merely by changing its depreciation method.

The principle of consistency does not mean that a company should ***never*** make a change in its accounting methods. In fact, a company ***should*** make a change if the new accounting method will provide more useful information than does the method presently in use. But when a significant change in accounting methods does occur, the fact that a change has been made and the dollar effects of the change should be ***fully disclosed*** in the financial statements. In audited financial statements, the disclosure of a change in accounting method is also incorporated in the CPA's opinion on the financial statements. A typical disclosure might read as follows: "During the current year the company changed from the declining-balance method of computing depreciation to the straight-line method. This change in method had the effect of increasing net income by $210,000."

Consistency applies to a single accounting entity and increases the comparability of financial statements from period to period. Different companies, even those in the same industry, may follow different accounting methods. For this reason, it is important to determine the accounting methods used by companies whose financial statements are being compared.

## The disclosure principle

Adequate disclosure means that all ***material*** and ***relevant facts*** concerning financial position and the results of operations ***are communicated to users.*** This can be accomplished either in the financial statements or in the notes accompanying the statements. Such disclosure should make the financial statements more useful and less subject to misinterpretation.

Adequate disclosure does not require that information be presented in great detail; it does require, however, that no important facts be withheld. For example, if a company has been named as defendant in a large lawsuit, this information must be disclosed. Other examples of information which should be disclosed in financial statements include:

**1** A summary of the accounting methods used in the preparation of the statements
**2** Dollar effects of any changes in these accounting methods during the current period
**3** Other significant events affecting financial position, including major new contracts for sale of goods or services, labor strikes, shortages of raw materials, and pending legislation which may significantly affect operations
**4** Identification of assets which have been pledged as collateral to secure loans
**5** Terms of major borrowing arrangements and existence of large contingent liabilities
**6** Contractual provisions relating to leasing arrangements, employee pension and bonus plans, and major proposed asset acquisitions

Even significant events which occur ***after*** the end of the accounting period but before the financial statements are issued may need to be disclosed.

Naturally, there are practical limits to the amount of disclosure that can be made in financial statements and the accompanying notes. The key point to bear in mind is that the supplementary information should be ***relevant to the users*** of the financial statements.

## Materiality

The term ***materiality*** refers to the ***relative importance*** of an item or event. Disclosure of relevant information is closely related to the concept of materiality; what is material is likely to be relevant. Accountants are primarily concerned with significant information and are not overly concerned with those items which have little effect on financial statements. For example, should the cost of a pencil sharpener, a wastepaper basket, or a stapler be recorded in asset accounts and depreciated over their useful lives? Even though more than one period will benefit from the use of these assets, the concept of materiality permits the immediate recognition of the cost of these items as an expense on grounds that it would be too expensive to undertake depreciation accounting for such low-cost assets and that the results would not differ significantly.

We must recognize that the materiality of an item is a relative matter; what is material for one business unit may not be material for another. Materiality of an item may depend not only on its ***amount*** but also on its ***nature.*** In summary, we can state the following rule: ***An item is material if there is a reasonable expectation that knowledge of it would influence the decisions of prudent users of financial statements.***

### Conservatism as a guide in resolving uncertainties

We have previously referred to the use of ***conservatism*** in connection with the measurement of net income and the reporting of accounts receivable and inventories in the balance sheet. Although the concept of conservatism may not qualify as an accounting principle, it has long been a powerful influence upon asset valuation and income determination. Conservatism is most useful when matters of judgment or estimates are involved. Ideally, accountants should base their estimates on sound logic and select those accounting methods which neither overstate nor understate the facts. When some doubt exists about the valuation of an asset or the realization of a gain, however, the accountant traditionally leans in the direction of caution and selects the accounting option which produces a lower net income for the current period and a less favorable financial position.

An example of conservatism is the traditional practice of pricing inventory at the lower of cost or market (replacement cost). Decreases in the market value of the inventory are recognized as a part of the cost of goods sold in the current period, but increases in market value of inventory are ignored. A judicious application of conservatism to the accounting process should produce more useful information; in contrast, the excessive use of conservatism or failure to apply conservatism may produce misleading information and result in losses to creditors and stockholders.

### CPAs' opinion on published financial statements

The annual financial statements of large corporations are used by great numbers of stockholders, creditors, government regulators, and members of the general public. What assurance do these people have that the information in these statements is reliable and is presented in conformity with generally accepted accounting principles? The answer is that the annual financial statements of large corporations are ***audited*** by independent certified public accountants (CPAs).

An audit is a thorough investigation of every item, dollar amount, and disclosure which appears in the financial statements. After completing the audit, the CPAs express their opinion as to the ***fairness*** of the financial statements. This opinion, called the ***auditors' report,*** is published with the statements in the company's annual report to its stockholders.

Considering the extensive investigation that precedes it, the audit opinion is surprisingly short. It usually consists of two brief paragraphs, unless the CPAs comment on unusual features of the financial statements. The first paragraph describes the ***scope*** of the auditors' examination; the second states their ***opinion*** of the financial statements. A report by a CPA firm might read as follows:

***Typical auditors' report***

> We have examined the balance sheet of American Oil Corporation as of December 31, 19___, and the related statements of income, retained earnings, and changes in financial position for the year then ended. Our examination was made in accordance with generally accepted auditing standards, and accordingly included such tests of the accounting records and such other auditing procedures as we considered necessary in the circumstances.

> ***In our opinion,*** the financial statements referred to above ***present fairly*** the financial position of American Oil Corporation at December 31, 19___, and the results of its operations and the changes in its financial position for the year then ended, ***in conformity with generally accepted accounting principles*** applied on a basis ***consistent with that of the preceding year.*** [Emphasis supplied.]

Over many decades, audited financial statements have developed an excellent track record of reliability. Note, however, that the CPAs ***do not guarantee*** the accuracy of financial statements; rather, they render their ***professional opinion*** as to the overall ***fairness*** of the statements. "Fairness," in this context, means that the financial statements are ***not misleading.*** However, just as a physician may make an error in the diagnosis of a particular patient, there is always a possibility that an auditor's opinion may be in error. The primary responsibility for the reliability of financial statements rests with the management of the issuing company, not with the independent CPAs.

## INFLATION—THE GREATEST CHALLENGE TO ACCOUNTING

***Inflation*** may be defined as either an increase in the general price level or a decrease in the purchasing power of the dollar. The ***general price level*** is the weighted average of the prices of all goods and services in the economy. Changes in the general price level are measured by a ***general price index*** with a base year assigned a value of 100. The index compares the level of current prices with that of the base year. Assume, for example, that Year 1 is the base year. If prices rise by 10% during Year 2, the price index at the end of Year 2 will be 110. At the end of Year 9 the price index might be 200, indicating that the general price level had doubled since Year 1.

The most widely recognized measure of the general price level in the United States is the Consumer Price Index (CPI), published monthly by the Bureau of Labor Statistics. The base year of the Consumer Price Index is 1967. In October 1978, the CPI passed the 200 level, indicating that prices (on the average) had doubled since 1967.

We often hear statements such as "Today's dollar is worth only 50 cents." The "worth" or "value" of a dollar lies in its ability to buy goods or services. This "value" is called ***purchasing power.*** The reciprocal of the general price index (100 divided by the current level of the index) represents the purchasing power of the dollar in the current year relative to that in the base year. For example, the reciprocal of the CPI in October 1978, was 100 ÷ 200, or .5. Therefore, we might say that $1 in that month was equivalent in purchasing power to 50 cents in 1967.

What effect do material changes in general price levels, and thus changes in the value of money, have on accounting measures? By combining transactions measured in dollars of various years, the accountant in effect ignores changes in the size of the measuring unit. For example, suppose that a company purchased land early in Year 1 for $200,000 and sold this land for $400,000 late in Year 10. Using the dollar as a measuring unit, we would recognize a gain of $200,000

($400,000 sales price − $200,000 cost) on the sale of the land. But if prices doubled during that 10-year period and the value of money was cut in half, we might say that the company was ***no better off*** as a result of buying and selling this land. The $400,000 received for the land in Year 10 represents the same command over goods and services as $200,000 did when invested in the land in Year 1.

We have experienced persistent inflation in the United States for almost 40 years; more importantly, the forces which have been built into our economic and political institutions almost guarantee that inflation will continue. The only question is how severe the inflationary trend will be. Our traditional accounting process is based upon the assumption of a stable dollar. This cost-based system works extremely well in periods of stable prices; it works reasonably well during prolonged but mild inflation; but it loses virtually all meaning if inflation becomes extreme. The greatest single challenge to the accounting profession today is to develop new accounting methods that will bring financial statements into accord with the economic reality of an inflationary environment.

### Profits—fact or illusion?

Corporate profits are watched closely by business managers, investors, and government officials. The trend of these profits plays a significant role in the allocation of the nation's investment resources, in levels of employment, and in national economic policy. As a result of the ***stable monetary assumption,*** however, a strong argument may be made that much of the corporate profit reported today is an illusion.

In the measurement of business income, a distinction must be drawn between profit and the recovery of costs. A business earns a profit only when the value of goods sold and services rendered (revenue) ***exceeds*** the value of resources consumed in the earning process (costs and expenses). Accountants have traditionally assigned "values" to resources consumed in the earning process by using historical dollar amounts. Depreciation expense, for example, may be based upon prices paid to acquire assets 10 or 20 years ago.

When the general price level is rising rapidly, such historical costs may significantly understate the current economic value of the resources being consumed. If costs and expenses are understated, it follows that reported profits are overstated. In other words, the stable monetary assumption may lead to reporting ***illusory*** profits; much of the net income reported by business enterprises actually may be a return of costs.

When reported profit is actually a return of costs, what we label as income taxes is in reality a tax upon invested capital. Moreover, dividends labeled as distributions of earnings are in fact being paid from capital. The reporting of large, but fictitious, profits also leads to demands for higher wages consistent with the reported profits.

In summary, the real world is one of inflation. If we continue to measure profits on the assumption that price levels do not change, financial statements will be misleading and out of touch with reality. Several broad social consequences appear to follow. For one, corporate liquidity (debt-paying ability) may fall so low as to bring an economic crisis. Secondly, since we allocate economic resources in large part on the basis of financial statements, poor allocation of resources may be the end consequence of ignoring inflation in our financial reporting. Finally, the overstatement of profits may lead to an unrecognized failure to maintain reasonable rates of capital formation. A nation with a declining rate of capital formation will find it difficult to hold its relative position in a competitive world economy or to achieve a rising standard of living.

### Two approaches to "inflation accounting"

Two alternative approaches to modifying our accounting process to cope with inflation have received much attention. These two approaches are:

1 **Constant dollar accounting** Under this approach, historical costs in the financial statements are adjusted to the ***number of current dollars representing an equivalent amount of purchasing power.*** Thus, all amounts are expressed in units (current dollars) of equal purchasing power. Since a general price index is used in restating the historical costs, constant dollar accounting shows the effects of changes in the ***general*** price level. Constant dollar accounting is also called ***general price level*** accounting.

2 **Current cost accounting** This method differs from constant dollar accounting in that assets and expenses are shown in the financial statements at the current cost to ***replace*** those specific resources. The ***current replacement cost*** of a specific asset may rise or fall at a different rate from the general price level. Thus, current cost accounting shows the effects of ***specific price changes,*** rather than changes in the general price level.

To illustrate these approaches to "inflation accounting," assume that in Year 1 you purchased 500 pounds of sugar for $100 when the general price index was at 100. Early in Year 2, you sold the sugar for $108 when the general price index was at 110 and the replacement cost of 500 pounds of sugar was $104. What is the amount of your profit or loss on this transaction? The amount of profit or loss determined under current accounting standards (unadjusted historical cost) and the two "inflation accounting" alternatives is shown below.

*Which "cost" of goods sold is most realistic?*

| | *Unadjusted Historical Cost* | *Adjusted for General Inflation (Constant Dollars)* | *Adjusted for Changes in Specific Prices (Current Costs)* |
|---|---|---|---|
| *Revenue* | *$108* | *$108* | *$108* |
| *Cost of goods sold* | *100* | *110* | *104* |
| *Profit (loss)* | *$ 8* | *$ (2)* | *$ 4* |

Under each method, an amount is deducted from revenue to provide for recovery of cost. However, the value assigned to the "cost" of goods sold differs under each of the three approaches.

**Unadjusted historical cost** This method is used in current accounting practice. The use of unadjusted historical cost is based upon the assumption that the dollar is a stable unit of measure. Profit is determined by comparing sales revenue with the ***historical cost*** of the asset sold. In using this approach to income determination, accountants assume that a business is as well off when it has recovered its ***original dollar investment,*** and that it is better off whenever it recovers more than the original number of dollars invested in any given asset.

In our example of buying and selling sugar, the profit figure of $8 shows ***how many dollars*** you came out ahead. However, this approach ignores the fact that Year 1 dollars and Year 2 dollars are ***not equivalent in terms of purchasing power.*** It also ignores the fact that the $100 deduction intended to provide for the recovery of cost is not sufficient to allow you to ***replace*** the 500 pounds of sugar.

**Constant dollar accounting** When financial statements are adjusted for changes in the general price level, historical amounts are restated as the number of current dollars ***equivalent in purchasing power*** to the historical cost. Profit is determined by comparing revenue with the ***amount of purchasing power*** (stated in current dollars) originally invested.

The general price index tells us that $110 in Year 2 is equivalent in purchasing power to the $100 invested in sugar in Year 1. But you do not have $110 in Year 2; you received only $108 dollars from the sale of the sugar. Thus, you have sustained a ***$2 loss in purchasing power.***

**Current cost accounting** In current cost accounting, profit is measured by comparing revenue with the ***current replacement cost*** of the assets consumed in the earning process. The logic of this approach lies in the concept of the going concern. What will you do with the $108 received from the sale of the sugar? If you are going to continue in the sugar business, you will have to buy more sugar. At current market prices, it will cost you $104 to replace 500 pounds of sugar; the remaining $4, therefore, is designated as profit.

Current cost accounting recognizes in the income statement the costs which a going concern actually has to pay to replace its expiring assets. The resulting profit figure, therefore, closely parallels the maximum amount which a business could distribute to its owners and still be able to maintain the present size and scale of its operations.

**Which approach measures income?** Which of these three approaches correctly measures income? The answer is that all three methods provide a correct measurement, but that each approach utilizes a different definition of "cost" and of "income." The real question confronting the accounting profession is which of these alternative measures of income is the ***most useful to decision makers?*** This question is being considered very carefully by the FASB, the SEC, and other interested parties. However, there is not yet widespread agreement as to the answer.

### FASB Statement No. 33—Is a big change coming?

Perhaps the day is coming when constant dollar or current cost information will replace the use of historical costs in financial statements. However, a change of this magnitude cannot be made without much planning and consideration of the possible consequences. Accounting information is used on a daily basis by millions of economic decision makers. A major change in the nature of this information is sure to affect the allocation of resources within our economy. Decision makers would have to learn to interpret the new information; capital would move out of some industries and into others; income tax laws and other government economic policies might change. In light of these considerations, careful experimentation with constant dollar and current cost information is needed before we abandon the use of historical costs as our basis for financial statements.

In 1979, the FASB issued ***Statement No. 33,*** which requires large corporations to include with their cost-based financial statements ***supplementary schedules*** showing certain constant dollar and current cost information. Note that this information is supplementary to the conventional financial statements and is not a substitute for them. This action by the FASB will introduce decision makers to constant dollar and current cost information on an experimental basis. If this experimentation leads to widespread use of constant dollar or current cost information, *Statement No. 33* will become a major milestone in the evolution of accounting principles.

### FASB requirements for disclosure of constant dollar and current cost information

*Statement No. 33* applies only to large corporations—those with total assets of $1 billion or total inventories and plant assets (before deducting accumulated depreciation) of more than $125 million. However, the FASB also encourages (but does not require) all business organizations of every size to comply with the provisions of the *Statement.*[5]

The supplementary disclosures required by ***Statement No. 33*** include:[6]

**1** Net income measured in constant dollars[7]
**2** The gain or loss in purchasing power which results from holding monetary assets or having monetary liabilities
**3** Net income on a current cost basis

---

[5] *FASB Statement No. 33,* "Financial Reporting and Changing Prices," FASB (Stamford, Conn: 1979), par. 23–25.
[6] Other disclosure requirements of *Statement No. 33,* including changes in current costs and five-year summaries, will be discussed in an intermediate level accounting course.
[7] When a company discontinues a segment of its operations or reports an extraordinary item in its income statement, the subtotal, Income from Continuing Operations, is disclosed instead of the net income figure. Income from continuing operations is discussed in Chapter 17.

The format which many companies use for making these disclosures is illustrated below. (The three required disclosures are identified by the numbered arrows.)

*Which income figure do you think is most realistic?*

***Supplement to financial statements:***

***FLATION COMPANY***

***Income Statement Adjusted for Changing Prices***

***For Year 10***

| | As Reported in the Primary Statements | Adjusted for General Inflation (Constant Dollars)* | Adjusted for Changes in Specific Prices (Current Costs) |
|---|---|---|---|
| Net sales | $300,000 | $300,000 | $300,000 |
| Costs and expenses: | | | |
| Cost of goods sold | $180,000 | $185,000 | $195,750 |
| Depreciation expense | 30,000 | 40,000 | 45,000 |
| Other expenses | 65,000 | 65,000 | 65,000 |
| Total | $275,000 | $290,000 | $305,750 |
| Net income | $ 25,000 | (1) → $ 10,000 | (3) → $ (5,750) |
| Net gain from decline in purchasing power of net amounts owed | | (2) → $ 4,000 | |

*Stated in dollars of average purchasing power during Year 10.

We shall now use the information in this illustration to demonstrate further the concepts of constant dollar and current cost accounting and to interpret these disclosures from the viewpoint of the financial statement user.

## Net income measured in constant dollars

A basic problem with the use of historical costs for measuring income is that revenue and expenses may be stated in dollars having different amounts of purchasing power. Sales revenue, for example, is recorded in current-year dollars. Depreciation expense, on the other hand, is based upon dollars spent to acquire assets in past years. As previously emphasized, dollars in the current year and dollars of past years are not equivalent in terms of purchasing power.

In a constant dollar income statement, expenses based on "old" dollars are ***restated*** at the number of current dollars representing the equivalent amount of purchasing power. When all revenue and expenses are stated in units of similar purchasing power, we can see whether the business is gaining or losing in terms of the amount of purchasing power it controls.

To restate a historical amount in terms of an equivalent number of current dollars, we multiply the historical amount by the ratio of the current price level to the historical price level, as illustrated below:

*Converting to current dollars*

$$\text{Historical cost} \times \frac{\text{Average price index for current period}}{\text{Index at date of historical cost}} = \text{Equivalent number of current dollars}$$

For example, assume that land was purchased for $10,000 when the price index stood at 100. If the price index is now 170, we may find the number of current dollars equivalent to the purchasing power originally invested in the land by multiplying the $10,000 historical cost by ***170/100.*** The result, $17,000, represents the number of current dollars equivalent in purchasing power to the 10,000 historical dollars.

**Price index levels for our illustration** The following changes in the general price index are assumed in our Flation Company illustration:

| *Date* | *Price Index* |
|---|---|
| *Beginning of Year 8 (acquisition date for depreciable assets)* | *150* |
| *End of Year 9* | *180* |
| *Average price level for Year 10** | *200* |
| *End of Year 10* | *216* |
| *Rate of inflation for Year 10†* | *20%* |

*The "average" price level for the year is computed as a monthly average and need not lie exactly halfway between the price levels at the beginning and end of the year.

†The inflation rate is computed by dividing the increase in the price index over the year by the price index at the beginning of the year: (216 − 180) ÷ 180 = 20%.

In restating historical dollars to current dollars, we shall use the ***average price level*** for Year 10 (200) to represent the purchasing power of current dollars.[8]

**Not all amounts are restated** Compare the constant dollar and historical cost income statements of the Flation Company for Year 10 (page 532). Note that only two items—depreciation expense and the cost of goods sold—have been restated in the constant dollar statement. Sales revenue and expenses other than depreciation consist of transactions occurring during the current year. Therefore, these amounts are ***already*** stated in current dollars. We need to adjust to current dollars only those expenses which are based on costs incurred in past years.

**Restating depreciation expense** Assume that Flation Company's depreciation expense all relates to equipment purchased early in Year 8 when the price level was 150. The equipment cost $300,000 and is being depreciated over 10 years by the straight-line method. Since the average price level in Year 10 is 200, the purchasing power originally invested in this equipment is equivalent to $400,000 current dollars ($\$300{,}000 \times \frac{200}{150} = \$400{,}000$). Thus, the amount of purchasing power expiring in Year 10, stated in current dollars, is $40,000 ($400,000 ÷ 10 years).

[8] An acceptable alternative is to use the year-end price level to represent the purchasing power of current dollars. However, use of the year-end price level means that all income statement amounts, including revenue and expense transactions conducted during the current year, must be restated. For this reason, the vast majority of companies presenting constant dollar information use the average price level for the current year.

A shortcut approach is simply to restate the historical depreciation expense, as follows:

| *Historical Dollars* | | *Conversion Ratio* | | *Equivalent Current Dollars* |
|---|---|---|---|---|
| *$30,000* | × | *200/150* | = | *$40,000* |

Since depreciable assets are long-lived, the price level prevailing when the assets were acquired may be substantially different from the current price level. In such cases, the amount of depreciation expense recognized becomes one of the most significant differences between historical dollar and current dollar financial statements.

**Restating the cost of goods sold** During Year 10, Flation Company sold merchandise with a historical cost of $180,000. Assume that $45,000 of these goods came from the beginning inventory, acquired at the end of Year 9 when the price level was 180; the remaining $135,000 of these goods were purchased during Year 10. The restatement of the cost of goods sold to average Year 10 dollars is shown below:

| | *Historical Dollars* | | *Conversion Ratio* | | *Equivalent Current Dollars* |
|---|---|---|---|---|---|
| *Beginning inventory* | *$ 45,000* | × | *200/180* | = | *$ 50,000* |
| *Purchased in Year 10* | *135,000* | | * | | *135,000* |
| *Cost of goods sold* | *$180,000* | | | | *$185,000* |

* No adjustment necessary—amount is already stated in current dollars.

## Interpreting the constant dollar income statement

The basic difference between historical dollar and constant dollar income statements is the unit of measure. Historical dollar income statements use the dollar as a basic unit of measure. The unit of measure in constant dollar income statements is the ***purchasing power of the current dollar.***

A conventional income statement shows how many dollars were added to owner's equity from the operation of the business. Identifying a dollar increase in owner's equity as "income" implies that owners are better off when they recover more than the original number of dollars they invested. No attention is given to the fact that a greater number of dollars may still have less purchasing power than was originally invested.

A ***constant dollar*** income statement shows whether the ***inflow of purchasing power*** from current operations is larger or smaller than the ***purchasing power consumed*** in the effort to generate revenue. In short, the net income figure tells us whether the amount of purchasing power controlled by the business has increased or decreased as a result of operations.

## Gains and losses in purchasing power

Constant dollar accounting introduces a new consideration in measuring the effects of inflation upon a business: gains and losses in purchasing power from holding monetary items. ***Monetary items*** are those assets and liabilities representing claims to a ***fixed number of dollars.*** Examples of monetary assets are cash, notes receivable, and accounts receivable; most liabilities are monetary, including notes payable and accounts payable.

Holding monetary assets during a period of rising prices results in a loss of purchasing power because the value of the money is falling. In contrast, owing money during a period of rising prices gives rise to a gain in purchasing power because debts may be repaid using dollars of less purchasing power than those originally borrowed.

To illustrate, assume that Flation Company held $40,000 in cash throughout Year 10, while the price level rose 20% (from 180 to 216). By the end of the year, this $40,000 cash balance will have lost 20% of its purchasing power, as demonstrated by the following analysis:

| | |
|---|---|
| *Number of dollars needed at year-end to represent the same purchasing power as $40,000 at the beginning of the year ($40,000 × 216/180)* | *$48,000* |
| *Number of dollars actually held at year-end* | *40,000* |
| *Loss in purchasing power as a result of holding monetary assets* | *$ 8,000* |

(We can also compute this loss simply by multiplying the amount of the monetary assets held throughout the year by the 20% inflation rate: $40,000 × 20% = $8,000.)

A similar analysis is applied to any monetary liabilities. Assume, for example, that Flation Company has a $60,000 note payable outstanding throughout Year 10. The resulting gain in purchasing power is computed as follows:

| | |
|---|---|
| *Number of dollars at year-end representing the same purchasing power as $60,000 owed at beginning of year ($60,000 × 216/180)* | *$72,000* |
| *Number of dollars actually owed at year-end* | *60,000* |
| *Gain in purchasing power as a result of owing a fixed number of dollars* | *$12,000* |

***FASB Statement No. 33*** requires disclosure of the ***net gain or loss*** from holding monetary assets and owing monetary liabilities. Flation Company has experienced a $4,000 net gain in purchasing power ($12,000 gain − $8,000 loss), because its monetary liabilities were greater than its monetary assets. The disclosure of this net gain is illustrated in the supplementary schedule on page 532.

[9] Some readers may notice that our net gain is stated in end-of-Year 10 dollars. To be technically consistent with the other constant dollar data on page 532, this net gain should be restated in dollars of average purchasing power for Year 10. The gain can be restated as follows: $4,000 \times \frac{200}{216} = \$3,704$. We have ignored this restatement because it is not material in dollar amount and is an unnecessary refinement for an introductory discussion.

### Interpreting the net gain or loss in purchasing power

In determining the change in the purchasing power represented by owner's equity, we must consider ***both*** the amount of constant dollar net income ***and*** the amount of any gain or loss resulting from monetary items. Thus, the purchasing power of the owner's equity in Flation Company increased by $14,000 during Year 10 ($10,000 net income + $4,000 gain in purchasing power from monetary items).

The purchasing power gain from monetary items is shown separately from the determination of net income to emphasize the special nature of this gain. The income statement shows the purchasing power created or lost ***as a result of business operations.*** The $4,000 net gain in purchasing power, however, is caused entirely by the ***effect of inflation*** upon the purchasing power of monetary assets and liabilities. A business that owns monetary assets or owes money may have a purchasing power gain or loss even if it earns no revenue and incurs no expenses.

In evaluating the effect of inflation upon a particular business, we must consider the effect of inflation upon operations and its effects upon the monetary assets and liabilities of the business. If a business must maintain high levels of cash or accounts receivable from customers, we should recognize that inflation will continually erode the purchasing power of these assets. On the other hand, if a business is able to finance its operations with borrowed capital, inflation will benefit the company by allowing it to repay smaller amounts of purchasing power than it originally borrowed.

### Net income on a current cost basis

Constant dollar accounting does not abandon historical costs as the basis for measurement but simply expresses these costs in terms of the current value of money. Current cost accounting, on the other hand, does represent a departure from the historical cost concept. The term "current cost" usually refers to the ***current replacement cost*** of assets. In a current cost income statement, expenses are stated at the estimated cost to ***replace the specific assets*** sold or used up. Thus, current cost accounting involves estimates of current market values, rather than adjustments to historical costs for changes in the general price level.

Of course, the replacement cost of an asset may fluctuate during the year. Since a cost such as depreciation expense occurs continually ***throughout*** the year, current cost measurements are based on the ***average*** replacement cost during the year, not on the replacement cost at year-end.

To illustrate, assume that the replacement cost of Flation Company's equipment was estimated to be $425,000 at the beginning of Year 10 and $475,000 at year-end. Current cost depreciation expense should be based upon the $450,000 average replacement cost of the equipment during the year. Since the equipment has a 10-year life, the depreciation expense appearing in the current cost income statement (page 532) is $45,000 ($450,000 ÷ 10 years).

Now let us consider the determination of the cost of goods sold on a current cost basis. All we need to know is (1) how many units of inventory were sold during the year, and (2) the average replacement cost of these units during Year 10. If Flation Company sold 145,000 units during the year, and the average replacement cost was $1.35 per unit, the cost of goods sold would be $195,750 on a current cost basis (145,000 units × $1.35). Note that the historical cost of units in the company's beginning inventory does not enter into the current cost computation.

### Interpreting a current cost income statement

A current cost income statement does ***not*** measure the flow of general purchasing power in and out of the business. Rather, it shows whether a company earns enough revenue to replace the goods and services used up in the effort to generate that revenue. The resulting net income figure closely parallels ***distributable profit***—the maximum amount that the business can distribute to its owners and still maintain the present size and scale of its operations.

Unfortunately, the financial statements of large corporations show that many companies in industries vital to our economy are reporting profits measured on a historical cost basis but are incurring large ***losses*** according to their supplementary current cost disclosures. Companies in the steel industry and utilities industry provide excellent examples. What does this mean to an informed reader of financial statements? In short, it means that these companies do not earn sufficient revenue to maintain their productive capacity. In the long run, they must either obtain capital from other sources or scale down the size of their operations.

### What direction will inflation accounting take?

The techniques for restating financial statements for changes in the general price level have been known for many years. Yet despite support from both the FASB and the APB, the preparation of constant dollar financial statements has not become a widespread practice.

Current cost accounting is a much newer idea and appears to be gaining acceptance in many countries. The British government has given approval to a System of Current Cost Accounting and has arranged for development of methods to implement it. In the Netherlands, large corporations are basing depreciation on replacement cost and determining cost of goods sold in terms of replacement values. In Australia, the Institute of Chartered Accountants has gone on record as favoring the valuation of assets at current cost and the measurement of profit by stating both revenue and expenses at current values.

One factor contributing to support for current cost accounting is that constant dollar financial statements are based upon the ***general*** price level and not upon the prices of ***specific*** goods and services. Any given company has inventories of specific commodities for which prices may be changing in quite a different manner from the general price level.

ILLUSTRATIVE CASE. In a recent year the wholesale price of sugar declined from over 60 cents a pound to approximately 12 cents a pound although the general price level was rising strongly. A company in the sugar industry would have presented a more realistic income statement by reducing its cost of goods sold to reflect the falling price of sugar than by increasing this cost upward for the change in the general price level.

On the other hand, a significant advantage of constant dollar accounting is its high degree of ***objectivity.*** Since all adjustments are made by using the same general price index, valuations are not based on estimates or personal opinion. The principal problem to be solved if current cost accounting is to succeed is the development of uniform standards for measuring the replacement cost of various types of assets. It appears likely that ***specific*** price indexes will be the most objective and satisfactory means of developing replacement cost data. However, these will be specialized indexes measuring ***specific types of commodities*** rather than a single index of the general price level.

It is important to remember, however, that constant dollar accounting and current cost accounting each convey different types of useful information. The two approaches are not mutually exclusive; that is, the use of one does not preclude use of the other. Both approaches may be used within a single set of financial statements. In all probability, the gradual modification of the accounting process to disclose more clearly the effects of inflation will involve continuing experimentation with both constant dollar and current cost accounting.

## KEY TERMS INTRODUCED OR EMPHASIZED IN CHAPTER 14

**Audit opinion** The report issued by a firm of certified public accountants after auditing the financial statements of a business. Expresses an opinion on the fairness of the financial statements and indicates the nature and limits of the responsibility being assumed by the independent auditors.

**Conservatism** A traditional practice of resolving uncertainties by choosing an asset valuation at the lower point of the range of reasonableness. Also refers to the policy of postponing recognition of revenue to a later date when a range of reasonable choice exists. Designed to avoid overstatement of financial strength and earnings.

**Consistency** An assumption that once a particular accounting method is adopted, it will not be changed from period to period. Intended to make financial statements of a given company comparable from year to year.

**Constant dollar accounting** The technique of expressing all financial statement amounts in dollars of equal purchasing power. This is accomplished by restating historical costs for subsequent changes in the general price level. Also called ***general price level accounting.***

**Cost principle** The traditional, widely used policy of accounting for assets at their historical cost determined through arm's-length bargaining. Justified by the need for objective evidence to support the valuation of assets.

**Current cost accounting** The valuation of assets and measurement of income in terms of current replacement costs rather than historical costs. This approach to inflation accounting indicates the ability of a business to replace its physical capital (specific inventory and plant assets) as it is sold or used up.

**Disclosure principle** Financial statements should disclose all material and relevant information about the financial position and operating results of a business. The notes accompanying financial statements are an important means of disclosure.

**Entity concept** Any legal or economic unit which controls economic resources and is accountable for these resources may be considered an accounting entity. The resources and the transactions of the entity are not to be intermingled with those of its owner or owners.

**General price level** The weighted-average price of all goods and services in the economy. Inflation may be defined as an increase in the general price level.

**Generally accepted accounting principles** Those accounting principles which have received substantial authoritative support, such as the approval of the FASB, the AICPA, or the SEC. Often referred to by the acronym GAAP.

**Going-concern assumption** An assumption that a business entity will continue in operation indefinitely and thus will carry out its existing commitments. If evidence to the contrary exists, then the assumption of liquidation would prevail and assets would be valued at their estimated liquidation values.

**Installment method** An accounting method used principally in the determination of taxable income. It provides for recognition of realized profit on installment contracts in proportion to cash collected.

**Matching principle** The revenue earned during an accounting period is compared or matched with the expenses incurred in generating this revenue in order to measure income. Fundamental to the accrual basis of accounting.

**Materiality** The relative importance of an amount or item. An item which is not important or significant enough to influence the decisions of prudent users of financial statements is considered as ***not*** material. The accounting treatment of immaterial items may be guided by convenience rather than by theoretical principles. For example, purchase of 10 gallons of gasoline is treated as the incurring of an expense rather than the acquisition of an asset.

**Monetary items** With respect to changes in price levels, monetary items include assets representing claims to a fixed number of dollars (such as cash and receivables) and most liabilities. Holding monetary assets during a period of rising prices results in a loss in purchasing power; conversely, owing monetary liabilities results in a gain in purchasing power.

**Monetary (stable-dollar) assumption** In using money as a measuring unit and preparing financial statements expressed in dollars, accountants make the assumption that the dollar is a stable unit of measurement. This assumption is obviously faulty as a result of continued inflation, and strenuous efforts are being made to change to current cost accounting or general price-level-adjusted measurements.

**Objectivity (objective evidence)** The valuation of assets and the measurement of income are to be based as much as possible on objective evidence, such as exchange prices in arm's-length transactions. Objective evidence is subject to verification by independent experts.

**Percentage-of-completion method** A method of accounting for long-term construction projects which recognizes revenue and profits in proportion to the work completed, based on an estimate of the portion of the project completed each accounting period.

**Purchasing power** The ability of money to buy goods and services. As the general price level rises, the purchasing power of the dollar declines. Thus, in periods of inflation, an ever-increasing number of dollars is necessary to represent a given amount of purchasing power.

**Realization principle** The principle of recognizing revenue in the accounts only when earned. Revenue is realized when the earning process is virtually complete, which is usually at the time of sale of goods or rendering service to customers.

## REVIEW QUESTIONS

1 What is the basic objective of financial statements?

2 To qualify as "generally accepted," accounting principles must receive substantial authoritative support. Name three groups or organizations in the United States which have been most influential in giving substantial authoritative support to accounting principles.

3 Explain what is meant by the expression "trade-off between ***reliability*** and ***relevance***" in connection with the preparation of financial statements.

4 Barker Company has at the end of the current period an inventory of merchandise which cost $500,000. It would cost $600,000 to replace this inventory, and it is estimated that the goods will probably be sold for a total of $700,000. If the firm were to terminate operations immediately, the inventory could probably be sold for $480,000. Discuss the relative reliability and relevance of each of these dollar measurements of the ending inventory.

5 Why is it necessary for accountants to assume the existence of a clearly defined accounting entity?

6 If the going-concern assumption were dropped, there would be no point in having current asset and current liability classifications in the balance sheet. Explain.

7 "The matching of costs and revenue is the natural extension of the time period principle." Evaluate this statement.

8 Define ***objectivity, consistency, materiality,*** and ***conservatism.***

9 Is the assumption that the dollar is a stable unit of measure realistic? What alternative procedures would you suggest?

10 **a** Why is it important that any change in accounting methods from one period to the next be disclosed?

**b** Does the concept of consistency mean that all companies in a given industry follow similar accounting methods?

11 Briefly define the principle of ***disclosure.*** List five examples of information that should be disclosed in financial statements or in notes accompanying the statements.

12 Publicly owned corporations are required to include in their annual reports a description of the accounting principles followed in the preparation of their financial statements. What advantages do you see in this practice?

13 List four stages of the productive process which might become the accountant's

basis for recognizing changes in the value of a firm's output. Which stage is most commonly used as a basis for revenue recognition? Why?

14 A CPA firm's standard audit opinion consists of two major paragraphs. Describe the essential content of each paragraph.

15 Define ***monetary assets*** and indicate whether a gain or loss results from the holding of such assets during a period of rising prices.

16 Why is it advantageous to be in debt during an inflationary period?

17 Evaluate the following statement: "During a period of rising prices, the conventional income statement overstates net income because the amount of depreciation recorded is less than the value of the service potential of assets consumed."

18 List the three supplementary disclosures required of large corporations by ***FASB Statement No. 33*** which were discussed in this chapter.

19 How does constant dollar accounting differ from current cost accounting? For which one would the Consumer Price Index be used?

20 Alpha Company sells pocket calculators which have been decreasing in cost while the general price level has been rising. Explain why Alpha Company's cost of goods sold on a constant dollar basis and on a current cost basis would be higher or lower than on a historical cost basis.

21 The latest financial statements of Boston Manufacturing Co. indicate that income measured in terms of constant dollars is much lower than income measured in historical dollars. What is the most probable explanation for this large difference?

22 What conclusion would you draw about a company that consistently shows large net losses when its income is measured on a current cost basis?

## EXERCISES

***Ex. 14-1*** For each situation described below, indicate the concept (or concepts) of accounting that is violated, if any. You may choose among the following concepts: Conservatism, consistency, disclosure, entity, going concern, matching, materiality, objectivity.

**Situations**

**a** A pencil sharpener acquired by a small business at a cost of $5 is estimated to have a useful life of 10 years and is recorded by a debit to the Office Equipment account.

**b** The owner of a small business used the business bank account in writing a check to a department store in payment for personal expenditures.

**c** The machinery used by a car wash business was shown in the balance sheet at its estimated scrap value which was far below the book value.

**d** The assets of a partnership are combined with the separate assets of the partners in preparing a balance sheet.

**e** The cost of merchandise purchased is recognized as expense before it is sold in order to report a less favorable financial position.

**f** Plans to dispose of a major segment of the business are not communicated to readers of the balance sheet.

**g** A portion of the cost of a major television promotional campaign in the month of May is deferred and arbitrarily allocated to expense over a five-year period.

**h** The method of depreciation is changed every two years and the change is disclosed in financial statements.

***Ex. 14-2*** The Clinton Corporation recognizes the profit on a long-term construction project as work progresses. From the information given below, compute the profit that should

| Year | Costs Incurred | Profit Considered Realized |
|---|---|---|
| 1 | $1,200,000 | $ ? |
| 2 | 3,000,000 | ? |
| 3 | 1,762,000 | ? |
| Total . . . . . . . . . . . . . . . | $5,962,000 | $1,538,000 |

be recognized each year, assuming that the original cost estimate on the contract was $6,000,000 and that the contract price is $7,500,000.

*Ex. 14-3* On September 15, Year 1, Susan Moore sold a piece of property which cost her $48,000 for $80,000, net of commissions and other selling expenses. The terms of sale were as follows: down payment, $8,000; balance, $3,000 on the fifteenth day of each month for 24 months, starting October 15, Year 1. Compute the gross profit to be recognized by Moore in Year 1, Year 2, and Year 3 **(a)** on the ***accrual basis*** of accounting and **(b)** on the ***installment basis*** of accounting.

*Ex. 14-4* This exercise emphasizes the significance of accrued and deferred revenue and expenses in applying the matching principle. Naylor Company reported net income for the period of $72,000, but failed to make adjusting entries for the following items:

(1) Included in the revenue account was the amount of $8,400 which should be considered as deferred revenue, as the services for which the customer had paid would not be rendered by Naylor Company until the following year.
(2) Accrued expense relating to unpaid salaries, $5,200.
(3) Accrued revenue for services rendered, $4,100.
(4) Included in the Rent Expense account was the amount of $3,800 of rent paid applicable to the following year.
(5) A payment of $4,100 for ordinary repairs to driveways and fences had been charged to the Land account.

Compute the corrected net income. Your answer should begin with "Net income as reported . . . $72,000," and show on a separate line the increase or decrease caused by each of the five items.

*Ex. 14-5* Three companies started business with $500,000 at the beginning of the current year when the general price index stood at 125. The First Company invested the money in a note receivable due in four years; the Second Company invested its cash in land; and the Third Company purchased a building for $2,000,000, assuming a liability for the unpaid balance of $1,500,000. The price level stood at 140 at the end of the year. Compute the purchasing power gain or loss on monetary items for each company during the year.

*Ex. 14-6* Empire Company paid $400,000 cash in Year 1 to acquire land as a long-term investment. At this time, the general price level stood at 100. In Year 5, the general price index stands at 140, but the price of land in the area in which Empire Company invested has doubled in value. Rental receipts for grazing and farming during the five-year period were sufficient to pay all carrying charges on the land.

Empire Company prepares a constant dollar income statement and discloses purchasing power gains and losses as supplementary information to its cost-based financial statements.

**a** How much of a purchasing power gain or loss relating to the land will be included in the supplementary disclosures over the five-year period? (Assume the land is still owned at the end of Year 5.)

**b** Assume the land is sold in Year 5 for $785,000. Compute the gain or loss on the sale on a basis of (1) historical cost and (2) constant dollars.

*Ex. 14-7* Western Showcase purchased equipment for $240,000 in Year 3 when the general price index stood at 120. The company depreciates the equipment over 15 years by the straight-line method, with no estimated salvage value. In Year 7, the general price level is 180 and the estimated replacement cost of the equipment is $387,000.

Compute the amount of depreciation expense for Year 7 on:

**a** A historical dollar basis
**b** A constant dollar basis
**c** A current cost basis

## PROBLEMS

### Group A

*14A-1* In each of the situations described below, the question is whether generally accepted accounting principles have been violated. In each case state the accounting principle or concept, if any, that has been violated and explain briefly the nature of the violation. If you believe the treatment ***is in accord with generally accepted accounting principles,*** state this as your position and briefly defend it.

**a** The Lynn Company has purchased a computer for $1.5 million. The company expects to use the computer for five years, at which time it will acquire a larger and faster computer. The new computer is expected to cost $3.5 million. During the current year the company debited $700,000 to the Depreciation Expense account to "provide for one-fifth of the estimated cost of the new computer."

**b** Bob Standish is president of Dutchman Mines. During the current year, geologists and engineers revised upward the estimated value of ore deposits on the company's property. Standish instructed the accountant for Dutchman Mines to record goodwill of $2 million, the estimated value of unmined ore in excess of previous estimates. The offsetting credit was made to revenue.

**c** Merchandise inventory which cost $2 million is reported in the balance sheet at $3 million, the expected sales price less estimated direct selling expenses.

**d** Jefferson Company reports net income for the current year of $1,300,010. In the audit report the auditors stated: "We certify that the results of operations shown in the income statement are a true and accurate portrayal of the company's operations for the current year."

**e** The Lee Oil Company reported on its balance sheet as an intangible asset the total of all wages, supplies, depreciation on equipment, and other costs related to the drilling of a producing oil well and then amortized this asset as oil was produced from the well.

*14A-2* Early in Year 1, Roadbuilders, Inc., was notified that it was the successful bidder on the construction of a section of state highway. The bid price for the project was $20 million. Construction is to begin in Year 1 and will take about 15 months to complete; the deadline for completion is in April of Year 2.

The contract calls for payments of $5 million per year to Roadbuilders, Inc., for four years, beginning in Year 1. (After the project is complete, the state will also pay a reasonable interest charge on the unpaid balance of the contract.) The company estimates that construction costs will total $16 million, of which $12 million will be incurred in Year 1 and $4 million in Year 2.

The controller of the company, Joe Morgan, recognizes that there are a number of ways he might account for this contract. He might recognize income at the time the contract is completed (sales method), in April of Year 2. Alternatively, he might recognize income during construction (production method), in proportion to the percentage of the total cost incurred in each of Years 1 and 2. Finally, he might recognize income in proportion to the percentage of the total contract price collected in installment receipts during the four-year period (installment method).

**Instructions**

**a** Prepare a schedule (in millions of dollars) showing the profit that would be recognized on this project in each of the next four years under each of the three accounting methods being considered by the controller. Assume that the timing and construction costs go according to plan. (Ignore the interest revenue relating to the unpaid balance of the contract.)

**b** Explain which accounting method you consider to be most appropriate in this situation. Also explain why you consider the other two methods less appropriate.

*14A-3* Air Services, a single proprietorship, has compiled the following information applicable to the year ended December 31, 19___.

| | *Balance, Jan. 1* | *Cash Receipts or (Payments)* | *Balance, Dec. 31* |
|---|---|---|---|
| *Accounts receivable—sale of merchandise* | *$17,000* | *$180,000* | *$25,500* |
| *Accounts payable* | *9,750* | *(88,200)* | *11,200* |
| *Prepaid supplies* | *1,360* | *(4,900)* | *750* |
| *Merchandise inventories* | *21,000* | | *23,600* |
| *Accrued wages payable* | *2,500* | *(39,000)* | *6,000* |

**Instructions**

**a** Prepare an "income statement" for the year on a cash basis of accounting. (A more accurate title would be a "Statement of Cash Receipts and Disbursements.") Disregard the fact that companies with inventories should not use the cash basis of accounting. Cost of goods sold is to be stated at the amount of cash payments on accounts payable during the year. The beginning and ending inventories are to be ignored in the cash basis statement.

**b** Prepare an income statement for the year on the accrual basis of accounting required by generally accepted accounting principles for a company with these characteristics. Hint: Sales equals cash receipts ($180,000) minus beginning balance of accounts receivable ($17,000) plus ending balance of accounts receivable ($25,500). Use a similar line of reasoning for the other items, considering first the cash receipt or payment during the year and then making adjustments for the beginning and ending balances.

*14A-4* The following supplementary schedule appears with the financial statements of Navigational Instruments for 19___:

*Income Statement Adjusted for Changing Prices*
*(in thousands of dollars)*

| | *As Reported in the Primary Statements* | *Adjusted for General Inflation (Constant Dollars)* | *Adjusted for Changes in Specific Prices (Current Costs)* |
|---|---|---|---|
| *Net sales* | *$600,000* | *$600,000* | *$600,000* |
| *Costs and expenses:* | | | |
| *Cost of goods sold* | *$400,000* | *$415,000* | *$410,000* |
| *Depreciation expense* | *50,000* | *65,000* | *95,000* |
| *Other expenses* | *110,000* | *110,000* | *110,000* |
| *Total* | *$560,000* | *$590,000* | *$615,000* |
| *Net income* | *$ 40,000* | *$ 10,000* | *$(15,000)* |
| *Loss from decline in purchasing power of net monetary assets owned* | | *$ 18,000* | |

**Instructions** Explain the reasoning behind your answer to each of the following questions:

**a** Has the replacement cost of the company's inventory increased faster or more slowly than the general price level during the year?

**b** Has the replacement cost of the company's depreciable assets increased faster or more slowly than the general price level since these assets were acquired?

**c** Were the average monetary assets held by the company during the year greater or smaller than the average monetary liabilities owed?

**d** What was the total change in the purchasing power of the owners' equity in this business during the year?

**e** Assuming that this is a typical year, are the company's earnings sufficient to maintain the present size and scope of its operations on a long-term basis?

*14A-5* Sandy Malone, the president of Sandstone Art Company, has asked you to prepare constant dollar and current cost income statements to supplement the company's financial statements. The company's accountant has provided you with the following data:

***Income Statement—Historical Cost***
***For the Current Year***

| | | |
|---|---|---|
| *Net sales* | | *$420,000* |
| *Costs and expenses:* | | |
| *Cost of goods sold* | *$210,000* | |
| *Depreciation expense* | *30,000* | |
| *Other expenses* | *160,000* | |
| *Total costs and expenses* | | *400,000* |
| *Net income* | | *$ 20,000* |

**Other Data**

(1) Changes in the general price index during the current year were as follows:

| | *Price Index* |
|---|---|
| *Beginning of current year* | *120* |
| *Average for current year* | *130* |
| *End of current year* | *138* |
| *Rate of inflation [(138 − 120) ÷ 120]* | *15%* |

Amounts in the constant dollar income statement are to be expressed in current-year dollars of average purchasing power.

(2) The company sells a single product and uses the first-in, first-out method to compute the cost of goods sold. The historical cost of goods sold includes the following unit sales at the following costs:

| | *Units* | × | *Average Unit Costs* | = | *Total* |
|---|---|---|---|---|---|
| *From beginning inventory* | *10,000* | | *$3.00* | | *$ 30,000* |
| *From current-year purchases* | *56,250* | | *3.20* | | *180,000* |
| *Cost of goods sold* | *66,250* | | *3.17* | | *$210,000* |

The $30,000 beginning inventory was purchased when the general price index stood at 120. (It is not necessary to know total purchases or ending inventory for the current year.)

(3) The company's depreciable assets consist of equipment acquired five years ago when the price index stood at 75. The equipment cost $450,000 and is being depreciated over a 15-year life by the straight-line method with no estimated salvage value.

The estimated replacement cost of the equipment was $600,000 at the beginning of the current year and $630,000 at year-end.

(4) Throughout the current year, the company has owned monetary assets of $90,000 and has owed monetary liabilities of $160,000.

**Instructions** Prepare a supplementary schedule in the format illustrated on page 532. Include comparative income statements prepared on the bases of historical costs, constant dollars, and current costs. Also show the net gain or loss from holding monetary items. Include supporting computations for the (1) cost of goods sold—constant dollar basis, (2) depreciation expense—constant dollar basis, (3) net gain or loss in purchasing power from holding monetary items, (4) cost of goods sold—current dollar basis, and (5) depreciation expense—current dollar basis.

## Group B

*14B-1* In each of the situations described below, the queston is whether generally accepted accounting principles have been properly observed. In each case state the accounting principle or concept, if any, that has been violated and explain briefly the nature of the violation. If you believe the treatment ***is in accord with generally accepted accounting principles,*** state this as your position and defend it.

**a** For a number of years the Waterman Company used the declining-balance method of depreciation both in its financial accounting records and in its income tax returns. During the current year the company decided to employ the straight-line method of depreciation in its accounting records but to continue to use the declining-balance method for income tax purposes.

**b** During the current year the Louis Company adopted a policy of charging purchases of small tools (unit cost less than $100) to expense as soon as they were acquired. In prior years the company had carried an asset account Small Tools which it had depreciated at the rate of 10% of the book value at the beginning of each year. The balance in the Small Tools account represented about 1% of the company's total plant and equipment, and depreciation on small tools was 0.4% of sales revenue. It is expected that purchases of small tools each year will run about the same as the depreciation that would be taken on these small tools.

**c** Ace Company printed a large mail-order catalog in July of each year, at a cost of $1.8 million. Customers ordered from this catalog throughout the year and the company agreed to maintain the catalog prices for 12 months after the date of issue. The controller charged the entire cost of the catalog to Advertising Expense in August when it was issued. The Ace Company's fiscal year ends on January 31 of each year. In defending this policy, the controller stated, "Once those catalogs are mailed they are gone. We could never get a nickel out of them."

*14B-2* Nantucket Boat Works builds custom sailboats. During the first year of operations, the company built four boats for Island Charter Company. The four boats had a total cost of $252,000 and were sold for a total price of $360,000, due on an installment basis. Island Charter Company paid $120,000 of this sales price during the first year, plus an additional amount for interest charges.

At year-end, work is in progress on two other boats which are 60% complete. The contract price for these two boats totals $220,000 and costs incurred on these boats during the year total $96,000 (60% of estimated total costs of $160,000).

**Instructions** Compute the gross profit for Nantucket Boat Works during its first year of operations under each of the following assumptions. (Interest earned from Island Charter Company does not enter into the computation of gross profit.)

**a** The entire profit is recognized on the four boats completed and profit on the two boats under construction is recognized on a percentage-of-completion basis.
**b** Profit on the four boats completed is recognized on the installment basis and no portion of the profit on the two boats under construction will be recognized until the boats are completed, delivered to customers, and cash is collected.

*14B-3* All sales by Fire Equipment are made on credit, with terms calling for payment 90 days after the date of sale. The company pays a commission of 10% of selling price to its sales staff as soon as the customers pay their accounts.

During the first three years of operations, the company reported sales on a cash basis; that is, it did not record the sale until the cash was collected. Commissions to the sales staff were recorded only when cash was collected from customers. Net income figures computed on this basis were:

| | |
|---|---|
| *Year 1* | *$ 60,000* |
| *Year 2* | *90,000* |
| *Year 3* | *135,000* |

An accountant, called in at the end of Year 3 to review the store's accounting system, suggested that a better picture of earnings would be obtained if both sales and commissions were recorded on the accrual basis. The accountant determined that accounts receivable at the end of each year were as follows:

| | |
|---|---|
| *Year 1* | *$62,000* |
| *Year 2* | *81,000* |
| *Year 3* | *44,200* |

Sales commissions should be accrued at the rate of 10% of accounts receivable.

**Instructions**

**a** On the basis of this information, prepare a schedule showing the amount of net income Fire Equipment would have reported in each of the three years if it had followed accrual accounting for its sales and sales commissions.
**b** Comment on the differences in net income under the two methods and the significance of the trend in the net income figures as revised.

*14B-4* The financial statements of Lagerbier for the current year include the following supplementary schedule showing the effects of inflation upon the company:

***Income Statement Adjusted for Changing Prices***
***(in thousands of dollars)***

| | *As Reported in the Primary Statements* | *Adjusted for General Inflation (Constant Dollars)* | *Adjusted for Changes in Specific Prices (Current Costs)* |
|---|---|---|---|
| *Net sales* | *$450,000* | *$450,000* | *$450,000* |
| *Costs and expenses:* | | | |
| *Cost of goods sold* | *$240,000* | *$245,000* | *$255,000* |
| *Depreciation expense* | *120,000* | *160,000* | *130,000* |
| *Other expenses* | *50,000* | *50,000* | *50,000* |
| *Total* | *$410,000* | *$455,000* | *$435,000* |
| *Net income (loss)* | *$ 40,000* | *$ (5,000)* | *$ 15,000* |
| *Gain from decline in purchasing power of net amounts owed* | | *$ 12,000* | |

**Instructions** Use the supplementary schedule to answer each of the following questions. Explain the reasoning behind your answers.

**a** Has the replacement cost of the company's inventory increased faster or more slowly than the general price index during the current year?

**b** Has the replacement cost of the company's depreciable assets increased faster or more slowly than the general price level since these assets were acquired?

**c** Were the average monetary assets held by the company during the year greater or smaller than the average monetary amounts owed?

**d** What was the total change in the purchasing power of the owners' equity in the business during the year?

**e** Assuming that this was a typical year, are the company's earnings sufficient to maintain the present size and scope of current operations on a long-term basis?

*14B-5* The accounting staff of Prescott Company has provided the following data to assist you in preparing constant dollar and current cost information to supplement the company's financial statements for the current year:

***Income Statement—Historical Cost***

***For the Current Year***

| | | |
|---|---|---|
| *Net sales* | | *$620,000* |
| *Costs and expenses:* | | |
| *Cost of goods sold* | *$310,000* | |
| *Depreciation expense* | *50,000* | |
| *Other expenses* | *200,000* | |
| *Total costs and expenses* | | *560,000* |
| *Net income* | | *$ 60,000* |

**Other data**

(1) Changes in the general price level during the current year were as follows:

| | *Price Index* |
|---|---|
| *Beginning of year* | *140* |
| *Average for year* | *150* |
| *End of year* | *161* |
| *Rate of inflation [(161 − 140) ÷ 140]* | *15%* |

Amounts in the constant dollar income statement are to be stated in current-year dollars of average purchasing power.

(2) The company sells a single product and uses the first-in, first-out method to compute the cost of goods sold. The historical cost of goods sold included the following unit sales at the following costs:

| | *Units* | × | *Average Unit Costs* | = | *Total* |
|---|---|---|---|---|---|
| *From beginning inventory* | *14,000* | | *$5.00* | | *$ 70,000* |
| *From current-year purchases* | *40,000* | | *6.00* | | *240,000* |
| *Cost of goods sold* | *54,000* | | *5.74* | | *$310,000* |

The $70,000 beginning inventory was purchased when the general price index stood at 140. (It is not necessary to know total purchases or ending inventory for the current year.)

(3) The company's depreciable assets consist of equipment acquired four years ago when the general price index stood at 80. The equipment cost $500,000 and is

being depreciated over a 10-year life by the straight-line method with no estimated salvage value.

The estimated replacement cost of the equipment was $980,000 at the beginning of the current year and $1,070,000 at year-end.

(4) Throughout the current year, the company owned monetary assets of $110,000 and owed monetary liabilities of $200,000.

**Instructions** Prepare a supplementary schedule in the format illustrated on page 532. Include comparative income statements prepared on the bases of historical cost, constant dollars, and current costs. Also show the net gain or loss resulting from monetary items. Show supporting computations for the (1) cost of goods sold stated in constant dollars, (2) depreciation expense stated in constant dollars, (3) net gain or loss in purchasing power from monetary items, (4) cost of goods sold measured in current costs, and (5) depreciation expense measured in current costs.

## BUSINESS DECISION PROBLEM 14

For many years, Festival Films used the lifo method of inventory valuation and the declining-balance method of depreciation in measuring the net income of its mail-order business. In addition, the company charged off all costs of catalogs as incurred. In Year 10, the company changed its inventory pricing method to fifo, adopted the straight-line method of depreciation, and decided to charge off catalog costs only as catalogs are distributed to potential customers.

The following information for the last three years is taken from the company's accounting records:

| | Year 10 | Year 9 | Year 8 |
|---|---|---|---|
| Sales (net) | $500,000 | $400,000 | $350,000 |
| Purchases (net) | 300,000 | 220,000 | 200,000 |
| Ending inventory—fifo | 50,000 | 45,000 | 40,000 |
| Ending inventory—lifo | 30,000 | 28,000 | 25,000 |
| Depreciation—declining-balance method | 27,500 | 30,000 | 35,000 |
| Depreciation—straight-line method | 20,000 | 20,000 | 20,000 |
| Operating expenses other than depreciation | 120,500 | 93,000 | 80,000 |
| Catalog costs included in operating expenses but considered applicable to future revenue | 18,500 | 8,000 | 5,000 |
| Net income as computed by Festival Films | 100,000 | 60,000 | 37,000 |

At the end of Year 10, Festival Films prepared the following comparative income statement and presented it to a banker in connection with an application for a substantial long-term loan:

**FESTIVAL FILMS**
**Comparative Income Statement**
**For Years Ended December 31**

| | Year 10 | Year 9 |
|---|---|---|
| Sales (net) | $500,000 | $400,000 |
| Cost of goods sold* | 278,000 | 217,000 |
| Gross profit on sales | $222,000 | $183,000 |
| Operating expenses | 122,000 | 123,000 |
| Net income | $100,000 | $ 60,000 |

* Based on lifo inventory method in Year 9; inventory at end of Year 10 was valued on fifo basis.

The loan officer for the Pacific National Bank, where Festival Films has applied for the loan, asks you to help decide whether to lend the money to Festival Films.

**Instructions**

**a** Prepare a more detailed comparative income statement for Years 9 and 10. For the cost of goods sold section, you should use the figures listed in the three-column schedule at the beginning of this problem to show as individual items the beginning inventory, net purchases, cost of goods available for sale, ending inventory, and cost of goods sold. In the section for operating expenses, show the depreciation expense separately from other operating expenses. Summary figures should be the same as those compiled by Festival Films.

Criticize the detailed comparative income statement in terms of generally accepted accounting principles. Indicate the dollar effect on net income of any violations of accounting principles.

**b** Prepare two comparative income statements for Years 9 and 10. First, prepare a comparative statement on the same accounting basis as in prior years. Second, prepare a comparative income statement on the revised basis of accounting decided upon by the company.

**c** What good feature is common to both of the comparative income statements called for in **b** above? Comment on the ***trend*** of net income shown in each income statement in **b** above, and also in the comparative income statement prepared by Festival Films.

# 15

# PARTNERSHIPS

Three types of business organization are common to American business: the single proprietorship, the partnership, and the corporation. In this chapter we shall concentrate on the accounting problems peculiar to a partnership. The Uniform Partnership Act, which has been adopted by most states to govern the formation and operation of partnerships, defines a partnership as "an association of two or more persons to carry on, as co-owners, a business for profit."

## Reasons for formation of partnerships

In the professions and in businesses which stress the factor of personal service, the partnership form of organization is widely used. In the fields of manufacturing, wholesaling, and retail trade, partnerships are also popular, because they afford a means of combining the capital and abilities of two or more persons. Perhaps the most common factor which impels an individual to seek a partner is the lack of sufficient capital to begin or to expand a business. A partnership is often referred to as a ***firm;*** the name of the firm often includes the word "company" as, for example, "Adams, Barnes, and Company."

## Significant features of a partnership

Before taking up the accounting problems peculiar to partnerships, it will be helpful to consider briefly some of the distinctive characteristics of the partnership form of organization. These characteristics (such as limited life and unlimited liability) all stem from the basic point that a partnership is not a separate legal entity in itself but merely a voluntary association of individuals.

**Ease of formation** A partnership can be created without any legal formalities. When two or more persons agree to become partners, such agreement constitutes a contract and a partnership is automatically created. The contract should be in writing in order to lessen the chances for misunderstanding and future disagreement. The voluntary aspect of a partnership agreement means that no one can be forced into a partnership or forced to continue as a partner.

ILLUSTRATIVE CASE Richard and Mike were friends and employees of the same large corporation. They became interested in forming a partnership to acquire a nearby small business being offered for sale for a down payment of $50,000. They felt that they could manage the business (which had two employees) in their spare time. Richard and Mike agreed that each would deposit $25,000 in a partnership bank account. There was no written agreement of partnership. Richard made his deposit from his personal savings; Mike had only $10,000 of his own but was able to obtain the other $15,000 from his brother-in-law, Joe, to whom he described the business with great enthusiasm. Mike then deposited $25,000 in the partnership bank account and the business was purchased. Richard had never met Joe and was not aware of his $15,000 investment.

A few months later, Joe became annoyed because he had received no return on his investment. He appeared suddenly at the business while Richard was there, stating that he was a partner and demanding to see the accounting records and the bank statements. Richard refused, and after an angry argument, Joe was forcibly ejected. The question of whether Joe was a "silent partner" caused bitter disagreement among all three of the principals. During this dispute, the business was forced to shut down because of lack of working capital. Richard, Mike, and Joe each retained an attorney to seek damages from the others.

Although a partnership may be at best a somewhat unstable form of organization, a written agreement of partnership might have avoided the problems encountered by Richard and Mike—and by Joe.

**Limited life** A partnership may be ended at any time by the death or withdrawal of any member of the firm. Other factors which may bring an end to a partnership include the bankruptcy or incapacity of a partner, the expiration of the period specified in the partnership contract, or the completion of the project for which the partnership was formed. The admission of a new partner or the retirement of an existing member means an end to the old partnership, although the business may be continued by the formation of a new partnership.

**Mutual agency** Each partner acts as an agent of the partnership, with authority to enter into contracts for the purchase and sale of goods and services. The partnership is bound by the acts of any partner as long as these acts are within the scope of normal operations. The factor of mutual agency suggests the need for exercising great caution in the selection of a partner. To be in partnership with an irresponsible person or one lacking in integrity is an intolerable situation.

**Unlimited liability** Each partner is personally responsible for all the debts of the firm. The lack of any ceiling on the liability of a partner may deter a wealthy person from entering a partnership.

A new member joining an existing partnership may or may not assume liability for debts incurred by the firm prior to his or her admission. A partner withdrawing from membership must give adequate public notice of withdrawal; otherwise the former partner may be held liable for partnership debts incurred subsequent to his or her withdrawal. The retiring partner remains liable for partnership debts existing at the time of withdrawal unless the creditors agree to a release of this obligation.

**Co-ownership of partnership property and profits** When a partner invests a building, inventory, or other property in a partnership, he or she does not retain any personal right to the assets contributed. The property becomes jointly owned by all partners. Each member of a partnership also has an ownership right in the profits.

Sometimes a store manager or other supervisory employee is allowed a certain percentage of the profits as a bonus, or in lieu of a fixed salary. This arrangement is merely a device for computing the bonus or salary; it does ***not*** give the employee an ownership right in the profits and does not make him a partner. Some retail stores rent their buildings under an agreement calling for a yearly rental computed as a percentage of profits. This type of rental agreement does not make the landlord a partner. To be a partner one must have an ***ownership*** right in the profits.

## Advantages and disadvantages of a partnership

Perhaps the most important advantage of most partnerships is the opportunity to bring together sufficient capital to carry on a business. The opportunity to combine special skills, as, for example, the specialized talents of an engineer and an accountant, may also induce individuals to join forces in a partnership. To form a partnership is much easier and less expensive than to organize a corporation. Operating as a partnership ***may*** in some cases produce income tax advantages as compared with doing business as a corporation. The partnership itself is not a legal entity and does not have to pay income taxes as does a corporation, although the individual partners pay taxes on their respective shares of the firm's income. Members of a partnership enjoy more freedom from government regulation and more flexibility of action than do the owners of a corporation; the partners may withdraw funds and make business decisions of all types without the necessity of formal meetings or legalistic procedures.

Offsetting these advantages of a partnership are such serious disadvantages as limited life, unlimited liability, and mutual agency. Furthermore, if a business is to require a large amount of capital, the partnership is a less effective device for raising funds than is a corporation. Many persons who invest freely in common stocks of corporations are unwilling to enter a partnership because of the unlimited liability imposed on partners.

## The partnership contract

Although a partnership can be formed by an oral agreement, it is highly desirable that a written contract of partnership be prepared by an attorney, setting forth the understanding between the partners on such points as the following:

1 The name, location, and nature of the business.
2 Names of the partners, and the duties and rights of each.
3 Amount to be invested by each partner. Procedure for valuing any noncash assets invested or withdrawn by partners.
4 Method of sharing profits and losses.
5 Withdrawals to be allowed each partner.
6 Provision for insurance on the lives of partners, with the partnership or the surviving partners named as beneficiaries.
7 The accounting period to be used.
8 Annual audit by certified public accountants.
9 Provision for arbitration of disputes.
10 Provision for dissolution. This part of the agreement may specify a method for computing the equity of a retiring or deceased partner and a method of settlement which will not disrupt the business.

## Partnership accounting

An adequate accounting system and an accurate measurement of income are needed by every business, but they are especially important in a partnership because the net income is divided among two or more owners. All partners need current, accurate information on profits so that they can make intelligent decisions on such questions as additional investments, expansion of the business, or sale of their respective interests in the partnership.

ILLUSTRATIVE CASE Crane and Davis were partners in an automobile dealership and auto repair shop. Crane was the active manager of the business, but Davis had supplied nearly all the capital. Aware that the firm was quite profitable, Crane devised a scheme to become the sole owner by buying out his partner. In order to persuade Davis to sell his interest at a bargain price, Crane deliberately began falsifying the accounting records and financial statements in a manner to understate the earnings of the business. Much of the revenue from auto repair work was not recorded at all; depreciation expense was overstated; ending inventories were understated; and the cost of new items of plant and equipment were charged to expense. The result was a series of monthly income statements which showed the business operating at a larger loss each month. Faced with these discouraging financial statements, Davis became pessimistic over the prospects for the business and was on the verge of selling his interest to Crane at a price far below the balance in his capital account.

However, a friend suggested that before selling out, Davis should insist upon an audit of the business by a CPA firm. An audit was performed and revealed that the business was in fact highly profitable. When confronted by Davis with the auditors' findings, Crane withdrew from the partnership and Davis became the sole owner.

Partnership accounting requires the maintenance of a separate capital account for each partner; a separate drawing account for each partner is also needed. The other distinctive feature of partnership accounting is the division of each year's net profit or loss among the partners in the proportions specified by the partnership agreement. In the study of partnership accounting, the new concepts are found in the owner's equity section; accounting for partnership assets and liabilities follows the same principles as for other forms of business organization.

## Opening the accounts of a new partnership

When a partner contributes assets other than cash, a question always arises as to the value of such assets. The valuations assigned to noncash assets should be their ***fair market values*** at the date of transfer to the partnership. The valuations assigned must be agreed to by all the partners.

To illustrate the opening entries for a newly formed partnership, assume that on January 1 John Blair and Richard Cross, who operate competing retail stores, decide to form a partnership by consolidating their two businesses. A capital account will be opened for each partner and credited with the agreed valuation of the ***net assets*** (total assets less total liabilities) he contributes. The journal entries to open the accounts of the partnership of Blair and Cross are as follows:

***Entries for formation of partnership***

| | | |
|---|---|---|
| *Cash* | *40,000* | |
| *Accounts Receivable* | *60,000* | |
| *Inventory* | *90,000* | |
| *Accounts Payable* | | *30,000* |
| *John Blair, Capital* | | *160,000* |
| *To record the investment by John Blair in the partnership of Blair and Cross.* | | |
| *Cash* | *10,000* | |
| *Land* | *60,000* | |
| *Building* | *100,000* | |
| *Inventory* | *60,000* | |
| *Accounts Payable* | | *70,000* |
| *Richard Cross, Capital* | | *160,000* |
| *To record the investment by Richard Cross in the partnership of Blair and Cross.* | | |

The values assigned to assets in the accounts of the new partnership may be quite different from the amounts at which these assets were carried in the accounts of their previous owners. For example, the land contributed by Cross and valued at \$60,000 might have appeared in his accounting records at a cost of \$20,000. The building which he contributed was valued at \$100,000 by the partnership, but it might have cost Cross only \$80,000 some years ago and might have been depreciated on his records to a net value of \$60,000. Assuming that market values of land and buildings had risen sharply while Cross owned this property, it is no more than fair to recognize the ***present market value*** of these assets at the time he transfers them to the partnership and to credit his capital account accordingly. Depreciation of the building in the partnership accounts will be based on the assigned value of \$100,000 at the date of acquisition by the partnership.

### Additional investments

Assume that after six months of operation the firm is in need of more cash, and the partners make an additional investment of $10,000 each on July 1. These additional investments are credited to the capital accounts as shown below:

*Entry for additional investment*

| | | |
|---|---|---|
| *Cash* | *20,000* | |
| *John Blair, Capital* | | *10,000* |
| *Richard Cross, Capital* | | *10,000* |
| *To record additional investments.* | | |

### Drawing accounts

The drawing account maintained for each partner serves the same purpose as the drawing account of the owner of a single proprietorship. The transactions calling for debits to the drawing accounts of partners may be summarized as follows:

1 Cash or other assets withdrawn by a partner
2 Payments from partnership funds of the personal debts of a partner
3 Partnership cash collected on behalf of the firm by a partner but retained by the partner personally

Credits to the drawing accounts are seldom encountered; one rather unusual transaction requiring such an entry consists of the payment of a partnership liability by a partner out of personal funds.

### Loans from partners

Ordinarily any funds furnished to the firm by a partner are recorded by crediting that partner's capital account. Occasionally, however, a partnership may be in need of funds but the partners do not wish to increase their permanent investment in the business, or perhaps one partner is willing to advance funds when the others are not. Under these circumstances, the advance of funds may be designated as a loan from the partner and credited to a partner's loan account. Partnership liabilities to outsiders always take precedence over any claims of partners.

### Closing the accounts of a partnership at year-end

At the end of the accounting period, the balance in the Income Summary account is closed to the partners' capital accounts, in accordance with the profit-sharing provisions of the partnership contract. If the partnership contract does not mention how profits are to be divided, the law assumes that the intention of the partners was for an equal division of profits and losses. If the partnership agreement specifies a method of dividing profits but does not mention the possibility of losses, any losses are divided in the proportions provided for sharing profits.

In the previous illustration of the firm of Blair and Cross, an equal sharing of profits was agreed upon. Assuming that a profit of $60,000 was realized during the first year of operations, the entry to close the Income Summary account would be as follows:

*Closing Income Summary: profits shared equally*

| | | |
|---|---|---|
| *Income Summary* | *60,000* | |
| *John Blair, Capital* | | *30,000* |
| *Richard Cross, Capital* | | *30,000* |
| *To divide net income for 19__ in accordance with partnership agreement to share profits equally.* | | |

The next step in closing the accounts is to transfer the balance of each partner's drawing account to his capital account. Assuming that withdrawals during the year amounted to $12,000 for Blair and $8,000 for Cross, the entry at December 31 to close the drawing accounts is as follows:

*Closing the drawing accounts to capital accounts*

| | | |
|---|---|---|
| *John Blair, Capital* | *12,000* | |
| *Richard Cross, Capital* | *8,000* | |
| *John Blair, Drawing* | | *12,000* |
| *Richard Cross, Drawing* | | *8,000* |
| *To transfer debit balances in partners' drawing accounts to their respective capital accounts.* | | |

**Working papers** The working papers for a partnership may include a pair of columns for each partner. These columns are placed between the Income Statement columns and the Balance Sheet columns of the work sheet. The net income or loss as shown in the Income Statement columns is also carried to the partners' capital columns and divided between them as provided in the partnership agreement. In all other aspects, the working papers for a partnership are identical to those for a single proprietorship as illustrated in Chapters 4 and 5.

**Income statement for a partnership** The income statement for a partnership differs from that of a single proprietorship in only one respect: a final section may be added to show the division of the net income between the partners, as illustrated on page 558 for the firm of Blair and Cross.

**Statement of partners' capitals** The partners will usually want an explanation of the change in their capital accounts from one year-end to the next. A supplementary schedule called a ***statement of partners' capitals*** is prepared to show this information. A statement of partners' capitals for Blair and Cross appears below the income statement on page 558.

The balance sheet of Blair and Cross would show the capital balance for each partner, as well as the total capital of $380,000.

**BLAIR AND CROSS**
*Income Statement*
*For the Year Ended December 31, 19__*

*Note distribution of net income*

| | | |
|---|---|---|
| Sales | | $600,000 |
| Cost of goods sold: | | |
| Inventory, Jan. 1 | $150,000 | |
| Purchases | 460,000 | |
| Cost of goods available for sale | $610,000 | |
| Less: Inventory, Dec. 31 | 210,000 | |
| Cost of goods sold | | 400,000 |
| Gross profit on sales | | $200,000 |
| Operating expenses: | | |
| Selling expenses | $100,000 | |
| General & administrative expenses | 40,000 | 140,000 |
| Net income | | $ 60,000 |
| Distribution of net income: | | |
| To John Blair (50%) | $ 30,000 | |
| To Richard Cross (50%) | 30,000 | $ 60,000 |

**BLAIR AND CROSS**
*Statement of Partners' Capitals*
*For the Year Ended December 31, 19__*

*Changes in capital accounts during the year*

| | Blair | Cross | Total |
|---|---|---|---|
| Investment, Jan. 1, 19__ | $160,000 | $160,000 | $320,000 |
| Add: Additional investment | 10,000 | 10,000 | 20,000 |
| Net income for the year | 30,000 | 30,000 | 60,000 |
| Subtotals | $200,000 | $200,000 | $400,000 |
| Less: Drawings | 12,000 | 8,000 | 20,000 |
| Balances, Dec. 31, 19__ | $188,000 | $192,000 | $380,000 |

## Partnership profits and income taxes

***Partnerships are not required to pay income taxes.*** However, a partnership is required to file an information tax return showing the amount of the partnership net income, and the share of each partner in the net income. Each partner must include his share of the partnership profit (after certain technical adjustments) on his individual income tax return. Partnership net income is thus taxable to the partners individually in the year in which it is earned. The income tax rules applicable to investment in a partnership are quite complex; those complexities are appropriate to advanced accounting courses.

Note that partners report and pay tax on their respective shares of the profits earned by the partnership during the year and not on the amounts which they have drawn out of the business during the year. ***The net income of the partner-***

***ship is taxable to the partners each year,*** even though there may have been no withdrawals. This treatment is consistent with that accorded a single proprietorship.

## The nature of partnership profits

The profit earned by a partnership, like that of a single proprietorship, may be regarded as consisting of three distinct elements: (1) compensation for the personal services rendered by the partners, (2) compensation (interest) for the use of invested capital, and (3) a "pure" profit or reward for the entrepreneurial functions of risk taking and policy making. Recognition of these ***three elements of partnership profits*** will be helpful in forming an equitable plan for the division of profits.

If one partner devotes full time to the business while another does not participate actively, the profit-sharing plan should give weight to this disparity in contributions of services. Any salaries authorized for partners ***are regarded as a preliminary step in the division of profits, not as an expense of the business.*** The partner is considered an owner, not an employee. The services which a partner renders to the firm are, therefore, considered to be rendered in anticipation of a share in profits, not in contemplation of a salary. The net profit reported by a partnership cannot be compared directly with the profit earned by a corporation of similar size, because the corporation treats as expense any payments to owner-managers for personal services rendered.

In the solution of problems in this book, the student should ***record withdrawals of assets by partners as debits to the partners' drawing accounts, regardless of whether or not the withdrawals are described as salaries.*** Some alternative treatments of salaries of partners can be explored in advanced accounting courses.

In the preceding illustrations of the partnership of Blair and Cross, we assumed that the partners invested equal amounts of capital, rendered equal services, and divided profits equally. We are now ready to consider cases in which the partners invest unequal amounts of capital and services.

## Dividing net income or loss

Partners can share net income or loss in any manner they decide upon; however, most profit-sharing agreements fall under one of the following types:

1 A fixed ratio. The fixed ratio method has already been illustrated in the example of the Blair and Cross partnership in which profits were shared equally, that is, 50% and 50%. Partners may agree upon any fixed ratio such as 60% and 40%, or 70% and 30%.
2 Salaries to partners, with remaining net income or loss divided in a fixed ratio.
3 Interest on partners' capitals, with remaining net income or loss divided in a fixed ratio.
4 Salaries to partners, interest on partners' capitals, and remaining net income or loss divided in a fixed ratio.

All these methods of sharing partnership income are intended to recognize differences in the personal services rendered by partners and in the amounts of capital invested in the firm. For example, if one partner invests twice as much capital as another, this needs to be considered in the plan for sharing profits. If one partner works full time in the business and the other only half time, this difference can be compensated for by setting different salaries. Different salaries to partners are also reasonable when one partner is more experienced or has a special skill not possessed by other partners.

In the illustrations which follow, it is assumed that beginning capitals were Arthur Adams, $160,000, and Ben Barnes, $40,000. At year-end, the Income Summary account showed a credit balance of $96,000, representing the net income for the year before any partners' salaries or interest on capital.

**Salaries to partners, with remainder in a fixed ratio** Because partners often contribute different amounts of personal services, partnership agreements often provide for partners' salaries as a factor in the division of profits.

For example, assume that Adams and Barnes agree that Adams will be allowed an annual salary of $24,000 and Barnes an annual salary of $48,000. Any remaining profits are to be divided equally. It is agreed that the salaries will be withdrawn in cash each month and recorded by debits to the drawing accounts.[1] The authorized salaries total $72,000 a year; this amount represents a first step in the division of the year's profit and is therefore subtracted from the net income of $96,000. The remaining profit of $24,000 will be divided equally.

*Profit sharing; salaries and fixed ratio as basis*

***Distribution of Net Income***

| | Adams | Barnes | Net Income |
|---|---|---|---|
| Net income to be divided | | | $96,000 |
| Salaries to partners | $24,000 | $48,000 | 72,000 |
| Remaining income after salaries | | | $24,000 |
| Allocated in a fixed ratio: | | | |
| Adams (50%) | 12,000 | | |
| Barnes (50%) | | 12,000 | 24,000 |
| Total share to each partner | $36,000 | $60,000 | $ -0- |

Under this agreement, Adams's share of the $96,000 profit amounts to $36,000 and Barnes's share amounts to $60,000. The entry to close the Income Summary account would be:

| | | |
|---|---|---|
| *Income Summary* | 96,000 | |
| *Arthur Adams, Capital* | | 36,000 |
| *Ben Barnes, Capital* | | 60,000 |
| *To close the Income Summary account by crediting each partner with his authorized salary and dividing the remaining profits equally.* | | |

[1] Salaries may be used as a device for dividing partnership net income, even though the partners do not wish to make any withdrawals of cash whatsoever. In this illustration, however, it is assumed that cash is withdrawn by each partner in an amount equal to his authorized salary.

**Interest on partners' capitals, with remainder in a fixed ratio** Next we shall assume a business situation in which the partners spend very little time in the business and net income depends primarily on the amount of money invested. The profit-sharing plan then might emphasize invested capital as a basis for the first step in allocating income.

For example, assume that Adams and Barnes agree that each partner is to be allowed interest at 15% on his beginning capital, with any remaining profit or loss to be divided equally. Net income to be divided is $96,000 and the beginning capitals are Adams, $160,000, and Barnes, $40,000, the same as in the preceding illustration.

*Profit sharing: interest on capitals and fixed ratio as basis*

***Distribution of Net Income***

| | Adams | Barnes | Net Income |
|---|---|---|---|
| Net income to be divided | | | $96,000 |
| Interest on beginning capitals: | | | |
| Adams ($160,000 × 15%) | $24,000 | | |
| Barnes ($40,000 × 15%) | | $ 6,000 | |
| Total allocated as interest | | | 30,000 |
| Remaining income after interest on capitals | | | $66,000 |
| Allocated in a fixed ratio: | | | |
| Adams (50%) | 33,000 | | |
| Barnes (50%) | | 33,000 | 66,000 |
| Total share to each partner | $57,000 | $39,000 | $ -0- |

The entry to close the Income Summary account in this example would be:

| | | |
|---|---|---|
| *Income Summary* | 96,000 | |
| *Arthur Adams, Capital* | | 57,000 |
| *Ben Barnes, Capital* | | 39,000 |
| *To close the Income Summary account by crediting each partner with interest at 15% on his beginning capital and dividing the remaining profits equally.* | | |

**Salaries, interest on capitals, and remainder in a fixed ratio** The preceding example took into consideration the difference in amounts of capital provided by Adams and Barnes but ignored any difference in personal services performed. In the next example, we shall assume that the partners agree to a profit-sharing plan providing for salaries and for interest on beginning capitals. Salaries, as before, are authorized at $24,000 for Adams and $48,000 for Barnes. Beginning capitals are $160,000 for Adams and $40,000 for Barnes. Each partner is to be allowed interest at 10% on his beginning capital balance, and any profits remaining after authorized salaries and interest allowances are to be divided equally.

**Distribution of Net Income**

*Profit sharing; salaries, interest, and fixed ratio as basis*

| | Adams | Barnes | Net Income |
|---|---|---|---|
| Net income to be divided | | | $96,000 |
| Salaries to partners | $24,000 | $48,000 | 72,000 |
| Income after salaries | | | $24,000 |
| Interest on beginning capitals: | | | |
| Adams ($160,000 × 10%) | 16,000 | | |
| Barnes ($40,000 × 10%) | | 4,000 | |
| Total allocated as interest | | | 20,000 |
| Remaining income after salaries and interest | | | $ 4,000 |
| Allocated in a fixed ratio: | | | |
| Adams (50%) | 2,000 | | |
| Barnes (50%) | | 2,000 | 4,000 |
| Total share to each partner | $42,000 | $54,000 | $ -0- |

The journal entry to close the Income Summary account in this case will be:

| | | |
|---|---|---|
| Income Summary | 96,000 | |
| Arthur Adams, Capital | | 42,000 |
| Ben Barnes, Capital | | 54,000 |
| To close the Income Summary account by crediting each partner with his authorized salary, interest at 10% on his beginning capital, and dividing the remaining profits equally. | | |

**Authorized salaries and interest in excess of net income** In the preceding example the total of the authorized salaries and interest was $92,000 and the net income to be divided was $96,000. Suppose that the net income had been only $80,000; how should the division have been made?

If the partnership contract provides for salaries and interest on invested capital, these provisions are to be followed even though the net income for the year is less than the total of the authorized salaries and interest. If the net income of the firm of Adams and Barnes amounted to only $80,000, this amount would be distributed as shown below.

**Distribution of Net Income**

*Authorized salaries and interest may exceed net income*

| | Adams | Barnes | Net Income |
|---|---|---|---|
| Net income to be divided | | | $ 80,000 |
| Salaries to partners | $24,000 | $48,000 | 72,000 |
| Income after salaries | | | $ 8,000 |
| Interest on beginning capitals: | | | |
| Adams ($160,000 × 10%) | 16,000 | | |
| Barnes ($40,000 × 10%) | | 4,000 | |
| Total allocated as interest | | | 20,000 |
| Residual loss after salaries and interest | | | $(12,000) |
| Allocated in a fixed ratio: | | | |
| Adams (50%) | (6,000) | | |
| Barnes (50%) | | (6,000) | 12,000 |
| Total share to each partner | $34,000 | $46,000 | $ -0- |

The residual loss of $12,000 is divided equally because the partnership contract states that profits and losses are to be divided equally after providing for salaries and interest. The entry to close the Income Summary account will be as follows:

| | | |
|---|---|---|
| *Income Summary* | *80,000* | |
| *Arthur Adams, Capital* | | *34,000* |
| *Ben Barnes, Capital* | | *46,000* |
| *To close the Income Summary account by crediting each partner with his authorized salary and with interest on invested capital and by dividing the residual loss equally.* | | |

## Admission of a new partner

An individual may gain admission to an existing partnership in either of two ways: (1) by buying an interest from one or more of the present partners, or (2) by making an investment in the partnership. When an incoming partner purchases an equity from a present member of the firm, the payment goes personally to the old partner, and there is no change in the assets or liabilities of the partnership. On the other hand, if the incoming partner acquires an equity by making an investment in the partnership, the assets of the firm are increased by the amount paid in by the new partner.

**By purchase of an interest** When a new partner buys an interest from a present member of a partnership, the only change in the accounts will be a transfer from the capital account of the selling partner to the capital account of the incoming partner.

Assume, for example, that L has a $50,000 equity in the partnership of L, M, and N. Partner L arranges to sell his entire interest to X for $80,000 cash. Partners M and N agree to the admission of X, and the transaction is recorded in the partnership accounts by the following entry:

*Incoming partner buys interest from present partner*

| | | |
|---|---|---|
| *L, Capital* | *50,000* | |
| *X, Capital* | | *50,000* |
| *To record the transfer of L's equity to the incoming partner, X.* | | |

Note that the entry in the partnership accounts was for $50,000, the recorded amount of Partner L's equity. ***The amount of this entry was not influenced by the price paid the retiring partner by the new member.*** The payment of $80,000 from X to L was a personal transaction between the two individuals; it did not affect the assets or liabilities of the partnership and is therefore not entered in the partnership accounting records.

As a separate but related example, assume that X is to gain admission to the firm of L, M, and N by purchasing one-fourth of the equity of each partner. The present capital accounts are as follows: Partner L, $80,000; Partner M, $80,000; and Partner N, $80,000. The payments by the incoming partner X are to go to the old partners personally and not to the partnership. The only entry required is the following:

*No change in total capital*

| | | |
|---|---|---|
| *L, Capital* | *20,000* | |
| *M, Capital* | *20,000* | |
| *N, Capital* | *20,000* | |
| *X, Capital* | | *60,000* |
| *To record admission of X to a one-fourth interest in the firm by purchase of one-fourth of the equity of each of the old partners.* | | |

**By an investment in the firm** An incoming partner may acquire an equity by making an investment in the firm. In this case the payment by the new partner goes to the partnership and not to the partners as individuals; the investment therefore increases the partnership assets and also the total owners' equity of the firm. As an example, assume that Ann Phillips and Judy Ryan are partners, each having a capital account of $100,000. They agree to admit Bart Smith to a one-half interest in the business upon his investment of $200,000 in cash. The entry to record the admission of Smith would be as follows:

*Investment in business by new partner*

| | | |
|---|---|---|
| *Cash* | *200,000* | |
| *Bart Smith, Capital* | | *200,000* |
| *To record the admission of Bart Smith to a one-half interest in the firm.* | | |

Although Smith has a one-half equity in the net assets of the new firm of Phillips, Ryan, and Smith, he is not necessarily entitled to receive one-half of the profits. Profit sharing is a matter for agreement among the partners; if the new partnership contract contains no mention of profit sharing, the assumption is that the three partners intended to share profits and losses equally.

**Allowing a bonus to former partners** If an existing partnership has exceptionally high earnings year after year, the present partners may demand a ***bonus*** as a condition for admission of a new partner. In other words, to acquire an interest of, say, $80,000, the incoming partner may be required to invest $120,000 in the partnership. The excess investment of $40,000 may be regarded as a bonus to the old partners and credited to their capital accounts in the established ratio for profit sharing.

To illustrate the recording of a bonus to the old partners, let us assume that Janet Rogers and Richard Steel are members of a highly successful partnership. As a result of profitable operations, the partners' capital accounts have doubled within a few years and presently stand at $100,000 each. David Taylor desires to join the firm and offers to invest $100,000 for a one-third interest. Rogers and Steel refuse this offer but extend a counteroffer to Taylor of $120,000 for a one-fourth interest in the capital of the firm and a one-fourth interest in profits. Taylor accepts these terms because of his desire to share in the unusually large profits of the business. The recording of Taylor's admission to the partnership is based on the following calculations:

*Calculation of bonus to old partners*

| | |
|---|---|
| ***Net assets (owners' equity) of old partnership*** | ***$200,000*** |
| ***Cash investment by Taylor*** | ***120,000*** |
| ***Net assets (owners' equity) of new partnership*** | ***$320,000*** |
| ***Taylor's one-fourth interest*** | ***$ 80,000*** |

To acquire an interest of $80,000 in the net assets of $320,000, Taylor has invested $120,000. His excess investment or bonus of $40,000 will be divided equally between Rogers and Steel, since their partnership agreement called for equal sharing of profits and losses.

The entry to record Taylor's admission to the partnership follows:

*Recording bonus to old partners*

| | | |
|---|---|---|
| ***Cash*** | ***120,000*** | |
| ***David Taylor, Capital*** | | ***80,000*** |
| ***Janet Rogers, Capital*** | | ***20,000*** |
| ***Richard Steel, Capital*** | | ***20,000*** |
| ***To record admission of David Taylor as a partner with a one-fourth interest in capital and profits.*** | | |

**Allowing a bonus to new partner** An existing partnership may sometimes be very anxious to bring in a new partner who can bring needed cash to the firm. In other instances the new partner may be a person of extraordinary ability or may possess advantageous business contacts that will presumably add to the profitability of the partnership. Under either of these sets of circumstances, the old partners may offer the new member a bonus in the form of a capital account larger than the amount of the incoming partner's investment.

Assume, for example, that A. M. Bryan and R. G. Davis are equal partners, each having a capital account of $36,000. Since the firm is in desperate need of cash, they offer to admit Kay Grant to a one-third interest in the firm upon her investment of only $24,000 in cash. The amounts of the capital accounts for the three members of the new firm are computed as follows:

| | | |
|---|---|---|
| ***Total capital of old partnership:*** | | |
| ***A. M. Bryan, capital*** | ***$36,000*** | |
| ***R. G. Davis, capital*** | ***36,000*** | ***$72,000*** |
| ***Cash invested by Kay Grant*** | | ***24,000*** |
| ***Total capital of new three-member partnership*** | | ***$96,000*** |
| ***Capital of each partner in the new firm:*** | | |
| ***A. M. Bryan ($96,000 × $\frac{1}{3}$)*** | ***$32,000*** | |
| ***R. G. Davis ($96,000 × $\frac{1}{3}$)*** | ***32,000*** | |
| ***Kay Grant ($96,000 × $\frac{1}{3}$)*** | ***32,000*** | ***96,000*** |

The following journal entry records the admission of Grant to a one-third interest in the business and also adjusts each capital account to the required level of $32,000.

*Entry for bonus to new partner*

| | | |
|---|---|---|
| *Cash* | *24,000* | |
| *A. M. Bryan, Capital* | *4,000* | |
| *R. G. Davis, Capital* | *4,000* | |
| *Kay Grant, Capital* | | *32,000* |
| *To record admission of Grant to a one-third interest, and the allowance of a bonus to her.* | | |

### Retirement of a partner

A partner interested in retirement may, with the consent of the other partners, sell his or her interest to an outsider. In this case the payment by the incoming partner goes directly to the retiring partner, and there is no change in the assets or liabilities of the partnership. The only entry required is to transfer the capital account of the retiring partner to an account with the new partner. This transaction is virtually the same as the one described on page 563 for the admission of a partner by purchase of an interest.

Next, let us change our assumptions slightly and say that Carol Coe, the retiring partner, has a $100,000 interest which she sells to her fellow partners, A and B, in equal amounts. A and B make the agreed payment to Coe from their personal funds, so again the partnership assets and liabilities are not changed. Regardless of the price agreed to for Coe's interest, the transaction can be handled in the partnership accounting records merely by transferring the $100,000 balance in Coe's capital account to the capital accounts of the other two partners.

*No change in total capital*

| | | |
|---|---|---|
| *Carol Coe, Capital* | *100,000* | |
| *A, Capital* | | *50,000* |
| *B, Capital* | | *50,000* |
| *To record the sale of Coe's interest in equal portions to A and B.* | | |

**Payment to retiring partner from partnership assets** The retiring partner, Carol Coe, may be paid from partnership funds an amount equal to her capital account or a larger or smaller amount. If the partnership has been in business for several years during a period of inflation, it is probable that the assets, especially land, have market values higher than their cost as shown in the accounting records. A partner retiring from the firm naturally expects to receive an amount related to current market values; consequently, the settlement is likely to be an amount higher than her capital account. It is sometimes suggested that upon the retirement of a partner, the assets should be revalued upward and the increase credited to the partners' capital accounts. However, this would be a departure from the cost principle. Although the increase in market value of assets logically should be used in computing the amount to pay the retiring partner, there is no reason that increases in asset values need be recorded in the accounting records. Any excess payment to the retiring partner may be treated as a bonus to her which must be charged against the capital accounts of the continuing partners in the agreed ratio for sharing profits and losses, as shown on page 567.

*Bonus paid to retiring partner*

| | | |
|---|---|---|
| *Carol Coe, Capital (retiring partner)* | *100,000* | |
| *A, Capital* | *20,000* | |
| *B, Capital* | *20,000* | |
| *Cash* | | *140,000* |
| *To record the retirement of partner Coe, and payment of her capital account plus a bonus of $40,000.* | | |

As a separate example, assume that Coe is to receive a settlement smaller than her capital account balance, because she agrees to take a loss in order to expedite the settlement. If Coe surrenders her $100,000 interest for $80,000, the entry will be:

*Payment to retiring partner of less than book equity*

| | | |
|---|---|---|
| *Carol Coe, Capital* | *100,000* | |
| *Cash* | | *80,000* |
| *A, Capital* | | *10,000* |
| *B, Capital* | | *10,000* |
| *To record the retirement of Coe, and settlement in full for $20,000 less than the balance of her capital account.* | | |

## Death of a partner

A partnership is dissolved by the death of any member. To determine the amount owing to the estate of the deceased partner, it is usually necessary to close the accounts and prepare financial statements. This serves to credit all partners with their individual shares of the net income earned during the fractional accounting period ending with the date of ***dissolution.***

The partnership agreement may prescribe procedures for making settlement with the estate of a deceased partner. Such procedures often include an audit by certified public accountants, appraisal of assets, and computation of goodwill. If payment to the estate must be delayed, the amount owed should be carried in a liability account replacing the deceased partner's capital account.

**Insurance on lives of partners** Members of a partnership often obtain life insurance policies which name the partnership as the beneficiary. Upon the death of a partner, the cash collected from the insurance company is used to pay the estate of the deceased partner. An alternative plan is to have each partner named as the beneficiary of an insurance policy covering the lives of the other partners. In the absence of insurance on the lives of partners, there might be insufficient cash available to pay the deceased partner's estate without disrupting the operation of the business.

## Liquidation of a partnership

A partnership is terminated or dissolved whenever a new partner is added or an old partner withdraws. The termination or dissolution of a partnership, however, does not necessarily indicate that the business is to be discontinued. Often the business continues with scarcely any outward evidence of the change in membership of the firm. Termination of a partnership indicates a change in the membership of the firm, which may or may not be followed by liquidation.

The process of breaking up and discontinuing a partnership business is called ***liquidation.*** Liquidation of a partnership spells an end to the business. If the business is to be discontinued, the assets will be sold, the liabilities paid, and the remaining cash distributed to the partners.

**Sale of the business** The partnershp of X, Y, and Z sells its business to the North Corporation. The balance sheet appears as follows:

*Partnership at time of sale*

***X, Y, AND Z***
***Balance Sheet***
***December 31, 19___***

| | | | |
|---|---|---|---|
| *Cash* | *$ 50,000* | *Accounts payable* | *$100,000* |
| *Inventory* | *200,000* | *X, capital* | *140,000* |
| *Other assets* | *150,000* | *Y, capital* | *120,000* |
| | | *Z, capital* | *40,000* |
| *Total assets* | *$400,000* | *Total liabilities & capitals* | *$400,000* |

The terms of sale provide that the partnership will retain the cash of $50,000 and will pay the liabilities of $100,000. The inventory and other assets will be sold to the North Corporation for a consideration of $230,000. The entries relating to the sale of the inventory and other assets are as follows:

*Entries for sale of business*

| | | |
|---|---|---|
| *Accounts Receivable, North Corporation* | *230,000* | |
| *Loss on Sale of Business* | *120,000* | |
| *Inventory* | | *200,000* |
| *Other Assets* | | *150,000* |
| *To record the sale of all assets other than cash to North Corporation.* | | |
| *Cash* | *230,000* | |
| *Accounts Receivable, North Corporation* | | *230,000* |
| *Collected the receivable from sale of assets.* | | |

***Division of the gain or loss from sale of the business*** The gain or loss from the sale of the business must be divided among the partners in the agreed profit- and loss-sharing ratio ***before*** any cash is distributed to them. The amount of cash to which each partner is entitled in liquidation cannot be determined until each capital account has been increased or decreased by the proper share of the gain or loss on disposal of the assets. Assuming that X, Y, and Z share profits and losses equally, the entry to allocate the $120,000 loss on the sale of the business will be as follows:

*Entry to divide loss on sale*

| | | |
|---|---|---|
| *X, Capital* | *40,000* | |
| *Y, Capital* | *40,000* | |
| *Z, Capital* | *40,000* | |
| *Loss on Sale of Business* | | *120,000* |
| *To divide the loss on the sale of the business among the partners in the established ratio for sharing profits and losses.* | | |

**Distribution of cash** The balance sheet of X, Y, and Z appears as follows after the loss on the sale of the assets has been entered in the partners' capital accounts:

*Balance sheet after sale of assets*

*X, Y, AND Z*
*Balance Sheet*
*(After the Sale of All Assets Except Cash)*

| *Assets* | | *Liabilities & Partners' Equity* | |
|---|---|---|---|
| *Cash* | *$280,000* | *Accounts payable* | *$100,000* |
| | | *X, capital* | *100,000* |
| | | *Y, capital* | *80,000* |
| | | *Z, capital* | *-0-* |
| *Total assets* | *$280,000* | *Total liabilities & capitals* | *$280,000* |

The creditors must be paid in full before cash is distributed to the partners. The sequence of entries is shown below.

*(1) Pay creditors*

| | | |
|---|---|---|
| *Accounts Payable* | *100,000* | |
| *Cash* | | *100,000* |
| *To pay the creditors in full.* | | |

*(2) Pay partners*

| | | |
|---|---|---|
| *X, Capital* | *100,000* | |
| *Y, Capital* | *80,000* | |
| *Cash* | | *180,000* |
| *To complete liquidation of the business by distributing the remaining cash to the partners according to the balances in their capital accounts.* | | |

Note that the equal division of the $120,000 loss on the sale of the business reduced the capital account of Partner Z to zero; therefore, Z received nothing when the cash was distributed to the partners. This action is consistent with the original agreement of the partners to share profits and losses equally. In working partnership liquidation problems, accounting students sometimes make the error of dividing the cash among the partners in the profit- and loss-sharing ratio. A profit- and loss-sharing ratio means just what the name indicates; it is a ratio for sharing profits and losses, ***not a ratio for sharing cash or any other asset.*** The amount of cash which a partner should receive in liquidation will be indicated by the balance in his or her capital account after the gain or loss from the disposal of assets has been divided among the partners in the agreed ratio for sharing profits and losses.

***Treatment of debit balance in a capital account*** To illustrate this situation, let us change our assumptions concerning the sale of the assets by the firm of X, Y, and Z, and say that the loss incurred on the sale of assets was $144,000 rather than the $120,000 previously illustrated. Z's one-third share of a $144,000 loss would be $48,000, which would wipe out the $40,000 credit balance in his capital account and create an $8,000 debit balance. After the liabilities had been paid, a balance sheet for the partnership would appear as follows:

***X, Y, AND Z***
***Balance Sheet***
***(After the Sale of All Assets Except Cash)***

*Z now owes $8,000 to the partnership*

| | | | |
|---|---|---|---|
| Cash | $156,000 | X, capital | $ 92,000 |
| Z, capital | 8,000 | Y, capital | 72,000 |
| Total assets | $164,000 | Total partners' capital | $164,000 |

To eliminate the debit balance in the capital account for Z, the partnership should collect from Z $8,000 in cash. If this collection is made, the capital balance for Z will become zero, and the cash on hand will be increased to $164,000, which is just enough to pay X and Y the balances shown by their capital accounts.

If Z is unable to pay the $8,000 due to the firm, how should the $156,000 of cash on hand be divided between X and Y, whose capital accounts stand at $92,000 and $72,000, respectively? Failure of Z to pay in the debit balance means an additional loss to X and Y; according to the original partnership agreement, X and Y are to share profits and losses equally. Therefore, each must absorb $4,000 additional loss thrown on them by Z's inability to pay the $8,000 due to the partnership. The $156,000 of cash on hand should be divided between X and Y in such a manner that the capital account of each will be paid down to $4,000, their respective shares of the additional loss. The journal entry to record this distribution of cash to X and Y is as follows:

*Entry to record distribution of cash on hand*

| | | |
|---|---|---|
| X, Capital | 88,000 | |
| Y, Capital | 68,000 | |
| Cash | | 156,000 |
| *To divide the remaining cash by paying down the capital accounts of X and Y to a balance of $4,000 each, representing the division of Z's loss between them.* | | |

After this entry has been posted, the only accounts still open in the partnership records will be the capital accounts of the three partners. A trial balance of the ledger will appear as follows:

*Trial balance after cash distribution*

**X, Y, AND Z**
***Trial Balance***
***(After Distribution of Cash)***

| | | |
|---|---|---|
| X, capital | | $4,000 |
| Y, capital | | 4,000 |
| Z, capital | $8,000 | |
| | $8,000 | $8,000 |

If Z is able later to pay in the $8,000 debit balance, X and Y will then receive the additional $4,000 each indicated by the credit balances in their accounts. If Z is not able to make good the debit balance, the distribution of cash to X and Y will have been equitable under the circumstances.

## KEY TERMS INTRODUCED OR EMPHASIZED IN CHAPTER 15

**Bonus to former partners** Portion of the investment by an incoming partner which may be credited to the capital accounts of the former partners. A premium paid to gain admission.

**Bonus to new partner** Excess of the capital account granted to a new partner over and above the amount of his investment. A special inducement to persuade an individual to join an existing partnership.

**Co-ownership of property and profits** The concept that all property of a partnership is owned by the partners as a group and that each partner has an ownership right in the profits.

**Information return** A partnership is not a taxable entity, but must file an information return with the IRS, showing the partnership net income and the share therein of each partner.

**Limited life** A partnership is legally dissolved by the death or withdrawal of any partner.

**Liquidation** The process of breaking up and discontinuing a partnership, including the sale of assets, payment of creditors, and distribution of remaining assets to the partners.

**Mutual agency** Authority of each partner to act as agent for the partnership within its normal scope of operations and to enter into contracts which bind the partnership.

**Partnership** An association of two or more persons to carry on as co-owners a business for profit.

**Partnership contract** An agreement among partners on the formation and operation of the partnership. Usually includes such points as a plan for sharing profits, amounts to be invested, and provision for dissolution.

**Profit sharing** A plan for division of partnership profits and losses among partners. May include salaries, allowances for interest on capital, and allowances for a fixed ratio. In the absence of an agreement on profit sharing, the law assumes an intention to share profits equally.

**Purchase of an interest** Transfer of all or part of the capital account of an existing partner to an incoming partner. Involves payment between individuals and not to the partnership.

**Salaries to partners** A method for division of a portion of partnership net income according to the agreed value of personal services rendered by individual partners. Not an expense, but a device for sharing profits.

**Statement of partners' capitals** A financial statement which shows for each partner and for the firm the amounts of beginning capitals, additional investments, net income, drawings, and ending capitals.

**Uniform Partnership Act** Uniform legislation enacted by most states. Governs the formation, operation, and liquidation of partnerships.

**Unlimited liability** Personal responsibility of each partner for all debts of the partnership.

## REVIEW QUESTIONS

1 Explain the difference between being admitted to a partnership by buying an interest from an existing partner and by making an investment in the partnership.

2 Is it possible that a partnership agreement containing interest and salary allowances as a step toward distributing income could cause a partnership net loss to be distributed so that one partner's capital account would be decreased by more than the amount of the entire partnership net loss?

3 Jane Miller is the proprietor of a small manufacturing business. She is considering the possibility of joining in partnership with Mary Bracken, whom she considers to be thoroughly competent and congenial. Prepare a brief statement outlining the advantages and disadvantages of the potential partnership to Miller.

4 Scott has land having a book value of $50,000 and a fair market value of $80,000 and a building having a book value of $70,000 and a fair market value of $60,000. The land and building become Scott's sole capital contribution to a partnership. What is Scott's capital balance in the new partnership? Why?

5 Allen and Baker are considering forming a partnership. What do you think are the two most important factors for them to include in their partnership agreement?

6 Partner X withdraws $25,000 from a partnership during the year. When the financial statements are prepared at the end of the year, X's share of the partnership income is $15,000. Which amount must X report on his income tax return?

7 Partner John Young has a choice to make. He has been offered by his partners a choice between no salary allowance and a one-third share in the partnership income or a salary of $16,000 per year and a one-quarter share of residual profits. Write a brief memorandum explaining the factors he should consider in reaching a decision.

8 What factors should be considered in drawing up an agreement as to the way in which income shall be shared by two or more partners?

**9** Shirley Bray and Carl Carter are partners who share profits and losses equally. The current balances in their capital accounts are: Bray, $50,000; Carter, $35,000. If Carter sells his interest in the firm to Deacon for $70,000 and Bray consents to the sale, what entry should be made in the partnership accounting records?

**10** What is meant by the term ***mutual agency?***

**11** If C is going to be admitted to the partnership of A and B, why is it first necessary to determine the current fair market value of the assets of the partnership of A and B?

**12** Describe how a ***dissolution*** of a partnership may differ from a ***liquidation*** of a partnership.

**13** What measure can you suggest to prevent a partnership from having insufficient cash available to pay the estate of a deceased partner without disrupting the operation of the business?

**14** What factors should be considered when comparing the net income figure of a partnership to that of a corporation of similar size?

**15** Upon the death of Robert Bell, a partner in the firm of Bell, Cross, and Davis, Charles Bell, the son of Robert Bell, demanded that he replace his father as a member of the partnership. Can Charles Bell enforce this demand? Explain.

**16** The partnership of X and Y is being dissolved. After the assets had been sold at a loss, the cash balance was $38,000. All creditors' claims, amounting to $14,000, were then paid. The capital account for X then showed a credit balance twice as large as that for Y. What must be the amount of Y's capital account? Explain.

## EXERCISES

*Ex. 15-1* A business owned by John Rogers was short of cash and Rogers therefore decided to form a partnership with Steve Wilson, who was able to contribute cash to the new partnership. The assets contributed by Rogers appeared as follows in the balance sheet of his business: cash, $900; accounts receivable, $18,900, with an allowance for doubtful accounts of $600; inventory, $42,000; and store equipment, $15,000. Rogers had recorded depreciation of $1,500 during his use of the store equipment in his single proprietorship.

Rogers and Wilson agreed that the allowance for doubtful accounts was inadequate and should be $1,000. They also agreed that a fair value for the inventory was its replacement cost of $46,000 and that the fair value of the store equipment was $12,000. You are to open the partnership accounts by making a general journal entry to record the investment by Rogers.

*Ex. 15-2* Explain briefly the effect of each of the transactions given below on a partner's capital and drawing accounts:

**a** Partner borrows funds from the business.

**b** Partner collects a partnership account receivable while on vacation and uses the funds for personal purposes.

**c** Partner receives in cash the salary allowance provided in the partnership agreement.

**d** Partner takes home merchandise (cost $80, selling price $120) for personal use.

**e** Partner has loaned money to the partnership. The principal together with interest at 15% is now repaid to the partner in cash.

*Ex. 15-3* On July 31, 19____, A and B agreed to combine their single proprietorships into a partnership. The partnership will take over all assets and assume all liabilities of A and B. The balance sheets for A and B are shown below:

| | A's Business | | B's Business | |
|---|---|---|---|---|
| | Book Value | Fair Value | Book Value | Fair Value |
| **Assets** | | | | |
| Cash | $ 2,500 | $ 2,500 | $ 9,000 | $ 9,000 |
| Accounts receivable | 12,000 | 11,600 | 30,000 | 29,000 |
| Inventory | 18,000 | 20,400 | 40,000 | 35,000 |
| Equipment (net) | 23,000 | 23,500 | 62,000 | 76,200 |
| Total | $55,500 | $58,000 | $141,000 | $149,200 |
| **Liabilities & Owner's Capital** | | | | |
| Accounts payable | $20,500 | $20,500 | $ 39,500 | $ 41,000 |
| Accrued wages payable | 600 | 600 | 1,000 | 1,000 |
| A, capital | 34,400 | 36,900 | | |
| B, capital | | | 100,500 | 107,200 |
| Total | $55,500 | $58,000 | $141,000 | $149,200 |

Accounts receivable of $1,400 are written off as uncollectible. This write-off explains the difference in amounts of accounts receivable shown in the Book Value and Fair Value column. The book value of B's accounts payable was less than fair value because liabilities of $1,500 had not been recorded.

Prepare a ***classified*** balance sheet in good form for the new entity of A-B Company immediately following formation of the partnership.

*Ex. 15-4* Redmond and Adams, both of whom are CPAs, form a partnership, with Redmond investing $40,000 and Adams $30,000. They agree to share net income as follows:

(1) Interest at 10% on beginning capital balances.
(2) Salary allowances of $45,000 to Redmond and $25,000 to Adams.
(3) Any partnership earnings in excess of the amount required to cover the interest and salary allowances to be divided 45% to Redmond and 55% to Adams.

The partnership net income for the first year of operations amounted to $97,000 before interest and salary allowances. Show how this $97,000 should be divided between the two partners. Use a three-column schedule with a separate column for each partner and a total column. List on separate lines the amounts of interest, salaries, and the residual amount divided.

*Ex. 15-5* Hal Jones, Carl Kent, and Dave Lawrence are partners and each has a capital account of $40,000. Kent, who owns another business, wishes to sell his equity in the partnership to his son, Charles, for $5,000 cash and a promissory note (without interest) for $15,000. Jones and Lawrence agree to the admission of Charles Kent as a partner. Prepare a general journal entry to record the transfer of Carl Kent's equity in the business.

*Ex. 15-6* A and B are partners having capital balances of $60,000 and $30,000. They share profits equally. The partnership has been quite profitable and has an excellent reputation. A and B agree to admit C to a one-third interest in the partnership for an investment of $54,000. The assets of the business are not to be revalued. Explain how the bonus to the old partners is computed and prepare a general journal entry to record the admission of C.

*Ex. 15-7* The capital accounts of the XYZ partnership are as follows: X, $120,000; Y, $60,000; Z, $90,000. Profits are shared equally. Partner Y is withdrawing from the partnership and it is agreed that he shall be paid $75,000 for his interest because the earnings of the business are high in relation to the assets of the firm. Assuming that the excess of the settlement over the amount of Y's capital account is to be recorded as a bonus to Y, prepare a general journal entry to record Y's retirement from the firm.

*Ex. 15-8* The CDE partnership is being liquidated. After all liabilities have been paid and all assets sold, the balances of the partners' capital accounts are as follows: C, $42,000 credit balance; D, $28,000 debit balance; E, $63,000 credit balance. The partners share profits equally.

**a** How should the available cash (the only remaining asset) be distributed if it is impossible to determine at this date whether D will be able to pay the $28,000 he owes the firm?

**b** Draft the journal entries to record a partial payment of $21,000 to the firm by D, and the subsequent distribution of this cash.

## PROBLEMS

### Group A

*15A-1* The partnership of Avery and Kirk was formed on July 1, when George Avery and Dinah Kirk agreed to invest equal amounts and to share profits and losses equally. The investment by Avery consists of $40,000 cash and an inventory of merchandise valued at $56,000.

Kirk also is to contribute a total of $96,000. However, it is agreed that her contribution will consist of the following assets of her business along with the transfer to the partnership of her business liabilities. The agreed values of the various items as well as their carrying values on Kirk's records are listed below. Kirk also contributes enough cash to bring her capital account to $96,000.

| | *Investment by Kirk* | |
|---|---|---|
| | *Balances on Kirk's Records* | *Agreed Value* |
| *Accounts receivable* | *$89,600* | *$89,600* |
| *Allowance for doubtful accounts* | *3,840* | *8,000* |
| *Inventory* | *9,600* | *12,800* |
| *Office equipment (net)* | *12,800* | *9,000* |
| *Accounts payable* | *28,800* | *28,800* |

**Instructions**

**a** Draft entries (in general journal form) to record the investments of Avery and Kirk in the new partnership.

**b** Prepare the beginning balance sheet of the partnership (in report form) at the close of business July 1, reflecting the above transfers to the firm.

**c** On the following June 30 after one year of operation, the Income Summary account showed a credit balance of $78,000 and the Drawing account for each partner showed a debit balance of $32,000. Prepare journal entries to close the Income Summary account and the drawing accounts at June 30.

*15A-2* The account balances of Adams Company, arranged in alphabetical order, at the end of the current year are as follows:

| | |
|---|---|
| *Accounts payable* | *$ 38,520* |
| *Accounts receivable* | *81,000* |
| *Accrued liabilities* | *2,880* |
| *Accumulated depreciation* | *18,000* |
| *Adams, capital (beginning of year)* | *70,000* |
| *Adams, drawing* | *10,080* |
| *Administrative expenses* | *91,620* |
| *Cash* | *32,620* |
| *Equipment* | *90,000* |
| *Finley, capital (beginning of year)* | *60,000* |
| *Finley, drawing* | *7,200* |
| *Inventory (beginning of year)* | *27,360* |
| *Notes payable* | *9,600* |
| *Purchases (including transportation-in)* | *391,800* |
| *Sales* | *648,960* |
| *Selling expenses* | *112,380* |
| *Short-term prepayments* | *3,900* |

There were no changes in partners' capital accounts during the year. The inventory at the end of the year was $28,200. The partnership agreement provided that partners are to be allowed 10% interest on invested capital as of the beginning of the year and that the residual net income is to be divided equally.

**Instructions**

**a** Prepare an income statement for the current year, using the appropriate accounts from the above list. At the bottom of the income statement, prepare a schedule showing the distribution of net income.

**b** Prepare a statement of partners' capitals for the current year.

**c** Prepare a balance sheet at the end of the current year.

*15A-3* River Train has three partners—A, B, and C. During the current year their capital balances were: A, $140,000; B, $100,000; and C, $60,000. The partnership agreement provides that partners shall receive salary allowances as follows: A, none, B, $48,000; and C, $40,000. The partners shall also be allowed 6% annually on their capital balances. Residual profits or loss are to be divided: A, $\frac{1}{2}$; B, $\frac{1}{3}$; and C, $\frac{1}{6}$.

**Instructions** Prepare separate schedules showing how income will be divided among the three partners in each of the following cases. The figure given in each case is the annual income available for distribution among the partners.

**a** Loss of $23,000

**b** Income of $37,000

**c** Income of $200,000 (Round amounts to the nearest even dollar.)

*15A-4* A condensed balance sheet for the partnership of Keystone Tools, owned by Hale and Kent, at September 30 is shown below. On this date the two partners agreed to admit a new partner, Lee. Hale and Kent have been dividing profits in a ratio of 3:2 (that is, 60% and 40%), and this ratio will continue between the two of them after the admission of Lee. In other words, the new partnership will have a profit- and loss-sharing ratio of Lee, 50%; Hale, 30% and Kent, 20%.

**KEYSTONE TOOLS**
**Balance Sheet**
**September 30**

| | | | | |
|---|---|---|---|---|
| Current assets | $180,000 | Liabilities | | $160,000 |
| Plant & equipment | | Partners' capitals | | |
| (net) | 420,000 | Hale, capital | $280,000 | |
| | | Kent, capital | 160,000 | 440,000 |
| Total assets | $600,000 | Total liabilities & capitals | | $600,000 |

**Instructions** Described below are four different situations under which Lee might be admitted to partnership. Considering each independently, prepare the journal entries necessary to record the admission of Lee to the firm.

**a** Lee purchases a one-half interest (50% of the entire ownership equity) in the partnership from Hale for $260,000. Payment is made to Hale as an individual.

**b** Lee purchases one-half of Hale's interest and one-half of Kent's interest, paying Hale $168,000 and Kent $96,000.

**c** Lee invests $300,000 in the partnership and receives a one-half interest in capital and income. It is agreed that there will be no change in the valuation of the present net assets. (Bonus to Lee is charged against Hale and Kent in a 3:2 ratio.)

**d** Lee invests $560,000 in the partnership and receives a one-half interest in capital and income. It is agreed that the allowance for doubtful accounts is currently overstated by $20,000. All other assets are carried at amounts approximating current fair value; therefore, no further revaluation is to be made. The bonus to the old partners indicated by the amount of the investment by Lee for a one-half interest will be divided between Hale and Kent in the 3:2 ratio. Prepare one journal entry for the adjustment of the Allowance for Doubtful Accounts and another entry to record the investment by Lee.

*15A-5* In the partnership of Kim, John, and Ray, the partners' capital accounts at the end of the current year were as follows: Kim, $224,000; John, $148,000; and Ray, $60,000. The partnership agreement provides that profits will be shared 40% to Kim, 50% to John, and 10% to Ray. At this time Kim decides to retire from the firm.

**Instructions** Described below are a number of independent situations involving the retirement of Kim. In each case prepare the journal entries necessary to reflect the withdrawal of Kim from the firm.

**a** Kim sells three-fourths of his interest to Ray for $208,000 and the other one-fourth to John for $64,000. The payments to Kim are made from the personal funds of Ray and John, not from the partnership.

**b** Kim accepts $88,000 in cash and a patent having a book value of $100,000 in full payment for his interest in the firm. This payment consists of a transfer of partnership assets to the retiring partner. The continuing partners agree that a revaluation of assets is not needed. The excess of Kim's capital account over the payment to him for withdrawal should be credited to John and Ray ($\frac{5}{6}$ and $\frac{1}{6}$).

**c** Kim receives $100,000 in cash and a 10-year, 12% note for $188,000 in full payment for his interest. Assets are not to be revalued. The bonus to Kim is to be charged against the capital accounts of the continuing partners ($\frac{5}{6}$ and $\frac{1}{6}$).

*15A-6* Ames Associates is a partnership and maintains its accounts on a calendar-year basis. At December 31 of the current year the revenue and expense accounts have been closed into the Income Summary account. The balances of selected accounts at year-end are shown on page 578.

| | December 31 Balance | |
|---|---|---|
| | Debit | Credit |
| Partner A, capital | | $120,800 |
| Partner A, drawing | $29,225 | |
| Partner B, capital | | 93,125 |
| Partner B, drawing | 24,650 | |
| Income summary | | 31,025 |

**Other data**

(1) During the year Partner B took out of stock for his personal use merchandise which cost the company $1,725 and had a retail value of $2,875. The bookkeeper credited Sales and charged Miscellaneous Expense for the retail value of all merchandise taken by B.

(2) Partner A paid $1,500 from his personal funds on November 18 to an attorney for legal services. Of this amount $625, which was for services relating to partnership business, should be treated as an additional investment by A.

(3) Partner B borrowed $13,500 from the partnership on September 1 of the current year, giving a six-month note with interest at 8%. The only record made of this transaction was a charge to B's drawing account for $13,500 at the time of the loan. B intends to repay the loan with interest at maturity.

(4) Partner A had the full-time use of a company-owned car. All operating expenses were paid by the partnership. It was agreed that A's drawing account would be charged 25 cents per mile for all miles driven for personal use. At the end of the year A reported that he had driven 3,000 miles for personal reasons, but the bookkeeper filed this information and made no entry.

(5) On March 31 Partner A invested an additional $25,000 in the business. The investment was properly recorded. Other than this, no changes in partners' capital accounts have been recorded during the year.

**Instructions**

**a** On the basis of the above information, make any adjusting or correcting entries necessary on December 31. The portion of any entry affecting revenue or expense accounts may be charged or credited directly to Income Summary.

**b** Prepare a schedule showing how the adjusted partnership income would be divided between the partners. The partnership agreement calls for salary allowances of $15,000 per year to A and $24,000 per year to B. The balance of profit (or loss) is to be shared in a 3:2 ratio.

**c** What effect did the adjustments have on A's share of the partnership income for the year? Determine the amount and explain briefly.

**d** Prepare a statement of changes in partners' capitals for the year. (Hint: In computing the beginning capital balances, consider the additional capital investment of $25,000 made by Partner A on March 31.)

***15A-7*** The December 31 balance sheet of Ranch Supply, a partnership, appears on page 579. In order to focus attention on the principles involved in liquidating a partnership, the balance sheet has been shortened by combining all assets other than cash under the caption of Other Assets.

Hand, Trent, and Dell share profits in a ratio of 3:2:1, respectively. At the date of the balance sheet the partners decided to liquidate the business.

***RANCH SUPPLY***
***Balance Sheet***
***December 31, 198X***

| | | | | |
|---|---|---|---|---|
| *Cash* | *$ 60,000* | *Liabilities* | | *$120,000* |
| *Other assets* | *300,000* | *Partners' capitals:* | | |
| | | *Hand, capital* | *$100,000* | |
| | | *Trent, capital* | *80,000* | |
| | | *Dell, capital* | *60,000* | *240,000* |
| *Total assets* | *$360,000* | *Total liabilities & capitals* | | *$360,000* |

**Instructions** Prepare schedules showing how the liquidation of the partnership would affect the various balance sheet items and how the cash would be distributed for each of the four independent cases listed below. Use six money columns in your schedules, as follows:

| *Cash* | *Other Assets* | *Lia-bilities* | *Hand, Capital* | *Trent, Capital* | *Dell, Capital* |
|---|---|---|---|---|---|

**a** Other assets are sold for $258,000.
**b** Other assets are sold for $96,000. All partners have personal assets and will contribute any necessary amounts to the partnership.
**c** Other assets are sold for $74,400. Trent has personal assets and will contribute any necessary amounts; Hand and Dell are both personally bankrupt.
**d** Other assets are sold for $48,000. Dell is personally solvent and will contribute any amount for which he is liable. Hand and Trent both have personal debts in excess of their personal assets.

## Group B

*15B-1* The partnership of Baker and Land was formed on January 1, when Ruth Baker and Susan Land agreed to invest equal amounts and to share profits equally. The investment by Baker consists of $50,000 cash and an inventory of merchandise valued at $76,000. Land is also to contribute a total of $126,000. However, it is agreed that her contribution will consist of the following assets of her business along with the transfer to the partnership of her business liabilities. The agreed value of the various items as well as their carrying values on Land's records are listed below:

| | ***Investment by Land*** | |
|---|---|---|
| | ***Balances on Land's Records*** | ***Agreed Value*** |
| ***Accounts receivable*** | ***$117,600*** | ***$117,600*** |
| ***Allowance for doubtful accounts*** | ***5,040*** | ***10,500*** |
| ***Inventory*** | ***12,600*** | ***16,800*** |
| ***Office equipment (net)*** | ***16,800*** | ***10,500*** |
| ***Accounts payable*** | ***37,800*** | ***37,800*** |

Land also contributed enough cash to bring her capital account to $126,000.

**Instructions**
**a** Draft general journal entries to record the investments of Baker and Land in the new partnership.

**b** Prepare the beginning balance sheet of the partnership (in report form) at the close of business January 1, reflecting the above transfers to the firm.
**c** On the following December 31 after one year of operations, the Income Summary account had a credit balance of $96,000 and the Drawing account for each partner showed a debit balance of $42,000. Prepare journal entries to close the Income Summary and the drawing accounts at December 31.

*15B-2* The accounts making up the trial balance of the partnership of Axe and Carr at the end of the current year are shown below arranged in alphabetical order.

| | |
|---|---|
| *Accounts payable* | *$ 90,000* |
| *Accounts receivable* | *103,000* |
| *Accrued liabilities* | *10,000* |
| *Accumulated depreciation: equipment* | *20,000* |
| *Administrative expenses* | *110,000* |
| *Allowance for doubtful accounts* | *2,000* |
| *Axe, capital* | *70,000* |
| *Axe, drawing* | *10,000* |
| *Carr, capital* | *90,000* |
| *Carr, drawing* | *18,000* |
| *Cash* | *28,000* |
| *Equipment* | *120,000* |
| *Inventory* | *36,000* |
| *Merchandise purchases* | *470,000* |
| *Sales* | *796,000* |
| *Selling expenses* | *160,000* |
| *Short-term prepayments* | *1,000* |
| *Transportation-in* | *22,000* |

**Other data** There were no changes in partners' capital accounts during the year.
The inventory at the end of the year was $32,000. The partnership agreement provides that partners are to be allowed 10% interest on invested capital as of the beginning of the year and are to divide residual profits in the ratio of Axe, 30%; Carr, 70%.

**Instructions**

**a** Prepare an income statement for the current year, using the appropriate accounts as given above. Also prepare a separate schedule showing the distribution of net income between the partners, as illustrated on page 558.
**b** Prepare a statement of partners' capital accounts for the year.
**c** Prepare a balance sheet as of the end of the year.

*15B-3* Rob King owns and operates a small business called London Shop. The business is in need of additional working capital and King is personally in need of $21,000 in cash. To meet these needs, King agreed on August 31 to join in partnership with John Hill in a business to be known as King-Hill. Hill will invest $56,000 cash in the business. King will contribute all assets of his business (except cash) to the partnership and the liabilities of King's business will be assumed by the partnership. It is also agreed that on August 31 King will withdraw (from funds invested by Hill) the sum of $21,000 in cash. The partnership contract provides that income will be divided 60% to King and 40% to Hill.

Information as to the assets and liabilities of King's business on August 31, 19___, and their agreed valuation is shown below. None of the receivables has been identified as definitely uncollectible.

| | Per King's Accounts | Agreed Valuation |
|---|---|---|
| Accounts receivable | $47,600 | |
| Allowance for doubtful accounts | 4,480 | $39,760 |
| Merchandise inventory | 92,960 | 75,600 |
| Store equipment | 17,360 | |
| Accumulated depreciation | 5,880 | 12,600 |
| Note payable | 33,600 | 33,600 |
| Interest payable | 588 | 588 |
| Accounts payable | 19,600 | 19,600 |

**Instructions**

**a** Make the necessary journal entries to record the formation of the King-Hill partnership at August 31. (Debit Accounts Receivable $47,600 and credit Allowance for Doubtful Accounts $7,840. Do not record accumulated depreciation.)

**b** At the end of September, after all adjusting entries, the Income Summary account of King-Hill shows a credit balance of $7,000. The partners' drawing accounts have debit balances as follows: King, $2,800; Hill, $1,400. Make the journal entries necessary to complete the closing of the partnership accounts at the end of September.

**c** Prepare a statement of partners' capitals for the month of September.

*15B-4* The partnership of Amos, Barth, & Co. was formed with Amos investing $40,000 and Barth investing $60,000. During the first year, net income amounted to $45,000.

**Instructions**

**a** Determine how the $45,000 net income would be divided under each of the following five independent assumptions as to the agreement for sharing profits and losses. Use schedules of the type illustrated in this chapter to show all steps in the distribution of net income between the partners.

(1) The partnership agreement does not mention profit sharing.

(2) Net income is to be divided in a fixed ratio: 40% to Amos and 60% to Barth.

(3) Interest at 15% to be allowed on beginning capital investments and balance to be divided equally.

(4) Salaries of $24,000 to Amos and $20,000 to Barth, balance to be divided equally.

(5) Salaries of $18,000 to Amos and $26,000 to Barth, interest at 15% to be allowed on beginning capital investments, balance to be divided equally.

**b** Prepare the journal entry to close the Income Summary account, using the division of net income developed in the last case (**a,** 5) above.

*15B-5* Pacific Traders is a partnership with a record of profitable operations. At the end of the current year the capital accounts of the three partners and the ratio for sharing profits and losses are as shown in the schedule on page 582. At this date, it is agreed that a new partner, Howard Sharp, is to be admitted to the firm.

| | Capital | Profit-Sharing Ratio |
|---|---|---|
| *Susan Abbot* | *$200,000* | $\frac{5}{8}$ |
| *Jill Riley* | *160,000* | $\frac{1}{4}$ |
| *David Kerr* | *120,000* | $\frac{1}{8}$ |

**Instructions** For each of the following situations involving the admission of Sharp to the partnership, give the necessary journal entry to record his admission.

**a** Sharp purchases one-half of Riley's interest in the firm, paying Riley personally $95,000.

**b** Sharp buys a one-quarter interest in the firm for $140,000 by purchasing one-fourth of the present interest of each of the three partners. Sharp pays the three individuals directly.

**c** Sharp invests $230,000 in the firm and receives a one-quarter interest in capital and profits of the business. Give the necessary journal entries to record Sharp's admission as a partner and the division of the bonus to the old partners in their established ratio for profit sharing.

*15B-6* Yankee Clipper is a partnership of three individuals. At the end of the current year, the firm had the following balance sheet.

***YANKEE CLIPPER***
***Balance Sheet***
***December 31, 19__***

| | | | | |
|---|---|---|---|---|
| *Cash* | *$ 65,000* | *Liabilities* | | *$ 99,000* |
| *Receivables* | *75,000* | *Partners' capitals:* | | |
| *Inventory* | *160,000* | *Bell, capital* | *$132,000* | |
| *Land* | *105,000* | *Cross, capital* | *90,000* | |
| | | *Dart, capital* | *84,000* | *306,000* |
| *Total assets* | *$405,000* | *Total liabilities & capitals* | | *$405,000* |

The partners share profits and losses in the ratio of 50% to Bell, 30% to Cross, and 20% to Dart. It is agreed that Dart is to withdraw from the partnership on this date.

**Instructions** Listed below are a number of different assumptions involving the withdrawal of Dart from the firm. For each case you are to prepare the general journal entry or entries needed to record Dart's withdrawal.

**a** Dart, with the permission of the other partners, gives his equity to his brother-in-law, Jones, who is accepted as a partner in the firm.

**b** Dart sells one-fourth of his interest to Cross for $24,000 cash and sells the other three-fourths to Bell for $72,000 cash. The payments are made by Cross and Bell personally and not by the partnership.

**c** Dart is paid $90,000 from partnership funds for his interest. The bonus indicated by this payment is charged against the continuing partners ($\frac{5}{8}$ against Bell and $\frac{3}{8}$ against Cross).

**d** Dart is paid $60,000 cash and given inventory having a book value of $66,000. These assets come from the firm. The partners agree that no revaluation of assets will be made. (Ratio for sharing profits and losses between Bell and Cross is 5:3.)

**e** The partners agree that land is worth $195,000 at present market prices. They do not wish to write up this asset in the accounts but believe that Dart is entitled to a settlement which includes his 20% interest in the increase in value. Dart is paid

$48,000 in cash and given a two-year, 12% note for $54,000. The bonus to Dart should be charged against Bell and Cross in the ratio of $\frac{5}{8}$ and $\frac{3}{8}$.

*15B-7* The partnership of Crystal Springs has ended its operations and is in the process of liquidation. All assets except for cash and accounts receivable have already been sold. The task of collecting the accounts receivable is now to be carried out as rapidly as possible. The general ledger balances are as follows:

| | Debit | Credit |
|---|---|---|
| Cash | $ 27,200 | |
| Accounts receivable | 116,800 | |
| Allowance for doubtful accounts | | $ 6,400 |
| Liabilities | | 36,800 |
| May, capital (profit–loss share 30%) | | 43,200 |
| Nix, capital (profit–loss share 50%) | | 33,600 |
| Peat, capital (profit–loss share 20%) | | 24,000 |

**Instructions** For each of the two independent situations shown below, prepare journal entries to record the collection or sale of the receivables, the payment of liabilities, and the distribution of all remaining cash to the partners. Support all entries with adequate explanation; the entries for distribution of cash to the partners should have explanations showing how the amounts were determined.

**a** Collections of $66,400 are made on receivables, and the remainder are deemed uncollectible. Use an account entitled Loss on Liquidation.

**b** Receivables are sold to a collection agency; the partnership receives in cash as a final settlement 30% of the gross amount of its receivables. The personal financial status of the partners is uncertain, but all available cash is to be distributed at this time. (Nix's deficiency will be charged to May and Peat in a 30:20 ratio.)

## BUSINESS DECISION PROBLEM 15

John and David are considering the formation of a partnership to engage in the business of aerial photography. John is a licensed pilot, is currently employed at a salary of $48,000 a year, and has $90,000 to invest in the business. David is a professional photographer who has been earning $20,000 a year managing a photographic shop. He has just inherited $200,000 which he plans to put into the partnership business. The two partners, after a careful study of their planned business operations, conclude that $100,000 of additional funds will be required, and they have been assured by a local investor, Ann Belton, that she will lend them this amount on a five-year note with interest at 12% annually. You may assume that 12% is a fair rate of return on capital invested in a business of this type.

Both partners will devote full time to the business and they have agreed to make no withdrawals during the first year. The forecasts prepared by the partners indicate that revenue during the first year will be $10,000 in excess of expenses, with the exception of the interest expense on the $100,000 loan from Belton. During the second year, the estimates indicate that revenue should exceed expenses (other than the interest expense on the loan) by $90,000. For the third year, it is believed that revenue will exceed expenses (other than the interest expense on the loan) by $168,000. (Bear in mind that these estimates of expenses do not include any salaries to the partners.)

**Instructions**

a On the basis of the above information, prepare a brief description of the ***income-sharing agreement*** you would recommend that the partners adopt. Explain the basis for your proposal. (Consider the value of personal services to be rendered by each partner and the amounts of capital provided. Assume that the present salaries of John and David are a fair measure of their earning ability.)

b Assume that the income estimates prepared by the partners are reasonable. Draw up a schedule showing for each of the three years how the partners will share in income (or loss) under the agreement you have proposed. Assume that no significant change occurs in capitals of partners. (This simplifying assumption makes it possible to ignore the possibility of changes in capital accounts resulting from the division of profits or losses, or from drawings and investments. Any such influences are assumed to counterbalance. In other words, it is arbitrarily assumed that the original capital balances for both partners remain unchanged throughout the first three years of operations.)

Your schedule should include three money columns, one for each year. On the first line list the expected operating income, then the interest expense on the note payable, and third the net income or loss for each year. Then show how the net income or loss of each year will be distributed between partners.

c Write a brief statement commenting on the difference between the income to the two partners and defending the results of the income-sharing plan you have devised.

# 16

# CORPORATIONS: ORGANIZATION AND STOCKHOLDERS' EQUITY

Who owns General Motors Corporation? The owners of a corporation are called ***stockholders.*** Stockholders in General Motors include over one million men and women, as well as many pension funds, mutual investment funds, employees' unions, banks, universities, and other organizations. Because a corporation can be used to pool the savings of any number of investors, it is an ideal means of obtaining the capital necessary for large-scale production.

Nearly all large businesses and many small ones are organized as corporations. There are still more single proprietorships and partnerships than corporations, but in dollar volume of business activity, corporations hold an impressive lead. Because of the dominant role of the corporation in our economy, it is important for everyone interested in business, economics, or politics to have an understanding of corporations and their accounting practices.

The growth of large corporations has led to a demand for information about their profitability and financial affairs from persons outside the corporate enterprise. Virtually everyone buys goods and services produced by our major corporations; a great many people also work for these companies, or receive dividends from them, or sell materials and supplies to them. Thus the general public and many special interest groups as well are concerned with the operations and financial stability of major corporations. Among the specific groups of outsiders demanding accounting information from large corporations are existing stockholders, prospective stockholders, creditors, banks, labor unions, financial analysts, consumer groups, government agencies, congressional committees, and news media of all types.

One result of the growth of the large corporation has been to expand greatly the role of the professional accountant and the reliance of society upon the validity and fairness of corporate accounting reports. In the past, the demand for accounting information came in large part from company management; now the demand for accounting information comes from virtually every sector of our society. This trend of rising public interest has created a new dimension for accounting and has led some CPAs who audit large corporations to say "The public is our client."

## What is a corporation?

A corporation is a legal entity having an existence separate and distinct from that of its owners. In the eyes of the law, a corporation is an artificial person having many of the rights and responsibilities of a real person.

A corporation, as a separate legal entity, may own property in its own name. Thus, the assets of a corporation belong to the corporation itself, not to the stockholders. A corporation has legal status in court, that is, it may sue and be sued as if it were a person. As a legal entity, a corporation enters into contracts, is responsible for its own debts, and pays income taxes on its earnings.

## Advantages of the corporate form of organization

The corporation offers a number of advantages not available in other forms of organization. Among these advantages are the following:

1 **No personal liability for stockholders** Creditors of a corporation have a claim against the assets of the corporation, not against the personal property of the stockholders. Thus, the amount of money which stockholders risk by investing in a corporation is ***limited to the amount of their investment.*** To many investors, this is the most important advantage of the corporate form.

2 **Ease of accumulating capital** Ownership of a corporation is evidenced by transferable ***shares of stock.*** The sale of corporate ownership in units of one or more shares permits both large and small investors to participate in ownership of the business. Some corporations actually have more than a million individual stockholders. For this reason, large corporations are often said to be ***publicly owned.*** Of course not all corporations are large. Many small businesses are organized as corporations and are owned by a limited number of stockholders. Such corporations are said to be ***closely held.***

3 **Ownership shares are readily transferable** Shares of stock may be sold by one investor to another without dissolving or disrupting the business organization. The shares of most large corporations may be bought or sold by investors in organized markets, such as the ***New York Stock Exchange.*** Investments in these shares have the advantage of ***liquidity,*** because investors may easily convert their corporate ownership into cash by selling their stock.

4 **Continuous existence** A corporation is a separate legal entity with a perpetual existence. The continuous life of the corporation despite changes in ownership is made possible by the issuance of transferable shares of stock. By way of

contrast, a partnership is a relatively unstable form of organization which is dissolved by the death or retirement of any of its members. The continuity of the corporate entity is essential to most large-scale business activities.

5 **Professional management** The stockholders own the corporation, but they do not manage it on a daily basis. To administer the affairs of the corporation, the stockholders elect a ***board of directors.*** The directors, in turn, hire a president and other corporate officers to manage the business. There is no mutual agency in a corporation; thus, an individual stockholder has no right to participate in the management of the business unless he or she has been hired as a corporate officer. The sharp separation between the functions of ownership and management leaves a corporation free to employ the best managerial talent available.

## Disadvantages of the corporate form of organization

Among the disadvantages of the corporation are:

1 **Heavy taxation** The income of a partnership or a single proprietorship is taxable only as personal income to the owners of the business. The income of a corporation, on the other hand, is subject to income taxes which must be paid by the corporation. The combination of federal and state corporate income taxes often takes about 50% of a corporation's before-tax income. If a corporation distributes its earnings to stockholders, the stockholders must pay personal income taxes on the amounts they receive. This practice of first taxing corporate income to the corporation and then taxing distributions of that income to the stockholders is sometimes called ***double taxation.***

2 **Greater regulation** A corporation comes into existence under the terms of state laws and these same laws may provide for considerable regulation of the corporation's activities. For example, the withdrawal of funds from a corporation is subject to certain limits set by law. Federal laws administered by the Securities and Exchange Commission require large corporations to make extensive public disclosure of their affairs.

3 **Separation of ownership and control** The separation of the functions of ownership and management may be an advantage in some cases but a disadvantage in others. On the whole, the excellent record of growth and earnings in most large corporations indicates that the separation of ownership and control has benefited rather than injured stockholders. In a few instances, however, a management group has chosen to operate a corporation for the benefit of insiders. The stockholders may find it difficult in such cases to take the concerted action necessary to oust the officers.

## Income taxes in corporate financial statements

Since a corporation is a separate legal entity subject to taxes upon its income, the ledger of a corporation should include accounts for recording income taxes. No such accounts are needed for a business organized as a single proprietorship or partnership.

attended by relatively few persons, often by less than 1% of the stockholders. Prior to the meeting, the management group will request stockholders who do not plan to attend in person to send in ***proxy statements*** assigning their votes to the existing management. Through this use of the proxy system, management may secure the right to vote as much as, perhaps, 90% or more of the total outstanding shares.

**Functions of the board of directors** The primary functions of the board of directors are to manage the corporation and to protect the interests of the stockholders. At this level, management may consist principally of formulating policies and reviewing acts of the officers. Specific duties of the directors include declaring dividends, setting the salaries of officers, reviewing the system of internal control with the internal auditors and with the company's independent auditors, authorizing officers to arrange loans from banks, and authorizing important contracts of various kinds.

The extent of participation in management by the board of directors varies widely from one company to another. In recent years increased importance has been attached to the inclusion on the boards of large corporations of individuals who were not officers of the company and who could thus have a view independent of that of corporate officers.

The official actions of the board are recorded in minutes of their meetings. The ***minutes book*** is the source of many of the accounting entries affecting the stockholders' equity accounts.

**Functions of corporate officers** Corporate officers usually include a president, one or more vice-presidents, a controller, a treasurer, and a secretary. A vice-president is often made responsible for the sales function; other vice-presidents may be given responsibility for such important functions as personnel, finance, and production.

The responsibilities of the controller, treasurer, and secretary are most directly related to the accounting phase of business operation. The ***controller,*** or chief accounting officer, is responsible for the maintenance of adequate internal control and for the preparation of accounting records and financial statements. Such specialized activities as budgeting, tax planning, and preparation of tax returns are usually placed under the controller's jurisdiction. The ***treasurer*** has custody of the company's funds and is generally responsible for planning and controlling the company's cash position. The ***secretary*** represents the corporation in many contractual and legal matters and maintains minutes of the meetings of directors and stockholders. Another responsibility of the secretary is to coordinate the preparation of the annual report, which includes the financial statements and other information relating to corporate activities. In small corporations, one officer frequently acts as both secretary and treasurer. The following organization chart indicates lines of authority extending from stockholders to the directors to the president and other officers.

*Typical corporate organization*

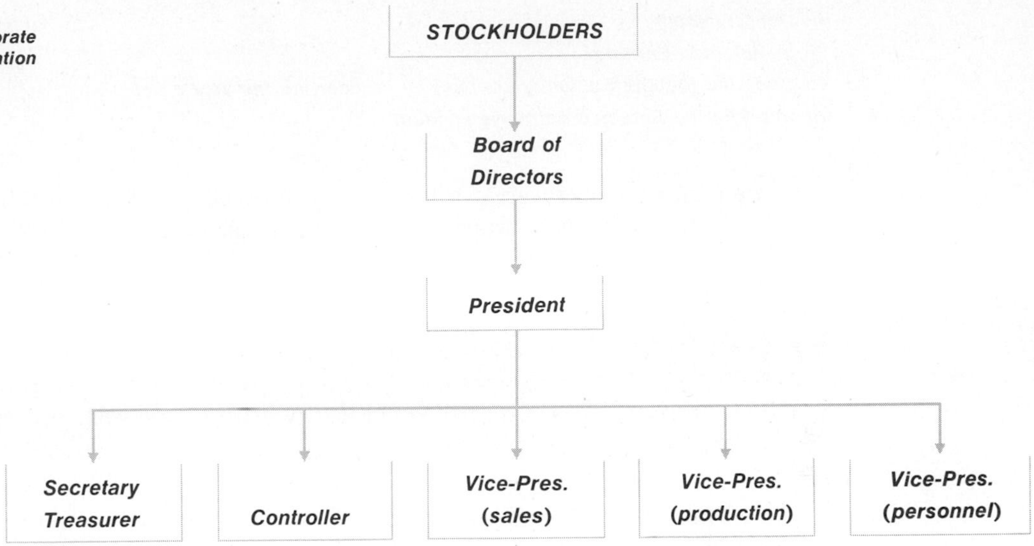


## Sources of corporate capital

The sections of the balance sheet showing assets and liabilities are much the same for a corporation as for a single proprietorship or partnership. The owner's equity section is the principal point of contrast. In a corporation the term ***stockholders' equity*** is used instead of owner's equity. The capital of a corporation, as for other types of business organizations, is equal to the excess of the assets over the liabilities. However, state laws require the capital of a corporation to be divided into several segments. Later in this chapter these various classifications of corporate capital will be considered in some detail, but at this point we will use a simpler model in which the capital of a corporation is carried in only two ledger accounts and shown on the balance sheet in two separate portions. These two classifications are (1) the capital invested by the stockholders (***paid-in capital***), and (2) the capital accumulated and retained through profitable operations (***earned capital***).

When stockholders invest cash or other assets in the business, the corporation issues in exchange shares of capital stock as evidence of the stockholders' equity ownership. In the simplest case, capital invested by the stockholders is recorded in the corporation's accounting records by a credit to an account entitled Capital Stock. The capital paid in by stockholders is regarded as permanent capital not ordinarily subject to withdrawal.

Capital accumulated through profitable operations is called ***retained earnings.*** At the end of the year the balance of the Income Summary account is closed into the Retained Earnings account. For example, if net income for the year is $70,000, the closing entry will be as follows:

| | | |
|---|---|---|
| *Income Summary* | *70,000* | |
| *Retained Earnings* | | *70,000* |
| *To close the Income Summary account by transferring the year's net income into the Retained Earnings account.* | | |

If the company operates at a loss of, say, $25,000, the Income Summary account will have a debit balance. The account must then be credited to close it. The closing entry will be:

| | | |
|---|---|---|
| *Retained Earnings* | *25,000* | |
| *Income Summary* | | *25,000* |
| *To close the Income Summary account by transferring the year's net loss into the Retained Earnings account.* | | |

If a corporation has sufficient cash, a distribution of profits may be made to stockholders. Distributions of this nature are termed ***dividends*** and decrease both total assets and total stockholders' equity. Since dividends are regarded as distributions of earned capital, the decrease in stockholders' equity is recorded in the Retained Earnings account. Thus, the amount of retained earnings at any balance sheet date represents the accumulated earnings of the company since the date of incorporation, minus any losses, and minus all dividends distributed to stockholders.

Some people mistakenly believe that retained earnings represent a fund of cash available to a corporation. ***Retained earnings are not assets; they are an element of stockholders' equity.*** Although the amount of retained earnings indicates the portion of total assets which were ***financed*** by earning and retaining net income, it does ***not*** indicate the ***form*** in which these resources are currently held. The resources generated by retaining profits may have been invested in land, buildings, equipment, or any other kind of asset. The total amount of cash owned by a corporation is shown by the balance of the Cash account, which appears in the asset section of the balance sheet.

**Stockholders' equity on the balance sheet** For a corporation with $100,000 of capital stock and $40,000 of retained earnings, the stockholders' equity section of the balance sheet (omitting certain details) will appear as follows:

*Paid-in capital and earned capital*

| | | |
|---|---|---|
| *Stockholders' equity:* | | |
| *Capital stock* | *$100,000* | |
| *Retained earnings* | *40,000* | *$140,000* |

If this same company had been unprofitable and had incurred losses aggregating $30,000 since its organization, the stockholders' equity section of the balance sheet would be as follows:

*Paid-in capital reduced by losses incurred*

| | | |
|---|---|---|
| ***Stockholders' equity:*** | | |
| *Capital stock* | *$100,000* | |
| *Less: Deficit* | *30,000* | *$70,000* |

This second illustration tells us that $30,000 of the original $100,000 invested by stockholders has been lost. Note that the capital stock in both illustrations remains at the fixed amount of $100,000, the stockholders' original investment. The accumulated profits or losses since the organization of the corporation are shown as ***retained earnings*** or as a ***deficit*** and are not intermingled with the paid-in capital. The term ***deficit*** indicates a negative amount of retained earnings.

## Cash dividends

The term ***dividend,*** when used by itself, is generally understood to mean a distribution of cash by a corporation to its stockholders. Dividends are stated as a specific amount per share of capital stock, as, for example, a dividend of $1 per share. The amount received by each stockholder is in proportion to the number of shares owned. A stockholder who owns 100 shares will receive a check for $100.

Dividends are paid only through action by the board of directors. The board has full discretion to declare a dividend or to refrain from doing so. Once the declaration of a dividend has been announced, the obligation to pay the dividend is a current liability of the corporation and cannot be rescinded.

Because a dividend is declared on one date by the board of directors and paid at a later date, two separate journal entries are necessary. To illustrate the entries for declaration and payment of a cash dividend, assume that a corporation declares a dividend of $1 a share on 100,000 shares of outstanding stock. The dividend is declared on December 15 and is payable on January 25. The two entries would be as follows:

| | | | |
|---|---|---|---|
| *Dec. 15* | *Retained Earnings* | *100,000* | |
| | *Dividends Payable* | | *100,000* |
| | *To record declaration by the board of directors of a cash dividend of $1 per share on the 100,000 shares of stock outstanding.* | | |
| *Jan. 25* | *Dividends Payable* | *100,000* | |
| | *Cash* | | *100,000* |
| | *To record payment of the $1 per share dividend declared Dec. 15 on the 100,000 shares of stock outstanding.* | | |

The account ***Dividends Payable,*** which was credited at the date of declaring the dividend, is a current liability. Some companies in recording the declaration of a dividend will debit an account entitled Dividends instead of debiting the Retained Earnings account. If a company has one or more issues of preferred stock as well as common stock, it may use a separate Dividends account for each issue. Whenever a Dividends account is used, a closing entry will be required at the end of the year to transfer the debit balance in the Dividends account into the Retained Earnings account. Under either method the end result is a reduction in retained earnings for the amount of the dividends declared.

### Authorization and issuance of capital stock

The articles of incorporation specify the number of shares of capital stock which a corporation is authorized to issue and the ***par value,*** if any, per share. Large issues of capital stock to be offered for sale to the general public must be approved by the SEC as well as by state officials. The corporation may choose not to issue immediately all the authorized shares; in fact, it is customary to secure authorization for a larger number of shares than presently needed. In future years, if more capital is needed, the previously authorized shares will be readily available for issue; otherwise, the corporation would be forced to apply to the state for permission to increase the number of authorized shares.

### Par value

The chief significance of par value is that it represents the ***legal capital*** per share, that is, the amount below which stockholders' equity cannot be reduced except by (1) losses from business operations or (2) legal action taken by a majority vote of stockholders. A dividend cannot be declared by a corporation if such action would cause the stockholders' equity to fall below the par value of the outstanding shares. Par value, therefore, may be regarded as a minimum cushion of capital existing for the protection of creditors.

Par value may be $1 per share, $5, $100, or any other amount decided upon by the corporation. The par value of the stock is ***no indication of its market value;*** the par value merely indicates the amount per share to be entered in the Capital Stock account. The par value of most common stocks is relatively low. Polaroid Corporation common stock, for example, has a par value of $1; Sears, Roebuck & Co. common stock has a par value of 75 cents, Avon Products stock has a par value of 50 cents per share. The market value of all these securities is far above their par value.

### Issuance of capital stock

Mere authorization of a stock issue does not bring an asset into existence, nor does it give the corporation any capital. The obtaining of authorization from the state for a stock issue merely affords a legal opportunity to obtain assets through the sale of stock.

When par value stock is ***issued,*** the Capital Stock account is credited with the par value of the shares issued, regardless of whether the issuance price is more or less than par. Assuming that 10,000 shares of $10 par value stock have been authorized and that 6,000 of these authorized shares are issued at a price of $10 each, Cash would be debited and Capital Stock would be credited for $60,000.

When stock is sold for more than par value, the Capital Stock account is credited with the par value of the shares issued, and a separate account, Paid-in Capital in Excess of Par Value, is credited for the excess of selling price over par. If, for example, the issuance price is $15, the entry is as follows:

***Stockholders' investment in excess of par value***

| | | |
|---|---|---|
| *Cash* | *90,000* | |
| *Capital Stock* | | *60,000* |
| *Paid-in Capital in Excess of Par Value* | | *30,000* |
| *Issued 6,000 shares of $10 par value stock at a price of $15 a share.* | | |

An alternative title for the account, Paid-in Capital in Excess of Par Value, is Premium on Capital Stock. The premium or amount received in excess of par value does not represent a profit to the corporation. It is part of the invested capital and it will be added to the capital stock on the balance sheet to show the total paid-in capital. The stockholders' equity section of the balance sheet is illustrated below. (The existence of $10,000 in retained earnings is assumed in order to have a complete illustration.)

***Corporation's capital classified by source***

| | |
|---|---|
| *Stockholders' equity:* | |
| *Capital stock, $10 par value, authorized 10,000 shares, issued and outstanding 6,000 shares* | *$ 60,000* |
| *Paid-in capital in excess of par value* | *30,000* |
| *Total paid-in capital* | *$ 90,000* |
| *Retained earnings* | *10,000* |
| *Total stockholders' equity* | *$100,000* |

If stock is issued by a corporation for less than par, the account Discount on Capital Stock should be debited for the difference between the issuance price and the par value. The issuance of stock at a discount is seldom encountered; it is illegal in many states.

## Capital stock outstanding

The basic unit of capital stock is called a ***share,*** but a corporation may issue capital stock certificates in denominations of 1 share, 100 shares, or any other number. The total number of shares of capital stock outstanding at any given time represents 100% ownership of the corporation. ***Outstanding*** shares are those in the hands of stockholders. The number of shares owned by an individual investor determines the extent of his or her ownership of the corporation.

Assume, for example, that Star Corporation issues a total of 50,000 shares of capital stock to investors in exchange for cash. If we assume further that Susan Morgan acquires 5,000 shares of the 50,000 shares outstanding, we may say that she has a 10% interest in the corporation. Suppose that Morgan now sells 2,000 shares to Evans. The total number of shares outstanding remains unchanged at 50,000, although Morgan's percentage of ownership has declined to 6% and a new stockholder, Evans, has acquired a 4% interest in the corporation. The transfer of 2,000 shares from Morgan to Evans had ***no effect*** upon the corporation's assets, liabilities, or amount of stock outstanding. The only way in which this transfer of stock affects the corporation is that the record of stockholders must be revised to show the number of shares held by each owner.

## No-par stock

In an earlier period of the history of American corporations, all capital stock had par value, but in more recent years state laws have permitted corporations to choose between par value stock and no-par value stock. However, most companies which issue no-par capital stock establish a stated value per share. From an accounting viewpoint, stated value and par value mean the same thing—both terms designate the legal capital per share and the amount to be credited to the Capital Stock account.

Assume that a corporation is organized in a state which permits the board of directors to establish a ***stated value*** on no-par stock, and that the board passed a resolution setting the stated value per share at $5. If a total of 80,000 shares were issued at $12 per share, the journal entry to record the issuance would be:

*Note stated value per share*

| | | |
|---|---|---|
| *Cash* | *960,000* | |
| *Common Stock* | | *400,000* |
| *Paid-in Capital in Excess of Stated Value* | | *560,000* |
| *Issued 80,000 shares of no-par value common stock at $12 each. Stated value set by directors at $5 per share.* | | |

In the absence of a stated value, the entire proceeds on the sale of stock ($960,000) would be credited to the Common Stock account and would be viewed as legal capital not subject to withdrawal.

## Preferred stock and common stock

In order to appeal to as many investors as possible, a corporation may issue more than one kind of capital stock. The basic type of capital stock issued by every corporation is called ***common stock.*** Common stock has the four basic rights previously mentioned. Whenever these rights are modified, the term ***preferred stock*** (or sometimes Class B Common) is used to describe this second type of capital stock. A few corporations issue two or more classes of preferred stock, each class having certain distinctive features designed to interest a particular type of investor. In summary, we may say that every business corporation has common stock; a good many corporations also issue preferred stock; and some companies have two or more types of preferred stock.

Common stock may be regarded as the basic, residual element of ownership. It carries voting rights and, therefore, is the means of exercising control over the business. Common stock has unlimited possibilities of increase in value; during periods of business expansion the market prices of common stocks of some leading corporations may rise to many times their former values. On the other hand, common stocks lose value more rapidly than other types of securities when corporations encounter periods of unprofitable business.

The following stockholders' equity section illustrates the balance sheet presentation for a corporation having both preferred and common stock; note that the item of retained earnings is not apportioned between the two groups of stockholders.

***Balance sheet presentation***

| | |
|---|---|
| *Stockholders' equity:* | |
| *8% cumulative preferred stock, $100 par value, authorized 100,000 shares, issued 50,000 shares* | *$ 5,000,000* |
| *Common stock, $5 par value, authorized 3 million shares, issued 2 million shares* | *10,000,000* |
| *Retained earnings* | *3,500,000* |
| *Total stockholders' equity* | *$18,500,000* |

## Characteristics of preferred stock

Most preferred stocks have the following distinctive features:

1 Preferred as to dividends
2 Preferred as to assets in event of the liquidation of the company
3 Callable at the option of the corporation
4 No voting power

Another very important but less common feature is a clause permitting the ***conversion*** of preferred stock into common at the option of the holder. Preferred stocks vary widely with respect to the special rights and privileges granted. Careful study of the terms of the individual preferred stock contract is a necessary step in the evaluation of any preferred stock.

**Stock preferred as to dividends** Stock preferred as to dividends is entitled to receive each year a dividend of specified amount before any dividend is paid on the common stock. The dividend is usually stated as a dollar amount per share. For example, the balance sheet of General Motors Corporation shows two types of preferred stock outstanding, one paying $5.00 a year and the other $3.75 a year, as shown below:

***Dividend stated as dollar amount***

| | |
|---|---|
| *Capital stock:* | |
| *Preferred, without par value (authorized 6 million shares):* | |
| *$5.00 series; stated value $100 per share, redeemable at $120 per share, outstanding 1,835,644 shares* | *$183,564,400* |
| *$3.75 series; stated value $100 per share, redeemable at $101 per share, outstanding 1,000,000 shares* | *100,000,000* |

Some preferred stocks state the dividend preference as a percentage of par value. For example, a 9% preferred stock with a par value of $100 per share would mean that $9 must be paid yearly on each share of preferred stock before any dividends are paid on the common. An example of the percentage method of stating the dividend on a preferred stock is found in the balance sheet of UAL, Inc. (United Airlines).

*Dividend stated as percentage of par*

***Shareholders' equity:***

***$5\frac{1}{2}$% cumulative prior preferred stock, $100 par value; authorized and outstanding 71,702 shares . . . . . . . . . . $7,170,200***

The holders of preferred stock have no assurance that they will always receive the indicated dividend. A corporation is obligated to pay dividends to stockholders only when the board of directors declares a dividend. Dividends must be paid on preferred stock before anything is paid to the common stockholders, but if the corporation is not prospering, it may decide not to pay dividends on either preferred or common stock. For a corporation to pay dividends, profits must be earned and cash must be available. However, preferred stocks in general offer more assurance of regular dividend payments than do common stocks.

**Cumulative preferred stock** The dividend preference carried by most preferred stocks is a ***cumulative*** one. If all or any part of the regular dividend on the preferred stock is omitted in a given year, the amount omitted is said to be ***in arrears*** and must be paid in a subsequent year before any dividend can be paid on the common stock. Assume that a corporation was organized January 1, Year 1, with 10,000 shares of $4 cumulative preferred stock and 50,000 shares of common stock. Dividends paid in Year 1 were at the rate of $4 per share of preferred stock and $2 per share of common. In Year 2, earnings declined sharply and the only dividend paid was $1 per share on the preferred stock. No dividends were paid in Year 3. What is the status of the preferred stock at December 31, Year 3? Dividends are in arrears in the amount of $7 a share ($3 omitted during Year 2 and $4 omitted in Year 3). On the entire issue of 10,000 shares of preferred stock, the dividends in arrears amount to $70,000.

Dividends in arrears ***are not listed among the liabilities of a corporation,*** because no liability exists until a dividend is declared by the board of directors. Nevertheless, the amount of any dividends in arrears on preferred stock is an important factor to investors and should always be disclosed. This disclosure is usually made by a note accompanying the balance sheet such as the following:

*Footnote disclosure of dividends in arrears*

***Note 6: Dividends in arrears***

***As of December 31, Year 3, dividends on the $4 cumulative preferred stock were in arrears to the extent of $7 per share and amounted in total to $70,000.***

In Year 4, we shall assume that the company earned large profits and wished to pay dividends on both the preferred and common stocks. Before paying a dividend on the common, the corporation must pay the $70,000 in arrears on the cumulative preferred stock plus the regular $4 a share applicable to the current year. The preferred stockholders would, therefore, receive a total of $110,000 in dividends in Year 4; the board of directors would then be free to declare dividends on the common stock.

For a ***noncumulative preferred stock,*** any unpaid or omitted dividend is lost forever. Because of this factor, investors view the noncumulative feature as an unfavorable element, and very few noncumulative preferred stocks are issued.

**Stock preferred as to assets** Most preferred stocks carry a preference as to assets in the event of liquidation of the corporation. If the business is terminated, the preferred stock is entitled to payment in full of its par value or a higher stated liquidation value before any payment is made on the common stock. This priority also includes any dividends in arrears.

**Callable preferred stock** Most preferred stocks include a ***call provision.*** This provision grants the issuing corporation the right to repurchase the stock from the stockholders at a stipulated ***call price.*** The call price is usually slightly higher than the par value of the stock. For example, $100 par value preferred stock may be callable at $105 or $110 per share. In addition to paying the call price, a corporation which redeems its preferred stock must pay any dividends in arrears. A call provision gives a corporation flexibility in adjusting its financial structure, for example, by eliminating a preferred stock and replacing it with other securities if future growth of the company makes such change advantageous.

**Convertible preferred stock** In order to add to the attractiveness of preferred stock as an investment, corporations sometimes offer a conversion privilege which entitles the preferred stockholders to exchange their shares for common stock in a stipulated ratio. If the corporation prospers, its common stock will probably rise in market value, and dividends on the common stock will probably be increased. The investor who buys a convertible preferred stock rather than common stock has greater assurance of regular dividends. In addition, through the conversion privilege, the investor is assured of sharing in any substantial increase in value of the company's common stock.

As an example, assume that Remington Corporation issued a 5%, $100 par, convertible preferred stock on January 1, at a price of $100 a share. Each share was convertible into four shares of the company's $10 par value common stock at any time. The common stock had a market price of $20 a share on January 1, and an annual dividend of 60 cents a share was being paid. During the next few years, Remington Corporation's earnings increased, the dividend on the common stock was raised to an annual rate of $1.50, and the market price of the common stock rose to $40 a share. At this point the preferred stock would have a market value of at least $160, since it could be converted at any time into four shares of common stock with a market value of $40 each. In other words, the market value of a convertible preferred stock will tend to move in accordance with the price of the common.

When the dividend rate is increased on the common stock, some holders of the preferred stock may convert their holdings into common stock in order to obtain a higher cash return on their investments. If the holder of 100 shares of the preferred stock presented these shares for conversion, Remington Corporation would make the following journal entry:

*Conversion of preferred stock into common*

| | | |
|---|---|---|
| ***5% Convertible Preferred Stock*** | ***10,000*** | |
| ***Common Stock*** | | ***4,000*** |
| ***Paid-in Capital in Excess of Par Value*** | | ***6,000*** |
| ***To record the conversion of 100 shares of preferred stock, par $100, into 400 shares of $10 par value common stock.*** | | |

Note that the issue price recorded for the 400 shares of common stock is based upon the carrying value of the preferred stock in the accounting records, not upon market prices at the date of conversion.

**Participating clauses in preferred stock** Since participating preferred stocks are very seldom issued, discussion of them will be brief. A fully participating preferred stock is one which, in addition to the regular specified dividend, is entitled to participate in some manner with the common stock in any additional dividends paid. For example, a $5 participating preferred stock would be entitled to receive $5 a share before the common stock received anything. After $5 a share had been paid to the preferred stockholders, a $5 dividend could be paid on the common stock. If the company desired to pay an additional dividend to the common, say, an extra $3 per share, the preferred stock would also be entitled to receive an extra $3 dividend. In brief, a fully participating preferred stock participates dollar for dollar with the common stock in any dividends paid in excess of the stated rate on the preferred stock.

It is important to remember that most preferred stocks are ***not*** participating. Although common stock dividends may increase year after year if the corporation prospers, the dividends on most preferred stocks are fixed in amount. The typical $6 preferred stock, for example, will never pay an annual dividend in excess of $6.

## The underwriting of stock issues

When a large amount of stock is to be issued, the corporation will probably utilize the services of an investment banking firm, frequently referred to as an ***underwriter.*** The underwriter guarantees the issuing corporation a specific price for the stock and makes a profit by selling the stock to the investing public at a higher price. The corporation records the issuance of the stock at the net amount received from the underwriter. The use of an underwriter assures the corporation that the entire stock issue will be sold without delay, and the entire amount of funds to be raised will be available on a specific date.

## Market price of common stock

The preceding sections concerning the issuance of stock at prices above and below par value raise a question as to how the market price of stock is determined. The price which the corporation sets on a new issue of stock is based on several factors including (1) an appraisal of the company's expected future earnings, (2) the probable dividend rate per share, (3) the present financial position of the company, and (4) the current state of the investment market.

After the stock has been issued, the price at which it will be traded among investors will rise and fall in response to all the forces of the marketplace. The market price per share will tend to reflect the progress of the company, with primary emphasis being placed on earnings and dividends. At this point in our discussion, the significant fact to emphasize is that market price is not related to par value, and that it tends to reflect current and future earnings and dividends.

### Stock issued for assets other than cash

Corporations generally sell their capital stock for cash and use the cash to buy the various types of assets needed in the business. Sometimes, however, a corporation may issue shares of its capital stock in a direct exchange for land, buildings, or other assets. Stock may also be issued in payment for services rendered by attorneys and promoters in the formation of the corporation.

When a corporation issues capital stock in exchange for services or for assets other than cash, the transaction should be recorded at the current ***market value*** of the goods or services received. Often, the best evidence as to the market value of these goods or services is the market value of the shares issued in exchange. For example, assume that a company issues 1,000 shares of its $1 par value common stock in exchange for land. Competent appraisers may have differing opinions as to the market value of the land. But let us assume that the company's stock is currently selling on a stock exchange for $90 per share. It is logical to say that the cost of the land to the company is $90,000, the market value of the shares issued in exchange.

Once the valuation has been decided, the entry to record the issuance of the stock in exchange for the land is as follows:

*How were dollar amounts determined?*

| | | |
|---|---|---|
| *Land* | *90,000* | |
| *Common Stock* | | *1,000* |
| *Paid-in Capital in Excess of Par Value* | | *89,000* |
| ***To record the issuance of 1,000 shares of $1 par value common stock in exchange for land. Current market value of stock ($90 a share) used as basis for valuing the land.*** | | |

### Subscriptions to capital stock

Small corporations sometimes sell stock on a subscription plan, in which the investor agrees to pay the subscription price at a future date or in a series of installments. For example, Subscriptions Receivable: Common would be debited and Common Stock Subscribed would be credited when the subscription contract was signed. Collections would be credited to Subscriptions Receivable: Common. When the entire subscription price had been collected and the stock issued, Common Stock Subscribed would be debited and Common Stock would be credited. The following illustration demonstrates the accounting procedures for stock subscriptions.

In this example, 10,000 shares of $10 par value stock are subscribed at a price of $15. Subscriptions for 6,000 of these shares are then collected in full. A partial payment is received on the other 4,000 shares.

*Subscription price above par*

| | | |
|---|---|---|
| ***Subscriptions Receivable: Common*** | ***150,000*** | |
| ***Common Stock Subscribed*** | | ***100,000*** |
| ***Paid-in Capital in Excess of Par Value*** | | ***50,000*** |
| ***Received subscriptions for 10,000 shares of $10 par value stock at price of $15 a share.*** | | |

When the subscriptions for 6,000 shares are collected in full, certificates for 6,000 shares will be issued. The following entries are made:

*Certificates issued for fully paid shares*

| | | |
|---|---|---|
| ***Cash*** | ***90,000*** | |
| ***Subscriptions Receivable: Common*** | | ***90,000*** |
| ***Collected subscriptions in full for 6,000 shares at $15 each.*** | | |
| ***Common Stock Subscribed*** | ***60,000*** | |
| ***Common Stock*** | | ***60,000*** |
| ***Issued certificates for 6,000 fully paid $10 par value shares.*** | | |

The subscriber to the remaining 4,000 shares paid only half of the amount of the subscription but promised to pay the remainder within a month. Stock certificates will not be issued until the subscription is collected in full, but the partial collection is recorded by the following entry:

*Partial collection of subscription*

| | | |
|---|---|---|
| ***Cash*** | ***30,000*** | |
| ***Subscriptions Receivable: Common*** | | ***30,000*** |
| ***Collected partial payment on subscription for 4,000 shares.*** | | |

From the corporation's point of view, Subscriptions Receivable is a current asset, which ordinarily will be collected within a short time. If financial statements are prepared between the date of obtaining subscriptions and the date of issuing the stock, the Common Stock Subscribed account is regarded as legal capital and will appear in the stockholders' equity section of the balance sheet.

## Donated Capital

On occasion, a corporation may receive assets as a gift. To increase local employment, for example, some cities have given corporations the land upon which to build factories. When a corporation receives such a gift, both total assets and total stockholders' equity increase by the market value of the assets received. ***No profit is recognized when a gift is received;*** the increase in stockholders' equity is regarded as paid-in capital. The receipt of a gift is recorded by debiting the appropriate asset accounts and crediting an account entitled ***Donated Capital.*** Donated capital appears in the stockholders' equity section of the balance sheet, as illustrated on page 607.

### Book value per share of common stock

Since each stockholders' equity in a corporation is determined by the number of shares he or she owns, an accounting measurement of interest to many stockholders is book value per share of common stock. Book value per share is equal to the ***net assets*** represented by one share of stock. The term ***net assets*** means total assets minus total liabilities; in other words, net assets are equal to total stockholders' equity. Thus in a corporation which has issued common stock only, the book value per share is computed by dividing total stockholders' equity by the number of shares outstanding.

For example, assume that a corporation has 4,000 shares of capital stock outstanding and the stockholders' equity section of the balance sheet is as follows:

*How much is book value per share?*

| | |
|---|---|
| *Capital stock, $1 par value* | *$ 4,000* |
| *Paid-in capital in excess of par value* | *40,000* |
| *Retained earnings* | *76,000* |
| *Total stockholders' equity* | *$120,000* |

The book value per share is $30; it is computed by dividing the stockholders' equity of $120,000 by the 4,000 shares of outstanding stock. In computing book value, we are not concerned with the number of authorized shares but merely with the outstanding shares, because the total of the outstanding shares represents 100% of the stockholders' equity.

**Book value when a company has both preferred and common stock** Book value is usually computed only for common stock. If a company has both preferred and common stock outstanding, the computation of book value per share of common stock requires two steps. First the redemption value or call price of the entire preferred stock issue and any dividends in arrears are deducted from total stockholders' equity. Secondly, the remaining amount of stockholders' equity is divided by the number of common shares outstanding to determine book value per common share. This procedure reflects the fact that the common stockholders are the residual owners of the corporate entity.

To illustrate, assume that the stockholders' equity is as follows:

*Two classes of stock*

| | |
|---|---|
| *8% preferred stock, $100 par, callable at $110* | *$1,000,000* |
| *Common stock, no-par; $5 stated value; authorized 100,000 shares, issued and outstanding 80,000 shares* | *400,000* |
| *Paid-in capital in excess of par value* | *800,000* |
| *Retained earnings* | *900,000* |
| *Total stockholders' equity* | *$3,100,000* |

All the capital belongs to the common stockholders, except the $1.1 million call price ($110 × 10,000 shares) applicable to the preferred stock (and any dividends in arrears on preferred stock). The calculation of book value per share of common stock can therefore be made as follows, assuming that there are no dividends in arrears:

*Compute book value per share of common stock*

| | |
|---|---|
| *Total stockholders' equity* | *$3,100,000* |
| *Less: Preferred stock (at call price of $110 per share)* | *1,100,000* |
| *Equity of common stockholders* | *$2,000,000* |
| *Number of shares of common stock outstanding* | *80,000* |
| *Book value per share of common stock* $\frac{\$2,000,000}{80,000}$ | *$25* |

The concept of book value is of vital importance in many contracts. For example, a majority stockholder might obtain an option to purchase the shares of the minority stockholders at book value at a specified future date. Many court cases have hinged on definitions of book value.

Book value is also used in judging the reasonableness of the market price of a stock. However, it must be used with great caution; the fact that a stock is selling at less than its book value does not necessarily indicate a bargain. The disparity between book value and market price per share is indicated by the following data currently available for three well-known corporations: International Paper, book value $54, market price $35; American Airlines, book value $26, market price $8; Johnson & Johnson, book value $32, market price $80. Current earnings, dividends per share, and prospects for future earnings are usually more important factors affecting market price than is book value.

Book value does ***not*** indicate the amount which the holder of a share of stock would receive if the corporation were to be dissolved. In liquidation, the assets would probably be sold at prices quite different from their carrying values in the accounts, and the stockholders' equity would go up or down accordingly.

**Changes in book value** Many events cause the book value per share of common stock to change. For example, earning net income increases total stockholders' equity, thereby increasing book value per share. Net losses and the declaration of dividends both reduce stockholders' equity and book value.

Another event which affects book value is the issuance of additional shares of common stock at a price either above or below the present book value per share. To illustrate, assume that a corporation has total stockholders' equity of $1,000,000, no preferred stock, and 100,000 shares of common stock outstanding. The book value per share is $10 ($1,000,000 ÷ 100,000 shares). If the company issues an additional 20,000 shares of common stock at $22 per share, total stockholders' equity will increase to $1,440,000. Note that the book value per share is now $12 ($1,440,000 ÷ 120,000 shares). Thus, the sale of additional common stock at a price above book value increases book value per share. Conversely, the sale of additional shares at a price below book value decreases the book value per share.

## Internal control over stock certificates and stockholder records

A large corporation with shares listed on the New York Stock Exchange usually has many millions of shares outstanding and several hundred thousand stockholders. Each day many stockholders sell their shares; the buyers of these shares become new members of the company's family of stockholders. Of course the corporation must have available an up-to-date record of the names and addresses of this constantly changing army of stockholders so that it can send dividend checks, financial statements, and voting forms to the right people. The corporation also must make sure that old stock certificates are canceled as new ones are issued so that no invalid or excess certificates become outstanding.

Large corporations establish excellent internal control over stock certificates by turning over the function of maintaining capital stock records to an independent ***stock transfer agent*** and an independent ***stock registrar.*** A bank or trust company serves as stock transfer agent and another bank acts as the stock registrar. When certificates are to be transferred from one owner to another, the certificates are sent to the transfer agent, who cancels them, makes the necessary entries in the stockholders' ledger, and signs new certificates which are forwarded to the stock registrar. The function of the registrar is to prevent any improper issuance of stock certificates. To accomplish this objective, the bank acting as registrar maintains records showing the total number of shares outstanding at all times. Note that the persons with custody of stock certificates and responsibility for maintaining stockholder records do not have access to assets of the corporation. The stock transfer agent is always able to provide a complete current list of names and addresses of stockholders for dividend payments and other communications by the corporation to its many owners.

Small corporations usually do not retain the services of an independent stock transfer agent and registrar. The small corporation typically orders blank stock certificates from a printer, usually in a bound book with stubs similar to a large checkbook. The certificates and the stubs are serially numbered by the printer, which aids the corporation in maintaining control over both the outstanding and the unissued certificates. At the time of issuance, a certificate is signed by the president and the secretary of the corporation, the number of shares is filled in on both the certificate and the stub, and the certificate is delivered to a stockholder. The open stubs in the stock certificate book represent total outstanding shares and should be reconciled with the capital stock account in the general ledger.

When a stockholder in a small corporation sells his or her shares, the certificate is endorsed, returned to the company, canceled, and attached to the stub. A new certificate is issued to the buyer of the shares.

A small corporation usually will maintain a stockholders' ledger as well as a stock certificate book. This subsidiary ledger contains a page for each stockholder; entries are made in number of shares rather than in dollars. Each stockholder's account shows the number of shares which he or she owns, the certificate numbers, the dates of acquisition, and the dates of sale.

Note how the records for capital stock are linked together to strengthen internal control. The total number of shares outstanding as shown by the stock certificate book (the open stubs) must agree with the total number of shares shown by the stockholders' ledger. This number multiplied by the par value per share ties in with the dollar balance of the capital stock account in the general ledger. Finally, as another internal control measure, we can make sure that no stock certificates are missing. We do this by accounting for all stock certificates by serial number, thereby identifying every certificate in the series as outstanding, canceled, or unissued.

### Balance sheet for a corporation illustrated

A fairly complete balance sheet for a corporation is illustrated on page 607. Note the inclusion in this balance sheet of liabilities for income taxes payable and dividends payable. These liabilities do not appear in the balance sheets of unincorporated businesses. Note also that each issue of capital stock is carefully described in the stockholders' equity section of the balance sheet. The caption for each capital stock account indicates the type of stock, the par value per share, and the number of shares authorized and issued. The caption for preferred stock also indicates the dividend rate, call price, and other important features of the stock issue.

In studying this balance sheet, bear in mind that current practice includes many alternatives in the choice of terminology and the arrangement of items in financial statements. Some of these alternatives are illustrated in Appendix A at the end of this book.

## KEY TERMS INTRODUCED OR EMPHASIZED IN CHAPTER 16

**Board of directors** Persons elected by common stockholders to direct the affairs of a corporation.

**Book value per share** The net assets per share of common stock, computed by dividing stockholders' equity by the number of common shares outstanding.

**Call price** The price to be paid by a corporation for each share of callable preferred stock if the corporation decides to call (redeem) the preferred stock.

**Capital stock** Transferable units of ownership in a corporation. A broad term which may refer to common stock, preferred stock, or both.

**Closely held corporation** A corporation owned by a small group of stockholders. The stock of closely held corporations is not traded on stock exchanges.

**Common stock** A type of capital stock which possesses the basic rights of ownership including the right to vote. Represents the residual element of ownership in a corporation.

**Convertible preferred stock** Preferred stock which entitles the owner to exchange his or her shares for common stock in a specified ratio.

**Corporation** A business organized as a legal entity separate from its owners. Chartered by the state with ownership divided into shares of transferable stock. Stockholders are not liable for debts of the corporation.

**Cumulative preferred stock** A class of stock with a provision that if divi-

**DEL MAR CORPORATION**
**Balance Sheet**
**December 31, Year 10**

| | | | |
|---|---|---|---|
| **Assets** | | | |
| Current assets: | | | |
| Cash | | | $ 305,600 |
| Accounts receivable (net of allowance for doubtful accounts) | | | 1,105,200 |
| Subscriptions receivable: common stock | | | 110,000 |
| Inventories (lower of fifo cost or market) | | | 1,300,800 |
| Short-term prepayments | | | 125,900 |
| Total current assets | | | $2,947,500 |
| Plant and equipment: | | | |
| Land | | $ 900,000 | |
| Buildings and equipment | $5,283,000 | | |
| Less: Accumulated depreciation | 1,250,000 | 4,033,000 | 4,933,000 |
| Other assets: Organization costs | | | 14,000 |
| Total assets | | | $7,894,500 |
| **Liabilities & Stockholders' Equity** | | | |
| Current liabilities: | | | |
| Accounts payable | | | $ 998,100 |
| Income taxes payable | | | 324,300 |
| Dividends payable | | | 109,700 |
| Interest payable | | | 20,000 |
| Total current liabilities | | | $1,452,100 |
| Long-term liabilities: Bonds payable, 12%, due Oct. 1, Year 20 | | | 1,000,000 |
| Total liabilities | | | $2,452,100 |
| Stockholders' equity: | | | |
| Cumulative 8% preferred stock, $100 par, callable at $104, authorized and issued 10,000 shares | | $1,000,000 | |
| Common stock, $1 par, authorized 1,000,000 shares, issued 600,000 shares | | 600,000 | |
| Common stock subscribed, 20,000 shares | | 20,000 | |
| Paid-in capital in excess of par: common | | 2,070,000 | |
| Donated capital | | 210,000 | |
| Total paid-in capital | | $3,900,000 | |
| Retained earnings | | 1,542,400 | |
| Total stockholders' equity | | | 5,442,400 |
| Total liabilities & stockholders' equity | | | $7,894,500 |

dends are reduced or omitted in any year, this amount accumulates and must be paid prior to payment of dividends on the common stock.

**Deficit** Accumulated losses incurred by a corporation. A negative amount of retained earnings.

**Dividend** A distribution of cash by a corporation to its stockholders.

**No-par stock** Stock without par value. Usually has a stated value, which is similar to par value.

**Organization costs** Costs incurred to form a corporation.

**Paid-in capital** The amounts invested in a corporation by its stockholders.

**Par value** The legal capital of a corporation. Also the face amount of a share of capital stock. Represents the minimum amount per share to be invested in the corporation when shares are originally issued.

**Preferred stock** A class of capital stock usually having preferences as to dividends and in the distribution of assets in event of liquidation.

**Publicly owned corporation** A corporation owned by a large number of people. The stock of publicly owned corporations generally is traded on organized stock exchanges.

**Retained earnings** That portion of stockholders' equity resulting from profits earned and retained in the business.

**Stated capital** That portion of capital invested by stockholders which cannot be withdrawn. Provides protection for creditors. Also called ***legal capital.***

**Stock certificate** A document issued by a corporation as evidence of the ownership of the number of shares stated on the certificate.

**Stock registrar** An independent fiscal agent, usually a large bank, retained by a corporation to control the issuance of stock certificates and provide assurance against overissuance.

**Stock transfer agent** A bank or trust company retained by a corporation to maintain its records of capital stock ownership and make transfers from one investor to another.

**Stockholders' ledger** A subsidiary record showing the number of shares owned by each stockholder.

**Subscriptions to capital stock** Formal promises to buy shares of stock from a corporation with payment at a later date. Stock certificates delivered when full payment received.

**Underwriter** An investment banking firm which handles the sale of a corporation's stock to the public.

## REVIEW QUESTIONS

1 Why are large corporations often said to be ***publicly owned?***

2 Distinguish between corporations and partnerships in terms of the following characteristics:
 **a** Owners' liability
 **b** Transferability of ownership interest

**c** Continuity of existence
**d** Federal taxation on income

**3** What are the basic rights of the owner of a share of corporate stock? In what way are these basic rights commonly modified with respect to the owner of a share of preferred stock?

**4** Explain the meaning of the term ***double taxation*** as it applies to corporate profits.

**5** Distinguish between ***paid-in capital*** and ***retained earnings*** of a corporation. Why is such a distinction useful?

**6** If the Retained Earnings account has a debit balance, how is it presented in the balance sheet and what is it called?

**7** Describe the usual nature of the following features as they apply to a share of preferred stock: **(a)** cumulative, **(b)** convertible, and **(c)** callable.

**8** Why is noncumulative preferred stock considered a very unattractive form of investment?

**9** When stock is issued by a corporation in exchange for assets other than cash, accountants face the problem of determining the dollar amount at which to record the transaction. Discuss the factors they should consider and explain their significance.

**10** State the classification (asset, liability, stockholders' equity, revenue, or expense) of each of the following accounts:

**a** Subscriptions receivable
**b** Organization costs
**c** Preferred stock
**d** Retained earnings
**e** Capital stock subscribed
**f** Paid-in capital in excess of par value
**g** Discount on preferred stock
**h** Income taxes payable

**11** What does ***book value per share*** of common stock represent? Does it represent the amount common stockholders would receive in the event that the corporation were liquidated? Explain briefly.

**12** How is book value per share of common stock computed when a company has both preferred and common stock outstanding?

**13** What would be the effect, if any, on book value per share of common stock as a result of each of the following independent events: **(a)** a corporation obtains a bank loan; **(b)** a dividend is declared (to be paid in the next accounting period); and **(c)** a corporation issues additional shares of common stock at a price above book value.

**14** A professional baseball team received as a gift from the city the land upon which to build a stadium. What effect, if any, will the receipt of this gift have upon the baseball team's balance sheet and income statement? Explain.

**15** Explain the following terms:

**a** Stock transfer agent
**b** Stockholders' ledger
**c** Underwriter
**d** Minutes book
**e** Stock registrar

## EXERCISES

*Ex. 16-1* Showboat Corporation has only one issue of capital stock, consisting of 40,000 outstanding shares. The net income in the first year of operations was $88,000. No dividends were paid in the first year. On January 15 of the second year, a dividend of 80 cents per share was declared by the board of directors payable February 15.

**Instructions**

a Prepare the journal entry at December 31 of Year 1 to close the Income Summary account.

b Prepare the journal entries for declaration of the dividend on January 15 and payment of the dividend on February 15.

*Ex. 16-2* In Year 1, Plastic Pipe Corporation earned net income of $186,000 and paid dividends of $1.50 per share on its 80,000 outstanding shares of capital stock. In Year 2, the corporation incurred a net loss of $90,000 and paid no dividends.

**Instructions**

a Prepare the journal entry to close the Income Summary account at December 31, Year 2.

b Compute the amount of retained earnings or deficit which will appear in the company's balance sheet at December 31, Year 2.

*Ex. 16-3* Heritage Corporation was organized on July 1, 19___. The corporation was authorized to issue 10,000 shares of $100 par value, 8% cumulative preferred stock, and 200,000 shares of no-par common stock with a stated value of $5 per share.

All the preferred stock was issued at par and 120,000 shares of the common stock were sold for $24 per share. Prepare the stockholders' equity section immediately after the issuance of the securities but prior to any operation of company.

*Ex. 16-4* Wolfe Company has outstanding two classes of $100 par value stock: 5,000 shares of 7% cumulative preferred and 25,000 shares of common. The company had a $50,000 deficit at the beginning of the current year, and preferred dividends had not been paid for two years. During the current year, the company earned $250,000. What will be the balance in retained earnings at the end of the current year, if the company pays a dividend of $1.10 per share on the common stock?

*Ex. 16-5* A portion of the stockholders' equity section from the balance sheet of Palermo Corporation appears below:

| | |
|---|---|
| ***Stockholders' equity:*** | |
| ***Preferred stock, 6% cumulative, $50 par, 40,000 shares authorized and issued*** | ***$2,000,000*** |
| ***Preferred stock, 9% noncumulative, $100 par, 8,000 shares authorized and issued*** | ***800,000*** |
| ***Common stock, $5 par, 400,000 shares authorized and issued*** | ***2,000,000*** |
| ***Total paid-in capital*** | ***$4,800,000*** |

**Instructions** Assume that all the stock was issued on January 1, 19___, and that no dividends were paid during the first two years of operations. During the third year, Palermo Corporation paid total cash dividends of $532,000.

a Compute the amount of cash dividends paid during the third year to each of the three classes of stock.

b Compute the dividends paid ***per share*** during the third year for each of the three classes of stock.

*Ex. 16-6* Presented below is the information necessary to compute the net assets (stockholders' equity) and book value per share of common stock for Ringside Corporation:

| | |
|---|---|
| ***9% cumulative preferred stock, $100 par (callable at $110)*** | ***$200,000*** |
| ***Common stock, $5 par, authorized 100,000 shares, issued 60,000 shares*** | ***300,000*** |
| ***Paid-in capital in excess of par*** | ***452,800*** |
| ***Deficit*** | ***126,800*** |
| ***Dividends in arrears on preferred stock, 2 full years*** | ***18,000*** |

**Instructions**

**a** Compute the amount of net assets (stockholders' equity).
**b** Compute the book value per share of common stock.

## PROBLEMS

### Group A

*16A-1* Presented below are two separate cases requiring preparation of the stockholders' equity section of a corporate balance sheet.

(1) Early in Year 3 Marine Corporation was formed with authorization to issue 320,000 shares of $5 par value common. The stock was issued at par, and the corporation reported a net loss of $96,000 for Year 3 and a net loss of $224,000 in Year 4. In Year 5 net income was $844,000.

(2) Pacific Corporation was organized early in Year 1 and authorized to issue 200,000 shares of $10 par value common and 32,000 shares of cumulative preferred stock. All the preferred and 192,000 shares of common were issued at par. The preferred stock was callable at 105% of its $100 par value and was entitled to dividends of 6% before any dividends were paid to common. During the first five years of its existence, the corporation earned a total of $2,304,000 and paid dividends of 50 cents per share each year on the common stock.

**Instructions** For each of the independent situations described, prepare in good form the stockholders' equity section of the balance sheet as of December 31, Year 5. Include a supporting schedule for each case showing your determination of the balance of retained earnings that should appear in the balance sheet.

*16A-2* The outstanding stock of Carni-Games, Inc., consists of 10,000 shares of common stock, which was issued at par value of $2 per share. On January 1, Year 5, the book value of the stock was $48 per share. During Year 5, the following transactions affecting the book value per share were completed by the corporation:

**Jan. 14** An additional 2,000 shares of stock were issued to P. T. Riley at a price of $42 per share.

**June 20** The board of directors declared a cash dividend of $1.80 per share.

**Aug. 19** An additional 3,000 shares of stock were issued to various investors at a price of $49.20 per share.

**Dec. 31** A net income of $81,000 was reported for Year 5.

**Instructions** Compute the successive book values per share of Carni-Games, Inc., common stock after each transaction. Organize your solution in three columns, showing after each transaction the amount of stockholders' equity, the number of shares of capital stock outstanding, and the book value per share.

*16A-3* The following information provides the basis for preparing journal entries and the stockholders' equity section of a corporate balance sheet.

Early in Year 10, Roger Gordon and several friends organized a corporation called Racquetball Courts, Inc. The corporation was authorized to issue 50,000 shares of $100 par value, $8 cumulative preferred stock and 400,000 shares of $1 par value common stock. The following transactions (among others) occurred during Year 10:

**Jan. 6** Issued for cash 25,000 shares of common stock at $12 per share. The shares were issued to Gordon and 14 other investors.

**Jan. 7** Issued an additional 500 shares of common stock to Gordon in exchange for his services in organizing the corporation. The stockholders agreed that these services were worth $6,000.

**Jan. 12** Issued 2,500 shares of preferred stock for cash of $250,000.

**June 4** Acquired land as a building site in exchange for 15,000 shares of common stock. In view of the appraised value of the land and the progress of the company, the directors of Racquetball Courts, Inc., agreed that the common stock was to be valued for purposes of this transaction at $15 per share.

**Nov. 15** The first annual dividend of $8 per share was declared on the preferred stock to be paid December 20 of Year 10.

**Dec. 20** Paid the cash dividend declared on November 15.

**Dec. 31** After the revenue and expenses (except income taxes) were closed into the Income Summary account, that account showed a before-tax profit of $114,000. Income taxes were determined to be $42,000.

**Instructions**

**a** Prepare journal entries for Year 10 in general journal form to record the above transactions. Include entries at December 31 to (1) record the income tax liability; (2) close the Income Tax Expense account into the Income Summary account; and (3) close the Income Summary account.

**b** Prepare the stockholders' equity section of the balance sheet at December 31, Year 10.

***16A-4*** The following case requires the preparation of the stockholders' equity section of a balance sheet at the end of Year 6.

North County Construction Co. was organized on January 31, Year 5, and was authorized to issue 320,000 shares of $10 par value common stock and 40,000 shares of $2 cumulative preferred stock, par value $40 per share. The corporation sold 95,000 shares of common stock for cash at $12 per share.

During Year 5, the first year of operation, the company incurred a loss of $100,000. At the beginning of Year 6, the company needed cash. In order to sell its preferred stock at par, the company added a convertible feature to the preferred stock by making it convertible into four shares of common stock. With this feature added, 12,000 shares of preferred stock were sold at par early in Year 6.

During Year 6, the company earned $380,000. The market price of the common stock rose, and holders of 10,000 shares of preferred stock converted these preferred shares, receiving in exchange 40,000 shares of common stock. A semiannual dividend of $1 per share had been declared and paid on all 12,000 shares of preferred stock prior to the conversion of any shares.

Late in Year 6, the company paid the second semiannual dividend of $1 on the preferred stock still outstanding and also declared a dividend of $1.50 per share on the common stock. All the 135,000 shares of common stock outstanding on December 31, Year 6, received the $1.50 dividend.

**Instructions** Prepare in good form the stockholders' equity section of the balance sheet at December 31, Year 6. Show in a separate supporting schedule how you arrived at the balance of retained earnings at that date.

***16A-5*** For several years, Linda Green has operated a successful business organized as a single proprietorship. In order to raise the capital to operate on a larger scale, she decided to organize a new corporation to continue in the same line of business. In January of Year 1, Green organized Far West Corporation, which was authorized to issue capital stock as follows:

50,000 shares of 8% cumulative preferred stock with a $50 par value per share
250,000 shares of $1 par value common stock

During January Far West Corporation completed the following transactions:

**Jan. 10** Issued 20,000 shares of common stock to various investors for cash at $11 per share.

**Jan. 10** Issued 40,000 shares of common stock to Green in exchange for assets with a current market value as follows:

| | |
|---|---|
| *Inventory* | *$ 90,000* |
| *Equipment* | *50,000* |
| *Building* | *160,000* |
| *Land* | *140,000* |

**Jan. 15** Received an invoice from an attorney for $7,000 for services relating to the formation of Far West Corporation. The invoice will be paid in 30 days.

**Jan. 17** Received subscriptions for 10,000 shares of preferred stock at $50 per share; 1,000 of the shares were subscribed by Green and 9,000 were subscribed by other investors.

**Jan. 31** Collected from Green the full amount of her subscription to 1,000 shares of preferred stock and issued a stock certificate for these shares. (No collection has yet been made from the subscribers to the other 9,000 shares of preferred stock.)

The corporation will begin operations in February; no revenue was earned and no expenses were incurred during January. No depreciation of plant assets and no amortization of organization cost will be recognized until February when operations get under way.

**Instructions**

**a** Prepare journal entries to record the transactions for January in the accounting records of Far West Corporation.

**b** Prepare a classified balance sheet for the corporation at January 31, Year 1.

*16A-6* The year-end balance sheet of Jamestown Corporation includes the following stockholders' equity section (with certain details omitted):

| | |
|---|---|
| ***Stockholders' equity:*** | |
| *$7.50 cumulative preferred stock, $100 par value, callable at $110, authorized 30,000 shares* | *$ 1,800,000* |
| *Common stock, $6 par value, authorized 500,000 shares* | *2,520,000* |
| *Paid-in capital in excess of par: common* | *5,250,000* |
| *Donated capital* | *500,000* |
| *Retained earnings* | *6,400,000* |
| *Total stockholders' equity* | *$16,470,000* |

**Instructions** On the basis of this information, answer the following questions and show any necessary supporting computations:

**a** How many shares of preferred stock are outstanding?

**b** What is the total dollar amount of the annual dividend requirement on preferred stock?

**c** How many shares of common stock are outstanding?

**d** What was the average issuance price of a share of common stock?

**e** What is the current book value per share of common stock?

**f** What is the total legal capital of the corporation?

**g** What is the total paid-in (or contributed) capital?

**h** Total dividends of $1,059,000 were declared on the preferred and common stock during the year, and the balance of retained earnings at the beginning of the year was $5,184,000. What was the amount of net income for the year?

*16A-7* Presented below are two independent cases requiring the preparation of the stockholders' equity section of a corporate balance sheet.

**Case A** In Year 1, Allan Jones organized SunRay Corporation to manufacture solar panels. The corporation was authorized to issue 100,000 shares of $10 par value common stock and 5,000 shares of 9% cumulative, $100 par value, preferred stock. All the preferred shares were issued at par and 30,000 shares of common stock were issued at $25 per share. During the first three years of its existence, SunRay Corporation earned a total of $346,000 and paid yearly dividends of $1.60 per share on the common stock, in addition to the regular dividends on the preferred stock. During Year 4, however, the corporation incurred a loss of $227,000 and paid no dividends.

**Case B** Nancy Monroe organized Monroe Furniture, Inc., in January, Year 1. The corporation issued at $18 per share one-half of its 100,000 authorized shares of $5 par common stock. On January 1, Year 2, the company sold at par the entire 10,000 authorized shares of $50 par value, 8% cumulative preferred stock. On January 1, Year 3, the company again needed money and issued 5,000 shares of an authorized 20,000 shares of $9, no-par, cumulative preferred stock for a total of $518,000. The company suffered losses and paid no dividends during Years 1 and 2, reporting a deficit of $300,000 at the end of Year 2. During Years 3 and 4 combined, the company earned a total of $1,100,000. Dividends of $1.50 per share were paid on common stock in Year 3 and $3.00 per share in Year 4.

**Instructions** For each of the independent cases described above, prepare in good form the stockholders' equity section of the balance sheet at December 31, Year 4. Include a supporting schedule for each case showing your determination of the balance of retained earnings or deficit at that date.

## Group B

*16B-1* The two cases described below are independent of each other. Each case provides the information necessary to prepare the stockholders' equity section of a corporate balance sheet.

**Case A** Crown Company was organized early in Year 3 with authorization to issue 80,000 shares of $5 par value common stock. All the shares were issued at par. The operations of the company resulted in a net loss of $20,000 for Year 3 and a net loss of $52,000 in Year 4. In Year 5 net income was $121,000. No dividends were declared during the three-year period.

**Case B** Royal Corporation was formed early in Year 1. Authorization was obtained to issue 100,000 shares of $10 par value common stock and 4,000 shares of $100 par value cumulative preferred stock. All the preferred and 80,000 shares of common were issued at par. The preferred stock was callable at $105 per share and was entitled to dividends of 6% before any dividends were paid to common. During the first five years of existence, the corporation earned a total of $560,000 and paid dividends of 20 cents per share each year on common stock.

**Instructions** For each of the situations described above, prepare in good form the stockholders' equity section of the balance sheet as of December 31, Year 5. Include a supporting schedule for each case showing your determination of the balance of retained earnings that should appear in the balance sheet.

*16B-2* Frost Corporation builds an excellent product, but the company is poorly managed. Maria Soto wants to acquire enough of the company's voting stock to elect a new board of directors which will hire new management. Soto has entered into contracts with several of Frost Corporation's stockholders to buy their common stock at a price equal to its book value at the end of Year 5. Because Frost Corporation has issued both preferred and common stock, Soto is not certain how the book value per share of common stock should be computed. She has come to you for assistance and has provided you with the following information.

At the end of Year 5, the total stockholders' equity of Frost Corporation is $1,230,000. The company was organized early in Year 1 and immediately issued 5,000 shares of 8%, $100 par, preferred stock and 30,000 shares of $5 par common stock. Except as explained below, there have been no changes in the number of shares outstanding.

**Instructions** Compute for Soto the book value per share of common stock at the end of Year 5 under each of the following independent assumptions:

**a** The preferred stock was redeemed by Frost Corporation in Year 4 and only the common stock remains outstanding.

**b** All shares of preferred and common stock are still outstanding. The preferred stock is callable at $105 and there are no dividends in arrears.

**c** The preferred stock is cumulative and callable at $108. The company paid the full preferred dividend in Years 1 and 2, but has paid no dividends in Years 3, 4, or 5.

**d** The preferred stock was convertible into common stock at a rate of four shares of common stock for each share of preferred. By the end of Year 5, all 5,000 shares of preferred stock had been converted into common stock.

***16B-3*** Jack Daniels organized Black Iron Corporation early in Year 1. On January 9, the corporation issued to Daniels and other investors 50,000 of its 200,000 authorized shares of $5 par value common stock at a price of $14 per share.

After the revenue and expense accounts (except income tax expense) were closed into the Income Summary account at the end of Year 1, that account showed a before-tax profit of $124,000. Income taxes for Year 1 were determined to be $44,000. No dividends were paid during Year 1.

On June 15, Year 2, the board of directors declared a cash dividend of 60 cents per share, payable July 31.

**Instructions**

**a** Prepare the journal entries for Year 1, to (1) record the issuance of the common stock, (2) record the income tax liability at December 31, (3) close the Income Tax Expense account into the Income Summary account, and (4) close the Income Summary account.

**b** Prepare the journal entries in Year 2 for the declaration of the dividend on June 15 and payment of the dividend on July 31.

**c** Assuming the operations for Year 2 resulted in a $19,700 net loss, prepare the journal entry to close the Income Summary account at December 31, Year 2.

**d** Prepare the stockholders' equity section of the balance sheet at December 31, Year 2. Include a supporting schedule showing your determination of retained earnings at that date.

***16B-4*** Cedar Products, Inc., was authorized to issue 500,000 shares of $5 par value common stock and 20,000 shares of $6 convertible and cumulative, no-par value, preferred stock. Each share of preferred stock is convertible, at the option of the shareholder, into four shares of common stock. All the preferred stock was issued at $103 per share, and 300,000 shares of common stock were issued at $15 per share. The balance in Retained Earnings at January 1, Year 10, is $670,000, and there are no dividends in arrears.

**Instructions**

**a** Prepare the stockholders' equity section of the balance sheet at January 1, Year 10.

**b** Assume that on January 1, Year 10, all the preferred stock is converted into shares of common stock. Prepare a journal entry to record the conversion.
**c** Prepare a revised stockholders' equity section of the balance sheet at January 1, Year 10, after the conversion of the preferred stock.

*16B-5* The following independent cases involve the issuance of capital stock in exchange for assets other than cash.

(1) Douglas Corporation, a successful, family-owned company, is in the process of acquiring a tract of land suitable for the construction of a factory. The Douglas Corporation has agreed to offer 52,000 shares of common stock in exchange for the land, which has an agreed fair market value of $1,300,000, based on two independent appraisals. Douglas Corporation stock is not traded on any stock exchange.

**Instructions** Give the journal entry that should be made to record this transaction under each of the following assumptions:
**a** The stock has a $2 par value.
**b** The stock has a $30 par value. (Disregard possible violation of state laws.)
**c** The stock is no par, with a stated value of $5.

(2) Hale Corporation, a well-established company, issued 5,200 shares of its $15 par value common stock in exchange for certain patents. The patents were entered in the accounts at $78,000. At this time, Hale common stock was quoted on the over-the-counter market at "25 bid and 27 asked"; that is, sellers were offering a given quantity of stock at $27 per share, and buyers were offering to buy certain quantities at $25 per share.

**Instructions** Comment on the company's treatment of this transaction. Write a brief statement explaining whether you agree or disagree, and why. What is the essential difference between the evidence available to the accountant as a basis for the record of Douglas Corporation and the evidence available for Hale Corporation?

*16B-6* Shown below is the stockholders' equity section of the balance sheet of Reno Corporation at the end of the current year.

***RENO CORPORATION***
***Stockholders' Equity***
***December 31, Current Year***

| | | |
|---|---|---|
| ***$2.75 preferred stock, $50 par value, authorized 40,000 shares:*** | | |
| ***Issued*** | ***$720,000*** | |
| ***Subscribed*** | ***360,000*** | ***$1,080,000*** |
| ***Common stock, no par, $5 stated value, authorized 320,000 shares:*** | | |
| ***Issued*** | ***$680,000*** | |
| ***Subscribed*** | ***140,000*** | ***820,000*** |
| ***Paid-in capital in excess of par or stated value:*** | | |
| ***On preferred*** | ***$108,000*** | |
| ***On common*** | ***164,000*** | ***272,000*** |
| ***Retained earnings (deficit)*** | | ***(300,000)*** |
| ***Total stockholders' equity*** | | ***$1,872,000*** |

Among the assets of the corporation appear the following items: Subscriptions Receivable: Preferred, $180,000; Subscriptions Receivable: Common, $91,000.

**Instructions** On the basis of this information, write a brief answer to the following questions, showing any necessary supporting computations.

**a** How many shares of preferred and common have been issued?
**b** How many shares of preferred and common have been subscribed?
**c** What was the average price per share received by the corporation on its preferred stock, including preferred stock subscribed?
**d** What was the average price per share received by the corporation on its common stock, including common stock subscribed?
**e** What is the average amount per share that subscribers of preferred stock have yet to pay on their subscriptions?
**f** What is the total paid-in capital of the Reno Corporation?
**g** What is the total legal or stated value of all capital stock of Reno Corporation?
**h** What is the average amount per share that common stock subscribers have already paid on their subscriptions? (Assume common subscribed at $6.)

*16B-7* The two independent cases presented below require preparation of the stockholders' equity section of a corporate balance sheet.

**Case A** In Year 1, Barbara Sterns organized Flowerland, Inc., a chain of retail nurseries. The corporation was authorized to issue 100,000 shares of $2 par value common stock and 10,000 shares of $5 cumulative, no-par value, preferred stock. All the preferred stock was issued for a total of $511,000, and 35,000 shares of common stock were issued at $20 per share. During the first three years of its existence, Flowerland, Inc., earned a total of $347,500 and paid yearly dividends of 90 cents per share on the common stock, in addition to the regular dividends on the preferred stock. During Year 4, however, the corporation incurred a loss of $204,000 and paid no dividends.

**Case B** Tom Martinez organized Urban Transport Company in January, Year 1. The corporation issued at $15 per share one-half of its 100,000 authorized shares of $5 par common stock. On January 1, Year 2, the corporation sold at par the entire 5,000 authorized shares of 8%, $100 par value, cumulative preferred stock. On January 1, Year 3, the company again needed money and issued 5,000 shares of an authorized 10,000 shares of $9, no-par, cumulative preferred stock for a total of $494,000. The company suffered losses in Years 1 and 2, reporting a deficit of $270,000 at the end of Year 2. During Years 3 and 4 combined, the company earned a total of $950,000. Dividends of $1 per share were paid on common stock in Year 3 and $3.50 per share in Year 4.

**Instructions** For each of the independent cases described, prepare in good form the stockholders' equity section of the balance sheet at December 31, Year 4. Include a supporting schedule for each case showing your determination of the balance of retained earnings at that date.

## BUSINESS DECISION PROBLEM 16

City Electric and Metropolitan Power are two utility companies with very stable earnings. City Electric consistently has a net income of approximately $96 million per year, and Metropolitan Power's net income consistently approximates $84 million per year. City Electric has 5,400,000 shares of 6% preferred stock, $50 par value, and 13,300,000 shares of $50 par value common stock outstanding. Metropolitan Power has 2,400,000 shares of 6% preferred stock, $100 par value, and 8,700,000 shares of $10 par value common stock outstanding. Assume that both companies distribute all net income as dividends every year, and will continue to do so. Neither company plans to issue additional shares of capital stock.

**Instructions**

**a** Compute the annual dividend which would be paid on the common stock of each company, assuming that City Electric has a net income of $96 million and Metropolitan Power has a net income of $84 million.

**b** Which company's common stock would you expect to have the higher ***market price per share?*** Support your answer with information provided in the problem.

# 17

# CORPORATIONS: OPERATIONS, EARNINGS PER SHARE, AND DIVIDENDS

The most important aspect of corporate financial reporting, in the view of most stockholders, is the determination of periodic net income. Both the market price of common stock and the amount of cash dividends per share depend to a considerable extent on the current level of earnings (net income). Even more important than the absolute amount of net income is the ***trend*** of earnings over time. Is net income increasing or decreasing from one year to the next? The common stocks of those companies which regularly achieve higher earnings year after year become the favorite securities of the investment community. Such stature helps greatly in raising new capital, in attracting and retaining highly competent management, and in many other ways.

## Public misconceptions of the rate of corporate earnings

Numerous public opinion surveys indicate that most people mistakenly believe that corporate earnings generally amount to somewhere between 20 and 50% of sales. College and university students should be better informed, but the authors have found, from questioning numerous classes at the beginning of the first course in accounting, that college students in guessing at the average rate of corporate earnings usually suggest far higher rates than actually exist. If you will look at the published annual reports of leading corporations, you will find that net income usually falls somewhere between 2 and 10% of sales. Remember that these financial statements have been audited by independent CPA firms, and also reviewed by the SEC. For all manufacturing companies a representative rate of earnings in recent years has been around 4 to 5%. Of course, there are exceptions. In the airline industry, for example, American Airlines, TWA, and Pan American each operated at a net loss for several years during the last decade. This question of the rate of corporate earnings will be considered more fully in Chapter 22.

### Developing predictive information

An income statement tells us a great deal about the performance of a company over the past year. For example, study of the income statement makes clear the rate of gross profit on sales, the net income for the year, the percentage of profit per dollar of sales, and the net income earned on each share of common stock. Can we expect the income statement for ***next year*** to indicate about the same level of performance? If the transactions summarized in the income statement for the year just completed were of a normal recurring nature, such as selling merchandise, paying employees, and incurring other normal expenses, we can reasonably assume that the operating results were typical and that somewhat similar results can be expected in the following year. However, in any business, unusual and nonrecurring events may occur which cause the current year's net income to be quite different from the income we should expect the company to earn in the future. For example, the company may have sustained large losses in the current year from an earthquake, a strike, or some other event which is not likely to recur in the near future.

Ideally, the results of unusual and nonrecurring transactions should be shown in a separate section of the income statement ***after*** the income or loss from normal business activities has been determined. Income from ***normal and recurring*** activities presumably should be a more useful figure for predicting future earnings than is a net income figure which includes the results of nonrecurring events. The problem in creating such an income statement, however, is in determining which events are so unlikely to recur that they should be excluded from the results of "normal" operations.

The question of how unusual an event should be to require separate presentation has long been debated by accountants and other interested parties. Current accounting practice recognizes four categories of unusual transactions and accords each category a different treatment in the income statement. These categories are (1) the results of discontinued operations, (2) extraordinary items, (3) other nonoperating gains and losses, and (4) the cumulative effect of an accounting change. The criteria which define these categories and the related income statement presentation are still being debated and may well change in future years.

### Discontinued operations

Assume that a corporation sells a major segment of its operations to another company late in the current year. A problem will arise in making the income statements comparable for this year and next year because the operations will be of different scope and magnitude after disposal of a segment of the business.

A ***segment of a business*** means "a component of a company whose activities represent a major line of business or class of customer."[1] The assets and operating results of a segment of a business should be clearly identifiable from the other assets and results of operations of the company. Some examples of segments of a business are:

1 An electronics division of a highly diversified manufacturing company
2 A professional sports team owned by a newspaper publishing company
3 A wholesale milk distributorship owned by a retail food chain

The income statement is more useful if the results of the ***continuing operations*** of a business entity are reported separately from the discontinued operations. The operating results of a discontinued segment of a business (including any gain or loss on the disposal of the segment) are listed separately in the income statement ***after*** determining the ***income from continuing operations.*** The purpose of such separate disclosure is to enable users of financial statements to make better predictive judgments as to the future earnings performance of the company.

For example, assume that Tanner Corporation reported a net income of $10 million for Year 10, including $4 million net income earned on sales of $100 million by an exporting division which was sold near the end of the year. Would Tanner Corporation be able to earn $10 million in Year 11 without the exporting business? Before answering this question, let us make an alternative assumption, that is, that the exporting division lost $8 million (after income taxes) in Year 10 instead of earning $4 million. What income might Tanner Corporation be expected to earn in Year 11 without the drain on earnings from the exporting business? The following partial income statement would be helpful to investors considering these two questions:

***TANNER CORPORATION***
***Partial Income Statement***
***For Year 10***

*Income or loss from discontinued operations in the income statement*

| | Assuming Exporting Division Earned $4 Million | Assuming Exporting Division Lost $8 Million |
|---|---|---|
| Income from continuing operations | $ 6,000,000 | $18,000,000 |
| Income (or loss) from discontinued operations* | 4,000,000 | (8,000,000) |
| Net income | $10,000,000 | $10,000,000 |

*The revenue in Year 10 from the discontinued segment was $100 million.

The ***income from continuing operations*** is a logical starting point for us to use in forecasting the probable earnings of Tanner Corporation for Year 11. Of

[1] *APB Opinion No. 30,* "Reporting the Results of Operations—Reporting the Effects of Disposal of a Segment of a Business, and Extraordinary, Unusual and Infrequently Occurring Events and Transactions," AICPA (New York: 1973).

course, other factors (such as price changes and increase in sales volume) may cause the income from continuing operations in Year 11 to differ from our forecast.

The ***revenue*** and ***expenses*** shown in an income statement for the year in which a segment of a business is eliminated should consist only of the ***revenue and expenses from continuing operations.*** The net income or loss from discontinued operations is reported separately in the income statement, and the revenue or total sales from the discontinued segment is disclosed in the notes to the financial statements. Any gain or loss on the disposal of a segment should be reported with the results of the discontinued operations.

**Allocation of income taxes between continuing and discontinued operations** When an income statement includes sections for both continuing and discontinued operations, the company's income tax expense should be ***allocated*** between these sections. Only the income tax expense applicable to continuing operations should be deducted as an expense in arriving at income from continuing operations. Remember that ***income from continuing operations*** is a net amount, computed by deducting all costs and expenses (including income taxes) from revenue. Income taxes relating to the discontinued operations should be considered, along with other expenses of the discontinued segment, in computing income (or loss) from discontinued operations.

To illustrate, assume that Alpha Corporation earns income ***before*** income taxes of $300,000 from continuing operations and $100,000 from operations discontinued during the year. If all income is taxable at a rate of 40%, the company's total income tax expense is 40% of $400,000, or $160,000. However, only $120,000 of this amount applies to continuing operations (computed as $300,000 × 40%); the remaining $40,000 of income tax expense stems from the discontinued operations. The following partial income statement illustrates the allocation of Alpha's total income tax expense.

***ALPHA CORPORATION***
***Partial Income Statement***
***For Year 6***

| | |
|---|---|
| *Income before taxes from continuing operations* | *$300,000* |
| *Income tax expense (total taxes are $160,000, of which $40,000 are attributable to discontinued operations)* | *120,000* |
| *Income from continuing operations* | *$180,000* |
| *Income from discontinued operations, net of taxes ($100,000 − $40,000)* | *60,000* |
| *Net income* | *$240,000* |

As a separate case, assume that Alpha's discontinued operations had incurred a before-tax ***loss*** of $50,000. Total before-tax income would be $250,000 ($300,000 − $50,000) and total income tax expense would be $100,000. The amount of income taxes applicable to the $300,000 before-tax income from continuing operations is still $120,000; however, the before-tax loss from discontinued operations creates a $20,000 ***tax savings*** (computed as $50,000 loss × 40%). This tax savings should be subtracted from the before-tax loss to show the loss from discontinued operations on an ***after-tax basis.*** The income statement presentation follows:

***ALPHA CORPORATION***
***Partial Income Statement***
***For Year 6***

| | |
|---|---|
| *Income before taxes from continuing operations* | *$300,000* |
| *Income tax expense (total taxes are $100,000 as a result of a $20,000 tax savings attributable to discontinued operations)* | *120,000* |
| *Income from continuing operations* | *$180,000* |
| *Loss from discontinued operations, net of tax savings ($50,000 − $20,000)* | *30,000* |
| *Net income* | *$150,000* |

Note that in both income statements for Alpha Corporation income from continuing operations is $180,000. ***The amount of income reported from continuing operations is not affected by the operating results of the discontinued operations.*** Thus, the subtotal Income from Continuing Operations should be a useful figure for evaluating the earning power of those segments of the company which are remaining in operation.

## Extraordinary items

Some gains and losses are so unusual in nature that it may be useful to include in the income statement a subtotal showing what net income ***would have been*** if these extraordinary events had not occurred. Such events are called ***extraordinary items,*** and the subtotal developed in the income statement is termed ***Income before Extraordinary Items.*** If an extraordinary item is segregated in the income statement, that is, shown separately from the results of normal recurring operations of the business, it will be easier for us to use the income statement as a meaure of "normal" performance.

An event or transaction must be ***material in dollar amount*** to warrant separate disclosure as an extraordinary item. For many years there was much argument over what kinds of events should be considered extraordinary. The definition was narrowed considerably by ***APB Opinion No. 30.*** Extraordinary items are now defined as material transactions and events that are both ***unusual in nature and occur infrequently*** in the operating environment of the business.

In order to be considered unusual in nature, the underlying event or transaction should be abnormal and clearly unrelated to the ordinary and typical activities of the entity. The scope of operations, lines of business, operating policies, and the environment in which an entity operates should be considered in applying this criterion. The environment of a business includes such factors as the characteristics of the industry, the geographic location of activities, and the degree of government regulation.

"Occurring infrequently," according to ***APB Opinion 30,*** means that the event or transaction is not reasonably expected to take place again in the foreseeable future. Past experience of the entity is generally a helpful guide in determining the frequency of an event or transaction.

To illustrate these criteria, assume that a manufacturing company suffers severe flood damage when a dam breaks at a nearby reservoir. The flood loss would qualify for presentation in the income statement as an extraordinary item, because it is highly unusual and is not likely to recur. On the other hand, consider the case of a farming enterprise located along river bottomland subject to severe flooding every few years. A large loss from a flood would not qualify as an extraordinary item in the income statement of this agricultural business, because it is not unusual and infrequent in the environment in which this particular business operates. Thus only those events which are both ***unusual and infrequent*** lead to extraordinary gains and losses. These qualitative standards are difficult to apply in practice, and differences of opinion still exist as to what is and what is not an extraordinary item. Listed below are some examples of gains or losses which are viewed as extraordinary and some which are not.

| *Extraordinary Items* | *Not Extraordinary Items* |
|---|---|
| *1 Effects of major casualties such as earthquake (if rare in the area)* | *1 Write-down or write-off of receivables, inventories, or intangible assets* |
| *2 Expropriation of assets by foreign governments* | *2 Gains or losses on disposal of a segment of a business or from sale or abandonment of plant assets* |
| *3 Effects of a prohibition under a newly enacted law or regulation* | *3 Effects of labor strikes or shortages of raw materials* |
| | *4 Changes in estimates of accumulated depreciation, accrued expenses, and profits or losses on long-term construction contracts* |

Few extraordinary items currently appear in corporate income statements as a result of the rigorous criteria established in ***APB Opinion No. 30.*** The presentation of extraordinary items in the income statement is illustrated below:

**COASTAL CORPORATION**
***Income Statement***
***For the Year Ended December 31, 19__***

| | | |
|---|---|---|
| Net sales | | $10,000,000 |
| Cost of goods sold | | 6,000,000 |
| Gross profit on sales | | $ 4,000,000 |
| Operating expenses: | | |
| Selling | $1,100,000 | |
| General and administrative | 700,000 | 1,800,000 |
| Income from operations | | $ 2,200,000 |
| Loss from settlement of lawsuit | | 200,000 |
| Income before income taxes | | $ 2,000,000 |
| Deduct: Income taxes (actual taxes are $600,000 as a result of a $200,000 tax savings attributable to extraordinary loss) | | 800,000 |
| Income before extraordinary item | | $ 1,200,000 |
| Extraordinary item: Loss from earthquake, net of reduction in income taxes ($500,000 − $200,000 tax savings) | | 300,000 |
| Net income | | $ 900,000 |

In the income statement illustrated, the nonoperating loss of $200,000 resulting from the settlement of a lawsuit was disclosed separately in the income statement but was ***not*** listed as an extraordinary item. This loss was important enough to bring to the attention of readers of the financial statements, but lawsuits are not so unusual or infrequent as to be considered extraordinary items. Since this lawsuit settlement is included in the "normal operations" section of the income statement, the $200,000 figure is a before-tax loss and the related tax effects are included in the $800,000 income tax expense relating to normal operations.

The income or loss from a discontinued segment of the business (including any gain or loss on disposal of the segment) is ***not*** an extraordinary item. When discontinued operations and an extraordinary item appear in the same income statement, the income or loss from the discontinued operations is presented ***before*** the extraordinary item. Thus, the subtotal Income before Extraordinary Items ***includes*** the operating results of any segments of the business which have been discontinued during the year.

**Allocation of income taxes between regular operations and extraordinary items** Coastal Corporation's income before extraordinary items represents what net income would have been without the extraordinary loss. Therefore, we must separate the tax effect of the earthquake loss from the income tax expense relating to regular operations. The amount of the earthquake loss is shown ***net of the related tax effects.*** In the preceding illustration, we have assumed the before-tax earthquake loss to be $500,000 and the related tax savings $200,000. This tax savings is deducted from the before-tax loss to show the extraordinary item in the income statement on an after-tax basis.

## Other nonoperating gains and losses

Some transactions are not typical of normal operations but also do not meet the criteria for separate presentation as extraordinary items. Among such events are settlements of lawsuits and the gains or losses resulting from the sale of plant assets. Such items, if material, should be individually listed as items of revenue or expense, rather than being combined with other items in broad categories such as sales revenue or general and administrative expenses.

## Cumulative effect of an accounting change

As a general rule, the ***principle of consistency*** requires that the same accounting methods be applied from one year to the next. However, a change in accounting methods is permissible if (1) the new method can be justified as being ***preferable*** to the old method, and (2) the effects of the change are ***adequately disclosed*** in the financial statements. Examples of a change in accounting methods are a change in the method used to depreciate assets or in the method of inventory valuation.

A description of the change, identification of the assets involved, and the effect of the change upon the net income of the current year should be disclosed in a note accompanying the financial statements. For many accounting changes, the ***cumulative effect*** which use of the new method ***would have had*** upon the income reported in prior years also must be reported in the current income statement.

To illustrate the effect of an accounting change upon the income of prior years, assume that a corporation buys a building in Year 2 and computes depreciation expense by the double-declining-balance method in Years 2, 3, and 4. At the beginning of Year 5, management decides to change to the straight-line method of depreciation. Also assume that if the straight-line method had been used in Years 2, 3, and 4, the combined depreciation expense for those three years would have been $210,000 less and net income for the three-year period would have been $210,000 greater than was actually reported. This $210,000 is the ***cumulative effect of the accounting change*** on the income of prior years.

Current rules of the FASB require recognition of this cumulative effect on prior years' income in the income statement for the year in which the accounting change is made.[2] Since the cumulative effect is actually an adjustment to the income of prior years, rather than relating to the operations of the current year, it is shown separately in the income statement, as illustrated on page 631.

## Earnings per share (EPS)

Perhaps the most widely used of all accounting statistics is ***earnings per share*** of common stock. Everyone who buys or sells stock in a corporation needs to know the annual earnings per share. Stock market prices are quoted on a per-share basis. If you are considering investing in General Motors stock at a price of, say, $70 per share, you need to know the earnings per share and the annual dividend per share in order to decide whether this price is reasonable. In other words, how much earning power and how much dividend income would you be getting for each share you buy?

To compute earnings per share, the annual net income available to the common stockholders is divided by the average number of common shares outstanding. The concept of earnings per share applies ***only to common stock;*** preferred stock has no claim to earnings beyond the stipulated preferred stock dividends.

Many financial analysts express the relationship between earnings per share and market price per share as a ***price-earnings ratio*** (p/e ratio). This ratio is computed by dividing the market price per share of common stock by the annual earnings per share.

**Weighted-average number of shares outstanding** The simplest example of computing earnings per share is found when a company has issued only common stock and the number of shares outstanding has not changed during the year. In this situation, the net income for the year divided by the number of shares outstanding at year-end equals earnings per share.

[2] Certain other accounting changes are disclosed by revising the financial statements of prior years rather than by recognition of the cumulative effect of the change in the current year. For a complete discussion of various types of accounting changes, see *APB Opinion No. 20,* "Accounting Changes." AICPA (New York: 1972).

In many companies, however, the number of shares of stock outstanding is changed one or more times during the year. When additional shares are issued in exchange for assets during the year, the computation of earnings per share is based upon the ***weighted-average*** number of shares outstanding.[3]

The weighted-average number of shares for the year is determined by multiplying the number of shares outstanding by the fraction of the year that said number of shares outstanding remained unchanged. For example, assume that 100,000 shares of common stock were outstanding during the first nine months of Year 1 and 140,000 shares during the last three months. Assume also that the increase in shares outstanding resulted from the sale of 40,000 shares for cash. The weighted-average number of shares outstanding during Year 1 would be 110,000, determined as follows:

| | |
|---|---|
| *100,000 shares × $\frac{3}{4}$ of a year* | *75,000* |
| *140,000 shares × $\frac{1}{4}$ of a year* | *35,000* |
| *Weighted-average number of common shares outstanding* | *110,000* |

This procedure gives more meaningful earnings per share data than if the total number of shares outstanding at the end of the year were used in the calculations. By using the weighted-average number of shares, we recognize that the proceeds from the sale of the 40,000 shares were available to generate earnings only during the last three months of the year. The contribution to earnings made by 40,000 shares outstanding during one-fourth of the year is equivalent to that of 10,000 shares outstanding for a full year. In other words, the weighted-average number of shares outstanding consists of 100,000 shares outstanding during the entire year plus the 10,000 share full-year equivalent of the shares issued during the year.

### Primary and fully diluted earnings per share

The computation of earnings per share is easily done for companies with common stock only, that is, companies not having convertible preferred stock or other obligations capable of being converted into additional common shares. In companies with such simple capital structures there is no risk of conversion which would increase the number of common shares and ***dilute*** (reduce) earnings per share of common stock.

When preferred stock is outstanding, the preferred stockholders participate in net income to the extent of the preferred stock dividends. To determine the portion of earnings ***applicable to common stock,*** we must deduct from net income the amount of any preferred stock dividends. To illustrate, let us assume that a company with a net income of $100,000 for Year 1 has 5,000 shares of $2 preferred

---

[3]When the number of shares outstanding changes as a result of a stock split or a stock dividend (discussed later in this chapter), the computation of the weighted-average number of shares outstanding should be adjusted ***retroactively*** rather than weighted for the period the new shares were outstanding. Earnings per share data for prior years thus will be consistently stated in terms of the current capital structure.

stock and 40,000 shares of common stock outstanding throughout the year. Earnings per share of common stock would be computed as follows:

*Earnings per share when preferred stock is outstanding*

| | |
|---|---|
| *Net income* | *$100,000* |
| *Less: Dividend on preferred stock for current period, 5,000 × $2* | *10,000* |
| *Income available for common stock* | *$ 90,000* |
| *Weighted-average number of common shares outstanding* | *40,000* |
| *Earnings per share of common stock, $90,000 ÷ 40,000 shares* | *$2.25* |

Let us now assume that each of the 5,000 shares of preferred stock is ***convertible*** into two shares of common stock. Conversion of the preferred stock would increase the number of common shares outstanding and might dilute earnings per share. Any common stockholder interested in the trend of earnings per share will want to know what effect conversion of the preferred stock would have upon this statistic.

To inform investors of the potential dilution which might occur, two earnings per share figures are presented. In computing the first figure, called ***primary*** earnings per share, we ignore the potential dilution represented by the convertible preferred stock.[4] In computing the second figure, called ***fully diluted*** earnings per share, we show the effect that conversion of the preferred shares would have had on primary earnings per share in the current year.

Primary earnings per share are computed in the same manner illustrated in our preceding calculation. In computing fully diluted earnings per share, ***we assume that the preferred stock was converted into common stock at the beginning of the current year.***[5] Under this assumption, there would have been no preferred stock dividends; however, there would have been an additional 10,000 shares of common stock outstanding throughout the year. The computation of primary earnings per share and fully diluted earnings per share is shown below:

*Primary and fully diluted earnings per share*

| | *Primary* | *Fully Diluted* |
|---|---|---|
| *Net income* | *$100,000* | *$100,000* |
| *Less: Dividends on preferred stock, 5,000 × $2* | *10,000* | *-0-* |
| *Earnings available for common stock* | *$ 90,000* | *$100,000* |
| *Number of shares of common stock outstanding:* | | |
| *In computing primary earnings per share* | *40,000* | |
| *In computing fully diluted earnings per share, 40,000 + (5,000 × 2)* | | *50,000* |
| *Earnings per share of common stock* | *$2.25* | *$2.00* |

[4] If certain criteria are met, convertible securities qualify as ***common stock equivalents*** and enter into the computation of primary earnings per share. Common stock equivalents and other complex issues relating to earnings per share are discussed in *APB Opinion No. 15,* "Earnings per Share," AICPA (New York, 1969).

[5] If the preferred stock had been issued during the current year, we would assume that it was converted into common stock on the date it was issued.

It is important to remember that fully diluted earnings per share represent a ***hypothetical case.*** The preferred stock actually was not converted during the year. The presentation of fully diluted earnings per share merely warns common stockholders what ***could*** have happened. When the difference between primary and fully diluted earnings per share is significant, investors should recognize the ***risk*** that future earnings per share may be diluted by conversions of other securities into common stock.

## Presentation of earnings per share in the income statement

All publicly owned corporations are required to present earnings per share data in their income statements.[6] If an income statement includes subtotals for income from continuing operations, income before extraordinary items, or the cumulative effect of an accounting change, per-share figures are shown for these amounts as well as for net income. The presentation of earnings per share for a company reporting discontinued operations and having a complex capital structure is illustrated below:

| | |
|---|---|
| *Income from continuing operations* | *$4,800,000* |
| *Loss from discontinued operations, net of related tax savings* | *1,200,000* |
| *Net income* | *$3,600,000* |
| *Earnings per share of common stock:* | |
| *Primary:* | |
| *Earnings from continuing operations* | *$2.20* |
| *Loss from discontinued operations* | *0.60* |
| *Net earnings for the year* | *$1.60* |
| *Fully diluted:* | |
| *Earnings from continuing operations* | *$2.00* |
| *Loss from discontinued operations* | *0.50* |
| *Net earnings for the year* | *$1.50* |

Note that both income from continuing operations and net income are expressed on a per-share basis. In addition, each of these amounts is shown on both a primary and a fully diluted basis. (We have also shown the amount of the loss from discontinued operations on a per-share basis, but this is merely a reconciling amount and may be omitted in a formal income statement.)

To informed users of financial statements, each of these figures has a different significance. Earnings per share from continuing operations represents the results of continuing and ordinary business activity. Presumably, this figure is the most useful one for predicting future operating results. ***Net earnings*** per share,

---

[6] In 1978 the FASB exempted closely held corporations (those not publicly owned) from the requirement of computing and reporting earnings per share. *See FASB Statement No. 23,* "Suspension of the Reporting of Earnings per Share and Segment Information by Nonpublic Enterprises" (Stamford, Conn.: 1978).

on the other hand, shows the overall operating results of the current year, including any discontinued operations or extraordinary items. The fully diluted per-share figures indicate the extent to which primary earnings per share could be diluted by the conversion of other securities into common stock.

Unfortunately the term ***earnings per share*** often is used without qualification in referring to various types of per-share data. When using per-share information, it is important to know exactly which per-share statistic is being presented. For example, the price-earnings ratios (market price divided by earnings per share) for common stocks listed on major stock exchanges are reported daily in the *Wall Street Journal* and many other newspapers. Which earnings per share figures are used in computing these ratios? Generally, these price-earnings ratios are based upon ***net earnings*** per share. If a company reports an extraordinary gain or loss, however, the ratio is computed using the per-share earnings ***before the extraordinary item.*** When a company reports both primary and fully diluted earnings per share, the price-earnings ratio is based upon the primary figure.

## Income statement for a corporation illustrated

In order to highlight important changes and trends in operating results, most corporations present ***comparative*** income statements in their quarterly and annual reports to stockholders. In a comparative income statement, the operating results of the current year are shown together with those of the preceding year.

A comparative income statement which includes losses from discontinued operations and extraordinary losses is illustrated on page 631. Fully diluted earnings per share are not presented because the company has a simple capital structure which does not create a potential for dilution of earnings per common share.

## Cash dividends

The prospect of receiving cash dividends is a principal reason for investing in the stocks of corporations. An increase or decrease in the established rate of dividends will usually cause an immediate rise or fall in the market price of the company's stock. Stockholders are keenly interested in prospects for future dividends and as a group are strongly in favor of more generous dividend payments. The board of directors, on the other hand, is primarily concerned with the long-run growth and financial strength of the corporation; it may prefer to restrict dividends to a minimum in order to conserve cash for purchase of plant and equipment or for other needs of the company. Many of the so-called "growth companies" plow back into the business most of their earnings and pay only very small cash dividends.

The preceding discussion suggests three requirements for the payment of a cash dividend. These are:

1 **Retained earnings** Since dividends represent a distribution of earnings to stockholders, the theoretical maximum for dividends is the total undistrib-

*Income statement with loss from discontinued operations and extraordinary items*

**DIVERSIFIED INDUSTRIES, INC.**
**Comparative Income Statement**
**For Years Ended December 31**

| | Year 5 | Year 4 |
|---|---|---|
| Net sales | $81,853,000 | $77,167,000 |
| Cost of goods sold | 58,649,000 | 56,111,000 |
| Gross profit on sales | $23,204,000 | $21,056,000 |
| Expenses: | | |
| Selling, administrative, and general | $10,072,000 | $ 9,493,000 |
| Interest | 1,504,000 | 1,325,000 |
| Other expense, net of miscellaneous income | 66,000 | 101,000 |
| Total expenses | $11,642,000 | $10,919,000 |
| Income (before income taxes) from continuing operations | $11,562,000 | $10,137,000 |
| Federal and state income taxes | 5,658,000 | 4,905,000 |
| Income from continuing operations | $ 5,904,000 | $ 5,232,000 |
| Loss from discontinued operations, net of income tax benefit of $1,328,000 | -0- | (1,344,000) |
| Income before extraordinary items | $ 5,904,000 | $ 3,888,000 |
| Extraordinary item: expropriation loss, net of income tax benefit of $1,048,000 | -0- | (1,200,000) |
| Cumulative effect on prior years' income (to Dec. 31, Year 4) of changing to a different depreciation method | 240,000 | -0- |
| Net income | $ 6,144,000 | $ 2,688,000 |
| Earnings per share of common stock: | | |
| Earnings from continuing operations | $4.92 | $4.36 |
| Loss from discontinued operations | -0- | (1.12) |
| Earnings before extraordinary items | $4.92 | $3.24 |
| Extraordinary loss | -0- | (1.00) |
| Cumulative effect of accounting change | .20 | |
| Net earnings | $5.12 | $2.24 |

uted net income of the company, represented by the credit balance of the Retained Earnings account. As a practical matter, many corporations limit dividends to somewhere near 40% of annual net income, in the belief that a major portion of the net income must be retained in the business if the company is to grow and to keep pace with its competitors.

2 **An adequate cash position** The fact that the company reports large earnings does not mean that it has a large amount of cash on hand. Earnings may have been invested in new plant and equipment, or in paying off debts, or in acquiring a larger inventory. There is no necessary relationship between the balance in the Retained Earnings account and the balance in the Cash account. The traditional expression of "paying dividends out of retained earnings" is misleading. Cash dividends can be paid only "out of" cash.

3 **Dividend action by the board of directors** Even though the company's net income is substantial and its cash position seemingly satisfactory, dividends are not paid automatically. A formal action by the board of directors is necessary to declare a dividend.

### Regular and special dividends

Many corporations establish a regular quarterly or annual dividend rate on common stock and pay this same amount for a period of years regardless of the year-to-year changes in earnings. Such a policy gives a higher investment quality to a company's stock. A strong cash position is necessary if a company is to be prepared to make regular dividend payments in the face of irregular earnings.

If earnings increase but the increase is regarded as a temporary condition, the corporation may decide to pay a ***special dividend*** in addition to the ***regular dividend.*** The implication of a special dividend is that the company is making no commitments as to a permanent increase in the amount of dividends to be paid. Of course, even a regular dividend may be reduced or discontinued at any time, but well-financed companies which have long-established regular dividend rates are not likely to omit or reduce regular dividend payments except in extreme emergencies.

### Dividend dates

Four significant dates are involved in the distribution of a dividend. These dates are:

1 **Date of declaration** On the day on which the dividend is declared by the board of directors, a liability to make the payment comes into existence.
2 **Date of record** The date of record always follows the date of declaration, usually by a period of two or three weeks, and is always stated in the dividend declaration. In order to be eligible to receive the dividend, a person must be listed as the owner of the stock on the date of record.
3 **Ex-dividend date** The ex-dividend date is significant for investors in companies with stocks traded on the stock exchanges. To permit the compilation of the list of stockholders as of the record date, it is customary for the stock to go "ex-dividend" three business days before the date of record. A stock is said to be selling ex-dividend on the day that it loses the right to receive the latest declared dividend. A person who buys the stock before the ex-dividend date is entitled to receive the dividend; conversely, a stockholder who sells shares before the ex-dividend date does not receive the dividend.
4 **Date of payment** The declaration of a dividend always includes announcement of the date of payment as well as the date of record. Usually the date of payment comes from two to four weeks after the date of record.

The journal entries to record the declaration and payment of a cash dividend were illustrated in Chapter 16 but are repeated here with emphasis on the date of declaration and date of payment.

| | | | | |
|---|---|---|---|---|
| *Entries made on declaration date and . . .* | *June 1* | *Retained Earnings* | *100,000* | |
| | | *Dividends Payable* | | *100,000* |
| | | *To record declaration of a cash dividend of $1 per share on the 100,000 shares of common stock outstanding. Payable July 10 to stockholders of record on June 20.* | | |
| *. . . on payment date* | *July 10* | *Dividends Payable* | *100,000* | |
| | | *Cash* | | *100,000* |
| | | *To record payment of $1 per share dividend declared June 1 to stockholders of record on June 20.* | | |

As mentioned in Chapter 16, some companies record the declaration of a dividend by debiting a Dividends account instead of debiting Retained Earnings. In this case, a closing entry is required at the end of the year to transfer the debit balance of the Dividends account into the Retained Earnings account. Under either method, the balance of the Retained Earnings account ultimately is reduced by the amount of all dividends declared during the period.

Most dividends are paid in cash, but occasionally a dividend declaration calls for payment in assets other than cash. A large distillery once paid a dividend consisting of a bottle of whiskey for each share of stock. When a corporation goes out of existence (particularly a small corporation with only a few stockholders), it may choose to distribute noncash assets to its owners rather than to convert all its assets into cash.

## Liquidating dividends

A ***liquidating*** dividend occurs when a corporation returns to stockholders all or part of their paid-in capital investment. Liquidating dividends are usually paid only when a corporation is going out of existence or is making a permanent reduction in the size of its operations. Normally dividends are paid as a result of profitable operations, and the recipients of a dividend are entitled to assume that the dividend represents a distribution of income unless they are specifically notified that the dividend is a return of invested capital.

## Stock dividends

***Stock dividend*** is a term used to describe a distribution of additional shares of stock to a company's stockholders in proportion to their present holdings. In brief, the dividend is payable in ***additional shares of stock*** rather than in cash. Most stock dividends consist of additional shares of common stock distributed to holders of common stock, and our discussion will be limited to this type of stock dividend.

A cash dividend reduces the assets of a corporation and reduces the stockholders' equity by the same amount. A stock dividend, on the other hand, causes no change in assets and no change in the ***total*** amount of the stockholders' equity. The only effect of a stock dividend on the accounts is to transfer a portion of the retained earnings into the Common Stock account and the Paid-in Capital from Stock Dividends account. In other words, a stock dividend merely "reshuffles" the stockholders' equity accounts, increasing the permanent capital accounts and decreasing the Retained Earnings account. A stockholder who receives a stock dividend will own an increased number of shares, but his or her total ownership equity in the company will be ***no larger than before.***

To illustrate this point, assume that a corporation with 2,000 shares of stock is owned equally by James Davis and Susan Miller, each owning 1,000 shares of stock. The corporation declares a stock dividend of 10% and distributes 200 additional shares (10% of 2,000 shares), with 100 shares going to each of the two stockholders. Davis and Miller now hold 1,100 shares apiece, but each still owns one-half of the business. The corporation has not changed; its assets and liabilities and its total stockholders' equity are exactly the same as before the dividend. From the stockholders' viewpoint, the ownership of 1,100 shares out of a total of 2,200 outstanding shares represents no more than did the ownership of 1,000 shares out of a total of 2,000 shares previously outstanding.

Assume that the market price of this stock was $110 per share prior to the stock dividend. Total market value of all the outstanding shares was, therefore, 2,000 times $110, or $220,000. What would be the market value per share and in total after the additional 200 dividend shares were issued? The 2,200 shares now outstanding should have the same total market value as the previously outstanding 2,000 shares, because the "pie" has merely been divided into more but smaller pieces. The price per share should have dropped from $110 to $100, and the aggregate market value of outstanding shares would consequently be computed as 2,200 shares times $100, or $220,000. Whether the market price per share will, in all cases, decrease in proportion to the change in number of outstanding shares is another matter. The market prices of stocks listed on a stock exchange are influenced daily by many different factors.

**Reasons for distribution of stock dividends** Many reasons have been given for the popularity of stock dividends; for example:

**1** To conserve cash. When the trend of earnings is favorable but cash is needed for expansion, a stock dividend may be an appropriate device for "passing along the earnings" to stockholders without weakening the corporation's cash position.[7]

**2** To reduce the market price of a corporation's stock to a more convenient trading range by increasing the number of shares outstanding. This objective is usually present in large stock dividends (25 to 100% or more).

**3** To avoid income tax on stockholders. For income tax purposes, stock dividends are not considered as income to the recipients; therefore, no income tax is payable.

[7] For example, the Standard Oil Company of California, in a letter to its stockholders, gave the following reason for the "payment" of a 5% stock dividend: "Payment of this stock dividend recognizes the continuing increase in your stockholders' equity in the Company's assets, resulting from reinvestment of part of the Company's earnings. Reinvestment of earnings has helped to sustain the Company's long-range program of capital and exploratory expenditures and investments aimed to increase future income and enhance further the value of your shareholding."

Some critics of stock dividends argue that a stock dividend is not really a dividend at all. These critics say that a company which cannot afford to pay a cash dividend should declare no dividends, rather than trying to deceive stockholders by increasing the number of outstanding shares. The popularity of stock dividends, according to such critics, is based on a lack of understanding on the part of stockholders.

Regardless of the merit of the arguments for and against stock dividends, most stockholders welcome these distributions. In many cases a small stock dividend has not caused the market price per share to decline appreciably; consequently, the increase in the number of shares in the hands of each stockholder has, regardless of logic, resulted in an increase in the total market value of his or her holdings.

**Entries to record stock dividends** Assume that a corporation had the following stockholders' equity accounts on December 15, Year 1, just prior to declaring a 10% stock dividend:

*Stockholders' equity before stock dividend*

| | |
|---|---|
| ***Stockholders' equity:*** | |
| ***Common stock, $10 par value, 300,000 shares authorized, 100,000 shares issued and outstanding*** | ***$1,000,000*** |
| ***Paid-in capital in excess of par*** | ***500,000*** |
| ***Retained earnings*** | ***2,000,000*** |
| ***Total stockholders' equity*** | ***$3,500,000*** |

Assume also that the closing market price of the stock on December 15, Year 1, was $30 a share. The company declares a 10% stock dividend, consisting of 10,000 common shares ($10\% \times 100{,}000 = 10{,}000$). The entry to record the ***declaration*** of the dividend is as follows:

*Stock dividend declared; note use of market price of stock*

| | | | |
|---|---|---|---|
| ***Year 1*** | | | |
| ***Dec. 15.*** | ***Retained Earnings*** | ***300,000*** | |
| | ***Stock Dividend to Be Distributed*** | | ***100,000*** |
| | ***Paid-in Capital from Stock Dividends*** | | ***200,000*** |
| | ***To record declaration of a 10% stock dividend consisting of 10,000 shares of $10 par value common stock. To be distributed on Feb. 9, Year 2, to stockholders of record on Jan. 15, Year 2. Amount of retained earnings transferred to permanent capital is based on market price of $30 a share on Dec. 15, 1 Year.*** | | |

The Stock Dividend to Be Distributed account is ***not a liability,*** because there is no obligation to distribute cash or any other asset. If a balance sheet is prepared between the date of declaration of a stock dividend and the date of distribution of the shares, this account, as well as Paid-in Capital from Stock Dividends, should be presented in the stockholders' equity section of the balance sheet.

The entry to record ***distribution*** of the dividend shares is as follows:

| | | | |
|---|---|---|---|
| *Stock dividend distributed* | *Year 2* | | |
| | *Feb. 9 Stock Dividend to Be Distributed* | *100,000* | |
| | *Common Stock* | | *100,000* |
| | *To record distribution of stock dividend of 10,000 shares.* | | |

Note that the amount of retained earnings transferred to permanent capital accounts by the above entries is not the par value of the new shares, but the ***market value,*** as indicated by the market price prevailing at the date of declaration. The reasoning behind this practice is simple: Since stockholders tend to measure the "worth" of a small stock dividend (say, 20 to 25% or less) in terms of the market value of the additional shares issued, then Retained Earnings should be reduced by this amount.

Large stock dividends (for example, those in excess of 20 to 25%) should be recorded by transferring only the par or stated value of the dividend shares from the Retained Earnings account to the Common Stock account. Large stock dividends generally have the effect of proportionately reducing the market price of the stock. For example, a 100% stock dividend would reduce the market price by about 50%, because twice as many shares would be outstanding. A 100% stock dividend is very similar to the 2 for 1 ***stock split*** discussed in the following section of this chapter.

## Stock splits

Most large corporations are interested in as wide as possible a distribution of their securities among the investing public. If the market price reaches very high levels as, for example, $150 per share, the corporation may feel that, by splitting the stock 5 for 1 and thereby reducing the price to $30 per share, the number of shareholders may be increased. The bulk of trading in securities occurs in 100-share lots and an extra commission is charged on smaller transactions. Many investors with limited funds prefer to make their investments in 100-share lots of lower-priced stocks. The majority of leading American corporations have split their stock; some have done so several times. Generally the number of shareholders has increased noticeably after the stock has been split.

A stock split consists of increasing the number of outstanding shares and reducing the par or stated value per share in proportion. For example, assume that a corporation has outstanding 1 million shares of $10 par value stock. The market price is $90 per share. The corporation now reduces the par value from $10 to $5 per share and increases the number of shares from 1 million to 2 million. This action would be called a 2 for 1 stock split. A stockholder who formerly owned 100 shares of the $10 par old stock would now own 200 shares of the $5 par new stock. Since the number of outstanding shares has been doubled without any change in the affairs of the corporation, the market price will probably drop from $90 to approximately $45 a share.

***A stock split does not change the balance of any ledger account;*** consequently, the transaction may be recorded merely by a memorandum notation in the general journal and in the Common Stock account.

**Distinction between stock splits and large stock dividends** What is the difference between a 2 for 1 stock split and a 100% stock dividend? There is very little difference; both will double the number of outstanding shares without changing total stockholders' equity, and both will serve to cut the market price of the stock in half. The stock dividend, however, will cause a transfer from the Retained Earnings account to the Common Stock account equal to the par or stated value of the dividend shares, whereas the stock split does not change the dollar balance of any account.

After an increase in the number of shares as a result of a stock split or stock dividend, earnings per share are computed in terms of the increased number of shares. In presenting five- or ten-year summaries, the earnings per share for earlier years are ***retroactively revised*** to reflect the increased number of shares currently outstanding and thus make the trend of earnings per share from year to year a valid comparison.

### Retained earnings

Throughout this book the term ***retained earnings*** is used to describe that portion of stockholders' equity derived from profitable operations. Retained earnings is a historical concept, representing the accumulated earnings (including prior period adjustments) minus dividends declared from the date of incorporation to the present. If we assume that there are no ***prior period adjustments,*** the major sources of entries in the Retained Earnings account will be (1) the periodic transfer of net income (or loss) from the Income Summary account and (2) the debit entries for dividend declarations.

### Prior period adjustments to the Retained Earnings account

On occasion, a company may discover that a material error was made in the measurement of net income in a prior year. Since net income is the source of retained earnings, an error in reported net income will cause an error in the amount of retained earnings shown in all subsequent balance sheets. When such an error comes to light, it should be corrected. However, if the error in measuring the net income of a prior year is corrected in the current period's income statement, net income for the current period will be distorted. Therefore, material errors in the amount of net income reported in prior periods are corrected by adjusting the balance of the Retained Earnings account. Such adjustments are called ***prior period adjustments.***

Material errors in the financial statements of prior years may arise as a result of mathematical errors, failure to interpret properly the accounting effects of transactions, or the use of inappropriate accounting principles and concepts. Assume, for example, that in Year 10 Vista Corporation is audited for the first time by a firm of certified public accountants. During the audit, the CPAs discover that in Year 6 land costing $120,000 had been written up in Vista Corporation's accounting records to an appraised value of $180,000 and a $60,000 gain had been included in net income. Since land should be valued in accounting records at cost rather than appraised value, the recognition of this $60,000 gain constitutes a material error in Vista Corporation's Year 6 financial statements.

What effect does this error have upon the Vista Corporation's financial statements in Year 10? Since the net income of Year 6 has been closed into the Retained Earnings account, both land and retained earnings are overstated in Year 10 by $60,000. The entry to correct this error is shown below:

| | | |
|---|---|---|
| *Retained Earnings* | *60,000* | |
| *Land* | | *60,000* |
| *Prior period adjustment to correct error made in the valuation of land and recognition of income in Year 6.* | | |

**Presentation of prior period adjustments in financial statements** Corrections of the operating results of prior years are ***not*** included in the income statement of the current year. Prior period adjustments are shown in the ***statement of retained earnings*** as an adjustment to the balance of retained earnings at the beginning of the current year. The amount of the prior period adjustment should be shown net of any related tax effects. The presentation of the prior period adjustment in the statement of retained earnings of Vista Corporation is illustrated on page 639.

Most companies present comparative financial statements; that is, financial statements of the preceding year are presented along with those of the current year. If the financial statements for the year in which the error occurred are being presented for comparative purposes, these statements should be ***revised to eliminate the error.*** A footnote to the comparative statements should explain that the financial statements for the earlier year have been revised to reflect correction of the error.

**New criteria make prior period adjustments rare** Until recently the items treated as prior period adjustments were not limited to the correction of errors. For example, when contract disputes, income tax disputes, or lawsuits were finally resolved, many companies reported the settlements as prior period adjustments. Other companies, however, viewed these events as affecting income for the current year. To resolve these differences, the FASB issued ***Statement of Financial Accounting Standards No. 16,*** which limits prior period adjustments to the correction of errors in prior years' financial statements and certain income tax adjustments.[8]

Under the criteria set forth in ***Statement No. 16,*** prior period adjustments in the financial statements of publicly owned corporations should be extremely rare. Publicly owned corporations audited annually by certified public accountants are not likely to have material errors in their financial statements which

[8] *FASB Statement No. 16,* "Prior Period Adjustments" (Stamford, Conn.: 1977).

subsequently will require correction by prior period adjustments. Such adjustments are much more likely to appear in the financial statements of closely held corporations which are not audited on an annual basis.

## Statement of retained earnings

In addition to the balance sheet and the income statement, most corporations include a statement of retained earnings and a statement of changes in financial position in their annual reports to stockholders. (The latter statement will be illustrated in Chapter 21.) If a company is audited by a CPA firm, all four of these basic financial statements are covered by the audit report. A simple example of a statement of retained earnings follows:

***SHORE LINE CORPORATION***
***Statement of Retained Earnings***
***For the Year Ended December 31, 19__***

| | |
|---|---|
| *Retained earnings at beginning of year* | *$620,000* |
| *Net income for the year* | *280,000* |
| *Subtotal* | *$900,000* |
| *Less: Dividends* | *100,000* |
| *Retained earnings at end of year* | *$800,000* |

In the published annual reports of publicly owned corporations, the statement of retained earnings is usually presented in ***comparative*** form covering two years. This format and the treatment of a prior period adjustment are illustrated below for Vista Corporation.

***VISTA CORPORATION***
***Statement of Retained Earnings***
***For Years Ended June 30***

*Statement of retained earnings shows prior period adjustments, net income, and dividends*

| | *Year 10* | *Year 9* |
|---|---|---|
| *Retained earnings at beginning of year:* | | |
| *As originally reported* | *$ 810,000* | *$780,000* |
| *Prior period adjustment—to correct error in valuation of land recorded in Year 6* | *(60,000)* | *(60,000)* |
| *As restated* | *$ 750,000* | *$720,000* |
| *Net income* | *360,000* | *210,000* |
| *Subtotal* | *$1,110,000* | *$930,000* |
| *Less: Cash dividends on common stock:* | | |
| *$2.40 per share in Year 10* | *240,000* | |
| *$1.80 per share in Year 9* | | *180,000* |
| *Retained earnings at end of year* | *$ 870,000* | *$750,000* |

The error in the Year 6 financial statements was discovered in Year 10 and is shown as a correction to the beginning balance in retained earnings for both Year 10 and Year 9, since both beginning amounts were overstated. The statement of retained earnings thus provides a useful vehicle for the disclosure of prior period adjustments and for the explanation of all changes in retained earnings during the accounting period.

An alternative presentation of net income and retained earnings is used by some companies. The reconciliation of retained earnings may be shown in the body of a ***combined statement of income and retained earnings,*** as illustrated below for Lacey Corporation.

**LACEY CORPORATION**
**Combined Statement of Income and Retained Earnings**
**For Years Ended December 31**

| | Year 5 | Year 4 |
|---|---|---|
| Net sales | $2,900,000 | $2,700,000 |
| Cost of goods sold | 1,730,000 | 1,650,000 |
| Gross profit on sales | $1,170,000 | $1,050,000 |
| Operating expenses | 620,000 | 590,000 |
| Income before income taxes | $ 550,000 | $ 460,000 |
| Income taxes | 260,000 | 215,000 |
| Net income | $ 290,000 | $ 245,000 |
| Retained earnings at beginning of year | 730,000 | 665,000 |
| | $1,020,000 | $ 910,000 |
| Dividends: $1 per share in Year 5 and $0.90 per share in Year 4 | 210,000 | 180,000 |
| Retained earnings at end of year | $ 810,000 | $ 730,000 |
| Earnings per share of common stock | $1.38 | $1.22 |

The statement for the Lacey Corporation emphasizes the close relationship of operating results and retained earnings. Some readers of financial statements, however, object to the fact that net income (or loss) is "buried" in the body of a combined statement of income and retained earnings rather than being prominently displayed as the final figure before reporting earnings per share.

## Appropriations and restrictions of retained earnings

A few corporations transfer a portion of their retained earnings into separate accounts called ***appropriations.*** The purpose of such appropriations is to indicate to users of financial statements that a portion of retained earnings is not available for the declaration of cash dividends. The limitation on cash dividends may be established voluntarily by the board of directors or it may be required by law or contract. An appropriation of retained earnings is recorded by a debit to Retained Earnings and a credit to the appropriation account such as Retained

Earnings Appropriated for Contingencies. Appropriation accounts are still a part of total retained earnings, as indicated by the following partial stockholders' equity section which appeared in a recent balance sheet of Wm. Wrigley Jr. Company:

***Appropriations in the balance sheet***

| | |
|---|---|
| ***Stockholders' equity:*** | |
| *Capital stock, no-par value—authorized and issued—2,000,000 shares* | *$ 19,200,000* |
| *Accumulated earnings retained for use in the business* | *109,130,000* |
| *Accumulated earnings appropriated for guarantees under employment assurance contracts* | *2,000,000* |

When the restriction on retained earnings is no longer needed, the appropriation account is eliminated by transferring its balance back to the Retained Earnings account.

Instead of establishing appropriations of retained earnings, most corporations disclose restrictions on the declaration of cash dividends in notes accompanying the financial statements.[9] An example of such disclosure is shown below.

***Alternative disclosure of restrictions placed on retained earnings***

*Rockwell International Corporation:*
Among other covenants, certain of the long-term debt agreements contain limitations on creation of additional long-term debt and restrictions on payment of dividends and acquisition of treasury stock. Retained earnings . . . not so restricted amounted to approximately $117,000,000.

Since the only purpose of appropriating retained earnings is to inform readers of the financial statements that a portion of the retained earnings is "reserved" for a specific purpose and is not available for declaration of cash dividends, this information can be conveyed more directly, with less danger of misunderstanding, by a note accompanying the financial statements.

## Treasury stock

Corporations frequently reacquire shares of their own capital stock by purchase in the open market. Paying out cash to reacquire shares will reduce the assets of the corporation and reduce the stockholders' equity by the same amount. One reason for such purchases is to have stock available to reissue to officers and employees under bonus plans. Other reasons may include a desire to increase the reported earnings per share or to support the current market price of the stock.

***Treasury stock*** may be defined as a corporation's own capital stock which has been issued, fully paid, and reacquired but not canceled. Treasury shares may be held indefinitely or may be issued again at any time. Shares of capital stock held in the treasury are not entitled to receive dividends, vote, or receive cash or other assets upon dissolution of the company. In the computation of earnings per share, shares held in the treasury are not regarded as outstanding shares.

[9] According to a recent issue of *Accounting Trends & Techniques* published by the AICPA, very few of the 600 annual reports surveyed showed appropriated retained earnings while a large majority of the annual reports referred to restrictions on retained earnings.

### Recording purchases and reissuance of treasury stock

Purchases of treasury stock should be recorded by debiting the Treasury Stock account with the cost of the stock. For example, if Torrey Corporation reacquires 150 shares of its own $5 par stock at a price of $100 per share, the entry is as follows:

***Treasury stock recorded at cost***

| | | |
|---|---|---|
| *Treasury Stock* | *15,000* | |
| *Cash* | | *15,000* |
| ***Purchased 150 shares of $5 par treasury stock at $100 per share.*** | | |

Note that the Treasury Stock account is debited for the ***cost*** of the shares purchased, not their par value.

**Treasury stock is not an asset** When treasury stock is purchased, the corporation is eliminating part of its stockholders' equity by paying off one or more stockholders. The purchase of treasury stock should be regarded as a ***reduction of stockholders' equity,*** not as the acquisition of an asset. For this reason, the Treasury Stock account should appear in the balance sheet ***as a deduction in the stockholders' equity section.***[10] The presentation of treasury stock in a corporate balance sheet is illustrated on page 644.

### Reissuance of treasury stock

When treasury shares are reissued, the Treasury Stock account is credited for the cost of the shares reissued and Paid-in Capital from Treasury Stock Transactions is debited or credited for any difference between ***cost*** and the reissue price. To illustrate, assume that 100 of the treasury shares acquired by Torrey Corporation at a cost of $100 per share are now reissued at a price of $115 per share. The entry to record the reissuance of these shares at a price above cost would be:

***Reissued at a price above cost***

| | | |
|---|---|---|
| *Cash* | *11,500* | |
| *Treasury Stock* | | *10,000* |
| *Paid-in Capital from Treasury Stock Transactions* | | *1,500* |
| ***Sold 100 shares of treasury stock, which cost $10,000, at a price of $115 per share.*** | | |

If treasury stock is reissued at a price below cost, paid-in capital from previous treasury stock transactions is reduced (debited) by the excess of cost over the reissue price. To illustrate, assume that Torrey Corporation reissues its remaining 50 shares of treasury stock (cost $100 per share) at a price of $90 per share. The entry would be:

---

[10] Despite a lack of theoretical support, a few corporations do classify treasury stock as an asset, on the grounds that the shares could be sold for cash just as readily as shares owned in another corporation. The same argument could be made for treating unissued shares as assets. Treasury shares are basically the same as unissued shares, and an unissued share of stock is definitely not an asset.

*Reissued at a price below cost*

| | | |
|---|---|---|
| *Cash* | *4,500* | |
| *Paid-in Capital from Treasury Stock Transactions* | *500* | |
| *Treasury Stock* | | *5,000* |
| *Sold 50 shares of treasury stock, which cost $5,000, at a price of $90 each.* | | |

If there is no paid-in capital from previous treasury stock transactions, the excess of the cost of the treasury shares over the reissue price may be recorded as a debit in any other paid-in capital account. If the company had no paid-in capital in excess of par from any source, the debit would be entered in the Retained Earnings account.

**No profit or loss on treasury stock transactions** Note that ***no gain or loss is recognized on treasury stock transactions,*** even when the shares are reissued at a price above or below cost. A corporation earns profits by selling goods and services to outsiders, not by issuing or reissuing shares of its own capital stock. When treasury shares are reissued at a price above cost, the corporation receives from the new stockholder a larger amount of paid-in capital than was eliminated when the corporation acquired the treasury shares. Conversely, if treasury shares are reissued at a price below cost, the corporation ends up with less paid-in capital as a result of the purchase and reissuance of the shares. Thus, any changes in stockholders' equity resulting from treasury stock transactions are regarded as changes in ***paid-in capital*** and are ***not*** included in the measurement of net income.

## Restriction of retained earnings when treasury stock is acquired

If a corporation is to maintain its paid-in capital intact, it must not pay out to its stockholders any more than it earns. As previously stated in the section dealing with dividends, the amount of dividends to be paid must not exceed the corporation's accumulated earnings, or the corporation will be returning a portion of the stockholders' original investment to them.

The payment of cash dividends and the acquisition of treasury stock have a good deal in common. In both transactions, the corporation is disbursing cash to its stockholders. Of course, the dividend payment is spread out among all the stockholders, whereas the payment to purchase treasury stock may go to only a few stockholders, but this does not alter the fact that the corporation is turning over some of its assets to its owners. The total amount which a corporation may pay to its stockholders without reducing paid-in capital is shown by the balance in the Retained Earnings account. Consequently, it is important that a corporation keep track of the total amount disbursed in payment for treasury stock and make sure that this amount plus any dividends paid does not exceed the company's accumulated earnings. This objective is conveniently accomplished by ***restricting*** the availability of retained earnings for dividends to the extent of the cost of treasury stock purchased. The restriction should be disclosed in a note accompanying the financial statements.

### Illustration of stockholders' equity section

The following illustration of a stockholders' equity section of a balance sheet shows a fairly detailed classification by source of the various elements of corporate capital:

*Compare with published financial statements*

***Stockholders' Equity***

| | | |
|---|---|---|
| *Capital stock:* | | |
| *9% preferred stock, $100 par value, authorized and issued 1,000 shares* | *$100,000* | |
| *Common stock, $5 stated value, authorized 100,000 shares, issued 60,000 shares, of which 1,000 are held in treasury* | *300,000* | |
| *Common stock subscribed, 6,000 shares* | *30,000* | *$430,000* |
| *Additional paid-in capital:* | | |
| *Paid-in capital from stock dividends* | *$ 50,000* | |
| *Paid-in capital in excess of stated value: common stock* | *290,000* | |
| *Paid-in capital from treasury stock transactions* | *5,000* | *345,000* |
| *Total paid-in capital* | | *$775,000* |
| *Retained earnings (of which $12,000, an amount equal to the cost of treasury stock purchased, is unavailable for dividends)* | | *162,000* |
| | | *$937,000* |
| *Less: Treasury stock, common, 1,000 shares at cost* | | *12,000* |
| *Total stockholders' equity* | | *$925,000* |

The published financial statements of leading corporations indicate that there is no one standard arrangement for the various items making up the stockholders' equity section. Variations occur in the selection of titles, in the sequence of items, and in the extent of detailed classification. Many companies, in an effort to avoid excessive detail in the balance sheet, will combine several related ledger accounts into a single balance sheet item. An example of published financial statements appears in the Appendix.

## KEY TERMS INTRODUCED OR EMPHASIZED IN CHAPTER 17

**Comparative financial statements** Financial statements of current year and the preceding year which are presented together to facilitate comparison.

**Date of record** The date on which a person must be listed as a shareholder in order to be eligible to receive a dividend. Follows the date of declaration of a dividend by two or three weeks.

**Discontinued operations** The operations (revenue and expenses) of a segment of a company which has been or is being sold.

**Earnings per share (EPS)** Net income available to the common stock divided by the weighted-average number of common shares outstanding during the year.

**Ex-dividend date** A date three days prior to the date of record specified in a dividend declaration. A person buying a stock prior to the ex-dividend date also acquires the right to receive the dividend. The three-day interval permits the compilation of a list of stockholders as of the date of record.

**Extraordinary items** Transactions and events that are both unusual in nature and occur infrequently; for example, a large earthquake loss.

**Fully diluted earnings per share** Net income available to the common stock divided by the weighted-average number of common shares outstanding during the year plus any other securities convertible into common shares (if conversion would decrease EPS).

**Price-earnings ratio** Market price of a share of common stock divided by annual earnings per share.

**Primary earnings per share** Net income available to the common stock divided by weighted-average number of common shares outstanding.

**Prior period adjustment** A correction of a material error in the earnings reported in the financial statements of a prior year. Prior period adjustments are recorded directly in the Retained Earnings account and are not included in the income statement of the current period.

**Restrictions of retained earnings** Action by the board of directors to classify a portion of retained earnings as unavailable for dividends.

**Segment of a business** A component of a business. The activities of the component represent a major line of business or class of customer.

**Statement of retained earnings** A basic financial statement showing the change in retained earnings during the year.

**Stock dividend** A distribution of additional shares to common stockholders in proportion to their holdings.

**Stock split** An increase in the number of shares outstanding with a corresponding decrease in par value per share. The additional shares are distributed proportionately to all common shareholders. Purpose is to reduce market price per share and encourage wider public ownership of the company's stock. A 2 for 1 stock split will give each stockholder twice as many shares as previously owned.

**Treasury stock** Shares of a corporation's own stock which have been issued, fully paid, and reacquired but not canceled.

## REVIEW QUESTIONS

1 Why is the reporting of the results of operations so important to users of financial statements?

2 Define a ***segment of a business*** and ***extraordinary items*** for purposes of reporting the results of operations.

3 Give some examples of ***segments of a business*** and ***extraordinary losses.***

4 Briefly describe how each of the following should be reported in the income statement for the current year.

**a** Write-off of a large account receivable from a bankrupt customer

**b** Large loss from sale of a major segment of a business
**c** Large gain from sale of one of many investments in common stock
**d** Large write-off of obsolete inventory
**e** Large uninsured loss from earthquake
**f** Correction of a material error in the reported net income of an earlier year

**5** How should the effect of a material event or transaction which is either unusual in nature or occurs infrequently, but not both, be disclosed?

**6** Explain what is meant by the ***cumulative effect on prior years' income of a change in accounting method.*** How and when is this item presented in a company's financial statements?

**7** Briefly define each of the following:
**a** Price-earnings ratio
**b** Primary earnings per share
**c** Fully diluted earnings per share

**8** Explain the significance of the following dates relating to dividends: date of declaration, date of record, date of payment, ex-dividend date.

**9** Distinguish between a ***stock split*** and a ***stock dividend.*** Is there any reason for the difference in accounting treatment of these two events?

**10** What are ***prior period adjustments?*** How are they presented in financial statements?

**11** What is the purpose of an appropriation of retained earnings? What are the arguments for and against the use of such appropriations?

**12** What type of transaction most frequently appears as a deduction in a statement of retained earnings?

**13** What is ***treasury stock?*** Why do corporations purchase their own shares? Is treasury stock an asset? How should it be reported in the balance sheet?

**14** In many states, the corporation law requires that retained earnings be restricted for dividend purposes to the extent of the cost of treasury shares. What is the reason for this legal rule?

**15** If a statement of retained earnings consisted of only four items, what would these four items most probably be?

**16** What is the most effective method of disclosing in financial statements the fact that a portion of the retained earnings is restricted by the terms of a long-term debt agreement and therefore not available for payment of dividends or acquisition of treasury stock?

**17** "In a long-established, successful corporation the Cash account would normally have a dollar balance equal to or larger than the Retained Earnings account." Do you agree with this quotation? Explain.

## EXERCISES

*Ex. 17-1* In Year 5, Salarno Company had net sales of $1,200,000, costs and other expenses (including income taxes) of $720,000, and an extraordinary loss (net of income tax) of $200,000. Prepare a condensed income statement (including earnings per share) for Year 5, assuming that an average of 100,000 shares of common stock were outstanding during Year 5.

*Ex. 17-2* Fred Johnson purchased 100 shares of stock in Mills Corporation at the time it was organized. At the end of the first year's operations, the corporation reported earnings (after taxes) of $6 per share, and declared a dividend of $3 per share. Johnson complains that he is entitled to the full distribution of the amount earned on his investment. Is there any reason why a corporation that earns $6 per share may not be able to pay a dividend of this amount? Are there any advantages to Johnson in the retention by the company of one-half of its earnings?

*Ex. 17-3* San Lorenzo Corporation has been in existence for three years and at the end of Year 3 intends to report earnings per share for each of the three years on a ***comparable basis.*** During Years 1 and 2 the common stock outstanding remained unchanged at 2,000,000 shares. In Year 3, the stock was split 3 for 1 on March 1, and 1,200,000 new shares were sold for cash on July 1. (Note that the company had the use of additional funds paid in by stockholders for the last half of Year 3.) The corporation had 7,200,000 shares outstanding at the end of Year 3.

**a** Compute the ***weighted-average number*** of shares outstanding for each year that should be used in reporting ***comparative earnings per share data*** in the financial statements at the end of Year 3. (Hint: For earnings per share to be comparable for all three years, the number of shares outstanding in Years 1 and 2 must be retroactively revised to reflect the stock split.)

**b** Assuming that net earnings were $22,500,000 in Year 1, $23,400,000 in Year 2, and $27,720,000 in Year 3, compute the earnings per share for each year to be reported on a comparable basis at the end of Year 3.

*Ex. 17-4* Lee Company has 180,000 shares of $10 par common stock and 10,000 shares of $6.60 cumulative preferred stock outstanding at the end of the current year. Each share of preferred stock is convertible into four shares of common stock. Net income for the current year is $660,000. Show how the primary and fully diluted earnings per share should appear in the income statement for the current year.

*Ex. 17-5* Old Oak Corporation declared a cash dividend of $500,000 on its common stock on September 15, payable on October 20 to stockholders of record on October 1. Prepare journal entries in general journal form (if an entry is needed) on each of the three dates.

*Ex. 17-6* Martin Corporation has a total of 20,000 shares of common stock outstanding and no preferred stock. The net assets of the Martin Corporation at the end of the current year are $750,000 and the market value of the stock is $48 per share. At year-end, the company declares a stock dividend of one share for each five shares held. If all parties concerned clearly recognized the nature of the stock dividend, what would you expect the market price per share of Martin's common stock to be on the ex-dividend date?

*Ex. 17-7* Glass Corporation has 1 million shares of $5 par value capital stock outstanding. You are to prepare the journal entries to record the following transactions:

**June 1** Declared a cash dividend of 80 cents per share.
**July 1** Paid the 80-cent cash dividend to stockholders.
**Aug. 1** Declared a 5% stock dividend. Market price of stock was $18 per share.
**Sept. 10** Issued 50,000 shares pursuant to the 5% stock dividend.
**Dec. 1** Declared a 50% stock dividend. Market price of stock was $20 per share.

*Ex. 17-8* Sharon Reed owns 1,000 out of a total of 20,000 outstanding common shares of McNerney Corporation. McNerney Corporation reports assets of $1,360,000 and total liabilities of $480,000 at the end of the current year, and at that time the board declares a stock dividend of one share for each 10 shares held. Compute the book value ***per share*** of Reed's stock and the total book value of Reed's investment in the corporation: **(a)** before the stock dividend; **(b)** after the stock dividend.

## PROBLEMS

### Group A

*17A-1* The operations for Replacement Parts, Inc., are summarized below for Year 10:

| | From Continuing Operations | From Discontinued Operations |
|---|---|---|
| Net sales | $14,000,000 | $3,000,000 |
| Costs and expenses (including applicable income tax effects) | 12,200,000 | 2,850,000 |
| Loss on disposal of discontinued segment, net of income taxes | | 450,000 |
| Extraordinary loss net of income tax effects | 520,000 | |

**Instructions** Assuming that the company had an average of 400,000 shares of a single class of capital stock outstanding during Year 10, prepare a condensed income statement (including earnings per share).

*17A-2* Katherine McCall, accountant for Alternative Energy Systems, Inc., was injured in a skiing accident at year-end, and a temporary employee was assigned responsibility for preparing the financial statements. The temporary employee had a limited knowledge of accounting and improperly prepared the following income statement:

**ALTERNATIVE ENERGY SYSTEMS, INC.**
**Income Statement**
**For Year 5**

| | | |
|---|---|---|
| Net sales | | $ 9,000,000 |
| Sale of treasury stock in Year 5 (cost, $780,000; proceeds $960,000) | | 180,000 |
| Excess of proceeds over par value of common stock issued in Year 5 | | 1,300,000 |
| Elimination of restriction upon retained earnings for treasury stock owned | | 780,000 |
| Total revenue | | $11,260,000 |
| Less: | | |
| Prior period adjustment to correct valuation of land | $ 610,000 | |
| Cost of goods sold | 4,950,000 | |
| Operating expenses | 2,040,000 | |
| Loss from tornado (before tax reduction of $180,000) | 420,000 | |
| Dividends declared on capital stock | 300,000 | |
| Estimated income taxes for Year 5 after reduction of $180,000 as a result of loss from tornado | 870,000 | 9,190,000 |
| Net income | | $ 2,070,000 |

The prior period adjustment is to correct the carrying value of land which was erroneously written up to its appraised value in Year 4. At the beginning of Year 5, the company's financial statements showed retained earnings of $3,130,000, of which $780,000 was unavailable for dividends because of treasury stock owned. However, this retained earnings figure was overstated by $610,000 because of the gain erroneously recorded in Year 4 from the write-up of the land to appraised value.

The total income taxes for Year 5 and the tax savings resulting from the tornado loss have been correctly estimated by an income tax advisor. The prior period adjustment and the treasury stock transaction have no income tax effect. The tornado loss should be reported in the income statement as an extraordinary item ***net of the income tax savings.***

**Instructions**

**a** Prepare a corrected income statement for Year 5. Show appropriate earnings per share figures in the income statement. Assume that the company had a weighted average of 200,000 shares of a single class of capital stock outstanding during the year.

**b** Prepare a statement of retained earnings for Year 5. The starting point for your statement should be retained earnings at the beginning of Year 5 as originally reported ($3,130,000).

*17A-3* Sea Quest Corporation operated both a fleet of commercial fishing vessels and a chain of six seafood restaurants. The restaurants continuously lost money and were discontinued during Year 6. The company's operating results for Year 6, before income taxes, were as follows:

| | |
|---|---|
| *Income before taxes from continuing operations* | *$6,500,000* |
| *Loss before taxes from discontinued operations* | *1,800,000* |
| *Extraordinary loss, before tax* | *1,200,000* |

The extraordinary loss resulted from the expropriation of a fishing vessel by a foreign government. All income is taxable at a rate of 40%. (The loss from discontinued operations and the extraordinary loss are deductible in determining the amount of taxable income.)

Sea Quest Corporation had 500,000 shares of common stock and 50,000 shares of 6%, $100 par value, convertible preferred stock outstanding throughout Year 6. Each share of the preferred stock is convertible into two shares of common stock.

**Instructions** Prepare a partial income statement for Year 6, beginning with Income before taxes from continuing operations . . . $6,500,000. The loss from discontinued operations and the extraordinary loss are to be shown net of income taxes. Include all appropriate earnings per share figures.

*17A-4* At the beginning of Year 5, Hydro-Spa Co. has total stockholders' equity of $660,000 and 20,000 outstanding shares of a single class of capital stock. During Year 5, the corporation completes the following transactions affecting its stockholders' equity accounts:

**Jan. 10** A 10% stock dividend is declared and distributed. (Market price, $40 per share.)

**Mar. 15** The corporation acquires 1,000 shares of its own capital stock at a cost of $40.50 per share.

**May 30** All 1,000 shares of the treasury stock are reissued at a price of $44.90 per share.

**July 31** The capital stock is split, two shares for one.

**Dec. 15** The board of directors declares a cash dividend of $1.10 per share, payable on January 15 of Year 6.

**Dec. 31** Net income of $127,600 (equal to $2.90 per share) is reported for Year 5.

**Instructions** Compute the amount of total stockholders' equity, the number of shares of capital stock outstanding, and the book value per share following each successive transaction. Organize your solution as a three-column schedule with separate column headings for (1) Total Stockholders' Equity, (2) Number of Shares Outstanding, and (3) Book Value per Share.

*17A-5* When Greg Martin was hired at the end of Year 12 as the new controller of Loma Vista Corporation, he was shown the following comparative statement of retained earnings which had been prepared by the corporation's part-time accountant:

| | Year 12 | Year 11 |
|---|---|---|
| Retained earnings, Jan. 1 | $754,000 | $621,000 |
| Net income | 214,000 | 228,000 |
| Subtotal | $968,000 | $849,000 |
| Less: Dividends | 95,000 | 95,000 |
| Retained earnings, Dec. 31 | $873,000 | $754,000 |

Because Loma Vista Corporation had never been audited by a firm of CPAs, Martin decided to make a careful investigation of the company's accounting records. His investigation disclosed the following errors made in prior years:

(1) In Year 6, land costing $220,000 had been written up to an appraised value of $425,000, and an "appraisal gain" of $205,000 had been included in net income of that year.

(2) In Year 11, the company had recorded no depreciation expense on machinery acquired in April of that year. The unrecorded depreciation expense for Year 11 amounted to $38,000. Depreciation expense for Year 12, however, had been computed and recorded correctly.

Neither of these errors had entered into the computation of the company's income taxes. Thus, income taxes expense had been correctly computed and recorded each year.

**Instructions**

**a** Prepare the journal entries necessary at December 31, Year 12, to correct the two errors made in Years 6 and 11. Prepare a separate entry to correct each error.

**b** Prepare a revised comparative statement of retained earnings for Years 11 and 12. Your statement should begin with the balance of retained earnings at the beginning of Years 11 and 12 ***as originally reported*** and should then show any necessary prior period adjustments to these balances. The net income for Year 11 should be shown at the corrected amount. (Hint: The error made in Year 11 does not cause an error in the amount of retained earnings at the beginning of Year 11.)

*17A-6* The stockholders' equity of Geothermal Resources, Inc., at January 1, Year 5, is as follows:

| | |
|---|---|
| Stockholders' equity: | |
| Common stock, $5 par value, 500,000 shares authorized, 240,000 issued | $1,200,000 |
| Paid-in capital in excess of par: common stock | 4,065,000 |
| Total paid-in capital | $5,265,000 |
| Retained earnings | 1,610,000 |
| Total stockholders' equity | $6,875,000 |

During Year 5, the following transactions relating to stockholders' equity occurred:

**Jan. 15** Paid a $2 per share cash dividend declared in December of Year 4. This dividend was properly recorded at the declaration date and was the only dividend declared during Year 4.

**June 10** Declared a 10% stock dividend to stockholders of record on June 30, to be distributed on July 15. At June 10, the market price of the stock was $35 per share.

**July 15** Distributed the stock dividend declared on June 10.

**Aug. 4** Purchased 5,200 shares of treasury stock at a price of $30 per share.

**Oct. 15** Reissued 2,200 shares of treasury stock at a price of $34 per share.

**Dec. 10** Reissued 1,000 shares of treasury stock at a price of $28.50 per share.

**Dec. 15** Declared a cash dividend of $2 per share to be paid on January 15 of Year 6 to stockholders of record on December 31.

**Dec. 31** The Income Summary account, showing net income of $890,000, was closed into the Retained Earnings account.

**Instructions**

**a** Prepare in general journal form the entries necessary to record these transactions.

**b** Prepare the stockholders' equity section of the balance sheet at December 31, Year 5. Include a note following your stockholders' equity section indicating any portion of retained earnings which is not available for dividends. Also include a supporting schedule showing your computation of the balance of retained earnings at year-end.

**c** Comment on whether Geothermal Resources, Inc., increased or decreased the total amount of cash dividends declared during Year 5 in comparison with dividends declared in the preceding year.

*17A-7* The Ramirez family decided early in Year 1 to incorporate their family-owned vineyards under the name Ramirez Corporation. The corporation was authorized to issue 200,000 shares of a single class of $10 par value capital stock. Presented below is the information necessary to prepare the stockholders' equity section of the company's balance sheet at the end of Years 1 and 2.

**Year 1** In January the corporation issued to members of the Ramirez family 84,000 shares of capital stock in exchange for cash and other assets used in the operation of the vineyards. The fair market value of these assets indicated an issue price of $30 per share. In December, Juan Ramirez died, and the corporation purchased 4,000 shares of its own capital stock from his estate at $35 per share. Because of the large cash outlay to acquire this treasury stock, the directors decided not to declare cash dividends in Year 1 and instead declared a 10% stock dividend to be distributed in January of Year 2. The stock price at the declaration date was $35 per share. (The treasury shares do not participate in the stock dividend.) Net income for Year 1 was $475,000.

**Year 2** In January the corporation distributed the stock dividend declared in Year 1, and in February, the 4,000 treasury shares were sold to Maria Ramirez at $39 per share. In June, the capital stock was split, two shares for one. (Approval was obtained to increase the authorized number of shares to 400,000.) On December 15, the directors declared a cash dividend of $2 per share, payable in January of Year 3. Net income for Year 2 was $542,000.

**Instructions** Prepare the stockholders' equity section of the balance sheet at

**a** December 31, Year 1

**b** December 31, Year 2

Show any necessary computations.

## Group B

*17B-1* Summarized below are the operations of Multi-Media, Inc., for Year 6:

| | From Continuing Operations | From Discontinued Operations |
|---|---|---|
| Net sales | $9,640,000 | $1,940,000 |
| Costs and expenses (including applicable income tax effects) | 8,650,000 | 2,100,000 |
| Loss on disposal of discontinued segment, net of income taxes | | 290,000 |
| Extraordinary loss, net of income tax effects | 310,000 | |

**Instructions** Assuming that the company had an average of 200,000 shares of a single class of capital stock outstanding during Year 10, prepare a condensed income statement (including earnings per share).

*17B-2* A new employee of Santa Rosa Corporation improperly prepared the following income statement for Year 3:

**SANTA ROSA CORPORATION**
**Income Statement**
**For Year 3**

| | | |
|---|---|---|
| Net sales | | $4,400,000 |
| Sales of treasury stock in Year 3 (cost $650,000; proceeds, $800,000) | | 150,000 |
| Excess of proceeds over par value of capital stock issued in Year 3 | | 960,000 |
| Elimination of restriction of retained earnings (for treasury stock owned) | | 650,000 |
| Total revenue | | $6,160,000 |
| Less: | | |
| Prior period adjustment to correct valuation of land | $ 250,000 | |
| Cost of goods sold | 2,480,000 | |
| Operating expenses | 1,020,000 | |
| Loss from earthquake (before tax reduction of $100,000) | 230,000 | |
| Dividends declared on capital stock | 150,000 | |
| Estimated income taxes for Year 3 after reduction of $100,000 as a result of the loss from earthquake | 320,000 | 4,450,000 |
| Net income | | $1,710,000 |

The prior period adjustment is to correct the carrying value of land which was erroneously written up to its appraised value in Year 2. At the beginning of Year 3, the financial statements of Santa Rosa Corporation showed retained earnings of $2,300,000, of which $650,000 was not available for dividends because of treasury stock owned. However, this beginning retained earnings figure was overstated by $250,000 because of the gain erroneously recognized in Year 2 from the write-up of the land to appraised value.

The total income taxes for Year 3 and the tax savings resulting from the earthquake loss have been correctly estimated by an income tax advisor. The prior period adjustment and the treasury stock transaction have no income tax effect. The earthquake loss should be reported in the income statement as an extraordinary item ***net of the income tax savings.***

**Instructions**

**a** Prepare a corrected income statement for Year 3, including appropriate earnings per share figures. Santa Rosa Corporation had a weighted average of 200,000 shares of a single class of capital stock outstanding during Year 3.

**b** Prepare a statement of retained earnings for Year 5. The starting point of this statement should be retained earnings at the beginning of Year 3 as originally reported ($2,300,000).

***17B-3*** Coastal Airlines, Inc., operated both an airline service and several motels located near airports. During Year 4, all motel operations were discontinued and the following operating results were reported:

| | |
|---|---|
| *Income before taxes from continuing operations* | *$4,500,000* |
| *Loss before taxes from discontinued operations* | *1,000,000* |
| *Extraordinary loss, before tax* | *400,000* |

All income is taxable at a rate of 40% (the loss from discontinued operations and the extraordinary loss are deductible in determining the amount of taxable income).

Coastal Airlines, Inc., had 400,000 shares of common stock and 50,000 shares of 6%, $100 par value, convertible preferred stock outstanding throughout Year 4. Each share of the preferred stock is convertible into two shares of common stock.

**Instructions** Prepare a partial income statement for Year 4, beginning with Income before taxes from continuing operations . . . $4,500,000. The loss from discontinued operations and the extraordinary loss are to be shown net of income taxes. Include all appropriate earnings per share figures.

***17B-4*** On January 1, Year 8, Electric Pump Company has total stockholders' equity of $4,400,000 and 50,000 outstanding shares of a single class of capital stock. During Year 8, the corporation completes the following transactions affecting its stockholders' equity accounts:

**Jan. 10** The board of directors delcares a cash dividend of $4.20 per share, payable on February 15.

**Apr. 30** The capital stock is split, two shares for one.

**June 11** The corporation acquires 2,000 shares of its own capital stock at a cost of $56.60 per share.

**July 21** All 2,000 shares of the treasury stock are reissued at a price of $61.60 per share.

**Nov. 10** A 5% stock dividend is declared and distributed (market value $60 per share).

**Dec. 31** Net income of $378,000 (equal to $3.60 per share) is reported for Year 8.

**Instructions** Compute the amount of total stockholders' equity, the number of shares of capital stock outstanding, and the book value per share following each successive transaction. Organize your solution as a three-column schedule with separate column headings for (1) Total Stockholders' Equity, (2) Number of Shares Outstanding, and (3) Book Value per Share.

***17B-5*** At the end of Year 9, Sandy Boone was hired as the new controller of Glen Allen Corporation, a successful family-owned business. Boone was shown the following comparative statement of retained earnings which had been prepared by the corporation's part-time accountant:

| | Year 9 | Year 8 |
|---|---|---|
| Retained earnings, Jan. 1 | $545,000 | $490,000 |
| Net income | 170,000 | 145,000 |
| Subtotal | $715,000 | $635,000 |
| Less: Dividends | 100,000 | 90,000 |
| Retained earnings, Dec. 31 | $615,000 | $545,000 |

Because Glen Allen Corporation had never been audited by a CPA firm, Boone decided to make a careful examination of the company's accounting records. Her investigation disclosed the following errors made in prior years:

(1) In Year 4, land costing $165,000 had been written up to an appraised value of $300,000 and a $135,000 "appraisal gain" had been included in net income in that year.

(2) In Year 8, the company had recorded no depreciation expense on new machinery placed in service in June of that year. The unrecorded depreciation expense for Year 8 amounted to $46,000. Depreciation expense for Year 9 was computed and recorded correctly.

Neither of these errors had entered into the computation of the company's income taxes. Thus, income taxes expense had been correctly computed and recorded each year.

**Instructions**

**a** Prepare the journal entries necessary at December 31, Year 9, to correct the errors made in Years 4 and 8. (Use a separate journal entry for correcting each error.)

**b** Prepare a revised comparative statement of retained earnings for Years 8 and 9. Your statement should begin with the balance of retained earnings at the beginning of Years 8 and 9 ***as originally reported*** and should then show any necessary prior period adjustments to these balances. The net income for Year 8 should be shown at the correct amount. (Hint: The amount of retained earnings reported at the beginning of Year 8 is not affected by the failure to record depreciation during Year 8.)

*17B-6* At the beginning of Year 12, Skyline Company showed the following amounts in the stockholders' equity section of its balance sheet:

| | |
|---|---|
| Stockholders' equity: | |
| Common stock, $10 par value, 500,000 shares authorized, 191,000 issued | $1,910,000 |
| Paid-in capital in excess of par | 1,540,000 |
| Total paid-in capital | $3,450,000 |
| Retained earnings | 986,000 |
| Total stockholders' equity | $4,436,000 |

The transactions relating to stockholders' equity accounts during Year 12 are as follows:

**Jan. 3** Declared a dividend of $1 per share to stockholders of record on January 31, payable on February 15.
**Feb. 15** Paid the cash dividend declared on January 3.
**Apr. 12** The corporation purchased 3,000 shares of its own capital stock at a price of $32 per share.
**May. 9** Reissued 2,000 shares of the treasury stock at a price of $36 per share.
**June 1** Declared a 5% stock dividend to stockholders of record at June 15, to be distributed on June 30. The market price of the stock at June 1 was $35 per share. (The 1,000 shares remaining in the treasury do not participate in the stock dividend.)
**June 30** Distributed the stock dividend declared on June 1.
**Aug. 4** Reissued 500 of the 1,000 remaining shares of treasury stock at a price of $30 per share.
**Dec. 31** The Income Summary account, showing net income for the year of $613,500, was closed into the Retained Earnings account.

**Instructions**

**a** Prepare in general journal form the entries to record the above transactions.
**b** Prepare the stockholders' equity section of the balance sheet at December 31, Year 12. Include a supporting schedule showing your computation of retained earnings at that date.
**c** Compute the maximum cash dividend per share which legally could be declared at December 31, Year 12, without impairing the paid-in capital of Skyline Company. (Hint: The availability of retained earnings for dividends is restricted by the cost of treasury stock owned.)

***17B-7*** David Klein was a free-lance engineer who developed and patented a highly efficient turbocharger for automotive engines. In Year 1, Klein and Scott Harris organized Performance, Inc., to manufacture the turbocharger. The corporation was authorized to issue 150,000 shares of $10 par value capital stock. Presented below is the information necessary to prepare the stockholders' equity section of the company's balance sheet at the end of Year 1 and Year 2.

**Year 1** On January 20, the corporation issued 80,000 shares of capital stock to Harris and other investors for cash at $32 per share. In addition, 5,000 shares of capital stock were issued on that date to Klein in exchange for his patents. In November, Klein was killed while auto racing in Europe. At the request of Klein's heirs, Performance, Inc., purchased the 5,000 shares of its capital stock from Klein's estate at $44 per share. Because of the unexpected cash outlay to acquire treasury stock, the directors decided against declaring any cash dividends in Year 1. Instead, they declared a 5% stock dividend which was distributed on December 31. The stock price at the declaration date was $42 per share. (The treasury shares did not participate in the stock dividend.) Net income for Year 1 was $415,000.

**Year 2** In March, the 5,000 treasury shares were reissued at a price of $52 per share. In August, the capital stock was split four shares for one, with a reduction in the par value to $2.50 per share and an increase in the number of shares authorized to 600,000. On December 20, the directors declared a cash dividend of 70 cents per share, payable in January of Year 3. Net income for Year 2 was $486,000.

**Instructions** Prepare the stockholders' equity section of the balance sheet at:
**a** December 31, Year 1
**b** December 31, Year 2
Show any necessary supporting computations

## BUSINESS DECISION PROBLEM 17

Near the end of the current year, the board of directors of the Shadetree Corporation is presented with the following statement of stockholders' equity:

| | |
|---|---|
| *Capital stock (120,000 shares issued)* | *$2,400,000* |
| *Paid-in capital in excess of par* | *1,440,000* |
| *Retained earnings* | *1,920,000* |
| *Total stockholders' equity* | *$5,760,000* |

Shadetree Corporation has paid dividends of $3.60 per share in each of the last five years. After careful consideration of the company's cash needs, the board of directors declared a stock dividend of 24,000 shares. Shortly after the stock dividend had been distributed and before the end of the year, the company declared a cash dividend of $3 per share.

John Joseph owned 10,000 shares of Shadetree Corporation's stock, acquired several years ago. The market price of this stock before any dividend action in the current year was $60 per share.

**Instructions** Based on the information given above, answer each of the following questions, showing all relevant computations.

**a** What is Joseph's share (in dollars) of the net assets as reported in the balance sheet of the Shadetree Corporation before the stock dividend action? What is his share after the stock dividend action? Explain why there is or is not any change as a result of the 20% stock dividend.

**b** What are the probable reasons why the market value of Joseph's stock differs from the amount of net assets per share shown in the accounting records?

**c** How does the amount of cash dividends that Joseph received in the current year compare with dividends received in prior years?

**d** On the day the stock went ex-dividend (with respect to the 20% stock dividend), its quoted market price fell from $60 to $50 per share. Did this represent a loss to Joseph? Explain.

**e** If the Shadetree Corporation had announced that it would continue its regular cash dividend of $3.60 per share on the increased number of shares outstanding after the 20% stock dividend, would you expect the market price of the stock to react in any way different from the change described in **d**? Why?

# 18

# CORPORATIONS: BONDS PAYABLE, LEASES, AND OTHER LIABILITIES

## BONDS PAYABLE

Financially sound corporations may arrange some long-term loans by issuing a note payable to a bank or an insurance company. But to finance a large project, such as building a refinery or acquiring a new fleet of jumbo jets, a corporation may need more long-term financing than any single lender can supply. When a corporation needs to raise a large amount of long-term capital—perhaps 10, 50, or 100 million dollars or more—it generally sells additional shares of capital stock or issues ***bonds payable.***[1]

The issuance of bonds payable is the equivalent of splitting a large loan into a great many units, called ***bonds.*** Each bond is, in essence, a long-term interest-bearing note payable, usually in the face amount of $1,000. The bonds are sold to the investing public, thus allowing many different investors to participate in the loan. An example of a corporate bond issue is the 8% sinking fund debentures of The Singer Company, due January 15, 1999. With this bond issue, The Singer Company borrowed $100 million by issuing 100,000 bonds of $1,000 each.

---

[1] Bonds payable also are issued by the federal government and by many other governmental units such as states, cities, and school districts. In this chapter, our discussion is limited to corporate bonds, although many of the concepts also apply to the bond issues of governmental agencies.

### Issuance of bonds payable

From the viewpoint of the issuing corporation, bonds payable constitute a long-term liability. Throughout the life of this liability, the corporation makes semiannual interest payments to the bondholders for the use of their money. A bondholder is a creditor of the corporation, not an owner. Therefore, bondholders generally do not have voting rights and do not participate in the earnings of the corporation beyond receiving the contractual, semiannual interest payments.

**Authorization of a bond issue** Formal approval of the board of directors and the stockholders is usually required before bonds can be issued. If the bonds are to be sold to the general public, approval must also be obtained from the SEC, just as for an issue of capital stock which is offered to the public.

The issuing corporation also selects a ***trustee*** to represent the interests of the bondholders. This trustee generally is a large bank or trust company. A contract is drawn up indicating the terms of the bond issue and the assets (if any) which are pledged as collateral for the bonds. Sometimes this contract places limitations on the payment of dividends to stockholders during the life of the bonds. For example, dividends may be permitted only when working capital is above specified amounts. If the issuing corporation defaults on any of the terms of this contract, the trustee may foreclose upon the assets which secure the bonds or may take other legal action on behalf of the bondholders.

**The role of the underwriter in marketing a bond issue** An investment banker or underwriter is usually employed to market a bond issue, just as in the case of capital stock. The corporation turns the entire bond issue over to the underwriter at a specified price; the underwriter sells the bonds to the public at a slightly higher price. By this arrangement the corporation is assured of receiving the entire proceeds on a specified date.

**Transferability of bonds** Corporation bonds, like capital stocks, are traded daily on organized securities exchanges. The holders of a 25-year bond issue need not wait 25 years to convert their investment into cash. By placing a telephone call to a broker, an investor may sell bonds within a matter of minutes at the going market price. This quality of liquidity is one of the most attractive features of an investment in corporation bonds.

**Quoted market prices** The market price of stocks is quoted in terms of dollars per share. Bond prices, however, are quoted as a ***percentage*** of their face value or ***maturity*** value, which is usually $1,000. The maturity value is the amount the issuing company must pay to redeem the bond at the date it matures (becomes due). A bond quoted at ***96*** would therefore have a market price of $960 (96% of $1,000). Bond prices are quoted at the nearest one-eighth of a percentage point. The following line from the financial page of a daily newspaper summarizes the previous day's trading in bonds of Sears, Roebuck and Co.

*What is the market value of this bond?*

| *Bonds* | *Sales* | *High* | *Low* | *Close* | *Net Change* |
|---|---|---|---|---|---|
| *Sears R $8\frac{5}{8}$ 95* | *45* | *86* | *$84\frac{1}{2}$* | *85* | *−1* |

This line of condensed information indicates that 45 of Sears, Roebuck and Co.'s $8\frac{5}{8}$, $1,000 bonds maturing in 1995 were traded. The highest price is reported as 86, or $860 for a bond of $1,000 face value. The lowest price was $84\frac{1}{2}$, or $845 for a $1,000 bond. The closing price (last sale of the day) was 85, or $850. This was one point below the closing price of the previous day, a decrease of $10 in the price of a $1,000 bond.

The primary factors which determine the market value of a bond are (1) the relationship of the bond's interest rate to other investment opportunities and (2) investors' confidence that the issuing company has the financial strength to make all future interest and principal payments promptly. Thus, a bond with a 10% interest rate will command a higher market price than an 8% bond with the same maturity date if the two companies issuing the bonds are of equal financial strength.

A bond selling at a market price greater than its maturity value is said to be selling at a ***premium;*** a bond selling at a price below its maturity value is selling at a ***discount.*** As a bond nears its maturity date, the market price of the bond moves toward the maturity value. At the maturity date the market value of the bond will be exactly equal to its maturity value, because the issuing corporation will redeem the bond for that amount.

**Types of bonds** Bonds secured by the pledge of specific assets are called ***mortgage bonds.*** An unsecured bond is called a ***debenture bond;*** its value rests upon the general credit of the corporation. A debenture bond issued by a very large and strong corporation may have a higher investment rating than a secured bond issued by a corporation in less satisfactory financial condition. For example, the $500 million of debenture bonds recently issued by IBM are rated AAA, the highest possible rating.

Some bonds have a single fixed maturity date for the entire issue. Other bond issues, called ***serial bonds,*** provide for varying maturity dates to lessen the problem of accumulating cash for payment. For example, serial bonds in the amount of $20 million issued in 1980 might call for $2 million of bonds to mature in 1990, and an additional $2 million to become due in each of the succeeding nine years. Almost all bonds are ***callable,*** which means that the corporation has the right to pay off the bonds in advance of the scheduled maturity date. To compensate the bondholders for being forced to give up their investments, the call price is usually somewhat higher than the face value of the bonds.

Most corporation bonds issued in recent years have been ***registered bonds;*** that is, the name of the owner is registered with the issuing corporation. Payment of interest is made by semiannual checks mailed to the registered owners. ***Coupon bonds*** were more popular some years ago and many are still outstanding. Coupon bonds have interest coupons attached; each six months during the life of the bond one of these coupons becomes due. The bondholder detaches the cou-

bonds were sold. In other words, the amount of the company's liability at the date of issuing the bonds is equal to the amount of money borrowed. Over the life of the bonds, however, we shall see that this carrying value gradually increases until it reaches the face value of the bonds at the maturity date.

**Bond discount as part of the cost of borrowing** In Chapter 9, we illustrated two ways in which interest charges can be specified in a note payable: the interest may be stated as an annual percentage rate of the face amount of the note, or it may be included in the face amount. Bonds issued at a discount include ***both*** types of interest charge. The $1,000,000 bond issue in our example calls for cash interest payments of $90,000 per year ($1,000,000 × 9% contract interest rate), payable semiannually. In addition to making the semiannual interest payments, the corporation must redeem the bond issue for $1 million on December 31, Year 10. This maturity value is $20,000 greater than the $980,000 received when the bonds were issued. Thus, the $20,000 discount in the issue price may be regarded as an ***interest charge included in the maturity value of the bonds.***

Although the interest charge represented by the discount will not be paid to bondholders until the bonds mature, the corporation benefits from this cost during the entire period that it has the use of the bondholders' money. Therefore, the cost represented by the discount should be allocated over the life of the bond issue. The process of allocating bond discount to interest expense is termed ***amortization*** of the discount.

In short, whenever bonds are issued at a discount, the total interest cost over the life of the bonds is equal to the total regular cash interest payments ***plus the amount of the discount.*** For the $1 million bond issue in our example, the total interest cost over the 10-year life of the bonds is $920,000, of which $900,000 represents the 20 semiannual cash interest payments and $20,000 represents the discount. The average annual interest expense, therefore, is $92,000 ($920,000 ÷ 10 years), consisting of $90,000 paid in cash and $2,000 amortization of the bond discount. This analysis is illustrated below:

| | | |
|---|---|---|
| *Total cash interest payments to bondholders ($1,000,000 × 9% × 10 years)* | | *$900,000* |
| *Add: Interest charge included in face amount of bonds:* | | |
| *Maturity value of bonds* | *$1,000,000* | |
| *Amount borrowed* | *980,000* | *20,000* |
| *Total cost of borrowing over life of bond issue* | | *$920,000* |
| *Average annual interest expense ($920,000 ÷ 10 years)* | | *$ 92,000* |

## Amortization of bond discount

The simplest method of amortizing bond discount is the ***straight-line method,*** which allocates an equal portion of the discount to Bond Interest Expense in each period.[3] In our example, the Discount on Bonds Payable account has an

[3] An alternative method of amortization, called the ***effective interest method,*** is illustrated later in this chapter. Although the effective interest method is theoretically preferable to the straight-line method, the resulting differences generally are not material in dollar amount.

initial debit balance of $20,000; each year one-tenth of this amount, or $2,000, will be amortized into Bond Interest Expense. Assuming that the interest payment dates are June 30 and December 31, the entries to be made each six months to record bond interest expense are as follows:

*Payment of bond interest and straight-line amortization of bond discount*

| | | |
|---|---|---|
| ***Bond Interest Expense*** | ***45,000*** | |
| ***Cash*** | | ***45,000*** |
| ***Paid semiannual interest on $1,000,000 of 9%, 10-year bonds.*** | | |

| | | |
|---|---|---|
| ***Bond Interest Expense*** | ***1,000*** | |
| ***Discount on Bonds Payable*** | | ***1,000*** |
| ***Amortized discount for six months on 10-year bond issue ($20,000 discount × $\frac{1}{20}$).*** | | |

The two entries shown above to record the cash payment of bond interest and to record the amortization of bond discount can conveniently be combined into one compound entry, as follows:

| | | |
|---|---|---|
| ***Bond Interest Expense*** | ***46,000*** | |
| ***Cash*** | | ***45,000*** |
| ***Discount on Bonds Payable*** | | ***1,000*** |
| ***To record payment of semiannual interest on $1,000,000 of 9%, 10-year bonds ($1,000,000 × 9% × $\frac{1}{2}$) and to amortize $\frac{1}{20}$ of the discount on the 10-year bond issue.*** | | |

Regardless of whether the cash payment of interest and the amortization of bond discount are recorded in separate entries or combined in one entry, the amount recognized as Bond Interest Expense is the same—$46,000 each six months, or a total of $92,000 a year. An alternative accounting procedure that will produce the same results is to amortize the bond discount only at year-end rather than at each interest-payment date.

Note that the additional interest expense resulting from amortization of the discount does not require any additional cash payment. The credit portion of the entry is to the contra-liability account, Discount on Bonds Payable, rather than to the Cash account. Crediting this contra-liability account ***increases the carrying value of bonds payable.*** The original $20,000 discount will be completely written off by the end of the tenth year, and the net liability (carrying value) will be the full face value of the bonds.

## Bonds sold at a premium

Bonds will sell above par if the contract rate of interest specified on the bonds is higher than the current market rate for bonds of this grade. Let us now change our basic illustration by assuming that the $1 million issue of 9%, 10-year bonds is sold at a price of 102 ($1,020 for each $1,000 bond). The entry is shown below:

*Issuing bonds at premium*

| | | |
|---|---|---|
| ***Cash*** | ***1,020,000*** | |
| ***Bonds Payable*** | | ***1,000,000*** |
| ***Premium on Bonds Payable*** | | ***20,000*** |
| ***Issued $1,000,000 face value of 9%, 10-year bonds at price of 102.*** | | |

If a balance sheet is prepared immediately following the sale of the bonds, the liability will be shown as follows:

*Carrying value increased by premium*

| | | |
|---|---|---|
| ***Long-term liabilities:*** | | |
| ***9% bonds payable, due Dec. 31, Year 10*** | ***$1,000,000*** | |
| ***Add: Premium on bonds payable*** | ***20,000*** | ***$1,020,000*** |

The amount of any unamortized premium is ***added*** to the maturity value of the bonds payable to show the current carrying value of the liability. Over the life of the bond issue, this carrying value will be reduced toward the maturity value of $1,000,000.

**Bond premium as reduction in the cost of borrowing** We have illustrated how issuing bonds at a discount increases the cost of borrowing above the amount of the regular cash interest payments. Issuing bonds at a premium, on the other hand, ***reduces the cost of borrowing below the amount of the regular cash interest payments.***

The amount received from issuance of the bonds is $20,000 greater than the amount which must be repaid at maturity. This $20,000 premium is not a gain but is to be offset against the periodic interest payments in determining the net cost of borrowing. Whenever bonds are issued at a premium, the total interest cost over the life of the bonds is equal to the regular cash interest payments ***minus the amount of the premium.*** In our example, the total interest cost over the life of the bonds is computed as $900,000 of cash interest payments minus $20,000 of premium amortized, or a net borrowing cost of $880,000. The annual interest expense will be $88,000, consisting of $90,000 paid in cash less an offsetting $2,000 transferred from the Premium on Bonds Payable account to the credit side of the Bond Interest Expense account.

The semiannual entries on June 30 and December 31 to record the payment of bond interest and amortization of bond premium are as follows:

*Payment of bond interest and straight-line amortization of bond premium*

| | | |
|---|---|---|
| ***Bond Interest Expense*** | ***45,000*** | |
| ***Cash*** | | ***45,000*** |
| ***Paid semiannual interest on $1,000,000 of 9%, 10-year bonds.*** | | |
| ***Premium on Bonds Payable*** | ***1,000*** | |
| ***Bond Interest Expense*** | | ***1,000*** |
| ***Amortized premium for six months on 10-year bond issue ($20,000 × $\frac{1}{20}$).*** | | |

## Year-end adjustments for bond interest expense

In the preceding illustration, it was assumed that one of the semiannual dates for payment of bond interest coincided with the end of the company's accounting year. In most cases, however, the semiannual interest payment dates will fall during an accounting period rather than on the last day of the year.

For purposes of illustration, assume that $1 million of 8%, 10-year bonds are issued at a price of 97 on October 1, Year 1. Interest payment dates are April 1 and October 1. The total discount to be amortized amounts to $30,000, or $1,500 in each six-month interest period. The company keeps its accounts on a calendar-year basis; consequently, the adjusting entries shown below will be necessary at December 31 for the accrued interest and the amortization of discount applicable to the three-month period since the bonds were issued.

| | | |
|---|---|---|
| *Bond Interest Expense* | *20,750* | |
|     *Bond Interest Payable* | | *20,000* |
|     *Discount on Bonds Payable* | | *750* |

*To adjust for accrued interest on bonds and to amortize discount for period from Oct. 1 to Dec. 31. Accrued interest: $\$1{,}000{,}000 \times .08 \times \frac{3}{12} = \$20{,}000$. Amortization: $\$30{,}000 \times \frac{3}{120} = \$750$.*

If the above bonds had been issued at a premium, similar entries would be made at the end of the period for any accrued interest and for amortization of premium for the fractional period from October 1 to December 31.

In the December 31, Year 1, balance sheet, the $20,000 of accrued bond interest payable will appear as a current liability; the long-term liability for bonds payable will appear as follows:

| | | |
|---|---|---|
| *Long-term liabilities:* | | |
|   *8% Bonds payable, due Oct. 1, Year 11* | *$1,000,000* | |
|   *Less: Discount on bonds payable* | *29,250* | *$970,750* |

When the bonds were issued on October 1, the net liability for bonds payable was $970,000. Note that the carrying value of the bonds has ***increased*** over the three months by the amount of discount amortized. When the entire discount has been amortized, the carrying value of the bonds will be $1,000,000, which is equal to their maturity value.

At April 1, Year 2, it is necessary to record interest expense and discount amortization only for the three-month period since year-end. Of the semiannual $40,000 cash payment to bondholders, one-half, or $20,000, represents payment of the liability for bond interest payable recorded on December 31, Year 1. The entry on April 1 is:

| | | |
|---|---|---|
| *Bond Interest Expense* | *20,750* | |
| *Bond Interest Payable* | *20,000* | |
|     *Discount on Bonds Payable* | | *750* |
|     *Cash* | | *40,000* |

*To record bond interest expense and amortization of discount for three-month period since year-end and to record semiannual payment to bondholders.*

### Straight-line amortization: a theoretical shortcoming

Although the straight-line method of amortizing bond discount or premium recognizes the full cost of borrowing over the life of a bond issue, the method has one conceptual weakness: the same dollar amount of interest expense is recognized each year. Amortizing a discount, however, causes a gradual increase in the liability for bonds payable; amortizing a premium causes a gradual decrease in the liability. If the uniform annual interest expense is expressed as a ***percentage*** of either an increasing or a decreasing liability, it appears that the borrower's cost of capital is changing over the life of the bonds.

This problem can be avoided by using the ***effective interest method*** of amortizing bond discount or premium. The effective interest method recognizes annual interest expense equal to a ***constant percentage of the carrying value of the related liability.*** This percentage is the effective rate of interest incurred by the borrower. For this reason, the effective interest method of amortization is considered theoretically preferable to the straight-line method. Whenever the two methods would produce ***materially different*** annual results, the Financial Accounting Standards Board requires the use of the effective interest method.

Over the life of the bonds, both amortization methods recognize the same total amount of interest expense. Even on an annual basis, the results produced by the two methods usually are very similar. Consequently, either method generally would meet the requirements of the FASB. Because of its simplicity, the straight-line method is widely used despite the theoretical arguments favoring the effective interest method.

### Effective interest method of amortization

When bonds are sold at a discount, the effective interest rate incurred by the issuing corporation is ***higher*** than the contract rate printed on the bonds. Conversely, when bonds are sold at a premium, the effective rate of interest is ***lower*** than the contract rate.

When the effective interest method is used, bond interest expense is determined by multiplying the ***carrying value of the bonds*** at the beginning of the period by the ***effective rate of interest*** for the bond issue. The amount of discount or premium to be amortized is the ***difference*** between the interest expense computed in this manner and the amount of interest paid (or payable) to bondholders for the period. The computation of effective interest expense and the amount of discount or premium amortization for the life of the bond issue is made in advance on a schedule called an ***amortization table.***

**Sale of bonds at a discount** To illustrate the effective interest method, assume that on May 1, Year 1, a corporation issues $1,000,000 face value, 9%, 10-year bonds with interest dates of November 1 and May 1. The bonds sell for $937,689,

***Amortization Table for Bonds Sold at a Discount***

***($1,000,000, 10-year bonds, 9% interest payable semiannually, sold at $937,689 to yield 10% compounded semiannually)***

| Six-Month Interest Period | (A) Interest Paid Semiannually ($4\frac{1}{2}$% of Face Value) | (B) Effective Semiannual Interest Expense (5% of Bond Carrying Value) | (C) Discount Amortization (B − A) | (D) Bond Discount Balance | (E) Carrying Value of Bonds, End of Period ($1,000,000 − D) |
|---|---|---|---|---|---|
| Issue date | | | | $62,311 | $ 937,689 |
| 1 | $45,000 | $46,884 | $1,884 | 60,427 | 939,573 |
| 2 | 45,000 | 46,979 | 1,979 | 58,448 | 941,552 |
| 3 | 45,000 | 47,078 | 2,078 | 56,370 | 943,630 |
| 4 | 45,000 | 47,182 | 2,182 | 54,188 | 945,812 |
| 5 | 45,000 | 47,291 | 2,291 | 51,897 | 948,103 |
| 6 | 45,000 | 47,405 | 2,405 | 49,492 | 950,508 |
| 7 | 45,000 | 47,525 | 2,525 | 46,967 | 953,033 |
| 8 | 45,000 | 47,652 | 2,652 | 44,315 | 955,685 |
| 9 | 45,000 | 47,784 | 2,784 | 41,531 | 958,469 |
| 10 | 45,000 | 47,923 | 2,923 | 38,608 | 961,392 |
| 11 | 45,000 | 48,070 | 3,070 | 35,538 | 964,462 |
| 12 | 45,000 | 48,223 | 3,223 | 32,315 | 967,685 |
| 13 | 45,000 | 48,384 | 3,384 | 28,931 | 971,069 |
| 14 | 45,000 | 48,553 | 3,553 | 25,378 | 974,622 |
| 15 | 45,000 | 48,731 | 3,731 | 21,647 | 978,353 |
| 16 | 45,000 | 48,918 | 3,918 | 17,729 | 982,271 |
| 17 | 45,000 | 49,114 | 4,114 | 13,615 | 986,385 |
| 18 | 45,000 | 49,319 | 4,319 | 9,296 | 990,704 |
| 19 | 45,000 | 49,535 | 4,535 | 4,761 | 995,239 |
| 20 | 45,000 | 49,761* | 4,761 | -0- | 1,000,000 |

* In the last period, interest expense is equal to interest paid to bondholders plus the remaining balance on the bond discount. This compensates for the accumulated effects of rounding amounts.

a price resulting in an effective interest rate of 10%.[4] An amortization table for this bond issue is shown above. (Amounts of interest expense have been rounded to the nearest dollar.)

This amortization table can be used to illustrate the concepts underlying the effective interest method of determining interest expense and discount amortization. Note that the "interest periods" in the table are the ***semiannual*** (six-month) interest periods. Thus, the interest payments (column A), interest

[4]Computation of the exact effective interest rate involves mathematical techniques beyond the scope of this course. A very close estimate of the effective interest rate can be obtained by dividing the ***average*** annual interest expense by the ***average*** carrying value of the bonds. Computation of average annual interest expense was illustrated on page 664. The average carrying value of the bonds is found by adding the issue price and the maturity value of the bond issue and dividing this sum by 2. Applying these procedures to the bond issue in our example provides an estimated effective interest rate of 9.93%, computed [($900,000 interest + $62,311 discount) ÷ 10 years] divided by [($937,689 + $1,000,000) ÷ 2].

expense (column B), and discount amortization (column C) are for six-month periods. Similarly, the balance of the Discount on Bonds Payable account (column D) and the carrying value of the liability (column E) are shown as of each semiannual interest payment date.

The original issuance price of the bonds ($937,689) is entered at the top of column E. This represents the carrying value of the liability throughout the first six-month interest period. The semiannual interest payment, shown in Column A, is $4\frac{1}{2}\%$ (one-half of the annual contract rate) of the $1,000,000 face value of the bond issue. The semiannual cash interest payment does not change over the life of the bonds. The interest expense shown in column B, however, ***changes every period.*** This expense is always a ***constant percentage*** of the carrying value of the liability as of the end of the preceding period. The "constant percentage" is the effective interest rate of the bond issue. The bonds have an effective annual interest rate of 10%, indicating a semiannual rate of 5%. Thus, the effective interest expense for the first six-month period is $46,884 (5% of $937,689). The discount amortization for period 1 is the difference between this effective interest expense and the contract rate of interest paid to bondholders.

After the discount is reduced by $1,884 at the end of period 1, the carrying value of the bonds in Column E ***increases*** by $1,884 (from $937,689 to $939,573). In period 2, the effective interest expense is determined by multiplying the effective semiannual interest rate of 5% by this new carrying value of $939,573 (5% × $939,573 = $46,979).

Semiannual interest expense may be recorded every period directly from the data in the amortization table. For example, the entry to record bond interest expense at the end of the first six-month period is:

| | | |
|---|---|---|
| ***Bond Interest Expense*** . . . . . . . . . . . . . . . . . . . . . . . . . . . . . . . . . | ***46,884*** | |
| ***Discount on Bonds Payable*** . . . . . . . . . . . . . . . . . . . . . . . . . | | ***1,884*** |
| ***Cash*** . . . . . . . . . . . . . . . . . . . . . . . . . . . . . . . . . . . . . . . . . | | ***45,000*** |
| ***To record semiannual interest payment and amortize discount for six months.*** | | |

Similarly, interest expense at the end of the fifteenth six-month period would be recorded by:

| | | |
|---|---|---|
| ***Bond Interest Expense*** . . . . . . . . . . . . . . . . . . . . . . . . . . . . . . . . . | ***48,731*** | |
| ***Discount on Bonds Payable*** . . . . . . . . . . . . . . . . . . . . . . . . . | | ***3,731*** |
| ***Cash*** . . . . . . . . . . . . . . . . . . . . . . . . . . . . . . . . . . . . . . . . . | | ***45,000*** |
| ***To record semiannual interest payment and amortize discount for six months.*** | | |

When bond discount is amortized, the carrying value of the liability for bonds payable ***increases*** every period toward the maturity value. Since the effective interest expense in each period is a constant percentage of this increasing carrying value, the interest expense also increases from one period to the next. This is the basic difference between the effective interest method and straight-line amortization.

**Sale of bonds at a premium** Let us now change our basic illustration by assuming that the $1,000,000 issue of 9%, 10-year bonds is sold on May 1, Year 1, at a price of $1,067,952, resulting in an effective interest rate of 8% annually (4% per six-month interest period). An amortization table for this bond issue is shown below.

***Amortization Table for Bonds Sold at a Premium***

***($1,000,000, 10-year bonds, 9% interest payable semiannually, sold at $1,067,952 to yield 8% compounded semiannually)***

| | (A) | (B) | (C) | (D) | (E) |
|---|---|---|---|---|---|
| Six-Month Interest Period | Interest Paid Semiannually ($4\frac{1}{2}$% of Face Value) | Effective Semiannual Interest Expense (4% of Bond Carrying Value) | Premium Amortization (A − B) | Bond Premium Balance | Carrying Value of Bonds, End of Period ($1,000,000 + D) |
| Issue date | | | | $67,952 | $1,067,952 |
| 1 | $45,000 | $42,718 | $2,282 | 65,670 | 1,065,670 |
| 2 | 45,000 | 42,627 | 2,373 | 63,297 | 1,063,297 |
| 3 | 45,000 | 42,532 | 2,468 | 60,829 | 1,060,829 |
| 4 | 45,000 | 42,433 | 2,567 | 58,262 | 1,058,262 |
| 5 | 45,000 | 42,330 | 2,670 | 55,592 | 1,055,592 |
| 6 | 45,000 | 42,224 | 2,776 | 52,816 | 1,052,816 |
| 7 | 45,000 | 42,113 | 2,887 | 49,929 | 1,049,929 |
| 8 | 45,000 | 41,997 | 3,003 | 46,926 | 1,046,926 |
| 9 | 45,000 | 41,877 | 3,123 | 43,803 | 1,043,803 |
| 10 | 45,000 | 41,752 | 3,248 | 40,555 | 1,040,555 |
| 11 | 45,000 | 41,622 | 3,378 | 37,177 | 1,037,177 |
| 12 | 45,000 | 41,487 | 3,513 | 33,664 | 1,033,664 |
| 13 | 45,000 | 41,347 | 3,653 | 30,011 | 1,030,011 |
| 14 | 45,000 | 41,200 | 3,800 | 26,211 | 1,026,211 |
| 15 | 45,000 | 41,048 | 3,952 | 22,259 | 1,022,259 |
| 16 | 45,000 | 40,890 | 4,110 | 18,149 | 1,018,149 |
| 17 | 45,000 | 40,726 | 4,274 | 13,875 | 1,013,875 |
| 18 | 45,000 | 40,555 | 4,445 | 9,430 | 1,009,430 |
| 19 | 45,000 | 40,377 | 4,623 | 4,807 | 1,004,807 |
| 20 | 45,000 | 40,193* | 4,807 | -0- | 1,000,000 |

* In the last period, interest expense is equal to interest paid to bondholders minus the remaining balance of the bond premium. This compensates for the accumulated effects of rounding amounts.

In this amortization table, the interest expense for each six-month period is equal to 4% of the carrying value at the beginning of that period. This amount of interest expense is less than the amount of cash being paid to bondholders, illustrating that the effective interest rate is less than the contract rate.

Based upon this amortization table, the entry to record the interest payment and amortization of the premium for the first six months of the bond issue is:

*Amortization of premium decreases interest expense*

| | | |
|---|---|---|
| **Bond Interest Expense** | **42,718** | |
| **Premium on Bonds Payable** | **2,282** | |
| **Cash** | | **45,000** |
| ***To record semiannual interest payment and amortization of premium.*** | | |

As the carrying value of the liability declines, so does the amount recognized as bond interest expense.

**Year-end adjusting entries** Since the amounts recognized as interest expense change from one period to the next, we must refer to the appropriate interest period in the amortization table to obtain the dollar amounts for use in year-end adjusting entries. To illustrate, consider our example of the bonds sold at a premium on May 1, Year 1. The entry shown above records interest and amortization of the premium through November 1, Year 1. If the company keeps its accounts on a calendar-year basis, two months' interest has accrued as of December 31, Year 1, and the following adjusting entry is made at year-end:

*Year-end adjustment*

| | | |
|---|---|---|
| **Bond Interest Expense** | **14,209** | |
| **Premium on Bonds Payable** | **791** | |
| **Bond Interest Payable** | | **15,000** |
| ***To record two months' accrued interest and amortize one-third of the premium for the interest period.*** | | |

This adjusting entry covers one-third (two months) of the second interest period. Consequently, the amounts shown as bond interest expense and amortization of premium are one-third of the amounts shown in the amortization table for the second interest period. Similar adjusting entries must be made at the end of every accounting period while the bonds are outstanding. The dollar amounts of these adjusting entries will vary, however, because the amounts of interest expense and premium amortization change in every interest period. The amounts applicable to any given adjusting entry will be the appropriate fraction of the amounts for the interest period then in progress.

Following the year-end adjusting entry illustrated above, the interest expense and premium amortization on May 1, Year 2, are recorded as follows:

*Interest payment following year-end adjustment*

| | | |
|---|---|---|
| **Bond Interest Expense** | **28,418** | |
| **Bond Interest Payable** | **15,000** | |
| **Premium on Bonds Payable** | **1,582** | |
| **Cash** | | **45,000** |
| ***To record semiannual interest payment, a portion of which had been accrued, and amortize remainder of premium applicable to interest period.*** | | |

## Retirement of bonds payable

Bonds are sometimes retired before the scheduled maturity date. The principal reason for retiring bonds early is to relieve the issuing corporation of the obligation to make future interest payments. If interest rates decline to the point that a corporation can borrow at an interest rate below that being paid on a particular bond issue, the corporation may benefit from retiring those bonds and issuing new bonds at a lower interest rate.

Most bond issues contain a call provision, permitting the corporation to redeem the bonds by paying a specified price, usually a few points above par. Even without a call provision, the corporation may retire its bonds before maturity by purchasing them in the open market. If the bonds can be purchased by the issuing corporation at less than their ***carrying value,*** a gain is realized on the retirement of the debt. If the bonds are reacquired by the issuing corporation at a price in excess of their carrying value, a loss must be recognized. In ***Statement No. 4,*** the FASB ruled that these gains and losses, if ***material*** in amount, should be shown separately in the income statement as extraordinary items.[5]

For example, assume that the Briggs Corporation has outstanding a $1 million bond issue with unamortized premium in the amount of $20,000. The bonds are callable at 105 and the company exercises the call provision on 100 of the bonds, or 10% of the issue. The entry would be as follows:

*Bonds called at price above carrying value*

| | | |
|---|---|---|
| *Bonds Payable* | *100,000* | |
| *Premium on Bonds Payable* | *2,000* | |
| *Loss on Retirement of Bonds* | *3,000* | |
| *Cash* | | *105,000* |
| *To record retirement of $100,000 face value of bonds called at 105.* | | |

The carrying value of each of the 100 called bonds was $1,020, whereas the call price was $1,050. For each bond called the company incurred a loss of $30, or a total loss of $3,000. Note that when 10% of the total issue was called, 10% of the unamortized premium was written off.

If bonds remain outstanding until the maturity date, the discount or premium will have been completely amortized and the accounting entry to retire the bonds (assuming that interest is paid separately) will consist of a debit to Bonds Payable and a credit to Cash.

One year before the maturity date, the bonds payable may be reclassified from long-term debt to a current liability in the balance sheet if payment is to be made from current assets rather than from a ***bond sinking fund.***

## Bond sinking fund

To make a bond issue attractive to investors, corporations may agree to create a sinking fund, exclusively for use in paying the bonds at maturity. A bond sinking

[5] *FASB, Statement No. 4,* "Reporting Gains and Losses from Extinguishment of Debt" (Stamford, Conn.: 1975).

fund is created by setting aside a specified amount of cash at regular intervals. The cash is usually deposited with a trustee, who invests it and adds the earnings to the amount of the sinking fund. The periodic deposits of cash plus the earnings on the sinking fund investments should cause the fund to equal approximately the amount of the bond issue by the maturity date. When the bond issue approaches maturity, the trustee sells all the securities in the fund and uses the cash proceeds to pay the holders of the bonds. Any excess cash remaining in the fund will be returned to the corporation by the trustee.

A bond sinking fund is not included in current assets because it is not available for payment of current liabilities. The cash and securities comprising the fund are usually shown as a single amount under a caption such as Long-Term Investments, which is placed just below the current asset section. Interest earned on sinking fund securities constitutes revenue to the corporation.

### Conversion of bonds payable into common stock

Convertible bonds represent a popular form of financing, particularly during periods when common stock prices are rising. The conversion feature gives bondholders an opportunity to profit from a rise in the market price of the issuing company's common stock while still maintaining their status of creditors rather than stockholders. Because of this potential gain, convertible bonds generally carry lower interest rates than nonconvertible bonds.

The conversion ratio is typically set at a price above the current market price of the common stock at the date the bonds are authorized. For example, if common stock with a par value of $10 a share has a current market price of $42 a share, the ***conversion price*** might be set at $50 per share, thus enabling a holder of a $1,000 par value convertible bond to exchange the bond for 20 shares of common stock.[6] Let us assume that $5 million of such bonds are issued at par, and that some time later when the common stock has risen in price to $60 per share, the holders of 100 bonds decide to convert their bonds into common stock. The conversion transaction would be recorded as follows:

***Conversion of bonds into common stock***

| | | |
|---|---|---|
| *Convertible Bonds Payable* | *100,000* | |
| *Common Stock, $10 par* | | *20,000* |
| *Paid-in Capital in Excess of Par* | | *80,000* |
| *To record the conversion of 100 bonds into 2,000 shares of common stock.* | | |

No gain or loss is recognized by the issuing corporation upon conversion of bonds; the carrying value of the bonds is simply assigned to the common stock issued in exchange. If the bonds had been issued at a price above or below par, the unamortized premium or discount relating to the bonds would be written off at the time of conversion in order to assign the carrying value of the bonds to the common stock.

[6] $1,000 ÷ $50 conversion price = 20 shares of common stock.

## LEASES

A company may purchase the assets needed for use in its business or it may choose to lease them. Examples of assets often acquired by lease include buildings, office equipment, automobiles, and factory machinery. A ***lease*** is a contract in which the ***lessor*** gives the ***lessee*** the right to use an asset in return for periodic rental payments. The lessor is the owner of the property; the lessee is the tenant or renter. Accounting for the many forms of lease transactions and the disclosure of lease obligations by lessees are among the more important issues facing accountants today.

### Operating lease

When the lessor gives the lessee the right to use the leased property for a limited period of time but retains the usual risks and rewards of ownership, the contract is known as an ***operating lease.*** In accounting for an operating lease, the lessor accounts for the monthly lease payments received as rental revenue. The lessee accounts for the lease payments as rental expense; no asset or liability (other than a short-term liability for accrued rent payable) relating to the lease is recorded in the lessee's accounts.

### Capital lease

When the objectives of the lease contract are to provide financing to the lessee for the eventual purchase of the property, or for use of the property over most of its useful life, the contract is referred to as a ***capital lease*** (or a ***financing lease***). Even though title to the leased property has not been transferred, capital leases are regarded as ***essentially equivalent to a sale*** of the property by the lessor to the lessee. Thus, a capital lease should be recorded as a ***sale*** of property by the lessor and as a ***purchase*** by the lessee. In such lease agreements, an appropriate interest charge usually is added to the regular sales price of the property in determining the total amount of the lease payments.

Some manufacturing companies frequently use capital lease agreements as a means of financing the sale of their products to customers. In accounting for merchandise "sold" through a capital lease, the lessor debits Lease Payments Receivable and credits Sales for an amount equal to the ***present value of the future lease payments.***[7] In most cases, the present value of these future payments is equal to the regular sales price of the merchandise. In addition, the lessor would transfer the cost of the leased merchandise from the Inventory account to the Cost of Goods Sold account (assuming a perpetual inventory system is in use). When lease payments are received, the lessor should recognize an appropri-

---

[7]We have elected to record the present value of the future lease payments by a single debit entry to Lease Payments Receivable. An alternative is to debit Lease Payments Receivable for the total amount of the future payments and to credit Discount on Lease Payments Receivable, a contra-asset account, for the unearned finance charges included in the contractual amount. Either approach results in the lessor recording a net receivable equal to the present value of the future lease payments.

ate portion of the payment as representing interest revenue and the remainder as a reduction in Lease Payments Receivable.

When equipment is acquired through a capital lease, the lessee should debit an asset account, Leased Equipment, and credit a liability account, Lease Payment Obligation, for the present value of the future lease payments. Lease payments made by the lessee are allocated between Interest Expense and a reduction in the liability, Lease Payment Obligation. No rent expense is involved. The asset account, Leased Equipment, is depreciated over the life of the equipment rather than the life of the lease. (The journal entries used in accounting for a capital lease are illustrated on page 697 of the appendix to this chapter.)

**Distinguishing between capital leases and operating leases** In ***Statement No. 13,*** the FASB required that a lease which meets at least one of the following criteria be accounted for as a capital lease:[8]

1 The lease transfers ownership of the property to the lessee at the end of the lease term.
2 The lease contains a "bargain purchase option."
3 The lease term is equal to 75% or more of the estimated economic life of the property.
4 The present value of the minimum lease payments is at least 90% of the fair value of the leased property.

Only those leases which meet none of the above criteria may be accounted for as operating leases.

**New standards reduce off-balance-sheet financing** Prior to the issuance of ***FASB Statement No. 13,*** the criteria defining capital leases were much narrower. As a result, a great number of long-term leases were accounted for as operating leases by the lessees. Operating leases often are called ***off-balance-sheet financing,*** because the obligation for future lease payments does not appear as a liability in the balance sheet of the lessee. As a result of the criteria set forth in ***Statement No. 13,*** the number of lease contracts qualifying as operating leases has been greatly reduced. In the opinion of the authors, accounting for long-term lease contracts as capital leases significantly improves the usefulness of the balance sheet in evaluating the resources and obligations of companies which lease substantial portions of their productive assets.

A number of more complex issues and special situations are involved in accounting for leases; these are covered in intermediate accounting.

## OTHER LIABILITIES

### Mortgage notes payable

Purchases of real estate and certain types of equipment often are financed by the issuance of mortgage notes payable. When a mortgage note is issued, the bor-

[8] *FASB Statement No. 13,* "Accounting for Leases" (Stamford, Conn.: 1976), pp. 9–10.

rower pledges title to specific assets as collateral for the loan. If the borrower defaults on the note, the lender may foreclose upon these assets. Mortgage notes usually are payable in equal monthly installments. These monthly installments may continue until the loan is completely repaid, or the note may contain a "due date" at which the remaining unpaid balance of the loan must be repaid in a single, lump-sum payment.

A portion of each monthly payment represents interest on the unpaid balance of the loan and the remainder of the monthly payment reduces the amount of the unpaid balance (principal). Since the principal is being reduced each month, the portion of each successive payment representing interest will ***decrease,*** and the portion of the payment going toward repayment of the principal will ***increase.*** To illustrate, assume that a company issues a $100,000 mortgage note to finance the purchase of a warehouse. The note requires monthly payments in the amount of $1,000 and bears interest at the annual rate of 9% (equal to $\frac{3}{4}$% per month). The following partial amortization table shows the allocation of the first three monthly payments between interest and principal:

*Monthly payments on a mortgage note*

| Payment Date | (A) Monthly Payment | (B) Monthly Interest Expense ($\frac{3}{4}$% of Unpaid Balance) | (C) Reduction in Principal (A − B) | (D) Unpaid Principal Balance |
|---|---|---|---|---|
| Sept. 11—Issuance date | | | | $100,000.00 |
| Oct. 11 . . . . . . . . . . . . . | $1,000.00 | $750.00 | $250.00 | 99,750.00 |
| Nov. 11 . . . . . . . . . . . . . | 1,000.00 | 748.13 | 251.87 | 99,498.13 |
| Dec. 11 . . . . . . . . . . . . . | 1,000.00 | 746.24 | 253.76 | 99,244.37 |

## Pension plans

A ***pension plan*** is a contract between a company and its employees under which the company agrees to pay retirement benefits to eligible employees. An employer company generally meets its obligations under a pension plan by making regular payments to an insurance company or other outside agency. As pension obligations accrue, the employer company records them by a debit to Pension Expense and a credit to Cash. If all required payments are made promptly to the pension fund trustee, no liability need appear on the employer company's financial statements. When employees retire, their retirement benefits are paid by the insurance company. This type of arrangement is called a ***funded pension plan.***

The Retirement Security Act of 1974 (ERISA) was a most complex piece of legislation requiring extensive reporting of pension plans to the federal government. The objectives included assuring that the enormous amounts of money in pension plans were properly accounted for, audited regularly, and available to meet obligations to retiring employees. The FASB is currently studying the need for new accounting standards to meet the requirements imposed by ERISA. Pension plans are considered in some detail in more advanced accounting courses.

### Estimated liabilities

An estimated liability is one known to exist, but for which the dollar amount is uncertain. A common example is the liability of a manufacturer to honor any warranty on products sold. For example, assume that a company manufactures and sells television sets which carry a two-year warranty. To achieve the objective of offsetting current revenue with all related expenses, the liability for future warranty repairs on television sets sold during the current period must be estimated at the balance sheet date. This estimate will be based upon the company's past experience.

### Loss contingencies

In Chapter 9, we discussed the ***contingent liability*** which arises when notes receivable are discounted at a bank. A contingent liability may be regarded as a ***possible*** liability, which may develop into a full-fledged liability or may be eliminated entirely by a future event. Contingent liabilities are also called ***loss contingencies.*** "Loss contingencies," however, is a broader term, encompassing the possible impairment of assets as well as the possible existence of liabilities.

A common loss contingency is the possibility of loss which arises when a lawsuit is filed against a company. Until the lawsuit is resolved, uncertainty exists as to the amount, if any, of the company's liability. Central to the definition of a loss contingency is the element of ***uncertainty***—uncertainty both as to the amount of loss and whether, in fact, a loss actually has occurred.

Loss contingencies are recorded in the accounting records at estimated amounts only when both of the following criteria are met: (1) it is ***probable*** that a loss has been incurred, and (2) the amount of loss can be ***reasonably estimated.***[9] An example of a loss contingency which meets these criteria and is recorded in the accounts is the estimated loss from doubtful accounts receivable. Loss contingencies which do not meet both of these criteria should be ***disclosed in footnotes*** to the financial statements whenever there is at least a ***reasonable possibility*** that a loss has been incurred. Pending lawsuits, for example, almost always are disclosed in footnotes, but the loss, if any, is not recorded in the accounting records until the lawsuit is settled.

When loss contingencies are disclosed in footnotes to the financial statements, the footnote should describe the nature of the contingency and, if possible, provide an estimate of the amount of possible loss. If a reasonable estimate of the amount of possible loss cannot be made, the footnote should include the range of possible loss or a statement that an estimate cannot be made. The following footnote is typical of the disclosure of the loss contingency arising from pending litigation:

*Footnote disclosure of a loss contingency*

***Note 8: Contingencies***

***In October of the current year, the Company was named as defendant in a lawsuit alleging patent infringement and claiming damages of $408 million. The Company denies all charges in***

[9] *FASB Statement No. 5,* "Accounting for Contingencies" (Stamford, Conn.: 1975).

***this case and is preparing its defenses against them. The Company is advised by legal counsel that it is not possible at this time to determine the ultimate legal and financial responsibility with respect to this litigation.***

Users of financial statements should pay close attention to the footnote disclosure of loss contingencies. Even though no loss has been recorded in the accounting records, some loss contingencies may be so material in amount as to threaten the continued existence of the company.

## KEY TERMS INTRODUCED OR EMPHASIZED IN CHAPTER 18

**Amortization of discount or premium on bonds payable** The process of systematically writing off a portion of bond discount to increase interest expense or writing off a portion of bond premium to decrease interest expense each period the bonds are outstanding.

**Bond sinking fund** Cash set aside by the corporation at regular intervals (usually with a trustee) to be used to pay the bonds at maturity.

**Capital lease** A lease contract which, in essence, finances the eventual purchase by the lessee of leased property. The lessor accounts for a capital lease as a sale of property; the lessee records an asset and a liability equal to the present value of the future lease payments. Also called a ***financing lease.***

**Carrying value of bonds** The face amount of the bonds plus any unamortized premium or minus any unamortized discount.

**Contract interest rate** The contractual rate of interest printed on bonds. The contract interest rate, applied to the face value of the bonds, determines the amount of the annual cash interest payments to bondholders. Also called the ***nominal interest rate.***

**Debenture bond** An unsecured bond, the value of which rests on the general credit of the corporation. Not secured by pledge of specific assets.

**Discount on bonds payable** Amount by which the face amount of the bond exceeds the price received by the corporation at the date of issuance. Indicates that the contractual rate of interest is lower than the market rate of interest.

**Effective interest method of amortization** Discount or premium on bonds is amortized by the difference between the contractual cash interest payment each period and the amount of interest computed by applying the effective interest rate to the carrying value of the bonds at the beginning of the current interest period. Causes bond interest expense to be a constant percentage of the carrying value of the liability.

**Effective interest rate** The actual rate of interest expense to the borrowing corporation, taking into account the contractual cash interest payments and the discount or premium to be amortized.

**Lessee** The tenant, user, or renter of leased property.

**Lessor** The owner of property leased to a lessee.

**Loss contingency** A situation involving uncertainty as to whether or not a loss has occurred. The uncertainty will be resolved by a future event. An example of a loss contingency is the possible loss related to a lawsuit pending against a company. Although loss contingencies are sometimes recorded in the accounts, they are more frequently disclosed only in footnotes in the financial statements.

**Off-balance-sheet financing** An arrangement in which the use of resources is financed without the obligation for future payments appearing as a liability in the balance sheet. An operating lease is the most common example of off-balance-sheet financing.

**Operating lease** A lease contract which is in essence a rental agreement. The lessee has the use of the leased property, but the lessor retains the usual risks and rewards of ownership. The periodic lease payments are accounted for as rent expense by the lessee and as rental revenue by the lessor.

**Premium on bonds payable** Amount by which the issuance price of a bond exceeds the face value. Indicates that the contractual rate of interest is higher than the market rate.

**Present value of a future amount** The amount of money that an informed investor would pay today for the right to receive the future amount, based upon a specific rate of return required by the investor. Bond prices are the present value to investors of the future principal and interest payments. Capital leases are recorded as an asset and a related liability in the accounting records of the lessee at the present value of the future lease payments.

## REVIEW QUESTIONS

**1** Distinguish between the two terms in each of the following pairs:
 **a** Mortgage bond; debenture bond
 **b** Contract (or nominal) interest rate; effective interest rate
 **c** Fixed-maturity bond; serial bond
 **d** Coupon bond; registered bond
 **e** Operating lease; capital lease
 **f** Estimated liability; contingent liability

**2** K Company has decided to finance expansion by issuing $10 million of 20-year debenture bonds and will ask a number of underwriters to bid on the bond issue. Discuss the factors that will determine the amount bid by the underwriters for these bonds.

**3** What is a ***convertible bond?*** Discuss the advantages and disadvantages of convertible bonds from the standpoint of **(a)** the investor and **(b)** the issuing corporation.

**4** The Computer Sharing Co. has paid-in capital of $10 million and retained earnings of $3 million. The company has just issued $1 million in 20-year, 8% bonds. It is proposed that a policy be established of appropriating $50,000 of retained earnings each year to enable the company to retire the bonds at maturity. Evaluate the merits of this proposal in accomplishing the desired result.

**5** The following excerpt is taken from an article in a leading business periodical: "In the bond market high interest rates mean low prices. Bonds pay out a fixed percentage of their face value, usually $1,000; an 8% bond, for instance, will pay $80 a year. In order for its yield to rise to 10%, its price would have to drop to $800." Give a critical evaluation of this quotation.

**6** Discuss the advantages and disadvantages of a ***call provision*** in a bond contract from the viewpoint of **(a)** the bondholder and **(b)** the issuing corporation.

**7** Explain why the effective rate of interest differs from the contract rate when bonds are issued **(a)** at a discount and **(b)** at a premium.

**8** When the effective interest method is used to amortize bond discount or premium, the amount of bond interest expense will differ in each period from that of the preceding period. Explain how the amount of bond interest expense changes from one period to another when the bonds are issued **(a)** at a discount and **(b)** at a premium.

**9** Explain why the effective interest method of amortizing bond discount or premium is considered to be theoretically preferable to the straight-line method.

**10** Explain how the lessee accounts for an operating lease and a capital lease. Why is an operating lease sometimes called ***off-balance sheet-financing?***

**11** A friend of yours has just purchased a house and has incurred a $50,000, 11% mortgage, payable at $476.17 per month. After making the first monthly payment, he received a receipt from the bank stating that only $17.84 of the $476.17 had been applied to reducing the principal amount of the loan. Your friend computes that at the rate of $17.84 per month, it will take over 233 years to pay off the $50,000 mortgage. Do you agree with your friend's analysis?

**12** Under what conditions are ***loss contingencies*** recorded at estimated amounts in the accounting records?

**13** A lawsuit has been filed against Telmar Corporation alleging violations of federal antitrust laws and claiming damages which, when trebled, total $1.2 billion. Telmar Corporation denies the charges and intends to contest the suit vigorously. Legal counsel advises the company that the litigation will last for several years and that a reasonable estimate of the final outcome cannot be made at this time.

Should Telmar Corporation include in its current balance sheet a liability for the damages claimed in this lawsuit? Explain fully.

**14** With reference to question **13** above, illustrate the disclosure of the pending lawsuit which should be included in the current financial statements of Telmar Corporation.

## EXERCISES

*Ex. 18-1* On December 31, Year 10, Wayne Corporation received authorization to issue $15,000,000 of 10%, 30-year debenture bonds. Interest payment dates were June 30 and December 31. The bonds were all issued at par on January 31, Year 11, one month after the interest date printed on the bonds.

**Instructions**

**a** Prepare the journal entry at January 31, Year 11, to record the sale of the bonds.

**b** Prepare the journal entry at June 30, Year 11, to record the semiannual bond interest payment.

*Ex. 18-2* Companies A and B have the same amount of operating income and the same number of outstanding shares of common stock. However, the two companies have different capital structures. Determine the amount earned per share of common stock for each of the two companies and explain the source of any difference.

| | *Company A* | *Company B* |
|---|---|---|
| *8% debenture bonds payable* | *$5,000,000* | *$ -0-* |
| *10% cumulative preferred stock, $100 par* | *1,000,000* | *6,000,000* |
| *Common stock, $50 par value* | *5,000,000* | *5,000,000* |
| *Retained earnings* | *2,500,000* | *2,500,000* |
| *Operating income, before interest and income taxes (assume a 40% tax rate)* | *3,500,000* | *3,500,000* |

*Ex. 18-3* Crest Company issued \$10,000,000 par value $9\frac{1}{2}$% bonds on July 1, Year 5, at $97\frac{1}{2}$. Interest is due on June 30 and December 31 of each year, and the bonds mature on June 30, Year 15. The fiscal year ends on December 31; bond discount is amortized by the straight-line method. Prepare the following journal entries:

**a** July 1, Year 5, to record the issuance of the bonds
**b** December 31, Year 5, to pay interest and amortize the bond discount
**c** June 30, Year 15, to pay interest, amortize the bond discount, and retire the bonds at maturity

*Ex. 18-4* North Company issued \$20 million of 11%, 10-year bonds on January 1, Year 1. Interest is payable semiannually on June 30 and December 31. The bonds were sold to an underwriting group at 105.

South Company issued \$20 million of 10%, 10-year bonds on January 1, Year 1. Interest is payable semiannually on June 30 and December 31. The bonds were sold to an underwriting group at 95.

Prepare journal entries to record all transactions during Year 1 for **(a)** the North Company bond issue and **(b)** the South Company bond issue. Assume that both companies amortize bond discount or premium by the straight-line method at each interest payment date.

*Ex. 18-5* The following liability appears on the balance sheet of the Sunrise Company on December 31, Year 1:

| | | |
|---|---|---|
| ***Long-term liabilities:*** | | |
| ***Bonds payable, $9\frac{3}{4}$%, due Dec. 31, Year 15*** . . . . . . . . . . . . | ***\$1,000,000*** | |
| ***Premium on bonds payable*** . . . . . . . . . . . . . . . . . . . . . . . . | ***42,000*** | ***\$1,042,000*** |

On January 1, Year 2, 20% of the bonds are retired at 98. Interest was paid on December 31, Year 1.

**a** Record the retirement of \$200,000 of bonds on January 1, Year 2.
**b** Record the interest payment for the six months ending December 31, Year 2, and the amortization of the premium on December 31, Year 2, assuming that amortization is recorded by the straight-line method only at the end of each year.

*Ex. 18-6* On April 1, Year 1, Basin Corporation issued \$1,000,000 of 10-year, 9% bonds payable and received proceeds of \$937,689, resulting in an effective interest rate of 10%. Interest is payable on September 30 and March 31. The effective interest method is used to amortize bond discount; an amortization table for this bond issue is illustrated on page 669.

**Instructions** Prepare the necessary journal entries (rounding all amounts to the nearest dollar) on:

**a** April 1, Year 1, to record the issuance of the bonds
**b** September 30, Year 1, to record the payment of interest and amortization of discount at the first semiannual interest payment date
**c** December 31, Year 1, to accrue bond interest expense through year-end
**d** March 31, Year 2, to record the payment of interest and amortization of bond discount at the second semiannual interest payment date.

*Ex. 18-7* Crown Point Corporation issued on the authorization date \$1,000,000 of 10-year, 9% bonds payable and received proceeds of \$1,067,952, resulting in an effective interest rate of 8%. The premium is amortized by the effective interest method; the amortization table for this bond issue is illustrated on page 671. Interest is payable semiannually.

**Instructions**

**a** Show how the liability for the bonds would appear on a balance sheet prepared immediately after issuance of the bonds.
**b** Show how the liability for the bonds would appear on a balance sheet prepared after 16 semiannual interest periods (two years prior to maturity).

**c** Show the necessary calculations to determine for this bond issue interest expense by the effective interest method for the first six-month period, the premium amortized at the end of that first period, and the cash interest payment. Your calculations should include use of the effective interest rate and also the contractual rate. Round all amounts to the nearest dollar.

*Ex. 18-8* Brand Corporation issued $1,000,000 of 7%, 10-year convertible bonds dated December 31, Year 8, at a price of 98. Semiannual interest payment dates were June 30 and December 31. The conversion rate was 20 shares of $10 par common stock for each $1,000 bond. Four years later on December 31, Year 12, bondholders converted $250,000 face value of bonds into common stock. Assume that unamortized discount on this date amounted to $12,000 for the entire bond issue. Prepare a journal entry to record the conversion on the bonds.

## PROBLEMS

### Group A

*18A-1* Seville Products, Inc., obtained authorization to issue $12,000,000 face value of 8%, 20-year bonds, dated April 30, Year 3. Interest payment dates were October 31 and April 30. Issuance of the bonds did not take place until July 31, Year 3. On this date all the bonds were sold at a price of 100 plus three months' accrued interest.

**Instructions** Prepare the necessary entries in general journal form on:
**a** July 31, Year 3, to record the issuance of the bonds
**b** October 31, Year 3, to record the first semiannual interest payment on the bond issue
**c** December 31, Year 3, to accrue bond interest expense through year-end and to close the Bond Interest Expense account
**d** April 30, Year 4, to record the second semiannual interest payment

*18A-2* On September 1, Year 1, American Farm Equipment issued $3 million in 9% debenture bonds. Interest is payable semiannually on March 1 and September 1, and the bonds mature on September 1, Year 11. Company policy is to amortize bond discount or premium by the straight-line method at each interest payment date; the company's fiscal year ends at December 31.

**Instructions**
**a** Make the necessary adjusting entries at December 31, Year 1, and the journal entry to record the payment of bond interest on March 1, Year 2, under each of the following assumptions:
(1) The bonds were issued at 98.
(2) The bonds were issued at 103.
**b** Compute the net bond liability at December 31, Year 1, under assumptions (1) and (2) above.

*18A-3* The items shown below appear in the balance sheet of Pilsner Breweries at December 31, Year 6:

| | | |
|---|---|---|
| ***Current liabilities:*** | | |
| ***Bond interest payable (for three months from Sept. 30 to Dec. 31)*** | | ***$ 200,000*** |
| ***Long-term debt:*** | | |
| ***Bonds payable, 8%, due Mar. 31, Year 17*** | ***$10,000,000*** | |
| ***Less: Discount on bonds payable*** | ***196,800*** | ***9,803,200*** |

The bonds are callable on any interest date. On September 30, Year 7, Pilsner Breweries called $2 million of the bonds at 103.

**Instructions**

**a** Prepare journal entries to record the semiannual interest payment on March 31, Year 7. Discount is amortized by the straight-line method at each interest payment date and was amortized to December 31, Year 6. Base the amortization on the 123-month period from December 31, Year 6, to March 31, Year 17.

**b** Prepare journal entries to record the amortization of bond discount and payment of bond interest at September 30, Year 7, and also to record the calling of $2 million of the bonds at this date.

**c** Prepare a journal entry to record the accrual of interest at December 31, Year 7. Include the amortization of bond discount to the year-end.

***18A-4*** Kentucky Coal Mines obtained authorization to issue $8,000,000 of 9%, 10-year bonds, dated May 1, Year 1. Interest payment dates were May 1 and November 1. Issuance of the bonds did not take place until July 1, Year 1. On this date, the entire bond issue was sold to an underwriter at a price which included the two months' accrued interest. Kentucky Coal Mines follows the policy of amortizing bond discount or premium by the straight-line method at each interest date as well as for year-end adjusting entries at December 31.

**Instructions**

**a** Prepare all journal entries necessary to record the issuance of the bonds and bond interest expense during Year 1, assuming that the sales price of the bonds on July 1 was $8,415,000 including accrued interest. (Note that the bonds will be outstanding for a period of only 9 years and 10 months.)

**b** Assume that the sales price of the bonds on July 1 had been $7,907,600, including accrued interest. Prepare journal entries for Year 1 parallel to those in part **a** above.

**c** Show the proper balance sheet presentation of the liability for bonds payable (including accrued interest) in the balance sheet prepared at December 31, ***Year 6,*** assuming that the original sales price of the bonds (including accrued interest) had been:

(1) $8,415,000, as described in part **a**

(2) $7,907,600, as described in part **b**

***18A-5*** On June 30, Year 4, King Cotton Company issued $4,000,000 par value of $9\frac{1}{2}$% bonds payable at a price of $103\frac{1}{4}$, resulting in an effective annual rate of interest of 9%. The semiannual interest payment dates are June 30 and December 31, and the bonds mature on June 30, Year 14. The company maintains its accounts on a calendar-year basis and amortizes bond premium by the effective interest method.

**Instructions**

**a** Prepare the required journal entries (with explanations) on:

(1) June 30, Year 4, to record the sale of the bonds.

(2) December 31, Year 4, for payment of interest and amortization of premium on bonds. (Use one compound entry.)

(3) June 30, Year 14, for payment of interest, amortization of the remaining premium, and to retire the bonds. Assume that the carrying value of the bonds at the beginning of this last six-month interest period is $4,009,569.

**b** Show how the accounts, Bonds Payable and Premium on Bonds Payable, would appear on the balance sheet at December 31, Year 4.

***18A-6*** On December 31, Year 10, Apache Corporation sold a $6,000,000 face value, 10%, 10-year bond issue to an underwriter at a price of 94. This price results in an effective annual interest rate of 11%. Interest is payable semiannually on June 30 and December 31. Apache Corporation amortizes bond discount by the effective interest method.

**Instructions**

**a** Prepare an amortization table for the first two years (four interest periods) of this bond issue. Round all amounts to the nearest dollar and use the following column headings for your table:

| Six-Month Interest Period | (A) Interest Paid Semi-annually ($6,000,000 × 5%) | (B) Effective Semi-annual Interest Expense (Carrying Value × $5\frac{1}{2}$%) | (C) Discount Amortization (B − A) | (D) Bond Discount Balance | (E) Carrying Value of Bonds, End of Period ($6,000,000 − D) |
|---|---|---|---|---|---|

**b** Using the information from your amortization table, prepare all journal entries necessary to record issuance of the bonds and bond interest for Year 11. (Use a compound entry for interest payment and amortization of bond discount at each semiannual interest payment date.)

**c** Show the proper balance sheet presentation of Bonds Payable and Discount on Bonds Payable at December 31, Year 12.

*18A-7* Roan Antelope, Inc., on September 1, Year 1, issued $9,000,000 par value, $8\frac{1}{2}$%, 10-year bonds payable with interest dates of March 1 and September 1. The company maintains its accounts on a calendar-year basis and follows the policy of amortizing bond discount and bond premium by the effective interest method at the semiannual interest payment dates as well as at the year-end adjusting of the accounts.

**Instructions**

**a** Prepare the necessary journal entries to record the following transactions, assuming that the bonds were sold for $8,700,000, a price resulting in an effective annual interest rate of 9%.
(1) Sale of the bonds on September 1, Year 1
(2) Adjustment of the accounts at December 31, Year 1, for accrued interest and amortization of adiscount
(3) Payment of bond interest and amortization of discount on March 1, Year 2

**b** Assume that the sales price of the bonds on September 1, Year 1, had been $9,300,000, resulting in an effective annual interest rate of 8%. Prepare journal entries parallel to those called for in **a** above at the dates of September 1, Year 1; December 31, Year 1; and March 1, Year 2.

**c** State the amounts of bond interest expense for Year 1 and the ***net*** amount of the liability for the bonds payable at December 31, Year 1, under the independent assumptions set forth in both **a** and **b** above. Show your computations.

*18A-8* Custom Truck Builders frequently uses long-term lease contracts to finance the sale of its trucks. On November 1, Year 1, Custom Truck Builders leased to Interstate Van Lines a truck carried in the perpetual inventory records at $33,520. The terms of the lease call for Interstate Van Lines to make 36 monthly payments of $1,400 each, beginning on November 30, Year 1. The present value of these payments, after considering a built-in interest charge of 1% per month, is equal to the regular $42,150 sales price of the truck. At the end of the 36-month lease, title to the truck will transfer to Interstate Van Lines.

**Instructions**

**a** Prepare journal entries in the accounts of Custom Truck Builders on:
(1) November 1 to record the sale financed by the lease and the related cost of

goods sold. (Debit Lease Payments Receivable for the $42,150 present value of the future lease payments.)
(2) November 30, to record receipt of the first $1,400 monthly payment. (Prepare a compound journal entry which allocates the cash receipt between interest revenue and reduction of Lease Payments Receivable. The portion of each monthly payment recognized as interest revenue is equal to 1% of the balance of the account Lease Payments Receivable, at the beginning of that month. Round all interest computations to the nearest dollar.)
(3) December 31, to record receipt of the second monthly payment.

**b** Prepare journal entries for Year 1 in the accounts of Interstate Van Lines on:
(1) November 1, to record acquisition of the leased truck.
(2) November 30, to record the first monthly lease payment. (Determine the portion of the payment representing interest expense in a manner parallel to that described in part **a.**)
(3) December 31, to record the second monthly lease payment.
(4) December 31, to recognize depreciation on the leased truck through year-end. Compute depreciation expense by the straight-line method, using a 10-year service life and an estimated salvage value of $6,150.

**c** Compute the net carrying value of the leased truck in the balance sheet of Interstate Van Lines at December 31, Year 1.

**d** Compute the amount of Interstate Van Lines' lease payment obligation at December 31, Year 1.

## Group B

***18B-1*** Texas Bus & Tractor Co. obtained all necessary approvals to issue $10,000,000 face value of 9%, 20-year bonds dated March 31, Year 4. Interest payment dates were September 30 and March 31. The bonds were not issued, however, until four months later, August 1, Year 4. On this date the entire bond issue was sold to an underwriter at a price of 100 plus accrued interest.

**Instructions** Prepare the required entries in general journal form on:

**a** August 1, Year 4, to record the issuance of the bonds
**b** September 30, Year 4, to record the first semiannual interest payment on the bonds
**c** December 31, Year 4, to accrue bond interest expense through year-end and to close the Bond Interest Expense account for the year
**d** March 31, Year 5, to record the second semiannual interest payment

***18B-2*** On October 31, Year 1, Perfect Racquet Mfg. Co. issued $12,000,000 face value of 11% debenture bonds, with interest payable on April 30 and October 31. The bonds mature 10 years from the date of issuance. Company policy is to amortize bond discount or premium by the straight-line method at each interest payment date; the company's fiscal year ends at December 31.

**Instructions**

**a** Make the necessary adjusting entries at December 31, Year 1, and the journal entry to record the payment of bond interest on April 30, Year 2, under each of the following assumptions:
(1) The bonds were issued at 97.
(2) The bonds were issued at 102.

**b** Compute the net bond liability at December 31, Year 1, under assumptions (1) and (2) above.

***18B-3*** The items shown on page 687 appear in the balance sheet of Key West Corporation at December 31, Year 10:

| | | |
|---|---|---|
| ***Current liabilities:*** | | |
| ***Bond interest payable (for three months from Sept. 30 to Dec. 31)*** | | ***$ 180,000*** |
| ***Long-term debt:*** | | |
| ***Bonds payable, 9%, due Sept. 30, Year 16*** | ***$8,000,000*** | |
| ***Less: Discount on bonds payable*** | ***68,400*** | ***7,931,600*** |

The bonds are callable on any interest date. On September 30, Year 11, Key West Corporation called $2 million of the bonds at 105.

**Instructions**

**a** Prepare journal entries to record the semiannual interest payment on March 31, Year 11. Discount is amortized by the straight-line method at each interest payment date and was amortized to December 31, Year 10. Base the amortization on the 57-month period from December 31, Year 10; to September 30, Year 15.

**b** Prepare journal entries to record the amortization of bond discount and payment of bond interest at September 30, Year 11, and also to record the calling of $2 million of the bonds at this date.

**c** Prepare a journal entry to record the accrual of interest at December 31, Year 11. Include the amortization of bond discount to the year-end.

***18B-4*** Country Recording Studios obtained the necessary approvals to issue $3 million of 10%, 10-year bonds, dated March 1, Year 1. Interest payment dates were September 1 and March 1. Issuance of the bonds did not occur until June 1, Year 1. On this date, the entire bond issue was sold to an underwriter at a price which included three months' accrued interest. Country Recording Studios follows the policy of amortizing bond discount or premium by the straight-line method at each interest date as well as for year-end adjusting entries at December 31.

**Instructions**

**a** Prepare all journal entries necessary to record the issuance of the bonds and bond interest expense during Year 1, assuming that the sales price of the bonds on June 1 was $3,309,000, including accrued interest. (Note that the bonds will be outstanding for a period of only 9 years and 9 months.)

**b** Assume that the sales price of the bonds on June 1 had been $2,899,500, including accrued interest. Prepare journal entries for Year 1 parallel to those in part **a** above.

**c** Show the proper balance sheet presentation of the liability for bonds payable (including accrued interest) in the balance sheet prepared at December 31, ***Year 5,*** assuming that the original sales price of the bonds (including accrued interest) had been:

(1) $3,309,000, as described in part **a**

(2) $2,899,500, as described in part **b**

***18B-5*** Red Sky Shipping maintains its accounts on a calendar-year basis. On June 30, Year 4, the company issued $6,000,000 face value of 7.6% bonds at a price of $97\frac{1}{4}$, resulting in an effective rate of interest of 8%. Semiannual interest payment dates are June 30 and December 31. Bond discount is amortized by the effective interest method. The bonds mature on June 30, Year 14.

**Instructions**

**a** Prepare the required journal entries on:

(1) June 30, Year 4, to record the sale of the bonds.

(2) December 31, Year 4, to pay interest and amortize the discount using the effective interest method.

(3) June 30, Year 14, to pay interest, amortize the discount, and retire the bonds. Assume that at the beginning of this last interest period, the carrying value of the bonds is $5,988,462. (Use a separate journal entry to show the retirement of the bonds.)

**b** Show how the accounts, Bonds Payable and Discount on Bonds Payable, should appear on the balance sheet at December 31, Year 4.

*18B-6* On December 31, Year 4, Napa Vineyards sold an $8,000,000, $9\frac{1}{2}$%, 12-year bond issue to an underwriter at a price of $103\frac{1}{2}$. This price results in an effective annual interest rate of 9%. The bonds were dated December 31, Year 4, and the interest payment dates were June 30 and December 31. Napa Vineyards follows a policy of amortizing the bond premium by the effective interest method at each semiannual payment date.

**Instructions**

**a** Prepare an amortization table for the first two years (four interest periods) of the life of this bond issue. Round all amounts to the nearest dollar and use the following column headings:

| Six-Month Interest Period | (A) Interest Paid Semi-annually ($8,000,000 × $4\frac{3}{4}$%) | (B) Effective Semi-annual Interest Expense (Carrying Value × $4\frac{1}{2}$%) | (C) Premium Amortization (A − B) | (D) Bond Premium Balance | (E) Carrying Value of Bonds, End of Period ($8,000,000 − D) |
|---|---|---|---|---|---|

**b** Using the information in your amortization table, prepare all journal entries necessary to record the bond issue and the bond interest expense during Year 5.

**c** Show the proper balance sheet presentation of the liability for bonds payable at December 31, Year 6.

*18B-7* On November 1, Year 8, Signal Electronics issued $11,900,000 face value of $8\frac{1}{2}$% 10-year bonds with interest dates of May 1 and November 1. The bonds were purchased by an underwriter for $11,500,000, resulting in an effective interest rate to Signal Electronics of 9%. Company policy calls for amortizing bond discount at each interest payment date as well as for year-end adjustment of the accounts. The accounting records are maintained on a calendar-year basis.

**Instructions**

**a** Prepare the journal entries required to:
(1) Record the sale of the bonds on November 1, Year 8.
(2) Adjust the accounts at December 31, Year 8, for accrued bond interest and amortization of discount. (Use one compound entry.)
(3) Record the semiannual payment of bond interest on May 1, Year 9, and amortize the bond discount. (Use one compound entry.)

**b** State the amounts to be reported on the financial statements at the end of Year 8 for:
(1) Bonds payable (face amount)
(2) Unamortized discount on bonds payable
(3) Net amount of liability for bonds payable
(4) Interest expense for Year 8

*18B-8* Beach Equipment Co. frequently uses long-term lease contracts as a means of financing the sale of its products. On November 1, Year 1, Beach Equipment Co. leased to Star Industries a machine carried in the perpetual inventory records at a cost of $18,120. The terms of the lease called for 48 monthly payments of $650 each, beginning November 30, Year 1. The present value of these payments, after considering a built-in interest charge of 1% per month, is equal to $24,680, the regular sales price of the machine. At the end of the 48-month lease, title to the machine will transfer to Star Industries.

**Instructions**

**a** Prepare journal entries for Year 1 in the accounts of Beach Equipment Co. on:
  (1) November 1 to record the sale financed by the lease and the related cost of goods sold. (Debit Lease Payments Receivable for the $24,680 present value of the future lease payments.)
  (2) November 30, to record receipt of the first $650 monthly payment. (Prepare a compound journal entry which allocates the cash receipt between interest revenue and reduction of Lease Payments Receivable. The portion of each monthly payment recognized as interest revenue is equal to 1% of the balance of the account Lease Payments Receivable, at the beginning of that month. Round all interest computations to the nearest dollar.)
  (3) December 31, to record receipt of the second monthly payment.

**b** Prepare journal entries for Year 1 in the accounts of Star Industries on:
  (1) November 1, to record acquisition of the leased machine.
  (2) November 30, to record the first monthly lease payment. (Determine the portion of the payment representing interest expense in a manner parallel to that described in part **a.**)
  (3) December 31, to record the second monthly lease payment.
  (4) December 31, to recognize depreciation on the leased machine through year-end. Compute the depreciation expense by the straight-line method, using a 10-year service life and an estimated salvage value of $6,680.

**c** Compute the net carrying value of the leased machine in the balance sheet of Star Industries at December 31, Year 1.

**d** Compute the amount of Star Industries' lease payment obligation at December 31, Year 1.

## BUSINESS DECISION PROBLEM 18

Marvelous Mattress Co. reported the balances given below at the end of the current year:

| | |
|---|---|
| *Total assets* | *$14,800,000* |
| *Current liabilities* | *3,600,000* |
| *Long-term liabilities* | *400,000* |
| *Stockholders' equity:* | |
| *Capital stock, $10 par value* | *4,000,000* |
| *Paid-in capital in excess of par* | *3,000,000* |
| *Retained earnings* | *3,800,000* |

The company is planning an expansion of its plant facilities, and a study shows that $12 million of new funds will be required to finance the expansion. Two proposals are under consideration:

***Stock Financing*** Issue 200,000 shares of capital stock at a price of $60 per share.

***Bond Financing*** Borrow $12 million on a 20-year bond issue, with interest at 7%.

The assets and liabilities of Marvelous Mattress Co. have remained relatively constant over the past five years, and during this period the earnings ***after*** income taxes have averaged 10% of the stockholders' equity as reported at the end of the current year. The company expects that its earnings ***before*** income taxes will increase by an amount equal to 12% of the new investment in plant facilities.

Past and future income taxes for the company may be estimated at 40% of income before income taxes.

**Instructions**

**a** Prove that the company's average income ***before*** income taxes during the past five years was $1,800,000

**b** Prepare a schedule showing the expected earnings per share of capital stock during the first year of operations following the completion of the $12 million expansion, under each of the two proposed means of financing.

**c** Evaluate the two proposed means of financing from the viewpoint of a major stockholder of Marvelous Mattress Co.

# APPENDIX

## APPLICATIONS OF PRESENT VALUE

The concept of present value has many applications in accounting, but it is most easily illustrated in the context of evaluating investment opportunities. In this context, the present value of an expected future cash receipt is the amount that a knowledgeable investor would pay ***today*** for the right to receive that future amount. The present value is always ***less*** than the future amount, because the investor will expect to earn a return on the investment. The amount by which the future cash receipt exceeds its present value represents the investor's profit; in short, this difference may be regarded as ***interest revenue*** included in the future amount.

The present value of a particular investment opportunity depends upon three factors: (1) the expected dollar amount to be received in the future, (2) the length of time until the future amount will be received, and (3) the rate of return (called the ***discount rate***) required by the investor. The process of determining the present value of a future cash receipt or payment is called ***discounting*** the future amount.

To illustrate the present value concept, assume that a specific investment is expected to result in a $1,000 cash receipt at the end of one year. An investor requiring a 10% annual rate of return would be willing to pay $909 today (computed as $1,000 ÷ 1.10) for the right to receive this future amount. This computation may be verified as follows (amounts rounded to the nearest dollar):

| | |
|---|---|
| *Amount to be invested (present value)* | $ 909 |
| *Required return on investment ($909 × 10%)* | 91 |
| *Amount to be received in one year (future value)* | $1,000 |

If the $1,000 is to be received ***two years*** in the future, the investor would pay only $826 for the investment today [($1,000 ÷ 1.10) ÷ 1.10]. This computation may be verified as follows (amounts rounded to the nearest dollar):

| | |
|---|---|
| *Amount to be invested (present value)* | *$ 826* |
| *Required return on investment in first year ($826 × 10%)* | *83* |
| *Amount invested after one year* | *$ 909* |
| *Required return on investment in second year ($909 × 10%)* | *91* |
| *Amount to be received in two years (future value)* | *$1,000* |

The amount that our investor would pay today, $826, is the ***present value*** of $1,000 to be received in two years, discounted at an annual rate of 10%. The $174 difference between the $826 present value and the $1,000 future amount may be regarded as the return (interest revenue) to be earned by the investor over the two-year period.

## Present value tables

Although we can compute the present value of future amounts by a series of divisions as illustrated above, a more convenient method is available. We can use a ***table of present values*** to find the present value of $1 at a specified discount rate and then multiply that value by the future amount. For example, in the table shown below, the present value of $1 to be received in two years, dis-

**Table 1** **Present Value of $1 Due in *n* Periods***

| Number of Periods (*n*) | Discount Rate 1% | 1½% | 5% | 6% | 10% | 12% | 15% | 20% |
|---|---|---|---|---|---|---|---|---|
| 1 | .990 | .985 | .952 | .943 | .909 | .893 | .870 | .833 |
| 2 | .980 | .971 | .907 | .890 | .826 | .797 | .756 | .694 |
| 3 | .971 | .956 | .864 | .840 | .751 | .712 | .658 | .579 |
| 4 | .961 | .942 | .823 | .792 | .683 | .636 | .572 | .482 |
| 5 | .951 | .928 | .784 | .747 | .621 | .567 | .497 | .402 |
| 6 | .942 | .915 | .746 | .705 | .564 | .507 | .432 | .335 |
| 7 | .933 | .901 | .711 | .665 | .513 | .452 | .376 | .279 |
| 8 | .923 | .888 | .677 | .627 | .467 | .404 | .327 | .233 |
| 9 | .914 | .875 | .645 | .592 | .424 | .361 | .284 | .194 |
| 10 | .905 | .862 | .614 | .558 | .386 | .322 | .247 | .162 |
| 20 | .820 | .742 | .377 | .312 | .149 | .104 | .061 | .026 |
| 24 | .788 | .700 | .310 | .247 | .102 | .066 | .035 | .013 |

* The present value of $1 is computed by the formula $p = 1/(1 + i)^n$, where $p$ is the present value of $1, $i$ is the discount rate, and $n$ is the number of periods until the future cash flow will occur. Amounts in this table have been rounded to three decimal places and are shown for a limited number of periods and discount rates.

counted at an annual rate of 10%, is $0.826. If we multiply .826 by the expected future cash receipt of $1,000, we get an answer of $826, the same amount produced by the series of divisions in our previous illustration.

### Selecting an appropriate discount rate

The ***discount rate*** may be viewed as the investor's required rate of return. All investments involve some degree of risk that actual future cash flows may turn out to be less than expected. Investors usually will expect a rate of return which justifies taking this risk. Under today's market conditions, investors require annual returns of between 8% and 12% on low-risk investments, such as government bonds and certificates of deposit. For relatively high-risk investments, such as the introduction of a new product line, investors may expect to earn an annual return of perhaps 20% or more.

In addition to the amount of risk involved, the "appropriate" discount rate for determining the present value of a specific investment depends upon the investor's cost of capital and the returns available from other investment opportunities. When a higher discount rate is used, the resulting present value will be lower and the investor, therefore, will be interested in the investment only at a lower price.

### Discounting annual cash flows

Let us now assume that an investment is expected to produce an annual net cash flow of $10,000 for each of the next three years. If Camino Company expects a 12% return on this type of investment, it may compute the present value of these cash flows as follows:

| *Year* | *Expected Net Cash Flow* | × | *Present Value of $1 Discounted at 12%* | = | *Present Value of Net Cash Flows* |
|---|---|---|---|---|---|
| *1* | *$10,000* | | *.893* | | *$ 8,930* |
| *2* | *10,000* | | *.797* | | *7,970* |
| *3* | *10,000* | | *.712* | | *7,120* |
| *Total present value of the investment* | | | | | *$24,020* |

This analysis indicates that the present value of the expected net cash flows from the investment, discounted at an annual rate of 12%, amounts to $24,020. This is the maximum amount that Camino Company could afford to pay for this investment and still expect to earn the 12% required rate of return.

In the preceding schedule, we multiplied each of the expected annual cash flows by the present value of $1 in the appropriate future period, discounted at 12% per year. The present values of the annual cash flows were then added to determine the total present value of the investment. Separately discounting each annual cash flow to its present value is necessary only when the cash flows vary in amount from one year to the next. Since the annual cash flows in our example are ***uniform in amount,*** there are two easier ways to compute the total present value.

One way is to add the three decimal figures representing the present value of \$1 in the successive years (.893 + .797 + .712) and then to multiply this total (2.402) by the \$10,000 annual cash flow. This approach produces the same result (\$10,000 × 2.402 = \$24,020) as we obtained by determining the present value of each year's cash flow separately and adding the results.

An even easier approach to determining the present value of uniform annual cash flows is to refer to an ***annuity table,*** which shows the present value of \$1 to be received periodically for a given number of periods. An annuity table is shown below:

***Table 2*** ***Present Value of \$1 to Be Received Periodically for n Periods***

| Number of Periods (n) | Discount Rate 1% | $1\frac{1}{2}$% | 5% | 6% | 10% | 12% | 15% | 20% |
|---|---|---|---|---|---|---|---|---|
| 1 | 0.990 | 0.985 | 0.952 | 0.943 | 0.909 | 0.893 | 0.870 | 0.833 |
| 2 | 1.970 | 1.956 | 1.859 | 1.833 | 1.736 | 1.690 | 1.626 | 1.528 |
| 3 | 2.941 | 2.912 | 2.723 | 2.673 | 2.487 | 2.402 | 2.283 | 2.106 |
| 4 | 3.902 | 3.854 | 3.546 | 3.465 | 3.170 | 3.037 | 2.855 | 2.589 |
| 5 | 4.853 | 4.783 | 4.329 | 4.212 | 3.791 | 3.605 | 3.352 | 2.991 |
| 6 | 5.795 | 5.697 | 5.076 | 4.917 | 4.355 | 4.111 | 3.784 | 3.326 |
| 7 | 6.728 | 6.598 | 5.786 | 5.582 | 4.868 | 4.564 | 4.160 | 3.605 |
| 8 | 7.652 | 7.486 | 6.463 | 6.210 | 5.335 | 4.968 | 4.487 | 3.837 |
| 9 | 8.566 | 8.361 | 7.108 | 6.802 | 5.759 | 5.328 | 4.772 | 4.031 |
| 10 | 9.471 | 9.222 | 7.722 | 7.360 | 6.145 | 5.650 | 5.019 | 4.192 |
| 20 | 18.046 | 17.169 | 12.462 | 11.470 | 8.514 | 7.469 | 6.259 | 4.870 |
| 24 | 21.243 | 20.030 | 13.799 | 12.550 | 8.985 | 7.784 | 6.434 | 4.937 |

Note that the present value of \$1 to be received periodically (annually) for three years, discounted at 12% per year, is 2.402. Thus, \$10,000 received annually for three years, discounted at 12%, is \$24,020 (\$10,000 × 2.402).

## Discount periods of less than one year

The interval between regular periodic cash flows is termed the ***discount period.*** In our preceding examples we have assumed annual cash flows and, therefore, discount periods of one year. Often a note or a contract may call for cash payments on a more frequent basis, such as monthly, quarterly, or semiannually. The illustrated present value tables can be used with discount periods of any length, ***but the discount rate must relate to the time interval of the discount***

***period.*** Thus, if we use the annuity table to find the present value of a series of monthly cash payments, the discount rate must be expressed as a monthly interest rate.

To illustrate, assume that StyleMart purchases merchandise from Western Fashions, issuing in exchange a $9,600 note payable to be paid in 24 monthly installments of $400 each. As discussed in Chapter 9, both companies should record this transaction at the present value of the note. If a reasonable ***annual*** interest rate for this type of note is 12%, we should discount the monthly cash payments at the ***monthly*** rate of 1%. The annuity table shows the present value of $1 to be received (or paid) for 24 monthly periods, discounted at 1% per month, is 21.243. Thus, the present value of the installment note issued by StyleMart is $8,497 ($400 × 21.243, rounded to the nearest dollar).

## Accounting applications of the present value concept

Accounting applications of the concept of present value have been discussed at appropriate points throughout this textbook. We will now demonstrate these applications with examples which make use of our present value tables.

**Valuation of long-term notes receivable and payable (Chapter 9)** When a long-term note receivable or payable does not bear a realistic stated rate of interest, a portion of the face amount of the note should be regarded as representing an interest charge. The amount of this interest charge can be determined by discounting the note to its present value using as a discount rate a realistic rate of interest.

To illustrate, consider our preceding example in which StyleMart purchases merchandise from Western Fashions by issuing an installment note payable with a face amount of $9,600 and no stated rate of interest. The present value of this note, discounted at the realistic market interest rate of 1% per month, was $8,497. The difference between the $9,600 face amount of the note and its present value of $8,497 is $1,103, which represents the interest charge included in the face amount. StyleMart should use the present value of the note in determining the cost of the merchandise and the amount of the related net liability, as shown by the following entry:

| | | |
|---|---|---|
| *Purchases* | *8,497* | |
| *Discount on Notes Payable* | *1,103* | |
| *Notes Payable* | | *9,600* |
| *Purchased merchandise by issuing a 24-month installment note payable with a 1% monthly interest charge included in the face amount.* | | |

Assuming that StyleMart uses the effective interest method to amortize the discount on the note, the entry to record the first monthly payment and the related interest expense is as follows:

| | | |
|---|---|---|
| *Notes Payable* | *400* | |
| *Interest Expense* | *85* | |
| *Discount on Notes Payable* | | *85* |
| *Cash* | | *400* |

*To record first monthly payment on installment note payable and recognize one month's interest expense ($8,497 × 1%, rounded to nearest dollar).*

**Estimating the value of goodwill (Chapter 12)** The asset goodwill may be defined as the present value of expected future earnings in excess of the normal return on net identifiable assets. One method of estimating goodwill is to estimate the annual amounts by which earnings are expected to exceed a normal return and then to discount these amounts to their present value.

For example, assume that John Reed is negotiating to purchase a small but very successful business. In addition to paying the fair market value of the company's net identifiable assets, Reed is willing to pay an appropriate amount for goodwill. He believes that the business will probably earn at least $40,000 in excess of "normal earnings" in each of the next five years. If Reed requires a 20% annual return on purchased goodwill, he would be willing to pay $119,640 for this expected five-year $40,000 annuity, computed as follows: $40,000 × 2.991 (from Table 2) = $119,640.

**Market prices of bonds (Chapter 18)** The market price of bonds may be regarded as the ***present value*** to bondholders of the future principal and interest payments. To illustrate, assume that a corporation issues $1,000,000 face value of 9%, 10-year bonds when the going market rate of interest is 10%. Since bond interest is paid semiannually, we must use 20 ***semiannual*** periods as the life of the bond issue and a 5% ***semiannual*** market rate of interest in our present value calculations. The expected issuance price of this bond issue may be computed as follows:

| | |
|---|---|
| ***Present value of future principal payments:*** | |
| ***$1,000,000 due after 20 semiannual periods, discounted at 5% per period:*** | |
| ***$1,000,000 × .377 (from Table 1)*** | ***$377,000*** |
| ***Present value of future interest payments:*** | |
| ***$45,000 per period ($1,000,000 × 9% × ½) for 20 semiannual periods,*** | |
| ***discounted at 5%: $45,000 × 12.462 (from Table 2)*** | ***560,790*** |
| ***Expected issuance price of bond issue**** | ***$937,790*** |

*The terms of this bond issue correspond with those of the bond issue illustrated in the amortization table on page 669 in Chapter 18. In the amortization table, however, the issuance price of the bonds is $937,689, or $101 less than indicated by our computations above. The difference results from our rounding the present value of $1 to only three decimal places. Rounding to three decimal places may cause an error of up to $500 per $1 mllion.

**Capital leases (Chapter 18)** A capital lease is regarded as a sale of the leased asset by the lessor to the lessee. At the date of this sale, the lessor recognizes sales revenue equal to the ***present value*** of the future lease payments receivable, discounted at a realistic rate of interest. The lessee also uses the present value of the future payments to determine the cost of the leased asset and the valuation of the related liability.

To illustrate, assume that on December 1, Kelly Grading Co. enters into a capital lease contract to finance the purchase of a bulldozer from Midwest Tractor Sales. The terms of the lease call for 24 monthly payments of $7,000 each, beginning on December 31. These lease payments include an interest charge of $1\frac{1}{2}\%$ per month. At the end of the 24-month lease, title to the bulldozer will pass to Kelly Grading Co.

The annuity table on page 694 shows that the present value of $1 to be received monthly for 24 months, discounted at $1\frac{1}{2}\%$ per month, is 20.030. Therefore, the present value of the 24 future lease payments is $7,000 × 20.030, or $140,210. Kelly Grading Co. (the lessee) should use this present value in determining the cost of the bulldozer and the amount of the related liability, as shown in the following entry:

*Entry by lessee*

| | | |
|---|---|---|
| ***Leased Equipment*** | ***140,210*** | |
|     ***Lease Payment Obligation*** | | ***140,210*** |
| ***To record acquisition of bulldozer from Midwest Tractor Sales on a capital lease. Lease terms call for 24 monthly payments of $7,000, which include a $1\frac{1}{2}\%$ monthly interest charge.*** | | |

Note that the cost assigned to the leased equipment is only $140,210, even though Kelly Grading Co. must actually pay $168,000 ($7,000 × 24 payments) over the life of the lease. The difference between these two amounts, $27,790, will be recognized by Kelly Grading Co. as interest expense over the next 24 months.

Midwest Tractor Sales (the lessor) should also use the present value of the future lease payments in determining the sales price of the bulldozer and the amount of the related receivable. Assuming that the bulldozer was carried in the perpetual inventory records at a cost of $110,000, the entry to record the sale is:

*Entry by lessor*

| | | |
|---|---|---|
| ***Lease Payments Receivable (net)*** | ***140,210*** | |
| ***Cost of Goods Sold*** | ***110,000*** | |
|     ***Inventory*** | | ***110,000*** |
|     ***Sales*** | | ***140,210*** |
| ***Financed sale of bulldozer to Kelly Grading Co. using a capital lease. Terms call for 24 monthly payments of $7,000, including a $1\frac{1}{2}\%$ monthly interest charge. Gross amount of the receivable is $168,000, of which $27,790 is unearned interest.*** | | |

## PRESENT VALUE PROBLEMS

***PV-1*** Use the tables on pages 692 and 694 to determine the present value of the following cash flows:

**a** $10,000 to be paid annually for seven years, discounted at an annual rate of 15%.

**b** $4,250 to be received today, assuming that money can be invested to earn 20% annually.

**c** \$350 to be paid monthly for 24 months, with an additional "balloon payment" of \$15,000 due at the end of the twenty-fourth month, discounted at a monthly interest rate of $1\frac{1}{2}\%$.

**d** \$30,000 to be received annually for the first three years, followed by \$20,000 to be received annually for the next two years (total of five years in which payments are made), discounted at an annual rate of 12%.

***PV-2*** On June 30 of the current year, Rural Gas & Electric Co. issued \$10,000,000 par value, 11%, 10-year bonds payable, with interest dates of December 31 and June 30. The bonds were issued at a discount, resulting in an effective semiannual interest rate of 6%. The company maintains its accounts on a calendar-year basis and amortizes the bond discount by the effective interest method.

**Instructions**

**a** Compute the issuance price for the bond issue which results in an effective semiannual interest rate of 6%. (Hint: Discount both the interest payments and the maturity value over 20 semiannual periods.)

**b** Prepare all journal entries necessary to record the issuance of the bonds and bond interest expense during Year 1, assuming that the sales price of the bonds on June 30 was the amount you computed in part **a.**

***PV-3*** On December 1, Showcase Interiors purchased a shipment of furniture from Colonial House by paying \$10,500 cash and issuing an installment note payable in the face amount of \$28,800. The note is to be paid in 24 monthly installments of \$1,200 each. Although the note makes no mention of an interest charge, the rate of interest usually charged to Showcase Interiors in such transactions is $1\frac{1}{2}\%$ per month.

**Instructions**

**a** Compute the present value of the note payable, using a discount rate of $1\frac{1}{2}\%$ per month.

**b** Prepare the journal entries in the accounts of Showcase Interiors on:

(1) December 1, to record the purchase of the furniture (debit Purchases).

(2) December 31, to record the first \$1,200 monthly payment on the note and to recognize interest expense for one month by the effective interest method. (Round interest expense to the nearest dollar.)

**c** Show how the liability for this note would appear in the balance sheet at December 31. (Assume that the note is classified as a current liability.)

***PV-4*** Metropolitan Transit District plans to acquire a large computer system by entering into a long-term lease agreement with the computer manufacturer. The manufacturer will provide the computer system under either of the following lease agreements:

**Five-year lease** MTD is to pay \$2,500,000 at the beginning of the lease (delivery date) and \$1,000,000 annually at the end of each of the next five years. At the end of the fifth year, MTD may take title to the system for an additional payment of \$3,000,000.

**Ten-year lease** MTD is to pay \$2,000,000 at the beginning of the lease and \$900,000 annually at the end of each of the next ten years. At the end of the tenth year, MTD may take title for an additional payment of \$1,300,000.

Under either proposal, MTD will buy the computer at the end of the lease. MTD is a governmental agency which does not seek to earn a profit and is not evaluating alternative investment opportunities. However, MTD does attempt to minimize its costs and it must borrow the money to finance either lease agreement at an annual interest rate of 12%.

**Instructions**

**a** Determine which lease proposal results in the lowest cost for the computer system when the future cash outlays are discounted at an annual interest rate of 12%.

**b** Prepare a journal entry to record the acquisition of the computer system under the lease agreement selected in part **a.** This journal entry will include the initial cash payment to the computer manufacturer required at the beginning of the lease.

***PV-5*** On December 31, Year 5, Richland Farms sold a tract of land, which had cost $300,000, to Skyline Developers in exchange for $50,000 cash and a four-year, 4%, note receivable for $400,000. Interest on the note is payable annually, and the principal amount is due on December 31, Year 9. The accountant for Richland Farms did not notice the unrealistically low interest rate on the note and made the following entry on December 31 to record the sale:

| | | |
|---|---|---|
| *Cash* | *50,000* | |
| *Notes Receivable* | *400,000* | |
| *Land* | | *300,000* |
| *Gain on Sale of Land* | | *150,000* |
| *Sold land to Skyline Developers in exchange for cash and a four-year note with interest due annually.* | | |

**Instructions**

**a** Compute the present value of the note receivable from Skyline Developers, assuming that a realistic rate of interest for this transaction is 20%. (Hint: Consider both the annual interest payments and the principal amount of the note.)

**b** Prepare the journal entry on December 31, Year 5, to record the sale of the land correctly. Show supporting computations for (1) the gain or loss on the sale, and (2) the discount on the note receivable.

**c** Explain what effects the error made by Richland Farms' accountant will have upon (1) the net income for Year 5, and (2) the combined net income for Years 6 through 9. Ignore income taxes.

# 19

# CORPORATIONS: INVESTMENTS IN CORPORATE SECURITIES

In the three preceding chapters, the issuance of corporate securities and such related transactions as the payment of dividends and interest have been considered primarily from the viewpoint of the issuing corporation. Now we will consider these transactions from the viewpoint of investors. Investors in corporate securities include other corporations, pension funds, banks, mutual funds, and millions of individuals.

## Securities exchanges

The stocks and bonds of most large corporations are listed on organized securities exchanges, such as the ***New York Stock Exchange.*** An investor may either buy or sell these listed securities through any brokerage house which is a member of the exchange. The brokerage company represents the investor and negotiates with other exchange members either to buy or sell the securities on behalf of its customer. The price at which the broker negotiates the transaction represents the current market value of the security and is immediately printed on the stock exchange ticker tape for reference by other investors. The financial pages of many newspapers report on a daily basis the highest, lowest, and closing (last) prices at which each listed security is exchanged.

At the time of issuance of stocks or bonds, the transaction is between the investor and the issuing corporation. The great daily volume of transactions in securities, however, consists of the sale of stocks and bonds by investors to other investors. On the New York Stock Exchange alone, 80 million or more shares of stock may be exchanged on a single day. The stocks and bonds of many smaller companies are not listed on an organized securities exchange, but brokerage firms also arrange for the purchase and sale of these unlisted or ***over-the-counter*** securities.

**Quoted market prices** The market price of stocks is quoted in terms of dollars per share. As illustrated in Chapter 18, corporate bond prices are quoted as a ***percentage*** of the bond's maturity value, which generally is $1,000. Thus, a bond quoted at 102 has a market value of $1,020 ($1,000 × 102%).

**Listed corporations report to a million owners** When a corporation invites the public to purchase its stocks and bonds, it accepts an obligation to keep the public informed on its financial condition and the profitability of operations. This obligation of disclosure includes public distribution of financial statements. The Securities and Exchange Commission is the government agency responsible for seeing that corporations make adequate disclosure of their affairs so that investors have a basis for intelligent investment decisions. The flow of corporate accounting data distributed through newspapers and financial advisory services to millions of investors is a vital force in the functioning of our economy; in fact, the successful working of a profit-motivated economy rests upon the quality and dependability of the accounting information being reported.

**Listed corporations are audited by certified public accountants** Corporations with securities listed on organized stock exchanges are required to have regular audits by independent public accountants. The financial statements distributed each year to stockholders are accompanied by a report by a firm of certified public accountants indicating that an audit has been made and expressing an opinion as to the fairness of the company's financial statements. It is the ***independent status*** of the auditing firm that enables investors to place confidence in audited financial statements.

## INVESTMENTS IN MARKETABLE SECURITIES

The term ***marketable securities*** refers primarily to U.S. government bonds and the bonds and stocks of large corporations. Because these securities can be quickly sold on securities exchanges, an investment in these securities is almost as liquid an asset as cash itself. In fact, investments in marketable securities are often called "secondary cash resources." If cash is needed for any operating purpose, these securities may quickly be converted into cash; in the meantime, investments in marketable securities are preferable to cash because of the interest or dividend revenue which they produce. Most companies watch their cash balances very carefully and invest any cash not needed for current operations in high-grade marketable securities.

When an investor owns several different marketable securities, the group of securities is termed an investment ***portfolio.*** In deciding upon the securities to include in the portfolio, the investor seeks to maximize return while minimizing risk. Risk often can be reduced by ***diversification,*** that is, by including in the portfolio a variety of securities, especially securities of companies in different industries.

Some investors own enough of a company's common stock to influence or control the company's activities through the voting rights of the shares owned. Such large holdings of common stock create an important business relationship between the investor and the issuing corporation. Since investments of this type cannot be sold without disturbing this relationship, they are not considered marketable securities. ***Investments for purposes of control*** will be discussed as a separate topic later in this chapter.

## Marketable securities as current assets

A recent balance sheet of International Business Machines Corporation (IBM) shows the following items listed first in the current asset section.

| | |
|---|---|
| ***Current assets:*** | |
| ***Cash*** | ***$ 208,607,210*** |
| ***Marketable securities, at lower of cost or market*** | ***5,947,653,848*** |

The large investment by IBM in marketable securities is in no way unusual; many corporations have large holdings of marketable securities. In the balance sheet, marketable securities are usually listed immediately after the asset Cash, because they are so liquid as to be almost the equivalent of cash.

In ***Statement No. 12,*** the Financial Accounting Standards Board indicated that a company may choose to separate its marketable securities into two groups: (1) temporary investments classified as current assets, and (2) long-term investments classified as noncurrent assets.[1]

If management intends to hold certain marketable securities on a long-term basis, these securities should be listed in the balance sheet just below the current asset section under the caption Long-Term Investments. In most cases, however, management stands ready to sell marketable securities whenever company needs or stock market trends make such action advantageous. Consequently, marketable securities are generally viewed as current assets.

## Accounting for investments in marketable securities

When securities are purchased, an account entitled Marketable Securities is debited for the entire purchase price, including any commissions to stockbrokers and any transfer taxes. A subsidiary ledger must also be maintained which shows for each security owned the acquisition date, total cost, number of shares (or bonds) owned, and cost per share (or bond). This subsidiary ledger provides the information necessary to determine the amount of gain or loss when an investment in a particular stock or bond is sold.

[1] *FASB Statement No. 12,* "Accounting for Certain Marketable Securities" (Stamford, Conn.: 1975).

The principal distinction between the recording of an investment in bonds and an investment in stocks is that interest on bonds accrues from day to day. When bonds are purchased between interest dates, the purchaser pays the quoted market price for the bond ***plus*** the interest accrued since the last interest payment date. By this arrangement the new owner becomes entitled to receive in full the next semiannual interest payment. An account called Bond Interest Receivable should be debited for the amount of interest purchased. Dividends on stock, however, ***do not accrue*** and the entire purchase price paid by the investor in stocks is recorded in the Marketable Securities account.

**Income on investments in bonds** To illustrate the accounting entries for an investment in bonds, assume that on August 1 an investor purchases ten 9%, $1,000 bonds which pay interest on June 1 and December 1. The investor buys the bonds on August 1 at a price of 98, plus a brokerage commission of $50 and two months' accrued interest of $150 ($\$10,000 \times 9\% \times \frac{2}{12} = \$150$). The entry on August 1 to record this investment is:

*Separate account for accrued bond interest purchased*

| | | |
|---|---|---|
| *Marketable Securities* | *9,850* | |
| *Bond Interest Receivable* | *150* | |
|     *Cash* | | *10,000* |
| *Purchased ten 9% bonds of Rider Co. at 98 plus a brokerage commission of $50 and two months' accrued interest.* | | |

On December 1, the semiannual interest payment date, the investor will receive an interest check for $450, which will be recorded as follows:

*Note portion of interest check earned*

| | | |
|---|---|---|
| *Cash* | *450* | |
|     *Bond Interest Receivable* | | *150* |
|     *Bond Interest Revenue* | | *300* |
| *Received semiannual interest on Rider Co. bonds.* | | |

The $300 credit to Bond Interest Revenue represents the amount actually earned during the four months the bonds were owned by the investor ($9\% \times \$10,000 \times \frac{4}{12} = \$300$).

If the investor's accounting records are maintained on a calendar-year basis, the following adjusting entry is required at December 31 to record bond interest earned since December 1:

| | | |
|---|---|---|
| *Bond Interest Receivable* | *75* | |
|     *Bond Interest Revenue* | | *75* |
| *To accrue one month's interest earned (Dec. 1–Dec. 31) on Rider Co. bonds ($\$10,000 \times 9\% \times \frac{1}{12} = \$75$).* | | |

**Amortization of bond discount or premium from the investor's viewpoint** We have discussed the need for the corporation issuing bonds payable to amortize any bond discount or premium to measure correctly the bond interest expense. But what about the ***purchaser*** of the bonds? Should an investor in bonds amortize any difference between the cost of the investment and its future maturity value in order to measure investment income correctly? The answer to this question depends upon whether the investor considers the bonds to be a ***short-term*** or a ***long-term*** investment.

A short-term investment in bonds generally is carried in the investor's accounting records at ***cost,*** and a gain or a loss is recognized when the investment is sold. Short-term investments in bonds usually will be sold before the bonds mature and the sales price will be determined by the current state of the bond market. Under these conditions, there is no assurance that amortization of premium or discount would give any more accurate measurement of investment income than would be obtained by carrying the bonds at cost.

When bonds are owned for the long term, however, it becomes more probable that the market price of the investment will move toward the maturity value of the bonds. At the maturity date, of course, the market value will be the maturity value of the bonds. Thus, companies making long-term investments in bonds ***should*** amortize any difference between the cost of the investment and its maturity value over the life of the bonds. If the effective interest method of amortization would produce results materially different from those obtained by the straight-line method, the effective interest method should be used.[2]

Amortization of the difference between cost and maturity value is recorded by direct adjustment to the Marketable Securities account. When a long-term investment in bonds is purchased at a discount, the amortization entries consist of a debit to Marketable Securities and a credit to Interest Revenue. When the bonds are purchased at a premium, amortization is recorded by debiting Interest Revenue and crediting Marketable Securities.

**Income on investments in stock** When should a cash dividend be recorded as income to the investor? Should it be the date the dividend is declared, the date of record, the ex-dividend date, or the date the dividend is received? Most investors record cash dividends as income on the date the dividend check arrives. The entry to record receipt of a cash dividend consists of a debit to Cash and a credit to Dividend Revenue.

Additional shares of stock received in stock splits or stock dividends ***are not income*** to the stockholder, and only a ***memorandum entry*** is used to record the increase in the number of shares owned. The ***cost basis per share*** is decreased, however, because of the larger number of shares comprising the investment after receiving additional "free" shares from a stock split or a stock dividend. As an example, assume that an investor paid $72 a share for 100 shares of stock, a total cost of $7,200. Later the investor received 20 additional shares as a stock dividend. The cost per share is thereby reduced to $60 a share, computed by dividing the total cost of $7,200 by the 120 shares owned after the 20% stock dividend. The memorandum entry to be made in the general journal would be as follows:

---

[2] *APB Opinion No. 21,* "Interest on Receivables and Payables," AICPA (New York: 1971), p. 423.

***July 10 Memorandum: Received 20 additional shares of Delta Co. common stock as a result of 20% stock dividend. Now own 120 shares with a cost basis of $7,200, or $60 per share.***

## Gains and losses from sale of investments in securities

The sale of an investment in stocks is recorded by debiting Cash for the amount received and crediting the Marketable Securities account for the carrying value of the securities sold. Any difference between the proceeds of the sale and the carrying value of the investment is recorded by a debit to Loss on Sale of Marketable Securities or by a credit to Gain on Sale of Marketable Securities.

At the date of sale of an investment in bonds, any interest accrued since the last interest payment date should be recognized as interest revenue. For example, assume that 10 bonds of the Elk Corporation carried in the accounts of an investor at $9,600 are sold at a price of 94 and accrued interest of $90. The commission on the sale is $50. The following entry should be made:

*Investment in bonds sold at a loss*

| | | |
|---|---|---|
| Cash | 9,440 | |
| Loss on Sale of Marketable Securities | 250 | |
| Marketable Securities | | 9,600 |
| Bond Interest Revenue | | 90 |
| Sold 10 bonds of Elk Corporation at 94 and accrued interest of $90 less broker's commission of $50. | | |

## Balance sheet valuation of marketable securities

Although the market price of a bond may fluctuate from day to day, we can be reasonably certain that when the maturity date arrives the market price will be equal to the bond's maturity value. Stocks, on the other hand, do not have maturity values. When the market price of a stock declines, there is no way we can be certain whether the decline will be temporary or permanent. For this reason, different valuation standards are applied in accounting for investments in marketable ***debt*** securities (bonds) and investments in marketable ***equity*** securities (stocks).

**Valuation of marketable debt securities** A short-term investment in bonds is generally carried in the accounting records at ***cost*** and a gain or loss is recognized when the investment is sold. If bonds are held as a long-term investment and the difference between the cost of the investment and its maturity value is substantial, the valuation of the investment is adjusted each year by amortization of the discount or premium.

**Valuation of marketable equity securities** The market values of stocks may rise or fall dramatically during an accounting period. An investor who sells an investment at a price above or below cost will recognize a gain or loss on the sale. But what if the investor continues to hold securities after a significant change in their market value? In this case, should any gain or loss be recognized in the financial statements?

In ***Statement No. 12,*** the FASB ruled that a portfolio of marketable equity securities should be shown in the balance sheet at the ***lower*** of aggregate cost or current market value. The effect of the ***lower-of-cost-or-market (LCM)*** rule is to recognize losses from drops in market value without recognizing gains from rising market prices.

Note that this rule does not accord the same treatment to market gains and losses. Accountants traditionally have applied different criteria in recognizing gains and losses. One of the basic principles in accounting is that gains shall not be recognized until they are ***realized,*** and the usual test of realization is the sale of the asset in question. Losses, on the other hand, are recognized as soon as objective evidence indicates that a loss has been incurred.

## Lower of cost or market (LCM)

In applying the lower-of-cost-or-market rule, the total cost of the portfolio of marketable equity securities is compared with its current market value, and the lower of these two amounts is used as the balance sheet valuation. If the market value of the portfolio is below cost, an entry is made to reduce the carrying value of the portfolio to current market value and to recognize an ***unrealized loss*** for the amount of the market decline. The write-down of an investment in marketable equity securities to a market value below cost is an end-of-period adjusting entry and should be based upon market prices at the balance sheet date.

To illustrate the lower-of-cost-or-market adjustment, assume the following facts for the investment portfolio of Eagle Corporation at December 31, Year 1:

| | *Cost* | *Market Value* |
|---|---|---|
| *Common stock of Adams Corporation* | *$100,000* | *$106,000* |
| *Common stock of Barnes Company* | *60,000* | *52,000* |
| *Preferred stock of Parker Industries* | *200,000* | *182,000* |
| *Other marketable equity securities* | *25,000* | *25,000* |
| *Totals* | *$385,000* | *$365,000* |

Since the total market value of the securities in our example is less than their cost to Eagle Corporation, the balance sheet valuation would be the lower amount of $365,000. This downward adjustment of $20,000 means that an unrealized loss of $20,000 will be included in the determination of the year's net income. The accounting entry would be as follows:

| *Year 1* | | | |
|---|---|---|---|
| *Dec. 31* | *Unrealized Loss on Marketable Securities* | *20,000* | |
| | *Valuation Allowance for Marketable Securities* | | *20,000* |
| | *To reduce the carrying value of the investment in marketable securities to the lower of cost or market.* | | |

The loss from the decline in the market value of securities owned is termed an ***unrealized loss*** to distinguish it from a loss which is realized by an actual sale of securities.

**The valuation account** The Valuation Allowance for Marketable Securities is a ***contra-asset*** account or ***valuation*** account. In the balance sheet, this valuation account is offset against the asset Marketable Securities in the same manner as the Allowance for Doubtful Accounts is offset against Accounts Receivable. The following partial balance sheet illustrates the use of the Valuation Allowance for Marketable Securities:

| | | |
|---|---|---|
| *Current assets:* | | |
| *Cash* | | *$ 80,000* |
| *Marketable securities* | *$385,000* | |
| *Less: Valuation allowance for marketable securities* | *20,000* | *365,000* |
| *Accounts receivable* | *$573,000* | |
| *Less: Allowance for doubtful accounts* | *9,000* | *564,000* |

**The valuation account is adjusted every period** At the end of every period, the balance of the valuation account is adjusted to cause marketable equity securities to be shown in the balance sheet at the lower of cost or current market value. If the valuation allowance must be increased because of further declines in market value, the adjusting entry will recognize an additional unrealized loss. On the other hand, if market prices have gone up since the last balance sheet date, the adjusting entry will reduce or eliminate the valuation allowance and recognize an ***unrealized gain.***

To illustrate the adjustment of the valuation account, let us assume that by the end of Year 2 the market value of Eagle Corporation's portfolio has increased to an amount greater than cost. Since market value is no longer below cost, the valuation allowance, which has a credit balance of $20,000, is no longer needed. Thus, the following entry would be made to eliminate the balance of the valuation allowance:

***Unrealized gain cannot exceed the former balance of the valuation account***

| | | | |
|---|---|---|---|
| *Year 2* | | | |
| *Dec. 31* | *Valuation Allowance for Marketable Securities* | *20,000* | |
| | *Unrealized Gain on Marketable Securities* | | *20,000* |
| | *To increase the carrying value of marketable securities to original cost following recovery of market value.* | | |

Note that the amount of unrealized gain recognized is limited to the amount in the valuation account. ***Increases in market value above cost are not recognized in the accounting records.*** In brief, when marketable securities have been written down to the lower of cost or market, they can be written back up ***to original cost*** if the market prices recover. However, current rules of the FASB do not permit recognition of a market rise above the original cost of the portfolio.

Because the valuation allowance is based upon a comparison of ***total*** portfolio cost and market value, the allowance cannot be directly associated with individual investments. The valuation allowance reduces the carrying value of the total portfolio but does not affect the individual carrying values of the investments which comprise the portfolio. Lower-of-cost-or-market adjustments, therefore, have ***no effect*** upon the gain or loss recognized when an investment is sold. When specific securities are sold, the gain or loss realized from the sale is determined by comparing the ***cost*** of the securities (without regard to lower-of-cost-or-market adjustments) to their selling price.[3]

**Income tax rules for marketable securities** The FASB rules described above are not acceptable in determining income subject to income tax. The only gains or losses recognized for income tax purposes are realized gains and losses resulting from sale of an investment.

### The argument for valuation at market value

A weakness in the position taken by the FASB is that some increases in the market value of securities owned are recognized in the financial statements while others are ignored. For this reason, many accountants believe that investments in marketable securities should be valued in the balance sheet at current market price regardless of whether this price is above or below cost. Increases and decreases in market value would then be recognized as gains or losses as these changes occur.

Several strong arguments exist for valuing marketable securities at market value:

1 Market value is a better indicator of the current debt-paying ability represented by the securities than is their original cost.
2 Market values may be objectively determined from market price quotations.
3 The market price may be realized at any time without interfering with the normal operations of the business.
4 Changes in market price may constitute a major portion of the economic benefit resulting from investments in marketable securities.

At this point it is important to stress that valuation of marketable securities at current market values which exceed cost is not in accordance with the present accounting practices of most companies.[4] However, the valuation of marketable securities is a controversial issue in the accounting profession and may be an area of forthcoming change in generally accepted accounting principles.

### Presentation of marketable securities in financial statements

Gains and losses on the sale of investments, as well as interest and dividend revenue, are nonoperating types of income. These items should be specifically

---

[3] The reader may notice that a decline in the market value of securities owned could be reported in the income statement on two separate occasions: first, as an unrealized loss in the period in which the price decline occurs; and second, as a realized loss in the period in which the securities are sold. However, after securities with market values below cost have been sold, the valuation allowance may be reduced or eliminated. The entry to reduce the valuation allowance involves the recognition of an unrealized gain which offsets the unrealized losses reported in earlier periods.

[4] Companies whose principal business activity includes investing in marketable securities (such as mutual funds and brokerage houses) currently use market values in accounting for their investment portfolios.

identified in the income statement and shown after the determination of operating income.

Although marketable securities are usually classified as current assets in the balance sheet, they may alternatively be classified as long-term investments if management has a definite intention to hold the securities for more than one year. Regardless of how marketable equity securities are classified in the balance sheet, they are shown at the lower-of-cost-or-market value.

The unrealized gains and losses resulting from application of the lower-of-cost-or-market rule, however, are presented differently in the financial statements depending upon whether the securities portfolio is classified as a current asset or a long-term investment. When the portfolio is viewed as a current asset, the unrealized gains and losses are closed into the Income Summary account and shown in the income statement along with other types of investment income.

In ***Statement No. 12,*** the FASB ruled that holding gains and losses on ***long-term*** investments should ***not*** be included in the measurement of the current year's income because management does not intend to sell these securities in the near future. Therefore, any unrealized loss recognized on long-term investments is shown in the balance sheet as a ***reduction in stockholders' equity*** instead of being closed into the Income Summary account.

### How should investors measure the performance of their investments?

The return on an investment includes both the periodic cash receipts of interest or dividends and the gain or loss when the investment is sold.

The earnings rate for the annual dividends or interest received may be computed as a percentage of cost or of current market value. Assume, for example, that an individual investor, Jane Morgan, bought 100 shares of Standard Company stock at $40 a share. The annual dividend was $3.20 a share, and therefore provided a yield of 8% on cost ($320 total yearly dividend ÷ $4,000 cost = 8% return on cost). The market price of the stock then rose to $80 without any change in the annual dividend. Although Morgan is still receiving a return of 8% on the cost of her investment ($4,000), the return expressed as a percentage of the present market value of her shares has dropped to 4% (computed as $320 ÷ $8,000). The return based on current market value is more useful as a basis for making investment decisions. Morgan may wish to sell her stock in Standard Company for $8,000 and invest this amount in some other stock which is currently paying dividends at a rate of 8% on its present market value. This would cause her investment income to rise from $320 a year to a higher level of $640, that is, $8,000 × 8%.

## INVESTMENTS FOR PURPOSES OF CONTROL

When an investor owns enough common stock to exercise a degree of control over the issuing company (called the ***investee***), the investment is not included in the portfolio of marketable securities. Such investments are shown in the balance sheet under the caption Long-Term Investments, which follows the current asset section.

If an investor is able to exercise significant control over the investee's management, dividends paid by the investee may no longer be a good measure of the investor's income from the investment. This is because the investor may control the investee's dividend policy. In such cases, dividends paid by the investee are likely to reflect the ***investor's*** cash needs and tax considerations, rather than the profitability of the investment.

For example, assume that Sigma Company owns all the common stock of Davis Company. For three years Davis Company is very profitable but pays no dividends, because Sigma Company has no need for additional cash. In the fourth year, Davis Company pays a large cash dividend to Sigma Company despite operating at a loss for that year. Clearly, it would be misleading for Sigma Company to report no investment income while the company it owns is operating profitably, and then to show large investment income in a year when Davis Company incurred a net loss.

The investor does not have to own 100% of the common stock of the investee to exercise a significant degree of control. An investor with much less than 50% of the voting stock may have effective control, since the remaining shares are not likely to vote as an organized block. In the absence of other evidence (such as another large stockholder), ownership of 20% or more of the investee's common stock is considered an investment for purposes of control. In such cases, the investor should account for the investment by using the ***equity method.***[5]

### The equity method

When the equity method is used, an investment in common stock is first recorded at cost but later is adjusted each year for changes in the stockholders' equity of the investee. As the investee earns net income, the stockholders' equity in the company increases. An investor using the equity method recognizes his ***proportionate share of the investee's net income*** as an increase in the carrying value of his investment. A proportionate share of a net loss reported by the investee is recognized as a decrease in the investment.

When the investee pays dividends, the stockholders' equity in the company is reduced. The investor, therefore, treats dividends received from the investee as a conversion of the investment into cash, thus reducing the carrying value of the investment. Investments accounted for by the equity method are ***not*** adjusted to the lower of cost or market value. In effect, the equity method causes the carrying value of the investment to rise and fall with changes in the book value of the shares.

**Illustration of the equity method** Assume that Cove Corporation purchases 25% of the common stock of Bay Company for $200,000, which corresponds to the un-

---

[5] *APB Opinion No. 18,* "The Equity Method of Accounting for Investments in Common Stock," AICPA (New York: 1971).

derlying book value. During the following year, Bay Company earns net income of $60,000 and pays dividends of $40,000. Cove Corporation would account for its investment as follows:

| | | |
|---|---|---|
| *Investment in Bay Company* | *200,000* | |
| *Cash* | | *200,000* |
| *To record acquisition of 25% of the common stock of Bay Company.* | | |
| *Investment in Bay Company* | *15,000* | |
| *Investment Income* | | *15,000* |
| *To increase the investment for 25% share of net income earned by Bay Company (25% × $60,000).* | | |
| *Cash* | *10,000* | |
| *Investment in Bay Company* | | *10,000* |
| *To reduce investment for dividends received from Bay Company (25% × $40,000).* | | |

The net result of these entries by Cove Corporation is to increase the carrying value of the investment in Bay Company account by $5,000. This corresponds to 25% of the increase reported in Bay Company's retained earnings during the period [25% × ($60,000 − $40,000) = $5,000].

In this illustration of the equity method, we have made several simplifying assumptions: (1) Cove Corporation purchased the stock of Bay Company at a price equal to the underlying book value; (2) Bay Company had issued common stock only and the number of shares outstanding did not change during the year; and (3) there were no intercompany transactions between Cove Corporation and Bay Company. If we were to change any of these assumptions, the computations in applying the equity method would become more complicated. Application of the equity method in more complex situations is discussed in advanced accounting courses.

## CONSOLIDATED FINANCIAL STATEMENTS

### Parent and subsidiary companies

A corporation which owns all or a majority of another corporation's capital stock is called a ***parent*** company, and the corporation which is wholly owned or majority-held is called a ***subsidiary.***[6] Through the voting rights of the owned shares, the parent company can elect the board of directors of the subsidiary company and thereby control the subsidiary's resources and activities. In effect, the ***affiliated companies*** (the parent and its subsidiaries) function as a ***single***

---

[6]Ownership of a majority of a company's voting stock means holding at least 50% plus one share.

***economic unit*** controlled by the directors of the parent company. This relationship is illustrated below:

*An economic entity may include more than one legal entity*

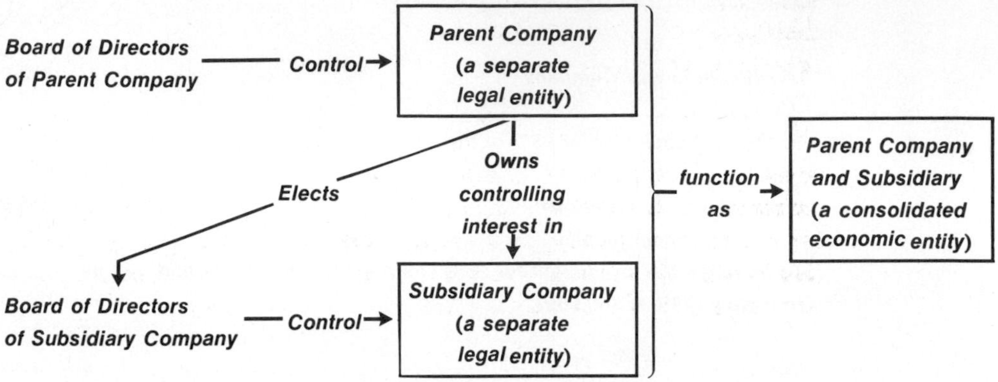


There are a number of economic, legal, and tax advantages which encourage large business organizations to operate through subsidiaries rather than through a single legal entity. Although we think of Sears, General Electric, or IBM as single companies, each of these organizations is really a group of affiliated corporations. Since the parent company in each case controls the resources and activities of its subsidiaries, it is logical for us to consider an affiliated group such as IBM as one ***economic*** entity.

### Financial statements for a consolidated economic entity

Because the parent company and its subsidiaries are separate legal entities, separate financial statements are prepared for each company. In the ***separate*** financial statements of the parent company, the subsidiaries appear only as investments accounted for by the ***equity method.*** Since the affiliated companies function as a single economic unit, the parent company also prepares financial statements which show the financial position and operating results of the entire group of companies. Such statements are called ***consolidated financial statements.***

The distinctive feature of consolidated financial statements is that the assets, liabilities, revenue, and expenses of ***two or more separate corporations are combined in a single set of financial statements.*** In a ***consolidated balance sheet,*** the assets of the entire group of affiliated companies are combined and reported as though only a single entity existed. For example, the amount shown as Cash on a consolidated balance sheet is the total of the cash owned by all of the affiliated companies. Liabilities of the various companies also are combined. Similarly, in a ***consolidated income statement,*** the revenue and expenses of the affiliated companies are combined to show the operating results of the consolidated economic entity.

Stockholders in the parent corporation have a vital interest in the financial results of all operations under the parent company's control, including those conducted through subsidiaries. Therefore, the parent company includes consolidated financial statements in its annual and quarterly reports to stockholders. Most of the companies listed on major stock exchanges are actually parent companies with one or more subsidiaries. Thus anyone using published financial statements will find it useful to understand the basic principles used in preparing consolidated financial statements.

## Principles of consolidation

Consolidated financial statements are prepared by combining the amounts that appear in the separate financial statements of the parent and subsidiary companies. In the combining process, however, certain adjustments are made to ***eliminate the effects of intercompany transactions*** and thus to reflect the assets, liabilities, and stockholders' equity from the viewpoint of a single economic entity.

**Intercompany transactions** The term ***intercompany transactions*** refers to transactions between affiliated companies. These transactions may include, for example, the sale of merchandise, the leasing of property, and the making of loans. When the affiliated companies are viewed separately, these transactions may create assets and liabilities for the individual companies. However, when the affiliated companies are viewed as a single business entity, these assets and liabilities are merely the result of internal transfers within the business organization and should not appear in the consolidated financial statements.

For example, if a subsidiary borrows money from the parent company, a note payable will appear as a liability in the balance sheet of the subsidiary company and a note receivable will appear as an asset in the separate balance sheet of the parent. When the two companies are viewed as a single consolidated entity, however, this "loan" is nothing more than a transfer of cash from one part of the business to another. Transferring assets between two parts of a single business entity does not create either a receivable or a payable for that entity. Therefore, the parent company's note receivable and the subsidiary's note payable should not appear in the consolidated financial statements.

**Preparing consolidated financial statements** Separate accounting records are maintained for each company in an affiliated group, but no accounting records are maintained for the consolidated entity. The amounts shown in consolidated financial statements ***do not come from a ledger;*** they are determined on a ***working paper*** by combining the amounts of like items on the financial statements of the affiliated companies. For example, the inventories of all the affiliated companies are combined into one amount for inventories. Entries to eliminate the effects of intercompany transactions are made ***only*** on this working paper. These elimination entries are ***not recorded in the accounting records*** of either the parent company or its subsidiaries.

## Consolidation at the date of acquisition

To illustrate the basic principles of consolidation, we will now prepare a consolidated balance sheet. Assume that on January 1, Year 10, Post Corporation purchases for cash 100% of the capital stock of Sun Company at its book value of $300,000. (The shares are purchased from Sun Company's former stockholders.) Also on this date, Post Corporation lends $40,000 cash to Sun Company, receiving a note as evidence of the loan. Immediately after these two transactions, the separate balance sheet accounts of Post Corporation and Sun Company are as shown in the following working paper:

***POST CORPORATION AND SUBSIDIARY***
***Working Paper—Consolidated Balance Sheet***
***January 1, Year 10 (Date of Acquisition)***

| | Post Corporation | Sun Company | Intercompany Eliminations Debit | Intercompany Eliminations Credit | Consolidated Balance Sheet |
|---|---|---|---|---|---|
| Cash | 60,000 | 45,000 | | | 105,000 |
| Notes receivable | 40,000 | | | (b) 40,000 | |
| Accounts receivable (net) | 70,000 | 50,000 | | | 120,000 |
| Inventories | 110,000 | 95,000 | | | 205,000 |
| Investment in Sun Company | 300,000 | | | (a) 300,000 | |
| Plant & equipment (net) | 210,000 | 180,000 | | | 390,000 |
| Totals | 790,000 | 370,000 | | | 820,000 |
| Notes payable | | 40,000 | (b) 40,000 | | |
| Accounts payable | 125,000 | 30,000 | | | 155,000 |
| Capital stock—Post Corporation | 400,000 | | | | 400,000 |
| Capital stock—Sun Company | | 200,000 | (a) 200,000 | | |
| Retained earnings—Post Corporation | 265,000 | | | | 265,000 |
| Retained earnings—Sun Company | | 100,000 | (a) 100,000 | | |
| Totals | 790,000 | 370,000 | 340,000 | 340,000 | 820,000 |

*Explanation of elimination:*
(*a*) To eliminate the Investment in Sun Company against Sun Company's stockholders' equity.
(*b*) To eliminate intercompany note receivable against related note payable.

## Intercompany eliminations

Before the balance sheet amounts of Post Corporation and Sun Company are combined, entries are made in the working paper to eliminate the effects of intercompany transactions. Intercompany eliminations may be classified into three basic types:

**1** Elimination of intercompany stock ownership
**2** Elimination of intercompany debt
**3** Elimination of intercompany revenue and expenses

The first two types of eliminations are illustrated in our example of Post Corporation and Sun Company. The elimination of intercompany revenue and expenses will be discussed later in this chapter.

To understand the need for elimination entries, we must adopt the viewpoint of the consolidated entity, in which Post Corporation and Sun Company are regarded as two departments within a single company.

**Entry (*a*): Elimination of intercompany stock ownership** The purpose of entry (*a*) in the illustrated working paper is to eliminate from the consolidated balance sheet both the asset account and the stockholders' equity accounts representing the parent company's ownership of the subsidiary.

Post Corporation's ownership interest in Sun Company appears in the ***separate*** balance sheets of both corporations. In the parent's balance sheet, this ownership interest is shown as the asset, Investment in Sun Company. In the separate balance sheet of the subsidiary, the parent company's ownership interest is represented by the stockholders' equity accounts, Capital Stock and Retained Earnings. In the ***consolidated*** balance sheet, however, this "ownership interest" is neither an asset nor a part of stockholders' equity.

From the viewpoint of the single consolidated entity, ***there are no stockholders in Sun Company.*** "Stockholders" are outside investors who have an ownership interest in the business. All of Sun Company's capital stock is "internally owned" by another part of the consolidated entity. A company's "ownership" of its own stock does not create either an asset or stockholders' equity. Therefore the asset account, Investment in Sun Company, and Sun Company's related stockholders' equity accounts must be eliminated from the consolidated balance sheet.

**Entry (*b*): Elimination of intercompany debt** When Post Corporation loaned $40,000 to Sun Company, the parent company recorded a note receivable and the subsidiary recorded a note payable. This "receivable" and "payable" exist only when Post Corporation and Sun Company are viewed as two separate entities. When both corporations are viewed as a single company, this "loan" is merely a transfer of cash from one part of the business to another. Such internal transfers of assets do not create either a receivable or a payable for the consolidated entity. Therefore, entry (*b*) is made to eliminate Post Corporation's note receivable and Sun Company's note payable from the consolidated balance sheet.

After the necessary eliminations have been entered in the working paper, the remaining balance sheet amounts of Post Corporation and Sun Company are combined to determine the assets, liabilities, and stockholders' equity of the consolidated entity. The consolidated balance sheet shown on page 716 is then prepared from the working paper.

## Acquisition of subsidiary stock at more (or less) than book value

When a parent corporation purchases a controlling interest in a subsidiary, it often pays a price for the shares that differs from their book value. In consolidating the financial statements of two affiliated corporations, we cannot ignore a

Note stockholders' equity is that of parent company

**POST CORPORATION AND SUBSIDIARY**
**Consolidated Balance Sheet**
**January 1, Year 10**

| | | |
|---|---|---|
| **Assets** | | |
| Current assets: | | |
| Cash | | $105,000 |
| Accounts receivable (net) | | 120,000 |
| Inventories | | 205,000 |
| Total current assets | | $430,000 |
| Plant & equipment (net) | | 390,000 |
| Total assets | | $820,000 |
| **Liabilities & Stockholders' Equity** | | |
| Current liabilities: | | |
| Accounts payable | | $155,000 |
| Stockholders' equity: | | |
| Capital stock | $400,000 | |
| Retained earnings | 265,000 | |
| Total stockholders' equity | | 665,000 |
| Total liabilities & stockholders' equity | | $820,000 |

difference between the cost of the parent company's investment in subsidiary shares and the book value of these shares on the statements of the subsidiary company. In consolidation, the parent's investment is offset against the stockholders' equity accounts of the subsidiary, and if the two amounts are not equal, we must determine what the difference between them represents.

To illustrate, suppose that at the end of the current year, C Company purchased ***all*** the outstanding shares of D Company for $680,000. At the date of acquisition, D Company reported on its balance sheet total stockholders' equity of $500,000, consisting of capital stock of $300,000 and retained earnings of $200,000. In preparing the elimination entry on the working papers for a consolidated balance sheet at the date of acquisition, we must determine what to do with the $180,000 difference between the price paid, $680,000, and the stockholders' equity of D Company, $500,000.

If we ask ourselves why C Company paid $680,000 for the stock of D Company, the answer must be that the management of C Company considered the net assets of D Company to be worth $180,000 more than their book value. C's management may believe that D Company's future earnings prospects are so favorable as to justify paying $180,000 for D Company's unrecorded ***goodwill.*** Or C's management may believe that the fair market value of certain specific assets of D Company (such as land or buildings) ***is in excess of book value.*** Since C Company paid $680,000 for a 100% interest in D Company in an arm's-length transaction, the accountant has ***objective evidence*** that unrecorded goodwill of $180,000 exists or that certain assets of D Company are undervalued. This evidence provides a basis for making the following elimination entry ***on the working papers*** for a consolidated balance sheet at the date of acquisition.

*Elimination entry when price paid for shares of subsidiary exceeds their book value*

| | | |
|---|---|---|
| *Capital Stock—D Company* | *300,000* | |
| *Retained Earnings—D Company* | *200,000* | |
| *Excess of Cost over Book Value of Investment in Subsidiary* | *180,000* | |
| *Investment in D Company (C Company's asset account)* | | *680,000* |
| *To eliminate the cost of C Company's 100% interest in D Company against D's stockholders' equity accounts and to recognize the excess of cost of the investment in D Company over the underlying book value.* | | |

The $180,000 Excess of Cost over Book Value of Investment in Subsidiary will appear as an asset in the consolidated balance sheet. This amount will be amortized over a period of years, depending on the type of undervalued asset which it represents.[7]

If the parent company ***pays less than book value*** for its interest in a subsidiary, a similar problem of interpretation exists. For example, suppose in the previous case that C Company had paid only $470,000 for all the outstanding shares of D Company, which have a book value of $500,000. This transaction indicates that because of poor earnings, or for other reasons, the book value of C's assets is in excess of fair market value. The elimination entry on the working papers to consolidate the financial statements of the two companies on the date of acquisition would be:

*Elimination entry when price paid for shares of subsidiary is less than their book value*

| | | |
|---|---|---|
| *Capital Stock—D Company* | *300,000* | |
| *Retained Earnings—D Company* | *200,000* | |
| *Investment in D Company (C Company's asset account)* | | *470,000* |
| *Excess of Book Value over Cost of Investment in Subsidiary* | | *30,000* |
| *To eliminate investment in D Company against D's stockholder's equity accounts, and to record the indicated reduction in D Company's assets.* | | |

This $30,000 credit, entitled Excess of Book Value over Cost of Investment in Subsidiary, is shown between the liabilities and the stockholders' equity section of the consolidated balance sheet. From a theoretical point of view, it may be considered a reduction in the balances of those asset accounts which are overvalued in D Company's separate balance sheet.

## Less than 100% ownership in subsidiary

If a parent company owns a majority interest in a subsidiary but less than 100% of the outstanding shares, a new kind of ownership equity known as the ***minority***

[7] For example, a recent annual report of Hilton Hotels Corporation included the following note accompanying its financial statements: "The $13,680,000 . . . cost of investment in excess of the net book value was attributable to the land and buildings. The portion allocated to the buildings is being amortized over the lives of the buildings." See also *APB Opinion No. 17,* "Intangible Assets," AICPA (New York: 1970).

***interest*** will appear in the consolidated balance sheet. This minority interest represents the ownership interest in the subsidiary held by stockholders other than the parent company.

When there are minority stockholders, only the portion of the subsidiary's stockholders' equity owned by the parent company is eliminated. The remainder of the stockholders' equity of the subsidiary is included in the consolidated balance sheet under the caption Minority Interest.

To illustrate, assume that at the end of Year 4, Park Company purchases 75% of the outstanding capital stock of Sims Company for $150,000 cash, an amount equal to the book value of the stock acquired. The working paper to prepare a consolidated balance sheet on the date that control of Sims Company is acquired appears below:

***PARK AND SUBSIDIARY***

***Working Paper—Consolidated Balance Sheet***

***December 31, Year 4 (Date of Acquisition)***

| | Park Company | Sims Company | Intercompany Eliminations | | Consolidated Balance Sheet |
|---|---|---|---|---|---|
| | | | Debit | Credit | |
| Cash | 200,000 | 50,000 | | | 250,000 |
| Other assets | 500,000 | 210,000 | | | 710,000 |
| Investment in Sims Company | 150,000 | | | (a) 150,000 | |
| Totals | 850,000 | 260,000 | | | 960,000 |
| Liabilities | 250,000 | 60,000 | | | 310,000 |
| Capital stock—Park Company | 500,000 | | | | 500,000 |
| Capital stock—Sims Company | | 120,000 | (a) 90,000<br>(b) 30,000 | | |
| Retained earnings—Park Company | 100,000 | | | | 100,000 |
| Retained earnings—Sims Company | | 80,000 | (a) 60,000<br>(b) 20,000 | | |
| Minority interest (25% of $200,000) | | | | (b) 50,000 | 50,000 |
| Totals | 850,000 | 260,000 | 200,000 | (b) 200,000 | 960,000 |

*Explanation of elimination:*
(*a*) To eliminate Park Company's investment in 75% of Sims Company's stockholders' equity.
(*b*) To classify the remaining 25% of Sims Company's stockholders' equity as a minority interest.

Entry (*a*) in this working paper offsets Park Company's asset, Investment in Sims Company, against ***75%*** of Sims Company's capital stock and retained earnings. The purpose of this entry is to eliminate intercompany stock ownership from the assets and stockholders' equity shown in the consolidated balance sheet. Entry (*b*) reclassifies the remaining 25% of Sims Company's capital stock and retained earnings into a special stockholders' equity account entitled Minority Interest. In the consolidated balance sheet, the minority interest appears in the stockholders' equity section as illustrated on page 719.

| | |
|---|---|
| ***Stockholders' equity:*** | |
| *Minority interest* | *$ 50,000* |
| *Capital stock* | *500,000* |
| *Retained earnings* | *100,000* |
| ***Total stockholders' equity*** | ***$650,000*** |

**Minority interest** Why is the minority interest shown separately in the consolidated balance sheet instead of being included in the amounts shown for capital stock and retained earnings? The reason for this separate presentation is to distinguish between the ownership equity of the controlling stockholders and the equity of the minority stockholders.

The stockholders in the parent company own the controlling interest in the consolidated entity. Because these stockholders elect the directors of the parent company, they control the entire group of affiliated companies. The minority interest, however, has ***no control*** over any of the affiliated companies. Because they own shares only in a subsidiary, they cannot vote for the directors of the parent company. Also, they can never outvote the majority stockholder (the parent company) in electing the directors or establishing the policies of the subsidiary.[8]

The minority stockholders receive 25% of the dividends declared by Sims Company but do not participate in dividends declared by the parent company. The controlling stockholders, on the other hand, receive all the dividends declared by Park Company but do not receive dividends declared by the subsidiary.

## Consolidated income statement

A consolidated income statement is prepared by combining the revenue and expense accounts of the parent and subsidiary. Revenue and expenses arising from ***intercompany transactions*** are eliminated because they reflect transfers of assets from one affiliated company to another and do not change the net assets from a consolidated viewpoint.

**Elimination of intercompany revenue and expenses** Some of the more common examples of intercompany items that should be eliminated in preparing a consolidated income statement are:

1 Sales to affiliated companies
2 Cost of goods sold resulting from sales to affiliated companies
3 Interest expense on loans from affiliated companies
4 Interest revenue on loans made to affiliated companies
5 Rent or other revenue received for services rendered to affiliated companies
6 Rent or other expenses paid for services received from affiliated companies

[8] Some companies emphasize the limited ownership role of the minority stockholders by showing the minority interest between the liabilities section and the stockholders' equity section of the consolidated balance sheet.

In its separate accounting records, the parent company uses the ***equity method*** to account for its investment in a subsidiary. Under the equity method, the parent company recognizes as Investment Income its share of the subsidiary's earnings. Because the individual revenue and expenses of the subsidiary are included in a consolidated income statement, the parent company's Investment Income (from subsidiary) account must be eliminated to avoid double counting this portion of the subsidiary's earnings.

Because of the complexity of the intercompany eliminations, the preparation of a consolidated income statement and a consolidated statement of retained earnings are topics appropriately deferred to an advanced accounting course.

## Purchase method and pooling-of-interests method: Two types of business combination

The transaction in which two corporations become affiliated is called a ***business combination.*** In our discussion of business combinations up to this point, we have assumed that the parent acquired a subsidiary company by paying cash for its shares. This kind of acquisition is accounted for by the ***purchase method.*** The purchase method is also used for cases in which the parent issues its own bonds payable or capital stock in payment for the subsidiary's shares. The term ***purchase method*** implies that the parent has acquired the subsidiary by purchase and that the former stockholders in the subsidiary have sold out. In addition to the purchase method which we have been discussing, there is an alternative called the ***pooling-of-interests method.*** We will now consider the type of business combination for which the pooling-of-interest method may be used.

If the stock of a subsidiary is acquired ***in exchange for shares of the parent company's common stock*** and if certain other criteria are met, a business combination may be treated as a pooling of interest.[9] A key aspect of such acquisitions is that the stockholders of the subsidiary company ***become stockholders of the parent corporation.*** The stockholders of the two companies are said to have ***pooled their interests,*** rather than one ownership group having sold its equity to the other.

When a subsidiary is acquired by a pooling of interests, no ownership interest is severed—in other words, no "purchase" or "sale" of the subsidiary's net assets occurs. Therefore, the net assets of the subsidiary are ***not revalued*** in the consolidated balance sheet, regardless of the market value of the securities issued in exchange. In the consolidated balance sheet, the assets of the subsidiary appear at their ***book values*** and no excess of cost over book value of the investment is recorded. Therefore, no amortization expense relating to this asset appears in the consolidated income statement.

---

[9] In addition to the parent company issuing only common stock in exchange for the subsidiary's shares, other specific criteria must be met for the affiliation to qualify as a pooling of interests. For example, at least 90% of the subsidiary's stock must be acquired within one year following the beginning of negotiations. For a more complete discussion of the differences between a purchase and a pooling of interests, see *APB Opinion No. 16,* "Business Combinations," AICPA (New York: 1970).

Another significant difference between the purchase and the pooling-of-interests methods is the treatment in the consolidated income statement of the subsidiary's earnings (revenue and expenses) in the year of affiliation. Under the purchase method, only the subsidiary's earnings ***after the date of acquisition*** are included in the consolidated income statement. Under the pooling-of-interests method, the consolidated income statement includes the earnings of the subsidiary ***for the entire year.***

To illustrate, let us assume that X Company acquired 100% of Y Company's stock on November 1, Year 1, and that each company earned \$600,000 during Year 1. Assuming the \$600,000 net income of Y Company was earned at a uniform rate during Year 1, the consolidated net income for the two companies under the purchase method would be \$700,000 (X Company's \$600,000 + 2/12 of Y Company's \$600,000). However, consolidated net income on a pooling basis would be \$1,200,000 even though \$500,000 ($\frac{10}{12}$ of \$600,000) of the earnings of Y Company were earned before the two companies became affiliated on November 1.

The following brief summary emphasizes some of the points of contrast between treating a corporate acquisition as a ***purchase*** or as a ***pooling of interests.***

| | *Purchase Method* | *Pooling-of-Interests Method* |
|---|---|---|
| 1 | *Subsidiary's assets are revalued in the consolidated balance sheet based upon the price paid by the parent for the subsidiary's stock. Excess of cost over book value (or book value over cost) may result.* | *Subsidiary's assets are shown in the consolidated balance sheet at their book values in the subsidiary's accounts. No excess of cost over book value (or book value over cost) is shown.* |
| 2 | *If excess of cost over book value appears in the consolidated balance sheet, consolidated net income in future periods is reduced by amortization expense relating to this asset.* | *Since no excess of cost over book value appears in the consolidated balance sheet, consolidated net income is not reduced by any related amortization expense.* |
| 3 | *Earnings of subsidiary are combined with the earnings of the parent only from the date of the affiliation.* | *Earnings of subsidiary for the entire year in which the affiliation occurs are included in the consolidated income statement.* |

In the opinion of the authors, the failure to revalue the assets of a subsidiary based upon the market value of the shares issued by the parent company is a serious weakness in the pooling-of-interests method. In many cases, the valuation of the subsidiary's assets at their book values results in significant understatement of consolidated assets and an overstatement of consolidated net income.

To illustrate, assume that S Company has total assets and stockholders' equity with a book value of \$6 million. (For simplicity, we will assume that S Company has no liabilities.) The ***market value*** of S Company's assets and stockholders' equity, however, is \$10 million, due to the existence of \$4 million in unrecorded goodwill.

Now assume that P Company issues \$10 million (market value) of its own shares in exchange for 100% of S Company's capital stock. If this acquisition is treated as a purchase, S Company's assets will appear in the consolidated balance sheet at \$10 million, including the \$4 million in goodwill.[10] As discussed in Chapter 12, goodwill must be amortized over a period of not more than 40 years. Therefore, consolidated net income will be reduced by at least \$100,000 per year (\$4 million ÷ 40 years) as the goodwill is amortized to expense.

If this affiliation is treated as a pooling of interests, the \$4 million in unrecorded goodwill will ***not appear*** in the consolidated balance sheet, and the assets of S Company will be shown at their book values of \$6 million. Also, there will be no amortization of goodwill in the consolidated income statement, thus causing net income to appear at a higher amount.

### When should consolidated statements be prepared?

Accounts of some subsidiary companies may not be included in consolidated statements. Consolidation of accounts is deemed appropriate only when effective control over the subsidiary is ***present*** and ***continuing*** and when the consolidated statements ***give a meaningful picture of financial position and results of operations.*** For example, a subsidiary's accounts should not be consolidated with those of the parent if control is likely to be temporary or if the subsidiary is facing bankruptcy. Similarly, if the assets of a foreign subsidiary cannot be withdrawn by the parent because of restrictions placed on such assets by foreign governments, consolidation of accounts should be avoided.

In other instances, consolidation of accounts may not be appropriate because the activities of the subsidiary are significantly different from those of the parent. For example, Sears, Roebuck and Co. does not consolidate its wholly owned subsidiary, Allstate Insurance Company. American Telephone and Telegraph Company (a public utility) does not consolidate Western Electric Company, which manufactures telephones and other electronic equipment. When the parent company controls a subsidiary but consolidation is not considered appropriate, the ***unconsolidated subsidiary*** appears in the financial statements as a long-term investment, accounted for by the equity method.

In this chapter, we have discussed investments in marketable securities, investments accounted for by the equity method, and investments in subsidiaries which are shown in the financial statements on a consolidated basis. The accounting treatment of an investment in stock depends primarily upon the ***degree of control*** which the investor is able to exercise over the issuing corporation. These relationships are summarized on page 723.

[10] The \$4 million of goodwill will appear in the consolidated balance sheet as Excess of Cost over Book Value of Investment in Subsidiary.

| *Degree of Control* | *General Practice* |
|---|---|
| *1 Controlling interest (ownership of more than 50% of voting stock)* | *Consolidate, except in situations where activities of subsidiary are significantly different from those of the parent or where assets of a foreign subsidiary cannot be withdrawn by the parent company. The equity method of accounting for unconsolidated subsidiaries would generally be used.* |
| *2 Influential but noncontrolling interest (ownership of between 20% and 50% of voting stock)* | *Show as a long-term investment, accounted for by the equity method.* |
| *3 Noninfluential interest (ownership of less than 20% of voting stock and investments in bonds and preferred stocks)* | *Show as a marketable security (may be classified as a current asset or long-term investment). Portfolio is valued at lower of cost or market.* |

## Who uses consolidated financial statements?

Millions of people invest in the securities of major corporations listed on the stock exchanges. All these people receive consolidated financial statements regularly informing them of the progress of the companies in which they have invested. The following tabulation of stock ownership in IBM gives some idea of the diversity of the groups which need an understanding of consolidated financial statements. Incidentally, note that more women than men are owners of IBM stock.

*Who owns IBM?*

| Type of Stockholder | Number of Accounts | Number of Shares* | Average per Stockholder | Percentage of Total Shares |
|---|---|---|---|---|
| Men | 120,239 | 12,711,524 | 106 | 8.5 |
| Women | 134,308 | 14,993,727 | 112 | 10.0 |
| Joint tenants | 84,435 | 2,537,055 | 30 | 1.7 |
| Fiduciaries | 94,732 | 5,228,291 | 55 | 3.5 |
| Brokers | 819 | 9,965,190 | 12,168 | 6.6 |
| Bank nominees | 3,722 | 88,292,185 | 23,722 | 58.8 |
| Partnerships and corporations | 3,681 | 3,748,864 | 1,018 | 2.5 |
| Insurance companies | 672 | 4,623,492 | 6,880 | 3.1 |
| Investment organizations | 847 | 165,235 | 195 | .1 |
| Banks and trust companies | 205 | 632,140 | 3,084 | .4 |
| Other organizations and associations | 8,336 | 2,504,064 | 300 | 1.7 |
| Employees and directors | 132,517 | 4,737,871 | 36 | 3.1 |
| Scrip | — | 15,637 | — | — |
| Totals | 584,513 | 150,155,275 | | 100.0 |

* Capital stock as of the record date for the annual meeting, Mar. 8, 1976.

The stockholders, managers, and members of the board of directors of the parent company have the primary interest in consolidated statements. The managers and directors are responsible for the entire resources under their control and for managing these resources profitably. Similarly, the stockholders of the parent company will prosper as the consolidated entity prospers. Their ownership interest is controlling, and they stand to benefit from strength anywhere in the entity and to suffer from weakness.

Long-term creditors of the parent company may find consolidated statements useful in assessing the general strength or weakness of the economic entity. In the long run, earning power is the primary source of safety for creditors. The operating performance of the affiliated group may be a significant safety index for creditors of the parent company.

Consolidated statements are not significant to the minority stockholders or creditors of a subsidiary company. A strong financial position shown in a consolidated balance sheet may conceal a very weak situation in the particular subsidiary company in which a creditor or minority stockholder has a legal interest. These groups should rely on the individual financial statements of the affiliate in which they have a legal claim.

Additional uses of consolidated financial statements and more complex problems encountered in preparing them are discussed in advanced accounting courses.

## KEY TERMS INTRODUCED OR EMPHASIZED IN CHAPTER 19

**Affiliated companies** A parent company and one or more subsidiary companies.

**Business combination** The combining of two or more companies into a single economic entity. A business combination may be brought about by the parent company purchasing a controlling interest in a subsidiary, or by a pooling of interests. Business combinations are often called ***mergers.***

**Consolidated financial statements** A set of statements presenting the combined financial position and operating results of affiliated corporations.

**Equity method** The method of accounting used when the investment by one corporation in another is large enough to influence the policies of the ***investee.*** The investor recognizes as investment income its proportionate share of the investee's net income, rather than considering dividends received as income.

**Intercompany debt** Amounts owed by one member of an affiliated group to another member of the affiliated group. Although intercompany debt is included in the separate financial statements of the debtor and the creditor companies, it should be eliminated when the two companies are viewed as a single economic entity.

**Intercompany transactions** Transactions between two affiliated companies. The effects of intercompany transactions, such as ***intercompany debt,*** are eliminated as a step in preparing consolidated financial statements.

**Investee** When an investor owns a sufficient amount (20% or more) of the voting stock in a company to exercise a significant degree of control over the company's policies, the controlled company is termed the investee. When the investor owns more than 50% of the investee's voting stock, the investee is called a ***subsidiary.***

**Lower of cost or market** The technique of valuing a portfolio of marketable equity securities in the balance sheet at the lower of cost or current market value. A write-down to a market value below cost involves recognition of an ***unrealized loss.***

**Marketable securities** A highly liquid type of investment which can be sold at any time without interfering with normal operation of the business. Usually classified as a current asset second only to cash in liquidity.

**Minority interest** The shares of a subsidiary company owned by persons other than the parent corporation.

**Parent company** A corporation which owns a controlling interest in another company.

**Pooling of interests** A method of accounting for a business combination in which assets and liabilities of the separate entities are combined at their existing carrying values. The stockholders of the combining companies are considered to have "pooled their interests," as opposed to an outright sale.

**Purchase method** A method of accounting for a business combination by recording assets at current market values as indicated by the price paid in the acquisition.

**Subsidiary company** A corporation in which a controlling stock interest is held by another corporation (the parent).

**Unrealized losses and gains** An unrealized loss results from writing down marketable equity securities to a market value below cost. An unrealized gain results from restoring a former write-down because of a recovery in market price. Securities cannot be written up above aggregate cost. Unrealized losses and gains on marketable securities classified as current assets are included in the determination of the year's net income. A net unrealized loss on marketable securities classified as long-term investments is excluded from the determination of net income and is shown in the balance sheet as a reduction in stockholders' equity.

**Valuation allowance for marketable securities** The contra-asset account used to reduce the carrying value of marketable equity securities from cost to a market value below cost. Adjusted at each balance sheet date.

## REVIEW QUESTIONS

1 Why are investments in marketable securities usually regarded as current assets?

2 Why must an investor who owns numerous marketable securities maintain a marketable securities subsidiary ledger?

3 If an investor buys a bond between interest dates, he or she pays as a part of the purchase price the accrued interest since the last interest date. On the other hand, if the investor buys a share of common or preferred stock, no "accrued dividend" is added to the quoted price. Explain why this difference exists.

4 Should stock dividends received be considered revenue to an investor? Explain.

5 Because of a decline in market prices, National Corporation had to write down the carrying value of its investment in marketable securities by $70,000 in the current year. In the determination of net income for the current year, does it make any difference if National Corporation's investment portfolio is classified as a current asset or a long-term investment? Explain fully.

6 In the current asset section of its balance sheet, Delta Industries shows marketable securities at a market value $12,000 below cost. If the market value of these securities rises by $19,000 during the next accounting period, how large an unrealized gain (if any) should Delta Industries include in its next income statement? Explain fully.

7 How does the financial reporting requirement of valuing marketable securities at the lower-of-cost-or-market value compare with income tax rules concerning marketable securities?

8 "To substitute current market value for cost as a basis for valuing marketable securities would represent a departure from traditional accounting practice." Discuss the case for and against using market value consistently as the basis of valuation in accounting for marketable securities.

9 When should investors use the equity method to account for an investment in common stock?

10 Dividends on stock owned are usually recognized as income when they are received. Does an investor using the ***equity method*** to account for an investment in common stock follow this policy? Explain fully.

11 Alexander Corporation owns 80% of the outstanding common stock of Benton Company. Explain the basis for the assumption that these two companies constitute a single economic entity operating under unified control.

12 What are consolidated financial statements? Explain briefly how these statements are prepared.

13 List the three basic types of intercompany eliminations which should be made as a step in the preparation of consolidated financial statements.

14 Explain why the price paid to acquire a controlling interest in a subsidiary company may be different from the book value of the equity acquired.

15 The following item appears on a consolidated balance sheet: "Minority interest in subsidiary . . . $620,000." Explain the nature of this item, and where you would expect to find it on the consolidated balance sheet.

16 Briefly explain the differences found in consolidated financial statements when a business combination is viewed as a ***pooling of interests*** rather than as a ***purchase.***

17 As a general rule, when should consolidated financial statements be prepared?

18 The annual report of Superior Manufacturing Company and Subsidiaries included the following note: "Accounts of all subsidiaries in which the Company owns more than 50% of the voting stock are shown on a consolidated basis, with three exceptions: Western Casualty and Indemnity Company, Consumer Credit Corporation, and Superior Manufacturing of Argentina, which are accounted for by the equity method."

Explain the probable reasons for not consolidating these three subsidiaries. Also explain how the investments in these unconsolidated subsidiaries will be shown in the consolidated balance sheet.

19 What groups of persons are likely to be primarily interested in consolidated financial statements? Why?

20 A creditor of Great Mining Company is concerned because the company is in financial difficulty and has reported increasingly large losses in the past three years. Great Mining Company is a 75%-owned subsidiary of Hannah Company.

When creditors examine the consolidated statements of the two companies they find that the earnings are satisfactory and that the consolidated entity is in a sound financial position. To what extent should the creditors be reassured by the consolidated statements, assuming that the information contained in them fairly presents the financial position of the consolidated entity?

## EXERCISES

*Ex. 19-1* Yamato Company purchased as a short-term investment $10,000 face value of the 9% bonds of Lorenzo, Inc., on March 31 of the current year, at a total cost of $10,125, including interest accrued since January 1. Interest is paid by Lorenzo, Inc., on June 30 and December 31. On July 31, four months after the purchase, Yamato Company sold the bonds and interest accrued since July 1 for a total price of $10,105.

Prepare all entries required in the accounting records of Yamato Company relating to the investment in Lorenzo, Inc., bonds. (Commissions are to be ignored.)

*Ex. 19-2* Prepare the journal entries in the accounting records of Axel Masters, Inc., to record the following transactions. Include a memorandum entry on July 9 to show the change in the cost basis per share.

**Jan. 7** Purchased as a temporary investment 1,000 shares of Reed Company common stock at a price of $41.50 per share, plus a brokerage commission of $500.

**Feb. 12** Received a cash dividend of $2.20 per share on the investment in Reed Company stock.

**July 9** Received an additional 50 shares of Reed Company common stock as a result of a 5% stock dividend.

**Aug. 14** Sold 500 shares of Reed Company common stock at a price of $44 per share, less a brokerage commission of $290.

*Ex. 19-3* The cost and market value of Edgebrook Corporation's portfolio of marketable securities at the end of Years 1 and 2 are shown below. The marketable securities are viewed as a current asset.

| | Cost | Market Value |
|---|---|---|
| Year 1 | $79,000 | $67,800 |
| Year 2 | 91,000 | 97,600 |

Show how the portfolio would appear in the balance sheet at the end of Year 1 and at the end of Year 2. If appropriate, use a valuation account in your presentation.

*Ex. 19-4* On January 1, Year 4, Travis Corporation purchases 40% of the common stock of Comoy, Inc., for $300,000, which corresponds to the underlying book value. Comoy, Inc., has issued common stock only. During Year 4, Comoy, Inc., earns net income of $70,000 and pays dividends of $30,000. Travis Corporation uses the equity method to account for this investment.

**Instructions**

**a** Prepare all journal entries in the accounting records of Travis Corporation relating to the investment during Year 4.

**b** During Year 5, Comoy, Inc., reports a net loss of $90,000 and pays no dividends. Compute the carrying value of Travis Corporation's investment in Comoy, Inc., at the end of Year 5.

*Ex. 19-5* Midtown Cafeterias has purchased all the outstanding shares of Ballpark Caterers for $270,000. At the date of acquisition, Ballpark Caterers' balance sheet showed total stockholders' equity of $240,000, consisting of $200,000 capital stock and $40,000 retained earnings.

In general journal entry form, prepare the eliminating entry necessary on the working paper to consolidate the balance sheets of these two companies.

*Ex. 19-6* Selected account balances from the separate balance sheets of Adams Company and its wholly owned subsidiary, Baker Company, are shown below:

| | Adams Company | Baker Company | Consolidated |
|---|---|---|---|
| Accounts receivable | $ 400,000 | $ 160,000 | $ |
| Accrued rent receivable—Adams Company | | 4,000 | |
| Investment in Baker Company | 1,240,000 | | |
| Accounts payable | 320,000 | 120,000 | |
| Accrued expenses payable | 11,000 | | |
| Bonds payable | 1,400,000 | 500,000 | |
| Capital stock | 2,000,000 | 1,000,000 | |
| Retained earnings | 1,820,000 | 240,000 | |

Adams Company owes Baker Company $4,000 in accrued rent payable and Baker Company owes Adams Company $30,000 on account for services rendered. Show the amount that should appear in the consolidated balance sheet for each of these selected accounts. If the account would not appear in the consolidated balance sheet, indicate "None" as the consolidated account balance.

*Ex. 19-7* On June 30 of Year 1, P Company ***purchased*** 80% of the stock of S Company for $480,000 in cash. The separate condensed balance sheets immediately after the purchase are shown below:

| | P Company | S Company |
|---|---|---|
| Cash | $ 140,000 | $ 90,000 |
| Investment in S Company | 480,000 | |
| Other assets | 2,180,000 | 710,000 |
| | $2,800,000 | $800,000 |
| Liabilities | $ 600,000 | $200,000 |
| Capital stock | 1,200,000 | 400,000 |
| Retained earnings | 1,000,000 | 200,000 |
| | $2,800,000 | $800,000 |

Prepare a consolidated balance sheet immediately after P Company acquired control of S Company.

## PROBLEMS

### Group A

*19A-1* On March 1, Year 7, Imperial Motors purchased $60,000 face value of the 9% bonds of Crest Theatres at a price of 96, plus accrued interest. The bonds pay interest semiannually on June 30 and December 31, and mature on June 30, Year 10 (40 months from the date of purchase). Imperial Motors views these bonds as a long-term investment and follows the policy of amortizing the difference between the cost of the bonds and their maturity value by the straight-line method at the end of each year.

**Instructions**

**a** Prepare the journal entries to record the following transactions in Year 7:
  (1) Purchase of the bonds on March 1
  (2) Receipt of semiannual bond interest on June 30
  (3) Receipt of semiannual bond interest on December 31 and amortization of the difference between cost of the bonds and their maturity value for 10 months.

**b** Assume that an unexpected need for cash forces Imperial Motors to sell the entire investment in Crest Theatres bonds for $57,850 plus accrued interest on January 31, Year 8. Prepare the journal entries to:
  (1) Accrue bond interest receivable at January 31, Year 8, and to amortize the difference between cost and maturity value for the one month since year-end.
  (2) Record the sale of the bonds on January 31.

***19A-2*** During the current year, Cherokee Company engaged in the following transactions relating to marketable securities:

**Feb. 28** Purchased 1,000 shares of National Products common stock for $63 per share plus a broker's commission of $600.

**Mar. 15** National Products paid a cash dividend of 50 cents per share which had been declared on February 20 payable on March 15 to stockholders of record on March 6.

**May 31** National Products distributed a 20% stock dividend.

**Nov. 15** National Products distributed additional shares as the result of a 2 for 1 stock split.

**Dec. 10** Cherokee Company sold 600 shares of its National Products stock at $28 per share, less a broker's commission of $150.

**Dec. 10** National Products paid a cash dividend of 25 cents per share. Dividend was declared November 20 payable December 10 to stockholders of record on November 30.

As of December 31, National Products common stock had a market value of $25 per share. Cherokee Company classifies its National Products stock as a current asset and owns no other marketable securities.

**Instructions** Prepare journal entries to account for this investment in Cherokee Company's accounting records. Include memorandum entries when appropriate to show changes in the cost basis per share. Also include the year-end adjusting entry, if one is necessary, to reduce the investment to the lower-of-cost-or-market value. For journal entries involving computations the explanation portion of the entry should include the computation.

***19A-3*** In the current asset section of its most recent balance sheet, Mirage Corporation showed marketable securities as follows:

| | | |
|---|---|---|
| *Marketable securities* | *$72,400* | |
| *Less: Valuation allowance for marketable securities* | *5,250* | *$67,150* |

Shortly after the above balance sheet date, Mirage Corporation sold for $44,000 marketable securities which had cost $42,600.

**Instructions**

**a** Prepare a journal entry to record the above sale for $44,000 of marketable securities which had cost $42,600.

**b** The following numbered items are ***independent*** assumptions as to the current market value of the equity securities which remain in Mirage Corporation's portfolio at the next balance sheet date after the sale recorded in part **a.** For each assumption, prepare the journal entry required to adjust the carrying value of the portfolio to the lower of cost or market as of the balance sheet date. Show computations supporting each entry.
(1) Assume current market value is $22,100.
(2) Assume current market value is $29,270.
(3) Assume current market value is $31,800.

*19A-4* The portfolio of marketable securities owned by Blue Marlin Corporation at January 1 of the current year consisted of the four securities listed below. All marketable securities are classfied as current assets.

| | |
|---|---|
| *$100,000 maturity value Bay Resort Corp. 7½% bonds due Dec. 31, 1986. Interest is payable on June 30 and Dec. 31 of each year. Cost basis $976 per bond* | *$97,600* |
| *$50,000 maturity value Copper Products Co. 9% bonds due Apr. 30, 1990. Interest is payable on Apr. 30 and Oct. 31 of each year. Cost basis $990 per bond* | *49,500* |
| *1,200 shares of Aztec Corporation common stock. Cost basis $38.50 per share* | *46,200* |
| *800 shares of Donner-Pass, Inc., $4.80 cumulative preferred stock. Cost basis $65 per share* | *52,000* |

Transactions relating to investments that were completed during the first six months of the current year follow:

**Jan. 10** Acquired 500 shares of Rhodes Co. common stock at $76 per share. Brokerage commissions paid amounted to $250.
**Jan. 21** Received quarterly dividend of $1.20 per share on 800 shares of Donner-Pass, Inc., preferred stock.
**Mar. 5** Sold 200 shares of Donner-Pass, Inc., preferred stock at $62 per share less commissions and transfer taxes amounting to $105.
**Apr. 1** Received additional 500 shares of Rhodes Co. common stock as a result of a 2 for 1 split.
**Apr. 20** Received quarterly dividend of $1.20 per share on 600 shares of Donner-Pass, Inc., preferred stock.
**Apr. 30** Received semiannual interest on Copper Products Co. 9% bonds. Accrued interest of $750 had been recorded on December 31 of last year in the Bond Interest Receivable account.
**May 1** Sold $25,000 face value of Copper Products Co. 9% bonds at 103, less a commission of $125.
**May 10** Received additional 120 shares of Aztec Corporation common stock as a result of 10% stock dividend.
**June 4** Received a cash dividend of 90 cents per share on Rhodes Co. common stock.
**June 24** Sold 800 shares of Aztec Corporation common stock at $38 per share, less a brokerage commission and transfer taxes amounting to $280.
**June 30** Received semiannual interest on Bay Resort Corp. 7½% bonds.

On June 30 of the current year, the quoted market prices of the marketable equity securities owned by Blue Marlin Corporation were as follows: Aztec Corporation common stock, $37; Donner-Pass, Inc., preferred stock, $62½; and Rhodes Co. common stock, $43.

**Instructions**

**a** Prepare journal entries to record the transactions listed above. Include an adjusting entry to record accrued interest on the remaining Copper Products Co.

bonds through June 30. (Do not consider a lower-of-cost-or-market adjustment in part **a**.)

**b** Prepare a schedule showing the cost and market value of the marketable equity securities owned by Blue Marlin Corporation at June 30. Prepare the adjusting entry, if one is required, to reduce the portfolio to the lower of cost or market. (At January 1, the market value of the portfolio was above cost and the Valuation Allowance for Marketable Securities account had a zero balance.)

*19A-5* Gremlin Village was organized on January 1, Year 4, to operate an amusement park. On this date, the corporation issued 400,000 shares of common stock at a price of $40 per share; 80,000 of these shares were issued to Video Productions, Inc.

Video Productions, Inc., regards its investment in Gremlin Village as long term. Shown below are the net income (or loss) earned and dividends paid by Gremlin Village during Years 4 and 5. Also shown is the market price per share of common stock at the end of each year.

| | Net Income (Loss) | Dividends Paid (at Dec. 31) | Market Price per Share (at Dec. 31) |
|---|---|---|---|
| Year 4 | $ (430,000) | None | $28 |
| Year 5 | 1,800,000 | $840,000* | 53 |

* $2.10 per share.

**Instructions**

**a** Prepare all journal entries relating to this investment in Years 4 and 5 in the accounting records of Video Productions, Inc. Assume that dividends are recognized as income when received and that the investment is valued at the lower of cost or market. (This is Video Production's only long-term investment.)

**b** Prepare all journal entries relating to this investment in Years 4 and 5 assuming that Video Productions, Inc., uses the ***equity method*** to account for its 20% ownership interest in Gremlin Village. Entries to recognize investment income or loss are made at year-end.

**c** For each ledger account used in parts **a** and **b**, explain briefly the nature of the account and where it will appear in the financial statements. Prepare a separate explanation for each account, but explain each account only once. You may omit an explanation of the Cash account.

An example of the type of explanation desired follows: "Marketable Securities—Long-Term: This is an asset account which appears in the balance sheet under the caption Long-Term Investments."

*19A-6* The information at the top of page 732 relates to Major Company and its subsidiary, the Minor Company.

Major Company acquired its controlling interest in Minor Company by issuing a combination of notes payable and additional shares of capital stock.

**Instructions**

**a** Was the acquisition of Minor Company viewed as a purchase or a pooling of interests? Why?

**b** What percentage of the outstanding stock of Minor Company is owned by Major Company? (Hint: First determine the percentage of Minor Company's stockholders' equity owned by the minority stockholders.)

**c** If Minor Company's accounts payable include $85,000 owed to Major Company, how much of Major Company's accounts payable are apparently owed to Minor Company?

**d** Explain the nature of the asset Excess of Cost over Book Value of Investment in Subsidiary.

| Assets | Major Company | Minor Company | Consolidated |
|---|---|---|---|
| Cash | $ 120,000 | $ 75,000 | $ 195,000 |
| Accounts receivable | 180,000 | 100,000 | 160,000 |
| Merchandise inventory | 360,000 | 230,000 | 590,000 |
| Investment in Minor Company | 900,000 | | |
| Other assets | 1,200,000 | 530,000 | 1,730,000 |
| Excess of cost over book value of investment in subsidiary | | | 220,000 |
| Total assets | $2,760,000 | $935,000 | $2,895,000 |
| **Liabilities & Stockholders' Equity** | | | |
| Accounts payable | $ 165,000 | $ 90,000 | $ 135,000 |
| Accrued liabilities | 30,000 | 45,000 | 75,000 |
| Notes payable (long-term) | 450,000 | | 450,000 |
| Capital stock | 1,000,000 | 300,000 | 1,000,000 |
| Paid-in capital in excess of par | 365,000 | 160,000 | 365,000 |
| Retained earnings | 750,000 | 340,000 | 750,000 |
| Minority interest | | | 120,000 |
| Total liabilities & stockholders' equity | $2,760,000 | $935,000 | $2,895,000 |

*19A-7* Osborne Electronics purchased 80% of the stock of Technical Instruments for cash. Shown below are the separate balance sheets of the two companies at the end of Year 10:

| Assets | Osborne Electronics | Technical Instruments |
|---|---|---|
| Cash | $ 35,000 | $ 18,000 |
| Note receivable from Technical Instruments | 50,000 | |
| Accounts receivable | 90,000 | 50,000 |
| Inventories | 100,000 | 145,000 |
| Investment in Technical Instruments (equity method) | 475,000 | |
| Plant and equipment | 350,000 | 450,000 |
| Accumulated depreciation | (140,000) | (83,000) |
| Total assets | $960,000 | $580,000 |
| **Liabilities & Stockholders' Equity** | | |
| Notes payable | $100,000 | $ 50,000 |
| Accounts payable | 120,000 | 60,000 |
| Accrued liabilities | 30,000 | 20,000 |
| Common stock, no par value | 400,000 | 200,000 |
| Retained earnings | 310,000 | 250,000 |
| Total liabilities & stockholders' equity | $960,000 | $580,000 |

**Additional information**

(1) Osborne Electronic's asset account, Investment in Technical Instruments, represents ownership of 80% of Technical Instruments stockholders' equity, which has a book value of $360,000 [80% × ($200,000 + $250,000) = $360,000]. The remain-

der of the Investment account balance represents an excess of the cost of the investment over its book value.

(2) The excess of cost over book value of investment in Technical Instruments cannot be allocated to any specific asset and should be reported at "Excess of Cost over Book Value of Investment in Subsidiary" in the consolidated balance sheet. Amortization of the excess of cost over book value has already been recorded through December 31, Year 10.

(3) During Year 10, Technical Instruments borrowed $50,000 from Osborne Electronics by issuing a one-year note payable. Interest on this note has been paid through December 31.

(4) The accounts payable of Osborne Electronics include $9,000 owed to Technical Instruments for services rendered during Year 10. This amount also is included in the accounts receivable of Technical Instruments.

**Instructions** Prepare a working paper for a consolidated balance sheet at the end of Year 10. Use the form illustrated on page 718. Include at the bottom of the working paper explanations of the elimination entries.

## Group B

*19B-1* Maria Mandella invested in $420,000 face value of 9%, 10-year bonds at a price of 95. The investment was made at the date of original issuance of the bonds and consequently involved neither accrued interest nor a broker's commission. Shortly after this transaction, the market price of the bonds dropped to 90. After holding the bonds exactly six years, Mandella sold them at a price of 102. The broker's commission charged was $1,500. There was no accrued interest at the date of sale because the sale occurred immediately after receipt of the semiannual interest payment.

**Instructions**

**a** Assume that Mandella at the date of purchase had no intention of holding the bonds to maturity and did not amortize the discount. Determine the total interest earned during the six-year period and the gain or loss on disposal.

**b** Assume that Mandella did intend to hold the bonds until maturity and did amortize the discount. When Mandella sold the bonds six years later, her carrying value for the investment was $411,600. Determine the total interest earned during the six-year period and the gain or loss on disposal.

**c** What is the most probable reason for the price of the bonds being above their face value at the date Mandella disposed of them? Would amortization of discount on the bonds have produced a more realistic measurement of yearly income in this case? Explain.

*19B-2* On March 31, Movie World purchased as a temporary investment 1,000 shares of Torch Company common stock at $63 per share plus broker's commission of $300. Torch Company had declared a cash dividend of 60 cents per share on March 18, payable on April 18 to stockholders of record on April 7.

On June 30, Torch Company distributed a 20% stock dividend. On December 1, the shares were split 2 for 1 and the additional shares distributed to stockholders. On December 5, a cash dividend of 50 cents per share was declared, payable on December 30 to stockholders of record on December 20. Movie World sold 600 shares of Torch Company stock at $40 a share on December 31. Commission charges on the sale amounted to $250.

**Instructions** Prepare journal entries to record the above events in Movie World's accounts. Include memorandum entries when appropriate, even though ledger accounts are not affected. For journal entries involving computations, the explanation portion of the entry should include the computations. No lower-of-cost-or-market adjustment is necessary.

*19B-3* Portofino Corporation acquired a portfolio of marketable equity securities in Year 1. The portfolio is regarded as a current asset, and securities are purchased and sold from the portfolio as part of the company's cash management program. The cost and market value of the portfolio at year-end is shown below for Years 1, 2, and 3:

| | Cost | Market Value |
|---|---|---|
| Year 1 | $118,000 | $110,200 |
| Year 2 | 109,600 | 104,700 |
| Year 3 | 115,300 | 116,800 |

**Instructions**

**a** For each of the three years, prepare the year-end adjusting entry to value the portfolio at the lower of cost or market.

**b** Show how the portfolio would appear in the balance sheet at the end of Year 2. (Use a valuation account in your presentation.)

*19B-4* Tom Jensen owned the following investments in marketable securities throughout the current year. He does not amortize discounts and premiums on bonds owned.

$100,000 in 10% Melton Corporation bonds, due four years and two months from date of purchase. Purchased at cost of $102,500, market price at end of current year, $101\frac{7}{8}$. (Market prices are customarily stated in eighths of a dollar. The fraction $\frac{7}{8}$ is expressed as .875 for purposes of computation.) Received two regular semiannual interest payments during current year.

$60,000 in 6% Chapel City bonds maturing eight years from date of purchase. Purchased for $56,120, market price on December 31 of current year, $94\frac{1}{2}$. Received regular semiannual interest payments during year.

1,600 shares of Webber Corporation $6 convertible preferred stock, $100 par value. Purchased for $159,800, market price at end of current year $$102\frac{3}{8}$ per share. Received regular dividends on March 1 and September 1 of current year.

1,000 shares of Lee Corporation common stock: cost $170 per share, market price at December 31, $290 per share. Received dividends of $5 per share on March 1, a 10% stock dividend on June 1, and $4 per share in cash on December 31 of current year.

**Instructions**

**a** Prepare a schedule showing the amount earned during the current year on each of these investments and the rate of return as a percentage of cost and of market value at the end of the year. Calculate the rate of return to the nearest hundredth of a percent. This schedule may be in columnar form with the following column headings:

| Name of Security | Original Cost | Year-End Market Value | Earnings This Year | Rate Earned on Cost, % | Rate Earned on Market Value, % |
|---|---|---|---|---|---|

**b** In a discussion with a business associate, Jensen commented on his average return for the year on the total cost of his investment. His friend replied that return on market value was a better measure of earning performance. Discuss the merits of the percentage earned on cost and the percentage earned on market value as measures of investment success.

*19B-5* Carolina Mills was organized on January 1, Year 1, to manufacture carpeting. On this date, the corporation issued 200,000 shares of common stock at a price of $25 per share; 40,000 of these shares were issued to Discount Carpet Sales, Inc.

Discount Carpet Sales, Inc., regards its investment in Carolina Mills as long term. Shown below are the net income (or loss) earned and dividends paid by Carolina Mills during Years 1 and 2. Also shown is the market price per share of common stock at the end of each year.

| | Net Income (Loss) | Dividends Paid (at Dec. 31) | Market Price per Share (at Dec. 31) |
|---|---|---|---|
| *Year 1* | *$420,000* | *$120,000** | *$37* |
| *Year 2* | *(270,000)* | *None* | *21* |

* 60 cents per share.

**Instructions**

**a** Prepare all journal entries relating to this investment in Years 1 and 2 in the accounting records of Discount Carpet Sales, Inc. Assume that dividends are recognized as income when received and that the investment is valued at the lower of cost or market. (This is Discount Carpet Sales, Inc.'s only long-term investment.)

**b** Prepare all journal entries relating to this investment in Years 1 and 2 assuming that Discount Carpet Sales, Inc., uses the ***equity method*** to account for its 20% ownership interest in Carolina Mills. Entries to recognize investment income or loss are made at year-end.

**c** For each ledger account used in parts **a** and **b**, explain briefly the nature of the account and where it will appear in the financial statements. Prepare a separate explanation for each account, but explain each account only once. You may omit an explanation of the Cash account.

An example of the type of explanation desired follows: "Marketable Securities—Long-Term: This is an asset account which appears in the balance sheet under the caption Long-Term Investments."

***19B-6*** Condensed balance sheets of Wheat and Pine Companies at the end of Year 1 are shown below:

| *Assets* | *Wheat Company* | *Pine Company* |
|---|---|---|
| *Current assets* | *$1,680,000* | *$240,000* |
| *Other assets* | *1,920,000* | *660,000* |
| *Total assets* | *$3,600,000* | *$900,000* |
| ***Liabilities & Stockholders' Equity*** | | |
| *Current liabilities* | *$ 840,000* | *$120,000* |
| *Long-term debt* | *600,000* | *84,000* |
| *Capital stock* | *1,200,000* | *360,000* |
| *Retained earnings* | *960,000* | *336,000* |
| *Total liabilities & stockholders' equity* | *$3,600,000* | *$900,000* |

**Instructions** Assume that, at the end of Year 1, Wheat Company purchased (using current assets) all the outstanding capital stock of Pine Company for $768,000. Prepare a consolidated balance sheet for Wheat and Pine Companies at the date of acquisition. (Use the title "Excess of cost over book value of investment in subsidiary" as an asset in the consolidated balance sheet.)

*19B-7* Given below are the balance sheet accounts for the London Company and the Pub Company at the end of Year 1:

| *Assets* | *London Company* | *Pub Company* |
|---|---|---|
| *Cash* | *$ 50,000* | *$ 20,000* |
| *Accounts receivable* | *85,000* | *30,000* |
| *Inventories* | *60,000* | *40,000* |
| *Investment in Pub Company stock (equity method)* | *162,000* | |
| *Plant and equipment* | *250,000* | *180,000* |
| *Accumulated depreciation* | *(50,000)* | *(40,000)* |
| *Total assets* | *$557,000* | *$230,000* |
| ***Liabilities & Stockholders' Equity*** | | |
| *Accounts payable* | *$ 40,000* | *$ 40,000* |
| *Accrued liabilities* | *25,000* | *10,000* |
| *Common stock, no par value* | *300,000* | *100,000* |
| *Retained earnings* | *192,000* | *80,000* |
| *Total liabilities & stockholders' equity* | *$557,000* | *$230,000* |

**Additional Information**

(1) London Company owns 90% of the capital stock of Pub Company, which was purchased for cash at a price equal to its book value.

(2) Pub Company owes London Company $7,000 in accrued rent payable. This amount is included in the accrued liabilities of the subsidiary and the accounts receivable of the parent company.

(3) London Company owes Pub Company $16,000 for services rendered. This amount is included in the parent company's accounts payable and the subsidiary's accounts receivable.

**Instructions** Prepare a working paper for a consolidated balance sheet at the end of Year 1. Use the form illustrated on page 718. Include at the bottom of the working paper explanations of the elimination entries.

## BUSINESS DECISION PROBLEM 19

On March 1, Year 1, Milton Paper Co. invested $4,698,000 cash in the capital stock of Travis Book Company. This represents 58% (58,000 shares) of the outstanding capital stock of Travis Book Company. The balance sheets of Travis Book Company at date of acquisition and at the end of Year 10 include the following:

| | *December 31 Year 10* | *March 1 Year 1* |
|---|---|---|
| *Current assets* | *$13,500,000* | *$7,500,000* |
| *Current liabilities* | *9,000,000* | *3,900,000* |
| *Other assets* | *15,000,000* | *9,000,000* |
| *Long-term liabilities* | *2,400,000* | *4,500,000* |
| *Capital stock, $5 stated value* | *3,000,000* | *3,000,000* |
| *Retained earnings* | *14,100,000* | *5,100,000* |

The balance sheet of the Milton Paper Co. at December 31, Year 10, is shown below:

**MILTON PAPER CO.**
**Balance Sheet**
**December 31, Year 10**

| | | |
|---|---|---|
| **Assets** | | |
| Current assets | | $22,500,000 |
| Investment in Travis Book Company (equity method) | | 9,918,000 |
| Other assets | | 21,582,000 |
| Total assets | | $54,000,000 |
| **Liabilities & Stockholders' Equity** | | |
| Current liabilities | | $12,000,000 |
| Bonds payable | | 18,000,000 |
| Total liabilities | | $30,000,000 |
| Stockholders' equity: | | |
| Capital stock, no par | $ 7,500,000 | |
| Retained earnings | 16,500,000 | |
| Total stockholders' equity | | 24,000,000 |
| Total liabilities & stockholders' equity | | $54,000,000 |

The accounts receivable of Milton Paper Co. include $7,500,000 due from Travis Book Company. The accounts of the two companies have never been consolidated because one manufactures a variety of paper products and the other publishes children's books. However, if a consolidated balance sheet were prepared at December 31, Year 10, the current assets would be $28,500,000 and the current liabilities would be $13,500,000.

Bonnie Bent, a director of Milton Paper Co., suggests that a consolidated balance sheet be prepared for the two companies in order to show a more meaningful financial position. "Through our ownership of 58% of Travis' voting stock, we control the resources and activities of Travis just as if it were a division of Milton Paper Co."

Louis Joseph, another director of Milton Paper Co., objects to Bent's suggestion in view of the poor working capital position of Travis Book Company and the low percentage of stock held in Travis Book Company. "Why should we hide our strong working capital position in consolidated statements? We only own 58% of the stock in Travis and I hate to see us show a liability to minority stockholders of $7,182,000 on our balance sheet. Besides, Travis is not in our kind of business, and I don't think we should include its earnings in our income statement because we haven't realized that profit. To recognize income from this investment before we receive cash dividends violates the accounting principle of conservatism."

**Instructions** Carefully evaluate the points made by Louis Joseph and give your recommendation whether or not the preparation of consolidated statements for the two companies would be appropriate. Your answer should discuss the following points:

(1) Does Milton Paper Co. control Travis Book Company and do the two companies engage in similar or unrelated types of business activity?
(2) Would a consolidated balance sheet show a weaker working capital position than does the separate balance sheet of Milton Paper Co.? In support of your answer, prepare a schedule showing the working capital and current ratio of Milton Paper Co., Travis Book Company, and the consolidated entity.
(3) Would the minority interest be shown as a liability in the consolidated balance sheet?
(4) Should Milton Paper Co. recognize as income its share of the annual earnings of Travis Book Company?

# 20

# INCOME TAXES AND BUSINESS DECISIONS

"A penny saved is a penny earned" according to an old saying credited to Benjamin Franklin. However, now that corporations (as well as some individuals) are subject to approximately a 50% income tax rate, we can modify this bit of folklore to read: "A dollar of income tax saved is worth two dollars of income earned."

In other words, about half of what a corporation earns, and half of what some individuals earn, must be paid to the federal government as income taxes. If advance tax planning will enable a corporation or an individual to save a dollar of income taxes, that dollar saved may be the equivalent of two dollars of before-tax earnings. Furthermore, there are a good many perfectly legal actions which can be taken to save or at least to postpone income taxes.

## Tax planning

Individuals who plan their business affairs in a manner that will result in the lowest possible income tax are acting rationally and legally. They are using the techniques called ***tax planning.*** In the words of a distinguished jurist, Judge Learned Hand:

> Over and over again courts have said that there is nothing sinister in so arranging one's affairs as to keep taxes as low as possible. Everybody does so, rich or poor; and all do right, for nobody owes any public duty to pay more than the law demands: taxes are enforced exactions, not voluntary contributions. To demand more in the name of morals is mere cant.

To minimize and to postpone income taxes are the goals of tax planning. Almost every business decision is a choice among alternative courses of action.

For example, should we lease or buy business automobiles; should we obtain needed capital by issuing bonds or preferred stock; should we use straight-line depreciation or an accelerated method? Some of these alternatives will lead to much lower income taxes than others. Tax planning, therefore, means ***determining in advance the income tax effect*** of every proposed business action and then making business decisions which will lead to the smallest tax liability. Tax practice is an important element of the services furnished to clients by CPA firms. This service includes not only the computing of taxes and preparing of tax returns, but also tax planning.

Tax planning must begin early. Unfortunately, some people wait until the end of the year and then, faced with the prospect of paying a large amount of income tax, ask their accountants what can be done to reduce the tax liability. If we are to arrange transactions in a manner that will lead to the minimum income tax liability, the tax planning must be carried out ***before*** the date of a transaction, not after it is an accomplished fact. Because it is important for everyone to recognize areas in which tax savings may be substantial, a few of the major opportunities for tax planning are discussed in the final section of this chapter.

## Tax avoidance and tax evasion

Newspaper stories tell us each year of some taxpayers who have deliberately understated their taxable income by failing to report a portion of income received or by claiming fictitious deductions such as an excess number of personal exemptions. Such purposeful understatement of taxable income is called ***tax evasion*** and is, of course, illegal. On the other hand, ***tax avoidance*** (the arranging of business and financial affairs in a manner that will minimize tax liability) is entirely legal.

## The critical importance of income taxes

Taxes levied by federal, state, and local governments are a significant part of the cost of operating a typical household, as well as a business enterprise. The knowledge required to be expert in taxation has made it a field of specialization among professional accountants. However, every manager who makes business decisions, and every individual who makes personal investments, urgently needs some knowledge of income taxes. A general knowledge of income taxes will help any business manager or owner to benefit more fully from the advice of the professional tax accountant.

Some understanding of income taxes will also aid the individual citizen in voting intelligently, because a great many of the issues decided in every election have tax implications. Such issues as pollution, inflation, foreign policy, and employment are quite closely linked with income taxes. For example, the offering of special tax incentives to encourage businesses to launch massive programs to reduce pollution is one approach to protection of the environment.

In terms of revenue generated, the four most important kinds of taxes in the United States are ***income taxes, sales taxes, property taxes,*** and ***excise taxes.***

Income taxes exceed all others in terms of the amounts involved, and they also exert a pervasive influence on all types of business decisions. For this reason we shall limit our discussion to the basic federal income tax rules applicable to individuals, partnerships, and corporations.

Income taxes are usually determined from information contained in accounting records. The amount of income tax is computed by applying the appropriate tax rates (as set by federal, state, and some local governments) to ***taxable income.*** As explained more fully later in this chapter, ***taxable income*** is not necessarily the same as ***accounting income*** even though both are derived from the accounting records. Although taxes are involuntary and often unrelated to benefits received, some degree of control over the amount of tax is usually attainable. Business managers can influence the amount of taxes they pay by their choice of form of business organization, methods of financing, and alternative accounting methods. Thus income taxes are inevitably an important factor in arriving at business decisions.

## The federal income tax: history and objectives

The present federal income tax dates from the passage of the Sixteenth Amendment to the Constitution in 1913.[1] This amendment, only 30 words in length,[2] removed all questions of the constitutionality of income taxes and paved the way for the more than 50 revenue acts passed by Congress since that date. In 1939 these tax laws were first combined into what is known as the Internal Revenue Code. The administration and enforcement of the tax laws are duties of the Treasury Department, operating through a division known as the Internal Revenue Service (IRS). The Treasury Department publishes its interpretation of the tax laws in Treasury regulations; the final word in interpretation lies with the federal courts.

Originally the purpose of the federal income tax was simply to obtain revenue for the government. And at first, the tax rates were quite low—by today's standards. In 1913 a married person with taxable income of $15,000 would have been subject to a tax rate of 1%, resulting in a tax liability of $150. Today, a married person with a $15,000 taxable income (worth far less in purchasing power) would pay over $1,600 in federal income tax. The maximum federal income tax rate in 1913 was 7%. Today it is 70%.

The purpose of federal income tax today includes a number of goals in addition to raising revenue. Among these other goals are to combat inflation, to influence the rate of economic growth, to encourage full employment, to favor small businesses, and to redistribute national income on a more equal basis.

[1] A federal income tax was proposed as early as 1815, and an income tax law was actually passed and income taxes collected during the Civil War. This law was upheld by the Supreme Court, but it was repealed when the need for revenue subsided after the war. In 1894 a new income tax law was passed, but the Supreme Court declared this law invalid on constitutional grounds.

[2] It reads "The Congress shall have power to lay and collect taxes on incomes, from whatever source derived, without apportionment among the several States, and without regard to any census or enumeration."

## Classes of taxpayers

In the eyes of the income tax law, there are four major classes of taxpayers: ***individuals, corporations, estates,*** and ***trusts.*** Proprietorships and partnerships are not taxed as business units; their income is taxed directly to the individual proprietor or partners, ***whether or not actually withdrawn from the business.*** A single proprietor reports his or her business income on an individual tax return; the members of a partnership include on their individual tax returns their respective shares of the partnership net income. An individual taxpayer's income tax return must include not only any business income from a proprietorship or partnership, but also any salary or other income and any deductions affecting the tax liability. A partnership must file an ***information return*** showing the computation of total partnership net income and the allocation of this income to each partner.

A corporation is a separate taxable entity; it must file a corporate income tax return and pay a tax on its annual taxable income. In addition, individual stockholders must report dividends received from corporations as part of their personal taxable income. The taxing of corporate dividends has led to the charge that there is "double taxation" of corporate income—once to the corporation and again when it is distributed to stockholders.

The ***income before taxes*** earned by a corporation may be subject to a federal corporate income tax rate of 46%. To illustrate, let us consider the tax impact on one dollar of corporate earnings. First the corporation pays 46%, or 46 cents, out of the dollar to the Internal Revenue Service. That leaves 54 cents for the corporation. Next, assume that the 54 cents is distributed as dividends to individual stockholders. The dividend will be taxed to the stockholders personally at rates varying from 14 to 70%, depending on their individual tax brackets. Thus, the 54 cents of after-tax income to the corporation could be reduced by 70%, or 38 cents of individual income tax, leaving 16 cents of the original dollar for the shareholder. In summary, ***federal income taxes can take as much as 84 cents out of a dollar earned by a corporation and distributed as a dividend to a shareholder.*** The remaining 16 cents could be reduced further by state income taxes.

Special and complex rules apply to the determination of taxable income for estates and trusts. These rules will not be discussed in this chapter.

## Cash basis of accounting for individual tax returns

Almost all individual tax returns are prepared on the cash basis of measuring income. Revenue is recognized when collected in cash; expenses are recognized when paid. The cash basis is advantageous for the individual taxpayer for several reasons. The income of most individuals comes in the form of salaries, interest, and dividends. At the end of each year, employers are required to inform each employee (and the IRS) of the salary earned and the income tax withheld during the year. This report (a W-2 form, illustrated on page 500) must be prepared on the cash basis without any accrual of unpaid wages. Companies paying interest and dividends also are required to use the cash basis in reporting the amounts paid during the year. Thus, most individuals are provided with reports prepared on a cash basis for use in preparing their individual tax returns.

The cash basis has other advantages for the individual taxpayer and for many professional firms and service-type businesses. It is simple, requires a minimum of record keeping, and often permits tax saving by deliberately shifting the timing of revenue and expense transactions from one year to another. For example, a dentist whose taxable income is higher than usual in the current year may decide in December to delay billing patients until January 1, and thus postpone the receipt of gross income to the next year. The timing of ***expense payments*** near the year-end is also controllable by a taxpayer using the cash basis. A taxpayer who has received a bill for a deductible expense item in December may choose to pay it before or after December 31 and thereby influence the amount of taxable income in each year. Further comparison of the cash basis with the accrual basis of income measurement is presented later in this chapter.

***Single Taxpayers***

| ***Taxable Income*** | | ***Tax*** | |
|---|---|---|---|
| ***Not over $2,300*** | | ***-0-*** | |
| ***Over—*** | ***But not over—*** | | ***of the amount over—*** |
| ***$2,300*** | ***$3,400*** | ***14%*** | ***$2,300*** |
| ***$3,400*** | ***$4,400*** | ***$154+16%*** | ***$3,400*** |
| ***$4,400*** | ***$6,500*** | ***$314+18%*** | ***$4,400*** |
| ***$6,500*** | ***$8,500*** | ***$692+19%*** | ***$6,500*** |
| ***$8,500*** | ***$10,800*** | ***$1,072+21%*** | ***$8,500*** |
| ***$10,800*** | ***$12,900*** | ***$1,555+24%*** | ***$10,800*** |
| ***$12,900*** | ***$15,000*** | ***$2,059+26%*** | ***$12,900*** |
| ***$15,000*** | ***$18,200*** | ***$2,605+30%*** | ***$15,000*** |
| ***$18,200*** | ***$23,500*** | ***$3,565+34%*** | ***$18,200*** |
| ***$23,500*** | ***$28,800*** | ***$5,367+39%*** | ***$23,500*** |
| ***$28,800*** | ***$34,100*** | ***$7,434+44%*** | ***$28,800*** |
| ***$34,100*** | ***$41,500*** | ***$9,766+49%*** | ***$34,100*** |
| ***$41,500*** | ***$55,300*** | ***$13,392+55%*** | ***$41,500*** |
| ***$55,300*** | ***$81,800*** | ***$20,982+63%*** | ***$55,300*** |
| ***$81,800*** | ***$108,300*** | ***$37,677+68%*** | ***$81,800*** |
| ***$108,300*** | ...... | ***$55,697+70%*** | ***$108,300*** |

| | | |
|---|---|---|
| ***Example:*** | ***Find the tax for a single person having taxable income of $21,000.*** | |
| ***Answer:*** | ***Tax on $18,200 as shown on tax rate schedule*** .................... | ***$3,565*** |
| | ***Tax on $2,800 excess at 34%*** .............................. | ***952*** |
| | ***Tax on $21,000 for a single person*** ........................ | ***$4,517*** |

### Tax rates

All taxes may be characterized as progressive, proportional, or regressive with respect to any given base. A ***progressive*** tax becomes a larger portion of the base as that base increases. Federal income taxes are ***progressive*** with respect to income, since a higher tax ***rate*** applies as the amount of taxable income increases. A ***proportional*** tax remains a constant percentage of the base no matter how that base changes. For example, a 6% sales tax remains a constant percentage of sales regardless of changes in the dollar amount of sales. A ***regressive*** tax becomes a smaller percentage of the base as the base increases. Regressive taxes, however, are extremely rare.

### Tax rate schedules

On these two facing pages we have tax rate schedules for single taxpayers and for married taxpayers filing joint returns. Tax rates for individuals at present vary from 14 to 70%, depending on the amount of income. Persons with very low

***Married Taxpayers Filing Joint Returns***

| *Taxable Income* | | *Tax* | |
|---|---|---|---|
| *Not over $3,400* | | *-0-* | |
| *Over—* | *But not over—* | | *of the amount over—* |
| *$3,400* | *$5,500* | *14%* | *$3,400* |
| *$5,500* | *$7,600* | *$294+16%* | *$5,500* |
| *$7,600* | *$11,900* | *$630+18%* | *$7,600* |
| *$11,900* | *$16,000* | *$1,404+21%* | *$11,900* |
| *$16,000* | *$20,200* | *$2,265+24%* | *$16,000* |
| *$20,200* | *$24,600* | *$3,273+28%* | *$20,200* |
| *$24,600* | *$29,900* | *$4,505+32%* | *$24,600* |
| *$29,900* | *$35,200* | *$6,201+37%* | *$29,900* |
| *$35,200* | *$45,800* | *$8,162+43%* | *$35,200* |
| *$45,800* | *$60,000* | *$12,720+49%* | *$45,800* |
| *$60,000* | *$85,600* | *$19,678+54%* | *$60,000* |
| *$85,600* | *$109,400* | *$33,502+59%* | *$85,600* |
| *$109,400* | *$162,400* | *$47,544+64%* | *$109,400* |
| *$162,400* | *$215,400* | *$81,464+68%* | *$162,400* |
| *$215,400* | . . . . . | *$117,504+70%* | *$215,400* |

***Example:*** ***Find the tax for a married couple filing a joint return and having a taxable income of $50,000.***

| | | |
|---|---|---|
| ***Answer:*** | ***Tax on $45,800 as shown on tax rate schedule*** . . . . . . . . . . . . . . . . | ***$12,720*** |
| | ***Tax on $4,200 excess at 49%*** . . . . . . . . . . . . . . . . . . . . . . . . . . . . . . | ***2,058*** |
| | ***Tax on $50,000 for a married couple filing a joint return*** . . . . . . . . . . . | ***$14,778*** |

incomes pay no income tax. Different tax rate schedules apply to (1) single taxpayers, (2) married taxpayers filing joint returns, (3) married taxpayers filing separate returns, and (4) single taxpayers who qualify as the head of a household. In computing the amount of the tax, the tax rates are applied to ***taxable income,*** a term which means gross income less certain exclusions and deductions specified in the tax law. Income tax rates are subject to ***frequent revision*** by Congress; in fact, a revision was under consideration by Congress at the time this was written.

### The steeply progressive nature of income taxes

To illustrate the steeply progressive nature of income taxes, let us compare two single taxpayers, one of whom has a relatively low income and the other a relatively high income. Assume that Tom Jones has taxable income of $4,000 a year and Mary Smith has taxable income of $40,000 a year. According to the tax rate schedule on page 742, Jones would owe tax of $250 and Smith would owe tax of $12,657. The tax owed by Jones is about 6% of his total taxable income of $4,000; the tax owed by Smith is about 32% of her total taxable income of $40,000.

Next, let us consider how much additional income tax each of these two individuals would have to pay on any additional income. According to the tax rate schedules, an increase of $100 in income for Jones would be taxed at 16%. However, an increase of $100 in income for Smith would be taxed at 49%. (For the sake of simplicity in this example, we have assumed that both taxpayers use the tax rate schedule. In practice, Jones would use the tax table discussed later in this chapter.)

Note that different and lower tax rates are applicable to the taxable income of married taxpayers who combine their income and deductions on a ***joint return.*** The schedules for married taxpayers filing separate returns and for heads of households are not shown in this chapter.

### Marginal tax rates compared with average tax rates

In any analysis of income taxes, it is important to distinguish the ***marginal*** rate of tax from the ***average*** rate. If a single person has taxable income of $28,800, his or her income tax will be $7,434, an average tax rate of about 26% of taxable income. On the next dollar of income, however, the tax is 44 cents because the individual is subject to a marginal tax rate of 44% on income over $28,800.

The marginal tax rate is especially important in making business decisions. Often the decision is whether to invest additional money or to expend additional time and effort in order to earn an increased amount of income. However, an increase in income will cause an increase in income taxes ***at the marginal rate.*** The ***after-tax*** result of a proposed investment must be estimated by using the marginal tax rate, and not the average tax rate. In other words, the attractiveness of an extra dollar of income depends on the marginal tax rate applicable to that particular dollar.

Assume that you are an unmarried executive with a taxable income of $28,800 and are considering a change to a new job that pays $5,000 more per year in salary. Using the tax rate schedules illustrated, your present tax is $7,434, but your marginal tax rate on the proposed $5,000 increase is 44%. Your decision with respect to the new job may well be affected by the fact that you would be able to keep only slightly more than half ($2,800) of the $5,000 increase in salary. Assume further that you live in a state with a relatively high state income tax. Some states have an income tax rate as high as 10% or more on income earned by a single person. Thus, you would be able to keep less than half of the proposed salary increase of $5,000.

Another way of looking at the impact of income taxes is from the viewpoint of the employer. A company that wants to increase the salary of an executive must pay about $2 for every $1 to be received by the executive in take-home pay.

### Maximum tax on personal service income (earned income)

The maximum federal tax on ***personal service income*** (***earned income***) is limited to 50%. Wages, salaries, and other compensation for personal services are defined as earned income. For example, a single person with an earned income of $110,000 is subject to a marginal tax rate of 50%. However, an individual who received this same amount of income from dividends or interest on investments would be subject to a marginal tax rate of 70%.

### Income taxes and inflation

As salaries and prices in general have risen sharply in recent years, people find themselves in higher income tax brackets even though their higher salaries represent no increase in purchasing power. Because income tax rates arc steeply progressive, this means that many people must pay a ***higher percentage*** of their earnings as income taxes solely as a result of inflation. Thus, income taxes are actually being increased in each year of inflation even though the schedule of tax rates remains unchanged. A $20,000 salary may buy no more today than a $10,000 salary some years ago, but a $20,000 salary is taxed at a much higher rate.

### Income tax formula for individuals

The federal government supplies standard income tax forms on which taxpayers are guided to a proper computation of their taxable income and the amount of the tax. It is helpful to visualize the computation in terms of an income tax formula. The general formula for the determination of taxable income for all taxpayers (other than corporations, estates, and trusts) is outlined on page 746.

The actual sequence and presentation of material on income tax forms differs somewhat from the arrangement in this formula. However, it is easier to understand the structure and logic of the federal income tax and to analyze tax rules and their effect by referring to the tax formula.

### Total income and gross income

Total income is an accounting concept; gross income is a tax concept. ***Total income*** includes, in the words of the law, "all income from whatever source derived." To determine whether an amount received by an individual taxpayer

***General Federal Income Tax Formula for Individuals***

*Use this formula to compute taxable income for individuals*

| | |
|---|---|
| ***Total Income*** | ***All income and gains from whatever source derived*** |
| ***minus*** | |
| ***Exclusions*** | ***Income excluded by law from taxation (see list of items on page 747*** |
| ***equals*** | |
| ***Gross Income*** | ***Income before deductions and exemptions listed below*** |
| ***minus*** | |
| ***Deductions to Arrive at Adjusted Gross Income*** | ***Generally business-related expenses and losses; 60% of net long-term capital gains (see discussion on pages 747–748)*** |
| ***equals*** | |
| ***Adjusted Gross Income*** | ***Significant because several subsequently deductible items are computed as or limited by some percentage of it*** |
| ***minus*** | |
| ***Excess Itemized Deductions from Adjusted Gross Income*** | ***Itemized deductions allowed by law (see pages 748–750) after being reduced by a standard amount*** |
| ***and minus*** | |
| ***Personal Exemptions*** | ***A deduction of $1,000 each for taxpayer, spouse, and dependents; an additional $1,000 for taxpayers over sixty-five years of age and for taxpayers who are blind*** |
| ***equals*** | |
| ***Taxable Income*** | ***Amount to which appropriate tax rates are applied*** |

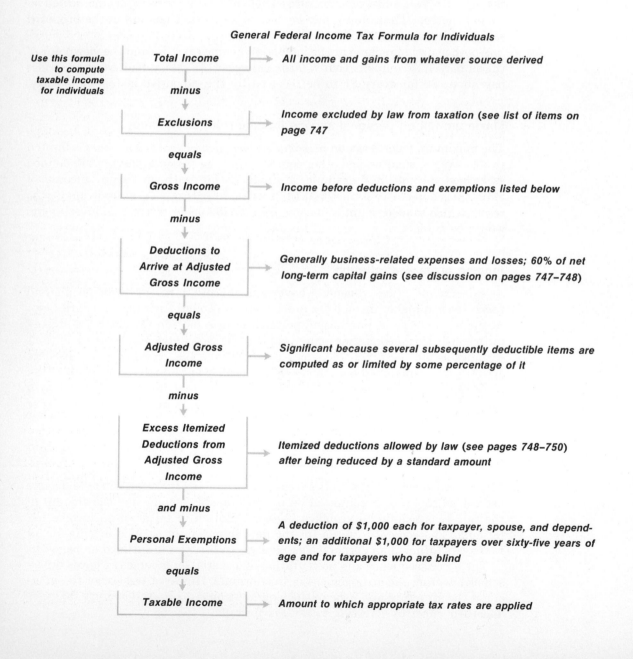

should be included in total income, one need only ask, "Is it income or is it a return of capital?"

***Gross income*** for tax purposes is all income not excluded by law. To determine whether any given income item is included in taxable gross income, one must ask, "Is there a provision in the tax law excluding this item of income from gross income?" Among the items ***presently excluded from gross income*** by statute are interest on state and municipal bonds, gifts and inheritances, life insurance proceeds, workmen's compensation and sick pay, social security benefits and the portion of receipts from annuities that represents return of cost, pensions to veterans, compensation for damages, and the first $200 of dividends or interest received ($400 on a joint tax return).

Among the items of miscellaneous income which must be ***included*** in gross income are prizes and awards won, tips received, and gains from sale of personal property. The fact that income arises from an illegal transaction does not keep it from being taxable. To identify exclusions from gross income, it is necessary to refer to the tax law and sometimes to Treasury regulations and court decisions.

## Deductions to arrive at adjusted gross income

The deductions from ***gross income*** allowed in computing ***adjusted gross income*** are discussed below:

1 **Business expenses of a single proprietorship** These include all ordinary and necessary expenses of carrying on a trade, business, or profession (other than as an employee). For the actual tax computation, business expenses are deducted from business revenue, and net business income is then included in adjusted gross income.

2 **Business expenses of an employee** Some expenses incurred by employees in connection with their employment are allowed as a deduction if the employees are not reimbursed by the employer. These include, for example, travel and transportation as part of employees' duties, expenses of "outside salespersons," and certain moving expenses. The costs of commuting from home to work are not deductible.

3 **Expenses attributable to rental properties** The owner of rental property, such as an apartment building, incurs a variety of operating expenses. Depreciation, property taxes, repairs, maintenance, interest on indebtedness related to property, and any other expense incurred in connection with the earning of rental income are allowed as a deduction. This means that only the ***net income*** derived from rental property is included in adjusted gross income.

4 **Losses from the sale of property used in business** The loss resulting from the sale of property used in a trade or business may be deducted against other items of gross income.[3]

---

[3]Losses arising from the sale of personal property, such as a home or personal automobile, are not deductible. On the other hand, gains from the sale of personal property are taxable. This appears inconsistent, until one realizes that a loss on the sale of personal property usually reflects depreciation through use, which is a personal expense.

5 **Net capital losses** Up to $3,000 of net capital losses may be deducted to arrive at adjusted gross income. Capital gains and losses are discussed on pages 751–753.

6 **Long-term capital gain deduction** Sixty percent of the excess of net long-term capital gains over net short-term capital losses is a deduction to arrive at adjusted gross income. In other words, only 40% of a long-term capital gain is taxable.

7 **Net operating loss carry-over** Taxable income may be either positive or negative. If positive income were taxed and no allowance made for operating losses, a taxpayer whose business income fluctuated between income and loss would pay a relatively higher tax than one having a steady income averaging the same amount. Therefore, the tax law allows the carry-back and carry-over of net operating losses as an offset against the income of other years. At the present time a loss may be carried back against the income of the three preceding years, and then forward against the income of the next seven years.

8 **Contributions to retirement plans** Individuals who are ***self-employed*** are permitted to deduct from gross income the amounts they contribute to a retirement plan. The present limit on such contributions is the lower of $7,500 or 15% of the self-employed person's annual earnings. By taking a deduction for this contribution, a self-employed person earning $50,000 or more can reduce adjusted gross income by as much as $7,500 each year. The amounts contributed plus earnings on the fund are taxable when the taxpayer retires and begins making withdrawals from the fund. This type of retirement plan (often referred to as a ***Keogh H.R.10 plan***) is intended to provide self-employed persons with opportunities similar to those of persons employed by organizations with well-defined pension or retirement plans.

Another type of retirement plan (distinct from the Keogh H.R.10 plan) is designed for ***employees*** who are not covered by a pension plan by the employing organization. This plan, called an ***individual retirement arrangement (IRA)*** permits an employee to contribute to the plan and to deduct from gross income 15% of compensation received, but not more than $1,500 a year.

### Deductions from adjusted gross income (itemized deductions)

Remember that there are two basic groups of deductions for individuals: (1) items deductible from gross income to arrive at adjusted gross income and (2) items deductible from adjusted gross income to arrive at taxable income. We are now considering the second group of items (such as charitable contributions, interest on home mortgage, and sales taxes) which an individual may deduct ***from*** adjusted gross income. These items are referred to as ***itemized deductions.***

The importance of itemizing deductions lies in the fact that every deduction reduces the income subject to tax. The taxpayer should retain documentary evidence supporting the deductions claimed.

**Zero bracket amount** For many years taxpayers were permitted to take a standard deduction computed as a percentage of adjusted gross income. This standard deduction was based on the concept that all taxpayers could be expected to claim some deductions, such as interest expense and charitable contributions. As an alternative to taking the standard deduction, taxpayers could ***itemize*** their deductions. The extra work to itemize deductions was worthwhile if the total was more than the standard deduction. In recent years the tax laws have been changed to provide a new ***zero bracket amount*** which replaced the standard deduction. This zero bracket amount was built into the tax tables in order to simplify the computation of tax liability. The result is to assure a given amount of tax-free income to all taxpayers. Presently, the zero bracket amount is $3,400 for married taxpayers filing a joint return, and $2,300 for single taxpayers. In effect, the law is assuming that every taxpayer could claim at least $2,300 of deductions ($3,400 if married); therefore the proof of those amounts need not be submitted. The zero bracket amount automatically allows for them.

**Excess itemized deductions** We have seen that the zero bracket amount is the equivalent of a standard deduction from adjusted gross income. The amount of income subject to tax can be reduced further by single taxpayers who itemize deductions in excess of $2,300 and by married taxpayers filing a joint return who itemize deductions in excess of $3,400. In other words, a reduction in tax is possible if a taxpayer has relatively large amounts of such items as contributions, interest, and property taxes, and the combined amount of these itemized deductions is in excess of the zero bracket amount. The term ***excess itemized deductions*** means the excess of itemized deductions over the zero bracket amount.

The major categories of itemized deductions allowable under the law are described below:

1 **Interest** Interest on any indebtedness, within certain limits.
2 **Taxes** State and local real and personal property taxes, state income taxes, and all sales taxes are deductible by the person on whom they are imposed. No federal taxes qualify as itemized deductions.
3 **Contributions** Contributions by individuals to charitable, religious, educational, and certain other nonprofit organizations are deductible, within certain limits. Gifts to friends, relatives, or other persons are not deductible.
4 **Medical expenses** Medical and dental expenses of the taxpayer and his or her family are deductible to the extent that they exceed 3% of adjusted gross income, subject to certain maximum limits, and limits on the deductibility of drugs and medicines. A taxpayer may deduct one-half of medical insurance costs up to $150 without regard to the 3% exclusion.
5 **Casualty losses** Losses in excess of $100 from any fire, storm, earthquake, shipwreck, theft, or other sudden, unexpected, or unusual causes are deductible.
6 **Expenses related to the production of income** In this category are included any necessary expenses in producing income or for the management of income-producing property, other than those deductible to arrive at adjusted gross income. Some examples of ***miscellaneous deductible expenses*** are union dues,

work clothes, professional dues, subscriptions to professional periodicals, investment advisers' fees, legal fees relating to investments, fees paid to employment agencies to get a job, and fees for income tax advice and for preparation of tax returns. Examples of ***miscellaneous nondeductible expenses*** are the cost of going to and from work, gifts to needy friends, most living expenses, babysitting expenses, the cost of school tuition, and gambling losses in excess of gambling winnings.

### Personal exemptions

In addition to itemized deductions, a deduction from adjusted gross income is allowed for ***personal exemptions.*** One exemption each is allowed for the taxpayer, the taxpayer's spouse, and each person who qualifies as a dependent of the taxpayer. At present the amount of each personal exemption is $1,000. The amount of the personal exemption may be changed by Congress at any time.

The term ***dependent*** has a particular meaning under tax law. Briefly stated, a dependent is a person who (1) receives over one-half of his or her support from the taxpayer, (2) is either closely related to the taxpayer or lives in the taxpayer's home, and (3) has gross income during the year of less than the current exemption amount unless he or she is a child of the taxpayer and is under nineteen years of age or is a full-time student.[4] A taxpayer and spouse may each claim an additional personal exemption if sixty-five years of age or over, and another exemption if blind. These additional exemptions do not apply to dependents.

Taxpayers who use the tax tables (illustrated later in this chapter) must determine the ***number*** of personal exemptions to which they are entitled in order to select the appropriate column in the tax tables. However they do not use the $1,000 deduction ***amount,*** because these amounts have been taken into account in constructing the tax tables. The personal exemption, unlike itemized deductions, does not require any record keeping as supporting evidence.

### Taxable income

We have now traced the steps required to determine the taxable income of an individual. In brief, this process includes:

1 Computation of total income
2 Exclusion of certain items specified by law to determine gross income
3 Deduction of business-related expenses to arrive at adjusted gross income
4 Deduction of excess itemized deductions and personal exemptions to arrive at the key figure of taxable income.

The concept of taxable income is most important because it is the amount to which the appropriate tax rate is applied to determine the tax liability.

---

[4] A child under nineteen or a full-time student who qualifies as a dependent in all other respects but who earns over the current exemption amount in any one year has, in effect, two personal exemptions. One may be taken by the taxpayer who claims him or her as a dependent; the other he will claim for himself on his own personal income tax return.

## Capital gains and losses

Certain kinds of property are defined under the tax law as capital assets.[5] The most common types of capital assets owned by individuals are securities and real estate (including a personal residence). Gains and losses from the sale of such assets are granted special treatment for income tax purposes. Anyone who studies federal income tax laws carefully in search of ways to save taxes will be impressed by the favorable tax treatment of ***long-term capital gains.*** Stated briefly, this favorable treatment causes long-term capital gains to be taxed at ***much lower rates*** than income from other sources (ordinary income). From the standpoint of tax planning, this situation calls for taxpayers to invest in properties that offer possible capital gains.

The rationale underlying special treatment of capital gains is to strengthen the economy by encouraging long-term investment in equities by individuals and by business concerns. If our future economy is to be strong and healthy, investment capital must flow into new growth industries. New growth industries are speculative. They do not offer investors assured low-risk income, but do offer the possibility of capital appreciation. Our tax laws can provide an incentive for risk-taking by investors, if capital gains are taxed at much lower rates than low-risk income such as interest on bonds and insured bank deposits.

**Amount of gain or loss** A gain from the sale of a capital asset occurs if the sales price exceeds the ***basis*** of the property sold. A loss occurs if the sales price is less than the basis of the asset. In general, the basis of purchased property is its ***cost*** reduced by the accumulated depreciation allowed or allowable in computing taxable income. The detailed rules for determining the basis of property are quite complex and will not be considered here. These rules depend in part on how the property was acquired (purchase, gift, or inheritance), whether it is personal or business property, and whether it is sold at a gain or a loss.

**Long-term versus short-term** Long and short are relative terms; in income taxation the dividing line is one year. Long-term capital gains (or losses) result from the sale of capital assets held for ***more than one year;*** short-term capital gains and losses result when capital assets are held one year or less.

Remember that long-term capital gains are the ones that receive favorable tax treatment; short-term capital gains are taxed as ordinary income. If an individual invests in a capital asset which rises greatly in market price, the classic mistake would be to sell it one day short of the holding period required to qualify the gain as long-term. That one-day error in timing would more than double the tax on the capital gain.

The term ***net short-term gain*** means short-term gains in excess of short-term losses. Net short-term gains must be reported in full and are taxed as ordinary income. Only 40% of long-term gains, reduced by any net short-term losses, are included in adjusted gross income.

---

[5] The Internal Revenue Code defines capital assets to include all items of property except: (a) business inventories; (b) accounts and notes receivable; (c) plant and equipment used in a business; (d) intangible assets such as copyrights and artistic compositions; and (e) government bonds and notes issued at a discount and due within one year.

ILLUSTRATIVE CASE Bob Savage, a taxpayer subject to a marginal tax rate of 30%, has a $1,000 net long-term capital gain and no net short-term capital loss. Savage would include only $400 (40% of the net long-term gain) in adjusted gross income and pay only a $120 tax on the $1,000 gain (30% of $400). The tax rate applicable to the $1,000 long-term gain is 12% (computed as $120 ÷ $1,000). This is less than half of Savage's marginal rate of 30%.

On the other hand, suppose that Savage has a marginal tax rate of 70%. If he were to include $400 (40% of the $1,000 net long-term gain) in adjusted gross income and apply the 70% marginal rate, the tax would be $280, or 28% of the total $1,000 net long-term gain. In this case the rate of tax applicable to the long-term capital gain is considerably less than one-half of the taxpayer's 70% marginal rate of tax on other income.

**Limited deductibility of capital losses** In general, capital ***losses,*** either long-term or short-term, are deductible only against capital gains. If total capital losses exceed gains, however, individual taxpayers (but not corporations) may deduct capital losses against other gross income up to a maximum of $3,000 a year. For example, if an individual incurred a capital loss of $100,000 but also had a salary of $50,000, he or she would have gross income subject to taxation of $47,000. The unused capital loss could be carried forward and offset against capital gains, if any, in future years, or against other income at the rate of $3,000 a year. Thus, a great many years would be required to offset the $100,000 capital loss against other income.

Critics of our present tax laws point out that persons who save and invest are taxed in a similar manner to those who gamble on horse races. (Gambling gains are taxable; gambling losses cannot be offset against other income.) Similarly, gains from investment are taxed heavily and losses from investments are generally not permitted as deductions if they exceed gains. This policy may be inconsistent with the national goal of encouraging investment. Although the United States formerly had worldwide recognition for its high productivity, the ratio of capital investment to gross national product has now fallen far below many other nations. The tax laws of some other countries are more conducive to investment; for example, no tax on capital gains.

Only 50% of a net long-term capital loss can be used in arriving at the maximum which can be offset against other income in a single year. In other words, a net long-term capital loss of $4,000 would be required to entitle the taxpayer to take a $2,000 deduction. Although capital losses not deductible in any given year may be carried forward to future tax years, it is apparent that a large capital loss as in the preceding example probably will not be utilized fully in future years unless the taxpayer is fortunate enough to have a large capital gain.

**Wash sales** When the prices of stocks or bonds drop sharply, some taxpayers may be inclined to sell their holdings in order to get the tax advantage of a capital loss to offset against other income. If a sale is made, the seller must not repurchase identical securities within 30 days or the capital loss will not be deductible. The IRS considers a "wash sale" to have occurred if substantially identical securities are purchased within 30 days before or after a sale.

**Business plant and equipment** Buildings, machinery, and other depreciable property used in a trade or business are not capital assets under the tax law. This means that a net loss realized on the sale or disposal of such business property is fully deductible. However, gains on such property held more than one year may be granted capital gains treatment under certain complex conditions. That portion of any gain resulting from reduction of an asset's basis through depreciation is taxable as ordinary income. This rule (called "recapture of depreciation") stems from the fact that depreciation offsets income taxed at ordinary rates. If the provision for recapture of depreciation did not exist, taxpayers would have a motivation to reduce ordinary income by depreciating assets as rapidly as possible and selling them at a gain taxable at less than the rates applicable to ordinary income. Gains on the sale of assets used in business and held one year or less are taxable as ordinary income.

## Tax tables

Earlier in this chapter we considered the ***tax rate schedules*** (pages 742–743) used by all single taxpayers with incomes in excess of $20,000 and all married taxpay-

***Tax Table for Single Persons***

The $2,300 zero bracket amount and your deduction for exemptions have been taken into account in figuring the tax shown in this table. **Do not take a separate deduction for them.** For single persons with income of $20,000 or less who claim 3 or fewer exemptions.

| *If line 34, Form 1040, or line 11, Form 1040A, is—* | | *And the total number of exemptions claimed is—* | | |
|---|---|---|---|---|
| | | *1* | *2* | *3* |
| *Over* | *But not over* | *Your tax is—* | | |
| *If $3,300 or less your tax is 0* | | | | |
| *3,300* | *3,350* | *4* | *0* | *0* |
| *3,350* | *3,400* | *11* | *0* | *0* |
| *3,400* | *3,450* | *18* | *0* | *0* |
| *3,450* | *3,500* | *25* | *0* | *0* |
| *13,900* | *13,950* | *2,066* | *1,825* | *1,585* |
| *13,950* | *14,000* | *2,079* | *1,837* | *1,597* |
| *14,000* | *14,050* | *2,092* | *1,849* | *1,609* |
| *14,050* | *14,100* | *2,105* | *1,861* | *1,621* |
| *19,700* | *19,750* | *3,744* | *3,423* | *3,123* |
| *19,750* | *19,800* | *3,761* | *3,438* | *3,138* |
| *19,800* | *19,850* | *3,778* | *3,453* | *3,153* |
| *19,850* | *19,900* | *3,795* | *3,468* | *3,168* |
| *19,900* | *19,950* | *3,812* | *3,483* | *3,183* |
| *19,950* | *20,000* | *3,829* | *3,498* | *3,198* |

***Tax Table for Married Persons Filing Jointly***

The $3,400 zero bracket amount and your deduction for exemptions have been taken into account in figuring the tax shown in this table. **Do not take a separate deduction for them.** For married persons filing joint returns with income of $40,000 or less.

| *If line 34, Form 1040, or line 11, Form 1040A, is—* | | *And the total number of exemptions claimed is—* | | | | | | | |
|---|---|---|---|---|---|---|---|---|---|
| | | *2* | *3* | *4* | *5* | *6* | *7* | *8* | *9* |
| *Over* | *But not over* | *Your tax is—* | | | | | | | |
| *If $5,400 or less your tax is 0* | | | | | | | | | |
| *5,400* | *5,450* | *4* | *0* | *0* | *0* | *0* | *0* | *0* | *0* |
| *5,450* | *5,500* | *11* | *0* | *0* | *0* | *0* | *0* | *0* | *0* |
| *5,500* | *5,550* | *18* | *0* | *0* | *0* | *0* | *0* | *0* | *0* |
| *5,550* | *5,600* | *25* | *0* | *0* | *0* | *0* | *0* | *0* | *0* |
| *20,000* | *20,050* | *2,751* | *2,511* | *2,271* | *2,060* | *1,850* | *1,640* | *1,430* | *1,247* |
| *20,050* | *20,100* | *2,763* | *2,523* | *2,283* | *2,071* | *1,861* | *1,651* | *1,441* | *1,256* |
| *20,100* | *20,150* | *2,775* | *2,535* | *2,295* | *2,081* | *1,871* | *1,661* | *1,451* | *1,265* |
| *20,150* | *20,200* | *2,787* | *2,547* | *2,307* | *2,092* | *1,882* | *1,672* | *1,462* | *1,274* |
| *39,800* | *39,850* | *9,291* | *8,861* | *8,431* | *8,023* | *7,653* | *7,283* | *6,913* | *6,543* |
| *39,850* | *39,900* | *9,312* | *8,882* | *8,452* | *8,042* | *7,672* | *7,302* | *6,932* | *6,562* |
| *39,900* | *39,950* | *9,334* | *8,904* | *8,474* | *8,060* | *7,690* | *7,320* | *6,950* | *6,580* |
| *39,950* | *40,000* | *9,355* | *8,925* | *8,495* | *8,079* | *7,709* | *7,339* | *6,969* | *6,599* |

ers with income in excess of $40,000. However, most taxpayers with incomes below these levels are required to compute their taxes by using the ***tax tables*** shown above and on page 753. Our interest is in the basic concepts of the income tax structure rather than in the mechanics of filling out tax returns; consequently, only small portions of these very lengthy tax tables are illustrated.

If you will compare the tax on single persons with the tax on married persons, you will find that when two salaried individuals marry, their combined tax increases. This fact has led to the criticism that the present federal tax structure penalizes matrimony.

## Tax credits

Tax credits differ from deductions. As previously explained, a deduction (such as charitable contributions) is subtracted from adjusted gross income and thus leads to a smaller amount of taxable income. A tax credit, however, is ***subtracted directly from the tax owed.*** Applying tax credits against the tax due is one of the concluding steps in preparation of the tax return.

One of the most important tax credits is the ***investment credit*** arising from purchase of certain depreciable business property. The investment credit is an example of efforts to provide tax incentives as a means of stimulating business investment and thus increasing the level of economic activity. When a business buys certain types of new long-lived equipment, such as office equipment or machinery, it can take a credit of 10% of the cost of the property as a deduction from the income tax for the year. The use of an investment credit does not affect the depreciation of the asset.

Among other types of tax credits currently available are the residential energy credit, the credit for wages paid in work incentive programs, foreign tax credit, credit for the elderly, credit for political contributions, and credit for child and dependent care expenses. Many restrictions limit the use of these credits to reduce income taxes.

## Quarterly payments of estimated tax

For self-employed persons such as doctors, dentists, and owners of small businesses, there is of course no salary and no withholding. Other examples of income on which no withholding occurs are rental income, dividends, and interest received. To equalize the treatment of employees and self-employed persons, the tax law requires persons who have taxable income in excess of a given amount, from which no withholding has been made, to file a ***declaration of estimated tax*** and to pay estimated income taxes in quarterly installments. Any underpayment or overpayment is adjusted when the annual tax return is filed.

A declaration of estimated tax is a statement which a taxpayer having ***income not subject to withholding*** must file with the IRS by April 15 each year. The declaration shows the taxable income expected for the current year and the quarterly payments of estimated tax to be made. The first of the quarterly payments must accompany the declaration.

Although salaried employees are subject to withholding, many have other income such as dividends which are not subject to withholding. These persons must therefore file a declaration of estimated tax and make quarterly payments if the income not subject to withholding is substantial.

## Tax returns, tax refunds, and payment of the tax

Whether you must file a tax return depends upon the amount of your income and your filing status. At present, a single person with income of $3,300 or more (the personal exemption plus the zero bracket amount) must file a return. A married couple filing jointly and having income of $5,400 or more must file. However, for a self-employed person, net earnings from self-employment of as little as $400 impose a requirement to file a return. These dollar limits, along with tax rates, are likely to be changed from year to year. The return must be filed within $3\frac{1}{2}$ months after the close of the taxable year. Most taxpayers are on a calendar-year basis; therefore, the deadline for filing is April 15.

**Withholding makes the system work** The payment of federal income taxes is on a "pay as you go" basis. The procedure by which employers withhold income taxes from the salaries of employees has been discussed previously in Chapter 13. Without the withholding feature, the present income tax system would probably be unworkable. The high rate of income taxes would pose an impossible collection problem if employees received their total earnings in cash and were later called upon at the end of the year to pay the government a major portion of a year's salary.

The amounts withheld from an employee's salary for income tax can be considered as payments on account. If the amount of income tax as computed by preparing a tax return at the end of the year is less than the amount withheld during the year, the taxpayer is entitled to a refund. On the other hand, if the tax as computed at year-end is more than the amount withheld, the balance must be paid with the tax return. Persons who are entitled to a refund because withholdings or payments of estimated tax exceed the tax liability will of course file a tax return to obtain a refund, even though they might not have sufficient income to make the filing of a tax return compulsory.

**The deceptive lure of a tax refund check** The majority of Americans receive tax refunds each year. Apparently these 60 million or more persons so enjoy receiving a refund check that they are willing to have the government withhold excessive amounts of tax from their paychecks throughout the year. The IRS reports that millions of individual taxpayers declare fewer personal exemptions than they expect to claim at year-end. The result is over-withholding of billions of dollars on which the government pays no interest. It seems strange during a period of inflation and high interest rates that American taxpayers would choose to have the government hold their money throughout the year with no interest in order to be paid back at year-end in dollars worth less in purchasing power than when earned.

## Computation of individual income tax illustrated

The computation of the federal income tax for Mary and John Reed is illustrated on page 757.

In this example it is assumed that the Reeds provide over one-half the support of their two children. John Reed is a practicing attorney who received $61,000 in gross fees from his law practice and incurred $32,000 of business expenses. Mary Reed earned $24,400 during the year as a CPA working for a national firm of accountants. During the year, $4,000 was withheld from her salary for federal income taxes. Just before the end of the year, John Reed contributed $3,000 to a Keogh H.R.10 retirement plan. The Reeds received $700 interest on municipal bonds, and $320 on savings accounts. Dividends received on stock jointly owned amounted to $26,000. During the year stock purchased several years ago by John Reed for $2,600 was sold for $3,600, net of brokerage fees, thus producing a $1,000 long-term capital gain.

The Reeds have total itemized deductions (contributions, interest expense, taxes, medical costs, etc.) of $17,120. They paid a total of $12,000 on their declaration of estimated tax during the year. John Reed is entitled to an investment credit of $1,000 on $10,000 worth of office equipment purchased during the year.

***MARY AND JOHN REED***
***Illustrative Federal Income Tax Computation***
***For the Year 198X***

| | | | |
|---|---|---|---|
| *Gross income (excluding $700 interest on municipal bonds):* | | | |
| *Gross fees from John Reed's law practice* | *$61,000* | | |
| *Less: Expenses incurred in law practice* | *32,000* | *$29,000* | |
| *Salary received by Mary Reed* | | *24,400* | |
| *Dividends received, $26,000, and interest earned, $320 (after combined exclusion of $400)* | | *25,920* | |
| *Long-term capital gain on stock held over one year* | | *1,000* | *$80,320* |
| *Deductions to arrive at adjusted gross income:* | | | |
| *Long-term capital gain deduction (60% of $1,000)* | | *$ 600* | |
| *Deduction for John Reed's contribution to a (Keogh H.R.10) retirement plan* | | *3,000* | *3,600* |
| *Adjusted gross income* | | | *$76,720* |
| *Deductions from adjusted gross income:* | | | |
| *Excess itemized deductions (itemized deductions, $17,120, minus $3,400 zero bracket amount)* | | *$13,720* | |
| *Personal exemptions (4 × $1,000)* | | *4,000* | *17,720* |
| *Taxable income* | | | *$59,000* |
| *Computation of tax (using tax rate schedule on page 743)* | | | |
| *Tax on $45,800 (joint return)* | | *$12,720* | |
| *Tax on $13,200 at 49%* | | *6,468* | *$19,188* |
| *Less: Investment tax credit (10% of $10,000)* | | | *1,000* |
| *Total tax* | | | *$18,188* |
| *Less: Advance payments and amounts withheld:* | | | |
| *Payments by Reeds on declaration of estimated tax* | | *$12,000* | |
| *Tax withheld from Mary Reed's salary* | | *4,000* | *16,000* |
| *Amount of tax remaining to be paid with return* | | | *$ 2,188* |

On the basis of these facts, the taxable income for the Reeds is shown to be $59,000. Since they file a joint return, the tax on this amount of taxable income may be computed from the tax rate schedules for married couples filing jointly and is $19,188. This tax is reduced by the $1,000 investment credit, producing a tax liability of $18,188. Taking withholdings and payments on declared estimated tax into account, the Reeds have already paid income taxes of $16,000 and thus owe $2,188 at the time of filing their tax return.

## Partnerships

A partnership was defined in Chapter 15 as an association of two or more persons to carry on as co-owners a business for profit. Partnerships are not considered taxable entities by income tax statutes. Under the federal income tax law, a partnership is treated as a conduit through which taxable income flows to the partners. Although a partnership pays no income tax, it must file an ***information***

***return*** showing the computation of net income or loss and the share of net income or loss allocable to each partner. The partners must include on their personal tax returns their respective shares of the net income or loss of the partnership.

Certain items of partnership income and deductions are segregated, and all partners are required to treat their respective shares of these items as if they had received or paid them personally. In general, these segregated items are those granted special tax treatment; they include tax-exempt interest, capital gains and losses, charitable contributions, and cash dividends received.

In certain types of business (motion pictures, oil and gas exploration, leasing, and farming), special rules apply when a partnership operates at a loss. The amount of the partnership loss which partners can deduct on their personal returns cannot exceed the amount which partners have placed ***at risk*** by investment in the partnership business. These "at risk" rules are intended to prevent partnerships from being used as tax-avoidance devices.

## Taxation of corporations

A corporation is a separate taxable entity. Our discussion is focused on the general business corporation and does not cover certain other types of corporations for which special tax treatment applies. Every corporation, unless specifically exempt from taxation, must file an income tax return whether or not it has taxable income or owes any tax.

The earning of taxable income inevitably creates a liability to pay income taxes. This liability and the related charge to expense must be entered in the accounting records before financial statements are prepared. The following journal entry is typical.

| | | |
|---|---|---|
| *Income Taxes Expense* | *60,000* | |
| *Income Taxes Payable* | | *60,000* |
| *To record corporate income taxes for the current period.* | | |

## Corporation tax rates

Tax rates for corporations are in a graduated five-step structure. The rates in effect at the time this was written are shown below. These rates are subject to frequent change by Congress.

***Corporations***

| *Taxable Income* | *Rates* |
|---|---|
| *Up to $25,000* | *17%* |
| *Over $25,000 but not over $50,000* | *20%* |
| *Over $50,000 but not over $75,000* | *30%* |
| *Over $75,000 but not over $100,000* | *40%* |
| *Over $100,000* | *46%* |

As indicated by the above table, taxable income of corporations is subject to graduated tax rates as follows: 17% of the first $25,000 of taxable income; 20% of taxable income over $25,000 and up to $50,000; 30% of taxable income over $50,000 and up to $75,000; 40% of taxable income over $75,000 and up to $100,000; and 46% of taxable income over $100,000. Note that above $100,000 the income tax on corporations is not progressive. No matter how large taxable income may be, the rate remains the same for amounts above $100,000.

## Computation of taxable income of corporations

The taxable income of corporations is computed in much the same way as for individuals: that is, by deducting ordinary business expenses from gross income. However, the following major differences from taxation of individuals must be considered:

1 **Dividends received** The dividends received by a corporation on its investments in stocks of other corporations are included in gross income, but 85% of such dividends can be deducted from gross income. The net result is that only 15% of dividend income is taxable to the receiving corporation. Corporations are not entitled to the dividend exclusion of $200 allowed to individual taxpayers.

2 **Capital gains and losses** Net long-term capital gains of corporations are subject to a maximum tax of 28%. A corporation is not entitled to the 60% long-term capital gain deduction as is an individual. If a corporation's taxable income (including any long-term capital gain) is below $50,000, the corporation pays only the regular rates of tax on the long-term capital gain rather than the 28% maximum capital gain tax rate.

The dividing line between long-term and short-term capital gains and losses is one year—the same as for individuals. Corporations may deduct capital losses only to the extent of capital gains. However, if capital losses exceed capital gains, the net loss may be offset against any capital gains of the three preceding years (carry-back) or the following five years (carry-forward).

3 **Other variations from taxation of individuals** The concept of adjusted gross income is not applicable to a corporation. There is no deduction for personal exemptions and no zero bracket amount. ***Gross income*** minus the deductions allowed to corporations equals ***taxable income.***

## Illustrative tax computation for corporation

To illustrate some of the features of the income tax law as it applies to corporations, a ***tax computation*** for Stone Corporation is shown on page 760. Remember that this illustration is not an income statement and does not show items in the sequence of an income statement.

A shortcut method of computing the tax for a corporation with taxable income above $100,000 consists of multiplying the ***entire amount*** of taxable income by 46% and then subtracting $19,250. The $19,250 figure is the excess of 46% of

*Note the difference between income per accounting records ($184,000) and taxable income ($180,000)*

**STONE CORPORATION**
**Illustrative Tax Computation**

| | | |
|---|---|---|
| *Revenue:* | | |
| *Sales* | | *$800,000* |
| *Dividends received from domestic corporations* | | *20,000* |
| *Total revenue* | | *$820,000* |
| *Expenses:* | | |
| *Cost of goods sold* | *$536,000* | |
| *Other expenses (includes capital loss of $13,000)* | *100,000* | *636,000* |
| *Income per accounting records* | | *$184,000* |
| *Add back (items not deductible for tax purposes):* | | |
| *Capital loss deducted as part of operating expenses** | | *13,000* |
| *Subtotal* | | *$197,000* |
| *Special deductions:* | | |
| *Dividends received credit (85% of $20,000)* | | *17,000* |
| *Taxable income* | | *$180,000* |
| *Tax computation:* | | |
| *17% of first $25,000* | *$ 4,250* | |
| *20% of second $25,000* | *5,000* | |
| *30% of third $25,000* | *7,500* | |
| *40% of fourth $25,000* | *10,000* | |
| *46% of $80,000 (taxable income above $100,000)* | *36,800* | |
| *Total income tax* | | *$ 63,550* |
| *Deduct: Quarterly payments of estimated tax* | | *60,000* |
| *Balance of tax payable with tax return* | | *$ 3,550* |

*The capital loss can be carried back three years and offset against capital gains if any.

$100,000 over the tax computed by applying the several rates of 17%, 20%, 30%, and 40% to the four $25,000 segments of the first $100,000.

For example, the shortcut method of computing the tax owed by Stone Corporation on its taxable income of $180,000 is as follows:

| | |
|---|---|
| *$180,000 × 46%* | *$82,800* |
| *Deduct* | *19,250* |
| *Total income tax* | *$63,550* |

The fact that tax rates on corporations are not as high as the top tax rates on individuals has caused some taxpayers to consider creating corporations as a means of avoiding taxes. In response, Congress has established two additional taxes to limit the use of closely held corporations as a device for holding property and avoiding individual income taxes. These two taxes are the ***accumulated earnings tax*** and the ***personal holding company tax.***

### Accumulated earnings tax

The stockholders of a closely held corporation may be tempted to avoid personal tax on dividends by retaining earnings in the corporation rather than distributing these earnings as dividends. To prevent such actions, a penalty surtax called the ***accumulated earnings tax*** is imposed on the income of a corporation in any year it accumulates earnings as a means of avoiding individual income tax on its shareholders. If a profitable corporation puts its earnings into bank savings accounts and marketable securities and has no specific plans for investing these amounts in operating assets, it might be subject to the accumulated earnings tax. The rate of the penalty surtax is $27\frac{1}{2}\%$ on the first \$100,000 and $38\frac{1}{2}\%$ on additional amounts. The tax is not imposed on a corporation that does not accumulate earnings beyond \$150,000. Remember that the accumulated earnings tax can be avoided by declaring dividends or by proving that the earnings have been accumulated to meet reasonable needs of the business.

### Personal holding company tax

A corporation with only a few stockholders and ***deriving its income mostly from investments*** may be classified as a personal holding company and subjected to a special tax of 70% of its undistributed income. This tax is in addition to regular income tax on corporations. The purpose of this tax is to discourage individuals from transferring income-producing property to corporations in order to avoid tax by reason of the difference between the rates of tax on individuals and corporations.

### Accounting income versus taxable income

In the determination of ***accounting income,*** the objective is to measure business operating results as accurately as possible in accordance with the generally accepted accounting principles summarized in Chapter 14. ***Taxable income,*** on the other hand, is a legal concept governed by statute and subject to sudden and frequent change by Congress. In setting the rules for determining taxable income, Congress is interested not only in meeting the revenue needs of government but in achieving certain public policy objectives. For example, the exclusion of interest on municipal bonds from taxable income is intended to make these bonds more attractive to investors and thus make it easier for the cities to borrow money. Since accounting income and taxable income are determined with different purposes in mind, it is not surprising that they often differ by material amounts. This distinction between accounting income and taxable income is important to every business, regardless of whether it is organized as a single proprietorship, a partnership, or a corporation.

### Cash basis versus accrual basis of accounting

The ***accrual basis*** of measuring business income has been discussed throughout the preceding chapters of this book, because it is the method used by most business enterprises in their accounting records and financial statements. Revenue is recognized when it is realized, and expenses are recorded when they are incurred, without regard to the timing of receipt or payment. Any taxpayer who maintains a set of accounting records may elect to use the accrual basis for tax purposes. When the production, purchase, or sale of merchandise is a significant factor in a business, the accrual method of accounting for these items is mandatory for income tax purposes as well.

The ***cash basis*** of accounting does not measure income in the accounting sense but has much merit in the area of taxation. Revenue is recognized when cash is received, and expenses are recorded when they are paid. This method is widely used for tax purposes because it is simple, requires a minimum of records, and provides reasonably satisfactory results for individuals not engaged in business and for businesses in which receivables, payables, and inventories are not a major factor. From the government's viewpoint, the logical time to collect tax on income is when the taxpayer receives the income in cash. At any earlier date the taxpayer may not have the cash to pay income taxes; at any later date the cash may have been used for other purposes.

The cash basis of accounting allowed for income tax purposes and used by individuals, most professional firms, and many service-type companies varies in two important ways from a simple offsetting of cash receipts and disbursements.

1 On the revenue side, a cash basis taxpayer must report revenue when it has been ***constructively received,*** even though the cash is not yet in his or her possession. Constructive receipt means that the revenue is so much within the control of the taxpayer as to be equivalent to receipt. For example, if a taxpayer has a bank savings account, the interest earned on that account is considered to be constructively received for income tax purposes even though the taxpayer does not draw it out.
2 On the expenditure side, the cost of acquiring depreciable property having a service life of more than one year is not deductible in the year of purchase. The taxpayer must treat such a purchase as the acquisition of an asset and deduct depreciation in appropriate years. A similar treatment must be given to major prepayments, such as rent paid in advance or insurance premiums which cover more than one year.

### Special tax treatment of revenue and expense

Even when the accrual method is used for tax purposes, differences between taxable income and accounting income may occur. Some differences result from special tax rules which are unrelated to accounting principles.

1 Some items included in accounting income are not taxable. For example, interest on state or municipal bonds is excluded from taxable income.
2 Some business expenses are not deductible. For example, goodwill is amortized in determining accounting income, but for income tax purposes goodwill is considered to have an indefinite life and amortization is not a deductible expense.

**3** Special deductions in excess of actual business expenses are allowed some taxpayers. For example, depletion deductions in excess of actual cost are allowed taxpayers in some mining industries. However, the ***statutory depletion*** (or ***percentage depletion***) allowance which formerly existed for income derived from oil and gas operations has been eliminated.

In addition, the ***timing*** of the recognition of certain revenue and expenses under tax rules differs from that under accounting principles. Some items of income received in advance may be taxed in the year of receipt while certain accrued expenses may not be deductible for income tax purposes until they are actually paid in cash.

## Alternative accounting methods offering possible tax advantages

You are already aware from your study of various methods of depreciation and various methods of inventory valuation that the choice of accounting methods can have considerable effect on the net income a company reports for a given year. The tax law permits taxpayers to follow certain accounting methods in the computation of taxable income which differ from the methods used in the accounting records and financial statements. Business executives therefore are faced with the challenge of choosing accounting methods for income tax purposes that will result in minimizing their tax burdens—usually by postponing the tax to later years.

For example, a company which uses straight-line depreciation for accounting purposes may choose to use the double-declining-balance method of depreciation in its income tax return. Taxpayers generally choose for income tax purposes those accounting methods which cause expenses to be recognized as soon as possible and revenue to be recognized as late as possible. However, the tax laws require that a business electing the lifo method of inventory valuation must also use this method for financial reporting.

There are many other examples of elective methods which postpone income taxes. Companies which sell merchandise on the installment basis may elect to report income on their tax returns in proportion to the cash received on the installment contracts rather that at the time of the sale of the merchandise. Taxpayers engaged in exploration for oil may charge the cost of drilling oil wells to expense as incurred rather than capitalizing these costs for later depreciation. Ranchers may treat the cost of cattle feed as expense in the year of purchase rather than in the year the feed is consumed.

## Interperiod income tax allocation

We have seen that differences between generally accepted accounting principles and income tax rules can be material. Some businesses might consider it more convenient to maintain their accounting records in conformity with the tax rules, but the result would be to distort financial statements. It is clearly preferable to maintain accounting records by the principles that produce relevant information about business operations. The data contained in the records can then be adjusted by use of work sheets to arrive at taxable income.

When a corporation follows one method in its accounting records and financial statements but uses a different method for its income tax return, a financial reporting problem arises. The difference in method will usually have the effect of postponing the recognition of income on the tax return (either because an expense deduction is accelerated or because revenue recognition is postponed). The question is whether the income tax expense should be accrued when the income is recognized in the accounting records, or when it is actually subject to taxation.

To illustrate the problem, let us consider a very simple case. Suppose the Pryor Company has before-tax accounting income of $200,000 in each of two years. However, the company takes as a tax deduction in Year 1 an expense of $80,000 which is reported for accounting purposes in Year 2. The company's accounting and taxable income, and the actual income taxes due (assuming for convenience an average tax rate of 40%) are shown below:

| | Year 1 | Year 2 |
|---|---|---|
| Accounting income (before income taxes) | $200,000 | $200,000 |
| Taxable income | 120,000 | 280,000 |
| Actual income taxes due each year, at assumed rate of 40% of taxable income | 48,000 | 112,000 |

Let us assume the Pryor Company reports in its income statement in each year the amount of income taxes due for that year as computed on the company's income tax returns. The effect on reported net income as shown in the company's financial statements would be as follows:

*Company reports actual taxes*

| | Year 1 | Year 2 |
|---|---|---|
| Accounting income (before income taxes) | $200,000 | $200,000 |
| Income taxes expense (amount actually due) | 48,000 | 112,000 |
| Net income | $152,000 | $ 88,000 |

The readers of Pryor Company's income statement might well wonder why the same $200,000 accounting income before income taxes in the two years produced such widely varying amounts of tax expense and net income.

To deal with this distortion between pretax income and after-tax income, an accounting policy known as ***interperiod income tax allocation*** is required for financial reporting purposes.[6] Briefly, the objective of income tax allocation is to accrue income taxes in relation to accounting income, whenever differences between accounting and taxable income are caused by differences in the ***timing*** of revenue or expenses. In the Pryor Company example, this means we would report in the Year 1 income statement a tax expense based on $200,000 of account-

[6] For a more complete discussion of tax allocation procedures, see *APB Opinion No. 11*, "Accounting for Income Taxes," AICPA (New York: 1967).

ing income even though a portion of this income ($80,000) will not be subject to income tax until Year 2. The effect of this accounting procedure is demonstrated by the following journal entries to record the income tax expense in each of the two years:

***Entries to record income tax allocation***

| | | | |
|---|---|---|---|
| *Year 1* | *Income Taxes Expense* | *80,000* | |
| | *Current Income Tax Liability* | | *48,000* |
| | *Deferred Income Tax Liability* | | *32,000* |
| | *To record current and deferred income taxes at 40% of accounting income of $200,000.* | | |
| *Year 2* | *Income Taxes Expense* | *80,000* | |
| | *Deferred Income Tax Liability* | *32,000* | |
| | *Current Income Tax Liability* | | *112,000* |
| | *To record income taxes of 40% of accounting income of $200,000 and to record actual income taxes due.* | | |

Using tax allocation procedures, Pryor Company's financial statements would report net income during the two-year period as follows:

***Company uses tax allocation procedure***

| | *Year 1* | *Year 2* |
|---|---|---|
| *Income before income taxes* | *$200,000* | *$200,000* |
| *Income taxes expense (tax allocation basis)* | *80,000* | *80,000* |
| *Net income* | *$120,000* | *$120,000* |

In this example, the difference between taxable income and accounting income (caused by the accelerated deduction of an expense) was fully offset in a period of two years. In practice, differences between accounting and taxable income may persist over extended time periods and deferred tax liabilities may accumulate to significant amounts. For example, in a recent balance sheet of Sears, Roebuck and Co., deferred taxes of $690 million were reported as a result of the use of the installment sales method for income tax purposes while reporting net income in financial statements on the usual accrual method.

In contrast to the example for the Pryor Company in which income taxes were deferred, income taxes ***may be prepaid*** when taxable income exceeds accounting income because of timing differences. The portion of taxes paid on income deferred for accounting purposes would be reported as prepaid taxes in the balance sheet. When the income is reported as earned for accounting purposes in a later period, the ***prepaid taxes are recognized as tax expense*** applicable to the income currently reported but ***taxed in an earlier period.***[7]

[7] A good example of this treatment is found in the annual report of the Ford Motor Company. A recent balance sheet showed "Income Taxes Allocable to the Following Year," $206.5 million, as a current asset. This large prepaid tax came about as a result of estimated car warranty expense being deducted from revenue in the period in which cars were sold; for income tax purposes, this expense is deductible only when it is actually incurred.

## TAX PLANNING

Federal income tax laws have become so complex that detailed tax planning has become a way of life for most business firms. Almost all companies today engage professional tax specialists to review the tax aspects of major business decisions and to develop plans for legally minimizing income taxes. Because it is important for everyone to recognize areas in which tax savings may be substantial, a few of the major opportunities for tax planning are discussed in the following sections of this chapter.

### Form of business organization

Tax factors should be carefully considered at the time a business is organized. As a single proprietor or partner, a business owner will pay taxes at individual rates, ranging currently from 14 to 70%, on the business income earned in any year ***whether or not it is withdrawn from the business.*** Corporations, on the other hand, are taxed on earnings at rates varying from 17 to 46%. In determining taxable income, corporations deduct salaries paid to owners for services but cannot deduct dividends paid to stockholders. Both ***salaries and dividends*** are taxable income to the persons receiving them.

These factors must be weighed in deciding in any given situation whether the corporate or noncorporate form of business organization is preferable. There is no simple rule of thumb, even considering only these basic differences. To illustrate, suppose that Able, a married man, starts a business which he expects will produce, before any compensation to himself and before income taxes, an average annual income of $80,000. Able plans to withdraw $20,000 yearly from the business. The combined corporate and individual taxes under the corporate and single proprietorship form of business organization are summarized on page 767.

Under these assumptions, the formation of a corporation is favorable from an income tax viewpoint. If the business is incorporated, the combined tax on the corporation and on Able personally will be $15,475. If the business is not incorporated, the tax will be $30,478, or almost twice as much. The key to the advantage indicated for choosing the corporate form of organization is that Able did not take much of the earnings out of the corporation.

If Able decides to operate as a corporation, the $47,750 of net income retained in the corporation will be taxed to Able as ordinary income ***when and if*** it is distributed as dividends. In other words, Able cannot get the money out of the corporation without paying personal income tax on it. An advantage of the corporation as a form of business organization is that Able can ***postpone*** payment of a significant amount of tax as long as the earnings remain invested in the business. However, if earnings are allowed to accumulate in the corporation beyond the $150,000 limit and beyond the reasonable needs of the business, the penalty of the undistributed earnings tax might be imposed.

**If all earnings of the business are to be withdrawn** Now let us change one of our basic assumptions and say that Able plans to withdraw all net income from the

*Which form of business organization produces a lower tax?*

**Form of Business Organization**

| | | Corporation | Single Proprietorship |
|---|---|---|---|
| Business income | | $80,000 | $80,000 |
| Salary to Able | | 20,000 | |
| Taxable income | | $60,000 | $80,000 |
| Corporate tax: | | | |
| 17% of first $25,000 | $4,250 | | |
| 20% of next $25,000 | 5,000 | | |
| 30% on excess of $10,000 | 3,000 | 12,250 | |
| Net income | | $47,750 | $80,000 |
| Combined corporate and individual tax: | | | |
| Corporate tax on $60,000 income (above) | | $12,250 | |
| Individual tax—joint return:* | | | |
| On Able's $20,000 salary | | 3,225 | |
| On Able's $80,000 share of business income | | | $30,478 |
| Total tax on business income | | $15,475 | $30,478 |

* Able's personal exemptions and deductions have been ignored, on the assumption that his other income equals personal exemptions and deductions. For convenience, we have used the tax rate schedule on page 743 to compute Able's personal tax rather than the tax tables. We have also omitted from consideration the possible impact of a maximum tax on personal service income.

business each year. Under this assumption the single proprietorship form of organization would be better than a corporation from an income tax standpoint. If the business is incorporated and Able again is to receive a $20,000 salary plus dividends equal to the $47,750 of corporate net income, the total tax will be much higher. The corporate tax of $12,250 plus personal tax of $23,863 (based on $20,000 salary and $47,750 in dividends) would amount to $36,113. This is considerably higher than the $30,478 which we previously computed as the tax liability if the business operated as a proprietorship.

We have purposely kept our example as short as possible. You can imagine some variations which would produce different results. Perhaps Able might incorporate and set his salary at, say, $75,000 instead of $20,000. If this salary were considered reasonable by the IRS, the corporation's taxable income would drop to $5,000 rather than the $60,000 used in our illustration. This and other possible assumptions should make clear that the choice between a corporation and a single proprietorship requires careful consideration of a number of factors in each individual case. Both the marginal rate of tax to which individual business owners are subject and the extent to which profits are to be withdrawn are always basic issues in studying the relative advantages of one form of business organization over another.

Under certain conditions, small, closely held corporations may elect to be Subchapter S corporations, in which case the corporation pays no tax but the individual shareholders are taxed directly on the corporation's earnings.

## Planning business transactions to minimize income taxes

Business transactions may often be arranged in such a way as to produce favorable tax treatment. For example, when real estate is sold under an installment contract covering several years, the taxable gain may be prorated over the period during which installment payments are received by the seller. To qualify for this treatment, payments received during the first year must not exceed 30% of the selling price. By arranging the transaction to meet these conditions, a substantial postponement of tax payments may be secured. For this reason farms, apartment buildings, and some other types of real estate are often offered for sale with a down payment of 29%.

Sometimes sellers try to arrange a transaction one way to their tax benefit and the buyers try to shape it another way to produce tax savings for them. ***Income tax effects*** thus become a part of price negotiations. For example, in buying improved real estate, the purchasers will try to allocate as much of the cost of the property to the building and as little to the land as possible, since building costs can be depreciated for tax purposes. Similarly, in buying a going business, the buyers will want as much as possible of the total purchase price to be attributed to inventories or to depreciable assets rather than to goodwill. The cost of goods sold and depreciation are deductible against ordinary income, whereas goodwill cannot be amortized for tax purposes. The point is, ***any failure to consider the tax consequences of major business transactions can be costly.***

Some examples of provisions of the federal tax laws clearly designed to affect business decisions include (1) accelerated depreciation, (2) additional first-year depreciation of 20% on assets of tangible personal property costing up to $10,000, (3) rapid depreciation on assets "critical to the public interest" such as pollution-control facilities and coal-mine safety equipment, (4) tax-free exchanges of certain types of assets or securities pursuant to a corporate merger, and (5) ***investment tax credits*** when certain types of depreciable assets are acquired.

## Tax planning in the choice of financial structure

In deciding upon the best means of raising capital to start or expand a business, consideration should be given to income taxes. Different forms of business financing produce different amounts of tax expense. Interest on debt, for example, is ***fully deductible,*** but dividends on preferred or common stock are not. This factor operates as a strong incentive to finance expansion by borrowing.

Let us suppose that a company subject to a 46% marginal tax rate needs $100,000 to invest in productive assets on which it can earn a 20% annual return. If the company obtains the needed money by issuing $100,000 in 16% preferred stock, it will earn ***after taxes*** only $10,800, which is not even enough to cover the $16,000 preferred dividend. (This after-tax amount is computed as $20,000 income less taxes at 46% of $20,000.)

Now let us assume on the other hand that the company borrowed $100,000 at 16% interest. The additional gross income would be $20,000 but interest expense of $16,000 would be deducted, leaving taxable income of $4,000. The tax on the

$4,000 at 46% would be $1,840, leaving after-tax income of $2,160. Analysis along these lines is also needed in choosing between debt financing and financing by issuing common stock.

The choice of financial structure should also be considered from the viewpoint of investors, especially in the case of a small, closely held corporation:

ILLUSTRATIVE CASE Assume that the owners of a small incorporated business decide to invest an additional $50,000 in the business to finance expanded operations. Should the owners make a $50,000 loan to the corporation or purchase $50,000 worth of additional capital stock? The loan may be advantageous because the $50,000 cash invested will be returned by the corporation at the maturity date of the loan without imposing any individual income tax on the owners. The loan may be designated to mature in installments or at a single fixed date. Renewal of the note is easily arranged if desired.

If the $50,000 investment were made by purchase of additional shares of capital stock, the return of these funds to the owners would be more difficult. If the $50,000 came back to the owners in the form of dividends, a considerable portion would be consumed by individual income taxes. If the corporation repurchased $50,000 worth of its own capital stock, the retained earnings account would become restricted by this amount. In summary, it is easier for persons in control of a small corporation to get their money back if the investment takes the form of a loan to the corporation rather than the purchase of additional capital stock.

### Income taxes as a factor in preparing cash budgets

Taxable income computed on the accrual basis is not necessarily matched by an inflow of cash. A healthy profit picture accompanied by a tight cash position is not unusual for a rapidly growing company. Income taxes are a substantial cash drain and an important factor in preparing cash budgets. In other words, a profitable growing business may find itself without the cash needed to pay its tax liability.

### Tax shelters

A tax shelter is an investment which produces a loss for tax purposes in the near term but hopefully proves profitable in the long run. Near the close of each year, many newspaper advertisements offer an opportunity to invest in a program which promises to reduce the investor's present tax liability yet produce future profits. These programs have a particular appeal to persons in very high tax brackets who face the prospect of paying most of a year's net income as taxes.

A limited partnership organization is often used, so that each investor may claim his or her share of the immediate losses. Typical of the types of ventures are oil and gas drilling programs and real estate investments offering high leverage and accelerated depreciation. Unfortunately, many so-called tax shelters have proved to be merely unprofitable investments, in which the investors saved taxes but lost larger amounts of capital. A sound approach to tax shelters should probably be based on the premise that if an investment does not appear ***worthwhile without the promised tax benefits, it should be avoided.***

Some tax shelters, on the other hand, are not of a high-risk nature. State and municipal bonds offer a modest rate of interest which is tax-exempt. Investment in real estate with deductions for mortgage interest, property taxes, and depreciation will often show losses which offset other taxable income, yet eventually prove profitable because of rising market value, especially in periods of inflation.

## KEY TERMS INTRODUCED OR EMPHASIZED IN CHAPTER 20

**Accumulated earnings tax** A penalty surtax designed to prevent corporations from retaining earnings beyond reasonable business needs so that shareholders could avoid individual income tax that would result from distribution of the earnings as dividends.

**Adjusted gross income** A subtotal in an individual's tax return computed by deducting from gross income any business-related expenses and other deductions authorized by law. A key figure to which many measurements are linked.

**Capital asset** Stocks, bonds, and real estate not used in a trade or business.

**Capital gain or loss** The difference between the cost basis of a capital asset and the amount received from its sale.

**Cash basis of accounting** Revenue is recorded when received in cash and expenses are recorded in the period in which payment is made. Widely used for individual tax returns and for tax returns of professional firms and service-type businesses. Gives taxpayers a degree of control over taxable income by deliberate timing of collections and payments. Not used in most financial statements because it fails to match revenue with related expenses.

**Declaration of estimated tax** Self-employed persons and others with income not subject to withholding must file by April 15 each year a declaration of estimated tax for the current year and must make quarterly payments of such tax.

**Excess itemized deductions** The excess of itemized deductions over the zero bracket amount.

**Gross income** All income and gains from whatever source derived unless specifically excluded by law, such as interest on state and municipal bonds.

**Interperiod tax allocation** Allocation of income tax expense among accounting periods because of timing differences between accounting income and taxable income. Causes income tax expense reported in financial statements to be in logical relation to accounting income.

**Itemized deductions** Personal expenses deductible from adjusted gross income, such as interest, taxes, contributions, medical expenses, casualty losses, and expenses incurred in production of income.

**Long-term capital gains and losses** Gains and losses resulting from sale of capital assets owned for more than a specified period (one year). A net long-term capital gain qualifies for a special lower tax rate.

**Marginal tax rate** The rate to which a taxpayer is subject on the top dollar of income received.

**Maximum tax on personal service income (earned income)** Under present law the maximum rate on earned income is 50%, whereas income from investments or other sources may be taxed at rates up to 70%.

**Personal exemption** A deduction (presently $1,000) from adjusted gross income for the taxpayer, the taxpayer's spouse, and each dependent.

**Tax credit** An amount to be subtracted from the tax itself. Examples are investment credit, residential energy credit, and credit for wages paid in work incentive programs.

**Tax planning** A systematic process of minimizing income taxes by considering in advance the tax consequences of alternative business or investment actions. A major factor in choosing the form of business organization and capital structure, in lease-or-buy decisions, and in timing of transactions.

**Tax shelters** Investment programs designed to show losses in the short term to be offset against other taxable income, but offering the hope of long-run profits.

**Taxable income** The computed amount to which the appropriate tax rate is to be applied to arrive at the tax liability.

**Zero bracket amount** A specified amount of income not subject to individual income tax. Presently $2,300 for single taxpayers and $3,400 for married taxpayers filing jointly. Replaced the standard deduction.

## DEMONSTRATION PROBLEM FOR YOUR REVIEW

Robert and Helen Sands have been engaged in various businesses for many years and have always prepared their own joint income tax return. In Year 11 the Sands decided to ask a certified public accountant to prepare their income tax returns.

Early in Year 12, the Sands presented the following tax information for Year 11 to the CPA:

| | |
|---|---|
| ***Personal revenue:*** | |
| *Salary from Sands Construction Company, after withholding of $3,168 federal income taxes and social security taxes of $1,140* | *$ 14,692* |
| *Dividends from Sands Construction Company (jointly owned)* | *16,875* |
| *Drawings from Northwest Lumber Company* | *6,000* |
| *Drawings from S & S Business Advisers* | *9,600* |
| *Interest income—City of Norwalk bonds* | *800* |
| *Interest income—savings account* | *1,150* |
| *Proceeds on sale of stock:* | |
| *Sale of stock acquired two years ago for $6,200* | *14,200* |
| *Sale of stock held for three months, cost $4,100* | *3,400* |
| *Sale of stock held for over six years, cost $3,500* | *1,800* |

| | |
|---|---|
| ***Personal expenses:*** | |
| *Contribution to St. Jerome's Church* | *$ 610* |
| *Interest on mortgage, $2,996; on personal note, $400* | *3,396* |
| *Property taxes, including $400 on vacant land in Arizona and a special assessment of $500 on residence for street widening* | *3,980* |
| *Sales taxes, including $580 paid on purchase of new automobile for personal use* | *850* |
| *Income taxes paid to state* | *2,100* |
| *Medical expenses* | *1,100* |
| *Subscription to investment advisory service* | *385* |
| ***Single proprietorship—wholesale lumber, doing business as Northwest Lumber Company:*** | |
| *Sales* | *118,000* |
| *Cost of goods sold* | *82,000* |
| *Operating expenses* | *38,800* |
| *Drawings by Sands* | *6,000* |
| ***Partnership—engaged in business consulting under the name of S & S Business Advisers:*** | |
| *Fees earned* | *76,300* |
| *Gain on sale of vacant lot acquired four years ago* | *4,400* |
| *Salaries paid to employees* | *32,400* |
| *Supplies expense* | *3,500* |
| *Contributions to charity* | *1,000* |
| *Rent expense* | *4,800* |
| *Miscellaneous business expenses* | *7,100* |
| *Drawings (Sands, $9,600 and Sims, $6,400)* | *16,000* |
| ***Corporation—engaged in construction under the name of Sands Construction Company:*** | |
| *Customer billings* | *230,000* |
| *Materials used* | *70,000* |
| *Construction labor* | *60,000* |
| *Officers' salaries expense* | *25,000* |
| *Legal and professional expense* | *3,500* |
| *Advertising expense* | *2,000* |
| *Other business expenses* | *19,800* |
| *Loss on sale of equipment* | *4,200* |
| *Cash dividends paid* | *22,500* |

The Sands have a 60% share in the profits of S & S Business Advisers and John Sims has a 40% share. The Sands own 75% of the stock of Sands Construction Company. Because of this controlling interest, they have assumed responsibility for the preparation of the income tax returns for these organizations.

The Sands are married, have three children, and support Robert's seventy-nine-year-old mother. Robert is fifty-five years old and Helen is younger but declines to give her date of birth. The oldest child, Bill, is twenty years old and attends school full time. The Sands provide all of their son's support, even though Bill earns approximately $1,400 per year from odd jobs and from investments inherited from his grandfather.

In April of Year 11, the Sands paid $3,100 balance due on their federal income tax return for Year 10. In addition to the income taxes withheld by the Sands Construction Company, Robert and Helen Sands made four quarterly payments of $1,500 each on their estimated tax for Year 11.

**Instructions** Using the tax rate schedule on page 743, prepare the joint return for Robert and Helen Sands for last year, showing the amount of tax due (or refund coming). You should also prepare in summary form the information for the partnership tax return for S & S Business Advisers and the corporation income tax return for the Sands Construction Company. Assume that a personal exemption is $1,000, that the corporate tax rate is 17% on the first $25,000 of taxable income and 20% on the next $25,000 and that Sands Construction Company has not paid any part of its income tax for Year 11.

## SOLUTION TO DEMONSTRATION PROBLEM

***S & S BUSINESS ADVISERS (a partnership)***
***Computation of Ordinary Income***
***For Year Ended December 31, Year 11***

| | | |
|---|---|---|
| *Fees earned* | | *$76,300* |
| *Operating expenses:* | | |
| *Salaries paid to employees* | *$32,400* | |
| *Supplies expense* | *3,500* | |
| *Rent expense* | *4,800* | |
| *Miscellaneous business expenses* | *7,100* | *47,800* |
| *Ordinary income* | | *$28,500* |

***Ordinary income and other items are to be included in partners' individual tax returns as follows:***

| | Sands (60%) | Sims (40%) |
|---|---|---|
| *Ordinary income, $28,500* | *$17,100* | *$11,400* |
| *Gain on sale of vacant lot, long-term capital gain, $4,400* | *2,640* | *1,760* |
| *Contributions to charity, $1,000* | *600* | *400* |

***SANDS CONSTRUCTION COMPANY***
***Income Tax Return***
***For Year Ended December 31, Year 11***

| | | |
|---|---|---|
| *Customer billings* | | *$230,000* |
| *Operating expenses:* | | |
| *Materials used* | *$70,000* | |
| *Construction labor* | *60,000* | |
| *Officers' salaries expense* | *25,000* | |
| *Legal and professional expenses* | *3,500* | |
| *Advertising expense* | *2,000* | |
| *Other business expenses* | *19,800* | |
| *Loss on sale of equipment* | *4,200* | *184,500* |
| *Taxable income* | | *$ 45,500* |
| *Total income tax: 17% of $25,000* | *$ 4,250* | |
| *20% of $20,500* | *4,100* | *$ 8,350* |

**Notes applicable to income tax return on page 755:**

(1) The loss from single proprietorship is properly deducted in arriving at adjusted gross income despite the fact that the Sands withdrew $6,000 from the business.

(2) The Sands' share of ordinary income from the partnership (S & S Business Advisers), $17,100, is fully taxable despite the fact that they withdrew only $9,600 from the partnership.

(3) The salary from the Sands Construction Company is included in gross income as $19,000, the gross salary before any deductions.

(4) The ordinary income for the partnership is determined without taking into account the contribution to charity of $1,000 or the long-term capital gain of $4,400. These items are reported by the partners on their personal income tax return on the basis of the profit- and loss-sharing ratio agreed upon by the partners.

(5) The special assessment on residence for street widening, $500, is not deductible in arriving at taxable income.

(6) Medical expenses are less than 3% of adjusted gross income, and therefore none is deductible.

(7) The oldest son, Bill, qualifies as a dependent even though he earned $1,400, because he is a full-time student.

(8) Interest on City of Norwalk bonds, $800, is not taxable.

**ROBERT AND HELEN SANDS**
**Joint Income Tax Return**
**For Year 11**

| | | | |
|---|---|---|---|
| **Gross income:** | | | |
| Salary from Sands Construction Company ($14,692 + $3,168 + $1,140) | | $19,000 | |
| Dividends from Sands Construction Company | $16,875 | | |
| Interest on savings account | 1,150 | | |
| Subtotal of dividends and interest | $18,025 | | |
| Less: Combined exclusion | 400 | 17,625 | |
| Income from S & S Business Advisers, a partnership | | 17,100 | |
| Net long-term capital gain: | | | |
| Stock acquired two years ago | $8,000 | | |
| Stock held over six years | (1,700) | | |
| Gain on sale of vacant lot—from partnership return | 2,640 | | |
| Total long-term capital gain | $8,940 | | |
| Less: Short-term loss on stock held for three months | 700 | 8,240 | $61,965 |
| **Deductions to arrive at adjusted gross income:** | | | |
| Loss incurred by Northwest Lumber Company, a single proprietorship ($118,000 − $82,000 − $38,800) | | $ 2,800 | |
| Long-term capital gain deduction (60% of $8,240) | | 4,944 | 7,744 |
| **Adjusted gross income** | | | $54,221 |
| **Deductions from adjusted gross income:** | | | |
| Itemized deductions: | | | |
| Contributions ($600 from partnership return and $610 to St. Jerome's Church) | | $ 1,210 | |
| Interest paid | | 3,396 | |
| Property taxes ($3,980 − $500) | | 3,480 | |
| Sales taxes | | 850 | |
| Income taxes paid to state | | 2,100 | |
| Subscription to investment advisory service | | 385 | |
| Total itemized deductions | | $11,421 | |
| Less: Zero bracket amount | | 3,400 | |
| Excess itemized deductions | | $ 8,021 | |
| Personal exemptions (6 × $1,000) | | 6,000 | 14,021 |
| **Taxable income for Year 11** | | | $40,200 |
| **Computation of tax for Year 11:** | | | |
| Tax on $35,200 on joint return (see page 743) | | $8,162 | |
| Tax on $5,000 excess at 43% | | 2,150 | $10,312 |
| **Deduct:** | | | |
| Tax withheld from salary | | $ 3,168 | |
| Payments on declaration of estimated tax ($1,500 × 4) | | 6,000 | 9,168 |
| **Tax payable with return for Year 11** | | | $ 1,144 |

## REVIEW QUESTIONS

1 List several ways in which business owners may legally alter the amount of taxes they pay.

2 What is meant by the expression "tax planning"?

3 What are the four major classes of taxpayers under the federal income tax law?

4 It has been claimed that corporate income is subject to "double taxation." Explain the meaning of this expression.

5 Taxes are characterized as ***progressive, proportional,*** or ***regressive*** with respect to any given base. Describe an income tax rate structure that would fit each of these characterizations.

6. State whether you agree with the following statements and explain your reasoning:

**a** A person in a very high tax bracket who makes a cash contribution to a college will reduce his or her tax liability by more than the amount of the gift.

**b** A decision as to whether a person is willing to undertake additional work in order to obtain additional income should be influenced more by a person's marginal tax rate than by his or her average tax rate.

7 State in equation form the federal income tax formula for individuals, beginning with total income and ending with taxable income.

8 Avery and Baker are both high-income single taxpayers who have exactly the same amount of taxable income. However, Avery is subject to a marginal tax rate far lower than the marginal rate for Baker. Neither of them has any capital gains or losses. What is the most probable explanation of the large difference in marginal tax rates for these two individuals?

9 List some differences in the tax rules for corporations in contrast to those for individuals.

10 Helen Bame, M.D., files her income tax return on a cash basis. During the current year she collected $12,600 from patients for medical services rendered in prior years, and billed patients $77,000 for services rendered this year. She has accounts receivable of $16,400 relating to this year's billings at the end of the year. What amount of gross income from her practice should Bame report on her tax return?

11 Joe Gilmore, a single man, files his income tax return on a cash basis. During the current year $800 of interest was credited to him on his savings account; he withdrew this interest on January 18 of the following year. No other interest and no dividends were received by Gilmore.

In December of the current year Gilmore purchased some business equipment having an estimated service life of five years. He also paid a year's rent in advance on certain business property on December 29 of the current year. Explain how these items would be treated on Gilmore's current year's income tax return.

12 From an individual taxpayer's viewpoint, it is better to have a $10,000 net long-term capital gain than $10,000 of ordinary income; however, ordinary losses are usually more advantageous than net capital losses. Explain.

13 Even when a taxpayer uses the accrual method of accounting, taxable income may differ from accounting income. Give four examples of differences between the tax treatment and accounting treatment of items that are included in the determination of income.

14 Under what circumstances is the accounting procedure known as ***income tax allocation*** appropriate? Explain the purpose of this procedure.

**15** List some tax factors to be considered in deciding whether to organize a new business as a corporation or as a partnership.

**16** Explain how the corporate income tax makes debt financing in general more attractive than financing through the issuance of preferred stock.

## EXERCISES

*Ex. 20-1* John and Mary are considering getting married. Each one is now single and each earns $20,000 a year. Each one has one personal exemption and no excess itemized deductions. Refer to the ***tax tables*** on pages 753–754 and determine how much tax John and Mary presently pay. If John and Mary get married, will their combined tax go up or down? By how much?

*Ex. 20-2* During the current year, Carl Davis, a bachelor, expects a taxable income of $45,000. Using the schedules on pages 742–743, determine how much federal income tax Davis would save were he to get married before the end of the year, assuming that his bride had no taxable income or itemized deductions and that the personal exemption is $1,000. (Assume that the 50% limitation on personal service income does not apply.)

*Ex. 20-3* From the tax rate schedules on pages 742–743, compute the tax for each of the following. (Assume that the 50% limitation on earned income does not apply.)

| | Taxable Income |
|---|---|
| a Single taxpayer | $ 16,000 |
| b Single taxpayer | 125,000 |
| c Married couple filing joint return | 16,000 |
| d Married couple filing joint return | 125,000 |

*Ex. 20-4* From the following information for William and Susan Jones, a married couple filing a joint tax return, compute the taxable income. (Use only the relevant information.)

| | |
|---|---|
| Total income, including gifts, inheritances, interest on municipal bonds, etc. | $49,200 |
| Exclusions (gifts, inheritances, interest on municipal bonds, etc.) | 17,520 |
| Deductions to arrive at adjusted gross income | 1,680 |
| Itemized deductions (assume zero bracket amount of $3,400) | 6,690 |
| Personal exemptions ($1,000 each) | 5,000 |
| Income taxes withheld from salary | 4,320 |

*Ex. 20-5* Some of the following items should be included in gross income; others on the list should be excluded. For each item listed, write the identifying letter and the word ***included*** or ***excluded*** to show whether the item belongs in gross income on the federal income tax return of an individual.

**a** Kickbacks received by automobile salespersons from insurance brokers to whom they referred customers
**b** Prize money received by participating in television quiz show
**c** Social security benefits
**d** Tips received by waiter
**e** Money inherited from estate of relative
**f** Interest received on investment in municipal bonds
**g** Profit on sale of sailboat purchased and renovated before being sold
**h** Gift from relative
**i** Dividends of $75 received from investment in General Motors stock (no other dividends or interest received during year)

**j** Interest of $90 received from investment in American Airlines bonds (no other interest or dividends during year)
**k** Vacation trip received as prize in lottery
**l** Compensation received for damages suffered in automobile accident

*Ex. 20-6* Shirley Jones is single, employed as an engineer, and has an adjusted gross income of $22,000. She is in the process of determining whether to itemize deductions on her federal tax return and has prepared a preliminary list of transactions from her checkbook and other records. For each item listed, write the identifying letter and the word ***deductible*** or ***nondeductible.*** Finally, state whether it will be advantageous for Jones to itemize deductions on her tax return and give figures to support your decision. Assume a zero bracket amount of $2,300.

| | |
|---|---|
| *a Interest paid on installment contract on automobile* | *$ 180* |
| *b Gift to an unemployed relative* | *300* |
| *c Professional dues* | *60* |
| *d Contribution to Red Cross* | *25* |
| *e Cost of commuting between home and work* | *800* |
| *f Property taxes* | *1,200* |
| *g Contributions to college fund drive* | *100* |
| *h State income taxes paid* | *1,300* |
| *i Medical expenses (not covered by insurance)* | *500* |
| *j Gasoline taxes* | *150* |
| *k Subscriptions to professional journals* | *40* |
| *l Cash stolen in a burglary* | *80* |

*Ex. 20-7* Malibu Corporation reports the following income during Year 1:

| | |
|---|---|
| *Operating income (income before extraordinary items and income taxes)* | *$550,000* |
| *Long-term capital gain* | *250,000* |
| *Extraordinary item:* | |
| *Loss (fully deductible)* | *50,000* |

Assume that corporate tax rates are as follows:

| | |
|---|---|
| *On first $25,000 of taxable income* | *17%* |
| *On second $25,000 of taxable income* | *20%* |
| *On third $25,000 of taxable income* | *30%* |
| *On fourth $25,000 of taxable income* | *40%* |
| *On taxable income over $100,000* | *46%* |
| *On long-term capital gains* | *28%* |

Compute the total tax liability for Malibu Corporation for Year 1.

*Ex. 20-8* Howard and Sara Wilson, a married couple, file a joint return and claim one exemption each plus two exemptions for dependents. (Assume that each personal exemption is $1,000.) They have gathered the following information in getting ready to prepare their tax return.

| | |
|---|---|
| *Federal income taxes withheld from salaries* | *$ 9,400* |
| *Payments of estimated tax* | *4,400* |
| *Itemized deductions (remember zero bracket amount)* | *3,480* |
| *Total income (including $800 interest on municipal bonds)* | *60,000* |
| *Business-related expenses* | *5,200* |

Compute **(a)** gross income, **(b)** adjusted gross income, **(c)** taxable income, and **(d)** amount of tax remaining to be paid. (Use the tax rate schedule for married individuals filing joint returns, page 743, and assume a zero bracket amount of $3,400.)

*Ex. 20-9* Mission Bay Corporation deducted on its tax return for Year 5 an expense of $100,000 which was not recognized as an expense for accounting purposes until Year 6. The corporation's accounting income before income taxes in each of the two years was $425,000. The company uses tax allocation procedures.

**a** Prepare the journal entries required at the end of Year 5 and Year 6 to record income tax expense. Use the shortcut method of computing tax as illustrated on page 760; multiply the entire amount of taxable income by 46% and then subtract $19,250.

**b** Prepare a two-column schedule showing the net income to appear on the financial statements for Years 5 and 6, assuming tax allocation procedures are used. Also prepare a similar schedule on the assumption that tax allocation procedures are not used.

## PROBLEMS

### Group A

*20A-1* **a** You are to consider the income tax status of each of the items listed below. List the numbers 1 to 15 on your answer sheet. For each item state whether it is ***included in gross income*** or ***excluded from gross income*** for federal income tax on individuals. Add explanatory comments if needed.

(1) Trip to Hawaii given by employer as reward for outstanding service.
(2) Taxpayer owed $1,500 on a note payable. During the current year the taxpayer painted a building owned by the creditor, and in return the creditor canceled the note.
(3) Gain on sale of Bart Corporation capital stock, held for five months.
(4) Salary received from a corporation by a stockholder who owns directly or indirectly all the shares of the company's outstanding stock.
(5) Amount received as damages for injury in automobile accident.
(6) Share of income from partnership in excess of drawings.
(7) Rent received on personal residence while on extended vacation trip.
(8) Value of U.S. Treasury bonds received as a gift from uncle.
(9) Tips received by a waitress.
(10) Proceeds of life insurance policy received on death of husband.
(11) Interest received on River City municipal bonds.
(12) Inheritance received on death of a rich uncle.
(13) Gain on the sale of an original painting.
(14) Value of a color TV set won as a prize in a quiz contest.
(15) Cash dividends of $500 received on stock of American Oil Company. (Assume taxpayer had no other dividend or interest income.)

**b** You are to determine the deductibility status, for federal income tax purposes, of each of the items listed below. List the numbers 1 to 10 on your answer sheet. For each item state whether the item ***is deducted to arrive at adjusted gross income; deducted from adjusted gross income;*** or ***not deductible.***

(1) Interest paid on mortgage covering personal residence.
(2) Carry-forward of an unused operating loss from previous year.
(3) Capital loss on the sale of securities.
(4) Damage in storm to motorboat used for pleasure.
(5) State sales tax paid on purchase of personal automobile.

(6) Expenses incurred in moving from Arlington to Houston to accept a new position with a different company, not reimbursed by employer.
(7) Travel expenses incurred by employee in connection with job, not reimbursed.
(8) Cost of traveling to and from home to place of employment.
(9) Fee paid to accountant for assistance in successfully contesting additional personal income taxes assessed by Internal Revenue Service.
(10) Taxpayer does maintenance work on rental property which he owns. This work would cost $500 if the taxpayer hired someone to do it.

*20A-2* The following two cases are independent of each other. See the instructions following the second case.

**Case A** The following information relates to the income tax situation of Rick Jones for the current year.

| | |
|---|---|
| *Total income* | *$96,000* |
| *Personal exemptions* | *1,000* |
| *Deductions to arrive at adjusted gross income* | *7,680* |
| *Itemized deductions* | *12,040* |
| *Exclusions from gross income* | *1,920* |

**Case B** Jill Friday, a psychiatrist, uses the accrual basis of accounting in maintaining accounting records for her business and in preparing financial statements, but uses cash basis accounting in determining her income subject to federal income tax. For the current year, her business net income (computed on an accrual basis) was $90,480. A comparison of the current balance sheet for the business with a balance sheet prepared a year earlier showed an increase of $14,400 in accounts receivable from clients during the current year. Current liabilities for rent, salaries owed to employees, and other operating expenses were $8,160 less at year-end than they were one year ago. The business income of $90,480 included $1,440 of interest received on municipal bonds.

Apart from the business, Friday has a personal savings account to which $864 was credited during the year, none of which was withdrawn. In addition to business expenses taken into account in computing net income of her business, Friday has $1,632 in deductions to arrive at adjusted gross income. Her personal exemptions amount to $1,000, and her itemized deductions are $11,000.

**Instructions** For each of the situations described above, determine the amount of the taxpayer's adjusted gross income and the taxable income for the year. Assume a zero bracket amount of $2,300 in each case.

*20A-3* During the year just ended, John Smith, a single taxpayer with one personal exemption and no itemized deductions, earned a salary of $24,000. During the year Smith had the following transactions resulting in capital gains and losses.
(1) Sold 200 shares of Lockport, Inc., for $5,400 after holding this investment for 9 months. The basis to Smith was cost of $4,900.
(2) Sold 100 shares of Gary, Inc., for $4,200, after holding these shares for 11 months. Cost was $6,000.
(3) Sold 100 shares of Lee Company for $4,800 after holding these shares for 13 months. Cost was $8,200.
(4) Sold 50 shares of Trent Company for $3,300 after holding these shares for 14 months. Cost was $2,700.

Assume that the personal exemption is in the amount of $1,000. Smith had no capital loss carry-over from prior years.

**Instructions**

**a** Compute Smith's net short-term capital gain or loss, his net long-term capital gain or loss, and his capital loss deduction (if any) for the year.

**b** Compute Smith's federal income tax for the year by referring to the tax rate schedule on page 742. Arrange your solution in good order and show among other things the adjusted gross income, taxable income, and calculation of the tax liability.

**c** Assuming that Smith could have sold the 100 shares of Lee Company stock two months sooner at the same price. Would this earlier sale have been better from a tax viewpoint? Explain.

***20A-4*** Ryan Corporation is completing its first year of operation. The company has been successful and a tentative estimate by the controller indicates an income before taxes of $250,000 for the year. Among the items entering into the calculation of the taxable income were the following:

(1) Inventories were reported on a first-in, first-out basis and amounted to $132,500 at year-end.

(2) Accounts receivable of $3,250 considered to be worthless were written off (direct charge-off method) and recorded as uncollectible accounts expense.

(3) Depreciation of $15,000 was recorded using the straight-line method.

Officers of the corporation are concerned over the large amount of income taxes to be paid and decide to change accounting methods for both financial reporting and tax purposes as follows:

(1) Inventories on a last-in, first-out basis would amount to $100,000.

(2) An acceptable allowance for doubtful accounts, after the write-off of $3,250 mentioned above, would be $10,000.

(3) Use of accelerated methods of depreciation would increase depreciation expense from $15,000 to $28,750.

**Instructions**

**a** Determine the ***taxable income*** of Ryan Corporation on the revised basis.

**b** Assume that the tax rates on corporations are 17% on the first $25,000; 20% on the second $25,000; 30% on the third $25,000; 40% on the fourth $25,000; and 46% on taxable income in excess of $100,000. Compute the income tax liability for Ryan Corporation (1) before the accounting changes, and (2) after the accounting changes. Also compute the reduction in the current year's income tax liability resulting from the accounting changes.

***20A-5*** Bill and Hannah Bailey own a successful small company, Bailey Corporation. The outstanding capital stock consists of 1,000 shares of $100 par value, of which 400 shares are owned by Bill and 600 by Hannah. In order to finance a new branch operation, the corporation needs an additional $100,000 in cash. Bill and Hannah have this amount on deposit with a savings and loan association and intend to put these personal funds into the corporation in order to establish the new branch. They will either arrange for the corporation to issue to them at par an additional 1,000 shares of stock, or they will make a loan to the corporation at an interest rate of 9%.

***Income before taxes*** of the corporation has been consistently averaging $150,000 a year, and annual dividends of $64,000 have been paid regularly. It is expected that the new branch will cause ***income before taxes*** to increase by $30,000. If new common stock is issued to finance the expansion, the total annual dividend of $64,000 will be continued unchanged. If a loan of $100,000 is arranged, the dividend will be reduced by $9,000, the amount of annual interest on the loan.

**Instructions**

**a** From the standpoint of the individual income tax return which Bill and Hannah file jointly, would there be any saving as between the stock issuance and the loan? Explain.

**b** From the standpoint of getting their money out of the corporation (assuming that the new branch is profitable), should Bill and Hannah choose capital stock or a loan for the infusion of new funds to the corporation?

**c** Prepare a two-column schedule, with one column headed If New Stock Is Used and the other headed If Loan Is Used. For each of these proposed methods of financing, show (1) the present corporate income ***before taxes;*** (2) the corporate income ***before taxes*** after the expansion; (3) the corporate income taxes after the expansion; and (4) the corporate net income after the expansion.

*20A-6* Bill and Shirley Grey own a hardware business and an apartment building. They file a joint federal income tax return. The Greys furnish over one-half the support of their son who attends college and who earned $2,560 in part-time jobs and summer employment. They also support Mr. Grey's father, who is seventy-two years old and has no taxable income of his own.

The depreciation basis of the apartment building is $160,000; depreciation is recorded at the rate of 4% per year on a straight-line basis. During the current year, the Greys had the following cash receipts and expenditures applicable to the hardware business, the apartment building, other investments, and personal activities.

| | |
|---|---|
| *Cash receipts:* | |
| *Cash withdrawn from hardware business (sales, $384,800; cost of goods sold, $284,800; operating expenses, $52,000)* | *$36,000* |
| *Gross rentals from apartment building* | *28,800* |
| *Cash dividends on stock owned jointly* | *3,160* |
| *Interest on River City bonds* | *976* |
| *Received from sale of stock purchased two years ago for $10,000* | *16,000* |
| *Received from sale of stock purchased four months previously for $6,600* | *4,600* |
| *Received from sale of motorboat purchased three years ago for $4,792 and used entirely for pleasure* | *2,712* |
| *Cash expenditures:* | |
| *Expenditures relating to apartment building:* | |
| *Interest on mortgage* | *7,200* |
| *Property taxes* | *4,720* |
| *Insurance (one year)* | *560* |
| *Utilities* | *2,368* |
| *Repairs and maintenance* | *3,872* |
| *Gardening* | *640* |
| *Other cash expenditures:* | |
| *Mortgage interest on residence* | *3,800* |
| *Property taxes on residence* | *1,700* |
| *Insurance on residence* | *400* |
| *State income tax paid* | *1,900* |
| *State sales taxes* | *700* |
| *Charitable contributions* | *1,200* |
| *Medical expenses* | *1,376* |
| *Payments on declaration of estimated tax for current year* | *10,000* |

**Instructions**

**a** Determine the amount of taxable income Bill and Shirley Grey would report on their federal income tax return for the current year. In your computation of taxable income, first list the revenue and expenses of the hardware business and show the net income from that business. Second, show the revenue and expenses of the apartment building and the amount of net income from this source. Third, show the data for dividends and capital gains. After combining the above amounts to determine adjusted gross income, list the itemized deductions and personal exemptions to arrive at taxable income. Assume that the zero bracket amount is $3,400 and that the personal exemption is $1,000 each.

**b** Compute the income tax liability for Bill and Shirley Grey using the tax rate schedule on page 743. Indicate the amount of tax due (for refund to be received).

*20A-7* The accounting records of Springfield Corporation included the following information for the current year:

| | |
|---|---|
| *Net sales* | *$7,500,000* |
| *Cost of goods sold* | *5,400,000* |
| *Dividends received from a domestic corporation* | *300,000* |
| *Dividends declared by board of directors on common stock of Springfield Corporation* | *600,000* |
| *Selling expenses* | *720,000* |
| *Administrative expenses* | *780,000* |
| *Earthquake loss (fully deductible for income tax purposes)* | *150,000* |

In December of the current year, Springfield Corporation spent $225,000 to move its corporate headquarters from one city to another. This expenditure was deducted in computing taxable income, but the company chose to defer it in the accounting records and charge it against revenue of the two subsequent years. The deferral was considered to achieve a better matching of costs with the increased revenue arising from the move. The company will follow income tax allocation procedures in reporting income taxes on the income statement during the current year.

**Instructions**

**a** Prepare an income statement for Springfield Corporation for the current year. At the bottom of the income statement show earnings per share data, including the effect of the extraordinary item (earthquake loss). The company has 300,000 shares of capital stock outstanding. In a separate schedule (Schedule A), show your computation of federal income taxes for the year, using the following rate structure:

| | |
|---|---|
| *First $25,000 of taxable income* | *17%* |
| *Second $25,000 of taxable income* | *20%* |
| *Third $25,000 of taxable income* | *30%* |
| *Fourth $25,000 of taxable income* | *40%* |
| *On excess over $100,000* | *46%* |

Hint: First prepare the top part of the income statement from Net sales down to "Income before income taxes . . . $900,000"; next prepare Schedule A, Federal income tax computation; and finally complete the income statement using data from Schedule A.

**b** Prepare the journal entry which should be made to record the income taxes expense and income tax liability (both current and deferred) at the end of the current year. Any tax effect resulting from the full deductibility of the earthquake loss should be offset against the Earthquake Loss account.

## Group B

*20B-1* **a** You are to consider the income tax status of each of the items listed below. List the numbers 1 to 15 on your answer sheet. For each item state whether it is ***included in gross income*** or ***excluded from gross income*** for federal income tax on individuals. Add explanatory comments if needed.

(1) Cash dividends received on stock of General Motors Corporation. (Assume taxpayer had no other dividend or interest income.)
(2) Value of a color TV set won as a prize in a quiz contest.
(3) Gain on the sale of an original painting.
(4) Inheritance received on death of a rich uncle.
(5) Interest received on Kansas City municipal bonds.
(6) Proceeds of life insurance policy received on death of husband.
(7) Tips received by a waitress.
(8) Value of U.S. Treasury bonds received as a gift from aunt.
(9) Rent received on personal residence while on extended vacation trip.
(10) Share of income from partnership in excess of drawings.
(11) Amount received as damages for injury in automobile accident.
(12) Salary received from a corporation by a stockholder who owns directly or indirectly all the shares of the company's outstanding stock.
(13) Gain on sale of Signal Company's capital stock.
(14) Taxpayer owed $1,000 on a note payable. During the current year the taxpayer painted a building owned by the creditor, and in return the creditor canceled the note.
(15) Las Vegas vacation given by employer as reward for outstanding service.

**b** Consider the deductibility status of each of the items listed below for the purpose of preparing an individual's income tax return. List the numbers 1 to 11 on your answer sheet. For each item state whether the item is ***deducted to arrive at adjusted gross income; deducted from adjusted gross income;*** or ***not deductible.***

(1) Dave Carter uses his vacation to paint a house (not his residence) which he owns and rents to others. A professional painter had bid $1,200 to do the job.
(2) Cost of commuting between home and place of employment.
(3) State sales tax paid on purchase of sailboat.
(4) Uninsured damage to roof of house caused by tornado.
(5) Interest paid on gambling debts.
(6) Capital loss on sale of investment in securities sold three months after purchase.
(7) Gambling losses. No gambling gains during the year.
(8) Expenses incurred in moving across country to accept position with different employer. Not reimbursed.
(9) Travel expense incurred by sales personnel in calling on various customers. Not reimbursed.
(10) Fee paid to CPA for services in contesting assessment of additional income taxes by IRS.
(11) Net operating loss carry-over by single proprietor.

*20B-2* James and Janet Baylor, a married couple with two minor children, had items of income and expense for the year just ended as shown on the upper part of page 785. Assume that James and Janet Baylor are both forty years of age, that a personal exemption is $1,000, and that the zero bracket amount is $3,400.

**Instructions** Compute the taxable income and the income tax liability for James and Janet Baylor who file a joint return. Use a format similar to that illustrated on page 757, but list itemized deductions in detail. Your solution should show the various elements of gross income, the adjusted gross income, itemized deductions, personal exemptions, and taxable income, followed by a section for computation of tax.

| | | |
|---|---|---|
| *Salaries from JB Corporation* | | *$60,000* |
| *Consulting fees (net of applicable expenses)* | | *4,200* |
| *Dividends (jointly owned)* | | *980* |
| *Interest on bonds of State of Maine* | | *252* |
| *Long-term capital gains* | | *6,700* |
| *Short-term capital losses* | | *2,800* |
| *Unused short-term capital loss carry-over from previous year* | | *2,100* |
| *Proceeds on insurance policy on life of uncle* | | *7,000* |
| *Casualty loss, interest, taxes, and other expenditures (see list below)* | | *52,700* |
| *Theft of furniture on July 20 while on vacation* | *$ 2,200* | |
| *Interest paid on loans* | *2,900* | |
| *Medical expenses* | *1,120* | |
| *Insurance on home* | *252* | |
| *Income taxes withheld from salary* | *16,000* | |
| *Miscellaneous deductible expenses* | *200* | |
| *Sales taxes* | *500* | |
| *Property taxes on home* | *1,100* | |
| *State income taxes* | *1,900* | |
| *Clothes, food, and other living expenses* | *26,528* | |
| *Total (as listed above)* | *$52,700* | |

Use the tax rate schedule on page 743 for married taxpayers filing joint returns.
Add a note identifying any items listed in the problem which are not deductible.

***20B-3*** John Brown earned a salary of $21,000 during Year 8 and also had the following sales transactions involving capital assets.

On August 10 of the current year (Year 8), Brown sold for $7,000 stock of Y Company which he had purchased January 10 of Year 8 for $8,600.

On October 1, Year 8, Brown sold for $14,000 stock of Drew Company which he had purchased two years earlier on October 1, Year 6, at a cost of $9,000.

On November 15, Year 8, Brown sold for $5,700 stock of Artco which he had purchased for $5,000 on January 15, Year 8.

On December 20, Year 8, Brown sold for $12,000 stock of Tee Company for which he had paid $13,100 on December 1, Year 1.

**Instructions**

**a** Compute the long-term capital gain or loss. (List securities by name and show the sales proceeds, cost, and gain or loss on each.)
**b** Compute the net short-term capital gain or loss.
**c** Compute the long-term capital gain deduction.
**d** Compute Brown's adjusted gross income. Start with salary, then include a section for capital gains and losses, showing separately the net long-term and net short-term gain or loss, the computation of the capital gain deduction, the net gain from sale of capital assets (after the capital gain deduction), and the adjusted gross income.

***20B-4*** In preliminary calculations the chief accountant of Dale Corporation computed income before income taxes to be $350,000 for the first year of operations. Some of the steps included in arriving at this figure are listed below.

(1) Depreciation of $21,000 was recognized under the straight-line method.
(2) The direct charge-off method of measuring uncollectible accounts expense was

followed. Accounts receivable of $4,550 were identified as uncollectible and were written off.

(3) The cost of ending inventories was determined on a first-in, first-out basis and amounted to $185,500.

The accountant pointed out to the president of the company that alternative accounting methods could be selected which would result in a smaller amount of taxable income. After some discussion it was agreed to make the following changes in accounting methods for both accounting and tax purposes:

(1) Accelerated depreciation was adopted and the revised figure for depreciation expense was $40,250.

(2) The allowance method of estimating uncollectible accounts expense was adopted. An aging of accounts receivable led to the conclusion that an allowance for uncollectible accounts of $14,000 was required with respect to customers' accounts other than the $4,550 of receivables which had already been written off as worthless.

(3) The last-in, first-out method of measuring inventory cost was adopted. Ending inventories amounted to $140,000 under this method.

**Instructions**

**a** Compute the ***taxable income*** of Dale Corporation after giving effect to the above changes.

**b** Assume that the tax rates on corporations are 17% on the first $25,000; 20% on the second $25,000; 30% on the third $25,000; 40% on the fourth $25,000; and 46% on taxable income in excess of $100,000. Compute the reduction in the current year's ***income tax liability*** for Dale Corporation resulting from the accounting changes. (Use a work sheet with two money columns; the first column should be headed "Before Accounting Changes" and the second column "After Accounting Changes.")

***20B-5*** The following two cases are independent of each other. The instructions for preparing your solution appear at the end of the second case.

**Case A** During the current year Robert Jensen has total income of $80,000. He has personal exemptions of $4,000, deductions to arrive at adjusted gross income of $6,400, itemized deductions of $8,200, and exclusions from gross income of $1,600. Jensen is married and the zero bracket amount is assumed to be $3,400.

**Case B** Ann Mason, an attorney conducting her own law practice, uses the accrual basis of accounting in maintaining accounting records and preparing financial statements. However, for income tax purposes, she uses the cash basis of accounting. During the current year, her business net income (computed on an accrual basis) was $75,400. Between the beginning and end of the current year, her financial statements showed that receivables from clients increased by $12,000, and current liabilities for rent and other operating expenses decreased by $6,800. The net income for the business included $1,200 of interest received on municipal bonds.

Mason has a personal savings account to which $920 in interest was credited during the year, none of which was withdrawn from the bank. In addition to business expenses taken into account in computing the net income of her law practice, Mason has $1,360 in deductions to arrive at adjusted gross income. Her personal exemption amounts to $1,000 and her itemized deductions are $5,900. The zero bracket amount is assumed to be $2,300. The first $200 of interest received is excluded from gross income.

**Instructions** For each of the two cases described above, prepare a separate schedule showing in appropriate order all the steps necessary to determine the taxpayer's ***adjusted gross income*** and the ***taxable income*** for the year. (For Case B, your solution

*20B-6* Riverbend Corporation had total income for the year of $304,000. Included in this amount were dividends of $6,000 received from domestic corporations. Expenses of the company for the year were as follows:

| | |
|---|---|
| *Advertising expense* | $ 18,800 |
| *Depreciation expense* | 6,400 |
| *Property taxes expense* | 4,500 |
| *Rent expense* | 34,000 |
| *Salaries expense* | 110,000 |
| *Travel expense* | 8,400 |
| *Utilities expense* | 6,900 |

**Instructions**

**a** Prepare an income statement for the corporation. Show dividend income as a separate item following Income from Operations. Reference the amount for Income Tax Expense to a separate supporting schedule as called for in **b** below.

**b** Compute Riverbend's total income tax for the year in a schedule which begins with "Income before income taxes," and shows all details of the tax computation.

**c** At a meeting of the board of directors of Riverbend Corporation late in December, the controller outlined the financial results for the year as shown above. A member of the board then offered the following suggestion.

"As I recall, the Corporation has an investment in General Motors stock which is presently worth about $15,000 less than we paid for it. Why don't we sell that stock on December 31 and buy back the same number of shares on the first business day in January? That will give us a capital loss this year, which will put us in a lower tax bracket and save several thousand dollars of income tax. By buying the stock back on January 2, we will maintain our investment position so if the stock goes up next year we won't have missed the boat."

Evaluate the director's suggestion from an income tax viewpoint.

*20B-7* The following information appears in the accounting records of the Valley Corporation for the current year:

| | |
|---|---|
| *Net sales* | $978,000 |
| *Cost of goods sold* | 697,200 |
| *Dividend revenue (on stock of domestic subsidiary corporation)* | 20,000 |
| *Dividends declared on common stock* | 50,000 |
| *Selling expenses* | 98,900 |
| *Administrative expenses* | 46,250 |
| *Gain on sale of capital asset acquired five years ago* | 8,800 |

During the current year the Valley Corporation incurred $30,000 of sales promotion expenses which may be deducted in computing taxable income, but which the company has chosen to defer on its accounting records and charge against revenue during the two subsequent years when the benefits of the sales promotion are expected to be reflected in revenue. The controller will follow tax allocation procedures in reporting the income taxes expense on the income statement during the current year.

should begin with business income on an accrual basis and show the adjustments necessary to compute business income on a cash basis.)

**Instructions**

**a** Prepare an income statement for Valley Corporation for the current year. In a separate supporting schedule show your computation of the provision for federal income taxes for the year, using the corporation rate schedule on page 758. (Remember the capital gain is taxed at 28%.)

**b** Prepare the journal entry which should be made to record the company's current income taxes expense, income tax liability, and deferred income tax liability as of the end of the year.

## BUSINESS DECISION PROBLEM 20

Gary and Joy Allen, a married couple, are in the process of organizing a business which is expected to produce, before any compensation to the Allens and before income taxes, an income of $72,000 per year. In deciding whether to operate as a single proprietorship or as a corporation, the Allens are willing to make the choice on the basis of the relative income tax advantage under either form of organization.

The Allens file a joint return, have no other dependents, and have itemized deductions that average around $11,200 per year.

If the business is operated as a single proprietorship, the Allens expect to withdraw the entire income of $72,000 each year.

If the business is operated as a corporation, the Allens will own all the shares; they will pay themselves salaries totaling $42,000 and will withdraw as dividends the entire amount of the corporation's net income after income taxes.

It may be assumed that the accounting income and the taxable income for the corporation would be the same and that the personal exemption is $1,000. Mr. and Mrs. Allen have only minor amounts of nonbusiness income, which may be ignored. The maximum tax rate on earned income of individuals is also to be ignored in working this problem.

**Instructions** Determine the relative income tax advantage to the Allens of operating either as a single proprietorship or as a corporation, and make a recommendation as to the form of organization they should adopt. Use the individual (joint return) and corporate tax rate schedules given on pages 743 and 758.

To provide a basis for this recommendation, you should prepare two schedules: one for operation as a single proprietorship, and one for operation as a corporation.

In the first schedule, compute the total income tax on the Allens' joint personal return when the business is operated as a proprietorship. Also show the Allens' disposable income, that is, the amount withdrawn minus personal income tax.

In the second schedule, compute the corporate income tax and the amount remaining for dividends. Also compute the Allens' ***personal*** income tax if the corporate form of business entity is used. From these two steps, you can determine the Allens' disposable income under the corporate form of operation.

# 21

# STATEMENT OF CHANGES IN FINANCIAL POSITION: CASH FLOWS

The business activities of a going concern may be viewed as cycles of investment, recovery of investment, and reinvestment. During the operating cycle, for example, the business invests cash in its inventories. These inventories are in turn sold to customers, often on credit. When customers pay their accounts, the company again has cash to apply against its debts and begin the operating cycle anew. Investments in plant and equipment also must be recovered through revenue at a rate fast enough to permit replacement of these assets as they wear out or become obsolete. If a business cannot recover the cash it has invested quickly enough to pay its debts as they become due, it must borrow or obtain cash from other sources in order to survive.

The balance sheet portrays the overall financial position of the business at a specific date during these recurring cycles of investment, recovery of investment, and reinvestment. The income statement shows the dollar amount of resources generated and consumed in business operations. In a sense, the fate of any given business enterprise is read in the income statement, since it tells whether revenue is larger or smaller during any period than the cost of the resources used up in generating this revenue. In this chapter we introduce a third major financial statement, the ***statement of changes in financial position***[1] and a related summary of cash movements, the ***cash flow statement.***

## STATEMENT OF CHANGES IN FINANCIAL POSITION

A statement of changes in financial position helps us to understand how and why the financial position of a business has changed during the period. This statement summarizes the long-term ***financing and investing activities*** of the business; it shows where the financial resources (funds) have come from and where they have gone. With this understanding of how funds have flowed into the business and how these funds have been used, we can begin to answer such important questions as: Do the normal operations of the business generate sufficient funds to enable the company to continue paying dividends? Did the company have to borrow to finance the acquisition of new plant assets, or was it able to generate the funds from current operations? Is the business becoming more or less solvent? And perhaps the most puzzling question: How can a ***profitable*** business be running low on cash and working capital? Even though a business operates profitably, its working capital may decline and the business may even become insolvent. If this situation occurs, many people will demand an explanation.

The statement of changes in financial position gives us answers to these questions, because it shows in detail the amount of funds received from each source and the amount of funds used for each purpose throughout the year. In fact, this financial statement used to be called a Statement of Sources and Applications of Funds. Many people still call it simply a ***Funds Statement.*** However, the name officially recommended by the FASB is the ***Statement of Changes in Financial Position.***

### "Funds" defined as working capital

In ordinary usage, the term ***funds*** usually means cash. Accountants and financial executives, however, think of "funds" in a broader sense. They view the funds available to a company as its ***working capital***—the difference between current assets and current liabilities.

Short-term credit is often used as a substitute for cash; notes and accounts payable as well as various accrued liabilities are used to meet the short-term financing needs of a business. Current assets are constantly being converted into cash, which is then used to pay current liabilities. The net amount of short-term liquid resources available to a business firm at any given time, therefore, is repre-

---

[1] In *Opinion No. 19,* "Reporting Changes in Financial Position," the Accounting Principles Board of the AICPA concluded (p. 373) that "information concerning the financing and investing activities of a business enterprise and the changes in its financial position for a period is essential for financial statement users, particularly owners and creditors, in making economic decisions. When financial statements purporting to present both financial position (balance sheet) and results of operations (statement of income and retained earnings) are issued, a statement summarizing changes in financial position should also be presented as a basic financial statement for each period for which an income statement is presented."

sented by its working capital—the difference between current assets and current liabilities. This explains why it is natural to think of working capital as a "fund" of liquid resources on hand at any given time.

If the amount of working capital increased during a given fiscal period, this means that more working capital was generated than was used for various business purposes; if a decrease in working capital occurred, the reverse is true. One of the key purposes of the statement of changes in financial position is to explain fully the increase or decrease in working capital during a fiscal period.[2] This is done by showing where working capital originated and how it was used.

## Sources and uses of working capital

Any transaction that increases the amount of working capital is a ***source of working capital.*** For example, the sale of merchandise at a price greater than its cost is a source of working capital, because the increase in cash or receivables from the sale is greater than the decrease in inventory.

Any transaction that decreases working capital is a ***use of working capital.*** For example, either incurring a current liability to acquire a noncurrent asset or using cash to pay expenses represents a decrease in working capital.

On the other hand, some transactions affect current assets or current liabilities but do ***not*** change the amount of working capital. For example, the collection of an account receivable (which increases cash and decreases an account receivable by an equal amount) is not a source of working capital. Similarly, the payment of an account payable (which decreases cash and decreases an account payable by an equal amount) does not change the amount of working capital.

The principal sources and uses of working capital are listed below:

### Sources of working capital:

1 **Current operations** If the inflow of funds from sales exceeds the outflow of funds to cover the cost of merchandise purchases and expenses of doing business, current operations will provide a net source of funds. If the inflow of funds from sales is less than these outflows, operations will result in a net use of funds. Not all expenses require the use of funds in the current period; therefore, the amount of funds provided by operations is ***not*** the same as the amount of net income earned during the period. Differences between the amount of ***working capital provided by operations*** and the amount of net income will be discussed later in the chapter.

In the long run, operations must result in a net source of funds if the business is to survive. A business cannot obtain funds through other sources indefinitely if those funds will only be consumed by business operations.

2 **Sale of noncurrent assets** A business may obtain working capital by selling

[2] In the preparation of a statement of changes in financial position, some companies define "funds" as cash, rather than as working capital. In these cases, the statement of changes in financial position becomes equivalent to the cash flow statement discussed later in this chapter. The vast majority of publicly owned corporations, however, use the working capital definition of "funds."

noncurrent assets, such as plant and equipment or long-term investments, in exchange for current assets. As long as current assets are received, the sale is a source of funds ***regardless of whether the noncurrent assets are sold at a gain or a loss.*** For example, assume that a company sells land which cost $80,000 for $60,000 in cash. Although the land was sold at a loss, the company has increased its current assets by $60,000. Thus, the transaction is a source of working capital.

3 **Long-term borrowing** Long-term borrowing, such as issuing bonds payable, results in an increase in current assets, thereby increasing working capital. ***Short-term borrowing,*** however, does ***not*** increase working capital. When a company borrows cash by signing a short-term note payable, working capital is unchanged because the increase in current assets is offset by an increase in current liabilities of the same amount.

4 **Sale of additional shares of stock** The sale of capital stock results in an inflow of current assets, thereby increasing working capital. In a similar manner, additional investments of current assets by owners represent sources of funds to single proprietorships and partnerships. The issuance of capital stock in conjunction with a stock dividend or a stock split, however, does not bring any new resources into the company and is not a source of funds.

**Uses of working capital:**

1 **Declaration of cash dividends** The declaration of a cash dividend results in a current liability (dividend payable) and is therefore a use of funds. Note that it is the ***declaration*** of the dividend, rather than the payment of the dividend, which is the use of funds. Actual payment of the dividend reduces current assets and current liabilities by the same amount and thus has no effect upon the amount of working capital. Stock dividends do not involve any distribution of assets and, therefore, are not a use of funds.

2 **Purchase of noncurrent assets** The purchase of noncurrent assets, such as plant and equipment, usually reduces current assets or increases current liabilities. In either case, working capital is reduced. Special situations in which noncurrent assets are acquired in exchange for other noncurrent assets or long-term liabilities are discussed later in this chapter.

3 **Repayment of long-term debt** Working capital is decreased when current assets are used to repay long-term debt. However, repayment of short-term debt is not a use of funds, since current assets and current liabilities decrease by the same amount.

4 **Repurchase of outstanding stock** When cash is paid out to repurchase outstanding shares of stock, working capital is reduced.

### Funds flow: a simple illustration

Assume that John Claire started a business, Claire Company, as a single proprietorship on April 30 by investing $40,000 cash; the company rented a building on

May 1 and completed the transactions shown below during the month of May.

(1) Claire invested an additional $20,000 cash in the business.
(2) Purchased merchandise costing $40,000 on credit and sold three-fourths of this, also on credit, for $58,000.
(3) Collected $45,000 on receivables; paid $32,000 on accounts payable.
(4) Paid $20,500 cash for operating expenses.
(5) Purchased land for the construction of a store. Gave $30,000 cash and a six-month note for $17,000 in payment for the land.
(6) Withdrew $2,000 from the business for personal use.

The financial statements at the end of May are shown below.

*Statements covering one month's operations of single proprietorship*

**CLAIRE COMPANY**
**Income Statement**
**For Month of May**

| | | |
|---|---|---|
| Sales | | $58,000 |
| Cost of goods sold: | | |
| Purchases | $40,000 | |
| Less: Ending inventory (one-fourth of purchases) | 10,000 | 30,000 |
| Gross profit on sales | | $28,000 |
| Operating expenses | | 20,500 |
| Net income for month of May | | $ 7,500 |

**CLAIRE COMPANY**
**Comparative Balance Sheet**

| Assets | May 31 | May 1 |
|---|---|---|
| Cash | $20,500 | $40,000 |
| Accounts receivable | 13,000 | |
| Inventory | 10,000 | |
| Land | 47,000 | |
| Total assets | $90,500 | $40,000 |
| **Liabilities & Owner's Equity** | | |
| Note payable | $17,000 | |
| Accounts payable | 8,000 | |
| John Claire, capital | 65,500 | $40,000 |
| Total liabilities & owner's equity | $90,500 | $40,000 |

The working capital amounted to $40,000 (consisting entirely of cash) on May 1 but was only $18,500 ($43,500 – $25,000) on May 31, a decrease of $21,500. In analyzing the six transactions completed during the month of May, we see that working capital was increased and decreased as follows:

*Land and the owner's capital accounts were increased as a result of these transactions*

**CLAIRE COMPANY**
**Effect of Transactions on Working Capital**
**For Month of May**

| | | |
|---|---|---|
| Increases: | | |
| Additional investment by owner | | $20,000 |
| Sale of merchandise for more than cost ($58,000 − $30,000) | | 28,000 |
| Total increases in working capital | | $48,000 |
| Decreases: | | |
| Payment of operating expenses | $20,500 | |
| Payment of cash for purchase of land | 30,000 | |
| Issuance of current note payable for purchase of land | 17,000 | |
| Withdrawal by owner | 2,000 | |
| Total decreases in working capital | | 69,500 |
| Decrease in working capital during May | | $21,500 |

A complete list of transactions for a fiscal period may not be readily available, and even if it were, analysis of such a list would be a laborious process. In practice, a statement of changes in financial position is prepared by analyzing the ***changes that occurred in the noncurrent accounts*** during the fiscal period. An analysis of the comparative balance sheet for Claire Company indicates that the Land account increased by $47,000. This increase indicates that land, a noncurrent asset was purchased during the period. Purchase of a noncurrent asset is a use of funds. Claire's capital account increased by $25,500 as a result of (1) additional investment of $20,000 (a source of funds), (2) net income of $7,500 (a source of funds), and (3) a withdrawal of $2,000 (a use of funds). We can therefore prepare the following statement of changes in financial position for the month of May, including a supporting schedule showing the changes in each component of working capital:

*A simple statement of changes in financial position*

**CLAIRE COMPANY**
**Statement of Changes in Financial Position**
**For Month of May**

| | | |
|---|---|---|
| Sources of working capital: | | |
| Operations (net income) | | $ 7,500 |
| Additional investment by owner | | 20,000 |
| Total sources of working capital | | $27,500 |
| Uses of working capital: | | |
| Purchase of land | $47,000 | |
| Withdrawal by owner | 2,000 | |
| Total uses of working capital | | 49,000 |
| Decrease in working capital | | $21,500 |

***Changes in Components of Working Capital***

| | End of May | Beginning of May | Increase or (Decrease) in Working Capital |
|---|---|---|---|
| *Current assets:* | | | |
| *Cash* | *$20,500* | *$40,000* | *$(19,500)* |
| *Accounts receivable* | *13,000* | *-0-* | *13,000* |
| *Inventory* | *10,000* | *-0-* | *10,000* |
| *Total current assets* | *$43,500* | *$40,000* | |
| *Current liabilities:* | | | |
| *Note payable* | *$17,000* | *$ -0-* | *(17,000)* |
| *Accounts payable* | *8,000* | *-0-* | *(8,000)* |
| *Total current liabilities* | *$25,000* | *$ -0-* | |
| *Working capital* | *$18,500* | *$40,000* | |
| *Decrease in working capital* | | | *$(21,500)* |

The differences between net income, net cash flow, and the change in working capital should be carefully noted in the foregoing example. Although Claire Company's net income for May was $7,500, its cash account ***decreased*** by $19,500 and its working capital ***decreased*** by $21,500.

## Effect of transactions on working capital

In preparing a statement of changes in financial position, it is convenient to view all business transactions as falling into three categories:

**1** Transactions which affect ***only current asset or current liability accounts.*** These transactions produce changes in working capital accounts but do not change the amount of working capital. For example, the purchase of merchandise increases inventory and accounts payable but has no effect on working capital; it may therefore be ignored in preparing a statement of changes in financial position.

**2** Transactions which affect a ***current asset or current liability account and a non-working capital account.*** These transactions bring about either an increase or a decrease in the amount of working capital. The issuance of long-term bonds, for example, increases current assets and increases bonds payable, a non-working capital account; therefore, the issuance of bonds payable is a source of working capital. Similarly, when the bonds approach maturity they are transferred to the current liability classification in the balance sheet. This causes a reduction (a use) of working capital. If changes in non-working capital accounts are analyzed, these events are brought to light, and their effect on working capital will be reported in the statement of changes in financial position.

**3** Transactions which affect ***only noncurrent accounts*** and therefore have no direct effect on the amount of working capital. The entry to record depreciation is an example of such a transaction. Other transactions in this category, such as the issuance of capital stock in exchange for plant assets, are called ***exchange transactions*** and are viewed as ***both a source and use of working capital,*** but do not change the amount of working capital.

**Exchange transactions** Suppose that equipment worth \$105,000 is acquired in exchange for 10,000 shares of \$5 par value capital stock. The entry to record this purchase would be:

*An exchange transaction*

| | | |
|---|---|---|
| *Equipment* | *105,000* | |
| *Capital Stock* | | *50,000* |
| *Paid-in Capital in Excess of Par* | | *55,000* |
| *Exchange of 10,000 shares of \$5 par value capital stock for equipment worth \$105,000.* | | |

This exchange transaction does not involve any current asset or current liability accounts and therefore has no ***direct*** effect upon working capital. However, the transaction may be viewed as consisting of two parts: (1) the sale of capital stock for \$105,000 and (2) the use of this \$105,000 to purchase equipment. Instead of being omitted from the statement of changes in financial position, an exchange transaction of this type is shown as ***both a source of funds*** (sale of capital stock) ***and a use of funds*** (purchase of equipment). This treatment is consistent with the objective of explaining in the statement of changes in financial position all the long-term financing activities of the business.

The acquisition of plant assets by issuing long-term debt and the conversion of bonds payable or preferred stock into common stock are other examples of exchange transactions which have no direct effect upon working capital. In the statement of changes in financial position, however, these transactions are shown as both a source and a use of working capital.

Most transactions affecting only long-term accounts are exchange transactions. Two exceptions, however, are stock splits and stock dividends. Stock splits and stock dividends do not involve an exchange and ***do not*** affect the financial position of the business. For this reason, stock splits and dividends ***are not shown*** in a statement of changes in financial position.

## Working capital provided by operations

Working capital provided by operations is the net increase or decrease in working capital resulting from the normal business activities of earning revenue and paying expenses. There are many similarities between the providing of working capital by operations and the earning of net income. For example, earning revenue increases net income and the related inflow of cash and receivables increases working capital. However, there also are significant differences between net income and the amount of working capital provided by operations.

**Some expenses do not reduce working capital** Some expenses, such as depreciation, amortization of intangible assets, and amortization of discount on bonds payable, reduce net income but have no immediate effect on the amount of working capital provided by normal operations.

To illustrate, assume that on December 31, Year 1, City Delivery Service buys three trucks at a cost of $30,000. As of January 1, Year 2, the company has no assets other than the trucks and has no liabilities. During Year 2 the company does business on a cash basis, collecting revenue of $40,000 and paying expenses of $22,000, thus showing an $18,000 increase in cash, which is its only working capital account. The company then records depreciation expense of $6,000 on its trucks, resulting in a $12,000 net income for Year 2. What is the amount of working capital provided by operations in Year 2? The recording of depreciation expense reduced net income, ***but it did not reduce working capital;*** working capital provided by operations remains at $18,000. The $12,000 net income figure therefore ***understates*** the amount of working capital provided by operations by the amount of depreciation expense recorded during the period.

One objective of the statement of changes in financial position is to explain any differences between net income and the amount of working capital provided by operations. If we are to convert the $12,000 net income of City Delivery Service to the amount of working capital provided by operations, we must ***add back*** the depreciation expense of $6,000. The computation of working capital provided by operations in the statement of changes in financial position of City Delivery Service for Year 2 is shown below:

| | |
|---|---|
| ***Sources of working capital:*** | |
| ***Operations:*** | |
| ***Net income*** | ***$12,000*** |
| ***Add: Depreciation expense*** | ***6,000*** |
| ***Working capital provided by operations*** | ***$18,000*** |

**Depreciation is not a source of funds** The addition of depreciation expense to the net income figure has led some people to view depreciation expense as a source of funds. It is important for the user of financial statements to understand that depreciation is neither a source nor a use of working capital. ***No funds flow into a business as a result of recording depreciation expense.*** It is shown in the statement of changes in financial position merely to explain one of the differences between the concept of net income and the concept of working capital provided by operations.

**Some items which increase income do not increase working capital** We have seen that some expenses do not reduce working capital. Similarly, some items in the income statement increase net income without increasing working capital; such items must be ***deducted*** from net income in arriving at working capital provided by operations. An example of such an item is the amortization of premium on bonds payable, which causes annual interest expense to be less than the cash payments of interest to bondholders.[3]

---

[3] The treatment of this item in the working paper and in the statement of changes in financial position is illustrated in the Demonstration Problem on pages 810–813.

**Nonoperating gains and losses** Extraordinary and nonoperating gains and losses, if material in amount, should be eliminated from net income in order to show the working capital provided by "normal" operations. For example, assume that land costing $100,000 is sold at a net gain of $50,000. In the statement of changes in financial position, the entire $150,000 in proceeds from the sale should be reported as "working capital provided by the sale of land." The $50,000 nonoperating gain, however, is included in the net income for the period. In determining the amount of working capital provided by operations, this $50,000 nonoperating gain must be ***deducted*** from the net income figure because the entire proceeds from the sale of the land are reported elsewhere in the statement of changes in financial position.

As a separate example, assume that the same land is sold for $70,000; then the nonoperating loss of $30,000 should be ***added*** to net income in arriving at working capital provided by operations, and the working capital provided through sale of land should be reported at $70,000.

**Computation of working capital provided by operations: a summary** The foregoing discussion relating to the measurement of working capital provided by operations can be summarized as follows:

***Computation of Working Capital Provided by Operations***

***Impact of operations on working capital***

**Working capital provided by operations = Net income + {Depreciation; Amortization of intangibles; Amortization of discount on bonds payable; Deferred income tax expense; Extraordinary and nonoperating losses (net)} − {Amortization of premium on bonds payable; Extraordinary and nonoperating gains (net)}**

## Preparation of more complex statement of changes in financial position

To illustrate the points just discussed, we shall prepare a statement of changes in financial position for the Allison Corporation from the comparative balance sheet and the condensed income statement shown on page 799. Note that the balance sheet is not classified, except for current assets and current liabilities.

A summary of the transactions completed by Allison Corporation which resulted in changes in ***noncurrent accounts*** during Year 4 follows:

**1 Changes in noncurrent assets:**

**a** Land costing $10,000 was sold for $30,000. Another parcel of land was acquired in exchange for bonds payable of $100,000.

*Can you give the reasons for the increase of $57,500 in working capital?*

**ALLISON CORPORATION**
**Comparative Balance Sheet**
**At December 31**

| Assets | Year 4 | Year 3 |
|---|---|---|
| Current assets: | | |
| Cash | $ 15,000 | $ 35,000 |
| Accounts receivable (net) | 105,000 | 85,000 |
| Inventory | 200,000 | 120,000 |
| Short-term prepayments | 25,000 | 12,000 |
| Total current assets | $345,000 | $252,000 |
| Land | 140,000 | 50,000 |
| Equipment | 290,000 | 230,000 |
| Less: Accumulated depreciation | (107,500) | (80,000) |
| Total assets | $667,500 | $452,000 |
| **Liabilities & Stockholders' Equity** | | |
| Current liabilities: | | |
| Notes payable to merchandise creditors | $ 60,000 | $ 40,000 |
| Accounts payable | 85,000 | 50,000 |
| Accrued liabilities | 22,500 | 42,000 |
| Total current liabilities | $167,500 | $132,000 |
| Notes payable, due Jan. 1, Year 17 | 15,000 | 10,000 |
| Bonds payable, due June 30, Year 20 | 160,000 | 100,000 |
| Capital stock, $5 par | 215,000 | 110,000 |
| Paid-in capital in excess of par | 50,000 | 30,000 |
| Retained earnings | 60,000 | 70,000 |
| Total liabilities & stockholders' equity | $667,500 | $452,000 |

**ALLISON CORPORATION**
**Condensed Income Statement**
**For Year Ended December 31, Year 4**

| | | |
|---|---|---|
| Sales (net) | | $900,000 |
| Cost of goods sold | | 585,000 |
| Gross profit on sales | | $315,000 |
| Operating expenses and income taxes | $255,000 | |
| Gain on sale of land | (20,000) | 235,000 |
| Net income | | $ 80,000 |

**b** Equipment was purchased for $60,000; the invoice was paid within ten days.
**c** Depreciation of $27,500 was recorded.

**2 Changes in noncurrent liabilities:**

**a** An additional $5,000 was borrowed on long-term notes due in Year 17.
**b** Bonds payable of $40,000 were retired at a price equal to par value and additional bonds of $100,000 were issued in exchange for land.

**3 Changes in stockholders' equity accounts:**

**a** A 50% stock dividend was declared in January, requiring a transfer of $55,000 from the Retained Earnings account to the Capital Stock account.

**b** In February, 10,000 shares of $5 par value stock were sold at $7 per share, thus increasing Capital Stock by $50,000 and Paid-in Capital in Excess of Par by $20,000.

**c** In addition to the $55,000 reduction in retained earnings as a result of the 50% stock dividend, cash dividends of $35,000 were declared.

**d** The net income for the year, $80,000 (including the nonoperating gain of $20,000), was transferred to the Retained Earnings account.

From the comparative balance sheets, the income statement, and the summary of the transactions during the year which changed noncurrent accounts, we can prepare a statement of changes in financial position by completing the following three steps:

1 Compute the change in working capital during the period.
2 Prepare a working paper for analysis of changes in noncurrent accounts.
3 Prepare the statement of changes in financial position.

**Computation of increase in working capital during the period** The first step in preparing a statement of changes in financial position is to determine the net increase or decrease in working capital during the period covered by the statement.

The working capital of the Allison Corporation increased by $57,500 during Year 4, determined as follows:

*Sources of working capital exceed uses by $57,500*

*Allison Corporation*
*Computation of Increase in Working Capital during Year 4*

| | Dec. 31, Year 4 | Dec. 31, Year 3 |
|---|---|---|
| Current assets | $345,000 | $252,000 |
| Less: Current liabilities | 167,500 | 132,000 |
| Working capital | $177,500 | $120,000 |
| Increase in working capital during Year 4 ($177,500 − $120,000) | | 57,500 |
| | $177,500 | $177,500 |

The purpose of the statement of changes in financial position is to explain the reasons for the change in working capital. This is accomplished by listing the specific sources and uses of working capital during the period. Since the working capital for the Allison Corporation increased by $57,500, the sources of working capital during Year 4 exceeded the uses by this amount. But before a statement of changes in financial position can be prepared, we must analyze the changes which took place during the year in the noncurrent accounts.

**Preparation of working paper for analysis of changes in noncurrent accounts** A working paper showing the analysis of changes in noncurrent accounts for the Allison Corporation is illustrated on page 801. The amount of working capital

## ALLISON CORPORATION

### Working Paper for Statement of Changes in Financial Position

### For Year Ended December 31, Year 4

| Debits | Account Balances, Jan. 1, Year 4 | Analysis of Transactions for Year 4: Debit | Analysis of Transactions for Year 4: Credit | Account Balances, Dec. 31, Year 4 |
|---|---|---|---|---|
| Working capital | 120,000 | (x) 57,500 | | 177,500 |
| Land | 50,000 | (4) 100,000 | (3) 10,000 | 140,000 |
| Equipment | 230,000 | (7) 60,000 | | 290,000 |
| Total | 400,000 | | | 607,500 |
| **Credits** | | | | |
| Accumulated depreciation | 80,000 | | (2) 27,500 | 107,500 |
| Notes payable, due Jan. 1, Year 17 | 10,000 | | (6) 5,000 | 15,000 |
| Bonds payable, due June 30, Year 20 | 100,000 | (8) 40,000 | (4) 100,000 | 160,000 |
| Capital stock, $5 par | 110,000 | | (5) 50,000<br>(10) 55,000 | 215,000 |
| Paid-in capital in excess of par | 30,000 | | (5) 20,000 | 50,000 |
| Retained earnings | 70,000 | (9) 35,000<br>(10) 55,000 | (1) 80,000 | 60,000 |
| Total | 400,000 | 347,500 | 347,500 | 607,500 |
| Sources of working capital: | | Sources | Uses | |
| Operations—net income | | (1) 80,000 | | (From operations, $87,500) |
| Add: Depreciation | | (2) 27,500 | | |
| Less: Gain on sale of land | | | (3) 20,000 | |
| Sale of land | | (3) 30,000 | | |
| Issuance of bonds payable | | (4) 100,000 | | |
| Sale of capital stock | | (5) 70,000 | | |
| Borrowed on notes payable, due Jan. 1, Year 17 | | (6) 5,000 | | |
| Uses of working capital: | | | | |
| Purchase of land in exchange for bonds payable | | | (4) 100,000 | |
| Purchase of equipment | | | (7) 60,000 | |
| Retirement of bonds payable | | | (8) 40,000 | |
| Cash dividends declared | | | (9) 35,000 | |
| Total sources and uses of working capital | | 312,500 | 255,000 | |
| Increase in working capital during Year 4 | | | (x) 57,500 | |
| | | 312,500 | 312,500 | |

Explanation of transactions for Year 4:

(1) Net income $80,000 (including a gain of $20,000 on sale of land) is transferred to Retained Earnings. This is a tentative source of working capital to be adjusted in (2) and (3) below.

(2) Depreciation for the year, $27,500, is added to net income in arriving at the working capital provided by operations because it did not reduce a current asset or increase a current liability.

(3) Sale of land for $30,000; the gain of $20,000 is deducted from net income in order that entire proceeds can be reported separately as a source of working capital.

(4) Issuance of $100,000 of bonds payable in exchange for land.

(5) Sale of capital stock, providing working capital of $70,000.

(6) Working capital was provided by borrowing $5,000 on long-term notes.

(7) Working capital was reduced through purchase of equipment, $60,000.

(8) Working capital of $40,000 was used to retire bonds payable.

(9) Cash dividends declared, $35,000; this is a use of working capital.

(10) Board of directors declared a 50% stock dividend; this transaction had no effect on working capital.

(x) Balance figure—increase in working capital during Year 4.

and the balances in noncurrent accounts at the beginning of the period are listed in the first column of the working paper; balances at the end of the year are listed in the last (right-hand) column. The two middle columns are used to ***explain the changes*** in each ***noncurrent*** account during the year and to indicate whether each change corresponds to a source or a use of funds. Transactions for the year (in summary form) are recorded in these middle columns and an offsetting entry is made in the lower section of the working papers indicating the effect of each transaction upon working capital.

**Explanation of transactions in working paper** By studying the changes in the noncurrent accounts during Year 4, we are able to find the specific reasons for the $57,500 increase in working capital. As previously stated, only changes in the noncurrent accounts represent sources and uses of working capital. The analyses of the transactions completed by the Allison Corporation during Year 4 are explained below:

(1) The net income of $80,000 is credited to the Retained Earnings account and is shown under "sources of working capital: operations." Net income represents an increase in stockholders' equity and is one of the major sources of working capital for most businesses. Net income, however, is only a tentative measure of the increase in working capital from operations because not all revenue and expense items represent sources and uses of working capital (depreciation, for example). Furthermore, any extraordinary and nonoperating items are eliminated from net income because the transactions giving rise to such items are reported separately if they generate or use working capital.

(2) Since depreciation expense does not reduce a current asset or increase a current liability, it has no effect on working capital. Therefore, the depreciation expense of $27,500 for the year is shown as an addition to net income in the working paper and is credited to Accumulated Depreciation. The net income, $80,000, plus depreciation expense, $27,500, or a total of $107,500, represents a ***tentative*** increase in working capital as a result of profitable operations. This $107,500 figure is viewed as tentative because it will be reduced in adjustment (3) by the amount of the gain on the sale of land ($20,000) which was included in the net income of $80,000; this gain will be included in the $30,000 source of working capital on the sale of land.

(3) The sale of land is recorded as a source of working capital of $30,000 because cash was generated when the land was sold. The cost of the land, $10,000, is credited to the Land account and the gain, $20,000, is shown as a reduction to the net income in order that the net proceeds on the sale of the land ($30,000) can be listed as a source of working capital. This adjustment gives us net "working capital provided by operations," $87,500, consisting of income ***before the gain on the sale of land,*** $60,000, plus depreciation, $27,500.

(4) The issuance of $100,000 par value bonds in exchange for land is an exchange transaction, representing both a source and a use of funds. First, an entry is made in the top portion of the working papers explaining the

$100,000 increase in the Bonds Payable account and an offsetting entry is made below showing a $100,000 source of funds. Next, a debit entry is made in the upper portion of the working papers explaining the $100,000 increase in the Land account and an offsetting entry is made below showing the $100,000 use of funds.

(5) The sale of capital stock in February for $70,000 is recorded in the upper portion of the working papers by credits to Capital Stock, $50,000 (10,000 shares with a $5 par value), and to Paid-in Capital in Excess of Par, $20,000. The issuance of capital stock is a source of funds; therefore, the offsetting entry in the lower section of the working papers is entered in the Sources column.

(6) An increase in long-term debt is a source of funds. Therefore, the borrowing of $5,000 on long-term notes payable is recorded in the working paper as a credit to Notes Payable and a source of working capital.

(7) Equipment was purchased for $60,000, causing a reduction in working capital. This is recorded in the working paper by a debit to Equipment and an offsetting entry describing the use of funds.

(8) During Year 4, Allison Corporation retired $40,000 of bonds payable at par. A reduction in long-term debt represents a use of working capital. The transaction is recorded in the working paper by a debit to Bonds Payable and an offsetting entry describing the use of funds. If a retirement of bonds payable results in a material loss or gain, the loss or gain would be reported in the income statement and would be eliminated from net income in the same manner as the gain on sale of land in transaction (3) above.

(9) Cash dividends declared on capital stock outstanding reduce both working capital and stockholders' equity and should be listed on a statement of changes in financial position as a use of working capital. The required working paper entry is a debit to Retained Earnings and an offsetting entry showing the use of funds. A cash dividend need not be paid in order to represent a reduction in working capital. The ***declaration*** of the cash dividend establishes a current liability and thus reduces working capital. The actual payment of the cash dividend has no effect on working capital because the payment merely reduces a current liability (Dividends Payable) and a current asset (Cash) by the same amount; ***a transaction which changes only current accounts cannot be a source or use of working capital.***

(10) The declaration of a stock dividend is merely a transfer from retained earnings to paid-in capital; a stock dividend has no effect on working capital because no working capital account is changed. The working paper entry to recognize the 50% stock dividend distributed by the Allison Corporation in January is a debit to Retained Earnings for $55,000 and a credit to Capital Stock for the same amount.

(x) After all changes in noncurrent accounts are analyzed in the working paper, the gross sources, $312,500, and uses, $255,000, of working capital are totaled. At this point, the increase in working capital during the year, $57,500, should be entered as a debit to Working Capital on the first line of the second column in the working paper and also as a balancing figure on the next to the last line of the third column in the working paper. The account balances at December 31, Year 4, can now be determined and totals obtained for the debits and credits in the top portion of the working paper. If the totals agree, we know that our analysis is correct, at least so far as the mechanics are concerned.

**Preparation of statement of changes in financial position** The preceding working paper analysis explained all changes in noncurrent accounts that took place during Year 4. In making this analysis, we listed the sources and uses of working capital in the lower section of the working paper on page 801. The increase of $57,500 in working capital has been confirmed and a statement of changes in financial position, including a schedule showing the changes in the components of working capital, can now be prepared as shown on page 805.

We can see that working capital provided by operations amounted to $87,500, and another $205,000 of working capital came from nonoperating sources (sale of land, sale of additional capital stock, and long-term borrowing). Working capital totaling $235,000 was used to purchase land and equipment, retire bonds payable, and declare cash dividends. These sources and uses resulted in a net increase of $57,500 in working capital. The statement of changes in financial position thus provides a concise view of the way in which the Allison Corporation generated and used its working capital during the year.

Investors and creditors find the statement of changes in financial position helpful not only in evaluating the past performance of a company but also in projecting its future movements of working capital and in evaluating probable ***liquidity*** (the ability to pay debts as they become due).

A statement of changes in financial position for a large listed corporation appears in the Appendix of this book.

## CASH FLOW ANALYSIS

While the statement of changes in financial position reports the inflow and outflow of working capital during an accounting period, management is often more concerned with having enough cash to meet its operating needs and to pay maturing liabilities. Cash is the most liquid asset, and the efficient use of cash is one of the most important tasks of management. A ***cash flow statement*** is often prepared in order to give a full and complete picture of cash receipts and disbursements for an accounting period. Such a cash flow statement may also be useful in preparing a cash budget.

A cash flow statement is definitely not a substitute for an income statement. Income statements, as we have shown in prior chapters, are prepared on an accrual basis. Accrual accounting was developed to overcome the limitations of cash movements as indicators of business performance. Cash outlays simply represent investments which may or may not prove sound. Cash receipts represent disinvestment and, taken by themselves, tell nothing about whether the inflow is beneficial or not. The accountant's measurement of net income is designed to tell something about the fate of a company's overall investment and disinvest-

**ALLISON CORPORATION**
**Statement of Changes in Financial Position**
**For Year Ended December 31, Year 4**

*Statement of changes in financial position shows sources and uses of working capital*

| | | |
|---|---|---|
| Sources of working capital: | | |
| Operations: | | |
| Net income | | $ 80,000 |
| Add: Expense not requiring the use of working capital— | | |
| depreciation | $27,500 | |
| Less: Nonoperating gain on sale of land | 20,000 | 7,500 |
| Total working capital provided by operations | | $ 87,500 |
| Sale of land | | 30,000 |
| Issuance of bonds payable | | 100,000 |
| Sale of capital stock | | 70,000 |
| Borrowed on long-term notes payable, due Jan. 1, Year 17 | | 5,000 |
| Total sources of working capital | | $292,500 |
| Uses of working capital: | | |
| Purchase of land in exchange for bonds payable | $100,000 | |
| Purchase of equipment | 60,000 | |
| Retirement of bonds payable | 40,000 | |
| Declaration of cash dividends | 35,000 | |
| Total uses of working capital | | 235,000 |
| Increase in working capital | | $ 57,500 |

**Changes in Composition of Working capital**

*This supporting schedule shows the change in each working capital account*

| | End of Year 4 | End of Year 3 | Increases or (Decreases) in Working Capital |
|---|---|---|---|
| Current assets: | | | |
| Cash | $ 15,000 | $ 35,000 | $(20,000) |
| Accounts receivable (net) | 105,000 | 85,000 | 20,000 |
| Inventory | 200,000 | 120,000 | 80,000 |
| Short-term prepayments | 25,000 | 12,000 | 13,000 |
| Total current assets | $345,000 | $252,000 | |
| Current liabilities: | | | |
| Notes payable to merchandise creditors | $ 60,000 | $ 40,000 | (20,000) |
| Accounts payable | 85,000 | 50,000 | (35,000) |
| Accrued liabilities | 22,500 | 42,000 | 19,500 |
| Total current liabilities | $167,500 | $132,000 | |
| Working capital | $177,500 | $120,000 | |
| Increase in working capital | | | $ 57,500 |

ment activities during a given period of time. Despite its imperfections, the income statement is still the best means we have for reporting operating performance of business enterprises.

However, there are occasions when one may wish to determine the amount of cash generated by operations. Reports of past cash flow may reveal a good deal about the financial problems and policies of a company. Forecasts of cash flows and cash budgets are useful managerial planning tools. The measurement of past and future cash flows from all sources, including operations, provides valuable information.

## Cash flow from operations

Suppose we wish to convert a company's income statement into a report of its cash flow from operations. How should we go about adjusting the data on the income statement to convert it into cash flow information?

To answer this question, we must consider the relationship between the amounts on an accrual basis income statement and the cash movements within the firm. For illustrative purposes, consider the income statement of the Allison Corporation for Year 4, which was presented earlier in this chapter.

*Condensed income statement: accrual basis*

***ALLISON CORPORATION***
***Condensed Income Statement***
***For Year Ended December 31, Year 4***

| | | |
|---|---|---|
| Sales (net) | | $900,000 |
| Cost of goods sold | | 585,000 |
| Gross profit on sales | | $315,000 |
| Operating expenses and income taxes | $255,000 | |
| Gain on sale of land | (20,000) | 235,000 |
| Net income | | $ 80,000 |

From our preceding discussion of Allison Corporation's transactions in Year 4, we already know that cash was received from the sale of land ($30,000), from the sale of capital stock ($70,000), and from borrowing on long-term notes ($5,000). We also know that cash was paid to acquire equipment ($60,000), to retire bonds payable ($40,000), and to pay cash dividends ($35,000). The remaining cash movements must consist of cash receipts from customers and cash payments for purchases and expenses, including income taxes.

**Cash receipts from customers** Sales on account are an important factor in most companies. The relationship between the amount of cash collected from customers and the net sales reported in the income statement depends on the change in accounts receivable between the beginning and end of any period. The relationship may be stated as follows:

*Converting sales to cash basis*

$$\text{Net sales} \left\{ \begin{array}{c} + \text{ decrease in accounts receivable} \\ \text{or} \\ - \text{ increase in accounts receivable} \end{array} \right\} = \text{cash receipts from customers}$$

In the Allison Corporation example, a glance at the comparative balance sheet on page 799 tells us that net accounts receivable increased from $85,000 to $105,000 during Year 4, an increase of $20,000. Therefore, the cash receipts from customers during Year 4 can be determined as follows:

*Net sales on cash basis*

| | |
|---|---|
| *Net sales* | *$900,000* |
| *Less: Increase in net accounts receivable during the year* | *20,000* |
| *Cash receipts from customers* | *$880,000* |

**Cash payments for purchases** The relationship between the cost of goods sold for a period and the cash payments for the purchase of merchandise depends both on the change in inventory and the change in notes and accounts payable to merchandise creditors during the period. The relationship may be stated, in two stages, as follows:

*Converting cost of goods sold to cash basis*

**Cost of goods sold** {**+ increase in inventory** **or** **− decrease in inventory**} **= net purchases** →

→ **net purchases** {**+ decrease in notes and accounts payable** **or** **− increase in notes and accounts payable**} **= cash payments for purchases**

Again referring to the Allison Corporation example, we can see that the company increased its inventory by $80,000 and that notes and accounts payable to merchandise creditors increased by $55,000 during the year. The cash payments for purchases during Year 4 would be computed as follows:

*Cost of goods sold on cash basis*

| | |
|---|---|
| *Cost of goods sold* | *$585,000* |
| *Add: Increase in inventory* | *80,000* |
| *Net purchases (accrual basis)* | *$665,000* |
| *Less: Increase in notes and accounts payable to creditors* | *55,000* |
| *Cash payments for purchases* | *$610,000* |

Let us review the logic behind this computation. If a company is increasing its inventory, it will be buying more merchandise than it sells during the period; furthermore, if the company is increasing its notes and accounts payable to merchandise creditors, it is not paying cash for all of these purchases.

**Cash payments for expenses** Expenses in the income statement arise from three major sources: cash expenditures, the write-off of prepayments, and incurring obligations for accrued expenses. The relationship between operating expenses and cash payments, therefore, depends on changes in asset accounts representing the prepayment of expenses, and on changes in accrued liability accounts.

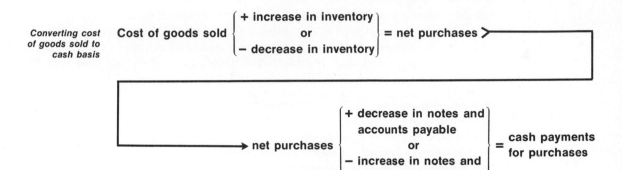

These relationships may be stated as follows:

*Converting an expense on accrual basis to cash basis*

$$\text{Expense}\begin{Bmatrix}+\text{ increase in related prepayment}\\ \text{or}\\ -\text{ decrease in related prepayment}\end{Bmatrix}\text{ and }\begin{Bmatrix}+\text{ decrease in related accrued liability}\\ \text{or}\\ -\text{ increase in related accrued liability}\end{Bmatrix}=\text{cash payments for expense}$$

In the case of a noncash expense such as depreciation, the decrease in the book value of a depreciable asset (a long-term prepayment) is exactly equal to the expense recorded, and the resultant cash payment is zero.

Using the information for the Allison Corporation, we can summarize the relationship between the operating expenses and income taxes reported in the income statement and cash payments for these expenses during Year 4 as follows:

*Expenses on cash basis*

| | |
|---|---|
| *Total operating expenses and income taxes in the income statement* | *$255,000* |
| *Add: Decrease in accrued liabilities* | *19,500* |
| *Increase in short-term prepayments* | *13,000* |
| *Less: Decrease in long-term prepayments (depreciation)* | *(27,500)* |
| *Cash payments for operating expenses and income taxes* | *$260,000* |

**Conversion of an income statement to cash basis** The conversion of the income statement of the Allison Corporation from an accrual to a cash basis is shown below. Note that this schedule incorporates the adjustments discussed in the preceding paragraphs.

*How much cash was generated from operations in Year 4?*

**ALLISON CORPORATION**

***Conversion of Income Statement from Accrual to Cash Basis***

***For Year Ended December 31, Year 4***

| | Income Statement (Accrual Basis) | Add (Deduct) | Cash Basis |
|---|---|---|---|
| Net sales | $900,000 | | |
| Less: Increase in accounts receivable | | $(20,000) | $880,000 |
| Cost of goods sold | 585,000 | | |
| Add: Increase in inventory | | 80,000 | |
| Less: Increase in notes and accounts payable to merchandise creditors | | (55,000) | 610,000 |
| Gross profit on sales | $315,000 | | $270,000 |
| Operating expenses and income taxes | 255,000 | | |
| Add: Decrease in accrued liabilities | | 19,500 | |
| Increase in short-term prepayments | | 13,000 | |
| Less: Depreciation expense | | (27,500) | 260,000 |
| Income before gain on sale of land (accrual basis) | $ 60,000 | | |
| Cash generated from operations | | | $ 10,000 |

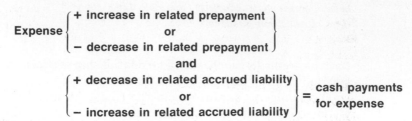

The cash flow from operations for the Allison Corporation, $10,000, is lower than the amount of income before the gain on the sale of land, $60,000, during Year 4. This difference is caused by a series of variations between revenue and expense transactions on the accrual basis and the related cash inflows and outflows during the year.

**Cash flow statement** The cash flow from operations computed above for the Allison Corporation does not tell the complete story of cash movements during the period. Let us now combine the $10,000 cash flow from operations with the information relating to cash receipts and payments obtained from the comparative balance sheet by way of the statement of changes in financial position. The result will be a statement that explains in full the $20,000 decrease in the cash balance during Year 4. Such a cash flow statement for the Allison Corporation is shown below:

***ALLISON CORPORATION***

***Cash Flow Statement***

***For Year Ended December 31, Year 4***

*Complete summary of cash movements for Year 4*

| | | |
|---|---|---|
| *Cash receipts:* | | |
| *Cash generated from operations (see schedule above)* | | *$10,000* |
| *Sale of land* | | *30,000* |
| *Sale of capital stock* | | *70,000* |
| *Borrowing on long-term notes* | | *5,000* |
| *Total cash receipts* | | *$115,000* |
| *Cash payments:* | | |
| *Purchase of equipment* | *$ 60,000* | |
| *Retirement of bonds payable* | *40,000* | |
| *Payment of cash dividends* | *35,000* | |
| *Total cash payments* | | *135,000* |
| *Decrease in cash during the year* | | *$ 20,000* |

The Allison Corporation example was sufficiently simple that we could develop cash flow information from a direct inspection of the income statement and comparative balance sheets. In more complex situations, the accountant will usually use a working paper to convert the income statement from an accrual to a cash basis and to develop cash flow information in a systematic fashion. Familiarity with these working-paper procedures is not necessary in order to be able to understand and interpret cash flow information; therefore, discussion of this process is reserved for more advanced accounting courses.

## KEY TERMS INTRODUCED OR EMPHASIZED IN CHAPTER 21

**Cash basis** A method of measuring operating results in terms of cash receipts and cash payments rather than revenue earned and expenses incurred.

**Cash flow statement** A statement showing the sources of cash receipts and purpose of cash payments during an accounting period. This statement is useful for explaining changes in the balance of the Cash account, but it is not a substitute for an income statement.

**Exchange transaction** In the context of a statement of changes in financial position, exchange transactions are financing or investing activities which do not directly affect working capital accounts. An example of such a transaction is the purchase of plant assets by issuing common stock. Such transactions should be shown in a funds statement as both a source and a use of working capital.

**Funds** In the context of a statement of changes in financial position, "funds" are usually defined as working capital.

**Noncurrent account** Any balance sheet account ***other than*** a current asset or a current liability. Noncurrent accounts include long-term investments, plant assets, intangible assets, long-term liabilities, and stockholders' equity accounts.

**Statement of changes in financial position** A financial statement showing the sources and uses of working capital during the accounting period. In addition, this statement shows financing and investing activities, such as exchange transactions, which do not directly affect working capital.

**Working capital** Current assets minus current liabilities. Working capital represents the net amount of liquid resources available to a business.

## DEMONSTRATION PROBLEM FOR YOUR REVIEW

The comparative financial data for Liquid Gas Company for the last two years are shown below:

| | December 31 | |
|---|---|---|
| *Debits* | *Year 2* | *Year 1* |
| *Cash* | *$ 39,220* | *$ 15,800* |
| *Receivables (net of allowance for doubtful accounts)* | *41,400* | *24,000* |
| *Inventories, lower of cost or market* | *27,600* | *36,800* |
| *Short-term prepayments* | *4,180* | *4,400* |
| *Land* | *9,000* | *19,000* |
| *Buildings* | *270,000* | *250,000* |
| *Equipment* | *478,600* | *450,000* |
| *Total debits* | *$870,000* | *$800,000* |
| *Credits* | *Year 2* | *Year 1* |
| *Accumulated depreciation: buildings* | *$ 95,000* | *$ 77,000* |
| *Accumulated depreciation: equipment* | *153,000* | *120,000* |
| *Accounts payable* | *59,200* | *30,000* |
| *Accrued liabilities* | *20,000* | *10,000* |
| *Bonds payable* | *90,000* | *90,000* |
| *Premium on bonds payable* | *2,800* | *3,000* |
| *Preferred stock ($100 par)* | *70,000* | *100,000* |
| *Common stock ($25 par)* | *260,000* | *250,000* |
| *Paid-in capital in excess of par* | *45,000* | *40,000* |
| *Retained earnings* | *75,000* | *80,000* |
| *Total credits* | *$870,000* | *$800,000* |

c

LIQUID GAS
Statement of Changes i
For Yea

Sources of working capital:
Operations:
Net income . . . . . . . . . . . . . . . . . . . . . .
Add: Expense not requiring the use of workin
depreciation . . . . . . . . . . . . . . . . .
Nonoperating loss on sale of land . . . .
Less: Increase in net income which did not p
capital—amortization of premium on bonds
Total working capital provided by operations .
Sale of land . . . . . . . . . . . . . . . . . . . . . .
Total sources of working capital . . . . . . . .
Uses of working capital:
Declaration of cash dividends . . . . . . . . . .
Purchase of buildings . . . . . . . . . . . . . .
Purchase of equipment . . . . . . . . . . . . .
Retirement of preferred stock . . . . . . . . . . .
Total uses of working capital . . . . . . . . . .
Decrease in working capital . . . . . . . . . . . . .

d

LIQUID GAS CO
Cash Flow Sta
For Year

Cash receipts:
Cash generated from operations (see Schedule A
Sale of land . . . . . . . . . . . . . . . . . . . . . .
Total cash receipts . . . . . . . . . . . . . . . .
Cash payments:
Payment of cash dividends . . . . . . . . . . . .
Purchase of buildings . . . . . . . . . . . . . .
Purchase of equipment . . . . . . . . . . . . .
Retirement of preferred stock . . . . . . . . . . .
Total cash payments . . . . . . . . . . . . . . . .
Increase in cash during the year . . . . . . . . . . .

Schedule A—Cash generated from operations:
Working capital provided by operations—part c . .
Add: Decrease in inventories . . . . . . . . . . . .
Decrease in short-term prepayments . . . . .
Increase in accounts payable . . . . . . . . .
Increase in accrued liabilities . . . . . . . . .
Less: Increase in receivables . . . . . . . . . . . .
Cash generated from operations . . . . . . . . . . .



**Other data**

(1) During Year 2, the board of directors of the company authorized a transfer of $15,000 from retained earnings to reflect a 4% stock dividend on the common stock.
(2) Cash dividends of $6,000 were paid on the preferred stock, and cash dividends of $50,000 were paid on the common stock.
(3) During Year 2, 300 shares of preferred stock were retired at par value.
(4) The only entries recorded in the Retained Earnings account were for dividends and to close the Income Summary account, which had a credit balance of $66,000 after the loss on the sale of the land.
(5) There were no sales or retirements of buildings and equipment during the year; land was sold for $8,000, resulting in a loss of $2,000.

**Instructions**

**a** Compute the change in working capital during Year 2. You may use totals for current assets and current liabilities.
**b** Prepare a working paper for a statement of changes in financial position for Year 2.
**c** Prepare a statement of changes in financial position for Year 2, without showing the composition of working capital.
**d** Prepare a cash flow statement, with a supporting schedule converting the net income from the accrual basis to the cash basis.

## SOLUTION TO DEMONSTRATION PROBLEM

**a** Computation of decrease in working capital:

| | As of December 31 Year 2 | Year 1 |
|---|---|---|
| Current assets | $112,400 | $81,000 |
| Less: Current liabilities | 79,200 | 40,000 |
| Working capital | $ 33,200 | $41,000 |
| Decrease in working capital during Year 2 | 7,800 | |
| | $ 41,000 | $41,000 |

b

**LIQUID GAS COMPANY**

**Working Paper for Statement of Changes in F**

**For Year 2**

| Debits | Account Balances Dec. 31, Year 1 | Tr |
|---|---|---|
| | | D |
| Working capital | 41,000 | |
| Land | 19,000 | |
| Buildings | 250,000 | (6) |
| Equipment | 450,000 | (7) |
| Total | 760,000 | |
| **Credits** | | |
| Accumulated depreciation: buildings | 77,000 | |
| Accumulated depreciation: equipment | 120,000 | |
| Bonds payable | 90,000 | |
| Premium on bonds payable | 3,000 | (8) |
| Preferred stock, $100 par | 100,000 | (9) 3 |
| Common stock, $25 par | 250,000 | |
| Paid-in capital in excess of par | 40,000 | |
| Retained earnings | 80,000 | (3) 1 |
| | | (4) 5 |
| Total | 760,000 | 14 |
| | | Sourc |
| Sources of working capital: | | |
| Operations—net income | | (1) 6 |
| Add: Depreciation | | (2) 51 |
| Loss on sale of land | | (5) 2 |
| Less: Amortization of premium on bonds payable | | |
| Sale of land | | (5) 8 |
| Uses of working capital: | | |
| Payment of cash dividends | | |
| Purchase of buildings | | |
| Purchase of equipment | | |
| Retirement of preferred stock | | |
| Total sources and uses of working capital | | 127, |
| Decrease in working capital | | (x) 7, |
| | | 134, |

Explanation of transactions for Year 2:
(1) Net income, $66,000, including a loss of $2,000 on sale of land, transferred to Ret
(2) Depreciation for the year, $51,000 (buildings, $18,000, and equipment, $33,000) is a which did not reduce working capital.
(3) Entry to record 4% stock dividend; no effect on working capital.
(4) Cash dividends declared, $56,000 (preferred stock, $6,000, and common, $50,000).
(5) To record sale of land for $8,000; the loss of $2,000 is added to net income because t on working capital.
(6) To record working capital used for purchase of buildings.
(7) To record working capital used for purchase of equipment.
(8) To record amortization of premium on bonds payable; the amortization increased net i
(9) To record working capital applied to retirement of preferred stock.
(x) Balancing figure—decrease in working capital during Year 2.



## REVIEW QUESTIONS

1 Why is working capital viewed as a "fund of liquid resources"?

2 What are the primary ways in which a firm generates working capital and the primary ways in which a firm uses working capital?

3 List four transactions which are neither a source nor a use of working capital and which are not disclosed in a statement of changes in financial position.

4 Sources of funds include borrowing, sale of noncurrent assets, operations, and sale of capital stock. Which of these possible sources of funds do you consider to be most important to the long-run survival of a business?

5 What information can a reader gain from a statement of changes in financial position that is not apparent from reading an income statement?

6 In preparing a statement of changes in financial position, business transactions may be classified into three categories. List these categories and indicate which category results in changes in working capital.

7 Give examples of expenses, other than depreciation expense, which reduce net income but which do not result in the use of working capital during the period.

8 Give an example of an increase in net income which does not result in an increase in working capital during the period.

9 The following quotation appeared in the annual report of a large corporation: "Depreciation, depletion, and amortization charges provide funds which cause our working capital provided by operations to consistently exceed our net income." Evaluate this quotation.

10 Although extraordinary and nonoperating gains and losses may be included in net income, what reason can you give for excluding such gains and losses in computing the working capital provided by operations? Use the following facts to illustrate your point: Net income including gain on sale of land, $100,000; sale of land, with a book value of $70,000, for $150,000.

11 Miller Corporation acquired a building for $300,000, paying $60,000 cash and issuing a long-term note payable for the balance. What is the effect of this transaction upon the working capital of Miller Corporation? How should the transaction be shown in a statement of changes in financial position?

12 During the year, holders of $4 million of Dallas Company convertible bonds converted their bonds into shares of Dallas Company common stock. The president of Dallas Company made the following statement: "By issuing common stock to retire these bonds, the company has saved $4 million in cash. Our statement of changes in financial position will not have to show the retirement of the bonds among the uses of working capital." Do you agree with this statement? Explain.

13 What is the major difference between the statement of changes in financial position and a cash flow statement?

14 Give several examples of transactions which can reduce the amount of cash generated by operations, as shown in a cash flow statement, without reducing working capital.

15 The president of Dexter Corporation was puzzled by the following statement made by the accountant: "Our working capital provided by operations amounted to $85,000 last year but our cash generated from operations was only $10,000 because of the increases in our inventory and receivables and the decrease in our accounts payable." Explain what the accountant meant.

16 An outside member of the board of directors of a small corporation made the following comment after studying the comparative financial statements for the past two years: "I have trouble understanding why our cash has increased stead-

ily during the past two years, yet our profits have been negligible; we have paid no dividends; and inventories, receivables, payables, cost of plant and equipment, long-term debt, and capital stock have remained essentially unchanged." Write a brief statement explaining how this situation might occur.

## EXERCISES

*Ex. 21-1* Indicate the amount of the increase or decrease (if any) in working capital as a result of each of the following events:

**a** Purchase and retirement of bonds payable, $1,000,000, at 96. The unamortized premium on bonds payable at the time of the retirement was $50,000.

**b** Declaration of a 25% stock dividend on $600,000 of par value capital stock outstanding.

**c** Purchase of equipment costing $400,000 for $100,000 cash and $75,000 (plus interest) payable every six months over the next two years.

**d** A $40,000 write-down of inventory to a market value below cost.

*Ex. 21-2* Briefly explain how each of the following situations should be reported in the statement of changes in financial position.

**a** Depreciation of $100,000 was recorded in Year 1; however, $25,000 of this amount is included in the ending inventory of finished goods.

**b** In July of Year 1, the 10,000 shares of $50 par value capital stock were split 3 for 1 and in November of Year 1, a 10% stock dividend was distributed.

**c** Cash of $10,000 was paid and capital stock with a market value of $90,000 was issued to acquire land worth $100,000.

*Ex. 21-3* The Tri-State Corporation reports a net loss of $80,000 on its income statement. In arriving at this figure, the following items among others were included:

| | |
|---|---|
| *Amortization of patents* | *$16,000* |
| *Amortization of premium on bonds payable* | *10,000* |
| *Gain on sale of land* | *40,000* |
| *Depreciation expense* | *50,000* |
| *Uninsured fire damage to building* | *88,400* |

What was the working capital increase or decrease as a result of ***operations?***

*Ex. 21-4* A summary of the comparative financial position for Landscape Consultants, Inc., for the current year appears below:

| | End of Current Year | Beginning of Current Year |
|---|---|---|
| Working capital | $110,000 | $125,000 |
| Land | 90,000 | 50,000 |
| Buildings | 160,000 | 100,000 |
| Less: Accumulated depreciation | (40,000) | (35,000) |
| | $320,000 | $240,000 |
| Notes payable, due in 5 years | $ 70,000 | $ -0- |
| Capital stock, no-par value | 200,000 | 200,000 |
| Retained earnings | 50,000 | 40,000 |
| | $320,000 | $240,000 |

The net income was $42,000 and included no nonoperating gains or losses. Depreciation expense for the current year was $5,000. A cash dividend was declared at the end of the current year.

Prepare a statement of changes in financial position for the current year without using a working paper.

*Ex. 21-5* The data below are taken from the records of the Ferraro Company:

| | End of Year | Beginning of Year |
|---|---|---|
| Accounts receivable | $ 20,200 | $10,200 |
| Inventories | 32,000 | 40,000 |
| Short-term prepayments | 2,300 | 1,500 |
| Accounts payable (merchandise creditors) | 28,000 | 25,000 |
| Accrued expenses payable | 1,000 | 1,200 |
| Net sales | 300,000 | |
| Cost of goods sold | 180,000 | |
| Operating expenses (includes depreciation of $10,000) | 80,000 | |

From the foregoing information, compute the following:
**a** Cash collected from customers during the year
**b** Cash paid to merchandise creditors during the year
**c** Cash paid for operating expenses during the year

*Ex. 21-6* The information below is taken from comparative financial statements for the Bear Corporation:

| | Year 10 | Year 9 |
|---|---|---|
| Net income (there were no extraordinary items) | $60,000 | $37,000 |
| Depreciation expense | 42,500 | 31,800 |
| Inventory at end of year | 15,000 | 28,000 |
| Accounts receivable at end of year | 9,000 | 12,000 |
| Accounts payable at end of year | 8,000 | 6,000 |
| Cash dividends declared in December of each year, payable Jan. 15 of following year | 22,500 | 15,000 |

From the data above, determine the following:
**a** The ***working capital*** provided by operations in Year 10
**b** The ***cash*** generated by operations in Year 10
**c** ***Working capital*** used for dividends in Year 10

## PROBLEMS

### Group A

*21A-1* Below is given a list of business transactions and adjustments. For each item you are to indicate the effect first on working capital, and second on cash. In each case the possible effects are an increase, a decrease, or no change.

(1) Payment of an account payable
(2) Depreciation recorded for the period
(3) Sale of long-term investment at a loss
(4) Payment of the current year's income tax liability, which was previously recorded in the accounting records
(5) Shares of common stock issued in exchange for convertible bonds converted by bondholders.

(6) An uncollectible account receivable written off against the Allowance for Doubtful Accounts
(7) Machinery sold for cash in excess of its carrying value
(8) Empty warehouse destroyed by fire; one-half of its carrying value covered by insurance and recorded as a receivable from the insurance company
(9) Amortization of discount on bonds payable
(10) Premium paid for a one-year insurance policy
(11) Declaration of a cash dividend
(12) Payment of previously declared cash dividend on common stock

**Instructions**

**a** List the numbers 1 to 12 on your answer sheet, and set up two columns headed "working capital effect" and "cash effect." For each transaction, write the words ***increase, decrease,*** or ***no change*** in the appropriate column to indicate the effect of the transaction on working capital and cash.

**b** Are any of the transactions listed above considered "exchange transactions" which would be listed as both a source and use of working capital in a statement of changes in financial position? Explain.

*21A-2* The following information is taken from the annual report of El Toro Corporation.

| | Year 2 | Year 1 |
|---|---|---|
| Current assets | $240,000 | $162,000 |
| Equipment | 360,000 | 252,000 |
| Less: Accumulated depreciation | (120,000) | (72,000) |
| Long-term investments | 48,000 | 60,000 |
| Current liabilities | 138,000 | 48,000 |
| Capital stock | 120,000 | 120,000 |
| Retained earnings | 270,000 | 234,000 |

Cash dividends declared amounted to $42,000; no equipment items were sold; investments were sold at a gain of $6,000; and net income (including the $6,000 nonoperating gain) for Year 2 was $78,000.

**Instructions** From the information given, prepare a statement of changes in financial position for Year 2, without using working papers.

*21A-3* Comparative account balances for Long Island Corporation at the end of Years 9 and 10 are listed below:

| | Year 10 | Year 9 |
|---|---|---|
| Cash | $ 60,000 | $ 100,000 |
| Accounts receivable (net) | 150,000 | 175,000 |
| Merchandise inventory | 325,000 | 250,000 |
| Land for future expansion | 75,000 | |
| Plant and equipment (see accumulated depreciation below) | 800,000 | 625,000 |
| Patents (net of amortization) | 90,000 | 100,000 |
| | $1,500,000 | $1,250,000 |
| Accumulated depreciation | $ 262,500 | $ 200,000 |
| Accounts payable | 152,500 | 75,000 |
| Dividends payable | 10,000 | |
| Notes payable due in Year 14 | 25,000 | |
| Capital stock, $10 par | 1,000,000 | 875,000 |
| Retained earnings | 50,000 | 100,000 |
| | $1,500,000 | $1,250,000 |

The following additional information is available for your consideration:
(1) The net loss for Year 10 amounted to $40,000.
(2) Cash dividends of $10,000 were declared.
(3) Land for future expansion was acquired.
(4) Equipment costing $175,000 was purchased for cash; $25,000 was borrowed for three years in order to pay for this equipment.
(5) Additional shares of capital stock were sold at par value.
(6) Other changes in noncurrent accounts resulted from the usual transactions recorded in such accounts.

**Instructions**

**a** Prepare a schedule showing the changes in components of working capital. Your schedule should show the balances of each current account at the beginning and at the end of Year 10 and the effect of the change in the account balance on working capital.
**b** Prepare working papers for a statement of changes in financial position for Year 10.
**c** Prepare a formal statement of changes in financial position for Year 10.

*21A-4* The following balance sheet data for Year 5 were obtained from the records of Augusta National Corporation:

| | Dec. 31 | Jan. 1 |
|---|---|---|
| Current assets | $298,700 | $202,500 |
| Plant and equipment (net) | 334,000 | 319,000 |
| Goodwill (amortized over 10 years) | 8,500 | 10,000 |
| Current liabilities | 150,000 | 81,500 |
| Bonds payable, 10% | 200,000 | -0- |
| Discount on bonds payable | 3,800 | -0- |
| Preferred stock, $100 par | -0- | 200,000 |
| Common stock, no par | 150,000 | 150,000 |
| Retained earnings | 145,000 | 100,000 |

**Additional data**

(1) The statement of retained earnings for Year 5 follows:

| | | |
|---|---|---|
| Beginning balance | | $100,000 |
| Add: Net income, including gain on disposal of land | | 80,000 |
| Subtotal | | $180,000 |
| Less: Amount paid to retire preferred stock in excess of carrying (book) value | $10,000 | |
| Cash dividends declared | 25,000 | 35,000 |
| Ending balance | | $145,000 |

(2) Ten-year bonds of $200,000 face value were issued on July 1 at 98; the proceeds and some additional cash were used to retire the entire issue of preferred stock at its call price of $105 per share.
(3) Land having a cost of $60,000 was exchanged at its fair value of $100,000 for equipment with a value of $120,000; the balance of $20,000 was paid in cash. A $40,000 gain was recognized on the exchange.
(4) Depreciation for the year was $45,000, amortization of goodwill was $1,500, and amortization of discount on bonds payable was $200.

**Instructions**

**a** Prepare a working paper for a statement of changes in financial position.

**b** Prepare a statement of changes in financial position. Report working capital provided from operations in a single amount as determined in the working paper.

*21A-5* A condensed balance sheet at Janury 1, Year 10, and the statement of changes in financial position for Year 10 for Intruder Alert, Inc., are shown below:

**INTRUDER ALERT, INC.**
**Balance Sheet**
**January 1, Year 10**

| | |
|---|---|
| **Assets** | |
| Current assets | $ 76,000 |
| Land | 50,000 |
| Equipment | 96,000 |
| Less: Accumulated depreciation | (30,000) |
| Patents (net of accumulated amortization) | 10,000 |
| Total assets | $202,000 |
| **Liabilities & Stockholders' Equity** | |
| Current liabilities | $ 36,000 |
| Capital stock, no-par value | 94,000 |
| Retained earnings | 72,000 |
| Total liabilities & stockholders' equity | $202,000 |

**INTRUDER ALERT, INC.**
**Statement of Changes in Financial Position**
**For Year 10**

| | | |
|---|---|---|
| Working capital, Jan. 1, Year 10 | | $ 40,000 |
| Sources of working capital: | | |
| Operations: | | |
| Net income | $48,000 | |
| Add: Depreciation expense | 20,000 | |
| Amortization of patents | 2,000 | |
| Less: Gain on disposal of equipment | (8,000) | |
| Working capital provided by operations | | 62,000 |
| Issuance of capital stock | | 22,000 |
| Disposal of equipment | | 14,000 |
| Subtotal | | $138,000 |
| Uses of working capital: | | |
| Dividends declared | $16,000 | |
| Purchase of land | 28,000 | |
| Purchase of equipment | 62,000 | 106,000 |
| Working capital, Dec. 31, Year 10 | | $ 32,000 |

Equipment costing $18,000, with accumulated depreciation of $12,000, was sold in Year 10. Current assets at December 31, Year 10, amounted to $80,000.

**Instructions** Using the information above, prepare a condensed balance sheet at December 31, Year 10. Show supporting computations.

*21A-6* When the controller of Trans-Alaska Corporation presented the following condensed comparative financial statements to the board of directors at the close of Year 2, the reaction of the board members was very favorable.

**TRANS-ALASKA CORPORATION**
**Comparative Income Statements**
**(in thousands of dollars)**

| | Year 2 | Year 1 |
|---|---|---|
| Net sales | $970 | $680 |
| Cost of goods sold | 590 | 480 |
| Gross profit on sales | $380 | $200 |
| Operating expenses, including depreciation of $80 in Year 2 and $60 in Year 1 | (180) | (140) |
| Income taxes | (90) | (25) |
| Net income | $110 | $ 35 |

**TRANS-ALASKA CORPORATION**
**Comparative Financial Position**
**As of December 31**
**(in thousands of dollars)**

| | | |
|---|---|---|
| Current assets | $ 410 | $395 |
| Less: Current liabilities | 200 | 225 |
| Working capital | $ 210 | $170 |
| Plant and equipment (net) | 970 | 650 |
| Total assets minus current liabilities | $1,180 | $820 |
| Financed by following sources of long-term capital: | | |
| Long-term liabilities | $ 250 | |
| Capital stock ($50 par value) | 500 | $500 |
| Retained earnings | 430 | 320 |
| Total sources of long-term capital | $1,180 | $820 |

Noting that net income rose from $3.50 per share of capital stock to $11 per share, one member of the board proposed that a substantial cash dividend be paid. "Our working capital is up by $40,000; we should be able to make a distribution to stockholders," he commented. To which the controller replied that the company's cash position was precarious and pointed out that at the end of Year 2, a cash balance of only $15,000 was on hand, a decline from $145,000 at the end of Year 1. The controller also reminded the board that the company bought $400,000 of new equipment during Year 2. When a board member asked for an explanation of the increase of $40,000 in working capital, the controller presented the following schedule (in thousands of dollars):

| | | Effect on Working Capital |
|---|---|---|
| *Increase in working capital:* | | |
| *Accounts receivable increased by* | | *$ 83* |
| *Inventories increased by* | | *45* |
| *Prepaid expenses increased by* | | *17* |
| *Accounts payable were reduced by* | | *62* |
| *Accrued expenses payable were reduced by* | | *28* |
| *Total increases in working capital* | | *$235* |
| *Decreases in working capital:* | | |
| *Cash decreased by* | *$130* | |
| *Income tax liability increased by* | *65* | *195* |
| *Increase in working capital during Year 2* | | *$ 40* |

After examining this schedule, the board member shook his head and said, "I still don't understand how our cash position can be so tight in the face of a tripling of net income and a substantial increase in working capital!"

**Instructions**

**a** Prepare a statement converting Trans-Alaska Corporation's income statement to a cash basis, determining the cash generated by operations during Year 2.

**b** From the information in **a** and an inspection of the comparative statement of financial position, prepare a cash flow statement for Year 2, explaining the $130,000 decrease in the cash balance.

**c** Prepare a statement accounting for the increase in working capital (statement of changes in financial position) for Trans-Alaska Corporation in a more acceptable form.

**d** Write a brief note of explanation to the board member.

## Group B

*21B-1* Below is given a list of business transactions and adjustments. For each item you are to indicate the effect first on working capital, and second on cash. In each case the possible effects are an increase, a decrease, or no change.

(1) Plant assets sold for cash at a price below their carrying values
(2) Declaration of a cash dividend
(3) Payment of a previously declared cash dividend
(4) One-year fire insurance policy paid in advance
(5) Inventory destroyed by fire; one-half of its carrying value covered by insurance and recorded as a receivable from the insurance company
(6) Amortization of the portion of prepaid insurance expense which expired during the current year
(7) An uncollectible account receivable written off against the Allowance for Doubtful Accounts
(8) Purchase of patent, giving 200 shares of the company's common stock in exchange
(9) Merchandise sold for cash at a price below cost
(10) Prior period adjustment made to reflect additional income taxes due on income of a prior period
(11) Marketable securities sold for cash at a price above cost
(12) Amortization of premium on bonds payable

**Instructions**

**a** List the numbers 1 to 12 on your answer sheet, and set up two columns headed "working capital effect" and "cash effect." For each transaction, write the words ***increase, decrease,*** or ***no change*** in the appropriate column to indicate the effect of the transaction on working capital and cash.

**b** Are any of the transactions listed above considered "exchange transactions" which would be listed as both a source and use of working capital in a statement of changes in financial position? Explain.

*21B-2* During Year 6 Wildcat Tractor Company showed the following ***changes*** in amount for the groups of accounts listed below. For example, current assets increased by $30,000 during Year 6, and this amount therefore appears in the "Debit" change column.

| | Changes during Year 6 | |
|---|---|---|
| | **Debit** | **Credit** |
| Current assets | $ 30,000 | |
| Plant and equipment | 160,000 | |
| Accumulated depreciation | | $ 40,000 |
| Current liabilities | 58,000 | |
| Capital stock, $10 par | | 128,000 |
| Paid-in capital in excess of par | | 32,000 |
| Retained earnings | | 48,000 |
| | $248,000 | $248,000 |

During Year 6 the company issued 12,800 shares of capital stock and applied the proceeds to the purchase of equipment. There were no retirements of plant and equipment during the year. Net income for Year 6 was $142,000 and cash dividends declared and paid during the year amounted to $94,000.

**Instructions** Prepare a statement of changes in financial position for Year 6, without using working papers.

*21B-3* Comparative post-closing trial balances for Home Port, Inc., are shown below:

| **Debits** | **Year 2** | **Year 1** |
|---|---|---|
| Cash | $ 72,000 | $ 78,000 |
| Marketable securities | | 96,000 |
| Accounts receivable | 120,000 | 228,000 |
| Inventories | 132,000 | 180,000 |
| Prepaid expenses | 36,000 | 24,000 |
| Land | 120,000 | |
| Buildings | 600,000 | |
| | $1,080,000 | $606,000 |
| **Credits** | | |
| Allowance for doubtful accounts | $ 6,000 | $ 12,000 |
| Accounts payable | 138,000 | 102,000 |
| Accrued liabilities | 102,000 | 78,000 |
| Long-term notes payable | 300,000 | 60,000 |
| Capital stock, $10 par | 396,000 | 246,000 |
| Retained earnings | 138,000 | 108,000 |
| | $1,080,000 | $606,000 |

During Year 1 Home Port, Inc., operated in rented space. Early in Year 2 the company acquired suitable land and made arrangements to borrow funds from a local bank on long-term notes to finance the construction of new buildings. The company also sold additional stock at par and all its marketable securities at book value. Construction of the buildings was not completed until the end of Year 2; therefore, no depreciation expense was recorded in Year 2. Net income for Year 2 was $78,000; cash dividends declared and paid during Year 2 amounted to $48,000.

**Instructions**

**a** Prepare a schedule of changes in components of working capital during Year 2. The schedule should show the balances of each current account at the beginning and at the end of Year 2 and the effect of the change in the account balance on working capital.

**b** Prepare working papers for a statement of changes in financial position.

**c** Prepare a formal statement of changes in financial position for Year 2, showing first the uses of working capital followed by sources of working capital.

*21B-4* Comparative balance sheets for Sierra Redwood Tub Co. at the end of Year 1 and Year 2 are shown below:

| | *Year 2* | *Year 1* |
|---|---|---|
| *Cash* | *$ 36,000* | *$ 60,000* |
| *Accounts receivable (net)* | *90,000* | *105,000* |
| *Merchandise inventory* | *195,000* | *150,000* |
| *Land for future expansion* | *45,000* | |
| *Plant and equipment (see accumulated depreciation below)* | *480,000* | *375,000* |
| *Patents (net of amortization)* | *54,000* | *60,000* |
| | *$900,000* | *$750,000* |
| *Accumulated depreciation* | *$157,500* | *$120,000* |
| *Accounts payable* | *91,500* | *45,000* |
| *Dividends payable* | *6,000* | |
| *Notes payable due in Year 5* | *15,000* | |
| *Capital stock, $10 par* | *600,000* | *525,000* |
| *Retained earnings* | *30,000* | *60,000* |
| | *$900,000* | *$750,000* |

**Additional data**

(1) The net loss for Year 2 amounted to $24,000.
(2) Cash dividends of $6,000 were declared.
(3) Land for future expansion was acquired.
(4) Equipment costing $105,000 was purchased for cash; $15,000 was borrowed for three years in order to pay for this equipment.
(5) Additional shares of capital stock were sold at par value.
(6) Other changes in noncurrent accounts resulted from the usual transactions recorded in such accounts.

**Instructions**

**a** Prepare a schedule computing the change in working capital during Year 2.

**b** Prepare working papers for a statement of changes in financial position for Year 2.

**c** Prepare a formal statement of changes in financial position for Year 2.

*21B-5* The accounting records of Earth Movers, Inc., showed the following balances at the end of Year 4 and Year 5:

| Debits | Year 5 | Year 4 |
|---|---|---|
| Cash | $ 93,000 | $ 120,000 |
| Accounts receivable | 165,000 | 105,000 |
| Merchandise inventory | 285,000 | 450,000 |
| Long-term investments | 45,000 | |
| Equipment | 1,170,000 | 675,000 |
| Accumulated depreciation | (240,000) | (180,000) |
| Land | 240,000 | 105,000 |
| | $1,758,000 | $1,275,000 |

| Credits | Year 5 | Year 4 |
|---|---|---|
| Accounts payable | $ 135,000 | $ 60,000 |
| Notes payable (current) | 15,000 | 90,000 |
| Bonds payable, due in Year 10 | 300,000 | 240,000 |
| Unamortized premium on bonds payable | 5,400 | 5,700 |
| Capital stock, $10 par | 600,000 | 450,000 |
| Paid-in capital in excess of par | 240,000 | 150,000 |
| Retained earnings | 462,600 | 279,300 |
| | $1,758,000 | $1,275,000 |

Net income for Year 5 amounted to $258,000. Cash dividends of $74,700 were declared and paid during Year 5. Additional purchases of investments, equipment, and land were completed during Year 5, financed in part through the sale of bonds at par and 15,000 shares of capital stock. Equipment costing $75,000 was sold at a price equal to its book value of $30,000.

**Instructions**

**a** Prepare a schedule of changes in working capital during Year 5.

**b** Prepare working papers for a statement of changes in financial position for Year 5. See the solution to the demonstration problem in this chapter for proper handling of the premium on bonds payable.

**c** Prepare a formal statement of changes in financial position for Year 5.

*21B-6* The financial statements shown on page 825 are presented to you by Linda Kahn, owner of Linda's Fashion Boutique.

Kahn is concerned over the decrease in her cash position during Year 2, especially in view of the fact that she invested an additional $33,000 in the business and had a net income of $39,500 during the year. She asks you to prepare a statement which will explain the decrease in the Cash account. You point out that while cash decreased by $30,000, the working capital increased by $60,000. You conclude that a statement of cash receipts and cash disbursements, showing cash collected from customers, cash paid to merchandise creditors, cash paid for operating expenses, etc., would give her the information she needs.

**Instructions**

**a** Prepare a schedule showing the conversion of the income statement from an accrual to a cash basis, thus determining the net cash outflow from operations.

**b** Prepare a cash flow statement which explains the decrease of $30,000 in cash during Year 2.

**c** Prepare a statement of changes in financial position without using a working paper. Include a supporting schedule showing changes in components of working capital.

*Balance Sheet*

| *Assets* | *Year 2* | *Year 1* |
|---|---|---|
| *Cash* | *$ 10,000* | *$ 40,000* |
| *Marketable securites* | *15,000* | *20,000* |
| *Accounts receivable (net)* | *100,000* | *35,000* |
| *Inventory* | *80,000* | *60,000* |
| *Equipment (net of accumulated depreciation)* | *35,000* | *45,000* |
| *Total assets* | *$240,000* | *$200,000* |
| ***Liabilities & Owner's Capital*** | | |
| *Accounts payable* | *$ 37,000* | *$ 40,000* |
| *Accrued liabilities* | *8,000* | *2,500* |
| *Note payable to bank (due early in Year 2)* | | *12,500* |
| *Linda Kahn, capital* | *195,000* | *145,000* |
| *Total liabilities & owner's capital* | *$240,000* | *$200,000* |

*Income Statement for Year 2*

| | | |
|---|---|---|
| *Sales (net)* | | *$400,000* |
| *Cost of goods sold* | | *300,000* |
| *Gross profit on sales* | | *$100,000* |
| *Operating expenses (including $10,000 depreciation)* | *$60,000* | |
| *Loss on sale of marketable securities* | *500* | *60,500* |
| *Net income* | | *$ 39,500* |
| *Drawings by owner* | | *22,500* |
| *Increase in owner's capital as a result of operations* | | *$ 17,000* |

## BUSINESS DECISION PROBLEM 21

Olympic Sportswear has working capital of $6,150,000 at the beginning of Year 5. Restrictions contained in bank loans require that working capital not fall below $6,000,000. The following projected information is available for Year 5:

(1) Budgeted net income (including nonoperating items) is $7,500,000. The following items were included in estimating net income: depreciation, $2,100,000; amortization of premium on bonds payable, $150,000; uncollectible accounts expense, $180,000; and income taxes, $6,300,000. The estimate of net income also included the nonoperating items described below.

(2) Sale of plant assets with a carrying value of $1,200,000 is expected to bring $1,500,000 net of income taxes.

(3) Additional plant assets costing $15,000,000 will be acquired. Payment will be as follows: 20% cash, 20% short-term note, and 60% through issuance of capital stock.

(4) Long-term investment will be sold at cost, $300,000.

(5) Bonds payable in the amount of $1,500,000, bearing interest at 11%, will be redeemed at 105 approximately 10 years prior to maturity in order to eliminate the high interest expense of $165,000 per year. The elimination of this interest and the gain or loss on the retirement of bonds payable were taken into account in estimating net income for Year 5. These bonds had been issued at par.

(6) Tentative planned cash dividend, $4,500,000.

**Instructions**

**a** Consider all the information given above and prepare a projected statement of changes in financial position (without showing the composition of working capital) in order to determine the estimated increase or decrease in working capital for Year 5. Some of the information given may be irrelevant.

**b** The planned cash dividend of $4,500,000 represents the same dividend per share as paid last year. The company would like to maintain dividends at this level. Does it appear likely that the past dividend policy can be maintained in Year 5? What factors other than working capital position should be considered in determining the level of cash dividends declared by the board of directors?

# 22

# ANALYSIS AND INTERPRETATION OF FINANCIAL STATEMENTS

Financial statements are the instrument panel of a business enterprise. They constitute a report on managerial performance, attesting to managerial success or failure and flashing warning signals of impending difficulties. To read a complex instrument panel, one must understand the gauges and their calibration to make sense out of the array of data they convey. Similarly, one must understand the inner workings of the accounting system and the significance of various financial relationships to interpret the data appearing in financial statements. To a reader with a knowledge of accounting, a set of financial statements tells a great deal about a business enterprise.

The financial affairs of a business may be of interest to a number of different groups; management, creditors, investors, politicians, union officials, and government agencies. Each of these groups has somewhat different needs, and accordingly each tends to concentrate on particular aspects of a company's financial picture.

### What is your opinion of the level of corporate profits?

As a college student who has completed (or almost completed) a course in accounting, you have a much better understanding of corporate profits than do people who have never studied accounting. The level of earnings of large corporations is a controversial topic, a favorite topic in many political speeches and at cocktail parties. Many of the statements one reads or hears from these sources are emotional rather than rational, and fiction rather than fact. Public opinion polls show that the public believes the average manufacturing company has an tainly, earnings should be compared with total assets and with invested capital as well as with sales. In this chapter we shall look at a number of ways of evaluating corporate profits and solvency.

## Sources of financial information

For the most part, this discussion will be limited to the kind of analysis that can be made by "outsiders" who do not have access to internal accounting records. Investors must rely to a considerable extent on financial statements in published annual and quarterly reports. In the case of large publicly owned corporations, additional information that must be filed with the Securities and Exchange Commission is available. Financial information for most corporations is also published by Moody's Investors Service, Standard & Poor's Corporation, and stock brokerage firms.

Bankers are usually able to secure more detailed information by requesting it as a condition for granting a loan. Trade creditors may obtain financial information for businesses of almost any size from credit-rating agencies such as Dun & Bradstreet, Inc.

**Comparative financial statements** The change in financial data over time is best exhibited in statements showing data for two or more years placed side by side in adjacent columns. Such statements are called ***comparative financial statements.***

The usefulness of comparative financial statements covering two or more years is well recognized. Published annual reports often contain comparative financial statements covering a period as long as 10 years. By observing the change in various items period by period, the analyst may gain valuable clues as to growth and other important trends affecting the business. A highly condensed comparative balance sheet is shown below.

*Condensed three-year balance sheet*

***BENSON CORPORATION***
***Comparative Balance Sheet***
***As of December 31***
***(in thousands of dollars)***

| | Year 3 | Year 2 | Year 1 |
|---|---|---|---|
| Assets: | | | |
| Current assets | $180 | $150 | $120 |
| Plant and equipment (net) | 450 | 300 | 345 |
| Total assets | $630 | $450 | $465 |
| Liabilities & Stockholders' Equity: | | | |
| Current liabilities | $ 60 | $ 80 | $120 |
| Long-term liabilities | 200 | 100 | -0- |
| Capital stock | 300 | 300 | 300 |
| Retained earnings (deficit) | 70 | (30) | 45 |
| Total liabilities & stockholders' equity | $630 | $450 | $465 |

## Tools of analysis

Few figures in a financial statement are highly significant in and of themselves. It is their relationship to other quantities, or the amount and direction of change since a previous date, that is important. Analysis is largely a matter of establishing significant relationships and pointing up changes and trends. Three widely used analytical techniques are (1) dollar and percentage changes, (2) component percentages, and (3) ratios.

**Dollar and percentage changes** The dollar amount of change from year to year is significant, but expressing the change in percentage terms adds perspective. For example, if sales this year have increased by $100,000, the fact that this is an increase of 10% over last year's sales of $1 million puts it in a different perspective than if it represented a 1% increase over sales of $10 million for the prior year.

The dollar amount of any change is the difference between the amount for a ***comparison*** year and for a ***base*** year. The percentage change is computed by dividing the amount of the change between years by the amount for the base year. This is illustrated in the tabulation below, using data from the comparative balance sheet above.

**Dollar and percentage changes**

| | *In Thousands* | | | *Increase or (Decrease)* | | | |
|---|---|---|---|---|---|---|---|
| | | | | *Year 3 over Year 2* | | *Year 2 over Year 1* | |
| | *Year 3* | *Year 2* | *Year 1* | *Amount* | *%* | *Amount* | *%* |
| *Current assets* . . . . . | *$180* | *$150* | *$120* | *$30* | *20%* | *$30* | *25%* |
| *Current liabilities* . . . . | *$ 60* | *$ 80* | *$120* | *($20)* | *(25%)* | *($40)* | *(33.3%)* |

Although current assets increased $30,000 in both Year 2 and Year 3, the percentage of change differs because of the shift in the base year from Year 1 to Year 2. These calculations present no problems when the figures for the base year are positive amounts. If a negative amount or a zero amount appears in the base year, a percentage change cannot be computed. For example, in the comparative balance sheet on page 830, there were no long-term liabilities in Year 1; therefore the percentage change from Year 1 to Year 2 for this liability cannot be calculated.

**Component percentages** The phrase "a piece of pie" is subject to varying interpretations until it is known whether the piece represents one-sixth or one-half of the total pie. The percentage relationship between any particular financial item and a significant total that includes this item is known as a ***component percentage;*** this is often a useful means of showing relationships or the relative importance of the item in question. Thus if inventories are 50% of total current assets, they are a far more significant factor in the current position of a company than if they are only 10% of total current assets.

One application of component percentages is to express each item on the balance sheet as a percentage of total assets. This shows quickly the relative importance of current and noncurrent assets, and the relative amount of financing obtained from current creditors, long-term creditors, and stockholders.

**Comparative income statement** Another application of component percentages is to express all items on an income statement as a percentage of net sales. Such a statement is sometimes called a ***common size*** income statement. A highly condensed income statement in dollars and in common size form is illustrated below.

*How successful was Year 2?*

*Income Statement*

| | Dollars | | Component Percentages | |
|---|---|---|---|---|
| | Year 2 | Year 1 | Year 2 | Year 1 |
| Net sales | $500,000 | $200,000 | 100.0% | 100.0% |
| Cost of goods sold | 350,000 | 120,000 | 70.0 | 60.0 |
| Gross profit on sales | $150,000 | $ 80,000 | 30.0% | 40.0% |
| Expenses (including income taxes) | 100,000 | 50,000 | 20.0 | 25.0 |
| Net income | $ 50,000 | $ 30,000 | 10.0% | 15.0% |

Looking only at the component percentages, we see that the decline in the gross profit rate from 40 to 30% was only partially offset by the decrease in expenses as a percentage of net sales, causing net income to decrease from 15 to 10% of net sales. The dollar amounts in the first pair of columns, however, present an entirely different picture. It is true that net sales increased faster than net income, but net income improved significantly in Year 2, a fact not apparent from a review of component percentages alone. This points out an important limitation in the use of component percentages. Changes in the component percentage may result from a change in the component, in the total, or in both. Reverting to our previous analogy, it is important to know not only the relative size of a piece of pie, but also the size of the pie; 10% of a large pie may be a bigger piece than 15% of a smaller pie.

**Ratios** A ratio is a simple mathematical expression of the relationship of one item to another. Ratios may be expressed in a number of ways. For example, if we wish to clarify the relationship between sales of $800,000 and net income of $40,000, we may state: (1) The ratio of net income to sales is 1 to 20 (or 1:20); (2) for every $1 of sales, the company has an average net income of 5 cents; (3) net income is $\frac{1}{20}$ of sales. In each case the ratio is merely a means of describing the relationship between sales and net income in a simple form.

In order to compute a meaningful ratio, there must be a significant relationship between the two figures. A ratio focuses attention on a relationship which is significant, but a full interpretation of the ratio usually requires further investigation of the underlying data. Ratios are an aid to analysis and interpretation; they are not a substitute for sound thinking.

## Standards of comparison

In using dollar and percentage changes, component percentages, and ratios, financial analysts constantly search for some standard of comparison against which to judge whether the relationships that they have found are favorable or unfavorable. Two such standards are (1) the past performance of the company and (2) the performance of other companies in the same industry.

**Past performance of the company** Comparing analytical data for a current period with similar computations for prior years affords some basis for judging whether the position of the business is improving or worsening. This comparison of data over time is sometimes called ***horizontal*** or ***dynamic*** analysis, to express the idea of reviewing data for a number of periods. It is distinguished from ***vertical*** or ***static*** analysis, which refers to the review of the financial information for only one accounting period.

In addition to determining whether the situation is improving or becoming worse, horizontal analysis may aid in making estimates of future prospects. Since changes may reverse their direction at any time, however, projecting past trends into the future is always a somewhat risky statistical pastime.

A weakness of horizontal analysis is that comparison with the past does not afford any basis for evaluation in absolute terms. The fact that net income was 2% of sales last year and is 3% of sales this year indicates improvement, but if there is evidence that net income ***should be*** 5% of sales, the record for both years is unfavorable.

**Industry standards** The limitations of horizontal analysis may be overcome to some extent by finding some other standard of performance as a yardstick against which to measure the record of any particular firm.[1] The yardstick may be a comparable company, the average record of several companies in the same industry, or some predetermined standard.

Suppose that Y Company suffers a 5% drop in its sales during the current year. The discovery that the sales of all companies in the same industry fell an average of 20% would indicate that this was a favorable rather than an unfavorable performance. Assume further that Y Company's net income is 2% of net sales. Based on comparison with other companies in the industry, this would be substandard performance if Y Company were an automobile manufacturer; but it would be a satisfactory record if Y Company were a grocery chain.

When we compare a given company with its competitors or with industry averages, our conclusions will be valid only if the companies in question are reasonably comparable. Because of the large number of diversified companies

---

[1] For example, the Robert Morris Associates publishes *Annual Statement Studies* which contains detailed data obtained from 27,000 annual reports grouped in 223 industry classifications. Assets, liabilities, and stockholders' equity are presented as a percentage of total assets; income statement amounts are expressed as a percentage of net sales; and key ratios are given (expressed as the median for each industry, the upper quartile, and the lower quartile). Measurements, within each of the 223 industry groups, are grouped according to the size of the firm. Similarly, Dun & Bradstreet, Inc., annually publishes *Key Business Ratios* in 125 lines of business divided by retailing, wholesaling, manufacturing, and construction. A total of 14 ratios are presented for each of the 125 industry groups.

formed in recent years, the term ***industry*** is difficult to define, and companies that fall roughly within the same industry may not be comparable in many respects. One company may engage only in the marketing of oil products; another may be a fully integrated producer from the well to the gas pump, yet both are said to be in the "oil industry."

Differences in accounting methods may lessen the comparability of financial data for two companies. For example, companies may employ different depreciation methods or estimates of the useful life of substantially similar assets; inventories may be valued by different methods; and the timing of revenue recognition may differ significantly among companies engaged in certain industries. Despite these limitations, studying comparative performances is a useful method of analysis if carefully and intelligently done.

## Objectives of financial analysis

Business decisions are made on the basis of the best available estimates of the outcome of such decisions. The purpose of financial analysis is to provide information about a business unit for decision-making purposes, and such information need not be limited to accounting data. While ratios and other relationships based on ***past performance*** may be helpful in predicting the future earnings performance and financial health of a company, we must be aware of the inherent limitations of such data. Financial statements are essentially summary records of the past, and we must go beyond the financial statements and look into the nature of the company, its competitive position within the industry, its product lines, its research expenditures, and, above all, the quality of its management.

The key objectives of financial analysis are to determine the company's earnings performance and the soundness and liquidity of its financial position. ***We are essentially interested in financial analysis as a predictive tool;*** accordingly, we want to examine both quantitative and qualitative data in order to ascertain the ***quality of earnings*** and the ***quality and protection of assets.*** In periods of recession when business failures are common, the balance sheet takes on increased importance because the question of liquidity is uppermost in the minds of many in the business community. When business conditions are good, the income statement receives more attention as people become absorbed in profit possibilities.

**Quality of earnings** Profits are the lifeblood of a business entity. No entity can survive for long and accomplish its other goals unless it is profitable. Continuous losses drain assets from the business, consume owners' equity, and leave the company at the mercy of creditors. For this reason, we are interested not only in the total ***amount*** of earnings but also in the ***rate*** of earnings on sales, on total assets, and on owners' equity. In addition, we must look to the ***stability*** and ***source*** of earnings. An erratic earnings performance over a period of years, for example, is less desirable than a steady level of earnings. A history of increasing earnings is preferable to a "flat" earnings record.

A breakdown of sales and earnings by ***major product lines*** is useful in evaluating the future performance of a company. In recent years publicly owned companies have broadened their reporting to include sales and profits by product lines, and the Securities and Exchange Commission now requires such reporting from large corporations.

Financial analysts often express the opinion that the earnings of one company are of higher quality than earnings of other similar companies. This concept of ***quality of earnings*** arises because each company management can choose from a variety of accounting principles and methods, all of which are considered generally acceptable. The financial analyst should ascertain whether the accounting principles and methods selected by management lead to a conservative measurement of earnings or tend to inflate current reported earnings by deferring certain costs and anticipating certain revenue. A company's management is often under heavy pressure to report rising earnings, and accounting policies may be tailored toward this objective. We have already pointed out the impact on current reported earnings of the choice between the lifo and fifo methods of inventory valuation and the choice of depreciation policies. In judging the quality of earnings, other appropriate questions are: What has been the effect on earnings of any accounting changes? How much of the net income is attributable to nonrecurring or nonoperating items? The very existence of a concept of ***quality of earnings*** is evidence that accountants still have some distance to travel in developing a body of accounting standards which will ensure a high degree of comparability of earnings reported by different companies.

**Quality of assets and the relative amount of debt** Although a satisfactory level of earnings may be a good indication of the company's long-run ability to pay its debts and dividends, we must also look at the composition of assets, their condition and liquidity, the relationship between current assets and current liabilities, and the total amount of debt outstanding. A company may be profitable and yet be unable to pay its liabilities on time; sales and earnings may be satisfactory but plant and equipment may be deteriorating because of poor maintenance policies; valuable patents may be expiring; substantial losses may be in prospect from slow-moving inventories and past-due receivables. Extensive use of credit and a liberal dividend policy may result in a low owners' equity and thus expose stockholders to substantial risks in case of a downturn in business.

## IMPACT OF INFLATION

During a period of severe inflation, financial statements which are prepared in terms of historical costs do not reflect fully the economic resources or the ***real income*** (in terms of purchasing power) of a business enterprise. We discussed in

Chapter 14 the requirements by the Financial Accounting Standards Board for large corporations to disclose both current cost and price-level-adjusted data in their annual reports. Financial analysts should therefore attempt to evaluate the impact of inflation on the financial position and operating results of the company being studied. They should raise such questions as: How much of the net income can be attributed to the increase in the general price level? Is depreciation expense understated in terms of current price levels? Are profits exaggerated because the replacement cost of inventories is higher than the cost of units charged to cost of goods sold? Is the company gaining or losing from inflation because of the composition of its assets and because its liabilities will be liquidated with "cheaper" dollars? Will the company be able to keep its "physical capital" intact by paying the higher prices necessary to replace plant assets as they wear out? The fundamental issues of modifying accounting information to cope with the impact of inflation were discussed in Chapter 14.

### Illustrative analysis for Seacliff Company

Keep in mind the above discussion of analytical principles as you study the illustrative financial analysis which follows. The basic information for our discussion is contained in a set of condensed two-year comparative financial statements for Seacliff Company shown on the following pages. Summarized statement data, together with computations of dollar increases and decreases, and component percentages where applicable, have been compiled. For convenience in this illustration, relatively small dollar amounts have been used in the Seacliff Company financial statements.

Using the information in these statements, let us consider the kind of analysis that might be of particular interest to (1) common stockholders, (2) long-term creditors, (3) preferred stockholders, and (4) short-term creditors.

***SEACLIFF COMPANY***

***Condensed Comparative Balance Sheet****

***December 31***

| | | | *Increase or (Decrease)* | | *Percentage of Total Assets* | |
|---|---|---|---|---|---|---|
| *Assets* | *Year 2* | *Year 1* | *Dollars* | *%* | *Year 2* | *Year 1* |
| *Current assets* | *$390,000* | *$288,000* | *$102,000* | *35.4* | *41.1* | *33.5* |
| *Plant and equipment (net)* | *500,000* | *467,000* | *33,000* | *7.1* | *52.6* | *54.3* |
| *Other assets (loans to officers)* | *60,000* | *105,000* | *(45,000)* | *(42.9)* | *6.3* | *12.2* |
| *Total assets* | *$950,000* | *$860,000* | *$ 90,000* | *10.5* | *100.0* | *100.0* |

| Liabilities & Stockholders' Equity | Year 2 | Year 1 | Increase or (Decrease) Dollars | % | Percentage of Total Assets Year 2 | Year 1 |
|---|---|---|---|---|---|---|
| *Liabilities:* | | | | | | |
| Current liabilities | $112,000 | $ 94,000 | $ 18,000 | (19.1) | 11.8 | 10.9 |
| Long-term liabilities | 200,000 | 250,000 | (50,000) | (20.0) | 21.1 | 29.1 |
| Total liabilities | $312,000 | $344,000 | $(32,000) | (9.3) | 32.9 | 40.0 |
| *Stockholders' equity:* | | | | | | |
| 9% preferred stock, $100 par, callable at $105 | $100,000 | $100,000 | | | 10.5 | 11.6 |
| Common stock, $50 par | 250,000 | 200,000 | $ 50,000 | 25.0 | 26.3 | 23.2 |
| Paid-in capital in excess of par | 70,000 | 40,000 | 30,000 | 75.0 | 7.4 | 4.7 |
| Retained earnings | 218,000 | 176,000 | 42,000 | 23.9 | 22.9 | 20.5 |
| Total stockholders' equity | $638,000 | $516,000 | $122,000 | 23.6 | 67.1 | 60.0 |
| Total liabilities & stockholders' equity | $950,000 | $860,000 | $ 90,000 | 10.5 | 100.0 | 100.0 |

*In order to focus attention on important subtotals, this statement is highly condensed and does not show individual asset and liability items. These details will be introduced as needed in the text discussion. For example, a list of Seacliff Company's current assets and current liabilities appears on page 847.

## SEACLIFF COMPANY
### Comparative Income Statement
### Years Ended December 31

| | Year 2 | Year 1 | Increase or (Decrease) Dollars | % | Percentage of Net Sales Year 2 | Year 1 |
|---|---|---|---|---|---|---|
| Net sales | $900,000 | $750,000 | $150,000 | 20.0 | 100.0 | 100.0 |
| Cost of goods sold | 530,000 | 420,000 | 110,000 | 26.2 | 58.9 | 56.0 |
| Gross profit on sales | $370,000 | $330,000 | $ 40,000 | 12.1 | 41.1 | 44.0 |
| *Operating expenses:* | | | | | | |
| Selling expenses | $117,000 | $ 75,000 | $ 42,000 | 56.0 | 13.0 | 10.0 |
| Administrative expenses | 126,000 | 95,000 | 31,000 | 32.6 | 14.0 | 12.7 |
| Total operating expenses | $243,000 | $170,000 | $ 73,000 | 42.9 | 27.0 | 22.7 |
| Operating income | $127,000 | $160,000 | $(33,000) | (20.6) | 14.1 | 21.3 |
| Interest expense | 24,000 | 30,000 | (6,000) | (20.0) | 2.7 | 4.0 |
| Income before income taxes | $103,000 | $130,000 | $(27,000) | (20.8) | 11.4 | 17.3 |
| Income taxes | 28,000 | 40,000 | (12,000) | (30.0) | 3.1 | 5.3 |
| Net income | $ 75,000 | $ 90,000 | $(15,000) | (16.7) | 8.3 | 12.0 |
| Earnings per share of common stock (see page 838) | $13.20 | $20.25 | $(7.05) | (34.8) | | |

**SEACLIFF COMPANY**
**Statement of Retained Earnings**
**Years Ended December 31**

| | Year 2 | Year 1 | Increase or (Decrease) Dollars | % |
|---|---|---|---|---|
| Balance, beginning of year | $176,000 | $115,000 | $61,000 | 53.0 |
| Net income | 75,000 | 90,000 | (15,000) | (16.7) |
| | $251,000 | $205,000 | $46,000 | 22.4 |
| Less: Dividends on common stock | $ 24,000 | $ 20,000 | $ 4,000 | 20.0 |
| Dividends on preferred stock | 9,000 | 9,000 | | |
| | $ 33,000 | $ 29,000 | $ 4,000 | 13.8 |
| Balance, end of year | $218,000 | $176,000 | $42,000 | 23.9 |

## Analysis by common stockholders

Common stockholders and potential investors in common stock look first at a company's earnings record. Their investment is in shares of stock, so ***earnings per share and dividends per share*** are of particular interest.

**Earnings per share of common stock** As indicated in Chapter 17, earnings per share of common stock are computed by dividing the income available to common stockholders by the number of shares of common stock outstanding. Any preferred dividend requirements must be subtracted from net income to determine income available for common stock, as shown in the following computations for Seacliff Company:

*Earnings related to number of common shares outstanding*

**Earnings per Share of Common Stock**

| | Year 2 | Year 1 |
|---|---|---|
| Net income | $75,000 | $90,000 |
| Less: Preferred dividend requirements | 9,000 | 9,000 |
| Income available for common stock (a) | $66,000 | $81,000 |
| Shares of common outstanding, during the year (b) | 5,000 | 4,000 |
| Earnings per share of common stock (a ÷ b) | $13.20 | $20.25 |

Earnings per share of common stock are shown in the income statement below the net income figure. When the income statement includes operations discontinued during the period, the earnings per share of common stock may be reported in the income statement in three amounts as follows: (1) income from continuing operations, (2) income (or loss) from discontinued operations, and (3) net income. Similar treatment may be appropriate for extraordinary items. Seacliff Company had no discontinued operations or extraordinary items and therefore the amount earned per share is computed by dividing the net income available for the common stock by the number of common shares outstanding during the year. The computation of earnings per share in more complicated situations was illustrated in Chapter 17.

**Dividend yield and price-earnings ratio** Dividends are of prime importance to some stockholders, but a secondary factor to others. In other words, some stockholders invest primarily to receive regular cash income, while others invest in stocks principally with the hope of securing capital gains through rising market prices. If a corporation is profitable and retains its earnings for expansion of the business, the expanded operations should produce an increase in the net income of the company and thus tend to make each share of stock more valuable.

As you know from your study of income taxes in Chapter 20, long-term capital gains are subject to much lower rates of income tax than ordinary income such as dividends. Consequently, some stockholders may prefer that a company retain and reinvest most of its earnings. However, most stockholders are interested in dividend income despite the relative tax disadvantage.

In comparing the merits of alternative investment opportunities, we should relate earnings and dividends per share to the ***market value*** of the stock. Dividends per share divided by market price per share determines the ***yield*** rate of a company's stock. Dividend yield is especially important to those investors whose objective is to maximize the dividend revenue from their investments.

Earnings performance of common stock is often expressed as a ***price-earnings ratio*** by dividing the market price per share by the annual earnings per share. Thus, a stock selling for $60 per share and earning $5 per share in the year just ended may be said to have a price-earnings ratio of 12 times earnings ($60 ÷ $5). The price-earnings ratio of the 30 stocks included in the Dow-Jones Industrial Average has varied widely in recent years, ranging from a low of about 6 for the group to a high of about 20.

Assume that the 1,000 additional shares of common stock issued by Seacliff on January 1, Year 2, received the full dividend of $4.80 paid in Year 2. When these new shares were issued, Seacliff Company announced that it planned to continue indefinitely the $4.80 dividend per common share currently being paid. With this assumption and the use of assumed market prices of the common stock at December 31, Year 1 and Year 2, the earnings per share and dividend yield may be summarized as follows:

***Earnings and dividends related to market price of common stock***

***Earnings and Dividends per Share of Common Stock***

| *Date* | *Assumed Market Value per Share* | *Earnings per Share* | *Price-Earnings Ratio* | *Dividends per Share* | *Dividend Yield, %* |
|---|---|---|---|---|---|
| *Dec. 31, Year 1* . . . . . . | *$125* | *$20.25* | *6* | *$5.00* | *4.0* |
| *Dec. 31, Year 2* . . . . . . | *$100* | *$13.20* | *8* | *$4.80* | *4.8* |

The decline in market value during Year 2 presumably reflects the decrease in earnings per share. Investors appraising this stock at December 31, Year 2, would consider whether a price-earnings ratio of 8 and a dividend yield of 4.8% represented a satisfactory situation in the light of alternative investment opportunities. They would also place considerable weight on estimates of the company's prospective future earnings and the probable effect of such estimated earnings on the market price of the stock and on dividend payments.

**Book value per share of common stock** The procedure for computing book value per share were fully described in Chapter 17 and will not be repeated here. We will, however, determine the book value per share of common stock for the Seacliff Company:

*Why did book value per share decrease?*

***Book Value per Share of Common Stock***

| | Year 2 | Year 1 |
|---|---|---|
| Total stockholders' equity | $638,000 | $516,000 |
| Less: Equity of preferred stockholders (1,000 shares at call price of $105) | 105,000 | 105,000 |
| Equity of common stockholders (a) | $533,000 | $411,000 |
| Shares of common stock outstanding (b) | 5,000 | 4,000 |
| Book value per share of common stock (a ÷ b) | $106.60 | $102.75 |

Book value per share was reduced by $9.35 in Year 2 as a result of dividend payments and the issuance of 1,000 additional shares of common stock at $80 per share, a figure significantly below the book value of $102.75 per share at the end of Year 1; book value was increased by earnings of $13.20 per share in Year 2, thus causing a net increase of $3.85 in the book value per share.

**Revenue and expense analysis** The trend of earnings of Seacliff Company is unfavorable and stockholders will want to know the reasons for the decline in net income. The comparative income statement on page 837 shows that despite a 20% increase in net sales, net income fell from $90,000 in Year 1 to $75,000 in Year 2, a decline of 16.7%. The ***net income as a percentage of net sales*** went from 12% to only 8.3%. The primary causes of this decline were the increases in selling expenses (56.0%), in general and administrative expenses (32.6%), and in the cost of goods sold (26.2%), all exceeding the 20% increase in net sales.

These observations suggest the need for further investigation. Suppose we find that Seacliff Company cut its selling prices in Year 2. This would explain the decrease in ***gross profit rate*** from 44% to 41.1% and would also show that sales volume in physical units rose more than 20%, since it takes proportionally more sales at lower prices to produce a given increase in dollar sales. Since the dollar amount of gross profit increased $40,000 in Year 2, the strategy of reducing sales prices to increase volume would have been successful if there had been little change in operating expenses. However, operating expenses rose by $73,000, resulting in a $33,000 decrease in operating income.

The next step would be to find which expenses increased and why. An investor may be handicapped here, because detailed operating expenses are not usually shown in published financial statements. Some conclusions, however, can be reached on the basis of even the condensed information available in the comparative income statement for Seacliff Company shown on page 837.

The substantial increase in selling expenses presumably reflects greater selling effort during Year 2 in an attempt to improve sales volume. However, the fact that selling expenses increased $42,000 while gross profit increased only $40,000 indicates that the cost of this increased sales effort was not justified in terms of results. Even more disturbing is the increase in general and administrative expenses. Some growth in administrative expenses might be expected to accompany increased sales volume, but because some of the expenses are fixed, the growth generally should be ***less than proportional*** to any increase in sales. The increase in general and administrative expenses from 12.7 to 14% of sales would be of serious concern to informed investors.

Management generally has greater control over operating expenses than over revenue. The ***operating expense ratio*** is often used as a measure of management's ability to control its operating expenses. The unfavorable trend in this ratio for Seacliff Company is shown below:

*Does a higher operating expense ratio indicate higher net income?*

***Operating Expense Ratio***

| | | Year 2 | Year 1 |
|---|---|---|---|
| Operating expenses | (a) | $243,000 | $170,000 |
| Net sales | (b) | $900,000 | $750,000 |
| Operating expense ratio (a ÷ b) | | 27.0% | 22.7% |

If management were able to increase the sales volume while at the same time increasing the gross profit rate and decreasing the operating expense ratio, the effect on net income could be quite dramatic. For example, if Seacliff Company increased its sales in Year 3 by 11% to $1,000,000, increased its gross profit rate from 41.1 to 44%, and reduced the operating expense ratio from 27 to 24%, its operating income would increase from $127,000 to $200,000 ($1,000,000 − $560,000 − $240,000), an increase of over 57%.

## Return on investment (ROI)

The rate of return on investment (often called ROI) is a test of management's efficiency in using available resources. Regardless of the size of the organization, capital is a scarce resource and must be used efficiently. In other words, management has a limited amount of dollars to work with, and a good manager is the one who can get the most out of the resources which are available. In judging the performance of branch managers or of company-wide management, it is reasonable to raise the question: What rate of return have you earned on the resources under your control? The concept of return on investment can be applied to a number of situations: for example, evaluating a branch, a total business, a product line, or an individual investment. A number of different ratios have been developed for the ROI concept, each well suited to a particular situation. We shall consider the return on total assets and the return on common stockholders' equity as examples of the return on investment concept.

**Return on total assets** An important test of management's ability to earn a return on funds supplied from all sources is the rate of return on total assets.

The income figure used in computing this ratio should be ***income before deducting interest expense,*** since interest is a payment to creditors for money used to ***acquire assets.*** Income before interest reflects earnings throughout the year and therefore should be related to the ***average*** investment in assets during the year. The computation of this ratio for Seacliff Company is shown below:

*Earnings related to investment in assets*

***Percentage Return on Total Assets***

| | | Year 2 | Year 1 |
|---|---|---|---|
| Net income | | $ 75,000 | $ 90,000 |
| Add back: Interest expense | | 24,000 | 30,000 |
| Income before interest expense | (a) | $ 99,000 | $120,000 |
| Total assets, beginning of year | | $860,000 | $820,000 |
| Total assets, end of year | | 950,000 | 860,000 |
| Average investment in assets | (b) | $905,000 | $840,000 |
| Return on total assets (a ÷ b) | | 10.9% | 14.3% |

This ratio shows that earnings per dollar of assets invested have fallen off in Year 2. If the same ratios were available for other companies of similar kind and size, the significance of this decline could be better appraised.

Management's effectiveness in the use of assets can be measured by dividing sales for the year by the average assets used in producing these sales. In computing this ***asset turnover*** rate, those assets not contributing directly to sales (such as long-term investments and loans to officers) should be excluded. A higher asset turnover suggests that management is making better use of assets, and if the ratio of income (before interest expense) to sales remains relatively constant, a higher rate of return on total assets will result.[2]

**Return on common stockholders' equity** Because interest and dividends paid to creditors and preferred stockholders are fixed in amount, a company may earn a

[2] In order to show that the return on total assets is dependent on both the asset turnover rate and the earnings rate on sales, we can develop the following formula:

$$\frac{\text{Sales}}{\text{Assets}} \times \frac{\text{Income before interest expense}}{\text{Sales}} = \text{Return on assets}$$

If we assume sales of $100, assets of $50, and net income of $10, the formula yields the following result:

$$\frac{\$100}{\$50} \times \frac{\$10}{\$100} = 20\%$$

The asset turnover (2 times) multiplied by earnings rate on sales (10%) results in a 20% return on assets. Assume that management is able to improve the asset turnover by increasing sales to $200 without increasing total assets and that the earnings rate on sales actually declines to 8%. Then the formula yields:

$$\frac{\$200}{\$50} \times \frac{\$16}{\$200} = 32\%$$

Despite a lower earnings rate on sales (8%), the return on total assets increased dramatically because assets were more effectively utilized, as indicated by the higher asset turnover rate of 4 times ($200 ÷ $50).

greater or smaller return on the common stockholders' equity than on its total assets. The computation of return on stockholders' equity for Seacliff Company is shown below:

***Does the use of leverage benefit common stockholders?***

**Return on Common Stockholders' Equity**

| | | Year 2 | Year 1 |
|---|---|---|---|
| *Net income* | | *$ 75,000* | *$ 90,000* |
| *Less: Preferred dividend requirements* | | *9,000* | *9,000* |
| *Net income available for common stock* | *(a)* | *$ 66,000* | *$ 81,000* |
| *Common stockholders' equity, beginning of year* | | *$416,000* | *$355,000* |
| *Common stockholders' equity, end of year* | | *538,000* | *416,000* |
| *Average common stockholders' equity* | *(b)* | *$477,000* | *$385,500* |
| *Return on common stockholders' equity (a ÷ b)* | | *13.8%* | *21.0%* |

In both years the rate of return to common stockholders was higher than the return on total assets, because the average combined rate of interest paid to creditors and dividends paid to preferred stockholders was less than the rate earned on each dollar of assets used in the business.

## Leverage

When the return on total assets is higher than the average cost of borrowed capital, as was the case in Seacliff Company, the common stockholders may benefit from the use of leverage. ***Leverage*** (or ***trading on the equity***) refers to buying assets with money raised by borrowing or by issuing preferred stock. If the borrowed capital can be invested to earn a return ***greater*** than the cost of borrowing, then the net income and the return on common stockholders' equity will ***increase.*** In other words, if you can borrow money at 12% and use it to earn 14%, you will benefit by doing so. However, leverage can act as a "double-edged sword"; the effects may be favorable or unfavorable to the holders of common stock. If the return on total assets should fall ***below*** the average cost of borrowed capital, leverage will ***reduce*** net income and the return on common stockholders' equity. When this unfavorable situation occurs, one possible solution would be to pay off the loans that carry high interest rates. However, most companies do not have sufficient amounts of cash to retire long-term debt or preferred stock on short notice. Therefore, the common stockholders may become "locked in" for a long period of time to the unfavorable effects of leverage.

When the return on assets exceeds the cost of borrowed capital, the extensive use of leverage can increase dramatically the return on common stockholders' equity. However, extensive leverage also increases the ***risk*** to common stockholders that their return may be reduced dramatically in future years. Furthermore, if a business incurs so much debt that it becomes unable to meet the required interest and principal payments, creditors may force liquidation or reorganization of the business, to the detriment of stockholders.

In deciding how much leverage is appropriate, the common stockholders

**Yield rate on bonds** T
cannot be computed i
because bonds, unlike
ownership of a 12%, 10
of 10 years and the rig
If the market price of
bond is the rate of inte
tual rights equal to $
*market price of the bo*
will fall; if interest rat
is above maturity valu
price of a bond is belo
interest rate.

**Number of times intere**
ence that one of the be
that, over the life of t
interest requirements
may have serious repe
A common measur
payment of interest to
This computation for

***Long-term creditors watch this ratio***

*Operating income (before i*
*Annual interest expense* .
*Times interest earned (a ÷*

The ratio remained unc
times interest earned
electric utilities industr
companies presently a
varying from 2 to 6.

**Debt ratio** Long-term c
in relation to the amou
is computed by dividin
Company.

***What portion of total assets is financed by debt?***

*Total liabilities* . . . . . . . .
*Total assets (or total liabilit*
*Debt ratio (a ÷ b)* . . . . . .

should consider the *stab*
relationship of this retu
should consider the amou
increase the return on t

Leverage most freque
current and long-term li
est payments are deducti
achieved through the issu
are *not* deductible for in
this respect will be muc

**Equity ratio** One indicat
equity ratio. This ratio n
stockholders, as distingu
stockholders' equity by t
of leverage, that is, a larg
equity ratio, on the other
leverage.

The equity ratio at ye

| Proportion of assets financed by stockholders | |
|---|---|
| | *Total stockholders' equity* . . |
| | *Total assets (or total liabilities* |
| | *Equity ratio (a ÷ b)* . . . . . |

Seacliff Company has a
favorable or unfavorable

From the viewpoint of
duce maximum benefits i
greater than the rate of i
can be very unfavorable
paid to creditors. Since t
has declined from 14.3% i
mon stockholders should
ment in Year 2 of retiring
common stockholders fro
on assets continue to dec

**Analysis by long-term cr**

Bondholders and other lo
tors: (1) the rate of retur
interest requirements, an
when it falls due.



From a creditor's viewpoint, the lower the debt ratio (or the higher the equity ratio) the better, since this means that stockholders have contributed the bulk of the funds to the business, and therefore the margin of protection to creditors against a shrinkage of the assets is high.

### Analysis by preferred stockholders

If preferred stock is convertible, the interests of preferred stockholders are similar to those of common stockholders. If preferred stock is not convertible, the interests of preferred stockholders are more closely comparable to those of long-term creditors.

Preferred stockholders are interested in the yield on their investment. The yield is computed by dividing the dividend per share by the market value per share. The dividend per share of Seacliff Company preferred stock is $9. If we assume that the market value at December 31, Year 2, is $60 per share, the yield rate at that time would be 15% ($9 ÷ $60).

The primary measurement of the safety of an investment in preferred stock is the ability of the firm to meet its preferred dividend requirements. The best test of this ability is the ratio of the net income available to pay the preferred dividend to the amount of the annual dividend, as follows:

*Times Preferred Dividends Earned*

| Is the preferred dividend safe? | | | Year 2 | Year 1 |
|---|---|---|---|---|
| | *Net income available to pay preferred dividends* . . . . . . . . . . . . . . | *(a)* | *$75,000* | *$90,000* |
| | *Annual preferred dividend requirements* . . . . . . . . . . . . . . . . . . . . | *(b)* | *$ 9,000* | *$ 9,000* |
| | *Times dividends earned (a ÷ b)* . . . . . . . . . . . . . . . . . . . . . . . . | | *8.3* | *10* |

Although the margin of protection declined in Year 2, the annual preferred dividend requirement still appears well protected.

**Weakness of preferred stocks when interest rates rise** Investors buy preferred stocks principally for the regular dividends they pay, just as investors buy bonds in order to receive regular interest payments. But what happens to the market price of an 8% preferred stock, originally issued at par of $100, if government policy and other factors cause interest rates to rise to, say, 18 or 20%? The market price of the preferred stock will decline to less than half its original issuance price. Unlike bonds, preferred stock does not have a maturity date. Bonds with relatively low interest rates tend to rise to their face value as they approach payoff at maturity. No such upward force affects preferred stocks.

In recent years new government bonds and U.S. Treasury bills, as well as corporate bonds and notes, have been offered at interest rates of 15% and more. Why should investors buy existing preferred stocks at prices and dividend rates that offer a lower yield than high-quality bonds and notes? The conclusion is that investors in preferred stocks should recognize the threat posed by a possible increase in interest rates.

## Analysis by short-term creditors

Bankers and other short-term creditors share the interest of stockholders and bondholders in the profitability and long-run stability of a business. Their primary interest, however, is in the current position of the firm—its ability to generate sufficient funds (working capital) to meet current operating needs and to pay current debts promptly. Thus the analysis of financial statements by a banker considering a short-term loan, or by a trade creditor investigating the credit status of a customer, is likely to center on the working capital position of the prospective debtor.

**Amount of working capital** The details of the working capital of Seacliff Company are shown below:

***SEACLIFF COMPANY***
***Comparative Schedule of Working Capital***
***As of December 31***

| | | | *Increase or (Decrease)* | | *Percentage of Total Current Items* | |
|---|---|---|---|---|---|---|
| | *Year 2* | *Year 1* | *Dollars* | *%* | *Year 2* | *Year 1* |
| *Current assets:* | | | | | | |
| *Cash* | *$ 38,000* | *$ 40,000* | *$ (2,000)* | *(5.0)* | *9.7* | *13.9* |
| *Receivables (net)* | *117,000* | *86,000* | *31,000* | *36.0* | *30.0* | *29.9* |
| *Inventories* | *180,000* | *120,000* | *60,000* | *50.0* | *46.2* | *41.6* |
| *Prepaid expenses* | *55,000* | *42,000* | *13,000* | *31.0* | *14.1* | *14.6* |
| *Total current assets* | *$390,000* | *$288,000* | *$102,000* | *35.4* | *100.0* | *100.0* |
| *Current liabilities:* | | | | | | |
| *Notes payable to creditors* | *$ 14,600* | *$ 10,000* | *$ 4,600* | *46.0* | *13.1* | *10.7* |
| *Accounts payable* | *66,000* | *30,000* | *36,000* | *120.0* | *58.9* | *31.9* |
| *Accrued liabilities* | *31,400* | *54,000* | *(22,600)* | *(41.9)* | *28.0* | *57.4* |
| *Total current liabilities* | *$112,000* | *$ 94,000* | *$ 18,000* | *19.1* | *100.0* | *100.0* |
| *Working capital* | *$278,000* | *$194,000* | *$ 84,000* | *43.3* | | |

The amount of working capital is measured by the ***excess of current assets over current liabilities.*** Thus, working capital represents the amount of cash, near-cash items, and cash substitutes (prepayments) on hand after providing for payment of all current liabilities.

This schedule shows that current assets increased $102,000, while current liabilities rose by only $18,000, with the result that working capital increased $84,000. There was a shift in the composition of the current assets and current liabilities; cash decreased from 13.9 to 9.7% of current assets, and inventory rose from 41.6 to 46.2%. Inventory is a less liquid resource than cash. Therefore, although the amount of working capital increased in Year 2, the quality of working capital is not as liquid as in Year 1. Although creditors want to see large and the average balance of inventories maintained throughout the year indicates the number of times that inventories "turn over" and are replaced each year.

Ideally we should total the inventories at the end of each month and divide by 12 to obtain an average inventory. This information is not always available, however, and the nearest substitute is a simple average of the inventory at the beginning and at the end of the year. This tends to overstate the turnover rate, since many companies choose an accounting year that ends when inventories are at a minimum.

Assuming that only beginning and ending inventories are available, the computation of inventory turnover for Seacliff Company may be illustrated as follows:

**What does inventory turnover mean?**

***Inventory Turnover***

| | | Year 2 | Year 1 |
|---|---|---|---|
| *Cost of goods sold* | (a) | $530,000 | $420,000 |
| *Inventory, beginning of year* | | $120,000 | $100,000 |
| *Inventory, end of year* | | 180,000 | 120,000 |
| *Average inventory* | (b) | $150,000 | $110,000 |
| *Average inventory turnover per year (a ÷ b)* | | 3.5 times | 3.8 times |
| *Average days to turn over (divide 365 days by inventory turnover)* | | 104 days | 96 days |

The trend indicated by this analysis is unfavorable, since the average investment in inventories in relation to the cost of goods sold is rising. Stating this another way, the company required on the average 8 days more during Year 2 to turn over its inventories than during Year 1. Furthermore, the inventory status ***at the end of the year*** has changed even more: At the end of Year 1 there were 104 days' sales represented in the ending inventory ($120,000/$420,000 × 365 days) compared with 124 days' sales contained in the ending inventory at the end of Year 2 ($180,000/$530,000 × 365 days).

The relation between inventory turnover and gross profit per dollar of sales may be significant. A high inventory and a low gross profit rate frequently go hand in hand. This, however, is merely another way of saying that if the gross profit rate is low, a high volume of business is necessary to produce a satisfactory return on total assets. Although a high inventory turnover is usually regarded as a good sign, a rate that is high in relation to that of similar firms may indicate that the company is losing sales by a failure to maintain an adequate stock of goods to serve its customers promptly.

**Accounts receivable turnover** The turnover of accounts receivable is computed in a manner comparable to that just described for inventories. The ratio between the net sales for the period and the average balance in accounts receivable is a rough indication of the average time required to convert receivables into cash. Ideally, a monthly average of receivables should be used, and only ***sales on credit***

should be included in the sales figure. For illustrative purposes, we shall assume that Seacliff Company sells entirely on credit and that only the beginning and ending balances of receivables are available:

***Accounts Receivable Turnover***

*Are customers paying promptly?*

| | | Year 2 | Year 1 |
|---|---|---|---|
| Net sales on credit | (a) | $900,000 | $750,000 |
| Receivables, beginning of year | | $ 86,000 | $ 80,000 |
| Receivables, end of year | | 117,000 | 86,000 |
| Average receivables | (b) | $101,500 | $ 83,000 |
| Receivable turnover per year (a ÷ b) | | 8.9 times | 9.0 times |
| Average age of receivables (divide 365 days by receivable turnover) | | 41 days | 41 days |

There has been no significant change in the average time required to collect receivables. The interpretation of the average age of receivables would depend upon the company's credit terms and the seasonal activity immediately before year-end. If the company grants 30-day credit terms to its customers, for example, the above analysis indicates that accounts receivable collections are lagging. If the terms were for 60 days, however, there is evidence that collections are being made ahead of schedule.

In Chapter 5 we defined the term ***operating cycle*** as the average time period between the purchase of merchandise and the conversion of this merchandise back into cash. In other words, the merchandise acquired for inventory is gradually converted into accounts receivable by selling goods to customers on credit, and these receivables are converted into cash through the process of collection. The word ***cycle*** refers to the circular flow of capital from cash to inventory to receivables to cash again.

The ***operating cycle*** in Year 2 was approximately 145 days (computed by adding the 104 days required to turn over inventory and the average 41 days required to collect receivables). This compares to an operating cycle of only 137 days in Year 1, computed as 96 days to dispose of the inventory plus 41 days to collect the resulting receivables. A trend toward a longer operating cycle suggests that inventory and receivables are increasing relative to sales and that profits may be hurt because of lower sales volume and an increasing investment in current assets.

## Summary of analytical measurements

The basic ratios and other measurements discussed in this chapter and their significance are summarized on page 852.

The student should keep in mind the fact that the full significance of any of the foregoing ratios or other measurements depends on the ***direction of its trend*** and on its ***relationship to some predetermined standard*** or industry average.

| Ratio or Other Measurement | Method of Computation | Significance |
|---|---|---|
| 1 Earnings per share of common stock | $\frac{\text{Net income} - \text{preferred dividends}}{\text{Shares of common outstanding}}$ | Gives the amount of earnings applicable to a share of common stock. |
| 2 Dividend yield | $\frac{\text{Dividend per share}}{\text{Market price per share}}$ | Shows the rate earned by stockholders based on current price for a share of stock. |
| 3 Price-earnings ratio | $\frac{\text{Market price per share}}{\text{Earnings per share}}$ | Indicates whether price of stock is in line with earnings. |
| 4 Book value per share of common stock | $\frac{\text{Common stockholders' equity}}{\text{Shares of common outstanding}}$ | Measures the recorded value of net assets behind each share of common stock. |
| 5 Operating expense ratio | $\frac{\text{Operating expenses}}{\text{Net sales}}$ | Indicates management's ability to control expenses. |
| 6 Return on total assets | $\frac{\text{Net income} + \text{interest expense}}{\text{Average investment in assets}}$ | Measures the productivity of assets regardless of capital structures. |
| 7 Return on common stockholders' equity | $\frac{\text{Net income} - \text{preferred dividends}}{\text{Average common stockholders' equity}}$ | Indicates the earning power of common stockholders' equity. |
| 8 Equity ratio | $\frac{\text{Total stockholders' equity}}{\text{Total assets}}$ | Shows the protection to creditors and the extent of leverage being used. |
| 9 Number of times interest earned | $\frac{\text{Operating income}}{\text{Annual interest expense}}$ | Measures the coverage of interest requirements, particularly on long-term debt. |
| 10 Debt ratio | $\frac{\text{Total liabilities}}{\text{Total assets}}$ | Indicates the percentage of assets financed through borrowing; it shows the extent of leverage being used. |
| 11 Times preferred dividends earned | $\frac{\text{Net income}}{\text{Annual preferred dividends}}$ | Shows the adequacy of current earnings to pay dividends on preferred stock. |
| 12 Current ratio | $\frac{\text{Current assets}}{\text{Current liabilities}}$ | Measures short-run debt-paying ability. |
| 13 Quick (acid-test) ratio | $\frac{\text{Quick assets}}{\text{Current liabilities}}$ | Measures the short-term liquidity of a firm. |
| 14 Inventory turnover | $\frac{\text{Cost of goods sold}}{\text{Average inventory}}$ | Indicates management's ability to control the investment in inventory. |
| 15 Accounts receivable turnover | $\frac{\text{Net sales on credit}}{\text{Average receivables}}$ | Indicates reasonableness of accounts receivable balance and effectiveness of collections. |

## KEY TERMS INTRODUCED OR EMPHASIZED IN CHAPTER 22

**Common size financial statement** All items are stated in percentages rather than dollar amounts. In the balance sheet each item is expressed as a percentage of total assets; in the income statement each item is expressed as a percentage of net sales.

**Comparative financial statements** Financial statement data for two or more successive years placed side by side in adjacent columns to facilitate study of changes.

**Component percentage** The percentage relationship of any financial statement item to a total including that item. For example, each type of asset as a percentage of total assets.

**Horizontal analysis** Comparison of the change in a financial statement item such as inventories during two or more accounting periods.

**Leverage** Refers to the practice of financing assets with borrowed capital. Extensive leverage creates the possibility for the rate of return on common stockholders' equity to be substantially above or below the rate of return on total assets. When the rate of return on total assets exceeds the average cost of borrowed capital, leverage increases net income and the return on common stockholders' equity. However, when the return on total assets is less than the average cost of borrowed capital, leverage reduces net income and the return on common stockholders' equity. Leverage is also called ***trading on the equity.***

**Quality of assets** The concept that some companies have assets of better quality than others, such as well-balanced composition of assets, well-maintained plant and equipment, and receivables that are all current. A lower quality of assets might be indicated by poor maintenance of plant and equipment, slow-moving inventories with high danger of obsolescence, past-due receivables, and patents approaching an expiration date.

**Quality of earnings** Earnings are said to be of high quality if they are stable, the source seems assured and the methods used in measuring income are conservative. The existence of this concept suggests that the range of alternative but acceptable accounting principles may still be too wide to produce financial statements that are comparable.

**Rate of return on investment (ROI)** The overall test of management's ability to earn a satisfactory return on the assets under its control. Numerous variations of the ROI concept are used such as return on total assets, return on total equities, etc.

**Ratios** See page 852 for list of ratios, methods of computation, and significance.

**Vertical analysis** Comparison of a particular financial statement item to a total including that item, such as inventories as a percentage of current assets, or operating expenses in relation to net sales.

## DEMONSTRATION PROBLEM FOR YOUR REVIEW

The accounting records of King Corporation showed the following balances at the end of Years 1 and 2:

| | Year 2 | Year 1 |
|---|---|---|
| Cash | $ 35,000 | $ 25,000 |
| Accounts receivable (net) | 91,000 | 90,000 |
| Inventory | 160,000 | 140,000 |
| Short-term prepayments | 4,000 | 5,000 |
| Investment in land | 90,000 | 100,000 |
| Equipment | 880,000 | 640,000 |
| Less: Accumulated depreciation | (260,000) | (200,000) |
| | $1,000,000 | $ 800,000 |
| Accounts payable | $ 105,000 | $ 46,000 |
| Income taxes payable and other accrued liabilities | 40,000 | 25,000 |
| Bonds payable—8% | 280,000 | 280,000 |
| Premium on bonds payable | 3,600 | 4,000 |
| Capital stock, $5 par | 165,000 | 110,000 |
| Retained earnings | 406,400 | 335,000 |
| | $1,000,000 | $ 800,000 |
| Sales (net of discounts and allowances) | $2,200,000 | $1,600,000 |
| Cost of goods sold | 1,606,000 | 1,120,000 |
| Gross profit on sales | $ 594,000 | $ 480,000 |
| Expenses (including $22,400 interest expense) | (330,000) | (352,000) |
| Income taxes | (91,000) | (48,000) |
| Extraordinary loss | (6,600) | -0- |
| Net income | $ 166,400 | $ 80,000 |

Cash dividends of $40,000 were paid and a 50% stock dividend was distributed early in Year 2. All sales were made on credit at a relatively uniform rate during the year. Inventory and receivables did not fluctuate materially. The market price of the company's stock on December 31, Year 2, was $86 per share; on December 31, Year 1, it was $43.50 (before the 50% stock dividend distributed in Year 2).

**Instructions** Compute the following for Year 2 and Year 1:

(1) Quick ratio
(2) Current ratio
(3) Equity ratio
(4) Debt ratio
(5) Book value per share of capital stock (based on shares outstanding after 50% stock dividend in Year 2)
(6) Earnings per share of capital stock (including extraordinary loss)
(7) Price-earnings ratio
(8) Gross profit percentage
(9) Operating expense ratio
(10) Income before extraordinary loss as a percentage of net sales
(11) Inventory turnover (Assume an average inventory of $150,000 for both years.)
(12) Accounts receivable turnover (Assume average accounts receivable of $90,000 for Year 1.)
(13) Times bond interest earned (before interest expense and income taxes)

## SOLUTION TO DEMONSTRATION PROBLEM

| | Year 2 | Year 1 |
|---|---|---|
| ***(1) Quick ratio:*** | | |
| *$126,000 ÷ $145,000* | *.9 to 1* | |
| *$115,000 ÷ $71,000* | | *1.6 to 1* |
| ***(2) Current ratio:*** | | |
| *$290,000 ÷ $145,000* | *2 to 1* | |
| *$260,000 ÷ $71,000* | | *3.7 to 1* |
| ***(3) Equity ratio:*** | | |
| *$571,400 ÷ $1,000,000* | *57%* | |
| *$445,000 ÷ $800,000* | | *56%* |
| ***(4) Debt ratio:*** | | |
| *$428,600 ÷ $1,000,000* | *43%* | |
| *$355,000 ÷ $800,000* | | *44%* |
| ***(5) Book value per share of capital stock:*** | | |
| *$571,400 ÷ 33,000 shares* | *$17.32* | |
| *$445,000 ÷ 33,000* shares* | | *$13.48* |
| ***(6) Earnings per share of capital stock (including extraordinary loss of $0.20 per share in Year 2):*** | | |
| *$166,400 ÷ 33,000 shares* | *$5.04* | |
| *$80,000 ÷ 33,000* shares* | | *$2.42* |
| ***(7) Price-earnings ratio:*** | | |
| *$86 ÷ $5.04* | *17 times* | |
| *$43.50 ÷ 1.5* = $29, adjusted market price; $29 ÷ $2.42* | | *12 times* |
| ***(8) Gross profit percentage:*** | | |
| *$594,000 ÷ $2,200,000* | *27%* | |
| *$480,000 ÷ $1,600,000* | | *30%* |
| ***(9) Operating expense ratio:*** | | |
| *($330,000 − $22,400) ÷ $2,200,000* | *14%* | |
| *($352,000 − $22,400) ÷ $1,600,000* | | *20.6%* |
| ***(10) Income before extraordinary loss as a percentage of net sales:*** | | |
| *$173,000 ÷ $2,200,000* | *7.9%* | |
| *$80,000 ÷ $1,600,000* | | *5%* |
| ***(11) Inventory turnover:*** | | |
| *$1,606,000 ÷ $150,000* | *10.7 times* | |
| *$1,120,000 ÷ $150,000* | | *7.5 times* |
| ***(12) Accounts receivable turnover:*** | | |
| *$2,200,000 ÷ $90,500* | *24.3 times* | |
| *$1,600,000 ÷ $90,000* | | *17.8 times* |
| ***(13) Times bond interest earned:*** | | |
| *($166,400 + $22,400 + $91,000) ÷ $22,400* | *12.5 times* | |
| *($80,000 + $22,400 + $48,000) ÷ $22,400* | | *6.7 times* |

*Adjusted retroactively for 50% stock dividend.

| | Harvest King | Industry Average |
|---|---|---|
| *Sales (net)* | $2,000,000 | 100% |
| *Cost of goods sold* | 1,440,000 | 68 |
| *Gross profit on sales* | $ 560,000 | 32% |
| *Operating expenses:* | | |
| *Selling* | $ 160,000 | 7% |
| *General and administrative* | 180,000 | 10 |
| *Total operating expenses* | $ 340,000 | 17% |
| *Operating income* | $ 220,000 | 15% |
| *Income taxes* | 55,000 | 6 |
| *Net income* | $ 165,000 | 9% |

**Instructions**

**a** Prepare a two-column common size income statement. The first column should show for Harvest King all items expressed as a percentage of net sales. (Round all figures to the nearest whole percent.) The second column should show as an industry average the percentage data given in the problem. The purpose of this common size statement is to compare the operating results of Harvest King for Year 1 with the average for the industry.

**b** Comment specifically on differences between Harvest King and the industry average with respect to gross profit on sales, selling expenses, general and administrative expenses, operating income, income taxes, and net income. Suggest possible reasons for the more important disparities.

*22A-3* Listed below is the working capital information for the Washington Corporation at the end of Year 1:

| | |
|---|---|
| *Cash* | $225,000 |
| *Temporary investments in marketable securities* | 120,000 |
| *Notes receivable—current* | 180,000 |
| *Accounts receivable* | 300,000 |
| *Allowance for doubtful accounts* | 15,000 |
| *Inventory* | 240,000 |
| *Prepaid expenses* | 30,000 |
| *Notes payable within one year* | 90,000 |
| *Accounts payable* | 247,500 |
| *Accrued liabilities* | 22,500 |

The following transactions are completed early in Year 2:

(0) Sold inventory costing $36,000 for $30,000.
(1) Declared a cash dividend, $120,000.
(2) Declared a 10% stock dividend.
(3) Paid accounts payable, $60,000.
(4) Purchased goods on account, $45,000.
(5) Collected cash on accounts receivable, $90,000.
(6) Borrowed cash on short-term note, $150,000.
(7) Issued additional shares of capital stock for cash, $450,000.
(8) Sold temporary investments costing $30,000 for $27,000 cash.
(9) Acquired temporary investments, $52,500. Paid cash.

(10) Wrote off uncollectible accounts, $9,000.
(11) Sold inventory costing $37,500 for $48,000.
(12) Acquired plant and equipment for cash, $240,000.

**Instructions**

**a** Compute the amount of quick assets, current assets, and current liabilities at the end of Year 1.

**b** Use the data compiled in part **a** to compute: (1) current ratio; (2) acid-test ratio; and (3) working capital.

**c** Indicate the effect (increase, decrease, none) of each transaction listed above for ***Year 2*** on the current ratio, acid-test ratio, and working capital. Use the following four-column format (item *0* is given as an example):

| | *Effect on* | | |
|---|---|---|---|
| ***Item*** | ***Current Ratio*** | ***Acid-Test Ratio*** | ***Working Capital*** |
| *0* | *Decrease* | *Increase* | *Decrease* |

*22A-4* The following information is taken from the records of Frost Corporation at the end of Year 1:

| | |
|---|---|
| *Sales (all on credit)* | *$600,000* |
| *Cost of goods sold* | *360,000* |
| *Average inventory (fifo method)* | *60,000* |
| *Average accounts receivable* | *100,000* |
| *Net income for Year 1* | *24,000* |
| *Total assets* | *$250,000* |
| *Total liabilities* | *140,000* |

The corporation did not declare dividends during the year and capital stock was neither issued nor retired. The liabilities consisted of accounts payable and accrued items; no interest expense was incurred.

**Instructions** From the information given, compute the following for Year 1: (Any answers expressed as percentages should be rounded to the nearest percent.)

**a** Inventory turnover.

**b** Accounts receivable turnover.

**c** Total operating expenses, assuming that income taxes amounted to $6,000.

**d** Gross profit percentage.

**e** Rate earned on average stockholders' equity. Average stockholders' equity should be computed as the average of two amounts: (1) stockholders' equity at the beginning of Year 1, and (2) stockholders' equity at the end of Year 1. Both these amounts can be derived from information given in the problem.

**f** Rate earned on total assets. (Use end-of-year total.)

**g** Frost Corporation has an opportunity to obtain a long-term loan at an annual interest rate of 9% and could use this additional capital at the same rate of profitability as indicated above. Would obtaining the loan be desirable from the viewpoint of the stockholders? Explain.

*22A-5* Given below are selected balance sheet items and ratios for the Metro Corporation at June 30, Year 8:

| | |
|---|---|
| *Total stockholders' equity (includes 100,000 shares of $6 par value capital stock issued at $6 per share, also retained earnings)* | *$1,000,000* |
| *Plant and equipment (net)* | *470,000* |
| *Asset turnover rate per year (sales ÷ total assets)* | *3 times* |
| *Inventory turnover rate per year* | *6 times* |
| *Average accounts receivable collection period (assuming a 360-day year)* | *30 days* |
| *Gross profit percentage* | *30%* |
| *Ratio of current liabilities to stockholders' equity (there is no long-term debt)* | *1.2 to 1* |
| *Acid-test ratio (quick ratio)* | *0.8 to 1* |

Assume that balance sheet figures did not change significantly during the year and that all sales are made on account.

**Instructions** From the foregoing information, construct a balance sheet for the Metro Corporation at June 30, Year 8, in as much detail as the data permit. It is suggested that you prepare the right-hand side of the balance sheet first. The following sequence of steps affords one convenient approach:

(1) List the capital stock (as given in the problem) in the stockholders' equity section.
(2) Compute the amount of retained earnings on the assumption that there are only two items comprising stockholders' equity.
(3) Use the ratio of 1.2 (given in the problem) between current liabilities and stockholders' equity to determine the amount of current liabilities. Then determine the balance sheet total for liabilities and stockholders' equity. Also record the total assets.
(4) Compute accounts receivable by two steps:
   (a) Compute sales by using asset turnover rate (given as 3).
   (b) Compute accounts receivable by relating the average collection period (given as 30 days) to the year's sales.
(5) Compute inventory by two steps:
   (a) Compute cost of goods sold (sales have been computed).
   (b) Use cost of goods sold and inventory turnover rate to compute inventory.
(6) Determine cash as a balancing amount (a plug figure).

*22A-6* The financial information given on page 863 for Continental Transfer Co. and American Van Lines (except market price per share of stock) is stated in ***thousands of dollars.*** The figures are as of the end of the current year. The two companies are in the same industry and are quite similar as to operations, facilities, and accounting methods. Assume that both companies pay income taxes equal to 50% of income before income taxes.

**Instructions**

**a** Compute for each company:
   (1) The number of times bond interest was earned during the current year. (Remember to use ***available income*** rather than net income in determining the coverage of interest expense.)
   (2) The debt ratio.

**b** In the light of the information developed in **a** above, write a paragraph indicating which company's bonds you think would trade in the market at the higher price.

| *Assets* | *Continental Transfer Co.* | *American Van Lines* |
|---|---|---|
| *Current assets* | *$ 97,450* | *$132,320* |
| *Plant and equipment* | *397,550* | *495,680* |
| *Less: Accumulated depreciation* | *(55,000)* | *(78,000)* |
| *Total assets* | *$440,000* | *$550,000* |
| ***Liabilities & Stockholders' Equity*** | | |
| *Current liabilities* | *$ 34,000* | *$ 65,000* |
| *Bonds payable, 8%, due in 15 years* | *120,000* | *100,000* |
| *Capital stock, no par* | *150,000* | *200,000* |
| *Retained earnings* | *136,000* | *185,000* |
| *Total liabilities & stockholders' equity* | *$440,000* | *$550,000* |
| *Analysis of retained earnings:* | | |
| *Balance, beginning of year* | *$125,200* | *$167,200* |
| *Net income for the year* | *19,800* | *37,400* |
| *Dividends* | *(9,000)* | *(19,600)* |
| *Balance, end of year* | *$136,000* | *$185,000* |
| *Market price of capital stock, per share* | *$30* | *$61* |
| *Number of shares of capital stock outstanding* | *6 million* | *8 million* |

Which would probably provide the higher yield? Explain how the ratios developed influence your answer. (It may be assumed that the bonds were issued several years ago and are traded on an organized securities exchange.)

**c** For each company compute the dividend yield, the price-earnings ratio, and the book value per share. (Show supporting computations to determine dividends per share. Remember that dollar amounts in the problem are in thousands of dollars, that is, three zeros omitted.) In determining the price-earnings ratios, you must first compute earnings per share. Show this computation in a supporting note.

**d** Express an opinion, based on the data developed in **c** above, as to which company's stock is a better investment at the present market price.

## Group B

*22B-1* The following information was developed from the financial statements of Quarry Tile, Inc.

| | *Year 11* | *Year 10* |
|---|---|---|
| *Net income* | *$ 46,000* | *$ 38,000* |
| *Net income as a percentage of sales* | *5%* | *4%* |
| *Gross profit on sales* | *$322,000* | *$342,000* |
| *Income taxes as a percentage of income before income taxes* | *20%* | *20%* |

**Instructions** (See page 864 for Parts *c, d,* and *e.*)

**a** Compute the net sales for each year.

**b** Compute the cost of goods sold in dollars and as a percentage of sales for each year.

c Compute the federal income taxes for each year.
d Prepare a comparative income statement for Years 10 and 11. Show the following items: Net sales, cost of goods sold, gross profit on sales, operating expenses, income before income taxes, income taxes, and net income.
e What favorable trends and unfavorable trends do you see in this year-to-year comparison of the income statement data of Quarry Tile, Inc.?

*22B-2* Listed in the left-hand column below is a series of business transactions and events relating to the activities of Potomac Mills. Opposite each transaction is listed a particular ratio used in financial analysis:

| Transaction | Ratio |
|---|---|
| (1) Purchased inventory on open account. | Quick ratio |
| (2) A larger physical volume of goods was sold at smaller unit prices. | Gross profit percentage |
| (3) Corporation declared a cash dividend. | Current ratio |
| (4) An uncollectible account receivable was written off against the allowance account. | Current ratio |
| (5) Issued additional shares of common stock and used proceeds to retire long-term debt. | Debt ratio |
| (6) Paid stock dividend on common stock, in common stock. | Earnings per share |
| (7) Conversion of bonds payable into common stock. | Times interest charges earned |
| (8) Appropriated retained earnings. | Rate of return on stockholders' equity |
| (9) During period of rising prices, company changed from fifo to lifo method of inventory pricing. | Inventory turnover |
| (10) Paid previously declared cash dividend. | Debt ratio |
| (11) Purchased factory supplies on open account. | Current ratio (assume that ratio is greater than 1:1) |
| (12) Issued shares of capital stock in exchange for patents. | Equity ratio |

**Instructions** What effect would each transaction or event have on the ratio listed opposite to it; that is, as a result of this event would the ratio increase, decrease, or remain unchanged? Your answer for each of the 12 transactions should include a brief explanation.

*22B-3* In the schedule at the top of page 865, certain items taken from the income statements of the Vincent Company for two fiscal years ending January 31 have been expressed as a percentage of net sales.

Net sales were $1 million in Year 1 and increased by 20% in Year 2.

**Instructions** Prepare a comparative income statement showing ***dollar amounts*** for Year 1 and Year 2. Follow the usual format showing net sales, a cost of goods sold section, gross profit on sales, an operating expense section, income before income

| | Percentage of Net Sales | |
|---|---|---|
| | Year 2 | Year 1 |
| Net sales | | |
| Beginning inventory | 10 | 16 |
| Net purchases | 68 | 60 |
| Ending inventory | 8 | 12 |
| Selling expenses | 13 | 15 |
| Administrative expenses | 8 | 9 |
| Income taxes | 4 | 5 |

taxes, income taxes expense, and net income. Use a four-column work sheet, with the first two columns for Year 2 and the last two columns for Year 1. The use of two columns for each year will enable you to use subtotals conveniently.

*22B-4* At the end of Year 5, the following information was obtained from the accounting records of Craftsman Clocks.

| | |
|---|---|
| Sales (all on credit) | $900,000 |
| Cost of goods sold | 540,000 |
| Average inventory (fifo method) | 90,000 |
| Average accounts receivable | 100,000 |
| Interest expense | 15,000 |
| Income taxes | 18,000 |
| Net income for Year 5 | 63,000 |
| Total assets | 600,000 |
| Total liabilities | 253,500 |

The company declared no dividends of any kind during the year and did not issue or retire any capital stock.

**Instructions** From the information given, compute the following for Year 1:

**a** Inventory turnover.
**b** Accounts receivable turnover.
**c** Total operating expenses. (Interest expense is a nonoperating expense.)
**d** Gross profit percentage.
**e** Rate earned on average stockholders' equity.
**f** Rate earned on total assets. (Use end-of-year total.)
**g** Craftsman Clocks has an opportunity to obtain a long-term loan at an annual interest rate of 11% and could use this additional capital at the same rate of profitability as indicated above. Would obtaining the loan be desirable from the viewpoint of the stockholders? Explain.

*22B-5* John Gale, the accountant for Southbay Corporation, prepared the financial statements for Year 1, including all ratios, and agreed to bring them along on a hunting trip with the executives of the corporation. To his embarrassment, he found that only certain fragmentary information had been placed in his briefcase and the completed statements had been left in his office. One hour before Gale was to present the financial statements to the executives, he was able to come up with the following information:

**SOUTHBAY CORPORATION**
**Balance Sheet**
**End of Year 1**
**(in thousands of dollars)**

| Assets | | | Liabilities & Stockholders' Equity | | |
|---|---|---|---|---|---|
| Current assets: | | | Current liabilities | | $ ? |
| Cash | | $ ? | Long-term debt, 8% interest | | ? |
| Accounts receivable (net) | | ? | Total liabilities | | $ ? |
| Inventory | | ? | Stockholders' equity: | | |
| Total current assets | | $ ? | Capital stock, $5 par | $300 | |
| Plant assets: | | | Retained earnings | 100 | |
| Machinery and equipment | $580 | | Total stockholders' equity | | 400 |
| Less: Accumulated depreciation | 80 | 500 | Total liabilities & stockholders' equity | | $ ? |
| Total assets | | $ ? | | | |

**SOUTHBAY CORPORATION**
**Income Statement**
**For Year 1**
**(in thousands of dollars)**

| | |
|---|---|
| Net sales | $ ? |
| Cost of goods sold | ? |
| Gross profit on sales (25% of net sales) | $ ? |
| Operating expenses | ? |
| Operating income (10% of net sales) | $ ? |
| Interest expense | 28 |
| Income before income taxes | $ ? |
| Income taxes—40% of income before income taxes | ? |
| Net income | $60 |

**Additional information**

(1) The equity ratio was 40%; the debt ratio was 60%.
(2) The only interest expense paid was on the long-term debt.
(3) The beginning inventory was $150,000; the inventory turnover was 4.8 times. (Inventory turnover = cost of goods sold ÷ average inventory.)
(4) The current ratio was 2 to 1; the acid-test ratio was 1 to 1.
(5) The beginning balance in accounts receivable was $80,000; the accounts receivable turnover for Year 1 was 12.8 times. All sales were made on account. (Accounts receivable turnover = net sales ÷ average accounts receivable.)

**Instructions** Using only the information available, the accountant asks you to help complete the financial statements for the Southbay Corporation. Present supporting computations and explanations for all amounts appearing in the balance sheet and the income statement. Hint: In completing the income statement, start with the net income figure (60% of income before income taxes) and work up.

*22B-6* Certain financial information relating to two companies, London Conspiracy and Coventry Clothiers, as of the end of the current year, is shown below. All figures (except market price per share of stock) are in ***thousands of dollars.***

| *Assets* | *London Conspiracy* | *Coventry Clothiers* |
|---|---|---|
| *Cash* | *$ 126.0* | *$ 180.0* |
| *Marketable securities, at cost* | *129.0* | *453.0* |
| *Accounts receivable, net* | *145.0* | *167.0* |
| *Inventories* | *755.6* | *384.3* |
| *Prepaid expenses* | *24.4* | *15.7* |
| *Plant and equipment, net* | *1,680.0* | *1,570.0* |
| *Intangibles and other assets* | *140.0* | *30.0* |
| *Total assets* | *$3,000.0* | *$2,800.0* |
| *Liabilities & Stockholders' Equity* | | |
| *Accounts payable* | *$ 344.6* | *$ 304.1* |
| *Accrued liabilities, including income taxes* | *155.4* | *95.9* |
| *Bonds payable, 7%, due in 10 years* | *200.0* | *500.0* |
| *Capital stock ($10 par)* | *1,000.0* | *600.0* |
| *Capital in excess of par* | *450.0* | *750.0* |
| *Retained earnings* | *910.0* | *550.0* |
| *Treasury stock (1,000 shares, at cost)* | *(60.0)* | *-0-* |
| *Total liabilities & stockholders' equity* | *$3,000.0* | *$2,800.0* |
| *Analysis of retained earnings:* | | |
| *Balance, beginning of year* | *$ 712.0* | *$ 430.0* |
| *Add: Net income* | *297.0* | *240.0* |
| *Less: Dividends* | *(99.0)* | *(120.0)* |
| *Balance, end of year* | *$ 910.0* | *$ 550.0* |
| *Market price per share of stock, end of year* | *$50* | *$40* |

**Instructions** London Conspiracy and Coventry Clothiers are generally comparable in the nature of their operations, products, and accounting procedures used. Write a short answer to each of the following questions, using whatever analytical computations you feel will best support your answer. Show the amounts used in calculating all ratios and percentages. Carry per-share computations to the nearest cent and percentages one place beyond the decimal point, for example, 9.8%.

**a** What is the book value per share of stock for each company?

**b** Prepare a four-column schedule showing for each company the component percentages represented by current liabilities, by long-term liabilities, and by stockholders' equity. Use the first two columns for London Conspiracy, showing dollar amounts in the first column and component percentages in the second column. Use the last two columns in the same way for Coventry Clothiers. On the basis of this analysis, express an opinion as to which company has a more conservative capital structure.

**c** Compute the price-earnings ratio and the dividend yield for each company. Use a work sheet with five money columns. Use the headings Market Price per Share, Earnings per Share, Price-Earnings Ratio, Dividends per Share, and Dividend Yield, %. Before computing the price-earnings ratio, you must compute earnings per share. Show all computations as supporting schedules.

**d** Compute (1) quick assets, (2) total current assets, and (3) working capital. Then compute the quick ratio and the current ratio. Finally, write a brief statement as to which company has the more liquid financial position. Base your answer on the above measurements.

## BUSINESS DECISION PROBLEM 22

Condensed comparative financial statements for Pacific Corporation appear below:

***PACIFIC CORPORATION***
***Comparative Balance Sheets***
***As of May 31***
***(in thousands of dollars)***

| Assets | Year 3 | Year 2 | Year 1 |
|---|---|---|---|
| Current assets | $ 3,960 | $ 2,610 | $ 3,600 |
| Plant and equipment (net of depreciation) | 21,240 | 19,890 | 14,400 |
| Total assets | $25,200 | $22,500 | $18,000 |
| **Liabilities & Stockholders' Equity** | | | |
| Current liabilities | $ 2,214 | $ 2,052 | $ 1,800 |
| Long-term liabilities | 4,716 | 3,708 | 3,600 |
| Capital stock ($10 par) | 12,600 | 12,600 | 8,100 |
| Retained earnings | 5,670 | 4,140 | 4,500 |
| Total liabilities & stockholders' equity | $25,200 | $22,500 | $18,000 |

***PACIFIC CORPORATION***
***Comparative Income Statements***
***For Years Ended May 31***
***(in thousands of dollars)***

| | Year 3 | Year 2 | Year 1 |
|---|---|---|---|
| Net sales | $90,000 | $75,000 | $60,000 |
| Cost of goods sold | 58,500 | 46,500 | 36,000 |
| Gross profit on sales | $31,500 | $28,500 | $24,000 |
| Operating expenses | 28,170 | 25,275 | 21,240 |
| Income before income taxes | $ 3,330 | $ 3,225 | $ 2,760 |
| Income taxes | 1,530 | 1,500 | 1,260 |
| Net income | $ 1,800 | $ 1,725 | $ 1,500 |
| Cash dividends paid (plus 20% in stock in Year 2) | $270 | $465 | $405 |
| Cash dividends per share | $0.21 | $0.37 | $0.50 |

### Instructions

**a** Prepare a three-year comparative balance sheet in percentages rather than dollars, using Year 1 as the base year.

**b** Prepare common size comparative income statements for the three-year period, expressing all items as percentage components of net sales for each year.

**c** Comment on the significant trends and relationships revealed by the analytical computations in **a** and **b.** Divide your comments into two sections—one on balance sheet trends and one on income statement trends. The balance sheet comments should cover current assets and current liabilities, plant and equipment, capital stock, retained earnings, and dividends. The income statement comments should cover the trend of gross profit and of operating expenses.

**d** If the capital stock of this company were selling at $11.50 per share, would you consider it to be overpriced, underpriced, or fairly priced? Consider such factors as book value per share, earnings per share, dividend yield, trend of sales, and trend of the gross profit percentage. Also consider the types of investors to whom the stock would be attractive or unattractive.

# 23

# RESPONSIBILITY ACCOUNTING: DEPARTMENTS AND BRANCHES

In most of our discussion thus far, we have viewed accounting as a system for information processing and measurement of assets, liabilities, and net income for a business unit as a whole. Considerable attention has been given to meeting the informational needs of outsiders, such as investors and creditors. In this and succeeding chapters, we shall focus closer attention on the ***uses of accounting information by management*** in planning and controlling the activities of a business unit.

The functions of planning and control involve formulating plans, taking action, measuring and reporting the results of the action, and evaluating these results. The evaluation of past actions is an important step in the formulation of new plans. The planning and control process can be illustrated as follows:

***Managers need information to plan, act, report, and evaluate performance***

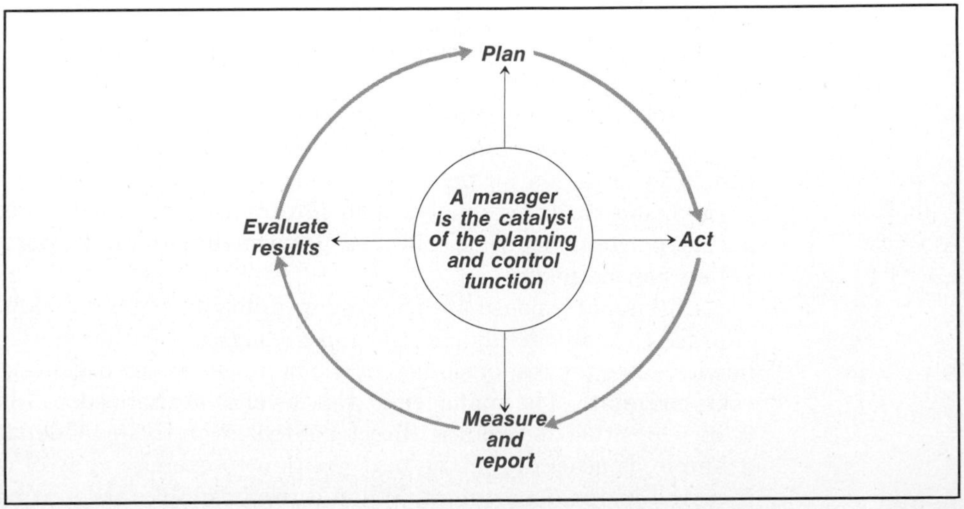

At the heart of this cycle is the manager, who must decide which actions to take, evaluate the results, and formulate the new plans. To meet the needs of management, an effective accounting system should yield information which is useful not only in arriving at decisions, but also in evaluating performance and in making managers more accountable for their actions.

## Responsibility accounting

Operating a business unit is a complex undertaking. Even in a small single proprietorship, the owner will benefit by setting goals such as expected sales volume, the expected amounts of related costs, and the planned amount of net income. The existence of these goals makes it possible to evaluate performance and identify trouble spots. In larger enterprises, with perhaps hundreds of managers and thousands of employees, the officers of the corporation must assign specific organizational responsibilities to different managers. An information system designed to measure the performance of that segment of a business for which a given manager is responsible is often referred to as a ***responsibility accounting system.***

A responsibility accounting system attempts to fit the functions of information gathering and internal reporting ***to the organizational structure of the business.*** In this way, the effectiveness of managers can be judged on the basis of expenses incurred (or revenue earned) which are ***directly under their control.*** To illustrate, assume that a chain of discount stores operates stores at six different locations and that each store is divided into four departments. A diagram depicting a ***partial*** responsibility accounting system for sales salaries incurred by this company might appear as shown on page 871.

This diagram indicates that the head of the grocery department is responsible for only the sales salaries incurred in that department; the manager of store no. 6 is accountable for all salaries paid within the store; and the vice-president in charge of sales has responsibility for all sales salaries for the company. In a responsibility accounting system all expenses and contributions to net income can be similarly traced from the income statement down through the various levels of responsibility.

A responsibility accounting system should reflect the plans and performance ***of each segment or activity*** of a business organization. It is designed to provide timely information for decision making and for the evaluation of performance. In addition to being timely, such information should highlight deviations of actual performance from planned performance so that appropriate corrective action can be taken.

All items of expense are the responsibility of some individual and should be charged to that individual at the ***point of origin.*** In other words, expenses should be viewed as the responsibility of the manager of the organizational unit where costs originate. The manager at this level is authorized to incur expenses and is in a position to exercise direct control over them. A department head, for example, is generally in the best position to exercise control over the expenses incurred in the department. When a responsibility accounting system is used, the amount of expenses the department head incurs in generating sales or in

*Who is responsible for total sales salaries of $8,100,000?*

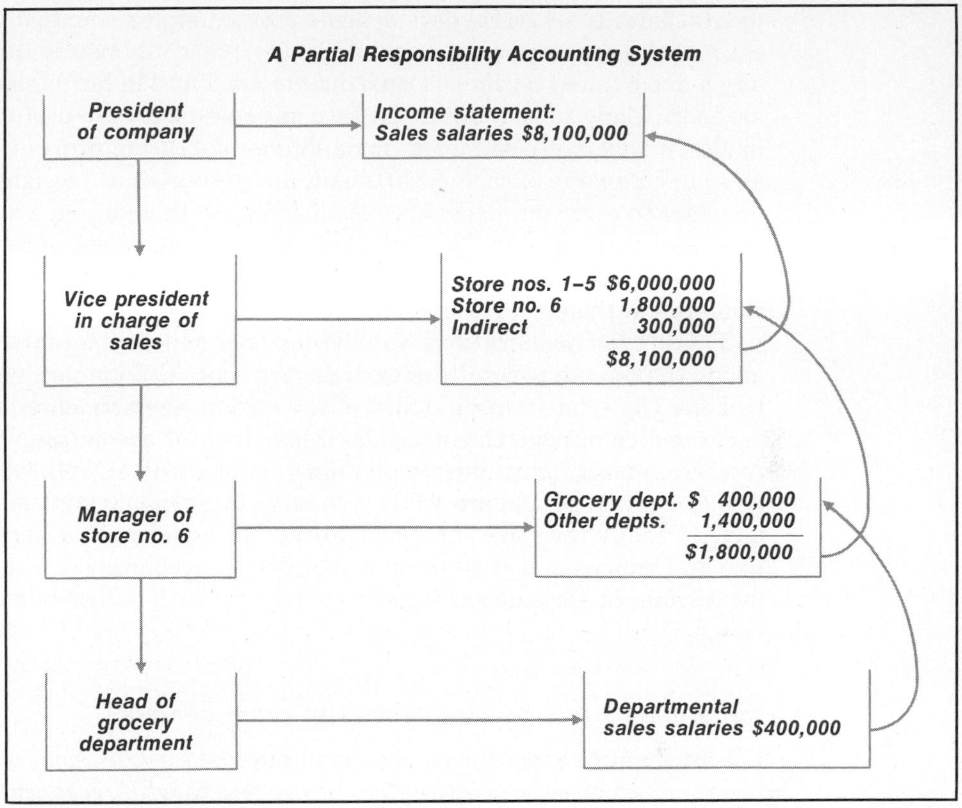


providing services to other segments of the business will be clearly reported. In this way the department head is ***held accountable for a specific area of responsibility*** without being able to pass the blame for poor overall company performance to other people.

Responsibility accounting systems may be developed at all levels of an organization where specific areas of authority and responsibility can be reasonably identified. Top management has the ultimate responsibility for overall profitability of a business enterprise; vice-presidents and different levels of "middle management" are responsible for generating revenue from various products or territories and for controlling costs incurred in generating such revenue; at lower levels, managers are charged with the responsibility of reaching the revenue goals and controlling costs incurred within the units which they supervise. In the remaining pages of this chapter we shall direct our attention to two types of accountability units—departments and branches.

## THE NEED FOR DEPARTMENTAL INFORMATION

If a business entity includes two or more segments, each providing a different service or handling different classes of merchandise, organization along departmental lines is a natural development. For example, a company consisting of a car rental service and an automobile repair shop could reasonably be operated as a two-department business. Departments are found in businesses of all sizes but are more likely to be found in larger companies; they are useful to service companies as well as to merchandising and manufacturing firms. A manager is usually put in charge of each department, and resources are assigned to enable the manager to carry out necessary responsibilities. In addition, a department manager may draw upon the general resources and staff talent of the entity for such services as accounting, financing, hiring, legal advice, advertising, transportation, and storage.

This kind of organizational subdivision creates a need for internal information about the operating results of each department. Top management can then determine the relative profitability of the various departments and evaluate the performance of department heads. Departmental accounting information also provides a basis for intelligent planning and control, as well as for assessing the effect of new ideas and procedures. To serve these managerial needs, accountants have to refine their measurement process. In addition to determining the revenue and expenses of the business as a whole, accountants face the problem of measuring the revenue and expenses attributable to each subdivision of the business.

## Departments may be cost centers or profit centers

For information processing and control purposes, subdivisions of a business may be organized as either cost centers or profit centers. A ***cost center*** is a unit of a business which incurs expenses (or costs) but which does not directly generate revenue. Examples of cost centers include such ***service departments*** as personnel, accounting, and public relations, which provide services to other departments. A ***profit center,*** on the other hand, is a segment of a business which not only incurs expenses (or costs) but also produces revenue that can be identified with such a segment. A profit center is expected to make a profit contribution to the business by earning a fair rate of return on the assets it employs. Examples of profit centers include a furniture department of a large retail store, a branch of a large bank, and the Chevrolet Motor Division of General Motors Corporation.

A manager is in charge of each cost or profit center. Managers of cost centers are typically evaluated in terms of their ability to keep costs and expenses within budgeted allowances; managers of profit centers are most frequently judged on their ability to generate earnings. In this chapter we are primarily concerned with units of a retail business (departments and branches) which are organized as profit centers for accounting purposes.

## The managerial viewpoint

The details of departmental revenue and expenses are not usually made available to the public, on the grounds that such information would be of considerable aid to competitors.[1] Departmental accounting information, therefore, is designed primarily to serve the needs of internal management. Among the major uses of such information are the following:

1 **As a basis for planning and allocating resources** Management wants to know how well various departments are performing in order to have a guide in planning future activities and in allocating the resources and talent of the firm to those areas that have the greatest profit potential. If one department is producing larger profits than another, this may indicate that greater effort should be made to expand and develop the activities in the more profitable department.

2 **As a basis for corrective action** A well-designed accounting system will throw a spotlight on troubled areas. A manager who is not doing a good job should be replaced; costs that are out of line should be more closely controlled; an unsuccessful department should be revamped or perhaps dropped altogether. Pointing up the areas that need managerial attention is an important function of responsibility accounting.

3 **As a basis for pricing decisions** If a business is to be successful, it must set the price of its products high enough to recover all operating expenses and also provide a reasonable profit. Therefore, departmental cost information is widely used in pricing decisions. Of course, costs are not the only factor to be considered in establishing the price of a product. Prices must be kept at competitive levels if the business is to attract customers. Sometimes a business may even elect to sell a few products at a loss in order to attract customers who also will buy other products.

This is not a complete list of the uses that might be made by management of departmental accounting information. It illustrates, however, the usefulness to management of an accounting system which allocates revenue and expenses among departments.

## Collecting information on departmental revenue and expenses

Two basic approaches may be used in developing ***departmental*** information for a business engaged in merchandising activities:

1 **Establish separate departmental accounts for various types of revenue and expense and identify individual transactions with a particular department.** This method is easily adapted for accounts such as sales, purchases, and inventories. For example, a business having three departments would use a separate sales account, a separate purchases account, and a separate inventory account for each department. In large companies most of this

---

[1] In *Statement No. 14,* the FASB requires publicly owned corporations to disclose in notes to their financial statements certain information about major *industry segments* of the business. The definition of an "industry segment" is much broader than that of a "department." Segment reporting requirements are discussed in intermediate accounting courses.

data gathering would be computerized. Department stores, for example, may use ***punched tags*** such as the one illustrated below:

***Punched tag used by department store***

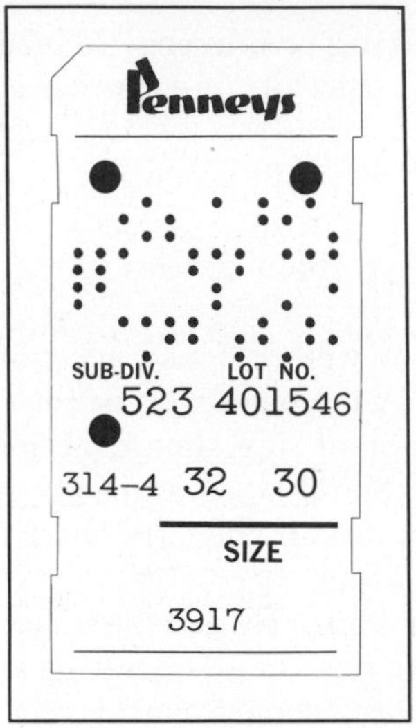


When an article of merchandise is sold, the tag is removed and machine processed to generate departmental sales and inventory information.

2 **Maintain only one general ledger account for a particular type of revenue or expense, and distribute the total amount among the various departments at the end of the accounting period.** When this procedure is used, distribution by departments is made on a work sheet at the end of the accounting period rather than in the ledger accounts. For example, rent might be recorded in a single expense account and the total allocated among departments. A simple departmental expense allocation sheet is illustrated on page 878.

Some companies carry departmentalization of operating results only as far as gross profit on sales; others extend the process to include certain direct operating expenses such as wages; a few go so far as to apportion ***all*** expenses among departments and compute net income on a departmental basis.

## Departmental gross profit on sales

In a merchandising business a figure of great interest to management is the gross profit realized over and above the cost of merchandise sold in any department. Gross profit on sales is a function of two variables: (1) the volume of goods sold and (2) the gross profit earned on each dollar of sales. The same total gross profit may be realized from a large volume of sales made at a low rate of gross profit, or from a smaller volume of sales made at a higher rate of gross profit.

Within any given business, department managers are constantly making decisions that affect the gross profit rate. Their goal is to maintain a sales volume

Note that the gross profit as a percentage of net sales is given for the business as a whole and by departments. (Earnings per share data have been omitted in the departmental income statements illustrated in this chapter because these statements are designed for internal use by management.)

If the number of departments were large, a horizontal expansion of the income statement in this fashion might become unwieldy, in which case separate statements of gross profit on sales for each department might be prepared and attached to the income statement for the business as a whole.

It is evident that Department A contributes a much higher rate of gross profit than Department B. By studying the reasons for this difference, management may be led to make changes in buying policies, selling prices, or the personnel of Department B in an effort to improve its performance. Whether Department A contributes more than B to the net income of the business, however, depends on the amount of operating expenses attributable to each department.

## Allocating operating expenses to departments

An analysis of expenses by departments provides information about the cost of departmental operations and makes it possible to prepare an income statement showing departmental net income. Two steps are generally involved in allocating operating expenses to departments: First, identify the expenses which are considered ***direct*** expenses of certain departments, and second, identify the expenses which are considered ***indirect*** departmental expenses and allocate these to the respective departments on some basis which will recognize the benefits received by each department.

***Direct expenses*** are those which may be ***identified by department,*** in the sense that if the department did not exist, the expense would not be incurred. For example, the cost of advertising a particular product is a direct expense of the department in which that product is sold. ***Indirect expenses*** are incurred ***for the benefit of the business as a whole;*** they cannot be identified readily with the activities of a given department. Indirect expenses would, for the most part, continue even though a particular department were discontinued. The cost of advertising the name and location of the business, rather than particular products, is an example of an indirect expense.

Some direct expenses may be charged to separate departmental expense accounts at the time they are incurred. Other expenses, even though they are direct in nature, may more conveniently be charged to a single account and allocated to departments at the end of the accounting period.

Indirect expenses, by their very nature, can be assigned to departments only by a process of allocation. For example, the salary of the president of the company is an expense not directly related to the activities of any particular department. If it is to be divided among the departments, some method of allocation is necessary which would charge each department with the approximate cost of the benefits it received.

Operating expenses may be allocated to departments through the use of a ***departmental expense allocation sheet*** similar to the one illustrated on page 878 for Day Corporation:



that will maximize the total dollar gross profit realized by their departments. This is not to say that operating expenses may be ignored; obviously a prime objective is to earn a satisfactory level of net income, the figure often referred to as the "bottom line."

**Departmental revenue** The first step in arriving at departmental gross profit is to departmentalize all revenue. To illustrate, assume that Day Corporation maintains in its general ledger separate departmental accounts for sales, sales returns and allowances, and sales discounts. As a convenient means of accumulating departmental revenue data, special columns may be added to the various journals. For example, Day Corporation's sales journal for a typical month might appear as shown below.

***Sales Journal***

| Date | | Invoice No. | Account Debited | LP | Accounts Receivable Dr | Sales | |
|---|---|---|---|---|---|---|---|
| | | | | | | Dept. A Cr | Dept. B Cr |
| 19__ | | | | | | | |
| Aug. | 1 | 4100 | Abar Co. | √ | 1,700 | 1,700 | |
| | | 4101 | Tilden Industries | √ | 2,180 | 1,470 | 710 |
| | 31 | | Totals | | 165,100 | 102,600 | 62,500 |
| | | | | | (5) | (200) | (300) |

**Electronic point-of-sale systems** If a business is divided into a large number of departments, the use of a separate journal column for each departmental account would result in journals of unmanageable size. One solution to this problem is the electronic cash registers now used in many large department stores. These electronic registers are actually computer terminals that enter departmental sales information directly into a central computer at the time each sale is rung up. Daily, weekly, or monthly summaries of departmental sales activity are then printed by the computer for use by management. The trend in modern accounting is to avoid journals with numerous columns by entering transaction data directly into a computerized accounting system. The great speed of the computer may then be used to prepare journals, ledgers, and special reports to management.

Regardless of the system used, the basic procedures are: (1) See that operating data are classified by departments on electronic cash registers, original invoices, credit memoranda, etc.; (2) sort and accumulate these individual transaction figures to arrive at subtotals for each departmental account; (3) enter this information in ledger accounts.

Since Day Corporation uses separate departmental accounts for sales, sales returns and allowances, and sales discounts, the net sales (as reported in the income statement below) can be determined directly from the balances in these accounts.

**Departmental cost of goods sold** We will assume that Day Corporation uses the periodic inventory system and keeps separate departmental accounts for each element of cost of goods sold.[2] Inventories, purchases, and purchase returns are readily identified by department. Purchase discounts and transportation-in must also be classified by department to determine the cost of goods sold by each department. This classification may be made at the time of each transaction, or the total purchase discounts and total transportation-in may be allocated to individual departments at the end of the accounting period. The cost of goods sold by departments for the current year is shown in the income statement illustrated in the following section.

**Income statement: Gross profit by departments** An income statement, departmentalized only through the gross profit on sales, is shown below.

***DAY CORPORATION***
***Income Statement***
***For the Current Year***

| | Total | Dept. A | Dept. B |
|---|---|---|---|
| Sales | $2,500,000 | $1,600,000 | $ 900,000 |
| Less: Sales returns and allowances | (25,000) | (11,500) | (13,500) |
| Sales discounts | (40,000) | (30,000) | (10,000) |
| Net sales | $2,435,000 | $1,558,500 | $ 876,500 |
| Cost of goods sold: | | | |
| Beginning inventory | $ 350,000 | $ 140,000 | $ 210,000 |
| Purchases | 1,800,000 | 1,026,000 | 774,000 |
| Transportation-in | 85,000 | 24,000 | 61,000 |
| Purchase returns | (50,000) | (28,500) | (21,500) |
| Purchase discounts | (30,500) | (15,000) | (15,500) |
| Merchandise available for sale | $2,154,500 | $1,146,500 | $1,008,000 |
| Less: Ending inventory | 450,000 | 180,000 | 270,000 |
| Cost of goods sold | $1,704,500 | $ 966,500 | $ 738,000 |
| Gross profit on sales | $ 730,500 | $ 592,000 | $ 138,500 |
| Gross profit as percentage of net sales (30% combined) | | 38% | 16% |
| Operating expenses (details omitted) | 627,500 | | |
| Operating income | $ 103,000 | | |
| Income taxes, 30% | 30,900 | | |
| Net income | $ 72,100 | | |

[2] When a perpetual inventory system is in use, separate Inventory and Cost of Goods Sold accounts are maintained for each department.



***Departmental Expense Allocation Sheet***
***For the Current Year***

| | | Total Operating Expenses | Department A | | Department B | |
|---|---|---|---|---|---|---|
| | | | Direct | Indirect | Direct | Indirect |
| Sales salaries expense | (1) | $135,000 | $ 84,500 | | $ 50,500 | |
| Advertising expense | (2) | 90,000 | 25,000 | 31,250 | 15,000 | 18,750 |
| Building expense | (3) | 80,000 | | 48,000 | | 32,000 |
| Buying expense | (4) | 134,000 | 70,000 | 14,250 | 39,000 | 10,750 |
| Delivery expense | (5) | 60,000 | | 15,000 | 10,000 | 35,000 |
| Administrative expense | (6) | 128,500 | 15,500 | 64,000 | 13,000 | 36,000 |
| Totals—direct and indirect | | $627,500 | $195,000 | $172,500 | $127,500 | $132,500 |
| Total for each department | | | $367,500 | | $260,000 | |

In order to keep this example short and simple, we have assumed that Day Corporation grouped its operating expenses into various functions or activities performed. For example, sales salaries expense includes all compensation and payroll-related costs of the sales staff and sales executives; delivery expense includes all costs of operating delivery trucks, wages of drivers, and all other costs relating to shipping merchandise to customers. The allocation of operating expenses in the departmental expense allocation sheet prepared by Day Corporation is explained in the following sections.

1 **Sales salaries expense** Day Corporation's salespeople work exclusively in either Department A or Department B. This is an example of a direct expense clearly identified with the departments involved and thus charged to departments on the basis of the personnel involved. The expense allocation sheet shows that direct sales force expense incurred was $84,500 for Department A and $50,500 for Department B.

2 **Advertising expense** Day Corporation advertises primarily through newspapers, with occasional spot advertisements on radio and television. Direct advertising expense amounts to $40,000 and represents the cost of newspaper space and time purchased to advertise specific products identified with each department. Indirect advertising expense amounts to $50,000 and includes the cost of administering the advertising program, plus advertising applicable to the business as a whole. Day Corporation allocated indirect advertising expense in proportion to the direct advertising expense, as shown below:

| | Direct Advertising Expense | Percentage of Total | Indirect Advertising Expense | Total Direct and Indirect |
|---|---|---|---|---|
| Department A | $25,000 | 62.5[a] | $31,250[c] | $56,250 |
| Department B | 15,000 | 37.5[b] | 18,750[d] | 33,750 |
| Total | $40,000 | 100.0 | $50,000 | $90,000 |

[a] $25,000 ÷ $40,000 = 62.5%
[b] $15,000 ÷ $40,000 = 37.5%
[c] $50,000 × 62.5% = $31,250
[d] $50,000 × 37.5% = $18.750

3 **Building expense** This includes all costs relating to the occupancy of the building. The Day Corporation allocates the building expense on the basis of square feet occupied by each department, 60% by Department A and 40% by Department B. Thus $48,000 (60% of $80,000) was allocated to Department A and $32,000 (40% of $80,000) was allocated to Department B. If the value of the floor space varies (as, for example, between the first floor and the second floor) then the allocation should be made on the basis of ***value of space*** rather than square footage.

4 **Buying expense** The compensation of departmental buyers, their travel expenses, and certain merchandise handling costs, amounting to $109,000, were considered direct expenses and assigned to the two departments on the basis of the personnel involved. Department A was charged with $70,000 of this direct expense and Department B absorbed $39,000. The indirect buying expense of $25,000 was allocated on the basis of total departmental purchases of $1,800,000 as follows: Department A, $1,026,000/$1,800,000 × $25,000, or $14,250; Department B, $774,000/$1,800,000 × $25,000 or $10,750. The possible defects of purchases as an allocation basis are obvious; there is no necessary reason why the cost of buying or handling an item of large dollar value is significantly greater than for a less costly item.

5 **Delivery expense** Department B shipped certain merchandise by common carriers at a cost of $10,000, a direct expense of this department. The $50,000 balance of the cost of maintaining a delivery service applies to both departments. A study covering several months of typical operation showed that on the average 70% of all delivery requests originated in Department B; therefore 30% ($15,000) of the indirect delivery expense was charged to Department A, and 70% ($35,000) to Department B.

6 **Administrative expense** Two direct expenses were included in the administrative expense category; the remainder were indirect:

| | *Total* | *Department A* | *Department B* |
|---|---|---|---|
| *Direct administrative expense:* | | | |
| *Uncollectible accounts expense* | *$ 18,500* | *$11,500* | *$ 7,000* |
| *Insurance on inventories* | *10,000* | *4,000* | *6,000* |
| *Total direct expenses* | *$ 28,500* | *$15,500* | *$13,000* |
| *Indirect administrative expense (allocated on basis of gross sales)* | *100,000* | *64,000* | *36,000* |
| *Total administrative expense* | *$128,500* | *$79,500* | *$49,000* |

The division of the $18,500 uncollectible accounts expense was made on the basis of an analysis of accounts charged off during the period. If this had not been feasible, allocation on the basis of credit sales in each department would have been reasonable. Insurance expense of $10,000 on inventories was charged to the departments on the basis of the average inventory in each department ($160,000 and $240,000, respectively), or a 40:60 ratio. Indirect administrative expense of $100,000 was allocated on the basis of gross sales, as follows:

| | |
|---|---|
| *Department A, $1,600,000/$2,500,000 × $100,000* | *$ 64,000* |
| *Department B, $900,000/$2,500,000 × $100,000* | *36,000* |
| *Total* | *$100,000* |

The following summary of operating expenses for Day Corporation will be useful to us in discussing the possibility of discontinuing Department B, which appears to be losing money:

| | Total | Department A | Department B |
|---|---|---|---|
| *Operating expenses:* | | | |
| *Direct* | *$322,500* | *$195,000* | *$127,500* |
| *Indirect* | *305,000* | *172,500* | *132,500* |
| *Total* | *$627,500* | *$367,500* | *$260,000* |

## Departmental income statement

On the basis of departmental data developed thus far, we can now prepare a statement showing the net income of the business and of each department, as shown below:

*DAY CORPORATION*
*Departmental Income Statement*
*For the Current Year*

*Should Department B be closed?*

| | Total | Department A | Department B |
|---|---|---|---|
| *Net sales* | *$2,435,000* | *$1,558,500* | *$ 876,500* |
| *Cost of goods sold* | *1,704,500* | *966,500* | *738,000* |
| *Gross profit on sales* | *$ 730,500* | *$ 592,000* | *$ 138,500* |
| *Operating expenses (from departmental expense allocation sheet on page 878):* | | | |
| *Sales salaries expense* | *$ 135,000* | *$ 84,500* | *$ 50,500* |
| *Advertising expense* | *90,000* | *56,250* | *33,750* |
| *Building expense* | *80,000* | *48,000* | *32,000* |
| *Buying expense* | *134,000* | *84,250* | *49,750* |
| *Delivery expense* | *60,000* | *15,000* | *45,000* |
| *Administrative expense* | *128,500* | *79,500* | *49,000* |
| *Total operating expenses* | *$ 627,500* | *$ 367,500* | *$ 260,000* |
| *Income (or loss) before income taxes* | *$ 103,000* | *$ 224,500* | *$(121,500)* |
| *Income taxes (or tax savings) 30%* | *30,900* | *67,350* | *(36,450)* |
| *Net income (or loss)* | *$ 72,100* | *$ 157,150* | *$ (85,050)* |

For the sake of simplicity, we are assuming that income taxes are paid by Day Corporation at the flat rate of 30%. To reflect clearly the relationship between income taxes and operating results, the income tax expense charged to Department A is 30% of the income before income taxes of that department, and this is offset by a tax savings of $36,450 equal to 30% of the loss before income taxes of $121,500 reported in Department B.

**When is a department unprofitable?** The first reaction of management, confronted with the departmental income statement shown above, might be that the corporation would be better off if Department B were dropped. The income statement appears to indicate that net income would have been $157,150 rather than $72,100 were it not for the existence of Department B. Is this true?

If we could, with a wave of the hand, blot Department B out of existence, the income statement of Day Corporation for the current year would probably appear as follows:

***DAY CORPORATION***

***Income Statement Reflecting Elimination of Department B***

***For the Current Year***

*Effect of eliminating Department B*

| | | |
|---|---|---|
| Net sales | | $1,558,500 |
| Cost of goods sold | | 966,500 |
| Gross profit on sales | | $ 592,000 |
| Operating expenses: | | |
| Direct expenses of Department A (from departmental allocation sheet on page 878) | $195,000 | |
| Indirect expenses (total originally allocated to both departments, $172,500 + $132,500) | 305,000 | 500,000 |
| Income before income taxes | | $ 92,000 |
| Income taxes (30%) | | 27,600 |
| Net income | | $ 64,400 |

Instead of improving the company's showing, the result is a *decrease* in income of $7,700 ($72,100 − $64,400). Apparently the information in the departmental income statement is misleading. The answer to this paradox is that ***the elimination of Department B would eliminate the entire gross profit on sales earned in that department but not any of the indirect expenses that were allocated to Department B.*** An explanation of the estimated $7,700 decline in net income which would result from eliminating Department B is summarized at the top of page 882.

It is apparent from this summary that reducing direct expenses by $127,500 and eliminating $3,300 in income taxes are not sufficient to offset the decrease in gross profit on sales of $138,500 that would follow from the elimination of Department B. If we compare the effect on expenses shown on this summary with the expenses allocated to Department B as shown on page 878, we see that only ***direct expenses*** of $127,500 were assumed to be eliminated as a result of the elimination of this department. This is no coincidence, since direct expenses were defined as those relating to the activities of a particular department that would be eliminated if the department did not exist. Thus compensation of sales and buying personnel, cost of direct advertising space, outbound transportation paid

***DAY CORPORATION***
***Estimated Effect of Elimination of Department B***
***For the Current Year***

*Is Department B unprofitable?*

| | Department B's share | Assuming Elimination of Department B: Not Eliminated (Indirect) | Eliminated (Direct) | Effect on Net Income |
|---|---|---|---|---|
| Gross profit on sales | $138,500 | | $138,500 | $(138,500) |
| Operating expenses | 260,000 | $132,500 | 127,500 | 127,500 |
| Effect on income before income taxes | | | | $ (11,000) |
| Reduction in income taxes (30% of $11,000 pretax loss) | | | | 3,300 |
| Reduction in net income if Department B is eliminated | | | | $ (7,700) |

to carriers, uncollectible accounts expense, and insurance on inventories would presumably disappear along with Department B.

The $132,500 of operating expenses that would ***not*** be eliminated is the amount of indirect expenses assigned to Department B. The assumption that indirect expenses are inescapable (fixed) and that they would remain unchanged is a convenient assumption but, realistically, some reduction in indirect expenses would probably occur if Department B were eliminated. The change in indirect expenses that follows from departmental changes will depend to some extent on the alternatives that are being considered. For example, the indirect expense, building expense, would continue largely unchanged whether Department B existed or not, since Day Corporation owns the entire building. However, if Day Corporation were to drop Department B and reduce the scale of its activities, it might rent the surplus space to outsiders and thus reduce building expense. On the other hand, if the question were whether Department B should be reorganized or a new kind of operation substituted for it, building expenses and other indirect expenses would probably not change by an amount large enough to influence the decision.

There is considerable wisdom in the phrase "different costs for different purposes." The allocation of costs for one purpose may not produce results that are significant for a different kind of decision; special cost studies are often necessary to answer particular questions. Some of these will be discussed in subsequent chapters.

### Departmental contribution to indirect expenses (overhead)

We have seen that the gross profit on sales by departments can be determined with good assurance that the results are reliable and useful. We have seen also that the division of direct expenses among departments is a fairly straightforward process. Sales revenue, cost of goods sold, and direct expenses are all operating elements that relate clearly to the existence of a given department and its activities.

On the other hand, most indirect expenses (***overhead***) are costs associated with the business as a whole, and in general they lie outside the control of department managers. Because of their indirect relationship to departmental activities, any basis of allocation used is somewhat arbitrary and the proper interpretation of the results is often in doubt.

Some accountants argue that the important benefits of departmental accounting can be gained by stopping short of a full allocation of all expenses to departments. They urge that each department be credited with revenues and charged with expenses that, in the opinion of management, would disappear if the department did not exist. This approach leads to a departmental income statement showing the ***contribution of each department to the indirect expenses of the business.*** Such a statement, using figures previously developed for Day Corporation, appears as follows:

**DAY CORPORATION**

**Departmental Income Statement Showing Contribution to Indirect Expenses**

**For the Current Year**

| | | Total | Department A | Department B |
|---|---|---|---|---|
| Net sales | | $2,435,000 | $1,558,500 | $876,500 |
| Cost of goods sold | | 1,704,500 | 966,500 | 738,000 |
| Gross profit on sales | | $ 730,500(30%) | $ 592,000(38%) | $138,500(16%) |
| Direct departmental expenses (see page 878) | | | | |
| Sales salaries expense | | $ 135,000 | $ 84,500 | $ 50,500 |
| Advertising expense | | 40,000 | 25,000 | 15,000 |
| Buying expense | | 109,000 | 70,000 | 39,000 |
| Delivery expense | | 10,000 | | 10,000 |
| Administrative expense | | 28,500 | 15,500 | 13,000 |
| Total direct expenses | | $ 322,500 | $ 195,000 | $127,500 |
| Contribution to indirect expenses | | $ 408,000 | $ 397,000 | $ 11,000 |
| Indirect expenses (see page 878) | | | | |
| Advertising expense | $ 50,000 | | | |
| Building expense | 80,000 | | | |
| Buying expense | 25,000 | | | |
| Delivery expense | 50,000 | | | |
| Administrative expense | 100,000 | | | |
| Total indirect expenses | | 305,000 | | |
| Income before income taxes | | $103,000 | | |
| Income taxes, 30% | | 30,900 | | |
| Net income | | $ 72,100 | | |

In contrast to the departmental net income statement on page 880 which shows that Department B suffered a net loss of $85,050, this statement shows that Department B ***contributed*** $11,000 (before income taxes) to the indirect expenses of the business. This figure agrees with the estimated reduction in net income ***before income taxes*** (see page 882) if Department B were discontinued.

The performance of department managers can be better judged by their ***contribution to indirect expenses*** than by the net income or loss for a department, because indirect expenses are generally ***outside the control of department managers.*** Furthermore, so long as a department is covering its direct expenses, it is probably contributing to the profitability of the business as a whole.

## ACCOUNTING SYSTEMS FOR BRANCH OPERATIONS

Merchandising companies often do business in more than one location by opening ***branch stores.*** As a business grows it may open branches in order to market its products over a larger territory and thus increase its profits. A branch is typically located at some distance from the ***home office*** and generally carries a stock of merchandise, sells the merchandise, makes collection on receivables, and pays some of its operating expenses. A branch is not a separate legal entity; it is simply a segment of a business which may be a single proprietorship, a partnership, or a corporation. From an accounting standpoint, a branch is a clearly identifiable ***profit center*** and offers an opportunity to implement the principles of responsibility accounting discussed earlier in this chapter.

An accounting system for a branch should generate information needed to measure the profitability of the branch and to ensure strong control over branch assets. Management needs information to answer questions such as: Is the branch yielding a satisfactory rate of return on the capital invested in it? Should the branch be expanded or closed? Are prices on merchandise sold by the branch too low? How much of a bonus should the branch manager receive? How much merchandise does the branch have in stock?

The home office may provide the branch with a cash ***working fund*** to be used for the payment of branch expenses. The merchandise handled by a branch may be obtained solely from the home office or a portion may be purchased from outside suppliers. Bills for merchandise purchases and certain operating expenses, such as wages and insurance, may be paid by the home office, or from the branch working fund. Cash receipts of the branch may be deposited either in a branch or a home office bank account. When a branch is authorized to have its own bank account, it will also generally pay its bills and remit any unneeded cash to the home office. The amount of operating independence given to a branch varies among companies and even among branches within the same company. Branch accounting systems are either ***centralized*** in the home office or ***decentralized*** at the branches.

### Branch records centralized in home office

In a ***centralized*** accounting system, the branch is provided with a small working fund (similar to a petty cash fund which is replenished periodically) to pay for small items of expense. The home office keeps most of the accounting records relating to the branch. Records of branch assets, liabilities, revenue, payrolls, and other expenses are maintained in the home office which processes the business documents (sales slips, deposit slips, invoices, etc.) received from the branch. The branch keeps very few accounting records and is generally instructed to deposit cash receipts in a home office account with a local bank. A centralized system is particularly appropriate when data processing equipment is located in the home office or when the branch is too small to hire a full-time accountant.

Separate records of revenue and expenses for each branch are maintained in the accounting records of the home office. In this way the operating results for each branch can be readily determined. Thus the three important features of a centralized accounting system for a branch are: (1) a working fund for the branch is established and is replenished as needed; (2) all business documents originating at the branch are transmitted to the home office; and (3) a separate record of branch assets, liabilities, revenue, and expenses is maintained by the home office.

## Records decentralized at the branch

As an alternative to centralizing all accounting work in the home office, a company may decide that a branch should maintain its own complete set of accounting records. Under such a ***decentralized*** accounting system, the branch accountant will prepare complete financial statements for the branch and forward them to the home office. The number and type of accounts, the system of internal control, the form and content of financial statements, and the accounting policies are generally prescribed by the home office. As a minimum, the transactions recorded by the branch include the expenses under the control of the branch manager and the revenue generated at the branch. At the end of the accounting period, the home office may notify the branch that certain expenses incurred at the home office have been allocated to the branch. Records of certain assets purchased by the home office and assigned to the branch, such as fixtures and equipment and the related depreciation accounts, are often maintained at the home office. Bank loans may be negotiated and recorded by the home office; the proceeds on such loans are advanced to the branch, or simply deposited in the branch bank account.

**Typical branch transactions illustrated** In order to illustrate the basic features of a decentralized branch accounting system, assume that on March 1, Homer & Company (a single proprietorship) opens a branch in the city of Brady. The company rents a fully equipped store and transfers cash of $10,000 and store supplies of $1,500 to the branch. The entries in the accounts of the Brady Branch and the home office to record this transfer, along with other ***branch*** transactions during March, are shown in summary form on page 886.

Only transactions (1), (4), and (8) are recorded in the home office accounting records, because these three transactions involve both the branch and the home office and thus require the use of the ***reciprocal*** accounts as shown on page 887.

| Summary of Transactions for March | Branch Accounting Records | | | Home Office Accounting Records | | |
|---|---|---|---|---|---|---|
| (1) Home office opened Brady Branch and transferred cash and store supplies to the branch | Cash | 10,000 | | Brady Branch | 11,500 | |
| | Store Supplies | 1,500 | | Cash | | 10,000 |
| | Home Office | | 11,500 | Store Supplies | | 1,500 |
| (2) Merchandise purchased by branch. Branch uses a perpetual inventory system.[1] | Inventory | 18,000 | | No entry | | |
| | Accounts Payable | | 18,000 | | | |
| (3) Expenses incurred by branch. | Selling Expense | 2,500 | | No entry | | |
| | General Expense | 1,900 | | | | |
| | Cash | | 3,200 | | | |
| | Accounts Payable | | 1,000 | | | |
| | Store Supplies | | 200 | | | |
| (4) General expense incurred by home office allocated to branch. | General Expense | 100 | | Brady Branch | 100 | |
| | Home Office | | 100 | General Expense | | 100 |
| (5) Sales made by branch. | Cash | 3,000 | | No entry | | |
| | Accounts Receivable | 17,000 | | | | |
| | Sales | | 20,000 | | | |
| (6) Collections by branch on accounts receivable. | Cash | 13,000 | | No entry | | |
| | Accounts receivable | | 13,000 | | | |
| (7) Payments by branch to merchandise creditors. | Accounts Payable | 14,500 | | No entry | | |
| | Cash | | 14,500 | | | |
| (8) Branch remits cash to home office at end of month. | Home Office | 5,000 | | Cash | 5,000 | |
| | Cash | | 5,000 | Brady Branch | | 5,000 |
| (9) To record the cost of goods sold by branch during the month. | Cost of Goods Sold | 12,000 | | No entry | | |
| | Inventory | | 12,000 | | | |

[1]See pp. 414–417 for a description of a perpetual inventory system.

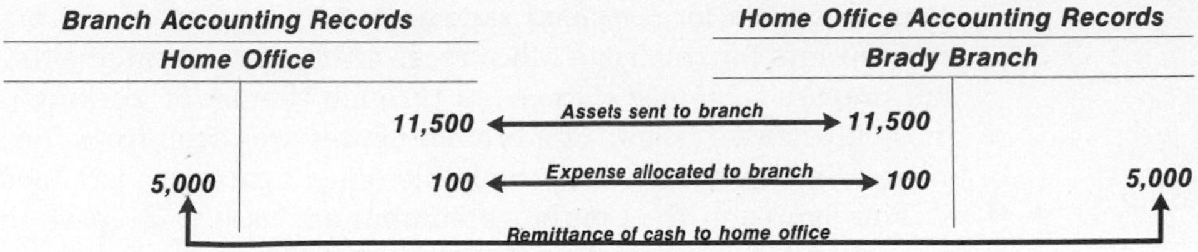


These accounts are called ***reciprocal accounts*** because they are used to record the same transactions from two opposite points of view. Note that the credit balance in the Home Office account, $6,600, is equal to the debit balance in the Brady Branch account, $6,600.

**Branch records** The Home Office account in the branch accounting records may be viewed as a "proprietorship" account which shows the net investment in the branch made by the home office. It is credited for assets transferred to the branch and for expenses allocated to the branch by the home office; it is debited when cash or other assets are remitted to the home office by the branch. At the end of the accounting period when the branch closes its accounts, the branch income or loss is closed into the Home Office account. A branch net income is debited to the Income Summary account and credited to the Home Office account; a loss reported by the branch would be debited to the Home Office account and credited to Income Summary.

**Home office records** In the accounting records of the home office, the Brady Branch account is viewed as an asset representing the net investment in the branch. This account is debited when assets are transferred to the branch or when expenses incurred at the home office are allocated to the branch; it is credited when cash or other assets are received from the branch. Income reported by the branch is debited to the Brady Branch account and credited to Income—Brady Branch; branch losses would be debited to Loss—Brady Branch and credited to the Brady Branch account.

**Statements for the branch** After the transactions illustrated on page 886 are recorded and summarized, the accountant for the Brady Branch submits the following statements to the home office:

***BRADY BRANCH***
***Income Statement***
***For Month of March***

| | | |
|---|---|---|
| *Sales* | | *$20,000* |
| *Cost of goods sold* | | *12,000* |
| *Gross profit on sales* | | *$ 8,000* |
| *Less: Selling expense* | *$2,500* | |
| *General expense* | *2,000* | *4,500* |
| *Net income* | | *$ 3,500* |

***BRADY BRANCH***
***Balance Sheet***
***March 31***

| | |
|---|---|
| *Cash* | *$ 3,300* |
| *Accounts receivable* | *4,000* |
| *Inventory* | *6,000* |
| *Store supplies* | *1,300* |
| *Total* | *$14,600* |
| *Accounts payable* | *$ 4,500* |
| *Home office ($6,600 + net income of $3,500)* | *10,100* |
| *Total* | *$14,600* |

**Working papers for combined statements for home office and branch** When the accountants for the home office receive the branch statements for March, they can prepare ***combined statements*** through the use of working papers similar to those illustrated below. The branch figures are taken from the statements submitted by the branch, and the home office figures are assumed.

The figures in the Combined column are used to prepare the income statement and the balance sheet for Homer & Company. Because there is nothing unusual about these statements, they will not be illustrated.

***HOMER & COMPANY***

***Working Papers for Combined Statements***

***For Month Ended March 31***

| | Adjusted Trial Balances | | Eliminations | | |
|---|---|---|---|---|---|
| | Home Office | Branch | Debit | Credit | Combined |
| **Debit balances:** | | | | | |
| Cash | 9,100 | 3,300 | | | 12,400 |
| Accounts receivable | 26,000 | 4,000 | | | 30,000 |
| Inventory | 34,000 | 6,000 | | | 40,000 |
| Store supplies | 3,000 | 1,300 | | | 4,300 |
| Land | 25,000 | | | | 25,000 |
| Buildings and equipment | 60,000 | | | | 60,000 |
| Brady Branch | 6,600 | | | (1) 6,600 | |
| Cost of goods sold | 50,000 | 12,000 | | | 62,000 |
| Selling expense | 6,500 | 2,500 | | | 9,000 |
| General expense | 5,800 | 2,000 | | | 7,800 |
| Interest expense | 300 | | | | 300 |
| Total debits | 226,300 | 31,100 | | | 250,800 |
| **Credit balances:** | | | | | |
| Notes payable | 40,000 | | | | 40,000 |
| Accounts payable | 22,500 | 4,500 | | | 27,000 |
| Accrued liabilities | 2,800 | | | | 2,800 |
| Home office | | 6,600 | (1) 6,600 | | |
| John Homer, capital | 75,000 | | | | 75,000 |
| Sales | 85,000 | 20,000 | | | 105,000 |
| Purchase discounts | 1,000 | | | | 1,000 |
| Total credits | 226,300 | 31,100 | 6,600 | 6,600 | 250,800 |

Explanation of elimination:

(1) Reciprocal accounts maintained by the home office and branch are eliminated. These accounts have no significance since the home office and the branch are a single entity. This elimination entry is made only on the working papers; it is not recorded in the accounting records of either the home office or the branch.

**Closing entries** At the end of the accounting period, the revenue and expense accounts at the branch are closed and the income of $3,500 is transferred to the Home Office account. The home office records the branch income in the Income—Brady Branch account; the balance in this account is then closed to Income Summary when the home office accounts are closed. These entries are illustrated below:

| *Branch Accounting Records* | | |
|---|---|---|
| *Sales* | *20,000* | |
| *Cost of Goods Sold* | | *12,000* |
| *Selling Expense* | | *2,500* |
| *General Expense* | | *2,000* |
| *Income Summary* | | *3,500* |
| *To close revenue and expense accounts.* | | |
| *Income Summary* | *3,500* | |
| *Home Office* | | *3,500* |
| *To transfer balance in Income Summary account to Home Office account.* | | |

| *Home Office Accounting Records* | | |
|---|---|---|
| *Brady Branch* | *3,500* | |
| *Income—Brady Branch* | | *3,500* |
| *To record branch income.* | | |
| *Income—Brady Branch* | *3,500* | |
| *Income Summary* | | *3,500* |
| *To close branch income to Income Summary.* | | |

## Interdepartmental and interbranch pricing policies

In order to obtain a better measure of departmental or branch profit performance, some companies bill the merchandise transferred to departments or branches at prices above cost. Of course, a company does not "make a profit" by simply transferring merchandise to one of its departments or branches; a profit on such transfers can only be realized when the merchandise is sold to customers. When end-of-period statements for the company as a whole are prepared, the ***unrealized profits*** on intracompany transfers of merchandise are eliminated. The ***actual*** cost of merchandise sold is deducted from revenue and the actual cost of merchandise on hand is included among the current assets in the balance sheet.

## KEY TERMS INTRODUCED OR EMPHASIZED IN CHAPTER 23

**Centralized accounting system** A system in which the branches of a company send information on daily transactions to the home office which maintains the accounting records for the entire company.

**Cost center** A unit of a business which incurs expenses or costs but does not directly generate revenue; for example, the personnel department.

**Decentralized accounting system** A system in which each branch of a company maintains its own complete set of accounting records.

**Departmental contribution to overhead** The excess of the gross profit of a given department over the operating expenses which would be eliminated if the department were discontinued. Even though a department is unprofitable when all expenses have been properly allocated, discontinuance of the department would cause the company's net income to decline if the department is making a contribution toward meeting overhead expenses.

**Departmental expense allocation** The process of allocating indirect expenses of a business among departments in order to measure the performance of each department. For example, building occupancy expense may be allocated on the basis of the square feet of space used by each department.

**Departmental income statement** An income statement showing the revenue, expenses, and net income of the business and of each department.

**Profit center** A unit of a business which produces revenue which can be identified with the unit; for example, the meat department of a supermarket.

**Reciprocal accounts** Offsetting accounts maintained by the home office and a branch. The home office maintains an asset account (with a debit balance) summarizing its investment in the branch. The branch maintains a Home Office account (with a credit balance) similar to a proprietorship account. Both of these accounts are eliminated (offset against each other) when combined financial statements are prepared for the home office and its branches.

**Responsibility accounting** A system designed to measure performance of each segment of a business for which a supervisor is responsible.

## REVIEW QUESTIONS

**1** What is a ***responsibility accounting*** system?

**2** Distinguish between a ***cost center*** and a ***profit center.***

**3** What are some uses that management may make of departmental accounting information?

**4** The College Bookstore has employed Kay Barton as its new manager. In the past the income statement of the bookstore has shown only total revenue and operating expenses. The new manager wants to introduce procedures for measuring gross profits for each of three departmental areas: textbooks, general books, and merchandise. Explain what changes in the accounting system will be required and what benefits Barton may expect to gain from the departmental information.

**5** Jill Stone, the manager of a retail store, states that the selling prices in her business are established by adding 50% to merchandise cost.

  **a** If this statement is factual, what rate of gross profit per dollar of gross sales should the company realize?

  **b** Assuming that the actual gross profit for one department of this firm for a given period is 28% of ***net*** sales, what reasons can you give to explain this?

**6** Give three examples of items representing indirect expenses to the departments within a large department store, such as Sears or Penneys. For each example of an indirect expense, indicate a reasonable basis for use in allocating this expense among the various departments.

**7** Explain the distinction between direct expenses and indirect expenses as these terms are used in relation to expense allocation among departments.

**8** Atwood Hardware has three operating departments. In its departmental income statement, building occupancy expenses are allocated among departments on the basis of sales. Explain why you do or do not agree that this procedure will produce useful information for management.

**9** After examining an income statement showing net income by departments, James Wood, the manager of one department, complains that the amount of income taxes allocated to his department is greater than the amount the business as a whole will have to pay, and he feels this is entirely unreasonable. Explain how this could happen, and whether or not you agree with the department manager's view.

**10** What is meant by the term ***contribution to indirect expenses?*** Explain why management may find information about the contribution to overhead of each department more useful than departmental net income figures.

**11** Briefly describe the type of information that management should obtain from a branch accounting system.

**12** Differentiate between a ***centralized*** and a ***decentralized*** accounting system for branch operations.

**13** Describe the nature of the Home Office account which appears in the records of the branch and the Branch account which appears in the records of the home office. Why are these two accounts referred to as ***reciprocal*** accounts?

**14** What is the reason for preparing working papers for combined statements of the home office and branch?

## EXERCISES

*Ex. 23-1* The floor space on the first floor is twice as valuable as the floor space on the second floor. Each of the two floors has 12,000 square feet and total monthly rental paid on the building is $15,000. How much of the monthly rental expense should be allocated to a department which occupies 4,800 square feet on the second floor?

*Ex. 23-2* The Rawton Company allocates indirect operating expenses to its two departments on the basis of sales. In Year 1, the following allocation was made:

| | Total | Dept. A | Dept. B |
|---|---|---|---|
| Sales | $500,000 | $300,000 | $200,000 |
| Indirect operating expenses | 140,000 | 84,000 | 56,000 |

Assume that in Year 2 sales in Department A remain at $300,000 but, as a result of a 50% increase in selling prices, sales in Department B increase to $300,000. If indirect operating expenses in Year 2 remain at $140,000, how much of these expenses will be allocated to each department? Is this result logical? Explain.

*Ex. 23-3* A given department shows an annual operating loss of $36,000 after deducting $54,000 of operating expenses. If $24,000 of the operating expenses allocated to this department are fixed and cannot be avoided, what would be the effect on the company's operating income if this particular department is closed?

*Ex. 23-4* The president of Dunbar Company wants to eliminate Department B "because it's losing money." The operating results for the latest year appear below:

| | Total | Dept. A | Dept. B |
|---|---|---|---|
| Sales | $900,000 | $600,000 | $ 300,000 |
| Operating expenses (40% of which remain constant at all levels of sales) | 810,000 | 360,000 | 450,000 |
| Operating income | $ 90,000 | $240,000 | $(150,000) |

What advice would you give the president, assuming that the indirect operating expenses of $324,000 would remain unchanged if Department B is eliminated?

*Ex. 23-5* Given below are the reciprocal interbranch accounts at the end of Year 1:

**Branch Records**
**Home Office**

| Date | Transaction | Dr | Cr | Balance |
|---|---|---|---|---|
| 12/1 | Balance | | | 91,600 |
| 12/10 | Cash remitted to home office | 14,000 | | 77,600 |
| 12/20 | Merchandise received from home office | | 10,000 | 87,600 |
| 12/31 | Net income | | 6,500 | 94,100 |

**Home Office Records**
**Jersey Branch**

| Date | Transaction | Dr | Cr | Balance |
|---|---|---|---|---|
| 12/1 | Balance | | | 91,600 |
| 12/12 | Cash received from branch | | 14,000 | 77,600 |
| 12/19 | Merchandise shipped to branch | 10,000 | | 87,600 |
| 12/29 | Equipment sent to branch | 2,000 | | 89,600 |

Prepare the entry required in **(a)** the branch records and **(b)** the home office records to bring each set of accounts up to date at the end of Year 1.

*Ex. 23-6* Refer to Exercise 23-5, above:

**a** What is the ***correct*** balance in each account at the end of Year 1?

**b** Show the elimination entry that would be required on the working papers at the end of Year 1 in preparing combined statements for the home office and the branch. (Show this entry in general journal form even though it would be made only on the working papers.)

## PROBLEMS

### Group A

*23A-1* A preliminary summary of the operating results for Dairymart for Year 1 follows:

| | Total | Department C | Department D |
|---|---|---|---|
| Net sales | $750,000 | $300,000 | $450,000 |
| Cost of goods sold and operating expenses other than advertising | (570,000) | (215,000) | (355,000) |
| Advertising expense (allocated on basis of net sales) | (100,000) | (40,000) | (60,000) |
| Operating income | $ 80,000 | $ 45,000 | $ 35,000 |

Advertising expense consists of $60,000 in direct product advertising (70% of which was applicable to Department C and 30% to Department D) and $40,000 in general advertising which promoted the image of the company. Bill Jay, the manager of Department D, thinks that his department was actually more profitable than Department C and argued that he was charged with an unreasonable amount of advertising expense. He maintains that the direct product advertising should be assigned to the departments on the basis of actual expenditures and that only the $40,000 of general (indirect) advertising should be allocated in proportion to net sales.

**Instructions** Prepare a departmental income statement for Year 1, following the expense allocation procedure suggested by the manager of Department D. Which department was more profitable? Why?

*23A-2* Maternity Shop offers its customers a 2% cash discount on all cash sales and adds a financing charge of 1% per month to all account balances that are not paid within 30 days of the invoice date. Cash discounts are allocated directly to its three operating departments at the time of sale. Revenues from financing charges are allocated to the departments on the basis of net *credit* sales.

These data are taken from the Maternity Shop accounts for the current year:

| | Total | Department X | Department Y | Department Z |
|---|---|---|---|---|
| Sales | $600,000 | $180,000 | $320,000 | $100,000 |
| Revenues from financing charges | 37,500 | | | |
| Cash discounts on sales | (4,500) | (1,000) | (2,900) | (600) |
| Net revenues from sales | $633,000 | | | |

**Instructions**

a Determine the amount of net credit sales for each of the three departments. (Hint: First determine the amount of cash sales in each department. Remember that cash discounts are equal to 2% of cash sales.)

b Determine the amount of financing charges that will be allocated to each department by the accountant of the Maternity Shop.

c Comment on the validity of the method used by this company in allocating financing charges to departments. Explain why you think it will or will not produce accurate results.

*23A-3* Joe Miller owns an apple orchard, from which he harvested and sold during the current year 200,000 pounds of apples. The price received varied in accordance with the grade of apple, as shown in the table below:

| Grade of Apple | Pounds | Price per Pound | Receipts |
|---|---|---|---|
| Superior | 40,000 | $0.24 | $ 9,600 |
| Medium | 100,000 | 0.108 | 10,800 |
| Cooking | 60,000 | 0.06 | 3,600 |
| | 200,000 | | $24,000 |

Miller's expenses for the year, as taken from his accounting records, are given on page 894.

| | | Dollars | Per Pound |
|---|---|---|---|
| *Indirect expenses:* | | | |
| *Growing expenses* | | *$ 6,000* | *$0.03* |
| *Harvesting expenses* | | *4,000* | *0.02* |
| *Direct expenses:* | | | |
| *Packing and shipping:* | | | |
| *Superior (40,000 pounds)* | *$2,000* | | *0.05* |
| *Medium (100,000 pounds)* | *4,000* | | *0.04* |
| *Cooking (60,000 pounds)* | *1,800* | *7,800* | *0.03* |
| *Total expenses* | | *$17,800* | |

Miller asked a friend, who was taking an accounting course at a nearby university, to determine his income from each grade of apple. The friend prepared the following schedule:

| | Total | Superior | Medium | Cooking |
|---|---|---|---|---|
| *Sales* | *$24,000* | *$9,600* | *$10,800* | *$ 3,600* |
| *Expenses:* | | | | |
| *Growing** | *$ 6,000* | *$1,200* | *$ 3,000* | *$ 1,800* |
| *Harvesting** | *4,000* | *800* | *2,000* | *1,200* |
| *Packing and shipping* | *7,800* | *2,000* | *4,000* | *1,800* |
| *Total expenses* | *$17,800* | *$4,000* | *$ 9,000* | *$ 4,800* |
| *Net income (or loss)* | *$ 6,200* | *$5,600* | *$ 1,800* | *$(1,200)* |

* Allocated to each grade on the basis of the number of pounds sold.

After studying this statement, Miller remarked to a neighbor, "I made a lot of money on my superiors and a little bit on the mediums, but I should have dumped the cooking apples in the river; they cost me more than I got for them!"

**Instructions**

**a** Prepare an income statement in a form that will show the contribution of each grade of apples to overhead (indirect expenses of growing and harvesting). Packing and shipping expenses should be considered direct expenses. Use separate columns for Total, Superior, Medium, and Cooking.

**b** Do you agree with Miller's remark to his neighbor? Discuss. Comment on the conclusion to be drawn as to the contribution of the cooking apples.

**c** Prepare an income statement showing ***net income*** for each grade of apple by allocating growing and harvesting expenses on the basis of the ***relative sales value*** of each grade.

*23A-4* Monique's is a retail business having three departments. Departmental expense accounts are maintained for some expenses, with the rest being allocated to the departments at the end of each accounting period. The operating expenses and other departmental data for the current year are shown on page 895.

| | Dept. K | Dept. L | Dept. M | Indirect Expenses |
|---|---|---|---|---|
| *Departmental operating expenses:* | | | | |
| Sales salaries (direct) | $ 30,000 | $ 25,750 | $19,250 | -0- |
| Indirect salaries | | | | $ 25,000 |
| Building rental | | | | 9,600 |
| Advertising (direct and indirect) | 1,800 | 1,200 | 600 | 1,500 |
| Supplies used (direct) | 600 | 700 | 500 | -0- |
| Payroll taxes (5% of salaries) | | | | 5,000 |
| Insurance expense | | | | 900 |
| Depreciation on equipment (direct) | 375 | 530 | 695 | -0- |
| Miscellaneous expense (direct and indirect) | 300 | 200 | 100 | 2,400 |

| | Dept. K | Dept. L | Dept. M | Total |
|---|---|---|---|---|
| *Other departmental data:* | | | | |
| Net sales | $212,500 | $127,500 | $85,000 | $425,000 |
| Cost of goods sold | 158,500 | 82,950 | 48,550 | 290,000 |
| Equipment (original cost) | 3,640 | 3,900 | 5,460 | 13,000 |
| Average inventory | 15,860 | 19,500 | 29,640 | 65,000 |
| Value of floor space | 50% | 30% | 20% | 100% |
| Floor space (square feet) | 1,600 | 1,600 | 800 | 4,000 |

Indirect expenses are allocated among the departments on the bases given below.

| Indirect Expense | Basis of Allocation |
|---|---|
| Indirect salaries | Amount of gross profit |
| Building rental | Value of floor space occupied |
| Advertising | Direct departmental advertising |
| Payroll taxes | Salaries, both direct and indirect |
| Insurance expense | Sum of equipment (original cost) and average inventory |
| Miscellaneous expense | Net sales |

**Instructions**

**a** Prepare a schedule showing the allocation of operating expenses among the three departments. Use four money columns headed: Total, Department K, Department L, and Department M. Give schedules for each expense item in support of the amounts allocated to departments.

**b** Prepare a summarized departmental income statement for Monique's, using the same column headings as in part **a.** Show summary figures for both total and departmental operating expenses, using totals from the schedule in **a.** Compute income taxes expense as 20% of income before taxes. (Omit computation of earnings per share.)

*23A-5* For many years the Colonial Furniture Company has operated a store in Kansas City. Early in Year 10, the company decided to open a branch store in Springfield and to use a decentralized accounting system for the branch. Both the branch and the home office use a perpetual inventory system. During the month of February the following transactions (given in summary form) were completed by the branch:

**Feb. 1** The home office sent $10,000 cash to the branch to be used as a working fund and authorized the branch manager to sign a lease on a store.

**Feb. 2** The branch manager paid store rent for February, $2,000 (debit Operating Expense on branch records).

**Feb. 3** Received merchandise from home office, $14,400 (debit Inventory on branch records; credit Inventory on home office records).

**Feb. 5** Purchased merchandise on credit from local factory, $13,600 (debit Inventory on branch records).

**Feb. 12** Borrowed $6,000 from local bank and deposited balance in branch checking account.

**Feb. 28** Sales during February: cash, $8,400; credit, $24,200.

**Feb. 28** Payments to merchandise creditors, $8,000.

**Feb. 28** Collections on accounts receivable, $11,500.

**Feb. 28** Paid operating expenses, $3,300.

**Feb. 28** Sent cash of $9,000 to home office. Returned to home office damaged sofa, which had been billed to the branch at $350. (Credit Inventory for return of sofa.)

**Feb. 28** Home office notified branch that operating expenses allocated to the branch for the month of February amounted to $840. This included advertising and other expenses paid by the home office. These expenses were originally recorded by the home office in the Operating Expense account.

**Feb. 28** Cost of goods sold by the Springfield Branch during February amounted to $22,400.

**Instructions**

**a** Record the foregoing transactions in journal entry form in the records of the branch. (Explanations may be omitted from all journal entries in this problem.) Also prepare closing entries. Compute the balance at February 28 in the Home Office account which appears in the accounts of the branch.

**b** Select the transactions which should be recorded in the records of the home office (including entry to record branch net income) and prepare entries to record them. Ignore closing entries. Compute the balance in the Springfield Branch account at February 28 which appears in the accounts of the home office.

## Group B

***23B-1*** Given below are the results for the two departments operated by Weber TV & Appliance Co. during Year 1:

| | Dept. X | Dept. Y |
|---|---|---|
| Sales | $612,000 | $350,000 |
| Sales returns and allowances | 12,000 | 20,000 |
| Cost of goods sold | 360,000 | 231,000 |
| Direct departmental expenses | 123,000 | 80,000 |
| Indirect departmental expenses (not allocated), $90,000 | | |
| Interest earned (not allocated), $10,000 | | |

**Instructions** Prepare a departmental income statement for Year 1 showing contribution to indirect expenses. Use three columns as follows: Total, Dept. X, and

Dept. Y. Assume that income taxes expense amounts to 25% of income before income taxes. (Omit computation of earnings per share.)

***23B-2*** Parkway Mall operates a retail business in a two-story building. Each floor has usable space of 20,000 square feet. The occupancy cost for the building per year averages $276,000. There are a number of separate departments in the store, and departmental income statements are prepared each year. Department no. 4 occupies 2,000 square feet of space on the first floor. Department no. 8 occupies 3,500 square feet of space on the second floor.

In allocating occupancy cost among the various departments, the accountant has determined that the average annual occupancy cost per square foot is $6.90 ($276,000 ÷ 40,000); therefore Department no. 4 has been charged with $13,800 of occupancy cost and Department no. 8 with $24,150, on the basis of space occupied.

Ellen Ward, the manager of Department no. 8, feels that this allocation is unreasonable. She has made a study of rental prices being charged for similar property in the area and finds the following:

| | *Average Yearly Rental per Square Foot* |
|---|---|
| *First-floor space* | *$10.00* |
| *Second-floor space* | *5.00* |

On the basis of this evidence, Ward argues that the charge to her department should be made on the ***relative value*** of space on each floor.

**Instructions**

**a** Comment on the validity of Ward's position.

**b** On the basis of Ward's findings, how much occupancy cost per year should be charged to Department no. 4 and to Department no. 8? Show computations. (Hint: Since first-floor space is twice as valuable as second-floor space, $66\frac{2}{3}$% of the total occupancy costs are applicable to the first floor.)

***23B-3*** Solana Sand & Gravel Co. has four operating departments. At the end of the current year the controller has computed departmental results in three ways, showing net income by departments, the departmental contribution to indirect expenses, and the gross profit on sales for each department, as shown below.

| | *Total* | *Dept. One* | *Dept. Two* | *Dept. Three* | *Dept. Four* |
|---|---|---|---|---|---|
| *Departmental net sales* | *$800,000* | *$320,000* | *$180,000* | *$220,000* | *$80,000* |
| *Departmental net income* | *21,200* | *68,300* | *(4,000)* | *(13,100)* | *(30,000)* |
| *Departmental contribution to indirect expenses* | *88,800* | *98,000* | *14,000* | *(2,200)* | *(21,000)* |
| *Departmental gross profit on sales* | *184,000* | *128,000* | *36,000* | *22,000* | *(2,000)* |
| *Gross profit as a percentage of sales* | *23%* | *40%* | *20%* | *10%* | *($2\frac{1}{2}$%)* |

Note: Parentheses indicate a loss.

**Instructions**

**a** On the basis of the above information, prepare a departmental income statement for Solana Sand & Gravel Co. It will be necessary to compute the following amounts: cost of goods sold, direct expenses, and indirect expenses. (Omit computation of earnings per share.)

**b** What conclusions would you reach about the operations of Departments One, Two, Three, and Four on the basis of the statement prepared in **a**? Should any of these departments be discontinued? Explain your reasoning.

***23B-4*** Turner & Cole, a retailing partnership, maintains departmental accounts for net sales and cost of goods sold. Operating expenses are allocated between the two departments of the business at the end of the year. The operating results for Year 2 are summarized below:

| | *Total* | *Dept. A* | *Dept. B* |
|---|---|---|---|
| ***Net sales*** | *$900,000* | *$540,000* | *$360,000* |
| ***Cost of goods sold*** | *540,000* | *297,000* | *243,000* |
| ***Gross profit*** | *$360,000* | *$243,000* | *$117,000* |
| ***(Gross profit percentage)*** | *(40%)* | *(45%)* | *(32½%)* |
| ***Operating expenses (not yet allocated)*** | *333,900* | | |
| ***Net income**** | *$ 26,100* | | |

*No income taxes expense appears because the business is organized as a partnership.

An analysis of operating expenses for Year 2 indicates that the following amounts in each class of expense are directly chargeable to the departments. (The allocation basis of the ***indirect*** portion of each class of expense is shown in brackets.)

| | *Direct Expenses* | | |
|---|---|---|---|
| | *Dept. A* | *Dept. B* | *Indirect Expenses* |
| ***Administrative expense (on basis of direct administrative expense)*** | *$18,000* | *$ 9,000* | *$42,900* |
| ***Advertising expense (on basis of net sales)*** | *21,000* | *15,000* | *16,800* |
| ***Buying expense (on basis of cost of goods sold)*** | *21,900* | *16,500* | *21,600* |
| ***Occupancy expense (equally)*** | *1,500* | *3,000* | *61,500* |
| ***Selling expense (on basis of net sales)*** | *35,400* | *21,600* | *28,200* |

**Instructions**

**a** Prepare a departmental expense allocation sheet for Year 2. Use the form illustrated on page 878.

**b** Prepare a departmental income statement for Year 2 showing contribution to indirect expenses. Use the form illustrated on page 883.

**c** Prepare a condensed income statement for Year 2, assuming that both direct and indirect expenses are allocated to the departments. Show a single figure for operating expenses. Based on the income statements prepared in parts **b** and **c**, do you believe that Department B should be eliminated? Explain.

***23B-5*** Auto Tune, Inc., operates several sales and service outlets (branches) throughout the metropolitan area of a large city. A decentralized accounting system is used by each branch. At the end of October, the following reciprocal accounts appear in the accounting records of the Central branch and the home office:

| *Branch Records* | | *Home Office Records* | |
|---|---|---|---|
| ***Home Office (credit balance)*** | *$17,970* | ***Central Branch (debit balance)*** | *$17,210* |

The reason for the discrepancy in the amounts shown in the two accounts is that the branch net income for October, $1,800, and a cash deposit made by the branch to the account of the home office, $1,040, have not been recorded by the home office. Both the branch and the home office use a perpetual inventory system.

During November, the following transactions affected the two accounts:

**Nov. 6** Home office shipped merchandise to branch, $7,250. Debit Inventory account on branch books; credit Inventory account on home office books.

**Nov. 12** Branch transferred $4,950 from its bank account to the bank account of the home office.

**Nov. 19** Branch returned shop supplies costing $610 to the home office. Shop supplies are carried in the Shop Supplies account in both sets of accounts.

**Nov. 30** Home office notified branch that operating expenses of $1,100 which had been recorded in the accounts of the home office in the Operating Expense account were chargeable to the Central branch.

**Nov. 30** The Income Summary account in the accounts of the branch showed a debit balance of $590 at the end of November.

**Instructions**

**a** Record the transactions listed above in the accounts of the Central branch. (Explanations may be omitted for all journal entries in this problem.)

**b** Record the two transactions relating to the month of October and all transactions for November in the accounts of the home office.

**c** Determine the balances in the Home Office account and the Central Branch account at the end of November.

## BUSINESS DECISION PROBLEM 23

Brit Dalby, owner of Dalby Drug Company, is considering the advisability of dropping all services that are not pharmaceutical in nature and concentrating on the drug business. At the present time, in addition to drugs, Dalby has a fountain and handles various general merchandise such as magazines, candy, toys, and cosmetics. During the past year, the sales and cost of goods sold for the store were as follows:

| | *Total* | *Drugs* | *Fountain* | *General Merchandise* |
|---|---|---|---|---|
| *Sales (net)* | *$531,000* | *$400,000* | *$45,000* | *$86,000* |
| *Cost of goods sold* | *300,500* | *200,000* | *36,000* | *64,500* |

Dalby has studied trade association studies summarizing the reports of other store owners who have made similar decisions. They report that after dropping fountain operations, drug sales declined an average of 10% and sales of general merchandise fell 8%. Reports from store owners who discontinued general merchandise operation, but continued to operate a fountain, indicate that drug sales fell by an average of 4% and fountain sales declined by $7\frac{1}{2}$%. If Dalby Drug Company discontinued general merchandise operation it could lease the surplus floor space for $2,500 per month to another business which would use it as a storage facility.

At the present time Dalby employs three pharmacists at combined annual salaries of $75,000, and a fountain man at $10,000 per year. The fountain man spends about 40% of his time stocking shelves and selling general merchandise items. If he were not there, one of the pharmacists would have to do this work and Dalby estimates that drug sales would decline an additional 2% (of present sales) as a result of inconvenience to customers.

The pharmacists have stated they would not be willing to take over the fountain operation, but Dalby believes that he could employ student help at a cost of $5,000 per year if the general merchandise sales were dropped. Dalby estimates that if the fountain were discontinued he might realize about $4,000 from the sale of fountain equipment, but he would have to spend about this amount in remodeling. He also considers that the effect on indirect operating expenses as a result of dropping either department would be negligible.

**Instructions**

**a** Determine the departmental contribution to indirect expenses during the past year.

**b** Prepare an analysis of the estimated dollar benefit or loss that might be expected to result if Dalby discontinued the fountain. Prepare a similar analysis assuming discontinuance of the general merchandise operation. What would be your advice to Dalby?

# 24

# ACCOUNTING FOR MANUFACTURING OPERATIONS

In preceding chapters we have considered accounting principles and procedures applicable to nonmanufacturing businesses—firms engaged in buying and selling merchandise, or in providing services. Another large and important category of business operation is ***manufacturing.*** All of the accounting principles and most of the accounting procedures we have discussed are equally applicable to manufacturers. Firms engaged in manufacturing, however, face some special accounting problems and require additional accounting procedures to measure, control, and report factory production costs.

## Manufacturers produce the goods they sell

The basic difference between a merchandising business and a manufacturer is that the merchant purchases merchandise in a ready-to-sell condition, whereas the manufacturer produces the goods it sells. In a merchandising business the cost of goods available for sale is based upon the ***cost to purchase*** this merchandise, as shown below:

***Dollar amounts based on purchase price***

**Beginning Inventory of Merchandise + Purchases of Merchandise = Cost of Goods Available for Sale**

In a manufacturing business, on the other hand, the cost of goods available for sale is based upon the ***cost to manufacture*** the finished goods, as indicated below:

***Dollar amounts based on manufacturing cost***

**Beginning Inventory of Finished Goods + Cost of Finished Goods Manufactured = Cost of Goods Available for Sale**

Comparison of these two similar computations shows that the ***cost of finished goods manufactured*** in a manufacturing company is in a sense the equivalent of ***purchases of merchandise*** in a merchandising business. This point is further emphasized by comparing the income statements of a merchandising company and a manufacturing company.

**Comparison of income statements for manufacturing and merchandising companies** The treatment of sales, selling expenses, general administrative expenses, and income taxes is the same in the income statement of a manufacturing company as for a merchandising company. The only difference in the two partial income statements shown below lies in the cost of goods sold section. In the income statement of Allied Manufacturing Company, the term Cost of Finished Goods Manufactured replaces the item labeled Purchases in the income statement of the merchandising company.

***APEX MERCHANDISING COMPANY***
***Partial Income Statement***
***For the Year Ended December 31, Year 5***

| | | |
|---|---|---|
| *Sales* | | *$1,300,000* |
| *Cost of goods sold:* | | |
| *Beginning inventory of merchandise* | *$150,000* | |
| → **Purchases** | *800,000* | |
| *Cost of goods available for sale* | *$950,000* | |
| *Less: Ending inventory of merchandise* | *170,000* | |
| *Cost of goods sold* | | *780,000* |
| *Gross profit on sales* | | *$ 520,000* |

***ALLIED MANUFACTURING COMPANY***
***Partial Income Statement***
***For the Year Ended December 31, Year 5***

| | | |
|---|---|---|
| *Sales* | | *$1,300,000* |
| *Cost of goods sold:* | | |
| *Beginning inventory of finished goods* | *$150,000* | |
| → ***Cost of finished goods manufactured (see supporting schedule)*** | *800,000* | |
| *Cost of goods available for sale* | *$950,000* | |
| *Less: Ending inventory of finished goods* | *170,000* | |
| *Cost of goods sold* | | *780,000* |
| *Gross profit on sales* | | *$ 520,000* |

In the illustrated income statement of Allied Manufacturing Company, our attention is focused on the item: "Cost of finished goods manufactured . . . $800,000." This amount was computed in a supplementary schedule prepared to accompany and support the income statement. The supplementary schedule is illustrated on page 909 and will be discussed later in this chapter.

Before we describe how the cost of finished goods manufactured is computed, let us first consider the ***types of costs*** which a manufacturer is likely to incur in producing a finished product.

## Manufacturing costs

A typical manufacturing firm buys raw materials and converts them into a finished product. The raw materials purchased by an aircraft manufacturer, for example, include sheet aluminum, steel, paint, and a variety of electronic gear and control instruments. The completed airplanes assembled from these components are the ***finished goods*** of the aircraft manufacturer. The terms ***raw materials*** and ***finished goods,*** as used in accounting, are defined from the viewpoint of each manufacturing firm. Sheet aluminum, for example, is a raw material from the viewpoint of an aircraft company, but it is a finished product of an aluminum company.

In converting raw materials into finished goods, the manufacturer employs factory labor, uses machinery, and incurs many other manufacturing costs, such as heat, light, and power, machinery repairs, and supervisory salaries. All manufacturing costs other than raw materials and direct factory labor are referred to as ***factory overhead.*** Thus, each unit of finished goods includes ***three basic types*** of manufacturing cost: (1) raw materials used, (2) direct labor, and (3) factory overhead. Each of these three cost elements will now be discussed in some detail.[1]

**Raw Materials** The cost of raw materials (also called ***direct materials***) represents the delivered cost of materials and parts which enter into and become part of the finished product. In thinking about the elements of manufacturing cost during a given period, we are interested in the cost of raw materials ***used*** rather than the amount of raw materials purchased. Purchases of raw materials flow into the raw materials warehouse, but the consumption or ***use*** of raw materials consists of the materials moved from the raw materials warehouse into the production process. The computation of the cost of raw materials used is illustrated below:

***Computing the cost of raw materials used***

| | |
|---|---|
| ***Raw materials used:*** | |
| *Beginning raw materials inventory* | *$ 50,000* |
| *Purchases of raw materials* | *160,000* |
| *Transportation-in (raw materials)* | *5,000* |
| *Cost of raw materials available for use* | *$215,000* |
| *Less: Ending raw materials inventory* | *45,000* |
| *Cost of raw materials used* | *$170,000* |

[1] The Committee on Terminology of the American Institute of Certified Public Accountants has recommended that ". . . items entering into the computation of cost of manufacturing, such as material, labor and overhead, should be described as *costs* and not as *expenses*."

Since the cost of raw materials used is computed by subtracting the amount of raw materials on hand at the end of the period from the total of the beginning inventory plus the purchases of raw materials during the period, any raw materials which were stolen, spoiled, or lost will be included automatically in the residual amount labeled "cost of raw materials used."

**Direct labor cost** The second major element of manufacturing costs is called ***direct labor*** and consists of the wages paid to factory employees ***who work directly on the product being manufactured.*** Direct labor costs include the payroll costs of machine operators, assemblers, and those who work on the product by hand or with tools, but not the wages of indirect workers such as plant watchmen, janitors, timekeepers, and supervisors.

What is the reason for separating the costs of direct labor and indirect labor? Direct labor is expended in converting raw materials into finished goods. If factory output is to be increased, it will be necessary to employ more direct workers and direct labor costs will rise. If factory output is to be reduced, any existing hours of overtime will be reduced and workers may be laid off. Direct labor costs vary directly with changes in the level of output; consequently, in planning operations for future periods, management can estimate the direct labor cost required for any desired volume of production.

Indirect labor, on the other hand, is much less inclined to rise and fall with changes in factory output. For example, an increase or decrease of 10% in the number of units being produced will ordinarily not cause any change in the salary of the factory superintendent or in the number of janitors or guards. A large change in the volume of production will, of course, have some impact upon indirect labor costs.

**Factory overhead** ***Factory overhead*** includes all costs incurred in the factory other than the costs of raw materials and direct labor. Included in factory overhead are such costs as the following:

**1 Indirect labor**
- **a** Supervision
- **b** Timekeeping
- **c** Janitorial and maintenance
- **d** Production scheduling and quality control
- **e** Plant security service

**2 Occupancy costs**
- **a** Depreciation of buildings
- **b** Insurance on buildings
- **c** Property taxes on land and buildings
- **d** Repairs and maintenance of buildings
- **e** Heat, light, and power

**3 Machinery and equipment costs**
- **a** Depreciation of machinery and equipment

**b** Insurance on machinery and equipment
**c** Property taxes on machinery and equipment
**d** Repairs and maintenance of machinery and equipment
**e** Small tools used in the factory

This is not a complete list of factory overhead costs; in fact, it is the impossibility of preparing a complete list that leads accountants to define factory overhead as ***all costs incurred in the factory other than raw material and direct labor.***

A significant characteristic of factory overhead is that these costs ***cannot be related directly to units of product*** as can the costs of direct labor and direct material. In a factory producing two different products such as radios and television sets, it is possible to measure fairly accurately the costs of raw material and direct labor applied to each product, but the nature of factory overhead costs (such as insurance and repairs to buildings) is such that they cannot be associated directly with the particular articles being produced. For this reason, raw materials and direct labor are sometimes referred to as the ***direct costs*** or ***prime costs*** of manufacturing in contrast to factory overhead, which may be regarded as an ***indirect cost.***

Certain costs such as insurance, property taxes, telephone, and salaries of executives may be applicable in part to factory operations and in part to administrative and selling functions of the company. In such cases these costs may be apportioned among factory overhead, general administrative expense, and selling expense accounts.

### The concept of product costs

Why is it important to associate such costs as factory wages and repairs to factory equipment with the cost of finished goods manufactured? Why not treat these costs as expenses of the current period? The answer to these questions is that manufacturing costs are ***product costs*** rather than ***period costs.***

Product costs are not viewed as expenses; rather, they are the cost of creating inventory. Thus, product costs ***represent an asset*** until the related goods are sold, at which time they are deducted from revenue as the ***cost of goods sold.*** In theory, product costs include all costs associated with the production and flow of manufactured goods up to the point where the goods are completed and ready for sale.

Costs that are charged to expense in the period in which they are incurred are called ***period costs.*** Such costs are ***not*** related to the production and flow of manufactured goods but are deducted from revenue on the assumption that the associated benefits are received in the same period as the expenditures are made. Period costs include all general and administrative expenses, selling expenses, and income taxes expense. Some specific examples are the salaries of the treasurer and controller and their staffs, commissions to salespeople, and advertising.

The flows of period costs and product costs through the financial statements are illustrated below:

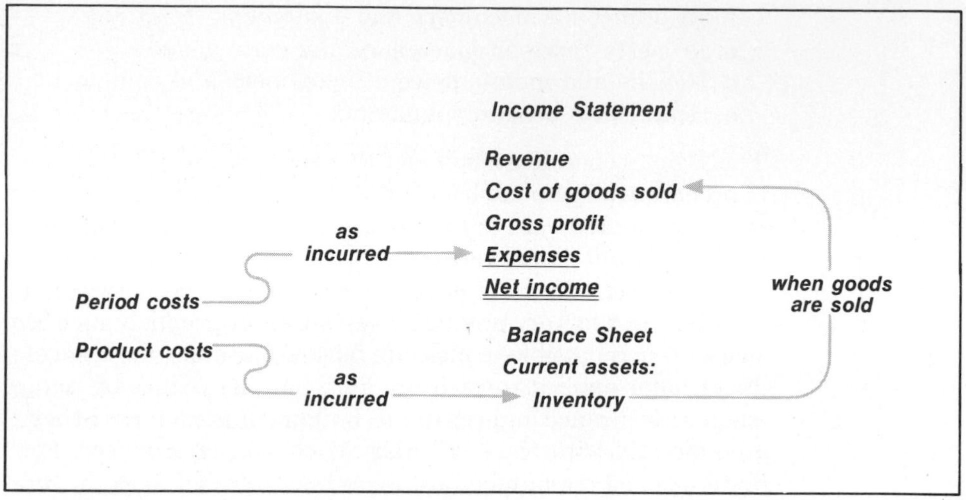


Depreciation on a raw materials warehouse is a product cost, because this cost relates to the manufacturing process. Depreciation on a finished goods warehouse, on the other hand, is a period cost because finished goods have been completed and are ready for sale.

The exact dividing line between product and period costs is not always clear. Traditionally, expenditures relating to the manufacturing function are considered product costs, and those relating to the selling and administrative functions are considered period costs. In some cases it is difficult to determine whether a particular cost relates to manufacturing or administrative functions. For example, the cost of maintaining a cost accounting department, or a personnel department, or a security service may be treated by some companies as factory overhead (product costs) and by other firms as administrative expense (period cost). These variations in accounting practice, however, stem from differences of interpretation rather than from theoretical distinctions.

## Product costs and the matching concept: an illustration

To illustrate the relationship between product costs and the generation of revenue, consider a real estate developer who starts construction on a tract of 10 homes in Year 1. During the year, the developer spends $90,000 on each house ($900,000 total) in materials, construction wages, and overhead. At the end of Year 1, all 10 houses are complete but none has yet been sold. How much of the $900,000 in construction costs should the developer recognize as expense in Year 1?

The answer is ***none.*** These costs are not related to any revenue earned by the developer in Year 1, but they are related to the revenue that will be earned in the period in which the houses are sold. Therefore, at the end of Year 1, the $900,000 of product costs should appear in the developer's balance sheet as inventory. As each house is sold, $90,000 will be deducted from the sales revenue as the cost of goods sold. In this way, the developer's Year 2 income statement will reflect properly both the revenue and the cost of each sale.

If any of the houses are still unsold at the end of Year 2, their cost should remain in the Inventory account on the balance sheet. By this time, however, the developer may need to consider making an adjustment to reduce the carrying value of this inventory to a market value below cost.

### Inventories for a manufacturing business

At any given moment, a manufacturer may have on hand three separate inventories: a stock of raw materials; partially completed products in various stages of manufacture; and finished goods awaiting sale. Inventories of each of these three classes of items must be taken at the end of each accounting period in order to determine the cost of inventories on hand and the cost of goods sold during the period.

In place of the single inventory account found on the balance sheet of a retail or wholesale business, a manufacturing concern has three separate inventory accounts, all of which are current assets.

1 **Raw materials inventory** This account represents the unused portion of the raw materials purchased. As a matter of convenience, factory supplies on hand (oil, grease, sweeping compounds) acquired for use in maintaining and servicing the factory building and machinery are often merged with raw materials.
2 **Goods in process inventory** This inventory consists of the ***partially completed*** goods on hand in the factory at year-end. The cost of these partially manufactured goods is determined by ***estimating*** the costs of the raw materials, direct labor, and factory overhead associated with these units.
3 **Finished goods inventory** This account shows the cost of finished goods on hand and awaiting sale to customers as of the end of the year. The cost of these finished units is composed of the factory costs of raw material, direct labor, and factory overhead.

### Cost of finished goods manufactured

In the partial income statement illustrated on page 902, we saw that a manufacturing company uses the cost of finished goods manufactured in determining the cost of goods available for sale and the cost of goods sold. Let us now see how a manufacturer would compute the cost of finished goods manufactured during the year.

Assume that Allied Manufacturing Company incurred the following manufacturing costs during Year 5:

| | |
|---|---|
| *Raw materials used in production* | *$170,000* |
| *Direct labor* | *400,000* |
| *Factory overhead (detail omitted)* | *240,000* |
| *Total manufacturing costs* | *$810,000* |

In addition to the manufacturing costs incurred in the current period, the cost of finished goods manufactured is affected by any costs assigned to the inventory of goods in process at either the beginning or end of the period. To illustrate, we will now compute the cost of finished goods manufactured by Allied Manufacturing Company during Year 5 under three alternative assumptions.

**Case 1:** First, let us assume that Allied has no inventory of goods in process at either the beginning or the end of Year 5. In this case, all the manufacturing costs incurred in Year 5 are applicable to goods started and completed in the year. The cost of finished goods manufactured, therefore, is $810,000, the sum of the manufacturing costs incurred during the year.

**Case 2:** Now assume that there was an inventory of goods in process of $30,000 at the beginning of Year 5, but no goods in process at the end of the year. This $30,000 beginning inventory of goods in process represents manufacturing costs incurred in Year 4 relating to goods still in process at the end of that year. Since the manufacture of these goods was ***completed in Year 5*** this $30,000 is part of the cost of goods ***finished*** in Year 5. Thus, the cost of finished goods manufactured during Year 5 is $840,000 ($30,000 beginning inventory of goods in process, plus $810,000 manufacturing costs incurred in Year 5).

**Case 3:** Finally, assume that Allied begins Year 5 with a $30,000 inventory of goods in process and ends the year with a $40,000 inventory of partially completed goods. The $40,000 ending inventory of goods in process represents the portion of Year 5's manufacturing costs which are applicable to ***partially*** completed goods rather than to finished goods. In this case, the cost of ***finished*** goods manufactured during Year 5 is computed as follows:

| | |
|---|---|
| *Goods in process inventory, beginning of year* | *$ 30,000* |
| *Total manufacturing costs incurred during year* | *810,000* |
| *Total cost of goods in process during year* | *$840,000* |
| *Less: Goods in process inventory, end of year* | *40,000* |
| *Cost of finished goods manufactured* | *$800,000* |

This third case is the normal situation; that is, most manufacturers have an inventory of partially completed goods at both the beginning and the end of each accounting period. Therefore, the cost of finished goods manufactured generally is computed as shown above.

It is important to distinguish between the terms ***cost of finished goods manufactured*** and ***total manufacturing costs.*** Cost of finished goods manufactured means the cost of the units of finished product ***completed*** during the period. Total manufacturing costs, on the other hand, include the cost of raw materials used, direct labor, and factory overhead for the period, whether the units worked on have been completed or are still in process at the end of the period. As an extreme example, consider a shipyard engaged in the construction of an aircraft carrier. During the first year of work on the ship, the manufacturing costs are as follows:

*Compare "total manufacturing costs" with "cost of goods manufactured"*

| | |
|---|---|
| *Cost of raw materials used* | *$12,000,000* |
| *Direct labor* | *10,000,000* |
| *Factory overhead* | *20,000,000* |
| *Total manufacturing costs* | *$42,000,000* |
| *Less: Goods in process inventory, ending* | *42,000,000* |
| *Cost of finished goods manufactured* | *$ -0-* |

The cost of finished goods manufactured is zero in the above illustration because no products (aircraft carriers) were ***completed*** during the year.

## Schedule of cost of finished goods manufactured

Manufacturing companies often show their computation of the cost of finished goods manufactured in a supplementary schedule which accompanies the income statement. A Schedule of Cost of Goods Manufactured for Allied Manufacturing Company in Year 5 is illustrated below. This schedule follows the same basic format as our computation in Case 3 (above) except that it is expanded to show separately each category of manufacturing cost, including the computation of the cost of raw materials used and the detail of factory overhead. (The amount of detail in a Schedule of Cost of Finished Goods Manufactured may vary greatly from one company to another.)

***ALLIED MANUFACTURING COMPANY***
***Schedule of Cost of Finished Goods Manufactured***
***For the Year Ended December 31, Year 5***

| | | | |
|---|---|---|---|
| *Goods in process inventory, beginning of year* | | | *$ 30,000* |
| *Raw materials used:* | | | |
| *Beginning raw materials inventory* | | *$ 50,000* | |
| *Purchases of raw materials (net)* | | *160,000* | |
| *Transportation-in (raw materials)* | | *5,000* | |
| *Cost of raw materials available for use* | | *$215,000* | |
| *Less: Ending raw materials inventory* | | *45,000* | |
| *Cost of raw materials used* | | *$170,000* | |
| *Direct labor* | | *400,000* | |
| *Factory overhead:* | | | |
| *Indirect labor* | *$120,000* | | |
| *Occupancy costs* | *35,000* | | |
| *Other factory overhead costs* | *85,000* | | |
| *Total factory overhead* | | *240,000* | |
| *Total manufacturing costs* | | | *810,000* |
| *Total cost of goods in process during the year* | | | *$840,000* |
| *Less: Goods in process inventory, end of year* | | | *40,000* |
| *Cost of finished goods manufactured* | | | *$800,000* |

The income statement for Allied Manufacturing Company in Year 5 is illustrated below. Note that the final amount of $800,000 computed in the schedule of cost of finished goods manufactured is carried forward to this income statement and is used in determining the cost of goods available for sale. Also note that no manufacturing costs are included in the operating expense section of the income statement. The item "Cost of goods sold . . . $780,000" represents the manufacturing costs applicable to goods sold in Year 5.

***ALLIED MANUFACTURING COMPANY***
***Income Statement***
***For the Year Ended December 31, Year 5***

| | | |
|---|---|---|
| Sales | | $1,300,000 |
| Cost of goods sold: | | |
| Beginning inventory of finished goods | $150,000 | |
| Cost of finished goods manufactured (see supporting schedule) | 800,000 | |
| Cost of goods available for sale | $950,000 | |
| Less: Ending inventory of finished goods | 170,000 | |
| Cost of goods sold | | 780,000 |
| Gross profit on sales | | $ 520,000 |
| Operating expenses: | | |
| Selling expenses | $185,000 | |
| General and administrative expenses | 215,000 | |
| Total operating expenses | | 400,000 |
| Income from operations | | $ 120,000 |
| Less: Interest expense | | 20,000 |
| Income before income taxes | | $ 100,000 |
| Income taxes expenses | | 30,000 |
| Net income | | $ 70,000 |
| Earnings per share of capital stock | | $2.80 |

## Valuation of inventories in a manufacturing business

Under the periodic inventory system, a manufacturer determines the inventory quantities on the basis of a physical count of raw materials, goods in process, and finished goods at the end of each period. (The use of a perpetual inventory system in a manufacturing business is discussed in Chapter 25.) When the physical quantity of raw materials on hand has been established, the cost of the raw materials inventory is determined in the same manner as for an inventory of merchandise in a trading company. Cost is readily determinable by reference to purchase invoices.

Determining the cost of an inventory of goods in process and an inventory of finished goods is usually a more difficult process. Cost cannot be derived merely by pulling a purchase invoice out of the files. If a manufacturing plant produces only a single product, the ***cost per unit*** for the finished goods inventory can be computed by dividing the cost of finished goods manufactured by the number of units produced. For example, if the cost of finished goods manufactured were $100,000 in a given year, during which the factory turned out 1,000 identical units, the cost per unit would be $100.

Most factories, however, produce more than one product, and the unit cost of each product must be determined by deriving from the accounting records the approximate amount of raw materials, direct labor, and factory overhead applicable to each unit. Determining the cost per unit of the work in process at year-end requires the following steps:

**1** Estimate the cost of the raw materials in the partially completed units.
**2** Add the estimated direct labor cost incurred per unit.
**3** Add an appropriate amount of factory overhead cost per unit.

This same procedure of computing a total cost per unit by combining the three elements of manufacturing cost is followed in pricing the finished goods inventory.

The raw material cost included in a unit of goods in process or a unit of finished goods may be established by reference to the engineering specification for the article. The cost of the direct labor embodied in each unit may be estimated on the basis of tests and observations by supervisors of the direct labor time required per unit of output. In other words, both raw material cost and direct labor cost ***are directly associated*** with units of product.

**Overhead application rate** The third element of manufacturing costs to be included in the pricing of inventories is factory overhead, and this cost element is ***not*** directly related to specific units of output. Therefore, a manufacturer must develop a reasonable method of estimating the appropriate amount of factory overhead per unit. One widely used method is to express total factory overhead costs for the period ***as a percentage*** of total direct labor costs. This percentage is called the ***overhead application rate.*** Factory overhead per unit is then estimated by applying this overhead application rate to the estimated direct labor cost per unit. This method assumes that the ratio of factory overhead to direct labor is the same for all units produced during the period.

For example, the schedule of cost of finished goods manufactured for Allied Manufacturing Company on page 909 shows total factory overhead costs of $240,000 and direct labor of $400,000, indicating an overhead application rate of ***60%*** ($240,000 ÷ $400,000). In other words, for every $1 of direct labor costs, the company incurred 60 cents of factory overhead. We would therefore estimate the factory overhead per unit at an amount equal to 60% of the direct labor cost per unit, as shown on page 912.

*Note the three cost elements in ending inventories*

**ALLIED MANUFACTURING COMPANY**
**Valuation of Ending Inventories**
**December 31, Year 5**

| Inventory | Components of Unit Cost: Prime Costs: Raw Materials | Direct Labor | Factory Overhead (60% of Direct Labor) | Total Unit Cost | Units in Inventory | Total Cost of Inventory |
|---|---|---|---|---|---|---|
| *Goods in process:* | | | | | | |
| Products D-3 | $8 | $10 | $ 6 | $24 | 1,000 | $ 24,000 |
| Product D-4 | 2 | 5 | 3 | 10 | 1,600 | 16,000 |
| Total | | | | | | $ 40,000 |
| *Finished goods:* | | | | | | |
| Product D-3 | $8 | $20 | $12 | $40 | 2,000 | $ 80,000 |
| Product D-4 | 6 | 15 | 9 | 30 | 3,000 | 90,000 |
| Total | | | | | | $170,000 |

## Additional ledger accounts needed by a manufacturing business

The accounting records of a manufacturer are more complex than those of a merchandising or service business. Accounts relating to sales, selling expenses, administrative expenses, liabilities, and stockholders' equity are handled in the same manner by manufacturers as by other companies. However, manufacturing requires some additional asset accounts, and a number of new accounts relating to manufacturing costs.

**Inventory and manufacturing cost accounts** As previously discussed, a manufacturing company uses three inventory accounts (raw materials, goods in process, and finished goods) in place of the single inventory account found in the balance sheet of a wholesale or retail business. In addition, the ledger of a manufacturing business must include accounts for recording each type of manufacturing cost. In recording factory overhead a separate account must be created for each type of indirect manufacturing cost (Depreciation of Machinery, Repairs, Timekeeping, etc.) as indicated on pages 904–905. If there are a great many of these factory overhead accounts, it is convenient to transfer them to a subsidiary ledger which will be controlled by a general ledger account entitled Factory Overhead.

**Plant and equipment accounts** Manufacturing companies generally invest a large part of their total capital in plant and equipment, including tools, dies, conveyors, etc. In recent years the trend toward automation of production has led to particularly heavy investment in manufacturing facilities. Depreciation of the plant and equipment is one of the costs included in factory overhead; the cost of the plant and equipment is thereby gradually transformed into the cost of finished goods manufactured. If a company rents or leases its plant and equipment, the monthly rentals paid would be included in factory overhead.

Because of the great variety of items of manufacturing equipment, it is customary to maintain a subsidiary plant ledger as described in Chapter 12. On the balance sheet the caption of Plant and Equipment, or Machinery and Equipment, is often used to summarize all types of productive facilities.

**The Manufacturing Summary account** Last in our list of ledger accounts unique to a manufacturing business is the Manufacturing Summary, which is used in the closing procedures at the end of each period to determine the cost of finished goods manufactured. The debit balances of the beginning inventories of goods in process and raw materials, the Materials Purchases and Transportation-in accounts, and all of the manufacturing cost accounts are closed (transferred) into the Manufacturing Summary account. Next, an entry is made recording the ending inventories of goods in process and raw materials and crediting the Manufacturing Summary. (These closing entries are illustrated on page 909.) Following these two closing entries, the Manufacturing Summary account has a debit balance ***equal to the cost of finished goods manufactured.*** The Manufacturing Summary account is then closed by transferring its debit balance to the Income Summary account, as shown in the illustration below:

*Note kinds of costs summarized in Manufacturing Summary account*

*Manufacturing Summary*

| | | | | | |
|---|---|---|---|---|---|
| *19__* | | | *19__* | | |
| *Dec. 31* | *Beginning goods in process inventory* | *30,000* | *Dec. 31* | *Ending goods in process inventory* | *40,000* |
| *31* | *Beginning raw materials inventory* | *50,000* | *31* | *Ending raw materials inventory* | *45,000* |
| *31* | *Purchases of raw materials* | *160,000* | *31* | *To close debit balance (cost of finished goods manufactured) to Income Summary* | *800,000* |
| *31* | *Transportation-in* | *5,000* | | | |
| *31* | *Direct labor* | *400,000* | | | |
| *31* | *Factory overhead (total)* | *240,000* | | | |
| | | *885,000* | | | *885,000* |

*Income Summary*

| | | | | | |
|---|---|---|---|---|---|
| *19__* | | | *19__* | | |
| *Dec. 31* | *Beginning finished goods inventory* | *150,000* | *Dec. 31* | *Sales* | *1,300,000* |
| *31* | *Selling expenses* | *185,000* | *31* | *Ending finished goods inventory* | *170,000* |
| *31* | *Gen. & adm. exp.* | *215,000* | | | |
| *31* | *Interest expense* | *20,000* | | | |
| *31* | *Income taxes* | *30,000* | | | |
| *31* | *Cost of finished goods manufactured* | *800,000* | | | |

The use of a Manufacturing Summary account accomplishes three related purposes:

1 The balances of the manufacturing cost accounts are returned to zero so that these accounts are ready for use in measuring the manufacturing costs of the next accounting period.
2 The product costs relating to ending inventories of raw materials and goods in process are recorded as assets to be shown in the balance sheet.
3 The cost of finished goods manufactured is determined for the period.

Note that the Manufacturing Summary account contains all the information which is needed to prepare a schedule of cost of finished goods manufactured.

## Work sheet for a manufacturing business

The work sheet for a merchandising business illustrated in Chapter 5 can be adapted for use in a manufacturing company merely by adding a pair of columns for the data which will appear in the schedule of cost of finished goods manufactured. An illustrative work sheet for Allied Manufacturing Company is presented on page 915. To emphasize the portions of this work sheet which are unique to a manufacturing business, we have omitted the columns containing the trial balance and adjustments and have begun the illustration with the Adjusted Trial Balance columns. Adjusting entries for a manufacturing business do not differ significantly from those previously described for a merchandising business.

**Treatment of inventories in the work sheet** Since the Manufacturing columns are the distinctive feature of this work sheet, they require close study, especially the handling of the inventory accounts.

1 The beginning inventory of raw materials and the beginning inventory of goods in process have become part of the cost of finished goods manufactured and are, therefore, carried from the Adjusted Trial Balance debit column to the Manufacturing debit column.
2 The ending inventories of raw materials and of goods in process must be recorded as assets and must be shown as a deduction in determining the cost of finished goods manufactured. This step requires the listing of the two inventories as debits in the Balance Sheet columns and as credits in the Manufacturing columns.

The nature of the Manufacturing columns may be clarified by a brief summary of the items placed in each column. The debit column includes the beginning inventories of raw materials and goods in process, plus all the manufacturing costs of the period. The credit column contains credits for the ending inventories of raw materials and goods in process. The total of the amounts in the debit column exceeds the total of the credit column by $800,000. This debit balance represents the cost of finished goods manufactured and is extended as a debit to the Income Statement columns.

Note that the beginning and ending inventories of finished goods appear in the Income Statement columns but ***not in the Manufacturing columns.*** A review

ALLIED MANUFACTURING COMPANY

Work Sheet

For the Year Ended December 31, Year 5

| | Adjusted Trial Balance | | Manufacturing | | Income Statement | | Balance Sheet | |
|---|---|---|---|---|---|---|---|---|
| | Dr | Cr | Dr | Cr | Dr | Cr | Dr | Cr |
| Cash | 62,000 | | | | | | 62,000 | |
| Accounts receivable (net) | 190,000 | | | | | | 190,000 | |
| Inventories, beginning | | | | | | | | |
| Raw materials | 50,000 | | 50,000 | | | | | |
| Goods in process | 30,000 | | 30,000 | | | | | |
| Finished goods | 150,000 | | | | 150,000 | | | |
| Plant and equipment | 535,000 | | | | | | 535,000 | |
| Accum. depr.: plant and equip. | | 175,000 | | | | | | 175,000 |
| Accounts payable | | 108,000 | | | | | | 108,000 |
| Accrued factory payroll | | 12,000 | | | | | | 12,000 |
| Income taxes payable | | 30,000 | | | | | | 30,000 |
| Note payable, 12%, due Year 10 | | 200,000 | | | | | | 200,000 |
| Capital stock, $10 par | | 250,000 | | | | | | 250,000 |
| Retained earnings, beginning | | 222,000 | | | | | | 222,000 |
| Dividends | 25,000 | | | | | | 25,000 | |
| Sales | | 1,300,000 | | | | 1,300,000 | | |
| Purchases of raw materials | 160,000 | | 160,000 | | | | | |
| Transportation-in (materials) | 5,000 | | 5,000 | | | | | |
| Direct labor | 400,000 | | 400,000 | | | | | |
| Indirect labor | 120,000 | | 120,000 | | | | | |
| Occupancy costs | 35,000 | | 35,000 | | | | | |
| Other factory overhead costs | 85,000 | | 85,000 | | | | | |
| Selling expenses | 185,000 | | | | 185,000 | | | |
| General and administrative expense | 215,000 | | | | 215,000 | | | |
| Interest expense | 20,000 | | | | 20,000 | | | |
| Income taxes expense | 30,000 | | | | 30,000 | | | |
| | 2,297,000 | 2,297,000 | | | | | | |
| Inventories ending | | | | | | | | |
| Raw materials | | | | 45,000 | | | 45,000 | |
| Goods in process | | | | 40,000 | | | 40,000 | |
| Finished goods | | | | | | 170,000 | 170,000 | |
| | | | 885,000 | 85,000 | | | | |
| Cost of finished goods manufactured | | | | 800,000 | 800,000 | | | |
| | | | 885,000 | 885,000 | 1,400,000 | 1,470,000 | | |
| Net income | | | | | 70,000 | | | 70,000 |
| | | | | | 1,470,000 | 1,470,000 | 1,067,000 | 1,067,000 |

of the schedule on page 909 shows that changes in the inventory of finished goods are ***not a factor*** in computing the cost of finished goods manufactured during the period.

### Closing the accounts at the end of the period

The entries to close the accounts of a manufacturing business can be taken directly from the work sheet. The first closing entry debits the Manufacturing Summary account with the total of all the amounts listed in the Manufacturing debit column on the work sheet. A second entry is made crediting the Manufacturing Summary account with the total of all the accounts listed in the Manufacturing credit column. These two entries serve to close all the manufacturing cost accounts and to record the ending inventories of raw materials and goods in process.

The next step in the closing procedure is to transfer the debit balance of the Manufacturing Summary account to the Income Summary. Note that this balance is the cost of finished goods manufactured. This entry is usually combined with the entry closing the beginning inventory of finished goods and the expense accounts into the Income Summary. Finally, the balances of the Income Summary and the Dividends accounts are closed into Retained Earnings. The closing entries at December 31, Year 5, for Allied Manufacturing Company are illustrated below and on page 917.

***Closing entries for a manufacturing firm***

| | | |
|---|---|---|
| *Manufacturing Summary* | *885,000* | |
| *Goods in Process Inventory (beginning)* | | *30,000* |
| *Raw Materials Inventory (beginning)* | | *50,000* |
| *Purchases of Raw Materials* | | *160,000* |
| *Transportation-in (raw materials)* | | *5,000* |
| *Direct Labor* | | *400,000* |
| *Indirect Labor* | | *120,000* |
| *Occupancy Costs* | | *35,000* |
| *Other Factory Overhead Costs* | | *85,000* |
| *To close manufacturing cost accounts to Manufacturing Summary.* | | |
| | | |
| *Goods in Process Inventory (ending)* | *40,000* | |
| *Raw Materials Inventory (ending)* | *45,000* | |
| *Manufacturing Summary* | | *85,000* |
| *To record ending inventories of goods in process and raw materials.* | | |
| | | |
| *Income Summary* | *1,400,000* | |
| *Finished Goods Inventory (beginning)* | | *150,000* |
| *Selling Expenses* | | *185,000* |
| *General and Administrative Expenses* | | *215,000* |
| *Interest Expense* | | *20,000* |
| *Income Taxes Expense* | | *30,000* |
| *Manufacturing Summary* | | *800,000* |
| *To close beginning inventory of finished goods, all expense accounts, and Manufacturing account to Income Summary.* | | |

| | | |
|---|---|---|
| *Sales (net)* | *1,300,000* | |
| *Finished Goods Inventory (ending)* | *170,000* | |
| *Income Summary* | | *1,470,000* |
| *To close Sales account and to record ending finished goods inventory.* | | |
| *Income Summary* | *70,000* | |
| *Retained Earnings* | | *70,000* |
| *To transfer balance in Income Summary (net income) to Retained Earnings* | | |
| *Retained Earnings* | *25,000* | |
| *Dividends* | | *25,000* |
| *To close the Dividends account to Retained Earnings.* | | |

## Cost accounting and perpetual inventory systems

In this chapter we have assumed the use of the periodic inventory system, although the concepts presented also apply to manufacturing companies which use perpetual inventory systems. Although many small manufacturers use the periodic inventory system, this system has several shortcomings for a manufacturing company, including the following:

1 Taking and pricing inventories is so time-consuming that it usually is done only once a year; consequently, operating statements are not available to management at sufficiently frequent intervals.
2 Cost data are averaged over all units produced during the period, so the system does not disclose changes in the unit cost of production occurring within the period.
3 The estimates used in computing the inventories of goods in process and finished goods are rough and inexact. Any inaccuracy in pricing the inventories causes a corresponding error in net income for the period.

The greater the number of products being manufactured, the more critical these deficiencies become. For these reasons, many manufacturing businesses use ***cost accounting systems*** designed to provide a steady flow of reports summarizing ***current*** production costs on a per-unit basis. Cost accounting is a specialized field of accounting, with the objective of providing management with a means of planning and controlling manufacturing operations. A cost accounting system is characterized by the maintenance of ***perpetual*** inventory records and by the development of cost figures for each unit manufactured. An introduction to the subject of cost accounting is presented in the following chapter.

## KEY TERMS INTRODUCED OR EMPHASIZED IN CHAPTER 24

**Cost of finished goods manufactured** Cost of units of finished product completed during the period. Beginning inventory of goods in process, plus cost of raw material used plus direct labor and factory overhead and minus ending inventory of goods in process, equals cost of finished goods manufactured during the period.

**Direct labor** Wages paid to factory employees who work directly on the products being manufactured.

**Factory overhead** All costs incurred in the manufacturing process other than the cost of raw materials and direct labor (for example, insurance, depreciation of machinery, and supervisors' salaries).

**Finished goods inventory** The completed units which have emerged from the manufacturing process and are on hand ready for sale to customers at year-end or any other specific date.

**Goods in process inventory** The inventory of partially completed goods in the process of manufacture as determined by a physical count at the year-end or other specific date.

**Indirect labor** Wages of employees in manufacturing operations who do not work directly with the product. Examples are wages of security guards and maintenance employees.

**Manufacturing Summary account** A summary account used in closing the accounts of a manufacturing business. All costs used in computing the cost of goods manufactured are transferred into the account, which is then closed to the Income Summary.

**Overhead application rate** Total factory overhead costs for the period expressed as a percentage of the total direct labor costs for the period. This rate is used in determining the amount of factory overhead applicable to each unit in the inventories of goods in process and finished goods.

**Period costs** Costs which are charged to expense in the period in which they are incurred. Generally include costs associated with selling and administrative functions.

**Product costs** Costs which become part of the inventory value of goods in process and finished goods. Deductible from revenue in the period the products in which they are included are sold.

**Raw (direct) materials inventory** The raw materials or purchased parts which are on hand and ready to be placed in production. Eventually become part of the units to be manufactured. Also includes factory supplies.

**Schedule of cost of finished goods manufactured** A supplementary schedule accompanying the income statement of a manufacturing company. Shows the various types of costs included in the cost of finished goods produced and becoming available for sale during the period.

**Total manufacturing costs** The total amount of the costs of raw materials used, direct labor, and factory overhead costs for a given period without regard to whether products are completed.

## REVIEW QUESTIONS

1 Explain how the content of the income statement of a manufacturing company differs from the items usually found in the income statement of a merchandising company.

2 A manufacturing company has more than one kind of inventory. Do all the types of inventories of a manufacturing company appear on its income statement? Explain.

3 What are the three major components of the cost of manufactured goods?

4 A manufacturing firm has three inventory control accounts. Name each of the accounts, and describe briefly what the balance in each at the end of any accounting period represents.

5 Into which of the three elements of manufacturing cost would each of the following be classified?
**a** Wages of assembly-line workers who package frozen food
**b** Briar used in the manufacture of pipes
**c** Wages paid by an automobile manufacturer to employees who test-drive completed automobiles
**d** Cost of making duplicate copies of blueprints in engineering department
**e** Cost of glue used to bind layers of plywood
**f** Property taxes on machinery
**g** Small tools used in the factory
**h** Wages of the factory payroll clerk

6 During a given period the cost of raw materials used by a manufacturing firm was \$22,000 and the raw material inventory decreased by \$4,500. What was the delivered cost of raw materials purchased?

7 Explain the distinction between ***product costs*** and ***period costs***. Why is this distinction important?

8 Indicate whether each of the following should be considered a product cost or a period cost:
**a** Depreciation on raw materials warehouse
**b** Salaries of office workers in credit department
**c** Cost of advertising finished products
**d** Christmas bonuses to sales personnel
**e** Salaries of factory timekeepers
**f** Depreciation on sales showroom fixtures
**g** Vacation pay to factory workers

9 Distinguish between ***total manufacturing costs*** and the ***cost of finished goods manufactured.***

10 What is meant by the term ***overhead application rate?***

11 Explain how the cost of the ending inventory of goods in process is determined at the end of the period under the periodic inventory system.

12 What does the balance in the Manufacturing Summary account represent, before the account is closed?

13 What are the major shortcomings of the periodic inventory system when used by a manufacturing company?

## EXERCISES

*Ex. 24-1* The information below is taken from the financial statements of Joe Trevino, Inc., at the end of Year 1:

| | |
|---|---|
| *Goods in process inventory, ending* | *$ 50,000* |
| *Cost of raw materials used* | *260,000* |
| *Cost of finished goods manufactured* | *620,000* |
| *Factory overhead, 75% of direct labor cost* | *150,000* |

Compute the cost of the goods in process inventory at January 1.

*Ex. 24-2* Factory overhead is 30% of cost of goods manufactured. Direct labor is 20% of sales and 40% of cost of goods manufactured. Ending raw materials inventory is $4,000 more than beginning raw materials inventory. Sales totaled $100,000 for the year. There was no inventory of goods in process at the beginning or end of the year. Compute the net cost of raw materials purchased during the year.

*Ex. 24-3* From the following account balances, prepare the entries required to close the manufacturing accounts at the end of Year 1. Include an entry to close the Manufacturing Summary account to the Income Summary account:

| | *End of Year* | *Beginning of Year* |
|---|---|---|
| *Raw materials inventory* | *$ 45,000* | *$52,500* |
| *Goods in process inventory* | *70,500* | *57,600* |
| *Purchases of raw materials (net)* | *240,000* | |
| *Direct labor* | *216,000* | |
| *Factory overhead (detail omitted)* | *149,400* | |

*Ex. 24-4* From the following account balances for the Dell Products Corporation, determine the overhead application rate based on direct labor cost:

| | |
|---|---|
| *Raw materials used* | *$240,000* |
| *Direct labor* | *200,000* |
| *Indirect labor* | *49,000* |
| *Factory maintenance* | *26,000* |
| *Depreciation on factory plant and machinery* | *19,500* |
| *Other factory overhead costs* | *25,500* |
| *Selling expenses (balance in controlling account)* | *40,000* |
| *General expenses (balance in controlling account)* | *60,000* |
| *Interest expense* | *10,000* |

*Ex. 24-5* Monroe Company produces a single product. At the end of the current year, the inventories of goods in process and finished goods are summarized below:

| | *Units* | *Raw Materials per Unit* | *Direct Labor per Unit* |
|---|---|---|---|
| *Goods in process* | *500* | *$6* | *$3* |
| *Finished goods* | *600* | *8* | *4* |

Factory overhead is applied to units produced at the rate of 110% of direct labor cost. Compute the cost of the ending inventory of goods in process and of finished goods.

## PROBLEMS

### Group A

*24A-1* The accounting records of Solar Manufacturing Co. show the following costs and expenses for the year ended December 31, Year 5:

| | |
|---|---|
| *Purchases of raw materials* | *$251,000* |
| *Transportation-in on raw materials* | *5,600* |
| *Indirect factory labor* | *92,600* |
| *Direct factory labor* | *230,000* |
| *Selling expenses (control)* | *177,200* |
| *Factory occupancy costs* | *85,400* |
| *General and administrative expenses (control)* | *203,600* |
| *Income taxes expense* | *90,000* |
| *Miscellaneous factory overhead* | *38,200* |

Inventories at the beginning and end of Year 5 were as follows:

| | *Dec. 31* | *Jan. 1* |
|---|---|---|
| *Raw materials* | *$ 44,300* | *$ 48,700* |
| *Goods in process* | *14,700* | *21,500* |
| *Finished goods* | *102,400* | *195,600* |

**Instructions**

**a** Prepare a schedule of cost of finished goods manufactured during the year.
**b** Prepare a schedule showing the cost of goods sold for the year.

*24A-2* The accounting records of Scott Mfg. Co. include the following information relating to the current year:

| | *Jan. 1* | *Dec. 31* |
|---|---|---|
| *Raw materials inventory* | *$ 95,000* | *$120,000* |
| *Goods in process inventory* | *40,000* | *37,500* |
| *Finished goods inventory, Jan. 1 (10,000 units)* | *190,000* | *?* |
| *Purchases of raw materials during year* | | *285,000* |
| *Direct labor cost during year* | | *395,000* |
| *Factory overhead costs during year* | | *242,500* |

The company manufactures a single product; during the current year, 45,000 units were manufactured and 40,000 units were sold.

**Instructions**

**a** Prepare a schedule of cost of finished goods manufactured for the current year.
**b** Compute the cost of producing a single unit during the current year.
**c** Compute the cost of goods sold during the year, assuming that the first-in, first-out method of inventory costing is used.
**d** Compute the cost of the inventory of finished goods at December 31 of the current year, assuming that the first-in, first-out method of inventory costing is used.

*24A-3* Marathon Motors manufactures three different models of outboard motors. The beginning inventories and manufacturing costs for the first quarter (January 1 through March 31) of Year 4 were as follows:

| | |
|---|---|
| *Inventories, Jan. 1, Year 4* | |
| *Raw materials* | *$ 629,500* |
| *Goods in process* | *165,500* |
| *Finished goods* | *919,000* |
| *Purchases of raw materials* | *1,860,000* |
| *Direct labor* | *2,660,000* |
| *Factory overhead* | *2,128,000* |

At March 31, Year 4, the following unit costs are applicable to the inventories of goods in process and finished goods:

| | *Units in Inventory* | *Cost per Unit* | |
|---|---|---|---|
| | | *Raw Materials* | *Direct Labor* |
| *Goods in process:* | | | |
| *Model 100* | *1,000* | *$45* | *$ 37.50* |
| *Model 200* | *750* | *50* | *50.00* |
| *Model 300* | *500* | *60* | *62.50* |
| *Finished goods:* | | | |
| *Model 100* | *2,500* | *45* | *75.00* |
| *Model 200* | *3,000* | *65* | *100.00* |
| *Model 300* | *2,000* | *85* | *125.00* |

The March 31 inventory of raw materials amounted to $613,000.

**Instructions**

**a** Prepare a schedule showing the cost of the inventories of goods in process and finished goods at March 31, Year 4. Use the form illustrated on page 912. Factory overhead is allocated to products on the basis of its relation to direct labor costs.
**b** Compute the cost of finished goods manufactured during the first quarter of Year 4.
**c** Compute the cost of goods sold for the first quarter of Year 4.

*24A-4* Early in Year 2, John Raymond founded Raymond Engineering Co. for the purpose of manufacturing a special flow control valve which he had designed. Shortly after year-end, the company's accountant was injured in a skiing accident, and no financial statements have been prepared for Year 2. However, the accountant had assembled the following information about the December 31 inventories of goods in process and finished goods:

| | Units in Inventory | Cost per Unit | |
|---|---|---|---|
| | | Raw Materials | Direct Labor |
| *Goods in process* | *1,500* | *$ 7* | *$ 8* |
| *Finished goods* | *3,000* | *11* | *12* |

Raw materials on hand at December 31 amounted to $46,000. (Since Year 2 is the first year of operations, there were no beginning inventories.)

While the accountant was in the hospital, Raymond prepared the following schedule from the balances in the company's ledger accounts:

| | | |
|---|---|---|
| *Sales* | | *$603,100* |
| *Cost of goods sold:* | | |
| *Purchases of raw materials* | *$181,000* | |
| *Direct labor costs* | *160,000* | |
| *Factory overhead* | *120,000* | |
| *Selling expenses* | *70,600* | |
| *Administrative expenses* | *132,000* | |
| *Total costs* | | *663,600* |
| *Net loss for year ended Dec. 31, Year 2* | | *$(60,500)* |

Raymond is very disappointed in these operating results. He states, "Not only did we lose more than $60,000 this year, but look at our unit production costs. We sold 10,000 units this year at a cost of $663,600; that amounts to a cost of $66.36 per unit. I know some of our competitors are able to manufacture similar valves for about $35 per unit. I don't need an accountant to know that this business is a failure."

**Instructions**

**a** Prepare a schedule showing the cost of the inventories of goods in process and finished goods at December 31, Year 2. Use the form illustrated on page 912. Determine the factory overhead cost per unit by using an overhead application rate based on direct labor costs.

**b** Compute the cost of finished goods manufactured during Year 2. After completing this computation, determine the average cost per finished unit manufactured. (This cost may differ from the cost per unit of the finished goods inventory, because it is an average unit cost of all finished goods produced throughout the year.)

**c** Prepare an income statement for Year 2. If the company has earned any operating income, assume an income tax rate of 30%. (Omit earnings per share figures.)

**d** Explain whether you agree or disagree with Raymond's remarks that the business is unprofitable and that its unit cost of production ($66.36, according to Raymond) is much higher than that of competitors (around $35). If you disagree with Raymond, explain any errors or shortcomings in his analysis.

***24A-5*** At December 31, Year 10, the following adjusted trial balance was prepared for Bridgeport Manufacturing Co.:

**BRIDGEPORT MANUFACTURING CO.**
***Adjusted Trial Balance***
***December 31, Year 10***

| | | |
|---|---|---|
| Cash | $ 92,000 | |
| Accounts receivable | 237,000 | |
| Allowance for doubtful accounts | | $ 12,000 |
| Raw materials inventory, Jan. 1, Year 10 | 61,200 | |
| Goods in process inventory, Jan. 1, Year 10 | 55,200 | |
| Finished goods inventory, Jan. 1, Year 10 | 130,000 | |
| Prepaid expenses | 13,000 | |
| Plant and equipment | 1,541,000 | |
| Accumulated depreciation: plant and equipment | | 480,600 |
| Patents | 56,600 | |
| Accounts payable | | 122,400 |
| Accrued liabilities | | 94,000 |
| Income taxes payable | | 130,500 |
| Capital stock, $20 par value | | 800,000 |
| Additional paid-in capital | | 200,000 |
| Retained earnings, Jan. 1, Year 10 | | 252,000 |
| Dividends | 88,000 | |
| Sales (net) | | 3,000,000 |
| Purchases of raw materials | 678,800 | |
| Transportation-in (materials) | 40,200 | |
| Direct labor | 941,000 | |
| Factory overhead (control) | 486,000 | |
| Selling expenses (control) | 284,600 | |
| Administrative expenses (control) | 256,400 | |
| Income taxes | 130,500 | |
| | $5,091,500 | $5,091,500 |

Inventories at December 31, Year 10, are shown below:

| | |
|---|---|
| Raw materials inventory | $ 64,400 |
| Goods in process inventory | 58,000 |
| Finished goods inventory | 126,500 |

**Instructions** Prepare the following:

a An 8-column work sheet, following the format illustrated on page 915, for the year ended December 31, Year 10. (Begin with the adjusted trial balance and include a pair of columns for Manufacturing, Income Statement, and Balance Sheet.)

b Closing entries for the year ended December 31, Year 10. (Use a Manufacturing Summary account to determine the cost of finished goods manufactured as part of your closing procedures.)

## Group B

*24B-1* Medallion Company prepared journal entries to close its accounts at December 31, Year 5. Two of these year-end closing entries are shown below:

| | | |
|---|---|---|
| *Manufacturing Summary* | *515,750* | |
| *Raw Materials Inventory (beginning)* | | *51,500* |
| *Goods in Process Inventory (beginning)* | | *27,250* |
| *Purchases of Raw Materials* | | *225,500* |
| *Transportation-in* | | *5,750* |
| *Direct Labor* | | *96,500* |
| *Indirect Labor* | | *53,500* |
| *Factory Occupancy Costs* | | *30,750* |
| *Miscellaneous Factory Overhead* | | *25,000* |
| *To close manufacturing cost accounts.* | | |
| | | |
| *Raw Materials Inventory (ending)* | *56,250* | |
| *Goods in Process Inventory (ending)* | *24,500* | |
| *Manufacturing Summary* | | *80,750* |
| *To record ending inventories of raw materials and goods in process.* | | |

**Instructions** Prepare a schedule of cost of finished goods manufactured for Year 5.

*24B-2* The adjusted trial balance and other records of Coast Manufacturing Company for the current year included the items listed below:

| | |
|---|---|
| *Goods in process inventory, beginning of year* | *$ 73,600* |
| *Direct labor* | *680,000* |
| *Indirect labor* | *254,000* |
| *Raw materials inventory, beginning of year* | *264,800* |
| *Raw materials inventory, end of year* | *236,800* |
| *Raw materials purchases* | *994,880* |
| *Maintenance and repairs* | *24,000* |
| *Heat, light, and power* | *34,400* |
| *Property taxes: factory buildings and equipment* | *30,400* |
| *Depreciation: factory buildings and equipment* | *76,320* |
| *Insurance on manufacturing operations* | *9,600* |
| *Amortization of patents on products manufactured* | *19,680* |
| *Other factory overhead costs* | *27,600* |

The factory superintendent reports that raw materials costing $48,000 and direct labor of $80,000 are applicable to uncompleted goods in process at the end of the current year.

**Instructions** (Part *c* appears on page 926.)

**a** Compute the overhead application rate for the current year based on direct labor cost.

**b** Determine the cost of the inventory of goods in process at the end of the current year.

c Prepare a schedule of cost of finished goods manufactured for the current year. Show one amount for factory overhead as computed in **a.**

*24B-3* The manufacturing costs of Palomar Corporation during the six-month period ended June 30, 19___, are summarized below:

| | |
|---|---|
| Raw materials used in production | $192,300 |
| Direct labor costs | 310,000 |
| Factory overhead | 248,000 |
| Total manufacturing costs | $750,300 |

Inventories of goods in process and finished goods at the beginning of this period were as follows:

| | |
|---|---|
| Inventories, Jan. 1, 19___: | |
| Goods in process | $ 32,400 |
| Finished goods | 134,000 |

An engineer in the production department has provided the following information relating to the cost of the inventories of goods in process and finished goods at June 30, 19___:

| | | Estimated Costs per Unit | |
|---|---|---|---|
| | Units in Inventory | Raw Materials | Direct Labor |
| Goods in process: | | | |
| Product #1 | 500 | $4.00 | $10.00 |
| Product #2 | 1,000 | 6.00 | 5.00 |
| Finished goods: | | | |
| Product #1 | 2,000 | 9.00 | 15.00 |
| Product #2 | 2,610 | 8.40 | 12.00 |

**Instructions**

a Prepare a schedule determining the cost of the June 30 inventories of goods in process and finished goods. Use the form illustrated on page 912. Determine the factory overhead cost per unit by using an overhead application rate based on direct labor costs.
b Compute the cost of finished goods manufactured during the six months ended June 30, 19___.
c Compute the cost of goods sold for the six months ended June 30, 19___.

*24B-4* William Nelson, the chief accountant of West Texas Guitar Company, was injured in an automobile accident shortly before the end of the company's first year of operations. At year-end, a clerk with a very limited understanding of accounting prepared the following income statement, which is unsatisfactory in several respects:

**WEST TEXAS GUITAR COMPANY**
**Income Statement**
**For First Year of Operations**

| | | |
|---|---|---|
| Sales (net) | | $960,000 |
| Cost of goods sold: | | |
| Purchases of raw materials | $260,000 | |
| Transportation-in | 12,000 | |
| Direct labor | 325,000 | |
| Indirect labor | 90,000 | |
| Depreciation on machinery—factory | 30,000 | |
| Rent | 24,000 | |
| Insurance | 6,000 | |
| Utilities | 18,000 | |
| Miscellaneous factory overhead | 27,600 | |
| Other operating expenses | 165,800 | |
| Dividends declared on capital stock | 36,000 | |
| Cost of goods sold | | 994,400 |
| Loss for year | | $(34,400) |

You are asked to help management prepare a corrected income statement for the first year of operations. Management informs you that 60% of rent, insurance, and utilities is applicable to the factory and that correct ending inventories consist of the following: Raw materials, $38,000; goods in process, $10,000; and finished goods, $110,400. (Since this is the first year of operations, there are no beginning inventories.)

**Instructions**

**a** Identify the shortcomings and errors in the above income statement. Based upon the shortcomings you have identified, explain whether you would expect the company's actual net income for the first year of operations to be higher or lower than the amount shown.

**b** Prepare a schedule of cost of finished goods manufactured during the year.

**c** Prepare a corrected income statement for the year. Assume that income taxes expense amounts to 30% of taxable income. (Omit earnings per share figures.)

*24B-5* Shown below is the adjusted trial balance of Green Bay Corporation at June 30, Year 5, the end of the company's fiscal year.

**GREEN BAY CORPORATION**
**Adjusted Trial Balance**
**June 30, Year 5**

| | | |
|---|---|---|
| Cash | $ 101,000 | |
| Accounts receivable | 141,000 | |
| Raw materials inventory, July 1, Year 4 | 38,200 | |
| Goods in process inventory, July 1, Year 4 | 34,500 | |
| Finished goods inventory, July 1, Year 4 | 218,000 | |
| Prepaid expenses | 8,000 | |
| Plant and equipment | 998,000 | |
| Accumulated depreciation: plant and equipment | | $ 300,500 |
| Accounts payable | | 76,500 |
| Accrued expenses payable | | 54,200 |
| Income taxes payable | | 116,000 |
| Notes payable (long-term) | | 150,000 |
| Capital stock, $10 par value | | 400,000 |
| Additional paid-in capital | | 125,000 |
| Retained earnings, July 1, Year 4 | | 250,700 |
| Dividends | 120,000 | |
| Sales | | 2,000,000 |
| Purchases of raw materials | 424,000 | |
| Transportation-in (materials) | 29,500 | |
| Direct labor | 600,500 | |
| Factory overhead (control) | 303,700 | |
| Selling expenses (control) | 180,000 | |
| Administrative expenses (control) | 160,500 | |
| Income taxes expense | 116,000 | |
| | $3,472,900 | $3,472,900 |

Inventories at June 30, Year 5, are as follows:

| | |
|---|---|
| Raw materials inventory | $ 40,200 |
| Goods in process inventory | 36,200 |
| Finished goods inventory | 200,500 |

**Instructions** Prepare:

a An 8-column work sheet for the year ended June 30, Year 5. (Follow the format illustrated on page 915; begin with the adjusted trial balance and include a pair of columns for Manufacturing, Income Statement, and Balance Sheet.)

b Closing entries for the year ended June 30, Year 5. (Use a Manufacturing Summary account to determine the cost of finished goods manufactured as part of your closing procedures.)

## BUSINESS DECISION PROBLEM 24

John Hall, a recent college graduate, is employed as assistant to the controller of Artcraft, Inc., a manufacturer of wood products. Manufacturing operations are carried on in the main plant in a large southern city and in two smaller plants in the nearby towns of Davis and Kingston. Each of the three plants manufactures a different line of products and each maintains a complete set of accounting records and determines its own cost of goods manufactured.

In studying the company's manufacturing costs, John Hall finds that certain factory overhead costs incurred in the main plant have not been allocated to the Davis and Kingston plants although these costs by their nature are clearly applicable to the two smaller plants. The costs in question include property taxes and insurance paid by the main plant and a portion of the salary of the production manager, who regularly makes trips to Davis and Kingston to solve production problems. John Hall recommends that the portion of factory overhead costs incurred at the main plant which are applicable to operations at the Davis and Kingston plants be allocated as manufacturing costs of the two smaller plants. In support of this recommendation, Hall emphasizes that the ending inventories of all three plants are incorrectly stated at the end of the current year, as was the case in prior years.

The controller is reluctant to adopt Hall's recommendation and argues as follows: "We have been handling these costs in the same way for fifteen years. All overhead costs have been charged to one plant or another, and it all ends up in cost of goods sold eventually anyway. Furthermore, for control purposes we want to record the indirect costs where the responsibility for their control lies, and the responsibility for the costs in question rests in the main plant."

In presenting his recommendation to the controller, John Hall had accumulated the following information:

| | |
|---|---|
| ***Factory overhead costs incurred in main plant during current year which are allocable to Davis and Kingston plants*** | ***$200,000*** |
| ***Percentage of current year's output included in ending inventories of finished goods and goods in process:*** | |
| ***Main plant*** | ***30%*** |
| ***Davis plant*** | ***10%*** |
| ***Kingston plant*** | ***5%*** |

### Instructions

**a** Assuming that John Hall's recommendation is carried out for the current year, what would be the dollar effect on total ending inventories? Show computations.

**b** Evaluate the position taken by John Hall and by the controller, and suggest a solution to the dispute.

# 25

# COST ACCOUNTING SYSTEMS

In Chapter 24 the financial statements for a manufacturing business were introduced. Among the matters emphasized were the cost of finished goods manufactured schedule and the several asset and factory cost accounts not found in the ledger of a merchandising business. In this chapter we are concerned with the more complex task of determining the ***cost of activities and products*** through the use of cost accounting systems.

## Cost accounting systems

A cost accounting system is a method of developing cost information within the framework of general ledger accounts. Because cost accounting systems are more widely used in manufacturing industries, we shall focus our attention on manufacturing costs. The need for cost information, however, is much broader than this. Many of the procedures used to obtain manufacturing costs are applicable to a variety of business situations and have been used by retailers, wholesalers, governmental agencies, and such service organizations as hospitals, public utilities, banks, and accounting firms to determine the cost of performing various service functions.

Cost accounting serves two important managerial objectives: (1) to determine the unit costs of production, and (2) to provide management with information useful in controlling the costs of business operations. Unit costs of production are determined by relating prices paid for materials, direct labor, and factory overhead to some unit of output, such as tons of steel produced. Unit cost information provides the basis for inventory valuation and measurement of the cost of goods sold. It also provides information useful in pricing decisions, bidding on production contracts, and evaluating the efficiency of operations.

***Control of costs*** is part of management's general responsibility for running the business efficiently and economically. Knowing the cost of making a product, performing a manufacturing operation, or carrying on some other function of the business is the starting point in controlling costs. The term ***management by exception*** refers to the common practice of managers devoting most of their attention to those areas of the business which are performing below expectation. By comparing actual unit costs with budgets, past performance, and other yardsticks, managers are able to identify those areas in which corrective actions are most needed.

ILLUSTRATIVE CASE Carter Electric had operated profitably for more than 30 years, specializing in the repair of electrical equipment used in industry. The company did no manufacturing but performed major electrical repairs for several utility companies and other large corporations. The business had been founded by John Carter as a tiny shop, but under his personal supervision had grown until it employed more than 200 people. Carter Electric had never used a cost accounting system and maintained only a minimum of accounting records. The setting of prices and making of bids on repair work was a matter of judgment by John Carter, who had long been regarded as an expert in this field.

On John Carter's seventy-fifth birthday, the company accepted its first manufacturing contract. It agreed to build a large number of new electronic communication devices for delivery over a three-year period under a contract with the U.S. Air Force. The contract price was negotiated personally by John Carter at $4,500 per unit, which was by far the lowest bid. After six months of intense production effort, financed partly by a bank loan, Carter Electric ran low on cash and asked the bank to increase its loan. The bank agreed after determining that the company was on schedule with the government contract. Representatives of the Air Force informed the bank that the units delivered thus far had been of excellent quality. Two months later the company was out of cash again and informed the bank that it must have a larger loan at once or it could not meet the current week's payroll.

Bank officials became alarmed and insisted on having a CPA firm make a quick review of Carter Electric's costs under the government contract. The CPA firm determined that the manufacturing costs per unit were in excess of $5,500. In other words, Carter Electric was keeping very busy turning out the new units at a loss of $1,000 each. The bank insisted that the company employ a capable cost accountant and install a cost accounting system. After a meeting with government procurement officers and analysis of the cost data, the contract was renegotiated at a higher price, which permitted Carter Electric to complete the contract and earn a modest profit.

## Problems of cost determination

A common misconception about accounting figures is that the cost of any product or unit of output can be measured with precision.

There are two reasons for the difficulty in measuring accurately ***the cost*** of anything: First, the relationship between the costs incurred and the output produced is often difficult to establish. Secondly, cost information may be assembled, combined, and reported in many different ways. The relevant "cost" information varies with the nature of the decision confronting management. No single definition of cost is ideally suited to all types of managerial decisions. Let us consider these two problems briefly.

**Relating costs to output** Costs are related to units of output in two stages. The first stage is to measure the cost of resources used up in the total productive effort of a given accounting period. Dividing the cost of assets or services among accounting periods is more a matter of judgment than arithmetic. For example, the services of long-lived assets such as plant and equipment are purchased in "bundles" and used up over a number of accounting periods. The amount of this "bundle of services' which is used up in any given accounting period cannot be determined with certainty. Thus, the portion of the total cost charged to the production of a given period is based upon assumptions as to the asset's total service life, its residual value, and the appropriate depreciation method.

The second stage in cost accounting is to allocate total manufacturing costs for the period among the varous products manufactured. Almost all total cost figures include some ***joint costs,*** which cannot be traced directly to given units of output. Joint costs are costs which apply jointly to ***two or more*** different products or departments. For example, the cost of a barrel of crude oil is a joint cost relating to each product (gasoline, heating oil, lubricating oil) that emerges from a refinery, but how should the cost of the crude oil be divided among these products? Similarly, some part of the salary of the plant manager is a cost of operating each department within the plant, but how much of this salary should be assigned to a particular department? Resolving these issues and assigning such costs to products or processes is the function of the cost accounting system.

**Different costs for different purposes** In addition to the inherent difficulties in measuring unit cost, we must recognize that different cost measurements are needed for different purposes. For example, consider the cost of heating a factory building. In arriving at inventory valuation and cost of goods sold, some portion of the total heating cost should be allocated to the various operations and in turn to the production of the period. In a study of the operating efficiency of factory supervisors, however, the cost of heating the building should be ignored because it is not subject to their control. If we are planning the addition of a wing to the building, the ***expected change*** in the heating cost as a result of the addition is the relevant cost figure. Thus for some purposes the entire heating cost is useful, for some only a part of the heating cost is relevant, and for still other purposes this cost may be omitted altogether.

If cost information is to be used intelligently, the user must understand that any cost figure has inherent limitations and that no single method of arriving at cost will serve equally well all the varied purposes for which such information is needed. Most cost systems are designed to meet the general purpose of income determination and to develop in the accounts the basic information from which cost studies for special purposes can be derived.

## Flow of costs through perpetual inventory accounts in cost systems

In Chapter 24 we saw that even when periodic inventories are used, the unit cost of finished goods manufactured can be determined. Under the periodic inventory system, however, much potentially useful information is buried in totals; cost data are available only at infrequent intervals; and the details of product or departmental costs are not available. The first step in setting up a cost system, therefore, is to establish ***perpetual*** inventories.

The cost elements that enter into the valuation of inventories are called ***product costs;*** costs that are not included in inventories but are deducted from revenue in the period in which they are incurred are called ***period costs.***

Product costs typically consist of manufacturing costs, as distinguished from selling and general administrative expenses. The flow of costs through perpetual inventories is therefore usually limited to direct materials, direct labor, and factory overhead.

Three perpetual inventory accounts are used to trace the flow of costs through the manufacturing operations and to associate costs with output:

1 Materials Inventory (raw materials and factory supplies)
2 Goods in Process Inventory (product in the process of manufacture)
3 Finished Goods Inventory (completed product)

To visualize basic cost flows, look at the diagram below. The arrows show the flow of costs through the perpetual inventory accounts; arrows connecting two items indicate the two sides of an accounting entry. Thus the use of raw materials reduces the Materials Inventory account and increases the Goods in Process Inventory.

*Arrows show flow of costs*

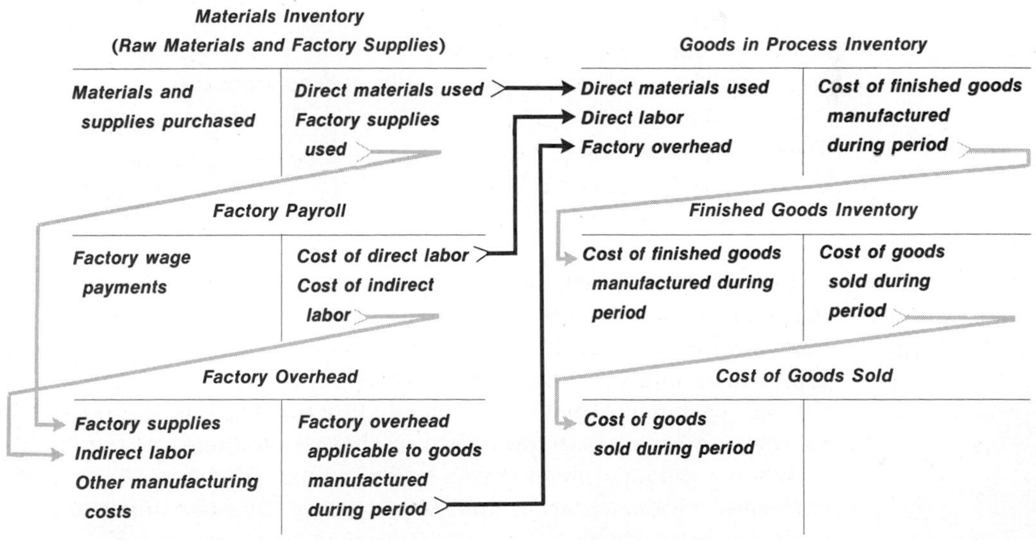


Note that when all the indicated entries have been made, the balances in the Materials Inventory, Goods in Process Inventory, and Finished Goods Inventory accounts represent the dollar valuation of these inventories. When a perpetual inventory system is used, the cost of goods sold can be taken directly from the ledger and placed in the income statement.

Even under a perpetual inventory system it is essential to take a physical inventory at various times to verify the accuracy of the ledger amounts and to disclose losses due to waste, theft, or breakage that were not recorded in the accounts.

## Two basic types of cost accounting systems

There are two distinct types of cost accounting systems: a job order cost system and a process cost system. In both systems the end product is the average unit cost of physical output.

Under a ***job order cost system,*** the key point of costing is a particular quantity of finished products which are manufactured together as a single ***job*** or ***lot.*** The cost of raw materials, direct labor, and factory overhead applicable to each job is compiled and divided by the number of finished units in the job to arrive at average unit cost, as illustrated below:

*Job Cost Sheet*

*Cost sheet for one job*

*Job Number:* 1101 | *Date Started:* 3/10/19__
*Product:* Model P Hand Drill | *Date Completed:* 4/15/19__
*Units Completed:* 2,000

| | |
|---|---|
| *Raw materials used* | *$ 7,500* |
| *Direct labor cost applicable to this job* | *10,000* |
| *Factory overhead applicable to this job, 125% of direct labor cost* | *12,500* |
| *Total cost of job no. 1101* | *$30,000* |
| *Average cost per unit ($30,000 ÷ 2,000)* | *$15* |

Under a ***process cost system,*** the key points in costing are the various ***departments or processes*** in the production cycle. First the cost of raw materials, direct labor, and factory overhead applicable to each department or process for ***a given period of time*** is compiled. Then the average cost of running a unit of product through each department is determined by dividing the total departmental cost by the number of units processed in that department during the period.

When a product moves through two or more departments, the total unit cost of finished product is accumulated by tracing the costs incurred in each department to the product as it moves from process to process. The process cost accounts for two departments are illustrated at the top of page 935.

Each kind of cost accounting system (job order and process) has advantages in particular manufacturing situations. Both are widely used. In the sections that follow we shall examine briefly the basic structure of the two cost accounting systems.

*Buildup of costs in two departments (processes)*

**Goods in Process, Assembly Department**

| | | | |
|---|---|---|---|
| *Raw material used* | *7,000* | *Transferred to Packing Dept.* | |
| *Direct labor* | *6,000* | *3,000 units @ $6* | |
| *Factory overhead applicable* | | *($18,000 ÷ 3,000)* | *18,000* |
| *to Assembly process* | *5,000* | | |

**Goods in Process, Packing Department**

| | | | |
|---|---|---|---|
| *From Assembly Dept. (3,000 units* | | *Transferred to finished goods* | |
| *@ $6)* | *18,000* | *inventory, 3,000 units @* | |
| *Additional materials used* | *2,000* | *$9 ($27,000 ÷ 3,000)* | *27,000* |
| *Direct labor* | *4,000* | | |
| *Factory overhead applicable* | | | |
| *to packing process* | *3,000* | | |

## JOB ORDER COST SYSTEM

In general, a job order cost system is applicable when each product or batch of product is significantly different. A job order cost system is used in the construction industry, for example, since each construction project is to some extent unique. Job order cost systems are also used in the aerospace, machine tool, job printing, motion picture, and shipbuilding industries for similar reasons.

An essential requirement of a job order cost system is that each product or batch of product can be identified in each step of the manufacturing operation. Through the use of various subsidiary cost records, the cost of raw materials, direct labor, and factory overhead applicable to each job is recorded on a ***job cost sheet,*** so that when the job is finished the total and the average unit cost of the job can be computed.

### Job order cost flow chart

A flow chart showing the accounts used in a simple job order cost system, together with lines indicating the flow of costs from one account to another, appears on pages 936 and 937.

The flow chart contains figures representing one month's operations for the Job Manufacturing Company. The company makes three products, identified as product A, product B, and product C. Two kinds of raw materials (materials Y and Z) are used. Each of the three perpetual inventory accounts (Materials Inventory, Goods in Process Inventory, and Finished Goods Inventory) is supported by subsidiary ledger records in which the details of the flow of costs are recorded.

*Job order cost flow chart*

**Factory Payroll**

| | | | |
|---|---|---|---|
| Wages paid | 70,000 | Direct labor | 60,000 |
| | | Indirect labor | 18,000 |
| | | (Bal., $8,000) | |

**Factory Overhead (Control)***

| | | | |
|---|---|---|---|
| Indirect labor | 18,000 | Applied (75% of direct labor) | 45,000 |
| Factory supplies | 6,500 | | |
| Other | 21,500 | | |
| (Bal., $1,000) | | | |

**Materials Inventory (Control)**

| | | | |
|---|---|---|---|
| Balance | 17,000 | Factory supplies | 6,500 |
| Purchases | 58,000 | Direct materials | 50,000 |
| (Bal., $18,500) | | | |

(For detail, see subsidiary ledger below)

**Subsidiary Materials Ledger**

**Factory Supplies**

| | | | |
|---|---|---|---|
| Balance | 4,000 | Used (factory overhead) | 6,500 |
| Purchases | 8,000 | | |
| (Bal., $5,500) | | | |

**Material Y**

| | | | |
|---|---|---|---|
| Balance | 6,000 | Used | 16,000 |
| Purchases | 13,000 | | |
| (Bal., $3,000) | | | |

**Material Z**

| | | | |
|---|---|---|---|
| Balance | 7,000 | Used | 34,000 |
| Purchases | 37,000 | | |
| (Bal., $10,000) | | | |

**Postings to Subsidiary Job Ledger as follows:**

*Direct labor, per time tickets:*

| | |
|---|---|
| Job no. 101 | $24,000 |
| Job no. 102 | 20,000 |
| Job no. 103 | 16,000 |
| Total | $60,000 |

Overhead ($45,000) at predetermined rate of 75% of direct labor

*Direct materials, per requisitions:*

| | |
|---|---|
| Job no. 101 | $ 8,000 |
| Job no. 102 | 25,000 |
| Job no. 103 | 17,000 |
| Total | $50,000 |

*Debit balance of $1,000 in this account represents underapplied factory overhead for the month.

**Goods in Process Inventory (Control)**

| | | | |
|---|---|---|---|
| Balance | 20,000 | Completed | |
| → Direct labor | 60,000 | (Job 101 & 102) | 130,000 → |
| → Factory overhead | 45,000 | | |
| → Raw materials | 50,000 | | |
| (Bal., $45,000) | | | |

(For detail, see subsidiary ledger below)

**Finished Goods Inventory (Control)**

| | | | |
|---|---|---|---|
| Balance | 25,000 | Sold | 125,000 → |
| → Completed | 130,000 | | |
| (Bal., $30,000) | | | |

(For detail, see subsidiary ledger below)

**Subsidiary Job Ledger**

| Job No. 101 | Product A |
|---|---|
| Balance | 20,000 |
| Direct labor | 24,000 |
| Factory overhead | 18,000 |
| Raw materials used | 8,000 |
| | 70,000 → |

| Job No. 102 | Product B |
|---|---|
| Direct labor | 20,000 |
| Factory overhead | 15,000 |
| Raw materials used | 25,000 |
| Total | 60,000 → |

| Job No. 103 | Product C |
|---|---|
| Direct labor | 16,000 |
| Factory overhead | 12,000 |
| Raw materials used | 17,000 |
| | Unfinished |

($45,000 ending inventory of Product C in process agrees with balance in Goods in Process Inventory control account)

**Subsidiary Finished Goods Ledger**

**Product A**

| | | | |
|---|---|---|---|
| Balance | 3,000 | Sold | 65,000 → |
| → Completed | 70,000 | | |
| (Bal., $8,000) | | | |

**Product B**

| | | | |
|---|---|---|---|
| → Completed | 60,000 | Sold | 40,000 → |
| (Bal., $20,000) | | | |

**Product C**

| | | | |
|---|---|---|---|
| Balance | 22,000 | Sold | 20,000 → |
| (Bal., $2,000) | | | |

**Cost of Goods Sold**

| | |
|---|---|
| → 125,000 | |

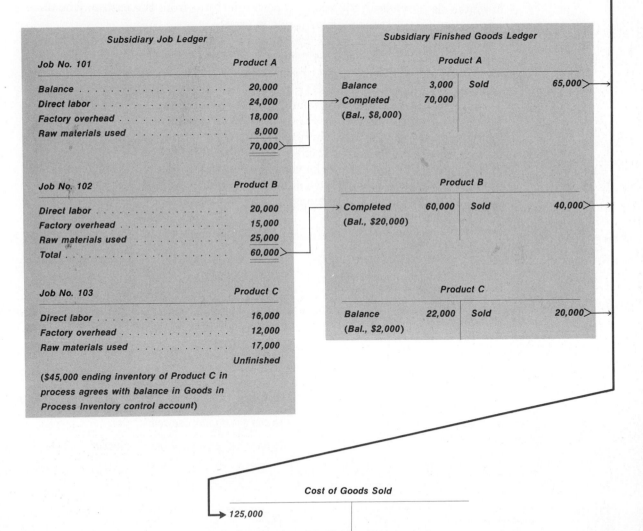

**Materials** Accounting for the purchase and use of raw materials and factory supplies is a straightforward application of the use of perpetual inventories. The summary entries in the Materials Inventory control account are matched by detailed entries in the subsidiary ledger accounts as follows:

1 The $17,000 beginning balance in the Materials Inventory account is equal to the beginning balances in the subsidiary ledger accounts for Factory Supplies, $4,000, Material Y, $6,000, and Material Z, $7,000.
2 The record in the subsidiary ledger accounts for the quantity and cost of materials purchased is made from information on suppliers' invoices. The cost of materials purchased, $58,000, was posted in total from the cash payments journal (or the voucher register if one is used).
3 Materials and factory supplies are issued on the basis of ***requisitions,*** which show the quantity needed and the identity of the job on which raw materials are to be used or the Factory Overhead account to which supplies should be charged. The ***direct materials cost*** is the cost of raw materials identified with specific jobs; ***factory supplies*** refers to materials or supplies charged to the Factory Overhead account.
4 The materials clerk refers to individual materials ledger cards to get the cost of each item requisitioned, and enters this on the requisition form. Since purchases are at different prices, the costing of materials used requires some systematic cost flow assumption such as lifo, fifo, or weighted average. A summary of the materials requisitions for the month becomes the basis for the

*Subsidiary ledger record for material Y*

***Materials Ledger Card***
***Material Y***

| | Purchased | | | Used | | | Balance | | |
|---|---|---|---|---|---|---|---|---|---|
| Ref.* | Quantity, Pounds | Unit Cost | Amount | Quantity, Pounds | Unit Cost† | Amount | Quantity, Pounds | Unit Cost† | Amount |
| Balance, beginning of month | | | | | | | 6,000 | $1.00 | $6,000 |
| Invoice no. 57 | 7,500 | $1.20 | $9.000 | | | | 6,000 | 1.00 | 6,000 |
| | | | | | | | 7,500 | 1.20 | 9,000 |
| Requisition no. 34 | | | | 6,000 | $1.00 | $6,000 | | | |
| | | | | 3,000 | 1.20 | 3,600 | 4,500 | 1.20 | 5,400 |
| Invoice no. 98 | 3,200 | 1.25 | 4,000 | | | | 4,500 | 1.20 | 5,400 |
| | | | | | | | 3,200 | 1.25 | 4,000 |
| Requisition no. 61 | | | | 4,500 | 1.20 | 5,400 | | | |
| | | | | 800 | 1.25 | 1,000 | 2,400 | 1.25 | 3,000 |

* Identifying number of invoice or requisition from which data were taken.
† Fifo basis.

entries crediting Materials Inventory ($56,500) and debiting Goods in Process Inventory ($50,000) for the cost of direct materials used and Factory Overhead ($6,500) with the cost of factory supplies used.

In the flow chart shown earlier, the subsidiary materials ledger accounts appear in T-account form only as a matter of convenience; in practice they would contain more detailed unit cost information and dates of entries. Illustrated below at the left is a materials ledger card for material Y.

**Factory labor** Payment of factory employees usually occurs after the services have been performed. During the pay period, detailed records of time, rates of pay, and the jobs on which employees worked must be kept in order to compile the necessary cost information. The wages earned by employees who work directly on job production are referred to as ***direct labor*** and are charged to each job. The wages earned by employees whose work is not directly associated with any particular job, known as ***indirect labor,*** are charged to Factory Overhead.

A number of mechanical and computerized means have been devised for compiling payroll information. A common system is to prepare ***time tickets*** for each employee, showing the time worked on each job, the employee's rate of pay, and the total cost chargeable to each job. These tickets, summarized periodically, become the basis for preparing the payroll and paying factory employees. They also become the basis for entries on various job cost sheets showing the direct labor cost incurred.

In the flow chart on pages 936 and 937, $60,000 of direct labor was charged to the three jobs in process and $18,000 of indirect labor was charged to Factory Overhead. Of the total wage cost of $78,000, only $70,000 was actually paid during the month. The balance of $8,000 in the Factory Payroll account represents the liability for unpaid wages at the end of the month.

**Factory overhead** Included in factory overhead are all manufacturing costs other than ***prime costs*** (direct materials and direct labor). Direct labor and factory overhead costs are often referred to as ***conversion*** or ***processing costs.*** The Factory Overhead account is usually a control account; details of individual factory overhead costs are kept in a subsidiary ledger. The source of individual overhead charges varies: indirect labor charges are summarized from payroll records; factory supplies used are summarized from materials requisitions; charges for such current services as electricity and water are posted from the cash payments journal (or the voucher register); depreciation on plant assets, the expiration of prepaid expenses, and overhead costs resulting from accrued liabilities (for example, property taxes) are recorded as adjusting entries at the end of the period.

Determining the total factory overhead cost for a given accounting period is relatively easy. The major problem is to relate overhead cost to physical output. The nature of factory overhead is such that the direct relation between cost and output, which exists in the case of direct labor and materials, is lacking. This problem is usually solved by relating factory overhead costs to some other cost factor which *can* be directly identified with units or lots of output. Many factory overhead costs either are a function of the passage of time (for example, building rent, foreman's salary) or tend to vary with the amount of labor or machine time involved in manufacture. For these reasons, charging factory overhead against units of output in proportion to the amount of ***direct labor cost, direct labor hours,*** or ***machine-hours*** involved in production is a reasonable and widely used procedure.

**Predetermined overhead application rates** Since many overhead costs tend to remain relatively fixed (constant) from month to month, total monthly overhead does not vary in proportion to seasonal or cyclical variations in factory output. Examples of ***fixed costs*** are property taxes and insurance on plant assets, straight-line depreciation on plant assets, and the monthly salary of the plant superintendent. ***Variable costs*** are those which change in direct proportion to output. If we allocate actual overhead costs incurred each month to the output of that month, the unit cost of production is likely to vary widely month by month. In months of high output, unit overhead costs would be low; in months of low output, unit overhead costs would be high. We can illustrate this for a company with a capacity to produce 10,000 units per month:

***Overhead Costs per Unit at Different Levels of Output***

*Overhead unit costs increase as volume decreases*

| | *Level of Output* | | | |
|---|---|---|---|---|
| | *100% of Capacity* | *75% of Capacity* | *50% of Capacity* | *25% of Capacity* |
| *Fixed overhead costs (constant at all levels)* | *$ 60,000* | *$ 60,000* | *$ 60,000* | *$60,000* |
| *Variable overhead costs* | *100,000* | *75,000* | *50,000* | *25,000* |
| *Total overhead costs* | *$160,000* | *$135,000* | *$110,000* | *$85,000* |
| *Number of units produced* | *10,000* | *7,500* | *5,000* | *2,500* |
| *Overhead cost per unit* | *$16* | *$18* | *$22* | *$34* |

Note that the ***fixed cost per unit increases as the level of output decreases*** and that the variable cost remains constant at $10 per unit. For most business purposes, it would be more confusing than helpful to have product cost figures that vary widely in response to short-run variations in the volume of output. Management needs product cost information for long-range product pricing decisions, income determination, and inventory valuation. For these purposes it is more useful to use what might be called "normal" costs than to have unit cost figures that reflect short-run variations in volume. For example, if we were determining the cost of two identical units of product in the finished goods inventory, it would not seem reasonable to say that one unit cost $30 because it was produced in a low-volume month and the other cost $20 because it was produced in a high-volume month.

The solution to this problem is to predetermine ***overhead application rates*** for an entire year in advance. To do this we first make an estimate of the total overhead costs for the year. This is called the ***budgeted overhead.*** Then we estimate the machine-hours, or direct labor hours, or direct labor cost, whichever is to be used as the ***overhead application base*** for the year. The predetermined overhead rate used in costing units of production is the budgeted overhead divided by the application base. For example, if factory overhead is budgeted at $600,000 for the coming year and it is estimated that the direct labor cost will amount to $500,000, the overhead application rate would be determined as follows:

*Predetermined overhead application rate*

| | |
|---|---|
| *Budgeted factory overhead for year* | *$600,000* |
| *Budgeted direct labor cost for year* | *500,000* |
| *Overhead application rate ($600,000 ÷ $500,000)* | *120%* |

The use of predetermined overhead rate has another advantage. Because the rate is estimated at the beginning of the year, "normal" product costs can be determined as various jobs are completed. ***It is not necessary to wait until the end of any period to know the factory overhead chargeable against goods produced.***

Assume that we are using direct labor cost as the overhead application base and that the predetermined application rate is 75% of direct labor cost. The actual overhead cost for any given period will be accumulated in the Factory Overhead control account. As production takes place and the direct labor cost is charged against jobs, overhead will also be applied to jobs at the predetermined rate of 75% of direct labor cost. As soon as a job is completed, we can determine the total cost and the unit cost of that job order. In the accounting records, the total amount of overhead applied to jobs during the period will be debited to Goods in Process and credited to Factory Overhead. In the flow chart on pages 936 and 937 for example, the total direct labor charged against the three jobs worked on during the month was $60,000, and 75% of this amount, or $45,000, was applied as the overhead cost applicable to these three jobs.

**Over- or underapplied overhead** We should not expect that applied overhead will ever exactly equal actual overhead, since the predetermined overhead application rate was based on estimates. A debit balance in the Factory Overhead account at the end of a period indicates that actual overhead exceeded the overhead applied to jobs; a credit balance shows that overhead applied was greater than the actual overhead costs incurred.

At the end of the year, if the overapplied or underapplied overhead is ***material in dollar amount,*** it should be apportioned among the Goods in Process Inventory, the Finished Goods Inventory, and Cost of Goods Sold on some reasonable basis to restate them at a more realistic cost. If the amount of over- or underapplied overhead is not material, it should be closed into Cost of Goods Sold, on the ground that most of the error applied to goods sold during the period.

The bases (such as direct labor cost) used in applying overhead vary with production but many elements of overhead do not. Therefore, overhead will tend to be ***underapplied*** during months of low production and ***overapplied*** during months of high production. The difference between actual and applied overhead is usually carried forward from month to month, and the overapplied overhead of one month is offset by the underapplied overhead of another. At the end of the year, any net balance of over- or underapplied overhead is then handled as described above.

**Goods in process inventory** The Goods in Process Inventory account is charged with the cost of direct materials, direct labor, and an estimate of the factory overhead costs applicable to all jobs. The supporting subsidiary ledger records for this control account are the job cost sheets relating to each job in process during the period. In the flow chart on pages 936 and 937, note that the balance in the goods in process inventory at the beginning of the month, $20,000, represents the cost incurred on job no. 101 during the previous month. During the current month additional costs of $155,000 were incurred. The flow of costs through subsidiary cost sheets and the Goods in Process Inventory control account is illustrated below.

***Subsidiary Job Cost Sheets***

*Flow of costs through job order cost sheets and control account*

| | *Job 101* | *Job 102* | *Job 103* | *Total (Control Account)* |
|---|---|---|---|---|
| *Goods in process inventory, beginning of month* | *$20,000* | | | *$ 20,000* |
| *Direct labor* | *24,000* | *$20,000* | *$16,000* | *60,000* |
| *Raw materials used* | *8,000* | *25,000* | *17,000* | *50,000* |
| *Factory overhead* | *18,000* | *15,000* | *12,000* | *45,000* |
| *Total costs incurred* | *$70,000* | *$60,000* | *$45,000* | *$175,000* |
| *Less: Cost of jobs completed—transferred to Finished Goods Inventory account* | *(70,000)* | *(60,000)* | *-0-* | *(130,000)* |
| *Goods in process inventory, end of month (job 103)* | *$ -0-* | *$ -0-* | *$45,000* | *$ 45,000* |

Note that the only job in process at the end of the month is job 103, and the cost of this job to date, $45,000, is equal to the balance in the control account, Goods in Process Inventory. The Goods in Process Inventory account includes all the information needed to prepare a statement of cost of goods manufactured at the end of an accounting period.

**Finished goods inventory** When a job is completed, the information on the job cost sheet is summarized and the total cost of that job becomes the basis for an entry crediting Goods in Process Inventory and debiting Finished Goods Inventory. Stock ledger cards are maintained as subsidiary ledger records for each type of finished product. When finished product is sold, Cash (or Accounts Receivable) is debited and Sales is credited. In addition, information on the stock ledger cards becomes the basis for removing the cost of these products from the Finished Goods Inventory account and charging the Cost of Goods Sold account. Once more some flow assumption (such as fifo or lifo) is required.

The relation between entries in the Finished Goods Inventory control account and the subsidiary finished stock ledger, as shown on the flow chart on pages 936 and 937, is summarized in the following schedule:

*Stock ledger supports entries in control account*

| *Finished Goods Inventory, Control Account* | | *Subsidiary Finished Goods Ledger* | | |
|---|---|---|---|---|
| *Beginning balance* | *$ 25,000* | *Product A* | *$ 3,000* | |
| | | *Product C* | *22,000* | *$ 25,000* |
| *Completed during period* | *130,000* | *Product A (job 101)* | | *70,000* |
| | | *Product B (job 102)* | | *60,000* |
| *Total goods available for sale* | *$155,000* | | | *$155,000* |
| *Less: Cost of goods sold during the period* | *(125,000)* | *Product A* | *$65,000* | |
| | | *Product B* | *40,000* | |
| | | *Product C* | *20,000* | *(125,000)* |
| | | *Product A* | *$ 8,000* | |
| | | *Product B* | *20,000* | |
| *Balance on hand at end of period* | *$ 30,000* | *Product C* | *2,000* | *$ 30,000* |

## PROCESS COST SYSTEM

Job order cost systems are appropriate when each batch of production is manufactured to different specifications. Many companies, however, produce a standardized product that flows on a relatively continuous basis through a series of production steps called ***processes.*** The natural focus of cost measurement in these situations is a ***cost center*** such as a manufacturing operation, department, or process. A process cost system is a method of accumulating cost information for such cost centers.

### Characteristics of a process cost system

In a process cost system, no attempt is made to determine the cost of particular lots of product as they move through the factory. Instead, the costs of materials, labor, and factory overhead during any given time period (such as a month) are traced to the various manufacturing processes or departments. The costs incurred in each process are accumulated in separate goods in process accounts, and a record is kept of the units produced in that process in each period. The ***average unit cost*** of performing each process is determined by dividing the departmental costs by the number of units processed during the period. The cost of a finished unit consists of the sum of the unit costs of performing each process involved in the unit's manufacture.

Process cost systems are particularly suitable for mass-production operations of all types. They are used in such industries as automobiles, appliances, cement, chemicals, lumber, steel, and petroleum. The process cost approach also may be used in the analysis of nonmanufacturing costs. Marketing activities, for example, may be divided into such functions as advertising, field calls by sales personnel, warehouse operations, and delivery of goods to customers. The cost per unit sold may then be computed for each of these marketing functions.

### Flow of costs in a process cost system

The basic features of a process cost system can best be illustrated by example. Assume that the Process Cost Company manufactures a standard-model tennis racquet. The company has two processing departments: In the Framing Department, wood strips are cut, shaped, and laminated together to form the racquet frame; in the Stringing Department, the racquet head is strung with nylon and a vinyl grip is placed on the handle. Finished racquets are stored in a warehouse and shipped to customers as orders are received.

The cost flow diagram on page 945 shows the basic process cost accounts and a summary of the manufacturing costs for the month of July. A careful study of the diagram will show that the Goods in Process account for each department contains all the information necessary to prepare a statement of the cost of goods manufactured.[1] Each cost flow in our illustration will now be examined to demonstrate the operation of a process cost system.

**Materials** There was a $4,000 balance in the Materials Inventory control account at the beginning of July. During the month of July purchases of materials were charged to the Materials Inventory account in the amount of $28,000. At the end of July a summary of direct materials requisitioned by each department and factory supplies used by all departments became the basis for the following entry:

*End-of-month entry: materials used*

| | | |
|---|---|---|
| *Goods in Process: Framing Department* | *18,800* | |
| *Goods in Process: Stringing Department* | *7,790* | |
| *Factory Overhead* | *2,000* | |
| *Materials Inventory* | | *28,590* |
| *To record materials used in July.* | | |

**Factory labor** The total cost of direct labor used by each department during July was determined from departmental payroll records. The wages of personnel (such as the factory superintendent, cost accountant, general maintenance employees) whose work is applicable to all departments were charged to Factory Overhead. The entry summarizing the payroll (ignoring various withholdings from wages) appears at the top of page 946.

[1] When a perpetual inventory system is used, it is unnecessary to show the beginning and ending inventories and purchases of materials in the statement of cost of goods manufactured; only the cost of materials used in production need be shown.

Cost flow diagram for process costing—compare with job order flow chart on pages 936 and 937

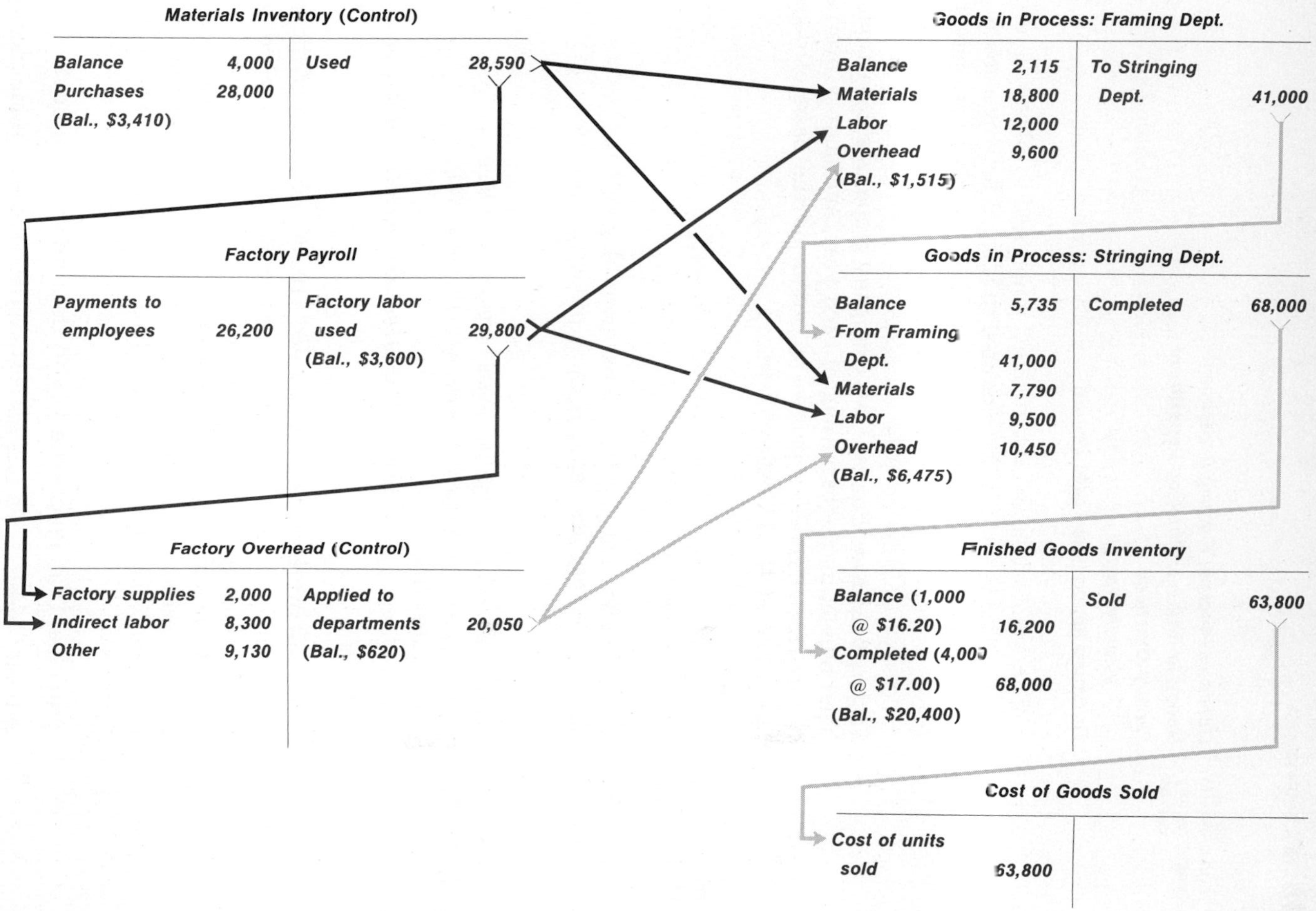

*End-of-month entry: factory payroll*

| | | |
|---|---|---|
| ***Goods in Process: Framing Department*** | ***12,000*** | |
| ***Goods in Process: Stringing Department*** | ***9,500*** | |
| ***Factory Overhead*** | ***8,300*** | |
| ***Factory Payroll*** | | ***29,800*** |
| ***To record factory labor used in July.*** | | |

Total factory labor cost incurred amounted to $29,800 and payments to employees during the month amounted to $26,200, leaving a credit balance of $3,600 in the Factory Payroll account, which represents wages payable at the end of July.

**Factory overhead** Process Cost Company prepares a departmental factory overhead budget at the beginning of each year, and factory overhead is applied to departmental goods in process accounts on the basis of departmental direct labor cost at the following rates:

*Predetermined overhead rates for our example*

| | |
|---|---|
| ***Framing Department*** | ***80% of direct labor cost*** |
| ***Stringing Department*** | ***110% of direct labor cost*** |

The entry charging the departmental goods in process accounts for their share of factory overhead, at these predetermined rates, may be summarized as follows:

*End-of-month entry: factory overhead applied*

| | | |
|---|---|---|
| ***Goods in Process: Framing Department (80% of $12,000)*** | ***9,600*** | |
| ***Goods in Process: Stringing Department (110% of $9,500)*** | ***10,450*** | |
| ***Factory Overhead*** | | ***20,050*** |
| ***To record factory overhead applied to production on basis of direct labor cost.*** | | |

Actual overhead for July totaled $19,430, leaving a credit balance of $620 in the Factory Overhead account, representing ***overapplied overhead*** for the month. This amount would be carried forward month to month, and any balance at the end of the year would be apportioned between ending inventories of goods in process and finished goods and the cost of goods sold during the year, or, if not material, simply closed out to the Cost of Goods Sold account.

## Equivalent full units—the key to determining unit cost

A basic objective of a process cost system is to determine the unit cost of materials, labor, and factory overhead for each manufacturing process or department. These unit costs become the basis for valuing inventories and for tracing the flow of costs through the departmental goods in process accounts and finally to Finished Goods Inventory and to Cost of Goods Sold.

If all units of product in a given department are completely processed (started and finished) during the period, computing unit cost is a simple matter of dividing the departmental costs by the number of units processed. In most cases, however, there are unfinished units of product on hand at the beginning as well as at the end of the accounting period. When some of the units on hand are unfinished, we cannot compute unit costs merely by dividing total costs by the number of units worked on, for this would assign the same unit cost to finished and unfinished goods. If completed and partially completed units of product are expressed in ***equivalent full units*** of completed product, however, this difficulty is overcome and meaningful unit costs can be determined by dividing the total cost by the equivalent full units produced. This computation is illustrated below for materials costs:

*Unit costs based on equivalent full units*

$$\text{Materials cost per unit} = \frac{\text{total cost of materials used during month}}{\text{equivalent full units produced during month}}$$

**What are "equivalent full units"?** Equivalent full units are a measure of the ***work done*** in a given accounting period. The concept of an equivalent full unit is based on the assumption that creating two units, each of which is 50% complete, represents the same amount of work as does producing one finished unit. Similarly, producing 1,000 units that are 25% complete is viewed as equivalent to 250 full units of production.

The work accomplished by a manufacturing department during a given accounting period may include (1) completing units which were already in process at the beginning of the period, (2) working on units started and completed during the current period, and (3) working on units which are still in process at the end of the current period. If we are to measure the work accomplished by the department, we must determine the equivalent full units of production represented ***by each of these three types of work effort.*** The computation of equivalent full units of production for a hypothetical company during the month of March is illustrated below:

***Computation of Equivalent Full Units***

*Equivalent full units—an index of productive effort for a period*

| | *Units* | × | *Portion Completed during March* | = | *Equivalent Full Units Completed (All Costs)* |
|---|---|---|---|---|---|
| *Beginning inventory in process (Mar. 1):* | | | | | |
| *80% completed in February but finished in March* | *20,000* | × | *20%* | = | *4,000* |
| *Units started and completed in March* | *50,000* | × | *100%* | = | *50,000* |
| *Units completed and transferred to storage* | *70,000* | | | | |
| *Ending inventory in process (Mar. 31), 40% completed in March* | *25,000* | × | *40%* | = | *10,000* |
| *Equivalent full units of production during March* | | | | | *64,000* |

Although 70,000 units were completed and transferred to storage in our example, the actual amount of work accomplished during March was equivalent to producing only 64,000 full units. The work performed in March consists of 4,000 equivalent full units of work (20% of 20,000) to complete the beginning inventory of goods in process, 50,000 equivalent full units to start and complete additional units during March, and 10,000 equivalent full units (40% of 25,000) on the goods still in process at the end of the month.

When materials and processing costs (direct labor and factory overhead) are applied at a ***uniform rate*** throughout the production process, the equivalent units of work done will be identical for all three cost elements. If the materials are placed in process at various stages (such as 100% at the beginning of production, or 40% at the beginning and 60% when most of the processing has been completed), the equivalent unit figure for materials will differ from that for processing costs. In such situations, the equivalent-unit computation for materials must be done separately from that for processing costs.

## Determination of unit costs and valuation of inventories: an example

We will now return to our example of the Process Cost Company to illustrate the computation of unit costs and the assignment of departmental costs to goods completed and goods in process at the end of the period. The costs incurred in the two processing departments during July appear in the departmental goods in process accounts, illustrated on page 945. The following production report shows the number of units processed in each department and provides information about the beginning and ending inventories of goods in process:

***Production report shows units only***

***Production Report for July***

| | Framing Dept. | Stringing Dept. |
|---|---|---|
| ***Units in process on July 1*** | 500[a] | 400[c] |
| ***Add: Units placed in production during July*** | 3,900 | 4,100 |
| ***Total units worked on during July*** | 4,400 | 4,500 |
| ***Less: Units in process on July 31*** | 300[b] | 500[d] |
| ***Units completed during July*** | 4,100 | 4,000 |

**a** 50% complete as to materials and processing costs on July 1.
**b** 50% complete as to materials and processing costs on July 31.
**c** 100% complete as to materials and 75% complete as to processing costs on July 1.
**d** 100% complete as to materials and 20% complete as to processing costs on July 31.

Using this information, we can now determine the unit costs in each of the two departments.

**Framing Department** From the information contained on the debit side of the departmental goods in process account (page 945) and in the production report above, a cost report for the Framing Department for July may be prepared as illustrated on page 949. The purposes of the cost report are (1) to summarize the units and cost charged to the department during the month, (2) to compute the unit costs of production during the month, and (3) to allocate the costs charged to the department between completed units and the ending inventory of goods in process.

***FRAMING DEPARTMENT***
***Cost Report for July***

| | Total Units | Total Costs ÷ | Equivalent Full Units* = | Unit Cost |
|---|---|---|---|---|
| ***Inputs:*** | | | | |
| *Units in process at beginning of month* | | | | |
| *(50% completed in June)* | *500* | *$ 2,115* | | |
| *Units placed in production during July* | *3,900* | | | |
| *Materials* | | *18,800* | *4,000* | *$ 4.70* |
| *Direct labor* | | *12,000* | *4,000* | *3.00* |
| *Factory overhead* | | *9,600* | *4,000* | *2.40* |
| ***Total inputs—units and costs*** | *4,400* | *$42,515* | | |
| ***Unit cost of work done in July*** | | | | *$10.10* |
| ***Outputs:*** | | | | |
| *Units in process at end of month, 50%* | | | | |
| *complete (300 units × 50% × $10.10)* | *300* | *$ 1,515* | | |
| *Units completed and transferred to* | | | | |
| *Stringing Dept. ($42,515 − $1,515)* | *4,100* | *41,000* | | *$10.00* |
| ***Total outputs—units and costs*** | *4,400* | *$42,515* | | |

* Computation of equivalent full units:

| | *Units* × | *Portion Completed during July* = | *Equivalent Full Units Produced* |
|---|---|---|---|
| Units in process at beginning of month | | | |
| (50% completed in June) | 500 | 50% | 250 |
| Units started and completed in July | 3,600† | 100% | 3,600 |
| Units completed and transferred to Stringing Dept. | 4,100 | | |
| Units in process at end of month (50% complete) | 300 | 50% | 150 |
| Equivalent full units of production during July | | | 4,000 |

† The number of units started and completed during July is found by subtracting the 300 units in process at July 31 from the 3,900 units placed in production during July.

The first section of the cost report (labeled Inputs) shows that total costs charged to the Framing Department during July amounted to $42,515, including the cost of $2,115 applicable to the beginning goods in process inventory which was carried forward from June. This total cost of $42,515 was incurred on the 4,400 units worked on during July. We could not, however, divide the total cost by 4,400 units to determine the manufacturing cost per unit for the month. Not all of these units were entirely processed in July; 500 units were already 50% complete at the beginning of the month, while another 300 units were only 50% complete at month-end. Therefore, we must compute the equivalent full units of production for July as a preliminary step toward determining unit cost.

In the Framing Department, materials and processing costs (labor and overhead) are applied to units of product at a uniform rate; that is, a unit that has received 50% of the required materials has also received 50% of the processing costs required to complete the unit. Therefore, the equivalent full units of production are the same for all three cost elements and may be determined by a single computation as shown at the bottom of the cost report on page 949. This computation shows that the work done in the Framing Department during July was equivalent to producing 4,000 full units.

We are now ready to determine the average unit cost of producing racquet frames during July. In the Inputs section of the cost report, the cost of materials used in July ($18,800) is divided by the equivalent full units of production (4,000) to give us a unit cost for materials of $4.70. The direct labor and factory overhead costs per unit are computed in a similar manner. The total of these three cost elements gives an average unit cost of $10.10 for the work performed by the Framing Department during July.

Once the unit manufacturing costs have been determined, the total costs charged to the department during July ($42,515) can be allocated between units completed and transferred to the Stringing Department in July and units still in process in the Framing Department at July 31. The easiest method of allocating these costs is to value the ending inventory of goods in process using the current unit cost figure, and then to assign the remainder of the costs to the units completed during the month.[2] This approach is illustrated in the Outputs section of the cost report on page 949.

Although 300 units are in process in the Framing Department at July 31, each unit is only 50% complete; therefore, the ending inventory of goods in process is assigned a cost of $1,515 (300 units × $10.10 × 50%). The remaining $41,000 ($42,515 − $1,515) represents the cost of the 4,100 units completed and transferred to the Stringing Department during July. The entry to transfer the cost of units completed in the Framing Department to the Stringing Department is illustrated below:

***Transfer of cost to next department***

| | | |
|---|---|---|
| ***Goods in Process: Stringing Department*** | ***41,000*** | |
|     ***Goods in Process: Framing Department*** | | ***41,000*** |
| ***To transfer cost of 4,100 completed racquet frames from Framing Department to Stringing Department. Average unit cost = $10.00.*** | | |

Note that the average unit cost of racquet frames ***completed*** in July is only $10.00, while the average unit cost of ***work done*** in July is $10.10. The reason for this difference is that some of the units completed in July received part of their processing during June. The cost of units ***completed*** in July, therefore, is a combination of manufacturing costs incurred in both June and July.[3]

---

[2] Using the current month's unit cost to value ending inventory conforms to the first-in, first-out method of inventory valuation. The use of other inventory methods (such as weighted average) in a process cost system is discussed in cost accounting courses.

[3] The $2,115 cost of goods in process at July 1 is the cost of 250 equivalent units of work performed in June (500 units, each 50% complete), indicating a June cost per unit of $8.46 ($2,115 ÷ 250). While 4,100 units were completed during July, 250 equivalent units of work was done on these units in June and the remaining 3,850 equivalent units of work was done in July. Thus, the cost of these units includes the following "layers":

| | |
|---|---|
| Costs brought forward from June: 250 equivalent units @ $8.46 | $ 2,115 |
| Costs incurred in July: 3,850 equivalent units @ $10.10 | 38,885 |
| Total cost of 4,100 units completed in July | $41,000 |
| Average unit cost ($41,000 ÷ 4,100) | $ 10.00 |

**Stringing Department** The July report of the Stringing Department is illustrated on page 952. In most respects, this report parallels that of the Framing Department. A few new features, however, appear in the cost report of the Stringing Department; these features will now be explained.

First, note that the cost inputs section of the report includes the cost of the ***racquet frames transferred*** into the Stringing Department from the Framing Department during July. From the viewpoint of the Stringing Department, these racquet frames are a form of "raw material" which will be processed into finished tennis racquets. (The $7,790 cost identified as "Materials added" represents only the nylon strings and vinyl grips attached to the racquet frames in the Stringing Department.) Obviously, the cost of finished tennis racquets would be understated if we did not include the cost of the racquet frames.

Second, notice that the equivalent full units of production figures are computed ***separately*** for materials and for processing costs. In our example involving the Framing Department, both materials and processing costs were applied to units of product uniformly throughout the production process, which meant that the equivalent full units of production was the same for each cost element. In the Stringing Department, however, 100% of the materials needed to complete each unit are placed in process at the beginning of production, while processing costs are applied uniformly throughout the production process. Since materials costs and processing costs are applied to units of product at ***different rates,*** the equivalent units figure for materials must be computed separately from that for processing costs.

The computations at the bottom of the cost report show that enough materials were used during July to produce 4,100 full units. Thus, the materials cost per unit is found by dividing the total materials cost, $7,790, by 4,100 equivalent full units of production. In terms of labor and overhead, however, the work accomplished during July was equivalent to fully processing only 3,800 units. Therefore, the 3,800 equivalent unit figure is used in determining the unit costs for direct labor and factory overhead. Note that the $17.15 unit cost of work performed in July ***includes the $10.00 unit cost*** of the racquet frames transferred in from the Framing Department.

A third new feature in the Stringing Department cost report is the itemizing of the various cost elements included in the ending inventory of units in process. Since these units are 100% complete as to materials but only 20% complete as to processing costs, the amount of each manufacturing cost included in the units must be computed separately. Also note that the cost of the racquet frames ($10.00 per unit) is included in the cost of the 500 units in process at July 31.

All of the $74,475 in costs charged to the Stringing Department during July are applicable either to the goods in process at July 31 or to units completed during the month. Since we have assigned $6,475 of these costs to the ending inventory of goods in process, the remaining $68,000 ($74,475 − $6,475) represents the cost of the 4,000 tennis racquets completed during July. The entry to transfer the cost of goods completed in the Stringing Department during July to the Finished Goods Inventory account appears at the top of page 953.

### *STRINGING DEPARTMENT*
### *Cost Report for July*

| | Total Units | Total Costs | ÷ Equivalent Full Units* | = Unit Cost |
|---|---|---|---|---|
| ***Inputs:*** | | | | |
| Units in process at beginning of month (100% complete as to materials and 75% as to processing costs) | 400 | $ 5,735 | | |
| Units transferred in from Framing Dept. | 4,100 | 41,000 | 4,100 | $10.00 |
| Materials added | | 7,790 | 4,100 | 1.90 |
| Direct labor | | 9,500 | 3,800 | 2.50 |
| Factory overhead | | 10,450 | 3,800 | 2.75 |
| Total inputs—units and costs | 4,500 | $74,475 | | |
| Unit cost of work done in July | | | | $17.15 |
| ***Outputs:*** | | | | |
| Units in process at end of month (100% complete as to materials and 20% as to processing): | | | | |
| Units transferred in from Framing Department (500 frames × $10.00) | 500 | $ 5,000 | | |
| Materials added (500 × 100%) | | 950 | | |
| Direct labor (500 × $2.50 × 20%) | | 250 | | |
| Factory overhead (500 × $2.75 × 20%) | | 275 | | |
| Cost of units in process, July 31 | | $ 6,475 | | |
| Units completed and transferred to Finished Goods Warehouse ($74,475 − $6,475) | 4,000 | 68,000 | | $17.00 |
| Total output—units and costs | 4,500 | $74,475 | | |

* Computation of equivalent full units:

| | Units | × Portion Completed during July | = Equivalent Full Units Produced |
|---|---|---|---|
| ***Materials:*** | | | |
| Units in process at beginning of month (100% completed as to materials in June) | 400 | -0- | -0- |
| Units started and completed in July | 3,600 | 100% | 3,600 |
| Units completed and transferred to Finished Goods Warehouse | 4,000 | | |
| Units in process at end of month (100% complete as to materials) | 500 | 100% | 500 |
| Equivalent full units of production—materials | | | 4,100 |
| ***Processing costs (labor and overhead):*** | | | |
| Units in process at beginning of month (75% complete as to processing costs in June) | 400 | 25% | 100 |
| Units started and completed in July | 3,600† | 100% | 3,600 |
| Units completed and transferred to Finished Goods Warehouse | 4,000 | | |
| Units in process at end of month (20% complete as to processing costs) | 500 | 20% | 100 |
| Equivalent full units of production—processing costs | | | 3,800 |

† The number of units started and completed in July is found by subtracting the 500 units still in process at July 31 from the 4,100 units transferred in from the Framing Department during July.

*Transfer of cost to finished goods inventory*

| | | |
|---|---|---|
| *Finished Goods Inventory* | *68,000* | |
| *Goods in Process: Stringing Department* | | *68,000* |
| *To transfer cost of 4,000 tennis racquets completed in Stringing Department during July to Finished Goods Inventory. Unit cost = $17.00* | | |

The entries to record the sale of goods by Process Manufacturing Company during July appear below:

*Entries to record sales and cost of goods sold*

| | | |
|---|---|---|
| *Accounts Receivable* | *84,000* | |
| *Sales* | | *84,000* |
| *To record sales on account during July.* | | |
| *Cost of Goods Sold* | *63,800* | |
| *Finished Goods Inventory* | | *63,800* |
| *To record cost of 3,800 tennis racquets sold during July, computed on a Fifo basis: 1,000 units @ $16.20 + 2,800 units @ $17.00.* | | |

## Summary of job order and process cost systems

Several simplifying assumptions have been made in developing the illustrations of job order and process cost systems; nevertheless, the essential features of the two types of cost systems were included. Both the job order and the process cost systems are essentially devices for collecting cost information. A job order cost system produces information about the cost of manufacturing a particular product or a batch of a given product; a process cost system produces information about the ***average cost*** of putting a homogeneous unit of product through various manufacturing operations for a given time period. A job order cost system usually involves more detailed cost accounting work and in return gives more specific cost information. A process cost system involves less detailed accounting work and accumulates costs in terms of major production processes or departmental cost centers. Both systems provide the information required to prepare a schedule of cost of finished goods manufactured, to arrive at unit costs, and to formulate business decisions.

## KEY TERMS INTRODUCED OR EMPHASIZED IN CHAPTER 25

**Cost report** A schedule prepared for each production process or department in a process cost system. Shows the costs charged to the department during the period, the computation of unit manufacturing costs, and allocates the departmental costs between units completed during the period and the ending inventory of goods in process.

**Equivalent full units of production** A measure of the work done during an accounting period. Includes work done on beginning and ending inventories of goods in process as well as work on units completely processed during the period.

**Factory overhead** All costs incurred in the manufacturing process other than the cost of raw materials and direct labor. Included in factory overhead are, for example, insurance, depreciation of machinery, and supervisors' salaries.

**Job cost sheet** A record used in a job order cost system to summarize the manufacturing costs (materials, labor, and overhead) applicable to each job, or batch or production. Job cost sheets may be viewed as a subsidiary ledger supporting the balance of the Goods in Process Inventory control account.

**Job order cost system** A cost accounting system under which the focal point of costing is a quantity of product known as a ***job*** or ***lot.*** Costs of raw materials, direct labor, and factory overhead applicable to each job are compiled to arrive at average unit cost.

**Joint cost** A cost which applies jointly to two or more different kinds of products or different departments. An example is depreciation on a factory building in which six different products are manufactured. Some logical basis must be found for allocating joint costs to the various products or departments which benefit from the cost.

**Over- or underapplied overhead** The difference between the actual factory overhead incurred during the period and the amount applied to goods in process by use of a predetermined factory overhead rate. A physical measure of production activity.

**Predetermined overhead rate** A rate estimated at the beginning of the year as the probable relationship of factory overhead expenses to a correlated factor such as direct labor cost, direct labor hours, or machine-hours. This predetermined rate is used to allocate factory overhead to goods in process, thus making it possible to determine the approximate complete cost of finished units as quickly as possible.

**Process cost system** A cost accounting system used mostly in industries such as petroleum or chemicals characterized by continuous mass production. Costs are not assigned to specific units but to a manufacturing process or department.

**Processing costs** The cost of processing raw materials into a finished product; includes both direct labor costs and factory overhead costs.

## DEMONSTRATION PROBLEM FOR YOUR REVIEW

The Diversified Mfg. Company started operations early in January with two production departments, Foundry and Blending. The Foundry Department produces special castings to customer specifications and the Blending Department produces an industrial compound which is sold by the pound. The company uses a job order cost system in the Foundry and a process cost system in the Blending Department.

The following schedule summarizes the operations for January:

| | Total Costs Incurred | Foundry | Blending | Inventory at Jan. 31 |
|---|---|---|---|---|
| *Materials* | *$40,000* | *$13,000* | *$23,000* | *$4,000* |
| *Direct labor* | *56,800* | *20,000* | *36,800* | |
| *Factory overhead* | *43,600* | *16,000* | *27,600* | |

Shown below is the schedule of the jobs in process in the Foundry Department at January 31:

| | Materials | Direct Labor |
|---|---|---|
| *Job no. 9* | *$600* | *$400* |
| *Job no. 10* | *580* | *500* |

All other jobs were shipped to customers at a billed price of $60,000. The factory overhead in the Foundry is applied on the basis of direct labor cost.

The January production report for the Blending Department shows the following:

| | Pounds |
|---|---|
| *Placed in production* | *95,000* |
| *Completed* | *80,000* |
| *In process at Jan. 31, 80% complete as to materials and processing costs* | *15,000* |

Of the units completed, 70,000 were sold for $92,500 and the other 10,000 are stored in the warehouse. Selling expenses for January amounted to $14,250 and general and administrative expenses amounted to $12,500.

**Instructions**

**a** Prepare the journal entries to record (1) materials purchases and the requisitions for the Foundry and Blending departments and (2) the labor and overhead costs (including allocation to the two departments).

**b** Determine the cost of the jobs in process in the Foundry Department at the end of January and prepare journal entries (1) to transfer the cost of jobs completed to Finished Goods Inventory and (2) to record the sales and cost of goods sold for the month.

**c** Prepare a cost report for the Blending Department and prepare journal entries (1) to transfer the cost of the finished product to the Finished Goods Inventory account and (2) to record the sales and cost of goods sold for the month.

**d** Prepare a condensed income statement for January. (Ignore income taxes.)

## SOLUTION TO DEMONSTRATION PROBLEM

a (1)

| | | |
|---|---|---|
| *Materials Inventory* | *40,000* | |
| *Accounts Payable* | | *40,000* |
| *To record purchase of materials.* | | |
| | | |
| *Goods in Process: Foundry Department* | *13,000* | |
| *Goods in Process: Blending Department* | *23,000* | |
| *Materials Inventory* | | *36,000* |
| *To record requisitions of materials.* | | |

(2)

| | | |
|---|---|---|
| *Factory Payroll* | *56,800* | |
| *Factory Overhead* | *43,600* | |
| *Cash, Accounts Payable, etc.* | | *100,400* |
| *To record factory payroll and overhead costs.* | | |
| | | |
| *Goods in Process: Foundry Department* | *36,000* | |
| *Goods in Process: Blending Department* | *64,400* | |
| *Factory Payroll* | | *56,800* |
| *Factory Overhead* | | *43,600* |
| *To allocate factory payroll and overhead costs to productive departments.* | | |

b Cost of jobs in process in Foundry Department at January 31:

| | Total | Job No. 9 | Job No. 10 |
|---|---|---|---|
| *Materials* | *$1,180* | *$ 600* | *$ 580* |
| *Direct labor* | *900* | *400* | *500* |
| *Factory overhead, 80% of direct labor* | *720* | *320* | *400* |
| | *$2,800* | *$1,320* | *$1,480* |

(1)

| | | |
|---|---|---|
| *Finished Goods Inventory* | *46,200* | |
| *Goods in Process: Foundry Department* | | *46,200* |
| *To record costs of jobs completed: Total costs charged to Foundry Dept., $49,000, less cost of jobs in process, $2,800, = $46,200.* | | |

(2)

| | | |
|---|---|---|
| *Accounts Receivable* | *60,000* | |
| *Sales* | | *60,000* |
| *To record sale of goods completed in Foundry Department.* | | |
| | | |
| *Cost of Goods Sold* | *46,200* | |
| *Finished Goods Inventory* | | *46,200* |
| *To record cost of goods sold from Foundry Department.* | | |

c

## BLENDING DEPARTMENT

### Cost Report for January

| | Total Units | Total Costs | ÷ Equivalent Full Units* | = Unit Cost |
|---|---|---|---|---|
| **Inputs:** | | | | |
| Materials | 95,000 | $23,000 | 92,000 | $0.25 |
| Direct labor | | 36,800 | 92,000 | 0.40 |
| Factory overhead | | 27,600 | 92,000 | 0.30 |
| Total inputs—units and costs | 95,000 | $87,400 | | |
| Unit cost for January | | | | $0.05 |
| **Outputs:** | | | | |
| Units in process at end of month (80% complete as to materials and processing costs) 15,000 × $0.95 × 80% | 15,000 | $11,400 | | |
| Transferred to Finished Goods Inventory ($87,400 − $11,400) | 80,000 | 76,000 | | $0.95 |
| Total outputs—units and costs | 95,000 | $87,400 | | |

*Computation of equivalent full units:

| | |
|---|---|
| Beginning inventory of goods in process | -0- |
| Units started and completed during January | 80,000 |
| Add: Full units of work done in January on ending inventory in process (15,000 × 80%) | 12,000 |
| Equivalent full units of production in January | 92,000 |

| | | |
|---|---|---|
| (1) Finished Goods Inventory | 76,000 | |
| Goods in Process: Blending Department | | 76,000 |
| To record cost of finished product. | | |
| (2) Accounts Receivable | 92,500 | |
| Sales | | 92,500 |
| To record sales from Blending Department. | | |
| Cost of Goods Sold | 66,500 | |
| Finished Goods Inventory | | 66,500 |
| To record cost of goods sold from Blending Department, 70,000 units @ $0.95 per unit. | | |

d

## DIVERSIFIED MFG. COMPANY

### Income Statement

### For January

| | | |
|---|---|---|
| Sales ($60,000 + $92,500) | | $152,500 |
| Cost of goods sold ($46,200 + $66,500) | | 112,700 |
| Gross profit on sales | | $ 39,800 |
| Operating expenses: | | |
| Selling expenses | $14,250 | |
| General and administrative expenses | 12,500 | 26,750 |
| Net income | | $ 13,050 |

## REVIEW QUESTIONS

1 What is a cost accounting system?

2 What are the two major objectives of cost accounting?

3 Why is it difficult to measure the precise cost of a product or a service produced by a business enterprise?

4 What is meant by the phrase, "different costs for different purposes"? Illustrate by explaining how a factory superintendent's salary might be treated differently, as a cost, for different purposes.

5 Differentiate between ***product costs*** and ***period costs.***

6 What factors should be taken into account in deciding whether to use a job order cost system or a process cost system in any given manufacturing situation?

7 Describe the three kinds of charges on a job cost sheet. For what general ledger control account do job cost sheets constitute supporting detail?

8 Explain why it is advantageous to use predetermined overhead rates in associating factory overhead with output.

9 Gerox Company applies factory overhead on the basis of machine-hours, using a predetermined overhead rate. At the end of the current year the factory overhead account has a credit balance. What are the possible explanations for this? What disposition should be made of this balance?

10 What are the characteristics of a process cost system?

11 What is meant by the term ***equivalent full units?*** How is this concept used in computing average unit costs?

12 When must the equivalent full units of production figure for materials be computed separately from that for processing costs? Explain.

13 If a department has no beginning inventory of goods in process but has 10,000 units in process at month-end, will the equivalent full units of work performed be greater or smaller than the number of units completed during the month? Explain.

14 Briefly describe the purposes of a cost report in a process cost system.

15 In a process cost system, is the average unit cost of ***work performed*** during the month always exactly equal to the average unit cost of ***goods completed*** during the month? Explain.

## EXERCISES

*Ex. 25-1* The information below is taken from the job order cost system used by the Gate Company:

| *Job Number* | *Balance, July 1* | *Production Costs in July* |
|---|---|---|
| *101* | *$1,400* | |
| *102* | *1,080* | |
| *103* | *300* | *$ 650* |
| *104* | *750* | *1,300* |
| *105* | | *1,900* |
| *106* | | *1,210* |

During July, jobs no. 103 and 104 were completed, and jobs no. 101, 102, and 103 were delivered to customers. From this information, compute the following:

**a** The goods in process inventory at July 1
**b** The finished goods inventory at July 1
**c** The cost of goods sold during July
**d** The goods in process inventory at July 31
**e** The finished goods inventory at July 31

*Ex. 25-2* The Snowplow Company, which used a job order cost system, completed the following transactions during the month of November:

**a** Direct labor, $15,000, and indirect labor, $5,000, were transferred from the Factory Payroll account to other appropriate accounts.
**b** Other factory overhead costs of $11,500 were incurred (credit Accounts Payable).
**c** Factory overhead costs were applied to goods in process at the rate of 80% of direct labor cost.
**d** Raw materials identified with specific jobs amounted to $8,200.
**e** Jobs with total accumulated costs of $30,000 were finished.
**f** The cost of units sold during the month amounted to $28,800; the sales price of units sold is $40,000.

Prepare entries in journal form to record the foregoing transactions. Explanations may be omitted.

*Ex. 25-3* Bar Stools, Inc., uses a job order cost system. The following information appears in the company's Goods in Process Inventory account for the month of January:

| | |
|---|---|
| *Debits to account:* | |
| *Balance Jan. 1* | *$ 20,000* |
| *Raw materials* | *48,000* |
| *Direct labor* | *80,000* |
| *Factory overhead (applied to jobs at 120% of direct labor cost)* | *96,000* |
| *Total debits to account* | *$244,000* |
| *Credits to account:* | |
| *Transferred to Finished Goods Inventory account* | *212,000* |
| *Balance, Jan. 31* | *$ 32,000* |

If the cost of raw materials relating to the jobs in process on January 31 amounts to $14,400, determine the amount of direct labor and of factory overhead which has been charged to these partially completed jobs.

*Ex. 25-4* The following relates to the Assembly Department of Lawncraft Mowers during the month of May:

| | |
|---|---|
| *Units in process at May 1 (60% completed in April)* | *2,000* |
| *Additional units placed in production during May* | *20,000* |
| *Units in process at May 31 (80% completed)* | *5,000* |

Determine the equivalent full units of production during the month of May, assuming that all costs are incurred uniformly as the units move through the production line.

*Ex. 25-5* Shamrock Industries uses a process cost system. Products are processed successively by Department A and Department B, and are then transferred to the finished goods warehouse. Shown below is cost information for Department B during the month of June:

| | | |
|---|---|---|
| *Cost of goods in process at June 1* | | *$ 19,000* |
| *Cost of units transferred in from Department A during June* | | *72,500* |
| *Manufacturing costs incurred in June:* | | |
| *Materials added* | *$44,000* | |
| *Direct labor* | *16,100* | |
| *Factory overhead* | *7,400* | *67,500* |
| *Total costs charged to Department B in June* | | *$159,000* |

The cost of goods in process in Department B at June 30 has been determined to be $22,700.

Prepare journal entries to record for the month of June (1) the transfer of production from Department A to Department B, (2) the manufacturing costs incurred by Department B, and (3) the transfer of completed units from Department B to the finished goods warehouse.

*Ex. 25-6* Given below are the production data for Department no. 1 for the first month of operation:

| | |
|---|---|
| *Inputs to department:* | |
| *Material, 1,000 units* | *$10,000* |
| *Direct labor* | *19,000* |
| *Factory overhead* | *14,250* |
| *Total* | *$43,250* |

During this first month, 1,000 units were placed into production; 800 units were completed and the remaining 200 units are 100% completed as to material and 75% completed as to direct labor and factory overhead.

You are to determine:

**a** Unit cost of material used
**b** Equivalent full units of production for direct labor and factory overhead
**c** Unit cost of direct labor
**d** Unit cost of factory overhead
**e** Total cost of 200 units in process at end of month
**f** Total cost of 800 units completed

## PROBLEMS

### Group A

*25A-1* Woodcrafters Cabinet Shop uses a job order cost accounting system. Factory overhead is charged to individual jobs through the use of a predetermined overhead rate based on direct labor costs. The following information appears in the company's Goods in Process Inventory account for the month of June:

| | |
|---|---|
| ***Debits to account:*** | |
| *Balance, June 1* | *$ 7,750* |
| *Raw materials* | *8,000* |
| *Direct labor* | *10,500* |
| *Factory overhead (applied to jobs as a percentage of direct labor cost)* | *8,400* |
| *Total debits to account* | *$34,650* |
| ***Credits to account:*** | |
| *Transferred to Finished Goods Inventory account* | *28,000* |
| *Balance, June 30* | *$ 6,650* |

**Instructions**

**a** Compute the predetermined overhead application rate used by the company.

**b** Assuming that the direct labor charged to the jobs still in process at June 30 amounts to $2,600, compute the amount of factory overhead and the amount of raw materials which have been charged to these jobs as of June 30.

**c** Prepare general journal entries to summarize:

(1) The manufacturing costs (materials, labor, and overhead) charged to production during June.

(2) The transfer of production completed during June to the Finished Goods Inventory account.

(3) The cash sale of 90% of the merchandise completed during June at a total sales price of $38,620. Show the related cost of goods sold in a separate journal entry.

*25A-2* Sunland Furniture Co. manufactures furniture to customers' specifications and uses a job order cost system. A predetermined overhead rate is used in applying factory overhead to individual jobs. In Department One overhead is applied on the basis of direct labor hours, and in Department Two on the basis of machine-hours. At the beginning of the current year, management made the following budget estimates to assist in determining the overhead application rate:

| | *Department One* | *Department Two* |
|---|---|---|
| *Direct labor cost* | *$300,000* | *$225,000* |
| *Direct labor hours* | *20,000* | *15,000* |
| *Factory overhead* | *$180,000* | *$90,000* |
| *Machine-hours* | *12,000* | *7,500* |

Production of a batch of custom furniture ordered by the City Furniture Chain (job no. 58) was started early in the year and completed three weeks later on January 29. The records for this job show the following cost information:

| | *Department One* | *Department Two* |
|---|---|---|
| ***Job order for City Furniture Chain (job no. 58):*** | | |
| *Direct materials cost* | *$10,100* | *$ 4,600* |
| *Direct labor cost* | *$16,000* | *$10,200* |
| *Direct labor hours* | *1,100* | *740* |
| *Machine-hours* | *750* | *500* |

Selected additional information for January is given below:

| | Department One | Department Two |
|---|---|---|
| *Direct labor hours—month of January* | *1,600* | *1,200* |
| *Machine-hours—month of January* | *1,100* | *600* |
| *Factory overhead incurred in January* | *$13,950* | *$7,470* |

**Instructions**

**a** Compute the predetermined overhead rate for each department.
**b** What is the total cost of the furniture produced for the City Furniture Chain?
**c** Prepare the entries required to record the sale (on account) of the furniture to the City Furniture Chain. The sales price of the order was $84,500.
**d** Determine the over- or underapplied overhead for each department at the end of January.

*25A-3* One of the primary products of Olympic Cameras is the Shutterbug, an automatic camera which is processed successively in the Assembly Department and the Lens Department, and then transferred to the company's sales warehouse. After having been shut down for three weeks as a result of a material shortage, the company resumed production of Shutterbugs on May 1. The flow of product through the departments during May is shown below.

| Assembly Department Goods in Process | |
|---|---|
| *Started in process— 30,000 units* | *To Dept. B— 25,000 units* |

| Lens Department Goods in Process | |
|---|---|
| *From Dept. A— 25,000 units* | *To warehouse— 21,000 units* |

Departmental manufacturing costs applicable to Shutterbug production for the month of May were as follows:

| | Assembly Department | Lens Department |
|---|---|---|
| *Units transferred from Assembly Department* | | *$ ?* |
| *Raw materials* | *$112,000* | *46,800* |
| *Direct labor* | *98,000* | *70,200* |
| *Factory overhead* | *70,000* | *140,400* |
| *Total manufacturing costs* | *$280,000* | *$ ?* |

Unfinished goods in each department at the end of May were on the average 60% complete, with respect to both raw materials and processing costs.

**Instructions**

**a** Prepare a production report for the Shutterbug for the month of May. Your production report should indicate for each of the two processing departments the number of units placed in production, in process at May 31, and completed during May.
**b** Determine the equivalent full units of production in each department during May.
**c** Compute unit production costs in each department during May.
**d** Prepare the necessary journal entries to record the transfer of product out of the Assembly Department and the Lens Department during May.

*25A-4* Shown below are the production report and a summary of the costs charged to a production department of Firebird Mfg. Co. for the month of July:

***Summary of Costs***

| | |
|---|---|
| *Costs brought forward from June (beginning inventory of goods in process)* | *$ 19,400* |
| *Materials used in July* | *91,600* |
| *Direct labor* | *56,000* |
| *Factory overhead (applied at 120% of direct labor cost)* | *67,200* |
| *Total costs to be accounted for* | *$234,200* |

***Production Report for July***

| | |
|---|---|
| *Units in process at July 1 (completed 40% as to materials and 60% as to processing costs in June)* | *2,000* |
| *Add: Units placed in production during July (of which 8,000 were completed during July)* | *11,000* |
| *Total units worked on during July* | *13,000* |
| *Less: Units in process at July 31 (75% complete as to materials and 80% complete as to processing costs)* | *3,000* |
| *Units completed and transferred to Finished Goods warehouse during July* | *10,000* |

**Instructions**

**a** Compute separately the equivalent full units of production during July for (1) materials and (2) processing costs.

**b** Prepare a cost report for July, as illustrated on page 949. Use the July unit cost figures in determining the cost of the ending inventory of goods in process and assign the remaining costs to units completed during July (a fifo assumption).

**c** Prepare journal entries to record (1) the manufacturing costs charged to the department during July, and (2) the transfer of completed units to the Finished Goods warehouse.

*25A-5* Chem-Tech manufactures an epoxy sealer, called Permacoat, in four sequential processes. The Fourth Process is the last step before the product is transferred to the warehouse as finished inventory.

All material needed to complete Permacoat is added at the beginning of the Fourth Process. The company accumulated the following cost information for the Fourth Process during the month of April:

| | |
|---|---|
| ***Cost inputs to the Fourth Process during April:*** | |
| *Costs brought forward from March (40,000 units which were 100% completed as to materials and 75% completed as to processing costs in March)* | *$ 357,400* |
| *Cost of 140,000 units transferred in from the Third Process during April (90,000 of these units were completed by Apr. 30)* | *560,000* |
| ***Manufacturing costs incurred in April:*** | |
| *Materials added* | *280,000* |
| *Direct labor* | *125,000* |
| *Factory overhead* | *375,000* |
| *Total costs to be accounted for* | *$1,697,400* |

During April, the 40,000 units in process at April 1 and 90,000 of the units transferred in from the Third Process were completed and transferred to the warehouse. The remaining 50,000 units transferred in from the Third Process were still in process at April 30 and were 100% complete as to materials and 50% complete as to direct labor and factory overhead.

**Instructions**

**a** Compute the equivalent full units of production during April. (Separate computations are required for materials and processing costs.)

**b** Prepare a cost report for the month of April. Use April unit cost figures to determine the cost of the goods in process at April 30; the remaining cost inputs apply to units completed during April (fifo method of inventory valuation).

**c** Prepare journal entries to record:
(1) Transfer of the 140,000 units from the Third Process into the Fourth Process.
(2) Manufacturing costs charged to the Fourth Process during April.
(3) Transfer of 130,000 completed units from the Fourth Process to the finished goods warehouse.

## Group B

*25B-1* Riverside Engineering is a machine shop which uses a job order cost accounting system. Overhead is applied to individual jobs at a predetermined rate based on direct labor costs. The job cost sheet for job no. 321 appears below:

***Job Cost Sheet***

*Job Number:* 321 | *Date Started:* May 10
*Product:* 2" brass check valves | *Date Completed:* May 21
*Units Completed:* 4,000

| | |
|---|---|
| *Raw materials used* | *$21,540* |
| *Direct labor* | *3,000* |
| *Factory overhead (applied as a percentage of direct labor)* | *3,900* |
| *Total cost of job no. 321* | *$28,440* |

**Instructions**

**a** Compute (1) the predetermined overhead application rate used by the company, and (2) the average unit cost of the valves manufactured in job no. 321.

**b** Prepare general journal entries to:
(1) Summarize the manufacturing costs charged to job no. 321.
(2) Record the completion of job no. 321.
(3) Record the credit sale of 2,100 units from job no. 321 at a unit sales price of $9.90. Record in a separate entry the related cost of goods sold.

*25B-2* Precision Instruments, Inc., uses a job order cost system and applies factory overhead to individual jobs by using predetermined overhead rates. In Department C overhead is applied on the basis of machine-hours, and in Department D on the basis of direct labor hours. At the beginning of the current year, management made the following budget estimates as a step toward determining the overhead application rates:

| | Department C | Department D |
|---|---|---|
| Direct labor | $210,000 | $384,000 |
| Factory overhead | $216,000 | $105,000 |
| Machine-hours | 36,000 | 900 |
| Direct labor hours | 18,000 | 25,000 |

Production order no. 399 for 2,000 units was started in the middle of January and completed two weeks later. The cost records for this job show the following information:

| | Department C | Department D |
|---|---|---|
| Job no. 399 (2,000 units of product): | | |
| Cost of materials used on job | $6,100 | $12,500 |
| Direct labor cost | $8,000 | $16,000 |
| Direct labor hours | 650 | 1,000 |
| Machine-hours | 1,200 | 100 |

**Instructions**

**a** Determine the overhead rate that should be used for each department in applying overhead costs to job no. 399.

**b** What is the total cost of job no. 399, and the unit cost of the product manufactured on this production order?

**c** Assume that actual overhead costs for the year were $215,000 in Department C and $107,600 in Department D. Actual machine-hours in Department C were 35,000, and actual direct labor hours in Department D were 26,000 during the year. On the basis of this information, determine the over- or underapplied overhead in each department for the year.

*25B-3* After having been shut down for two months during a strike, Sunray Appliances resumed operations on August 1. One of the company's products is a dishwasher which is successively processed by the Tub Department and the Motor Department before being transferred to the finished goods warehouse. Shown below are the production reports and cost data for the two departments:

**Production Report for August**

| | Tub Department | Motor Department |
|---|---|---|
| Units placed in production | 1,700 | 900 |
| Less: Goods in process, Aug. 31 | 800 | 400 |
| Units completed during August | 900 | 500 |

**Departmental Cost Summary**

| | | |
|---|---|---|
| Transferred in from Tub Department | | $ ? |
| Materials | $54,000 | 57,600 |
| Direct labor | 30,000 | 10,400 |
| Factory overhead | 16,500 | 6,400 |

Due to the strike, there were no goods in process at August 1 in either department. The units in process in both departments at August 31 are 75% complete with respect to both materials and processing costs.

**Instructions**

**a** Compute the equivalent full units of production in August for each department.
**b** Compute the unit production costs for August in each department. (Include in the production costs of the Motor Department the cost of the 900 units transferred in from the Tub Department.)
**c** Use the August unit cost figures to determine the cost of the ending inventory of goods in process in each department at August 31.
**d** Prepare the journal entries required to record the transfer of completed units out of each of the two departments during August.

*25B-4* Aladdin Electric manufactures several products, including an electric garage door opener called the Door Tender. Door Tenders are completely processed in one department and are then transferred to the finished goods warehouse. All manufacturing costs are applied to Door Tender units at a uniform rate throughout the production process. The following information is available for July:

| | |
|---|---|
| ***Inputs during July:*** | |
| *Beginning inventory of goods in process* | *$ 21,220* |
| *Manufacturing costs incurred in July:* | |
| *Materials used* | *53,400* |
| *Direct labor* | *32,040* |
| *Factory overhead* | *21,360* |
| *Total costs to be accounted for* | *$128,020* |

The beginning inventory consisted of 400 units which had been 90% completed during June. In addition to completing these units, the department started and completed another 1,500 units during July and started work on 300 more units which were 80% completed at July 31.

**Instructions**

**a** Compute the equivalent full units of production in July.
**b** Prepare a cost report for the department for the month of July, as illustrated on page 952. Use the July unit cost figures to determine the cost of the ending inventory of goods in process.
**c** Prepare journal entries to record (1) the manufacturing costs charged to the department during July, and (2) the transfer of 1,900 completed units to the finished goods warehouse.

*25B-5* Saf-T-File, Inc., manufactures metal filing cabinets and uses a process cost system. The filing cabinets pass through a series of production departments, one of which is the Lock Assembly Department. The production report and a summary of the costs charged to the Lock Assembly Department during the month of April follow:

***Production Report for April***

| | |
|---|---|
| *Units in process at Apr. 1 (100% completed as to materials, 80% completed as to processing costs in March)* | *500* |
| *Add: Units transferred in from Drawer Assembly Dept. during April (of which 1,600 were completed by Apr. 30)* | *2,000* |
| *Total units worked on during April* | *2,500* |
| *Less: Units in process at Apr. 30 (100% complete as to materials, 50% complete as to processing costs)* | *400* |
| *Units completed and transferred to Painting Dept. during April* | *2,100* |

***Summary of Costs Charged to Lock Assembly Department***

| | |
|---|---|
| *Costs brought forward from March (beginning inventory of goods in process)* | *$ 29,840* |
| *Costs transferred in from Drawer Assembly Dept.* | *104,000* |
| *Materials added* | *8,200* |
| *Direct labor added* | *3,800* |
| *Factory overhead (applied at 150% of direct labor cost)* | *5,700* |
| *Total costs to be accounted for* | *$151,540* |

**Instructions**

**a** Compute separately the equivalent full units of production during April for (1) materials and (2) processing costs (direct labor and factory overhead).

**b** Prepare a cost report for April, as illustrated on page 949. Use April unit cost figures to determine the cost of goods in process at April 30; the remaining cost inputs apply to units transferred from the Lock Assembly Department to the Painting Department during April.

**c** Prepare journal entries to record:
(1) Transfer of the 2,000 units from the Drawer Assembly Department into the Lock Assembly Department.
(2) Manufacturing costs charged to the Lock Assembly Department during April.
(3) Transfer of 2,100 completed units from the Lock Assembly Department to the Painting Department.

## BUSINESS DECISION PROBLEM 25

John Park is the founder and president of Park West Engineering. One of the company's principal products is sold exclusively to BigMart, a national chain of retail stores. BigMart buys a large quantity of the product in the first quarter of each year, but buys successively smaller quantities in the second, third, and fourth quarters. Park West cannot produce in advance to meet the big first quarter sales requirement, because BigMart frequently makes minor changes in the specifications for the product. Therefore, Park West must adjust its production schedules to fit BigMart's buying pattern.

In Park West's cost accounting system, unit costs are computed quarterly on the basis of actual material, labor, and factory overhead costs charged to goods in process at the end of each quarter. At the close of the current year, Park received the following cost report, by quarters, for the year. (Fixed factory overhead represents items of manufacturing costs that remain relatively constant month by month; variable factory overhead includes those costs that tend to move up and down in proportion to changes in the volume of production.)

| | *First Quarter* | *Second Quarter* | *Third Quarter* | *Fourth Quarter* |
|---|---|---|---|---|
| *Raw materials* | *$ 78,000* | *$ 60,000* | *$ 42,000* | *$ 22,000* |
| *Direct labor* | *80,000* | *60,000* | *40,000* | *20,000* |
| *Fixed factory overhead* | *30,000* | *30,000* | *30,000* | *30,000* |
| *Variable factory overhead* | *48,000* | *39,000* | *29,000* | *14,000* |
| *Total manufacturing cost* | *$236,000* | *$189,000* | *$141,000* | *$ 86,000* |
| *Equivalent full units produced* | *40,000* | *30,000* | *20,000* | *10,000* |
| *Unit production cost* | *$ 5.90* | *$ 6.30* | *$ 7.05* | *$ 8.60* |

Park is concerned about the steadily rising unit costs. He states, "We have a contract to produce 50,000 units for BigMart next quarter at a unit sales price of $8.50. If this sales price won't even cover our unit production costs, I'll have to cancel the contract. But before I take such drastic action, I'd like you to study our method of computing unit costs to see if we might be doing something wrong."

**Instructions**

**a** As the first step in your study, determine the unit cost of each cost element (materials, labor, fixed factory overhead, and variable factory overhead) in the first quarter and in the fourth quarter of the current year.

**b** Based on your computation in part **a,** which cost element is primarily responsible for the increase in unit production costs? Explain why you think the unit cost for this cost element has been rising throughout the year.

**c** Compute an overhead application rate for Park West Engineering which expresses total factory overhead for the year (including both fixed and variable overhead) as a percentage of direct labor costs.

**d** Redetermine the unit production cost for each quarter using the overhead application rate to apply factory overhead costs.

**e** Determine the expected unit cost of producing 50,000 units next quarter. (Assume that unit costs for materials and direct labor remain the same as in the fourth quarter and use the overhead application rate to determine the unit cost of applied overhead.)

**f** Explain to Park how Park West might improve its procedures for determining unit production costs. Also explain whether Park West reasonably can expect to recover its production costs next quarter if it sells 50,000 units to BigMart at a unit sales price of $8.50.

# 26

# MANAGERIAL CONTROL: STANDARD COSTS AND BUDGETING

The two basic objectives of a cost accounting system are to determine the unit cost of production and to provide management with information useful in controlling the cost of business operations. In the preceding chapter, we saw that unit cost information can be developed in process cost or job order cost systems. In this chapter, we discuss how these cost accounting systems can be expanded to better assist management in controlling costs and in evaluating the efficiency of departmental operations. Specifically, we will explore the use of standard costs and budgets as aids to managerial control.

## STANDARD COSTS FOR PRODUCT COSTING AND CONTROL

The usefulness of a cost accounting system is increased when ***predetermined cost estimates*** for materials, labor, and factory overhead are included in the system to serve as bench marks against which actual costs may be compared. These predetermined cost estimates are called ***standard costs.*** A standard cost is the cost that ***should be incurred*** to produce a product or to perform an operation ***under relatively ideal conditions.***

Comparison of actual costs to the predetermined standard costs serves to direct managers' attention to those areas in which actual costs appear excessive. This is known as ***management by exception*** because managers should not spend time on areas of activity which are running according to plans. Effective managers focus attention on those activities which are "off target," that is, those not meeting the established standards of performance. For example, if a standard cost to produce a given product is set at $10 per unit and the actual cost is $12.50 per unit, management would want to know why actual cost exceeded standard cost by such a large margin and would strive to attain tighter control over production costs.

Standard costs may be included in both process cost and job order cost accounting systems.

## Establishing and revising standard costs

To provide a reasonable basis for comparison, ***standard costs should be set at realistic and achievable levels.*** If the standard costs are too low, an excess of actual costs over standard costs becomes a normal condition, rather than an indication of inefficiency. On the other hand, if standard costs are too high, they may be easily achieved and inefficient operations will not be brought to management's attention.

In establishing the standard cost for a manufactured product, the manufacturing process and the current prices of materials, labor, and factory overhead must be carefully studied. The standard cost which is then established should be achievable under existing conditions, as long as the production departments operate in an efficient manner.

Once cost standards are set, they should be reviewed periodically and changed whenever production methods change, products are redesigned, or the prices paid for materials, labor, and factory overhead change. When actual costs exceed standard costs because of waste or inefficiency, however, the standard costs should ***not*** be revised upward. A standard cost for materials, for example, would not be changed if 10% of material placed in production has been spoiled because of carelessness by employees. The standard cost for material would be changed, however, if the price for materials is increased by suppliers. Similarly, the standard cost for labor would not be changed if too many hours of labor are wasted; but it would be changed if laborsaving equipment is installed or if new contracts with labor unions call for increased wage rates.

## Cost variances

Even though standard costs may be carefully set and revised as conditions change, actual costs will still vary from standard costs. The differences between standard costs and actual costs are known as ***cost variances.*** Cost variances for materials, direct labor, and factory overhead result from a wide variety of causes which must be carefully measured and analyzed. As might be expected, different individuals within an organization are responsible for different cost variances.

It is possible to use standard costs only for cost control purposes and for the preparation of various internal reports for management's use. In most cases, however, standard costs and cost variances actually are recorded in the accounts. Under standard cost procedures, the costs charged to Goods in Process, Finished Goods, and Cost of Goods Sold are the ***standard costs*** of materials, direct labor, and factory overhead, not the actual costs. Any differences between the actual costs and the standard costs of goods produced are accumulated in a number of ***variance accounts.***

A cost variance is said to be ***unfavorable*** when actual costs exceed standard costs. When actual costs are less than standard costs, the cost variance is said to be ***favorable.***

### Illustration of the use of standard costs

To illustrate the use of standard costs and the computation of cost variances, assume that Standard Manufacturing Company has a normal monthly capacity to work 10,000 direct labor hours and to produce 10,000 units of product M. The standard cost for a unit of product M is shown below:

*Standard cost for a unit of product M*

| | | |
|---|---|---|
| *Materials, one pound at $5 per pound* | | *$ 5* |
| *Direct labor, one hour at $10 per hour* | | *10* |
| *Factory overhead, based on direct labor hours:* | | |
| *Fixed ($20,000 ÷ 10,000 units monthly capacity)* | *$2* | |
| *Variable ($10,000 ÷ 10,000 units monthly capacity)* | *1* | *3* |
| *Standard cost per unit of product M* | | *$18* |

During the month of March, the following actual costs were incurred in producing 9,500 units of product M. There was no work in process either at the beginning or at the end of March.

*Were standard cost targets achieved?*

| | | |
|---|---|---|
| *Materials, 9,400 pounds at $5.20 per pound* | | *$ 48,880* |
| *Direct labor, 9,600 hours at $10.40 per hour* | | *99,840* |
| *Factory overhead:* | | |
| *Fixed* | *$20,000* | |
| *Variable* | *12,480* | *32,480* |
| *Total actual costs incurred in March* | | *$181,200* |

By comparing these actual costs to the standard cost of product M, we can determine the net cost variance for March:

*Who is responsible for the apparent waste of $10,200?*

| | |
|---|---|
| *Total actual costs (see above)* | *$181,200* |
| *Total standard costs for units produced, 9,500 units at $18 per unit* | *171,000* |
| *Net unfavorable cost variance (excess of actual over standard costs)* | *$ 10,200* |

In planning corrective action, management will want to know the specific causes of this $10,200 net unfavorable cost variance. By comparing each element of manufacturing cost (materials, labor, and overhead) to the related standard costs, we can explain the net cost variance for March in greater detail. Let us begin by determining the portion of this variance which is attributable to the price and the quantity of materials used in March.

**Material price and material quantity variances** In establishing the standard material cost for each unit of product, two factors were considered: (1) the quantity of material that should have been used in making a unit of finished product, and (2) the prices that should have been paid in acquiring this quantity of material. Therefore, the total material cost variance may result from differences between standard and actual material usage, or between standard and actual prices paid for materials, or from a combination of these two factors. This can be illustrated by the following diagram:

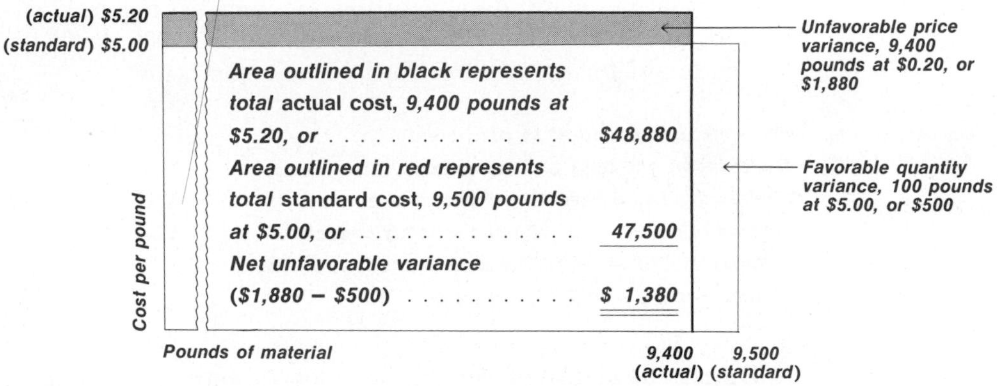


The variances for materials and the journal entry required to record the cost of material incurred by the Standard Manufacturing Company in the month of March may be summarized as follows:

*Why was actual material cost higher than standard?*

***Material Price and Quantity Variances***

| | | | | |
|---|---|---|---|---|
| *Actual quantity of materials used at actual cost per pound, 9,400 × $5.20* | *$48,880* | | | |
| | | *$1,880* | *Unfavorable price variance* | |
| *Actual quantity of materials used at standard cost per pound, 9,400 × $5.00* | *47,000* | | | |
| | | *(500)* | *Favorable quantity variance* | |
| *Standard quantity of materals at standard cost per pound, 9,500 × $5.00* | *47,500* | | | |
| *Excess of actual over standard cost (unfavorable)* | | *$1,380* | | |
| *Journal entry:* | | | | |
| *Goods in Process (standard cost)* | | *47,500* | | |
| *Material Price Variance* | | *1,880* | | |
| *Material Quantity Variance* | | | | *500* |
| *Materials (actual cost)* | | | | *48,880* |
| *To record materials used in March.* | | | | |

The excess of actual cost of materials over standard cost was caused by two factors: The unfavorable ***material price variance*** of $1,880 resulted from the fact that each pound of material used cost 20 cents more than the standard price of $5; this portion of the total material variance is the responsibility of the person placing orders for materials. The favorable ***material quantity variance*** of $500 resulted from using 100 fewer pounds of materials than the standard allowed; this variance indicates that the shop supervisors are doing a good job because they are responsible for seeing that materials are not wasted or spoiled.

Note that in the example above the Goods in Process account is debited for the standard cost of materials used and that the Materials account is reduced by an amount equal to the actual cost of materials used. An alternative procedure would be to record materials purchased in the Materials account at standard cost, thus recording the price variance at the time of purchase. The unfavorable material price variance is recorded as a debit (a loss) and the favorable material quantity variance is recorded as a credit (a gain).

**Labor rate and labor usage variances** Labor cost standards are also a product of two factors: (1) the hours of labor that should be used in making a unit of product, and (2) the wage rate that should be paid for that labor. An analysis of the total labor variance will indicate whether the variance was due to the fact that more (or less) than standard time was required in production, or that more (or less) than standard wage rates were paid, or some combination of these two factors. The computation of the labor variances for the Standard Manufacturing Company and the journal entry required to record the direct labor cost for March are illustrated below.

***Labor cost exceeded standard because of a wage increase and because 100 hours of labor were wasted***

***Labor Rate and Usage Variances***

| | | | |
|---|---|---|---|
| *Actual labor hours used at actual hourly rate, 9,600 × $10.40* | *$99,840* | | |
| | | *$3,840* | *Unfavorable rate variance* |
| *Actual labor hours used at standard hourly rate, 9,600 × $10.00* | *96,000* | | |
| | | *1,000* | *Unfavorable usage variance* |
| *Standard labor hours at standard hourly rate, 9,500 × $10.00* | *95,000* | | |
| *Excess of actual over standard cost (unfavorable)* | | *$4,840* | |
| *Journal entry:* | | | |
| *Goods in Process (standard cost)* | | *95,000* | |
| *Labor Rate Variance* | | *3,840* | |
| *Labor Usage Variance* | | *1,000* | |
| *Accrued Factory Labor (actual cost)* | | | *99,840* |
| *To record direct labor incurred in March.* | | | |

The foregoing tabulation indicates that both the ***labor rate variance*** and the ***labor usage variance*** are unfavorable. The causes of these variances should be carefully investigated. If the rate increase of 40 cents per labor hour resulted from a new union contract, the $10 per hour standard cost figure should be revised; however, if the increase resulted from using higher-rated employees on the production line or from unnecessary overtime work, corrective action on the part of the shop foreman may be in order. The supervisor should also be asked to explain the reason why 100 hours of labor in excess of standard were used during the month.

**Factory overhead variances** The difference between actual factory overhead costs incurred and the standard factory overhead costs charged to the units produced during the period is called the ***overhead variance.*** Two factors can contribute to the overhead variance. First, ***expenditures*** for factory overhead may differ from the standard amounts. Secondly, fixed factory overhead per unit will vary inversely with the ***number of units produced.*** Since fixed factory overhead remains relatively constant in dollar amount, the fewer units produced during the period, the higher the amount of fixed overhead per unit.

In computing the standard cost of fixed overhead per unit ($2 in our example), it was necessary to assume some normal volume of production. ***Normal volume*** is the expected average utilization of plant capacity over many years. In the computation of the standard cost of product M (page 971), a normal volume of 10,000 units per month was used in determining the standard cost of fixed overhead. It follows that whenever actual production is less than 10,000 units per month, an unfavorable cost variance will result; when actual production exceeds 10,000 units per month, there will be a favorable cost variance. The portion of the overhead variance which results from a difference between actual and normal volume is called the ***volume variance.***

Production managers generally are not responsible for the volume variance, because production volume depends upon such factors as sales demand and inventory levels. On the other hand, they can exercise considerable control over the level of expenditures for variable overhead. Therefore, the portion of the overhead variance caused by variations in the dollar amount of overhead expenditures is called the ***controllable variance.***

The computation of the two elements of the overhead variance for the Standard Manufacturing Company and the journal entry to record factory overhead for March are shown on page 975.

The controllable variance is the difference between actual expenditures for factory overhead and the factory overhead ***budgeted*** for the actual volume of production. The reason for this $2,980 unfavorable variance is that expenditures for variable factory overhead amounted to $12,480 in March compared to standard variable overhead of $9,500 (9,500 units × $1) at the 9,500-unit production level. This unfavorable controllable variance should alert management to the need to exercise greater control over variable factory overhead.

The volume variance is the difference between the factory overhead ***budgeted*** for the actual volume of production (9,500 units) and the ***standard*** overhead cost ($3 per unit) for that volume. Actual fixed overhead for March was $20,000.

***Factory Overhead Variances***

*Actual factory overhead exceeded standard. Can you explain why this happened?*

| | | | | |
|---|---|---|---|---|
| *Actual factory overhead incurred (see page 971)* | | *$32,480* | | |
| *Factory overhead budgeted for level of production attained, 9,500 units:* | | | *$2,980* | *Unfavorable controllable variance* |
| *Fixed* | *$20,000* | | | |
| *Variable, 9,500 × $1.00* | *9,500* | *29,500* | | |
| | | | *1,000* | *Unfavorable volume variance* |
| *Standard factory overhead, 9,500 × $3.00* | | *28,500* | | |
| *Excess of actual over standard cost (unfavorable)* | | | *$3,980* | |

*Journal entry:*

| | | |
|---|---|---|
| *Goods in Process (standard cost)* | *28,500* | |
| *Controllable Factory Overhead Variance* | *2,980* | |
| *Volume Variance* | *1,000* | |
| *Factory Overhead (actual overhead incurred)* | | *32,480* |
| *To transfer factory overhead incurred in March to goods in process and variance accounts.* | | |

Since fixed overhead is charged to the Goods in Process account at the standard cost of $2 per unit (page 971), a production volume of 9,500 units results in only $19,000 of fixed overhead being charged to production. The remaining $1,000 of fixed overhead is therefore recorded as an unfavorable volume variance.

An unfavorable volume variance necessarily occurs when actual production is less than normal volume (10,000 units). Similarly, a favorable volume variance necessarily results when actual volume exceeds normal volume. As mentioned earlier, the scheduled volume of production depends on many factors, such as inventory levels and sales demand. Therefore, production managers generally are ***not*** responsible for volume variances. An unfavorable volume variance may be viewed as an ***idle capacity loss***—the cost of maintaining a plant with a capacity greater than current production levels.

**Transfer of cost of units completed to finished goods inventory** At the end of March, the entry to record the transfer of cost of goods completed from the Goods in Process account to the Finished Goods Inventory account is shown below:

*Entry to record goods completed*

| | | |
|---|---|---|
| *Finished Goods Inventory (at standard cost)* | *171,000* | |
| *Goods in Process (at standard cost)* | | *171,000* |
| *To record transfer of completed goods to finished goods inventory at standard cost (9,500 units × $18 = $171,000).* | | |

## Disposition of variance accounts

Under a standard cost system, monthly inventories of goods in process and finished goods may be priced at standard cost. Cost variances are allowed to accumulate from month to month; hopefully, only a small total variance will remain because unfavorable variances in one month are offset by favorable variances in other months. At the end of the fiscal year, however, a net unfavorable cost variance would be added to Cost of Goods Sold, as illustrated below:

***RAQUEL MFG. COMPANY***
***Partial Income Statement***
***Year 1***

*Unfavorable cost variance is added to cost of goods sold*

| | | |
|---|---|---|
| *Sales (net)* | | *$450,000* |
| *Cost of goods sold, at standard* | *$300,000* | |
| *Add: Net unfavorable cost variance* | *3,000* | |
| *Cost of goods sold and net unfavorable cost variance* | | *303,000* |
| *Gross profit on sales* | | *$147,000* |

A net favorable cost variance would be deducted from Cost of Goods Sold at the end of the fiscal year.

However, if the total cost variance (either favorable or unfavorable) for the year is large, it would be more appropriate to prorate the total cost variance between Goods in Process, Finished Goods, and Cost of Goods Sold in order to restate these accounts to ***actual cost.*** This would be particularly appropriate when the cost variance is caused by unrealistic standards rather than from outright waste or idle capacity losses. However, a large variance resulting from waste, inefficiency, or idle capacity generally is charged against income in the period in which it is incurred. To assign a portion of such a variance to the inventory accounts would amount to treating waste and inefficiency as an asset.

### Summary of advantages of standard cost system

Among the advantages accruing to management from the use of a standard cost system are the following:

1 The setting of standards requires a thorough analysis of operations; this tends to uncover inefficiencies and helps management maximize profits.
2 A standard cost system assists in the establishment of clearly defined organizational lines of authority and responsibility; this may result in less day-to-day confusion and higher employee morale.
3 Analysis of variances from standard costs helps management control costs in future periods.
4 Standard cost information is often useful in formulating pricing decisions concerning products and services.
5 Standard costs are useful in designing an effective system of responsibility accounting and budgetary controls throughout the organization.

## BUDGETING AS AN AID TO PLANNING AND CONTROL

A ***budget*** is a summary statement of plans expressed in quantitative terms; it guides individuals or an accounting entity in reaching financial or operational goals. If standard costs are used in the accounting system for a company engaged in manufacturing activities, such costs are also used in the preparation of budgets.

Most college students have at one time or another drawn up plans for the effective use of their time to secure a balance between academic and extracurricular activities. This is a ***time budget*** expressed in days or hours. Similarly, students with limited financial resources find it helpful to write down a plan for spending available money which will see them through a semester or year of schooling. This is an ***expenditure budget*** expressed in monetary terms.

The problem that plagues college students—planning the efficient use of limited resources—also faces managers of organizations of every type. Business executives must plan to attain profit objectives and meet their financial obligations as they become due. Administrators of nonprofit organizations and government agencies must plan to accomplish objectives of programs with the resources available to them. Budgets are as universal as the concept of planning; as a matter of fact, a budget is often viewed as a comprehensive ***financial plan***—a kind of compass designed to guide managers through the turbulent waters of business activity.

### The purpose of budgeting

Every budget is a ***forecast of future events.*** Business budgets show anticipated revenue, expenses, and the financial position of the company at some future point in time, assuming that the budget estimates are met. Systematic forecasting serves the control function in two major ways:

First, by showing what results will be if present plans are put into effect, a budget discloses areas that require attention or ***corrective action.*** For example, the college student whose budget shows potential expenditures of $6,000 for the year and who has only $4,000 in financial resources is forewarned. By knowing this in advance, the student may be able to find ways of augmenting resources or reducing expenses. Similarly, a business budget showing that profit objectives will not be met or that working capital will not be sufficient may enable management to act in advance to alter the revenue and cost picture or to obtain additional financing.

The second use of budgets for control purposes is in ***evaluating performance.*** Organizational plans are carried out by people. Control is thus exercised not over operations, revenue, and costs, but over the ***persons responsible*** for those operations and the related revenue and expenses. Budgets provide a yardstick against which a manager's actual performance may be compared.

It is this latter feature—performance evaluation—that accounts for the general unpopularity of budgets. Managers are human, and few of us are overjoyed about techniques which enable our boss to check our performance. Furthermore, some disagreement always arises as to the dollar amounts included in the budget. Departmental managers naturally want high levels of expenditures and low levels of output budgeted for their departments. This would increase the resources available to the departmental manager and make it easier to meet the budgeted level of performance. Top management, on the other hand, wants the budget to promote high levels of output and low levels of expenditure by each department manager.

The delicate task of human relations is an important part of effective budgeting. A budget is most effective when the people whose performance is being evaluated recognize the budgeted amounts as realistic standards for performance. This recognition is best achieved when managers at all levels of the business are invited to participate in the preparation of the budget.

### The budget period

As a general rule, the period covered by a budget should be long enough to show the effect of managerial policies but short enough so that estimates can be made with reasonable accuracy. This suggests that different types of budgets should be made for different time spans.

A ***master budget*** is an overall financial and operating plan for a forthcoming fiscal period. It is usually prepared on a quarterly or an annual basis. Long-range budgets, called ***capital budgets,*** which incorporate plans for major expenditures for plant and equipment or the addition of product lines, might be prepared to cover plans for as long as 5 to 10 years. ***Responsibility budgets,*** which are segments of the master budget relating to the aspect of the business that is the responsibility of a particular manager, are often prepared monthly. ***Cash budgets*** may be prepared on a day-to-day basis. Some companies follow a ***continuous budgeting*** plan whereby budgets are constantly reviewed and updated. The updating is accomplished, for example, by extending the annual budget one additional month at the end of each month. A review of the budget may also suggest that the budget be changed as a result of changing business and operating conditions.

### Preparing a master budget

The major steps in developing a master budget may be outlined as follows:

1 Establish basic goals and long-range plans for the company.
2 Prepare a sales forecast for the budget period. The sales forecast, of course, will be based on the forecast of general business and economic conditions anticipated during the budget period. This is a starting point because to a significant extent production or purchases, inventory levels, cash requirements, and operating expenses are governed by the expected volume of sales.
3 Estimate the cost of goods sold and operating expenses. These estimates will depend directly on the sales budget and a thorough knowledge of the relation between costs and volume of activity. Production costs used to estimate cost of goods sold are often based on standard costs for the products manufactured.
4 Determine the effect of budgeted operating results on asset, liability, and ownership equity accounts. The cash budget is the largest part of this step, since changes in many asset and liability accounts will depend on cash flow forecasts.
5 Summarize the estimated data in the form of a projected income statement for the budget period and a projected (sometimes called a ***pro forma***) balance sheet as of the end of the budget period.

### Master budget illustrated

Master budgets are the culmination of the entire planning process throughout an organization. The detailed mechanics of a master budget may become quite complex. To illustrate master budgeting in an introductory fashion, it is necessary to assume a very simple budgeting situation and to condense detail as much as possible.

We shall assume a manufacturing company that makes and sells a single product. The balance sheet for the Berg Company as of January 1 is shown below. Management has asked for a master budget that will provide an estimate of net income for the first and second quarters of the coming year and a projected balance sheet at the end of each of the first two quarters. The company has notes payable of $160,000 due in quarterly installments of $40,000, starting on March 31 of the current year. Sales of the company's product are seasonal; sales during the second quarter are expected to exceed first-quarter sales by 50%. However, the economy of stabilizing production and a very tight labor supply have led management to plan for stable production of 120,000 units during the first and second quarters. This will require an increase in inventory during the first quarter to meet second-quarter sales demand. Management is concerned about its ability to finance the inventory buildup during the first quarter and meet the quarterly payments on the bank loan.

**BERG COMPANY**
**Actual Balance Sheet**
**January 1, Current Year**
**Assets**

| | | |
|---|---|---|
| *Current assets:* | | |
| Cash | | $ 75,000 |
| Receivables | | 82,000 |
| Inventories: | | |
| Materials | $ 25,000 | |
| Finished goods (fifo method) | 52,000 | 77,000 |
| Prepayments | | 21,000 |
| Total current assets | | $255,000 |
| *Plant and equipment:* | | |
| Buildings and equipment | $970,000 | |
| Less: Accumulated depreciation | 420,000 | |
| Total plant and equipment | | 550,000 |
| Total assets | | $805,000 |

**Liabilities & Stockholders' Equity**

| | | |
|---|---|---|
| *Current liabilities:* | | |
| Notes payable, 16% ($40,000 payable quarterly) | | $160,000 |
| Other current payables | | 78,000 |
| Income taxes payable | | 50,000 |
| Total current liabilities | | $288,000 |
| *Stockholders' equity:* | | |
| Capital stock, no par, 100,000 shares outstanding | $350,000 | |
| Retained earnings | 167,000 | 517,000 |
| Total liabilities & stockholders' equity | | $805,000 |

**BERG COMPANY**
**Operating Budget Estimates**
**First and Second Quarters of Current Year**

| Schedule | | 1st Quarter | 2d Quarter |
|---|---|---|---|
| A1 | Sales budget: | | |
| | Selling price per unit | $ 3.00 | $ 3.00 |
| | Sales forecast in units | 100,000 | 150,000 |
| | Budgeted sales | $300,000 | $450,000 |
| A2 | Production budget (in units): | | |
| | Planned production | 120,000 | 120,000 |
| | Inventory at beginning of quarter | 30,000 | 50,000 |
| | Units available for sale | 150,000 | 170,000 |
| | Estimated sales (A1) | 100,000 | 150,000 |
| | Inventory at end of quarter | 50,000 | 20,000 |

| | | Per Quarter |
|---|---|---|
| A3 | Cost estimates: | |
| | Variable costs: | |
| | Per unit manufactured: | |
| | Materials | $ 0.50 |
| | Direct labor | 0.60 |
| | Variable factory overhead | 0.30 |
| | Per unit sold: | |
| | Selling and administrative expense | 0.30 |
| | Fixed costs (per quarter): | |
| | Factory overhead | $ 42,000 |
| | Selling and administrative expense | 70,000 |
| A4 | Budgeted cost of finished goods manufactured (120,000 units): | |
| | Materials used ($0.50 per unit) | $ 60,000 |
| | Direct labor ($0.60 per unit) | 72,000 |
| | Variable factory overhead ($0.30 per unit) | 36,000 |
| | Fixed factory overhead | 42,000 |
| | Total cost of finished goods manufactured | $210,000 |
| | Cost per unit ($210,000 ÷ 120,000 units) | $1.75 |

| | | 1st Quarter | 2d Quarter |
|---|---|---|---|
| A5 | Ending finished goods inventory: | | |
| | 50,000 units at $1.75 | $ 87,500 | |
| | 20,000 units at $1.75 | | $ 35,000 |
| A6 | Selling and administrative expense budget: | | |
| | Variable expenses ($0.30 × units sold) | $ 30,000 | $ 45,000 |
| | Fixed expenses | 70,000 | 70,000 |
| | Total selling and administrative expense | $100,000 | $115,000 |

**Operating budget estimates** The operating data estimates needed to prepare a projected income statement for each of the first two quarters are shown on page 980:

Estimates of unit sales and sales price per unit (Schedule A1) are based on marketing plans and pricing policy in the light of past experience. The production budget (Schedule A2) reflects not only the decision to stabilize production, but the decision to reduce the inventory of finished goods from its January 1 level of 30,000 units to 20,000 units at the end of June to minimize funds tied up in finished goods and thus help meet the second-quarter loan repayment. The cost estimates (Schedule A3) provide the basis for attaching dollars to production and for budgeting operating expenses. Details of operating expenses are omitted. ***Note that variable factory overhead is stated in terms of units manufactured, and variable selling and administrative expenses in terms of units sold.*** Schedules A4 and A6 show the determination of budgeted costs of goods manufactured and operating expenses. The ending finished goods inventory is computed in Schedule A5.

**Projected income statement** The projected income statement shown below is based on the operating budget estimates in Schedules A1 to A6. Schedule numbers are indicated parenthetically on the statement. Two items need further comment:

*Here is what quarterly income should be*

***BERG COMPANY***
***Projected Income Statement***
***First Two Quarters of Current Year***

| | 1st Quarter | 2d Quarter |
|---|---|---|
| Sales | $300,000 | $450,000 |
| Cost of goods sold: | | |
| Finished goods, beginning inventory | $ 52,000 | $ 87,500 |
| Cost of goods manufactured (A4) | 210,000 | 210,000 |
| Cost of goods available for sale | $262,000 | $297,500 |
| Less: Finished goods, ending inventory (A5) | 87,500 | 35,000 |
| Cost of goods sold | $174,500 | $262,500 |
| Gross profit on sales | $125,500 | $187,500 |
| Expenses: | | |
| Selling and administrative expense (A6) | $100,000 | $115,000 |
| Interest expense | 6,400 | 4,800 |
| Total expenses | $106,400 | $119,800 |
| Income before income taxes | $ 19,100 | $ 67,700 |
| Income taxes (50% of income before income taxes) | 9,550 | 33,850 |
| Net income | $ 9,550 | $ 33,850 |
| Earnings per share* | $0.10 | $0.34 |

* Rounded to nearest cent.

Interest on the $160,000 bank loan is estimated on the assumption that the $40,000 installment will be paid at the end of the first quarter. Interest at 16% per year, or 4% per quarter, is computed on the outstanding balance of $160,000 during the first quarter and on $120,000 during the second quarter.

Income tax expense is budgeted on the assumption that combined federal and state income taxes will amount to 50% of income before income taxes. We shall assume that last year's tax liability of $50,000 will be paid in two equal installments in the first two quarters of the current year.

**Financial budget estimates** The estimates and data necessary to prepare a cash budget and projected balance sheet for each quarter are shown below and on page 983. A forecast of the Berg Company's financial position at the end of each

***BERG COMPANY***
***Financial Budget Estimates***
***First and Second Quarters of Current Year***

| Schedule | | 1st Quarter | 2d Quarter |
|---|---|---|---|
| B1 | Budgeted materials purchased and inventory: | | |
| | Materials used (A4) | $ 60,000 | $ 60,000 |
| | Desired ending inventory | 40,000 | 40,000 |
| | Materials available for use | $100,000 | $100,000 |
| | Less: Inventory at beginning of quarter | 25,000 | 40,000 |
| | Budgeted material purchases | $ 75,000 | $ 60,000 |

B2 *Source of budgeted operating costs:*

| | Total | Current Payables | Expiration of Prepayments | Depreciation |
|---|---|---|---|---|
| First quarter: | | | | |
| Material purchases (B1) | $ 75,000 | $ 75,000 | | |
| Direct labor (A4) | 72,000 | 72,000 | | |
| Factory overhead (A4) | 78,000 | 64,000 | $ 4,400 | $ 9,600 |
| Selling and administrative expense (A6) | 100,000 | 94,600 | 3,000 | 2,400 |
| Total | $325,000 | $305,600 | $ 7,400 | $ 12,000 |
| Second quarter: | | | | |
| Material purchases (B1) | $ 60,000 | $ 60,000 | | |
| Direct labor (A4) | 72,000 | 72,000 | | |
| Factory overhead (A4) | 78,000 | 64,400 | $ 4,000 | $ 9,600 |
| Selling and administrative expense (A6) | 115,000 | 109,500 | 3,100 | 2,400 |
| Total | $325,000 | $305,900 | $ 7,100 | $ 12,000 |

| Schedule | | 1st Quarter | 2d Quarter |
|---|---|---|---|
| B3 | *Payments on current payables:* | | |
| | Balance at beginning of quarter | $ 78,000 | $101,500 |
| | Increase in payables during quarter (B2) | 305,600 | 305,900 |
| | Total payables during quarter | $383,600 | $407,400 |
| | Estimated balance at end of quarter (given) | 101,500 | 91,000 |
| | Payments on current payables during quarter | $282,100 | $316,400 |
| B4 | *Prepayments budget:* | | |
| | Balance at beginning of quarter | $ 21,000 | $ 15,600 |
| | Estimated cash expenditure during quarter | 2,000 | 5,000 |
| | Total prepayments | $ 23,000 | $ 20,600 |
| | Expiration of prepayments (B2) | 7,400 | 7,100 |
| | Prepayments at end of quarter | $ 15,600 | $ 13,500 |
| B5 | *Debt service budget:* | | |
| | Liability to bank at beginning of quarter | $160,000 | $120,000 |
| | Interest expense for the quarter | 6,400 | 4,800 |
| | Total principal plus accrued interest | $166,400 | $124,800 |
| | Cash payments (principal and interest) | 46,400 | 44,800 |
| | Liability to bank at end of quarter | $120,000 | $ 80,000 |
| B6 | *Budgeted income taxes:* | | |
| | Income tax liability at beginning of quarter | $ 50,000 | $ 34,550 |
| | Estimated income taxes for the quarter (income statement) | 9,550 | 33,850 |
| | Total accrued income tax liability | $ 59,550 | $ 68,400 |
| | Cash outlay (one-half of last year's tax liability) | 25,000 | 25,000 |
| | Income tax liability at end of quarter | $ 34,550 | $ 43,400 |
| B7 | *Estimated cash collections on receivables:* | | |
| | Balance of receivables at beginning of year | $ 82,000 | |
| | Collections on first-quarter sales of $300,000 ($\frac{2}{3}$ in first quarter and $\frac{1}{3}$ in second) | 200,000 | $100,000 |
| | Collections on second-quarter sales of $450,000 ($\frac{2}{3}$ in second quarter) | | 300,000 |
| | Total cash collections by quarter | $282,000 | $400,000 |
| B8 | *Budgeted accounts receivable:* | | |
| | Balance at the beginning of the quarter | $ 82,000 | $100,000 |
| | Sales on open account during quarter (A1) | 300,000 | 450,000 |
| | Total accounts receivable | $382,000 | $550,000 |
| | Less: Estimated collections on accounts receivable (B7) | 282,000 | 400,000 |
| | Estimated accounts receivable balance at end of quarter | $100,000 | $150,000 |

quarter requires that the account balances on the January 1 balance sheet be adjusted to reflect projected revenue and expenses and the resulting changes in assets and liabilities. Since cash is the most active financial account in a business, the key to preparing a financial budget is a forecast of cash flows, leading to a cash budget by quarters.

The starting point in this process is to convert the operating budget data into cash flows and changes in financial accounts. We begin by scheduling the source of budgeted operating costs (Schedule B2). It is first necessary to convert the materials used figure in the cost of goods manufactured statement into materials purchased, which requires an estimate of the materials inventories at the end of each quarter. The production supervisor feels that the January 1 materials inventory of $25,000 is too low. To meet the production schedule, the supervisor would like to have on hand at the end of the first quarter and throughout the second quarter about two-thirds of the materials usage for the second quarter. The desired ending inventory in Schedule B1 is therefore set at $40,000, which is two-thirds of the $60,000 projected materials usage in the second quarter.

The three primary sources of operating costs are current payables (accounts payable and accrued liabilities), the write-off of prepaid expenses, and depreciation of plant and equipment. The analysis of the source of manufacturing, selling, and administrative costs in Schedule B2 provides the key to estimates of the required outlays for current payables in Schedule B3. The estimate of the ending balance of current payables ($101,500 at the end of the first quarter and $91,000 at the end of the second quarter) has been made by the company treasurer on the basis of past experience and knowledge of suppliers' credit terms and the wage payment policies of the company. The treasurer has also estimated the amount of cash which will be used each quarter to prepay expenses (Schedule B4).

The quarterly payments of $40,000 on the bank loan, plus $6,400 interest in the first quarter and $4,800 interest in the second quarter, are summarized in Schedule B5.

The Berg Company sells to customers entirely on account. Therefore, the sole source of cash receipts for this company during the two quarters is the collection of accounts receivable. Losses from uncollectible accounts and cash discounts are ignored in this example. The credit manager estimates that two-thirds of the sales in any quarter will be collected in that quarter, and the remaining one-third of the quarter's sales will be collected in the following quarter. The forecast of cash collections (B7) and estimated balance of receivables (B8) are based on these estimates.

**Cash budget** The information derived from the financial budget schedules on pages 982 and 983 is the basis for the following quarterly cash budget. (The figures used in the preparation of the cash budget have been highlighted in black in the financial budget schedules.)

The cash budget is an important tool for forecasting whether the company will be able to meet its obligations as they mature. Often the cash budget may indicate a need for short-term borrowing or other measures to generate or conserve cash in order to keep the company solvent. Remember that one of the

**BERG COMPANY**
**Cash Budget**
**First Two Quarters of Current Year**

*Projected cash flow and ending cash balance*

| | 1st Quarter | 2d Quarter |
|---|---|---|
| Cash balance at beginning of quarter | $ 75,000 | $ 1,500 |
| Receipts: | | |
| Collections on receivables (B7) | 282,000 | 400,000 |
| Total cash available | $357,000 | $401,500 |
| Disbursements: | | |
| Payment of current payables (B3) | $282,100 | $316,400 |
| Prepayments (B4) | 2,000 | 5,000 |
| Payments on notes, including interest (B5) | 46,400 | 44,800 |
| Income tax payments (B6) | 25,000 | 25,000 |
| Total disbursements | $355,500 | $391,200 |
| Cash balance at end of the quarter | $ 1,500 | $ 10,300 |

principal reasons for preparing budgets is to give advance warning of potential problems such as cash shortages.

**Projected balance sheet** We now have the necessary information to forecast the financial position of the Berg Company at the end of each of the next two quarters. The projected balance sheets are illustrated below and on page 986. Budget schedules from which various figures on the balance sheet have been derived are indicated parenthetically on the statement.

**BERG COMPANY**
**Projected Balance Sheet**
**As of the End of First Two Quarters of Current Year**

*Projected quarterly balance sheet*

| | 1st Quarter | 2d Quarter |
|---|---|---|
| **Assets** | | |
| Current assets: | | |
| Cash (per cash budget) | $ 1,500 | $ 10,300 |
| Receivables (B7) | 100,000 | 150,000 |
| Inventories: | | |
| Materials (B1) | 40,000 | 40,000 |
| Finished goods (A5) | 87,500 | 35,000 |
| Prepayments (B4) | 15,600 | 13,500 |
| Total current assets | $244,600 | $248,800 |
| Plant and equipment: | | |
| Buildings and equipment | $970,000 | $970,000 |
| Less: Accumulated depreciation (B2) | (432,000) | (444,000) |
| Total plant and equipment | $538,000 | $526,000 |
| Total assets | $782,600 | $774,800 |

| | | |
|---|---|---|
| ***Liabilities & Stockholders' Equity*** | | |
| *Current liabilities:* | | |
| *Notes payable, 16% ($40,000 due quarterly)* | *$120,000* | *$ 80,000* |
| *Other current payables (B3)* | *101,500* | *91,000* |
| *Income taxes payable (B6)* | *34,550* | *43,400* |
| *Total current liabilities* | *$256,050* | *$214,400* |
| *Stockholders' equity:* | | |
| *Capital stock, no par, 100,000 shares issued and outstanding* | *$350,000* | *$350,000* |
| *Retained earnings, beginning of quarter* | *167,000* | *176,550* |
| *Net income for the quarter* | *9,550* | *33,850* |
| *Total stockholders' equity* | *$526,550* | *$560,400* |
| *Total liabilities & stockholders' equity* | *$782,600* | *$774,800* |

## Using budgets effectively

The process of systematic planning would probably be of some value even if a budget, once prepared, were promptly filed away and forgotten. In preparing a budget managers are forced to look into all aspects of a company's activity, and this in itself will often enable them to do a better job of managing. The primary benefits of budgeting, however, stem from uses made of budgeted information after it is prepared. We have noted three ways in which budgets serve management: (1) as a plan or blueprint for accomplishing a set of objectives, (2) as a warning system for anticipating conditions that require advance remedial action, and (3) as a means of evaluating the performance of company personnel.

Let us consider briefly how the master budget we have just demonstrated might serve these three functions.

**A plan for accomplishing objectives** A number of operating objectives were incorporated in the budget estimates of the Berg Company. A primary objective was to achieve management's profit goals. Secondary objectives were to stabilize production throughout the first two quarters and to reduce the inventory of finished goods by the end of the second quarter. The operating budget is a set of plans for doing these things.

The projected income statement (page 981) shows an improved net income during the second quarter, reflecting the favorable effect of increased sales volume in relation to the existence of certain fixed costs. The responsibility for securing the volume of sales revenue budgeted in each quarter rests with the sales department. The problem of scheduling the production of 120,000 units each quarter and of seeing that production costs do not exceed budget estimates is the responsibility of the manufacturing department. General management is responsible for maintaining control over administrative expenses.

In order to relate budgeted information to these various responsibilities, it is desirable to rearrange the overall master budget figures in terms of responsibility centers. In broad outline, such a rearrangement might be accomplished by preparing quarterly budget estimates for major centers of responsibility, such as sales by territories, factory overhead costs, cash receipts and disbursements, personnel requirements, research expenditures, etc.

Dividing the total budget plan into responsibility segments ensures that each executive knows the goals and his or her part in achieving them. The use of responsibility budgets requires a carefully designed system of ***responsibility accounting***[1] in order that the results of a given responsibility center can be compared with the budget plan.

**An advance warning of potential trouble** One of the major concerns of the management of the Berg Company was the ability of the company to meet the quarterly payments on its loan obligation. The cash budget for the first two quarters of the year indicates that the cash position of the company at the end of each quarter will be precariously low. A cash balance of $1,500 is forecast at the end of the first quarter, and a balance of $10,300 at the end of the second quarter (see page 985). This indicates that if all goes well the payments ***can*** be met, but there is little margin for error in the estimates.

Management, when confronted with such a forecast, should take steps in advance to prevent the cash balance from dropping as low as the budgeted amounts. It may be possible to obtain longer credit terms from suppliers and thus reduce payments on accounts payable during the first two quarters. The company may decide to let inventories fall below scheduled levels in order to postpone cash outlays. An extension of the terms of the note payable might be sought, or the possibility of long-term financing might be considered. If any or all of these steps were taken, it would be necessary to revise the budget estimates accordingly. The fact that management is ***forewarned*** of this condition several months before it happens, however, illustrates one of the prime values of budgeting.

**A yardstick for appraising performance** The effective use of budgets in gauging performance is not an easy task. It is not feasible to discuss all facets of this problem here, but let us briefly consider two important points.

The first point is the importance of basing performance evaluations only upon those costs and revenues which are under the control of the person being evaluated. For example, Mike Jones, the foreman of a manufacturing department, can influence labor costs in his department through his control over idle time, overtime hours, and the number of employees to be hired. He may also exert some control over such overhead costs as equipment maintenance, supplies used, and power expenses. On the other hand, Jones probably has no influence on either the salary of the plant superintendent or the amount of building depreciation, some portion of which might be charged to his department.

The view that a manager should not be charged with costs over which he or she has no control is widely used in modern budgeting practice, with the result

[1]See Chap. 23 for a discussion of responsibility accounting, which serves as a basis for the preparation of responsibility budgets.

that responsibility budgets commonly include only ***controllable costs.*** An alternative is to segregate noncontrollable costs in a separate section of a manager's budget and to use only the figures that are in the "controllable" section of the budget in appraising the manager's performance.

The second point is that even controllable costs may be affected by factors over which a manager has little influence. An example is the effect of significant differences between the volume of production originally budgeted and the volume actually attained. The fact that actual volume varied from budgeted volume might cause many departmental costs to differ significantly from the budgeted amounts. Some method must be devised for evaluating the department manager's performance ***given the level of production which was actually attained.*** This can be done through the use of ***flexible budgets.***

## Flexible budget—a more effective control tool

Suppose, for example, that Harold Stone, production manager of Berg Company, is presented with the following schedule of budgeted and actual results at the end of the first quarter's operations:

*Is this a good or a bad performance?*

**BERG COMPANY**
**Production Costs—Budgeted and Actual for First Quarter**
**(Master Budget)**

| | Budgeted | Actual | Over or (under) Budget |
|---|---|---|---|
| Production costs: | | | |
| Materials used | $ 60,000 | $ 63,800 | $ 3,800 |
| Direct labor | 72,000 | 76,500 | 4,500 |
| Variable factory overhead | 36,000 | 38,000 | 2,000 |
| Fixed factory overhead | 42,000 | 42,400 | 400 |
| Total production costs | $210,000 | $220,700 | $10,700 |

At first glance it appears that the production manager's cost control performance is bad, since his production costs are $10,700 in excess of budget. However, one piece of information has been deliberately omitted from the above schedule. ***Instead of the 120,000 units of production planned for the first quarter, 130,000 units were actually manufactured.***

Under these circumstances, the above comparison of budgeted and actual costs becomes meaningless as a measure of the production manager's performance. There is no point in comparing actual costs for one level of output with budgeted cost performance at a different level of output.

One solution is to base performance evaluation on a ***flexible budget.*** A flexible budget consists of advance estimates of costs and expenses for ***each of several possible levels of activity,*** such as 100,000 units, 120,000 units, and 130,000 units. As the year progresses, the actual level of production will become known and the ***estimated costs for that level*** will be compared with the ***actual costs*** to determine how well management has performed. On this basis, a comparison of the production manager's budgeted and actual performance might be made as follows:

***BERG COMPANY***
***Production Costs—Budgeted and Actual for First Quarter***
***(Flexible Budget)***

*Flexible budget shows a different picture*

| | Originally Budgeted | Flexible Budget | Actual Costs | Actual Costs over or (under) Flexible Budget |
|---|---|---|---|---|
| Units of production | 120,000 | 130,000 | 130,000 | |
| Production costs: | | | | |
| Materials used | $ 60,000 | $ 65,000 | $ 63,800 | $(1,200) |
| Direct labor | 72,000 | 78,000 | 76,500 | (1,500) |
| Variable factory overhead | 36,000 | 39,000 | 38,000 | (1,000) |
| Fixed factory overhead | 42,000 | 42,000 | 42,400 | 400 |
| Total production costs | $210,000 | $224,000 | $220,700 | $(3,300) |

This comparison gives quite a different picture of the production manager's cost performance. On the basis of actual volume, Stone has done better than budgeted costs in all categories except fixed factory overhead, most of which is probably outside his control.

Many well-managed companies prepare a flexible budget for different levels of production and sales. A flexible budget is in reality a series of budgets for ***different levels of activity.*** The preparation of a flexible budget rests on the ability to predict the probable cost behavior at different activity levels. The installation of a standard cost system is generally quite useful for this purpose.

## KEY TERMS INTRODUCED OR EMPHASIZED IN CHAPTER 26

**Budget** A plan or forecast for a future period expressed in quantitative terms. Intends to establish objectives and aid in achieving these objectives with the resources available.

**Capital budget** Plans for major expenditures for plant and equipment or product lines for perhaps 5 to 10 years in the future.

**Cash budget** A forecast of expected cash receipts, payments, and periodic balances.

**Controllable factory overhead variance** The difference between actual factory overhead and the budgeted factory overhead for the level of output achieved.

**Favorable cost variance** The amount by which actual costs are ***less*** than standard costs. Recorded by a credit entry to the variance account.

**Fixed costs** Those costs which do not change with changes in volume of output.

**Flexible budget** A series of budgets for different possible levels of production. Facilitates evaluation of performance.

**Idle capacity loss** An unfavorable volume variance—the portion of fixed overhead costs which are not assigned to units of production as a result of actual production volume being less than normal volume. Fixed overhead costs not charged to production may be viewed as the cost of maintaining idle plant capacity.

**Labor rate variance** The difference between the standard labor rate and actual rate multiplied by the actual hours.

**Labor usage variance** The difference between standard labor hours and actual labor hours used multiplied by the standard hourly rate.

**Master budget** An overall financial and operating plan, including a sales forecast, estimated cost of goods sold, operating expenses, and projected financial statements.

**Material price variance** The difference between the standard price and actual price of material used multiplied by the standard quantity.

**Material quantity variance** The difference between standard quantity and actual quantity of material used multiplied by the standard price of the material.

**Normal volume** The expected average volume of production from existing plant facilities over a long period of time. This is the assumed volume of production used in determining standard fixed costs per unit.

**Standard costs** Predetermined costs that should be incurred to produce a unit of product or perform a particular operation under ideal conditions.

**Variable costs** Costs that vary proportionately with volume of output.

**Volume variance** The difference between the factory overhead budgeted for the actual volume of production and the standard overhead cost for that volume. Volume variances necessarily result whenever the actual volume of production differs from the normal volume which was used to compute the standard cost of fixed overhead per unit. For this reason, volume variances generally are beyond the control of production managers. Also called ***idle capacity loss.***

## REVIEW QUESTIONS

**1** Define ***standard costs*** and briefly indicate how they may be used by management in planning and control.

**2** Briefly list some of the advantages of using a standard cost system.

**3** What is wrong with the following statement: "There are three basic kinds of cost systems: job order, process, and standard."

**4** Once standard costs are established, what conditions would require that standards be revised?

**5** List the variances from standard cost that are generally computed for materials, direct labor, and factory overhead.

**6** What is meant by a favorable labor usage variance? How is the labor usage variance computed?

7 Define each of the following terms: ***normal volume, fixed costs,*** and ***idle capacity loss.***

8 Explain the cause of an unfavorable and of a favorable overhead volume variance.

9 Why is an unfavorable overhead volume variance sometimes called an idle capacity loss?

10 Would a production foreman be equally responsible for an unfavorable materials price variance and an unfavorable materials quantity variance? Explain.

11 "The cost of waste and inefficiency cannot be regarded as an asset." Explain how this statement supports the use of standard costs in the valuation of goods in process and finished goods inventories.

12 What would be the purposes of preparing a budget for a business of any size?

13 An article in *Business Week* stated that approximately one-third of the total federal budget is considered "controllable." What is meant by a budgeted expenditure being controllable? Give two examples of government expenditures that may be considered "noncontrollable."

14 Describe the major steps in the preparation of a master budget.

15 Describe three ways in which budgets serve management.

16 What is a ***flexible budget?*** Explain how a flexible budget increases the usefulness of budgeting as a means of evaluating performance.

## EXERCISES

*Ex. 26-1* The standard for materials in manufacturing item Z is one pound at $4.00. During the current month, 5,000 units of item Z were produced and 5,100 pounds of materials costing $21,420 were used. Analyze the $1,420 variance between actual cost and standard cost in such a way as to show how much of it was attributable to price change and how much to excess quantity of materials used. Indicate whether the variances are favorable or unfavorable.

*Ex. 26-2* From the following information for the Fitch Corporation, compute the controllable factory overhead variance and the volume variance and indicate whether the variances are favorable or unfavorable.

| | | |
|---|---|---|
| *Standard factory overhead based on normal monthly volume:* | | |
| *Fixed ($80,000 ÷ 10,000 units)* | *$ 8.00* | |
| *Variable ($120,000 ÷ 10,000 units)* | *12.00* | *$20.00* |
| *Units actually produced in current month* | | *9,000 units* |
| *Actual factory overhead costs incurred (including $80,000 fixed)* | | *$184,400* |

*Ex. 26-3* The standard costs and variances for direct materials, direct labor, and factory overhead for the month of April are given below:

| | Standard Cost | Variances: Unfavorable | Variances: Favorable |
|---|---|---|---|
| Direct materials | $ 60,000 | | |
| Price variance | | | $3,000 |
| Quantity variance | | | 1,800 |
| Direct labor | 120,000 | | |
| Rate variance | | $1,200 | |
| Usage variance | | | 5,400 |
| Factory overhead | 180,000 | | |
| Controllable variance | | 2,400 | |
| Volume variance | | 3,600 | |

Determine the actual costs incurred during the month of April for direct materials, direct labor, and factory overhead.

*Ex. 26-4* The flexible budget at the 70 and 80% levels of activity is shown below:

| | At 70% | At 80% | At 90% |
|---|---|---|---|
| Sales | $700,000 | $800,000 | $ |
| Cost of goods sold | 420,000 | 480,000 | |
| Gross profit on sales | $280,000 | $320,000 | $ |
| Operating expenses ($45,000 fixed) | 185,000 | 205,000 | |
| Operating income | $ 95,000 | $115,000 | $ |
| Income taxes, 30% | 28,500 | 34,500 | |
| Net income | $ 66,500 | $ 80,500 | $ |

Complete the flexible budget at the 90% level of activity. Assume that the cost of goods sold and variable operating expenses vary directly with sales and that income taxes remain at 30% of operating income.

*Ex. 26-5* Sales on account for the first quarter are budgeted as follows:

| | |
|---|---|
| January | $200,000 |
| February | 250,000 |
| March | 300,000 |

All sales are made on terms of 2/10, n/30; collections on accounts receivable are typically made as follows:

| | |
|---|---|
| In month of sale: | |
| Within discount period | 50% |
| After discount period | 20% |
| In month following sale: | |
| Within discount period | 15% |
| After discount period | 10% |
| Returns, allowances, and uncollectibles | 5% |
| Total | 100% |

Compute the estimated cash collections on accounts receivable for the month of March.

*Ex. 26-6* The cost accountant for the Modern Molding Co. prepared the following monthly report relating to the Grinding Department:

| | Budget (10,000 hours) | Actual (11,000 hours) | Variances: Unfavorable | Variances: Favorable |
|---|---|---|---|---|
| Direct materials | $30,000 | $32,000 | $2,000 | |
| Direct labor | 20,000 | 21,500 | 1,500 | |
| Variable factory overhead | 25,000 | 27,850 | 2,850 | |
| Fixed factory overhead | 15,000 | 14,950 | | $50 |

Prepare a revised report of production costs in which the variances are computed by comparing the actual costs incurred with estimated costs ***using a flexible budget*** for 11,000 hours. Assume that direct materials, direct labor, and variable factory overhead would all be 10% higher when 11,000 hours are worked than when only 10,000 hours are worked.

## PROBLEMS

### Group A

*26A-1* Wall Systems Corporation uses standard costs in its cost accounting system. The standard cost for a certain product at a normal volume of 1,000 units per month is as follows:

| | | |
|---|---|---|
| Lumber, 100 feet at $300 per 1,000 feet | | $30.00 |
| Direct labor, 5 hours at $8.00 per hour | | 40.00 |
| Factory overhead (applied at $22.00 per unit produced): | | |
| Fixed ($10,000 ÷ 1,000 units) | $10.00 | |
| Variable | 12.00 | 22.00 |
| Total standard unit cost | | $92.00 |

The actual unit cost for a given month in which 800 units were produced is shown below.

| | |
|---|---|
| Lumber, 110 feet at $280 per 1,000 feet | $30.80 |
| Direct labor, $5\frac{1}{2}$ hours at $7.80 per hour | 42.90 |
| Factory overhead, $18,000 ÷ 800 units | 22.50 |
| Total actual unit cost | $96.20 |

At the end of the month, the company's accountant submitted the following cost report to management relating to the 800 units produced:

| | Total | Per Unit |
|---|---|---|
| Excess lumber used in production | $ 640 | $0.80 |
| Excess labor cost incurred | 2,320 | 2.90 |
| Actual factory overhead in excess of standard: | | |
| $18,000 − (800 × $22.00) | 400 | 0.50 |
| Actual cost in excess of standard | $3,360 | $4.20 |

**Instructions** Prepare a schedule which would give management a better understanding of the reasons for the $3,360 excess cost incurred. This schedule should include the following:
**a** Material price variance and material quantity variance
**b** Labor rate variance and labor usage variance
**c** Controllable factory overhead variance and volume variance
Indicate whether each variance is favorable or unfavorable.

*26A-2* Mossberg Company produces a machine part which is processed successively by Department X and Department Y. Factory overhead is applied to units of production at the following standard costs:

| | Factory Overhead per Unit | | |
|---|---|---|---|
| | Fixed | Variable | Total |
| Department X | $4.00 | $6.50 | $10.50 |
| Department Y | 2.00 | 5.00 | 7.00 |

These standard factory overhead costs per unit are based on a normal volume of production of 1,000 units per month. In January, variable factory overhead is expected to be 5% above standard because of scheduled repairs to equipment. The company plans to produce 800 units during January.

**Instructions** Prepare a budget for factory overhead costs in January. Use column headings as follows: Total, Department X, and Department Y.

*26A-3* Yard Care Products manufactures an insecticide and uses standard costs in its job cost system. The insecticide is processed in 400-pound batches. You are engaged to explain any differences between standard and actual costs incurred in producing 100 batches during the first month of operation. The following additional information is available:
(1) The standard costs for a 400-pound batch are as follows:

| | Quantity | Price | Total Cost |
|---|---|---|---|
| Materials: | | | |
| Various chemicals | 400 pounds | $0.30 | $120 |
| Direct labor: | | | |
| Preparation, blending, etc. | 20 hours | 5.00 | 100 |
| Factory overhead: | | | |
| Variable costs | 20 hours | 3.00 | 60 |
| Fixed costs | 20 hours | 1.00 | 20 |
| Total standard cost per 400-pound batch | | | $300 |

(2) During the first month, 41,000 pounds of chemicals were purchased for $11,480, an average cost of 28 cents per pound. All the chemical was used during the month, resulting in a price variance of $820 and a quantity variance of $300.
(3) Average wage paid for 1,900 hours of direct labor was $4.80 per hour and amounted to $9,120. The labor rate variance was $380 and the labor usage variance was $500.
(4) The standards were established for a normal production volume of 125 batches

per month. At this level of production, variable factory overhead was budgeted at \$7,500 per month and fixed factory overhead was budgeted at \$2,500 per month. During the first month, actual factory overhead amounted to \$8,800, including \$2,500 fixed costs. The controllable factory overhead variance was \$300 and the volume variance was \$500.

**Instructions**

**a** Prepare schedules showing how the variances from standard for materials, labor, and factory overhead were computed. Indicate whether the variances are favorable or unfavorable.

**b** Prepare journal entries to record the variances and costs incurred (at standard) in the Goods in Process account for (1) materials, (2) labor, and (3) factory overhead.

***26A-4*** Helen Barnes, owner of the Barnes Company, is negotiating with her bank for a \$100,000, 12%, 90-day loan effective July 1 of the current year. If the bank grants the loan, the proceeds will be \$97,000, which Barnes intends to use on July 1 as follows: pay accounts payable, \$75,000; purchase equipment, \$8,000; add to bank balance, \$14,000.

The current working capital position of the Barnes Company, according to financial statements as of June 30, is as follows:

| | |
|---|---|
| *Cash in bank* | *\$ 10,000* |
| *Receivables (net of allowance for doubtful accounts)* | *80,000* |
| *Merchandise inventory* | *45,000* |
| *Total current assets* | *\$135,000* |
| *Accounts payable (including accrued operating expenses)* | *75,000* |
| *Working capital* | *\$ 60,000* |

The bank loan officer asks Barnes to prepare a forecast of her cash receipts and disbursements for the next three months, to demonstrate that the loan can be repaid at the end of September.

Barnes has made the following estimates, which are to be used in preparing a three-month cash budget: Sales (all on open account) for July, \$150,000; August, \$180,000; September, \$135,000; and October, \$100,000. Past experience indicates that 80% of the receivables generated in any month will be collected in the month following the sale, 19% in the second month following the sale, and 1% will prove uncollectible. Barnes expects to collect \$60,000 of the June 30 receivables in July, and the remaining \$20,000 in August.

Cost of goods sold has averaged consistently about 65% of sales. Operating expenses are budgeted at \$18,000 per month plus 8% of sales. With the exception of \$2,200 per month depreciation expense, all operating expenses and purchases are on open account and are paid in the month following their incurrence.

Merchandise inventory at the end of each month should be sufficient to cover the following month's sales.

**Instructions**

**a** Prepare a monthly cash budget showing estimated cash receipts and disbursements for July, August, and September, and the cash balance at the end of each month. Supporting schedules should be prepared for estimated collections on receivables, estimated merchandise purchases, and estimated payments for operating expenses and of accounts payable for merchandise purchases.

**b** On the basis of this cash forecast, write a brief report to Barnes explaining whether she will be able to pay the \$100,000 loan at the bank at the end of September.

*26A-5* Rimfire Rifle Corporation uses departmental budgets and performance reports in planning and controlling its manufacturing operations. The following performance report for the production department for Year 1 was presented to the president of the company:

| | Budgeted Costs for 10,000 Units | | Actual Costs Incurred | Over or (Under) Budget |
|---|---|---|---|---|
| | Per Unit | Total | | |
| *Variable manufacturing costs:* | | | | |
| Direct materials | $15.00 | $150,000 | $171,500 | $21,500 |
| Direct labor | 24.00 | 240,000 | 264,000 | 24,000 |
| Indirect labor | 7.50 | 75,000 | 97,500 | 22,500 |
| Indirect materials, supplies, etc. | 4.50 | 45,000 | 49,500 | 4,500 |
| Total variable manufacturing costs | $51.00 | $510,000 | $582,500 | $72,500 |
| *Fixed manufacturing costs:* | | | | |
| Lease rental | $ 4.50 | $ 45,000 | $ 45,000 | None |
| Salaries of foremen | 12.00 | 120,000 | 125,000 | $ 5,000 |
| Depreciation and other | 7.50 | 75,000 | 77,500 | 2,500 |
| Total fixed manufacturing costs | $24.00 | $240,000 | $247,500 | $ 7,500 |
| Total manufacturing costs | $75.00 | $750,000 | $830,000 | $80,000 |

Although a production volume of 10,000 guns was originally budgeted for Year 1, the actual volume of production achieved for the year was 12,000 guns. The company does not use standard costs; materials and direct labor are charged to production at actual cost. Factory overhead is applied to production at the predetermined rate of 150% of the actual direct labor cost.

After a quick glance at the performance report showing an unfavorable manufacturing cost variance of $80,000, the president said to the accountant: "Fix this thing so it makes sense. It looks as though our production people really blew the budget. Remember that we exceeded our budgeted production schedule by a significant margin. I want this performance report to show a better picture of our ability to control costs."

**Instructions**

a Prepare a revised performance report on a flexible budget basis for Year 1. Use the same format as the production report above, but revise the budgeted cost figures to reflect the actual production level of 12,000 guns.

b In a few sentences compare the original performance report with the revised report.

c What is the amount of over- or underapplied factory overhead for Year 1? (Note that a standard cost system is not used.)

## Group B

*26B-1* The accountants for Optical Products have developed the following information regarding the standard cost and the actual cost of a product manufactured in June:

| | Standard Cost | Actual Cost |
|---|---|---|
| *Materials:* | | |
| *Standard: 10 ounces at $0.15 per ounce* | *$1.50* | |
| *Actual: 11 ounces at $0.16 per ounce* | | *$1.76* |
| *Direct labor:* | | |
| *Standard: .50 hour at $10.00 per hour* | *5.00* | |
| *Actual: .45 hour at $10.40 per hour* | | *4.68* |
| *Factory overhead:* | | |
| *Standard: $5,000 fixed cost and $5,000 variable cost for 10,000 units normal monthly volume* | *1.00* | |
| *Actual: $5,000 fixed cost and $4,600 variable cost for 8,000 units actually produced in June* | | *1.20* |
| *Total unit cost* | *$7.50* | *$7.64* |

The normal volume is 10,000 units per month, but only 8,000 units were manufactured in June.

**Instructions** Compute the following cost variances for the month of June and indicate whether each variance is favorable or unfavorable:
**a** Material price variance and material quantity variance
**b** Labor rate variance and labor usage variance
**c** Controllable factory overhead variance and volume variance

*26B-2* Coast Company manufactures a product which is first refined and then packed for shipment to customers. The standard direct labor cost per 100 pounds in each process follows:

| *Process* | *Direct Labor Hours per 100 Pounds* | *Standard Direct Labor Cost per Hour* |
|---|---|---|
| *Refining* | *2* | *$6.00* |
| *Packing* | *1* | *4.80* |

The budget for October calls for the production of 100,000 pounds of product. The expected labor cost in the refinery is expected to be 8% above standard for the month of October as a result of higher wage rates and inefficiencies in the scheduling of work. The expected cost of labor in the packing room is expected to be 5% below standard because of a new arrangement of equipment.

**Instruction** Prepare a budget for direct labor costs for October. Use column headings as follows: Total, Refining, and Packing.

*26B-3* Safari Outfitters uses standard costs in a process cost system. At the end of the current month, the following information is prepared by the company's cost accountant:

| | Materials | Direct Labor | Factory Overhead |
|---|---|---|---|
| Actual costs incurred | $96,000 | $82,500 | $123,240 |
| Standard costs | 90,000 | 84,000 | 115,500 |
| Material price variance (favorable) | 2,400 | | |
| Material quantity variance (unfavorable) | 8,400 | | |
| Labor rate variance (favorable) | | 3,000 | |
| Labor usage variance (unfavorable) | | 1,500 | |
| Controllable factory overhead variance (unfavorable) | | | 3,240 |
| Volume variance (unfavorable) | | | 4,500 |

The total standard cost per unit of finished product is $30. During the current month, 9,000 units were completed and transferred to the finished goods inventory and 8,800 units were sold. The inventory of goods in process at the end of the month consists of 1,000 units which are 65% completed. There was no inventory in process at the beginning of the month.

**Instructions**

**a** Prepare journal entries to record all variances and the costs incurred (at standard) in the Goods in Process account. Prepare separate compound entries for (1) materials, (2) direct labor, and (3) factory overhead.

**b** Prepare journal entries to record (1) the transfer of units finished to the Finished Goods Inventory account and (2) the cost of goods sold (at standard) for the month.

**c** Assuming that the company operated at 90% of its normal capacity during the current month, what is the amount of the fixed factory overhead per month? (Hint: The unfavorable overhead volume variance represents the fixed factory overhead charged to idle capacity rather than to units of product.)

*26B-4* Rogers Company wants a projection of cash receipts and disbursements for the month of November. On November 28, a note will be payable in the amount of $40,400, including interest. The cash balance on November 1 is $18,100. Accounts payable to merchandise creditors at the end of October were $77,500.

The company's experience indicates that 60% of sales will be collected during the month of sale, 30% in the month following the sale, and 8% in the second month following the sale; 2% will be uncollectible. The company sells various products at an average price of $8 per unit. Selected sales figures are shown below:

| | Units |
|---|---|
| September—actual | 20,000 |
| October—actual | 30,000 |
| November—estimated | 40,000 |
| December—estimated | 25,000 |
| Total estimated for Year 1 | 400,000 |

Because purchases are payable within 15 days, approximately 50% of the purchases in a given month are paid in the following month. The average cost of units purchased is $5 per unit. Inventories at the end of each month are maintained at a level of 1,000 units plus 10% of the number of units that will be sold in the following month. The inventory on October 1 amounted to 4,000 units.

Budgeted operating expenses for November are $85,000. Of this amount, $30,000 is considered fixed (including depreciation of $12,000). All operating expenses, other than depreciation, are paid in the month in which they are incurred.

The company expects to sell fully depreciated equipment in November for $9,500 cash.

**Instructions** Prepare a cash budget for the month of November, supported by schedules of cash collections on accounts receivable and cash disbursements for purchases of merchandise.

*26B-5* After several years of unprofitable operations, Vogue West, a retail department store, retained a CPA firm to design better cost controls. The following flexible budget was prepared for the current year:

| | Yearly Fixed Expenses | Variable Expenses per Sales Dollar |
|---|---|---|
| *Cost of merchandise sold* | | *$0.700* |
| *Selling and promotion expense* | *$ 70,000* | *0.082* |
| *Building occupancy expense* | *62,000* | *0.022* |
| *Buying expense* | *50,000* | *0.040* |
| *Delivery expense* | *37,000* | *0.010* |
| *Credit and collection expense* | *24,000* | *0.002* |
| *Administrative expense* | *177,000* | *0.003* |
| *Totals* | *$420,000* | *$0.859* |

Management expected to attain a sales level of $4 million during the current year. At the end of the year the actual results achieved by the company were as follows:

| | |
|---|---|
| *Net sales* | *$3,500,000* |
| *Cost of goods sold* | *2,380,000* |
| *Selling and promotion expense* | *340,000* |
| *Building occupancy expense* | *140,000* |
| *Buying expense* | *198,000* |
| *Delivery expense* | *61,000* |
| *Credit and collection expense* | *30,000* |
| *Administrative expense* | *188,000* |

**Instructions**

**a** Prepare a statement comparing the actual and budgeted revenues and expenses for the current year, showing variations between actual and budgeted amounts. Use a flexible budget procedure to determine budgeted revenues and expenses.

**b** Write a brief statement evaluating the company's performance in relation to planning as reflected in the flexible budget.

## BUSINESS DECISION PROBLEM 26

Armstrong Chemical began operations in January of Year 1. The company manufactures an acrylic floor wax called Tough-Coat. The following standard cost estimates were developed several months before the company began its actual operations:

| | Estimated Standard Cost per Unit |
|---|---|
| *Material X-1 (one ounce)* | *$1.00* |
| *Material X-2 (one pound)* | *.50* |
| *Direct labor* | *.80* |
| *Factory overhead* | *.40* |
| *Total estimated cost per unit* | *$2.70* |

The estimated factory overhead cost per unit was determined by dividing budgeted factory overhead for Year 1 by the 1,000,000 units scheduled to be produced in Year 1.

During Year 1, 1,000,000 units of Tough-Coat were actually produced and 900,000 units were sold. Actual costs incurred during Year 1 were:

| | |
|---|---|
| *Material X-1 purchased, 1,200,000 ounces @ $0.70* | *$ 840,000* |
| *Material X-2 purchased, 1,150,000 pounds @ $0.50* | *575,000* |
| *Direct labor* | *880,000* |
| *Factory overhead* | *400,000* |
| *Total production costs incurred in Year 1* | *$2,695,000* |

At the end of Year 1, the following variance accounts appeared in the company's accounting records:

| | |
|---|---|
| *Favorable price variance on all material X-1 purchased, 1,200,000 ounces (credit)* | *$(360,000)* |
| *Unfavorable materials quantity variance, 50,000 pounds of material X-2 spoiled in production (debit)* | *25,000* |
| *Unfavorable direct labor rate variance because of 10% wage increase at beginning of Year 1 (debit)* | *80,000* |
| *Net favorable cost variance* | *$(255,000)* |

The company's inventories at the end of Year 1, stated at standard cost, were as follows:

| | | |
|---|---|---|
| *Materials:* | | |
| *Material X-1, 200,000 ounces @ $1.00* | *$200,000* | |
| *Material X-2, 100,000 pounds @ $0.50* | *50,000* | *$250,000* |
| *Finished goods:* | | |
| *Tough-Coat, 100,000 units @ $2.70* | | *270,000* |
| *Total inventory at Dec. 31, Year 1* | | *$520,000* |

The independent certified public accountant, who has been engaged to audit the company's financial statements, wants to adjust this inventory to "a revised standard cost" which would take into account the favorable price variance on material X-1 ($0.30 per ounce) and the 10% wage increase at the beginning of Year 1. The president of the company objects on the following grounds: "Such a revision is not necessary because the cost of material X-1 already shows signs of going up and the wage increase was not warranted because the productivity of workers did not increase one bit. Furthermore, if we revise our inventory figure of $520,000, our operating income will be reduced from the current level of $100,000." You are called in by the president to help resolve the controversy.

**Instructions** Do you agree with the president? Assuming that you conclude that the standards for July should be revised, what value should be assigned to the inventory at the end of Year 1? What effect would this revaluation of inventory have upon the company's $100,000 net income?

# 27

# COST-VOLUME-PROFIT ANALYSIS

In addition to standard costs and budgeting discussed in Chapter 26, management uses many other aids to plan and control the activities of a business. One of the more important analytical tools used by management is cost-volume-profit analysis. ***Cost-volume-profit*** analysis is a means of learning how costs and profits behave in response to changes in the level of business activity. An understanding of the relationships between costs and the volume of activity is useful to management in predicting the effects of various decisions and strategies upon the net income of the business.

## Uses of cost-volume-profit analysis

Cost-volume-profit analysis may be used by management to answer questions such as the following:

1 What level of sales must be reached to cover all expenses, that is, to break even?
2 How many units of a product must be sold to earn a given net income per year?
3 What will happen to our net income if we expand capacity and thereby add $50,000 to our annual fixed costs?
4 What will be the effect of changing compensation of sales personnel from fixed monthly salaries to a straight commission of 10% on sales?
5 If we increase our spending on advertising to $100,000 per month, what increase in sales volume will be required to maintain our current level of net income?

Cost-volume-profit relationships are useful not only to management but also to creditors and investors. The ability of a business to pay its debts and to increase its dividend payments, for example, depends largely upon its ability to generate earnings. Assume that a company's sales volume is expected to increase by 10% during the next year. What will be the effect of this increase in sales volume upon the company's net income? The answer depends upon how the company's costs behave in response to this increase in the level of business activity.

The concepts of cost-volume-profit analysis may be applied to the business as a whole, to individual segments of the business such as a division, a branch, a department, or to a particular product line.

### Cost-volume relationships

To illustrate the relationships between costs and the level of activity, we shall first consider cost behavior in a simple and familiar setting, the cost of operating a personal automobile. Suppose that someone tells you that the average annual cost of owning and operating an automobile is $2,700. Obviously, each individual driver does not incur an annual cost of exactly $2,700. In large part, the annual cost of owning an automobile depends upon how much you drive.

**The volume index** In studying cost behavior, we first look for some measurable concept of volume or activity that has a strong influence on the amount of cost incurred, and we then try to find out how costs change in response to changes in volume. The unit of measure used to define "volume" is called the ***volume index.*** A volume index may be based upon production inputs, such as tons of peaches processed, direct labor hours used, or machine-hours worked; or it may be based upon outputs, such as equivalent full units of product manufactured, units sold, or the dollar value of sales revenue generated. Semester or quarter credit hours is a significant volume index in analyzing educational costs; passenger miles flown is a useful volume index in airline operations; dollar sales is an important volume meaure for a department store.

In our example, we shall use ***miles driven*** as the volume index of operating a personal automobile. Once an appropriate volume index has been found, we can classify all costs into three general categories:

**Variable costs** A ***variable*** cost increases and decreases directly and proportionately with changes in volume. If, for example, volume increases 10%, a variable cost will also increase by approximately 10%. Gasoline is an example of a variable automobile cost, since fuel consumption is directly related to miles driven.

**Semivariable (or mixed) costs** Costs which change in response to changes in volume but by less than a proportionate amount are called ***semivariable*** or ***mixed*** costs. A 10% increase in volume, for example, may result in a 6% increase in a semivariable cost. Automobile maintenance and repair costs rise as miles driven increase, but a certain amount of such costs will be incurred without regard to mileage. For example, tire and battery deterioration occurs in response to both miles driven and the passage of time.

**Fixed (or nonvariable) costs** Costs which remain unchanged despite changes in volume are called ***fixed*** or ***nonvariable.*** Usually such costs are incurred as a function of some other factor such as time. For example, the annual insurance premium and license fee on an automobile are fixed costs since they are independent of the number of miles driven.

***Automobile costs—graphic analysis*** To illustrate automobile cost-volume behavior, we shall assume the following somewhat simplified data to describe the cost of owning and operating a typical mid-sized automobile:

***Three classes of automobile costs***

| *Type of Cost* | *Amount* |
|---|---|
| *Variable costs:* | |
| *Gasoline, oil, and servicing* | *8 cents per mile* |
| *Semivariable costs:* | |
| *Maintenance and repairs* | *$200 per year plus 2 cents per mile* |
| *Depreciation* | *$800 per year plus 2 cents per mile* |
| *Fixed costs:* | |
| *Insurance* | *$380 per year* |
| *License fee* | *$120 per year* |

We can express these cost-volume relationships graphically. The relation between volume (miles driven per year) and the three types of cost both separately and combined is shown in the following diagrams:

***Graphic Analysis of Automobile Costs***

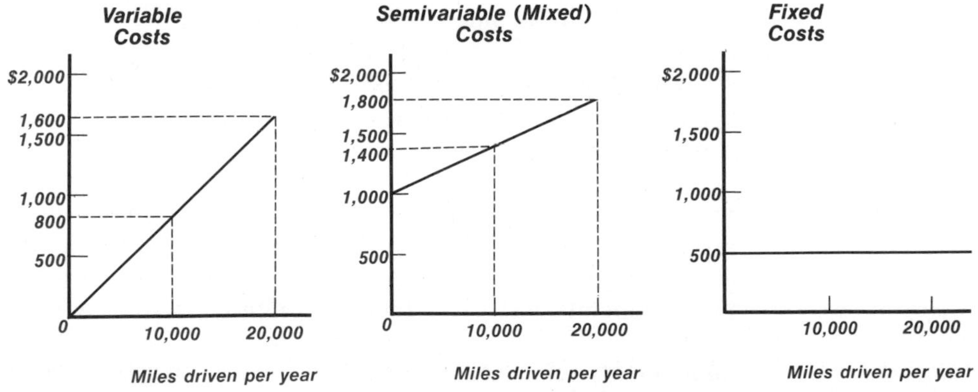

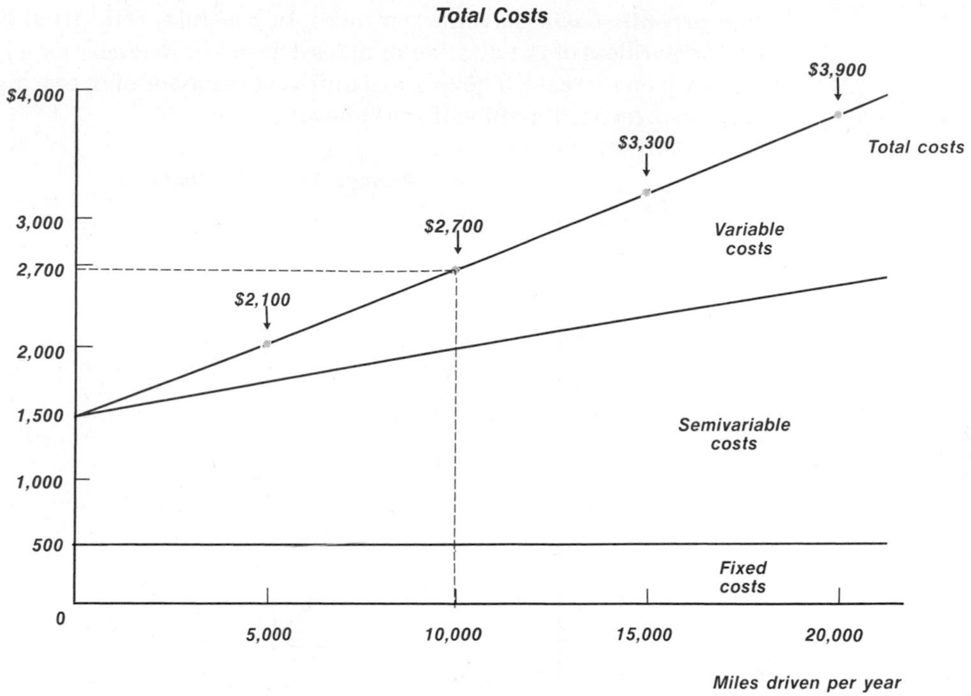


We can read from the total costs graph the estimated annual automobile cost for any assumed mileage. For example, an owner who expects to drive 10,000 miles in a given year may estimate the total cost at $2,700, or 27.0 cents per mile. By combining all the fixed and variable elements of cost, we can generalize the cost-volume relationship and state simply that the cost of owning an automobile is $1,500 per year plus 12 cents per mile driven during the year.

The effect of volume on unit (per-mile) costs can be observed by converting total cost figures to average unit costs as follows:

*Note decrease in cost per mile as use increases*

***Cost per Mile of Owning and Using an Automobile***

| | | | | |
|---|---|---|---|---|
| *Miles driven* | 5,000 | 10,000 | 15,000 | 20,000 |
| *Costs:* | | | | |
| *Fully variable (8 cents per mile)* | $ 400 | $ 800 | $1,200 | $1,600 |
| *Semivariable:* | | | | |
| *Variable portion (4 cents per mile)* | 200 | 400 | 600 | 800 |
| *Fixed portion ($200 + $800)* | 1,000 | 1,000 | 1,000 | 1,000 |
| *Completely fixed ($380 + $120)* | 500 | 500 | 500 | 500 |
| *Total costs* | $2,100 | $2,700 | $3,300 | $3,900 |
| *Cost per mile* | $ 0.42 | $ 0.27 | $ 0.22 | $0.195 |

It should be noted that the variable portion of the costs incurred in operating an automobile increases in total as miles driven increase but ***remains constant***

***on a per-mile basis*** (12 cents per mile). In contrast, total fixed costs remain the same regardless of the number of miles driven but ***decrease on a per-mile basis*** as miles driven increase. The average unit-cost behavior of operating an automobile may be presented graphically as shown below:

***Average cost per mile for driving a car***

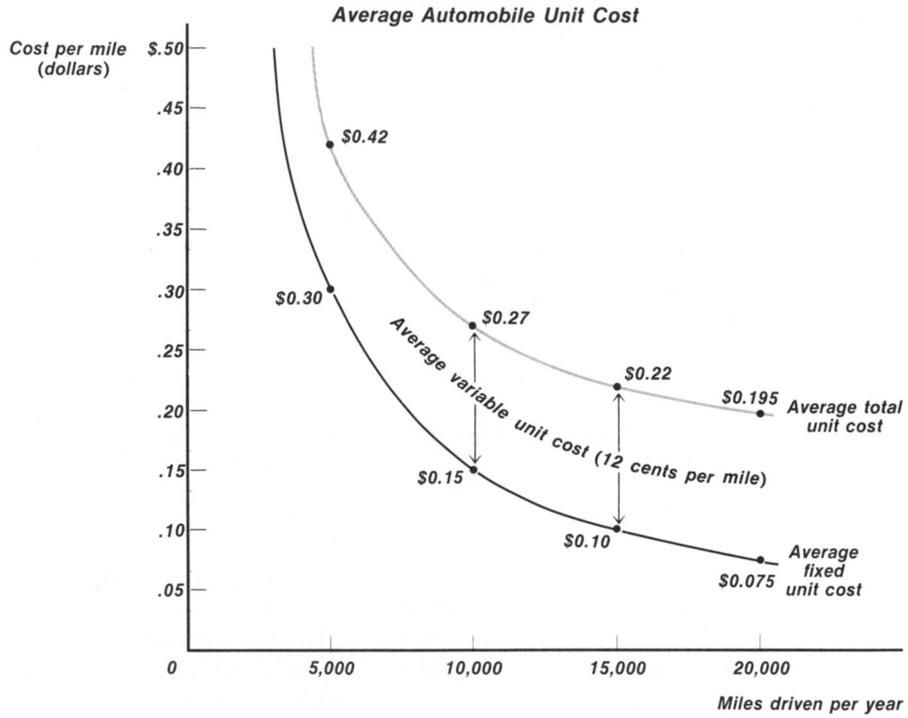


## Cost behavior in businesses

Cost relationships in a business are seldom as simple as those in our automobile example. Given a suitable index of volume (or activity), however, the operating costs of all businesses exhibit variable, semivariable, and fixed characteristics.

Some business costs increase in lump-sum steps rather than continuous increments, as shown in graph **(a)** on page 1007. For example, when production reaches a point where another supervisor and crew must be added, a lump-sum addition to labor costs occurs at this point. Other costs may vary along a curve rather than a straight line, as in graph **(b).** For example, when overtime must be worked to increase production, the labor cost per unit may rise more rapidly than volume because of the necessity of paying overtime premium to employees.

Taking all the possible variations of cost behavior into account would add greatly to the complexity of cost-volume analysis. How far from reality are the assumed straight-line relationships? Fortunately, there are two factors that make straight-line approximations of cost behavior useful for analytical purposes.

*"Stair-step" and curvilinear costs*

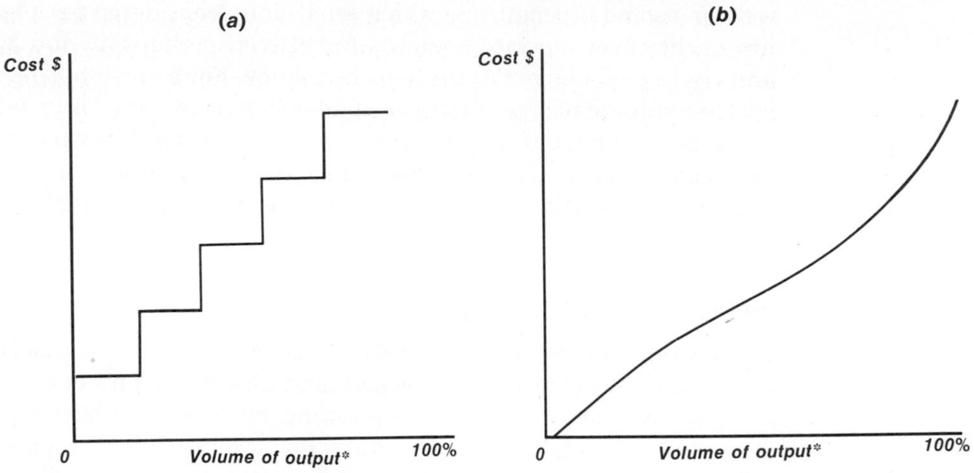


*Stated as a percentage of plant capacity.

First, unusual patterns of cost behavior tend to offset one another. If we were to plot actual total costs incurred by a business over a time period in which volume changes occurred, the result might appear as in the cost-volume graph **(a)** below:

*Are straight-line cost patterns realistic?*

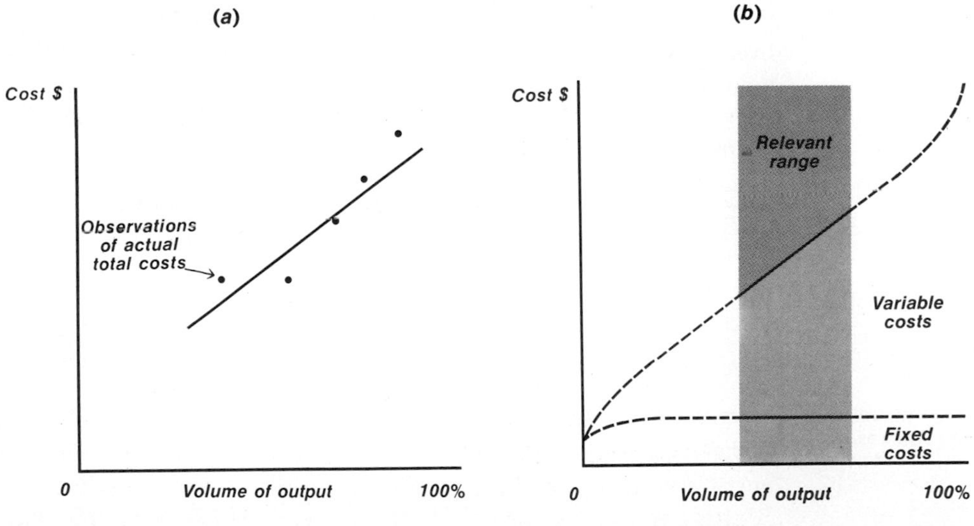


Total cost often moves in close approximation to a straight-line pattern when the various "stair-step" and curvilinear cost patterns of individual costs are combined.

Second, unusual patterns of cost behavior are most likely to occur at extremely high or extremely low levels of volume. For example, if output were increased to near 100% of plant capacity, variable costs would curve sharply upward because of payments for overtime. An extreme decline in volume, on the other hand, might require shutting down plants and extensive layoffs, thereby reducing some expenditures which are usually considered fixed costs. Most businesses, however, operate somewhere between perhaps 45 and 80% of capacity, and try to avoid large fluctuations in volume. For a given business, the probability that volume will vary outside of a fairly narrow range is usually remote. The range over which output may reasonably be expected to vary is called the ***relevant range.*** Within this relevant range, the assumption that total costs vary in straight-line relation to changes in volume is reasonably realistic for most companies.

## Profit-volume relationships

Business managers continually study the effect of internal decisions and external conditions on revenue, expenses, and ultimately on net income. Revenue is affected by the actions of competitors, by a firm's pricing policies, and by changes in the market demand for a firm's products or services. Expenses are affected by the prices paid for inputs, the volume of production or business activity, and the efficiency with which a firm translates input factors into salable output.

An important aspect of planning to meet given profit objectives is the analysis of the effect of volume changes on net income. The study of business profit-volume relationships is sometimes called ***break-even analysis,*** in honor of the point at which a business moves from a loss to a profit position. Since the objective of business endeavor is to earn a fair rate of return on investment, the break-even point (that is, the point of zero income) is of course not a planned goal. However, the knowledge of revenue and cost behavior necessary to determine the break-even point carries with it valuable insights that are useful in planning and control.

*Note variable and fixed expense elements*

***HANNIGAN'S ICE CREAM COMPANY***
***Monthly Operating Data—***
***Typical Retail Store***

| | Fixed Expenses | Variable Expenses per Gallon | Variable Expenses as Percentage of Sales Price |
|---|---|---|---|
| Average selling price | | $4.00 | 100% |
| Cost of ice cream (including delivery) | | $2.20 | 55.0% |
| Monthly operating expenses: | | | |
| Manager's salary | $2,200 | | |
| Wages | 4,200+ | .14 | 3.5 |
| Store rent | 1,600 | | |
| Utilities | 180+ | .04 | 1.0 |
| Miscellaneous | 820+ | .02 | .5 |
| Total expenses | $9,000+ | $2.40 | 60.0% |
| Contribution to fixed expenses | | $1.60 | 40.0% |

**Cost-volume-profit analysis—an illustration** A simple business situation will be used to illustrate the kinds of information that can be derived from cost-volume-profit analysis. Hannigan's Ice Cream Company (a single proprietorship) has a chain of stores located throughout a large city, selling ice cream in various flavors. Although the company sells to customers in packages of different size, we shall assume that volume of business is measured in gallons of ice cream sold. The company buys its ice cream from a dairy at a price of $2.20 per gallon. Retail sales prices vary depending on the quantity purchased by a customer, but revenue per gallon of ice cream sold *averages* $4 per gallon and does not vary significantly from store to store or from period to period. Monthly operating statistics for a typical store are shown on page 1008.

**Graphic analysis** A ***profit-volume*** (or ***break-even***) graph for the typical retail store of Hannigan's Ice Cream Company, based on the above data, is shown below. The horizontal scale represents volume in thousands of gallons of ice cream per month. Since none of the company's stores sells more than 10,000

***HANNIGAN'S ICE CREAM COMPANY***
***Monthly Profit—Volume Graph***
***Typical Retail Store***

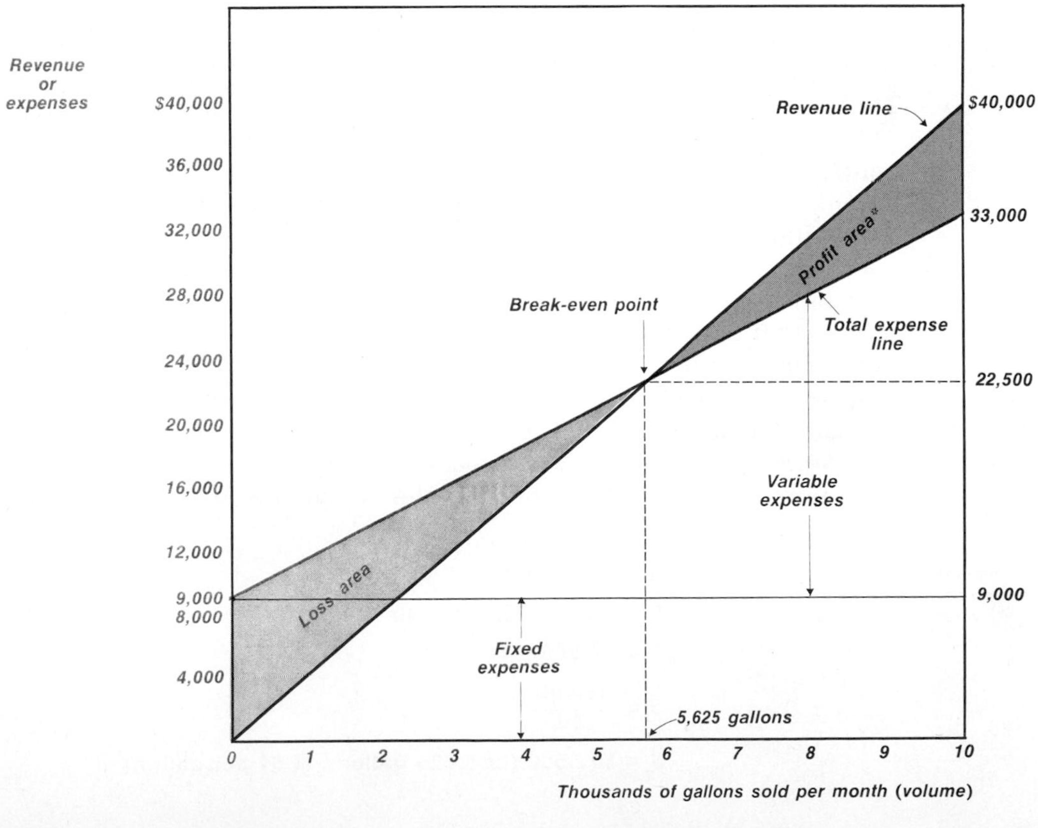

gallons per month, this is assumed to be the upper limit of the relevant volume range. The vertical scale is in dollars of revenue or expenses. The steps in plotting this profit-volume graph are as follows:

1 First the revenue line is plotted, running from $0 at zero volume of sales to $40,000, representing 10,000 gallons of sales per month at $4 per gallon.
2 The fixed (nonvariable) monthly operating expenses are plotted as a horizontal line at the level of $9,000 per month.
3 Starting at the $9,000 fixed expense line, the variable expense of $2.40 per gallon is plotted. Note that this line also becomes the total expense line since it is added on top of the fixed expense line.

The monthly profit or loss that may be expected at any sales volume level per store may be read from the profit-volume graph. For example, the break-even point (zero profit) is 5,625 gallons per month, or $22,500 of sales per month. Sales below 5,625 gallons per month will result in a net loss, and sales above 5,625 gallons per month will result in net income. Income taxes are not relevant in our example because Hannigan's Ice Cream Company is a single proprietorship.

**Profit-volume formula** A formula may be developed for general use in analyzing profit-volume behavior. The formula is based on the factors that make up the computation of net income.

**Sales (*S*) = Variable expense (*V*) + Fixed expense (*F*) + Net income (*I*)**

We are usually looking for a "target sales volume" in profit-volume analysis. For example, we want to know the sales volume necessary to break even, or the volume necessary to earn a given net income, or the effect of a change in variable or fixed expenses on the volume necessary to produce a given net income. In our profit-volume formula, *S* represents the target sales volume.

To illustrate, we shall use this formula to compute the monthly sales volume necessary for a typical Hannigan's Ice Cream Company store to break even. At the break-even point, the target net income is zero; our analysis on page 1008 shows that monthly fixed expenses amount to $9,000. Since we do not yet know the monthly sales volume, however, we do not know the amount of variable expenses. Our analysis on page 1008 shows that variable expenses amount to 60% of sales; therefore, we shall use .60*S* to represent the amount of variable expenses. By expressing variable expenses as a percentage of sales, we have only one unknown, *S*, and the monthly sales volume needed to break even can be computed as follows:

***Computing break-even sales volume***

$$S = V + F + I$$

$$S = .60S + \$9,000 + \$0$$

$$.40S = \$9,000$$

$$S = \frac{\$9,000}{.40}$$

$$S = \$22,500 \text{ (or 5,625 gallons at \$4 per gallon)}$$

**Contribution margin approach** The *contribution margin,* in profit-volume analysis, is the excess of sales over variable expenses. The *contribution margin ratio* is the percentage of sales (in dollars) available to cover fixed expenses and yield a net income. The contribution margin ratio is computed as follows:

*A key to profit-volume analysis*

$$\text{Contribution margin ratio} = \frac{\text{Sales} - \text{Variable costs}}{\text{Sales}}$$

The contribution margin ratio does not vary with changes in sales volume; it represents the average contribution that each dollar of sales makes to the recovery of fixed expenses and toward generating a net income. Therefore, we can simplify our profit-volume formula by expressing the target sales volume in terms of the contribution margin ratio, as follows:

*Simplified profit-volume formula*

$$\text{Target sales volume} = \frac{\text{Fixed costs} + \text{Target income (before taxes)}}{\text{Contribution margin ratio}}$$

To illustrate, in terms of our ice cream store example, suppose that we want to know the sales volume per store necessary to produce a monthly net income of $2,000. (Since our example involves a single proprietorship, income before taxes is equal to net income.) The contribution margin ratio is 40% ($1.60 ÷ $4.00), as shown in the operating data on page 1008. Therefore, the sales volume necessary to produce $2,000 in monthly net income may be computed as follows:

$$\text{Target sales volume} = \frac{\$9{,}000 + \$2{,}000}{.40} = \$27{,}500$$

To achieve a monthly sales volume of $27,500, a Harrigan's Ice Cream Company store must sell 6,875 gallons of ice cream per month ($27,500 ÷ $4 per gallon).

**Profit-volume planning** Once profit-volume relationships have been established, it is possible to provide planning information that is useful in arriving at a variety of decisions. To illustrate the process, consider a number of different questions that might be raised by the management of Hannigan's Ice Cream Company:

*1* ***Question.*** To increase volume, management is considering a policy of giving greater discounts on gallon and half-gallon packages of ice cream. It is estimated that the effect of this pricing policy would be to reduce the average selling price per gallon by 16 cents (that is, from $4 per gallon to $3.84). Management is interested in knowing the effect of such a price reduction on the monthly break-even volume per store.
**Analysis.** The proposed change in average sales price changes the contribution margin ratio from .40 to .375, as shown below:

$$\frac{\$3.84 - \$2.40}{\$3.84} = .375 \text{ (or } 37\tfrac{1}{2}\%)$$

The cost of ice cream and fixed operating expenses remain unchanged by this pricing decision. Therefore, the monthly target sales volume to break even under the new pricing situation would be:

$$\text{Target sales volume} = \frac{\$9{,}000 + \$0}{.375} = \$24{,}000 \text{ per month}$$

In terms of gallons sold per month, the break-even volume would be $24,000 ÷ $3.84 = 6,250 gallons, or more than 11% higher than the present 5,625 gallon break-even volume. Thus management should be advised that the proposed pricing policy is desirable only if the unit sales volume per store can be expected to increase more than 11% per month as a result of the lower sales prices on gallon and half-gallon packages.

2 ***Question.*** Management is considering a change in the method of compensating store managers. Instead of a fixed salary of $2,200 per month, it is proposed that managers be put on a salary of $660 per month plus a commission of 24 cents per gallon of sales. The present average monthly net income per store is $2,400 on sales of $28,500 ($28,500 × 40% − $9,000 = $2,400). What sales volume per store will be necessary to produce the same monthly net income under the proposed incentive compensation arrangement?
***Analysis.*** This proposal involves a change in both the contribution margin ratio and the fixed monthly operating expenses. Adding 24 cents per gallon to variable costs raises the total variable cost to $2.64 per gallon and reduces the contribution margin ratio to 34%, as computed below:

$$\frac{\$4.00 - \$2.64}{\$4.00} = 34\%$$

Cutting the manager's salary from $2,200 to $660 per month will reduce monthly fixed expenses from $9,000 to $7,460. The sales volume required to produce a monthly net income of $2,400 may be computed as follows:

$$\text{Target sales volume} = \frac{\$7{,}460 + \$2{,}400}{.34} = \$29{,}000 \text{ per month}$$

To produce the same $2,400 per month net income under the new compensation plan, sales volume per store would have to be increased by $500 (or 125 gallons) over the current monthly sales volume of $28,500. The issue thus boils down to whether the incentive compensation arrangement will induce store managers to increase volume by more than 125 gallons per month. Profit-volume analysis does not answer this question, but it provides the information which enables management to exercise its judgment intelligently.

3 ***Question.*** Hannigan's Ice Cream Company stores are now open 12 hours each day (from 9 A.M. to 9 P.M.). Management is considering a proposal to decrease store hours by opening two hours later each morning. It is estimated that this policy would reduce sales volume by an average of 500 gallons per month and would cut fixed expenses (utilities and wages) by $1,000 per month. Assuming a present average net income of $2,400 per store, would it pay the company to change its store hours?
***Analysis.*** The loss of 500 gallons of sales per month would decrease revenue by $2,000 (500 × $4). This would result in the loss of contribution margin of $800 ($2,000 × 40%). Therefore, whether the reduction in store hours would increase net income per store may be determined by direct ***incremental analysis*** as follows:

| | |
|---|---|
| ***Reduction in fixed operating expenses*** | ***$1,000*** |
| ***Less: Loss of contribution margin ($2,000 × 40%)*** | ***800*** |
| ***Prospective increase in monthly net income per store*** | ***$ 200*** |

Note that the present average monthly net income of $2,400 per store is not considered relevant in making this analysis. Incremental analysis indicates that reducing store hours will decrease any net loss by $200 or add $200 to any net income figure. The incremental approach to cost and revenue analysis is discussed in more detail in Chapter 28.

### Other uses of a profit-volume graph

The profit-volume graph is a flexible planning and control tool; its form can be changed to meet various decision-making needs of management. An example is presented below.

**Profit-volume graph showing total contribution margin and margin of safety** A profit-volume graph may be prepared in such a way that it shows the total contribution margin at any level of activity (sales volume) and the margin of safety sales volume. For example, assume that Dash Company has total fixed expenses of $180,000 per year, that the contribution margin ratio is 45%, and that sales at full capacity would be $800,000 per year. A profit-volume graph may be prepared as follows:

*Profit-volume graph, showing contribution margin and margin of safety sales volume*

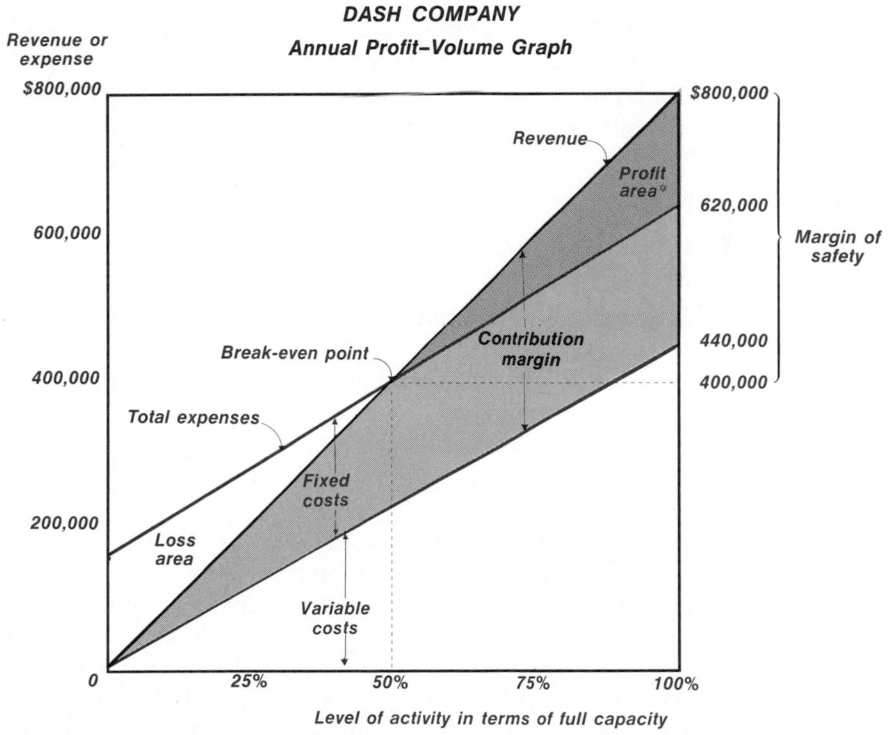


*Profit area represents income before income taxes.

When the profit-volume graph is prepared in this form, it is easy to determine the total contribution margin (the difference between total revenue and variable expenses) at any level of activity. We can see that at the break-even point the total contribution margin is equal to total fixed expenses ($180,000); at any level beyond the break-even point, the profit area is equal to the difference between the total contribution margin and total fixed expenses. For example, at full capacity the profit is equal to $180,000, which is the excess of the contribution margin, $360,000 ($800,000 – $440,000), over total fixed expenses, $180,000.

The ***margin of safety*** is the dollar amount by which actual sales exceed break-even sales volume. It measures the amount by which sales can decrease (assuming that expense relationships remain unchanged) without producing a loss. In the graph illustrated above, the margin of safety sales volume at 100% level of activity is $400,000; at the 75% level, the margin of safety sales volume is $200,000 ($600,000 – $400,000). If you study the graph carefully, you will see that the amount of operating income (before income taxes) may be determined as follows:

$$\text{Operating income} = \frac{\text{Margin of safety}}{\text{sales volume}} \times \frac{\text{Contribution}}{\text{margin ratio}}$$

This relationship gives us a quick tool in projecting operating income at various levels of sales. For example, if sales are expected to be $500,000 and the break-even point is $400,000, the operating income will be $45,000 when the contribution margin ratio is 45%. This is determined by simply multiplying the margin of safety sales volume, $100,000 ($500,000 – $400,000), by the contribution margin ratio, 45%.

## Assumptions underlying profit-volume analysis

In preparing a profit-volume graph, accountants assume the following:

1 Sales price per unit remains constant.
2 If more than one product is sold, the proportion of the various products sold (sales mix) is assumed to be constant.
3 Fixed expenses remain constant at all levels of sales within the assumed relevant range of activity.
4 Variable expenses remain constant as a percentage of sales revenue.
5 For a business engaged in manufacturing, the number of units produced is assumed to be equal to the number of units sold.

These assumptions simplify profit-volume analysis. In actual practice, however, some of these assumptions may not hold true. However, profit-volume analysis is still a useful planning and control tool for management. As changes take place in selling prices, sales mix, expenses, and production levels, management should incorporate such changes into profit-volume analysis and revise any previous estimates of probable results. The assumptions underlying profit-volume analysis suggest that this management tool should be continuously monitored and revised as conditions change.

## Importance of sales mix in profit-volume analysis and management decisions

In our example of Hannigan's Ice Cream Company, we assumed that the contribution margin ratio ***averaged*** 40% of sales expressed in dollars and that the ***average*** selling price was $4 per gallon of ice cream sold. Let us now change our example and assume that a detailed analysis indicates that ice cream is actually sold in three packages as follows:

*Why would you prefer to sell only the gallon size?*

| | Quart | Half-Gallon | Gallon |
|---|---|---|---|
| Sales price per package | $1.20 | $2.00 | $3.60 |
| Less: Variable expense per package | 0.84 | 1.10 | 1.80 |
| Contribution margin per package | $0.36 | $0.90 | $1.80 |
| Contribution margin ratio (contribution margin ÷ sales price) | 30% | 45% | 50% |
| Break-even sales volume, assuming that only the one size package was sold (fixed expenses, $9,000, divided by contribution margin ratio) | $30,000 | $20,000 | $18,000 |

Earlier in this chapter we stated that Hannigan's Ice Cream Company is now selling a certain ***mix*** of the three sizes and that a sales volume of $22,500 is required to break even ($9,000 ÷ average contribution margin of .40). If ice cream were sold exclusively in quarts, sales of $30,000 would be required to break even; if only half-gallon packages were sold, the break-even sales volume would be $20,000; if only gallon packages were sold, the break-even sales volume would be $18,000. The reason the break-even sales volume differs for each size is because each size yields a different contribution margin per dollar of sales (contribution margin ratio). ***The larger the contribution margin ratio, the lower the sales volume that is required to cover a given amount of fixed expenses.***

The amount of net income earned by a business unit depends not only on the volume of sales and the ability to control expenses, but also on the quality of sales. Sales yielding a high contribution margin are more profitable than sales yielding a low contribution margin. Thus, sales with a high contribution margin percentage are said to be ***high-quality sales.*** A shift from low-margin sales to high-margin sales can materially increase net income even though total sales decrease; on the other hand, a shift from high-margin to low-margin sales can turn a net income into a loss despite an increase in total sales.

## Contribution margin per unit of scarce resource

The contribution margin approach is useful to management in deciding what products to manufacture (or purchase for resale) and what products to eliminate when certain factors of production are available only in limited quantity. One of the important functions of management is to develop the most profitable uses of such scarce resources as raw materials, skilled labor, high-cost equipment, and factory floor space.

Assume that you are offered two equally satisfactory jobs, one paying $6 per hour and one paying $9 per hour. Since your time is scarce and you wish to maximize the pay that you receive for an hour of your time, you would naturally choose the job paying $9 per hour. For the same reason, if a company has the capacity to utilize only 100,000 direct labor hours per year, management would want to use this capacity in such a way as ***to produce the maximum contribution margin per hour of direct labor.*** To illustrate this concept, assume that the Maximus Corporation is considering the production of three products. The contribution margin per direct labor hour required to produce each of the three products is estimated as follows:

***MAXIMUS CORPORATION***

***Contribution Margin per Hour of Direct Labor***

*Should production of product C be expanded?*

| Product | Sales Price per Unit | − | Variable Costs per Unit | = | Contribution Margin per Unit | ÷ | Direct Labor Hours Required to Produce One Unit | = | Contribution Margin per Hour of Direct Labor |
|---|---|---|---|---|---|---|---|---|---|
| A . . . . . | $100 | | $60 | | $40 | | 10 | | $ 4 |
| B . . . . . | 80 | | 50 | | 30 | | 5 | | 6 |
| C . . . . . | 60 | | 40 | | 20 | | 2 | | 10 |

Even though a unit of product A yields the highest contribution margin ($40) and the highest contribution margin ratio (40%), it is ***the least profitable product in terms of contribution margin per hour of direct labor.*** If sales of products B and C do not depend on the sales of product A and there are no operational problems involved in varying the production mix of the three products, the production of product A should be kept to a minimum. This would be particularly appropriate if the Maximus Corporation could not meet the demand for all three products because of inability to expand plant capacity beyond 100,000 direct labor hours.

We can see that a unit of product A requires 10 hours of direct labor and generates $40 in contribution margin; a unit of product B requires only 5 hours of direct labor and yields $30 in contribution margin; and a unit of product C requires only 2 hours of direct labor and yields $20 in contribution margin. In summary, 10 hours of effort on product A yields $40 in contribution margin while 10 hours of effort on product B yields $60 in contribution margin, and 10 hours of effort on product C generates a whopping $100 in contribution margin. If the entire capacity of 100,000 direct labor hours were used to produce ***only a single product,*** the following total contribution margin would result:

*Why should we continue to produce product A?*

| Product | Total Capacity (hours) | × | Contribution Margin per Hour of Direct Labor | = | Total Contribution Margin If Only One Product Is Manufactured |
|---|---|---|---|---|---|
| A . . . . . . . . . . . . | 100,000 | | $ 4 | | $ 400,000 |
| B . . . . . . . . . . . . | 100,000 | | 6 | | 600,000 |
| C . . . . . . . . . . . . | 100,000 | | 10 | | 1,000,000 |

This schedule does not mean that the production of product A can be discontinued. While product C is clearly the most profitable, perhaps the demand for it is not enough to keep the plant working at full capacity; or the sales of product C may to some extent depend on sales of products A and B. In most cases, a company is not in a position to manufacture only the product which yields the highest contribution margin and let other less alert business executives manufacture the low-margin products. A company should, however, try to sell as much of the high-margin products as possible in order to maximize its net income.

One of the key functions of business organizations is to employ scarce economic resources in ways which will best serve the needs of society. The net income earned by a business is, in a way, a reward for producing the goods needed by a society at the lowest possible cost. Sales mix and contribution margin analyses are useful in realizing the twin goals of producing goods at low cost and at the same time earning a satisfactory net income in order for a business unit to survive and thus to continue to meet social needs.

### Summary of basic cost-volume-profit relationships

In this chapter we have demonstrated a number of ratios and mathematical relationships which are useful in cost-volume-profit analysis. For your convenience, these relationships are summarized below:

| *Measurement* | *Method of Computation* |
|---|---|
| *Contribution margin per unit* | *Unit sales price − variable costs per unit* |
| *Contribution margin ratio* | $\dfrac{\textit{Sales − variable costs}}{\textit{Sales}}$ |
| *Break-even sales volume* | $\dfrac{\textit{Fixed costs}}{\textit{Contribution margin ratio}}$ |
| *Break-even sales volume (in units)* | $\dfrac{\textit{Fixed costs}}{\textit{Contribution margin per unit}}$ |
| *Target sales volume* | $\dfrac{\textit{Fixed costs + target income (before taxes)}}{\textit{Contribution margin ratio}}$ |
| *Margin of safety sales volume* | *Actual sales volume − break-even sales volume* |
| *Operating income (before taxes)* | *Margin of safety sales volume × contribution margin ratio* |

## KEY TERMS INTRODUCED OR EMPHASIZED IN CHAPTER 27

**Break-even point** The level of sales and output at which a company neither earns a profit nor incurs a loss. Revenue exactly covers expenses.

**Contribution margin** Sales minus variable expenses.

**Contribution margin ratio** The percentage of sales available to cover fixed expenses and yield a net income.

**Cost-volume-profit analysis** The study of how costs and net income respond to changes in the level of business activity.

**Fixed (or nonvariable) costs** Costs that remain unchanged despite changes in volume of output.

**Margin of safety** Amount by which actual sales exceed the break-even point.

**Profit-volume formula** Sales = variable expenses + fixed expenses + net income.

**Relevant volume range** The span or range of output over which output is likely to vary and assumptions about cost behavior are generally valid. Excludes extreme volume variations.

**Semivariable costs** Costs that respond to change in volume of output by less than a proportionate amount.

**Variable costs** Costs that increase and decrease directly and proportionately to changes in volume of output.

## DEMONSTRATION PROBLEM FOR YOUR REVIEW

The management of the Fresno Processing Company has engaged you to assist in the development of information to be used for managerial decisions.

The company has the capacity to process 20,000 tons of cottonseed per year. The yield from a ton of cottonseed is as shown below.

| *Product* | *Average Yield per Ton* of Cottonseed* | *Average Selling Price* | *Total Revenue* |
|---|---|---|---|
| *Oil* | *400 pounds* | *$ 0.14 per pound* | *$56* |
| *Meal* | *600 pounds* | *60.00 per ton* | *18* |
| *Hulls* | *800 pounds* | *30.00 per ton* | *12* |
| *Lint* | *200 pounds* | *0.02 per pound* | *4* |
| *Totals* | *2,000 pounds* | | *$90* |

* There are 2,000 pounds in a ton.

A special marketing study revealed that the company can expect to sell its entire output for the coming year at the average selling prices listed above.

You have determined the company's cost structure to be as follows:

| | |
|---|---|
| *Processing costs:* | |
| *Variable:* | *$13 per ton of cottonseed placed into process* |
| *Fixed:* | *$70,000 per year at all levels of production* |
| *Marketing costs:* | *All variable, $27 per ton of all products sold* |
| *Administrative costs:* | *All fixed, $110,000 per year at all levels of production and sales activity* |

### Instructions

**a** Assuming that the company pays $30 per ton of cottonseed, how many tons of raw cottonseed must be processed and sold if the company is to break even?

**b** Assuming that the company has 10,000 shares of stock and that the income tax rate is 50%, how many tons of raw cottonseed must the company process and sell, if it pays $30 per ton of cottonseed, in order to report earnings of $8 per share?

**c** Compute the average maximum amount that the company can afford to pay for a ton of raw material (cottonseed) if it is to break even by processing and selling 15,000 tons of cottonseed during the current year.

## SOLUTION TO DEMONSTRATION PROBLEM

**a** Computation of number of tons that must be processed and sold in order to break even, if cottonseed is purchased for $30 per ton:

| | | |
|---|---|---|
| *Total revenue per ton of cottonseed* | | *$90* |
| *Less: Variable costs:* | | |
| *Processing* | *$13* | |
| *Marketing* | *27* | |
| *Cottonseed* | *30* | *70* |
| *Contribution margin per ton* | | *$20* |

Break-even sales volume:

*Fixed costs, $180,000 ($70,000 processing costs + $110,000 administrative costs) ÷ $20 contribution margin per ton = 9,000 tons.*

**b** Sales volume necessary to earn $8 per share:

| | |
|---|---|
| *Fixed costs, $110,000 + $70,000* | *$180,000* |
| *Required pretax income (10,000 × $8) ÷ .5* | *160,000* |
| *Total contribution margin required* | *$340,000* |
| *Contribution margin per ton—see part a* | *$20* |

*Number of tons that must be processed and sold in order to earn $8 per share: $340,000 ÷ $20 = 17,000 tons.*

**c** Computation of average maximum amount that the company can afford to pay for a ton of cottonseed:

| | | |
|---|---|---|
| *Total revenue per ton of cottonseed* | | *$90* |
| *Less: Costs per ton other than cottonseed:* | | |
| *Processing* | *$13* | |
| *Marketing* | *27* | |
| *Fixed costs ($180,000 ÷ 15,000 tons)* | *12* | *52* |
| *Balance, maximum amount that can be paid for a ton of cottonseed and still break even at 15,000-ton volume* | | *$38* |

## REVIEW QUESTIONS

1 Why is it important for management to focus attention on cost-volume-profit relationships?

2 What is a ***volume index*** and why is it important in analyzing cost behavior?

3 A is a variable cost; B is a fixed (nonvariable) cost; and C is a semivariable cost. How would you expect each of these total dollar costs to vary with changes in production volume? How would they vary with changes in production if they were expressed in ***dollars per unit*** of production?

4 The simplifying assumption that costs and volume vary in straight-line relationships makes the analysis of cost behavior much easier. What factors make this a reasonable and useful assumption in many cases?

5 What important relationships are shown on a profit-volume (break-even) graph?

6 Kris Company has an average contribution margin of 35%. What target sales volume per month is necessary to produce a monthly operating income of $22,000, if fixed (nonvariable) expenses are $118,000 per month?

7 Why is the profit-volume formula a more flexible analytical tool than a profit-volume graph?

8 Define ***margin of safety*** and ***relevant range*** of activity.

9 A top executive of a major steel company was recently quoted as follows: "The industry finds itself at the highest break-even point in our history. In the past we could make a profit operating at 50% of our plant capacity, but now that has gone up 20 points." List some reasons why the break-even point probably increased to 70% of capacity for the steel industry.

10 An executive of U.S. Steel Corporation put the blame for lower net income for a recent fiscal period on the "shift in product mix to higher proportion of export sales." Sales for the period increased slightly while net income declined by 28%. Explain how a change in product (sales) mix to a higher proportion in export sales would result in a lower level of net income.

11 Why is it helpful to know the approximate amount of contribution margin generated from the use of a scarce resource such as a machine-hour or an hour of direct labor?

12 The president of an airline blamed a profit squeeze on "unwise and unjustifiable promotional fares." He pointed out that 50% of the company's revenue came from "discount fares." Explain why discount fares tend to reduce net income and point out circumstances in which a discount from the regular price of a plane fare could possibly increase net income.

13 An economist writing in the *Wall Street Journal* stated that inflation is caused by a shortage of supply in relation to demand. The article suggested that business executives should try to maintain profits by increasing sales volume and reducing prices rather than by increasing prices. Evaluate this argument.

14 In a recent report to stockholders, the management of a large corporation stated that lower sales volume, coupled with higher material and labor costs, resulted in a first-quarter loss of $131,000, compared with a profit of $525,000 in the first quarter of the preceding year. In order to keep costs and expenses in line with anticipated volume, budgeted fixed costs and expenses for the current year were reduced from $28.3 million to $25 million, thus reducing the break-even sales level from $80.4 million to "a more comfortable $76 million."

List some ways that fixed costs and expenses can be reduced and mention several other actions which were probably taken by management to attain a lower break-even point.

## EXERCISES

*Ex. 27-1* The information shown below relates to the only product sold by Portland Company:

| | |
|---|---|
| *Selling price per unit* | *$ 10* |
| *Variable costs per unit* | *8* |
| *Fixed costs per year* | *200,000* |

**a** Compute the contribution margin ratio and the sales volume required to break even.
**b** Assuming that the company sells 125,000 units during the current year, compute the margin of safety sales volume.

*Ex. 27-2* Information concerning a product manufactured by Ames Brothers appears below:

| | |
|---|---|
| *Sales price per unit* | *$70.00* |
| *Variable cost per unit* | *$42.00* |
| *Total fixed production and operating costs* | *$280,000* |
| *Maximum capacity with present facilities* | *20,000 units* |

Determine the following:
**a** The contribution margin per unit
**b** The number of units that must be sold to break even
**c** The sales level that must be reached in order to earn $224,000 before income taxes

*Ex. 27-3* Lake Corporation has a break-even sales volume of $60,000 per month. Because of an increase of $3,600 in fixed expenses, the sales volume required to break even increased to $72,000. The sales price and the variable expenses of the single product produced did not change. Based on the foregoing information compute:
**a** Variable expenses as a percentage of sales
**b** Total fixed expenses before the $3,600 increase

*Ex. 27-4* Malibu Corporation has fixed expenses of $30,000 per month. It sells two products as follows:

| | Sales Price | Variable Expense | Contribution Margin |
|---|---|---|---|
| *Product no. 1* | *$10* | *$4* | *$6* |
| *Product no. 2* | *10* | *7* | *3* |

**a** What sales volume is required to break even if two units of product no. 1 are sold with one unit of product no. 2?
**b** What sales volume is required to break even if one unit of product no. 1 is sold with two units of product no. 2?

*Ex. 27-5* For each of the six independent situations below, compute the missing amounts:
**a** Only one product is manufactured:

| | Sales | Variable Expenses | Contribution Margin per Unit | Fixed Expenses | Income (before Taxes) | Units Sold |
|---|---|---|---|---|---|---|
| *(1)* | *$_____* | *$120,000* | *$18* | *$_____* | *$24,000* | *4,000* |
| *(2)* | *180,000* | _____ | ___ | *45,000* | *30,000* | *5,000* |
| *(3)* | *600,000* | _____ | *30* | *150,000* | *90,000* | _____ |

**b** Many products are manufactured:

| Sales | Variable Expenses | Contribution Margin, % | Fixed Expenses | Income (before Taxes) |
|---|---|---|---|---|
| (1) $900,000 | $720,000 | __% | $ ______ | $78,000 |
| (2) 600,000 | ______ | 40% | ______ | 45,000 |
| (3) ______ | ______ | 30% | 105,000 | 30,000 |

## PROBLEMS

### Group A

*27A-1* The following information relates to the single product sold by Pinapple Pak, Inc.

| | |
|---|---|
| *Selling price per unit* | $ 20 |
| *Variable costs per unit* | 12 |
| *Fixed costs per year* | 360,000 |

**Instructions** Determine the following, showing as part of your answer the formula which you used in your computation. For example, the formula used to determine the contribution margin ratio (part **a**) is:

$$\text{Contribution margin ratio} = \frac{\text{Sales} - \text{Variable costs}}{\text{Sales}}$$

(Hint: Refer to the summary of key formulas on page 1017.)

**a** Contribution margin ratio. (Use per-unit amounts in your computation.)
**b** Sales volume required to break even.
**c** Sales volume required to earn an annual income before taxes of $150,000.
**d** The margin of safety sales volume if annual sales total 75,000 units.
**e** Income before taxes if annual sales total 75,000 units.

*27A-2* Stop-n-Shop operates a downtown parking lot containing 800 parking spaces. The lot is open 2,500 hours per year. The parking charge per car is 40 cents per hour; the average customer parks two hours. Stop-n-Shop rents the lot for $4,750 per month. The lot supervisor is paid $16,000 per year. Five employees who handle the parking of cars are paid $250 per week for 50 weeks, plus $500 each for the two-week vacation period. Employees rotate vacations during the slow months when four employees can handle the reduced load of traffic. Lot maintenance, payroll taxes, and other fixed expenses amount to $2,000 per month, plus 4 cents per parking hour sold.

**Instructions**

**a** Draw a profit-volume graph for Stop-n-Shop on an annual basis. Use parking-space hours as the measure of volume of activity and show fixed expenses on the bottom of the graph.
**b** What is the contribution margin ratio? What is the annual break-even point in dollars of parking revenue?
**c** Suppose that the five employees were taken off the hourly wage basis and paid 24 cents per car parked, with the same vacation pay as before. (1) How would this change the contribution margin per parking-space hour sold and total fixed expenses? (2) What annual sales revenue would be necessary to produce $44,500 per year income before taxes under these circumstances?

*27A-3* Offshore Sports Products manufactures fishing rods. The rods are sold by a manufacturer's representative who receives a sales commission equal to 10% of the sales price. For the coming year, the company has budgeted the following costs (excluding the 10% sales commission and income taxes) for the production and sale of 40,000 rods:

| | Budgeted Costs (Other Than Sales Commission and Income Taxes) | Budget Costs per Unit | Percentage of Costs Considered Variable |
|---|---|---|---|
| Direct materials | $400,000 | $10 | 100% |
| Direct labor | 320,000 | 8 | 100 |
| Factory overhead (fixed and variable) | 160,000 | 4 | 40 |
| Administrative expenses | 80,000 | 2 | 20 |
| Totals | $960,000 | $24 | |

**Instructions**

**a** Compute the sales price per unit that would result in an annual income before taxes of $210,000, assuming that the company produces and sells 40,000 fishing rods. (Hint: Remember that income before taxes and estimated costs other than the sales commission amount to only 90% of sales revenue. The remaining 10% must be paid to the manufacturer's representative.)

**b** Assuming that the company decides to sell the rods at a unit price of $40, compute the following:

(1) Total fixed costs budgeted for the year.

(2) Variable costs per unit, ***excluding*** the 10% sales commission.

(3) The contribution margin per unit, ***after considering the 10% sales commission.***

(4) The number of units that must be produced and sold annually to break even at a sales price of $40 per unit.

*27A-4* Landry Knife Company manufactures three different products. The estimated demand for the products for Year 4 is such that production will not be able to keep pace with incoming orders. Some pertinent data for each product are listed below:

| Product | Estimated Sales for Year 4, Units | Sales Price | Direct Material Cost | Direct Labor Cost | Variable Factory Overhead |
|---|---|---|---|---|---|
| A | 16,000 | $15.00 | $3.00 | $8.00 | $1.00 |
| B | 2,400 | 13.00 | 2.00 | 8.00 | 1.00 |
| C | 8,000 | 8.50 | 1.00 | 4.00 | 1.00 |

Direct labor costs an average of $8.00 per hour.

**Instructions**

**a** Prepare a schedule showing the contribution margin per one unit of each product and also the contribution margin per one hour of direct labor applied to the production of each class of product.

**b** If you were to reduce the production of one of the products in order to meet the demand for the others, what would that product be? Why? Assume that available direct labor hours represent the scarce resource which limits total output.

**c** Assume that the 16,000 hours of direct labor hours now used to produce product A are used to produce additional units of product C. What would be the effect on total contribution margin?

*27A-5* Audio Electronics manufactures tape decks and currently sells 9,250 units annually to producers of sound reproduction systems. Jay Wilson, president of the company, anticipates a 15% increase in the cost per unit of direct labor on January 1 of next year. He expects all other costs and expenses to remain unchanged. Wilson has asked you to assist him in developing the information he needs to formulate a reasonable product strategy for next year.

You are satisfied that volume is the primary factor affecting costs and expenses and have separated the semivariable costs and expenses into their fixed and variable segments. Beginning and ending inventories generally remain at a level of 1,000 units.

Below are the current-year data assembled for your analysis:

| | | |
|---|---|---|
| *Selling price per unit* | | *$200* |
| *Variable costs and expenses per unit:* | | |
| *Materials* | *$60* | |
| *Direct labor* | *40* | |
| *Factory overhead and selling and administrative expenses* | *20* | *120* |
| *Contribution margin per unit (40%)* | | *$ 80* |
| *Fixed costs and expenses (factory and other)* | | *$400,000* |

**Instructions**

**a** What increase in the selling price is necessary to cover the 15% increase in direct labor cost and still maintain the current contribution margin ratio of 40%?

**b** How many tape decks must be sold to maintain the current operating income of $340,000 if the sales price remains at $200 and the 15% wage increase goes into effect? Disregard income taxes.

**c** Wilson believes that an additional $600,000 of machinery (to be depreciated at 20% annually) will increase present capacity (10,000 units) by 40%. If all tape decks produced can be sold at the present price of $200 per unit and the wage increase goes into effect, how would the estimated operating income before capacity is increased compare with the estimated operating income after capacity is increased? Prepare schedules of estimated operating income at full capacity ***before*** and ***after*** the expansion. Disregard income taxes.

## Group B

*27B-1* Shown below is information relating to the only product sold by Southwind Corporation:

| | |
|---|---|
| *Selling price per unit* | *$ 40* |
| *Variable costs per unit* | *28* |
| *Fixed costs per year* | *180,000* |

Instructions Determine the following, showing as part of your answer the formula or relationships you used in your computations. For example, the formula used to determine the contribution margin ratio (part **a**) is:

$$\textbf{Contribution margin ratio} = \frac{\textbf{Sales} - \textbf{Variable costs}}{\textbf{Sales}}$$

(Hint: A summary of key relationships appears on page 1017.)

**a** Contribution margin ratio. (Use per-unit amounts in this computation.)
**b** Sales volume required to break even.
**c** Sales volume required to earn an annual income before taxes of $75,000.
**d** The margin of safety sales volume if annual sales total 20,000 units.
**e** Income before taxes if annual sales total 20,000 units

*27B-2* Rainbow Paints operates a chain of retail paint stores. Although the paint is sold under the Rainbow label, it is purchased from an independent paint manufacturer. Guy Walker, president of Rainbow Paints, is studying the advisability of opening another store. His estimates of monthly expenses for the proposed location are:

| | |
|---|---|
| *Fixed expenses:* | |
| *Occupancy costs* | *$3,160* |
| *Salaries* | *3,640* |
| *Other* | *1,200* |
| *Variable expenses (including cost of paint)* | *$6 per gallon* |

Although Rainbow stores sell several different types of paint, monthly sales revenue consistently averages $10 per gallon sold.

**Instructions**

**a** Compute the contribution margin ratio and the break-even point in dollar sales and in gallons sold for the proposed store.
**b** Draw a monthly profit-volume graph for the proposed store, assuming 3,000 gallons per month as the maximum sales potential. Show fixed expenses on the bottom of the graph.
**c** Walker thinks that the proposed store will sell between 2,200 and 2,600 gallons of paint per month. Compute the amount of income (before taxes) that would be earned per month at each of these sales volumes.

*27B-3* Bolt Industries is a newly organized manufacturing business which plans to manufacture and sell 100,000 units per year of a new product. The following estimates have been made of the company's costs and expenses (other than income taxes):

| | *Fixed* | *Variable per Unit* |
|---|---|---|
| *Manufacturing costs:* | | |
| *Direct materials* | | *$ 6.00* |
| *Direct labor* | | *4.00* |
| *Factory overhead* | *$170,000* | *2.00* |
| *Period expenses:* | | |
| *Selling expenses* | | *1.50* |
| *Administrative expenses* | *100,000* | |
| *Totals* | *$270,000* | *$13.50* |

**Instructions**

**a** What should the company establish as the sales price per unit if it sets a target of earning an income of $180,000 before taxes by producing and selling 100,000 units during the first year of operations? (Hint: First compute the required contribution margin per unit.)

**b** At the unit sales price computed in part **a**, how many units must the company produce and sell to break even? (Assume all units produced are sold.)
**c** What will be the margin of safety if the company produces and sells 100,000 units at the sales price computed in part **a**?

*27B-4* Optical Instruments produces two models of binoculars. Information for each model is shown below:

| | Model 100 | | Model 101 | |
|---|---|---|---|---|
| Sales price per unit | | $180 | | $120 |
| Costs and expenses per unit: | | | | |
| Direct materials | $51 | | $33 | |
| Direct labor | 33 | | 30 | |
| Factory overhead (applied at the rate of $18 per machine-hour) | 36 | | 18 | |
| Variable selling expenses | 30 | | 15 | |
| Total costs and expenses per unit | | 150 | | 96 |
| Profit per unit | | $ 30 | | $ 24 |
| Machine-hours required to produce one unit | | 2 | | 1 |

Total factory overhead amounts to $180,000 per month, one-third of which is fixed. The demand for either product is sufficient to keep the plant operating at full capacity of 10,000 machine-hours per month. Assume that ***only one product is to be produced in the future.***

**Instructions**

**a** Prepare a schedule showing the contribution margin per machine-hour for each product.
**b** Explain your recommendation as to which of the two products should be discontinued.

*27B-5* James Denny is considering investing in a vending machine operation involving 25 vending machines located in various plants around the city. The machine manufacturer reports that similar vending machine routes have produced a sales volume ranging from 1,000 to 2,000 units per machine per month. The following information is made available to Denny in evaluating the possible profitability of the operation.

(1) An investment of $50,000 will be required, $14,000 for merchandise and $36,000 for the 25 machines.
(2) The machines have a service life of five years and no salvage value at the end of that period. Depreciation will be computed on the straight-line basis.
(3) The merchandise (candy and soft drinks) retails for an average of 30 cents per unit and will cost Denny an average of 15 cents per unit.
(4) Owners of the buildings in which the machines are located are paid a commission of 3 cents per unit of candy and soft drinks sold.
(5) One man will be hired to service the machines. He will be paid $1,400 per month.
(6) Other expenses are estimated at $400 per month. These expenses do not vary with the number of units sold.

**Instructions**

**a** Determine the break-even volume in dollars and in units per month.
**b** Draw a monthly profit-volume graph for sales volume up to 2,000 units per machine per month. The graph should be similar to the one illustrated on page 1013 which shows the total contribution margin and the margin of safety.

**c** What sales volume per month will be necessary to produce a return of 30% (before taxes) on Denny's investment during his ***first year*** of operation?

**d** Denny is considering offering the building owners a flat rental of $30 per machine per month in lieu of the commission of 3 cents per unit sold. What effect would this change in commission arrangement have on his ***monthly*** break-even volume in terms of units?

## BUSINESS DECISION PROBLEM 27

Purple Cow Drive-Ins operates a chain of drive-ins selling only ice cream products. The following information is taken from the records of a typical drive-in now operated by the company:

| | | |
|---|---|---|
| *Average selling price of ice cream per gallon* | | $ 6.40 |
| *Number of gallons sold per month* | | 7,500 |
| *Variable expenses per gallon:* | | |
| *Ice cream* | $3.60 | |
| *Supplies (cups, cones, toppings, etc.)* | 1.20 | |
| *Total variable expenses per gallon* | | $ 4.80 |
| *Fixed expenses per month:* | | |
| *Rent on building and parking lot* | | $1,200.00 |
| *Utilities and upkeep* | | 760.00 |
| *Wages, including payroll taxes* | | 4,540.00 |
| *Manager's salary, including payroll taxes but excluding any bonus* | | 1,800.00 |
| *Other fixed expenses* | | 700.00 |
| *Total fixed expenses per month* | | $9,000.00 |

Based on these data, the monthly break-even sales volume is determined as follows:

$$\frac{\$9{,}000 \text{ (fixed expenses)}}{\$1.60 \text{ (contribution margin per unit)}} = 5{,}625 \text{ gallons (or } \$36{,}000)$$

**Instructions**

**a** Assuming that the manager has a contract calling for a bonus of 20 cents per gallon for each gallon sold beyond the break-even point, compute the number of gallons of ice cream that must be sold per month in order to earn a monthly income (before income taxes) of $2,800.

**b** In order to increase monthly income, the company is considering the following two alternatives:

(1) Reduce the selling price to $6.00 per gallon. This action is expected to increase the number of gallons sold by 40%. The manager would be paid a salary of $1,800 per month without a bonus.

(2) Spend $1,000 per month on advertising without any change in selling price. This action is expected to increase the number of gallons sold by 20%. The manager would be paid a salary of $1,800 per month without a bonus.

Which of these two alternatives would be more profitable for a typical drive-in store now selling 7,500 gallons? How many gallons must be sold per month under each alternative in order to break even? Give complete schedules in support of your answers and indicate to management which of the two alternatives it should adopt.

# 28

# CAPITAL BUDGETING AND OTHER AIDS TO MANAGERIAL DECISIONS

## Deciding among alternatives

All business decisions involve a choice among alternative courses of action. The criteria for such choices may be subjective, such as attitudes of employees, or the criteria may be objective, such as dollars of cost and revenue. Most decisions are influenced by a combination of both subjective and objective factors. In most situations it is possible to analyze some of the consequences of alternative actions in quantitative terms and to use the results of this analysis in making a decision.

If two alternative actions are under consideration, quantitative analysis will generally show which action will lead to the higher profit, or if an investment is involved, to the higher return on investment. ***Return on investment*** may be expressed as the ratio of income per period to the average investment for the period. Since income is influenced by both revenue and cost (expenses), any expected change either in revenue or in cost is relevant to the decision.

If a decision involves a new investment that will be recovered through increased net revenue or cost savings over a period of several years, an analysis of cash flows over time is appropriate, an analysis which requires the use of present value computations.

**Outline of an alternative-choice problem** The solution to most alternative-choice problems is formulated through the following steps:

1 Define the problem and identify the alternative solutions to be considered.
2 Measure and compare the consequences of each alternative, insofar as these consequences can be expressed quantitatively.
3 Evaluate the subjective factors and consider the extent to which they offset quantitative considerations.
4 Arrive at a decision.

Often the need for a managerial decision begins with a proposal to change what is now being done. Once the issue is raised, however, the alternatives to consider may be more numerous than simply making a choice between what is now being done and the specific proposed change. For example, suppose that the installation of a certain computer for data processing has been proposed. If we are seriously considering this computer, the alternatives may be to: (1) continue our present data processing system; (2) buy the computer in question; (3) buy some other type of computer; (4) lease the computer selected; or (5) improve the present data processing system by eliminating unnecessary steps. If too many alternatives are considered, the analysis becomes hopelessly complex. Fortunately, it is usually possible to rule out certain choices on the basis of a rough analysis, leaving only a few alternatives for serious consideration.

Measuring the outcome or consequences of alternative courses of action involves a forecast of the future, and some degree of error is always present. We may decide to estimate what will probably happen and proceed with our analysis on the assumption that our expectations will be fully realized. On the other hand, we may formulate two or more possible outcomes, assess the ***probability*** of each and arrive at an expected outcome which is a weighted average of the probability of a number of outcomes. It is clearly advantageous to express as many consequences of a decision in quantitative terms as possible because it is easy to find the net effect of quantitative factors. ***Costs*** and ***cost additions*** can be subtracted from ***revenue*** and ***cost savings*** to produce a net numerical representation of the advantage or disadvantage associated with a given course of action.

A few of the more common applications of alternative-choice decisions are discussed in the following sections.

## Illustration of an alternative-choice decision: unprofitable product line

The Suncraft Company manufactures household mixers in three models: Deluxe, Standard, and Economy. Below is an income statement showing product

***SUNCRAFT COMPANY***
***Income Statement—Last Year***

*Should the Deluxe and Economy models be dropped?*

| | Total | Deluxe Model | Standard Model | Economy Model |
|---|---|---|---|---|
| Sales (units) | 34,000 | 4,000 | 20,000 | 10,000 |
| Sales revenue | $960,000 | $160,000 | $600,000 | $200,000 |
| Manufacturing costs | 730,000 | 138,000 | 412,000 | 180,000 |
| Gross profit on sales | $230,000 | $ 22,000 | $188,000 | $ 20,000 |
| Operating expenses | 213,200 | 36,200 | 120,000 | 57,000 |
| Income or (loss) before taxes | $ 16,800 | $(14,200) | $ 68,000 | $(37,000) |

results. The overall profit margins for the last few years have been unsatisfactory, and the issue has been raised as to whether one or more of the models should be dropped from production.

This information suggests that if the company were to drop both the Deluxe and Economy models and produce only the Standard model it might expect earnings of around $68,000 per year—a striking improvement. On the other hand, it might be argued that the Deluxe model contributes $22,000 of gross profit and the Economy model $20,000, and that they should be continued since this is a positive contribution to operating expenses. The trouble with both these conclusions is that they are based on irrelevant information. The fact that a given expense is ***allocated*** to a particular product, for example, ***does not mean that this cost would disappear if the product were dropped.***

A first step in obtaining information more useful for decision-making purposes is to determine the contribution margin of each product. ***Contribution margin*** per unit is the difference between unit sales price and all variable costs per unit. The contribution margin per unit, based on the Suncraft Company data, is shown below:

*All models are covering their variable costs*

***SUNCRAFT COMPANY***

***Per-Unit Contribution Margin by Models—Last Year***

| | Deluxe Model | Standard Model | Economy Model |
|---|---|---|---|
| Selling price per unit | $40 | $30 | $20 |
| Variable costs per unit: | | | |
| Variable manufacturing costs | $30 | $18 | $15 |
| Variable operating expenses | 6 | 4 | 4 |
| Total variable costs per unit | $36 | $22 | $19 |
| Contribution margin per unit | $ 4 | $ 8 | $ 1 |

The per-unit contribution margins may be reconciled with the income statement figures as follows:

*Total contribution margin by products*

***SUNCRAFT COMPANY***

***Total Contribution Margin by Models—Last Year***

| | Total | Deluxe Model | Standard Model | Economy Model |
|---|---|---|---|---|
| Number of units sold (a) | 34,000 | 4,000 | 20,000 | 10,000 |
| Contribution margin per unit (b) | | $4 | $8 | $1 |
| Total contribution margin (a × b) | $186,000 | $ 16,000 | $160,000 | $ 10,000 |
| Less: All fixed costs | 169,200 | 30,200 | 92,000 | 47,000 |
| Income or (loss) before taxes | $ 16,800 | $(14,200) | $ 68,000 | $(37,000) |

The contribution margin analysis begins to sharpen the picture. Apparently each of the three models makes some contribution to fixed costs. Dropping the Deluxe model would reduce income by $16,000 and dropping the Economy model would reduce income by $10,000. Before accepting this conclusion, however, we should ask ourselves whether the assumptions used in dividing costs into their fixed and variable components are sound.

Two assumptions, inherent in the fixed and variable cost data, are important to our tentative conclusions. First, we have assumed that the variable and fixed relationship of cost to volume holds for variations in output all the way down to zero for a particular model. In our discussion of cost-volume relationships in Chapter 27, we noted that the division of costs into fixed and variable components is usually valid for variations in output somewhat above and below the normal scale of production. If manufacture of a product is discontinued entirely, however, the nature of operations may be changed so that some fixed costs can be eliminated in their entirety.

Secondly, the use of contribution margin data rests on the assumption that the sales of any particular model are independent of the sales of the other two models. It is entirely possible that dropping either the Deluxe or Economy model ***will result in an increase in sales of the other models;*** it is also possible that dropping one model ***may adversely affect the sale of the other models.***

Let us see how these two factors might affect our analysis. In view of its low contribution margin, the Economy model seems the most likely candidate for elimination. Assume that a careful study of fixed costs is made and indicates that the elimination of this model would enable the Suncraft Company to reduce certain fixed costs by $7,000.

It seems likely that some buyers of the Economy model might shift to the Standard model if the Economy model were no longer offered. When asked for an estimate of this factor, the sales manager presented the following report:

*Sales manager's estimate of shift in sales*

| Number of Economy Model Sales That Might Shift to Standard Model (per Year) | × | My Estimate of the Probability That This Many Would Shift | = | Expected Shift in Sales |
|---|---|---|---|---|
| 1,000 | | .05 | | 50 |
| 2,000 | | .10 | | 200 |
| 3,000 | | .30 | | 900 |
| 4,000 | | .40 | | 1,600 |
| 5,000 or more | | .15 | | 750 |
| | | | | 3,500 units |

By incorporating the expected reduction in fixed costs and shift in sales into our analysis, we can prepare the schedule shown below:

*Complete analysis of decision variables*

**SUNCRAFT COMPANY**

**Estimate of Annual Change in Income from Dropping Economy Model**

| | | |
|---|---|---|
| Increase in annual income from dropping Economy model: | | |
| Estimated reduction in costs presently classified as fixed | | $ 7,000 |
| Gain in contribution margin because of shift in sales from Economy model to Standard model: | | |
| Sales manager's expected sales shift to Standard model | 3,500 | |
| Contribution margin per unit of Standard model | ×$8 | 28,000 |
| Total increase in annual income | | $35,000 |
| Less: Reduction in annual income from dropping Economy model: | | |
| Contribution margin on Economy models now sold: 10,000 units × $1 contribution margin per unit | | 10,000 |
| **Estimated net increase in annual income if Economy model is dropped** | | **$25,000** |

We have now isolated the data relevant to the decision. If our assumptions and estimates are realized, we can increase the annual income (before taxes) of the Suncraft Company by $25,000 (from $16,800 to $41,800) by dropping the Economy model from the line.

## Accepting special orders

In many business decisions, the relevant factors are the ***differences*** between the costs incurred and the revenue earned under alternative courses of action. These differences are often called ***incremental*** (or ***differential***) costs and revenue. Costs which do not vary among alternative courses of action are not relevant in making alternative-choice decisions.

The decision of whether to accept an order for an additional volume of business at special terms may be used to illustrate the concept of incremental analysis. Assume, for example, that Sports Supply Company estimates its production of golf balls for the coming year at 200,000 dozen, although its plant capacity is approximately 275,000 dozen golf balls per year. The company receives an order from a foreign company for 50,000 dozen golf balls to be used for sales promotion efforts. The foreign company would pay all shipping costs and wants a special imprint on the ball. The company normally sells golf balls for $12 per dozen and the foreign company's offer is for $8 per dozen. If the order is accepted, the company will have to spend $15,000 in cash to design and set up the special imprint on the golf balls. A summary of estimated results for the coming year is presented below:

*A special order is profitable if revenue from it exceeds incremental costs*

| | Planned Output (200,000 Dozen) | With Special Order (250,000 Dozen) | Incremental Analysis |
|---|---|---|---|
| Sales: $12 per dozen | $2,400,000 | $2,400,000 | |
| $8 per dozen | | 400,000 | $400,000 |
| Variable costs: | | | |
| $6 per dozen | (1,200,000) | (1,500,000) | (300,000) |
| Fixed costs | (900,000) | (900,000) | |
| Special imprint costs | | (15,000) | (15,000) |
| Estimated operating income | $ 300,000 | $ 385,000 | $ 85,000 |

Note that the average cost of producing golf balls without the special order is $10.50 per dozen [($1,200,000 + $900,000) ÷ 200,000 dozen]. If a decision were made based on this average cost, the special order would probably be rejected. Incremental analysis, however, shows that ***incremental revenue*** from accepting the special order amounts to $400,000, while the ***incremental cost*** is only $315,000. Thus, accepting the special order will increase Sports Supply Company's operating income by $85,000.

The relevant factors in this type of decision are the incremental revenue that will be earned and the additional (incremental) cost that will be incurred by accepting the special order. ***The average cost of production is not relevant to the decision.***

In evaluating the merits of a special order such as the one received by the Sports Supply Company, we must give particular attention to the effect that such an order may have on the company's regular sales volume and selling prices. Obviously, it would not be wise for the Sports Supply Company to sell 50,000 dozen golf balls to a domestic company which might try to sell the golf balls to the regular customers of Sports Supply Company for, say, $10 per dozen.

### Make or buy decisions

In many manufacturing situations, companies are often faced with decisions whether (1) to produce a certain component part required in the assembly of its finished products or (2) to buy the part from outside suppliers. If a company produces a part which can be purchased at a lower cost, it may be more profitable for the company to buy the part and utilize its productive resources for other purposes.

For example, if a company can buy a part for $5 per unit which costs the company $6 per unit to produce, the choice seems to be clearly in favor of buying. But the astute reader will quickly raise the question, "What is included in the cost of $6 per unit?" Assume that the $6 unit cost of producing 10,000 units was determined as follows:

*What is the variable cost per unit for this company?*

| | *Cost of Part* |
|---|---|
| *Direct materials* | *$ 8,000* |
| *Direct labor* | *12,500* |
| *Variable factory overhead* | *10,000* |
| *Fixed factory overhead* | *29,500* |
| *Total costs* | *$60,000* |
| *Cost per unit ($60,000 ÷ 10,000 units)* | *$6* |

A careful review of operations indicates that if the production of this part were discontinued, all the cost of direct materials and direct labor and $9,000 of the variable factory overhead would be eliminated. In addition, $2,500 of the fixed factory overhead can be eliminated. These, then, are the relevant costs in producing the 10,000 parts, and we can summarize them as follows:

*Incremental costs ($32,000) exceed the variable cost ($30,500); however, it would cost $50,000 to buy the part from outside suppliers*

| | *Make the Part* | *Buy the Part* | *Incremental Analysis* |
|---|---|---|---|
| *Manufacturing costs for 10,000 units:* | | | |
| *Direct materials* | *$ 8,000* | | *$ 8,000* |
| *Direct labor* | *12,500* | | *12,500* |
| *Variable factory overhead* | *10,000* | *$ 1,000* | *9,000* |
| *Fixed factory overhead* | *29,500* | *27,000* | *2,500* |
| *Purchase price of part, $5 per unit* | | *50,000* | *(50,000)* |
| *Totals* | *$60,000* | *$78,000* | *$(18,000)* |

It appears that the company should continue to produce this part. The incremental cost per unit is only $3.20 [($8,000 + $12,500 + $9,000 + $2,500) ÷ 10,000 units], and it would cost the company $1.80 per unit (or $18,000) ***more*** to buy the part than it is costing to produce. If, however, in place of this particular part, the company had an opportunity to manufacture another product which would produce a contribution margin greater than $18,000, then the part should be purchased.

Note that, in the foregoing analysis, not all the variable factory overhead costs incurred in producing the part would be eliminated if the part were not produced and that only $2,500 of fixed factory costs would be eliminated. We have assumed these facts in order to illustrate that not all variable costs are necessarily incremental and that ***some fixed costs may be incremental*** in a given situation.

## Sunk costs and opportunity costs

The only costs relevant to a decision are those costs which vary among the alternative courses of action being considered. A ***sunk cost*** is one which has been irrevocably incurred by past actions. Sunk costs are not relevant to decisions because they cannot be changed regardless of what decision is made. The term ***out-of-pocket cost*** is often used to describe costs which have not yet been incurred and which may vary among the alternative courses of action. Out-of-pocket costs, therefore, are relevant in making decisions.

**Scrap or rebuild defective units** To illustrate the irrelevance of sunk costs, assume that 500 television sets which cost $80,000 to manufacture are found to be defective and management must decide what to do with them. These sets may be sold "as is" for $30,000, or they can be rebuilt and placed in good condition at an additional out-of-pocket cost of $60,000. If the sets are rebuilt, they can be sold for the regular price of $100,000. Should the sets be sold as is or rebuilt?

Regardless of whether the sets are sold or rebuilt, the $80,000 sunk cost has already been incurred. The relevant considerations in the decision to sell the sets as is or rebuild are the incremental revenue and the incremental cost. By rebuilding the sets, the company will realize $70,000 more revenue than if the sets are sold as is. The incremental cost necessary to obtain this incremental revenue is the $60,000 cost of rebuilding the sets. Thus, the company will be $10,000 ($70,000 − $60,000) better off if it rebuilds the sets.

**Opportunity costs** At this stage, we should give consideration to the concept of ***opportunity costs.*** An opportunity cost is the benefit which could be obtained by ***pursuing another course of action.*** As a simple illustration, assume that a student passes up a summer job that pays $1,800 in order to attend summer school. The $1,800 may be viewed as an opportunity cost of attending summer school.

Opportunity costs are not recorded in the accounting records, but they are an important factor in many business decisions. Ignoring opportunity costs is a common source of error in making cost analyses. In our example involving the defective television sets, we determined that the company could earn an additional $10,000 by rebuilding the sets rather than by selling them as is. Suppose, however, that rebuilding the sets would require the use of production facilities which would otherwise be used to manufacture new sets worth $20,000 in excess of their cost. Obviously, the company should not forego a $20,000 profit in order to earn $10,000. When this $20,000 opportunity cost is considered, it becomes evident that the company should sell the defective sets as is and use its production facilities for the manufacture of new sets.

## CAPITAL BUDGETING

Perhaps the most common alternative-choice problems involve decisions for replacement of plant assets or expansion of productive facilities. The process of planning and evaluating proposals for investment in plant assets is called ***capital budgeting.*** Capital budgeting decisions are complicated by the fact that the decision must be made from estimates of future operating results, which by their nature involve a considerable degree of uncertainty. Yet these decisions are crucial to the long-run financial health of a business enterprise. Not only are large amounts of money committed for long periods of time, but many capital budgeting decisions are difficult or impossible to reverse once the funds have been committed and the project has begun. Thus, companies may benefit from good capital budgeting decisions and suffer from poor ones for many years.

Many nonfinancial factors are considered in making capital budgeting decisions. For example, many companies give high priority to creating new jobs and avoiding layoffs. However, it is also essential that investments in plant assets earn a satisfactory return on the funds invested. Without this return, investors will not be willing to make funds available to finance the project and the company will not be able to generate sufficient funds for future investment projects.

Capital budgeting is a broad field, involving many sophisticated techniques for evaluating the financial and nonfinancial considerations. We shall limit our discussion in this area to three of the most common techniques of evaluating investment opportunities: payback period, return on average investment, and discounted cash flow analysis.

To illustrate these techniques, let us assume that Tanner Corporation is considering several alternative investments, including the purchase of equipment to produce a new product. The equipment costs $45,000, has a 10-year service life, and an estimated salvage value of $5,000. Tanner Corporation estimates that production and sale of the new product will increase the company's net income by $5,000 per year, computed as follows:

| | | |
|---|---|---|
| *Estimated sales of new product* | | *$40,000* |
| *Deduct estimated expenses:* | | |
| *Depreciation on new equipment [($45,000 − $5,000) ÷ 10 years]* | *$ 4,000* | |
| *Manufacturing costs other than depreciation* | *20,000* | |
| *Additional selling and general expenses* | *6,000* | *30,000* |
| *Estimated increase in before-tax income* | | *$10,000* |
| *Less: Additional income taxes (50%)* | | *5,000* |
| *Estimated increase in net income* | | *$ 5,000* |

Most capital budgeting techniques involve analysis of the estimated annual net cash flows pertaining to the investment. Annual net cash flow is the excess of cash receipts over cash payments in a given year. In our example, assume that all revenue is received in cash and all expenses other than depreciation are paid in cash. Tanner Corporation should expect an annual ***net cash flow of $9,000*** (\$40,000 – \$20,000 – \$6,000 – \$5,000) from sales of the new product. Note that annual net cash flow exceeds estimated net income (\$5,000) by the amount of the depreciation expense (\$4,000). This is because none of the cash received as revenue is paid out as depreciation expense. Other differences which may exist between net income and net cash flow were discussed in Chapter 21.

## Payback period

The ***payback period*** is the length of time necessary to recover the entire cost of an investment from the resulting annual net cash flow. In our example, the payback period is computed as follows:

$$\frac{\text{Amount to be invested}}{\text{Estimated annual net cash flow}} = \frac{\$45{,}000}{\$9{,}000} = 5 \text{ years}$$

In selecting among alternative investment opportunities, a short payback period is considered desirable because the sooner the amount of the investment is recovered, the sooner the funds may be put to other use. A short payback period also reduces the risk that changes in economic conditions will prevent full recovery of the investment. Before an investment can be considered profitable, the life of the investment must exceed the payback period. However, the payback period ignores the total life and, therefore, the total profitability of the investment. For this reason, the payback period should never be the only factor considered in a major capital budgeting decision.

## Return on average investment

The ***rate of return on average investment*** is the average annual net income from an investment expressed as a percentage of the ***average*** amount invested. Tanner Corporation will have to invest \$45,000 in the new equipment, but each year depreciation will reduce the carrying value of this asset by \$4,000. Since the annual net cash flow will exceed net income by this amount, we may view depreciation expense as providing for the recovery of the amount originally invested. Thus, the amount invested in the equipment at any given time is represented by the carrying value (cost less accumulated depreciation) of the asset.

When straight-line depreciation is used, the carrying value of an asset decreases uniformly over the asset's life. Thus, the average carrying value is equal to an amount halfway between the asset's original cost and its salvage value. (When the expected salvage value is zero, the average investment is simply one-half of the original investment.) Mathematically, the average amount invested over the life of an asset may be determined as follows:

$$\text{Average investment} = \frac{\text{Original cost} + \text{Salvage value}}{2}$$

Thus, Tanner Corporation will have an average investment in the new equipment of ($45,000 + $5,000) ÷ 2, or $25,000. We may compute the expected rate of return on this average investment as follows:

$$\frac{\text{Average estimated net income}}{\text{Average investment}} = \frac{\$5{,}000}{\$25{,}000} = 20\%$$

In deciding whether 20% is a satisfactory rate of return, Tanner Corporation should consider such factors as the rate of return available from alternative investment opportunities, the risk involved in actually realizing the expected rate of return, the corporation's cost of capital, and the nonfinancial factors relating to the investment. In comparing alternative investment opportunities, management usually prefers the investment with the lowest risk, highest rate of return, and shortest payback period. Of course, the same investment is seldom superior to all others in every respect. Thus, managers must consider many subjective factors in making their decisions.

A weakness in the concept of return on average investment is the failure to consider the ***timing*** of the future cash flows. Computing the average annual net income, for example, ignores the question of whether the cash receipts will occur early or late in the life of the investment. Also, computing the average investment in the equipment fails to consider whether the purchase price of the equipment must be paid in advance or in installments stretching over a period of years. A technique which does take into account the timing of cash flows is called ***discounting*** future cash flows.

## Discounting future cash flows

As explained in Chapter 18, the present value of a future cash flow is the amount that a knowledgeable investor would pay today for the right to receive that future amount. The exact amount of the present value depends upon (1) the amount of the future payment, (2) the length of time until the future amount will be received, and (3) the rate of return required by the investor. ***Discounting*** is the process of determining the present value of cash flows.

The use of present value tables to discount future cash flows was demonstrated in the appendix, entitled Applications of Present Value, at the end of Chapter 18. (Readers who are not familiar with the concept of present value and with the use of present value tables should review that appendix, beginning on page 691, before continuing with this chapter.) The two present value tables presented in the appendix are repeated on page 1038 for your convenience.

Table 1 shows the present value of a single lump-sum payment of $1 to be received $n$ periods (years) in the future. Table 2 shows the present value of a $1 annuity—that is, $1 to be received each year for $n$ consecutive years. For illustrative purposes, both tables have been kept short and include only selected discount rates and extend for a limited number of periods. However, the tables

Table 1

**Present Value of $1 Due in n Periods**

| Number of Periods (n) | Discount Rate 1% | 1½% | 5% | 6% | 10% | 12% | 15% | 20% |
|---|---|---|---|---|---|---|---|---|
| 1 | .990 | .985 | .952 | .943 | .909 | .893 | .870 | .833 |
| 2 | .980 | .971 | .907 | .890 | .826 | .797 | .756 | .694 |
| 3 | .971 | .956 | .864 | .840 | .751 | .712 | .658 | .579 |
| 4 | .961 | .942 | .823 | .792 | .683 | .636 | .572 | .482 |
| 5 | .951 | .928 | .784 | .747 | .621 | .567 | .497 | .402 |
| 6 | .942 | .915 | .746 | .705 | .564 | .507 | .432 | .335 |
| 7 | .933 | .901 | .711 | .665 | .513 | .452 | .376 | .279 |
| 8 | .923 | .888 | .677 | .627 | .467 | .404 | .327 | .233 |
| 9 | .914 | .875 | .645 | .592 | .424 | .361 | .284 | .194 |
| 10 | .905 | .862 | .614 | .558 | .386 | .322 | .247 | .162 |
| 20 | .820 | .742 | .377 | .312 | .149 | .104 | .061 | .026 |
| 24 | .788 | .700 | .310 | .247 | .102 | .066 | .035 | .013 |

Table 2

**Present Value of $1 to Be Received Periodically for n Periods**

| Number of Periods (n) | Discount Rate 1% | 1½% | 5% | 6% | 10% | 12% | 15% | 20% |
|---|---|---|---|---|---|---|---|---|
| 1 | 0.990 | 0.985 | 0.952 | 0.943 | 0.909 | 0.893 | 0.870 | 0.833 |
| 2 | 1.970 | 1.956 | 1.859 | 1.833 | 1.736 | 1.690 | 1.626 | 1.528 |
| 3 | 2.941 | 2.912 | 2.723 | 2.673 | 2.487 | 2.402 | 2.283 | 2.106 |
| 4 | 3.902 | 3.854 | 3.546 | 3.465 | 3.170 | 3.037 | 2.855 | 2.589 |
| 5 | 4.853 | 4.783 | 4.329 | 4.212 | 3.791 | 3.605 | 3.352 | 2.991 |
| 6 | 5.795 | 5.697 | 5.076 | 4.917 | 4.355 | 4.111 | 3.784 | 3.326 |
| 7 | 6.728 | 6.598 | 5.786 | 5.582 | 4.868 | 4.564 | 4.160 | 3.605 |
| 8 | 7.652 | 7.486 | 6.463 | 6.210 | 5.335 | 4.968 | 4.487 | 3.837 |
| 9 | 8.566 | 8.361 | 7.108 | 6.802 | 5.759 | 5.328 | 4.772 | 4.031 |
| 10 | 9.471 | 9.222 | 7.722 | 7.360 | 6.145 | 5.650 | 5.019 | 4.192 |
| 20 | 18.046 | 17.169 | 12.462 | 11.470 | 8.514 | 7.469 | 6.259 | 4.870 |
| 24 | 21.243 | 20.030 | 13.799 | 12.550 | 8.985 | 7.784 | 6.434 | 4.937 |

contain the appropriate rates and periods for all problem material in this chapter.

The discount rate may be viewed as the investor's required rate of return. The present value of the future cash flows is the maximum amount that the investor may pay for the investment and still expect to earn the required rate of return. Therefore, an investment is considered desirable when its cost is less than the present value of the expected future cash flows. Conversely, an investment is undesirable when its cost is greater than the present value of expected future cash flows.

The higher the discount rate being used, the lower will be the resulting present value. Therefore the investor will be interested in the investment only at a lower price. The "appropriate" discount rate for determining the present value of a specific investment depends upon the nature of that investment, the alternative investment opportunities available, and the investor's cost of capital.

Let us now apply the concept of discounting cash flows to our continuing example of the Tanner Corporation. We shall assume that Tanner Corporation requires a 15% annual rate of return on investments in new plant assets. The $45,000 investment in equipment is expected to produce annual net cash flows of $9,000 for 10 years. Table 2 on page 1038 shows that the present value of $1 to be received annually for 10 years, discounted at an annual rate of 15%, is 5.019. Therefore, the present value of $9,000 received annually for 10 years is $9,000 × 5.019, or $45,171.

In addition to the annual cash flows, Tanner Corporation expects to receive $5,000 in salvage value for the equipment at the end of the tenth year. Referring to Table 1 on page 1038, we see that the present value of $1 due in 10 years, discounted at 15% per year, is .247. Thus, the present value of $5,000 to be received 10 years hence is $5,000 × .247, or $1,235. We may now analyze the proposal to invest in the equipment as follows:

| | |
|---|---|
| *Present value of expected annual cash flows ($9,000 × 5.019)* | *$45,171* |
| *Present value of proceeds from disposal of equipment ($5,000 × .247)* | *1,235* |
| *Total present value of future cash flows* | *$46,406* |
| *Amount to be invested (payable in advance)* | *45,000* |
| *Net present value of proposed investment* | *$ 1,406* |

This analysis indicates that the present value of the expected net cash flows from the investment, discounted at an annual rate of 15%, amounts to $46,406. This is the maximum amount which Tanner Corporation could afford to invest in the project and still expect to earn the required 15% annual rate of return. Since the actual cost of the investment is only $45,000 Tanner Corporation can expect to earn more than 15%.

The ***net present value*** of the proposal is the difference between the total present value of the net cash flows and the cost of the investment. When the net present value is equal to zero, the investment provides a rate of return exactly equal to the rate used in discounting the cash flows. A ***positive*** net present value means that the investment provides a rate of return ***greater than the discount rate;*** a ***negative*** net present value means that the investment yields a return of ***less*** than the discount rate. Since the discount rate is usually the minimum rate of return required by the investor, proposals with a positive net present value are considered acceptable and those with a negative net present value are viewed as unacceptable.

### Replacement of old equipment

A problem often facing management is whether it should buy new and more efficient equipment or whether it should continue to use existing equipment. Assume, for example, that the Ardmore Company is meeting increasing competition in the sale of product Q. The sales manager believes the source of the trouble is that competitors have installed more efficient equipment, which has enabled them to reduce prices. The issue raised therefore is whether Ardmore Company should: (1) buy new equipment at a cost of $120,000, or (2) continue using its present equipment. We will make the simplifying assumption that both the new and present equipment have a remaining useful life of five years and neither will have any residual value. The new equipment will produce substantial savings in direct labor, direct materials, and factory overhead costs. The company does not believe the use of new equipment will have any effect on sales volume, so the decision rests entirely on whether cost savings are possible.

The old equipment has a book value of $100,000 but can be sold for only $20,000 if it is replaced. At first glance, the resulting $80,000 loss on disposal appears to be a good reason for not replacing the old equipment. However, the cost of the old equipment is a ***sunk cost*** and is not relevant to the decision. If the old machinery is sold, its book value contributes to the amount of the loss; if the old machinery is retained, its book value will be recognized as expense through future charges to depreciation. Thus, this cost cannot be avoided by Ardmore Company regardless of which decision is made. From a present value standpoint, there is some benefit to recognizing this sunk cost as a loss in the current period inasmuch as the related tax reduction will occur this year rather than over the remaining life of the equipment.

In deciding whether to replace the old equipment, Ardmore Company should determine the ***present value of the incremental net cash flows*** resulting from replacement of the old machinery. This present value may then be compared with the cost of the new equipment to determine whether the investment will provide the required rate of return. To compute the incremental annual net cash flow from replacing the old equipment, management must consider both the annual cash savings in manufacturing costs and the difference in annual income taxes. Income taxes will differ under the alternative courses of action because of differences in (1) variable manufacturing costs and (2) annual depreciation expense.

Let us assume that the new machinery will result in a $34,000 annual cash savings in variable manufacturing costs. However, annual depreciation on the new equipment will be $24,000 ($120,000 ÷ 5 years), whereas annual depreciation on the old equipment is $20,000 ($100,000 ÷ 5 years). This $4,000 increase in depreciation expense means that purchase of the new equipment will ***increase*** taxable income by $30,000 ($34,000 cost savings less $4,000 additional depreciation). Assuming a tax rate of 40%, purchase of the new equipment will increase annual income tax expense by $12,000 ($30,000 × .40). The incremental annual net cash flow from owning the new machinery, therefore, amounts to $22,000 ($34,000 cost savings less $12,000 additional income tax expense).

We shall assume that Ardmore Company requires a 12% return on investments in plant assets. Referring to the annuity table on page 1038, we see that the present value of $1 received annually for five years is 3.605. Therefore, $22,000 received annually for five years, discounted at an annual rate of 12%, has a present value of $79,310 ($22,000 × 3.605). In addition to the present value of the annual net cash flows, however, we must consider two other factors: (1) the proceeds from sale of the old equipment and (2) the tax savings resulting from the loss on disposal.

The $20,000 proceeds from sale of the old equipment will be received immediately and, therefore, have a present value of $20,000. The $80,000 loss on disposal results in a $32,000 reduction ($80,000 × .4) in income taxes payable at the end of the first year. The present value of $32,000 one year hence discounted at 12% is $28,576 ($32,000 × .893), as determined from a present value table.

We may now determine the net present value of the proposal to replace the old equipment with new as follows:

| | |
|---|---|
| *Present value of incremental annual cash flows ($22,000 × 3.605)* | *$ 79,310* |
| *Present value of proceeds from sale of old equipment* | *20,000* |
| *Present value of tax savings from loss on disposal ($32,000 × .893)* | *28,576* |
| *Total present value* | *$127,886* |
| *Amount to be invested* | *120,000* |
| *Net present value* | *$ 7,886* |

Since the total present value of all future cash flows from acquiring the new equipment exceeds the cost of the investment, Ardmore Company should replace the old equipment with new.

## VARIABLE (DIRECT) COSTING AS AN AID TO MANAGEMENT

The discussion in Chapter 25 dealing with job order and process cost systems was based on the assumption that the actual manufacturing costs incurred in any given period are assigned to the units produced in that period. Manufacturing costs (fixed and variable) were ultimately associated with the goods in process inventory, the finished goods inventory, and the cost of goods sold. This procedure is known as ***full costing*** or ***absorption costing.*** An alternative costing assumption which can be useful to management is called ***variable costing*** (or ***direct costing***).

The three basic features of variable costing are:

1 All manufacturing costs are first divided into those which are variable and those which are fixed.
2 Variable manufacturing costs are treated as ***product costs*** and are assigned to the goods produced. Some of the goods produced are found in ending inventories (goods in process and finished goods) and the rest become a part of cost of goods sold during the current period.
3 Fixed manufacturing costs, along with all selling and administrative expenses, are treated as ***period costs*** and are charged to revenue of the period in which they are incurred.

The flow of costs under variable and full costing is illustrated in the diagram below:

***Flow of Costs under Variable and Full Costing***

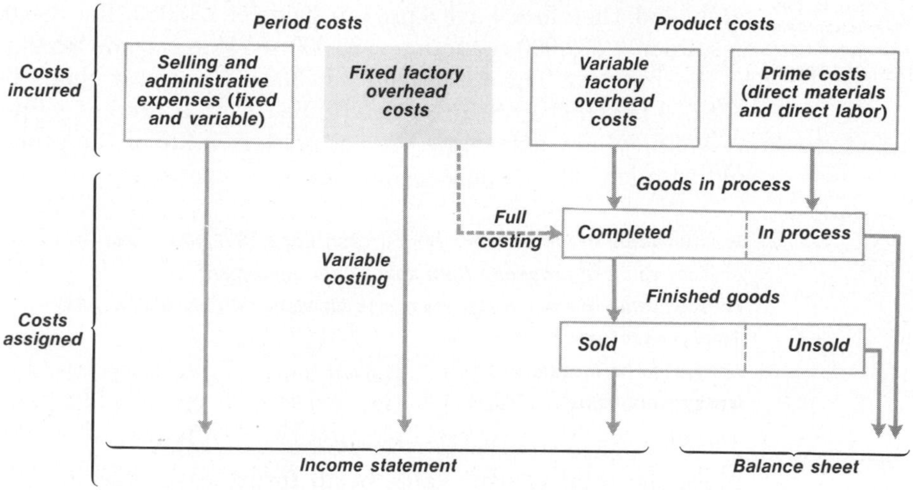


The diagram shows that selling and administrative expenses and fixed factory overhead costs are charged to revenue of the current period when variable costing is used. As a result, the Goods in Process account is charged only with variable manufacturing costs, and the ending inventories of goods in process and finished goods include only variable manufacturing costs. When full costing is used, fixed factory overhead costs are treated as product costs, a portion of which is assigned to the ending inventories of goods in process and finished goods.

## Illustration of variable costing

The differences between variable costing and full costing may be illustrated by preparing an income statement under each method, using the following information for the Hamilton Corporation:

*Data for Year 1*

| | |
|---|---|
| *Production—Year 1 (assume no goods in process)* | *40,000 units* |
| *Sales—Year 1* | *30,000 units* |
| *Sales price per unit* | *$10* |
| *Variable manufacturing costs per unit* | *$4* |
| *Variable selling and administrative expenses per unit* | *$1* |
| *Fixed costs:* | |
| *Manufacturing* | *$40,000* |
| *Selling and administrative expenses* | *$30,000* |

A partial income statement based on this information, using the variable cost assumption, appears below:

*Fixed factory overhead costs excluded from inventory—Year 1*

**HAMILTON CORPORATION**

*Partial Income Statement—Variable Costing*

*Year 1*

| | | |
|---|---|---|
| *Sales (30,000 units @ $10)* | | *$300,000* |
| *Cost of goods sold (30,000 units @ $4 variable manufacturing costs)* | | *120,000* |
| *Manufacturing margin* | | *$180,000* |
| *Variable selling and administrative expenses (30,000 units @ $1)* | | *30,000* |
| *Contribution margin* | | *$150,000* |
| *Fixed costs:* | | |
| *Manufacturing* | *$40,000* | |
| *Selling and administrative expenses* | *30,000* | *70,000* |
| *Income from operations* | | *$ 80,000* |

*(Ending inventory of finished goods, 10,000 units @ $4 = $40,000)*

In the partial income statement using variable costing, the variable manufacturing costs of the units sold are deducted from sales in arriving at the ***manufacturing margin.*** When variable selling and administrative expenses are deducted from the manufacturing margin we have the ***contribution margin*** which is available to cover all fixed (or period) costs. Income from operations is then determined by subtracting all fixed costs from the contribution margin.

A partial income statement using the same information but following the traditional full cost assumption is presented on page 1044.

## Effect of variable costing on income and inventory

Comparing the partial income statements above and on page 1044 shows that the income from operations using full costing exceeds by $10,000 the income using variable costing. This difference is explained by analyzing the disposition of fixed manufacturing costs under the two costing methods. Under variable costing the fixed manufacturing costs, $40,000, are recognized as expenses in the current period; under full costing, fixed manufacturing costs are apportioned between the ending inventory of finished goods and the cost of goods sold. Since only 75%

of units produced were sold, only $30,000 of the fixed manufacturing costs were included in the cost of goods sold figure.

*Fixed factory overhead costs included in inventory—Year 1*

**HAMILTON CORPORATION**
**Partial Income Statement—Full Costing**
**Year 1**

| | |
|---|---|
| Sales (30,000 units @ $10) | $300,000 |
| Cost of goods sold* | 150,000 |
| Gross profit on sales | $150,000 |
| Selling and administrative expenses (fixed and variable) | 60,000 |
| Income from operations | $ 90,000 |

*Computation of cost of goods sold:

| | |
|---|---|
| Variable manufacturing costs (40,000 units @ $4) | $160,000 |
| Fixed manufacturing costs | 40,000 |
| Full cost of production (40,000 units @ $5) | $200,000 |
| Less: Ending inventory of finished goods (10,000 units @ $5) | 50,000 |
| Cost of goods sold (30,000 units) | $150,000 |

When ***inventories are increasing*** (that is, units produced exceed units sold), the use of variable costing will result in a smaller net income than when full costing is used because under variable costing fixed manufacturing costs are charged immediately to expense. Under full costing, fixed manufacturing costs are included in inventories. As inventories increase, some fixed costs expensed under variable costing will remain in inventories under full costing. When ***inventories are decreasing*** (that is, units sold exceed units produced), the income under variable costing will be larger than the income under full costing, because the decrease in inventory will be charged against revenue at less than full cost.

To illustrate one possible case (an increase in inventories), assume that the sales volume for the Hamilton Corporation in Year 2 remained unchanged at 30,000 units at $10 per unit, and that the level of production increased to 50,000, thus increasing the ending inventory of finished goods from 10,000 units to 30,000 units. The following information is available for Year 2. (***Note that unit variable costs and total fixed costs are exactly the same as in Year 1.***)

*Data for Year 2*

| | |
|---|---|
| Production—Year 2 (assume no goods in process) | 50,000 units |
| Sales—Year 2 | 30,000 units |
| Sales price per unit | $10 |
| Variable manufacturing costs per unit | $4 |
| Variable selling and administrative expenses per unit | $1 |
| Fixed costs: | |
| Manufacturing | $40,000 |
| Selling and administrative expenses | $30,000 |

A partial income statement for Year 2, using the variable cost assumption, is illustrated on page 1045.

*Fixed factory overhead excluded from inventory—Year 2*

**HAMILTON CORPORATION**
**Partial Income Statement—Variable Costing**
**Year 2**

| | | |
|---|---|---|
| Sales (30,000 @ $10) | | $300,000 |
| Cost of goods sold (30,000 units @ $4 variable manufacturing costs) | | 120,000 |
| Manufacturing margin | | $180,000 |
| Variable selling and administrative expenses (30,000 units @ $1) | | 30,000 |
| Contribution margin | | $150,000 |
| Fixed costs: | | |
| Manufacturing | $40,000 | |
| Selling and administrative expenses | 30,000 | 70,000 |
| Income from operations | | $ 80,000 |

(Ending inventory of finished goods, 30,000 units @ $4 = $120,000)

A full costing partial income statement for Year 2 appears below:

*Fixed factory overhead costs included in inventory—Year 2*

**HAMILTON CORPORATION**
**Partial Income Statement—Full Costing**
**Year 2**

| | |
|---|---|
| Sales (30,000 @ $10) | $300,000 |
| Cost of goods sold* | 146,000 |
| Gross profit on sales | $154,000 |
| Selling and administrative expenses (fixed and variable) | 60,000 |
| Income from operations | $ 94,000 |

*Computation of cost of goods sold:

| | |
|---|---|
| Beginning inventory, 10,000 units (from Year 1) | $ 50,000 |
| Add: Variable manufacturing costs (50,000 units @ $4) | 200,000 |
| Fixed manufacturing costs, Year 2 | 40,000 |
| Goods available for sale (60,000 units) | $290,000 |
| Less: Ending inventory on fifo basis, 30,000 units @ $4.80 ($240,000 ÷ 50,000 units) | 144,000 |
| Cost of goods sold (30,000 units) | $146,000 |

Briefly, we can summarize the results for the two years using variable costing and full costing as follows:

*Results using variable and full costing compared*

| | Income from Operations | | | Ending Inventory | | |
|---|---|---|---|---|---|---|
| | Sales | Variable Costing | Full Costing | Variable Costing | Full Costing | Difference |
| Year 1 | $300,000 | $80,000 | $90,000 | $ 40,000 | $ 50,000 | $10,000* |
| Year 2 | 300,000 | 80,000 | 94,000 | 120,000 | 144,000 | 24,000† |

*Income for the first year was $10,000 higher under full costing because ending inventory is higher by this amount.

†Two-year income in total is $24,000 higher under full costing because cumulative ending inventory is higher by this amount.

When variable costing is used, the income from operations for Year 2 remained unchanged at $80,000—a perfectly logical result since sales volume, selling price, variable costs per unit, and fixed costs were all unchanged. Using full costing, however, the income from operations increased from $90,000 in Year 1 to $94,000 in Year 2, ***despite the fact that the sales volume remained at the same level*** as in Year 1. This apparently illogical result probably represents a strong argument in favor of the use of variable costing for decision-making purposes by management; ***when variable costing is used, income from operations changes in concert with changes in sales volume rather than with changes in production volume.***

Proponents of variable costing also argue that fixed manufacturing costs are not a part of the cost of goods produced during a given period but are the ***costs of having the capacity to produce.*** They believe that fixed manufacturing costs are ***period*** or ***capacity*** costs which should be charged against the revenue of the period in which they are incurred, without regard to the level of production. Critics of variable costing, however, point out that fixed manufacturing costs ***add value to the goods produced*** and are no less essential in the production of goods than variable costs. They argue that a profit on the sale of any product emerges only after recovery of the total cost of bringing that product to the point of sale.

Segregating variable and fixed costs in the accounts produces data that are useful to management in studying cost-volume-profit relationships and in arriving at decisions involving pricing, production planning, and cost control. On the other hand, exclusion of fixed manufacturing costs from inventory valuation understates the full cost of inventories and makes variable costing of doubtful validity for income measurement purposes. For this reason, ***variable costing is not an accepted procedure for income determination.***[1] When variable costing is used for internal decision-making purposes, inventory costs must be restated on a full cost basis for external reporting and for income tax purposes.

## Summary of advantages and disadvantages of variable costing

Some of the advantages and disadvantages generally associated with the use of variable costing procedures may be summarized as follows:

***Advantages***

1. ***Installation of a variable costing system requires a careful analysis of costs; this may result in more effective planning and cost control throughout the entire organization.***
2. ***Information needed for cost-volume-profit analysis is readily available from statements prepared on a variable costing basis.***

***Disadvantages***

1. ***Financial statements prepared on the variable costing basis are not acceptable for financial reporting or income tax purposes.***
2. ***Inventories, working capital, and stockholders' equity tend to be understated when variable costing is used for financial reporting purposes.***

[1] American Institute of Certified Public Accountants, *Accounting Research and Terminology Bulletins,* Final Edition (New York: 1961), pp. 28–29.

| *Advantages* | *Disadvantages* |
| --- | --- |
| *3 Because variable and fixed costs are segregated, the variable costing income statement may be more useful to management in arriving at certain decisions.* | *3 Segregation of factory overhead costs into fixed and variable components is often difficult.* |
| *4 Since fixed costs are not allocated to departments or products under variable costing, it is easier for management to determine the contribution margin on product lines and sales territories.* | *4 Exclusion of fixed factory overhead costs from inventory tends to make long-run pricing decisions less effective because prices may be set at a level sufficient to recover the variable costs but not all the fixed costs. Net income can only result after all costs are recovered.* |
| *5 Operating income under variable costing will generally increase when sales increase and decrease when sales decrease; this may not be true when full costing is used.* | |

## Concluding comments

The information needed by managers is sometimes significantly different from that collected in the ordinary processes of financial accounting. Managers are primarily concerned with the possible outcomes of future courses of action. This means that they must have reliable estimates of costs which will be incurred and revenue which will be earned as a result of a business decision. Effective decision making generally includes the following steps:

1 A clear definition of the problem or proposed action is prepared, and the relevant information (both quantitative and subjective) is gathered.
2 The decision is made and the actions and resources required to carry out the decision are spelled out.
3 A feedback system is designed which will evaluate the decision against actual results.

Although managers are responsible for making decisions, accountants provide inputs needed to implement each of these steps. Examples of business decisions which would not require some form of accounting information are not easy to find.

We have merely scratched the surface in discussing the possible kinds of analyses that might be prepared in making decisions. The brief treatment in this chapter, however, has been sufficient to establish the basic principles that lie behind such analyses. The most profitable course of action is determined by studying the costs and revenue that are ***incremental*** to the particular alternatives under consideration. The relevant information generally involves making ***estimates*** about the future. As a result, such information is subject to some degree of error. Of course it is important to remember that subjective factors may be brought into the decision picture after the quantitative analysis has been made.

## KEY TERMS INTRODUCED OR EMPHASIZED IN CHAPTER 28

**Capital budgeting** The process of planning and evaluating proposals for investments in plant assets.

**Discount rate** The required rate of return used by an investor to discount future cash flows to their present value.

**Discounted cash flows** The present value of expected future cash flows.

**Full (absorption) costing** The traditional method of product costing in which both fixed and variable manufacturing costs are treated as product costs and charged to inventories.

**Incremental (or differential) cost** The difference between the total cost of alternative courses of action.

**Net present value** The excess of the present value of the net cash flows expected from an investment over the amount to be invested. Net present value is one method of ranking alternative investment opportunities.

**Opportunity cost** The benefit foregone by not pursuing an alternative course of action. Opportunity costs are not recorded in the accounting records, but are important in making many types of business decisions.

**Payback period** The length of time necessary to recover the cost of an investment through the cash flows generated by that investment. Payback period is one criterion used in making capital budgeting decisions.

**Present value** The amount of money today which is considered equivalent to a cash inflow or outflow expected to take place in the future. The present value of money is always less than the future amount, since money on hand today can be invested to become the equivalent of a larger amount in the future.

**Relevant cost** A cost which should be given consideration in making a specific decision.

**Return on average investment** The average annual net income from an investment expressed as a percentage of the average amount invested. Return on average investment is one method of ranking alternative investment opportunities according to their relative profitability.

**Sunk cost** A cost which has irrevocably been incurred by past actions. Sunk costs are irrelevant to decisions regarding future actions.

**Variable costing** The technique of product costing in which variable manufacturing costs are charged to inventories produced and fixed manufacturing costs are treated as period expenses.

## REVIEW QUESTIONS

1 Comment on the following position taken by a business executive: "Since relevant quantitative information is difficult to obtain and is subject to some degree of error, I'd rather make decisions on the basis of subjective factors and my many years of business experience."

2 What is the difference between a ***sunk cost*** and an ***out-of-pocket cost?***

3 Define ***opportunity costs*** and explain why they represent a common source of error in making cost analyses.

4 Briefly discuss the type of information you would want before deciding to discontinue the production of a major line of products.

5 Explain why the book value of existing equipment is not relevant in deciding whether the equipment should be scrapped (without realizing any proceeds) or continued in use.

6 The Calcutta Corporation produces a large number of products. The costs per unit for one product, a fishing reel, are shown below:

| | |
|---|---|
| *Prime costs (direct materials and direct labor)* | *$7.00* |
| *Variable factory overhead* | *4.00* |
| *Fixed factory overhead* | *2.00* |

The company recently decided to buy 10,000 fishing reels from another manufacturer for $12.50 per unit because "it was cheaper than our cost of $13.00 per unit." Evaluate the decision only on the basis of the cost data given.

7 A company regularly sells 100,000 washing machines at an average price of $250. The average cost of producing these machines is $180. Under what circumstances might the company accept an order for 20,000 washing machines at $175 per machine?

8 What is ***capital budgeting?*** Why are capital budgeting decisions crucial to the long-run financial health of a business enterprise?

9 A company invests $100,000 in plant assets with an estimated 20-year service life and no salvage value. These assets contribute $10,000 to annual net income when depreciation is computed on a straight-line basis. Compute the payback period and explain your computation.

10 What is the major shortcoming of using the payback period as the only criterion in making capital budgeting decisions?

11 What factors should an investor consider in appraising the adequacy of the rate of return from a specific investment proposal?

12 Discounting a future cash flow at 15% results in a lower present value than does discounting the same cash flow at 10%. Explain why.

13 What factors determine the present value of a future cash flow?

14 Discounting cash flows takes into consideration one characteristic of the earnings stream which is ignored in the computation of return on average investment. What is this characteristic and why is it important?

15 List the three basic features of ***variable (direct) costing.***

16 During the current year the inventory of finished product of a manufacturing firm declined. In which case would the company's reported income be larger: if it used variable costing, or if it used full costing? Explain your reasoning.

17 The Bombay Company reports an amount labeled ***manufacturing margin*** in its income statement. The income statement is stamped "for management's use

only." Explain what is meant by "manufacturing margin" and why the income statement containing this term is not issued to outsiders.

18 List three advantages and three disadvantages of using variable (direct) costing.

## EXERCISES

*Ex. 28-1* Shown below is the typical monthly operating data of Arrow Hardware Store:

| | Hardware | Sporting Goods | Total |
|---|---|---|---|
| Sales | $120,000 | $ 6,000 | $126,000 |
| Cost of goods sold: | | | |
| Variable | (42,000) | (3,600) | (45,600) |
| Fixed | (12,000) | (1,200) | (13,200) |
| Gross profit on sales | $ 66,000 | $ 1,200 | $ 67,200 |
| Operating expenses: | | | |
| Variable | (30,000) | (1,800) | (31,800) |
| Fixed | (18,000) | (2,400) | (20,400) |
| Operating income (before taxes) | $ 18,000 | $(3,000) | $ 15,000 |

The store manager is considering discontinuing the sale of sporting goods in order to improve the profitability of the store. Prepare a schedule showing the effect upon monthly operating income of eliminating the sale of sporting goods. Assume that no fixed costs will be eliminated and that hardware sales will not change as a result of discontinuing sporting goods sales.

*Ex. 28-2* Auto Parts Company has 20,000 units of a defective product on hand which cost $43,200 to manufacture. The company can either sell this product as scrap for $1.08 per unit or it can sell the product for $4.20 per unit by reworking the units and correcting the defects at a cost of $26,400. What should the company do? Prepare a schedule in support of your recommendation.

*Ex. 28-3* Bowman Corporation is considering an investment in special-purpose equipment to enable the company to obtain a four-year government contract for the manufacture of a special item. The equipment costs $300,000 and would have no salvage value when its use is discontinued at the end of the four years. Estimated annual operating results of the project are:

| | | |
|---|---|---|
| Revenue from contract sales | | $325,000 |
| Expenses other than depreciation | $225,000 | |
| Depreciation (straight-line basis) | 75,000 | 300,000 |
| Increase in net income from contract work | | $ 25,000 |

All revenue and all expenses other than depreciation will be received or paid in cash in the same period as recognized for accounting purposes. Compute for the proposal to undertake the contract work the following:

**a** Payback period.
**b** Return on average investment.
**c** Net present value of proposal to undertake contract work, discounted at an annual rate of 12%. (Refer to annuity table on page 1038.)

*Ex. 28-4* The cost to Ellis Company of manufacturing 10,000 units of item X is $240,000, including $80,000 of fixed costs and $160,000 of variable costs. The company can buy the part from an outside supplier for $18.00 per unit, but the fixed factory overhead now allocated to the part will remain unchanged. Should the company buy the part or continue to manufacture it? Prepare a comparative schedule in the format illustrated on page 1033.

***Ex. 28-5*** Given below are the production and sales data for the Aluminum Products Company at the end of its first year of operations:

| | |
|---|---|
| *Sales (6,000 units × $77)* | *$462,000* |
| *Production costs (10,000 units):* | |
| *Variable* | *350,000* |
| *Fixed* | *210,000* |
| *Selling and administrative expenses (all fixed)* | *70,000* |

Compute income from operations for the year using **(a)** full costing and **(b)** variable costing.

***Ex. 28-6*** Using the tables on page 1038, determine the present value of the following cash flows, discounted at an annual rate of 15%:

**a** $35,000 to be received 20 years from today
**b** $12,000 to be received annually for 5 years
**c** $42,000 to be received annually for 7 years, with an additional $30,000 salvage value due at the end of the seventh year
**d** $30,000 to be received annually for the first 3 years, followed by $20,000 received annually for the next 2 years (total of 5 years in which cash is received)

## PROBLEMS

### Group A

***28A-1*** A partial income statement for the Platte River Company for the first year of its operations, prepared in conventional (full costing) form, is shown below. During the year 125,000 units were manufactured, of which 100,000 units were sold.

***PLATTE RIVER COMPANY***
***Income Statement***
***For First Year of Operations (in thousands)***

| | | |
|---|---|---|
| *Sales (100,000 units at $100 per unit)* | | *$10,000* |
| *Cost of goods sold:* | | |
| *Direct material* | *$3,500* | |
| *Direct labor* | *2,750* | |
| *Variable factory overhead* | *250* | |
| *Fixed factory overhead* | *2,000* | |
| *Total manufacturing costs* | *$8,500* | |
| *Less: Ending finished goods inventory (25,000 units)* | *1,700* | |
| *Cost of goods sold ($68 per unit)* | | *6,800* |
| *Gross profit on sales* | | *$ 3,200* |
| *Less: Operating expenses:* | | |
| *Variable* | *$1,000* | |
| *Fixed* | *1,200* | |
| *Total operating expenses* | | *2,200* |
| *Income from operations* | | *$ 1,000* |

**Instructions**

**a** Revise the statement using the variable (direct) costing approach. Briefly explain the difference in the income from operations reported in the two statements. (Note that income statement amounts are shown in thousands of dollars.)

**b** Prepare a schedule showing whether it would be profitable for the Platte River Company to accept an offer from a foreign customer to purchase 25,000 units for $60 per unit. This special order would have no effect on fixed factory overhead or on operating expenses.

*28A-2* Solar Systems manufactures a check valve which is used in several of its products. The vice president of production is considering whether to continue manufacturing these valves, or whether to buy them from an outside source at a cost of $9.40 per valve. Solar Systems uses 50,000 of the valves each year. The cost to manufacture the valves is $10.60 per unit, as shown below:

| | |
|---|---|
| *Direct materials* | *$150,000* |
| *Direct labor* | *190,000* |
| *Factory overhead:* | |
| *Variable* | *80,000* |
| *Fixed* | *110,000* |
| *Annual manufacturing costs for 50,000 valves* | *$530,000* |
| *Unit cost ($530,000 ÷ 50,000 units)* | *$10.60* |

If the valves are purchased, all of the direct materials and direct labor costs will be eliminated, and 80% of the variable overhead will be eliminated. In addition, some of the equipment used in the manufacture of the valves will be sold at its book value. The sale of this equipment will reduce fixed factory overhead costs by $7,900 for depreciation and $200 for property taxes. No other reduction in fixed factory overhead will result from discontinuing production of the valves.

**Instructions**

**a** Prepare a schedule in the format illustrated on page 1053 to determine the incremental cost or benefit of buying the valves from the outside supplier. Based on this schedule, would you recommend that Solar Systems manufacture the valves or buy them from the outside source?

**b** Assume that if the valves are purchased from the outside source, the factory space previously used to manufacture valves can be used to manufacture an additional 2,000 solar collectors per year. Solar collectors have an estimated contribution margin of $70 per unit. Manufacturing the additional solar collectors would not increase fixed factory overhead. Would this new assumption change your recommendation as to whether to make or buy the check valves? In support of your conclusion, prepare a schedule showing the incremental cost or benefit of buying the valves from the outside supplier and using the factory space to produce more solar collectors.

*28A-3* Cardiff Corporation is considering two alternative proposals for modernizing its production facilities. To provide a basis for selection, the cost accounting department has developed the data shown on page 1053 regarding the expected annual operating results for the two proposals.

**Instructions**

**a** For each proposal, compute the (1) payback period, (2) return on average investment, and (3) net present value, discounted at an annual rate of 12%. (Round the payback period to the nearest tenth of a year and the return on investment to the nearest tenth of a percent.)

| | Proposal 1 | Proposal 2 |
|---|---|---|
| Required investment in equipment | $360,000 | $350,000 |
| Estimated service life of equipment | 8 years | 7 years |
| Estimated salvage value | -0- | $ 14,000 |
| Estimated annual cost savings (net cash flow) | $ 75,000 | $ 76,000 |
| Depreciation on equipment (straight-line basis) | $ 45,000 | $ 48,000 |
| Estimated increase in annual net income | $ 30,000 | $ 28,000 |

**b** Based on your analysis in part **a**, state which proposal you would recommend and explain the reasons for your choice.

*28A-4* The management of Metro Printers is considering a proposal to replace some existing printing equipment with a new highly efficient laser printer. The existing equipment has a current book value of $2,200,000 and a remaining life (if not replaced) of 10 years. The laser printer has a cost of $1,300,000 and an expected useful life of 10 years. The laser printer would increase the company's annual cash flow by reducing operating costs and by increasing the company's ability to generate revenue. Susan Mills, controller of Metro Printers, has prepared the following estimates of the laser printer's effect upon annual earnings and cash flow:

| | | |
|---|---|---|
| Estimated increase in annual cash flow (before income taxes): | | |
| Incremental revenue | $140,000 | |
| Cost savings (other than depreciation) | 110,000 | $250,000 |
| Reduction in annual depreciation expense: | | |
| Depreciation on existing equipment | $220,000 | |
| Depreciation on laser printer | 130,000 | 90,000 |
| Estimated increase in income before income taxes | | $340,000 |
| Increase in annual income taxes (40%) | | 136,000 |
| Estimated increase in annual net income | | $204,000 |
| Estimated increase in annual net cash flow ($250,000 − $136,000) | | $114,000 |

Don Adams, a director of Metro Printers, makes the following observation: "These estimates look fine, but won't we take a huge loss in the current year on the sale of our existing equipment? After the invention of the laser printer, I doubt that our old equipment can be sold for much at all." In response, Miller provides the following information about the expected loss on the sale of the existing equipment:

| | |
|---|---|
| Book value of existing printing equipment | $2,200,000 |
| Estimated current sales price, net of removal costs | $200,000 |
| Estimated loss on sale, before income taxes | $2,000,000 |
| Reduction in current year's income taxes as a result of loss (40%) | 800,000 |
| Loss on sale of existing equipment, net of tax savings | $1,200,000 |

Adams replies, "Good grief, our loss would be almost as great as the cost of the laser printer. If we have to take a $1,200,000 loss and pay $1,300,000 for the laser printer, we'll be into the new equipment for $2,500,000. I'd go along with a cost of $1,300,000, but $2,500,000 is just too high a price to pay."

**Instructions**

**a** Compute the net present value of the proposal to sell the existing equipment and buy the laser printer, discounted at an annual rate of 15%. In your computation, make the following assumptions regarding the timing of cash flows:

(1) The purchase price of the laser printer will be paid in cash immediately.

(2) The $200,000 sales price of the existing equipment will be received in cash immediately.

(3) The income tax benefit from selling the existing equipment will be realized one year from today.

(4) The annual net cash flows may be regarded as received at year-end for each of the next ten years.

**b** Is the cost to Metro Printers of acquiring the laser printer $2,500,000, as Adams suggests? Explain fully.

*28A-5* Advance Electronics opened its new Jefferson Plant at the beginning of the current year to manufacture a burglar alarm. During the year, the Jefferson Plant manufactured 60,000 burglar alarms, of which 50,000 were sold and 10,000 remain on hand as finished goods inventory. There was no goods in process inventory at year-end. A partial income statement for the Jefferson Plant, prepared in conventional (full costing) form, is shown below:

***JEFFERSON PLANT***
***Partial Income Statement***
***For First Year of Operations***

| | | |
|---|---|---|
| *Sales (50,000 units @ $60)* | | *$3,000,000* |
| *Cost of goods sold:* | | |
| *Manufacturing costs (60,000 units @ $42)* | *$2,520,000* | |
| *Less: Ending inventory (10,000 units @ $42)* | *420,000* | *2,100,000* |
| *Gross profit on sales* | | *$ 900,000* |
| *Operating expenses:* | | |
| *Variable ($8 per unit sold)* | *$ 400,000* | |
| *Fixed* | *425,000* | *825,000* |
| *Income from operations* | | *$ 75,000* |

The $2,520,000 in total manufacturing costs consisted of the following cost elements:

| | | |
|---|---|---|
| *Direct materials* | | *$ 900,000* |
| *Direct labor* | | *720,000* |
| *Factory overhead:* | | |
| *Variable* | *$300,000* | |
| *Fixed* | *600,000* | *900,000* |
| *Total manufacturing costs* | | *$2,520,000* |

The manager of the Jefferson Plant is proud of the $75,000 operating income reported for the first year of operations. However, the controller of Advance Electronics, an advocate of variable costing, makes the following statement: "The only reason that the Jefferson Plant shows a profit is that $100,000 of fixed costs are carried in the ending inventory figure. Actually, a sales volume of 50,000 units is below the break-even point."

**Instructions**

**a** Prepare a schedule showing each manufacturing cost on a per-unit basis. As a subtotal in your schedule, show the variable manufacturing cost per unit. The final total in your schedule will be the total manufacturing cost per unit ($42).

**b** Prepare a revised partial income statement for the Jefferson Plant using the variable (direct) costing approach.

**c** Briefly explain the difference in the amount of operating income reported in the two statements. Is the controller correct about the $420,000 ending inventory in the full costing income statement including $100,000 of fixed manufacturing costs?

**d** Compute the contribution margin per unit sold. (Use as a starting point the total contribution margin shown in your variable costing income statement.)

**e** How many units must be produced and sold each year for the Jefferson Plant to break even—that is to cover its fixed expenses? (In computing the break-even point, assume all units produced are sold.) Is the controller correct that the Jefferson Plant failed to achieve the break-even point in unit sales volume during its first year of operations?

## Group B

*28B-1* The Magic Game Company sells 600,000 game sets per year at $9.00 each. The current unit cost of the game sets is broken down as follows:

| | |
|---|---|
| *Direct materials* | *$1.50* |
| *Direct labor* | *2.70* |
| *Variable factory overhead* | *0.60* |
| *Fixed factory overhead* | *1.20* |
| *Total* | *$6.00* |

At the beginning of the current year the company receives a special order for 10,000 game sets per month ***for one year only*** at $5.40 per unit. A new machine with an estimated life of five years would have to be purchased for $30,000 to produce the additional units. Management thinks that it will not be able to use the new machine beyond one year and that it will have to be sold for approximately $19,500.

**Instructions** Compute the estimated increase or decrease in annual operating income that will result from accepting this special order.

*28B-2* Toro Equipment Co. manufactures an electric motor which it uses in several of its products. Management is considering whether to continue manufacturing the motors, or whether to buy them from an outside source. The following information is available:

(1) The company needs 10,000 motors per year. The motors can be purchased from an outside supplier at a cost of $20 per unit.

(2) The cost of manufacturing the motors is $24 per unit, computed as follows:

| | |
|---|---|
| *Direct materials* | *$ 80,000* |
| *Direct labor* | *40,000* |
| *Factory overhead:* | |
| *Variable* | *70,000* |
| *Fixed* | *50,000* |
| *Total manufacturing costs* | *$240,000* |
| *Cost per unit ($240,000 ÷ 10,000 units)* | *$24* |

(3) Discontinuing the manufacture of motors will eliminate all of the direct materials and direct labor costs, but will eliminate only 60% of the variable factory overhead costs.

(4) If the motors are purchased from an outside source, certain machinery used in the production of motors will be sold at its book value. The sale of this machinery will reduce fixed factory overhead costs by $3,600 for depreciation and $400 for property taxes. No other reductions in fixed factory overhead will result from discontinuing production of the motors.

**Instructions**

**a** Prepare a schedule in the format illustrated on page 1033 to determine the incremental cost or benefit of buying the motors from the outside supplier. Based on this schedule, would you recommend that the company manufacture the motors or buy them from the outside source?

**b** Assume that if the motors are purchased from the outside source, the factory space previously used to produce motors can be used to manufacture an additional 7,000 power trimmers per year. Power trimmers have an estimated contribution margin of $9 per unit. The manufacture of the additional power trimmers would have no effect upon fixed factory overhead. Would this new assumption change your recommendation as to whether to make or buy the motors? In support of your conclusion, prepare a schedule showing the incremental cost or benefit of buying the motors from the outside source and using the factory space to produce additional power trimmers.

*28B-3* Ortega Company is evaluating two alternative investment opportunities. The controller of the company has prepared the following analysis of the two investment proposals:

| | *Proposal A* | *Proposal B* |
|---|---|---|
| *Required investment in equipment* | *$220,000* | *$240,000* |
| *Estimated service life of equipment* | *5 years* | *6 years* |
| *Estimated salvage value* | *$ 10,000* | *-0-* |
| *Estimated annual net cash flow* | *$ 60,000* | *$ 60,000* |
| *Depreciation on equipment (straight-line basis)* | *$ 42,000* | *$ 40,000* |
| *Estimated annual net income* | *$ 18,000* | *$ 20,000* |

**Instructions**

**a** For each proposed investment, compute the (1) payback period, (2) return on average investment, and (3) net present value, discounted at an annual rate of 12%. (Round the payback period to the nearest tenth of a year and the return on investment to the nearest tenth of a percent.)

**b** Based upon your computations in part **a**, which proposal do you consider to be the best investment? Explain.

*28B-4* Rothmore Appliance Company is planning to introduce a built-in blender to its line of small home appliances. Annual sales of the blender are estimated at 10,000 units at a price of $35 per unit. Variable manufacturing costs are estimated at $16 per unit, incremental fixed manufacturing costs (other than depreciation) at $30,000 annually, and incremental selling and general expenses relating to the blenders at $50,000 annually.

To build the blenders, the company must invest $240,000 in molds, patterns, and special equipment. Since the company expects to change the design of the blender every four years, this equipment will have a four-year service life with no salvage value. Depreciation will be computed on a straight-line basis. All revenue and expenses other than depreciation will be received or paid in cash. The company's combined state and federal income tax rate is 50%.

**Instructions**

**a** Prepare a schedule showing the estimated annual net income from the proposal to manufacture and sell the blenders.

**b** Compute the annual net cash flow expected from the proposal.

**c** Compute for this proposal (1) payback period (round to the nearest tenth of a year), (2) return on average investment (round to the nearest tenth of a percent), and (3) net present value, discounted at an annual rate of 15%.

***28B-5*** At the beginning of the current year, Audio Corporation opened its Windville Plant to manufacture a new model stereo speaker. During the year, 100,000 speakers were manufactured, of which 80,000 were sold at a unit sales price of $90. Variable manufacturing costs for the year amounted to $3,600,000, and fixed manufacturing costs totaled $1,200,000. Variable operating expenses were $720,000, and fixed operating expenses were $924,000.

**Instructions**

**a** Prepare a schedule showing variable, fixed, and total manufacturing costs per unit.

**b** Prepare partial income statements (ending with income from operations) for the Windville Plant for the current year using:
(1) Full costing
(2) Variable costing

**c** Briefly explain the difference in the amount of income from operations reported in the two partial income statements.

**d** Using the data contained in the variable costing income statement, compute (1) the contribution margin per unit sold, and (2) the number of speakers which must be manufactured and sold annually for the Windville Plant to cover its fixed manufacturing costs and fixed operating expenses—that is, to break even.

## BUSINESS DECISION PROBLEM 28

Cornbelt Cereal Company is engaged in manufacturing a breakfast cereal. You are asked to advise management on sales policy for the coming year.

Two proposals are being considered by management which will (1) increase the volume of sales, (2) reduce the ratio of selling expense to sales, and (3) decrease manufacturing cost per unit. These proposals are as follows:

**Proposal no. 1: Increase advertising expenditures by offering premium stamps**
It is proposed that each box of cereal will contain premium stamps which will be redeemed for cash prizes. The estimated cost of this premium plan is estimated at $0.10 per box of cereal sold. The new advertising plan will take the place of all existing advertising expenditures and the current selling price of $1.00 per unit will be maintained.

**Proposal no. 2: Reduce selling price of product**
It is proposed that the selling price of the cereal be reduced to $0.95 per box, and that advertising expenditures be increased over those of the current year. This plan is an alternative to Proposal no. 1, and only one will be adopted by management.

Management has provided you with the following information as to the current year's operations:

| | |
|---|---|
| *Sales (5,000,000 boxes at $1.00 per box)* | *$5,000,000* |
| *Manufacturing costs (5,000,000 boxes at $0.60 per box)* | *3,000,000* |
| *Selling expenses, 20% of sales (one-fourth of which was for newspaper advertising)* | *1,000,000* |
| *Administrative expenses* | *420,000* |

Estimates for the coming year for each proposal are shown below:

| | Proposal No. 1 | Proposal No. 2 |
|---|---|---|
| *Increase in unit sales volume* | *50%* | *30%* |
| *Decrease in manufacturing cost per unit* | *10%* | *5%* |
| *Newspaper advertising* | *None* | *10% of sales* |
| *Other selling expenses* | *8% of sales* | *8% of sales* |
| *Premium plan expense* | *$0.10 per box* | *None* |
| *Administrative expenses* | *$515,000* | *$475,000* |

**Instructions** Which of the two proposals should management select? In support of your recommendation, prepare a statement comparing the income from operations for the current year with the anticipated income from operations for the coming year under Proposal no. 1 and under Proposal no. 2. In preparing the statement use the following three column headings: Current Year, Proposal No. 1, and Proposal No. 2.

# Appendix

## FINANCIAL STATEMENTS OF A PUBLICLY OWNED COMPANY

The financial statements of General Motors Corporation, a company listed on the New York Stock Exchange, are presented on the following pages. These financial statements have been audited by Deloitte Haskins & Sells, an international firm of certified public accountants. The audit report is attached. This particular company was selected becuase its financial statements provide realistic illustrations of many of the financial reporting issues discussed in this book.

Notice that several pages of explanatory notes are included with the basic financial statements. These explanatory notes supplement the condensed information in the financial statements and are designed to carry out the disclosure principle discussed in Chapter 14 of this book. As indicated in Chapter 14, the disclosure principle means that all material and relevant facts should be communicated to the users of financial statements.

The final two pages of this section illustrate the impact of inflation on financial statements. Data adjusted for general inflation and current cost data as well are presented by General Motors in accordance with requirements of the Financial Accounting Standards Board.

## Consolidated Financial Statements

General Motors Corporation
and Consolidated Subsidiaries

## Responsibilities for Financial Statements

The following financial statements of General Motors Corporation and Consolidated Subsidiaries were prepared by the management which is responsible for their integrity and objectivity. The statements have been prepared in conformity with generally accepted accounting principles and, as such, include amounts based on judgments of management.

Management is further responsible for maintaining a system of internal accounting controls, designed to provide reasonable assurance that the books and records reflect the transactions of the companies and that its established policies and procedures are carefully followed. The system is continually reviewed for its effectiveness and is augmented by written policies and guidelines, the careful selection and training of qualified personnel, and a strong program of internal audit.

Deloitte Haskins & Sells, independent certified public accountants, are engaged to examine the financial statements of General Motors Corporation and its subsidiaries and issue reports thereon. Their examination is conducted in accordance with generally accepted auditing standards and includes a review of internal accounting controls and a test of transactions. The Accountants' Report appears on page 25.

The Board of Directors, through the Audit Committee of the Board, is responsible for: (1) assuring that management fulfills its responsibilities in the preparation of the financial statements; and (2) for engaging the independent public accountants with whom the Committee reviews the scope of the audits and the accounting principles to be applied in financial reporting. The Audit Committee, which is composed entirely of non-employe Directors, meets regularly (separately and jointly) with the independent public accountants, representatives of management, and the internal auditors to review the activities of each and to ensure that each is properly discharging its responsibilities. To ensure complete independence, Deloitte Haskins & Sells have full and free access to meet with the Audit Committee, without management representatives present, to discuss the results of their examination and their opinions on the adequacy of internal accounting controls and the quality of financial reporting.

Chairman

Chief Financial Officer

## Statement of Consolidated Income

For The Years Ended December 31, 1979 and 1978
(Dollars in Millions Except Per Share Amounts)

| | 1979 | 1978 |
|---|---|---|
| **Net Sales** | $66,311.2 | $63,221.1 |
| Equity in earnings of nonconsolidated subsidiaries and associates (dividends received amounted to $112.8 in 1979 and $123.7 in 1978) | 218.3 | 253.0 |
| Other income less income deductions—net (Note 2) | 191.9 | ( 141.4) |
| **Total** | 66,721.4 | 63,332.7 |
| **Costs and Expenses** | | |
| Cost of sales and other operating charges, exclusive of items listed below | 55,848.7 | 51,275.7 |
| Selling, general and administrative expenses | 2,475.5 | 2,255.8 |
| Depreciation of real estate, plants and equipment | 1,236.9 | 1,180.6 |
| Amortization of special tools | 1,950.4 | 1,855.7 |
| Provision for the Bonus Plan (Note 3) | 133.8 | 168.4 |
| United States, foreign and other income taxes (Note 5) | 2,183.4 | 3,088.5 |
| **Total** | 63,828.7 | 59,824.7 |
| **Net Income** | 2,892.7 | 3,508.0 |
| Dividends on preferred stocks | 12.9 | 12.9 |
| **Earned on Common Stock** | $ 2,879.8 | $ 3,495.1 |
| Average number of shares of common stock outstanding (in millions) | 286.8 | 285.5 |
| **Earned Per Share of Common Stock** (Note 6) | $10.04 | $12.24 |

Reference should be made to notes on pages 1063 through 1067.

# Consolidated Balance Sheet

December 31, 1979 and 1978
(Dollars in Millions)

| Assets | 1979 | 1978 |
|---|---|---|
| **Current Assets** | | |
| Cash | $ 247.1 | $ 177.3 |
| United States Government and other marketable securities and time deposits—at cost, which approximates market: | | |
| Held for payment of income taxes | 373.0 | 791.3 |
| Other | 2,366.3 | 3,086.2 |
| Accounts and notes receivable (Note 7) | 5,030.4 | 5,638.7 |
| Inventories | 8,076.3 | 7,576.7 |
| Prepaid expenses | 463.4 | 729.3 |
| **Total Current Assets** | 16,556.5 | 17,999.5 |
| **Investments and Miscellaneous Assets** (Note 8) | 3,828.2 | 2,812.1 |
| **Common Stock Held for the Incentive Program** (Note 3) | 192.9 | 181.1 |
| **Property** | | |
| Real estate, plants and equipment (Note 10) | 24,879.4 | 22,052.0 |
| Less accumulated depreciation (Note 10) | 14,298.2 | 13,438.8 |
| Net real estate, plants and equipment | 10,581.2 | 8,613.2 |
| Special tools—less amortization | 1,057.0 | 992.4 |
| **Total Property** | 11,638.2 | 9,605.6 |
| **Total Assets** | $32,215.8 | $30,598.3 |

| Liabilities and Stockholders' Equity | | |
|---|---|---|
| **Current Liabilities** | | |
| Accounts, drafts and loans payable | $ 4,305.4 | $ 4,612.4 |
| United States, foreign and other income taxes payable | 478.6 | 944.8 |
| Accrued liabilities | 5,084.3 | 4,493.4 |
| **Total Current Liabilities** | 9,868.3 | 10,050.6 |
| **Long-Term Debt**—less unamortized discount (Note 11) | 880.0 | 978.9 |
| **Other Liabilities** | 1,551.6 | 1,384.4 |
| **Deferred Investment Tax Credits** | 651.7 | 519.9 |
| **Other Deferred Credits** | 84.9 | 94.6 |
| **Stockholders' Equity** (Notes 3 and 12) | | |
| Preferred stock ($5.00 series, $183.6; $3.75 series, $100.0) | 283.6 | 283.6 |
| Common stock | 487.4 | 480.1 |
| Capital surplus (principally additional paid-in capital) | 1,034.6 | 792.0 |
| Net income retained for use in the business | 17,373.7 | 16,014.2 |
| **Total Stockholders' Equity** | 19,179.3 | 17,569.9 |
| **Total Liabilities and Stockholders' Equity** | $32,215.8 | $30,598.3 |

Reference should be made to notes on pages 1063 through 1067.

## Statement of Changes in Consolidated Financial Position

For The Years Ended December 31, 1979 and 1978
(Dollars in Millions)

| | 1979 | 1978 |
|---|---|---|
| **Source of Funds** | | |
| Net income | $2,892.7 | $3,508.0 |
| Depreciation of real estate, plants and equipment | 1,236.9 | 1,180.6 |
| Amortization of special tools | 1,950.4 | 1,855.7 |
| Deferred income taxes, undistributed earnings of nonconsolidated subsidiaries and associates, etc.—net | ( 321.2) | ( 64.6) |
| Total current operations | 5,758.8 | 6,479.7 |
| Proceeds from issuance of long-term debt | 41.3 | 111.9 |
| Proceeds from disposals of property—net | 166.9 | 125.5 |
| Proceeds from sale of newly issued common stock | 249.9 | 20.5 |
| Other—net | 125.4 | 273.8 |
| **Total** | 6,342.3 | 7,011.4 |
| **Application of Funds** | | |
| Dividends paid to stockholders | 1,533.2 | 1,725.5 |
| Expenditures for real estate, plants and equipment | 3,371.8 | 2,737.8 |
| Expenditures for special tools | 2,015.0 | 1,826.7 |
| Investments in nonconsolidated subsidiaries and associates | 542.8 | 201.6 |
| Retirements of long-term debt | 140.2 | 201.2 |
| **Total** | 7,603.0 | 6,692.8 |
| Increase (Decrease) in working capital | ( 1,260.7) | 318.6 |
| Working capital at beginning of the year | 7,948.9 | 7,630.3 |
| Working capital at end of the year | $6,688.2 | $7,948.9 |
| **Increase (Decrease) in Working Capital by Element** | | |
| Cash, marketable securities and time deposits | ($1,068.4) | $ 814.8 |
| Accounts and notes receivable | ( 608.3) | 957.6 |
| Inventories | 499.6 | 401.0 |
| Prepaid expenses | ( 265.9) | ( 131.1) |
| Accounts, drafts and loans payable | 307.0 | ( 893.3) |
| United States, foreign and other income taxes payable | 466.2 | ( 57.3) |
| Accrued liabilities | ( 590.9) | ( 773.1) |
| Increase (Decrease) in working capital | ($1,260.7) | $ 318.6 |

Reference should be made to notes on pages 1063 through 1067.

# Notes to Financial Statements

## Note 1. Significant Accounting Policies

*Principles of Consolidation*

The consolidated financial statements include the accounts of the Corporation and all domestic and foreign subsidiaries which are more than 50% owned and engaged principally in manufacturing or wholesale marketing of General Motors products. General Motors' share of earnings or losses of nonconsolidated subsidiaries and of associates in which at least 20% of the voting securities is owned is generally included in consolidated income under the equity method of accounting. Intercompany items and transactions between companies included in the consolidation are eliminated and unrealized intercompany profits on sales to nonconsolidated subsidiaries and to associates are deferred.

*Income Taxes*

Investment tax credits are deducted in determining taxes estimated to be payable currently and are deferred and amortized over the lives of the related assets. The tax effects of timing differences between pretax accounting income and taxable income (principally related to depreciation, sales and product allowances, undistributed earnings of subsidiaries and associates, and benefit plans expense) are deferred, except that the tax effects of certain expenses charged to income prior to 1968 have not been deferred but are recognized in income taxes provided at the time such expenses become allowable deductions for tax purposes. Provisions are made for estimated United States and foreign taxes, less available tax credits and deductions, which may be incurred on remittance of the Corporation's share of subsidiaries' undistributed earnings less those deemed to be permanently reinvested. Possible taxes, beyond those provided, would not be material.

*Inventories*

Inventories are stated generally at cost, which is not in excess of market. The cost of substantially all domestic inventories was determined by the last-in, first-out (LIFO) method, which was adopted in 1976. If the first-in, first-out (FIFO) method of inventory valuation had been used by the Corporation for U.S. inventories, it is estimated they would be $1,603.1 million higher at December 31, 1979, compared with $1,097.7 million higher at December 31, 1978. The cost of inventories outside the United States was determined generally by the FIFO or the average cost method.

*Property, Depreciation and Amortization*

Property is stated at cost. Maintenance, repairs, rearrangement expenses, and renewals and betterments which do not enhance the value or increase the basic productive capacity of the assets are charged to costs and expenses as incurred.

Depreciation is provided on groups of property using, with minor exceptions, an accelerated method which accumulates depreciation of approximately two-thirds of the depreciable cost during the first half of the estimated lives of the property. The annual group rates of depreciation are as follows:

| *Classification of Property* | *Annual Group Rates* |
|---|---|
| Land improvements | 5% |
| Buildings | 3½% |
| Machinery and equipment | 8⅓% (Average) |
| Furniture and office equipment | 6% (Average) |

Expenditures for special tools are amortized, with the amortization applied directly to the asset account, over short periods of time because the utility value of the tools is radically affected by frequent changes in the design of the functional components and appearance of the product. Replacement of special tools for reasons other than changes in products is charged directly to cost of sales.

*Pension Program*

The Corporation and its subsidiaries have a number of pension plans covering substantially all employes. Benefits under the plans are generally related to an employe's length of service, wages and salaries, and, where applicable, contributions. The costs of these plans are determined on the basis of actuarial cost methods and include amortization of prior service cost over periods not exceeding 30 years. With the exception of certain overseas subsidiaries, pension costs accrued are funded.

*Product Related Expenses*

Expenditures for advertising and sales promotion and for other product related expenses are charged to costs and expenses as incurred; provisions for estimated costs related to product warranty are made at the time the products are sold.

Expenditures for research and development are charged to expenses as incurred and amounted to $1,949.8 million in 1979 and $1,633.1 million in 1978.

*Foreign Exchange*

All exchange and translation activity is included in cost of sales and amounted to gains of $83.7 million in 1979 and $62.7 million in 1978.

## Note 2. Other Income Less Income Deductions (Dollars in Millions)

| | 1979 | 1978 |
|---|---|---|
| Other income: | | |
| Interest income | $507.0 | $358.6 |
| Other | 72.2 | 66.1 |
| Income deductions: | | |
| Interest on long-term debt | ( 95.4) | ( 90.0) |
| Other interest | ( 273.0) | ( 265.9) |
| Other | ( 18.9) | ( 210.2)(1) |
| Net | $191.9 | ($141.4) |

(1) Principally provision for cost of liquidation of Argentine automotive operations and discontinuance of appliance manufacturing at Frigidaire.

## Note 3. Incentive Program

The Incentive Program consists of the General Motors Bonus Plan, first approved by stockholders in 1918, and the General Motors Stock Option Plans, adopted in 1957 and 1977. The By-Laws provide that the Plans shall be presented for action at a stockholders' meeting at least once in every five years. The Incentive Program was last approved by stockholders at the 1977 Annual Meeting.

## Notes to Financial Statements (continued)

**Note 10. Real Estate, Plants and Equipment and Accumulated Depreciation** (Dollars in Millions)

| | 1979 | 1978 |
|---|---|---|
| Real estate, plants and equipment: | | |
| Land | $ 304.4 | $ 268.0 |
| Land improvements | 808.3 | 719.3 |
| Leasehold improvements—less amortization | 25.4 | 22.3 |
| Buildings | 5,498.7 | 4,975.4 |
| Machinery and equipment | 16,131.0 | 14,434.1 |
| Furniture and office equipment | 392.6 | 317.9 |
| Construction in progress | 1,719.0 | 1,315.0 |
| Total | $24,879.4 | $22,052.0 |
| Accumulated depreciation: | | |
| Land improvements | $ 463.8 | $ 430.6 |
| Buildings | 3,132.0 | 2,964.9 |
| Machinery and equipment | 10,461.0 | 9,832.3 |
| Furniture and office equipment | 192.1 | 161.7 |
| Extraordinary obsolescence | 49.3 | 49.3 |
| Total | $14,298.2 | $13,438.8 |

**Note 11. Long-Term Debt (Excluding Current Portion)** (Dollars in Millions)

| | | 1979 | 1978 |
|---|---|---|---|
| GM—U.S. dollars: | | | |
| 8.05% Notes | 1985 | $300.0 | $300.0 |
| 8⅝% Debentures | 2005 | 300.0 | 300.0 |
| Other | 1981-2000 | 75.0 | 77.7 |
| Consolidated subsidiaries: | | | |
| United States dollars | 1981-86 | 128.5 | 231.9 |
| British pounds | 1987-92 | 33.2 | 30.6 |
| Australian dollars | 1981-83 | 24.9 | 34.5 |
| Other currencies | 1981-2004 | 23.8 | 10.0 |
| Total | | 885.4 | 984.7 |
| Less unamortized discount | | 5.4 | 5.8 |
| Total | | $880.0 | $978.9 |

Maturities of long-term debt at December 31, 1979 for each of the five years through 1984 are (in millions): 1980—$41.2 (included in current liabilities); 1981—$57.9; 1982—$53.1; 1983—$44.0; and 1984—$17.4.

**Note 12. Stockholders' Equity** (Dollars in Millions Except Per Share Amounts)

| | 1979 | 1978 |
|---|---|---|
| **Capital Stock:** | | |
| **Preferred Stock,** without par value, cumulative dividends (authorized, 6,000,000 shares), no change during the year: | | |
| $5.00 series, stated value $100 per share, redeemable at Corporation option at $120 per share (issued, 1,875,366 shares; in treasury, 39,722 shares; outstanding, 1,835,644 shares) | $ 183.6 | $ 183.6 |
| $3.75 series, stated value $100 per share, redeemable at Corporation option at $100 per share (issued and outstanding, 1,000,000 shares) | 100.0 | 100.0 |
| **Common Stock,** $1⅔ par value (authorized, 500,000,000 shares): | | |
| Issued at beginning of the year (288,069,840 shares in 1979 and 287,704,811 shares in 1978) | 480.1 | 479.5 |
| Newly issued stock sold under provisions of the Stock Option Plans, Employe Stock Ownership Plan and Savings-Stock Purchase Program (4,402,659 shares in 1979 and 365,029 shares in 1978) | 7.3 | .6 |
| Issued at end of the year (292,472,499 shares in 1979 and 288,069,840 shares in 1978) | 487.4 | 480.1 |
| Total capital stock at end of the year | 771.0 | 763.7 |
| **Capital Surplus (principally additional paid-in capital):** | | |
| Balance at beginning of the year | 792.0 | 772.1 |
| Proceeds in excess of par value of newly issued common stock sold under provisions of the Stock Option Plans, Employe Stock Ownership Plan and Savings-Stock Purchase Program | 242.6 | 19.9 |
| Balance at end of the year | 1,034.6 | 792.0 |
| **Net Income Retained for Use in the Business:** | | |
| Balance at beginning of the year | 16,014.2 | 14,231.7 |
| Net income | 2,892.7 | 3,508.0 |
| Total | 18,906.9 | 17,739.7 |
| Cash dividends: | | |
| Preferred stock, $5.00 series, $5.00 per share | 9.2 | 9.2 |
| Preferred stock, $3.75 series, $3.75 per share | 3.7 | 3.7 |
| Common stock, $5.30 per share in 1979 and $6.00 per share in 1978 | 1,520.3 | 1,712.6 |
| Total cash dividends | 1,533.2 | 1,725.5 |
| Balance at end of the year | 17,373.7 | 16,014.2 |
| **Total Stockholders' Equity** | $19,179.3 | $17,569.9 |

## Notes to Financial Statements (concluded)

**Note 13. Segment Reporting**

General Motors is a highly vertically-integrated business operating primarily in a single industry consisting of the manufacture, assembly, and sale of automobiles, trucks and related parts and accessories. Net sales, net income, total assets and average number of employes in the U.S. and in locations outside the U.S. for 1979 and 1978 are summarized below. Net income is after provisions for deferred income taxes applicable to that portion of the undistributed earnings deemed to be not permanently invested, less available tax credits and deductions, and appropriate consolidating adjustments for the geographic areas set forth below. Interarea sales are made at negotiated selling prices.

| 1979 | United States | Canada | Europe | Latin America | All Other | Total[1] |
|---|---|---|---|---|---|---|
| | | | (Dollars in Millions) | | | |
| **Net Sales:** | | | | | | |
| Outside | $49,559.9 | $4,611.8 | $8,338.2 | $2,023.8 | $1,777.5 | $66,311.2 |
| Interarea | 5,454.9 | 3,432.9 | 276.9 | 109.0 | 34.4 | — |
| Total net sales | $55,014.8 | $8,044.7 | $8,615.1 | $2,132.8 | $1,811.9 | $66,311.2 |
| **Net Income** | $ 2,320.5 | $ 224.1 | $ 338.2 | $ 14.5 | $ 13.9 | $ 2,892.7 |
| **Net Assets:** | | | | | | |
| Total current assets | $11,468.2 | $1,277.4 | $2,575.0 | $ 683.4 | $ 630.3 | $16,556.5 |
| Real estate, plants and equipment | 19,941.1 | 1,056.2 | 2,700.2 | 605.1 | 576.8 | 24,879.4 |
| Accumulated depreciation | ( 11,495.3) | ( 593.0) | ( 1,598.4) | ( 212.8) | ( 398.7) | ( 14,298.2) |
| Special tools—less amortization | 765.4 | 31.3 | 203.4 | 12.8 | 44.1 | 1,057.0 |
| Other assets | 3,373.3 | 112.3 | 293.1 | 149.4 | 221.2 | 4,021.1 |
| Total assets | 24,052.7 | 1,884.2 | 4,173.3 | 1,237.9 | 1,073.7 | 32,215.8 |
| Loans payable | 2.8 | — | 529.8 | 209.2 | 182.3 | 924.1 |
| Other current liabilities | 6,317.3 | 630.5 | 1,472.8 | 323.6 | 201.1 | 8,944.2 |
| Total current liabilities | 6,320.1 | 630.5 | 2,002.6 | 532.8 | 383.4 | 9,868.3 |
| Long-term debt | 664.4 | — | 34.4 | 111.7 | 69.5 | 880.0 |
| Other liabilities and deferred credits | 1,521.8 | 103.7 | 681.9 | 39.8 | 67.8 | 2,288.2 |
| Total liabilities | 8,506.3 | 734.2 | 2,718.9 | 684.3 | 520.7 | 13,036.5 |
| Allied accounts | 926.0 | ( 395.1) | ( 208.5) | ( 186.8) | ( 135.6) | — |
| Net assets | $16,472.4 | $ 754.9 | $1,245.9 | $ 366.8 | $ 417.4 | $19,179.3 |
| **Average Number of Employes** (in thousands) | 618 | 39 | 131 | 33 | 32 | 853 |

| 1978 | United States | Canada | Europe | Latin America | All Other | Total[1] |
|---|---|---|---|---|---|---|
| | | | (Dollars in Millions) | | | |
| **Net Sales:** | | | | | | |
| Outside | $49,048.8 | $3,362.9 | $7,421.0 | $1,784.5 | $1,603.9 | $63,221.1 |
| Interarea | 4,450.0 | 3,412.8 | 245.7 | 94.0 | 4.8 | — |
| Total net sales | $53,498.8 | $6,775.7 | $7,666.7 | $1,878.5 | $1,608.7 | $63,221.1 |
| **Net Income (Loss)** | $ 3,073.2 | $ 157.5 | $ 376.2 | ($ 96.2)[2] | $ 15.6 | $ 3,508.0 |
| **Total Assets** | $24,260.5 | $1,343.7 | $3,854.4 | $1,142.3 | $ 876.1 | $30,598.3 |
| **Net Assets** | $15,921.6 | $ 601.2 | $1,219.7 | $ 217.2 | $ 246.7 | $17,569.9 |
| **Average Number of Employes** (in thousands) | 611 | 38 | 126 | 34 | 30 | 839 |

(1) After elimination of interarea transactions. (2) Due principally to cost of liquidation of Argentine automotive operations.

**Note 14. Contingent Liabilities**

There are various claims and pending actions against the Corporation and its subsidiaries with respect to commercial matters, including warranties and product liability, governmental regulations including environmental and safety matters, civil rights, patent matters, taxes and other matters arising out of the conduct of the business. Certain of these actions purport to be class actions, seeking damages in very large amounts. The amounts of liability on these claims and actions at December 31, 1979 were not determinable but, in the opinion of the management, the ultimate liability resulting will not materially affect the consolidated financial position or results of operations of the Corporation and its consolidated subsidiaries.

## Accountants' Report

Deloitte Haskins & Sells
Certified Public Accountants

1114 Avenue of the Americas
New York 10036

General Motors Corporation, its Directors and Stockholders:

February 13, 1980

We have examined the Consolidated Balance Sheet of General Motors Corporation and consolidated subsidiaries as of December 31, 1979 and 1978 and the related Statements of Consolidated Income and Changes in Consolidated Financial Position for the years then ended. Our examinations were made in accordance with generally accepted auditing standards and, accordingly, included such tests of the accounting records and such other auditing procedures as we considered necessary in the circumstances.

In our opinion, these financial statements present fairly the financial position of the companies at December 31, 1979 and 1978 and the results of their operations and the changes in their financial position for the years then ended, in conformity with generally accepted accounting principles applied on a consistent basis.

*Deloitte Haskins & Sells*

# Supplementary Information

## Lines of Business

General Motors is a highly vertically-integrated business operating primarily in the manufacture, assembly and sale of automobiles, trucks and related parts and accessories classified as automotive products. Substantially all of General Motors' products are marketed through retail dealers and through distributors and jobbers in the United States and Canada and through distributors and dealers overseas. To assist in the merchandising of General Motors' products, General Motors Acceptance Corporation and its subsidiaries offer financial services and certain types of automobile insurance to dealers and customers. The amount of net sales attributable to United States, Canadian and overseas operations, and by class of product is summarized for the five years ended December 31, 1979 as follows:

| *Net Sales Attributable to:* | 1979 | 1978 | 1977 | 1976 | 1975 |
|---|---|---|---|---|---|
| | | | (Dollars in Millions) | | |
| United States operations | | | | | |
| Automotive products | $51,093.5 | $49,603.0 | $44,317.0 | $37,069.6 | $26,137.3 |
| Nonautomotive products | 3,389.8 | 3,391.3 | 2,795.2 | 2,277.0 | 2,392.8 |
| Defense and space | 531.5 | 504.5 | 438.8 | 438.1 | 387.7 |
| Total United States operations | 55,014.8 | 53,498.8 | 47,551.0 | 39,784.7 | 28,917.8 |
| Canadian operations | 8,044.7 | 6,775.7 | 5,743.9 | 5,263.0 | 4,263.3 |
| Overseas operations | 12,394.4 | 10,975.0 | 8,399.1 | 7,495.2 | 7,227.3 |
| Elimination of interarea sales | ( 9,142.7) | ( 8,028.4) | ( 6,732.7) | ( 5,361.9) | ( 4,683.5) |
| Total | $66,311.2 | $63,221.1 | $54,961.3 | $47,181.0 | $35,724.9 |
| Worldwide automotive products | $62,006.6 | $58,985.5 | $51,429.5 | $44,106.3 | $32,536.0 |
| Worldwide nonautomotive products | $ 4,304.6 | $ 4,235.6 | $ 3,531.8 | $ 3,074.7 | $ 3,188.9 |

Because of the high degree of integration, substantial interdivisional and intercompany transfers of materials and services are made. Consequently, any determination of income by areas of operations or class of products shown above is necessarily arbitrary because of the allocation and reallocation of costs, including corporate costs, benefiting more than one division or product. Within these limitations, the Corporation estimates that the percentage of net income attributable to the United States, Canadian and overseas operations, and by class of product for the five years ended December 31, 1979 is as follows:

| *Percentage of Net Income Attributable to:* | 1979 | 1978 | 1977 | 1976 | 1975 |
|---|---|---|---|---|---|
| United States operations | 79% | 87% | 89% | 82% | 85% |
| Canadian operations | 8 | 5 | 3 | 6 | 9 |
| Overseas operations | 13 | 8 | 8 | 12 | 6 |
| Total | 100% | 100% | 100% | 100% | 100% |
| Automotive products | 90% | 96% | 95% | 97% | 90% |
| Nonautomotive products | 10% | 4% | 5% | 3% | 10% |

## Selected Quarterly Data

| | 1979 Quarters | | | | 1978 Quarters | | | |
|---|---|---|---|---|---|---|---|---|
| | 1st | 2nd | 3rd | 4th | 1st | 2nd | 3rd | 4th |
| Dollars in Millions | | | | | | | | |
| Net sales | $17,897.7 | $18,982.3 | $13,313.5 | $16,117.7 | $14,867.2 | $17,026.1 | $13,583.3 | $17,744.5 |
| Net income | 1,257.2 | 1,188.0 | 21.4 | 426.1 | 869.6 | 1,106.3 | 527.9 | 1,004.2 |
| Per Share Amounts | | | | | | | | |
| Earned | 4.39 | 4.13 | .06 | 1.46 | 3.03 | 3.86 | 1.84 | 3.51 |
| Dividends | 1.00 | 1.65 | 1.15 | 1.50 | 1.00 | 1.50 | 1.00 | 2.50 |
| Stock Price Range* | | | | | | | | |
| High | 59.38 | 61.75 | 65.88 | 64.88 | 62.50 | 66.88 | 66.50 | 65.50 |
| Low | 53.13 | 56.38 | 54.88 | 49.38 | 57.13 | 59.25 | 58.00 | 53.75 |

*The principal market is the New York Stock Exchange and prices are based on the Composite Tape.

## Supplementary Information (concluded)

| **Summary of Operations** (Dollars in Millions Except Per Share Amounts) | 1979 | 1978 | 1977 | 1976 | 1975 |
|---|---|---|---|---|---|
| Net sales | $66,311.2 | $63,221.1 | $54,961.3 | $47,181.0 | $35,724.9 |
| Equity in earnings of nonconsolidated subsidiaries and associates, and other income—net | 410.2 | 111.6 | 277.0 | 211.9 | 21.0 |
| Cost of sales and selling, general and administrative expenses, exclusive of items listed below | 58,324.2 | 53,531.5 | 46,425.2 | 39,546.4 | 31,255.5 |
| Depreciation of real estate, plants and equipment | 1,236.9 | 1,180.6 | 974.0 | 939.3 | 906.1 |
| Amortization of special tools | 1,950.4 | 1,855.7 | 1,406.4 | 1,296.9 | 1,180.1 |
| Provision for the Bonus Plan | 133.8 | 168.4 | 161.0 | 139.7 | 32.9 |
| United States, foreign and other income taxes | 2,183.4 | 3,088.5 | 2,934.2 | 2,567.8 | 1,118.2 |
| Net income | 2,892.7 | 3,508.0 | 3,337.5 | 2,902.8 | 1,253.1 |
| Dividends on preferred stocks | 12.9 | 12.9 | 12.9 | 12.9 | 12.9 |
| Earned on common stock | 2,879.8 | 3,495.1 | 3,324.6 | 2,889.9 | 1,240.2 |
| Dividends on common stock | 1,520.3 | 1,712.6 | 1,944.8 | 1,590.5 | 688.4 |
| Net income retained in the year | $ 1,359.5 | $ 1,782.5 | $ 1,379.8 | $ 1,299.4 | $ 551.8 |
| Net income—percent of sales | 4.4% | 5.5% | 6.1% | 6.2% | 3.5% |
| —percent of stockholders' equity | 15.1% | 20.0% | 21.2% | 20.2% | 9.6% |
| Earned on common stock—per share | $ 10.04 | $ 12.24 | $ 11.62 | $ 10.08 | $ 4.32 |
| Dividends on common stock—per share | 5.30 | 6.00 | 6.80 | 5.55 | 2.40 |
| Net income retained in the year—per share | $ 4.74 | $ 6.24 | $ 4.82 | $ 4.53 | $ 1.92 |
| Total taxes—per share | $ 15.72 | $ 18.69 | $ 16.58 | $ 14.16 | $ 8.14 |
| Average shares of common stock outstanding (in millions) | 286.8 | 285.5 | 286.1 | 286.7 | 286.8 |
| Dividends on capital stock as a percentage of net income | 53.0% | 49.2% | 58.7% | 55.2% | 56.0% |

Management's discussion and analysis of operations for 1979, 1978 and 1977 appear on pages 14 through 17.

| **Additional Statistics** (Dollars in Millions Except Per Share Amounts) | | | | | |
|---|---|---|---|---|---|
| Expenditures for real estate, plants and equipment | $ 3,371.8 | $ 2,737.8 | $ 1,870.9 | $ 998.9 | $ 1,200.9 |
| Expenditures for special tools | $ 2,015.0 | $ 1,826.7 | $ 1,775.8 | $ 1,308.4 | $ 1,035.6 |
| Worldwide average number of employes (in thousands) | 853 | 839 | 797 | 748 | 681 |
| Worldwide payrolls (includes financing and insurance subsidiaries) | $18,851.0 | $17,195.5 | $15,270.8 | $12,908.5 | $10,028.4 |
| Common and preferred stockholders—Number (in thousands) | 1,237 | 1,268 | 1,245 | 1,251 | 1,323 |
| —Equity | $19,179.3 | $17,569.9 | $15,766.9 | $14,385.2 | $13,082.4 |
| Book value per share of common stock | $ 64.61 | $ 60.01 | $ 53.82 | $ 49.02 | $ 44.50 |
| Working capital | $ 6,688.2 | $ 7,948.9 | $ 7,630.3 | $ 7,556.6 | $ 6,394.0 |

| **Worldwide Factory Sales of Cars and Trucks** (Units in Thousands) | | | | | |
|---|---|---|---|---|---|
| Manufactured in the United States | | | | | |
| Passenger cars | 5,084 | 5,292 | 5,259 | 4,883 | 3,680 |
| Trucks and coaches | 1,361 | 1,586 | 1,436 | 1,335 | 978 |
| Total manufactured in the United States | 6,445 | 6,878 | 6,695 | 6,218 | 4,658 |
| Manufactured in Canada | 843 | 853 | 777 | 715 | 595 |
| Manufactured overseas* | 1,705 | 1,751 | 1,596 | 1,635 | 1,376 |
| Total factory sales of cars and trucks—all sources | 8,993 | 9,482 | 9,068 | 8,568 | 6,629 |

*Includes units manufactured by Isuzu Motors Limited under contract for and marketed by GM.

# The Impact of Inflation on Financial Data

In recent years, the accounting profession has given a great deal of consideration to the question of reporting the impact of inflation on financial data. Many complex theories have been proposed and studied but none has received general acceptance. Nevertheless, all interested parties agree that inflation has an impact on financial data. Thus, in September 1979 the Financial Accounting Standards Board (FASB) issued Statement No. 33, *Financial Reporting and Changing Prices.* Statement No. 33 establishes standards for reporting certain effects of price changes on financial data. No one method is required by the Statement; instead, alternative methods are required in order to display various effects. The Statement is intended to help readers of financial data assess results in the following specific areas:

a. The erosion of general purchasing power,
b. Enterprise performance,
c. The erosion of operating capability, and
d. Future cash flows.

The accompanying Schedules display the basic historical cost financial data adjusted for general inflation (constant dollar) and also for changes in specific prices (current cost) for use in such assessments.

In reviewing these Schedules, the following comments may be of assistance in understanding the reasons for the different "income" amounts and the uses of the data.

**Financial statements—historical cost base**

The objective of financial statements, and the primary purpose of accounting, is to furnish, to the fullest extent practicable, objective, quantifiable summaries of the results of financial transactions to those who need or wish to judge management's ability to manage. The data are prepared by management and independently verified by the independent public accountants.

The present accounting system in general use in the United States and the financial statements prepared by major companies from that system were never intended to be measures of relative economic value, but instead are basically a history of transactions which have occurred and by which current and potential investors and creditors can evaluate their expectations. There are many subjective, analytical, and economic factors which must be taken into consideration when evaluating a company. Those factors cannot be quantified objectively. Just as the financial statements cannot present in reasonable, objective, quantifiable form all of the data necessary to evaluate a business, they also should not be expected to furnish all the data needed to evaluate the impact of inflation on a company.

**Data adjusted for general inflation—constant dollar base**

Financial reporting is, of necessity, stated in dollars. It is generally recognized that the purchasing power of a dollar has deteriorated in recent years, and the costs of raw materials and other items as well as wage rates have increased and can be expected to increase further in the future. It is not as generally recognized, however, that profit dollars also are subject to the same degree of reduction in purchasing power. Far too much attention is given to the absolute level of profits rather than the relationship of profits to other factors in the business and to the general price level. For example, as shown in the accompanying Schedule A, adjusting the annual amount of sales and net income to a constant 1967 dollar base, using the U.S. Bureau of Labor Statistics' Consumer Price Index for Urban Consumers, demonstrates that constant dollar profits have not increased in recent years in line with the changes in sales volume. This is reflected in the general decline in the net income as a percent of sales over that period as well as the decrease in the dividend paid in terms of constant dollars of purchasing power.

**Data adjusted for changes in specific prices—current cost**

Another manner in which to analyze the impact of inflation on financial data (and thus the business) is by adjusting the historical cost data to the current costs for the major balance sheet items which have been accumulated through the accounting system over a period of years and which thus reflect different prices for the same commodities and services.

The purpose of this type of restatement is to furnish estimates of the impact of price increases for replacement of inventories and property on the potential future net income of the business and thus assess the probability of future cash flows. Although these data may be useful for this purpose, they do not reflect specific plans for the replacement of property. A more meaningful estimate of the impact of such costs on future earnings is the estimated level of future capital expenditures which is set forth in the Letter to Stockholders on page 3.

**Summary**

In the accompanying Schedules, the effects of the application of the preceding methods on the past five years' and the current year's operations are summarized. Under both the constant dollar and the current cost methods, the net income of the business is lower than that determined under the historical cost method. What does this mean? It means that business, as well as individuals, is affected by inflation and that the purchasing power of business dollars also has declined. In addition, the costs of maintaining the productive capacity, as reflected in the current cost data (and estimate of future capital expenditures), have increased. Of particular concern is the effect of a fixed income tax rate on such data. Since present tax laws do not allow deductions for the current costs of depreciation, the taxes levied on the company exceed statutory rates after the data are adjusted for the impact of inflation. This is reflected on Schedule B in which the effective tax rate rises from 44.9% under the historical cost base to 58.4% and 57.9% under the 1979 constant dollar and current cost bases, respectively. Management must seek ways to cope with the impact of inflation on accounting through accounting methods such as the last-in, first-out (LIFO) method of inventory valuation, which matches current costs with current revenues, and through accelerated methods of depreciation.

In comparing these data to those of other companies for the current year, it should be kept in mind that under the Federal income tax law, the LIFO basis for inventory valuation is recognized *only* if it is also followed in the financial statements. Since Statement No. 33 specifically prohibits the restatement of taxes in the current year, the effective tax rates for those companies using first-in, first-out (FIFO) and straight-line depreciation in their accounts will be even higher than those companies that use the LIFO and accelerated depreciation methods in their accounting.

Another significant adjustment is the restatement of stockholders' equity—the investment base. The adjustment for general inflation (constant dollar) puts all the expenditures for these items on a consistent purchasing power basis—the average 1967 dollar. This adjustment decreases the historical stockholders' equity, as represented by net assets in Schedule A, of about $19.2 billion to a constant dollar basis of $12.2 billion. In other words, the $19.2 billion represented in the financial statements has only $12.2 billion of purchasing power expressed in 1967 dollars. The net assets adjusted for specific prices (current cost restated in 1967 dollars), as shown in Schedule A, amounted to $13.0 billion. This is $0.8 billion higher than that shown on a constant dollar basis due to the fact that the CPI-U index is accelerating more rapidly than the indices of specific prices applicable to General Motors.

Finally, it must be emphasized that there is a critical need for national monetary and fiscal policies designed to control inflation and to provide adequate capital for future business growth which, in turn, will mean increased productivity and employment.

**Schedule A**

**Comparison of Selected Data Adjusted for Effects of Changing Prices**

(Dollars in Millions Except Per Share Amounts)

Historical cost data adjusted for general inflation (constant dollar) and changes in specific prices (current cost). (A)

| | 1979 | 1978 | 1977 | 1976 | 1975 |
|---|---|---|---|---|---|
| Net Sales—as reported | $66,311.2 | $63,221.1 | $54,961.3 | $47,181.0 | $35,724.9 |
| —in constant 1967 dollars | 30,501.9 | 32,354.7 | 30,281.7 | 27,672.1 | 22,161.8 |
| Net Income—as reported | $ 2,892.7 | $ 3,508.0 | $ 3,337.5 | $ 2,902.8 | $ 1,253.1 |
| —in constant 1967 dollars | 817.0(B) | 1,384.5 | 1,580.9 | 1,485.4 | 283.9 |
| —in current cost 1967 dollars | 829.5(B) | | | | |
| Earned per share of common stock—as reported | $ 10.04 | $ 12.24 | $ 11.62 | $ 10.08 | $ 4.32 |
| —in constant 1967 dollars | 2.83(B) | 4.83 | 5.50 | 5.15 | 0.96 |
| —in current cost 1967 dollars | 2.87(B) | | | | |
| Dividends per share of common stock—as reported | $ 5.30 | $ 6.00 | $ 6.80 | $ 5.55 | $ 2.40 |
| —in constant 1967 dollars | 2.44 | 3.07 | 3.75 | 3.26 | 1.49 |
| Net income as a percent of sales—as reported | 4.4% | 5.5% | 6.1% | 6.2% | 3.5% |
| —in constant 1967 dollars | 2.7 | 4.3 | 5.2 | 5.4 | 1.3 |
| —in current cost 1967 dollars | 2.7 | | | | |
| Net income as a percent of stockholders' equity—as reported | 15.1% | 20.0% | 21.2% | 20.2% | 9.6% |
| —in constant 1967 dollars | 6.7 | 11.2 | 13.1 | 14.8 | 3.2 |
| —in current cost 1967 dollars | 6.4 | | | | |
| Net assets at year-end—as reported | $19,179.3 | $17,569.9 | $15,766.9 | $14,385.2 | $13,082.4 |
| —in constant 1967 dollars | 12,163.4 | 12,351.3 | 12,041.4 | 10,007.7 | 8,921.8 |
| —in current cost 1967 dollars | 12,982.7 | | | | |
| Unrealized gain from decline in purchasing power of dollars of net amounts owed | $ 83.8 | | | | |
| Increase in specific prices of inventory and property over increase in the general price level—net decrease | ($ 221.8) | | | | |
| Market price per common share at year-end—unadjusted | $ 50.00 | $ 53.75 | $ 62.88 | $ 78.50 | $ 57.63 |
| —in constant 1967 dollars | 23.00 | 27.51 | 34.64 | 46.04 | 35.75 |
| Average Consumer Price Index | 217.4 | 195.4 | 181.5 | 170.5 | 161.2 |

(A) Adjusted data have been determined by applying the Consumer Price Index—Urban to the data with 1967 (CPI-100) as the base year as specified by SFAS No. 33. Depreciation has been calculated on a straight-line basis for this calculation.

(B) These amounts will differ from those shown for constant dollar and current cost in Schedule B because a different base year has been used (1967 in Schedule A and 1979 in Schedule B) in order to illustrate the impact of changing prices in alternative forms.

**Schedule B**

**Schedule of Income Adjusted for Changing Prices**

For The Year Ended December 31, 1979

(Dollars in Millions Except Per Share Amounts)

| | As Reported in the Financial Statements (Historical Cost) | Selected Data Adjusted for General Inflation (1979 Constant Dollar) | Adjusted for Changes in Specific Prices (1979 Current Cost) |
|---|---|---|---|
| Net Sales | $66,311.2 | $66,311.2 | $66,311.2 |
| Cost of sales | 55,848.7 | 56,462.2 | 56,107.5 |
| Depreciation and amortization expense | 3,187.3 | 3,690.4 | 4,017.8 |
| Other operating items—net | 2,199.1 | 2,199.1 | 2,199.1 |
| United States and other income taxes | 2,183.4(A) | 2,183.4(A) | 2,183.4(A) |
| Total costs and expenses | 63,418.5 | 64,535.1 | 64,507.8 |
| Net Income | $ 2,892.7 | $ 1,776.1(B) | $ 1,803.4(B) |
| Earned per share of common stock | $ 10.04 | $ 6.15(B) | $ 6.24(B) |
| Effective income tax rate | 44.9%(A) | 58.4%(A) | 57.9%(A) |
| Unrealized gain from decline in purchasing power of dollars of net amounts owed | | $ 182.2 | $ 182.2 |
| Increase in specific prices of inventory and property over increase in the general price level—net decrease | | | ($ 482.1)(C) |

(A) In accordance with SFAS No. 33, no adjustment has been made to the provision for income taxes. The effect is to increase the effective tax rate as shown.

(B) These amounts will differ from those shown for constant dollar and current cost in Schedule A because a different base year has been used (1967 in Schedule A and 1979 in Schedule B) in order to illustrate the impact of changing prices in alternative forms.

(C) At December 31, 1979, current cost of inventory was $9,679.4 million and current cost of real estate, plant and equipment, net of accumulated depreciation, was $19,079.2 million. The current cost of property owned and the related depreciation expense were calculated by applying selected producer price indices to historical book values of machinery and equipment, the Marshall Valuation Service index to buildings and the use of assessed values for land.

# INDEX

# INDEX

(continued from front cover)

**15A-6** (b) Adjusted net income, $33,235; B's capital, $101,944
**15A-7** (b) Cash To Dell, $26,000
**15B-1** (b) Total assets, $289,800
**15B-2** (a) Net income, $30,000
**15B-3** (c) Hill, capital, Sept. 30, $57,400
**15B-4** (a) (5) Share to Barth, $28,000
**15B-5** (c) Bonus to old partners, $52,500
**15B-6** No key figure
**15B-7** (b) Cash to May, $18,144
Bus. Dec. Prob. 15: No key figure

**16A-1** Stockholders' equity, (1) $2,124,000; (2) $5,984,000
**16A-2** Stockholders' equity, June 20, $542,400
**16A-3** (b) Stockholders' equity, $833,000
**16A-4** Retained earnings, Dec. 31, Year 6, $63,500
**16A-5** (b) Total assets, $1,167,000
**16A-6** No key figure
**16A-7** Stockholders' equity, Case A, $1,090,000; Case B, $2,383,000
**16B-1** Stockholders' equity, Case A, $449,000; Case B, $1,560,000
**16B-2** No key figure
**16B-3** (d) Stockholders' equity, $730,300
**16B-4** (a) Stockholders' equity, $7,230,000; (c) Stockholders' equity, $7,230,000
**16B-5** No key figure
**16B-6** No key figure
**16B-7** Stockholders' equity, Case A, $1,110,000; Case B, $1,989,000
Bus. Dec. Prob. 16: Dividends paid on common stock by City Electric, $79,800,000

**17A-1** Income before extraordinary items, $1,500,000
**17A-2** (a) Net income, $720,000
**17A-3** Income before extraordinary items, $2,820,000
**17A-4** Book value per share, May 30, $30.20
**17A-5** (b) Retained earnings, Jan. 1, Year 12, as restated, $511,000
**17A-6** (b) Total paid-in capital, $6,112,300
**17A-7** (a) Total paid-in capital, $2,800,000; (b) retained earnings, $369,000

**17B-1** Income before extraordinary items, $540,000
**17B-2** (a) Net income, $350,000
**17B-3** Income before extraordinary items, $2,100,000
**17B-4** Book value per share, July 21, $42
**17B-5** (b) Retained earnings, Jan. 1, Year 9, as restated, $364,000
**17B-6** (b) Total paid-in capital, $3,789,500
**17B-7** (a) Total paid-in capital, $2,888,000; (b) Retained earnings, $483,800
Bus. Dec. Prob. 17: (a) Joseph's share of net assets, $480,000

**18A-1** (c) Closing entry, $400,000
**18A-2** (b) (1) Discount on bonds payable, $58,000
**18A-3** (b) Loss on retirement of bonds, $96,480
**18A-4** (c) (1) Premium on bonds payable, $130,000
**18A-5** (b) Net long-term liability, $3,874,150
**18A-6** (a) Carrying value of bonds, June 30, Year 11, $5,650,200
**18A-7** (c) Interest expense, issued at discount, $261,000; issued at premium, $248,000
**18A-8** (d) Lease payment obligation, $40,184
**18B-1** (c) Closing entry, $375,000
**18B-2** (b) (1) Discount on bonds payable, $354,000
**18B-3** (b) Loss on retirement of bonds, $114,400
**18B-4** (c) (1) Premium on bonds payable, $124,000
**18B-5** (b) Net long-term liability, $5,840,400
**18B-6** (a) Carrying value of bonds, June 30, Year 5, $8,272,600
**18B-7** (b) (4) Interest expense, $172,500
**18B-8** (d) Lease payment obligation, $23,870
Bus. Dec. Prob. 18: (b) Earnings per share, stock financing, $3.24

**PV-1** (c) Present value, $17,511
**PV-2** (b) Amortization of discount at Dec. 31, $15,710
**PV-3** (c) Net liability, Dec. 31, $23,197
**PV-4** (a) Present value under 5-year lease, $7,806,000
**PV-5** (b) Discount on note receivable, $165,776

**19A-1** (b) Loss on sale, $410
**19A-2** Unrealized loss on marketable securities, $2,700
**19A-3** (b) (1) Unrealized loss on marketable securities, $2,450
**19A-4** (b) Market value at June 30, $99,740
**19A-5** (b) Investment loss, Year 4, $86,000
**19A-6** (b) Percentage owned, 85%
**19A-7** Consolidated total assets, $1,121,000
**19B-1** (b) Gain on sale of bonds, $15,300
**19B-2** Gain on sale, Dec. 31, $7,925
**19B-3** (b) Net carrying value, $104,700
**19B-4** (a) Total earnings this year, $32,600
**19B-5** (b) Investment income Year 1, $84,000
**19B-6** Total assets, $3,804,000
**19B-7** Consolidated total assets, $602,000
Bus. Dec. Prob. 19: Current ratio (consolidated basis) 2.1 to 1

**20A-1** No key figure
**20A-2** Adjusted gross income, Case A, $86,400; Case B, $65,712
**20A-3** Capital loss deduction, $2,700
**20A-4** Taxable income, $193,750
**20A-5** (c) Net income if new stock is used, $116,450
**20A-6** Adjusted gross income, $55,400
**20A-7** Income taxes, $277,450
**20B-1** No key figure
**20B-2** Adjusted gross income, $65,500
**20B-3** (c) Long-term capital gain deduction, $1,800
**20B-4** Taxable income on revised basis, $271,250
**20B-5** Adjusted gross income, Case A, $72,000; Case B, $54,760
**20B-6** (b) Total income tax, $31,304
**20B-7** (a) Actual income taxes payable this year, $33,193
Bus. Dec. Prob. 20: Disposable income under single proprietorship form, $51,134